e-
e-
FO

Deitel™
Books, Cyber Classrooms and Complete Training Courses
published by
Prentice Hall

For Managers Series
e-Business and e-Commerce for Managers

How to Program Series
e-Business and e-Commerce How to Program
Internet and World Wide Web How to Program
Visual Basic® 6 How to Program
XML How to Program
Perl How to Program
Java™ How to Program, 3/E
C How to Program, 3/E
C++ How to Program, 3/E

Multimedia Cyber Classroom Series
e-Business and e-Commerce Multimedia Cyber Classroom
Internet and World Wide Web Multimedia Cyber Classroom
Visual Basic® 6 Multimedia Cyber Classroom
XML Multimedia Cyber Classroom
Perl Multimedia Cyber Classroom
Java™ Multimedia Cyber Classroom, 3/E
C++ Multimedia Cyber Classroom, 3/E

The Complete Training Course Series
The Complete e-Business and e-Commerce Programming Training Course
The Complete Internet and World Wide Web Programming Training Course
The Complete Visual Basic® 6 Training Course
The Complete XML Training Course
The Complete Perl Training Course
The Complete Java™ 2 Training Course, 3/E
The Complete C++ Training Course, 3/E

Visual Studio® Series
Visual Basic® 6 How to Program
Getting Started with Microsoft® Visual C++™ 6 with an Introduction to MFC
Getting Started with Microsoft® Visual J++® 1.1

For continuing updates on Prentice Hall and Deitel & Associates, Inc. publications visit the Prentice Hall Web site

www.prenhall.com/deitel

To communicate with the authors, send email to:

deitel@deitel.com

For information on corporate on-site seminars and public seminars offered by Deitel & Associates, Inc. worldwide, visit:

www.deitel.com

e-Business and
e-Commerce
FOR MANAGERS

H. M. Deitel
Deitel & Associates, Inc.

P. J. Deitel
Deitel & Associates, Inc.

K. Steinbuhler
Deitel & Associates, Inc.

DEITEL™

PRENTICE HALL
Upper Saddle River,
New Jersey 07458

Prentice
Hall

Library of Congress Cataloging-in-Publication Data
E-business and e-commerce for managers / H.M. Deitel, P.J. Deitel, K. Steinbuhler
         p. cm.
    Includes bibliographical references and index.
    ISBN 0-13-032364-0
         1. Electronic Commerce. 2. Business enterprises--Computer networks--Management
    I. Title: E-business and e-commerce for managers. II. Deitel, Paul J. III. Steinbuhler, K. (Kate)
    IV. Title.
    HF5548.32 .D45 2000
    658.8'4--dc21   00-051667

Vice President and Editorial Director, ECS: *Marcia Horton*
Acquisitions Editor: *Petra J. Recter*
Assistant Editor: *Sarah Burrows*
Project Manager: *Crissy Statuto*
Editorial Assistant: *Karen Schultz*
Vice President of Production and Manufacturing, ESM: *David W. Riccardi*
Executive Managing Editor: *Vince O'Brien*
Managing Editor: *David A. George*
Senior Production Editor: *Camille Trentacoste*
Production Editor: *Penny Cox*
Director of Creative Services: *Paul Belfanti*
Creative Director: *Carole Anson*
Art Director: *Heather Scott*
Chapter Opener and Cover Designer: *Tamara Newnam Cavallo*
Manufacturing Manager: *Trudy Pisciotti*
Manufacturing Buyer: *Pat Brown*
Marketing Manager: *Jennie Burger*

 © 2001 by Prentice-Hall, Inc.
Upper Saddle River, New Jersey 07458

10 9 8 7 6 5 4 3 2 1

ISBN 0-13-032364-0

Prentice-Hall International (UK) Limited, *London*
Prentice-Hall of Australia Pty. Limited, *Sydney*
Prentice-Hall Canada Inc., *Toronto*
Prentice-Hall Hispanoamericana, S.A., *Mexico*
Prentice-Hall of India Private Limited, *New Delhi*
Prentice-Hall of Japan, Inc., *Tokyo*
Pearson Education Asia Pte. Ltd., *Singapore*
Editora Prentice-Hall do Brasil, Ltda., *Rio de Janeiro*

To

Michael M. Tulman:

> Thank you for your love of business,
> and for your love of teaching and
> writing that you shared with us.
>
> We dedicate this book to you,
> our friend and mentor, to whom we owe
> our teaching and writing careers.
>
> *Harvey and Paul Deitel*

To my parents for their love, infinite patience and support.
   Kate Steinbuhler

Contents

Preface   xxvii

Part 1
Introduction

1   Introduction to e-Business and e-Commerce   2
1.1   Introduction: Transitioning to the Web   3
1.2   History of the Internet   5
1.3   History of the World Wide Web   6
1.4   Internet and World Wide Web Development   7
1.5   e-Business and e-Commerce Overview   7
1.6   A Word of Caution   12
1.7   Tour of the Book   12
1.8   Internet and World Wide Web Resources   20

Part 2
Constructing an e-Business

2   e-Business Models   27
2.1   Introduction   28
2.2   Storefront Model   28
2.2.1   Shopping-Cart Technology   29
2.2.2   Online Shopping Malls   31

2.3	Auction Model	32
2.4	Portal Model	35
2.5	Dynamic-Pricing Models	37
	2.5.1 Name-Your-Price Model	38
	2.5.2 Comparison-Pricing Model	39
	2.5.3 Demand-Sensitive Pricing Model	40
	2.5.4 Bartering Model	40
	2.5.5 Rebates	40
	2.5.6 Offering Free Products and Services	40
2.6	B2B E-Commerce and EDI	41
2.7	Click-and-Mortar Businesses	44
2.8	Internet and World Wide Web Resources	46

3   Building an e-Business: Design, Development and Management   54

3.1	Introduction	55
3.2	Getting Started	56
	3.2.1 Generating e-Business Ideas	56
	3.2.2 Growth of e-Business: Evaluating Risk	57
	3.2.3 Finding Funding and Going Public	57
3.3	Putting Your Plan Into Action	60
	3.3.1 Choosing a Domain Name	60
	3.3.2 Supply-Chain Management: Distributors, Vendors and Shipment Providers	61
	3.3.3 Web-Site Hosting	62
	3.3.4 Web Design	67
	3.3.5 Enhancing the User Experience	69
	3.3.6 Protecting Your e-Business	72
	3.3.7 Streaming Media: How Much Is Too Much?	73
	3.3.8 Preparing for New Technologies	73
3.4	e-Business Solutions	73
	3.4.1 End-to-End e-Business Solutions	74
	3.4.2 Other e-Business Solutions	76
	3.4.3 Maintaining and Monitoring Your Web Site	77
	3.4.4 e-Commerce Consulting	79
3.5	Internet and World Wide Web Resources	80

4   Online Monetary Transactions   91

4.1	Introduction	92
4.2	Credit-Card Transactions	92
	4.2.1 Anatomy of an Online Credit-Card Transaction	94
	4.2.2 Credit-Card Transaction Enablers	95
4.3	Online Credit-Card Fraud	96
4.4	Digital Currency	97
4.5	e-Wallets	98
4.6	Alternate Consumer Payment Options	99

4.7	Peer-to-Peer Payments	100
4.8	Smart Cards	101
4.9	Micropayments	102
4.10	Business-to-Business (B2B) Transactions	104
4.11	e-Billing	108
4.12	Developing Payment Standards	111
4.13	Internet and World Wide Web Resources	112

Part 3
e-Business and e-Commerce

5	**Internet Hardware, Software and Communications**		**123**
5.1	Introduction		124
5.2	Structure of the Internet		125
5.3	Hardware		125
	5.3.1	Servers	126
	5.3.2	Communications Media	126
	5.3.3	Storage Area Networks (SANs)	127
5.4	Connecting to the Internet		127
	5.4.1	Digital Subscriber Line (DSL)	128
	5.4.2	Broadband	130
	5.4.3	Integrated Services Digital Network (ISDN)	130
	5.4.4	T-1 and T-3 Lines	130
5.5	Internet2®		131
5.6	Software		131
	5.6.1	Application Service Providers (ASPs)	131
	5.6.2	Databases	132
5.7	Operating Systems		133
	5.7.1	UNIX®	133
	5.7.2	Microsoft Windows®	134
	5.7.3	Linux®	135
	5.7.4	Mac® OS X	136
5.8	Enhancing Business Communication		138
	5.8.1	Intranets and Extranets	138
	5.8.2	Streaming Audio and Video	138
	5.8.3	Internet Telephony	139
	5.8.4	Webcasting and Web Conferencing	140
5.9	Internet and World Wide Web Resources		141
6	**Wireless Internet and m-Business**		**151**
6.1	Introduction		152
6.2	Wireless Devices		152
6.3	m-Business		153
6.4	Wireless Internet Access		156

6.5		Wireless Web Technology	158
	6.5.1	Web Clipping	158
	6.5.2	WAP™ and WML	160
6.6		Software Applications for Wireless Devices	163
6.7		Wireless Local Area Networks (WLANs)	166
6.8		Bluetooth™	167
6.9		Wireless Communications	168
6.10		Location Tracking	168
	6.10.1	Global Positioning System (GPS)	168
	6.10.2	E911 Act	169
6.11		Future of Wireless Internet	170
	6.11.1	Implications for Disabled People	170
	6.11.2	Ultimate Wireless Device	170
6.12		Internet and World Wide Web Resources	171

7   Internet Security   181

7.1		Introduction	182
7.2		Ancient Ciphers to Modern Cryptosystems	183
7.3		Secret-key Cryptography	184
7.4		Public-key Cryptography	186
7.5		Key Agreement Protocols	188
7.6		Key Management	188
7.7		Digital Signatures	189
7.8		Public-key Infrastructure, Certificates and Certification Authorities	191
7.9		Cryptanalysis	193
7.10		Security Protocols	193
	7.10.1	Secure Sockets Layer (SSL)	193
	7.10.2	Secure Electronic Transaction™ (SET™)	194
7.11		Security Attacks	196
7.12		Network Security	199
	7.12.1	Firewalls	199
	7.12.2	Kerberos	200
	7.12.3	Biometrics	201
7.13		Steganography	201
7.14		Internet and World Wide Web Resources	203

Part 4
Internet Marketing

8   Internet Marketing   218

8.1	Introduction	219
8.2	Branding	220
8.3	Internet Ma\rketing Research	220
8.4	e-Mail Marketing	222

8.5   Promotions   224
8.6   e-Business Advertising   225
        8.6.1   Banner Advertising   226
        8.6.2   Buying and Selling Banner Advertising   228
        8.6.3   Media-Rich Advertising   230
        8.6.4   Wireless Advertising   231
8.7   e-Business Public Relations   232
8.8   Business-to-Business (B2B) Marketing on the Web   233
8.9   Search Engines   234
        8.9.1   META Tags   234
        8.9.2   Search-Engine Registration   234
8.10   Internet and World Wide Web Resources   236

9   Affiliate Programs   246
9.1   Introduction   247
9.2   How an Affiliate Program Works   248
9.3   Selecting An Affiliate-Program Reward Structure   248
        9.3.1   Pay-Per-Click Model   249
        9.3.2   Pay-Per-Lead Model   249
        9.3.3   Pay-Per-Sale Model   249
        9.3.4   Multi-Tiered Model   249
        9.3.5   Hybrid Model   250
        9.3.6   CPM (Cost-Per-Thousand) Model   250
9.4   Attracting Affiliates   251
9.5   Monitoring An Affiliate Program   251
9.6   Affiliate Solution Providers   252
        9.6.1   Commission Junction   252
        9.6.2   LinkShare   253
        9.6.3   Be Free   254
        9.6.4   ClickTrade   254
        9.6.5   PlugInGo.com   256
9.7   Web-site "Stickiness"   256
9.8   Becoming an Affiliate   257
9.9   Examples of Affiliate Programs   260
9.10   Examples of Affiliate Programs by Industry   261
9.11   Costs and Taxation of Affiliate Programs   265
9.12   Affiliate-Program Directories and Search Engines   265
9.13   Internet and World Wide Web Resources   266

10   e-Customer Relationship Management   272
10.1   Introduction   273
10.2   Tracking and Analyzing Data   274
        10.2.1   Log-File Analysis   275
        10.2.2   Data Mining   275
        10.2.3   Customer Registration   278
        10.2.4   Cookies   278

10.3	Personalization	279
	10.3.1	Intelligent Agents	280
	10.3.2	Personalization vs. Privacy	280
10.4	Contact Centers	280
	10.4.1	Frequently Asked Questions (FAQs)	281
	10.4.2	e-Mail	282
	10.4.3	Online Text Chatting	282
	10.4.4	Speech Synthesis and Recognition; Natural Language Processing	283
	10.4.5	Voice Communications	285
	10.4.6	Sales-Force Automation	287
10.5	Business-to-Business e-CRM	289
10.6	Complete e-CRM Solutions	289
10.7	Internet and World Wide Web Resources	290

Part 5
Legal, Ethical, Social and Global Issues

11	Legal and Ethical Issues; Internet Taxation	302
11.1	Introduction	303
11.2	Legal Issues: Privacy on the Internet	303
	11.2.1	Right to Privacy	304
	11.2.2	Internet and the Right to Privacy	304
	11.2.3	Network Advertising Initiative	306
	11.2.4	Employer and Employee	307
	11.2.5	Protecting Yourself as a User	309
	11.2.6	Protecting Your Business: Privacy Issues	310
11.3	Legal Issues: Other Areas of Concern	311
	11.3.1	Defamation	312
	11.3.2	Sexually Explicit Speech	313
	11.3.3	Children and the Internet	314
	11.3.4	Alternative Methods of Regulation	315
	11.3.5	Intellectual Property: Copyright and Patents	316
	11.3.6	Trademark and Domain Name Registration	320
	11.3.7	Unsolicited Commercial e-Mail (Spam)	321
	11.3.8	Online Auctions	322
	11.3.9	Online Contracts	323
	11.3.10	User Agreements	323
11.4	Cybercrime	324
11.5	Internet Taxation	324
11.6	Internet And World Wide Web Resources	327

12	Globalization	339
12.1	Introduction	340
12.2	Regulating the Internet on an International Level	341

12.2.1   Accounting for Legal and Cultural Differences   341
12.2.2   International Internet Regulations   342
12.3   Creating an e-Business with Global Capabilities   344
12.3.1   Choosing an International Market   344
12.3.2   Obtaining a Local Internet Address   346
12.3.3   Internationalization and Localization   346
12.3.4   Partnering and Hiring   352
12.3.5   Payment Systems   353
12.3.6   Distribution   354
12.3.7   Legal and Taxation Systems   355
12.3.8   Promotions   356
12.4   Canada   357
12.5   Mexico and Central and South America   358
12.6   Europe   359
12.7   Africa   360
12.8   Middle East   361
12.9   Asia   362
12.10   Australia   363
12.11   Future of Global e-Business   364
12.12   Internet and World Wide Web Resources   364

13   Social and Political Issues   375
13.1   Introduction   376
13.2   Health, Social Interaction and the Internet   376
13.2.1   Social Health   376
13.2.2   Children and the Internet   377
13.3   Socio-Economic Segregation   378
13.4   New Economic Workplace   379
13.5   Online Communities   380
13.5.1   Online Communities: Defining the Difference   380
13.5.2   Communication Tools   383
13.5.3   Online Activism   385
13.6   Online Charities and Non Profit Organizations on the Web   388
13.7   Internet and World Wide Web Resources   389

14   Accessibility   397
14.1   Introduction   398
14.2   Web Accessibility   398
14.3   Web Accessibility Initiative   400
14.4   Providing Alternatives for Multimedia Content   400
14.4.1   Readability   401
14.4.2   Using Voice Synthesis and Recognition with VoiceXML™   401
14.5   Accessibility in Microsoft® Windows® 2000   402
14.5.1   Tools for Visually Impaired People   402
14.5.2   Tools for Hearing-Impaired People   406
14.5.3   Tools for Users Who Have Difficulty Using the Keyboard   407

14.5.4	Microsoft Narrator	411
14.5.5	Microsoft On-Screen Keyboard	413
14.5.6	Accessibility Features in Microsoft Internet Explorer 5.0	413
14.6	Other Accessibility Tools	415
14.7	Internet and World Wide Web Resources	417

Part 6
e-Business and e-Commerce
Case Studies

15   Online Industries   424

15.1	Introduction	425
15.2	Retailing on the Web	425
15.3	Medical Services Online; Health and Nutrition	426
15.4	Online Travel	428
15.5	Transportation and Shipping	429
15.6	Online Automotive Sites	431
15.7	Energy Online	432
15.8	Selling Brainpower Online	434
15.9	Online Art Dealers	435
15.10	Online Grocery Stores	436
15.11	Online Real Estate	437
15.12	Online Legal Services	441
15.13	Government Online	442
15.14	Insurance Online	443
15.15	Children Online	444
15.16	Purchasing Event Tickets Online	446
15.17	Genealogy Online	447
15.18	Internet and World Wide Web Resources	447

16   Online Banking and Investing   455

16.1	Introduction	456
16.2	Online Banking Services	456
16.2.1	Hybrid Banks	457
16.2.2	Internet-Only Banks	459
16.3	Online Loans	461
16.4	How the Web Is Changing the Investment Community	463
16.4.1	Electronic Communication Networks (ECNs)	463
16.4.2	Online Trading	465
16.4.3	Online Bond Trading	472
16.5	Merging Financial Services	472
16.6	Financial Aggregation Services	473
16.7	Wireless Banking and Trading	474

16.8   Financial Planning Online   477
16.9   Internet and World Wide Web Resources   478

17   e-Learning   489
17.1   Introduction   490
17.2   e-Learning Technologies and Infrastructure.   491
17.3   e-Learning Overview   492
17.4   E-Learning Solution Providers   493
17.5   Training Marketplaces   495
17.6   Information Technology (IT) Training Online   495
17.7   Traditional Education Online   499
17.8   Studying Online   501
17.9   Educational Supplies and Resources Online   503
17.10   Internet and World Wide Web Resources   503

18   e-Publishing   511
18.1   Introduction   512
18.2   Electronic Publishing   512
18.3   Self-Publishing   515
18.4   Print on Demand   518
18.5   e-Publishing: Related Hardware and Technologies   519
        18.5.1   XrML   519
        18.5.2   e-Books   520
18.6   Online News Sources   521
18.7   e-Zines and Online Magazines   521
18.8   Future of e-Publishing   523
18.9   Internet and World Wide Web Resources   525

19   Online Entertainment   530
19.1   Introduction   531
19.2   Online Entertainment   532
19.3   Entertainment and Technology   533
19.4   MP3 and File-Transfer Technology   534
19.5   Amateur and Independent Artist Opportunities   534
19.6   Interactive Web TV   536
19.7   Music and the Web   537
19.8   Web Radio   537
19.9   Sports on the Web   538
19.10   Comedy on the Web   540
19.11   Online Games   541
19.12   Online Hollywood   542
        19.12.1   Talent Scouting   544
        19.12.2   Screen Writing   545
        19.12.3   Distribution and Supplies   545
19.13   The Future of Entertainment   545
19.14   Internet and World Wide Web Resources   547

20   Online Career Services   553

20.1   Introduction   554
20.2   Resources for the Job Seeker   555
20.3   Online Opportunities for Employers   556
        20.3.1   Posting Jobs Online   558
        20.3.2   Problems with Recruiting on the Web   560
        20.3.3   Diversity in the Workplace   560
        20.3.4   Recruiting Services   562
        20.3.5   Testing Potential Employees Online   563
20.4   Career Sites   563
        20.4.1   Comprehensive Career Sites   564
        20.4.2   Technical Positions   565
        20.4.3   Contracting Online   566
        20.4.4   Executive Positions   567
        20.4.5   Students and Young Professionals   568
        20.4.6   Other Online Career Services   569
20.5   Internet and World Wide Web Resources   569

Part 7
Appendices

A   Microsoft® Internet Explorer 5.5   578

A.1   Introduction to the Internet Explorer 5.5 Web Browser   579
        A.1.1   Connecting to the Internet   579
        A.1.2   Features of Internet Explorer 5.5   580
        A.1.3   File Transfer Protocol (FTP)   583
        A.1.4   Outlook Express and Electronic Mail   585
        A.1.5   Outlook Express and Newsgroups   589
        A.1.6   NetMeeting and MSN Messenger Service   591
        A.1.7   Controlling the Details   594

B   Building an e-Business:
Internet and Web Programming   599

B.1   Introduction   600
B.2   Problem Statement   600
B.3   Three–Tier Architecture   600
        B.3.1   Top Tier: The User Interface   601
        B.3.2   Middle Tier: Business Processes (The Server)   601
        B.3.3   Bottom Tier: Database   602
B.4   Introduction to the **Bug2Bug.com** Bookstore   602

C Introduction to HyperText Markup Language 4 (HTML 4) **614**

C.1 Introduction 615
C.2 Markup Languages 615
C.3 Editing HTML 616
C.4 Common Tags 617
C.5 Headers 619
C.6 Text Styling 620
C.7 Linking 622
C.8 Images 625
C.9 Formatting Text With **\<FONT\>** **629**
C.10 Special Characters, Horizontal Rules and More Line Breaks 631
C.11 Internet and WWW Resources 634

D Intermediate HTML 4 **639**

D.1 Introduction 640
D.2 Basic HTML Tables 640
D.3 Intermediate HTML Tables and Formatting 643
D.4 Basic HTML Forms 646
D.5 More Complex HTML Forms 649
D.6 Internet and WWW Resources 655

E Introduction to HTML, ASP, XML and JavaScript Syntax **660**

E.1 Introduction 661
E.2 Introduction to HTML 661
E.3 Introduction to ASP 661
E.4 Introduction to XML 665
E.5 Introduction to JavaScript 666

F The Client Tier: The User Interface **672**

F.1 The Client Tier 673
F.2 HTML 674
F.3 XML and XSL 679

G The Middle Tier: Business Processes **685**

G.1 Introduction 686
G.2 Active Server Pages (ASP) 686
G.3 Adding and Viewing Cart contents 701
G.4 Check Out 707

H The Bottom Tier: The Database **722**

H.1 Introduction 723
H.2 Bottom Tier: Database 723
H.3 Access Database 723

I   Accessibility Programming   **725**
I.1   Introduction   726
I.2   Providing Alternatives for Multimedia Content   726
I.3   Maximizing Readability by Focusing on Structure   729
I.4   Accessibility in HTML Tables   729
I.5   Accessibility in HTML Frames   733
I.6   Accessibility in XML   733
I.7   Using Voice Synthesis and Recognition with VoiceXML™   734
7.6   Internet and World Wide Web Resources   741

J   Installing a Web Server   **746**

K   Setting Up a Microsoft ODBC Data Source   **747**

       Glossary   **748**

       Index   **770**

Illustrations

Part 1
Introduction

1 Introduction to e-Business and e-Commerce

1.1 Works cited.   4

1.2 **Campusfood.com** home page.
(Courtesy of **Campusfood.com**, Inc.)   9

1.3 Growth on the Internet. (Courtesy of Jupiter Research, Spring 2000.)   10

Part 2
Constructing an e-Business

2 e-Business Models

2.1 eBay home page. (These materials have been reproduced by Prentice Hall with the permission of eBay, Inc. COPYRIGHT © EBAY, INC. ALL RIGHTS RESERVED.)   33

2.2 Placing a bid on eBay. (These materials have been reproduced by Prentice Hall with the permission of eBay, Inc. COPYRIGHT © EBAY, INC. ALL RIGHTS RESERVED.)   34

2.3 Customers have the benefit of comparison shopping at Yahoo! Shopping. (Reproduced with Permission of Yahoo!© by Yahoo! Inc. YAHOO! and the YAHOO! logo are trademarks of Yahoo! Inc.)   37

2.4 A sampling of B2B exchange sites by industry. (Reprinted by Permission of Forbes Magazine © 2000 Forbes 2000.)   44

3   Building an e-Business: Design, Development and Management

3.1   Business plan overview.   57
3.2   Rare Medium's incubation methodology. (Courtesy of Rare Medium.)   59
3.3   e-Commerce based shipping options.   62
3.4   **GoCargo.com** shipping bid. (Courtesy of **GoCargo.com**.)   63
3.5   Web-site hosts.   63
3.6   **Websiteforfree.com**'s Web-site design. (Courtesy of **WebsiteforFREE.com**.)   67
3.7   Homestead site tour. (Courtesy of **Homestead.com**© Incorporated. All Rights Reserved.)   68
3.8   ImagePump zoom technology. (Courtesy of Xippix, Inc.)   70
3.9   Enhanced view with the Magnifier. (Courtesy of Xippix, Inc.)   70
3.10   **MyEvents.com** calendar feature. (Courtesy of MyEvents.)   71
3.11   **MyEvents.com** contacts feature. (Courtesy of MyEvents.)   71
3.12   Secure Assure's example Privacy Profile™. (Courtesy of Secure Assure, LLC.)   72
3.13   Other e-business solution providers.   75
3.14   Holistix Web Manager. (Courtesy of Holitix, Inc.)   78
3.15   e-Business consulting companies   79

4   Online Monetary Transactions

4.1   Basic steps in an online credit-card transaction.   94
4.2   CyberCash FraudPatrol. (Courtesy of CyberCash™ Inc. CyberCash is a trademark or registered trademark of CyberCash Inc., in the United States and other countries.)   96
4.3   Using eCash on the Web. (Courtesy of eCash Technologies, Inc. and ©2000 eCash.)   98
4.4   EntryPoint Internet Toolbar. (Courtesy of EntryPoint Incorporated.)   100
4.6   QPass transaction process. (Courtesy of QPass, Inc.)   103
4.7   TradeCard contract. (Courtesy of TradeCard Inc.)   106
4.8   Clareon online transaction service. (All Rights Reserved, Clareon Corporation 2000.)   107
4.9   PAYTRU$T SmartBalance™ screen shot. (Courtesy of Paytrust, Inc.)   109

Part 3
e-Business and e-Commerce

5   Internet Hardware, Software and Communications

5.1   Internet connection comparison chart. (Courtesy of GLINK, LLC.)   128
5.2   Internet Service Providers (ISPs) that offer free Internet access.   129
5.3   Table of a relational database.   133
5.4   Popular Linux vendors.   137
5.5   **RealPlayer** dialog. (Copyright© 1995-2000 RealNetworks, Inc. All Rights Reserved. RealNetworks, **Real.com**, RealPlayer are trademarks or registered trademarks of RealNetworks, Inc.)   139

6 Wireless Internet and m-Business

6.1   BlackBerry home page. (Courtesy of Research In Motion Limited. The
        BlackBerry and RIM families of related marks, images and symbols are the
        exclusive properties of, and trademarks of Research In Motion Limited,
        used by permission.)   154
6.2   Palm Web clipping applications library. (Courtesy of Palm, Inc.)   159
6.3   Palm VII handheld. (Courtesy of Palm, Inc.)   160
6.5   Rendering a WML document using Nokia's browser. (© 2000
        Nokia Mobile Phones.)   162
6.6   Microsoft Pocket PC devices. (Courtesy of Microsoft Corporation,
        Casio Computer Co., Ltd., Compaq Corporation, Hewlett Packard
        and Symbol Technologies, Inc.)   164
6.7   Microsoft's Pocket Internet Explorer. (Courtesy of Microsoft
        Corporation and Compaq Corporation.)   165
6.8   Demo of a video delivered to a wireless device using PacketVideo.
        (Courtesy of PacketVideo Corporation.)   166

7 Internet Security

7.1   Encrypting and decrypting a message using a symmetric secret key.   184
7.2   Distributing a session key with a key distribution center.   185
7.3   Encrypting and decrypting a message using public-key cryptography.   187
7.4   Authentication with a public-key algorithm   188
7.5   Creating a digital envelope.   189
7.6   A portion of the VeriSign digital certificate. (Courtesy of VeriSign, Inc.)   191
7.7   Example of a conventional watermark. (Courtesy of Blue Spike, Inc.)   202
7.8   An example of steganography: Blue Spike's Giovanni digital
        watermarking process. (Courtesy of Blue Spike, Inc.)   203

Part 4
Internet Marketing

8 Internet Marketing   218

8.1   Banner advertisements. (Courtesy of **GaryCohn.com** Marketing.)   226
8.2   Example of a panel ad. (Courtesy of Venture Capital Online, Inc.)   227
8.3   ValueClick's home page. (Courtesy of ValueClick, Inc.)   229
8.4   Search engines and their registration processes.   235

9 Affiliate Programs

9.1   Affiliate-program operation for a program that pays commissions on sales.   248
9.2   Diagram of a two-tiered affiliate-program model.   250
9.3   LinkShare's home page. (Courtesy of LinkShare Corporation.)   253
9.4   Be Free's performance-marketing page for merchants.
        (Courtesy of Be Free, Inc.)   255
9.5   Be Free demonstration: How promotions work, step 1.
        (Courtesy of Be Free, Inc.)   255
9.6   Sample store from **vstore.com**. (Courtesy of Vcommerce Corporation.)   258

9.7	Adbility's specific segments within an industry. (Courtesy of **Adbility.com**.)	259
9.8	Adbility's listing of affiliate programs for books in the "general" segment. (Courtesy of **Adbility.com**.)	260
9.9	Companies that use affiliate programs.	262
9.10	Associate-It home page (Courtesy of iSeed Inc.)	266

10   e-Customer Relationship Management

10.1	WebTrends home page. (Courtesy of © 2000 WebTrends Corporation. All rights reserved. WebTrends is a registered trademark of WebTrends Corporation.)	276
10.2	Example analysis from a WebTrends product. (Courtesy of © 2000 WebTrends Corporation. All rights reserved. WebTrends is a registered trademark of WebTrends Corporation.)	277
10.3	CLICKiCHAT's online text chatting. (Courtesy of StartCall Corporation.)	284
10.4	Ask Jeeves™ home page with a sample query. (Courtesy of Ask Jeeves, Inc.)	285
10.5	Ask Jeeves™ results page from sample query. (Courtesy of Ask Jeeves, Inc.)	286
10.6	RealCall Alert Demonstration. (Courtesy of RealCall, Inc.)	288

Part 5
Legal, Ethical, Social and Global Issues

11   Legal and Ethical Issues; Internet Taxation

11.1	**PrivacyBot.com**. (Courtesy of Invisible Hand Software, LLC.)	311
11.2	Net Nanny home page. (Courtesy of Net Nanny Software International Inc.)	315
11.3	FTC "dummy" site for NordiCaLite. (Courtesy of Federal Trade Commission.)	325
11.4	FTC warning page. (Courtesy of Federal Trade Commission.)	326

12   Globalization

12.1	Type of information found at Global Reach's Web site. (Courtesy of Global Reach.)	345
12.2	Logos dictionary query page with sample query. (Courtesy of Logos Group, Italy.)	347
12.3	Logos query results page with sample query result. (Courtesy of Logos Group, Italy.)	348
12.4	**Aquarius.net** translator search. (Courtesy of Language Networks BV.)	349
12.5	eBay's Chinatown site uses a red background signifying celebration and good luck. (These materials have been reproduced with the permission of eBay Inc. COPYRIGHT © EBAY INC. ALL RIGHTS RESERVED.)	350
12.6	Various America Online icons. (AOL screenshots copyright © 2000 America Online, Inc. Used with permission.)	351
12.7	First Tuesday provides jobs in the European Information Technology market. (Courtesy of First Tuesday, Ltd.)	353
12.8	Africa Online Ghana site. (Courtesy of Africa Online, Inc.)	361
12.9	Australia's InFARMation (Courtesy of **inFARMation.com.au**.)	363

13 Social and Political Issues

13.1   Ethnic Web communities.   381
13.2   Interest-based online communities   381
13.3   Sample of gender-specific sites on the Internet.   382
13.4   Person-to-person and conference calls through Firetalk. (Courtesy of
       FireTalk Communications, Inc.)   384
13.5   Firetalk's Instant Messaging interface. (Courtesy of FireTalk
       Communications, Inc.)   384
13.6   Firetalk Web-based tour. (Courtesy of FireTalk Communications, Inc.)   385
13.7   YouthActivism home page. (Courtesy of Activism Project 2000.)   386
13.8   Non-profit organizations online.   388

14 Accessibility

14.1   Acts designed to protect access to the Internet for people with disabilities.   399
14.2   We Media home page. (Courtesy of We Media Inc.)   399
14.3   **Text Size** dialog.   403
14.4   **Display Settings** dialog.   403
14.5   **Accessibility Wizard** initialization options.   404
14.6   **Scroll Bar** and **Window Border** Size dialog.   404
14.7   Setting window element sizes.   405
14.8   **Display Color Settings** options.   405
14.9   **Accessibility Wizard** mouse cursor adjustment tool.   406
14.10 **SoundSentry** dialog.   406
14.11 **Show Sounds** dialog.   407
14.12 **StickyKeys** dialog.   408
14.13 **BounceKeys** dialog.   408
14.14 **ToggleKeys** dialog.   409
14.15 **Extra Keyboard Help** dialog.   409
14.16 **MouseKeys** window.   410
14.17 **Mouse Button Settings** window.   410
14.18 **Mouse Speed** dialog.   411
14.19 **Set Automatic Timeouts**.   411
14.20 Saving new accessibility settings with the **Save Settings to File** dialog.   412
14.21 **Narrator** window.   412
14.22 **Narrator** reading **Notepad** text.   413
14.23 Microsoft **On-Screen Keyboard**.   414
14.24 Microsoft Internet Explorer 5.0's **Accessibility** options.   414
14.25 Advanced accessibility settings in Microsoft Internet Explorer 5.0.   415
14.26 Accessing the **Text Size** menu in Microsoft Internet Explorer 5.0.   415

Part 6
e-Business and e-Commerce Case Studies

15 Online Industries

15.1   WebMD Home page (Copyright © 2000 WebMD Corporation. Reprinted with
       permission.)427
15.2   **Travelocity** Home page. (Courtesy of Travelocity.)   431

15.3   Webvan Home page. (Courtesy of Webvan Group, Inc.)   437
15.4   **Apartments.com** can help you find an apartment.
        (Courtesy of Apartments.com.)   440
15.5   The CyberSettle Home Page (Courtesy of Cybersettle.com)   442
15.6   **ebix.com** Home page (Courtesy of ebix.com, Inc.).   445
15.7   **Ticketmaster.com** Home page. (Used under permission of
        Ticketmaster Online-CitySearch, Inc.)   446

16   Online Banking and Investing

16.1   Internet-only banks and online banking information sites.   460
16.2   E-LOAN's E-TRACK demo. (Courtesy of E-LOAN, Inc.)   462
16.3   Archipelago order routing and execution example. (Courtesy of
        Archipelago Holdings, L.L.C.)   465
16.4   E*TRADE offers investing and financial services. (Courtesy of
        E*TRADE Securities, Inc.)   467
16.5   Dollar-based investing through ShareBuilder. (Courtesy of
        Netstock Corporation.)   469
16.6   ShareBuilder example of sample investments. (Courtesy of
        Netstock Corporation.)   469
16.7   Online Brokerages.   470
16.8   **Tradebonds.com**'s zero coupon bond query. (Courtesy
        of **Tradebonds.com**.)   473
16.9   Example of Yodlee's service through Citibank's myciti.
        (Courtesy of Yodlee, Inc.)   475
16.10   Example of Yodlee's charting capability. (Courtesy of Yodlee, Inc.) 476

17   e-Learning

17.1   e-Learning SWOT analysis.   490
17.2   e-learning solution providers.   494
17.3   Online IT training.   496
17.4   Quisic Corporate Programs. (Courtesy of © Quisic. All Rights Reserved.) 497
17.5   PreMBA Course Outline. (Courtesy of © Quisic. All Rights Reserved.) 498
17.6   Graduate and professional degrees available online.   500
17.7   Examples of online ventures by college and universities.   501
17.8   **Tutor.com**'s whiteboard. (Courtesy of **tutor.com**, Inc.)   502

18   e-Publishing

18.1   Analysis of e-publishing.   514
18.2   Steven King self published his second e-Book, The Plant.
        (Courtesy of Stephen King.)   516
18.3   Mightywords gives authors a chance to publish their works online.
        (Courtesy of MightyWords.com, Inc.)   517
18.4   eBook is one of many electronic book readers available.
        (Courtesy of Gemstar-TV Guide International.)   520
18.5   E Ink is made up of microcapsules. (Courtesy of E Ink
        Corporation - October 2000.)   524

19 Online Entertainment

19.1   Entertainment activities have varied among online adults in the summer of 2000. Note: chat data reflects the period beginning 30 days prior to initial publication. All other data reflects the three month period prior to publication.[3] (Reprinted by permission of The Industry Standard.)   533

19.2   Superhero Roommate is just one of many original series at **icebox.com.** (Courtesy of Icebox, Inc.)   535

19.3   **WindowsMedia.com** allows you to find your favorite radio station. (Courtesy of FNX Radio Network and Microsoft Corporation).   539

19.4   You never know what to expect at the **Onion.com.** (Courtesy of Onion, Inc.)   540

19.5   The Hollywood Stock Exchange. (Courtesy of the Hollywood Stock Exchange®. Copyright © 1996-2000. All Rights Reserved.)   542

19.6   The **Inside.com** home page. (Courtesy of Powerful Media Inc./**Inside.com**.)   544

20 Online Career Services

20.1   The **Monster.com** home page. (Courtesy of Monster.com.]   556

20.2   **FlipDog.com** job search. (Courtesy of **FlipDog.com**.)   557

20.3   List of a job seeker's criteria.   559

20.4   Career opportunities at BlackVoices. (Courtesy of **BlackVoices.com**.)   561

20.5   Advantage Hiring, Inc.'s Net-Interview™ service. (Courtesy of Advantage Hiring, Inc.)   562

20.6   Cruel World online career services. (Courtesy of Cruel World, Inc.)   565

20.7   **eLance.com** request for proposal (RFP) example. (Courtesy of eLance, Inc.]   567

Part 7
Appendices

A Microsoft® Internet Explorer 5.5

A.1   Using the **Internet Connection Wizard** to get on the Internet.   580

A.2   Deitel & Associates, Inc., Web site. (Courtesy of Deitel & Associates, Inc.)   581

A.3   Capturing a picture from a Web site. (Courtesy of Pearson Education.)   582

A.4   AutoComplete address-bar options.   583

A.5   **History** options. (Courtesy of Pearson Education.)   584

A.6   Using IE5.5 to access FTP sites.   585

A.7   Outlook Express opening screen and the **Internet Accounts** dialog box.   586

A.8   Adding e-mail and news accounts in Outlook Express.   587

A.9   Outlook Express e-mail main screen.   588

A.10   Adding and modifying names in your **Address Book**.   589

A.11   E-mail message in **Outlook Express**.   590

A.12   Using **Outlook Express** to browse newsgroups.   591

A.13   Using NetMeeting to "speak" with people on the Internet.   592

A.14   Chatting using MSN Messenger.   593

A.15   Changing your **Internet Options** in IE5.5. (Courtesy of
       Pearson Education.)   594
A.16   "The Deitel Buzz" newsletter, displayed with Adobe Acrobat.
       (Courtesy of Pearson Education.)   596

B   Building an e-Business: Internet and Web Programming

B.1   Three-tier architecture for the **Bug2Bug.com** online bookstore.   601
B.2   Technologies used by **Bug2Bug.com** and their descriptions.   603
B.3   **Bug2Bug.com**'s home page (**Welcome.html**).   604
B.4   List of available books (**books.asp**).   605
B.5   Visual Basic information page (**book1.asp**).   605
B.6   Contents of the shopping cart (**viewCart.asp**).   606
B.7   User attempting to submit order with empty field (**order.html**).   607
B.8   User trying to submit order with State field empty (**order.html**).   608
B.9   User attempting to check-out form with an invalid state abbreviation
       (**order.html**).   609
B.10   Order confirmation (**process.asp**).   610
B.11   Table of books on back order (**backOrder.xml**).   610
B.12   Shopping cart documents and their interactions.   611
B.13   Summary of **Bug2Bug.com**'s documents.   611

C   Introduction to HyperText Markup Language 4 (HTML 4)

C.1   Basic HTML file.   617
C.2   Header elements **H1** through **H6.**   619
C.3   Stylizing text on Web pages.   621
C.4   Linking to other Web pages.   623
C.5   Linking to an email address.   624
C.6   Placing images in HTML files.   625
C.7   Using images as link anchors.   627
C.8   Using the **FONT** element to format text.   629
C.9   Inserting special characters into HTML.   631
C.10   Using horizontal rules.   632

D   Intermediate HTML 4

D.1   HTML table.   640
D.2   A complex table with formatting and color.   643
D.3   Simple form with basic fields and a text box.   646
D.4   Form including textareas, password boxes and checkboxes.   650
D.5   HTML form including radio buttons and pulldown lists.   652

E   Introduction to HTML, ASP, XML and JavaScript Syntax

E.1   **Enter** button of **welcome.html**.   661
E.2   List of available books from **books.asp**.   662
E.3   View of shopping cart contents from **viewCart.asp**.   663
E.4   Some VBScript variant subtypes.   664
E.5   Some VBScript functions.   665

E.6   Listing of **backOrder.xml**   **665**
E.7   HTML table created by values from **backOrder.xml**.   666
E.8   A first program in JavaScript.   667
E.9   Validation script and output windows from **order.html**.   669

F   The Client Tier: The User Interface
F.1   **Bug2Bug.com** documents presented in this appendix.   673
F.2   Listing for **welcome.html**.   674
F.3   HTML output generated by **books.asp**.   677
F.4   Listing for **backOrder.xml**.   680
F.5   Listing for **books.xsl**.   681

G   The Middle Tier: Business Processes
G.1   **Bug2Bug.com** documents presented in this appendix.   687
G.2   Some built-in ASP objects.   687
G.3   Listing for **books.asp**.   688
G.4   Two ADO object and collection types.   693
G.5   Two SQL keywords.   694
G.6   Listing for **book1.asp**.   696
G.7   Listing for **addToCart.asp**.   701
G.8   Listing for **viewCart.asp**.   703
G.9   Listing for **order.html**.   707
G.10   Listing for **process.asp**.   717

H   The Bottom Tier: The Database
H.1   **Products** table for the **Bug2Bug.com** Access database.   724

I   Accessibility Programming
I.1   Using the **alt** attribute of the **img** tag.   727
I.2   HTML table without accessibility modifications.   730
I.3   Table optimized for screen reading using attribute **headers**.   731
I.4   A home page written in VoiceXML.   734
I.5   Publication page of Deitel's VoiceXML page.   736
I.6   Elements in VoiceXML.   740

Preface

Live in fragments no longer. Only connect.
Edward Morgan Forster

Welcome to the exciting world of the Internet, the World Wide Web, e-business and e-commerce. This book is by an old guy, a young guy, a young lady and the Deitel & Associates, Inc. writing team she heads, known collectively as "The PACK." The old guy (HMD; Massachusetts Institute of Technology 1967) has been in the computer field for 40 years. The young guy (PJD; MIT 1991) has been programming and/or teaching programming for 19 years. The young lady (Kate Steinbuhler; Boston College 2000) majored in English and communications and studied Web development. Kate's team, the PACK—for "Paul," "Abbey," "Christy" and "Kate"—consists of Paul Brandano (Boston College School of Management 2000; majored in marketing), Abbey Deitel (Carnegie Mellon University 1995; majored in industrial administration), Christy Connolly (Boston College School of Management; majored in marketing and finance), and, of course Kate Steinbuhler. Together, our experience includes Internet, World Wide Web, e-business and e-commerce software technologies, as well as academic study and industry experience in computer science, information technology, finance, marketing, management, English and communications.

Ideally, we want this book to speak to students in all areas of interest; we hope you will find it informative, challenging and entertaining. This is not a computer programming book, but it does include an optional case study (in Appendices B through H) on building a storefront e-business that sells books online.

E-business and e-commerce are evolving rapidly, if not explosively. This creates tremendous challenges for us as authors, for our publisher (Prentice Hall), for instructors, for students and for professional people. This book, *e-business & e-commerce for Managers*, is designed to meet these challenges.

Why We Wrote *e-Business and e-Commerce for Managers*

Today, e-business and e-commerce are exploding; businesses everywhere are creating Web presences and reaching their markets in ways that were never before possible. College professors are eager to incorporate e-business and e-commerce into their undergraduate and graduate Internet, Web and business curricula. Professionals are eager to incorporate e-business and e-commerce technology into their organizations. Students want to learn these leading-edge technologies that will be immediately useful to them as they leave the college environment and head into a world where the Internet and World Wide Web have a massive prominence.

Our goal was clear: produce a textbook for college-level courses in e-business and e-commerce for students with little or no programming experience, and to explore the tremendous opportunities afforded by the Web. To meet this goal, we produced a comprehensive book that explains the different elements of e-business and e-commerce and provides abundant real-world applications to encourage students to learn from examples currently on the Web. We performed extensive research for this book and located hundreds of Internet and Web resources to help students learn about building and managing e-businesses. These links include general information, tutorials and demonstrations. Many of the demos are fun, such as the E*TRADE investing game in which students can win cash prizes for participating. The resources also point students to lots of free stuff on the Internet, including free Internet access.

This book is appropriate for students and professionals who wish to create their own e-businesses. Many of the Internet and Web resources we include point students to turnkey solutions (some for a fee and others for free) for creating e-businesses. Students will also be able to use the programming technologies presented in the appendices to create e-businesses themselves (they will also need to set up merchant accounts with banks and use an industrial-strength database system). The tour of the book in Chapter 1 outlines the elements we present for building real e-businesses.

Teaching Approach

e-Business and e-Commerce for Managers contains a rich collection of examples, exercises and projects drawn from many fields to gives students an opportunity to solve interesting real-world problems. The book concentrates on the principles of good e-business management, and provides opportunities for class discussion and scores of Web-based exercises. The text emphasizes good pedagogy.

World Wide Web Access

The installation instructions for the case study for *e-Business and e-Commerce for Managers* (and our other publications) is free for download at the Deitel & Associates, Inc. Web site:

    www.deitel.com

Objectives

Each chapter begins with a statement of *Objectives*. This tells students what to expect and gives them an opportunity, after reading the chapter, to determine if they have met these objectives.

Quotations

The learning objectives are followed by quotations. Some are humorous, some are philosophical and some offer interesting insights. Our students enjoy relating the quotations to the chapter material. Many of the quotations are worth a "second look" *after* reading each chapter.

Outline

The chapter *Outline* helps students approach the material in top-down fashion. This, too, helps students anticipate what is to come and set a comfortable and effective learning pace.

Illustrations/Figures

The illustrations and figures provide visual examples of business concepts, or feature actual businesses on the Web. Charts and tables offer lists of additional resources, and break information into an organized, easy-to-read format.

e-Facts

The *e-Facts* offer the student an interesting break from the text. They are tied into the current discussion, providing interesting facts and statistics on the effects of the Internet, current trends and future projections.

Summary

Each chapter ends with additional pedagogical devices. We present a thorough, bullet-list-style *Summary* of each chapter, to help the student review and reinforce key concepts.

Terminology

We include in the *Terminology* section an alphabetized list of the important terms defined in the chapter—again for further reinforcement.

Self-Review Exercises and Answers

Self-Review Exercises and Answers are included for self-study. This gives the student a chance to build confidence with the material and prepare for the regular exercises. Students should attempt all the self-review exercises and check their answers.

Exercises

The chapter exercises include simple recall of important terminology and concepts, issues for class discussion, Web-based demonstrations and group and semester projects. The large number of exercises across a wide variety of areas enables instructors to tailor their courses to the unique needs of their audiences, and to vary course assignments each semester. Instructors can use these exercises to form homework assignments, short quizzes and major examinations. The solutions for most of the exercises are included in the *Instructor's Manual*. **[NOTE: Please do not write to us requesting the instructor's manual. Distribution of this publication is strictly limited to college professors teaching from the book. Instructors may obtain the solutions manual only from their regular Prentice Hall representatives. We regret that we cannot provide the solutions to professionals.]**

Optional Case Study Using the Deitel™ Live-Code™ Approach

The optional case study, "Building an e-Business," in the appendices completely implements a simplified version of an e-business storefront that sells books. Please take a moment now and read about this case study in the Tour of the Book at the end of Chapter 1; the case study is summarized in the descriptions of Appendices B through H. In the case study, each new concept is presented in the context of a complete, working program immediately followed by one or more windows showing the program's input/output dialog. We call this style of teaching and writing our ***live-code approach***™. *We use real, working programs to teach programming languages.* Reading these programs is much like entering and running them on a computer. All the code in the case study is free for download at our Web site, **www.deitel.com**. If you choose to do the case study, please download this code and carefully read the installation and setup instructions in Appendices J and K on our Web site.

Glossary

The extensive glossary summarizes the key terms in each chapter to provide a quick reference for students while working on a homework assignment or preparing for an exam.

Index Entries

We have included an extensive *Index* at the back of the book. This helps the student find any term or concept by keyword. The terms in the *Terminology* sections generally appear in the *Index* (along with many more index items from each chapter). Students can use the *Index* in conjunction with the *Terminology* sections to be sure they have covered the key material of each chapter.

Recommended Readings

An extensive bibliography of books, articles and online documentation is included at the close of several chapters to encourage further reading.

Acknowledgments

One of the great pleasures of writing a textbook is acknowledging the efforts of the many people whose names may not appear on the cover, but whose hard work, cooperation, friendship and understanding were crucial to the production of the book.

Many other people at Deitel & Associates, Inc. devoted long hours to this book.

- Barbara Deitel managed the preparation of the manuscript, coordinated the production of the book with Prentice Hall and spent long hours researching the quotations at the beginning of each chapter. She did all this in parallel with handling her extensive financial and administrative responsibilities at Deitel & Associates, Inc., including serving as Chief Financial Officer.

- Abbey Deitel, a graduate of Carnegie Mellon University's Industrial Management program, and President of Deitel & Associates, Inc., co-authored Chapters 5, 6, 7 and Appendix A and actively participated in the development of the other chapters.

- Paul Brandano, a graduate of the Boston College Carroll School of Management, and Director of Marketing and Corporate Training at Deitel & Associates, Inc., co-authored Chapters 2, 15, 18 and 19 and actively participated in the development of the other chapters. He would like to thank, Mr. Tom Pollock who provided insights for Chapter 19.

- Christine Connolly, a graduate of Boston College Carroll School of Management and Director of Public Relations and Advertising at Deitel & Associates, Inc., co-authored Chapters 8, 9, 10 and 16 and actively participated in the development of the other chapters. She would like to acknowledge Vicky Crittenden, Chair and Associate Professor of Marketing at the Carroll School of Management at Boston College, for support as a mentor and friend.

- Peter Brandano, a graduate of Boston College with a major in computer science, co-authored Chapter 14 and Appendix I, and validated the case study in Appendices B through H.

- Sean Santry, a computer science and philosophy graduate of Boston College, and Director of Software Development at Deitel & Associates, Inc., co-authored Chapter 5 and served as an advisor on the programming appendices.

We would also like to acknowledge contributions of several people who contributed to the case study in Appendices B through H.

- Tem Nieto, a graduate of the Massachusetts Institute of Technology, and the Director of Product Development at Deitel & Associates, Inc., was the chief architect of the case study appendices. He has co-authored several books and multimedia packages with the Deitels and has contributed over the years to virtually every Deitel & Associates, Inc. publication.

- Matt R. Kowalewski, a graduate of Bentley College with a major in accounting information systems, was the chief implementer and writer of the programming appendices. He also co-authored Chapter 5.

- Carlo Garcia, a senior majoring in computer science at Boston University, participated in the development of the programming appendices.

- Marina Zlatkina, a senior majoring in computer science at Brandeis University, edited the case study.

- Peter Lavalle, a junior majoring in computer information systems at Bentley College, edited the case study.

- Jacob Ellis, a freshman at the University of Pennsylvania, and David Gusovsky, a freshman at Berkeley, co-authored with us Chapters 3 and 4 in our *Internet and World Wide Web How to Program* book. Appendices C and D evolved from these chapters.

The Deitel & Associates, Inc. *College Internship Program* offers a limited number of salaried positions to Boston-area college students majoring in Computer Science, Information Technology, Marketing, English and technical writing. Students work at our corporate headquarters in Sudbury, Massachusetts full-time in the summers and/or part-time during the academic year. Full-time positions are available to college graduates. For more information about this competitive program, please contact Abbey Deitel at **deitel@deitel.com** and check our Web site, **www.deitel.com**. Deitel & Associates, Inc. student interns who worked on this book include:

- Neil Agarwal, a Harvard student majoring in Mathematics, co-authored Chapter 7.

- Rudolf Faust, a freshman at Stanford University, co-authored Chapter 1 and the Preface.

- Jaimee Lederman, a graduate of Brown University, co-authored Chapter 4.

- Lauren Trees, a senior majoring in English at Brown University, co-authored Chapter 12. We would especially like to thank Lauren for her extraordinary research efforts and participation in designing the outline of the book.

- Jeni Jefferson, a senior at Boston College, helped research the quotes and co-authored the glossary.

- Melissa Jordan, a senior majoring in graphic design at Boston University, created the artwork for the chapters.

- Jason Rosenfeld, a junior majoring in computer science at Northwestern University, edited Chapter 14 and Appendix I.

- Christina Carney, a senior at Framingham State College, researched the quotes and helped develop the glossary.

- Fletcher Boland, a senior at Lincoln-Sudbury Regional High School, researched many of the Internet and World Wide Web Resource sections.

We are fortunate to have been able to work on this project with the talented and dedicated team of publishing professionals at Prentice Hall. We especially appreciate the extraordinary efforts of our computer science editor, Petra Recter, our project manager, Crissy Statuto, our assistant editor, Sarah Burrows, and their boss—our mentor in publishing—Marcia Horton, Editor-in-Chief of Prentice-Hall's Engineering and Computer Science Division. Vince O'Brien and Camille Trentacoste did a marvelous job managing production.

We owe special thanks to the creativity of Tamara Newnam Cavallo (**smart_art@earthlink.net**) who did the art work the cover, the chapter-opener art and the e-Fact icon.

We wish to acknowledge the efforts of our reviewers and to give a special note of thanks to Crissy Statuto of Prentice Hall who managed this extraordinary review effort:

Graham Peace (Duquesne University)
Kenton Walker (University of Wyoming)
Jane Mackay (Texas Christian University)
Elizabeth Erickson (University of San Francisco)
Ted Pawlicki (University of Rochester)
Anne Marie Smith (La Salle University)
Bobbie Hyndman (West Texas A&M University)
Clint Bickmore (Front Range Community College)
Shirley Becker (Florida Institute of Technology)
Q. B. Chung (Villanova University)
Edmund Lam (University of California)
Jeff Laird (Northeast Technical Community College)
Richard Platt (University of West Florida)
Clive Sanford (University South Florida)
Robert Mills (Utah State University)
Joe Bell (University of Northern Colorado)
Peter Alexander (University of California)
Phillip Gordon (University of California- Berkeley)
Biao Wang (Boston University)

Roger Rongxin Chen (University of San Francisco)
Mark Cannice (University of San Francisco)
Stuart Brian (Holy Family College)
Peter Cammick (University of Tampa)
Antonis Stylianou (University of North Carolina at Charlotte)
Gopal Iyer (Florida Atlantic University)
Babita Gupta (California State University at Monterey Bay)
Ken Tachibana (iMind Education Systems)
Stephen Cocconi (Los Medanos College)
Marios Koufaris (Baruch College)
Scott Schneberger (University of West Ontario)
Frank Fish (Auto Leisure Products)
Steve Burnett (RSA Security)
Duke Butler (marchFirst)
John Daly (Verizon Wireless)
Brian O'Donahue (Verizon Wireless)
Jeremy Kurtz (Stark State College of Technology)
Jonathan Earl (Technical Training and Consulting)
Craig Peterson (Utah State University)

Under a tight time schedule, these reviewers scrutinized the text and made countless suggestions for improving the accuracy and completeness of the presentation.

We would sincerely appreciate your comments, criticisms, corrections and suggestions for improving the text. Please address all correspondence to our email address:

`deitel@deitel.com`

We will respond immediately. Well, that's it for now. Our best wishes to you as you enter the exciting world of e-business and e-commerce.

Dr. Harvey M. Deitel
Paul J. Deitel
Kate Steinbuhler

About the Authors

Dr. Harvey M. Deitel, CEO of Deitel & Associates, Inc., has 40 years in the computing field including extensive industry and academic experience. He is one of the world's leading computer science instructors and seminar presenters. Dr. Deitel earned B.S. and M.S. degrees from the Massachusetts Institute of Technology and a Ph.D. from Boston University. He has 20 years of college teaching experience including earning tenure and serving as the Chairman of the Computer Science Department at Boston College before founding Deitel & Associates, Inc. with Paul J. Deitel. He is author or co-author of several dozen books and multimedia packages and is currently writing many more. With translations published in Japanese, Russian, Spanish, Elementary Chinese, Advanced Chinese, Korean, French, Polish and Portuguese, Dr. Deitel's texts have earned international recognition. Dr. Deitel has delivered professional seminars internationally to major corporations, government organizations and various branches of the military.

Paul J. Deitel, Executive Vice President of Deitel & Associates, Inc., is a graduate of the Massachusetts Institute of Technology's Sloan School of Management where he studied Information Technology. Through Deitel & Associates, Inc. he has delivered Internet and World Wide Web courses and programming language classes for industry clients including Compaq, Sun Microsystems, White Sands Missile Range, Rogue Wave Software, Computervision, Stratus, Fidelity, Cambridge Technology Partners, Lucent Technologies, Adra Systems, Entergy, CableData Systems, NASA at the Kennedy Space Center, the National Severe Storm Laboratory, IBM and many other organizations. He has lectured on for the Boston Chapter of the Association for Computing Machinery, and has taught satellite-based courses through a cooperative venture of Deitel & Associates, Inc., Prentice Hall and the Technology Education Network. He and his father, Dr. Harvey M. Deitel, are the world's best-selling Computer Science textbook authors.

Kate Steinbuhler, Editorial Director at Deitel & Associates, Inc. and a graduate of Boston College with majors in English and communications, served as project manager and primary author of Chapters 3, 11, 12, 17 and 20. She co-authored Chapters 1, 4, 12 and 14, and served as project manager and co-author for six business chapters in *e-Business and e-Commerce for Managers'* sister book, *e-Business and e-Commerce How To Program*. She would like to acknowledge the other members of the PACK (the PACK consists of Paul Brandano, Abbey Deitel, Christy Connolly and Kate Steinbuhler) for their hard work and devotion to the project, and extend a special thank you to Greg Friedman and Alyssa Clapp for their support. She would also like to thank Dale Herbeck, Chair and Associate Professor of Communications at Boston College, who provided insights for Chapter 11.

The Deitels are co-authors of the best-selling introductory college computer-science programming language textbooks, *Internet and World Wide Web How to Program* and *e-Business and e-Commerce How to Program*. The Deitels are also co-authors the *Internet and World Wide Web Programming Multimedia Cyber Classroom* and the *e-Business and e-Commerce Programming Multimedia Cyber Classroom*. The Deitels are authors of the world's #1 selling college text books in Java, C and C++.

e-Business and e-Commerce How to Program: A Sister Book Intended for Programming Courses

e-Business & e-Commerce for Managers is one of two e-Business/e-Commerce books that we developed for Prentice Hall this year; this book—intended primarily for managers and nonprogrammers—and its sister book, *e-Business & e-Commerce How to Program*—is intended for information technology and computer science majors. Here is the table of contents for *e-Business & e-Commerce How to Program*:

Chapter 1 Introduction to Computers, the Internet and the Web
Chapter 2 Introduction to Internet Explorer 5 and the World Wide Web
Chapter 3 e-Business Models
Chapter 4 Internet Marketing
Chapter 5 Online Monetary Transactions
Chapter 6 Legal, Ethical and Social Issues; Internet Taxation
Chapter 7 Computer and Network Security
Chapter 8 Hardware, Software and Communications

Chapter 9 Introduction to Hypertext Markup Language 4 (HTML 4)
Chapter 10 Intermediate HTML 4
Chapter 11 Ultimate Paint
Chapter 12 Microsoft Frontpage Express
Chapter 13 JavaScript/ JScript: Introduction to Scripting
Chpater 14 JavaScript/ JScript: Control Structures I
Chapter 15 JavaScript/ JScript: Control Structures II
Chapter 16 JavaScript/ JScript: Functions
Chapter 17 JavaScript/ JScript: Arrays
Chapter 18 JavaScript/ JScript: Objects
Chapter 19 Dynamic HTML: Cascading Style Sheets™ (CSS)
Chapter 20 Dynamic HTML: Object Model and Collections
Chapter 21 Dynamic HTML: Event Model
Chapter 22 Dynamic HTML: Filters and Transitions
Chapter 23 Dynamic HTML: Data Binding with Tabular Data Control
Chapter 24 Dynamic HTML: Client-Side Scripting with VBScript
Chapter 25 Active Server Pages (ASP)
Chapter 26 ASP Case Studies
Chapter 27 XML (Extensible Markup Language)
Chapter 28 Case Study: An Online Bookstore
Chapter 29 Perl 5 and CGI (Common Gateway Interface)
Chapter 30 Dynamic HTML: Structured Graphics ActiveX Control
Chapter 31 Dynamic HTML: Path, Sequencer and Sprite ActiveX Controls
Chapter 32 Multimedia: Audio, Video, Speech Synthesis and Recognition
Chapter 33 Macromedia® Flash™: Building Interactive Animations
Chapter 34 Accessibility
Appendix A: HTML Special Characters
Appendix B: HTML Colors
Appendix C: ASCII Character Set
Appendix D: Operator Precedence Charts

e-Business and e-Commerce Programming Multimedia Cyber Classroom: An Interactive Multimedia Version of *e-Business and e-Commerce How to Program*

We have prepared an optional, interactive CD-ROM-based, software version of *e-Business and e-Commerce How to Program* called the *e-Business and e-Commerce Programming Multimedia Cyber Classroom*. It is loaded with features for learning and reference. The *Cyber Classroom* is wrapped with the textbook at a discount in *The Complete e-Business and e-Commerce Programming Training Course*. If you already have the book and would like to purchase the *e-Business and e-Commerce Programming Multimedia Cyber Classroom* separately, please call 1-800-811-0912 and ask for ISBN# 0130895407.

The CD has an introduction with the authors overviewing the *Cyber Classroom's* features. The 258 live-code example Web documents in the textbook truly "come alive" in the *Cyber Classroom*. If you are viewing a document and want to execute it, simply click on the lightning bolt icon and the document will be loaded into a Web browser and rendered.

You will immediately see—and hear for the audio-based multimedia Web pages—the program's outputs. If you want to modify a document and see and hear the effects of your changes, simply click the floppy-disk icon that causes the source code to be "lifted off" the CD and "dropped into" one of your own directories so that you can edit the document and try out your new version. Click the speaker icon for an audio that talks about the document and "walks you through" the code.

The *Cyber Classroom* also provides navigational aids including extensive hyperlinking. The *Cyber Classroom* remembers in a "history list" recent sections you have visited and allows you to move forward or backward in that history list. The thousands of index entries are hyperlinked to their text occurrences. You can key in a term using the "find" feature and the *Cyber Classroom* will locate occurrences of that term throughout the text. The *Table of Contents* entries are "hot," so clicking a chapter name takes you to that chapter.

Students like the hundreds of solved problems from the textbook that are included with the *Cyber Classroom*. Studying and running these extra programs is a nice way for students to enhance their learning experience.

Students and professional users of our *Cyber Classrooms* tell us they like the interactivity and that the *Cyber Classroom* is an effective reference because of the extensive hyperlinking and other navigational features. We recently had an e-mail from a person who said that he lives "in the boonies" and cannot take a live course at a university, so the *Cyber Classroom* was a good solution to his educational needs.

Professors tell us that their students enjoy using the *Cyber Classroom*, spend more time on the course and master more of the material than in textbook-only courses. Also, the *Cyber Classroom* helps shrink lines outside professors' offices during office hours. We have also published the *C++ Multimedia Cyber Classroom (3/e)*, the *Visual Basic 6 Multimedia Cyber Classroom, the Java 2 Multimedia Cyber Classroom (3/e)* and the *Internet and World Wide Web Programming Multimedia Cyber Classroom*.

About Deitel & Associates, Inc.

Deitel & Associates, Inc. is an internationally recognized corporate training and content creation organization specializing in Internet/World Wide Web software technology, e-business/e-commerce software technology and computer programming languages education. Deitel & Associates, Inc. is a member of the World Wide Web Consortium. The company provides courses on Internet and World Wide Web programming, e-business and e-commerce programming, Object Technology and major programming languages. The principals of Deitel & Associates, Inc. are Dr. Harvey M. Deitel and Paul J. Deitel. The company's clients include many of the world's largest computer companies, government agencies, branches of the military and business organizations. Through its publishing partnership with Prentice Hall, Deitel & Associates, Inc. publishes leading-edge programming textbooks, professional books, interactive CD-ROM-based multimedia *Cyber Classrooms*, satellite courses and Web-based training courses. Deitel & Associates, Inc. and the authors can be reached via email at

`deitel@deitel.com`

To learn more about Deitel & Associates, Inc., its publications and its worldwide corporate on-site curriculum, see the last few pages of this book and visit:

www.deitel.com

Individuals wishing to purchase Deitel books, Cyber Classrooms, Complete Training
Courses and Web-based training courses can do so through

www.deitel.com

Bulk orders by corporations and academic institutions should be placed directly with Prentice Hall. See the last few pages of this book for worldwide ordering details.

The World Wide Web Consortium (W3C)

W3C® Deitel & Associates, Inc. is a member of the *World Wide Web Consortium*
MEMBER *(W3C)*. The W3C was founded in 1994 "to develop common protocols for
the evolution of the World Wide Web." As a W3C member, we hold a seat
on the W3C Advisory Committee (our Advisory Committee representa-
tive is our Chief Technology Officer, Paul Deitel). Advisory Committee members help provide "strategic direction" to the W3C through meetings around the world (the Spring 2000
meeting was held in Amsterdam). Member organizations also help develop standards recommendations for Web technologies (such as HTML, XML and many others) through participation in W3C activities and groups. Membership in the W3C is intended for companies
and large organizations. For information on becoming a member of the W3C visit
www.w3.org/Consortium/Prospectus/Joining.

Part 1

Introduction

Outline

Chapter 1   Introduction to e-Business and
             e-Commerce

1

Introduction to e-Business and e-Commerce

Objectives

- To examine the growth of e-business and e-commerce.
- To explore the opportunities and challenges to creating an online business.
- To understand how the Internet and World Wide Web are revolutionizing business.
- To explore the success of an Internet entrepreneur.
- To issue a word of caution to aspiring online entrepreneurs.
- To present a tour of the book.

From the most ancient subject we shall produce the newest science.
Ebbinghaus, Hermann

The simple opposition between the people and big business has disappeared because the people themselves have become so deeply involved in big business.
Walter Lippmann

By 2010, the only big company will be an e-company.
John Chambers, CEO Cisco Systems[1]

Cautiousness in judgment is nowadays to be recommended to each and every one: if we gained only one incontestable truth every ten years from each of our philosophical writers the harvest we reaped would be sufficient.
G. C. Lichtenberg

Outline

1.1   Introduction: Transitioning to the Web
1.2   History of the Internet
1.3   History of the World Wide Web
1.4   Internet and World Wide Web Development
1.5   e-Business and e-Commerce Overview
1.6   A Word of Caution
1.7   Tour of the Book
1.8   Internet and World Wide Web Resources

Summary • Terminology • Self-Review Exercises • Answers to Self-Review Exercises • Exercises • Works Cited

1.1 Introduction: Transitioning to the Web

Welcome to the World of e-business and e-commerce. In the last decade, the Internet and World Wide Web have changed the way people communicate, conduct business and manage their daily lives. This text, *e-Business & e-Commerce for Managers* is designed to offer a clear perspective on the new Internet economy and introduce the basic principles of e-business and e-commerce. We have worked hard to create a text that is user-friendly to both business students and non-business students.

The book offers extensive Web resources, connecting readers to some of the most important businesses on the Web. These resources include companies offering turnkey solutions to help entrepreneurs set up full-scale e-business Web sites, as well as examples of companies that have used the Web to reach global markets. We have included solutions that are suitable to the needs of multinational corporations, as well as to start-up e-businesses. For those who want to build an e-business site from scratch, we have included an optional, extensive programming appendix, which offers an introduction to some of the most widely used Web technologies. These technologies include *HTML, XML, XSL, JavaScript, Structured Query Language (SQL), ActiveX Data Objects (ADO), HTTP Protocol, VBScript* and *Active Server Pages (ASP)*. The appendix is designed for the non-programmer and provides a detailed overview of each topic. Each line of programming code is accompanied by a thorough explanation to ensure even nonprogrammers understand each concept. Once you have finished the case study, you will have built a basic shopping-cart-enabled e-business. More experienced programmers may consider using our book *e-Business & e-Commerce How to Program* (Prentice Hall, 2001) and other programming texts.

We have worked hard to include the latest and most important developments in e-business and e-commerce. We have conducted extensive research to ensure that we approach each issue accurately and that the information is timely. We reference scores of newspapers, journals, case studies and academic publications (Fig 1.1). In many cases we have included Web links to demonstrations and product walk-throughs to give readers an opportunity for deeper understanding. We have also included extensive World Wide Web resources in each of the chapters—the reader is strongly encouraged to visit these Web sites.

In this chapter, we introduce the terms e-business and e-commerce and discuss how the Internet has revolutionized business. We explore the online success of a young entrepreneur who began his e-business from a college campus. We issue a healthy dose of caution in light of the many e-business ventures that have failed, but we remain upbeat and optimistic.

Resources

Affiliate Selling (John Wiley & Sons)
Boston Business Journal
Building Cyberstores (McGraw-Hill)
Business 2.0
Business Week
C@LL CENTER CRM Solutions™
Certification Magazine
Chattanooga Times
Code and Other Laws of Cyberspace
    (Basic Books)
Computer Reseller News
Computer Shopper
Computer World
Customers.com
Cyber Rules: Strategies for Excelling At
    E-Business (Doubleday)
Digital Age
e-Business Advisor
eCompany
ENT
eWeek
Fast Company
Financial Times
Forbes
Fortune Small Business
Global Business Technology
Information Hiding: Techniques for
    Steganography and Digital Watermarking
    (Artech House)
Information Week
Infoworld
Inside Technology Training

Intelligent Enterprise
Inter@ctive Week
Internet.com
InternetWeek
Legal Backgrounder
Drudge Manifesto (New American Library)
Mass High Tech
Messaging Magazine
Money
Net Commerce Magazine
Network World
Newsweek
Operating Systems, Second Edition
PC Magazine
PC Novice
PC Week
Performance Computing
Presentations
Principles of Internet Marketing (South-
    Western College Publishing)
Programming Application With the Wireless
    Application Protocol (John Wiley and Sons)
Revolution
RSA Security, Inc.
Siliconindia
Technology Review
The Boston Globe
The Complete Guide to Associate and Affiliate
    Programs on the Net (McGraw-Hill)
The Denver Post
The Independent (London)
The Industry Standard

Fig. 1.1 Works cited (part 1 of 2).

Resources

The New York Times

The One to One Field Book: The Complete
    Toolkit for Implementing a 1 to 1 Marketing
    Program (Bantam Doubleday Dell
    Publishing Group)

The Portable MBA

The Wall Street Journal

Time

Toronto Star

Understanding WAP (Artech House)

Upside

USA Today

Webtechniques

Yahoo! Internet Life

ZDNet

Fig. 1.1   Works cited (part 2 of 2).

1.2 History of the Internet

In the late 1960s, one of the authors (HMD) was a graduate student at MIT. His research at
MIT's Project Mac (now the Laboratory for Computer Science—the home of the World
Wide Web Consortium) was funded by ARPA—the Advanced Research Projects Agency
of the Department of Defense. ARPA sponsored a conference at which several dozen
ARPA-funded graduate students were brought together at the University of Illinois at Ur-
bana-Champaign to meet and share ideas. During this conference, ARPA rolled out the
blueprints for networking the main computer systems of about a dozen ARPA-funded universities and research institutions. They were to be connected with communications lines
operating at a then-stunning 56KB (1K=1024 bits per second; a bit is a single piece of
data—either a zero or a one), at a time when most people (of the few who could be) were
connecting over telephone lines to computers at a rate of 110 bits per second. HMD vividly
recalls the excitement at that conference. Researchers at Harvard talked about communicating with the Univac 1108 supercomputer across the country at the University of Utah to
handle calculations related to their computer graphics research. Many other intriguing possibilities were raised. Academic research was about to take a giant leap forward. Shortly
after this conference, ARPA proceeded to implement what quickly became called the *AR-
PAnet*, the grandparent of today's *Internet*.

Things worked out differently than originally planned. Although the ARPAnet did
enable researchers to share each others' computers, its chief benefit proved to be the capability of quick and easy communication via what came to be known as *electronic mail (e-
mail)*. This is true even today on the Internet, with e-mail facilitating communication
among hundreds of millions of people worldwide.

e-Fact 1.1

Statistics suggest that e-mail usage is now ten times greater than postal mail.[2]

One of ARPA's primary goals for the network was to allow multiple users to send and
receive information at the same time over the same communications paths (such as phone
lines). The network operated with a technique called *packet switching* in which digital data
was sent in small packages called *packets*. The packets contained data, address information,
error-control information and sequencing information. The address information was used

to route the packets of data to their destination, and the sequencing information was used to help reassemble the packets (which—because of complex routing mechanisms—could actually arrive out of order) into their original order for presentation to the recipient. This packet-switching technique greatly reduced transmission costs from those of dedicated communications lines.

The network was designed to operate without centralized control. This meant that if a portion of the network should fail, the remaining working portions would still be able to route packets from senders to receivers over alternate paths.

The protocols for communicating over the ARPAnet became known as *TCP—the Transmission Control Protocol*. TCP ensured that messages were properly routed from sender to receiver and that those messages arrived intact.

In parallel with the early evolution of the Internet, organizations worldwide were implementing their own networks for both intra-organization (i.e., within the organization) and inter-organization (i.e., between organizations) communication. A huge variety of net-working hardware and software appeared. One challenge was to get these to intercommunicate. ARPA accomplished this with the development of *IP—the Internetworking Protocol*), truly creating a "network of networks," the current architecture of the Internet. The combined set of protocols is now commonly called *TCP/IP*.

Initially, use of the Internet was limited to universities and research institutions; then the military became a big user. Eventually, the government decided to allow access to the Internet for commercial purposes. Initially there was resentment among the research and military communities—it was felt that response times would become poor as "the net" became saturated with so many users.

In fact, the exact opposite has occurred. Businesses rapidly realized that, by making effective use of the Internet they could tune their operations and offer new and better services to their clients, so they started spending vast amounts of money to develop and enhance the Internet. This generated fierce competition among the communications carriers and hardware and software suppliers to meet this demand. The result is that *bandwidth* (i.e., the information carrying capacity of communications lines) on the Internet has increased tremendously and costs have plummeted. It is widely believed that the Internet has played a significant role in the economic prosperity that the United States and many other industrialized nations have enjoyed over the last decade and are likely to continue enjoying for many years.

1.3 History of the World Wide Web

The *World Wide Web* allows computer users to locate and view multimedia-based documents (i.e., documents with text, graphics, animations, audios and/or videos) on almost any subject. Even though the Internet was developed more than three decades ago, the introduction of the *World Wide Web* was a relatively recent event. In 1990, *Tim Berners-Lee* of CERN (the European Laboratory for Particle Physics) developed the World Wide Web and several communication protocols that form the backbone of the World Wide Web.

The Internet and the World Wide Web will surely be listed among the most important and profound creations of humankind. In the past, most computer applications ran on *stand-alone computers*, i.e., computers that were not connected to one another. Today's applications can be written to communicate among the world's hundreds of millions of computers. The Internet mixes computing and communications technologies. It makes our work easier.

It makes information instantly and conveniently accessible worldwide. It makes it possible for individuals and small businesses to get worldwide exposure. It is changing the nature of the way business is done.

1.4 Internet and World Wide Web Development

Computer use is increasing in almost every field of endeavor. In an era of steadily rising costs, computing costs have decreased dramatically because of the rapid developments in both hardware and software technology. Computers that might have filled large rooms and cost millions of dollars just two decades ago can now be inscribed on the surfaces of silicon chips smaller than a fingernail, costing perhaps a few dollars each. Ironically, silicon is one of the most abundant materials on earth—it is an ingredient in common sand. Silicon-chip technology has made computing so economical that hundreds of millions of general-purpose computers are in use worldwide, helping people in business, industry, government and in their personal lives. That number could easily double in a few years.

Advances in hardware and software have led to the explosion of the Internet and World Wide Web. Propelling the wave of innovation is a constant demand for new and improved technology. People want to transmit pictures and they want those pictures to be in color. They want to transmit voices, sounds and audio clips. They want to transmit full-motion color video. And at some point, they will insist on three-dimensional, moving-image transmission. Our current flat, two-dimensional televisions will eventually be replaced with three-dimensional versions that turn our living rooms into "theaters-in-the-round" or sports stadiums. Our business offices will enable 3D video conferencing among colleagues half a world apart as if they were sitting around one conference table. Consumers who want to buy products from electronic storefronts will be able to see perfect 3D images of these products beforehand. The possibilities are intriguing and the Internet is sure to play a key role in making many of these possibilities become reality.

There have been predictions that the Internet will eventually replace the telephone system. Why stop there? It could also replace radio and television as we know them today. It is not hard to imagine the Internet and the World Wide Web replacing newspapers with completely electronic news media. Many newspapers and magazines already offer Web-based versions, some fee based and some free. Over 95 percent of printed material is currently not online, but in the future it may be. The e-book, an electronic text that is encryption-protected by the publisher, is on the rise and could well supplant the paper book. With a chemistry e-book, students could watch animations of chemical reactions, and a history e-book could be updated to include current events. Increased bandwidth is making it possible to stream good quality audio and video over the Web. Companies and even individuals already run their own Web-based radio and television stations. Just a few decades ago, there were only a few television stations. In a few more years, we will have access to thousands of stations broadcasting over the Web worldwide. This textbook you are reading may someday appear in a museum alongside radios, TVs and newspapers in an "early media of ancient civilization" exhibit.

1.5 e-Business and e-Commerce Overview

We have recently entered the *Age of Knowledge*. Often you might hear the phrases, "knowledge is power" and "content is king" when discussing business on the Internet. Events in the short course of e-business and e-commerce history have demonstrated that successful e-businesses are those that recognize the needs of their target audienceS and match those needs with relevant content. Building an e-business to accomplish this is not limited to seasoned professionals—many successful online ventures have been started by students on college campuses (see the `Campusfood.com` feature).

The terms e-business and e-commerce, often confused with one another, are different. According to Andrew Bartel, vice president and research leader of e-commerce trends at Giga Information Group, Inc., *e-commerce* involves exchanges among customers, business partners and the vendor. For example, a supplier interacts with a manufacturer, customers interact with sales representatives and shipment providers interact with distributors. *E-business* is composed of these same elements, but also includes operations that are handled within the business itself. For example, production, development, corporate infrastructure and product management.[3]

E-business and e-commerce have increased the speed and ease of business transactions and, as a result, competition is intense. Businesses must adjust constantly to new technologies, integrate newer and faster systems and meet the needs of people around the world. Inventories are no longer kept in preparation for orders; rather, products are prepared specifically for consumers. Good employees are hard to find and even harder to keep. Competing entities must now collaborate to survive, and must realize that customers do not have far to go to buy from the next available vendor.

Campusfood.com: Meeting the Needs of the College Campus[5,5]

Originally launched to serve the students at the University of Pennsylvania, `Campusfood.com` now serves students from approximately 150 universities and colleges around the United States (Fig. 1.2). The site provides interactive menus to local eating establishments, allowing students to place orders over the Internet. Students receive discounts on local restaurants, and can easily find restaurant contact information including hours of operation, locations and phone numbers. Digitally transmitted orders also reduce mistakes, benefitting both restaurants and students.

Founder Michael Saunders began developing the site while a junior at the University of Pennsylvania. With the help of some classmates, the site was launched in 1998. Almost immediately after graduation, the `Campusfood.com` team began visiting universities on the East coast in an effort to build their customer base. This involved registering schools, attracting students and generating a list of the local restaurants from which the students could order food to be delivered. Currently, this activity is outsourced to a marketing firm and schools nationwide are being added to the list.

Financed through private investors, friends and family members, the site was built on an investment of less than one million dollars. Another company, with services also reaching the college-student market, has investments totaling upwards of $100 million. Revenue is generated through transaction fees; the site takes a 5 percent commission on each order.

Still under development is an electronic payment system that will work like a debit account on a student's meal plan. Students can browse registered schools and order online by visiting **www.campusfood.com**.

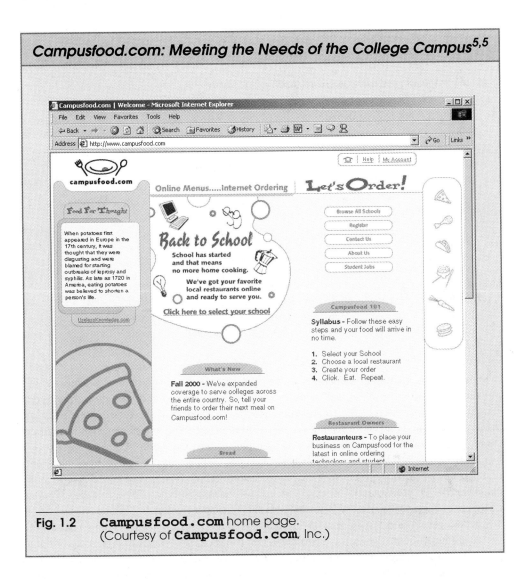

Campusfood.com: Meeting the Needs of the College Campus[5,5]

Fig. 1.2   Campusfood.com home page.
(Courtesy of **Campusfood.com**, Inc.)

As more people begin using the Web, all companies, whether they are currently established online or planning to conduct some of their business transactions online, must consider the impact that Web-enabled business will have on them. Women, the elderly and people with modest incomes are appearing online.[6] Figure 1.3, further demonstrates the growth of e-business and e-commerce. For a look at the Internet, its history and its population, visit the Web site: **www.gccgroup.com/internet/facts1.htm**.

Setting up and running an e-business, especially one that processes a large number of transactions, requires technical, marketing and advertising expertise. Customers want access to products and services on a 24-by-7 basis (24 hours-per-day, 7 days-per-week) and the easiest way to provide that is to move operations online. The businesses that provide the most reliable, most functional, most user-friendly and fastest services will be the ones that succeed.

Before	After
In 1999, 54.5 million users were ages 19-49.	By 2005, users between the ages of 19-49 are expected to number 84.0 million.
Users over the age of 50 numbered 17.3 million in 1996.	Jupiter Research estimates 49.6 million Internet users will by over the age of 50 in 2005.
By the end of 1999, 45.4 million households were online.	More than 80.2 million households will be online by 2005.
In 1999, teenagers spent $129 million online.	By 2002, research estimates that teenagers will spend approximately $1.2 billion online.

Fig. 1.3   Growth on the Internet. (Courtesy of Jupiter Research, Spring 2000.)

Banks are moving all their operations online, as it becomes clear that the Web, unconstrained by geographic boundaries, is a more efficient vehicle for their services and allows them to operate on a truly global scale. Real-time trading in foreign markets has been made possible, as has instantaneous currency conversion. Soon, global data on financial activity will be available online in real time and global transactions through the Internet will become the norm.

People can pay their bills, write and cash checks, trade stocks, take out loans, mortgage their homes and manage their assets online. Money as we know it may cease to exist, replaced by more convenient technologies such as smart cards and digital cash. Intelligent programs will take care of the financial and logistical aspects of the interactions between the individuals and corporations that populate the Internet. All that a person will need to go shopping is a connection, a computer and a digital form of payment.

Traditional "brick and mortar" stores are already being supplemented by a multitude of electronic storefronts populating the World Wide Web. No single brick-and-mortar store can offer 50,000 products, but an online store has the capability to offer a limitless number of them. Services exist that will comparison shop for consumers, finding the best deal on any product or service. An increasing amount of consumer information is being made available, leading to better deals for customers. For instance, Web sites that post car invoice prices have made it possible for auto buyers to circumvent the sticker price. Internet shopping is already beginning to eclipse more traditional modes, according to research done during the Christmas season of 1999, which found higher satisfaction rates for shopping online than it did for shopping at brick-and-mortar stores or through catalogs.

In addition to business-to-consumer operations such as electronic stores and business-to-business marketplaces, services are also taking their place on the Internet. A business that orders products from a supplier online not only completes the transaction with greater speed and convenience compared to its offline counterpart, but also can keep track of the shipments. Business-to-business Web sites are also channels that permit close cooperation between different businesses as well as the outsourcing services that are, and will continue to be, so crucial to the Internet economy.

The transition from *brick-and-mortar* businesses (businesses that have only a physical presence) to *click-and-mortar* businesses (businesses that have both an online and an offline presence) is happening in all sectors of the economy. It is now possible for a business to operate effectively without an office, because the employees can conduct all communications via phone, voice mail, fax, e-mail and the emerging capabilities of the Internet. There are already Internet services that integrate phone, fax, voice and e-mail, and in the future, new technologies will further facilitate the *virtual office*. Some businesses have already divested themselves of all their bricks-and-mortar and gone completely online. Despite the shift online, the brick-and-mortar segments of many businesses will not become obsolete. They will still have their uses and purposes, but to work effectively, they must be integrated with their online counterparts, as the Internet economy requires integration to facilitate the transfer of information.

Many e-businesses can personalize users' browsing experiences, tailoring Web pages to their users' individual preferences and letting users bypass irrelevant content. This is done by tracking the consumer's movement through the Internet and combining that data with information provided by the consumer, which could include billing information, interests and hobbies, among other things. *Personalization* is making it easier and more pleasant for many people to surf the Internet and find what they want.

Hand in hand with the promise of personalization, however, comes the problem of *privacy invasion*. What if the e-business to which you give your personal data sells or gives that data to another organization without your knowledge? What if you do not want your movements on the Internet to be tracked by unknown parties? What if an unauthorized party gains access to your private data, such as credit-card numbers, medical history or even criminal history? These are some of the many questions that must be addressed by consumers, e-businesses and lawmakers alike.

Personalization is just the tip of the privacy iceberg, as there are many other ways that privacy can be compromised on the Internet. However, there are many organizations and companies that crusade for privacy and provide privacy software. *Pretty Good Privacy (PGP)*, an encryption program written in 1991, was so strong that the U.S. government could not crack it.

The unprecedented information-transfer capabilities, unregulated nature, and breakneck growth of the Internet have fostered rampant copyright infringement and piracy of intellectual property. Innovative new technologies such as MP3 have been used in an illicit manner to transfer music over the Internet—touching off litigation by the recording industry against companies whose technologies can be used to facilitate the transfer of illegal copies of recordings. Electronic piracy of books and printed material is also common, yet it does not seem to concern the publishing industry as much, as sales of paper books have not yet been noticeably affected. The demand for the security of intellectual property is helping drive the development of new technologies including digital signatures, digital certificates and digital steganography. These technologies, which are constantly advancing to higher degrees of security, are becoming standard for online transactions and communications.

e-Fact 1.2

According to Jupiter Communications, just over one-third of Internet shoppers in 1999 were making a purchase online for the first time.[7]

People with disabilities form one of the largest online communities, as the Internet and Web have enabled them to take advantage of computing and communication technologies. Things that were once difficult for people with disabilities, such as buying goods at a store, are made easier by e-commerce technologies. However, at the time of this writing, 95 to 99 percent of all Web sites are still inaccessible to people with visual, hearing or mobility impairments. In this regard, the World Wide Web Consortium (W3C) is pursuing its *Web Accessibility Initiative* (information about the Web Accessibility Initiative is available at **www.w3.org/WAI**). [Every Deitel book now has an accessibility chapter.]

To enable people with disabilities to author their own Web sites, the WAI is instituting the *ATAG (Authoring Tools Accessibility Guidelines)*, which contains specifications for software developers to follow. The goal of the WAI is to transform the Web into a medium which all people are able to access.

1.6 A Word of Caution

Despite the rapid growth and stories of success, we must advise caution. We firmly believe that e-business and e-commerce are unstoppable trends that will bring success to a great many businesses. But poor management, ineffective marketing, ill-designed logistics, un-realistic expectations, intense competition and sheer greed in a "Gold-Rush" frenzy have caused many e-business failures.

e-Fact 1.3

During a shakeout period in Fall, 2000, in which a great many e-businesses failed, it is particularly interesting that **domcomfailures.com**—*a business that keeps track of e-business failures—failed.*[8]

Financing presents one of the biggest challenges to growing e-businesses. Despite the turmoil generated by the initial scramble to go public, many Internet start-ups are small organizations (fewer than 15 percent have 50 or more employees) struggling to get off the ground. According to studies conducted by *The Industry Standard*, just under half of Internet start-ups have not acquired their first round of financing, and less than 10 percent have gone to their third round. In fact, *The Industry Standard* found that of the 2.5 million e-business entrepreneurs only 600 went public—and this is over the course of 6 years (1994-2000).[9]

e-Fact 1.4

In the year 2000, it was widely reported that there were approximately seven billion people in the world and one billion Web pages.[10]

It is imperative to fully understand the challenges and opportunities inherent in building e-businesses. The relatively low cost of entry and access to turnkey solutions—some of which are free—allow anyone to build an e-business, but to build an **Amazon.com** (or many of the other significant e-businesses we review in this book), much of that energy must be devoted to laying the groundwork—building the business plan. A solid business plan is essential, so much so that in Silicon Valley a landlord might request to read it before agreeing to rent office space.[11] We discuss business plans, finding funding, turnkey solutions and other important topics throughout this book.

1.7 Tour of the Book

In this section, we take a tour of the material you will study in *e-Business and e-Commerce for Managers*. All of the chapters end with an Internet and World Wide Web Resources section that provides a listing of Web sites you should visit to enhance your knowledge of e-business and e-commerce. Many chapters also include a recommended readings section. Also, you may want to visit our Web sites (**www.deitel.com** and **prenhall.com/deitel**) to stay informed of the latest information, corrections and additional resources.

Chapter 1—Introduction and Tour of the Book

In this chapter, we introduce the Internet and the World Wide Web and the profound implications they are having on the business world. A brief introduction to the history of the Internet and the World Wide Web is included. Also, we discuss how e-business and e-commerce enhance and replace our traditional methods of conducting business transactions. An exploration of challenges and opportunities presented to the aspiring e-business is also included.

Chapter 2—e-Business Models

The Internet, and especially the Web, are causing profound rethinking and restructuring of the way in which the world's business is conducted. Every major organization and most smaller groups are working hard to incorporate Internet and Web technology into existing systems and new information systems designs. In this chapter, we discuss the fundamentals of conducting business on the Internet and the Web. We present a number of case studies, with the key goal of highlighting the common core of technologies needed to implement e-business systems. We emphasize the importance of Internet and Web technology, database technology, security technology and others. The Internet and the Web "level the playing field" making it possible even for small companies to establish a business presence in worldwide markets quickly, something that was extraordinarily difficult to do just a few years ago.

Chapter 3—Building an e-Business: Design, Development and Management

Building an e-business requires more than setting up an electronic storefront and waiting for customers to arrive. There are many steps along the way, and you must weigh the benefits against the potential risks. An aspiring e-business owner must be prepared for the responsibilities that building an e-business entails. In this chapter, we discuss turnkey solutions, shipping and fulfillment options, Web-site monitoring and maintenance services and end-to-end e-business solutions. We discuss generating e-business ideas, writing a business plan and finding financing. Choosing a domain name, preparing for new technologies and selecting a Web-site host are also discussed. Examples, demonstrations, online tours and helpful links are included to enhance the learning experience.

Chapter 4—Online Monetary Transactions

Chapter 4 describes the techniques and technologies used to process online payments. Some of them, such as e-wallets, bill paying and online banking are Internet extensions of conventional methods of payment. New paradigms for financial transactions are also emerging in the form of smart cards, digital cash and micropayments. Many, if not all, of these payment models will be important to e-business in the future, especially since some of them are in a position to supplant traditional payment mechanisms. Some companies focus on specific aspects of online monetary transactions, and others, such as CyberCash, function as comprehensive platforms for electronic payment. Each approach to handling money online has its own advantages and disadvantages, as well as uses for which it is particularly well-suited. Case studies on leaders in online financial services are presented. Trends toward standards for online payment processing are also examined.

Chapter 5—Internet Hardware, Software and Communications

Often e-business owners have a limited understanding of the technologies and equipment needed to implement successful e-businesses. Chapter 5 offers an introduction to the communications media and hardware used to connect computers to the Internet, as well as a brief introduction to how the Internet works. We discuss connection media (dial-ups, DSL and cable), their costs and connection speeds. Enhancing business communication, also important to business owners, is also discussed in Chapter 5. Topics include intranets and extranets, streaming audio and video, Internet telephone and Web-conferencing. A discussion on application service providers (ASPs), a Web-enabled substitution for software development and implementation, is included, as well as an overview of the most popular operating systems, Microsoft Windows, MacIntosh, Unix and Linux.

Chapter 6—Wireless Internet and m-Business

The hottest topic in e-business and e-commerce is wireless technology. Often referred to as m-Business, mobile business allows anyone, anywhere, at any time to conduct online transactions, make purchases and send e-mail. Business owners can manage their responsibilities while they are away from the office and, in the future, employees and other interested individuals can enhance their skills by taking Web-based courses anytime, anywhere, even while on the train to work. The advantages and limitations of this promising new technology are discussed in Chapter 6. We discuss how wireless technology is currently used and some of the applications we will see in the near future. We also introduce the Wireless Application Protocol (WAP) which is the standard for the wireless industry. We discuss Wireless Mark-up Language (WML). Bluetooth™ technology, which is used in limited areas such as within homes or offices, is presented in the chapter. Bluetooth-enabled devices could lead to completely wireless offices, eliminating even the wire that connects your mouse to your computer. We also discuss the GPS-based wireless location industry.

Chapter 7—Internet Security

To have a successful online business, it is essential to protect consumer information and ensure secure transactions. This requires authentication of the parties involved, verification of the information's integrity, privacy of the information and proof that the information was sent and properly received. Chapter 7 examines security systems and technologies—including Public Key Cryptography, SSL, SET, digital signatures, digital certificates, digital steganography and the cutting-edge technology of biometrics—used to meet these requirements. Other network security topics, such as firewalls and antivirus programs are also covered in detail, and common security threats such as cryptanalytic attacks, DoS attacks, viruses, worms and Trojan Horses are discussed. Security breaches and network attacks can cause immense damage, loss of productivity and loss of credibility to the affected individuals or organizations, making it essential for e-businesses to protect their customers and for customers to protect their own interests.

Chapter 8—Internet Marketing

An effective marketing strategy is important to the success of a business. Chapter 8 discusses branding and the different online methods that can improve brand awareness and recognition. A discussion of various Internet marketing research methods including online surveys, focus groups and industry research and the advantages and disadvantages of each are included. Various online advertising methods are covered, including a section on cross-media advertising which emphasizes the collaboration of both online and offline media. Chapter 8 also examines online public relations, including creating and delivering online press releases, using e-mail to communicate with consumers, building customer trust and managing crisis situations. To increase traffic to a site, we review search engine ranking, and the use of META tags to increase the likelihood of appearing high on the search engine result lists. We examine methods of promotion and using direct e-mail marketing to target customers. Business-to-business marketing and its differences from business-to-consumer marketing are also included.

Chapter 9—Affiliate Programs

Generating traffic to a site is critical to the success of an e-business. Chapter 9 reviews the various affiliate and partnering models and how they work. Program models include pay-per-click, pay-per-sale, pay-per-lead, multi-tiered and hybrid. We discuss the advantages and disadvantages of each model to assist e-business owners in choosing a program that is right for them. We highlight examples of successful affiliate programs and explain how to create and build your own. Monitoring the success of your affiliate program and maintaining a high level of Web-site "stickiness" is discussed, as well as program taxation issues. This chapter also provides extensive coverage of leading affiliate solution providers.

Chapter 10—e-Customer Relationship Management

Integrating the Internet into your customer relationship management system is important to establish lasting relationships and is crucial to an e-business's success. This chapter discusses the necessity of good online customer service. Topics include personalization, visitor tracking, call centers, online text chatting and other related services that can help your e-business gain a competitive advantage through effective customer service. Sales-force automation and full-service e-CRM solutions are also discussed. We examine developing technologies that will continue to enhance customer relationship management. Topics include speech synthesis, speech recognition and natural language processing. Links to demonstrations of these technologies are included to supplement the reader's understanding. The sections include company features and URLs to direct students to applicable Web sites to try online customer relationship management techniques.

Chapter 11—Legal and Ethical Issues; Internet Taxation

The explosive growth of the Internet, the increasing access that it provides to all types of information and its nature as a largely unregulated medium have raised many legal and ethical issues. What happens when things that can be found and bought on the Internet are legal in one region or country and illegal in another? Where should the line be drawn between personalization and consumer privacy? Chapter 11 takes an in-depth look at the ways in which the Internet challenges traditional law and includes many relevant cases and their outcomes. We introduce the privacy side of the privacy vs. personalization debate. Real-world examples of this conflict are included. We discuss issues regarding defamation, trademark infringement, pornography, obscenity and patents. Copyright infringement, involving publishers and the entertainment industry and companies such as **MP3.com** and Napster are also discussed. With e-business and e-commerce undergoing explosive growth, taxation of goods and services provided via the Internet has also become a complex dilemma. While most Internet purchases are not taxed, many states and countries argue for a standard taxation method to protect the funding of social programs, such as education. We provide an overview of the opposing views and the complications that arise when Internet sales are taxed.

Chapter 12—Globalization

The Internet enables businesses to reach an international audience more efficiently and at a lower cost than ever before; even small businesses can reach a global market. For many businesses, globalization is crucial to remaining competitive in their market niche. Chapter

12 addresses many of the issues facing businesses that are considering worldwide marketing of their products and services.

We discuss what international markets are most lucrative, how to make your Web site available in multiple languages and how to address international shipping and taxation. Operating your e-business according to the often conflicting legal parameters of different nations is also addressed. In addition, we offer a brief overview of various world regions, their current Internet use, estimates of their future Internet use and how e-business and e-commerce is regarded among their populations.

Chapter 13—Social Issues

The Internet has profound implications on social issues. In this chapter, we examine the "digital divide" and how to accommodate people who do not have the economic means to connect to the Internet and use its services. We explore how businesses, communities and the government are working to bring the Internet into the schools, as well as considering the advantages and disadvantages of electronic education. This issue is also addressed in Chapter 17, e-Learning. Our system of government in the United States and our means of collaborating on issues that are important to us also reflect the influence of the Internet. Chapter 13 examines what changes have already occurred and what might be possible in the future. For example, our means of researching issues, our voting system and our ability to express our opinions have all been affected by the Internet. We also explore online communities and activist groups, and examine how the Web is enabling them to organize and focus their efforts.

Chapter 14—Web Accessibility

Currently, the World Wide Web presents serious challenges to people with disabilities. Multimedia-rich Web sites often present difficulty to text readers and other programs designed to help people with visual disabilities. The increasing amount of audio on the Web is inaccessible to people with auditory disabilities. To resolve this situation, the World Wide Web Consortium (W3C) created the Web Accessibility Initiative (WAI), which provides guidelines on how to make Web sites accessible to people with disabilities. We provide an overview of the laws already in place and how they affect business on the Web. We also address many of the methods used to meet these requirements, such as voice recognition software. We walk through the setup for the Windows 2000 accessibility tools and examine accessibility features of Internet Explorer. Two of the most popular text readers, Microsoft Narrator and Henter-Joyce JAWS, are discussed as well.

Chapter 15—Online Industries

In Chapter 2, e-Business Models, we discussed the options an entrepreneur has when designing an online business. In this chapter, we explore various industries, providing examples of how some businesses have already modified themselves to take advantage of this new medium. Industries discussed include travel, medicine, law, energy, transportation and consulting. The chapter explains how to use the Web effectively to improve business practices and grow into new areas. Scores of URLs, online demonstrations and tutorials supplement the text.

Chapter 16—Online Banking and Investing

Online banking and investing are two of the most popular online industries. Online bankers can pay bills, check account history and make transfers over the Internet. The benefit of online banking is convenience, as customers have access to their account information from anywhere at anytime. The advantages and disadvantages of Internet-only and clicks-and-mortar banks are discussed in detail and supported with case studies. Chapter 16 also explains how the Web is changing the lending, trading and financial planning industries by covering important topics such as the aggregation of financial services, electronic communication networks (ECNs) and wireless banking and trading. Links to demonstrations and tutorials direct students to the Web to participate in trading games and to learn more about managing their money. The chapter also advises caution and includes a brief discussion about the risks of trading and investing online.

Chapter 17—e-Learning

Online learning is one of the fastest growing industries on the Web. It provides a means for businesses to increase the "stickiness" of their Web sites, corporations to reduce the cost of training their employees and individuals to advance their learning according to their own schedules. It also helps elementary, high-school and college students find tutors, and hosts online portals for buying and selling school supplies. We explore various education models available on the Internet, including traditional education, elementary and secondary education, information technology (IT), personal interest and corporate training. We also discuss the social implications of obtaining an education online, such as reduced human-to-human interaction and the effects of the digital divide (people who do not have the economic means to connect to the Internet and use its services vs. people who can afford the equipment and connection services). Links to demonstrations and tutorials allow students to sample online courses and explore tutorial services.

Chapter 18—e-Publishing

Electronic publishing is just beginning to emerge as a new medium for content creators. Technologies such as the electronic book readers, and XrML—a copyright protection technology—are discussed in detail. Many authors do not have the technical expertise to self-publish their material; this chapter presents electronic publishing opportunities available to these writers. These opportunities include self-publishing, subsidy e-publishing, and print-on-demand. Many content creators have used the Web to start special interest magazines or e-Zines that are distributed through e-mail. We discuss e-zines in detail and give examples of some of the popular electronic publications. Online content providers are also taking advantage of the Web as a means to distribute news. *The Wall Street Journal* and **CNN.com** are among those with a Web presence. Chapter 18 overviews the current state of electronic publishing and offers some interesting predictions.

Chapter 19—Online Entertainment

The Web is dramatically changing the entertainment industry. Creators, directors and producers can get their start on the Internet. This chapter outlines the effect the Internet and World Wide Web had on the entertainment industry, and explores the future possibilities. We discuss each major entertainment genre including film, music, sports, radio and television, and how it is responding to recent developments in technology. Case studies are presented in each section. The chapter also discusses how Web sites have used the Internet to improve entertainment as we currently know it. Streaming media, copyright issues, distribution, convergence and the future of technologies likely to be used in the entertainment industry are among the many topics covered.

Chapter 20—Online Career Services

For the job seeker and the employer, the Internet presents valuable resources and services. Automatic searching features allow both employees and employers to search the Web for open positions and job candidates according to specific requirements. This greatly reduces the amount of time spent preparing and reviewing resumes, as well as travel expenses for distance recruiting and interviewing. In this chapter, we explore career services on the Web from both the job seeker's and the employer's perspectives. We introduce comprehensive job sites, industry-specific sites and contracting opportunities, as well as additional resources and career services designed to meet the needs of specific demographics.

Appendix A: Microsoft Internet Explorer 5.5

This appendix is a walkthrough of Microsoft's Internet Explorer 5.5 browser. It will help students become familiar with the features of IE5.5 including browsing the Web, using Outlook Express to send and receive e-mail and using NetMeeting to have online conferences. We recommend students read this appendix immediately after reading Chapter 1 of *e-Business and e-Commerce for Managers.*

Appendices—B through H; Building an e-Business: Introduction to Web Programming

Appendices B through H carefully walk the reader through the design and implementation of an online e-business that sells books. This case study has been carefully designed for students with little or no programming experience. This unique case-study introduces students to real e-business programming technologies such as HyperText Markup Language (HTML), JavaScript, Active Server Pages (ASP), Extensible Markup Language (XML), Extensible Stylesheet Language (XSL), VBScript, ActiveX Data Objects (ADO), Structured Query Language (SQL) and Microsoft Access databases. Students are also introduced to real e-business implementations such as shopping carts, database access and validation. The case study walks the student through the three "tiers" of a typical e-business implementation: the client, the server and business processes and the database.

Appendix B—Building an e-Business: Introduction to Internet and Web Programming

Appendix B presents the problem statement and overviews the case study. The reader is carefully guided through the case study using a series of screen images that clearly illustrate the interactions between the user and the online bookstore. We present a table that summarizes the various Web technologies used in the case study. Each technology and its role in the case study is explained.

Web-based applications, such as the online bookstore, involve many interacting documents. Non-programmers often have a difficult time visualizing how the documents relate. To help the student, we provide two key illustrations that show how all the documents we present in the case study interact with one another and a high-level diagram that illustrates the relationship between the three tiers (i.e., client, server/business processes and database) of a Web-based application.

Appendix C—Introduction to HTML 4

Appendix C is the first of two appendices that begin unlocking the power of the Web by introducing HTML (Hypertext Markup Language). The material presented here is derived from the extensive treatment in our Internet and Web Programming book *e-Business & e-Commerce How to Program.* HTML is a markup language for identifying the elements of an HTML document (Web page) so that a browser, such as Microsoft's Internet Explorer can render (i.e., display) that page on your computer screen. We introduce the basics of creating Web pages in HTML using a technique we call the live-code™ approach. Every concept is presented in the context of a complete working HTML document (or Web page) that is immediately followed by the screen output produced when that HTML document is rendered by Internet Explorer 5. We write many simple Web pages. The next appendix introduces more sophisticated HTML techniques, such as tables, which are particularly useful for presenting and manipulating information from databases.

Appendix D—Intermediate HTML 4
In Appendix D, we provide a deeper discussion of HTML through the intermediate level. The material presented is also derived from our book *e-Business & e-Commerce How to Program*. In this appendix, we demonstrate how to format information in lists and tables. We discuss how to collect information from users browsing a Web site. We explain how to use internal linking and image maps to make Web pages easier to navigate. By the end of this chapter, the student will be familiar with most commonly used HTML tags and features and will be able to create more interesting and visually appealing Web sites.

Appendix E—Introduction to HTML, JavaScript, XML, XSL and ASP Syntax
This appendix overviews the technologies used in the case study. The student is carefully introduced to each technology using illustrations and short code segments. For example, we illustrate a button and provide a side-by-side listing of the HTML that creates the button. This appendix gives the students the opportunity to become familiar with the technologies at the programmatic level in a controlled manner. Key lines of code from the case study are presented for each technology. In Appendices F through H, we present the entire code for our bookstore e-business and provide a clear discussion of it.

Appendix F—Top Tier: The Client
Appendix F is the first of three appendices that walk the reader through the program files that comprise this case study. This appendix introduces the graphical user interface that our bookstore e-business presents to the client. In a three-tier, Web-based application, the user interface tier or top tier is called the client. For our application, Internet Explorer 5 is the client. Technologies, such as HTML, are top-tier technologies because they are used by the client. We introduce and discuss the majority of the HTML files used by the case study in this appendix. XML and XSL, which can be used on the top tier, are also discussed.

Appendix G—Middle Tier: The Server and Business Processes
Appendix G introduces the student to the middle tier, also called the server, where the business logic resides. The middle tier is often the most complex tier. In this appendix, we carefully introduce the reader to Microsoft Active Server Pages (ASP) which handle requests from the top tier and interacts with the bottom tier (i.e., the database). We implement our Active Server Pages using VBScript—the most popular scripting language for ASP. We interact with the database using ActiveX Data Objects (ADO) and the universal Structured Query Language (SQL).

Appendix H—Bottom Tier: The Database
In this appendix, we introduce the bottom tier—the database—which provides long-term storage of data. The bottom tier is the foundation of an e-business. We discuss the specific database used in the case study and introduce the student to fundamental database concepts.

Appendix I—Accessibility Programming

Currently, the World Wide Web presents challenges to people with disabilities. Multimedia-rich Web sites present difficulties to text readers and other programs designed to help people with vision impairments, and the increasing amount of audio on the Web is inaccessible people who are deaf. The World Wide Web Consortium's Web Accessibility Initiative (WAI) provides guidelines on how to make the Web accessible to people with disabilities. This appendix builds upon programming concepts introduced earlier by illustrating how HTML documents can be modified for accessibility. An example of VoiceXML, which can be used to increase accessibility with speech synthesis and speech recognition, is also provided. We examine a VoiceXML Web home page and how it generates a speech dialog with the user. The chapter concludes with an extensive list of accessibility Web resources.

Appendix J—Setup Instructions [Web site]

Appendix I, which is available at **www.deitel.com** (at the "Download/Resource" page) presents step-by-step setup and installation instructions for the online bookstore case study.

Appendix K—Registering an ODBC System Data Source Name (DSN) [Web site]

Appendix K, which is available at **www.deitel.com**, provides step-by-step instructions for setting up the bottom tier for the online bookstore case study.

Well—there you have it. We have worked hard to create what we hope will be an interesting, challenging and rewarding experience for you. The future is now! As you read the book please check our Web sites for regular updates, errata and additional learning resources. Please send your comments, criticisms, suggestions and questions to the authors at **deitel@deitel.net**. We look forward to hearing from you and will respond promptly.

1.8 Internet and World Wide Web Resources

www.deitel.com

Please check this site for daily updates, corrections and additional resources for all Deitel & Associates, Inc. publications.

www.learnthenet.com/english/index.html

Learn the Net is a Web site containing a complete overview of the Internet, the World Wide Web and the underlying technologies. The site contains information that can help Internet and Web novices get started.

www.w3.org

The W3C home page is a comprehensive description of the Web and where it is headed. The World Wide Web Consortium is an international joint effort with the goal of overseeing the development of the World Wide Web. The goals of the W3C are divided into categories: User Interface Domain, Technology and Society Domain, Architecture Domain and Web Accessibility Initiatives. For each Internet technology with which the W3C is involved, the site provides a description of the technology and its benefits to Web designers, the history of the technology and the future goals of the W3C in developing the technology. Topics discussed on the site include Hypertext Markup Language (HTML), Cascading Style Sheets (CSS), Document Object Model (DOM), multimedia, graphics, Hypertext Transfer Protocol (HTTP), Extensible Markup Language (XML) and Extensible Stylesheet Language (XSL). This site is of great benefit for understanding the standards of the World Wide Web. Each of these topics is discussed (at various levels of depth) in this book.

www.gccgroup.com/internet/facts1.htm

This site provides an overview of the Internet and its population.

SUMMARY

- ARPAnet, is the predecessor to the modern Internet.

- The Internet and electronic mail (e-mail) allow for instant worldwide communication.

- Statistics suggest that e-mail usage is now ten times greater than postal mail.[2]

- Early networks operated using packet switching in which digital data was sent in small packages called packets. The packets contained data, address information, error-control information and sequencing information. The address information was used to route the packets of data to their destinations, and the sequencing information was used to help reassemble the packets (which, because of complex routing mechanisms could actually arrive out of order) into their original order for presentation to the recipient.

- The Internet is designed to operate without centralized control. This means that if a portion of the Internet should fail, the remaining working portions are still be able to route packets from senders to receivers over alternate paths.

- The protocols for communicating over the ARPAnet became known as TCP—the Transmission Control Protocol. TCP ensures that messages are properly routed from sender to receiver and that those messages arrives intact.

- The Internetworking Protocol (IP) creates a "network of networks. The combined set of protocols is now commonly called TCP/IP.

- Initially, use of the Internet was limited to universities and research institutions; then the military became a big user. Eventually, the government decided to allow access to the Internet for commercial purposes.

- When the Internet was made available to commercial interests, businesses quickly realized that they needed faster more reliable connections to operate effectively. As a result, bandwidth (i.e., the information carrying capacity of communications lines) on the Internet increased tremendously and with competition, costs plummeted.

- In 1990, Tim Berners-Lee of CERN (the European Laboratory for Particle Physics) developed the World Wide Web and several communication protocols that form the backbone of the Web.

- The World Wide Web allows computer users to locate and view multimedia-based documents (i.e., documents with text, graphics, animations, audios and/or videos) on almost any subject.

- In the past, most computer applications ran on stand-alone computers, i.e., computers that were not connected to one another.

- In an era of steadily rising costs, computing costs have decreased dramatically because of the rapid developments in both hardware and software technology. Computers that might have filled large rooms and cost millions of dollars just two decades ago can now be inscribed on the surfaces of silicon chips smaller than a fingernail, costing perhaps a few dollars each.

- Over 95 percent of printed material is currently not online, but in the future it may be.

- The e-book, an electronic text that is encryption-protected by the publisher, is on the rise and could well supplant the paper book.

- Increased bandwidth is making it possible to stream good quality audio and video over the Web.

- Many refer to our current state of business and technology as the Age of Knowledge.

- According to Andrew Bartel, vice president and research leader of e-commerce trends at Giga Information Group, Inc., e-commerce involves exchanges among customers, business partners and the vendor. For example, a supplier interacts with a manufacturer, customers interact with sales representatives and shipment providers interact with distributors.

- Also according to Bartal's definition, e-business is composed of e-commerce elements, but also includes operations that are handled within the business itself., for example, production, development, corporate infrastructure and product management.

- E-business and e-commerce have increased the speed and ease of business transactions and, as a result, competition is intense. Competing entities must now collaborate to survive, and must realize that customers do not have far to go to buy from the next available vendor.

- Businesses must constantly adjust to new technologies, integrate newer and faster systems and meet the needs of people around the world. Inventories are no longer kept in preparation for orders; rather, products are prepared specifically for consumers.

- In 1999, 54.5 million users were ages 19-49. By 2005, users between the ages of 19-49 are expected to number 84.0 million.

- By the end of 1999, 45.4 million households were online. More than 80.2 million households will be online by 2005.

- The businesses that provide the most reliable, functional, user-friendly and fastest services will be the ones that succeed. Customers want access to products and services on a 24-by-7 basis (24 hours-per-day, 7 days-per-week) and the easiest way to provide that is to move operations online.

- Banks are moving all their operations online, as it becomes clear that the Web, unconstrained by geographic boundaries, is a more efficient vehicle for their services. The Web also enables banks to operate on a truly global scale.

- People can pay their bills, write and cash checks, trade stocks, take out loans, mortgage their homes and manage their assets online. Money as we know it may cease to exist, replaced by more convenient technologies such as smart cards and digital cash.

- Traditional "brick and mortar" stores are already being supplemented by a multitude of electronic storefronts populating the World Wide Web.

- In addition to business-to-consumer operations such as electronic stores and business-to-business marketplaces, services are also taking their place on the Internet.

- It is now possible for businesses to operate effectively without offices, because employees can conduct all communications via phone, voice mail, fax, e-mail and the Internet.

- Many e-businesses can personalize users' browsing experiences, tailoring Web pages to their users' individual preferences and letting them bypass irrelevant content. Personalization is making it easier and more pleasant for many people to surf the Internet and find what they want.

- Hand in hand with the promise of personalization comes the problem of privacy invasion.

- The unprecedented information-transfer capabilities, unregulated nature, and breakneck growth of the Internet have fostered rampant copyright infringement and piracy of intellectual property.

- At the time of this writing, 95 to 99 percent of all Web sites are inaccessible to people with visual, hearing or mobility impairments. The World Wide Web Consortium (W3C) is pursuing its Web Accessibility Initiative to improve Web accessibility for the disabled.

- Financing presents one of the biggest challenges to growing e-businesses. According to studies conducted by The Industry Standard, just under half of Internet start-ups have not acquired their first round of financing, and less than 10 percent have gone to their third round.

- In the year 2000, it was widely reported that there were approximately seven billion people in the world and one billion Web pages.

TERMINOLOGY

24-by-7   ARPA
Age of Knowledge   ARPANet

Authoring Tools Accessibility Guidelines (ATAG)
bandwidth
Berners-Lee, Tim
Bluetooth
brick-and-mortar
business plan
business-to-business (B2B)
business-to-consumer (B2C)
CERN
click-and-mortar
dedicated communications lines
digital cash
digital certificate
digital divide
digital signature
digital steganography
domain name
e-book
e-business
e-commerce
electronic mail
electronic piracy
ethical issues
European Laboratory for Particle Physics
e-wallet
globalization
HTML (Hypertext Markup Language)
HTTP protocol
Internet
Internetworking Protocol (IP)
Intranets

legal issues
micropayments
network of networks
online banking
online financial services
online payment
packet switching
packets
personalization
Pretty Good Privacy (PGP)
privacy
Project Mac
scalability
security
smart card
steganography
TCP
TCP/IP
Tim Berners-Lee
Transmission Control Protocol (TCP)
verification
virtual office
VoiceXML
Web
Web Accessibility Initiative (WAI)
Wireless Applications Protocol (WAP)
World Wide Web (WWW)
World Wide Web Consortium (W3C)
XML
XSL

SELF-REVIEW EXERCISES

1.1 State whether each of the following is true or false; if false, explain why.
  a) Initially, use of the Internet was limited to the military.
  b) In an era of steadily rising costs, computing costs have been decreasing dramatically because of the rapid developments in both hardware and software technology.
  c) People are currently able to pay their bills, write and cash checks, trade stocks, take out loans, mortgage their homes and manage their assets online.
  d) The engineers at ARPAnet have been credited with creating the World Wide Web.
  e) A business plan is a crucial part of the business-building process.

1.2 Fill in the blanks in each of the following statements.
  a) The _____ is also known as the grandparent of today's Internet.
  b) In the past, most computer applications ran on _____ computers, i.e., computers that were not connected to one another.
  c) An _____ is defined as a company that has an online presence.
  d) At the time of this writing, _____ percent of Web sites are inaccessible to people with visual, hearing or mobility impairments.
  e) The original speed of the ARPANet was _____.

ANSWERS TO SELF-REVIEW EXERCISES

1.1   a) False. Initially the Internet was used by academics and researchers. b) True. c) True. d) False. Tim Berners Lee and the W3C have been credited with creating the architecture of the World Wide Web. e) True.

1.2   a) ARPAnet. b) Stand-alone. c) e-business. d) 90 to 95.

EXERCISES

1.3   State whether each of the following is true or false; if false, explain why.
   a) Most e-businesses are owned and managed by large organizations.
   b) Poor management, ineffective marketing and ill-designed logistics have caused many dot-com failures.
   c) The Web was created two decades before the Internet.
   d) Silicon, the material used to make computer chips, is an abundant material.
   e) The Internet is designed to operate without centralized control

1.4   Fill in the blanks in each of the following statements.
   a) _____ e-commerce Web sites are channels that permit close cooperation between two or more businesses.
   b) Customers want access to products and services on a constant or _____ basis, and the easiest way to provide that is to move operations online.
   c) The chief benefit of ARPAnet proved to be the capability of quick and easy communication via _____ .
   d) The small packages containing data, address information, error control information and sequencing information transmitted across the Internet are called _____ .
   e) The World Wide Web was developed by _____ in 1990.

1.5   Define the following.
   a) e-business
   b) packet switching
   c) e-commerce
   d) ARPA's role in the development of the Internet.
   e) Pretty Good Privacy (PGP)

1.6   In this chapter, we suggest that an e-business can be created by anyone with an idea and the energy. Research recent newspapers and magazine articles to find individuals who have emerged as e-business leaders and answer the following questions:
   a) How did they get started?
   b) What challenges have they faced?
   c) What successes have they achieved?
   d) Do they offer any advice to aspiring e-business owners?

1.7   Visit **Campusfoods.com** and answer the following questions.
   a) Is the site easily navigable? Explain.
   b) How does **campusfoods.com** generate revenue?
   c) With how many restaurants is Campus Foods currently affiliated?
   d) Would you use **campusfoods.com**? Why or Why not?

1.8   In this chapter, we briefly discuss failed dot-coms. Search recent newspaper editions and magazine articles and answer the following questions:
   a) Make a list of failed or failing dot-coms. Did you find it difficult to generate a list of failed dot-coms?
   b) What were some of the reasons for failure?

      c) What would you have done differently?

      d) Given the volatility recently seen in the Internet economy, what are your predictions for the future of e-commerce?

1.9   E-business and e-commerce is a rapidly growing industry. New business models, marketing tactics and technologies are introduced almost daily. Many of the resources listed in Figure 1.1 have online editions. Use a search engine (e.g., **www.altavista.com**, **www.google.com**, **www.yahoo.com**, etc.) to find these editions. Once at these sites, prepare a list of recently introduced business models, marketing tactics and technologies. Search the archives to find answers to the following questions. Prepare a presentation.

      a) Did you find it difficult to generate this list?

      b) Which items were most interesting to you?

      c) What capabilities to these items offer?

      d) Do you think they will be successful?

      e) Suggest your own additional items.

WORKS CITED

The notation <**www.domain-name.com**> indicates that the citation is for information found at the Web site.

1. "Businesses Need to Speed if They Want to Succeed," *USA Today* 26 October 2000: 6B.

2. NetWork Commerce Advertisement," *The Wall Street Journal* 8 November 2000: C17.

3. A. Bartels, "The Difference Between E-Business and e-Commerce," *Computer World* 30 October 2000: 41.

4. <**www.campusfood.com**>

5. M. Prince, "Easy Doesn't Do It," *The Wall Street Journal* 17 July 2000: R6-R13.

6. C. Guglielmo, "E-Commerce: There to Here," *Inter@ctive Week* 15 November 1999: 106.

7. C. Guglielmo, "E-Commerce: There To Here," *Inter@ctive Week* 15 November 1999: 106.

8. "DotCom Doldrums," *Time* 16 October 2000: 133.

9. A. Hamilton, et.al., "State of the Start-Up," *The Industry Standard* 12 June 2000: 187, 191.

10. E. Zahner, "Ahoy, Internet Companies," *USA Today* 7 June 2000: 15A.

11. A. Hamilton, et.al.,"State of the Start-Up," *The Industry Standard* 12 June 2000: 187, 191.

Part 2

Constructing an e-Business

Outline

Chapter 2 e-Business Models

Chapter 3 Building an e-Business: Design, Development and Management

Chapter 4 Online Monetary Transactions

2

e-Business Models

Objectives

- To understand the different business models implemented on the Internet.
- To explore the transition from brick-and-mortar businesses to e-businesses.
- To understand the many options available to entrepreneurs online.
- To review both B2C and B2B e-business models.

The Road to the City of Emeralds is paved with yellow brick.
Lyman Frank Baum

Ye shall no more give the people straw to make brick.
The Old Testament

I can't work without a model.
Vincent Van Gogh

The propensity to truck, barter and exchange one thing for another … is common to all men, and to be found in no other race of animals.
Adam Smith

Method goes far to prevent trouble in business.
William Penn

To business that we love we rise betime,
And go to't with delight.
William Shakespeare

Outline

2.1 Introduction

2.2 Storefront Model

    2.2.1   Shopping-Cart Technology

    2.2.2   Online Shopping Malls

2.3 Auction Model

2.4 Portal Model

2.5 Dynamic-Pricing Models

    2.5.1   Name-Your-Price Model

    2.5.2   Comparison-Pricing Model

    2.5.3   Demand-Sensitive Pricing Model

    2.5.4   Bartering Model

    2.5.5   Rebates

    2.5.6   Offering Free Products and Services

2.6 B2B E-Commerce and EDI

2.7 Click-and-Mortar Businesses

2.8 Internet and World Wide Web Resources

Summary • Terminology • Self-Review Exercises • Answers to Self-Review Exercises • Exercises • Works Cited • Recommended Reading

2.1 Introduction

There are many benefits of bringing a business to the Internet. An e-business can offer personalization, high-quality customer service and improved *supply-chain management*—the strategic management of distribution channels and the processes that support them. In this chapter, we explore the different types of businesses operating on the Internet, as well as the technologies needed to build and run an e-commerce Web site.

    Amazon.com, eBay™, Yahoo! and other e-commerce sites have helped to define industry categories and business models on the Web. Entrepreneurs starting e-businesses and people interested in e-commerce should be aware of the many e-business models. In this chapter, we review the storefront model, the auction model, dynamic-pricing models, the portal model and other Web-business models. Businesses operating within a particular model can leverage their technologies to differentiate themselves from the competition.

2.2 Storefront Model

The move toward e-commerce presents many benefits, as well as a number of new considerations. The *storefront model* is what many people think of when they hear the word "e-business." The storefront model combines transaction processing, security, online payment and information storage to enable merchants to sell their products online. This model is a basic form of e-commerce in which the buyer and the seller interact directly.

e-Fact 2.1

Shopping online is an increasingly popular activity. At the close of 1999, nearly 55 million people (60 percent of Internet users) were shopping online.[1]   2.1

To conduct storefront e-commerce, merchants need to organize online catalogs of products, take orders through their Web sites, accept payments securely, send merchandise to customers and manage customer data (such as customer profiles). They must also market their sites to potential customers—a topic further explored in Chapter 8, Internet Marketing.

Although the term "e-commerce" is fairly new, large corporations have been conducting e-commerce for decades, by networking their systems with those of business partners and clients. For example, the banking industry uses *Electronic Funds Transfer* (*EFT*) to transfer money between accounts. (This system will be discussed in greater detail in Chapter 4, Online Monetary Transactions.) Many companies also use a standard communications protocol called *Electronic Data Interchange* (*EDI*), in which business forms, such as purchase orders and invoices, are standardized, so that companies can share information with customers, vendors and business partners electronically. EDI is discussed in detail in Section 2.6, B2B E-Commerce and EDI.

Until recently, e-commerce was feasible only for large companies. However, the Internet and the World Wide Web make it possible for small businesses to use EDI as well. E-commerce also allows companies to conduct business *24-by-7*—all day, everyday—on a worldwide basis.

Some of the most successful e-businesses use the storefront model. Many of the leading storefront model companies are *B2C* (business-to-consumer) companies. For example, **More.com** is a health and beauty e-commerce site that uses an electronic shopping cart to allow customers to shop, buy and arrange shipment. Its products include skin-care products, eye-care products, pharmaceuticals and many other health and wellness products.

Moviefone.com uses the Internet to improve its offline customer service. Through its Web site, customers have access to movie tickets, reviews, movie clips and trailers. Moviefone uses shopping-cart technology to offer its tickets, an advanced database system to store customer and inventory data and a strong supporting infrastructure to make its Internet operations possible.

2.2.1 Shopping-Cart Technology

One of the most commonly used e-commerce enablers is the *shopping cart*. This order-processing technology allows customers to accumulate items they wish to buy as they continue to shop. Supporting the shopping cart is a product catalog, which is hosted on the *merchant server* in the form of a *database*. The merchant server is the data storage and management system employed by the merchant. It is often a system of computers that conduct all of the functions necessary for running a Web site. A database is a part of the merchant server designed to store and report on large amounts of information. For example, a database for an online clothing retailer would typically include such product specifications as item description, size, availability, shipping information, stock level and on-order information. Databases also store customer information such as names, addresses, credit-card data and past purchases. The **Amazon.com** feature explains the these technologies and their implementation.

Amazon.com and the Storefront Model

Perhaps the most widely recognized example of an e-business that uses shopping-cart technology is **Amazon.com**.[2, 3] Founded in 1994, the company has rapidly grown to become one of the world's largest online retailers. **Amazon.com** offers millions of products to more than 17 million customers in 160 countries. **Amazon.com** also offers online auctions.

In its first few years, **Amazon.com** served as a mail-order book retailer. Its line product line has since expanded to include music, videos, DVDs, electronic cards, consumer electronics, hardware, tools, beauty items and toys. **Amazon.com**'s catalog is constantly growing and the site allows you to navigate among millions of products.

Amazon.com uses a database on the *server-side* (the merchant's computer systems) that allows customers on the *client-side* (the customer's computer, handheld device, etc.) to search for products in a variety of ways. This system is an example of a *client/server application*. The **Amazon.com** database consists of product specifications, availability, shipping information, stock levels, on-order information and other data. Book titles, authors, prices, sales histories, publishers, reviews and in-depth descriptions are also stored in the database. This extensive database makes it possible for **Amazon.com** to cross-reference products. For example, a novel may be listed under various categories, including fiction, best-sellers and recommended titles.

Amazon.com personalizes its site to service returning customers; a database keeps a record of all previous transactions, including items purchased, shipping and credit-card information. Upon returning to the site, customers are greeted by name and presented with lists of recommended titles, based on the customers' previous purchases. **Amazon.com** searches the customer database for patterns and trends among its clientele. By monitoring such customer data, the company provides personalized service that would otherwise need to be handled by sales representatives. Amazon's computer system drives sales of additional items without human interaction.

Buying a product at **Amazon.com** is simple. You begin at the **Amazon.com** home page and decide on the type of product you would like to purchase. For example, if you are looking for our book *e-Business & e-Commerce How to Program*, you can find the book by using the **Search Box** in the top-left corner of the home page. Select **Books** in the **Search Box**, then type the title of the book into the window. You will then be taken directly to the product page for the book. To purchase the item, select **Add to Shopping Cart**, on the top-right corner of the page. The shopping-cart technology processes the information and displays a list of the products you have placed in the shopping cart. You then have the option to change the quantity of each item, remove an item from the shopping cart, check out or continue shopping.

When you are ready to place your order, you proceed to checkout. As a first-time visitor, you will be prompted to fill out a personal-identification form with information including your name, billing address, shipping address, shipping preference and credit-card information. You will also be asked to enter a password that you will use to access your account data for all future transactions. Once you confirm your information, you can place your order.

Amazon.com and the Storefront Model (Cont.)

Customers returning to **Amazon.com** can use its *1-Click*[SM] *system*, which allows the customer to reuse previously entered payment and shipping information to place an order with just one click of the mouse. It is an example of how an intelligently designed database application can make online business transactions faster and easier.

When you have finished placing your order, **Amazon.com** sends a confirmation to you by e-mail. It sends a second e-mail when the order is shipped. A database monitors the status of all shipments. You can track the status of your purchase until it leaves the **Amazon.com** shipping center by selecting the **Your Account** link at the bottom of the page and entering your password. This will bring you to an **Account Maintenance** page. You can cancel your order at any time before the product is shipped, which usually occurs within 24 to 48 hours of purchase. **Amazon.com** has regional warehouses from which it ships a majority of packages overnight without having to use express delivery services.[4]

Amazon.com operates on secure servers that protect your personal information. If you feel uncomfortable using your credit card on the Web, you can initiate your order through Amazon's Web site using the last five digits of your credit card and later complete your order by calling Amazon's Customer Service Department to provide the remaining numbers. We discuss Web security in Chapter 7, Internet Security.

For more examples of e-businesses that use shopping-cart technology, visit **www.etoys.com**, **www.eddiebauer.com**® and **www.cdnow.com**. In Chapter 3, Building an e-Business, we discuss the important methods and techniques for building an e-business.

While shopping-cart technology offers consumers the convenience of quick and easy transactions, it creates problems regarding consumer privacy and online security. These issues are discussed at length in Chapter 7, Internet Security and Chapter 11, Legal and Ethical Issues; Internet Taxation.

2.2.2 Online Shopping Malls

Online shopping malls present consumers with a wide selection of products and services. They offer more convenience than does searching and shopping at independent online storefronts, for a number reasons. For example, consumers can find products from a wide variety of vendors, and rather than making several separate purchases, they can use the mall's shopping-cart technology to purchase items from many stores in a single transaction. Often, these online shopping-mall sites act as shopping portals, directing traffic to the leading shopping retailers for a specific product.

An example of a leading online mall is **Mall.com**, which features many of the same vendors you will find in your local brick-and-mortar mall—offline retailers such as JCrew, The Gap (**www.gap.com**), The Sports Authority and the Sharper Image. **Shopnow.com**® and **www.DealShop.com** are other online malls.

2.3 Auction Model

The Web offers many kinds of auction sites in addition to sites that search other auction sites to pinpoint the lowest prices on an available item. Usually, auction sites act as forums through which Internet users can assume the role of either seller or bidder. As a seller, you are able to post an item you wish to sell, the minimum price you require to sell your item and a deadline to close the auction. Some sites allow you to add features such as a photograph or a description of the item's condition. As a bidder, you may search the site for the availability of the item you are seeking, view the current bidding activity and place a bid— usually in designated increments. Some sites allow you to submit a maximum bidding price, and an automated system will continue bidding for you. Auction technology is explained in depth in the eBay feature.

e-Fact 2.2

Forrester Research has revealed that an estimated $3.8 billion will have been spent on online person-to-person auctions in the year 2000 alone. This number is dwarfed by the $52 billion that is projected to be spent on business-to-business auctions in 2002.[5]   *2.2*

The *reverse-auction model* allows the buyer to set a price that sellers compete to match, or even beat. One example of a reverse-auction site is **Liquidprice.com**, which processes your auction bid within two days. A faster option is available when the buyer sets a *reserve price*. A reserve price is the lowest price that the seller will accept. Sellers can set the reserve price higher than the minimum bid. If no bid meets the reserve price, the auction is unsuccessful. If a seller sets a reserve price at **Liquidprice.com**, the seller will receive a series of bids within six hours of the initial posting. However, in this faster option, if a successful bid is made, the buyer and seller must commit.

Although auction sites usually require a commission on sales, these sites are only a forum for online buying and selling. After an auction has been completed, both the seller and the bidder are notified, and the method of payment and the delivery is then worked out between the two parties. Most auction sites do not involve themselves in payment or delivery, but they might do so if delivery and payment services could be used to generate revenue and profit.

eBay™ and the Online Auction Model

Online auctions have become an enormously successful method of e-commerce. The leading company in this business is *eBay (Fig. 2.1)*.[6] eBay is one of the most profitable e-businesses. The successful online auction house has its roots in a 50-year-old novelty item—Pez® candy dispensers. Pam Omidyar, an avid collector of Pez® dispensers, came up with the idea of trading them over the Internet. When she expressed this idea to her boyfriend, Pierre Omidyar (now her husband), he was instantly struck with the soon-to-be-famous e-business auction concept. In 1995, the Omidyars created a company called AuctionWeb. The company was renamed eBay and has since become the premier online auction house, with as many as 4 million unique auctions in progress and 450,000 new items added each day.[7]

eBay^TM and the Online Auction Model (Cont.)

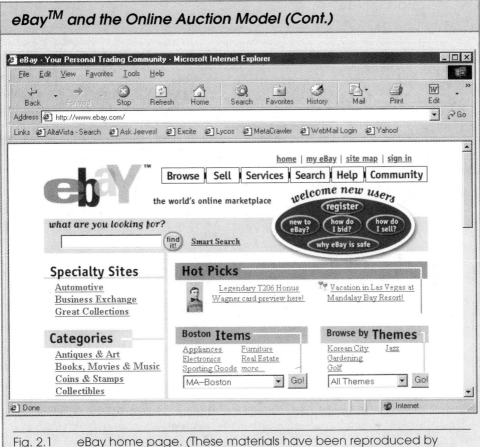

Fig. 2.1   eBay home page. (These materials have been reproduced by Prentice Hall with the permission of eBay, Inc. COPYRIGHT © EBAY, INC. ALL RIGHTS RESERVED.)

On eBay, people can buy and sell just about anything. The company collects a submission fee, plus a percentage of the sale amount. The submission fee is based on the amount of exposure you want your item to receive, with a higher fee required if you would like to be among the "featured auctions" in your specific product category, and an even higher fee if you want your item to be listed on the eBay home page under **Featured Items**. Listings are shown on the home page periodically. Another attention-attracting option is to publish the product listing in a boldface font (for an additional charge).

eBay uses a database to manage the millions of auctions it offers. This database evolves dynamically as sellers and buyers enter personal identification and product information. The seller entering a product to be auctioned, provides a description of the product, keywords, an initial price, a closing date for the auction and personal information. This data is used to produce the product profile seen by potential buyers (Fig. 2.2).

---

eBay™ and the Online Auction Model (Cont.)

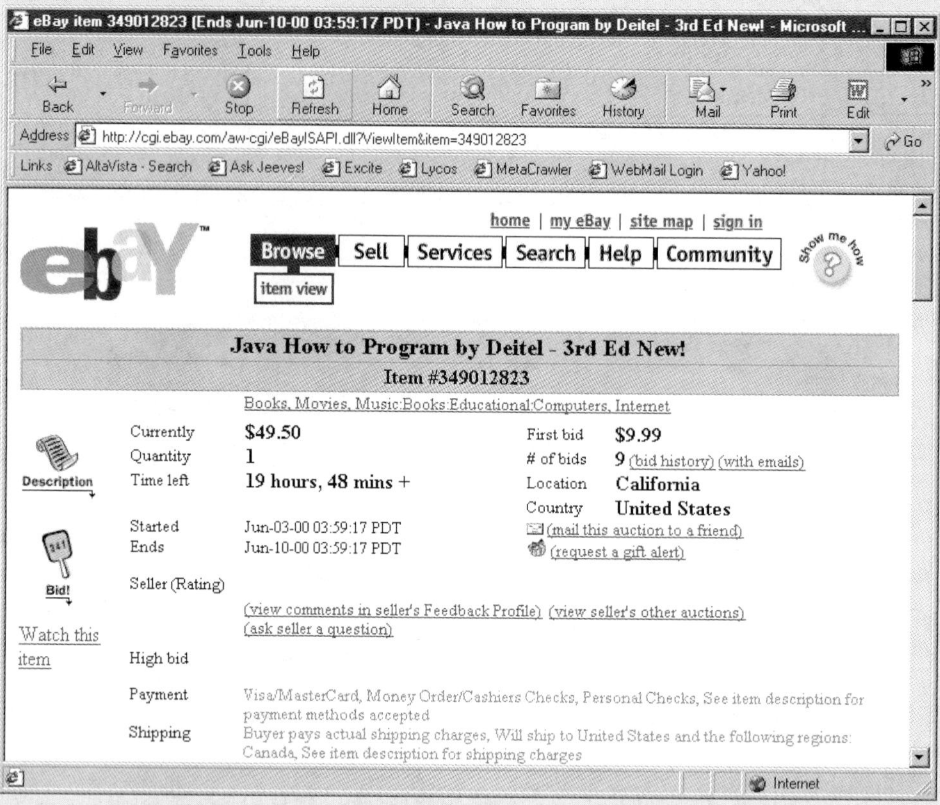

eBay item 349012823 (Ends Jun-10-00 03:59:17 PDT) - Java How to Program by Deitel - 3rd Ed New! - Microsoft ...

File   Edit   View   Favorites   Tools   Help

Back | Forward | Stop | Refresh | Home | Search | Favorites | History | Mail | Print | Edit

Address http://cgi.ebay.com/aw-cgi/eBayISAPI.dll?ViewItem&item=349012823   Go

Links AltaVista - Search   Ask Jeeves!   Excite   Lycos   MetaCrawler   WebMail Login   Yahoo!

home | my eBay | site map | sign in

ebaY

| Browse | Sell | Services | Search | Help | Community |

item view

Java How to Program by Deitel - 3rd Ed New!
Item #349012823

Books, Movies, Music:Books:Educational:Computers, Internet

Description	Currently	$49.50	First bid	$9.99
	Quantity	1	# of bids	9 (bid history) (with emails)
	Time left	19 hours, 48 mins +	Location	California
			Country	United States
	Started	Jun-03-00 03:59:17 PDT	(mail this auction to a friend)	
Bid!	Ends	Jun-10-00 03:59:17 PDT	(request a gift alert)	
	Seller (Rating)			
Watch this item		(view comments in seller's Feedback Profile) (view seller's other auctions) (ask seller a question)		
	High bid			
	Payment	Visa/MasterCard, Money Order/Cashiers Checks, Personal Checks, See item description for payment methods accepted		
	Shipping	Buyer pays actual shipping charges, Will ship to United States and the following regions: Canada, See item description for shipping charges		

Internet

Fig. 2.2   Placing a bid on eBay. (These materials have been reproduced by Prentice Hall with the permission of eBay, Inc. COPYRIGHT © EBAY, INC. ALL RIGHTS RESERVED.)

The auction process begins when the seller posts a description of the item for sale and fills in the appropriate registration information. The seller must specify a minimum opening bid. If potential buyers feel this price is too high, the item may not receive any bids. In many cases, a *reserve price* is also set. Sellers might set the opening bid lower than the reserve price to generate bidding activity.

If a successful bid is made, the seller and the buyer negotiate the shipping details, warranty and other particulars. eBay serves as a liaison between the parties; it is the interface through which sellers and buyers can conduct business. eBay does not maintain a costly physical inventory or deal with shipping, handling or other services that businesses such as Amazon and other retailers must provide.

eBay has spawned a number of businesses that use the site as their means of selling products. These businesses depend on eBay to remain up and running. Because downtime can be costly to an online business, companies like eBay make investments in *high-availability computing* and *continuous-availability computing*.

---

eBay™ and the Online Auction Model (Cont.)

High-availability computing attempts to minimize downtime; continuous-availability computing attempts to eliminate it completely. One key to such technologies is *fault-tolerant systems* that use *redundancy*. Every crucial piece of hardware—processors, disks and communications channels—has one or more levels of backup, so that, in a failure, the system shifts from a failed component to a backup component. This procedure enables the system to keep running while the failed component is fixed or replaced. The same is true of data: Because companies cannot afford to lose their business data, the data are also maintained redundantly. Tandem (**www.tandem.com**) and Stratus (**www.stratus.com**) build continuous-availability and high-availability computing systems.

The impact of eBay on e-business has been profound. Its founders took a limited-access offline business model and, by using the Internet, were able to bring it to the desktops of consumers worldwide. This business model consistently generates a profit on the Web. *Business Week* states, "The bidding and close interaction between buyers and sellers promotes a sense of community—a near addiction that keeps them coming back." [8] By implementing traditional marketing strategies and keeping the process simple, eBay has offered a successful alternative to storefront-style e-commerce.

There are several other online auction sites, including Yahoo! Auctions (**auctions.yahoo.com**), Amazon Auctions (**www.amazon.com**), FairMarket, Inc. (**www.fairmarket.com**) and Sotheby's (**www.sothebys.com**). If you prefer to see an auction as it happens, visit the demo at **www.ibidlive.com**.

Auctions are also being employed by *business-to-business* (B2B) Web sites. In these auctions, the buyers and the sellers are companies. Companies use online auctions to sell excess inventory and gain access to new, price-sensitive customers. Three examples of B2B auction sites are DoveBid, Inc. (**www.dovebid.com**), WorldCall Exchange (**www.worldcallexchange.com**) and **U-Bid-It.com**.

2.4 Portal Model

Portal sites give visitors the chance to find almost everything they are looking for in one place. They often offer news, sports and weather information, as well as the ability to search the Web. When most people hear the word "portal," they think of search engines. *Search engines* are *horizontal portals*, or portals that aggregate information on a broad range of topics. Other portals are more specific, offering a great deal of information pertaining to a single area of interest; these portals are called *vertical portals*.

Online shopping is a popular addition to the major portals. Sites such as **Hotbot.com**, **About.com**®, **altavista.com** and **Yahoo.com**® provide users with a shopping page that links them to thousands of sites carrying a variety of products.

Portals linking consumers to online merchants, online shopping malls and auction sites provide several advantages. These portals help users collect information on an item for which they are looking and allow users to browse independently owned storefronts, unlike some online shopping malls. (See the feature on Yahoo! for an example of a shopping portal.) Yahoo! permits users to browse a variety of sites while maintaining the convenience of paying through their Yahoo! account.

`About.com` offers its users an individualized experience through *GuideSite*, a service that acts as a personal shopper for the user. `About.com`'s "guides," each specializing in a particular product type, are continually updated and are accessible via e-mail for consumer comments and questions.[9]

Consumers must be savvy when using portals to do their online shopping. Each portal structures its online shopping experience a little differently. Some portals charge merchants for a link; others do not. For example, `GoTo.com` bills merchants per consumer click-through. The more a business is willing to pay for each consumer click, the higher that business will appear in `GoTo.com`'s ranks. Portals that charge a listing fee limit the number of merchants accessible to customers.[10] Other sites—`About.com` and `altavista.com`, for example—do not charge merchants to appear in some locations on their sites (`About.com`'s *GuideSite* and `Altavista.com`'s *Shopping and Services Categories*), but reserve the top of the page and other prime site locations for paying customers.

Yahoo! and the Web Portal Model

Yahoo! is a horizontal portal with an enormous number of site links and subject categories (Fig. 2.3). It also provides consumers with shopping-cart capabilities. Through Yahoo!, consumers can link to a variety of online stores, adding items to their Yahoo! shopping cart as they shop. Once users are registered with Yahoo!, they may begin searching for products. After selecting a product and a merchant, users have the option of adding the item to their shopping cart or putting it on their wish list. The wish list is a personalized Web page that aggregates and stores all items you wish to purchase at a later date. It can also be used to build a Christmas list or a wedding registry.

To participate in Yahoo!'s shopping offering, a consumer clicks on the **Shopping** link at the top of Yahoo!'s home page. From there, a consumer can search for a product by selecting a category, conducting a keyword search or visiting one of the **Featured Stores**. Other features included on this page are gift registration, **Hot Products**, **What's Selling Now** and the *Yahoo! Points* reward system. Signing up for gift registration or the reward system is a simple process, completed by clicking on the **Sign-In** link and creating a username and password.

When consumers are ready to check out, they can purchase all their items through Yahoo!, rather than purchasing at each store. This simplifies the purchasing process by limiting the number of registration and billing forms the customer must complete.

Yahoo! Shopping is just one of the many sections within Yahoo! A visitor to the site can search the Web for any product. To improve the quality of its Web-searching capabilities, Yahoo! has partnered with the search engine `Google.com`. When Web surfers enter a keyword using Google search technology, they receive a list of links based on the popularity of each site; the Web links are returned in descending order based on the number of people who link to each site.[11]

Yahoo! and the Web Portal Model (Cont.)

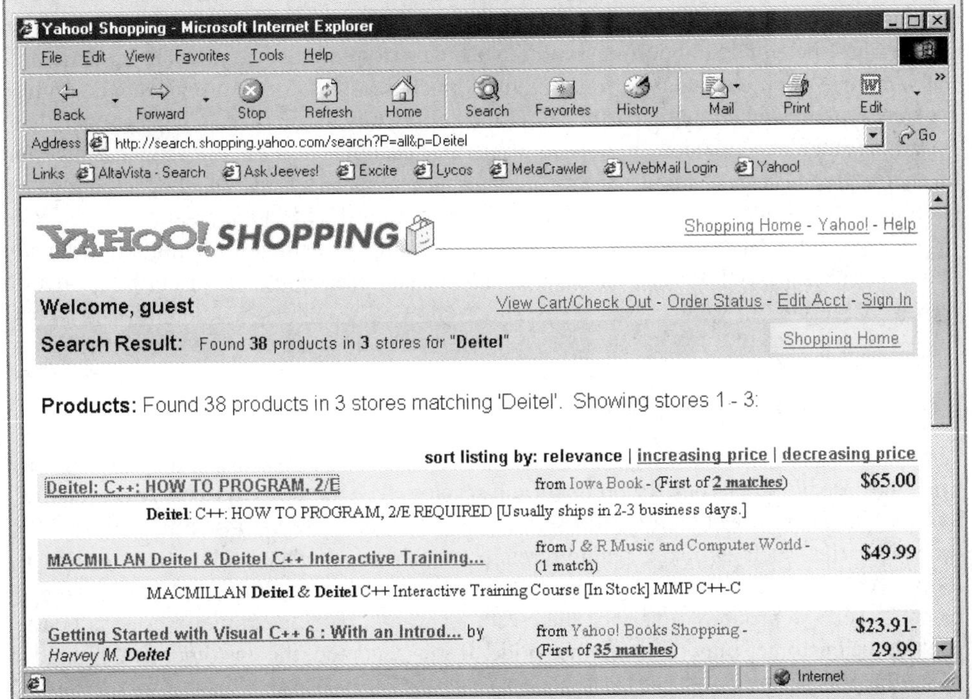

Fig. 2.3   Customers have the benefit of comparison shopping at Yahoo! Shopping. (Reproduced with Permission of Yahoo!© by Yahoo! Inc. YAHOO! and the YAHOO! logo are trademarks of Yahoo! Inc.)

Other leading horizontal portals include Ask Jeeves! (**www.ask.com**) and AltaVista (**www.av.com**). Ask Jeeves! uses *natural-language processing* technology to understand a customer's question and generate an answer. Natural-language processing is discussed in detail in Chapter 10, e-Customer Relationship Management. This enables search engine users to enter their queries as simple english sentences—other search engines base their searches on keywords entered ny the user. Ask Jeeves! queries all of the major search engines to provide customers with links to sites relating to their question. AltaVista links to all areas of the Web and offers free Internet access, shopping, affiliate opportunities and breaking news. Other search engines include **www.google.com**, **www.metacrawler.com**, **www.dogpile.com** and **www.gomez.com**.

2.5 Dynamic-Pricing Models

In the past, bargain hunters had to search for deals by visiting numerous local retailers and wholesalers. In this section, we describe in depth the many ways in which creative pricing is being used to generate business. Many of these methods would not be possible without the Internet. Some companies enable customers to name the prices they are willing to pay for travel, homes, automobiles and consumer goods.

Buying in bulk has always driven prices down, and there are now Web sites that allow you to find lower prices by joining with other buyers to purchase products in large quantities. Another pricing strategy used by many e-businesses is to offer products and services for free. By forming strategic partnerships and selling advertising (see Chapter 9, Affiliate Programs) many companies are able to offer their products at a greatly reduced rate, and often for free. Bartering and offering rebates are other ways in which companies are keeping prices down on the Internet (see Chapter 8, Internet Marketing).

The Web has also improved the customer's ability to compare pricing among many vendors. Sites like **Deja.com** and **bottomdollar.com** aggregate pricing information on a wide variety of products sold across the Web.

2.5.1 Name-Your-Price Model

The *name-your-price* business model empowers customers by allowing them to state the price they are willing to pay for products and services (see the **Priceline.com** feature). Many of the businesses that offer this service have formed partnerships with leaders of various industries, such as travel, lending, retail, etc. These industry leaders receive the customer's desired price from the business, which acts as an intermediary, and decide whether or not to sell the product or service the customer wants. If the customer's price is not accepted, the customer may offer another price. If it is accepted, the customer is obligated to make the purchase.

Priceline.com and the Comparison-Pricing Model

Employing the *name-your-price business model* has catapulted **Priceline.com** into the spotlight. Through its system, you can name your price for airline tickets, hotel rooms, rental cars and mortgages. Its patented business mechanism, called the *demand-collection system*, is a *shopping bot* that takes customers' bids to the Priceline partners to see whether they will accept the prices for the requested products and services. Many e-businesses are using *intelligent agents* (such as shopping bots) to enhance their Web sites. Intelligent agents are programs that search and arrange large amounts of data and report answers based on that data. Shopping bots are often used to scour data contained within a single database or across the Web to find answers to specific questions. (Intelligent-agent and shopping-bot technology are discussed in Chapter 10, e-Customer Relationship Management.)

The buying process is easy at **Priceline.com**. For example, when looking for a domestic flight, you first enter your departure location, destination, bid price and the number of tickets you would like to purchase. You then select the travel dates and airports in or near the departure or arrival cities. The more flexible you are with your travel arrangements, the greater your chance of getting the air ticket at your stated price.

Priceline.com and the Comparison-Pricing Model (Cont.)

The **Priceline.com** bot presents your bid to the airlines and attempts to negotiate a fare below the customer's bid price. If the bid is accepted, **Priceline.com** retains the difference between the customer's bid and the actual fare. The markup percentage varies with the price that is accepted by the airline. For domestic flights, the whole process takes about an hour.

Priceline.com is another example of how the Internet and Web are profoundly changing the way business is conducted. In the case of airlines, hundreds of thousands of airline seats go empty each day. **Priceline.com** helps airlines sell those seats. By facilitating the sale of excess inventory at a discount, **Priceline.com** allows airlines to realize increased revenue and helps passengers save money.

Last-minute travel is expensive. Airlines and accommodations are often priced at a premium. With **Priceline.com** and similar services, you can often travel at reduced rates far below the retail price. However, waiting until the last minute is also risky, as there is no guarantee that seating will be available.

2.5.2 Comparison-Pricing Model

The *comparison-pricing model* allows customers to poll a variety of merchants and find a desired product or service at the lowest price (see the **BottomDollar.com** feature). These sites often generate revenue from partnerships with particular merchants. You need to be careful when using these services, though, because you may not necessarily be getting the best price available on the entire Web.

BottomDollar.com Will Help You Find the Lowest Price[13]

BottomDollar.com uses intelligent-agent technology to search the Web and find the products you want at the best available prices. A customer can use **BottomDollar.com** to search for a product or to browse the various categories on the site. The service searches the catalogs of over 1,000 online retailers to find the products you want. The search usually takes less than a minute. Imagine trying to call or visit 1,000 different stores one by one.

Shopping bots and intelligent agents are changing the ways in which people shop. Rather than going directly to the stores with established brand names, customers are using services like **BottomDollar.com** to get the best available prices. This situation pressures online retailers to keep their prices competitive.

Similar comparison pricing sites include **Dealtime.com**, **Deja.com** and **MySimon.com**. DealTime (**www.dealtime.com**) selects merchants based on customer popularity, reliability and reviews. **Deja.com** is a multifaceted Web site offering shopping, discussion groups, customer ratings and comparison shopping. Users of the service can write their own opinions in the sections for discussions and reviews. MySimon (**www.mysimon.com**) offers a comparison-pricing search from a small number of better known retailers.

2.5.3 Demand-Sensitive Pricing Model

The Web has enabled customers to demand better, faster service at cheaper prices. It also empowers buyers to shop in large groups to obtain group discounts. The concept behind the demand-sensitive-pricing business model is that the more people who buy a product in a single purchase, the lower the cost per person becomes. Selling products individually can be expensive because the vendor must price a product so that it covers selling and overhead costs while still generating a profit. When customers buy in bulk, these costs are shared among products, and the profit margin is increased. Mercata™ (**www.mercata.com**) sells products for the home, electronics, computers and peripherals using the demand-sensitive pricing model. MobShop^SM (**www.mobshop.com**) offers comparable services. Because pricing and products vary between these and other, similar sites, customers should visit several such sites before making a purchase.

2.5.4 Bartering Model

Another popular method of conducting e-business is *bartering*, or offering one item in exchange for another. **Ubarter.com™** is a site that allows individuals and companies wishing to sell a product to post their listings. The seller makes an initial offer with the intention of bartering to reach a final agreement with the buyer. A broad range of products and services is available for barter.

If a business is looking to get rid of an overstocked product, iSolve^SM (**www.isolve.com**) can help sell it. Products can be sold directly or on a barter basis. Potential customers send their pricing preferences to the merchant, who evaluates the offer. Deals are often part barter and part cash. Examples of items typically bartered are overstocked inventory items, factory surplus and unneeded assets.

2.5.5 Rebates

Rebates can help attract customers to your site. Many companies offer "everyday low prices" and specials to keep customers coming back. **eBates.com** is a shopping site where customers receive a rebate on every purchase. **eBates.com** has formed partnerships with wholesalers and retailers who offer discounts; the company passes these discounts to customers in the form of rebates. By adding value to a customer's visit, eBates builds customer satisfaction and loyalty. eBates retains a portion of the savings.

eCentives.com offers a similar service. During the eCentives registration process, customers are asked to describe their interests, needs, hobbies, etc. This information allows **eCentives.com** to tailor rebates and product promotions directly to the customer. The site forms partnerships with vendors, who, in turn, offer their rebates and promotions on the site.

2.5.6 Offering Free Products and Services

Many entrepreneurs are forming their business models around advertising-driven revenue streams. Television networks, radio stations, magazines and print media use advertising to fund their operations and make a profit. The sites discussed in this section offer their products for free on the Web. Many of the sites also form partnerships with companies to exchange products and services for advertising space and vice versa.

The Hollywood Stock Exchange (**www.hsx.com**) is a free gaming site where visitors become traders of entertainment stocks and Hollywood star bonds. Traders are able to track the value of their movie and music stocks and bonds as they fluctuate. The strongest portfolios are rewarded with prizes. Although no actual money is traded, real prizes are awarded. The company is able to offer its services for free by selling advertising to sponsors.

iWon.com™ is a portal site that rewards users with raffle points as they browse the site's content. **iWon.com** has the appearance of a traditional search engine, offering links to news, sports, weather, and other topics. However, users registering and surfing the site become eligible for daily, weekly, monthly and annual prizes. Every advertisement and link has a point value, and as points accrue, so does a customer's chances of winning. **iWon.com** supports its free contests through advertising revenue and partnerships.

Freelotto.com also offers free contests supported by advertising revenue. After registering with **Freelotto.com**, you can enter a free lottery. FreeLotto awards tens of millions of dollars in cash and prizes through its online lottery system. However, you must visit sponsoring Web sites in exchange for an entry into the daily **Freelotto.com** contest. **Freelotto.com** generates its income from these sponsors.

Freemerchant.com offers free hosting, a free store builder, a free shopping cart, free traffic logs, free auction tools and all of the necessary elements for running an e-commerce storefront or auction site. **Freemerchant.com** makes money from its strategic partnerships and referrals. **Freemerchant.com** partners are companies that can help small businesses establish a presence on the Web. These partners offer their services free of charge in exchange for advertising.

At **Startsampling.com**, you can earn prizes for trying and reviewing products. The site allows you to request free samples from companies across the country. Web sites offering similar services include **free-programs.com**, **freestuffcenter.com** and **emazing.com**.

2.6 B2B E-Commerce and EDI

B2B, the acronym for "business-to-business," refers to the relationship between two or more companies. Online or offline, the term "B2B" can be applied to simple relationships between a single buyer and a single seller, as well as to complex distribution and fulfillment systems that link hundreds of suppliers and manufacturers. Electronic Data Interchange (EDI) systems help businesses manage their supply chains. A company's supply chain refers to the relationship between original equipment manufacturers (OEMs), secondary manufacturers, distributors, shipping companies, retailers and consumers.

Traditional EDI systems are made up of a combination of computers and communications equipment that give businesses the ability to conduct secure, reliable transactions electronically. Traditional EDI, as opposed to Internet-based EDI, uses a *value-added network*, or VAN. The VAN is a closed network that includes all members of a production process. Every supplier, manufacturer and distributor is linked to the EDI system through the VAN. EDI systems track and document the daily accounting and inventory data for a business. For example, an airplane manufacturer may have an EDI system in place to manage its supply and distribution relationships. In a given day, the airline manufacturer might receive thousands of yards of sheet metal, countless shipments of electronics equipment and dozens of engines from various suppliers worldwide. Each of these shipments must pass through complex distribution channels. Since the shipments are essential to the timely completion of an airplane, the manufacturer must make every effort to ensure that the products will be delivered on time. Operations personnel at the manufacturing plant use the EDI system to buy supplies, track shipments and keep an accurate inventory count. This process is done through a standardized transfer of electronic documentation that verifies each party in a transaction, records the terms and conditions of the transaction and processes the order. Purchase orders and invoices are commonly processed through EDI systems.[14]

Although EDI systems improve efficiency and promote better accounting practices, they can be costly to operate. Many suppliers and distributors are small machine shops and shipping companies, which do not have the technology to link themselves into a traditional EDI system. Suppliers and distributors also have to consider their other customers. If a supplier standardizes its information systems with a single manufacturer, it may become more difficult to do business with other, "incompatible" manufacturers. In this instance, the manufacturer can either incur the cost of integrating the supplier into the system or exclude the supplier from the EDI system and manage the relationship manually. Either way, the benefits of the EDI system are compromised, and expenses increase. The Internet is improving EDI standards by making it more accessible to a broader group of manufacturers, distributors and retailers.

Since the transfer of data is conducted through a common system (the Web), compatibility is less of an issue. In the past, companies with incompatible information management systems might have had difficulty conducting transactions. XML (eXtensible Markup Language) can now be used to improve compatibility between disparate systems, creating new market opportunities. XML is a development technology similar to HTML (Hypertext Markup Language). HTML is a language used to format the content and appearance of Web sites. It has been a de facto Web development standard since its creation. XML takes the language one step further and defines the meaning of data.[15] For example, an XML developer can code the data in a product catalog with XML. Each product in the catalog is assigned tags describing its size, color, price, supplier, estimated lead time and discounting policy. Since XML can be used with a wide range of systems and platforms, the company could then offer its catalog data on multiple B2B exchange sites. The product name, price and other descriptive data are formatted automatically to fit the look and feel of each site.[16]

ebXML.com is the Web presence of the *United Nations body for the Facilitation of Electronic Commerce* (*UN/CEFACT*) and the *OASIS*, a nonprofit organization dedicated to the standardization of electronic business. The goal of the group is to create and support an XML-based standard, *ebXML*, for business communication and operations on the Web. The site is a source of documentation for the ebXML standard and the latest news and updates on the progress of the standard.[17]

B2B exchange sites offer this new form of EDI. These exchange sites have been established in almost every major industry and provide a method of buying, selling, bartering and partnering in a standardized environment. Some of the most successful automobile, energy, health care and construction organizations use B2B exchanges to conduct business with their suppliers and customers. The typical B2B exchange site allows manufacturers, wholesalers, retailers and end consumers to buy, sell and barter over the Web (Fig 2.4). By aggregating these relationships into a single marketplace, B2B exchange sites can provide secure, reliable and more accessible forms of EDI.

Many B2B exchanges and Internet-based EDI systems enable businesses to link their current information systems with those of other businesses. For instance, an automobile exchange can give an automobile manufacturer access to hundreds of suppliers, each competing for its business. This competitive environment leads to lower prices for the automobile manufacturer. Once a purchase has been made, the manufacturer pays for the product and arranges shipment through the site. Once the cars are assembled, the manufacturer can use the exchange to form relationships with various dealerships and auctions.

B2B e-commerce and the use of exchange sites allow businesses to reach their markets faster and more efficiently. By shortening *lead time*, or the time it takes to receive a product from a supplier after an order has been placed, businesses can lower their inventory costs and gain competitive advantage. Long lead times increase inventory costs, increase worker stress levels and strain relationships between the manufacturer and the supplier.[18]

Companies can arrange shipment of supplies at the exact time they are needed, thereby limiting any unnecessary inventory expense. In many cases, a company's inventory management system will place a supply order automatically when inventory levels drop below critical levels. This eliminates the need for a stockroom, as parts are delivered from the truck directly to the production floor. This system is often referred to as *JIT (just-in-time) inventory management*. JIT inventory management has been practiced for decades, but a fully integrated e-commerce infrastructure can improve a company's ability to operate under such protocols. The Web can help reduce supplier delays, which traditionally are a major risk for manufacturers.[19]

e-Fact 2.3

Goldman Sachs has estimated that B2B e-commerce will generate as much as $1.5 trillion in revenues by 2004, with some estimates running even higher.[20]   2.3

The process of integrating traditional EDI systems with the Web is often referred to as *Enterprise Application Integration (EAI).*[21] There are a number of companies that use XML and similar technologies to help other companies integrate their current systems with the Web. These companies, called *business-to-business integrators (B2Bi)*, include Excara (`www.excara.com`), `Webmethods.com®`, Commerce One® (`www.commerceone.com`), Tibco Software, Inc. (`www.tibco.com`), `Freemarkets.com®` and Mercator®, (`www.mercator.com`). They help a brick-and-mortar business develop an online presence with e-commerce capabilities, enabling the business' products to be distributed through its site, B2B exchanges and corporate intranets. They will help convert a company's paper or CD-ROM-based catalog into a dynamically enhanced digital catalog. B2B integrators will also improve a company's supply-chain management efforts by standardizing its electronic data interchange protocols and product-listing procedures. Many integrators also help companies improve their marketing and promotional efforts.

The ItoI exchange site, located at `www.itoi.com`, is designed for inter-industry trading and offers services in the chemical, retail, construction and energy industries. The business provides a marketplace for raw materials, chemicals, equipment and services. Visitors have the option of buying through traditional methods, auctioning or conducting exchanges—in an exchange, customers make requests, and merchants attempt to fill the requests at the best available price.

`BidGov.com` is an exchange site for the U.S. government. This intra-government exchange site fosters economic growth by generating new business for government agencies and related groups. `BidGov.com` operates with a reverse auction model. An agency looking to make a purchase must first submit a *request for proposal (RFP)*—a formal statement of need that allows vendors to sell their products and services to the agency. Once this request is made, the agency will post classified ads and receive bids from other individuals and agencies capable of fulfilling the request. Customers can also make purchases through a traditional auction. Figure 2.4 gives examples of additional B2B exchanges, listed by industry.

2.7 Click-and-Mortar Businesses

In this section, we explore the advantages and the disadvantages of developing an online presence, and the ways in which traditional businesses are implementing Internet strategies to enhance their brick-and-mortar operations. We also consider the decision to create an Internet-only business.

Industry	Key Benefits	Exchange Sites
Automotive	• Combined supplier base. • Connects automobile manufacturers, dealers and consumers in a single marketplace. • Decreases lead time and production costs.	Covisint.com IStarXchange.com Autovia.com
Electronics	• Provides access to thousands of components from hundreds of electronics suppliers. • Provides ability to search by part number, product type or manufacturer. • Increases competitive pricing.	FastParts.com avnet.com chipcenter.com
Energy	• Provides real-time pricing data on energy commodities. • Provides access to hundreds of energy commodities. • Allows regional energy providers to gain access to a worldwide market.	enrononline.com altra.com houstonstreet.com
Food	• Reduced lead times preserve perishables. • Provides access to real-time pricing data. • Online auction technology allows for alternative pricing.	gofish.com globalfoods.com foodtrader.com
Chemical	• Access to millions of chemical products from thousands of suppliers. • Integrated supply chains promote faster, more reliable transactions.	chemdex.com chemconnect.com e-chemicals.com
Construction	• Contracting and subcontracting are made simpler by online bidding. • Construction companies can find raw materials from suppliers worldwide.	Bidcom.com buildscape.com e-builder.com

Fig. 2.4   A sampling of B2B exchange sites by industry. (Reprinted by Permission of Forbes Magazine © 2000 Forbes 2000.)

Internet-only establishments face several challenges, particularly those businesses offering business-to-consumer services, such as e-retailers and online banking services. One problem facing Internet-only businesses is customer relations. As we will see in Chapter 16, Online Banking and Investing, Internet-only banks can struggle to build a customer base, because many consumers demand human-to-human communication when managing their money. In Chapter 10, e-Customer Relationship Management, we explore online methods of improving communication and customer service.

While Internet-only businesses offer the convenience of home shopping and often reduce costs for the consumer, they also face the challenges of name recognition and customer satisfaction. Branding is discussed in Chapter 8, Internet Marketing. Internet shoppers must rely on a screen image of a product when they are making purchasing decisions. Texture, true color and quality are often difficult to determine. Many click-and-mortar businesses allow customers to purchase products online and pick them up at the brick-and-mortar store. Many of these companies also allow online purchases to be returned at physical locations. This adds convenience for the customer, but adds a another level of accounting complexity for the merchant. In the next chapter, we explore choosing a domain name, as well as features that can be added to your site to address your customers' concerns about quality. Trust and confidence are two key issues that often impede an e-business in its beginning stages.

There are many circumstances when it is more beneficial to operate as an Internet-only business. For example, the *overhead costs* (or the costs of operation, including rents, utilities, storage and taxes) of Internet-only businesses are generally lower than those of traditional brick-and-mortar businesses. However, e-business owners must also be aware of the costs of computer equipment and of managing a *24-by-7 business (i.e.,* a business that functions round the clock every day of the year).

Businesses must also consider the ability of their organizations to function online. Restaurants, for example, cannot exist solely on the Web, but they can offer a Web site for providing directions and making reservations. Menus, entertainment and special events can also be posted on the site. The same might be true for many other businesses in service industries. Auto and home repair, beauty and medical assistance are among the industries that cannot provide their services online.

e-Fact 2.4

Click-and-mortar retailers accounted for 59 percent of online retail sales, compared with 41 percent for Internet-only retailers, in 1999.[22]   *2.4*

One of the most highly publicized transitions from brick-and-mortar operations to click-and-mortar operations was that of Charles Schwab. Facing competition from E*TRADE and other online stock-trading Web sites, Charles Schwab (`www.schwab.com`) moved its brokerage services to the Web. The Internet has allowed customers to trade at lower commission rates and has given them a chance to become more informed investors. Schwab has found that its customers value the security and service they receive from a traditional broker, but also enjoy the convenience of trading on the Web.[23] Chapter 16, Online Banking and Investing, discusses these and related issues in detail.

Barnes & Noble (`www.bn.com`) has established itself as a leader in the booksellers' market, both online and offline. Customers have access to the same inventory online as they do in the actual stores. In the event that a customer is dissatisfied with a purchase made online, the product can be returned to a local brick-and-mortar Barnes & Noble store.

1-800-Flowers (**www.1800flowers.com**) offers its flower and gift delivery service both online and offline. The Web has given a major boost the gift and floral industry by making it easier for customers to make purchases. One of the problems with offering an order-by-phone service only is that the customer does not get to see the product before it is sent. Other online flower dealers include Winston Flowers (**www.winston-flowers.com**), **FTD.com** and **flowersdirect.com**.

CircuitCity (**www.circuitcity.com**) specializes in consumer electronics, appliances, audio and video. It has effectively integrated its online and offline entities. CircuitCity has tied its offline stores to its online stores, allowing customers to order online and pick up the products at their local stores, though shipping is still available.

In this chapter, we have examined the various business models used on the Internet. In the next chapter, we discuss building e-businesses. We explore writing a business plan, choosing a domain name, finding a Web-site host and Web-site design. We outline many turnkey solutions available to entrepreneurs (several of which are free) and give future e-business owners a better understanding of the fundamental technologies needed to operate a business online.

2.8 Internet and World Wide Web Resources

Storefront Model

barnesandnoble.com
One of the first brick-and-mortar companies to make a large-scale commitment to the Web, Barnes & Noble sells books, e-books, CDs and software on their Web site using the shopping cart technology.

Moviefone.com
Moviefone enhances its offline efforts by allowing people to buy advance tickets to movies from its Web site. Visitors can also view movie trailers, read cast interviews and get the latest movie reviews.

Half.com
This company sells new, used a refurbished its often at half the cost from its Web site. You can buy products from the site or sell used items to **Half.com**.

Auction Model

eBay.com
This site is one of the most well known and successful sites on the Web. The site give average people the chance to sell their items on the Internet.

auctiontalk.com
This site is an auction portal, providing links to other auctions and specific products being auctioned at various sites online.

fsauctions.co.uk
Freeserve is one of the UK's most popular Web sites. FSauctions is the freeserve auction site.

Portal Model

google.com
Google is an advanced search engine that rank search results based on the true popularity of the Web site. The more people that follow a link to a particular site, the higher the site will appear in a search.

yahoo.com
Yahoo is a full scale portal allowing people to search the Web using a traditional search engine, by browsing specific categories. Yahoo! also offers games, e-business solutions and free e-mail.

altavista.com
AltaVista is one of the most widely visited sites on the Web. It is a full-scale search portal providing targeted links and a search bar.

Name-Your-Price Model

priceline.com
The originator and patent holder of the name-your-price model, **Priceline.com** gives customers the ability to name their price for travel arrangements and scores of other products and services.

ticketsnow.com
Finding low-priced tickets to concerts and theater is often difficult, this site gives people the ability to bid for a lower price on their tickets.

allbooks4less.com
Textbooks can be expensive, this site allows people to name-their-price for text books.

Comparison-Pricing Model

www.deja.com
Deja.com uses the comparison pricing model to sell products through its Web site. The site also hosts newsgroups on a broad range of topics.

www.pricewatch.com
People interested in building a computer or upgrading their current system will find the lowest prices on computer equipment on this price comparison Web site.

www.bottomdollar.com
Bottomdollar.com was one of the first sites to offer comparison-pricing services. The site will find lower prices on a broad range of retail products including consumer electronics, software, books, camera equipment, toys and more.

Demand-Sensitive Pricing Model

www.mercata.com
One of the originators of the group-buying model on the Internet, this site will drop the price as the number of its sold to the group increases.

www.mobshop.com
A competitor of Mercata, Mobshop also lowers prices as group buying increases.

www.shop2gether.com
This site gives visitors a chance to buy products at a lower price buy buying with a group.

Bartering Model

www.ubarter.com
This site facilitates B@B transactions by allowing members to trade assets through the **ubarter.com** Web site.

www.bigvine.com
This site allows business to sell virtually any product in return for Trade dollars. These Trade dollars can be used to purchase other products on the Bigvine Web site.

www.bartertrust.com
Automotive parts and equipment, advertising, office supplies and retail products are among the products available to trade on this Web site.

Rebates

www.ebates.com

This site provides electronic rebates on popular products available on its site.

www.ecentives.com

This site is a competitor to ebates and allows customers to get rebates and incentives on purchase made through the eCentives Web site.

Free Products and Services

2000freebies.com

This search engine offers visitors links to thousands of free products and services on the Web.

www.killerfreebies.com

Killerfreebies offers links to free software, clothing, wedding supplies, server space and a large number of free products and services.

www.startsampling.com

Startsampling will send members free product samples in return for filling out short questionnaires. People can also win free samples by participating in contests and quizzes.

Click-and-Mortar Businesses

www.compusa.com

Compusa combines its online and offline efforts to provide the best possible service to its customers. A full product catalog is available from the Web site.

www.circuitcity.com

Circuit City allows customers to pick up products purchased online in its brick-and-mortar stores.

SUMMARY

- An e-business can offer personalized service, high-quality customer service and improved supply-chain management.

- An e-business is defined as a company that has an online presence. Selling, trading, bartering and engaging in transactions over the Web is referred to as e-commerce.

- The storefront model combines transaction processing, security and information storage, to allow merchants to sell their products on the Web.

- The banking industry uses Electronic Funds Transfer (EFT) to transfer money between accounts.

- Many companies use Electronic Data Interchange (EDI), in which business forms, such as purchase orders and invoices, are standardized so that companies can share information with customers, vendors and business partners electronically.

- E-commerce enables companies to conduct business 24 hours a day, 7 days a week (24-by-7), worldwide.

- B2C stands for "business to consumer."

- The merchant server is the data storage and management system employed by the merchant.

- A database is a part of the merchant server designed to store and report on large amounts of information. Databases also store customer information, such as names, addresses, credit-card data and past purchases.

- Online shopping malls present consumers with a wide selection of products and services. Consumers can search and shop for a variety of products; rather than making separate purchases, they can use the mall's shopping-cart technology to purchase items from many stores in a single transaction.

- Forrester Research has revealed that an estimated $3.8 billion will have been spent on online person-to-person auctions in the year 2000 alone. This number is dwarfed by the $52 billion that is projected to be spent on business-to-business auctions in 2002.

- Reverse auctions, or auctions that allow the buyer to set a price as sellers compete to match, or even beat it, are becoming more popular.

- eBay uses a database to manage the millions of auctions that it offers. This database evolves dynamically as sellers and buyers enter personal identification and product information.

- High-availability computing attempts to minimize downtime; continuous-availability computing attempts to eliminate it completely.

- Fault-tolerant systems use redundancy. Every crucial piece of hardware—processors, disks and communications channels—has one or more levels of backup, so, in a failure, the system simply shifts from a failed component to a backup component. The system keeps running while the failed component is fixed or replaced.

- In the past, bargain hunters had to search out deals by visiting numerous local retailers and wholesalers. Today, a few mouse clicks are all you need to find the lowest price available.

- Buying in bulk has always driven prices down, and there are now sites on the Web that allow you to lower the price of a product by waiting for others to purchase the product at the same time.

- A pricing strategy used by many e-businesses is to offer products and services for free.

- Bartering and offering rebates are ways in which companies are keeping prices down on the Internet.

- The name-your-price business model empowers customers by allowing them to choose their price for products and services.

- Shopping bots are often used to scour data contained within a single database or across the Web to find answers to specific questions.

- The comparison-pricing model allows customers to poll merchants and find a desired product or service at the lowest price. These sites often take their revenue from partnerships with merchants.

- The Web has allowed customers to demand better, faster service at cheaper prices. It has also empowered buyers to shop in large groups to achieve a group rate on products.

- The concept behind the demand-sensitive pricing business model is that the more people who buy a product in a single purchase, the lower the cost per person becomes.

- Another popular method of conducting e-business is bartering, or offering an item you do not want or need in exchange for something for which you have a need.

- Rebates are a good way to attract customers to your site. Many companies offer everyday low prices and specials to keep customers coming back.

- B2B e-commerce is defined as buying, selling, partnering, bartering or trading, conducted between two or more businesses. Goldman Sachs has estimated that B2B e-commerce will generate as much as $1.5 trillion in revenues by 2004, with some estimates running even higher.

- The B2B marketplace is one of the fastest growing segments of e-commerce. Industry leaders have begun using B2B marketplaces and exchanges to improve their business methods on the Web.

- Procurement, or acquiring goods or services, and effective supply-chain management can be difficult and costly aspects of running a business.

- B2B service providers make business-to-business transactions on the Internet easier. These e-businesses help other businesses improve policy and procedure, customer service and general operations.

- Brick-and-mortar companies that wish to add a Web presence must determine the level of cooperation and integration the two separate entities will share.

- A company that can offer its services online and offline can add value to the customer's experience.

TERMINOLOGY

1-Click^(SM) system
24-by-7
auction model
B2B exchange
B2C (business-to-consumer)
bartering
brick-and-mortar business
business to business (B2B)
business-to-business integrators (B2Bi)
click-and-mortar business
client/server application
comparison-pricing model
continuous-availability computing
database
demand collection system
dynamic-pricing model
e-books
e-business
ebXML
e-commerce
EAI (Enterprise Application Integration)
EDI (Electronic Data Interchange)
EFT (Electronic Funds Transfer)

fault-tolerant systems
high-availability computing
horizontal portal
industry to industry (ItoI)
intelligent agent
JIT (just-in-time) inventory management
lead time
merchant server
name-your-price model
procurement
redundancy
request for proposal (RFP)
reserve price
reverse-auction model
search engine
shopping bot
shopping cart
storefront model
supply-chain management
toolbook
value-added network
vertical portal

SELF-REVIEW EXERCISES

2.1 State whether the following are true or false. If the answer is false, explain why.

a) A shopping cart allows customers to continue to browse after selecting each item they wish to purchase.

b) In a reverse auction, the seller sets a price and customers make individual bids to buy an item.

c) A reserve price is the highest bid a customer is willing to make.

d) In the demand-sensitive-pricing model, the price decreases as more people buy.

e) The name-your-price model is an auction-based model.

2.2 Fill in the blanks in each of the following statements:

a) A business with a presence off, but not on, the Web is described as a _____ company.

b) The _____ model is designed to bring prices down by increasing the number of customers who buy a particular product at once.

c) Customers can shop for products and store them for later purchase using a _____.

d) Reserve prices are set by a seller in an _____.

e) The two types of portals are called _____ and _____.

ANSWERS TO SELF-REVIEW EXERCISES

2.1 a) True. b) False. This statement expresses the concept of a true auction. c) False. A reserve price is the lowest price a seller will accept in an auction. d) True. e) False. The name-your price model allows customers to get a lower price by clearing the price with a number of vendors. This model does not involve an auction.

2.2 a) brick-and-mortar. b) demand-sensitive pricing model. c) shopping cart. d) auction. e) vertical, horizontal.

EXERCISES

2.3   State whether the following are true or false. If the answer is false, explain why.

   a) eBay began as using the storefront model, but eventually introduced the auction model.

   b) Shopping bots are often used to scour data contained within a single database or across the Web to find answers to specific questions.

   c) A B2B exchange allows businesses to conduct transactions online despite having disparate information systems.

   d) Businesses with both a physical and an online presence are referred to as brick-and-mortar businesses.

   e) Just-in-time inventory management is used to authenticate the shipper and receiver of products in a warehouse.

2.4   Fill in the blanks in each of the following statements:

   a) _____ computing attempts to minimize downtime; _____ computing attempts to eliminate it completely.

   b) A _____ is a formal statement of need that allows vendors to solicit their products and services to the government.

   c) _____ sites allows customers to search several Web sites to find a desired product or service at the lowest price.

   d) Integrating traditional EDI systems with the Web is often referred to as _____.

   e) _____ can be used to improve compatibility between disparate systems, creating new market opportunities.

2.5   Categorize each of the following items as it best relates to the storefront model, the auction model or dynamic-pricing models:

   a) reserve price
   b) liquid price
   c) shopping cart
   d) catalog
   e) Mercata
   f) BottomDollar.com

2.6   Define each of the following terms:

   a) Web-based training
   b) name-your-price model
   c) shopping cart
   d) reverse auction
   e) redundancy
   f) high-availability computing
   g) merchant server

2.7   (*Class Discussion*) Visit **Amazon.com**, eBay, Yahoo! and **Priceline.com**. How do each of these companies generate a majority of their revenues? Visit each site and comment on the sites navigability. Which model would you be most likely to use when making a purchase? Why?

2.8   Visit **Bottomdollar.com**, **Pricewatch.com** and **Deja.com** each of these sites offers a comparison-pricing service. At each site, search for a digital camera, a photo scanner and a printer. Find the lowest price on each of these products at each site. Try to use the same brand and model in each case. Make a chart with five columns and place the names of each product type vertically in the first column. In the header row, list the name of each site. Under each company write the appropriate product name and price for each specific product type. Add up your total for each site. Now visit a traditional retailer such as **circuitcity.com** or **compusa.com**, find the same products on one of these sites and list them in the fifth column. Find a total cost of the products on from the retailers Web site. Which of the sites was able to provide the lowest price on these products? Which site was able to offer price quotes from the largest number of sources?

2.9   **Enrononline.com** is a B2B exchange for the energy industry. Take the free tour available on the sites home page. How many energy products does **enrononline.com** offer? According to the tour, how does a person initiate a bid on an energy commodity? What is the "All or Nothing" option as described in the tour? Enron offers an alternative to the B2B exchange at the end of the tour, what is this alternative buying method?

2.10   Spend one hour searching the Web for free products and services. List as many free resources as possible. Estimate the value of each free item you find. Determine the total value of all of the free resources you discovered. Write a short essay summarizing your search efforts and discussing your findings. If you are working with a group, compare your findings with those of others.

2.11   Make a spreadsheet containing a column for each of the following business models: storefront model, auction model, name-your-price-model and B2B exchange model. In each column, list three e-businesses that operate in the corresponding model. Visit the Web site of each of the companies you have selected. Answer the following questions:
  a) Do the companies operate with more than one of the defined business models (e.g., storefront and auction)? If, so which models do they implement?
  b) Are the companies Internet-only companies, or brick-and-mortar businesses?
  c) How do the companies generate revenue?

WORKS CITED

The notation <**www.domain-name.com**> indicates that the citation is for information found on that Web site.

1.   J. Dodd, "Avoid the Hustle," *PC Novice* 11 May 2000: 4.
2.   F. Hayes, "Amazoned," *Computer World* 17 May 1999: 116.
3.   L. Himelstein and R. Hof, "eBay vs. **Amazon.com**," *Business Week* May 1999: 128.
4.   D.K. Berman, H. Green, "Cliff-Hanger Christmas,"*Business Week e.biz*, 23 October 2000: 33.
5.   **"**When the Auction Is -- The B2B market hits $52 billion in 2002," <**www.iconocast.com**> 23 March 2000.
6.   F. Hayes, 116.
7.   L. Himelstein and R. Hof, 128.
8.   L. Himelstein and R. Hof, 128.
9.   M. Nelson "Portals to the Products You Need." *PC Novice*, 11 May 2000: 24.
10.   M. Nelson, 24.
11.   T. Foremski, "Google Spins Web of Success," *Financial Times* 6 July 2000: 12.
12.   S. Burke, "AOL Time Warner Merger: A New Model For Partnerships," *Computer Reseller News* <**www.technweb.com/wire/finance/story/INV20000110S0008**>.
13.   <**www.bottomdollar.com**>.
14.   "E-Business Technology Forecast," PriceWaterhouseCoopers 1999:120.
15.   "E-Business Technology Forecast," 45.
16.   "Business-to-Business Integration for the New Network Economy," Active Software, <**www.activesoftware.com**> 2000:6.

17. R. Drummond, "Are Portals Just Another Integration Problem?," *e-Business Advisor* July 2000: 48-49.

18. R. F. Bruner et al., *The Portable MBA* (New York: John Wiley & Sons, Inc. 1998) 146-147

19. C.W. Lamb, J.F. Hair, C. McDaniel, *Marketing* (Cincinnati: South-Western College Publishing, 1998) 400-401.

20. "Where the Money Is: B2B—Money is in the profiling B2B buyers," 6 January 2000 `<www.iconocast.com/issue/2000010603.html>`.

21. M. Duvall, "Integrators Make B2B Exchanges Easier," *Inter@ctive Week* 27 March 2000: 30.

22. D.K. Berman, H. Green, 36.

23. T. Perkins, "The Red Eye: The Year of Clicks and Mortar," *Red Herring* 23 October 2000.

RECOMMENDED READINGS

Batcheldor, B. "Auction Site Offers New Consumer Electronics." *InformationWeek* 31 January 2000: 82.

Dragan, R. "Microsoft Site Server 3.0 Commerce Edition." *PC Magazine* 14 December 1998: `<www.zdnet.com/filters/printerfriendly/0,6061,374713-3,00.html>`.

Copage, E. "Web Sites Clamor for Teens Attention." *The New York Times* 13 April 2000: E10.

Fletcher, J. "The Great E-Mortgage Bake-Off." *The Wall Street Journal* 2 June 2000: 12.

Goncalves, M. "Consortium Aims for Standards for E-Business." *Mass High Tech* 28 August 1999: 17.

Goodison, D. "`Kozmo.com` Wraps up Food deal, and Faces Redlining Rap." *Boston Business Journal* 28 April 2000: 27.

Guglielmo, C. "Don't Write Off Barnes & Noble." *Upside*: 132-137.

Guthrie, B. "When Trouble Strikes." *PC Novice* 11 May 2000: 17.

King, J. "How to B2B." *ComputerWorld* 28 February 2000.

Kosiur, D. *Understanding Electronic Commerce.* Redmond, WA: Microsoft Press, 1997.

Kwon, R. "Delivering Medical Records, Securely." *Internet World* 10 August 1998: 23.

McNamara, P. "Emerging Electronic Commerce Standard Passes First Big Test." *Network World* 6 October 1997: 55.

Methvin, D. W. "How to Succeed in E-Business." *Windows Magazine* August 1999: 98–108.

Nemzow, M. *Building CyberStores.* New York: McGraw-Hill, 1997.

Price, D.L. *Online Auctions at eBay: Bid with Confidence, Sell with Success.* Rocklin, CA: PRIMA TECH a Division of PRIMA Publishing, 1999.

Ranjay G. and Garino J. "Bricks to Clicks." *Siliconindia* June 2000: 75-78.

Symoens, J. "Site Server is a Fine Set of Tools for Web Site Building." *InfoWorld* 26 January 1998: `<www.infoworld.com>`.

Wagner, M. "Google Bets Farm on Linux." *InternetWeek* 5 June 2000: 1, 84.

Walker, R. "Get Big Fast." *PC Novice* 11 May: 210-212.

Weber, J. "Clicks and Mortar." *The Industry Standard* 2 August 1999: 5.

Wilson, T. "Up Next: An Exchange Of Exchanges." *Internet Week* 10 April 2000: 25.

3

Building an e-Business: Design, Development and Management

Objectives

- To discuss the decision to build an e-business.
- To review the importance of good Web-site design.
- To introduce Web-site features that can enhance a visitor's experience.
- To review the various types of e-business solutions.
- To explore e-consulting services on the Web.
- To introduce various turnkey solutions for building your own e-businesses.

Ah, to build, to build!
That is the noblest art of all the arts.
Henry Wadsworth Longfellow

Money itself doesn't interest me. But you must make money to go on building the business.
Rupert Murdoch

A good name is better than precious ointment.
Hebrew Bible

Merchants have no country. The mere spot they stand on does not constitute so strong an attachment as that from which they draw their gains.
Thomas Jefferson

In real life, unlike in Shakespeare, the sweetness of the rose depends upon the name it bears. Things are not only what they are. They are, in very important respects, what they seem to be.
Hubert H. Humphrey

Outline

3.1   **Introduction**
3.2   **Getting Started**
    3.2.1   **Generating e-Business Ideas**
    3.2.2   **Growth of e-Business: Evaluating Risk**
    3.2.3   **Finding Funding and Going Public**
3.3   **Putting Your Plan Into Action**
    3.3.1   **Choosing a Domain Name**
    3.3.2   **Supply-Chain Management: Distributors, Vendors and Shipment Providers**
    3.3.3   **Web-Site Hosting**
    3.3.4   **Web Design**
    3.3.5   **Enhancing the User Experience**
    3.3.6   **Protecting Your e-Business**
    3.3.7   **Streaming Media: How Much Is Too Much?**
    3.3.8   **Preparing for New Technologies**
3.4   **e-Business Solutions**
    3.4.1   **End-to-End e-Business Solutions**
    3.4.2   **Other e-Business Solutions**
    3.4.3   **Maintaining and Monitoring Your Web Site**
    3.4.4   **e-Commerce Consulting**
3.5   **Internet and World Wide Web Resources**

Summary • Terminology • Self-Review Exercises • Answers to Self-Review Exercises • Exercises • Works Cited

3.1 Introduction

There are numerous ways to approach designing, developing and maintaining an e-business. Some businesses can establish an online presence by using a *turnkey solution* (a pre-packaged e-business). Other options include e-business templates that outline the basic structure, but allow the design to be determined by the owner. Larger corporations, or businesses with substantial funding, can outsource the project to an organization offering e-business solution packages or choose to build the e-business in-house through an application platform.

In this chapter, we explore the various options available to help you construct your own e-business, choose an effective design by adding features to enhance your visitors' experiences and select a domain name to attract visitors. We discuss integrating both *front-end systems* (that portion of your e-business that is visible to the consumer) and *back-end systems* (usually your database management, payment processing and logistics). We also explore several solutions available on the Web to help you manage and monitor your e-business. We provide scores of URLs that offer access to online tutorials and demonstrations, where you can learn more about online services.

3.2 Getting Started

There are many things you must consider before beginning an e-business. Building, managing and maintaining a Web site involves advertising, marketing, customer relationship management, accepting online payments, providing and continuously updating content, recognizing cultural differences and legal parameters and providing security features for your visitors and your business. Ultimately, this can become an expensive venture depending on the degree of sophistication. In this section, we discuss briefly the decision to build an e-business.

e-Fact 3.1

Its graduates, normally leaning toward management consulting and Wall Street careers, Harvard University's MBA program saw 40 percent of its 1999 graduates pursue careers in the Internet industry.[1]

3.2.1 Generating e-Business Ideas

Before beginning to build an e-business, you must have a solid idea of the products and services you want to offer via the Web. Surf the Web to discover what exists. Are the Web sites you find providing exceptional services, or could they be offering more? Also, visit other sites offering different services and determine their best features. Ask yourself if these features could be adjusted to meet the needs of your viewers. We provide numerous examples of e-businesses throughout the book, particularly in Chapter 2, Business Models, and Chapter 15, Online Industries.

Above all, a solid *business plan* is essential. A business plan enables you to envision your e-business on paper for evaluation purposes (Fig. 3.1). It serves as a presentation of your business' objectives and long-term expectations, forcing prospective e-businesses to state their goals clearly prior to beginning the project. When presenting your idea to others, it exhibits professionalism and purpose.

A brief introduction to the business plan should be presented first. Introduce your readers to the layout, what you will discuss and when you will discuss it. This should be followed by an overview of the business premise including the primary issues. Headings and sub-headings should categorize the content of your business plan, making it easy for the reader to reference.

For a tutorial on business plan writing, visit Synrgistics' *Small Business and Business Start-Ups* Web site at **www.synrgistic.com/busplan/busplan.htm**. *Mindspring Biz* also provides a helpful tutorial, including sample questions you need to ask yourself when developing your business plan. This tutorial is found at **www.businesstown.com/ mindspring/planning/creating-developing.asp**. For individuals who are unfamiliar with the development of a business plan, free software on the subject can be downloaded from **www.adarus.com/html/demos.html**. The software provides step-by-step processes and will generate financial reports.

Focusing on what makes your e-business unique is important. Internet incubators, discussed in Section 3.2.3, discusses how a good idea and a well-designed business plan can help you find venture capital funding for your e-business.

Sections	How to define your business plan.
Primary Purpose	You must define the purposes of your business. What do you intend to sell? What services will you provide?
Strategy	Describe how your product or service fits into the market. How is it different from existing products or services, and how will it be profitable?
Support	Provide evidence that supports the idea of your business. How do you justify these as support to the idea? Have you conducted research? What is your market? Who are your customers? Who is on your management team and what are their credentials? How will you generate revenue? What are your expenses?
Business Model	What model will you implement? How will you conduct transactions?
Process	List the steps you feel are necessary to build your e-business. Does more research need to be conducted before you can move forward? Investors will want to know where their money is being allocated.

Fig. 3.1   Business plan overview.

3.2.2 Growth of e-Business: Evaluating Risk

In the past few years, many Internet companies have experienced rapid growth. However, many others have struggled to get off the ground, to find funding and, especially, to make a profit. It is important to review the current market. What businesses are successful? Which are struggling? Research will play a crucial role in the development of your e-business.

e-Fact 3.2

Successful Internet start-ups have led to the most rapid accumulation of wealth in history.[2]

Technological advancements usually lead to growth in industry. Similar to the advent of the railroad, which greatly revolutionized the transportation industry in the 19th century, the Internet has produced new industries and altered and enhanced existing industries. The Internet, however, is developing at a rate that greatly exceeds technological advancements of the past.[3] This rapid growth requires careful consideration. Even e-businesses that target a specific market first must be aware of the changing technologies and their costs and be able to grow with them.

e-Fact 3.3

Recent surveys indicate that, after reviewing several online industries, 59 percent of total business online was conducted through businesses having both an Internet presence and physical locations, and 41 percent of online business was conducted through Internet-only businesses.[4]

3.2.3 Finding Funding and Going Public

Building an e-business can be an expensive and risky venture, whether it be an extension of a large brick-and-mortar business or a new business. Competition is intense, determining your market niche and reaching your target audience often require significant financial backing. An *Internet incubator* is a company that specializes in the development of Internet businesses. Often, incubators will serve as the financiers, as well as work with the development team for creating e-businesses. E-business ventures such as Disappearing Inc.™, eToys, NetZero and **ConnectedCampus.com**™ are incubator clients.

e-Fact 3.4

Forrester Research estimates that the cost to bring a business online ranges from $2—$40 million.

For their effort, incubators often receive a stake in the developing e-business, typically 50 percent or more. This usually gives the incubator control of the business.[5] After several months, the incubator's team members play a smaller role in the business. However, because of its stake in the company, the incubator typically remains active in decision making and the direction of the company, offering advice to an e-business as it grows.[6]

Some incubators will finance and manage a growing dot-com without requiring ownership or payment upfront. This is usually a government agency or an educational institution. Rather, they simply provide assistance, hoping that the successful e-businesses will compensate them at a later date.

e-Fact 3.5

According to the National Business Incubator Association, the growth of the Internet has caused the number of incubators in the United States to go from 12 to 850.[7]

Incubators are focused on getting e-businesses established as quickly as possible. E-business owners can also profit from an incubator's previous experience. For many struggling e-businesses, incubators can make the difference between success and failure.

When choosing an incubator, there are many things to consider. First, the incubator might decide to reassign corporate responsibilities. For this reason, it is important to gather information on the services you will receive and the reputation of the incubator. In addition, e-proprietors and organizations should also be aware of the incubator's success rate—e-businesses supported by an incubator do not necessarily succeed.

Rare Medium[8]: Funding Your Online Venture

With an international presence, Rare Medium (**www.raremedium.com**) provides Internet incubator services designed to assist e-businesses in all stages of their development (Fig. 3.2). E-businesses seeking an incubator can submit their business plans to Rare Medium at **ventures@raremedium.com**.

Rare Medium provides e-commerce services called *Custom e-Commerce Planning* and *Development* and *Managed E-commerce Services*. Planning and developing services include business-to-business (B2B) transactions, *m-Commerce* (wireless, or mobile, commerce), online sales and supply-chain management. Managed E-commerce Services offers end-to-end e-business solutions and consultation.

Other Rare Medium services include branding, broadband and wireless technologies, Internet services and strategic planning. Clients of Rare Medium include **Regards.com**, **LivePerson.com** and **ePrize.com**. For more information, visit Rare Medium at **www.raremedium.com**.

Rare Medium[8]: Funding Your Online Venture (Cont.)

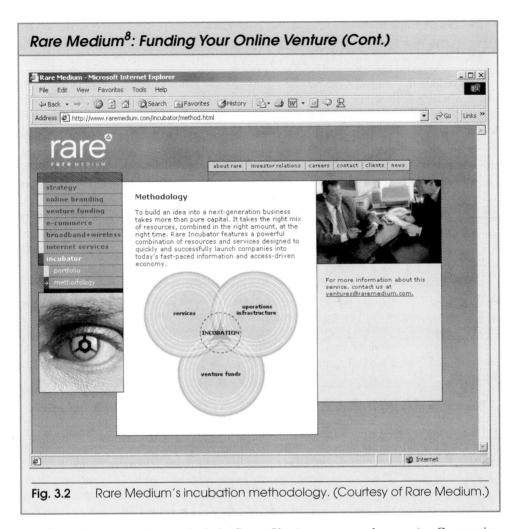

Fig. 3.2   Rare Medium's incubation methodology. (Courtesy of Rare Medium.)

Other Internet incubators include Camp Six (**www.campsix.com**), eCorporation (**www.ecorporation.com**), idealab (**www.idealab.com**) and eHatchery (**www.ehatchery.com**).

Venture capitalists (individuals or groups that generate the financial support of a growing enterprise, usually in exchange for ownership in the company), angel investors (wealthy investors with business experience) and acquiring the expertise of a parent company can also help fund e-businesses. For example, **Angelclubs.com** serves as a forum to introduce angel investors to business start-ups. Investors can visit the site to explore the various ideas posted by potential partners.

Ultimately, e-businesses look to make an *Initial Public Offering* (IPO). The money generated from public investors can be used to grow the company further and establish it at the forefront of its market. This is not an easy task, Internet start-ups must first sell the business premise to investors. They present company facts, figures and assumed risk in a business plan. Interested investors will then fund the IPO, claiming a pre-determined percentage of the ownership when the company goes public.

e-Fact 3.6

According to Hoover's Inc., 231 companies went public in the first half of 1999, an average of two companies per business day.[9]

Once launched publicly, a business must try to maintain its stock value at, or above, its initial offering price. In the early months of 2000, stock values were considerably greater than their original offering prices. For example, in the 52 week period prior to publication, **Priceline.com**, experienced a high stock value of $104.25 a share and a low stock value of $3.00 a share. [10]

3.3 Putting Your Plan Into Action

After you have reviewed your business plan, carefully considered starting an e-business and (if you needed to) sought venture funding, you can begin building your e-business. In this section, we explore managing distribution, shipping, enhancing the user experience and preparing for new technologies.

There are many important issues that must also be addressed when creating an e-business. These issues are discussed in separate chapters which include accepting online payments (see Chapter 4, Online Monetary Transactions), setting up communications, hardware and software (see Chapter 5, Internet Hardware, Software and Communications), marketing your Web site (see Chapter 8, Internet Marketing) and managing your consumers (see Chapter 10, e-Customer Relationship Management).

3.3.1 Choosing a Domain Name

How many advertisements for various Web sites have you heard or seen recently? From television commercials to the sides of buses, Internet domain names are everywhere. Do the people who see your advertisements remember your name? Do these people return to your site regularly? If your advertisements do not register in the minds of your target market, your advertising campaign may not be the problem; the problem may be a poorly chosen domain name.[11] A *domain name* is the name that you use in the URL for your Web site. Choose a concise name that people will be able to recognize and type easily. Because your Web site will be accessible worldwide, it is important to consider how your domain name will be interpreted in many different languages and cultures.

The fully qualified host name of a computer on the Internet, such as **www.deitel.com**, has three major parts: the host name, the domain name and the *top-level domain* (*TLD*). Most Web servers use **www** as the host name. A domain name is often the name of the company that owns a site or a word or phrase that otherwise describes the site. The TLD usually describes the type of organization that owns the domain name. For example, the **com** TLD usually refers to a commercial business, whereas the **org** TLD usually refers to a nonprofit organization. Each country also has its own TLD, such as **us** for the United States, **ca** for Canada and **uk** for the United Kingdom. International domain name registration is discussed in Chapter 12, Globalization.

e-Fact 3.7

Finding an unused domain name can be difficult. According to a 1999 survey of 25,000 standard English-language dictionary words, 93 percent are registered as domain names.[12]

As available domain names with the dot-com (**.com**) extension are becoming rare, companies are beginning to use dot-net (**.net**) and dot-org (**.org**). Dot-net is usually used for network-related sites, while dot-org normally denotes a non-profit organization.[13] With the number of available domain names decreasing, ICANN (Internet Corporation for Assigned Names and Numbers) is considering the possibility of introducing new suffixes, such as **.movie**, **.inc**, **.info** and **.web**.[14][15] The following sites assist you in searching for, registering and purchasing domain names: **www.domainit.com**, **www.register.com** and **www.networksolutions.com**. The cost to register a domain name depends on the extension. For example, in some cases it is more costly to register a **.com.uk** (for the United Kingdom) than it is to register **.com**. Usually, ownership of a domain name requires a one-time registration fee followed by recurring annual fees. These generally fall between $30 and $200 per name.

e-Fact 3.8

*The tiny island country Tuvala, located between Australia and Hawaii, received $50 million from a Canadian company for its TLD, **.tv**, a valuable TLD for the entertainment industry. The initial payment of $18 million has increased the country's gross domestic product by 50 percent.*[16]

3.3.2 Supply-Chain Management: Distributors, Vendors and Shipment Providers

The Internet can also help an e-business owner manage *fulfillment* (i.e. warehouse storage, shipping, inventory management and return procedures). For example, businesses are no longer required to keep large inventories. Instead, through the online management of fulfillment, these companies can rely on a *manufacturer* (the direct producer of the product) or a *distributor* (the supplier who acts as a middleman to manufacturers and vendors, often reducing the price of an item by buying in bulk) to supply them with products as needed. This also allows e-businesses and brick-and-mortar businesses with Web-enabled supply chains to accept made-to-order requests. For example, Dell (**www.dell.com**) allows consumer to select the features they want included in their PCs.[17] This is an advantageous procedure, however, one that must be carefully managed. During the 1998 Christmas season, when many companies were fined for failing to deliver gifts in time for the holidays, the need for timely delivery became apparent.[18]

The ability for members of the supply chain to view the fulfillment status increases efficiency. For example, a Web merchant can serve customers better by knowing the status of each order. Web-based fulfillment mechanisms will demonstrate if the product is available, if it has left the warehouse or if it has been delivered (and who signed for it). Wireless Internet access (see Chapter 6, Wireless Internet and m-Business) has also enhanced this process by allowing fulfillment status to be checked from any location at any time.[19] B2B supply-chain management and EDI is discussed in Chapter 2, e-Business Models.

ChangePoint™ (**www.changepoint.com**) offers a hosted supply-chain management solution that can be viewed by visiting **www.changepoint.com/index2.html** and clicking on the appropriate link. The demonstration allows users to select one particular area in which they wish to learn more, or to select a full tour. The full tour walks users through the service features, providing an example screen capture and commentary. It highlights solutions, such as storing and sorting customer relationship management information, managing employees, billing procedures and marketing.

For Web merchants keeping an inventory (vs. distributor direct shipment), a shipping service must be selected. Many of the shipping services have started to offer e-business solutions in addition to their regular shipping services (Fig. 3.3).

GoCargo.com offers a reverse-auction platform where importers and exporters may auction their ocean container shipments. Service providers (carriers and intermediaries) may bid on these auctions. **GoCargo.com** charges a commission to the winning bidder of the auction. In addition to an online demonstration of the auction process, account managers operate a trading floor 24 hours a day to assist shippers and carriers all over the world (Fig. 3.4). Other Web-based services offering logistics support include Evolve™ (**www.evolve.com**), Atlas Commerce™ (**www.ebusinessevolved.com/get_there**) and **SubmitOrder.com**™.

3.3.3 Web-Site Hosting

W*eb-hosting* companies provide products, services and support for companies, organizations and individuals to help them create and maintain Web sites (Fig. 3.5). Many Web-hosting companies offer customers space on a Web server where they can build a Web site.

 e-Fact 3.9

According to Forrester Research, the Web-hosting market will be valued at $19.8 billion by 2004.[20]

Company	URL	Services	Description of Services
UPS	**www.ups.com**	UPS Online™ Tracking	Allows consumers to track shipping progress from your Web site.
		UPS Online™ Rates and Service Selection	Allows consumers to view shipping options and fees from your Web site.
		UPS Online™ Time in Transit	Allows consumers to estimate the time between shipment and delivery.
		UPS Online™ Address Validation	Checks entered shipping information for validity.
USPS	**www.usps.gov**	NetPost™ Mailing Online (MOL)	Allows you to prepare your mail and mailing list on your computer to be distributed to the U.S. Postal Service over the Web.
		Shipping Online™	Allows business owners to order shipping supplies, prepare shipping labels, track mail and determine postage costs.
		PosteCS™	Allows business owners to send documents securely over the Internet.
FedEx	**www.fedex.com**	FedEx Ship Manager™	Allows consumers to manage shipments online.

Fig. 3.3   e-Commerce based shipping options.

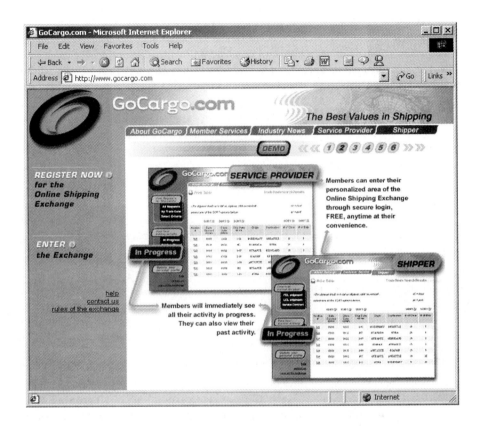

Fig. 3.4 **GoCargo.com** shipping bid. (Courtesy of **GoCargo.com**.)

Web-site Host	URL
LoudCloud	`www.loudcloud.com`
Hostopia	`www.hostopia.com`
DedicatedHosting.com	`www.dedicatedhosting.com`
HostPro®	`www.hostpro.com`
Global Crossing™	`www.globalcrossing.com`
Exodus™	`www.exodus.com`
Digital Island	`www.digitalisland.com`
Digex	`www.digex.com`
ValueWeb	`www.valueweb.com`

Fig. 3.5   Web-site hosts.

For businesses, Web-hosting companies offer more advanced services, including *dedicated servers* and *colocation*. A dedicated server is assigned one specific purpose. This ensures that the function that the server was intended to manage is not interrupted by other responsibilities, offering the advantage of consistent download times. Colocation services provide a secure physical location for a business' server hardware. Typical colocation services include dedicated Internet connections and protection from power outages, fire and other disasters.

Each level of service provided by a Web host (see DellHost feature) offers different amounts of storage space and data transfers. Basic plans allot small amounts of both, providing sufficient resources for a small-content site—a site that attracts only a small number of visitors and does not involve high levels of interactivity—to operate. Larger e-commerce sites require more resources to handle the intense activity they receive each day.

DellHost: Dell's Web-Site Hosting Service[21]

Dell's Web-hosting service, DellHost (`www.dellhost.com`), is able to accommodate everything from small Web sites to large e-commerce sites. DellHost provides its customers with basic, enhanced and premium e-commerce options. The basic package offers 100 MB of storage capacity, 5 GB of transfers a month, 10 e-mail accounts and a shopping cart using *Mercantec Softcart,* DellHost's shopping technology. This package is sufficient for a small e-commerce site with up to 50 products in its catalog. The premium package provides 300 MB of storage, 25 GB of transfers per month, 100 e-mail accounts and Mercantec Softcart. The premium package has the ability to handle an e-commerce site with an unlimited number of products in its catalog.

Users are given 24-hour access, so they can update their site at any time. DellHost guarantees 99.9 percent uptime for all of the Web sites it hosts. For marketing purposes, DellHost reports on all site traffic and performance. The service also includes Secure Socket Layer (SSL) support, for secure online transactions. (SSL is discussed in Chapter 7, Internet Security.) Unlimited e-mail forwarding and e-mail autoresponders are also provided. Users can apply *Common Gateway Interface (CGI),* a program that allows input to be received and output to be sent through a Web browser; programs for processing data from forms submitted on the Web and up to five streams of audio or video.

DellHost also provides site-designing and site-promotion services. Merchants can make changes to their sites once they are built. *Trellix Web*, another available feature, is site-building software. This resource is free and requires no HTML or graphics experience.

DellHost offers a range of services that help merchants reach a wide customer base and attract visitors to their Web sites. For example, DellHost can help the merchant register with search engines to increase the chance of customers visiting the site through Internet searches. Press releases can also be created. Using existing *opt-in e-mail lists* (i.e. or lists of individuals who request specific information on products and services in which they may be interested to be sent via e-mail), DellHost can send standard e-mails to potential customers. DellHost also provides services for building advertising banners and placing them on other Web sites in order to encourage customers to visit your site.

Some e-business owners may choose to host their own sites. This requires the purchase of the necessary hardware, such as a Web server, a database server, an Internet connection (for example, a T1 or DSL line) and a Web-site administrator to manage the site. This could be a costly endeavor, be sure to research equipment prices and other expenses thoroughly.

e-Fact 3.10

According to Forrester Research, 90 percent of Web hosting will be done through Web-host providers (versus shared and colocation services) by 2005.[22]

Several companies offer services and software for creating Web sites (see the feature "Using Yahoo! Store to set Up an Online Store."). Freemerchant (**www.freemerchant.com**) provides a free turnkey solution for building an online store. The site offers hosting, store-building capabilities and a shopping-cart model at no cost to the user. Once the user gets the store up and running, Freemerchant supplies other tools to enhance the business. These tools include online auction tools, package tracking and free technical support. Merchants are, however, required to pay for a *merchant account*, which allows them to accept credit-card payments. Merchant accounts and accepting online payments are discussed in detail in Chapter 4, Online Monetary Transactions.[23]

Using Yahoo! Store to Set Up an Online Store

There are many online *store-builder* solutions that allow merchants to set up online storefronts complete with catalogs, shopping carts and order-processing capabilities. These fixed-price options are available to businesses of all sizes, but they are ideal for small businesses that cannot afford custom solutions or do not have secure merchant servers. *Yahoo! Store* is one of the most popular e-commerce store-builder solutions.[28] Yahoo! Store is available at **store.Yahoo.com**.

Yahoo! Store charges a monthly fee based on the number of items you want to sell. This turnkey solution is designed to simplify the process of creating an online store. All the features you need to set up a complete e-commerce site are included.

To set up your own demo store, go to **store.yahoo.com** and click on the **Create a Store** link. Under **I'm a New User**, click on **Sign me up!** You will need to enter the address and name for your site. Then click on **Create**. You will be presented with the Yahoo! Store Merchant Service Agreement, which you must accept before you can proceed to build your demo store. Setting up a demo store is free, but you cannot accept orders through a demo store. After accepting the agreement, Yahoo! Store provides detailed directions to help merchants set up active online storefronts.

You can change the style of your Web site by clicking on the **Look** button. There are several style templates. If you do not like the templates, you can select **Random** to change the colors and fonts. Each time you do this, you will see a new "look" for your site. Yahoo! Store automatically sets up the shopping cart and secure order forms so customers can purchase products through your new Web store.

To set up a working storefront where you can accept orders, you must sign on with Yahoo! Store and set up a merchant account with a bank, enabling your site to accept credit-card payments. Generally, merchant banks and credit-card companies charge a small percentage of each transaction as their fee.

Using Yahoo! Store to Set Up an Online Store (Cont.)

Yahoo! Store e-commerce sites are hosted on Yahoo! secure servers. Yahoo! maintains the servers on a 24-by-7 basis. Yahoo! backs up all the information needed to run your store and provides SSL technology to encrypt all credit-card transactions. We discuss SSL in Chapter 7, Internet Security.

Yahoo! Store merchants can track sales, see how customers are getting to their sites, and use the Yahoo! wallet; such e-wallets are discussed in Chapter 4, Online Monetary Transactions. Also, each Yahoo! Store is included in Yahoo! Shopping, allowing customers to access your store through a link at the Yahoo! Web site.[29]

BigStep.com walks a user through the process of building a Web site. It covers building a home page, registering with search engines and accepting credit-card transactions. **Bigstep.com** also provides status and activity reports. An animated demonstration that walks you through the process can be viewed at **www.bigstep.com/foyer/examples.jhtml**. Steps include selecting colors, fonts and background. Examples of sites constructed through BigStep can be found at **www.bigstep.com/foyer/examples.jhtml**. Most services offered through BigStep are free; however, to accept online credit-card payments, merchants must pay to set up a merchant account. BigStep also charges a small transaction fee for each purchase made through the Web site.[24]

Tripod.com offers its *SiteBuilder* tool for creating Web sites. Tripod provides several preset page layouts. Once a layout is chosen, Tripod provides another page with sample text and graphics. The user can change text, insert graphics and create new links. Tripod also supports the construction of product catalogs in which users can display photos of products, assign product numbers, list prices and provide product descriptions. Tripod merchants are required to purchase a merchant account and register a domain name.[25]

Commerce One (**www.commerceone.com**) offers B2B e-commerce solutions. *BuySite* is a commercial solution that allows companies to set up their own B2B exchanges. Users are able to offer full services to their customers, including buyers, vendors, dealers and distributors, and other supplementary services associated with B2B e-commerce.[26]

Virtual Spin (**www.virtualspin.com**) offers a full range of e-commerce services. The company designs and implements all of the infrastructure necessary to run an e-business. Virtual Spin can also help you build and manage an affiliate program (see Chapter 9, Affiliate Programs). Virtual Spin merchants are charged by the number of items in their store and for the support services they use.[27]

AbleCommerce's *AuctionBuilder* 1.0 software (**www.auctionbuilder.com**) allows users to build their own online auction sites. The software can be customized to meet the needs of specific e-businesses. AuctionBuilder is a low-cost e-business auction-building solution.[30]

Similarly, **Bidland.com** offers *AuctionSite*™, which allows users to build an auction site. Site construction is free, and there is no monthly fee, but a fee is charged to the seller for each transaction. A *Guided Tour* of the service is available at **www.bidland.com**. The tour demonstrates the prompting menus that allow users to customize the site to meet their needs and maintain a unique identity. The walkthrough is divided into four categories. A demonstration site is available at **www.bidland.com/@/auctionblock07**.

Websiteforfree.com allows users to begin setting up e-businesses. The free portion of the site's services include home-page design, the ability to make site corrections and use of the site's educational resources. Modular packages, including accepting credit-card payments, building a catalog, online recruiting and search capabilities can be added to the site for a fee. Users can choose from four packages: Service Basic, Service Premium, Products Basic and Products Premium. Sample sites can be viewed at **www.websiteforfree.com** and an online demonstration of this service can be found by clicking on the appropriate link (Fig. 3.6).[31]

Similarly, Homestead® (**www.homestead.com**) provides users with seven different Web-site templates for building a "starter" Web site up for free. Templates are available for small-business Web sites, personal Web pages, nonprofit organizations, etc. An online tour walks the users through a simulated Web-site construction (Fig. 3.7), showing users how to choose their template and then personalize it with images, colors, fonts and content. An online tour can be found at **www.tutorial.homestead.com**.

3.3.4 Web Design

A well-designed, easy-to-navigate Web site is a crucial element in a successful e-business. While elaborate design and graphics might attract customers initially, content should be the foundation. Web services such as **www.eprise.com** help businesses update their content regularly. This is particularly important for e-businesses offering timely information. For example, online retailers might not want to reorganize their layout, but will want to update consistently. Content management is discussed in greater detail in Section 3.4.2.

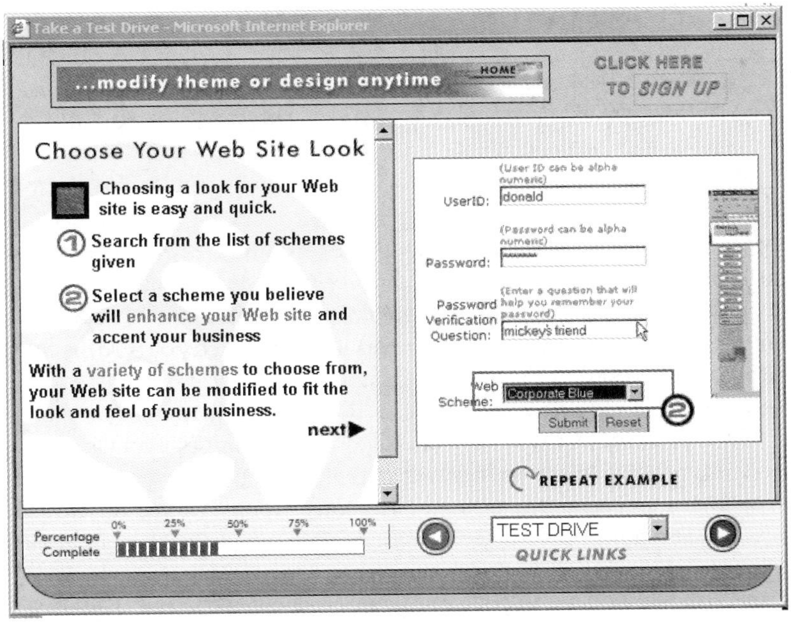

Fig. 3.6   **Websiteforfree.com**'s Web-site design. (Courtesy of **WebsiteforFREE.com**.)

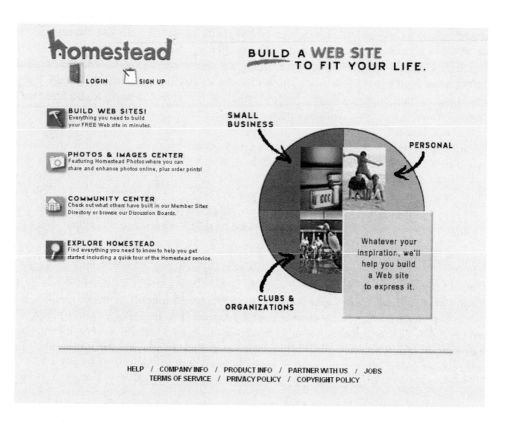

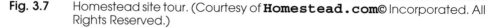

Fig. 3.7   Homestead site tour. (Courtesy of **Homestead.com**© Incorporated. All Rights Reserved.)

Design consistency, or uniformity among the sections, is also important. Your Web site should be well connected, in terms of both content and design. International design elements are discussed in Chapter 12, Globalization. **Webtechniques.com** suggests visiting **www.cooking.com**, **www.apple.com** and **www.crayola.com** for examples of well-designed Web sites.[32] Other good examples of well-designed e-commerce sites include **Amazon.com** and **eBay.com**. These sites exemplify strong branding; their logos and color schemes appear on every Web page. Contact information is easily located. Crayola® lists its privacy policy and contact links at the bottom of every page. Dell® organizes its site to accommodate the different customer groups—home offices, small businesses, large corporations, government customers and educational institutions are each provided links to additional resources.

Customers should be able to find and price products and services easily. For every business category, there are scores of e-businesses offering their services on the Web. As a result, products and services must be priced competitively. Low *switching costs*, or the costs of changing vendors, make e-commerce a fiercely competitive field.[33] Because online shoppers have access to a large number of different stores, they will spend less time at your site if it is not conveniently organized. Other factors that might discourage consumers include poor customer service and weak return policies.

Web sites should be designed with consumers' preferences in mind. Market research (see Chapter 8, Internet Marketing) will allow you to discover preferences by region and by demographic. Understanding these preferences will enable you to strategize and create more effective Web sites.

3.3.5 Enhancing the User Experience

In addition to designing your site to meet your consumers' preferences, there are a number of other features you can implement to enhance their experience. In this section, we review searching capabilities, intelligent agents, community-building features and product viewing technology.

Some of the problems associated with site layout can be solved by adding a search engine. Searching features to make it easy to find items on your site can be added for free through **www.freefind.com**. You submit your e-mail address and URL, and the site then sends you the HTML code via e-mail for implementing the search feature on your site.

Intelligent agents (software programs that communicate with end users and recognizes the users' preferences), when employed on your site, can help you meet the needs of your customers by comparing their previous behavior and adjusting the site's offerings to match that behavior. **Amazon.com** is a good example of this. Registered users are greeted to the site by name and offered books, music and other products that relate to their most recent purchases. For example, if you bought a mystery novel at **Amazon.com**, on your next visit you would probably be presented with a list of popular mystery novels. Intelligent agents make this personalization possible. Personalization and the ongoing debate about consumer privacy, two issues closely related to the use of intelligent agents are discussed in depth in Chapter 10, e-Customer Relationship Management and Chapter 11, Legal and Ethical Issues; Taxation.

There are a variety of features you can add to your site to enhance the consumer's shopping experience. For example, *ZOOM™ Server software* (**www.mgisoft.com**) allows consumers to take a closer look at your merchandise. By zooming in by degrees, shoppers can see texture and quality. *ImagePump™* (**www.xippix.com**) offers a similar technology. Figures 3.8 and 3.9 show the ImagePump interface that allows the user to focus on a particular area, zoom in, zoom out and rotate the image.

Community-building tools can also enhance your visitors' experience and increases the possibility they will visit the site frequently. For example, your e-business can provide a place where people can ask questions and find answers or locate an event near them. **MyEvents.com** is an application service provider (see Chapter 5, Internet Hardware, Software and Communications) that offers both Internet and wireless access to common files, including calendars, reminders and bulletin boards (Figs. 3.10 and 3.11).

Answers to common questions can be made available by including a *frequently asked questions* (*FAQs*) link. Company contact information is another important element; users should be supplied with an e-mail address, a phone number and a postal address. This information should be clearly identified and easy to locate. FAQs are discussed in Chapter 10, e-Customer Relationship Management.

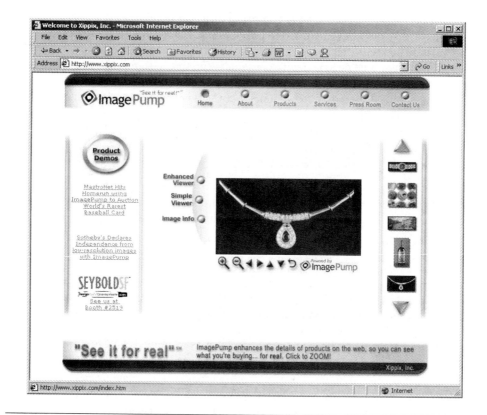

Fig. 3.8   ImagePump zoom technology. (Courtesy of Xippix, Inc.)

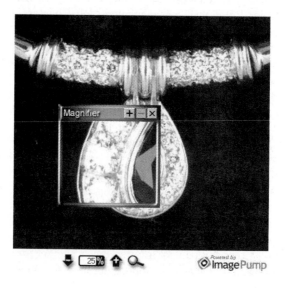

Fig. 3.9   Enhanced view with the Magnifier. (Courtesy of Xippix, Inc.)

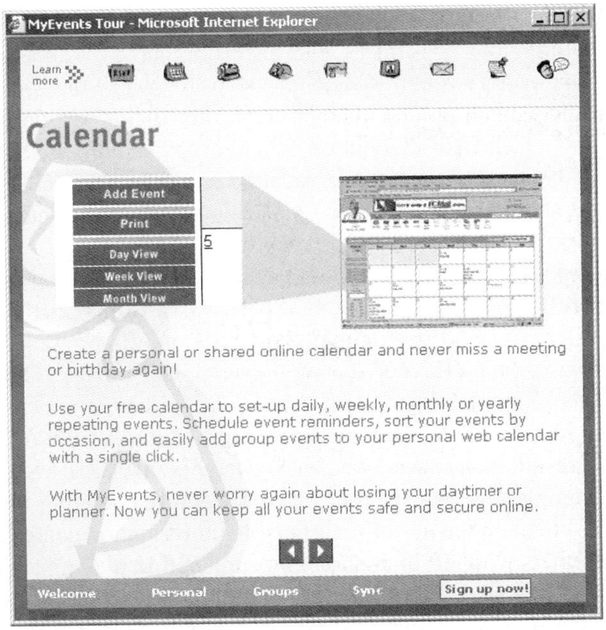

Fig. 3.10 **MyEvents.com** calendar feature. (Courtesy of MyEvents.)

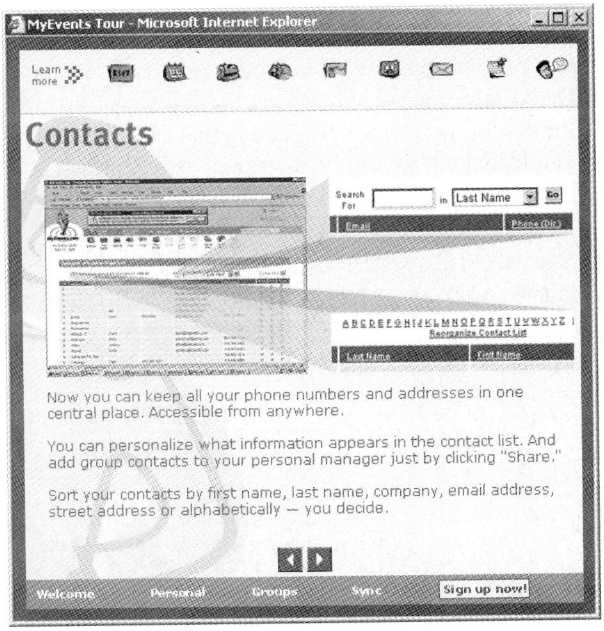

Fig. 3.11 **MyEvents.com** contacts feature. (Courtesy of MyEvents.)

3.3.6 Protecting Your e-Business

In addition to providing your consumers with a well-organized Web site, timely shipping and effective personalization, you must also take steps to protect the consumer and your e-business from misunderstandings and misinterpretations. In this section, we discuss implementing a privacy policy and a disclaimer on your Web site. Additional legal issues are discussed in depth in Chapter 11, Legal and Ethical Issues; Internet Taxation.

Your Web site should include a *privacy policy* detailing the intended uses of consumers' private information. Consumer privacy on the Internet and resources for developing your privacy policy are discussed in detail in Chapter 11, Legal and Ethical Issues; Internet Taxation. Telling consumers how their personal information is used can influence their decision to visit your site. For example, Staples™, an office supplies store, requested that consumers provide their ZIP code during the shopping process. The ZIP code was to be used to determine the availability of a product, based on the consumer's proximity to the nearest warehouse. In a simple oversight, Staples neglected to inform users of the purpose of the request. As a result, many users, when asked to enter their ZIP code, abandoned their purchases before completing the checkout process. Simply changing the phrasing of the request to alert consumers to the use of their personal information decreased by 75 percent the number of customers who left their shopping carts before making a purchase.[34]

There are many Web sites that will help you build a privacy policy. Often, these sites provide you with their seal, which demonstrates your concern for consumer privacy. Figure 3.12 is an example of Secure Assure's *Privacy Profile*™. Users (i.e., e-business owners) can visit the site and submit their use of personal information into a questionnaire. The Web site then generates a graph in HTML that e-business owners can plug into their code, making it easier for users to educate themselves on the site's policies.

E-businesses should also host disclaimers on their sites to provide users with the limits of their products and services. For example, small spelling or editing errors, such as an inaccurate statistic or product price could result in product misrepresentation, angry consumers and lost business. Dated information and inaccurate links can also lead to problems for Web-site owners. Similar to privacy policies and contact information, disclaimers should be easy to locate and information should be presented in a clear and concise manner.[35]

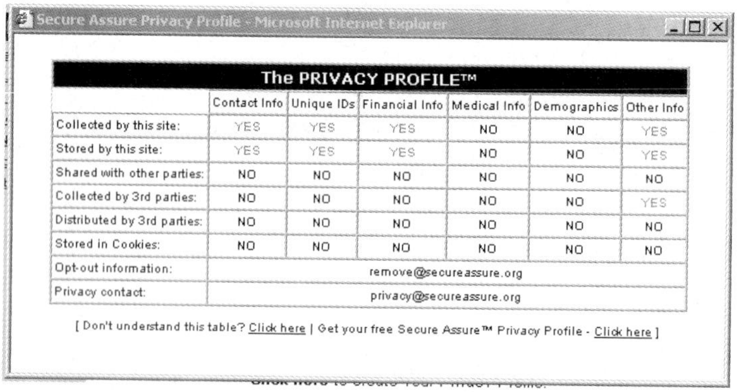

The PRIVACY PROFILE™					
	Contact Info	Unique IDs	Financial Info	Medical Info	Demographics	Other Info
Collected by this site:	YES	YES	YES	NO	NO	YES
Stored by this site:	YES	YES	YES	NO	NO	YES
Shared with other parties:	NO	NO	NO	NO	NO	NO
Collected by 3rd parties:	NO	NO	NO	NO	NO	YES
Distributed by 3rd parties:	NO	NO	NO	NO	NO	NO
Stored in Cookies:	NO	NO	NO	NO	NO	NO
Opt-out information:	remove@secureassure.org					
Privacy contact:	privacy@secureassure.org					

[Don't understand this table? Click here | Get your free Secure Assure™ Privacy Profile - Click here]

Fig. 3.12   Secure Assure's example Privacy Profile™.
(Courtesy of Secure Assure, LLC.)

`Egghead.com` recognized the need for a disclaimer when it mislabeled a product at $34.85 when it was valued at $335. In the few hours that the lower price was on the site, dozens of orders were submitted. Egghead cancelled orders for the product at the $34.85 price, suggesting that it reserved the right to correct and cancel faulty orders. The site's disclaimer reads, "`Egghead.com` reserves the right to cancel a bid or order... that is advertised in error...."[36]

3.3.7 Streaming Media: How Much Is Too Much?

It is important to recognize that, while multimedia such as streaming video and audio can enhance content, not all users have the capabilities to download this kind of information efficiently—or even at all. Your site should be able to provide such consumers with simpler, but nevertheless effective Web pages. One way to test this is to run trial downloads of your site through a standard dial-up connection prior to launch. Several services are available to help you do this. They are discussed in Section 3.4.3, Maintaining and Monitoring Your Web Site. Streaming media, download speeds and enhancing technologies are discussed in greater detail in Chapter 5, Hardware, Software and Network Communications.

3.3.8 Preparing for New Technologies

Building a Web site for your e-business is only the beginning. By keeping new technologies in mind when designing your site, you can reduce the cost of incorporating these technologies later. For example, what might fit well on a full-sized computer screen might not work well on the face of a cell phone, pager or personal digital assistant. The information sent to each device must be appropriate for that particular device.[37]

It is important to begin thinking about employing new technologies to make your e-business accessible to mobile devices. Wireless Application Protocol (WAP) is discussed in Chapter 6, Wireless Internet and m-Business.

3.4 e-Business Solutions

E-business owners may have the skills to manage a business, but they typically do not know how to program and design a Web site. Web-site building services, e-consulting and marketing can all be outsourced to an e-business solution provider. In this section, we explore various e-business solution packages.

Microsoft Site Server Commerce Edition

Large companies that need custom e-commerce solutions may choose to build and maintain their own e-commerce sites. *Microsoft Site Server Commerce Edition* (`www.microsoft.com/catalog`) is a popular software package that allows companies to manage transactions, offer secure payment services using both the SSL and SET security protocols (see Chapter 7, Internet Security), support a large catalog of products, keep records of online transactions and even design Web sites.[38] [39] [40] Site Server Commerce Edition, which can be installed on a company's own servers, offers more options for an online business do than prepackaged e-commerce *turnkey solutions,* such as Yahoo! Store or iCat Web Store.

Microsoft Site Server Commerce Edition (Cont.)

Site Server Commerce Edition is designed for use with Microsoft Windows NT and Microsoft SQL Server. Microsoft Windows NT is an operating system that allows companies to build relatively secure computer networks. Microsoft SQL Server is a powerful, commercial-quality database management system that allows large organizations to store massive amounts of information, such as consumer profiles. Microsoft Site Server Commerce Edition also includes Visual InterDev, which is Microsoft's high-end Web application development software.

Microsoft Site Server Commerce Edition is more powerful than most prepackaged store-builder solutions, but it is also more costly to license, manage, develop and support. To run successful online stores, merchants must maintain their own 24-by-7 support. Many companies will not have the technical expertise and resources to implement their Web sites with Site Server Commerce Edition and will prefer hiring outside groups to provide complete solutions.

3.4.1 End-to-End e-Business Solutions

An *end-to-end e-business solution provider* offers services to build Web sites from conception to implementation. In addition to providing design, development and deployment services such companies provide capabilities such as accepting payments online, implementing new technologies and monitoring their services. An end-to-end solution should also provide for easy adaptation to your back-end systems, fulfillment (payment authorization and account settlement, distribution and shipping) and data management. Online organizations such as Microsoft's bCentral (see the bCentral feature) provide such services.

Webvision (**www.webvision.com**)—a comprehensive e-business solution—builds, connects and maintains your Web site. Designed to meet the needs of larger organizations, *WEBtropolis ORDERnet*, a service offered by Webvision, builds a series of integrated features to create and enhance e-businesses. WEBtropolis includes storefront construction, searching features, database, a B2B turnkey solution, marketing strategies and the ability to accept payments online. *WEBtropolis AUCTIONnet* and *BIDtropolis, Reverse Auction Solution* are comprehensive building solutions for e-businesses requiring the auction business model. Through *iCom Site Design*, sites are given a unique interface to reinforce corporate identity.

Webvision's deployment services include DSL, storage and information protection, domain-name registration and monitoring services. These features provide businesses with the ability to use videoconferencing, synchronized communication and multimedia. *WebVision ICOMVideo* allows businesses to capture, convert, compress and stream video over the Internet. Colocation services provide a secure physical location for a business' server hardware.

Once a Web site has been constructed, Webvision can provide a variety of 24-by-7 management services. Members receive notification and reports as problems arise. Services include *Website Monitoring*, which reports visitor information and reliability issues, and *ProActive Monitoring*, which reports backup, capacity and system information.

End-to-End Solution Provider—Microsoft bCentral

Microsoft's bCentral (**www.bcentral.com**) provides aspiring small e-businesse owners with a list of products and services necessary to building an e-business. For a nominal monthly fee, users receive a domain name, Web-site construction services and an e-mail account for managing business communications.

Other services offered through bCentral to help e-business owners get started include assistance in writing a business plan, comparison and purchasing information for connection media and insurance coverage. Internet marketing (see Chapter 8, Internet Marketing) including business listings, advertising networks, banner advertisement exchange and search-engine registration is also available. To further meet your consumer's needs, *Privacy Wizard* will generate a privacy statement to reflect the uses of a consumer's personal information.

ROIDirect.com is another end-to-end solution provider. ROIDirect's *ECommerce* solution offers building, branding, maintenance and management services. Navigation tools, customer service, reward structures and referrals are available when building a Web site through ROIDirect. A complete list of its Web-site building features and services can be viewed in the online demonstration found at **www.roidirect.com/ecommerce/tour01.htm**. It provides users with a walk-through of ROIDirect's services. There are many companies on the Web offering e-business solutions (Fig. 3.13).

Dell E Works[41]

Dell E Works (**www.delleworks.com**) provides products and services for the development of e-businesses. Dell offers Internet infrastructure design, development and testing services and advanced hardware and software capabilities. The service also include site hosting and promotion. Dell E Works consulting services help e-businesses plan for future developments in technology and increases in traffic. Dell partnerships include Intel®, Oracle® and Microsoft®. These partnerships provide E Works's clients with the most current technologies. Financing and support services are also available to participating e-businesses. Web users interested in using Dell E Works must complete a questionnaire. Users are then contacted by a Dell representative to further discuss their e-business plan. The service is fee based.

Provider	URL
Genuity™	www.genuity.com
Interland	www.interland.com
Appnet™	www.appnet.com

Fig. 3.13   Other e-business solution providers (part 1 of 2).

Provider	URL
Sapient	www.sapient.com/home
Scient®	www.scient.com
Viant	www.viant.com
Proxicom®	www.proxicom.com
Inforte	www.inforte.com
Aspect	www.aspect.com
Global Commerce™	www.commerce.com
Telegea	www.telegea.com
IBM® WebSphere™	www.ibm.com

Fig. 3.13   Other e-business solution providers (part 2 of 2).

3.4.2 Other e-Business Solutions

In addition to end-to-end e-business solutions, there are a variety of other options that assist in e-business development, operation and management. **Openair.com** is a Web-based project management, expense-tracking and time-management service provider. The service is available to one employee of a company for free; each subsequent employee of the company is charged a nominal monthly fee.[42]

Online accounting application service providers (ASPs) offer small organizations the opportunity to operate with current technologies at reasonable costs. Through these ASPs, financial management can be done remotely at any time. These services do present challenges, however; you must evaluate factors such as security, service disruptions and a limited feature set.[43] ASPs are discussed in greater detail in Chapter 5, Hardware, Software and Communications.

Intacct™ (**www.intacct.com**) provides online accounting and auditing services. Reports are offered in graphical form and can be organized by department. It offers an 18-step setup process to help businesses get started. A free 14-day trial is available at **www.intacct.com/trial**. An online demonstration detailing the features of the service can be viewed at **www.intacct.com**. The demo walks the user through the accounting services offered and the benefits they provide. It also discusses the user's ability to customize the service. At any point, the user can follow the links to a more detailed description of the product or to the sign-up page for the free trial.[44] Other Web-based accounting services include BAport Accounting (**www.baport.com**), Netledger™ (**www.netledger.com**) offering a free thirty-day trial and BizTone Financials (**www.biztone.com**).

Content management is another type of e-business solution. Many Web-site hosting services are supplying *content-delivery networks* (CDNs) to help e-businesses manage their content (see Akamai feature). This type of solution enables you to manage information on your site in an efficient manner, allowing for regular site updates—a feature that increases the frequency of return visits—and improved site consistency. For example, if you want to alter your logo, you should be able to apply the changes all at once to the many places the logo appears on the site and have it updated instantly. As a result, consumers receive a higher rate of exposure to your brand. Large businesses can use content management to control business and employee relations and product development, decreasing *time-to-market* (the speed at which a company can begin to sell its products or services). This allows them to keep information on the Web current across intranets, extranets and the Internet.

Allaire Spectra™ (`www.allaire.com/products/spectra`) offers content management services. Users can visit the Web site and apply for a free trial. Other content management providers include Mediasurface™ (`www.mediasurface.com`), InfoOffice™ (`www.infooffice.com`) and ITKnowledge.com[SM] (`www.itknowledge.com/reference/dir.contentmanagement.ecommerce1.html`).

3.4.3 Maintaining and Monitoring Your Web Site

In addition to a *balanced scorecard* (`<www.bscol.com>`) a method used to measure the success of a business by its performance in customer satisfaction, integration capabilities and potential for growth, an e-business must also consider its use of current technologies for management and production purposes. Outsourcing testing and monitoring services can greatly reduce the cost of maintaining your e-business.[46] Knowing the limits of your site's capabilities, such as average download times and user capacities, can reduce the number of consumer complaints.

Companies such as Mercury Interactive (`testyourlimits.mercuryinteractive.com`) measure the capacity of Web sites. This information can then be used to determine areas that need to be enhanced. For example, knowing that your Web site can handle only so many visitors at one time might help you decide to upgrade your services to accommodate a larger capacity. Similarly, eBSure, Inc. (`www.ebsure.com`) offers its software suite of *eBWatch™*, *eBTracker™* and *eBRobot™*. The suite's features allow Web-site owners to measure the amount of time transactions take, gather information about visitors on the site and register the pages visited (i.e. the time spent waiting for downloads on a particular page and the actions taken by the user).

Akamai: Content Delivery[45]

Akamai (`www.akamai.com`) provides an enhanced *content delivery service* for Web sites. Typical Web pages are composed of many different types of data, including text, images and multimedia objects. When a user visits a Web site, all of these images and multimedia objects must be downloaded from a Web server. If a company's Web server is located in Australia and a user in the United States visits the Web site, the images and multimedia content of the site have to be transmitted half-way around the globe. Akamai's *FreeFlow* technology speeds the delivery of images, multimedia and other Web content by placing that content on servers worldwide. Using the FreeFlow Launcher, Web site designers "Akamaize" their site by marking content to be delivered using the Akamai network. FreeFlow takes this content and stores it on Akamai Web servers around the world. When a user visits a Web site that has been "Akamaized," the images and multimedia content are downloaded from an Akamai server near the user for faster content delivery. Akamai also provides *FreeFlow Streaming,* which employs similar content-delivery techniques for streaming video and audio over the Internet.

`iSharp.com` (`www.isharp.com`) provides Web-site testing, monitoring and consulting services. Interested users can subscribe to iSharp, requesting only the services they require. Testing services monitor the amount of traffic your site will be able to handle, enabling you to prepare for increases in traffic. For example, hiring iSharp to run a pretest before you open your site for business could indicate that the site takes too long to download via a specific medium, such as a dial-up modem. As a result, you might decide to reduce the number of images that appear on the site.[47][48]

iSharp also monitors user activity, such as the amount of time spent completing a transaction and the type of transaction, and notifies Web-site owners of pressing problems. Design, development, auditing and certification are available through iSharp's consulting services. For more information, visit **`www.isharp.com`**.

Holistix™, Inc. offers two testing solutions for e-businesses. Holistix *Web Manager* monitors Web-site performance and offers solutions for problems as they occur (Fig. 3.14). The product provides internal alerts if problems occur within the firewall. Firewalls and other security issues are discussed in detail in Chapter 7, Internet Security. Holistix *Remote Monitor* records the activity of the site from outside the firewall. This service allows e-businesses to view the site from the user's perspective. Holistix Remote Monitor is available for a free trial and Holistix Web Manager offers an online demonstration at **`www.holistix.net/products/solutions2.htm`**. The demonstration presents several scenarios and indicates how various problems might be corrected using the Holistix technology.

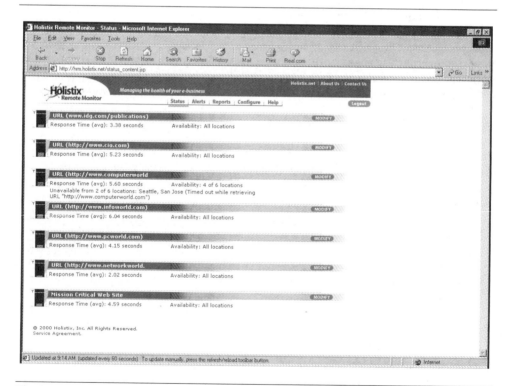

Fig. 3.14   Holistix Web Manager. (Courtesy of Holitix, Inc.)

Keynote.com, which offers a free trial and an online demonstration, available at

`www.keynote.com/services/downloads/downloads_demos.html`

also offers online monitoring services. The demonstration allows users to select a commonly asked question about site reliability, industry comparisons or user accessibility. The tour then produces the graphic image of this information in a simulated test. Other similar services include SiteRock[SM] (`mii.siterock.com/home.html`), Red Alert (`www.redalert.com`) and Web Assure (`www.webassure.com`).

3.4.4 e-Commerce Consulting

Consulting firms guide developing e-businesses. Some operate as advisors, while others provide building and maintenance services similar to those provided by end-to-end providers. Figure 3e.15 lists e-business consulting companies.

Andersen Consulting (*Accenture* as of 01.01.01) devotes one section of its Web site to the discussion of e-commerce. The e-commerce home page contains several articles anticipating the future of e-commerce and how to survive as a dot-com, as well as strategies for building e-businesses. The *e-Commerce Defined* page offers the *e-Intelligence Quiz* (`www.ac.com/ecommerce/define.html`) to help users determine how much they know about the industry and to help them to learn more. Users can explore the Andersen Consulting (Accenture) Web site to find the answers.

Company Name	URL
Accenture (formerly Anderson Consulting)	`www.ac.com`
iPlanet	`iplanet.com/index.html`
KPMG Consulting	`webevents.broadcast.com/kpmg/building050300`
SAP.com	`mysap.com`
Sun Microsystems	`www.sun.com/service/sunps/jdc/intovw.html`
Kintana	`www.kintana.com`
Xpedior	`www.xpedior.com`
Ernst & Young	`www.ey.com/ebusiness`
eRunway	`www.erunway.com`
Deloitte and Touche	`www.us.deloitte.com`
Answerthink Consulting Group	`www.answerthink.com`

Fig. 3.15   e-Business consulting companies.

SAP™ (Systems, Applications and Products in Data Processing) is a software solutions provider. ***MySap.com***™ allows individuals and corporations to create an online forum in which e-business solutions can be used for all types of business transactions. A common Web browser allows users to access their information from remote locations. *Workplace management*—the management of people and projects on a daily basis—is among the many solutions offered through mySAP. This solution allows users to organize their responsibilities, correct and change their personal information, make scheduling adjustments, send and receive e-mail and manage documents. An interactive demonstration of this service, located at **mysap.com/solutions/workplace/index.htm**, presents a character with three primary responsibilities. It then presents three scenarios in which this character can use the workplace management solution to increase efficiency.

Other solutions provided by mySAP (many with interactive demonstrations) include mobile workplace (**mysap.com/solutions/mobile_workplace/index.htm**), e-commerce (**mysap.com/solutions/e-commerce/index.htm**), customer relationship management (**mysap.com/solutions/crm/index.htm**) (also discussed in detail in Chapter 10, e-Customer Relationship Management), product lifecycle management (**mysap.com/solutions/plm/index.htm**), human capital management (**mysap.com/solutions/hr/index.htm**), business intelligence, financials and collaborative business and industry solutions. Similar to the workplace management demo, the interactive tours for these solutions walk the user through the service, based on a given scenario.[49]

3.5 Internet and World Wide Web Resources

Writing a Business Plan

www.synrgistic.com/busplan/busplan.htm
This site offer the *Small Business and Business Start-Ups* tutorial, designed to help students develop a business plan.

www.businesstown.com/mindspring/planning/creating-developing.asp
Mindspring Biz offers a tutorial with sample questions to ask yourself when designing a business plan.

www.adarus.com/html/demos.html
Adarus offers free business plan development software.

Web Hosting

www.hostopia.com
This site provides Web-hosting services.

www.dedicatedhosting.com
This site provides Web-site hosting on a server completely dedicated to your site.

www.hostpro.net
This site provides 30 days of free Web-site hosting. It offers colocation and redundant connections. Servers and facilities are monitored on a 24-by-7 basis. A facility tour (Flash or RealPlayer) is provided.

www.interland.com
This site provides dedicating and shared Web-site hosting.

www.intelonlineservices.com/info
This is Intel's Web hosting and e-business services site.

`www.rackspace.com`
This site provides managed Web-site hosting with 24-by-7 support.

`www.datareturn.com`
DataReturn provides advanced Web hosting, application hosting and Microsoft Exchange hosting.

Directory of Web-site Hosting Services

`www.ibm.com/smallbusiness/4me/wc411`
IBM's small-business Web-hosting, Web-access and e-mail site.

e-Business Consulting

`www.ac.com`
The Anderson Consulting (Accenture) Web site has one section dedicated to the international development of e-commerce. This site provides a large number of statistics.

`www.us.deloitte.com`
The Deloitte and Touche consulting services Web site.

`www.plural.com`
The Web site for a consulting and development firm called Plural.

`www.oneco.net`
This company provides e-business strategy, a call center, customer profiling, direct marketing and content management services.

`www.capgemini.com`
This is the Cap Gemini management consulting, systems transformation and information systems management Web site.

`www.mysap.com`
mySAP is an e-business solutions provider. Users can access daily activities, responsibilities and information. Online demonstrations are available for most services.

Strategy/Marketing Solutions

`www.kmgi.com`
KMGI provides interactive media for e-commerce sites. Presentations and demonstrations are available for viewing.

`www.eprise.com`
This site provides content management services.

`www.mgisoft.com`
This site hosts the ZOOM Server Software, allowing users to view pictures of products in more detail.

`www.xippix.com`
This site hosts the ImagePump Software, which operates in a manner similar to ZOOM.

`www.bitlocker.com`
This site provides Web-based database applications. An online tutorial to help you build your own database is available.

`www.openpages.com`
This site provides Internet content management services.

`www.genuity.com`
Genuity is an e-business solutions provider of networking, hosting and security applications. It was formerly known as GTE Internetworking and BBN.

www.answerthink.com

Answerthink helps businesses evolve with technical advancements. It provides marketing and branding, Web development and e-commerce services.

e-Business Solutions

www.bcentral.com

This end-to-end e-business solution includes everything from building an e-business and choosing domain name, to finding an insurance package and automating payroll.

www.webvision.com

This site provides end-to-end e-business solutions. Marketing, online payments and searching capabilities are among the solutions provided.

www.openair.com

OpenAir's PSA (Professional Services Automation) Service automates scheduling, expenses, invoicing and other essential business tasks.

www.livevault.com

This site provides automatic real-time database and file backup services.

www.hp.com/go/webqos

Hewlett-Packard's WebQoS (Quality of Service) prevents slow service and denial-of-service attacks. Security is discussed in greater detail in Chapter 7, Internet Security.

www.accpac.com

This site provides accounting and business management solutions.

www.sagasoftware.com

This site provides e-business integration software that supports information exchange and transactions.

www.internosis.com

This site provides e-commerce, knowledge management and assistance for Microsoft products.

www.allaire.com

The services offered by this site include e-business software that provides a complete infrastructure for online business.

www.netsetgo.com

NetSetGo is a provider of Internet professional services, such as application design, marketing strategies and Web-site hosting.

www.ospreyus.com

This site provides service solutions for designing, constructing and extending business.

www.upshot.com

This site provides Web-based sales management, allowing users to share sales information.

www.sitesmith.com

This site offers services that help improve the performance, reliability and security of large, complex Web sites.

www.fullecom.com

This site provides credit-card processing, product distribution, customer-service management and Web content services.

www.sterlingcommerce.com

This site provides e-business marketplace solutions, integration and consulting.

www.vignette.com

Vignette makes software that assists businesses in managing and publishing content on the Internet.

www.vitts.net
Vitts provides high-speed Internet access, Web-site hosting, outsourcing and network services.

www.level8.com
Level8's software integrates IT systems to increase organization and corporate efficiency.

www.siterock.com
SiteROCK manages your Web site on a 24-by-7 basis to keep it up and running.

Free Turnkey Solutions

www.websiteforfree.com
The free portion of the site's services include home-page design, the ability to make site corrections and use of the site's educational resources.

www.freemerchant.com
This site provides a free turnkey solution for building an online store and offers hosting, store-building capabilities and a shopping-cart model at no cost to the user.

www.bigstep.com
BigStep walks a user through the process of building a Web site. It covers building a home page, registering with search engines and accepting credit-card transactions.

Fee-Based Turnkey Solutions

www.tripod.com
This site offers its SiteBuilder tool for creating Web sites and provides several preset page layouts.

www.commerceone.com
CommerceOne offers a commercial solution that allows companies to set up their own B2B exchanges.

www.virtualspin.com
Virtual Spin offers a full range of e-commerce services including designing and implementing all of the infrastructure necessary to run an e-business.

www.auctionbuilder.com
AbleCommerce's AuctionBuilder 1.0 software allows users to build their own online auction sites. The software can be customized to meet the needs of specific e-businesses.

www.yahoostore.com
Yahoo! Store charges a monthly fee based on the number of items you want to sell. It simplifies the process of creating an online store. All the features you need to set up a complete e-commerce site are included.

Building and Managing a Web Site

www.homestead.com
Homestead allows users to select a template and add features to design their own free starter site.

www.estoremanager.com
This site hosts an application that allows users to build their own storefronts in a few hours. There is a monthly fee for hosting the sites.

www.webvision.com
Webvision will help you build your Web site as well as manage and maintain it.

www.allbusiness.com
This site is a small-business portal site, with links to localized business journals.

www.broadvision.com
Broadvision offers support and consulting services, such as customer relationship management (Chapter 10, e-Customer Relationship Management), billing and transaction automation.

www.newmediary.com
New Mediary helps Internet businesses locate one another. It provides free listings for your business.

www.channelweb.com
Channel Web is a portal for solution providers. The site offers B2B product pricing, news and reviews.

www.isharp.com
iSharp provides online testing services, including tests of transaction times and site traffic.

www.testyourlimits.mercuryinteractive.com
Mercury Interactive offers Web-site monitoring services that track the site from the viewer's perspective, examining aspects such as download times and transaction times.

www.holistix.net
Holistix provides Web-site management services and operates as a solutions provider.

www.outsourcegroup.com
Outsource Group allows users to monitor their human resources services.

www.employease.com
Employease helps businesses manage their employees. An online demonstration, that walks the user through screen shots of the service is available.

www.service911.com
This site provides technical support to your employees or your customers, both on your Web site and off-line. A free tour of its services is provided.

www.register.com/corporate
This site is a corporate domain-name registration service. The site provides Domain Lockdown™, an additional security feature that helps to prevent hackers or other third parties from altering your registration information.

Domain-Name Registration

www.register.com
This site enables users to search for, and register a domain name.

www.networksolutions.com
NetworkSolutions allows users to choose a domain name, as well as build and maintain a Web site.

www.greatdomains.com
When visiting this site, users can buy, sell or receive an appraisal on the value of their Web site.

www.domainit.com
Internet users can visit this site to register a domain name.

Incubators

www.raremedium.com
Rare Medium offers a variety of e-business solutions in addition to its incubation services.

www.campsix.com
Camp Six offers B2B incubation services.

www.ecorporation.com
eCorporation offers a variety of design and development incubation services.

`www.idealab.com`
This incubator has launched eBay, Refer.com and Netzero as well as many other successful online ventures.

`www.ehatchery.com`
eHatchery offers full-service incabation services.

SUMMARY

- Building, managing and maintaining a Web site involves advertising, marketing, customer relationship management, accepting online payments, providing and continuously updating content, recognizing cultural and legal parameters, providing security features for your visitors and your business and many other considerations.

- A solid business plan is essential. A business plan enables you to envision your e-business on paper for evaluation purposes.

- An Internet incubator is a company that specializes in the development of Internet businesses.

- Some incubators will finance and manage a growing dot-com without requiring ownership or payment up front. Rather, they provide assistance with the hopes that the successful e-businesses will compensate them at a later date.

- While elaborate design and graphics might attract customers initially, content should be the foundation of good Web-site design.

- Customers should be able to find and price products and services easily. Low switching costs, or the costs of changing vendors make e-commerce a fiercely competitive field.

- Web sites should be designed with consumers' preferences in mind. Market research can help you determine preferences by region and by demographic. Understanding these preferences will help you strategize and create more effective Web sites.

- Your Web site should also display a privacy policy detailing the intended uses of consumers' private information. Telling consumers how their personal information is used can influence their decision to visit your site.

- Answers to common questions can be made available by including a frequently asked questions (FAQs) link. Company contact information is another important element. Users should be supplied with an e-mail address, a phone number and a postal address.

- It is important to recognize that while multimedia such as streaming video and audio can enhance content, not all users have the capabilities to download this kind of information efficiently—or even at all.

- A domain name is the name that you use in the URL for your Web site. Choose a name that people will be able to recognize and type easily. Because your Web site will be accessible worldwide, it is important to consider how different groups of people will interpret your domain name.

- As domain names with the dot-com (`.com`) extension are becoming rare, people are beginning to use dot-net (`.net`) and dot-org (`.org`). Dot-net is usually used for network-related sites, while dot-org is normally used to denote nonprofit organizations.

- The fully qualified host name of a computer on the Internet has three major parts: the host name, the domain name and the top-level domain (TLD). Most Web servers use www as a host name.

- A domain name is often the name of the company that owns a site, or it is a word or phrase that otherwise describes the site.

- It is important to begin thinking about making e-businesses accessible to mobile devices.

- The Internet can also help an e-business owner manage fulfillment (i.e. warehouse storage, shipping, inventory management and return procedures).

- A manufacturer is the direct producer of the product and a distributor is the supplier who acts as a middleman to manufacturers and vendors, often reducing the price of an item by buying in bulk.

- Online supply-chain management also allows e-businesses and brick-and-mortar businesses with Web-enabled supply chains to accept made-to-order requests.

- Web-based fulfillment mechanisms will demonstrate if the product is available, if it has left the warehouse or if it has been delivered (and who signed for it).

- E-business owners may have the skills to manage a business, but typically do not know how to program and design a Web site. Web-site building services, human resources, e-consulting and marketing can all be outsourced to e-business solutions providers.

- An end-to-end e-business solution offers services to build a Web site from conception to implementation.

- An end-to-end solution should also provide for easy adaptation to your back-end systems, as well as fulfillment (payment authorization and account settlement, distribution and shipping) and data management.

- The Internet can help an e-business owner manage logistics.

- Fulfillment includes warehouse storage, shipping, inventory management and return procedures.

- Content management allows you to update information on your site in an efficient manner. It includes the ability to frequently update content, which can increase the frequency of return visits, and improved site consistency.

- Consulting firms guide developing e-businesses. Some operate as advisors, while others provide building and maintenance services similar to those provided by end-to-end providers.

- Creating an appealing employment package enables new companies to meet the needs of their current employees and serves as an incentive for prospective employees.

- Web-hosting companies provide products, services and support for companies, organizations and individuals to help them create and maintain Web sites. Many Web-hosting companies offer customers space on a Web server where they can build a Web site.

- A dedicated server is used by a Web-hosting company to serve only one customer's Web site.

- Colocation services provide a secure physical location for a business' server hardware. Typical colocation services include dedicated Internet connections and protection from power outages, fire and other disasters.

TERMINOLOGY

application service provider (ASP)
back-end systems
balanced scorecard
brick-and-mortar business
business plan
click-and-mortar business
colocation
content delivery networks
content delivery service
content management
dedicated server
deployment
design consistency
distributor

domain name
domain name system (DNS)
end-to-end e-business solution providers
frequently asked questions (FAQs)
front-end systems
fulfillment
fully qualified host name
host name
incubator
Initial Public Offering (IPO)
intelligent agents
Internet
Internet Corporation for Assigned Names
        and Numbers (ICANN)

m-commerce
manufacturer
merchant account
overhead cost
privacy policy
registrars
streaming audio and video

switching costs
time to market
top-level domain (TLD)
turnkey solution
venture capitalist
workplace management
zooming

SELF-REVIEW EXERCISES

3.1   State whether each of the following is true or false; if false, explain why.
  a) Internet incubators will usually receive less than 20 percent of a business when becoming investors in the business.
  b) Most Web servers use **http://** as a host name.
  c) Typical colocation services include dedicated Internet connections and protection from power outages and fire.
  d) Businesses that offer Internet services as a supplement to their physical presence are referred to as Web-and-mortar businesses.
  e) Including complex graphics, movie clips and audio on your Web site always makes the experience more enjoyable for the user.

3.2   Fill in the blanks in each of the following statements.
  a) An Internet _____ is a company that specializes in the development of Internet businesses.
  b) _____, or the ability to select one brand over another easily, makes e-commerce a fiercely competitive field.
  c) A fully qualified host name of a computer has three major parts: the _____ , the domain name and the TLD.
  d) A _____ server is used to host only one customer's Web site.
  e) It is important to include a _____ that details the intended uses of consumers' private information.

ANSWERS TO SELF-REVIEW EXERCISES

3.1   a) False. Internet incubators will often assume half the ownership in an e-business when investing in it. b) False. Most Web servers use **www** as a host name. c) True. d) False. They are referred to as click-and-mortar businesses. e) False. Not always; many users will not have the technical capabilities or computing power to download the site.

3.2   a) incubator. b) Low switching costs. c) host name. d) dedicated server. e) privacy policy.

EXERCISES

3.3   State whether each of the following is true or false; if false, explain why.
  a) The Internet can help an e-business owner manage logistics.
  b) **Freemerchant.com** offers Web site-building services including a merchant account for accepting credit-card payment for free.
  c) It is important to measure the amount of traffic a Web site can manage before launching the site.
  d) SAP is an acronym for: Systems, Applications and Providers of Digital Processing.
  e) Fulfillment usually includes warehouse storage, shipping, inventory management and return procedures.

3.4   Fill in the blanks in each of the following statements.
a) Typical _____ services include dedicated Internet connections and protection from power outages, fire and other disasters.
b) A domain name represents a group of hosts on the Internet; it combines with a host name and top-level domain (TLD) to form a _____, which provides a unique, user-friendly way to identify a site on the Internet.
c) _____ are responsible for managing the registration of domain names with individuals and businesses.
d) An _____ offers services to build a Web site from conception to implementation.

3.5   Define the following and provide an example of each:
a) incubator
b) manufacturer
c) distributer
d) design consistency

3.6   Pick 10 words that you think would be great domain names for an e-business. Go to any of the Internet name registration sites mentioned in this chapter. Which of the names are available? What percentage of the names on your list were available? What conclusions can you draw?

3.7   In this chapter, we discussed the importance of good Web-site design. Find a site on the Web that you feel could be designed better. Plan the layout of the home page and three other pages on the site—for example, a contact page, a products page, an "about us" page or a services page. You do not need to fully develop the content, as you are concerned only with design here. What links will you provide? What resources will be listed? Where will you put them? Then, choose a more effective domain name for this site. Why did you choose it? Visit **register.com** to see if the domain name of your choice is available.

3.8   *(Semester project)* In the beginning of this chapter (Section 3.2), we discussed the importance of having a well-structured business plan. Visit the tutorials mentioned, and download the free business plan software. Begin to familiarize yourself with the information necessary to develop a business plan. What questions do you need to ask yourself? Divide into groups of three to four people and brainstorm ideas for your own e-business. Assign people to conduct the necessary research. When you have accumulated enough information, begin working your ideas into a business plan for your new e-business. Present your business plan to the class, imagine that they are a group of possible investors. Be prepared to answer their questions, supporting your answer with the evidence you found in your research.

3.9   *(Project)* In this chapter, we explored several services on the Web that allow users to build their own Web sites. Many of these services are free to use. Visit one of the sites listed and begin to build your own site. Keep in mind design and layout. Add links and other features to make your site easier to navigate. Have others visit your site and provide you with feedback.

WORKS CITED

The notation <**www.domain-name.com**> indicates that the citation is for information found at that Web site.
1.   M. Lewis, "Boom or Bust," Business 2.0 April 2000: 195.
2.   J. Fallows, "The Other Divide," *The Industry Standard* 10-17 January 2000: 48.
3.   J. Fallows, 74.
4.   W. Bulkeley, "Clicks and Mortar," *The Wall Street Journal* 17 July 2000: R4.
5.   P. Carbonara and M. Overfelt, "The Dot-Com Factories," *Fortune Small Business* July/August 2000: 48.

6. P. Carbonara and M. Overfelt, 48.

7. P. Carbonara and M. Overfelt, 48.

8. `<www.raremedium.com>`

9. G. Saveri, "Inside an Internet IPO," *Business Week* 6 September 1999.

10. `<www.fool.com>`.

11. D. Tynan, "What to Name the Baby," *The Industry Standard* 24 April 2000: 158+.

12. D. Tyron, 160.

13. K. Kaplan, "New Competitors for Dot-com," `<Latimes.com>` 10 July 2000.

14. Kaplan,"New Competitors for Dot-com".

15. P. Loftus, "Internet Registry Firms Await Decision on Broad Expansion of Domain Names," *The Wall Street Journal* 23 October 2000: C26.

16. J. Black, "Tiny Tuvalu Profits From Web Name," *The New York Times* 4 September 2000: C2.

17. N. Moran, "How Supply Chains Will Become Dynamic Arteries," *Financial Times* 1 November 2000: VIII.

18. "Business-to-Consumer Fulfillment Raises the Bar," *Business Week* 26 June 2000.

19. "Logistics and Fulfillment: e-Commerce Meets the Material World," *Business Week* 26 June 2000.

20. "The Rise of MSPs," *Internet World* 15 October 2000: 30.

21. `<www.dell.com>`

22. "The Rise of MSPs," *Internet World* 15 October 2000: 30.

23. `<www.freemerchant.com>`

24. `<www.bigstep.com>`.

25. `<www.tripod.com>`. Tripod is owned by Lycos, Inc., and is part of the Lycos Network of sites.

26. `<www.commerceone.com>`.

27. `<www.virtualspin.com>`

28. M. Nemzow, *Building Cyberstores* New York: McGraw-Hill, 1997.

29. `<www.yahho.com>`

30. J. Rapoza, "AuctionBuilder capable, economical," *eWeek* 7 August 2000: 69.

31. `<www.websiteforfree.com>`.

32. J. Cunningham, "Ten Reasons Your Site Isn't Selling," *Web Techniques* August 2000: 18.

33. J. Nielson and D. Norman, "Usability on the Web Isn't a Luxury," *Information Week* 14 February 2000: 65.

34. M. Schwartz, "Sharper Staples," *Computer World* 12 June 2000: 76.

35. S. Kalara, "Disclaimer and the Dot-Coms," *Siliconindia* June 2000: 82.

36. `<www.egghead.com>`.

37. L. Downes, "Deconstructing the Web," *The Industry Standard* 14 August 2000: 186.

38. H. Bethoney and J. Repoza, "Microsoft Bundles Basics for E-Commerce," *PC Week Online* `<www.zdnet.com/pcweek/reviews/0216/26site.html>` 26 January 1998.

39. R. Dragan, "Microsoft Site Server 3.0 Commerce Edition," *PC Magazine* <www.zdnet.com/products/stories/reviews/0,4161,374713,00.html> 14 December 1998.

40. J. Symoens, "Site Server is a fine set of tools for Web site building," *Infoworld* <www.infor-world.com> 26 January 1998.

41. <www.dell.com>

42. <www.openair.com>.

43. S. McKie, "A Balance Sheet for Online Accounting," *Business Finance* July 2000: 76.

44. <www.intacct.com>

45. <www.akamai.com>

46. C. Henrie, "Command Performance," *Intelligent Enterprise* 5 June 2000: 34.

47. <www.isharp.com>

48. M, Songini, "Service lets users stress-test Web sites," *Network World* 31 July 2000: 36.

49. <www.sap.com

4

Online Monetary Transactions

Objectives

- To explore various methods of conducting online monetary transactions.
- To review the application of traditional payment models to the Internet.
- To discuss the role of security in support of online monetary transactions.
- To understand Internet-based monetary transaction models: e-billing, micropayments, peer-to-peer payments and digital currency.

Alas, how deeply painful is all payment.
Lord Byron

Cash payment is not the sole nexus of man with man.
Thomas Carlyle

Ah, take the Cash, and let the Credit go...
Edward Fitzgerald

So far as my coin would stretch; and where it would not, I have used my credit.
William Shakespeare

Beautiful credit! The foundation of modern society.
Mark Twain

O Gold! I still prefer thee unto paper,
Which makes bank credit like a bark of vapour.
Lord Byron

Outline

4.1   Introduction
4.2   Credit-Card Transactions
    4.2.1   Anatomy of an Online Credit-Card Transaction
    4.2.2   Credit-Card Transaction Enablers
4.3   Online Credit-Card Fraud
4.5   e-Wallets
4.6   Alternate Consumer Payment Options
4.4   Digital Currency
4.7   Peer-to-Peer Payments
4.8   Smart Cards
4.9   Micropayments
4.10   Business-to-Business (B2B) Transactions
4.11   e-Billing
4.12   Developing Payment Standards
4.13   Internet and World Wide Web Resources

Summary • Terminology • Self-Review Exercises • Answers to Self-Review Exercises • Exercises • Works Cited • Recommended Reading

4.1 Introduction

Secure electronic funds transfer is crucial to e-commerce. In this chapter, we examine how individuals and organizations conduct monetary transactions on the Internet. Credit-card transactions, digital cash and e-wallets, smart cards, micropayments and electronic bill presentment and payment are discussed. Also in this chapter, we list many of the companies that are playing important roles in online payment technology. We describe the products, software and services that these companies produce, and we direct you to their Web sites for further information. Many of these Web sites include animated demos. Security, a crucial element to the implementation and acceptance of online payment technology, is discussed in depth in Chapter 7, Internet Security.

 e-Fact 4.1

According to Forrester Research, the United States is expected to spend $1.4 trillion dollars online by 2004.[1]

4.2 Credit-Card Transactions

Although credit cards are a popular form of payment for online purchases, many people resist the appeal and simplicity of credit-card transactions due to security concerns. Customers fear credit-card fraud by merchants and other parties. Some credit cards, such as the Prodigy Internet® Mastercard® and American Express, have features enabling them to accommodate online and offline payments (see American Express feature). The Prodigy card also provides online fraud protection, as well as a point-based reward program that allows card holders to redeem points for Prodigy Internet access.[2]

American Express®: Enabling Secure Payments on the Web

American Express offers several online services to small businesses (**www.ameri-canexpress.com/homepage/smallbusiness.shtml**). Quarterly management reports, online account access and applications for accepting the American Express card can all be managed via the Internet. Business planning, travel planning, accepting international payments and global expansion are also among the services and solutions provided through the American Express Web site.

Blue for Business (**www18.americanexpress.com/blueforbusiness**) offers several features to enhance online business transactions. American Express's smart card, *Blue*, allows business owners to carry a balance and conduct secure online and offline transactions. The computer chip embedded on the face of the Blue card contains the cardholder's certificate of authenticity. When used in making online purchases, the card is used with a corresponding card reader. The user is also asked to enter a PIN number to enable the system to certify ownership of the card.

The American Express *Purchase Protection Program* protects buyers against damaged goods and the *Buyers Assurance Plan* offers an extended warranty on purchases made with the Blue card. American Express also offers the *Online Wallet*[SM], which works with the Blue card and smart-card reader. Through the Online Wallet, users can access *ExpressForm*[SM], which helps users fill out forms on the Web, and *Autobuy*[SM], a service that completes purchasing information for the user. Bill payment, online account access and e-commerce purchasing discounts are also available through Blue for Business. Interested users can take an online tour by visiting the Blue for Business home page.

For regular card holders, American Express offers *Private Payments*[SM]. Designed to protect user privacy, the Private Payments system provides a unique account number for each individual purchase. This number expires within 30 to 67 days of issue date, reducing the possibility of the number being stolen. Private Payments can be used on all Web sites accepting American Express, but it is limited by a few, specific transactions. For example, American Express recommends that the card not be used for recurring charges or purchases where the actual card must be presented, such as theater tickets. A tutorial (**www26.americanexpress.com/privatepayments/tutorial.jsp**) explains the purchasing process when using Private Payments. An animated demo enhances the tutorial.[3]

American Express @ Work[SM] is designed to facilitate larger corporations with enhanced integration technologies. The *Online Program Management* plan allows corporations to manage the corporate accounts of a large number of employees. Card authorization, cancellations and address changes can all be managed through the program. Corporate card reports are also available online. Businesses are notified by e-mail when the report has been posted. These reports can be downloaded, and saved and printed from the Web.

e-Fact 4.2

According to Cyber Dialogue, Inc., approximately 88 percent of the $53 billion dollars spent online in 2000 will be via credit cards.[4]

4.2.1 Anatomy of an Online Credit-Card Transaction

To accept credit-card payments, a merchant must have a *merchant account* with a bank. Traditional merchant accounts accept only *POS (point-of-sale) transactions*, or those that occur when you present your credit card at a store. With the growth in e-commerce, specialized Internet merchant accounts have been established to handle online credit-card transactions. These include *card-not-present* (CNP) transactions. For example, when purchasing on the Web, the card number and expiration dates can be provided, but the merchant does not see the actual card being used in the purchase. A merchant account can be established through either a bank or a third party service.[5]

When making a purchase online using a credit card (Fig. 4.1), the buyer will be required to submit their credit-card number, expiration date and shipping and billing information. This information is sent securely over the Internet to the merchant (Step 1 in the diagram). Issues of *authentication* (the person is, in fact, who they say they are), *authorization* (the money is available to complete the transaction), Secure Socket Layer (SSL) and Secure Electronic Transaction (SET) technologies are discussed in Chapter 7, Internet Security. The merchant then submits the credit card information to the *acquiring bank* (i.e. the bank with which the merchant holds an account) (Step 2). From there, the buyer's account information is verified. This involves the *issuing bank* (i.e. the bank from which the buyer obtained the credit card, and the credit-card association) (Step 3). Verification is received by the acquiring bank and is passed on to the merchant (Step 4), who then ships the product (Step 5). Payment cannot be issued to the merchant until the product has been shipped.

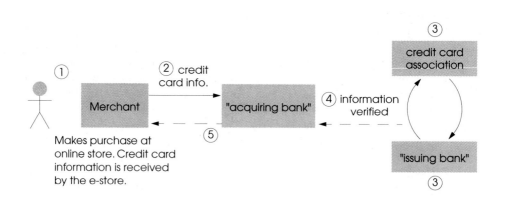

Fig. 4.1   Basic steps in an online credit-card transaction.

4.2.2 Credit-Card Transaction Enablers

Companies like CyberCash (**www.cybercash.com**) and iCat™ (**www.icat.com**) enable merchants to accept credit-card payments online (see the Cybercash feature). These companies have established business relationships with financial institutions that will accept online credit-card payments for merchant clients. iCat acts as a third party that receives consumer-credit information and securely interacts with both the consumer and merchant bank accounts to verify the sale and make monetary transfers.[6]

Trintech® offers online credit-card transaction capabilities. The *Payware*® product suite enables companies to process electronic transactions. The suite includes the *eMerchant* program, which enables merchants to accept online payments; *eHost*, which can accommodate transactions from multiple stores; and *eIssuer,* which issues the consumer a *virtual credit card* that is stored on the user's computer, providing one-click shopping at participating merchants. Trintech is also developing a *mobile payments* option that can be used from mobile phones.[7]

NextCard, Inc.® (**www.nextcard.com**) enables secure online credit-card transactions. The site offers a shopping portal, *GoShopping!,* allowing users to search for the lowest prices and an instant-payment option, *NextCard Concierge*[SM].

CyberCash[8]

CyberCash enables businesses to receive payments over the Web. *CashRegister*, an online service created by CyberCash, makes it possible for merchants to receive credit-card numbers, offer the numbers to the appropriate financial institution for validation and accept credit-card payments in a secure environment over the Web. Most major credit cards, such as Visa, Mastercard, Discover/Novus and some debit cards, can be processed by CashRegister. In addition to its CashRegister technology, CyberCash also offers affiliate-marketing services (see Chapter 9, Affiliate Programs) and payment solutions for offline businesses.

The CashRegister system works by establishing a direct connection between its Web servers and the Web sites of its e-business customers. A software application called the *Merchant Connection Kit (MCK)* is used to make this connection; the kit includes HTML files and sample scripts to use when adding CashRegister to an existing e-commerce site. [Note: HTML and scripting technologies for building Web sites are discussed in the computer programming case study in Appendices C through I.] In most cases, CashRegister can be built into generic shopping carts and storefronts, eliminating the need for customized software (shopping cart technology is discussed in Chapter 2, e-Business Models).

The CashRegister process begins once a customer is finished shopping on a merchant's Web site. The customer completes a form, entering credit-card and shipping information, and is presented with a screen containing items selected, prices and billing information. This information is then sent to CyberCash for validation. Once validation is received, the purchase can be completed, and funds are transferred electronically from the customer's account to the merchant's account.

CyberCash[8]

CashRegister offers convenience and security to its users. Using a complete set of *redundant servers* (i.e. identical servers for back up if one server fails), CyberCash is able to maintain continuous service and minimize downtime. CashRegister also keeps track of all transactions completed through a merchant's Web site and produces reports to assist the merchant with record keeping and customer tracking. To protect users' private information, all financial information transmitted via the Internet is encrypted and digitally signed. (Encryption and digital signatures are discussed in Chapter 7, Internet Security).

Cybercash, an e-commerce enabler, offers *FraudPatrol*™ in an effort to reduce online credit-card fraud. An animated demonstration of the service can be found at **www.cybercash.com/fraudpatrol/howitworks.html**.   FraudPatrol works with Cybercash's Merchant Connection Kit, sending an encrypted version of the transaction to FraudPatrol, where it is matched to collected data. If the transaction is suspect—or example, the same credit-card number has been used 20 times during that day—then the merchant can reject the sale (Fig. 4.2). There is an initiation fee (which varies for member and nonmembers) and each time FraudPatrol is used a transactional fee is charged.

To view an extensive list of CashRegister e-commerce software products, visit **cybercash.com/cashregister/solutions_software.html**.

Fig. 4.2   CyberCash FraudPatrol. (Courtesy of CyberCash™ Inc. CyberCash is a trademark or registered trademark of CyberCash Inc., in the United States and other countries.)

4.3 Online Credit-Card Fraud

Credit-card fraud is a significant problem for many e-businesses. When a credit-card holder claims a purchase was made by an unauthorized individual, or when a purchase was not received, it results in a *chargeback*. When this occurs, the charges in question are not the responsibility of the credit-card holder. In brick-and-mortar transactions, the merchant scans the card to produce proof of the sale and this is signed by the consumer. Should a chargeback occur, the merchant is protected against fines and reimbursement fees by having acquired this information. On the Internet, neither a scan of the card nor a signature is registered. When a chargeback occurs, it is most often the merchant who has to incur the cost.

e-Fact 4.3

According to First Data Group, 1.25 percent of transactions on the Internet result in a chargeback. This is approximately four times the percentage of catalog transaction chargebacks and nine times the percentage of brick-and-mortar chargebacks.[9]

In an effort to combat this, Visa established a list of high-risk business models. Businesses following these models are subject to high levels of credit-card fraud and, as a result, are highly penalized when their chargeback rates climb to a specified percentage of the total number of transactions. This percentage generally falls between 1–2 percent. Opponents argue that the method is overbroad, often deterring business owners from accepting online payments. The list includes travel and direct-marketing industries.[10]

VISA has also developed a list of "best practices" to be used by merchants when conducting credit-card transactions. The list includes implementing a firewall, using encryption (see Chapter 7, Internet Security) and anti-virus software, and incorporating inter-company security practice. The protocols are mandatory: merchants failing to meet the requirements may not be able to accept Visa credit cards as a method of payment.[11]

Most credit cards have a three-digit code on the back of the card. Mastercard has increased security by requesting this code when purchases are made. This number does not appear on receipts of transactions, so it cannot be lifted from discarded or stolen credit-card receipts.[12]

Nochargebacks.com provides merchants with a solution for preventing online credit-card fraud. Site members can access the site's database containing credit-card numbers, e-mail addresses and postal addresses used for purchases that resulted in a chargeback.[13] **Verifyfraud.com** offers similar fraud-protection services.

4.4 Digital Currency

Digital cash is one example of digital currency. It is stored electronically and can be used to make online electronic payments. Digital-cash accounts are similar to traditional bank accounts: consumers deposit money into their digital-cash accounts to be used in their digital transactions. Digital cash is often used with other payment technologies, such as digital wallets. Aside from alleviating some of the security concerns many people have about online credit-card transactions, digital cash allows people who do not have credit cards to shop online.

eCash Technologies, Inc. (**www.ecash.net**) provides software solutions that extend physical-world payment methods into cyberspace. eCash Technologies' product suite enables financial institutions and other businesses worldwide to offer a variety of secure, private and easy-to-use payment options. These include person-to-person (P2P), debit, business-to-business (B2B), prepaid and mobile payment options. The Monneta product suite also enables merchant-specific payment solutions, including electronic gift certificates and customer loyalty programs (Fig. 4.3). Demonstrations found at **www.ecash.net/Demo** describe how to obtain, use and give (as a gift) eCash currency.

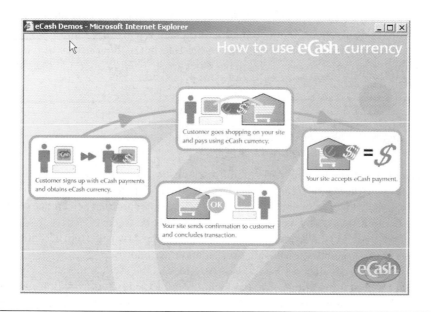

Fig. 4.3   Using eCash on the Web. (Courtesy of eCash Technologies, Inc. and ©2000 eCash.)

Gift cash, often sold as "points," is another form of digital currency that can be redeemed at leading shopping sites. It is an effective way of giving teen shoppers or those without credit cards the ability to make purchases on the Web. Flooz® (**www.flooz.com**) is an example of gift currency. *Flooz* can be used at online stores including **toysrus.com** and **barnesandnoble.com**.[14]

Some companies offer points-based rewards paid for completing specified tasks. These tasks may include visiting Web sites (which exposes the visitor to advertising), registering or buying products. One such reward scheme, *beenz*® (**www.beenz.com**), is an international, points-based currency system. Through a partnership with beenz, vendors can offer promotional systems. For instance, a retail site on the Web could offer beenz for registering with the Web site. As beenz are accumulated the customer can earn prizes, discounts or other rewards.[15]

Many companies are developing methods for teenagers to shop online (see VISA Buxx feature). **Internetcash.com** offers a digital-cash model for teenagers. It sells cards in various monetary denominations at convenience stores and gas stations. These cards are activated over the Internet and can be used to shop at teen-oriented member stores.[16]

4.5 e-Wallets

To facilitate the credit-card order process, many companies are introducing *electronic wallet* services. *E-wallets* allow you to keep track of your billing and shipping information so that it can be entered with one click at participating merchants' sites. E-wallets also store e-checks, e-cash and your credit-card information for multiple cards.

Visa Buxx: Developing Good Spending Habits[17]

The Visa Buxx card helps to develop healthy spending habits among teenagers. Parents and teenagers can register to use the card by visiting the Visa Buxx Web site (**www.visabuxx.com**). An online tour describes the service and highlights the benefits to both teens and parents. The card is accepted at more than 18 million merchants and can also be used as an ATM card. Similar to a debit card, the Visa Buxx card has a pre-determined balance that cannot be exceeded in any transaction. Security is administered through a PIN number determined by the card holder and each transaction is certified by the merchant through the credit-card association.

The Web site also provides *Money Tools*, a section dedicated to teaching teenagers how to manage their money. Discussions cover investing, banking, establishing credit and guidelines for shopping online. Parents and students can access account balances by visiting the site and typing in the correct usernames and passwords.

Credit-card companies, such as Visa, offer a variety of e-wallets (**www.visa.com/ pd/ewallet/main.html**). Some Visa e-wallets are co-sponsored by specific banks; for example, the *bankonewallet*[SM] is available to Bank One customers for use with only a Visa/Mastercard credit or check card. MBNA offers an e-wallet that allows the consumer to perform one-click shopping at member sites. Its e-wallet automatically fills in transfer, shipping and payment information on the forms of nonmember merchants.[18]

Entrypoint.com™ offers a free, personalized desktop toolbar that includes an e-wallet to facilitate one-click shopping at its affiliate stores (Fig. 4.4). The toolbar's features include news reports, sports scores and a stock ticker. Similar to MNBA, the Entrypoint e-wallet facilitates automatic form completion at nonmember stores. For a product demonstration, visit **www.entrypoint.com**. The demonstration highlights each function of the toolbar and provides an interactive demonstration of the various features. Users can also read through a commentary that further describes the product.[19]

There are many digital wallets on the market that are not accepted by all vendors. Visa, Mastercard and a group of e-wallet vendors have standardized the technology with the *Electronic Commerce Modeling Language (ECML)*. Since the standard was unveiled in June 1999, many of the leading online vendors have adopted it.[20]

4.6 Alternate Consumer Payment Options

Although *electronic payment* is more convenient, Internet merchants that do not accept credit cards can accept payments such as checks or money orders through the mail. Cash-on-delivery (COD), although rarely used in the United States, is another possible option for those who are hesitant to pay electronically. (Internationally preferred payment options are discussed in Chapter 12, Globalization).

Debit cards offer an alternative for credit-card holders to access their savings, checking and other accounts. These cards can be used in the same manner as credit cards, but instead of the customer paying a monthly bill, the funds are deducted directly from the customer's checking account. Customers are also able to withdraw cash from their accounts through *Automatic Teller Machines* (ATMs).

Fig. 4.4   EntryPoint Internet Toolbar. (Courtesy of EntryPoint Incorporated.)

Banks and businesses are also creating options for online payment that do not involve credit cards. Companies such as AmeriNet (**www.debit-it.com**) allow merchants to accept a customer's checking account number as a valid form of payment. AmeriNet provides authorization and account settlement, handles distribution and shipping (known as *fulfillment*) and manages customer service inquiries (Fig. 4.5).[21]

Other companies offering alternative methods of payment include **DoughNET.com**, which allows individuals under the age of 18 to establish an account for online shopping, and **RocketCash.com**, which redeems different types of online currency (i.e. beenz and cybergold) and allows them to be spent at participating merchants.[22]

4.7 Peer-to-Peer Payments

Peer-to-peer transactions allow online monetary transfers between consumers. eCash runs a peer-to-peer payment service that allows the transfer of digital cash via e-mail between two people who have accounts at eCash-enabled banks.

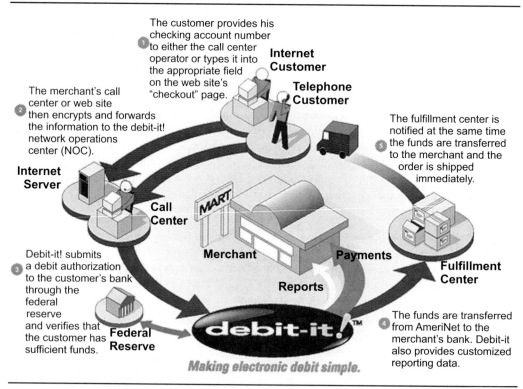

Fig. 4.5   Amerinet debit-it process flow. (Courtesy of **www.debit-it.com**.)

PayPal offers a digital-payment system. PayPal allows a user to send money to anyone with an e-mail address, regardless of what bank either person uses, or whether or not the recipient is pre-registered with the service. People wishing to send money to others can log on to PayPal at **www.x.com**, open an account and register the amount to be sent. That amount is billed to the person's credit card. Payment notification is sent to the recipient, and an account is established in the recipient's name. When the person to whom the payment is sent receives the e-mail notification, he or she simply registers with PayPal and has access to an account containing the payment. The funds in this account can be transferred to the recipient's bank account by direct deposit or mailed by check from PayPal.

Transactions through PayPal are instantaneous, the service is free for individuals sending money to one another and the payee is not required to enter any credit-card information. Businesses pay a small transaction fee.

The Paypal system can also be used to enable credit-card payment for auction items in *real time*. Credit card information is checked before a transaction is initiated. This means that the transaction begins processing immediately after it is initiated, reducing the risk of fraud or overdrawn accounts. The buyer or the seller can initiate the service. If you refer someone to PayPal, you will receive a small monetary reward. A visual demo of the service can be viewed at **www.pay.x.com/cgi-bin/webscr?cmd=p/auc/work-out-side**.[23]

eBay and Wells Fargo offer another form of peer-to-peer payment called *BillPoint*. It allows buyers to submit electronic payments to sellers' checking accounts.[24] Prior to this technology, buyers were required to send checks or money orders. Sellers can choose to include BillPoint as a payment option on their auction pages, so anyone can use the service without registering. Sellers pay a flat fee for the transaction and a percentage fee on the sale price above a given amount. In the future, eBay and Wells Fargo plan to sell this technology for use on other sites. To view a tutorial on the Billpoint system, visit **www.billpoint.com/help/tutorial.html.** This animated demo includes a detailed commentary, as it walks the user through the step-by-step payment process. Screen shots of the forms and services are highlighted.[25]

Another peer-to-peer payment company, **Tradesafe.com™**, accommodates the larger amounts typically involved in B2B transactions. **Tradesafe.com** offers peer-to-peer credit-card transactions and also provides its services to electronic merchants. If a purchase exceeds a certain amount, **Tradesafe.com** acts as an intermediary and withholds payment to the seller until the goods arrive in acceptable condition. **Tradesafe.com** also accepts personal checks, money orders and wire transfers.[26]

4.8 Smart Cards

Smart cards, cards with computer chips embedded on their faces, are able to hold more information than ordinary credit cards with magnetic strips. Smart-card technology can be used to hold information on health care, transportation, identification, retail, loyalty programs and banking, to name a few. Smart cards enable information for different purposes to be stored in one location.

There are *contact* and *contactless* smart cards. In order to read the information on the smart card and update information on the computer chip, contact smart cards need to be placed in a *smart card reader.* A contactless smart card has both a coiled antenna and a computer chip inside, enabling the card to transmit information. The contactless card enables faster information exchange than is possible using a contact smart card. For example, contactless cards are convenient for transportation services, such as an automatic toll payment. A contactless smart card can be placed in a device in your car to charge your account as you drive through toll booths.[27]

Smart cards can require the user to have a password, giving the smart card a security advantage over credit cards. Information can be designated as "read only" or as "no access." Security measures such as encryption (discussed in Chapter 7, Internet Security) can also be used. To address security concerns, the card can have a picture on its face to identify the user.

Similar to the smart card, eConnect (**www.econnectholdings.com**) provides solutions to make Internet transactions more secure through hardware devices. The company allows customers to use ATM cards to make purchases over the Internet. eConnect also has technology for securing credit-card payments. eConnect's product, *eCashPad*, is a device that connects to your computer and scrambles financial data, making it secure to send that data over the Internet. *ePocketPay* is another product developed by eConnect and will allow a consumer to make secure purchases from the ePocketPay portable device. This device acts as a cell phone with a card reader built into it.[28]

Financial institutions employ smart cards to provide benefits for their members. Visa has created *Visa Cash*, a smart card used to store money and make purchases. When you need to make purchases, you can place your Visa Cash card into the smart-card reader and view the balance before and after the purchase on your computer. Visa makes both disposable Visa Cash cards, which can be thrown out after the funds have been depleted, and reloadable cards, to which money can be added. (Additional information can be found at **www.visa.com/nt/chip/info.html**.) For more information about smart-card technology and smart-card companies, visit the Smart Card Industry Association at **www.scia.org**.

4.9 Micropayments

Merchants must pay a fee for each credit-card transaction that they process; this can become costly when customers purchase inexpensive items. The cost of some items could actually be lower than the standard transaction fees, causing merchants to incur losses. *Micropayments*, or payments that generally do not exceed $10, offer a way for nominally priced products and services (music, pictures, text or video) to be sold over the Web. Millicent (see the Millicent feature in this section) is a micropayment technology provider.

e-Fact 4.4

According to Gartner Group, in an ongoing study of online retailers, only a small percentage offered a payment option for items priced under $10.[29]

To offer the option of micropayments, some companies have formed strategic partnerships with utility companies. For instance, a phone bill is essentially an aggregation of micropayments that are charged at the end of a particular period of time in order to justify the transaction fees. The eCharge™ system gives companies the ability to offer this option to their customers.

eCharge uses *ANI (Automatic Number Identification)* to verify the identity of the customer and the purchases they make. The eCharge software can only be used with a dial-up connection. In order for your payments to be charged to your phone bill, a 1-900 number must be called. eCharge temporarily disconnects the user from the Internet to do this. Once the payment is complete, the user is reconnected. This process is completed quickly, with little inconvenience to the user.[30]

A number of companies will allow you to outsource your payment-management systems. Many of these systems can handle multiple payment methods including micropayments. Qpass is an example of a company that can manage micropayments for pay-per-download, subscription-based and pay-per-click systems. Qpass enables periodicals such as *The New York Times* and *The Wall Street Journal* to offer subscriptions over the Web. Customers who buy products and services through a Qpass-enabled company receive monthly bills that include descriptions of all purchases made during that month.

Additional services offered by Qpass include the Qpass *PowerWallet*, which registers passwords, credit-card information and other preferences necessary to make online transactions more efficient; customer service; marketing and sales assistance (Fig. 4.6). Visit Qpass at **www.qpass.com**.[31]

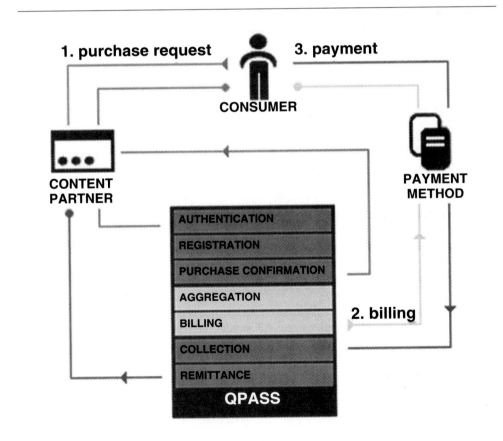

Fig. 4.6   QPass transaction process. (Courtesy of QPass, Inc.)

Millicent™: Enabling Micropayments[32]

Millicent is a micropayment technology provider. Companies that use Millicent payment technology allow their customers to make micropayments using credit or debit cards, prepaid purchasing cards or by adding purchases to a monthly Internet Service Provider (ISP) bill or phone bill. The customer uses any one of these payment methods to prepay a sum of money that can be used to make micropayments.

Millicent handles all of the payment processing needed for the operation of an e-business, including customer support and distribution services. Vendors can direct the transactions to Millicent, or the vendors can install the Millicent processing software on their own systems.

Millicent's services are especially useful to companies that offer subscription fees and small pay-per-download fees for digital content. This content may include text, audio, video, software applications or Web-based training products. Millicent payment technology can also be used with affiliate programs; the Millicent system will generate a payment to the affiliate once earnings exceed a predetermined minimum. Affiliate programs are discussed in Chapter 9, Affiliate Programs.

Millicent is a product of Compaq. The product currently is available in Japan; North American and European service will be available soon. Visit Millicent at **www.millicent.com**.

4.10 Business-to-Business (B2B) Transactions

The fastest growing sector of e-commerce payments is *business-to-business (B2B) transactions*. These payments are often much larger than B2C transactions and involve complex business accounting systems.[33] In this section, we explore many of the available B2B payment solutions and the services they offer (see the Tradecard feature).

Paymentech™ (**www.paymentech.com**) is one of the largest payment solutions providers for point-of-sale transactions on the Internet. Its systems are used by companies such as CyberCash, CyberSource® and AT&T SecureBuy. Brick-and-mortar and electronic merchants can choose from many transaction-processing options, including debit cards, credit cards, bank cards, checks and EBT authorization and settlement. *EBT (Electronic Benefits Transfer)* is defined by the USDA as the electronic transfer of government funds to retailers for the benefit of the needy.[36] The service also provides reporting and processing tools and services to help manage a merchant account and electronic check processing. Paymentech supports all types of credit and debit cards and conducts all transactions in a secure environment. Paymentech's online authorization systems, available on a 24-by-7 basis, enable merchants to initiate, transmit and receive authorizations in one phone call. Address verification can also be performed online.

Merchants using Paymentech can customize their payment-processing plans. For corporate use, Paymentech offers a Mastercard/Visa credit card, which enables electronic checking and billing and access to its *PaymentNet* online reporting service. PaymentNet allows merchants to track their expenses in a secure environment on a 24-by-7 basis. Its features include custom reporting, e-billing and cross-compatibility with other third-party expense reporting tools.[37]

ViaPay (**www.viapay.com**) offers debit-card and credit-card transactions with eCredit (**www.ecredit.com**) provides real-time, credit-transaction capabilities of B2B size. Using its *Global Financing Network* ™, eCredit customers can have access to automated credit approval and financing. eCredit's linked system of financing agencies and information networks makes large-scale commercial transactions convenient. eCredit establishes a relationship with a business and integrates automated systems at all levels of business transactions.

eCredit services such as *InstantDecision*™ and *BusinessVerify*™ allow businesses to access databases that check the credit and validity of new customers. More comprehensive **ecredit.com** services, such as *DecisionDesktop,* integrate financial information with the customer's credit policy to approve or deny transactions. eCredit also provides services that integrate the company's existing financial systems and automate the collections process.[38]

TradeCard™[34]

The TradeCard network provides a complete global B2B e-commerce infrastructure, expanding current e-commerce capabilities to the international level. Particular attention is paid to the complexity of cross-border data management and payment. Trade-Card attempts to provide an inexpensive and comprehensive solution that expedites all phases of global commerce.

Before using the TradeCard system, buyers and sellers must become TradeCard members. TradeCard's alliances, Coface Group and Thomas Cook, evaluate potential members to determine a credit score and perform anti-money laundering and *Office of Foreign Assets Control (OFAC)* checks. OFAC is responsible for enforcing international trade sanctions.[35] The buyer creates a preformatted electronic purchase order on the TradeCard system and presents the document to the seller for negotiation and agreement. The purchase order data is stored electronically in the TradeCard database, and electronic invoices and packing slips are produced from this data. All of these documents are available online to the relevant parties involved in the transaction. TradeCard uses a patented "data compliance engine" to check the information on the documents against the original purchase order (Fig. 4.7). If any discrepancies are found, concerned parties are notified immediately and can negotiate to resolve the conflict.

TradeCard then awaits delivery confirmation from a *third-party logistics services provider* (3PL), which is the industry terminology for a shipping company. When such confirmation is received and compliance is met, TradeCard completes the financial transaction by sending a request for payment to the buyer's financial institution. The actual monetary transfer to the seller's account is performed by Thomas Cook, a travel and financial services firm that is an alliance of TradeCard. Thus, TradeCard enables large-scale and large-dollar commerce without credit-card payment through direct interaction with existing financial institutions. For a demonstration of the TradeCard process, visit **www.tradecard.com**. The demo walks the user through the procurement, fulfillment, compliance and settlement services for both the buyer's and seller's point of view. Access to the demo requires the user to submit a limited amount of personal information. As a value-added service, TradeCard provides customers with access to a wide variety of integral trade service providers, such as logistics and international inspection companies.

TradeCard™[34]

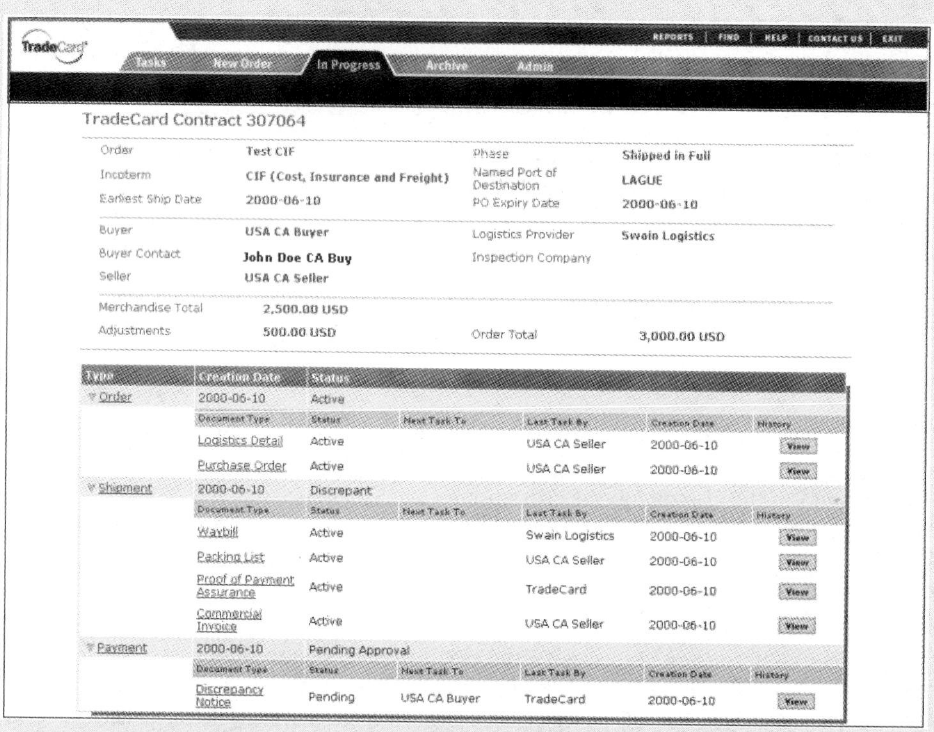

Fig. 4.7   TradeCard contract. (Courtesy of TradeCard Inc.)

Tradecard and Mastercard have also developed a method for conducting payment for large business-to-business transactions. Geared for overseas payments, the service will expedite the transaction process by implementing participating businesses' back-end systems. The service will operate on Mastercard's verification processes and Tradecard's international integration capabilities.

Clareon also facilitates B2B transactions by providing digital payment and settlement services (Fig. 4.8). Payment is digitally signed, secured and authenticated via *digital payment authentication (DPA)*. Unlike traditional EDI, Clareon is compatible with all *enterprise resource planning (ERP)* (i.e. a software system that integrates and automates manufacturing, distribution, management issues, projects and employees) systems and can adapt electronic records for companies, banks and each member of a given transaction. Clareon software downloads the DPA and remittance data and converts it into an XML format. (We introduce XML briefly in Chapter 5, Hardware, Software and Communications and then incorporate a more in-depth treatment of XML in the programming case study, Building an e-Business, in Appendices B through I.) From there, the information is again converted; the remittance data is sent to the seller and the DPA is forwarded to the bank. Both the buyer and the seller have access to the payment status.[39]

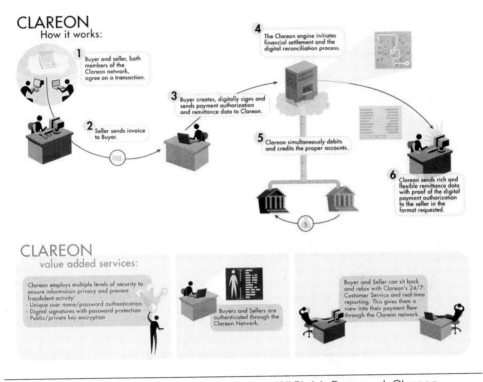

Fig. 4.8   Clareon online transaction service. (All Rights Reserved, Clareon Corporation 2000.)

Aside from enabling electronic payment, many business-oriented services are aimed at electronic consolidation and reconciliation of the business transaction process. By consolidating information from all entities involved in a business transaction and by accessing this information from a central portal, companies can track an entire transaction from "order-to-cash"—ordering, invoicing and settlement—while reducing administrative costs, errors, waste and complexity in the supply chain. eTime Capital (**www.etimecapital.com**) offers software applications with a simple Web-based interface to track payment and delivery systems. By supplying all parties with details of both the financial and logistical aspects of the transaction, eTime Capital facilitates smooth coordination of shipping and payments. The service also provides a forum for all parties to settle disputes that may arise over obligation fulfillment, thereby shortening delivery time and reducing costs.[40]

Other firms are *order-fulfillment providers*. Now that it has become so easy to open an electronic storefront, many companies suddenly find themselves dealing with *logistics*, or management details, and distribution. **SubmitOrder.com**™ attempts to bring its supply chain expertise and logistical services to small Internet businesses, providing a distribution network for smaller merchants. **SubmitOrder.com** can receive shipments at its warehouses directly from the merchant's manufacturers; the service then keeps track of the inventory and communicates electronically with the merchant. Orders are received directly at its shipping centers, where products are then packaged and shipped.[41]

Overall, many see Internet-based electronic B2B transactions as a convenience that will augment, but not replace, traditional *Electronic Data Interchange (EDI)* systems. EDI remains a useful technology for standard orders and business transactions between firms with established business relationships. Internet-based B2B seems to be gaining popularity in auction-type marketplaces and for sharing transaction documents over the Internet.

4.11 e-Billing

B2C market transactions are less complicated than B2B transactions. Using *Electronic Bill Presentment and Payment* (EBPP) a company can display a bill on multiple platforms on-line and offer actual payment processes. Payments are generally electronic transfers from consumer checking accounts. This is conducted through the ACH (*Automated Clearing House*), the current method for processing electronic monetary transfers (see the Check-Free feature).

e-Fact 4.5

Electronic Bill Presentment and Payment (EBPP) was estimated to be a $30 million market in 1999, with 5% of high-volume billers offering such services, and an additional 25% planning to do so within a year.[42]

e-Fact 4.6

According to the International Data Group, online payment processing is estimated to be a $1 billion market by 2004.[46]

CheckFree™[43]

CheckFree is a *consolidation service* that can service any biller and present consumers with all their bills in one interactive online environment. Many financial institutions that offer EBPP use Checkfree technology, including Yahoo! and most major U.S. banks.[44] If a biller has a partnership with CheckFree, the bill will arrive electronically in the recipient's CheckFree inbox.

If the company or person you wish to pay does not offer electronic billing, you can still set up payment to them from any bank account using the *Pay Everyone* service. All that is necessary is the recipient's address. CheckFree will print out a hardcopy check against your account and send it to anyone you wish to pay.

For billers, the e-billing option can add convenience and lower costs. While it costs anywhere between 50 cents and $2 to process a paper bill, e-bills cost 35 to 50 cents each.[45] For financial institutions, CheckFree offers its technology and services to enable a bank's site to become a comprehensive bill-payment portal.

All payments and outstanding bills can be tracked online and consumers have interactive access to their entire payment histories. Users can postdate payments as with paper checks and set up automatic recurring payments for mortgage payments and insurance premiums. CheckFree will alert you if there is a problem with any of your payments. Records of transactions can be exported to financial software such as Intuit's Quicken and Microsoft Money. A demo of the user experience can be found at **www.checkfree.com**. The animated demo walks the user through check writing, bill payment and payment tracking services.

Paytrust (**www.paytrust.com**), which has recently consolidated services with **PayMyBills.com**, has a consumer-focused approach to e-billing. First, customers indicate to Paytrust which bills they would like to pay through the service. Those billers are contacted and the bills are redirected to Paytrust. If the biller has the capability, Paytrust then receives the bills electronically from the biller. Otherwise, billers send the paper bill to one of Paytrust's biller distribution centers where the bills are scanned. Paytrust e-mails the customer announcements of newly arrived bills (paper or electronic) and impending payment due dates. The subscriber then logs on to the secure, password-protected, Paytrust Web site where they can review and pay their bill from their pre-existing checking account(s). A subscriber can set up automatic payments and recurring payments. An automatic payment is one that can be set up to be made on a recurring basis without requiring approval each time. Subscribers can indicate to pay the full bill, pay the minimum due or pay a fixed amount. A recurring payment is a payment that can be issued regularly for a fixed amount, without receiving a bill. An e-mail notice will be generated each time a recurring bill is about to be paid. Paytrust offers users the option to pay their bills anywhere using the Palm VII™ hand-held computer. Paytrust also offers *SmartBalance*™, which enables secure integration of users' Paytrust activity with their online bank account balances (Fig. 4.9).[47] For a demo visit, **www.paytrust.com/htmlu/tryitout.htm**. The demo walks the user through screen captures of bill-payment status, payment information and balance sheets.

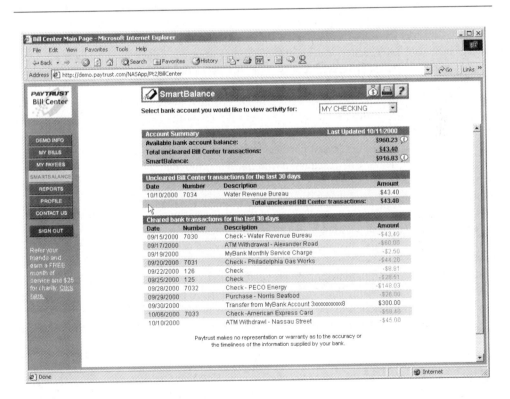

Fig. 4.9   PAYTRU$T SmartBalance™ screen shot. (Courtesy of Paytrust, Inc.)

The U.S. Postal Service offers online payment capabilities. The service is available for a free 6-month trial. After six months, users are charged a small monthly fee for the first 20 transactions then a nominal fee for each additional transaction. Registered users can pay anyone in the United States from any location. Payments are protected through a username and password. As an additional security measure, a *Payment Activation Code* is issued by the Postal Service and delivered to the user via postal mail. The user is required to enter this information before transaction capabilities are enabled. An online demonstration (**www.usps.com/ebpp/ebpp_demo/welcome.htm**) walks the user through registration and payment processes.

Yahoo! offers a similar service called Bill Pay. A free 3-month trial of the service is available. Users can then choose to continue the service for a nominal fee. An online demo is available at **help.yahoo.com/help/fin/bills/tour/tour-01.html**. It walks the user through the bill payment process, illustrating the screens that would appear to the user. An upcoming payments page reminds the user of scheduled payments and a message center allows the user to contact customer service representatives directly from the payment service. Yahoo! also offers online bill presentment, reducing the number of paper bills received by the consumer.[48]

Other companies accommodate billers, presenting them with services to enable EBPP. One such company is Derivion[SM] (**www.derivion.com**), which entered a partnership with Paytrust to accelerate consumer adoption of EBPP. Derivion provides billers with electronic capabilities in conjunction with Paytrust's service. Derivion offers billing companies the technology and expertise needed to transfer from paper to electronic billing, through a product known as *inetBiller*[SM], which also allows the billing company to maintain control over its e-bills. Billers can continue using customized bills including their logo and style to maintain their corporate identity. This increases cross-marketing possibilities and individual access to consumers. For example, a credit-card bill could include a link to upgrade the card level if the bill exceeds a predetermined threshold. Another example is a phone bill including a link to wireless services offered by the same provider. A demo can be found at **www.derivion.com**.[49]

Encirq (**www.encirq.com**) partners with banks that issue credit cards, presenting the consumer with what Encirq calls an *illuminated statement.* The illuminated statement is interactive, placing special offers from retail merchants to correspond with the itemized charges on a credit-card statement. Encirq's product offers even more cross-marketing possibilities than those previously mentioned, in that both the financial institution and the merchant are able to target customers with promotions. Encirq does this by building and updating a highly specific customer profile each time a new set of charges is received. Then the customer is categorized and matched with advertisers and specific advertisements. All of this is done in a secure environment where neither the merchant nor Encirq itself is privy to the customer's statement. The Encirq program is loaded onto the customer's desktop and advertisements are matched to the customer's purchasing profile.[50]

Encirq receives revenue from merchant ads and splits the profits with the financial institutions that host the illuminated statements.[51] This allows financial institutions to put to use the valuable marketing information they have about their customers without violating their privacy. This service is optional. If customers are happy with the service and take advantage of the merchant's offers, the result is greater use of the financial institution's credit cards, increasing profits and customer loyalty.[52]

Gerling, an international insurance company, offers debt protection to e-businesses participating in business-to-business transactions. *Tradecover* helps to ensure that payment will be received when international business is conducted. The service works with the database containing a list of high-risk companies.

4.12 Developing Payment Standards

The standardization of payment mechanisms on the Internet is essential to the success of e-commerce. Businesses offering domestic and international services must have assurance that payment will be received, that it is secure and that it is valid. Addressing security issues is crucial to the acceptance of online payment standards; consumers and merchants must be able to trust that their information is kept intact and remains secure during transmission. SET and SSL are two standards that protect the integrity of online transactions—these standards and other security issues are discussed in depth in Chapter 7, Internet Security.

Transaction information also needs to be standardized so that all parties are able to accept and read the information. The *Open Financial Exchange* (OFX) (`www.ofx.net/ofx/default.asp`) was developed and presented by Intuit, Microsoft and Checkfree in 1997 to serve as a standard mechanism for the exchange of financial information.[53] Small businesses, large corporations and private consumers can all use this technology to communicate financial information securely over the Internet. Private organizations are also developing online payment standards (see the Jalda feature).

Jalda™ Developing Standards of Payment[54]

Jalda, developed by Ericsson, is an open standard online payment system that connects *content providers* (anyone selling a good or service on the Internet) with an *Internet Payment Provider* (IPP). IPPs (network operators, ISPs, payment-card companies, banks or utility companies) aggregate the sum payment of content transactions, billing the consumer periodically. Often, when downloading music, text, etc., the sum cost of the download is too small to justify the transaction fees when processing a credit card. Jalda's technology has been designed to accommodate this.

By employing this standard of payment, users (both consumers and businesses) will be able to make purchases on the Web and through wireless devices (Wireless capabilities are discussed in depth in Chapter 6, Wireless Internet and m-Business). For example, a user can purchase a can of soda from a soda machine, travel through a toll booth and play a video game on the Internet and have all transactions placed on the same bill. Users enter a PIN code into their wireless device, which authenticates the transaction.

Jalda's Application Programming Interface presents the payment standard on the content provider's site. This is connected to a server managed by the IPP. When a transaction is made, it travels from the consumer to the content provider's API and then to the IPP. Jalda's API is downloadable over the Net. Payment for use of the service occurs between the IPP and the content provider.

In this chapter, we introduced the payment processes currently available on the Web. We discussed the advantages of offering payment options, as well as briefly discussing security issues related to online payments. In Chapter 5, Internet Hardware, Software and Communications, we explore the communications media and hardware used to connect computers to the Internet, as well as a brief introduction to how the Internet works.

4.13 Internet and World Wide Web Resources

General

www.thestandard.net
This site is an online magazine devoted to the Internet economy. E-commerce is among the subject headings and it provides a list of links to various electronic payment systems.

ganges.cs.tcd.ie/mepeirce/Project/oninternet.html
A list of links to various electronic payment systems is provided at this site.

www.internetindicators.com
This site provides Internet economic data. It is intended for people interested in learning about the Internet economy.

www.ofx.net/ofx/ab_main.asp
The Open Financial Exchange (OFX) Web site.

Credit–Card Payment

www.cybercash.com
CyberCash enables e-merchants to accept credit-card payments online. The company also offer an e-wallet technology and an online bill-paying service.

www.icat.com
iCat enables merchants to accept credit cards online. It will host your Web site and aid in site design.

www.trintech.com
Trintech offers a secure credit-card payment system that enables simultaneous purchases from multiple stores. This is used in virtual shopping malls.

shopping.altavista.com/home.sdc
This is the site of AltaVista's shopping mall. It uses the Payware eIssuer technology.

www.intellicharge.com
Intellicharge specializes in merchant-account management. It settles merchant accounts on the day of the request.

www.onlineorders.net
Onlineorders provides links and factual information regarding online payments and the methods of implementing payment systems.

E-Wallets

www.visa.com/pd/ewallet/main.html
Visa offers various e-wallets for use with Visa credit cards. These wallets are backed by a specific financial institution that issues the Visa card.

www.entrypoint.com
Entrypoint's product is a personalized desktop toolbar that offers easy access to news, sports, finance, travel and shopping. It includes an e-wallet feature for use at affiliate Internet stores.

`www.MBNAwallet.com`

MBNA wallet allows you to make all of your online purchases quickly and easily.

`www.brodia.com`

Brodia promises e-wallet services that enable users to store their credit-card numbers and other purchasing information for shopping online.

Checking Account Payment

`www.debit-it.com`

This site allows merchants to draw against the balance in their checking account as a valid form of payment over the Internet.

`www.netchex.com`

Netchex allows customers to set up an online debit-card system, where all purchases are deducted from a single Netchex account. This enables people to shop without using a credit card.

Digital Cash

`www.ecash.net`

eCash offers digital cash services for both online purchases and peer-to-peer payment.

`www.flooz.com`

Flooz is a form of digital cash that is used as a gift currency. Customers buy Flooz currency with their credit cards and then establish gift accounts. The recipient can then spend the Flooz account at participating stores.

`www.beenz.com`

beenz is an international, points-based currency system. It allows vendors to offer a promotional system on their Web site.

`www.giftcertificates.com`

This site allows Internet users to purchase gift certificates online.

`www.internetcash.com`

Internetcash is a digital currency that is aimed at teenagers. The currency is purchased through prepaid cards at convenience stores. Affiliated merchants are targeted to a young demographic.

`abracad.users.netlink.co.uk/emoney.html`

This is a link to a general resource page on digital-cash technology.

`www.rocketcash.com`

This service is designed for individuals under the age of 18. It provides them with an online spending account.

`www.doughnet.com`

Similar to RocketCash, this site provides an online spending account, particularly for users under the age of 18.

Peer-To-Peer Payment

`www.paypal.com/cgi-bin/webscr?cmd=index`

PayPal offers a peer-to-peer payment system that enables anyone to receive payment from anyone else via e-mail. Payments can be made by credit card or checking account.

`www.billpoint.com`

This site offers a peer-to-peer credit-card payment system designed by eBay and Wells Fargo and used on the eBay auction site.

www.tradesafe.com

Tradesafe is a credit-card peer-to-peer payment system that is aimed at business-to-business transactions. They provide B2B services and special security for large transactions.

www.moneyzap.com

The digital cash system offered through Western Union.

Smart Cards

www.scia.com

The Smart Card Industry Association Web site provides information on smart-card technology and services.

www.visa.com/nt/chip/info.html

This page contains information on the forthcoming smart card being offered by Visa, which will contain a digital-cash application and e-wallet services.

www.smart-card.com

A monthly e-magazine that contains comprehensive information on smart-card technology, as well as links to other sites.

www.nextcard.com

Nextcard has developed a credit card specifically designed for the Web. Online payments can be made with a built-in digital wallet.

www.americanexpress.com

American Express offers the Blue smart card (personal and corporate) and related services through its Web site.

Micropayments

www.hut.fi/~jkytojok/micropayments

This is a paper on electronic-payment systems with a focus on micropayments.

www.echarge.com

eCharge partners with AT&T to provide micropayment services billed to the user's phone bill.

www.ipin.com

iPin allows charges from micropayment purchases to appear on the customer's ISP bill.

www.trivnet.com

Trivnet's technology bills micropayment purchases to the customer's ISP bill.

www.qpass.com

Qpass is an e-commerce enabler. It allows companies to sell products and conduct secure transactions over the Web. It can provide the infrastructure needed to run your e-business.

www.millicent.digital.com

Millicent allows customers and e-businesses to conduct transactions using micropayments.

B2B

www.ecredit.com

eCredit helps entrepreneurs and established businesses find credit to support their online operations. eCredit will also help you manage your money.

www.clareon.com

Clareon provides end-to-end e-commerce solutions connecting buyers and sellers with a secure payment system.

www.etimecapital.com
eTimeCapital provides a solution for accounts receivable and cash-flow management on the Web.

www.tradecard.com
Tradecard handles international trade and e-commerce over the Web. Tradecard provides secure on-line payments.

www.swift.com
Swift's site offers secure, online, international credit-card transactions.

EBPP

www.checkfree.com
Checkfree allows you to receive and pay your bills online.

www.paytrust.com
Paytrust is a an online bill-payment system. Paytrust allows you to access and pay your bills with the *Palm VII* organizer.

www.derivion.com
Derivion provides bill-payment capabilities.

www.encirq.com
Encirq allows bill payment sites to add targeted advertising to online customer statements.

www.usps.gov
The U.S. Postal service offers bill-paying services.

bills.yahoo.com
Yahoo! offers bill payment and presentment services through its Web site. The service includes message delivery and payment updates. The first three months are free.

www.c2it.com
This free, online service offered through Citibank enables peer-to-peer payments.

SUMMARY

- The electronic transfer of funds is crucial to e-commerce.
- The major online payment schemes include payments by credit card, cash, and check, payments to businesses, peer-to-peer payments, banking and bill paying.
- Customers are concerned about the possibility of credit-card fraud by merchants or other parties.
- When making a purchase online using a credit card, the buyer will be required to submit their credit card number, expiration date and shipping and billing information.
- The merchant submits the credit card information to the *acquiring bank* or to the bank with which the merchant holds an account. From there, the buyer's account information is verified. This involves the *issuing bank*, or the bank from which the buyer obtained the credit card, and the credit-card association. Verification is received by the acquiring bank and is then passed on to the merchant, who will ship the product. Payment cannot be issued to the merchant until the product has been shipped.
- To accept credit card payments, a merchant must have a merchant account with a bank.
- E-wallets allow you to keep track of your billing and shipping information, so that it can be entered with one click at participating merchants' sites. They also store e-checks, e-cash and your credit-card information for multiple cards.
- IAlthough electronic payment is more convenient, Internet merchants that do not accept credit cards can accept payments in the form of checks or money orders through the mail.

- Debit cards offer an alternative for card holders to access their savings, checking and other accounts. These cards can be used in the same way as a credit card, but instead of paying a monthly bill, the charge is automatically deducted from the customer's checking account.

- There are many forms of digital currency; digital cash is stored electronically and can be used to make online electronic payments.

- Digital-cash accounts are similar to traditional bank accounts; consumers deposit money into their digital-cash accounts to be used in their digital transactions.

- Aside from alleviating some of the security fears that many people have about online credit-card transactions, digital cash allows people who do not have credit cards to shop online, and merchants who accept digital cash payments avoid credit-card transaction fees.

- Gift cash, often sold as points, is another form of digital currency that can be redeemed at leading shopping sites. It is an effective way of giving teen shoppers, or those without credit cards, the ability to make purchases on the Web.

- Some companies offer points-based rewards offered in exchange for completing specified tasks. These tasks may include visiting Web sites, registering or buying products.

- Peer-to-peer transactions allow the online transfer of money between consumers.

- PayPal allows a user to send money to anyone with an e-mail address, regardless of what bank either person uses or whether or not the recipient is preregistered with the service.

- The X Payment system can be used to enable credit-card payment for auction items in real time. This means that the transaction begins processing immediately after it is initiated, reducing the risk of fraud or overdrawn accounts.

- eBay and Wells Fargo offer another form of peer-to-peer payment called BillPoint. It allows buyers to submit electronic payments to sellers' checking accounts.

- Another peer-to-peer payment company, **Tradesafe.com**, accommodates the larger amounts typically involved in B2B transactions.

- A smart card, a card with a computer chip embedded on its face, is able to hold more information than an ordinary credit card with a magnetic strip.

- Smart-card technology has many applications. Smart cards can be used to store health care, transportation, identification, purchasing, loyalty programs and banking information, to name a few.

- There are contact and contactless smart cards. Contact smart cards need to be placed in a smart card reader. A contactless smart card has both a coiled antenna and a computer chip inside, enabling the card to transmit information.

- eConnect's product, eCashPad is a device that connects to your computer and scrambles financial data, making it secure to send over the Internet.

- Visa has created Visa Cash, a smart card used to store money and make purchases.

- Micropayments, which generally do not exceed $10, provide a way for companies offering nominally priced products and services (music, pictures, text or video) to receive payments online without the use of a credit card.

- The fastest growing sector of e-commerce payments is business-to-business (B2B) transactions. These payments are often much larger in size than B2C transactions and involve complex business accounting systems.

- EBT (Electronic Benefits Transfer) is defined by the USDA as the electronic transfer of government funds to retailers for the benefit of the needy.

- eCredit provides real-time, credit-transaction capabilities of B2B size.

- Aside from enabling electronic payment, many business-oriented services are aimed at integrating business transaction processes.

- E-billing technologies are finding success in the B2C market, where transactions are less complicated than B2B transactions.

- Paytrust has a consumer-focused approach to e-billing. Users send their bills directly to Paytrust, which then scans them and places them online for the consumer to view.

- Encirq's illuminated statement is interactive and includes special offers from retail merchants that correspond with the itemized charges on a credit-card statement.

- The *Open Financial Exchange* (OFX) was presented by Intuit, Microsoft and Checkfree in 1997 to serve as a standard mechanism for the exchange of financial information.

TERMINOLOGY

ACH (Automated Clearing House)
acquiring bank
Advanced Fraud Detection
Amerinet
ANI (Automatic Number Identification)
authentication
authorization
AutoBuy
Automatic Teller Machines (ATMs)
bankonewallet
business-to-business (B2B)
BusinessVerify
card not present transactions (CNP)
chargeback
consolidation service
contact smart card
contactless smart card
content provider
CyberCash CashRegister
CyberCash Instabuy
debit card
DecisionDesktop
digital cash
digital payment authentication (DPA)
eCashPad
Electronic Benefits Transfer (EBT)
Electronic Bill Presentment and Payment (EBPP)
Electronic Commerce Modeling Language
    (ECML)
Electronic Data Exchange (EDI)
electronic payment
eMerchant
enterprise resource planning (ERP)

e-PocketPay
e-wallet
fulfillment
Global Financing Network
illuminated statement
inetBiller
Internet Payment Provider (IPP)
issuing bank
logistics
merchant account
Merchant Connection Kit (MCK)
micropayment
mobile payment
Office of Foreign Assets Control (OFAC)
Open Financial Exchange
order-fulfillment provider
pay-everyone services
PaymentNet
peer-to-peer payment
point-of-sale (POS) transactions
PowerWallet
real time
redundant servers
SmartBalance
smart card
smart-card reader
Standard Fraud Detection
third-party logistics service provider
Trintech eHost
Trintech eIssuer
virtual credit card
Visa Cash
X Payments

SELF-REVIEW EXERCISES

4.1　State whether the following are true or false. If the answer is false, explain why.
　　a)　An e-commerce site must establish a merchant account with a bank before credit-card orders can be processed online.

b) When purchasing on the Web, the card number and expiration dates can be provided, but the merchant does not see the actual card being used in the purchase. This is called a card-not-present (CNP) transaction.

c) eCash is accepted by all e-commerce Web sites as a form of payment.

d) eCharge is a micropayments system that is billed through your e-mail account.

e) Micropayments are small sums of money that can be charged to a user for products and services bought online.

4.2   Fill in the blanks in each of the following:

a) Millicent offers a cost effective system of collecting small sums of money over the Internet. These small sums are called _____.

b) Traditional merchant accounts accept only _____, or those that occur when you present your credit card at a store.

c) The _____ is the bank with which the merchant holds an account.

d) The _____ is the bank from which the buyer obtained the credit card.

e) The _____ payment system allows for monetary transactions over the Internet between two consumers.

ANSWERS TO SELF-REVIEW EXERCISES

4.1   a) True. b) True. c) False. Only participating stores accept eCash. The customer, merchant and bank must all be able to use the eCash system d) False. eCharge is a micropayments system that automatically places charges on your home phone bill. e) True.

4.2   a) Micropayments. b) POS (point-of-sale) transactions. c) acquiring bank. d) issuing bank. e) Instabuy.

EXERCISES

4.1   State whether the following are true or false. If the answer is false, explain why.

a) InetBiller is a peer-to-peer payment system.

b) Smart cards can be used only to make online purchases.

c) A contactless smart card has both a coiled antenna and a computer chip inside.

d) EBPP stands for electronic bill presentment and payment.

e) In order to make a credit-card purchase on the Web, the consumer must be 21.

4.2   Fill in the blanks in each of the following:

a) iPin offers micropayments that are billed to the client within their _____ bill.

b) A _____ stores information on the user's computer, providing one-click shopping at participating merchants.

c) _____, an online service created by CyberCash, makes it possible for merchants to receive credit-card numbers, offer the numbers to the appropriate financial institution for validation and accept them as a form of payment in a secure environment over the Web.

d) Visa, Mastercard and a group of e-wallet vendors have standardized e-wallet technology with the _____.

e) _____ is the online payment system offered by Visa to help young consumers manage their money and make purchases on the Web.

4.3   Categorize each of the following items as either e-billing or peer-to-peer payment:

a) PayPal

b) CheckFree

c) Encirq

d) BillPoint

e) TradeSafe

4.4   Define the following:
  a) digital cash
  b) peer-to-peer payment
  c) e-wallet
  d) micropayments
  e) EBPP
  f) merchant account
  g) smart card

4.5   (*Class Discussion*).In this chapter, we discuss online payment processes and some of the concerns related to making purchases over the Internet. Security, privacy and accuracy are among the greatest concerns. Poll your friends, family and professors. What percentage of people you talked to had made a purchase online. Did they have any problems? Using the information provided and additional research, decide which mechanisms are best suited for protecting credit-card information. Consider both Visa and Mastercard's approach. How do they compare? Be prepared to discuss your answers.

4.6   In this chapter we discuss peer-to-peer payments. Visit the BillPoint demonstration at **www.billpoint.com/help/tutorial.html** and answer the following questions.
  a) According to the tutorial, which two links are necessary to use BillPoint Online Payments?
  b) What is the action taken by the seller at the close of the auction?
  c) Name three of the items required in the BillPoint invoice.
  d) What are the two methods that can be chosen by the bidder for initiating payment?

4.7   In this chapter, we discuss e-billing. Visit the CheckFree demo at **www.checkfree.com** and answer the following questions.
  a) What are the four fields that must be filled out in the check payment process?
  b) What feature allows you to make several payments at once?
  c) What feature allows you to make repeated payments?
  d) In the Payment Histories feature, what are the three status indicators?
  e) What are the two programs that payment histories can be exported into?

4.8   In this chapter, we introduced the EBPP service offered through the U.S. Postal Service. Visit the online demonstration and answer the following questions.
  a) Name the four ways you can add a new payee to your payee list.
  b) How is the Payment Activation Code distributed to the user?
  c) A list of your paid, cancelled and failed checks can be viewed at what location?

WORKS CITED

The notation <**www.domain-name.com**> indicates that the citation is for information found at that Web site.
1. ViaPay advertisement. *Worth* Nov. 2000.
2. <**www.prodigycard.com/About.html**>.
3. M. Trombly, "Amex Unveils Disposable Credit Numbers," *Computer World* 11 September 2000: 4.
4. R. Crocket, "No Plastic? No Problem," *Business Week E.Biz* 23 October 2000: 18.
5. <**www.online-commerce.com/tutorial2.html**>.
6. <**www.icat.com**>.
7. <**www.trintech.com**>.
8. <**www.cybercash.com**>.

9. J. Angwin, "Credit-Card Scams Bedevil E-Stores," *The Wall Street Journal* 19 September 2000: B1.

10. R. Barrett, "E-Tailers Caught in Card," *Inter@ctive Week* 10 April 2000: 10.

11. E. Messmer, "Online card fraud targeted," *Network World* 21 August 2000: 1, 72.

12. E. Messmer, "Online card fraud targeted," *Network World* 21 August 2000: 1, 72.

13. <www.nochargebacks.com>.

14. <www.flooz.com>.

15. <www.beenz.com>.

16. <www.internetcash.com>.

17. <www.visa.com>.

18. <www.visa.com/pd/ewallet/main.html>.

19. <www.entrypoint.com>.

20. M. Barnett, "Credit Card Heavies Unveil E-Wallet Standard," **TheStandard.com** 14 June 1999.

21. <www.debit-it.com>.

22. R. Crockett, "No Plastic? No Problem?" *Business Week E.Biz* 23 October 2000: 18.

23. <www.x.com>.

24. G. Naders, "EBay, Wells Team Up On Web Payments," *The Wall Street Journal* 1 March 2000

25. <www.billpoint.com>.

26. <www.tradesafe.com>.

27. <www.gemplus.com/basics/what.html>.

28. <www.econnectholdings.com/econ_intro.html>.

29. M. Solomon, "Micropayments," *Computer World* 1 May 2000: 62.

30. <www.echarge.com>.

31. <www.qpass.com>.

32. <www.millicent.com>.

33. J. Vijayan, "Business-to-Business Billing No Easy Task," *Computer World* 13 March 2000: 20.

34. <www.tradecard.com>.

35. <www.treas.gov/ofac>.

36. <www.usda.com>.

37. <www.paymentech.com>

38. <www.ecredit.com> and conversation with customer service representative.

39. <www.clareon.com>.

40. <www.etimecapital.com>.

41. <www.submitorder.com>.

42. <www.treas.gov/fac>.

43. <www.checkfree.com> and customer service representative.

44. M. Richey, "A Checklist For CheckFree," **MotleyFool.com** 23 May 2000.

45. [C. Le Beau, "The Big Payoff," **TheStandard.com** 8 May 2000.

46. L. Rosencrance, "IDC: More People Paying Bills Online," *Computer World* 17 April 2000: 26.

47. <**www.paytrust.com**>.

48. <**bills.yahoo.com**>.

49. <**www.derivon.com**>.

50. <**www.encirq.com**>.

51. M. Charski, "Extending Credit-Card Bills," *Inter@ctive Week* 22 May 2000: 63.

52. <**www.encirq.com**>.

53. <**www.ofx.net/ofx/default.asp**>.

54. <**www.jalda.com**>.

Part 3

e-Business and e-Commerce

Outline

Chapter 5   Internet Hardware, Software and
             Communications
Chapter 6   Wireless Internet and m-Business
Chapter 7   Internet Security

5

Internet Hardware, Software and Communications

Objectives

- To explore how the Internet works.
- To introduce some of the communications media and hardware used to connect computers on the Internet.
- To introduce technologies used for high-speed Internet connections, such as fiber optics, DSL and broadband.
- To introduce new Internet-related initiatives, including Internet2® and Microsoft® .NET.
- To explore technologies used to enhance online business communications.

"Now! Now!" cried the Queen. "Faster! Faster!"
Lewis Carroll

In the future, you're going to get computers as prizes in breakfast cereals. You'll throw them out because your house will be littered with them.
Robert Lucky

It took five months to get word back to Queen Isabella about the voyage of Columbus, two weeks for Europe to hear about Lincoln's assassination and only 1.3 seconds to get the word from Neil Armstrong that man can walk on the moon.
Isaac Asimov, Isaac Asimov's Book of Facts

A new beauty has been added to the splendor of the world— the beauty of speed.
Fillippo Tommaso Marinetti

Outline

5.1   Introduction
5.2   Structure of the Internet
5.3   Hardware
        5.3.1   Servers
        5.3.2   Communications Media
        5.3.3   Storage Area Networks (SANs)
5.4   Connecting to the Internet
        5.4.1   Digital Subscriber Line (DSL)
        5.4.2   Broadband
        5.4.3   Integrated Services Digital Network (ISDN)
        5.4.4   T-1 and T-3 Lines
5.5   Internet2®
5.6   Software
        5.6.1   Application Service Providers (ASPs)
        5.6.2   Databases
5.7   Operating Systems
        5.7.1   UNIX®
        5.7.2   Microsoft Windows®
        5.7.3   Linux®
        5.7.4   Mac® OS X
5.8   Enhancing Business Communication
        5.8.1   Intranets and Extranets
        5.8.2   Streaming Audio and Video
        5.8.3   Internet Telephony
        5.8.4   Webcasting and Web Conferencing
5.9   Internet and World Wide Web Resources

Summary • Terminology • Self-Review Exercises • Answers to Self-Review Exercises • Exercises •
Works Cited • Recommended Reading

5.1 Introduction

In this chapter, we explore the technology of the Internet, including hardware, software and communications. We discuss technologies such as fiber optics, which enables high-speed data transfers over the Internet. We introduce new technologies that provide relatively inexpensive, high-speed Internet service to homes and businesses, such as digital subscriber lines (DSL) and broadband Internet media. We discuss streaming media (audio and video), Internet telephony and other technologies used to enhance online business communications.

Years ago, application development was expensive, due to the high costs of hardware, software and communications. Computers and communications were much slower than they are today. Now, with advancements in technology, these costs are rapidly decreasing, speeds are increasing, and, with fiber optics, the volume of data transfers over the Internet is becoming virtually unlimited.

e-Fact 5.1

Moore's Law: In 1965, Gordon Moore, cofounder of Intel, observed that the number of transistors per square inch on integrated circuits had doubled every year since the integrated circuit was invented. He predicted that this trend would continue. Data density has doubled approximately every 18 months. It is expected that this trend will continue for at least 20 more years.[1]

5.2 Structure of the Internet

The Internet is a network of interconnected *host computers*, or *hosts*. Each host is assigned a unique address called an *IP address* (IP stands for *Internet Protocol*). Just as people use street addresses to locate houses or businesses in a city, computers use IP addresses to locate other computers on the Internet.

Computers on the Internet communicate with each other by sending *packets* of data across the network. A packet is much like a letter sent through the post office. A letter consists of an envelope with the address of the person who sent the letter, a delivery address and the letter's contents. Similarly, packets sent across the Internet contain a *source address*, a *destination address*, *sequencing information*, *error-control information* and the *data* to be delivered to the destination address. The source address is the IP address of the computer that sent the packet, and the destination address is the IP address of the computer to which the data was sent. When a computer sends data across the Internet, the data is usually divided into multiple packets. The packets may arrive at the destination host out of order. The host that receives the packets uses the sequencing information to rearrange the data into their proper order. In Chapter 7, Internet Security, we discuss how communications are kept secure.

Packets are generally not sent directly to the destination address. The Internet is a large, complex network; each host could not possibly know the best route by which a packet should be sent to any other host on the Internet. Therefore, a special kind of host, called a *router*, is used to move packets across the Internet efficiently. A packet may pass through many routers before it reaches its destination. Sending a packet through many computers may seem inefficient, but the Internet was designed so that if one part of the network fails, the remaining parts can still function. Routers are responsible for redirecting packets around portions of the network that may have failed and for ensuring that packets are delivered to the proper destination hosts.

5.3 Hardware

The Internet employs many advanced hardware technologies. In this section, we discuss the various communications media used to connect hosts, as well as the roles hosts play on the Internet.

5.3.1 Servers

A *server* is a host on the Internet that manages network resources and fulfills requests from *clients*. There are many types of servers, including *Web servers, e-mail servers, database servers* and *file servers*. A single server may provide multiple services. For example, one server may act as both a Web server and a file server.

A Web server stores Web pages and delivers the pages to clients upon request. A Web browser uses the *hypertext transfer protocol* (*HTTP*) to request and transfer pages from a Web server. A *protocol* defines the steps necessary for computers to communicate over the Internet. Other common protocols include the *file transfer protocol* (*FTP*) for sending large files and documents, the *post office protocol* (*POP*) for receiving e-mail and the *simple mail transfer protocol* (*SMTP*) for sending e-mail.

Most requests to a Web server from a browser are requests for HTML documents. We present a thorough introduction to HTML in Appendices C and D.

5.3.2 Communications Media

A *communications medium* is the hardware that connects computers and other digital equipment. The most important measure for a communications medium is its *bandwidth*, which indicates how much data can be transferred through the medium in a fixed amount of time. If we were plumbers, we might measure the number of gallons of water that could flow through a pipe in one second. A wide pipe allows more water to flow through per second than a narrow pipe. Likewise, a high-bandwidth communications medium allows more data to flow through per second than a low-bandwidth communications medium. Bandwidth is usually measured in *bits per second* (*bps*) (bits are "binary digits"—pieces of data that can have the value 0 or 1), *kilobits per second* (*Kbps*) or *megabits per second* (*Mbps*). A kilobit is about 1000 bits per second (actually, 1024), and a megabit is about a million bits per second (actually, 1024 multiplied by 1024). A medium that can transmit data at a rate of 1.5 Mbps is able to transfer approximately 1,500,000 bits of data in one second. Communications media have become so fast that we even talk about *gigabits per second* (*gbps*)—about a billion bits per second and terabits-per-second (i.e., trillion-bits-per-second) communications media (check out Metromedia at **www.mmfn.com**)!

For many years, *copper wire* has been the primary communications medium. The *plain old telephone system* (*POTS*), used for voice telephone calls around the world, was built with copper wire. There are many advantages to using copper wire, including wide availability, reliability and ease of installation. However, copper wire has proven inadequate for handling ultra-high-speed data transmission between computers.

Fiber-optic cable, which is composed of flexible glass fiber, is thinner and lighter than traditional copper wire, yet has much wider bandwidth. Traditional copper wire carries electronic signals that are interpreted by computers as bits. Fiber-optic cable uses short bursts of light to represent bits. An *optical modem* (modem stands for *modulator and demodulator*) translates digital signals from computers into light through a process called *modulation*. The light is transmitted over the fiber-optic cable to the receiver's optical modem, which converts the light back into electrical signals through a process called *demodulation*.

Recently, an advanced optical technology called the *opto-chip* was developed. The opto-chip is able to convert the most basic particle of light, the photon, into an electric current. This process allows tremendous amounts of data to be sent over fiber-optic networks through particles 100 times smaller than the diameter of a human hair.[2] Further enhancements to fiber-optic technology allow multiple wavelengths of light to be transmitted over a single fiber. Each additional wavelength greatly increases the data-carrying capacity of fiber-optic technology.

The strength of a signal transmitted over a communications medium, such as copper wire or fiber-optic cable, is reduced as the signal travels farther and farther. Copper wire and fiber-optic cable are therefore limited by the distances over which they can transmit signals reliably. *Repeaters* can be used to alleviate this problem by amplifying and retransmitting the signal across segments of copper wire or fiber-optic cable. Fiber-optic cable is able to maintain a stronger signal than copper wire over longer distances and therefore requires fewer repeaters.

For many applications, fiber-optic technology is cost prohibitive. Fiber-optic cable is more expensive than copper wire, and installation of fiber-optic cable is more complicated than installation of copper wire. Because fiber-optic cable transmits light, it must be carefully cut and polished to ensure proper signal transmission.[3] Copper wire is already widely used, so switching to fiber-optic cable requires rewiring and purchasing new hardware.

5.3.3 Storage Area Networks (SANs)

Companies produce large volumes of data to support sales analysis tools, enterprise resource planning (ERP) systems, multimedia Web sites and e-commerce systems. The complexities of maintaining these data in a reliable and fault-tolerant way becomes increasingly difficult as the volume of data increases. A *storage area network* (*SAN*) provides high-capacity, reliable data storage and delivery on a network. Using a SAN allows network administrators to collect data in logical groups on data servers distributed throughout the network. *SAN devices* store large volumes of data and may also provide backup and recovery services. Using *mirroring* technology, a SAN device stores *redundant* copies of data, so that if one copy is lost or damaged, a mirrored copy can be used to recover the lost data. SANs use *fiber-channel* technology to connect computers on the network to SAN devices. Fiber channel is a high-speed communications medium based on fiber-optic technology that provides transfer rates of 100 Mbps.

Companies such as EMC (`www.emc.com`), Compaq (`www.compaq.com`), IBM (`www.ibm.com`) and Hewlett-Packard (`www.hp.com`) all provide high-capacity *network storage devices* for use in SANs. StorageNetworks (`www.storagenetworks.com`) also provides SANs as a service to companies. For a fee, StorageNetworks will store multiple *terabytes* (one terabyte equals one trillion bytes) of a company's data in its data centers worldwide. StorageNetworks provides access to the data through a high-speed fiber-optic line connected directly between the StorageNetworks data center and its client companies.

5.4 Connecting to the Internet

There are many ways for computers to connect to the Internet. Figure 5.1 summarizes common types of Internet connections and their comparative speeds and availability. Most home users subscribe to an *Internet Service Provider* (*ISP*) to connect to the Internet (see feature WebTV®). Typical ISPs allow customers to connect to the Internet using normal telephone lines. Using an *analog modem*, a user connects to an ISP, which then connects the user to the Internet. A modem takes *digital* signals from the computer and turns them into analog signals. These *analog signals* can be transmitted over a telephone line just like a human voice. A modem at the ISP then converts the sound back into a digital signal that can be transmitted over the Internet.

Most ISPs charge fixed monthly fees for Internet access. Some ISPs offer free Internet access (Fig. 5.2) in return for personal demographic data, such as your age, address, interests and income level. These ISPs then display advertisements on the Web pages you view. This type of service is similar to the business arrangement of public broadcast television.

5.4.1 Digital Subscriber Line (DSL)

A *Digital Subscriber Line (DSL)* offers high-bandwidth Internet access over existing copper telephone lines. The abbreviation xDSL is used to describe the many types of DSL that are available, such as *asymmetric DSL (ADSL), symmetric DSL (SDSL), high-speed DSL (HDSL)* and *very high-speed DSL (VDSL)*.

Method	Speed (Kbps)	Send Speed = Receive Speed	Cost	Availability for Businesses
Modem	33–56	No	Very low	Universal
Cable modem	64–1500	No	Medium	Very limited
ISDN	56–128	Yes	High	Widely available
xDSL	384–55,000	No	Low	Limited
Frame relay/T1	64–1544	Yes	Very high	Widely available

Fig. 5.1   Internet connection comparison chart. (Courtesy of GLINK, LLC.)

WebTV®

WebTV® is a low-cost technology for connecting to the Internet through the user's television, instead of a PC. WebTV users can dial into an ISP through a modem to surf the Web, send and receive e-mail and chat with other people on the Internet. When sending e-mail, the user can add pictures and audio clips using a video camera, digital camera or VCR. WebTV also enhances television programming by allowing the user to pause, fast forward and replay both live and recorded programs as they watch.

The basic WebTV system includes a wireless keyboard, an 8.6-GB (i.e., "gigabytes"; one gigabyte of storage can hold one billion characters of data, where a character is typically composed of eight bits) hard drive and a 56-Kbps modem. It provides the capability to record up to 6 hours of television programming. A more expensive version of the WebTV system allows users to record up to 12 hours of television programming, by adding a larger, 17-GB hard drive. For more information, visit **www.webtv.com**.

Company	URL
NetZero®	`www.netzero.com`
isFree.com™	`www.isfree.com`
ACI	`www.dialfree.net`
Address.com	`www.address.com`
NetZero®	`www.freeinternet.com`

Fig. 5.2   Internet Service Providers (ISPs) that offer free Internet access.

DSL transforms standard copper telephone wires into high-speed digital connections. Since this wiring is already in place in most homes and offices, millions of users can start using DSL service without any additional rewiring, which helps lower the cost of DSL services. DSL takes advantage of the portion of the bandwidth not used for voice calls and splits your phone line into three information-carrying channels. One channel carries data from the Internet to your home computer. Another channel transports data from your home computer to the Internet. The third channel handles regular phone calls and faxes.

In terms of bandwidth, DSL connections offer transfer speeds of up to 55 Mbps. These speeds are much faster than the speeds obtained using a modem over regular telephone lines. However, DSL connections require special hardware at the local telephone company's *central office* and at the user's location. Also, because of limitations on DSL technology, the speed of a DSL connection decreases over distance. Therefore, the fastest DSL connections are available only to homes and businesses located within a few thousand feet of a central office. Lower speed DSL connections are available up to approximately 20,000 feet from a central office.[4]

ADSL connections are referred to as asymmetric because the connection speed for sending data to the Internet (*upstream*) is slower than the connection speed for receiving data from the Internet (*downstream*). ADSL is popular with home users, since the data these users send upstream consist mostly of e-mail messages and requests for Web pages, whereas the data they receive downstream often include Web pages, download files, graphics and multimedia content, which can be of considerable size.

Unlike ADSL, SDSL is *symmetric*, meaning that it transfers data at the same speed both upstream and downstream. SDSL can transmit data at rates of up to 3 Mbps. HDSL also provides equal bandwidth for upstream and downstream transfers at rates of up to 1.544 Mbps. For users within 4500 feet of a central office, VDSL offers symmetric transfer rates of between 13 Mbps and 55 Mbps.[5]

The high-bandwidth capabilities of DSL allow DSL providers to offer enhanced services to their customers. For example, *voice-over DSL* (*VoDSL*) promises to be a cost-efficient technology for managing data and voice services for small businesses and home offices. VoDSL takes advantage of the high bandwidth of a DSL connection to provide voice telephone services and high-speed data access over a single standard telephone line. An *integrated access device* (*IAD*) installed at the customer's location provides network connections for high-speed Internet access, as well as connections for multiple voice telephone lines. The IAD transmits voice data over DSL to a *gateway* device at the DSL provider. The gateway takes the voice data transmitted by the IAD and sends it across the standard telephone system. Both voice data and high-speed network data can be transmitted over DSL simultaneously. Since these technologies use a single standard telephone line, the cost of providing the services is dramatically reduced. Packaging voice and data services over a single telephone line will help DSL providers reduce the cost of these services for consumers and businesses. To find out what DSL services are available in your area, visit **www.getspeed.com**.

5.4.2 Broadband

Broadband is a category of high-bandwidth Internet service provided mainly by cable television and telephone companies to home users. Broadband communication can handle voice, data and video information. Adding broadband capabilities to a network enables videoconferencing, real-time voice and streaming-media applications. Like DSL, broadband service is always connected, eliminating the need to dial into an ISP to use the Internet.

A *cable modem* translates digital signals for transmission over the same cables that bring cable television to homes and businesses. Unlike with DSL, the bandwidth delivered to cable-modem connections is shared among many users. This attribute can reduce the amount of bandwidth available to each user when there are many people in one neighborhood or building using the system at once. Cable modems typically offer downstream transfer speeds of between 384 Kbps and 1.5 Mbps and upstream speeds of 128 Kbps. Using a cable modem in your home eliminates the need for an extra phone line for your computer or, if you only have one phone line, allows you to use the Internet without tieing up the phone line.

5.4.3 Integrated Services Digital Network (ISDN)

Integrated Services Digital Network (*ISDN*) provides high-speed connections to the Internet over both digital and standard telephone lines, with transfer speeds of up to 128 Kbps. A specialized piece of hardware called a *terminal adaptor* (*TA*) and an ISP that provides ISDN service are needed. Because of these restrictions, ISDN availability is limited, and the service is costly.

ISDN bandwidth is divided into three channels that each perform different tasks, using *Basic Rate Interface* (*BRI*). Two *bearer* (*B*) channels each support data transfers at 64 Kbps, while the *data* (*D*) channel is used to transmit routing information. Each B channel can be used for either voice or data communications. The B channels may also be combined to provide the maximum ISDN transfer rate of 128 Kbps. For more information about ISDN, visit **www.isdnzone.com**.

5.4.4 T-1 and T-3 Lines

A *T-1 line* is a dedicated connection that supports data rates of 1.544 Mb per second. T-1 lines are made up of 24 *channels*. Each channel supports 64 Kbps. A *T-3 line* support data rates of 43Mbps and is made up of 672 channels that each support 64Kbps. T-1 and T-3 lines can be used for both voice and data communication. T-1 and T-3 lines are popular in many large organizations. For more information about T-1 and T-3 lines, visit **www.everythingt1.com**.

5.5 Internet2®

Internet2® (**www.internet2.edu**) is a consortium working to develop the next generation of the Internet. The consortium, which is composed of 180 universities, along with a number of industry and government organizations, is developing advanced technologies and network applications.[6] One of the major developments of Internet2 will be increased bandwidth. *Abeline*, a high-speed network currently used by Internet2 consortium members, will soon be able to transfer 2.4 gigabits of data per second. That rate is 10 to 15 times faster than that provided by the current technology.[7]

The Internet2 consortium is working on several advanced applications that will enable interactive access over the Internet. One of these applications, *teleimmersion*, allows users in different locations to share information in real time—even 3D images. For example, tele-immersive computers can project realistic 3D images of people. This technology will allow doctors to view 3D images of a patient's brain from remote locations and thereby treat the patient remotely. It will also allow manufacturers and designers to meet and share 3D images of models from locations around the world.

Another advanced application is the *virtual laboratory*, which will enable researchers worldwide to collaborate on projects, allowing them to share massive computing power, databases, simulations and software.

Digital libraries are another advanced application for Internet2. Currently, much of the information stored electronically and on the Internet is text based. Digital libraries will be able to store audio and video files. This will make it possible, for example, to search for a movie by a line from its soundtrack. To learn more about Internet2 and some of its intended applications, visit **www.internet2.edu**.

5.6 Software

In Chapter 3, Building an e-Business, we discussed the types of software available for developing and maintaining a business on the Internet. In this section, we explore some of the software technologies and services used to run an e-business, such as *application service providers* (*ASPs*), *operating systems* and *databases*. Marketing software, another key resource for developing a successful Web site, is discussed in Chapter 8, Internet Marketing.

5.6.1 Application Service Providers (ASPs)

Traditionally, large companies needing software to manage business processes, such as project management, order processing and sales calculations, would develop these applications in their own *information technology* (*IT*) departments. Alternatively, some companies would hire outside consulting firms to build these applications for them. *Application service providers* (*ASPs*) provide customized business software applications over the Internet. ASPs develop a single set of commonly used applications and customize those applications to each customer. While many companies need the same applications to manage projects, individual companies may manage projects differently from one another. As part of the services they provide, many ASPs will enhance their applications to take into account the needs of individual customers. The ASP has the responsibility of maintaining the applications and updating them as necessary. By using an ASP for business applications, companies can eliminate the costs associated with developing and maintaining business applications themselves. Instead, each company pays a fee that allows its users to access the applications over the Internet. Applications provided by ASPs are also available for use more immediately than applications developed by an IT departments or outside consulting firms, because ASPs have already built and tested the applications. Companies such as Corio™ (**www.corio.com**), Breakaway Solutions (**www.breakaway.com**), Adgrafix (**www.adgrafix.com**) and Verio™ (**home.verio.com**) are among the many companies that provide application services.

Security is a major concern for companies that outsource their business applications to ASPs. The data managed by these applications are stored on servers owned by the ASP and then transferred over the Internet. Consequently, ASPs provide *virtual private networks* (*VPNs*) that allow customers to connect to their applications securely over the Internet. VPNs use the *point-to-point tunneling protocol* (*PPTP*) to create a secure channel of communication between the customer and the ASP. For more information about security, see Chapter 7, Internet Security.

5.6.2 Databases

Most computerized information is stored in databases. A *database* is an integrated collection of data. A *database management system* (*DBMS*) involves the data itself and the software that controls the storage and retrieval of data. Database management systems provide mechanisms for storing and organizing data in a manner that facilitates satisfying sophisticated queries and data manipulations.

The most popular database systems in use today are *relational databases*. A language called *Structured Query Language* (*SQL*, pronounced "sequel") is almost universally used with relational database systems to make *queries* (i.e., to request information that satisfies given criteria) and manipulate data. Some of the more popular enterprise-level relational database systems include Microsoft SQL Server (**www.microsoft.com/sql**), Oracle (**www.oracle.com**), Sybase (**www.sybase.com**), DB2 (**www.ibm.com/db2**) and Informix (**www.informix.com**). A popular personal relational database is Microsoft Access, which we use for simplicity in our case study on building an e-business at the end of this book.

The *relational database model* is a logical representation of the data that allows the relationships between the data to be considered independently of the physical implementation of the data structures.

A relational database is composed of *tables*. Figure 5.3 illustrates a sample table that might be used in a personnel system. The name of the table is **Employee**; it illustrates the attributes of six employees. The purpose of this illustration is to show how a relational database stores two dimensional information about employees. Any particular row of the table is called a *record* (or *row*). Each column of the table represents a different *field* (or *column* or *attribute*). This table consists of six records and six fields. A record represents attributes of a particular employee, and a field represents an attribute that is associated with all employees. The **Number** field of each record is used as the *primary key* for referencing data in the table. The records in Fig. 5.3 are listed in ascending order by the primary key. Primary-key fields in a table cannot contain duplicate or null values as they are used to identify a particular record. In this example, the **Number** identifies each employee. If the **Number** field were left blank, that employee would not be found when searching the table.

Particular values within a field may be duplicated between records. For example, three different records in the **Employee** table's **Department** field contain number 413. A primary key may also be composed of more than one field in the database.

Table: Employee

	Number	Last Name	Department	Salary	Location
	23603	JONES	413	1100	NEW JERSEY
	24568	KERWIN	413	2000	NEW JERSEY
A record	34589	LARSON	642	1800	LOS ANGELES
	35761	MYERS	611	1400	ORLANDO
	47132	NEUMANN	413	9000	NEW JERSEY
	78321	STEPHENS	611	8500	ORLANDO

Primary key   A column

Fig. 5.3   Table of a relational database.

5.7 Operating Systems

An *operating system* (OS) is software that manages the resources on a computer, such as the *central processing unit* (*CPU*), *random access memory* (*RAM*), various *input/output devices* (*I/O*) and the data stored on hard disks, CD-ROMS and other storage media.

There are several types of operating systems, including *multiuser, multiprocessor, multitasking and multithreading*. A multiuser OS allows more than one user to run programs simultaneously. A multiprocessor OS controls a computer that has many hardware CPUs. A multitasking OS allows multiple applications to run simultaneously. For example, a user may have both a spreadsheet application and a word processor open while using an e-mail application to send and receive messages. A multithreading OS allows an individual program to specify that several activities should be performed in parallel.

A *software platform* provides the basic services that *applications* need to run. Applications are programs such as spreadsheets, word processors and Web browsers. The major operating systems used in desktop computers are *UNIX®, Linux®, Macintosh®* and *Windows®*. There are also modified operating systems for devices designed specifically for browsing the Internet (see feature Internet Appliances).

5.7.1 UNIX®

From 1965 through 1969, Bell Laboratories participated with General Electric (later called Honeywell) and Project MAC (at the Massachusetts Institute of Technology) in the development of the Multics system. Multics was a large and complex system. The designers of Multics envisioned a general-purpose computer utility that could essentially be "all things to all people."[8]

As the effort progressed, it became clear that although Multics was likely to deliver a variety of the services envisioned, it would be a huge, expensive and ponderous system. For these reasons, Bell Laboratories withdrew from the effort in 1969. Some members of Bell's research staff began to work on a far less ambitious system. The group was led by Ken Thompson, who sought to create a simple computing environment for programming research and development. The first version of UNIX was written in assembly language.

In 1970, Brian Kernighan coined the name "UNIX" as a pun on Multics; indeed, in the sense that Multics was "multi," UNIX systems were "uni" limited computing services.

Dennis Ritchie joined the development effort and helped rewrite UNIX systems in C, which helped make UNIX systems software more portable and understandable. The fact that the first version of the UNIX operating system was built in just a few years primarily by two people, and the fact that the people who built the system were major users of it, contributed to much of UNIX's unique design and coherence.

AT&T, before its deregulation by the Federal Trade Commission, was not allowed to compete in the computer industry. Since it was unable to sell UNIX, it made UNIX systems available to universities essentially for free. AT&T also distributed the source code, thus encouraging further development and innovation. Thousands of students who used UNIX in college entered the computer industry and encouraged their organizations and companies to make major UNIX systems commitments.

UNIX systems met the needs of programmers who were building software and of administrators who control software development efforts. They were not, however, designed to replace "heavy-duty" commercial operating systems; hardware performance was not one of the design precepts in early UNIX systems. Security, reliability, recoverability and other critical issues in commercial systems were also downplayed in early UNIX systems.

The UNIX Time-Sharing System, Seventh Edition, released in 1979, brought UNIX systems closer to becoming valid commercial products. The system was made more portable and powerful.

In 1980, the University of California at Berkeley was funded by the Defense Department to evolve UNIX systems from small timesharing operating systems into systems appropriate for studying distributed computing environments. Sun Microsystems® later modeled its SunOS version of UNIX after the system developed at Berkeley. Sun wanted a system for supporting a network of workstations. Sun enhanced the Berkeley system to include facilities for supporting a graphics, window-based, mouse-oriented interface. It also provided facilities for diskless workstations to use the network for file storing, sharing and paging. Sun's latest operating system, Solaris, is one of the most commercially successful UNIX-based operating systems; another is IBM's AIX.

The Open Group standards organization controls the specification for UNIX and holds the trademark. The organization seeks to promote open systems standards. Visit The Open Group's UNIX site at **www.unix-systems.org** for more information about UNIX.

5.7.2 Microsoft Windows®

The most popular operating system in the world is *Microsoft Windows®*. The Windows operating system is based on an older operating system called *MS-DOS*. In 1985, Microsoft introduced Windows, which essentially added the *graphical user interface (GUI)* to the DOS system. This version achieved little success, due to performance problems and the lack of applications designed to run on the system. Windows 2.0, though improved, also failed to make a large impact in the market. Users running these early versions of Windows suffered from the same problems as users trying to browse the Web using a slow modem connection: It took too long to open applications, change screens, etc.

Windows 3.0, released in 1990, finally achieved widespread success and, with MS-DOS embedded within it, became the best-selling operating system in the world. The performance of the system was much improved over previous versions, and it supported numerous software applications. Windows 95, released in 1995, introduced a new graphical user interface and increased performance; with its many new and improved features, Windows 95 quickly dominated the market for personal-computer and business-desktop operating systems. Windows 98 and Windows NT have maintained Microsoft's dominance in the operating-systems market. Windows 2000, based on Windows NT, is a more powerful and more secure operating system, typically used on computer networks and servers. Various versions of Windows are currently used on approximately 90 percent of desktop computers. To learn more about Microsoft's future plans for Windows, see the feature Microsoft .NET.

For a detailed history of Windows, visit **www.zdnet.com/pcmag/features/windows98/history2.html**. For more information about Microsoft Windows, visit **www.microsoft.com/windows2000/default.asp**.

5.7.3 Linux®

One of the most popular software platforms for hosting Web sites and applications is *Linux®* (**www.linux.com** and **www.linux.org**). Linux is a UNIX-like operating system that has been developed by volunteers worldwide, though it was initially developed by one person, Linus Torvalds. Linux has enjoyed its greatest success on the *server-side* versus on desktops (referred to as the *client side*). Many people use Linux on the client side (where Windows currently dominates)—that number will increase as more versions of Linux with user-friendly graphical user interfaces (GUIs) become available. Version 1.0 of the Linux operating system was released in 1994, and it has quickly gained market share to become one of the world's most widely used operating systems. Its staggering growth is attracting attention from industry and investors. VA Linux Systems, which provides Linux solutions for the Web, had one of the biggest initial public offerings (IPOs) of stock ever: The company's stock price jumped 698 percent in its first day.[10]

Microsoft .NET

The *Microsoft® .NET* initiative (**www.microsoft.com/net**) is changing the way in which Microsoft applications interact with the Web and with each other. .NET weaves together the operating system, the Internet and each device to create applications and services to be accessed anytime, anywhere, from any device. .NET could potentially support UNIX and Linux as well.[9] Rather than storing applications on each individual system, .NET applications are available over the Web, thus giving you access to the latest version of the software at all times. Also, your data is stored on the Internet and can be accessed from multiple devices, including desktop computers and wireless devices.

The four main tools used to build and maintain .NET components are Windows.NET, the Visual Studio.NET integrated development environment (IDE), .NET Enterprise Servers and the .NET framework. Microsoft .NET services include Passport.NET (for user authentication), a calendar, personalization and other services that allow users to customize content and collaborate with other users. .NET applications will be built with XML, allowing them to interact with each other and share information. The result will be a highly customizable solution that will allow users to tailor applications and information to their unique needs.

e-Fact 5.2

A study by International Data Corporation showed that 1.3 million copies of Linux were shipped in 1999, making it the second most popular server operating system, behind Microsoft's Windows NT.[11]

The *Gnome Foundation* (**www.gnome.org**)—which is supported by many large companies, including IBM®, Sun Microsystems®, Compaq and Hewlett-Packard—was founded to develop a free Linux-based desktop environment and a free application framework to compete with Microsoft Office for the desktop-computer environment.[12]

Linux is one of many *open-source software* projects. Open-source software has freely available source code, so that anyone can use and make updates to the software. It also allows you to customize the program to meet your specific needs. All of the source code for the Linux *kernel*, which is the core of the operating system, and for most of the applications that run on Linux is freely available over the Internet and on many CD-ROM distributions. Although the source code for open-source software is made public, most open-source software products have licensing agreements that govern the use of the source code. One of the most widely used open-source licenses is the *GNU General Public License* (*GPL*). The GPL requires, among other things, that the source code for GPL-licensed software, as well as the source code for any modifications or improvements to that software, is made freely available to the public. Details about the GPL are available at **www.fsf.org/copyleft/gpl.html**. One of the most popular Web servers on the Internet, Apache (**www.apache.org**), is also an open-source software.

e-Fact 5.3

According to a study by International Data Corporation, the number of Linux users is doubling or tripling each year.[13]

Even though open-source software is freely available to the public, many companies are able to profit from products and services based on open-source software. A number of companies, including Red Hat (**www.redhat.com**) and Caldera (**www.caldera.com**), sell complete Linux software packages on CD-ROM as well as customer service and support (Fig. 5.4). Other companies, including VA Linux (**www.valinux.com**) and Dell (**www.dell.com**), sell computer hardware with the Linux operating system pre-installed.

Application software companies are also beginning to sell commercial software that is compatible with Linux. Corel has a free, downloadable (but not open-source) version of the popular WordPerfect word processor available for the Linux platform, in addition to a commercial version available for purchase. Oracle's database products are available for purchase on the Linux platform. Also, Sun Microsystems offers a free Linux-based office suite called Star Office.

5.7.4 Mac® OS X

In 1984, Apple Computer, Inc., announced the Macintosh®, an affordable desktop computer with a graphical user interface. This computer was one of the first widely available systems to use a window-based (i.e., a GUI) interface, a mouse and icons. The Macintosh operating system achieved great success in the 1980s, dominating the market for GUI-based personal computers. The Macintosh Consortium allowed colleges to purchase discounted computers. As a result, the Macintosh was widely used in computer labs at schools throughout the United States.

Company Name	URL
Caldera Systems	www.caldera.com
Red Hat	www.redhat.com
SuSE	www.suse.com
TurboLinux	www.turbolinux.com
VA Linux Systems	www.valinux.com

Fig. 5.4   Popular Linux vendors.

Apple maintained complete control over the Macintosh operating system. It was available only on computers manufactured by Apple. When Microsoft Windows was released and licensed to multiple PC manufacturers, Macintosh sales quickly began to decline. By the mid-1990s, the Macintosh accounted for only a small portion of the market, mostly in creative fields, such as publishing, advertising and graphics. In the late 1990s, sales of Apple Macintosh personal computers started to increase again with the introduction of the attractively designed iMac personal computer and a powerful new operating system.

The *Mac OS X operating system* (pronounced "O S Ten") (**www.apple.com/macosx**) was unveiled by Steve Jobs, CEO of Apple Computer, Inc., at Apple Expo 2000. OS X version 1.0 is expected to be available in early 2001. Darwin, the core of Mac OS X, was built using industry open standards based on Unix. The result is a more powerful, stable system that is interoperable with UNIX systems and applications. Mac OS X uses the Apache Web server for personal file sharing.

The new operating system also has enhanced the Macintosh's graphics capabilities. Aqua, the new Mac OS X interface, has the color, motion and translucence of water. Windows fade away rather than closing abruptly. Buttons have motion that can help users navigate. The icons are of photo quality and are intuitive. For more information about Aqua, visit **www.apple.com/macosx/technologies/aqua.html**.

Internet Appliances

Internet appliances are desktop devices designed specifically for connecting to the Internet. Two popular Internet appliances include the *iPAQ Home Internet Appliance* and the *Netpliance i-opener*. These devices allow you to browser the Web, send and receive e-mail and access streaming media online. Since these devices have limited functionality (they do not include many common desktop applications such as word processors), they are significantly less expensive than personal computers.

iPAQ is a line of Internet devices from Compaq which include wireless, handheld devices (see Chapter 6, Wireless Internet and m-Business) and the iPAQ Home Internet Appliance, which comes pre-loaded with all of the required software. The iPAQ Home Internet Appliance has a 15-inch color screen, a keyboard, built-in speakers and a 56K modem. It runs on the MSN™ Companion Operating System with Microsoft's Internet Explorer 4 browser. Internet service is provided by MSN for a monthly fee. For more information about iPAQ products, visit **www5.compaq.com/products/iPAQ**.

Internet Appliances (Cont.)

The i-opener from Netpliance comes with a 10-inch screen, a built-in 56K modem, plus a keyboard with a built-in mouse and keys to access email, your address book and some of the most popular Web sites. The system handles four separate e-mail accounts. It comes with a custom browser and runs the QNX operating system. Internet access is provided by Netpliance for a monthly fee which must be pre-paid in three-month, six-month or one-year increments. For more information about the i-opener, visit `www.netpliance.com`.

5.8 Enhancing Business Communication

Business communication is benefitting from Internet technologies. Technologies such as intranets, extranets and streaming audio and video allow businesses to send clients detailed and impressive sales presentations, post product demonstrations on Web sites and more. Internet telephony makes PC-to-PC and PC-to-phone calls possible, dramatically reducing the cost of communication. Finally, Web casting and virtual conferencing make it possible to meet with clients around the world right from your own office.

Wireless technology is also enhancing e-business communication. In Chapter 6, Wireless Internet and m-Business, we discuss how wireless technology is changing the way businesses communicate with each other and with their customers.

5.8.1 Intranets and Extranets

An *intranet* is an organization's internal network that uses the *TCP/IP* protocols of the Internet. Generally, only authorized parties, such as the organization's employees, have access to an organization's intranet. The intranet is used to store internal information, such as files, databases, policies and procedures. This information can be available through internal Web sites, which are similar to regular World Wide Web sites, but can be accessed only by authorized users.

An *extranet* is an intranet that is also accessible by authorized external parties who are not members or employees of the organization. An extranet provides multiple levels of access. For example, members or employees might have unrestricted access to information on the extranet, whereas customers or vendors might have access to a limited subset of that information. Extranets help enhance business communication because they enable integration across organizations. For example, a manufacturing company can have direct access to the inventory database of its vendors through the vendors' extranets. The manufacturing company can then use that information to place orders without first having to communicate with a sales person, speeding delivery for the finished product and potentially increasing sales.

5.8.2 Streaming Audio and Video

Streaming technologies allow you to send and process audio and video data continuously. Rather than making you wait for an entire audio or video file to download completely, streaming technology allows you to start playing the audio or video file while it is still downloading. Using streaming technology, you can play music over the Internet, watch a small video on a Web site and more (see the feature RealPlayer). Streaming technologies are enhancing the Web, transforming it from a static medium to an interactive experience.

5.8.3 Internet Telephony

Internet telephony enables communication over the Internet, allowing you to use your PC as a telephone. You can place phone calls over the Internet, and send faxes and voice-mail messages to people worldwide. The result is a cost-efficient communications medium that helps to improve e-business communication (see feature Net2Phone®).

RealPlayer®

One of the most versatile programs for streaming media is *RealPlayer®*, developed by RealNetworks (Fig. 5.5). You can download the most recent version of **RealPlayer** by clicking on the **Download Now** link at `www.real.com`. It is capable of playing live or prerecorded sound files and even videos (with a fast enough connection). There are also a number of *channels* that you can access, including news, sports, comedy, talk shows and live events.

Many Internet sites allow you to take advantage of **RealPlayer**. For example, the `www.npr.org`, `internetradio.about.com` and `wmbr.mit.edu/sta-tions/list.html` all feature either live Internet radio programs and sound or links to sites with live radio and sound events.

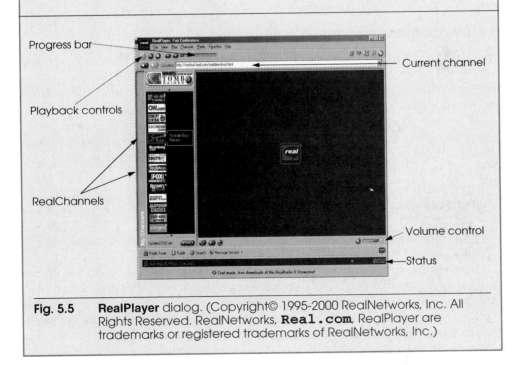

Fig. 5.5   RealPlayer dialog. (Copyright© 1995-2000 RealNetworks, Inc. All Rights Reserved. RealNetworks, **Real.com**, RealPlayer are trademarks or registered trademarks of RealNetworks, Inc.)

Net2Phone®

The Net2Phone® Internet telephony service allows you to make free PC-to-telephone calls within the United States, and international calls at discounted rates (**www.net2phone.com**). Users download the Net2Phone software. System requirements include Microsoft Windows 95/98/2000/NT, a PC sound card, a microphone and speakers or a headset. To place a call, users dial with the on-screen keypad. *Net2Phone Pro*™ allows you to make PC-to-PC or PC-to-phone calls. You can also send faxes using the service. *Net2Phone Direct*™ is a phone-quality Internet telephony service.

Net2Phone and other Internet telephony services are not always compatible with systems running firewalls (see Chapter 7, Internet Security), which monitor and limit access into and out of a network. As a result, you may not be able to send or receive calls if you are using such a system.

Net2Phone's *ClickTogether* service allows companies to add personalized voice capabilities to a Web site, enabling one-on-one interaction with visitors to the site. To initiate a conversation, the visitor clicks on the **Contact** button and enters the contact information. The company can return the call over the phone or using Internet telephony capabilities. ClickTogether allows the company representative and the visitor to initiate a real-time chat session through the site. It also includes cobrowsing, pointing and highlighting features that allow the visitor and the company representative to navigate a Web page together, highlighting areas of the page. For more information about ClickTogether and for a live demo, visit **www.net2phone.com/ecommerce/ clicktogether.html**.

5.8.4 Webcasting and Web Conferencing

Webcasting and *Web conferencing* enhance business communication. Webcasting is essentially broadcasting over the Web. Businesses can stream seminars, conferences, shows, sales presentations and more though their Web sites. One of the most famous Webcasts is the annual Victoria's Secret lingerie fashion show. Business can conduct live Webcasting events or store prerecorded Webcasts on their site to be viewed at any time. Web conferencing allows businesses to meet and collaborate online, in real time from anywhere in the world (see the feature Webcasting and Web Conferencing: Evoke Communications).

Webcasting and Web Conferencing: Evoke

Evoke Communications is an Internet communications service provider specializing in Webcasting and Web conferencing services (**www.evoke.com**).

Evoke Webcasting allows you to stream live or recorded audio, video and other visual media over the Internet or a corporate Intranet. It is a vehicle for presenting demonstrations, conferences and other live or recorded events. To learn more about how businesses are using Evoke Webcasting, visit **www.evoke.com/Webcasting/ busiuse.htm**. Click on the **Demo** link to see how the services work.

Webcasting and Web Conferencing: Evoke (Cont.)

Evoke Webconferencing allows businesses to meet and communicate online with people worldwide. Presentation slides and other visual tools, such as pictures and graphs, may be uploaded to the Web and viewed by all participants in the conference. Users can also access Web conferences by using wireless devices (see Chapter 6, Wireless Internet and M-Business). The moderator speaks using a telephone, and the audio is broadcast through the site. Conference attendees post written messages to the site to communicate with the moderator and other attendees. To view an animated demonstration of Evoke Webconferencing, go to **www.evoke.com/webconferencing/index.html** and click on the **Demo** link.

Evoke Collaboration allows businesses to conduct online meetings and seminars. Users can share applications and communicate in real time by using the chat capability. Evoke offers different collaboration products with varying features, security and customization capabilities. To view a demonstration of Evoke Collaboration products, go to **www.evoke.com/collaboration/index.html** and click on the **Demo** link.

5.9 Internet and World Wide Web Resources

Internet Access

www.bellatlantic.com/infospeed
This is Bell Atlantic's DSL information site.

www.dsl.net
DSL.net provides DSL solutions, from Internet access to Web hosting and e-commerce capabilities.

www.getspeed.com
To find out what DSL services are available in your area, visit this site.

dsl.gte.net
This site explains the advantages of DSL, its uses and how it works. It also offers pricing information and comparisons with other, similar technologies.

www.sorenson-usa.com/dsl-mac.html
This site offers information about DSL Internet access for Macintosh users.

www.nwfusion.com/dsl
NetworkWorldFusion provides resources, such as tutorials and information, on the different types of DSL for both DSL users and people interested in acquiring DSL. This site also distributes newsletters and provides newsgroups on various DSL topics.

www.alliancedatacom.com/paradyne-dsl-tutorial.asp
The tutorial on this site helps users become more familiar with DSL service. It starts with the basics and moves on to more in-depth subjects, including DSL networks. The tutorial also includes a DSL glossary.

www.2wire.com/dsl/dsl_tutorial.html
2Wire provides a low-level tutorial on DSL that discusses how to find a provider. This site also discusses the applications of DSL for telecommuters and businesses.

www.dslprime.com
DSL Prime provides news and technical information related to DSL.

www.dslreports.com
This site provides news, product reviews and product information related to DSL.

www.alliedriser.com
Allied Riser offers a range of broadband services on its fiber-optic networks inside office buildings.

www.everythingt1.com
This site includes information about T-1 and T-3 lines including a FAQ, a glossary, links to related Web sites and links to service providers.

www.cidera.com
Cidera provides satellite-based broadband services as an alternative to land lines for content providers and distributors on the Internet.

www.globix.com
This company provides broadband services via its nationwide fiber-optic network and offers many e-business solutions, including Web hosting and security.

www.qwest.com
Qwest is a leading provider of broadband Internet connections for home users, as well as small and large businesses.

www.isdnzone.com
This site provides information about ISDN, including demos, links to other sites and plug-ins.

www.webtv.com
WebTV® is a low-cost technology for connecting to the Internet through the user's television.

Free Internet Access

dslforfree.homepage.com
This site provides free Internet access, along with free DSL services. This site also provides links to other free services related to the Internet.

www.freedsl.com
In exchange for anonymous demographic information about your use of their service, FreeDSL provides you with free DSL services at speeds as high as 144Kbps.

www.dialfree.net
DialFree provides its subscribers with free Internet access. It is able to do so by requiring its subscribers to fill out a monthly survey. DialFree then passes this information on to its partners to help them better understand the views and behavior of Internet users.

download.freeinternet.com
By placing banner ads on the viewing window of its users' browser, Freeinternet is able to provide free Internet access through advertising revenue.

freelane.excite.com
Freelane provides free Internet access through a navigation bar that is downloaded from the Internet by using any browser.

www.isfree.com
ISfree offers Internet access for a flat monthly fee. Why, then, do they call themselves free? Through a referral program, your monthly fees may go down to zero, or you may even end up getting paid to be a subscriber: For every person who signs up for the service and cites you as a referral, you get a credit against your fees. After four referrals, you get a free month of service.

Operating Systems

www.unix-systems.org
The Open Group maintains the specification for the UNIX operating system. Visit this site to view the latest UNIX specification, news and white papers.

www.microsoft.com/windows/default.asp
The Microsoft Windows site includes product downloads, information and support.

www.apple.com/macosx
The Apple Mac OS X site includes product information, downloads and details about the technologies used in the operating system. You can also view samples of the new graphical user interface.

www.linux.com
This resource site provides news, development information, games, job listings and other information related to Linux.

www.linux.org
Linux Online! is a resource site with links to news, documentation, support, applications, hardware, user groups and more.

www.ibm.com/linux
IBM is a major Linux supporter. Visit this site for information about IBM Linux-enabled servers and software support.

www.linux-center.org/en
This site is an excellent resource for information on Linux. It provides links to news, applications, support and development sites.

Fiber Optics

www.sff.net/people/Jeff.Hecht/history.html
This site provides a short history of fiber optics and references a more in-depth explanation that is included in the author's book.

www.commspecial.com/fiberguide.htm
Communications Specialties, Inc., provides a detailed introduction to fiber-optic technology and concepts.

www.fiberopticsonline.com
Fiber Optics Online is an industry portal with information about fiber-optic products and technology.

Streaming Media

www.broadcast.com
This is a comprehensive site for streaming audio and video. Hundreds of live events are available daily for listening with RealPlayer.

internetradio.about.com
Internet Radio offers many live broadcasts from radio stations throughout the country, covering a broad range of topics and types of music.

Application Service Providers

www.corio.com
This application service provider offers products and services related to customer relationship management, financial management, human resources and other key business functions.

www.breakaway.com
Breakaway Solutions hosts business applications on its servers for a monthly fee.

www.adgrafix.com
Adgrafix offers applications for discussion boards, lead management, chat and more.

home.verio.com
Verio offers applications for collaboration, e-mail, e-commerce, databases and FrontPage 2000.

SUMMARY

- The Internet is a network of interconnected host computers, or hosts. Each host is assigned a unique address called an IP address.

- Computers on the Internet communicate with each other by sending packets of data across the network.

- Packets sent across the Internet contain a source address, a destination address, sequencing information, error-control information and the data to be delivered to the destination address.

- Routers are responsible for redirecting packets around any areas of the network that may have failed and ensuring that packets are delivered to the proper destination hosts.

- A server is a host on the Internet that manages network resources and fulfills requests from clients. There are many types of servers, including Web, e-mail, database and file servers.

- A Web browser uses the hypertext transfer protocol (HTTP) to request and transfer pages from a Web server. A protocol defines the steps necessary for computers to communicate over the Internet.

- The most important measure for a communications medium is its bandwidth, which indicates how much data can be transferred through the medium in a fixed amount of time. Bandwidth is usually measured in bits per second (bps), kilobits per second (Kbps) or megabits per second (Mbps).

- For many years, copper wire has been the primary communications medium.

- Fiber-optic cable, which is composed of flexible glass fiber, is thinner and lighter than traditional copper wire, yet has much wider bandwidth. Fiber-optic cable uses short bursts of light to represent bits.

- An optical modem (modem stands for modulator and demodulator) translates digital signals from computers into light through a process called modulation. The light is transmitted over the fiber-optic cable to the receiver's optical modem, which converts the light back into an electrical signal through a process called demodulation.

- Repeaters can be used to alleviate the problem of signal strength decreasing over distance by amplifying and retransmitting the signal across segments of copper wire or fiber-optic cable.

- A storage area network (SAN) provides high-capacity, reliable data storage and delivery on a network.

- SAN devices store large volumes of data and may also provide backup and recovery services.

- Using mirroring technology, a SAN device stores redundant copies of data so that if one copy is lost or damaged, a mirrored copy can be used to recover the lost data.

- Most home users subscribe to an Internet Service Provider (ISP) to connect to the Internet.

- Using an analog modem, a user connects to an ISP, which then connects the user to the Internet.

- A modem takes digital signals from a computer and turns them into analog signals.

- A T-1 line is a dedicated connection that supports data rates of 1.544 Mb per second. T-1 lines are made up of 24 channels. Each channel supports 64 Kbps.

- T-3 lines support data rates of 43Mb per second and are made up of 672 channels.

- A Digital Subscriber Line (DSL) offers high-bandwidth Internet access over existing copper telephone lines.

- DSL takes advantage of the portion of the bandwidth not used for voice calls and splits phone lines into three information-carrying channels.

- In terms of bandwidth, DSL connections offer transfer speeds of up to 55 Mbps.

- The speed of a DSL connection decreases over distance. Therefore, the fastest DSL connections are available only to homes and businesses located within a few thousand feet of a central office.

- VoDSL takes advantage of the high bandwidth of a DSL connection to provide voice telephone services and high-speed data access over a single standard telephone line.

- Both voice data and high-speed network data can be transmitted over DSL simultaneously.

- Broadband is a category of high-bandwidth Internet service provided mainly by cable television and telephone companies to home users.

- Broadband communication can handle voice, data and video information.

- A cable modem translates digital signals for transmission over the same cables that already bring cable television to homes and businesses. Cable modems typically offer downstream transfer speeds of between 384 Kbps and 1.5 Mbps and upstream speeds of 128 Kbps.

- Integrated Services Digital Network (ISDN) provides high-speed connections to the Internet over both digital and standard telephone lines, with transfer speeds of up to 128 Kbps.

- Internet2® is a consortium working to develop the next generation of the Internet. Abeline, the high-speed network currently used by Internet2 consortium members, will soon be able to transfer 2.4 gigabits of data per second.

- Teleimmersion allows users in different locations to share information in real time—even 3D images.

- Digital libraries will be able to store audio and video files.

- Application Service Providers (ASPs) provide customized business software applications over the Internet.

- ASPs provide virtual private networks (VPNs) that allow customers to connect to their applications securely over the Internet.

- A database is an integrated collection of data. A database management system (DBMS) involves the data itself and the software that controls the storage and retrieval of data.

- The most popular database systems in use today are relational databases.

- A language called Structured Query Language (SQL—pronounced "sequel") is almost universally used with relational database systems to make queries (i.e., to request information that satisfies given criteria) and manipulate data.

- The relational database model is a logical representation of the data that allows the relationships between the data to be considered independently of the physical implementation of the data structures.

- An operating system (OS) is software that manages the resources on a computer, such as the central processing unit (CPU), random-access memory (RAM), input/output devices (I/O) and the data stored on hard disks.

- A multiuser OS allows more than one user to run a program at the same time. A multiprocessor OS controls a computer that has many hardware CPUs. A multitasking OS allows multiple applications to run simultaneously.

- Applications are programs such as spreadsheets, word processors and Web browsers.

- The most popular operating system in the world is Microsoft Windows.

- Windows 95, released in 1995, introduced a new graphical user interface. With many new and improved features, Windows 95 quickly dominated the market for operating systems.

- Windows NT is a powerful and secure operating system often used in computer networks and to run servers.

- Different versions of Windows are currently used on over 90 percent of desktop computers.

- Version 1.0 of the Linux operating system was released in 1994, and it has quickly gained market share to become one of the most widely used operating systems.

- The Gnome Foundation—which is supported by many companies, including IBM, Sun Microsystems, Compaq and Hewlett-Packard—was founded to develop a free Linux-based desktop environment and a free application framework to compete with Microsoft Office for the desktop computer environment.

- Open-source software has freely available source code, so that anyone can use and make updates to the software. It also allows you to customize the program to meet your specific needs.

- One of the most widely used open-source licenses is the GNU General Public License (GPL). The GPL requires, among other things, that the source code for GPL-licensed software, as well as the source code for any modifications or improvements to that software, is made freely available to the public.

- In 1984, Apple Computer, Inc., announced the Macintosh—an affordable desktop computer with a graphical user interface. This computer was one of the first widely available systems to use a windows-based interface, a mouse and icons.

- In the late 1990s, sales of Apple Macintosh computers started to increase with the introduction of the iMac personal computer and a powerful new operating system.

- An intranet is an organization's internal network that uses the TCP/IP protocols of the Internet.

- An extranet is an intranet that is also accessible by authorized external parties who are not members or employees of the organization.

- Streaming technologies allow you to send and process data continuously.

- Internet telephony enables communication over the Internet, allowing you to use your PC as a telephone. You can place phone calls over the Internet and send faxes and voice mail messages to people worldwide.

- Web casting is essentially broadcasting over the Web. Businesses can stream seminars, conferences, shows, sales presentations and more though their Web sites.

- Web conferencing allows businesses to meet and collaborate online, in real time from anywhere in the world.

TERMINOLOGY

24 by 7
Abeline
analog modem
Application Service Provider (ASP)
Asymmetric Digital Subscriber Line (ADSL)
attribute
bandwidth
Basic Rate Interface (BRI)
bearer channel
bits per second (bps)
broadband
business-to-business (B2B)
cable modem
central office
central processing unit (CPU)
channels
ClickTogether
client side
Code Division Multiple Access (CDMA)

column in a relational database table
Common Gateway Interface (CGI)
communications medium
content delivery service
copper wire
data channel
database
database management system (DBMS)
database server
dedicated connection
dedicated server
demodulation
destination address
digital cellular phone
digital libraries
Digital Subscriber Line (DSL)
Domain Name System (DNS)
downstream
error-control information

fiber channel
fiber optics
fiber-optic cable
file server
fully qualified host name
gateway
gigabits per second (gbps)
Gnome Foundation
GNU Public License (GPL)
graphical user interface (GUI)
High-speed Digital Subscriber Line (HDSL)
host computer
hosts
information technology (IT)
input/output devices
Integrated Access Device (IAD)
Integrated Services Digital Network (ISDN)
Internet appliances
Internet Protocol (IP)
Internet Service Provider (ISP)
Internet telephony
Internet2
IP address
iPAQ Home Internet Appliance
kernel
kilobits per second (Kbps)
Linux
Mac OS X
megabits per second (Mbps)
merchant account
modem
modulation
modulator and demodulator
MS-DOS
multiprocessor
multitasking
multithreading
multiuser
Net2Phone Direct
Net2Phone Pro
Netpliance i-opener
network storage device
open-source software
operating system (OS)
optical modem
opto chip
packet
plain old telephone system (POTS)

platform
point-to-point tunneling protocol (PPTP)
post office protocol (POP)
primary key
processor speed
protocol
random-access memory (RAM)
record
redundant
registrar
relational database
repeater
router
row in a relational database table
sequencing information
server
server side
Simple Mail Transfer Protocol (SMTP)
software platform
source address
storage area network (SAN)
storage devices
Structured Query Language (SQL)
symmetric
Symmetric Digital Subscriber Line (SDSL)
T-1 line
T-3 line
tables
TCP/IP
teleimmersion
terabyte
terminal adapter (TA)
turnkey solution
UNIX
upstream
uptime
Very high-speed Digital Subscriber Line (VDSL)
virtual laboratory
Virtual Private Network (VPN)
Voice over Digital Subscriber Line (VoDSL)
Web conferencing
Web hosting
Web server
Webcasting
WebTV
Windows
xDSL

SELF-REVIEW EXERCISES

5.1   Fill in the blanks in each of the following statements:

a) A _____ is a computer that is connected to the Internet.

b) Every computer on the Internet is assigned a unique _____ address.

c) _____ is a high-bandwidth communications medium made of flexible strands of glass.

d) _____ is a measure of the amount of data that can flow through a communications medium in a fixed amount of time.

e) DSL is an acronym for _____.

f) An _____ provides business applications for use over the Internet.

g) A _____ provides a user-friendly address for a company's computers on the Internet.

h) Open source software makes the _____ for programs freely available to the public.

5.2   State whether the following are *true* or *false*. If the answer is *false*, explain why.

a) DSL offers a lower bandwidth connection to the Internet than does an analog modem.

b) The connection speed of DSL is limited by the distance from the telephone company's central office.

c) Cable modems are used to connect a computer to the Internet.

d) The bandwidth delivered over cable television systems is shared among users in a neighborhood or apartment building.

e) A database is an integrated collection of data.

ANSWERS TO SELF-REVIEW EXERCISES

5.1   a) host. b) IP. c) Fiber-optic cable. d) Bandwidth. e) digital subscriber line. f) ASP (application service provider. g) domain name. h) source code.

5.2   a) False. DSL offers much higher bandwidth than is available through analog modems. b) True. c) True. d) True. e) True. f) True. g) True.

EXERCISES

5.3   Expand the following acronyms:

a) HTTP

b) FTP

c) ISDN

d) WWW

e) ISP

5.4   (*Class Discussion*). The costs of hardware, software and communications are decreasing dramatically each year. In the past, applications developers and e-business designers were held back by these costs. In the future, these costs may be so low as to be insignificant. The one area where we seem to have a difficult time reducing costs is software development; salaries, employee benefits and real estate costs are all built into the expense of developing software. Therefore, many people believe the key to future systems is to reduce software development costs and cleverly conceptualize the premises of these businesses.

a) How will these trends affect the development of future e-businesses and applications?

b) What types of applications do you think will become successful in the future given these parameters?

5.5   Check out three of the Internet Service Providers listed in Fig. 5.2 that provide free Internet access.

a) Compare the features of their service with that of one or more fee-based Internet services.

b) What do these sites companies require of you in exchange for free service?

5.6   Go to **www.evoke.com/webconferencing/index.html** and click on the **Demo** link to watch the animated demo of Evoke Communications' Webconferencing service.

a) How do you start a Webconference?

b) How do you upload your presentation?

c) How do participants submit a question to the moderator of the Webconference?

d) What information is provided in the Webconferencing report after a Webconference is completed?

5.7   Investigate the availability and price of each of the following Internet access services in your area:

a) T1

b) T3

c) DSL

d) ISDN

e) Broadband cable Internet access.

5.8   Visit the GNU General Public License Web site, at **www.fsf.org/copyleft/ gpl.html**. What do you perceive to be the advantages and disadvantages of distributing software under this licensing agreement?

WORKS CITED

The notation <**www.domain-name.com**> indicates that the citation is for information found at the Web site.

1.   <**www.webopedia.com**>.

2.   A. Boyle, "Opto-chip Broadband Breakthrough," <**www.zdnet.com/zdnn/stories/ news/0,4586,2523487,00.html**> 6 April 2000.

3.   S. Strange, "Transition Networks-Fiber White Paper," <**www.ttransition.com/prod- ucts/fiber_wp.html**>.

4.   <**www.real-time.com/Services/Connectivity/DSL/DSL_Fact_Sheet/ dsl_fact_sheet.html**>.

5.   <**www.vectris.com/Vectris_New_Web/corporate/cpt_reference/ cpt_reference_center.cfm?Page_Title=Reference**>.

6.   <**www.internet2.edu/html/about.html**>.

7.   Y. Li-Ron, "Special Advertising Section: This Will Change Everything," *Digital Age*: 4, 8.

8.   H. Deitel, *Operating Systems, Second Edition* (Reading: Addison-Wesley, 1990) 571-573.

9.   M. Otey, "Untangling Microsoft .NET," *SQL Server Magazine* November 2000: 43-46.

10. A. Lucchetti and P.W. Tam, "VA Linux IPO Soars a Record 698%," *The Wall Street Journal* 10 December 1999: C1, C7.

11. P. Hochmuth, "Big Boys Give Linux Push Toward Enterprise," *Network World* 21 August 2000: 1, 16.

12. J. Markoff, "Linux Backers Plan Assault on Microsoft," *The New York Times* 14 August 2000: C1, 8.

13. A. H. Johnson, "Global IT Watch," *Global Technology Business* March 1999: 60.

RECOMMENDED READING

Alexander, S. "Wireless Web Access." *ComputerWorld* 5 June 2000: 84.

Armstrong, L. "Changing the Cyber House Rules." *Business Week* 7 Feb 2000: 46.

Borella, M. "Protocol Helps Stretch IPv4 Addresses." *Network World* 17 Jan 2000: 43.

Cauley, L. "A Speed Bump to the Wire Web." *The Wall Street Journal* 17 Feb 2000: B1+.

Cole-Gomolosky, B. "E-Commerce Education Brings IT, Business Together in Classroom." *ComputerWorld* 2 Aug 1999: 32.

Duvall, M. "E-Marketplaces Getting Connected" *Inter@ctive Week* 10 Jan 2000: 40-46.

"Everything You Always Wanted to Know About Connecting to the Internet but Were Afraid to Ask." *The Boston Globe* 20 Jan 2000: D5.

Greene, T. "Voice-Over-DSL Turns Heads at ComNet." *Network World* 31 Jan 2000: 8.

Hendrickson, D. "All Aboard the E-Commerce Express" *Mass Tech High* 7-13 Feb 2000: 15.

Howe, P.J. "Setting Net on Its Ear." *Boston Globe* 14 Feb 2000:

Keen, P.G. "E-Commerce: Chapter 2." *ComputerWorld* 13 Sep 1999: 48.

McGarvey, J. "E-Commerce Drives Bandwidth Needs." *Inter@ctive Week* 8 Nov 1999: 16.

Riggs, B. "Convergence Culture Shock." *Information Week* 13 Dec 1999: 143.

Stedman, C. "Moving to Web Applications? Don't Forget Bandwidth." *ComputerWorld* 31 Jan 2000: 59.

Whyman, B. "Crossing the Fault Line." *The Industry Standard* 21 Feb 2000: 129.

Zimmerman, C. "Akamai's Intervu Deal Bolsters Content-Delivery Capabilities" *Internet Week* 14 Feb. 2000: 8.

6

Wireless Internet and m-Business

Objectives

- To understand the technology of wireless devices.
- To understand the Wireless Application Protocol and the Wireless Mark-up Language (WML).
- To learn how wireless technology is currently used.
- To explore the great variety of wireless applications already in place.
- To understand mobile commerce.
- To explore the future of wireless technology.

Strong and content I travel the open road.
Walt Whitman

To see a world in a grain of sand
And a heaven in a wild flower,
Hold infinity in the palm of your hand
And eternity in an hour.
William Blake

You will never be alone with a poet in your pocket.
John Adams

Many attempts to communicate are nullified by saying too much.
Robert Greenleaf

Information is the oxygen of the modern age.
Ronald Reagan

Outline

6.1   Introduction
6.2   Wireless Devices
6.3   m-Business
6.4   Wireless Internet Access
6.5   Wireless Web Technology
       6.5.1   Web Clipping
       6.5.2   WAP™ and WML
6.6   Software Applications for Wireless Devices
6.7   Wireless Local Area Networks (WLANs)
6.8   Bluetooth™
6.9   Wireless Communications
6.10   Location Tracking
       6.10.1   Global Positioning System (GPS)
       6.10.2   E911 Act
6.11   Future of Wireless Internet
       6.11.1   Implications for Disabled People
       6.11.2   Ultimate Wireless Device
6.12   Internet and World Wide Web Resources

Summary • Terminology • Self-Review Exercises • Answers to Self-Review Exercises • Exercises •
Works Cited • Recommended Reading

6.1 Introduction

The hottest topic today in e-business and e-commerce is wireless Internet technology. Wireless technology turns e-business into *m-business*, or *mobile business*. It allows you to connect to the Internet any time from virtually any place. You can use it to conduct online transactions, make purchases, trade stocks and send e-mail. New technologies will lead to the wireless office, where computers, phones and other office equipment are all networked without cables. The advantages and limitations of promising new wireless technologies are discussed in this chapter. We also discuss how wireless technology is currently used and its future applications.

e-Fact 6.1

According to one industry estimate, 80 percent of wireless devices will have Internet access, and there will be over one billion users worldwide by 2004.[1]

6.2 Wireless Devices

The first-generation wireless technology was the cellular phone. These phones were initially quite bulky and expensive, though the size and the cost have declined dramatically. Second generation wireless technology, which includes digital cellular phones, is currently in use worldwide. Third generation, or *3G* technology will enable wireless devices to send and receive data as much as seven times faster than a standard 56K modem.[2] 3G technology will help fuel the growth of m-business over the next several years.

The proliferation of consumer devices, such as *personal digital assistants* (*PDAs*), *digital cellular phones* and *two-way pagers* is driving the demand for m-business (see feature Research In Motion: The BlackBerry Handheld). PDAs are handheld devices that are often used as personal organizers, store contact information and run numerous other applications; many PDAs have mobile Internet access capabilities. Two-way pagers are small paging devices capable of sending and receiving text messages.

Wireless devices enabled with Internet access allow users to manage their information while away from their desktop computers. Through PDAs, such as the *Palm* handheld computer and the *Pocket PC*, and through digital cellular phones and laptop computers, users are able to buy airline tickets and groceries, trade stocks and check their e-mail remotely.[3] These examples represent only a small fraction of the conveniences provided by wireless Internet access. In fact, outside the United States, mobile phones are the preferred medium for getting information and making e-business transactions.[4]

e-Fact 6.2

According to a recent study, there were approximately 200 million Internet users and 400 million mobile phone users in 1999. As more Internet-enabled mobile phones become available, the base of e-commerce customers will grow.[5]

Wireless devices and the current wireless technologies still present many obstacles to m-business. Wireless services are not available everywhere. For example, cellular service is not available on ships in the middle of the ocean, on airplanes or in unpopulated areas; satellite service, which requires line-of-sight to the satellite, does not work indoors or in the shadow of a building. Also, wireless Internet service is still relatively expensive; most wireless Internet service providers charge per-use fees. As a result, it is usually more cost effective to use wired connections. Limited bandwidth for wireless transmissions restricts the amount of data that can be sent over the wireless network, as well as the speed of the transmissions. As a result, wireless technology does not provide the same level of service as wired connections. Small screens on wireless devices make it difficult to browse the Web. Wireless devices also have significantly smaller memory capacity and less powerful processors than desktop computers. There are also issues of security and safety. Wireless transmissions are easy to tap. There is also concern about the radiation generated by some wireless devices, particularly mobile phones. Researchers are currently studying whether the radiation generated by these phones is significant enough to be a health hazard when the device is held next to your ear.

Although numerous obstacles to m-business remain, wireless technology is growing rapidly. It is only a matter of time before we see significant improvements to wireless capabilities that will result in a literal explosion of m-business worldwide.

6.3 m-Business

One of the most important new applications on the Web will be *mobile business*, known as *m-business*. M-Business is e-business using wireless devices with Internet access. M-Business will have significant implications for both the B2C and B2B marketplaces.

Research In Motion: The BlackBerry™ Handheld

The *BlackBerry* handheld device from Research In Motion Limited (RIM) is the most popular wireless e-mail solution (Fig. 6.1).[6]   Available in both pager-size and palm-size units, the devices include a keypad, making it easy to type messages quickly. E-mails are sent and retrieved automatically; you do not need to dial into a provider for access.

RRIM has developed wireless handhelds that support both industry-leading wide-area wireless data network protocols: *DataTAC® Network* and *Mobitex Network*. Both DataTAC and Mobitex are *personal communications services* (*PCS*) networks that enable wide-area wireless data communication. Both protocols provide in-building penetration, roaming, messaging services, guaranteed delivery and reliability.

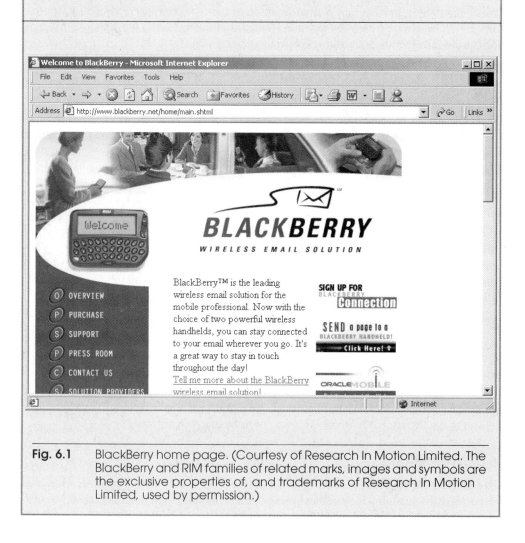

Fig. 6.1   BlackBerry home page. (Courtesy of Research In Motion Limited. The BlackBerry and RIM families of related marks, images and symbols are the exclusive properties of, and trademarks of Research In Motion Limited, used by permission.)

Research In Motion: The BlackBerry™ Handheld (Cont.)

There are a variety of services available for the BlackBerry handhelds. The *Black-Berry Exchange Edition* is a secure, wireless e-mail service for businesses using *Microsoft Exchange* (**www.microsoft.com/exchange**). Some of the features of this service include e-mail and organizer software, desktop software, optional server software, the ability to integrate a mailbox with Microsoft Exchange and flat-rate airtime. The *BlackBerry Internet Edition* allows mobile users to access e-mail anytime, anywhere. Some of the features of this service include organizer software and single-mailbox integration with an Internet e-mail account. (Visit **www.rim.net/products/handhelds/service.html#Exchange** for information about other BlackBerry services.)

The *RIM Developer Zone* (**www.developers.rim.net**) provides information for software developers interested in building applications to be used on RIM devices. The Web site has links to tools, discussions, FAQs, downloads and documentation.

---

e-Fact 6.3

According to a study by International Data Corporation, mobile commerce in Europe is expected to reach over $30 billion by 2004.[7]

In the B2C marketplace, m-business will result in increased conveniences for consumers. Imagine being able to use your mobile phone to purchase a can of soda from a vending machine or gas for your car.[8] Consumers are currently using mobile devices for information such as news, sports scores and e-mail. They are also using wireless devices to trade stocks and make some purchases. In the future, consumers will use wireless devices to make frequent, small transactions. In Section 6.10 we discuss location-based services which will also impact B2C m-business, allowing companies to send advertisements, coupons and more to consumers' wireless devices based on their locations. One company currently taking advantage of wireless technology is Progressive Casualty Insurance Company (**www.progressive.com**). Customers can use wireless devices to find a local insurance agent or get a price quote. In the future, the company plans to add the ability to make payments, check account information and access automobile recall information.

In the B2B marketplace, wireless applications for sales and service professionals provide one of the largest opportunities for m-business. Using wireless applications, salespeople can access product databases and place orders while they are on the road. Service professionals can address customer needs immediately, even when they are not in the office. Also, wireless devices currently have a limited ability to access word-processor files and spreadsheets.[9] In the near future, company databases and billing systems will enable ordering and billing to be conducted remotely. More advanced applications, such as direct advertising based on location, are currently under development. Companies taking advantage of wireless technologies will have a real advantage.

Wireless technology is attracting interest from virtually every industry, and creating interesting competitive and partnership opportunities. Internet service providers are facing competition from mobile phone companies providing wireless Internet access and e-commerce solutions. Sprint, for example, offers numerous e-commerce products and services for business of all sizes (**www.sprint.com/e-commerce**). Mobile-phone companies are at risk of losing market share to manufacturers of PDAs that are building digital cellular phone capabilities into their devices. Some of the these companies may begin to partner to combine their services, or the companies may merge as they pursue the "ultimate wireless device."

Wireless technology is receiving so much attention that even automobile manufacturers, such as Toyota are forming divisions devoted to the development of wireless technology.[10] Some automobiles in Japan are already built with wireless devices to send and receive e-mail right from the dashboard. In September 2000, Toyota Motor Corporation announced that it will establish the Toyota InfoTechnology Center Co., Ltd. Realizing the importance of wireless information and communication, Toyota formed the new company as a research and development center for mobile and Internet technologies. Toyota Motor Corporation is already involved in automotive multimedia and e-commerce businesses.

6.4 Wireless Internet Access

The *mobile Internet* is by far one of the most exciting areas of wireless technology. Currently, mobile phone services, such as *Sprint PCS* (PCS stands for "personal communications service"), offer limited Internet and Web access through digital phones (see feature Sprint PCS). Now, digital-phone companies, electronics companies and Internet service providers are racing to establish themselves as leaders in this exciting new area (see feature GoAmerica: Wireless Internet Service).

Code Division Multiple Access (*CDMA*) is a technology currently used for digital wireless communications. With CDMA, each transmission is assigned a specific channel, giving the transmission the benefit of the entire bandwidth within that channel and reducing the possibility that a connection will be broken. To ensure security, CDMA technology is able to assign each transmission on the network a unique code. The *Global System for Mobile Communications* (*GSM*) is another technology used for digital cellular communication and is particularly popular in Europe and Asia. GSM uses a technology called *Time Division Multiple Access* (*TDMA*) which takes multiple calls and assigns each call to a different time slot on the same radio frequency. Up to eight calls can simultaneously use the same frequency. One of the features of GSM is the *short messaging service* (*SMS*) which allows mobile phones to receive text messages.

These technologies may soon be replaced with 3G technologies including *EDGE*, *cdma2000* and *W-CDMA*. EDGE, a standard currently being developed by AT&T and Nokia, combines TDMA and GSM technologies. EDGE will enable high-speed wireless Internet access, e-mail, streaming audio and video and more.[11] 3Com and Samsung are developing cdma2000, which is an improved version of CDMA technology with increased bandwidth. W-CDMA, or wideband CDMA, is being developed by NTT DoCoMo, the largest wireless service provider in Japan. W-CDMA will be approximately 40 times faster than the technology DoCoMo currently uses for its wireless service.

Each of these technologies will subscribe to the guidelines for 3G as established by the *International Telecommunications Union* (*ITU*). For more information about 3G and the ITU, visit **www.itu.org**.

Feature: Sprint PCS^{SM}

Sprint PCS (**sprintpcs.com**) is a nationwide network that offers an array of wireless solutions for both business and personal applications. The main technology driving the PCS network is CDMA.

CDMA is a technology used for digital wireless communications. With CDMA, each transmission is assigned a specific channel, giving the transmission the benefit of the entire bandwidth within that channel and reducing the possibility that a connection will be broken. To ensure security, CDMA technology is able to assign each transmission on the PCS network a unique code.

Sprint's *Wireless Web Browser*, *Wireless Web Connection* and *Wireless Web Messaging* allow users to access information on the Internet remotely. Sprint's Wireless Web Browser, called the *UP.Browser*™, from **Phone.com**, acts like the browsers used on a connected desktop. Through the UP.Browser, users can view Web sites designed specifically for wireless Web browsers. These sites include Yahoo!, **Amazon.com**, Ameritrade, **MapQuest.com**, AOL, **CNN.com**, eBay and many others. (Users with Shockwave software can view a demonstration of the Wireless Web Browser by visiting **www.sprintpcs.com/wireless/wwbrowsing.html** and following the links. Shockwave software is available free for download at **www.shockwave.com**.)

The Sprint Wireless Web Connection Kit allows customers to use their PCS phone as a modem to connect their laptop to the Internet over the Sprint PCS network. Users can browse the Web, send and receive e-mail and access electronic schedules.

Through Sprint *Wireless Web Updates* and Yahoo!, users can view weather information, stock quotes, current news and forwarded e-mail messages, all delivered directly to their PCS phones.

Sprint PCS has partnered with several software companies to provide additional features for corporate customers. Customers can use their Sprint PCS phones to connect to their corporate e-mail accounts, contact lists and calendars. Using Sprint PCS enabled with Seibel wireless applications (**www.seibel.com**), salespeople can access important customer information, check the status of an order and respond to customer service requests. Sprint PCS phones enabled with *PeopleSoft Mobile Company Directory* (**www.peoplesoft.com**) allow employees to search their companies' global directories wirelessly. To learn more about Sprint PCS Wireless Web for Business, visit **www.sprintpcs.com/aboutsprintpcs/buzz/articles/ 092200_wwforbiz_summary.html**.

GoAmerica: Wireless Internet Service

GoAmerica (**goamerica.com**) is a wireless Internet service provider. Its services include Internet access, Web browsing and e-mail capabilities for a variety of wireless devices, including PDAs and two-way pagers.

> ### GoAmerica: Wireless Internet Service (Cont.)
>
> The *Go.Web™* wireless Web browser allows users access to e-mail and the Web. It includes a large collection of content, such as news, financial information, entertainment and more from many popular sites. Go.Web allows you to view real Web pages rather than small sections of content "clipped" from the sites. It compresses the sites to reduce download time. Using Go.Web, you can make purchases, trade stocks and more—from your wireless device, anytime and anywhere.
>
> Users who want customized content can use *MyGo.Web™*, which allows users to access information specific to their needs. For example, salespeople in the field can access their product catalogs over the network, check for information about competitors online and send proposals to their clients via e-mail.
>
> GoAmerica enables you to access your corporate network, monitor your competitors online and e-mail your colleagues and clients. The GoAmerica-supported RIM wireless handheld device allows salespeople to communicate using real-time, two-way text messaging. The RIM device also contains the Go.Web™ service, which gives users access to e-mail and the World Wide Web. (For more information about GoAmerica, visit **www.goamerica.com**.)

6.5 Wireless Web Technology

Three technologies used to provide Web access to wireless devices include *Wireless Application Protocol* (*WAP™*), *Web clipping* and Microsoft's *Pocket Internet Explorer*, part of Pocket PC.[12]

6.5.1 Web Clipping

Web clipping allows you to take relevant pieces of a Web site and deliver it to your wireless device, eliminating excess content and graphics that can make browsing the site on a wireless device cumbersome. For example, you can clip the headlines from an online news portal, clip sports scores or clip stock quotes for specific companies. Palm™, the leading manufacturer of PDAs, has designed Web-clipping applications for many of the most popular Web sites. Palm Web clipping uses a *proxy server* to respond to queries for Web pages. A proxy server lies between the client (such as a Web browser) and the regular Web server. It stores all queries for a period of time. First, the query is received by a proxy server controlled by the wireless Internet service provider. Next, the proxy server goes to the Web site and "clips" the necessary data. Finally, the proxy server transmits the data back to your wireless device. When a user makes a query, the proxy server checks to see if it has the information saved already. If the proxy server does not have the information, it passes the request to the regular server. Using proxy servers increases performance, saving the time needed to go to the Web site and download the information from the regular server. For more information and to see an automated demo of how Web clipping works, visit **www.palm.com/products/palmvii/webclipping.html**. You can find a list of Web clipping applications at **www.palm.net/apps/index.html** (Fig. 6.2). A few of the most popular applications include ThinAirMail, E*TRADE and FedEx.

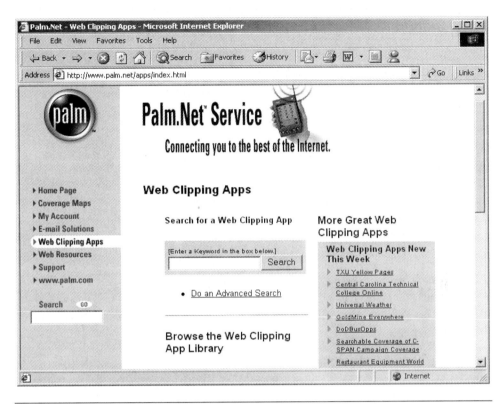

Fig. 6.2   Palm Web clipping applications library. (Courtesy of Palm, Inc.)

Personal Digital Assistants: The Palm™ Handheld

With the Palm™ VII wireless handheld computer (Fig. 6.3), Palm, Inc. (**palm.net**) introduced Web-clipping technology for displaying Web content. Using the *Query Application Builder* (*QAB*), Web designers build *Palm Query Applications* (*PQAs*) to be installed on users' Palm handheld computers. With a PQA for a particular Web site installed on a Palm VII handheld, a user can view the tailored content for that Web site. A tutorial covering PQA can be found at **palm.com/devzone/palmvii/tutorials/tutorial_palm.html**.[13]

The *Mobile Internet Kit*, supplied by Palm, Inc., provides wireless capabilities to Palm III and Palm V series handheld computers through the use of a snap-on modem or wireless phone. *Multimail* (by ActualSoft), allows users to access any standard e-mail account from their Palm handheld computer. The Mobile Internet Kit also provides Palm handhelds with the ability to view Web pages.

OmniSky (**omnisky.com**) adds wireless capabilities to the Palm V and Vx handhelds with the *Wireless Minstrel V* modem, which allows users to check e-mail and browse the Web wirelessly.

Personal Digital Assistants: The Palm™ Handheld (Cont.)

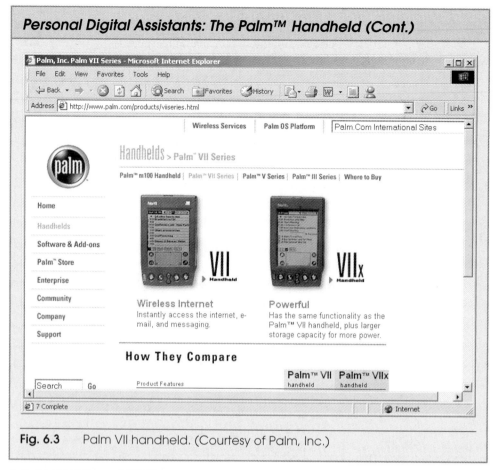

Fig. 6.3   Palm VII handheld. (Courtesy of Palm, Inc.)

6.5.2 WAP™ and WML

One of the most important approaches to wireless communication is standard accessibility. In 1997, the *Wireless Application Protocol (WAP)* was developed by Nokia, Ericsson, Motorola and others to foster the emergence of the wireless Internet.[14] The WAP is a set of communication protocols designed to enable different kinds of wireless devices to communicate and access the Internet. WAP is designed to standardize development across different wireless technologies worldwide. The WAP, which is intended primarily for Internet-enabled digital phones, pagers and other handheld devices, uses Web sites specifically designed for wireless handheld devices that have small screens and low-bandwidth constraints.

The *Wireless Markup Language (WML)* is the scripting language used to create Web content to be delivered to wireless handheld devices. WML, which is based on XML (discussed in the Web programming Appendices), removes "unnecessary" content from Web pages, such as graphics and animations. WML tags are used to "mark up" a Web page to specify how the page should be formatted on a wireless device (Fig. 6.4). *Microbrowsers*, designed with limited bandwidth and limited memory requirements, access the Web via the wireless Internet. Without graphics and animations, the transmission consumes less bandwidth and memory and it becomes easier to view on the small screens of wireless devices.

WML works with the WAP to deliver the content. WML is similar to HTML, but it does not require input devices, such as a keyboard or mouse for navigation.

Consider a digital phone that requests a Web page on the Internet. A WAP gateway, which acts as a proxy server, receives the request, translates it and sends it to the appropriate Internet server. The server responds by sending the requested WML document. The WAP gateway parses this document's WML (i.e., it analyzes the WML document, checking it for correctness) and sends the proper text to the digital phone.

A WML document is called a *deck* and contains static parts called *cards*. Each card consists of one user interaction, providing the WML browser with a small, self-contained document for browsing. Since the amount of memory available for browsing is small, only one document can be loaded at a time. For the same reason, the WML tag set is compact. It includes telephony tags so that secure telephone functionality can be implemented with WML/WMLScript. For instance, a voice-mail service can have a WML user interface that gives users choices for their mailboxes. WML also has image support for devices that can display bit-mapped graphics.

Figure 6.4 is an example of a WML document. To view this example, you will need a WML browser and server, such as the *Nokia WAP Developer Toolkit*, which is available free for download from **www.nokia.com/corporate/wap/sdk.html**. [*Note*: You must register at this Web site in order to download the WAP Developer Toolkit.] Figure 6.5 shows how the WML document is rendered using a WML browser on a Nokia phone.

```
1   <?xml version = "1.0"?>
2   <!DOCTYPE wml PUBLIC "-//WAPFORUM//DTD WML 1.1//EN"
3           "http://www.wapforum.org/DTD/wml_1.1.xml">
4
5   <!-- Fig. 20.8 : payBill.wml -->
6   <!-- Simple WML example      -->
7
8   <wml>
9      <card id = "paybill" title = "Welcome">
10        <p>
11           Welcome to Pay your bill from your cell!
12        </p>
13
14        <p>
15           Enter the amount:
16           <input type = "text" name = "amount" format = "*N"/>
17        </p>
18
19        <do type = "accept" label = "Submit amount">
20           <go href = "#pay"/>
21        </do>
22     </card>
23
24     <card id = "pay" title = "PAID">
25        <p>
26           You have paid $$$(amount). Thank you!
27        </p>
28     </card>
```

Fig. 6.4   WML document for paying a bill (part 1 of 2).

```
29
30   </wml>
```

Fig. 6.4   WML document for paying a bill (part 2 of 2).

Value of **title** attribute   **text** box

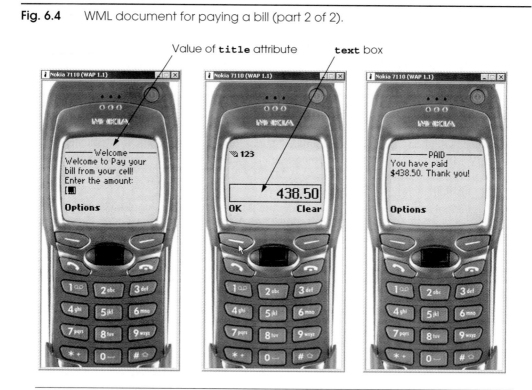

Fig. 6.5   Rendering a WML document using Nokia's browser. (© 2000 Nokia Mobile Phones.)

The following optional information is intended for the more technically inclined reader. Readers who do the optional case study in the appendices on programming an e-business will be able to understand this walkthrough of the WML code. This walkthrough is a line-by-line explanation of the code is Fig. 6.4.

Line 8 contains the **wml** element, which can contain any number of **card** elements. Recall that a **card** is essentially one document page. Lines 9 through 21

```
<card id = "paybill" title = "Welcome">
```

represent the first **card**, which has a unique identifier of **paybill** and a **title**, **Welcome**. The **title** attribute specifies the document's title in a manner similar to HTML's **title** element. This **card** is rendered in the left-most Nokia browser window (Fig. 6.5).

Lines 10 through 12

```
<p>
   Welcome to Pay your bill from your cell!
</p>
```

use element **p** to mark up text for display. This element is similar to a paragraph element in HTML.

Line 16

```
<input type = "text" name = "amount" format = "*N"/>
```

is an input element that specifies the document will present a **text** box (**named amount**) for user input. This **text** box accepts numeric values only, because attribute **format** is set to ***N**.

Lines 18 through 20

```
<do type = "accept" label = "Submit amount">
   <go href = "#pay"/>
</do>
```

set an action for the page using element **do**. The contents of the **do** element are performed when the user **accept**s the data input into the text box (in this case by clicking **OK** as shown in middle screen capture of Fig. 6.5). In this particular case, element **go**'s **href** attribute references the **card** with and **id** of **pay** (line 22).

Line 22

```
<card id = "pay" title = "PAID">
```

is the **pay card** requested when the user a accepts the input in the **text** box. We display the amount entered into the **text** box by preceding the **text** box name with a dollar sign (**$**) character. To actually display a dollar sign, two dollar signs are needed (i.e., **$$**). So, on line 23

```
You have paid $$$(amount). Thank you!
```

we display a dollar sign, output the value entered into the **amount text** box and the message **Thank you!**. This output is shown in the right-most screen capture of Fig. 6.4.

For more information about the WAP, visit **www.wapforum.org**. For additional information on WML, visit **www.xml.com/pub/Guide/WML** and **oasis-open.org/cover/wap-wml.html**.

e-Fact 6.4

According to a recent study by the Yankee Group, the number of people using the wireless Web will increase to over 40 million by 2002 and over 200 million by 2005.[15]

6.6 Software Applications for Wireless Devices

Wireless technology is creating many new opportunities in entertainment (see feature PacketVideo: Wireless Video Technology). Nokia, for example, is working on applications that will allow you to play video games on your cell phones, competing against players worldwide. **MP3.com** announced users will soon be able to download music files to wireless devices including PDAs and mobile phones.[17]

Software developers face a challenge when designing applications for wireless devices. Currently, there are a variety of wireless devices—cellular phones, PDAs, pagers, etc.—and no widely accepted standard for applications. As a result, developers may have to write an application many times, customizing it for each different type of device with which the application may communicate.[19]

Microsoft® Pocket Internet Explorer

Microsoft's *Pocket PC* platform takes a different approach to displaying Web content on hand-held devices (Fig. 6.6). Pocket PCs include *Pocket Internet Explorer*, which reformats complete Web pages as they are downloaded from the Internet for display on the Pocket PC (Fig. 6.7). This process allows Pocket PC users to access most of the content currently available on the Web and eliminates the need to tailor Web content for delivery to handheld devices.[16] Pocket Internet Explorer supports HTML, XML and other popular standards used in Web development. Users sync (or network) their Pocket PC with their desktops and download their favorite Web sites to their Pocket PC. This gives users access to information on the sites, even when they are not online. (For more information about Pocket Internet Explorer, visit **www.microsoft.com/ mobile/pocketpc/features/pie.asp**.)

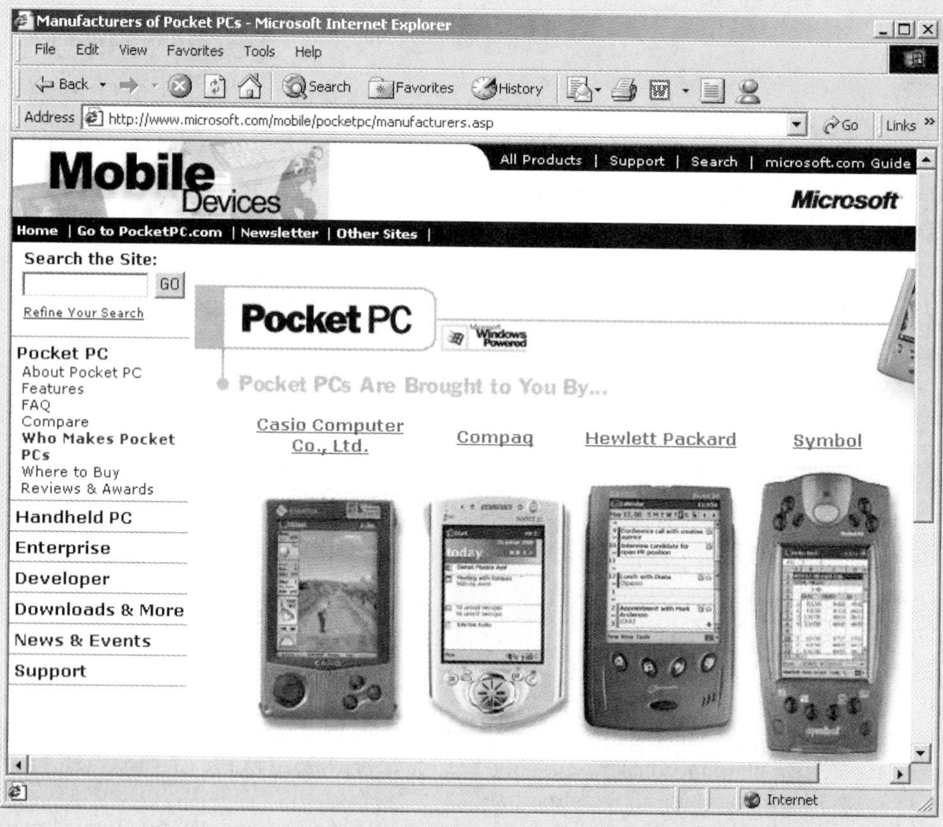

Fig. 6.6   Microsoft Pocket PC devices. (Courtesy of Microsoft Corporation, Casio Computer Co., Ltd., Compaq Corporation, Hewlett Packard and Symbol Technologies, Inc.)

Microsoft® Pocket Internet Explorer (Cont.)

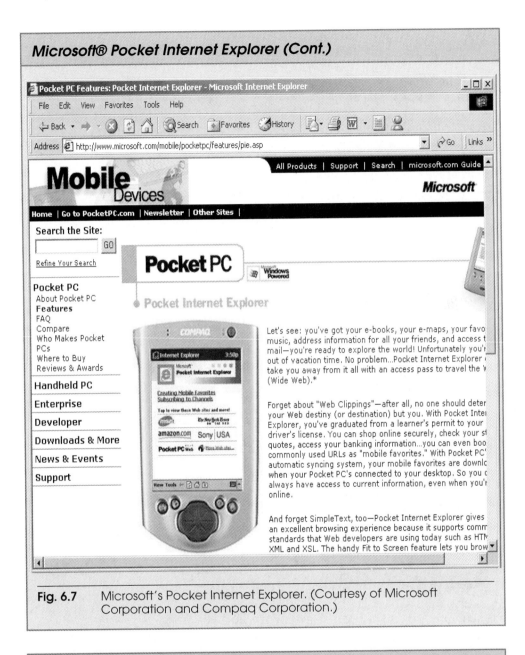

Fig. 6.7   Microsoft's Pocket Internet Explorer. (Courtesy of Microsoft Corporation and Compaq Corporation.)

PacketVideo: Wireless Video Technology

PacketVideo (**packetvideo.com**) specializes in wireless video technology for mobile devices. The technology will have huge implications for e-business, e-commerce and online entertainment. It will enhance mobile communications with the addition of streaming video and rich multimedia.

PacketVideo: Wireless Video Technology (Cont.)

PacketVideo was the first company in the world to transmit full audio and video over a cellular network with a bandwidth of only 9.6 Kbps to a wireless device (Fig. 6.8).[18] It is an *open platform*, which means that it allows third-party developers to create and distribute their own wireless video and multimedia applications.

PacketVideo technology is used worldwide. Its *PVPlatform* includes encoding, using the *PVAuthor*; serving, using the *PVServer;* and decoding using the *PVPlayer*. Some of the current applications include movie previews, video e-mail and a remote "babycam." (Check out the animated demo of PacketVideo by going to **www.pack-etvideo.com/products_overview.html#** and following the links.)

PacketVideo is currently developing additional applications for its technology, including targeted advertising, e-commerce and two-way video communications. The technology is already being built into the next generation of wireless devices.

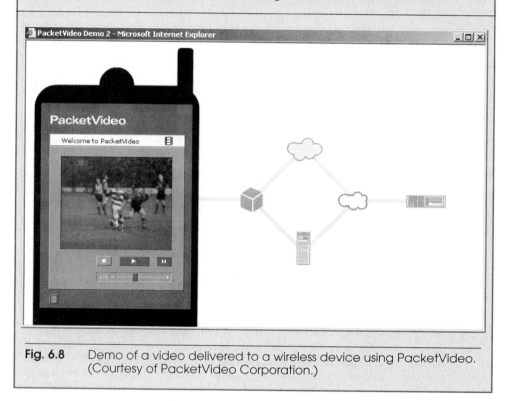

Fig. 6.8   Demo of a video delivered to a wireless device using PacketVideo. (Courtesy of PacketVideo Corporation.)

6.7 Wireless Local Area Networks (WLANs)

Consider all the wires in an office. There are wires connecting each mouse, keyboard and monitor to a computer. There are networking wires connecting each terminal and printer to a server. Wires are everywhere and can become cumbersome to maintain. Technologies such as *radio frequency*, *laser*, *infrared* and *Bluetooth*™ (see section 6.8) can be used to create wireless local area networks, called *WLANs*.

There are many benefits to using wireless technology for networks. First, wireless networks are easier to install and maintain without disrupting an office. Also, computers can easily be moved without having to install a new network connection in each location. In addition, wireless networks are also portable, allowing organizations to relocate quickly and efficiently.

Radio Frequency WLANs (*RF WLANs*) are often used to network devices at a distance. They are limited because they use radio frequencies, that are also used by cellular phones, radio broadcasts and other systems. Radio frequencies in the United States are regulated by the Federal Communications Commission (FCC). One of the major problems with radio frequency is interference, making this solution less secure than some other alternatives (security is discussed in Chapter 7, Internet Security).

Unlike RF WLANs, infrared and laser WLANs do not require FCC approval, nor do they have the same interference issues. However, infrared and laser WANs can be used only for short distances, generally within an office or between two nearby buildings. Infrared technology, which is already used by Palm devices and WebTV, can be used to create wireless networks within an office or even between nearby offices. Infrared technology is more cost efficient than laser technology, the equipment has a longer lifespan and the technology is less susceptible to weather.[20] Laser technology is used for building-to-building connections. It is reliable and easy to install, and the system is portable. *Transceivers* are set up on the rooftops of the two buildings where the offices are located. The transceivers, which send the signal between the buildings, are then linked to the network using fiber-optic cable.[21]

For more information about infrared networking systems, visit **www.jolt.co.il**, **www.levcom.co.il/olencom/navigator/index.htm** and **www.plaintree.com/wire_pro.htm**. To learn more about laser WLANs, visit **www.lsainc.com/products/connectivitysolutions/highperflacomm/products.html** and **www.astroterra.com**.

6.8 Bluetooth™

Bluetooth™ is a wireless technology that provides short-range, high-speed voice and data communication between digital devices. The technology was conceived by Ericsson in 1994. In 1998, the *Bluetooth Special Interest Group*—initially comprising Ericsson, IBM, Intel, Toshiba and Nokia—was formed to develop an open specification for the technology and to encourage cross-platform capabilities for the different wireless devices.[22] Currently, over 2000 companies are supporting the standard and Bluetooth-enabled devices.

Bluetooth provides up to 1 Mbps (megabits per second) of data transfer capability between devices as much as 30 feet apart. It is expected that future versions of the standard will work at distances of up to 300 feet and will provide 2Mbps transfers. Many types of devices, such as PCS phones, PDAs and laptop computers can incorporate Bluetooth technology and use it to communicate with one another.[23] The technology does not consume a large amount of power, making it suitable for small, battery-operated wireless devices.

Bluetooth can also be used to create wireless offices, linking computers via a wireless LAN, connecting mice and keyboards to desktop computers without cumbersome cables and even connecting PCs to printers. Bluetooth uses a radio frequency band that is available worldwide, allowing for global compatibility.

Bluetooth technology allows you to use the same phone as an interoffice intercom at work, a portable phone with fixed-line charges at home and a mobile phone with standard cellular phone charges when you are on the move.[24]

Bluetooth uses encryption and authentication techniques to ensure the security of communications (see Chapter 7, Internet Security). However, researchers discovered flaws in the technology that would allow a third party to obtain the encryption key or the user's identity.[25] At the time of publication, members of the Bluetooth technical standards group expected the security problems to be fixed quickly. For more information about Bluetooth, visit **www.bluetooth.com**.

6.9 Wireless Communications

Wireless devices have several limitations, including occasionally unreliable connections and slow connection speeds. For example, a cellular connection could easily be interrupted before the completion of a transaction. Wireless-device bandwidth ranges from 9.6 Kbps to 14.4 Kbps, about one fifth of the capabilities of a standard dial-up connection.[26] As a result, many businesses are tailoring their content to meet the capabilities of wireless devices, deciding which services and products offered are best suited for wireless access.

In the future, *general packet radio services* (*GPRS*) will enable wireless devices to transmit data at speeds of up to 114 kbps. The offering of these services will be closely followed by the launch of the *universal mobile telecommunications standard* (*UMTS*), which will offer transfer speeds of up to 2 Mbps for wireless devices.[27] Other developments for wireless Internet access include the use of *smart phones* for secure mobile transactions. Smart phones are mobile phones that can send and receive both voice and data messages.[28]

6.10 Location Tracking

A significant development in wireless technology and m-business is *location tracking*. Location tracking can be used for navigation, such as *GPS* (*Global Positioning System*) devices installed in cars; it can be used by shipping companies to track delivery trucks, giving customers more accurate tracking information and expected delivery time; it can also be used for targeted marketing. Web sites like **Go2systems.com** even use location information to provide a list of nearby restaurants, hotels and coffee shops.[29]

e-Fact 6.5

Strategy Analytics predicts the market for personal location services and location-based mobile commerce will reach approximately $7 billion in 2005.[30]

NEAR magazine focuses on the wireless location industry.[31] The magazine features articles from many experts and executives in the wireless industry. You can view the magazine online at **www.nearmagazine.com**.

6.10.1 Global Positioning System (GPS)

The *Global Positioning System* (*GPS*) was developed by the United States Department of Defense for military purposes and is now used in numerous commercial devices. GPS uses satellites to track a user's position (vertical and horizontal), velocity and the time in their location. It can be used virtually anywhere in the world, including on airplanes and ships.

GPS uses 24 satellites in six circular orbits (four satellites per orbit), plus five ground stations and three antennas that check the satellites and communicate information to them using radio signals. The ground stations are able to track a satellite's location based on the amount of time it takes for the signal to be sent from the satellite to the ground station. If a satellite is not positioned correctly in its orbit, the ground station sends a signal to the satellite to reposition itself. Location and time are computed using a formula called *triangulation*. A GPS receiver receives radio signals from four different satellites, orbiting thousands of miles above the Earth. Three of the satellites are used to determine the latitude, longitude and altitude of the receiver. The fourth satellite is used to check for errors in the triangulation.

Originally, the government had two levels of GPS service. The *Standard Positioning Service* (*SPS*) was available for public use. SPS was accurate to approximately 100 meters horizontal and 156 meters vertical. The *Precise Positioning Service* (*PPS*), originally only available to the military and now available commercially, is precise to within a few meters. For an online tutorial explaining how GPS works, visit **www.trimble.com/gps**.

6.10.2 E911 Act

The *E911 Act*, put forth by the Federal Trade Commission (FTC) and signed into law, was designed to standardize and enhance 911 service across mobile devices. Its goal is to improve emergency response time to 911 calls placed using cellular phones. The *Disabilities Issues Task Force* of the FCC is also working to make sure that hearing- and speech-impaired people have access to 911 service through mobile devices. Although the bill will improve safety, it also raises concerns about users' privacy.

e-Fact 6.6

According to the Cellular Telecommunications Industry Association (CTIA), approximately 118,000 emergency calls are made using cell phones every day.[32]

The first phase of the E911 Act (the "E" stands for "Enhanced") requires all wireless cellular carriers to provide *Automatic Number Information* (*ANI*)—the phone numbers of cellular phones calling in 911 emergencies. The carriers must also provide the locations of cell sites or base stations receiving the 911 calls, which give indications of the callers' locations. The second phase of the bill mandates that all mobile-phone carriers provide *Automatic Location Identification* (*ALI*) of a caller to the emergency dispatcher. ALI consists of specific latitudinal and longitudinal location information.

There are several benefits to the E911 Act. In many cases, drivers are not always sure of their exact location. This new information can help emergency response teams accurately locate callers, improving response time. Also, if a call is breaking up or the emergency operator cannot understand the caller, emergency response teams will still be able to locate the caller.[33] The ability to track a digital cellular phone call to a precise location will help save lives.

A side effect of the E911 Act is that cellular-phone users can be tracked at all times. This situation is great for safety reasons, but it can be an invasion of privacy. The FCC has ruled that mobile-phone carriers can provide caller location information to advertisers and other third-party organizations. As a result, you may soon find that you are receiving advertisements from stores as you walk through a mall. However, it will also enable you to locate friends nearby, to obtain up-to-the-minute traffic information and more.[34] For more information about privacy issues, see Chapter 11, Legal and Ethical Issues; Internet Taxation.

For more information about the E911 bill, visit the FCC's site at **www.fcc.gov/ e911**. For details about the automatic location identification specification of the bill, visit **www.fcc.gov/Bureaus/Wireless/Public_Notices/2000/ da002099.html**.

6.11 Future of Wireless Internet

Imagine the implications of wireless technology on everyday life. The cost of mobile phones and other wireless devices is decreasing each year; these devices are getting smaller, and the technology is improving rapidly. Virtually any device could become wireless. Plus, the cost of wireless communications is decreasing rapidly. Given the enormous opportunity to take advantage of wireless technology, venture capitalists are investing aggressively in wireless companies. Experts predict explosive growth in this area over the next few years.

e-Fact 6.7

Currently, less than 1 percent of all cars sold in Japan have built-in computers with wireless Internet access. Matsushita Communication Industrial predicts that number will grow to 40 percent by 2003. It has also been predicted that the market for the hardware and software components of these computers, which currently totals approximately $8 billion, will grow to over $60 billion by 2015.[35]

6.11.1 Implications for Disabled People

Wireless technology will profoundly improve the lives of people with disabilities. For example, wireless technology may be used to help visually impaired people navigate. Consider a visually impaired person trying to cross a busy intersection. The traffic light could be equipped with Bluetooth technology to broadcast messages to Bluetooth-enabled GPS wireless devices. The wireless device would receive a signal that the crossing sign says "Walk" and would then convert that message to audio for the person to hear. The device could also warn the person about cars that are jumping the light and tell the person when it is safe to walk.

Wireless technology may also help hearing-impaired people. For example, a hearing-impaired person shopping in a mall cannot hear an announcement about a sale in a store. Using Bluetooth technology, the mall could broadcast the announcement to the person's Bluetooth-enabled PDA device, which would convert the speech to text and display the text message for the hearing-impaired person. The same technology could be used to connect the PDA wirelessly to a television or radio to provide closed captioning for broadcasts.

Alzheimer's patients could also benefit from wireless technology. In the early stages of the disease, patients can suddenly find themselves lost. By using a handheld device with GPS technology, Alzheimer's patients can get their exact location, the location of the nearest police station and contact information for family members. The same technology could be used as a tracking device, which could be built into a wristband for Alzheimer's patients or small children, allowing family members to find them immediately.

6.11.2 Ultimate Wireless Device

Currently, wireless devices include PDAs, mobile phones, GPS devices, two-way pagers and a few others. In the future, these devices may converge into one ultimate wireless device.

The ultimate wireless device will combine all of the features of a mobile phone, PDA and two-way pager. It will also include a camera for video telephony and photography. You will be able to use it to make calls from anywhere in the world. You also will be able to send and receive e-mail in real-time, without having to dial into a service provider. It will maintain your address book, schedules, to-do lists and more. It will have a built-in GPS system that not only will help you get directions, but it will also notify you when you are near a store that sells an item you have on your shopping list. It will automatically update you with the latest traffic reports so you can immediately change your route. It will also automatically check you in at hotels or airports so you will not have to wait in line. You will even be able to download and play MP3 music files.

The possibilities for wireless technologies and m-business are exciting. In the exercises at the end of this chapter, we encourage you to design your version of the ultimate wireless device and compare your designs with those of your classmates. One major concern with current generation wireless technology and the future 3G wireless technology is security. In Chapter 7, Internet Security, we discuss how to secure transactions over an insecure medium such as the Internet.

6.12 Internet and World Wide Web Resources

Wireless Internet Service Providers

www.goamerica.com
GoAmerica is a wireless Internet service provider, supplying Internet access, Web browsing and e-mail capabilities for a variety or wireless devices such as PDAs and two-way pagers.

www.avantgo.com
AvantGO is a free mobile Internet service that allows you to browse Web pages using a Palm or Windows CE device. They also have a service for WAP-enabled phones to surf the Web.

www.nttdocomo.com
DoCoMo is one of the largest wireless product and service providers in Japan.

www.att.com/wireless/
AT&T offers mobile phone and Web services for individuals and businesses.

www.nortelnetworks.com/products/01/umts/frame.htmlwww.pinpoint.com
This is an automated demo of Nortel's 3G (third generation) wireless services.

www.verizon.com
Verizon offers mobile phone and Web services including e-mail and other WAP applications.

Wireless Phones and Modems

www.nokia.com
Visit this site to learn about some of the most popular mobile phones on the market. You will also find information on WAP applications for mobile business.

www.motorola.com
Motorola offers numerous Web-enabled mobile phone and paging devices.

www.ericsson.com
Visit this site to learn more about Ericsson's Web-ready phones and wireless devices.

www.ephones.com
This site has information about wireless phones, prices and technical information. You will also find a background on the wireless industry including historical and technical information.

www.samsung.com/products/index.html#
Check out some of Samsung's innovative wireless devices, including a smart phone that incorporates e-mail, Web browsing and data management. The smart phone also has hand-writing recognition, making it easier to compose messages.

www.wap.siemens.sportal.com
Using a Siemens WAP-enabled phone, you can visit this site to download the latest news, scores and statistics about your favorite European football (soccer) teams.

www.omnisky.com/
Watch the interactive demo which shows Omnisky's wireless modem, e-mail and Web services devices at work.

www.ricochet.net
Visit this site to learn about wireless modems and Internet access.

www.neopoint.com
Check out the interactive demo showing you all the features of the NeoPoint mobile phone with wireless modem, wireless Internet and data-storage capabilities.

www.globalstar.com
Visit this site to learn about the Globalstar satellite wireless phone. These phones can be used in remote areas where cellular service is not available, however they require line of site to the satellite.

Wireless e-Mail and Messaging

www.skytel.com
Check out various models of two-way pagers and wireless e-mail devices.

www.blackberry.net
BlackBerry two-way pagers from Research in Motion, Ltd. (RIM) are the world's most popular wireless e-mail devices. E-mails are sent and retrieved automatically.

www.etrieve.com
This service allows you to listen to your e-mail, converting the text to speech. You can also respond to e-mail by sending a voice message that is sent to the receiver as an attached **.wav** audio file.

www.bellsouthwd.com/ip26
This site has a demo showing you how to use an interactive messaging device for wireless e-mail.

Personal Digital Assistants

www.handspring.com
The Handspring Visor™ handheld computer can be used as a GPS system, an e-book or a personal organizer.

www.palm.com
The Palm is currently the most widely used PDA. It can be used for wireless Internet access and more.

www.pocketpc.com
This site is a portal for Microsoft Pocket PC news, information, downloads and more.

www.pctechguide.com/25mob3.htm
This site describes the history of PDAs.

WML and WAP

www.wapforum.org
WAP Forum is the industry association working to develop a standard for communication on wireless devices. This site includes news, information, FAQs, events, developer information and protocol specifications.

www.wapland.com
This site includes news, reviews, product information, a WAP FAQ and other resources related to the wireless Internet.

www.ericsson.com
This site has extensive information on WAP. including a tutorial, FAQ and links. Ericsson also manufactures mobile phones with WAP browsers.

www.oasis-open.org/cover/wap-wml.html
This site contains an extensive list of WML and WAP articles and other resources.

www.webreference.com/js/column61
This site contains an in-depth WML tutorial.

www.wirelessdevnet.com/
The Wireless Developer network is an excellent resource for news, tutorials and technical information. This site has excellent introductions to Bluetooth and Palm Query Application Development.

www.w3scripts.com/wap
Check out the interactive WAP demo (requires Internet Explorer 5 or higher) and the WAP/WML tutorial.

Wireless Applications

www.aethersystems.com
Check out the wireless commerce solutions from Aether Systems including the Personal Commerce Portal, Aether M Wallet, wireless bill paying and more.

www.ic.siemens.com/mobile-business/en/welcome/flash/index.html
Visit this site for more information about Siemen's mobile business products and solutions.

www.junglesoft.com
Download Jungleport, an application for Palm devices that includes city maps, dining guides and yellow pages.

www.smartserv.com
This application service provider offers a variety of wireless applications, such as a wireless information services portal, using the WAP and Windows CE platform.

www.everypath.com
This wireless applications provider takes Web content, databases, and other business applications and "mobilizes" them for a variety of wireless devices. Check out the Macromedia Flash-enabled demo that includes interesting industry estimates and details about the company's products and services.

www.pinpoint.com
This company offers a search engine designed for wireless devices.

Global Positioning Systems

www.gpsy.com/gpsinfo
This site contains links to numerous GPS-related Web sites including FAQs, news, satellite information, mapping programs and government GPS sites.

www.artivity.com/gps/index_eng.htm
This GPS resource guide includes links to hardware and software vendors, FAQs, newsgroups, a glossary of GPS terms and more.

www.navtech.com
Navtech is a manufacturer of in-vehicle navigation systems.

www.magellangps.com
This GPS manufacturer offers several models including portable and in-vehicle devices.

SUMMARY

- New technologies will lead to the wireless office, where computers, phones and other office equipment are all networked without any cables.
- The proliferation of consumer devices such as personal digital assistants (PDAs), digital cellular phones and two-way pagers is driving the demand for m-business.
- Outside the United States, mobile phones are the preferred medium for getting information and making e-business transactions.
- Wireless navigation systems help travelers find directions using the Global Positioning System (GPS).
- Limited bandwidth restricts the amount of data that can be transmitted over the wireless network.
- Small screens on wireless devices make it difficult to browse the Web.
- Wireless devices have significantly smaller memory capacity and less powerful processors than desktop computers.
- Wireless transmissions are easy to tap. There is also concern about the radiation generated by some wireless devices, particularly mobile phones.
- Wireless applications for sales and service professionals is one of the largest opportunities on the Web.
- With CDMA technology, each transmission is assigned a specific channel, giving the transmission the benefit of the entire bandwidth within that channel and reducing the possibility that a connection will be broken.
- Three technologies used to provide Web access to wireless devices include Wireless Application Protocol (WAP™), Web clipping and Microsoft's Pocket Internet Explorer, part of Pocket PC.
- A proxy server lies between the client (such as a Web browser) and the regular Web server. It stores all queries for a period of time.
- Using the Query Application Builder (QAB), Web designers build Palm Query Applications (PQAs) to be installed on users' Palm handheld devices.
- WAP is a set of communication protocols for wireless devices to enable different kinds of wireless devices to communicate and access the Internet.
- The Wireless Markup Language (WML) is the scripting language used to design Web content to be delivered to wireless handheld devices. It removes "unnecessary" content from Web pages, such as graphics and animations.
- WML works with the WAP to deliver the content. WML is similar to HTML but does not require input devices such as a keyboard or mouse for navigation.
- A WML document is called a deck and contains static parts called cards.
- Developers may have to write an application many times, customizing it for each different type of device with which the application may communicate.
- PacketVideo was the first company in the world to transmit full audio and video over a cellular network with a bandwidth of only 9.6 Kbps to a wireless device.
- Technologies such as radio frequency, laser, infrared and Bluetooth™ can be used to create wireless local area networks called WLANs.
- Radio Frequency WLANs (RF WLANs) are often used to network devices at a distance.
- Radio frequencies are regulated by the Federal Communications Commission.
- Unlike RF WLANs, infrared and laser WLANs do not require FCC approval, nor do they have some of the same interference issues.

- Infrared technology, which is already used by Palm devices and WebTV, can be used to create wireless networks within an office or even between nearby offices.

- Laser technology is used for building-to-building connections. It is reliable, easy to install and the system is portable.

- Bluetooth™ is a wireless technology that provides short-range, high-speed voice and data communication between digital devices.

- Bluetooth provides up to 1 Mbps (megabytes per second) of data transfer capability between devices as much as 30 feet apart. It is expected that future versions of the standard will work at distances of up to 300 feet.

- Bluetooth uses a radio frequency band that is available worldwide allowing for global compatibility.

- Bluetooth technology will allow you to use the same phone as an interoffice intercom at work, a portable phone with fixed line charges at home and a mobile phone with standard cellular phone charges when you are on the move.

- Bluetooth uses encryption and authentication techniques to ensure the security of communications.

- In the future, general packet radio services (GPRS) will enable wireless devices to transmit data at speeds of up to 114 Kbps. This will be closely followed by the launch of the universal mobile telecommunications standard (UMTS), which will offer transfer speeds up to 2 Mbps for wireless devices.

- The E911 Act, put forth by the Federal Trade Commission (FCC) and passed by the United States Senate in August, 1999, was designed to standardize and enhance 911 service across mobile devices.

- The Disabilities Issues Task Force of the FCC is also working to make sure that hearing- and speech-impaired people have access to 911 using mobile devices.

- A side affect of the E911 Act is that cellular phone users can be tracked at all times. The FCC ruled that mobile phone carriers can provide caller location information to advertisers and other third-party organizations.

TERMINOLOGY

3G
Automatic Location Identification (ALI)
Automatic Number Information (ANI)
BlackBerry™ Exchange Edition
BlackBerry Internet Edition
BlackBerry two-way pager
Bluetooth™
Bluetooth Special Internet Group
cards (in WML)
cdma2000
Code-Division Multiple Access (CDMA)
DataTAC® network (wireless data network protocol)
deck (in WML)
Disabilities Issues Task Force (of the FCC)
E911 Act
EDGE
Federal Trade Commission (FTC)
general packet radio services (GPRS)
Global Positioning System (GPS)
Global System for Mobile Communications (GSM)
GoAmerica
Go.Web™
Handspring
infrared
International Telecommunications Union (ITU)
laser
m-business
microbrowsers
Microsoft Exchange
Microsoft's Pocket PC
mobile business
Mobile Company Directory (PeopleSoft)
mobile Internet
Mobitex network (wireless data network protocol)
Nokia WAP Developer Toolkit
open platform
PacketVideo
Palm

Palm Query Applications (PQAs)
personal communications services (PCS)
personal digital assistants (PDAs)
Pocket Internet Explorer (Microsoft)
Pocket PC (Microsoft)
Precise Positioning Service (PPS)
proxy server
Query Application Builder (Palm)
Radio Frequency WLAN (RF WLAN)
RIM Developer Zone
short messaging service
smart phones
Sprint PCS
Standard Positioning Service (SPS)
Time Division Multiple Access (TDMA)
transceiver

triangulation
two-way pager
universal mobile telecommunications standard (UMTS)
UP.Browser™ (**Phone.com**)
W-CDMA
WAP Developer Tool Kit (Nokia)
WAP Forum™
Web clipping
Wireless Application Protocol (WAP)
Wireless Local Area Network (WLAN)
Wireless Markup Language (WML)
Wireless Web Browser (Sprint)
Wireless Web Connection Kit (Sprint)
Wireless Web Messaging (Sprint)
Wireless Web Updates (Sprint)

SELF-REVIEW EXERCISES

6.1   State whether the following are *true* or *false*. If the answer is *false*, explain why.
   a) Code Division Multiple Access (CDMA) assigns multiple calls to different time slots on the same radio frequency.
   b) GPS uses information from two satellites to track a user's exact location.
   c) Radio Frequency WLANs are regulated by the Federal Communications Commission.
   d) The E911 Act will require mobile-phone services to provide tracking information for users placing emergency calls.
   e) WML tags are used to mark up a Web page to specify how the page should be formatted on a wireless device.

6.2   Fill in the blanks in each of the following statements:
   a) _____ is e-business conducted using wireless devices.
   b) _____ is a set of communications protocols for wireless devices to allow different types of wireless devices to communicate and access the Internet.
   c) Four technologies used to create WLANs include _____, _____, _____, and _____.
   d) A WML document is called a _____, and it contains static parts called _____.
   e) The _____ was designed to standardize and enhance 911 service across mobile devices.

ANSWERS TO SELF-REVIEW EXERCISES

6.1   a) False. CDMA is a technology that assigns each transmission to a specific channel, giving the transmission the benefit of the entire bandwidth within that channel. b) False. GPS uses three satellites, plus information from a fourth satellite for error checking, to measure a user's location. c) True. d) True. e) True.

6.2   a) m-Business. b) Wireless Applications Protocol (WAP). c) Radio Frequency, laser, infrared and Bluetooth. d) deck, cards. e) E911 Act.

EXERCISES

6.3   Define the following terms:
   a) Bluetooth

b) WAP
c) Web clipping
d) m-commerce
e) WML

6.4   (*Group Project*). Design your "ultimate wireless device."
a) Describe how will it look.
b) What services will it perform?
c) What technologies are required for it to perform those services?

6.5   In this chapter, we presented a few examples of how wireless technology will help disabled people. Describe three other ways in which the technologies will help disabled people in their everyday activities.

6.6   Try the demonstration of the Sprint PCS Wireless Web Browser at **www.sprint-pcs.com/wireless/wwbrowsing.html**, and note the functions that are available through it. What do you perceive to be the major obstacles in conducting m-business using a mobile phone connected to the Internet?

6.7   Review the differences between the WAP using WML, Web clipping and Microsoft's Pocket Internet Explorer. Which technology do you perceive to be the best solution for wireless Web browsing, and why?

6.8   (*Class Discussion*). The E911 Act will increase safety for cellular phone users; however, it may also infringe on their privacy. Come to class prepared to discuss the following questions:
a) What are some of the benefits of this tracking technology?
b) What are some of the significant drawbacks?
c) Should the FCC allow commercial vendors to access tracking information? Explain why or why not.

6.9   Study the Bluetooth Web site at **www.bluetooth.com**. Describe how the technology will be used in the near future.

6.10   Describe how GPS technology can be used in the following devices:
a) clock
b) PDA
c) car
d) car keys
e) pen
f) mobile phone
g) laptop computer

6.11   Go to **www.w3scripts.com/wap**.

6.12   (*Class Discussion*). Read e-Fact 6.1. Come to class prepared to discuss the following:
a) How will the proliferation of wireless Internet access impact business and our personal lives?
b) What are some of the major concerns related to privacy, security, accuracy and dependability of the wireless Internet?

WORKS CITED

The notation **<www.domain-name.com>** indicates that the citation is for information found at the Web site.

1. R. Gerber, "The Mobility Revolution," *The New York Times* 21 August 2000: 1-2.

2. A. Walker, "WAP," *NEAR* Volume 1 Issue 1: 5-7.

3.   B. Issberner, "How 'Context Switch Radios' Will Streamline with Personal Area Networks," *Wireless Integration* `<wi.pennwellnet.com/home/articles>` 1 March 2000.

4.   P. Seybold, "Dial M for Commerce," *Business 2.0* April 2000: 113-114.

5.   H. Simon, "Sinking Your Teeth Into M-Commerce," *Intelligent Enterprise* 18 August 2000: 60-63.

6.   `<www.rim.net>`.

7.   S. Baker, "Goliath vs. Goliath: In the Battle for Europe's Mobile Web, the Small May Not Last," *Business Week* 29 May 2000: 152-154.

8.   L. Rogak, "Commerce Adds an M," `<www.business2.com/content/channels/technology/2000/06/13/12410>`, 27 June 2000.

9.   S. Neil, "Walking the Wireless Web," *PC Week* 20 March 2000: 80.

10.   "Announcing the Toyota InfoTechnology Center," `<www.toyota.com/times/corporate/docs/2000rel/09techcenter.html>` 25 September 2000.

11.   "AT&T Wireless Services And Nokia Agree To Develop And Test Advanced Enhancements To All IP-Edge Network," `<www.att.com/press/item/0,1354,3021,00.html>`, 26 June 2000.

12.   S. Alexander, "Wireless Web Access," *Computerworld* 5 June 2000: 84.

13.   T. Powell and J. Lima, "The Challenges of a Wireless Web," *Network World* 20 March 2000: 81.

14.   T. Hughes, "The Web unwired," *Global Technology Business* December 1999: 33.

15.   M. Cleary, "Content Sites Vie for Wireless," *Interactive Week* 31 July 2000: 42.

16.   S. Alexander, "Wireless Web Access," *Computerworld* 5 June 2000: 84.

17.   `<mp3.boston.com/spotlight/articles/20001107_synch.shtml>`.

18.   `<www.packetvideo.com/introduction.html>`.

19.   A. Radding, "Developers Brace for Wireless Boom," *Informationweek* 27 March 2000: 175-180.

20.   `<www.jolt.co.il, www.levcom.co.il/olencom/navigator/index.htm>`.

21.   `<www.lsainc.com/products/connectivitysolutions/highperflacomm/products.html>`.

22.   C. Bisbikian and B. A. Miller, "Bluetooth: Get Wired Without the Wires," *e-Business Advisor*, October 2000: 14-17.

23.   T. Hughes, "The Web Unwired," *Global Technology Business* December 1999: 32.

24.   `<www.bluetooth.com/#>`.

25.   J. Markoff, "Flaws in Digital Wireless Technology Said to Allow Eavesdropping," *The New York Times* 2 September 2000: B3.

26.   T. Hughes, "The Web unwired," *Global Technology Business* December 1999: 32.

27.   T. Hughes, "The Web unwired," *Global Technology Business* December 1999: 32.

28.   A. Walker, "WAP," *NEAR* Volume 1 Issue 1: 5-7.

29.   L. Vaas, "Going 2 the Wireless World," *PC Week* 20 March 2000: 68.

30.   S. Marek, "Connecting the Dot-Coms," *NEAR* Volume 1 Issue 2: 15-17, 57.

31.   `<www.nearmagazine.com>`.

32.   "Recently Pinpointed: Industry News from Around the Globe," *NEAR* Volume 1 Issue 2: 49.

33.   S. A. Pignone, "When Cell Phones Save Lives," *NEAR* Volume 1 Issue 2: 11-14.

34. I. Gale, "The Phone as a Tracking Device," *The Industry Standard's Grok* November 200: 32.

35. E. Thornton, "Digital Wheels," *Business Week* 10 April 2000: 114-124.

RECOMMENDED READING

J. Adam, "Internet Everywhere," *Technology Review* September/October 2000: 87-93.

D. Barney, "Wireless: On the Verge of Greatness," *Network World* 18 September 2000: 18-19.

S. Berinato and C. Nobel, "Unplugged and Insecure," *eWeek* 3 July 2000, 2000: 27.

J. Bort, "Preventing a WAP," *The Buzz Issue* 11 September 2000: 56-62.

J. Boyd, "The Web Goes Wireless," *Internet Week* 11 September 2000: 27-28.

R. Buckman, "Microsoft, Advertisers Target the Wireless Web," *The Wall Street Journal* 24 July 2000: B1; B8.

D. Cannon, "Wireless- Not Just Another Way to Connect Your PC to the Network," *Messaging Magazine* March/April 2000: 26-28.

J. Champy, "Wireless Dreams," *Computerworld* 22 May 2000: 47.

S. Cleary, "Location Services Enter the Mobile-Phone Game," *The Wall Street Journal* 11 September 2000: B9A.

S. Crenshaw, "Technology Still Lags for Safe Wireless e-Commerce," *Masshightech* 31 July-6 August 2000: 26.

J. Gantz, "Wireless Protocol Is Coming. Are you ready?" *Computerworld* 17 April 2000: 29.

M. Hamblen, "Wireless Insecurity," *Computer World* 4 September 2000: 72.

M. Hamblen, "Wireless Meets Web," *Computer World* 28 February 2000: 14.

M. Hicks, "Wireless Intranets: Proceed With Caution," *PC Week* 20 march 2000: 74.

P. Howe, "Wireless Done Cheap," *The Boston Globe* 15 May 2000: C2.

T. Hughes, "The Web Unwired," *Global Business Technology* December 1999: 32-36.

J. Krause, "Free Access Spreads Its Wings," *The Industry Standard* 8 May 2000: 67.

P. Lewis, "Heading North to the Wireless Future," *The New York Times* 1 June 2000: E1; E3.

K. Maney, "Cell Phones Could Be Secret Decoder Rings of the Future," *USA Today* 21 September 2000: 3B.

D. McVIcker, "So Where Is the Wireless Web," *Upside* April 2000: 257-262.

B. Moran, "Suddenly, Wireless Net Access Is the Next Big Thing," *Mass High Tech* 15-21 May 2000: 30.

S. Neil, "Walking the Wireless Web," *PC Week* 20 March 2000: 67-80.

V. Nijhawan, "Look Ma, No Wires," *Siliconindia* July 2000: 32-36s.

W. Rash, "Death, The Internet and the Need for WIreless Communications," *Internet Week* 29 May 2000: 61.

W. Rash, "The Future Is Now for Wireless e-Commerce," *Internet Week* 14 February 2000: 69.

B. Reid, "US Could Be Left Behind In m-Commerce," *Financial Times* 17 August 2000: 14.

J. Rewick, "Upoc Goes After Generation Wireless's Gabbers," *The Wall Street Journal* 14 September 2000: B8.

S. Romero, "Wireless Internet Casts Its Shadow, and Substance, in New York," *The New York Times* 21 August 2000: C1, C6.

M. Saylor, "Newspapers Go Wireless," *The New York Times* 8 May 2000: 6.

H. Simon, "Sinking Your Teeth Into m-Commerce," *Intelligent Enterprise* 18 August 2000: 60-63.

C. Soule, "One Company WAP's Out to Revitalize Its Business," *Mass High Tech* 15-21 May 2000: 29.

T. Sullivan, "A World Without Wires," *ENT* 22 March 2000: 30-31.

E. Thornton, "Digital Wheels," *Business Week* 10 April 2000: 114-124.

L. Vaas, "Going2 the Wireless World," *PC Week* 20 March 2000: 68.

B. Wallace, "Wireless Ventures Promise More Services, Lower Prices," *Information Week* 10 April 2000: 30.

T. Weiss, "Wireless Internet Initiative Advances," *Computer World* 18 September 2000: 31.

S. Wildstrom, "Wireless Gets Easier and Faster," *Business Week* 29 May 2000: 34.

7

Internet Security

Objectives

- To understand the basic concepts of security.
- To understand public-key/private-key cryptography.
- To learn about popular security protocols, such as SSL and SET.
- To understand digital signatures, digital certificates and certification authorities.
- To become aware of various threats to secure systems, such as viruses and denial-of-service attacks.
- To understand emerging security techniques, such as biometrics and steganography.

Three may keep a secret, if two of them are dead.
Benjamin Franklin

Attack—Repeat—Attack.
William Frederick Halsey, Jr.

Private information is practically the source of every large modern fortune.
Oscar Wilde

There must be security for all—or not one is safe.
The Day the Earth Stood Still, screenplay by Edmund H. North

No government can be long secure without formidable opposition.
Benjamin Disraeli

Outline

7.1   Introduction

7.2   Ancient Ciphers to Modern Cryptosystems

7.3   Secret-key Cryptography

7.4   Public-key Cryptography

7.5   Key Agreement Protocols

7.6   Key Management

7.7   Digital Signatures

7.8   Public-key Infrastructure, Certificates and Certification Authorities

7.9   Cryptanalysis

7.10   Security Protocols

       7.10.1   Secure Sockets Layer (SSL)

       7.10.2   Secure Electronic Transaction™ (SET™)

7.11   Security Attacks

7.12   Network Security

       7.12.1   Firewalls

       7.12.2   Kerberos

       7.12.3   Biometrics

7.13   Steganography

7.14   Internet and World Wide Web Resources

Summary • Terminology • Self-Review Exercises • Answers to Self-Review Exercises • Exercises • Works Cited • Recommended Reading

7.1 Introduction

The explosion of e-business and e-commerce is forcing businesses and consumers to focus on Internet security. Consumers are buying products, trading stocks and banking online. They are providing their credit-card numbers, social-security numbers and other highly confidential information through Web sites. Businesses are sending confidential information to clients and vendors over the Internet. At the same time, we are experiencing increasing numbers of security attacks. Individuals and organizations are vulnerable to data theft and hacker attacks that can corrupt files and even shut down e-businesses. Security is fundamental to e-business.

e-Fact 7.1

According to a study by International Data Corporation (IDC), organizations spent $6.2 billion on security consulting in 1999, and IDC expects the market to reach $14.8 billion by 2003.[1]

Modern computer security addresses the various problems and concerns of protecting electronic communications and maintaining network security. There are four fundamental requirements of a successful, secure transaction: *privacy, integrity, authentication* and *non-repudiation. The privacy issue is the following*: How do you ensure that the information you transmit over the Internet has not been captured or passed on to a third party without your knowledge? *The integrity issue is the following*: How do you ensure that the information you send or receive has not been compromised or altered? *The authentication issue is the following*: How do the sender and receiver of a message prove their identities to each other? *The nonrepudiation issue is the following*: How do you legally prove that a message was sent or received?

In addition to these requirements, network security addresses the issue of *availability*: How do we ensure that the network and the computer systems to which it connects will stay in operation continuously?

In this chapter, we will explore Internet security, from secure electronic transactions to secure networks, and the fundamentals of secure business, known as *s-business*. We will discuss how e-commerce security is achieved using current technologies. We encourage you to visit the Web resources provided in Section 7.14 to learn more about the latest developments in e-commerce security. These resources include many demos that you will find to be informative and entertaining.

7.2 Ancient Ciphers to Modern Cryptosystems

The channels through which data pass over the Internet are not secure; therefore, any private information that is being passed through these channels must be protected. To secure information, data can be encrypted. *Cryptography* transforms data by using a *key*—a string of digits that acts as a password—to make the data incomprehensible to all but the sender and the intended receivers. Unencrypted data are called *plaintext*; encrypted data are called *ciphertext*. Only the intended receivers should have the corresponding key to decrypt the ciphertext into plaintext. A *cipher*, or *cryptosystem*, is a technique or algorithm for encrypting messages.

Cryptographic ciphers were used as far back as the time of the ancient Egyptians. In ancient cryptography, messages were encrypted by hand, usually with a method based on the alphabetic letters of the message. The two main types of ciphers were *substitution ciphers* and *transposition ciphers*. In a substitution cipher, every occurrence of a given letter is replaced by a different letter; for example, if every "a" is replaced by a "b," every "b" by a "c," etc., the word "security" would encrypt to "tfdvsjuz." In a transposition cipher, the ordering of the letters is shifted; for example, if every other letter, starting with "s," in the word "security" creates the first word in the ciphertext and the remaining letters create the second word in the ciphertext, the word "security" would encrypt to "scrt euiy." Complicated ciphers were created by combining substitution and transposition ciphers. For example, using the substitution cipher first, then the transposition cipher, the word "security" would encrypt to "tdsu fvjz." The problem with many historical ciphers is that their security relied on the sender and receiver to remember the encryption algorithm and keep it secret. Such algorithms ("algorithm" is a computer science term for "procedure") are called *restricted algorithms*. Restricted algorithms are not feasible to implement among a large group of people. Imagine if the security of U.S. government communications relied on every U.S. government employee to keep a secret; the encryption algorithm would easily be compromised.

Modern cryptosystems are digital. Their algorithms are based on the individual *bits* of a message rather than letters of the alphabet. A computer stores data as a *binary string*, which is a sequence of ones and zeros. Each digit in the sequence is called a bit. Encryption and decryption keys are binary strings with a given *key length*. For example, 128-bit encryption systems have a key length of 128 bits. Longer keys have stronger encryption; it takes more time and computing power to "break the code."

Until January 2000, the U.S. government placed restrictions on the strength of crypto-systems that could be exported from the United States, by limiting the key length of the encryption algorithms. Today, the regulations on exporting cryptosystems are less stringent. Any cryptosystem may be exported as long as the end user is not a foreign government or from a country with embargo restrictions on it.[2]

7.3 Secret-key Cryptography

In the past, organizations wishing to maintain a secure computing environment used *symmetric cryptography*, also known as *secret-key cryptography*. Secret-key cryptography uses the same symmetric secret key to encrypt and decrypt a message (Fig. 7.1). In this case, the sender encrypts a message using the symmetric secret key, then sends the encrypted message and the symmetric secret key to the intended recipient. A fundamental problem with secret-key cryptography is that before two people can communicate securely, they must find a way to exchange the symmetric secret key and securely. One approach is to have the key delivered by a courier, such as a mail service or Federal Express. While this approach may be feasible when two individuals communicate, it is not efficient for securing communication in a large network, nor can it be considered completely secure. The privacy and the integrity of the message could be compromised if the key is intercepted as it is passed between the sender and the receiver over unsecure channels. Also, since both parties in the transaction use the same key to encipher and decipher a message, you cannot authenticate which party created the message. Finally, to keep communications private with each receiver, a different key is required for each receiver, so organizations could have huge numbers of symmetric secret keys to maintain.

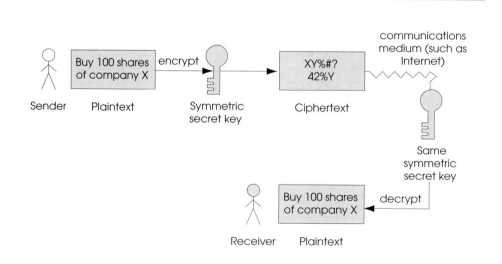

Fig. 7.1   Encrypting and decrypting a message using a symmetric secret key.

An alternative approach to the key-exchange problem is to have a central authority, called a *key distribution center* (*KDC*). The key distribution center shares a (different) symmetric secret key with every user in the network. In this system, the key distribution center generates a *session key* to be used for a transaction (Fig. 7.2). Next, the key distribution center distributes the session key to the sender and receiver, encrypted with the symmetric secret key they each share with the key distribution center. For example, say a merchant and a customer want to conduct a secure transaction. The merchant and the customer each have unique symmetric secret keys they share with the key distribution center. The key distribution center generates a session key for the merchant and customer to use in the transaction. The key distribution center then sends the session key for the transaction to the merchant, encrypted using the symmetric secret key the merchant already shares with the center. The key distribution center sends the same session key for the transaction to the customer, encrypted using the symmetric secret key the customer already shares with the key distribution center. Once the merchant and the customer have the session key for the transaction, they can communicate with each other, encrypting their messages using the shared session key.

Using a key distribution center reduces the number of courier deliveries (again, by means such as mail or Federal Express) of symmetric secret keys to each user in the network. In addition, users can have a new symmetric secret key for each communication with other users in the network, which greatly increases the overall security of the network. However, if the security of the key distribution center is compromised, then the security of the entire network is compromised.

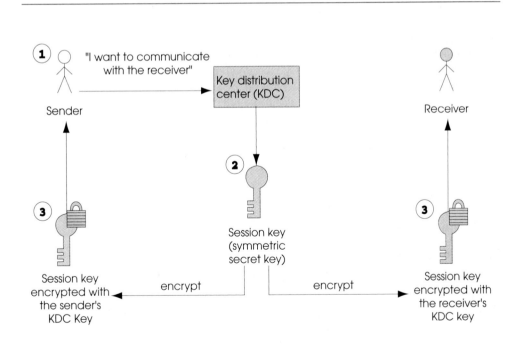

Fig. 7.2   Distributing a session key with a key distribution center.

One of the most commonly used symmetric encryption algorithms is the *Data Encryption Standard* (*DES*), which was developed by the National Security Agency (NSA) and IBM in the 1950s. DES has a key length of 56 bits. For many years, DES has been the standard set by the U.S. government and the American National Standards Institute (ANSI). However, cryptanalysts today believe that DES is not completely secure, because the key length is too short, making it easy to crack. As a result, the current standard of symmetric encryption is *Triple DES*, a variant of DES that is essentially three DES systems in a row, each having its own secret key. The United States government is in the process of selecting a new, more secure standard for symmetric encryption. The new standard will be called the *Advanced Encryption Standard* (*AES*). The *National Institute of Standards and Technology* (*NIST*), which sets the cryptographic standards for the U.S. government, is currently evaluating algorithms from five finalists, based on strength, efficiency, speed and a few other characteristics.[3]

7.4 Public-key Cryptography

In 1976, *Whitfield Diffie* and *Martin Hellman*, researchers at Stanford University, developed *public-key cryptography* to solve the problem of exchanging keys securely. Public-key cryptography is asymmetric. It uses two inversely related keys: a *public key* and a *private key*. The private key is kept secret by its owner. The public key is freely distributed. If the public key is used to encrypt a message, only the corresponding private key can decrypt it, and vice versa (Fig. 7.3). Each party in a transaction has both a public key and a private key. To transmit a message securely, the sender uses the receiver's public key to encrypt the message. The receiver decrypts the message using his or her unique private key. No one else knows the private key, so the message cannot be read by anyone other than the intended receiver; this system ensures the privacy of the message. The defining property of a secure public-key algorithm is that it is computationally infeasible to deduce the private key from the public key. Although the two keys are mathematically related, deriving one from the other would take enormous amounts of computing power and time, enough to discourage attempts to deduce the private key. An outside party cannot participate in communication without the correct keys. Thus, the security of the entire process is based on the secrecy of the private keys. If a third party obtains the decryption key, then the security of the whole system is compromised. If the integrity of a system is compromised, you can simply change the key, instead of changing the whole encryption or decryption algorithm.

Either the public key or the private key can be used to encrypt or decrypt a message. For example, if a customer uses a merchant's public key to encrypt a message, only the merchant can decrypt the message, using the merchant's private key. Thus, the merchant's identity can be authenticated, since only the merchant knows the private key. However, the merchant has no way of validating the customer's identity, since the encryption key the customer used is publicly available.

If the decryption key is the sender's public key and the encryption key is the sender's private key, the sender of the message can be authenticated. For example, suppose a customer sends a merchant a message encrypted using the customer's private key. The merchant decrypts the message using the customer's public key. Since the customer encrypted the message using his or her private key, the merchant can be confident of the customer's identity. This systems works as long as the merchant can be sure that the public key with which the merchant decrypted the message belongs to the customer, not a third party posing as the customer. The problem of proving ownership of a public key is discussed in Section 7.8.

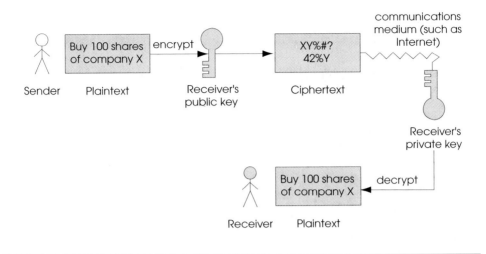

Fig. 7.3   Encrypting and decrypting a message using public-key cryptography.

These two methods of public-key encryption can actually be used together to authenticate both participants in a communication (Fig. 7.4). Suppose that a merchant wants to send a message securely to a customer so that only the customer can read it, and suppose also that the merchant wants to provide proof to the customer that the merchant (not an unknown third party) actually sent the message. First, the merchant encrypts the message using the customer's public key. This step guarantees that only the customer can read the message. Then the merchant encrypts the result using the merchant's private key, which proves the identity of the merchant. The customer decrypts the message in reverse order. First, the customer uses the merchant's public key. Since only the merchant could have encrypted the message with the inversely related private key, this step authenticates the merchant. Then the customer uses the customer's private key to decrypt the next level of encryption. This step ensures that the content of the message was kept private in the transmission, since only the customer has the key to decrypt the message.

The most commonly used public-key algorithm is *RSA*, an encryption system developed by Ron Rivest, Adi Shamir and Leonard Adleman in 1977. These three MIT professors founded *RSA Security, Inc.,* in 1982. Today, their encryption and authentication technologies are used by most Fortune 1000 companies and leading e-commerce businesses. With the emergence of the Internet and the World Wide Web, their security work has become even more significant and plays a crucial role in e-commerce transactions. Their encryption products are built into hundreds of millions of copies of the most popular Internet applications, including Web browsers, commerce servers and e-mail systems. Most secure e-commerce transactions and communications on the Internet use RSA products. For more information about RSA, cryptography and security, visit **www.rsasecurity.com**.

Pretty Good Privacy (PGP) is a public-key encryption system used to encrypt e-mail messages and files. It is freely available for noncommercial use. PGP is based on a "web of trust;" each client in a network can vouch for another client's identity to prove ownership of a public key. The "web of trust" is used to authenticate each client. To learn more about PGP and to download a free copy of the software, go to the MIT Distribution Center for PGP, at **web.mit.edu/network/pgp.html**.

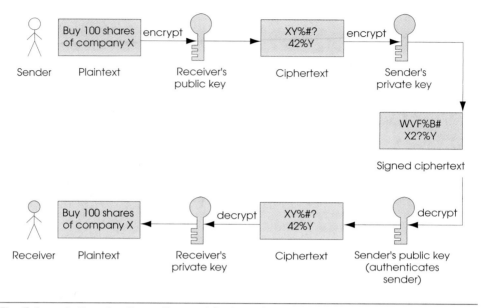

Fig. 7.4   Authentication with a public-key algorithm.

7.5 Key Agreement Protocols

A drawback of public-key algorithms is that they are not efficient for sending large amounts of data. They require significant computer power, which slows down communication. Thus, public-key algorithms should not be thought of as a replacement for symmetric secret-key algorithms. Instead, public-key algorithms can be used to allow two parties to agree upon a key to be used for symmetric secret-key encryption over an unsecure medium. The process by which two parties can exchange keys over an unsecure medium is called a *key agreement protocol*. A *protocol* sets the rules for communication: Exactly what encryption algorithm(s) is (are) going to be used?

The most common key agreement protocol is a *digital envelope* (Fig. 7.5). Using a digital envelope, the message is encrypted using a symmetric secret key, and then the symmetric secret key is encrypted using public-key encryption. For example, a sender encrypts a message using a symmetric secret key. The sender then encrypts that symmetric secret key using the receiver's public key. The sender attaches the encrypted symmetric secret key to the encrypted message and sends the receiver the entire package. The sender could also digitally sign the package before sending it to prove the sender's identity to the receiver (Section 7.7). To decrypt the package, the receiver first decrypts the symmetric secret key using the receiver's private key. Then, the receiver uses the symmetric secret key to decrypt the actual message. Since only the receiver can decrypt the encrypted symmetric secret key, the sender can be sure that only the intended receiver can read the message.

7.6 Key Management

Maintaining the secrecy of private keys is crucial to keeping cryptographic systems secure. Most compromises in security result from poor *key management* (e.g., the mishandling of private keys, resulting in key theft) rather than attacks that attempt to decypher the keys.[4]

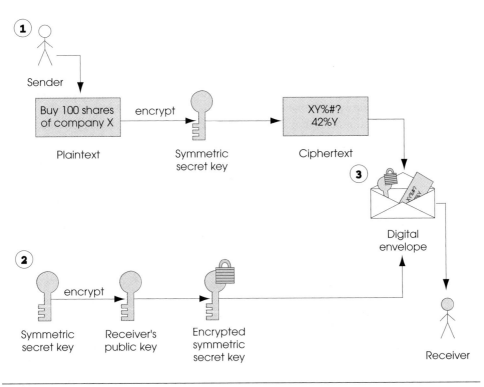

Fig. 7.5   Creating a digital envelope.

A main component of key management is *key generation*—the process by which keys are created. A malicious third party could try to decrypt a message by using every possible decryption key. Keys are made secure by choosing a key length so large that it is computationally infeasible to try all such combinations.

Key-generation algorithms are sometimes unintentionally constructed to choose only from a small subset of possible keys. If the subset is small enough, then it may be possible for a malicious third party to try every possible key to crack the encryption (see Section 7.9, on cryptanalysis). Therefore, it is important to have a key-generation program that is truly random.

7.7 Digital Signatures

Digital signatures, the electronic equivalent of written signatures, were developed to be used in public-key cryptography to solve the problems of authentication and integrity. A digital signature authenticates the sender's identity, and, like a written signature, digital signatures are difficult to forge. To create a digital signature, a sender first takes the original plaintext message and runs it through a *hash function*, which is a mathematical calculation that gives the message a *hash value*. For example, you could take the plaintext message "Buy 100 shares of company X," run it through a hash function and get a hash value of 42. The hash function could be as simple as adding up all the 1s in a message, though it is usually more complex. The hash value is also known as a *message digest*. The chance that two different messages will have the same message digest is statistically insignificant. *Collision* occurs when multiple messages have the same hash value. It is computationally infeasible to compute a message from its hash value or to find two messages with the same hash value.

Next, the sender uses the sender's private key to encrypt the message digest. This step creates a digital signature and authenticates the sender, since only the owner of that private key could encrypt it the message. The original message, encrypted with the receiver's public key, the digital signature and the hash function, is sent to the receiver. The receiver uses the sender's public key to decipher the original digital signature and reveal the message digest. The receiver then uses the his or her own private key to decipher the original message. Finally, the receiver applies the hash function to the original message. If the hash value of the original message matches the message digest included in the signature, then there is *message integrity*; the message has not been altered in transmission.

There is a fundamental difference between digital signatures and handwritten signatures. A handwritten signature is independent of the document being signed. Thus, if someone can forge a handwritten signature, they can use that signature to forge multiple documents. A digital signature is created using the contents of the document. Therefore, your digital signature is different for each document you sign.

Digital signatures do not provide proof that a message has been sent. Consider the following situation: A contractor sends a company a digitally signed contract, which the contractor later would like to revoke. The contractor could do so by releasing its private key and then claiming that the digitally signed contract came from an intruder who stole the contractor's private key. *Timestamping*, which binds a time and date to a digital document, can help solve the problem of nonrepudiation. For example, suppose the company and the contractor are negotiating a contract. The company requires the contractor to digitally sign the contract and then have the document digitally timestamped by a third party called a *timestamping agency*. The contractor sends the digitally signed contract to the timestamping agency. The privacy of the message is maintained since the timestamping agency sees only the encrypted, digitally signed message (as opposed to the original plaintext message). The timestamping agency affixes the time and date of receipt to the encrypted, signed message and digitally signs the whole package with the timestamping agency's private key. The timestamp cannot be altered by anyone except the timestamping agency, since no one else possesses the timestamping agency's private key. Unless the contractor reports its private key to have been compromised before the document is timestamped, the contractor cannot legally prove that the document was signed by a third party. The sender could also require the receiver to digitally sign and timestamp the message as proof of receipt. To learn more about timestamping, visit **AuthentiDate.com (www.authentidate.com)**.

The U.S. government's digital-authentication standard is called the *Digital Signature Algorithm* (*DSA*). The U.S. government recently passed digital-signature legislation that makes digital signatures as legally binding as handwritten signatures. This legislation will result in an increase in e-business. For the latest news about U.S. government legislation in information security, visit **www.itaa.org/infosec**. For more information about the bills, visit the following government sites:

```
thomas.loc.gov/cgi-bin/bdquery/z?d106:hr.01714:
thomas.loc.gov/cgi-bin/bdquery/z?d106:s.00761:.
```

7.8 Public-key Infrastructure, Certificates and Certification Authorities

One problem with public-key cryptography is that anyone with a set of keys could potentially assume another party's identity. For example, say a customer wants to place an order with an online merchant. How does the customer know that the Web site being accessed indeed belongs to that merchant and not to a third party that posted a site and is masquerading as the merchant to steal credit-card information? *Public Key Infrastructure (PKI)* integrates public-key cryptography with *digital certificates* and *certification authorities* to authenticate parties in a transaction.

A digital certificate is a digital document issued by a *certification authority (CA)*. A digital certificate includes the name of the subject (the company or individual being certified), the subject's public key, a serial number, an expiration date, the signature of the trusted certification authority and any other relevant information (Fig. 7.6). A CA is a financial institution or other trusted third party, such as *VeriSign*. The CA takes responsibility for authentication, so it must carefully check information before issuing a digital certificate. Digital certificates are publicly available and are held by the certification authority in *certificate repositories*.

Fig. 7.6   A portion of the VeriSign digital certificate. (Courtesy of VeriSign, Inc.)

The CA signs the certificate by encrypting either the subject's public key or a hash value of the public key using the CA's own private key. The CA has to verify every subject's public key. Thus, users must trust the public key of a CA. Usually, each CA is part of a *certificate authority hierarchy*. A certificate authority hierarchy is a chain of certificate authorities, starting with the *root certification authority*, which is the Internet Policy Registration Authority (IPRA). The IPRA signs certificates using the *root key*. The root signs certificates only for *policy creation authorities*, which are organizations that set policies for obtaining digital certificates. In turn, policy creation authorities sign digital certificates for CAs. CAs sign digital certificates for individuals and organizations.

VeriSign, Inc., is a leading certificate authority. For more information about VeriSign, visit **www.verisign.com**. For a listing of other digital-certificate vendors, please see Section 7.14.

e-Fact 7.2

It can take a year and cost from $5 million to $10 million for a financial firm to build a digital certificate infrastructure, according to Identrus, a consortium of global financial companies that is providing a framework for trusted business-to-business e-commerce.[5]

Periodically changing key pairs is helpful in maintaining a secure system in case your private key is compromised without your knowledge. The longer you use a given key pair, the more vulnerable the keys are to attack. As a result, digital certificates are created with an expiration date, to force users to switch key pairs. If your private key is compromised before its expiration date, you can cancel your digital certificate and get a new key pair and digital certificate. Canceled and revoked certificates are placed on a *certificate revocation list* (*CRL*). CRLs are stored with the certification authority that issued the certificates.

Many people still perceive e-commerce to be unsecure. In fact, transactions using PKI and digital certificates are more secure than exchanging private information over phone lines, through the mail or even paying by credit card in person. After all, when you go to a restaurant and the waiter takes your credit card in back to process your bill, how do you know the waiter did not write down your credit-card information? In contrast, the key algorithms used in most secure online transactions are nearly impossible to compromise. By some estimates, the key algorithms used in public-key cryptography are so secure that even millions of today's computers working in parallel could not possibly break the code in a century. However, as computing power rapidly increases, key algorithms that are considered strong today could be easily breakable in the near future.

To obtain a digital certificate to digitally sign your personal e-mail messages, visit **www.verisign.com** or **www.thawte.com**. VeriSign offers a free 60-day trial, or you can purchase the service for a yearly fee. Thawte offers free digital certificates for personal e-mail. Web server certificates may also be purchased through Verisign and Thawte; however, they are more expensive than e-mail certificates.

Digital-certificate capabilities are built into many e-mail packages. For example, in Microsoft Outlook, you can go to the **Tools** menu and select **Options**. Then click on the **Security** tab. At the bottom of the dialog box, you will see the option to obtain a digital ID. Selecting the option will take you to a Microsoft Web site with links to several worldwide certification authorities. Once you have a digital certificate, you can digitally sign your e-mail messages.

7.9 Cryptanalysis

Even if keys are kept secret, it may be possible to compromise the security of a system. Trying to decrypt ciphertext without knowledge of the decryption key is known as *cryptanalysis*. Commercial encryption systems are constantly being researched by cryptologists to ensure that the systems are not vulnerable to a cryptanalytic attack. The most common form of cryptanalytic attacks are those in which the encryption algorithm is analyzed to find relations between bits of the encryption key and bits of the ciphertext. Often, these relations are only statistical in nature and incorporate outside knowledge about the plaintext. The goal of such an attack is to determine the key from the ciphertext.

Weak statistical trends between ciphertext and keys can be exploited to gain knowledge about the key if enough ciphertext is known. Proper key management and expiration dates on keys help prevent cryptanalytic attacks. Also, using public-key cryptography to securely exchange symmetric secret keys allows you to use a new symmetric secret key to encrypt every message.

7.10 Security Protocols

Everyone using the Web for e-business and e-commerce needs to be concerned about the security of their personal information. There are several protocols that provide transaction security, such as *Secure Sockets Layer* (*SSL*) and *Secure Electronic Transaction*™ (*SET*™). We discuss these security protocols in the next two subsections.

7.10.1 Secure Sockets Layer (SSL)

The *Secure Sockets Layer* (*SSL*) *protocol*, developed by Netscape Communications, is a nonproprietary protocol commonly used to secure communication on the Internet and the Web.[6, 7] SSL is built into many Web browsers, including Netscape Communicator, Microsoft Internet Explorer and numerous other software products. It operates between the Internet's TCP/IP communications protocol and the application software.

In a standard correspondence over the Internet, a sender's message is passed to a *socket* (which transmits information in a network); the socket interprets the message in Transmission Control Protocol/Internet Protocol (TCP/IP). TCP/IP is the standard set of protocols used for communication between computers on the Internet. Most Internet transmissions are sent as sets of individual message pieces, called *packets*. At the sending side, the packets of one message are numbered sequentially, and error-control information is attached to each packet. TCP/IP routes packets to avoid traffic jams, so each packet might travel a different route over the Internet. At the receiving end, TCP/IP makes sure that all of the packets have arrived, puts them in sequential order and determines if the packets have arrived without alteration. If the packets have been altered, TCP/IP retransmits them. TCP/IP then passes the message to the socket at the receiver end. The socket translates the message back into a form that can be read by the receiver's application. In a transaction using SSL, the sockets are secured using public-key cryptography.

SSL uses public-key technology and digital certificates to authenticate the server in a transaction and to protect private information as it passes from one party to another over the Internet. SSL transactions do not require client authentication. To begin, a client sends a message to a server. The server responds and sends its digital certificate to the client for authentication. Using public-key cryptography to communicate securely, the client and server negotiate *session keys* to continue the transaction. Session keys are symmetric secret keys that are used for the duration of that transaction. Once the keys are established, the communication proceeds between the client and the server by using the session keys and digital certificates.

Although SSL protects information as it is passed over the Internet, it does not protect private information, such as credit-card numbers, once the information is stored on the merchant's server. When a merchant receives credit-card information with an order, the information is often decrypted and stored on the merchant's server until the order is placed. If the server is not secure and the data are not encrypted, an unauthorized party can access the information. Hardware devices called *peripheral component interconnect (PCI) cards* designed for SSL transactions can be installed on Web servers to secure data for an entire SSL transaction from the client to the Web server.[8] The PCI card processes the SSL transactions, freeing the Web server to perform other tasks. Visit **www.phobos.com/Products/infamily.htm** for more information about these devices. For more information about the SSL protocol, check out the Netscape SSL tutorial at **developer.netscape.com/tech/security/ssl/protocol.html** and the Netscape Security Center site at **www.netscape.com/security/index.html**.

7.10.2 Secure Electronic Transaction™ (SET™)

The *Secure Electronic Transaction (SET) protocol*, developed by Visa International and MasterCard, was designed specifically to protect e-commerce payment transactions.[9, 10] SET uses digital certificates to authenticate each party in an e-commerce transaction, including the customer, the merchant and the merchant's bank. Public-key cryptography is used to secure information as it is passed over the Web.

Merchants must have a digital certificate and special SET software to process transactions. Customers must have a digital certificate and *digital wallet* software. A digital wallet is similar to a real wallet; it stores credit (or debit) card information for multiple cards, as well as a digital certificate verifying the cardholder's identity. Digital wallets add convenience to online shopping; customers no longer need to reenter their credit-card information at each shopping site.[11]

When a customer is ready to place an order, the merchant's SET software sends the order information and the merchant's digital certificate to the customer's digital wallet, thus activating the wallet software. The customer selects the credit card to be used for the transaction. The credit-card and order information are encrypted by using the merchant's bank's public key and sent to the merchant along with the customer's digital certificate. The merchant then forwards the information to the its bank to process the payment. Only the merchant's bank can decrypt the message, since the message was encrypted using the bank's public key. The merchant's bank then sends the amount of the purchase and its own digital certificate to the customer's bank to get approval to process the transaction. If the customer's charge is approved, the customer's bank sends an authorization back to the merchant's bank. The merchant's bank then sends a credit-card authorization to the merchant. Finally, the merchant sends a confirmation of the order to the customer.

In the SET protocol, the merchant never sees the client's proprietary information. Therefore, the client's credit-card number is not stored on the merchant's server, considerably reducing the risk of fraud.

Although SET is designed specifically for e-commerce transactions and provides a high level of security, it has yet to become the standard protocol used in the majority of transactions. Part of the problem is that SET requires special software on both the client and server side; that requirement increases transaction costs. Also, the transactions are more time consuming than transactions using other protocols, such as SSL. Both Visa and MasterCard have taken steps to reduce the financial burden to merchants, in an effort to encourage more merchants to use SET. However, with higher transaction fees and little pressure from customers, many businesses are still reluctant to switch.[13]

SET Secure Electronic Transaction LLC is an organization formed by Visa and MasterCard to manage and promote the SET protocol. For more information about SET, visit **www.setco.org**, **www.visa.com** and **www.mastercard.com**. Visa has a demonstration of an online shopping transaction using SET at **www.visa.com/nt/ecomm/security/main.html**. GlobeSet, a digital-wallet software vendor, also offers a tutorial of a SET transaction that uses a digital wallet, which may be found at **www.globeset.com**.

Microsoft Authenticode

How do you know that the software you ordered online is safe and has not been altered? How can you be sure that you are not downloading a computer virus that could wipe out your computer? Do you trust the source of the software? With the emergence of e-commerce, software companies are offering their products online, so that customers can download software directly onto their computers. Security technology is used to ensure that the downloaded software is trustworthy and has not been altered. *Microsoft Authenticode*, combined with VeriSign digital certificates (or *digital IDs*), authenticates the publisher of the software and detects whether the software has been altered. Authenticode is a security feature built into Microsoft Internet Explorer.

To use Microsoft Authenticode technology, each software publisher must obtain a digital certificate specifically designed for the purpose of publishing software; such certificates may be obtained through certification authorities, such as VeriSign (Section 7.8). To obtain a certificate, a software publisher must provide its public key and identification information and sign an agreement that it will not distribute harmful software. This requirement gives customers legal recourse if any downloaded software from certified publishers causes harm.

Microsoft Authenticode uses digital-signature technology to sign software (Section 7.5). The signed software and the publisher's digital certificate provide proof that the software is safe and has not been altered.

When a customer attempts to download a file, a dialog box appears on the screen displaying the digital certificate and the name of the certificate authority. Links to the publisher and the certificate authority are provided so that customers can learn more about each party before they agree to download the software. If Microsoft Authenticode determines that the software has been compromised, the transaction is terminated.

To learn more about Microsoft Authenticode, visit the following sites:

```
msdn.microsoft.com/workshop/security/authcode/signfaq.asp
msdn.microsoft.com/workshop/security/authcode/authwp.asp
```

7.11 Security Attacks

Recent cyberattacks on e-businesses have made the front pages of newspapers worldwide. *Denial-of-service attacks*, *viruses* and *worms* have cost companies billions of dollars. Denial-of-service attacks usually require the power of a network of computers working simultaneously; the attacks cause networked computers to crash or disconnect from the network, making services unavailable. Denial-of-service attacks can disrupt service on a Web site and can even shut down critical systems such as telecommunications or flight-control centers.

Viruses are computer programs—often sent as an attachment or hidden in audio clips, video clips and games—that attach to, or overwrite, other programs to replicate themselves. Viruses can corrupt your files or even wipe out your hard drive. Before the Internet, viruses spread through files and programs (such as video games) transferred to computers by removable disks. Today, viruses are spread over a network simply by sharing "infected" files embedded in e-mail attachments, documents or programs. A worm is similar to a virus, except that it can spread and infect files on its own over a network; worms do not need to be attached to another program to spread. Once a virus or worm is released, it can spread rapidly, often infecting millions of computers worldwide within minutes or hours.

A denial-of-service attack occurs when a network's resources are taken up by an unauthorized individual, leaving the network unavailable for legitimate users; typically, the attack is performed by flooding servers with data packets. This action greatly increases the traffic on the network, overwhelming the servers and making it impossible for legitimate users to download information.

Another type of denial-of-service attack targets the *routing tables* of a network. Routing tables are essentially the road map of a network, providing directions for data to get from one computer to another. This type of attack is accomplished by modifying the routing tables, thus disabling network activity. For example, the routing tables can be changed to send all data to one address in the network. In a *distributed denial-of-service attack*, the packet flooding does not come from a single source, but from many separate computers. Actually, such an attack is rarely the concerted work of many individuals. Instead, it is the work of a single individual who has installed viruses on various computers, gaining illegitimate use of the computers to carry out the attack. Distributed denial-of-service attacks can be difficult to stop, since it is not clear which requests on a network are from legitimate users and which are part of the attack. In addition, it is particularly difficult to catch the culprit of such attacks, because the attacks are not carried out directly from the attacker's computer.

Who is responsible for viruses and denial-of-service attacks? Most often the responsible parties are referred to as *hackers*. Hackers are usually skilled programmers. Some hackers break into systems just for the thrill of it, without causing any harm to the compromised systems (except, perhaps, humbling and humiliating their owners); others have malicious intent. Either way, hackers are breaking the law by accessing or damaging private information and computers. In February 2000, distributed denial-of-service attacks shut down a number of high-traffic Web sites, including Yahoo!, eBay, CNN Interactive and Amazon. In this case, a hacker used a network of computers to flood the Web sites with traffic that overwhelmed the sites' computers. Although, denial-of-service attacks merely shut off access to a Web site and do not affect the victim's data, they can be extremely costly. For example, when eBay's Web site went down for a 24-hour period on August 6, 1999, its stock value declined dramatically.[12]

Viruses, one of the most dangerous threats to network security, are typically malicious programs. There are many classes of computer viruses. A *transient virus* attaches itself to a specific computer program. The virus is activated when the program is run and deactivated when the program is terminated. A more powerful type of virus is a *resident virus*, which, once loaded into the memory of a computer, operates for the duration of the computer's use. Another type of virus is the *logic bomb*, which triggers when a given condition is met, such as a *time bomb* that is triggered when the clock on the computer matches a certain time or date.

A *Trojan horse* virus is a malicious program that hides within a friendly program or simulates the identity of a legitimate program or feature, while actually causing damage to the computer or network in the background. The Trojan horse virus gets its name from Greek history and the story of the Trojan War. In this story, Greek warriors hid inside a wooden horse, which the Trojans took within the walls of the city of Troy. When night fell and the Trojans were asleep, the Greek warriors came out of the horse and opened the gates to the city, letting the Greek army enter the gates and destroy the city of Troy. Trojan horse viruses can be particularly difficult to detect, since they appear to be legitimate, useful programs. In June 2000, news spread of a Trojan horse virus disguised as a video clip sent as an e-mail attachment. The Trojan horse virus was designed to give the attacker access to the infected computers, potentially to launch a denial-of-service attack against Web sites.[16]

Two of the most famous viruses to date are *Melissa*, which struck in March 1999, and the *ILOVEYOU virus* that hit in May 2000. Both viruses cost organizations and individuals billions of dollars. The Melissa virus spread in Microsoft Word documents sent via e-mail. When the document was opened, the virus was triggered. Melissa accessed the Microsoft Outlook address book on that computer and automatically sent the infected Word attachment by e-mail to the first 50 people in the address book. Each time another person opened the attachment, the virus would send out another 50 messages. Once into a system, the virus infected any subsequently saved files.

The ILOVEYOU virus was sent as an attachment to an e-mail posing as a love letter. The message in the e-mail said "Kindly check the attached love letter coming from me." Once opened, the virus accessed the Microsoft Outlook address book and sent out messages to the addresses listed, helping to spread the virus rapidly worldwide. The virus corrupted all types of files, including system files. Networks at companies and government organizations worldwide were shut down for days trying to remedy the problem and contain the virus.

 e-Fact 7.3

Estimates for damage caused by the ILOVEYOU virus were as high as $10 billion to $15 billion, with the majority of the damage done in just a few hours.

Viruses and worms are not just limited to computers. In June 2000, a worm named *Timofonica* that was propagated through e-mail quickly made its way into the cellular phone network in Spain, sending prank calls and leaving text messages on the phones. No serious damage was done, nor did the worm infect the cell phones, but experts predict that we will see many more viruses and worms spread to cell phones in the future.[17] Also, viruses spread through handheld devices are starting to appear.

Why do these viruses spread so quickly? One reason is that many people are too willing to open executable files from unknown sources. Have you ever opened an audio clip or video clip from a friend? Have you ever forwarded that clip to other friends? Do you know who created the clip and if any viruses are embedded in it? Did you open the ILOVE YOU file to see what the love letter said?

Most antivirus software is reactive, going after viruses once they are discovered, rather than protecting against unknown viruses. New antivirus software, such as Finjan Software's SurfinGuard® (**www.finjan.com**), looks for executable files attached to e-mail and runs the executables in a secure area to test if they attempt to access and harm files. For more information about antivirus software, see the feature on **McAfee.com** antivirus utilities.

Web defacing is another popular form of attack by hackers, wherein the hackers illegally enter an organization's Web site and change the contents. CNN Interactive has issued a special report titled "Insurgency on the Internet," with news stories about hackers and their online attacks. Included is a gallery of hacked sites. One notable case of Web defacing occurred in 1996, when Swedish hackers changed the Central Intelligence Agency Web site (**www.odci.gov/cia**) to read "Central Stupidity Agency." The hackers put obscenities, messages and links to adult-content sites on the page. Many other popular and large Web sites have been defaced.

McAfee.com Antivirus Utilities

McAfee.com provides a variety of antivirus utilities (and other utilities) for users whose computers are not continuously connected to a network, for users whose computers are continuously connected to a network (such as the Internet) and for users connected to a network via wireless devices, such as personal digital assistants and pagers.

For computers that are not continuously connected to a network, McAfee provides its antivirus software *VirusScan*®. This software is configurable to scan files for viruses on demand or to scan continuously in the background as the user does his or her work.

For computers that are network and Internet accessible, McAfee provides its online **McAfee.com** Clinic. Users with a subscription to McAfee Clinic can use the online virus software from any computer they happen to be using. As with VirusScan software on stand-alone computers, users can scan their files on demand. A major benefit of the Clinic is its *ActiveShield* software. Once installed, ActiveShield can be configured to scan every file that is used on the computer or just the program files. It can also be configured to check automatically for virus definition updates and notify the user when such updates become available. The user simply clicks on the supplied hyperlink in an update notification to connect to the Clinic site and clicks on another hyperlink to download the update. Thus, users can keep their computers protected with the most up-to-date virus definitions at all times. For more information about McAfee, visit **www.mcafee.com**. Also, check out Norton security products from Symantec, at **www.symantec.com**. Symantec is a leading security software vendor. Its product Norton™ Internet Security 2000 provides protection against hackers, viruses and threats to privacy for both small businesses and individuals.

Cybercrime can have significant financial implications on an organization.[14] Companies need to protect their data, intellectual property, customer information, etc. Implementing a *security policy* is key to protecting your organization's data and network. When developing a security plan, organizations must assess their vulnerabilities and the possible threats to security. What information do they need to protect? Who are the possible attackers and what is their intent—data theft or damaging the network? How will the organization respond to incidents?[15] For more information about security and security plans, visit **www.cerias.com** and **www.sans.org**. Visit **www.baselinesoft.com** to check out books and CD-ROMs on security policies. Baseline Software's book *Information Policies Made Easy: Version 7* includes over 1000 security policies. This book is used by numerous Fortune 200 companies.

The rise in cybercrimes has prompted the U. S. government to take action. Under the National Information Infrastructure Protection Act of 1996, denial-of-service attacks and distribution of viruses are federal crimes punishable by fines and jail time. For more information about the U. S. government's efforts against cyber crime or to read about recently prosecuted cases, visit the U.S. Department of Justice Web site, at **www.usdoj.gov/criminal/cybercrime/compcrime.html**. Also check out **www.cybercrime.gov**, a site maintained by the Criminal Division of the U. S. Department of Justice.

The *CERT®* (*Computer Emergency Response Team*) *Coordination Center* at Carnegie Mellon University's Software Engineering Institute responds to reports of viruses and denial-of-service attacks and provides information on network security, including how to determine if your system has been compromised. The site provides detailed incident reports of viruses and denial-of-service attacks, including descriptions of the incidents, their impact and the solutions. The site also includes reports of vulnerabilities in popular operating systems and software packages. The *CERT Security Improvement Modules* are excellent tutorials on network security. These modules describe the issues and technologies used to solve network security problems. For more information, visit the CERT Web site, at **www.cert.org**.

To learn more about how you can protect yourself or your network from hacker attacks, visit AntiOnline™, at **www.antionline.com**. This site has security-related news and information, a tutorial titled "Fight-back! Against Hackers," information about hackers and an archive of hacked sites. You can find additional information about denial-of-service attacks and how to protect your site at **www.irchelp.org/irchelp/nuke**.

7.12 Network Security

The goal of network security is to allow authorized users access to information and services, while preventing unauthorized users from gaining access to, and possibly corrupting, the network. There is a trade-off between network security and network performance: Increased security often decreases the efficiency of the network.

7.12.1 Firewalls

A basic tool in network security is the *firewall*. The purpose of a firewall is to protect a *local area network* (*LAN*) from intruders outside the network. For example, most companies have internal networks that allow employees to share files and access company information. Each LAN can be connected to the Internet through a gateway, which usually includes a firewall. For years, one of the biggest threats to security came from employees inside the firewall. Now that businesses rely heavily on access to the Internet, an increasing number of security threats are originating outside the firewall—from the hundreds of millions of people connected to the company network by the Internet.[18] A firewall acts as a safety barrier for data flowing into and out of the LAN. Firewalls can prohibit all data flow not expressly allowed, or can allow all data flow that is not expressly prohibited. The choice between these two models is up to the network security administrator and should be based on the need for security versus the need for functionality.

There are two main types of firewalls: *packet-filtering firewalls* and *application-level gateways*. A packet-filtering firewall examines all data sent from outside the LAN and automatically rejects any data packets that have local network addresses. For example, if a hacker from outside the network obtains the address of a computer inside the network and tries to sneak a harmful data packet through the firewall, the packet-filtering firewall will reject the data packet, since it has an internal address, but originated from outside the network. A problem with packet-filtering firewalls is that they consider only the source of data packets; they do not examine the actual data. As a result, malicious viruses can be installed on an authorized user's computer, giving the hacker access to the network without the authorized user's knowledge. The goal of an application-level gateway is to screen the actual data. If the message is deemed safe, then the message is sent through to the intended receiver.

Using a firewall is probably the single most effective and easiest way to add security to a small network.[19] Often, small companies or home users who are connected to the Internet through permanent connections, such as DSL lines, do not employ strong security measures. As a result, their computers are prime targets for hackers to use in denial-of-service attacks or to steal information. It is important for all computers connected to the Internet to have some degree of security on their systems. There are numerous firewall software products available. Several products are listed in the Web resources in Section 7.14.

7.12.2 Kerberos

Firewalls do not protect you from internal security threats to your local area network. Internal attacks are common and can be extremely damaging. For example, disgruntled employees with network access can wreak havoc on an organization's network or steal valuable, proprietary information. It is estimated that 70 percent to 90 percent of attacks on corporate networks are internal.[20] *Kerberos* is a freely available, open-source protocol developed at MIT. It employs symmetric secret-key cryptography to authenticate users in a network and to maintain the integrity and privacy of network communications.

Authentication in a Kerberos system is handled by a main Kerberos system and a secondary *Ticket Granting Service* (*TGS*). This system is similar to key distribution centers, which were described in Section 7.3. The main Kerberos system authenticates a client's identity to the TGS; the TGS authenticates client's rights to access specific network services.

Each client in the network shares a symmetric secret key with the Kerberos system. This symmetric secret key may be used by multiple TGSs in the Kerberos system. The client starts by entering a login name and password into the Kerberos authentication server. The authentication server maintains a database of all clients in the network. The authentication server returns a *Ticket-Granting Ticket* (*TGT*) encrypted with the client's symmetric secret key that it shares with the authentication server. Since the symmetric secret key is known only by the authentication server and the client, only the client can decrypt the TGT, thus authenticating the client's identity. Next, the client sends the decrypted TGT to the Ticket Granting Service to request a *service ticket*. The service ticket authorizes the client's access to specific network services. Service tickets have a set expiration time. Tickets may be renewed by the TGS.

7.12.3 Biometrics

An innovation in security is likely to be *biometrics*. Biometrics uses unique personal information, such as fingerprints, eyeball iris scans or face scans, to identify a user. This system eliminates the need for passwords, which are much easier to steal. Have you ever written down your passwords on a piece of paper and put the paper in your desk drawer or wallet? These days, people have passwords and PIN codes for everything—Web sites, networks, e-mail, ATM machines and even for their cars. Managing all of those codes can become a burden. Recently, the cost of biometric devices has dropped significantly. Keyboard-mounted fingerprint scanning devices are being used in place of passwords to log into systems, check e-mail or access secure information over a network. Each user's iris scan, face scan or fingerprint is stored in a secure database. Each time a user logs in, his or her scan is compared with the database. If a match is made, the login is successful. Two companies that specialize in biometric devices are IriScan (**www.iriscan.com**) and Keytronic (**www.keytronic.com**). For additional resources, see Section 7.14.

Currently, passwords are the predominant means of authentication; however, we are beginning to see a shift to smart cards and Biometrics. Microsoft recently announced that it will include the *Biometric Application Programming Interface* (*BAPI*) in future versions of Windows, which will make it possible for companies to integrate biometrics into their systems.[21] *Two-factor authentication* uses two means to authenticate the user, such as biometrics or a smart card used in combination with a password. Though this system could potentially be compromised, using two methods of authentication is more secure than just using passwords alone.

One of the major concerns with biometrics is the issue of privacy. Implementing fingerprint scanners means that organizations will be keeping databases with each employee's fingerprint. Do people want to provide their employers with such personal information? What if those data are compromised? To date, most organizations that have implemented biometric systems have received little, if any, resistance from employees. For more information on privacy issues, see Chapter 11, Legal and Ethical Issues; Internet Taxation.

7.13 Steganography

Steganography is the practice of hiding information within other information. The term literally means "covered writing." Like cryptography, steganography has been used since ancient times. Steganography allows you to take a piece of information, such as a message or image, and hide it within another image, message or even an audio clip. Steganography takes advantage of insignificant space in digital files, in images or on removable disks.[22] Consider a simple example: If you have a message that you want to send secretly, you can hide the information within another message, so that no one but the intended receiver can read it. For example, if you want to tell your stockbroker to buy a stock and your message must be transmitted over an unsecure channel, you could send the message "BURIED UN-

DER YARD." If you have agreed in advance that your message is hidden in the first letters of each word, the stock broker picks these letters off and sees "BUY."

An increasingly popular application of steganography is *digital watermarks* for intellectual property protection. An example of a conventional watermark is shown in Fig. 7.7. A digital watermark can be either visible or invisible. It is usually a company logo, copyright notification or other mark or message that indicates the owner of the document. The owner of a document could show the hidden watermark in a court of law, for example, to prove that the watermarked item was stolen.

Digital watermarking could have a substantial impact on e-commerce. Consider the music industry. Music publishers are concerned that MP3 technology is allowing people to distribute illegal copies of songs and albums. As a result, many publishers are hesitant to put content online, as digital content is easy to copy. Also, since CD-ROMs are digital, people are able to upload their music and share it over the Web. Using digital watermarks, music publishers can make indistinguishable changes to a part of a song at a frequency that is not audible to humans, to show that the song was, in fact, copied.

Blue Spike's Giovanni™ digital watermarking software uses cryptographic keys to generate and embed steganographic digital watermarks into digital music and images (Fig. 7.8). The watermarks can be used as proof of ownership to help digital publishers protect their copyrighted material. The watermarks are undetectable by anyone who is not privy to the embedding scheme, and thus the watermarks cannot be identified and removed. The watermarks are placed randomly.

Fig. 7.7   Example of a conventional watermark. (Courtesy of Blue Spike, Inc.)

Fig. 7.8   An example of steganography: Blue Spike's Giovanni digital
watermarking process. (Courtesy of Blue Spike, Inc.)

Giovanni incorporates cryptography and steganography. It generates a symmetric secret key based on an encryption algorithm and the contents of the audio or image file that will carry the watermark. The key is then used to place (and eventually decode) the watermark. The software identifies the perceptually insignificant areas of the image or audio file, enabling a digital watermark to be embedded inaudibly, invisibly and in such a way that if the watermark is removed, the content is likely to be damaged.

Digital watermarking capabilities are built into some image-editing software applications, such as Adobe PhotoShop 5.5 (**www.adobe.com**). Companies that offer digital watermarking solutions include Digimarc (**www.digimark.com**) and Cognicity (**www.cognicity.com**).

In the last few chapters, we discussed the technologies involved in building and running an e-business, and how to secure online transactions and communications. In Chapter 8, Internet Marketing, we discuss how to attract customers to your e-business Web site and build your customer base. We discuss the components of an Internet marketing campaign, including marketing, promotions and public relations.

7.14 Internet and World Wide Web Resources

Security Resource Sites

www.securitysearch.net
This is a comprehensive resource for computer security. The site has thousands of links to products, security companies, tools and more. The site also offers a free weekly newsletter with information about vulnerabilities.

www.esecurityonline.com
This site is a great resource for information on online security. The site has links to news, tools, events, training and other valuable security information and resources.

www.epic.org
The *Electronic Privacy Information Center* deals with protecting privacy and civil liberties. Visit this site to learn more about the organization and its latest initiatives.

theory.lcs.mit.edu/~rivest/crypto-security.html
The *Ronald L. Rivest: Cryptography and Security* site has an extensive list of links to security resources, including newsgroups, government agencies, FAQs, tutorials and more.

www.w3.org/Security/Overview.html
The *W3C Security Resources* site has FAQs, information about W3C security and e-commerce initiatives and links to other security related Web sites.

web.mit.edu/network/ietf/sa
The Internet Engineering Task Force (IETF), which is an organization concerned with the architecture of the Internet, has working groups dedicated to Internet Security. Visit the *IETF Security Area* to learn about the working groups, join the mailing list or check out the latest drafts of the IETF's work.

dir.yahoo.com/Computers_and_Internet/Security_and_Encryption
The *Yahoo Security and Encryption* page is a great resource for links to Web sites security and encryption.

www.counterpane.com/hotlist.html
The Counterpane Internet Security, Inc., site includes links to downloads, source code, FAQs, tutorials, alert groups, news and more.

www.rsasecurity.com/rsalabs/faq
This site is an excellent set of FAQs about cryptography from RSA Laboratories, one of the leading makers of public key cryptosystems.

www.nsi.org/compsec.html
Visit the National Security Institute's *Security Resource Net* for the latest security alerts, government standards, and legislation, as well as security FAQs links and other helpful resources.

www.itaa.org/infosec
The Information Technology Association of America (ITAA) *InfoSec* site has information about the latest U.S. government legislation related to information security.

staff.washington.edu/dittrich/misc/ddos
The *Distributed Denial of Service Attacks* site has links to news articles, tools, advisory organizations and even a section on security humor.

www.infoworld.com/cgi-bin/displayNew.pl?/security/links/
security_corner.htm
The Security Watch site on **Infoword.com** has loads of links to security resources.

www.antionline.com
AntiOnline has security-related news and information, a tutorial titled "Fight-back! Against Hackers," information about hackers and an archive of hacked sites.

www.microsoft.com/security/default.asp
The Microsoft security site has links to downloads, security bulletins and tutorials.

www.grc.com
This site offers a service to test the security of your computer's Internet connection.

Magazines, Newsletters and News sites

www.networkcomputing.com/consensus
The *Security Alert Consensus* is a free weekly newsletter with information about security threats, holes, solutions and more.

www.infosecuritymag.com
Information Security Magazine has the latest Web security news and vendor information.

www.issl.org/cipher.html
Cipher is an electronic newsletter on security and privacy from the Institute of Electrical and Electronics Engineers (IEEE). You can view current and past issues online.

securityportal.com
The *Security Portal* has news and information about security, cryptography and the latest viruses.

www.scmagazine.com
SC Magazine has news, product reviews and a conference schedule for security events.

www.cnn.com/TECH/specials/hackers
Insurgency on the Internet from CNN Interactive has news on hacking, plus a gallery of hacked sites.

rootshell.com/beta/news.html
Visit Rootshell for security-related news and white papers.

Government Sites for Computer Security

www.cit.nih.gov/security.html
This site has links to security organizations, security resources and tutorials on PKI, SSL and other protocols.

cs-www.ncsl.nist.gov
The *Computer Security Resource Clearing House* is a resource for network administrators and others concerned with security. This site has links to incident-reporting centers, information about security standards, events, publications and other resources.

www.cdt.org/crypto
Visit the Center for Democracy and Technology for U. S. legislation and policy news regarding cryptography.

www.epm.ornl.gov/~dunigan/security.html
This site has links to loads of security-related sites. The links are organized by subject and include resources on digital signatures, PKI, smart cards, viruses, commercial providers, intrusion detection and several other topics.

www.alw.nih.gov/Security
The *Computer Security Information* page is an excellent resource, providing links to news, newsgroups, organizations, software, FAQs and an extensive number of Web links.

www.fedcirc.gov
The Federal Computer Incident Response Capability deals with the security of government and civilian agencies. This site has information about incident statistics, advisories, tools, patches and more.

axion.physics.ubc.ca/pgp.html
This site has a list of freely available cryptosystems, along with a discussion of each system and links to FAQs and tutorials.

www.ifccfbi.gov
The Internet Fraud Complaint Center, founded by the Justice Department and the FBI, fields reports of Internet fraud.

`www.disa.mil/infosec/iaweb/default.html`
The Defense Information Systems Agency's *Information Assurance* page includes links to sites on vulnerability warnings, virus information and incident-reporting instructions, as well as other helpful links.

Internet Security Vendors

`www.rsasecurity.com`
RSA is one of the leaders in electronic security. Visit its site for more information about its current products and tools, which are used by companies worldwide.

`www.ca.com/protection`
Computer Associates is a vendor of Internet security software. It has various software packages to help companies set up a firewall, scan files for viruses and protect against viruses.

`www.checkpoint.com`
Check Point™ Software Technologies Ltd. is a leading provider of Internet security products and services.

`www.mycio.com`
MyCIO provides Internet security software and services.

`www.opsec.com`
The Open Platform for Security (OPSEC) has over 200 partners that develop security products and solutions using the OPSEC to allow for interoperability and increased security over a network.

`www.baltimore.com`
Baltimore is an e-commerce security solutions provider. Its most popular product is UniCERT, a digital certificate product that is used in PKI. It also offers SET, public-key cryptography and digital certificate solutions.

`www.ncipher.com`
nCipher is a vendor of hardware and software security products. Its products include an SSL accelerator that speeds up transaction of SSL Web servers and a secure key management system.

`www.entrust.com`
Entrust Technologies provides e-security products and services.

`www.tenfour.co.uk`
TenFour provides software for secure e-mail.

`www.antivirus.com`
ScanMail® is an e-mail virus detection program for Microsoft Exchange.

`www.contenttechnologies.com/ads`
Content Technologies is a security software provider. Its products include firewall and secure e-mail programs.

`www.zixmail.com`
Zixmail™ is a secure e-mail product that allows you to encrypt and digitally sign your messages using different e-mail programs.

`www.pgp.com/scan`
PGP Security software protects your site from denial-of-service attacks.

`web.mit.edu/network/pgp.html`
At this site you can download *Pretty Good Privacy*® freeware, which allows you to send messages, files, etc., securely.

`www.radguard.com`
Radguard provides large-scale security solutions for e-businesses.

www.certicom.com
Certicom provides security solutions for the wireless Internet.

www.raytheon.com
Raytheon Corporation's *SilentRunner* monitors activity on a network to find internal threats, such as data theft or fraud.

SSL and SET

developer.netscape.com/tech/security/ssl/protocol.html
This Netscape page has a brief description of SSL, plus links to an SSL tutorial and FAQs.

www.netscape.com/security/index.html
The Netscape Security Center is an extensive resource for Internet and Web security. You will find news, tutorials, products and services on this site.

psych.psy.uq.oz.au/~ftp/Crypto
This FAQs page has an extensive list of questions and answers about SSL technology.

www.setco.org
The Secure Electronic Transaction LLC was formed through Visa and MasterCard to work on the SET specification. Visit this Web site to learn more about SET and the companies using SET in their products, and check out the brief FAQs list and glossary.

www.visa.com/nt/ecomm/security/main.html
Visa International's security page includes information on SSL and SET. The page includes a demonstration of an online shopping transaction, which explains how SET works.

www.mastercard.com/shoponline/set
The *MasterCard SET* Web site includes information about the SET protocol, a glossary of SET-related terms, the latest developments and a demonstration walking you through the steps of a purchase using SET technology.

www.openssl.org
The *Open SSL Project* provides a free, open source toolkit for SSL.

Public-key Cryptography

www.entrust.com
Entrust produces effective security software products using Public Key Infrastructure (PKI).

www.cse.dnd.ca
The Communication Security Establishment has a short tutorial on Public Key Infrastructure (PKI) that defines PKI, public-key cryptography and digital signatures.

www.magnet.state.ma.us/itd/legal/pki.htm
The Commonwealth of Massachusetts Information Technology page has loads of links to sites related to PKI that contain information about standards, vendors, trade groups and government organizations.

www.ftech.net/~monark/crypto/index.htm
The Beginner's Guide to Cryptography is an online tutorial and includes links to other sites on privacy and cryptography.

www.faqs.org/faqs/cryptography-faq
The *Cryptography FAQ* has an extensive list of questions and answers.

www.pkiforum.org
The PKI Forum promotes the use of PKI.

www.counterpane.com/pki-risks.html
Visit the Counterpane Internet Security, Inc.'s site to read the article "Ten Risks of PKI: What You're Not Being Told About Public Key Infrastructure."

Digital Signatures

www.ietf.org/html.charters/xmldsig-charter.html
The *XML Digital Signatures* site was created by a group working to develop digital signatures using XML. You can view the group's goals and drafts of their work.

www.elock.com
E-Lock Technologies is a vendor of digital-signature products used in Public Key Infrastructure. This site has an FAQs list covering cryptography, keys, certificates and signatures.

www.digsigtrust.com
The Digital Signature Trust Co. is a vendor of Digital Signature and Public Key Infrastructure products. It has a tutorial titled "Digital Signatures and Public Key Infrastructure (PKI) 101."

Digital Certificates

www.verisign.com
VeriSign creates digital IDs for individuals, small businesses and large corporations. Check out its Web site for product information, news and downloads.

www.thawte.com
Thawte Digital Certificate Services offers SSL, developer and personal certificates.

www.silanis.com/index.htm
Silanis Technology is a vendor of digital-certificate software.

www.belsign.be
Belsign issues digital certificates in Europe. It is the European authority for digital certificates.

www.certco.com
Certco issues digital certificates to financial institutions.

www.openca.org
Set up your own CA using open-source software from The OpenCA Project.

Digital Wallets

www.globeset.com
GlobeSet is a vendor of digital-wallet software. Its site has an animated tutorial demonstrating the use of an electronic wallet in an SET transaction.

www.trintech.com
Trintech digital wallets handle SSL and SET transactions.

wallet.yahoo.com
The Yahoo! Wallet is a digital wallet that can be used at thousands of Yahoo! Stores worldwide.

Firewalls

www.interhack.net/pubs/fwfaq
This site provides an extensive list of FAQs on firewalls.

www.spirit.com/cgi-bin/report.pl
Visit this site to compare firewall software from a variety of vendors.

www.zeuros.co.uk/generic/resource/firewall
Zeuros is a complete resource for information about firewalls. You will find FAQs, books, articles, training and magazines on this site.

www.thegild.com/firewall
The *Firewall Product Overview* site has an extensive list of firewall products, with links to each vendor's site.

`csrc.ncsl.nist.gov/nistpubs/800-10`
Check out this firewall tutorial from the U.S. Department of Commerce.

`www.watchguard.com`
WatchGuard® Technologies, Inc., provides firewalls and other security solutions for medium to large organizations.

`www.networkice.com`
BlackICE Defender, from Network ICE, combines a firewall with intrusion detection.

Kerberos

`www.nrl.navy.mil/CCS/people/kenh/kerberos-faq.html`
This site is an extensive list of FAQs on Kerberos from the Naval Research Laboratory.

`web.mit.edu/kerberos/www`
Kerberos: The Network Authentication Protocol is a list of FAQs provided by MIT.

`www.contrib.andrew.cmu.edu/~shadow/kerberos.html`
The Kerberos Reference Page has links to several informational sites, technical sites and other helpful resources.

`www.pdc.kth.se/kth-krb`
Visit this site to download various Kerberos white papers and documentation.

Biometrics

`www.iosoftware.com/products/integration/fiu500/index.htm`
This site describes a security device that scans a user's fingerprint to verify identity.

`www.identix.com/flash_index.html`
Identix specializes in fingerprinting systems for law enforcement, access control and network security. Using its fingerprint scanners, you can log on to your system, encrypt and decrypt files and lock applications.

`www.iriscan.com`
Iriscan's *PR Iris*™ can be used for e-commerce, network and information security. The scanner takes an image of the user's eye for authentication.

`www.keytronic.com`
Key Tronic manufactures keyboards with fingerprint recognition systems.

Steganography and Digital Watermarking

`www.bluespike.com/giovanni/giovmain.html`
Blue Spike's *Giovanni* watermarks help publishers of digital content protect their copyrighted material and track their content that is distributed electronically.

`www.outguess.org`
Outguess is a freely available steganographic tool.

`www.cl.cam.ac.uk/~fapp2/steganography/index.html`
The Information Hiding Homepage has technical information, news and links related to digital watermarking and steganography.

`www.demcom.com`
DemCom's *Steganos Security Suite* software allows you to encrypt and hide files within audio, video, text or HTML files.

`www.digimarc.com`
Digimarc is a leading provider of digital-watermarking software solutions.

www.cognicity.com
Cognicity specializes in digital-watermarking solutions for the music and entertainment industries.

Newsgroups

news:comp.security.firewalls

news:comp.security.unix

news:comp.security.misc

news:comp.protocols.kerberos

SUMMARY

- There are four fundamental requirements of a successful, secure transaction: privacy, integrity, authentication and nonrepudiation.
- Cryptography transforms data by using a key—a string of digits that acts as a password—to make the data incomprehensible to all but the sender and the intended receivers.
- Unencrypted data are called plaintext; encrypted data are called ciphertext.
- A cipher, or cryptosystem, is a technique or algorithm for encrypting messages.
- Longer keys have stronger encryption; it takes more time and computing power to break the encryption code.
- Secret-key cryptography uses the same symmetric secret key to encrypt and decrypt a message.
- In a network with a key distribution center, each user shares one symmetric secret key with the key distribution center.
- One of the most commonly used symmetric encryption algorithms is the Data Encryption Standard (DES), which was developed by the National Security Agency (NSA) and IBM in the 1950s.
- The current standard of symmetric encryption is Triple DES, a variant of DES that is essentially three DES systems in a row, each having its own secret key.
- The U. S. government is in the process of selecting a new, more secure standard for symmetric encryption. The new standard will become the Advanced Encryption Standard (AES).
- In 1976, Whitfield Diffie and Martin Hellman, two researchers at Stanford University, developed public-key cryptography to solve the problem of exchanging keys securely.
- Public-key cryptography is asymmetric. It uses two inversely related keys: a public key and a private key. The private key is kept secret by its owner. The public key is freely distributed.
- If the public key is used to encrypt a message, only the corresponding private key can decrypt it, and vice versa.
- If the user's decryption key is the public key and his or her encryption key is private, the sender of the message can be authenticated.
- The most commonly used public-key algorithm is RSA, an encryption system developed by Ron Rivest, Adi Shamir and Leonard Adleman in 1977.
- The process by which two parties can exchange keys over an unsecure medium is called a key agreement protocol.
- The most common key agreement protocol is a digital envelope.
- Digital signatures, the electronic equivalent of written signatures, were developed to be used in public-key cryptography to solve the problems of authentication and integrity.
- A digital signature authenticates the sender's identity, and, like a written signature, it is difficult to forge.

- A timestamping agency affixes the time and date of receipt to the encrypted, signed message and digitally signs the whole package with the timestamping agency's private key.
- The digital authentication standard of the U.S. government is called the Digital Signature Algorithm (DSA).
- Public Key Infrastructure (PKI) adds digital certificates to the process of authentication.
- A digital certificate includes the name of the subject (the company or individual being certified), the subject's public key, a serial number, an expiration date, the authorization of the trusted certification authority and any other relevant information.
- A certification authority (CA) is a financial institution or other trusted third party, such as VeriSign.
- Digital certificates are publicly available and are held by the certification authority in certificate repositories.
- By some estimates, the key algorithms used in public-key cryptography are so secure that even millions of computers working in parallel could not possibly break the code in a century.
- Trying to decrypt ciphertext without knowledge of the decryption key is known as cryptanalysis.
- SSL uses public-key technology and digital certificates to authenticate the server in a transaction and to protect private information as it passes from one party to another over the Internet.
- Session keys are symmetric secret keys that are used for the duration of a transaction.
- SET uses digital certificates to authenticate each party in an e-commerce transaction, including the customer, the merchant and the merchant's bank.
- A digital wallet is similar to a real wallet; it stores credit (or debit) card information for multiple cards, as well as a digital certificate verifying the cardholder's identity.
- In the SET protocol, the merchant never actually sees the client's proprietary information. Therefore, the client's credit-card number is not stored on the merchant's server, considerably reducing the risk of fraud.
- Microsoft Authenticode uses digital-signature technology to sign software. The signed software and the publisher's digital certificate provide proof that the software is safe and has not been altered.
- Viruses are computer programs—usually sent as an attachment or hidden in audio clips, video clips and games—that attach to or overwrite other programs to replicate themselves.
- A worm is similar to a virus, except that it can spread and infect files on its own over a network; worms do not need to be attached to another program to spread.
- A denial-of-service attack occurs when a network's resources are taken up by an unauthorized individual, leaving the network unavailable for legitimate users; typically, the attack is performed by flooding servers with data packets.
- A logic bomb triggers when a given condition is met, such as when the clock on the computer matches a certain time or date.
- A Trojan horse virus is a malicious program that hides within a friendly program or simulates the identity of a legitimate program or feature, while actually causing damage to the computer or network in the background.
- Web defacing is another popular form of attack by hackers, wherein the hackers illegally enter an organization's Web site and change the contents.
- A firewall protects a local area network (LAN) from intruders outside the network.
- A packet-filtering firewall examines all data sent from outside the LAN and automatically rejects any data packets that have local network addresses.

- The goal of a application-level gateway is to screen the actual data. If the message is deemed safe, then the message is sent through to the intended receiver.

- Kerberos is a freely available, open-source protocol developed at MIT. It employs symmetric secret-key cryptography to authenticate users in a network and to maintain the integrity and privacy of network communications.

- Biometrics uses unique personal information, such as fingerprints, eyeball iris scans or face scans, to identify a user. This system eliminates the need for passwords, which are much easier to steal.

- Steganography is the practice of hiding information. The term literally means "covered writing."

TERMINOLOGY

ActiveShield
Advanced Encryption Standard (AES)
application-level gateway
asymmetric algorithms
authentication
Authenticode (from Microsoft)
availability
binary string
biometrics
bit
CERT (Computer Emergency Response Team)
CERT Security Improvement Modules
certification authority (CA)
certificate authority hierarchy
certificate repository
certificate revocation list (CRL)
cipher
ciphertext
collision
cryptanalysis
cryptography
cryptosystem
Data Encryption Standard (DES)
data packets
decryption
denial-of-service attack
Diffie-Hellman Key Agreement Protocol
digital certificate
digital envelope
digital IDs
Digital Signature Algorithm (DSA)
digital signature
digital wallet
digital watermarking
distributed denial-of-service attack
encryption
firewall
hacker
hash function

hash value
ILOVEYOU Virus
integrity
Internet Policy Registration Authority (IPRA)
Kerberos
key
key agreement protocol
key distribution center
key generation
key length
key management
local area network (LAN)
logic bombs
Melissa Virus
message digest
message integrity
Microsoft Authenticode
National Institute of Standards and Technology
network security
nonrepudiation
one-way hash functions
packet-filtering firewall
packets
PCI (peripheral component interconnect) cards
plaintext
policy creation authorities
privacy
private key
protocol
public key
public-key algorithms
public-key cryptography
Public Key Infrastructure (PKI)
resident virus
restricted algorithms
root certification authority
root key
routing tables
RSA Security, Inc.

s-business
secret key
Secure Electronic Transactions (SET)
Secure Sockets Layer (SSL)
service ticket
session keys
SET Secure Electronic Transaction LLC
socket
steganography
substitution cipher
symmetric encryption algorithms
TCP/IP (Transmission Control Protocol/Internet
    Protocol)

Ticket Granting Ticket (TGT)
time bombs
timestamping
timestamping agency
timofonica
transient virus
transposition cipher
Triple DES
Trojan horse virus
VeriSign
virus
Web defacing
worm

SELF-REVIEW EXERCISES

7.1   State whether the following are *true* or *false*. If the answer is *false*, explain why.
    a) In a public-key algorithm, one key is used for both encryption and decryption.
    b) Digital certificates are intended to be used indefinitely.
    c) Secure Sockets Layer protects data stored on a merchant's server.
    d) Secure Electronic Transaction is another name for Secure Sockets Layer.
    e) Digital signatures can be used to provide undeniable proof of the author of a document.
    f) In a network of 10 users communicating using public-key cryptography, only 10 keys are needed in total.
    g) The security of modern cryptosystems lies in the secrecy of the algorithm.
    h) Users should avoid changing keys as much as possible, unless they have reason to believe that the security of the key has been compromised.
    i) Increasing the security of a network often decreases its functionality and efficiency.
    j) Firewalls are the single most effective way to add security to a small computer network.
    k) Kerberos is an authentication protocol that is used over TCP/IP networks.

7.2   Fill in the blanks in each of the following statements:
    a) Cryptographic algorithms in which the message's sender and receiver both hold an identical key are called _____.
    b) A _____ is used to authenticate the sender of a document. In a _____, a document is encrypted using a symmetric secret key and sent with that symmetric secret key, encrypted using a public-key algorithm.
    c) A certificate that needs to be revoked before its expiration date is placed on a _____.
    d) The recent wave of network attacks that have hit companies such as eBay, and Yahoo are known as _____.
    e) A digital fingerprint of a document can be created using a _____.
    f) The four main issues addressed by cryptography are _____, _____, _____ and _____.
    g) A customer can store purchase information and data on multiple credit cards in an electronic purchasing and storage device called a _____.
    h) Trying to decrypt ciphertext without knowing the decryption key is known as _____.
    i) A barrier between a small network and the outside world is called a _____.

ANSWERS TO SELF-REVIEW EXERCISES

7.1   a) False. The encryption key is different from the decryption key. One is made public, and the other is kept private. b) False. Digital certificates are created with an expiration date to encourage users to periodically change their public/private-key pair. c) False. Secure Sockets Layer is an Internet security protocol, which secures the transfer of information in electronic communication. It does not protect data stored on a merchant's server. d) False. Secure Electronic Transaction is a security protocol designed by Visa and MasterCard as a more secure alternative to Secure Sockets Layer. e) False. A user who digitally signed a document could later intentionally give up his or her private key and then claim that the document was written by an imposter. Thus, timestamping a document is necessary, so that users cannot repudiate documents written before the pubic/private-key pair is reported as invalidated. f) False. Each user needs a public key and a private key. Thus, in a network of 10 users, 20 keys are needed in total. g) False. The security of modern cryptosystems lies in the secrecy of the encryption and decryption keys. h) False. Changing keys often is a good way to maintain the security of a communication system. i) True. j) True. k) True.

7.2   a) symmetric key algorithms. b) digital signature. c) digital envelope. d) certificate revocation list. e) distributed denial-of-service attacks. f) hash function. g) privacy, authentication, integrity, nonrepudiation. h) electronic wallet. i) cryptanalysis. j) firewall.

EXERCISES

7.3   What can online businesses do to prevent hacker attacks, such as denial-of-service attacks and virus attacks?

7.4   Define the following security terms:
   a) digital signature
   b) hash function
   c) symmetric key encryption
   d) digital certificate
   e) denial-of-service attack
   f) worm
   g) message digest
   h) collision
   i) triple DES
   j) session keys

7.5   Define each of the following security terms, and give an example of how it is used:
   a) secret-key cryptography
   b) public-key cryptography
   c) digital signature
   d) digital certificate
   e) hash function
   f) SSL
   g) Kerberos
   h) firewall

7.6   Write the full name and describe each of the following acronyms:
   a) PKI
   b) RSA
   c) CRL
   d) AES
   e) SET

7.7   (*Class Discussion*). The Internet and the wireless Internet are inherently unsecure, yet we are heading in a direction where many government, military and business operations will be conducted online. In that context, discuss the importance of security. Are you satisfied the Internet can be made secure enough to handle these transactions?

7.8   List the four problems addressed by cryptography, and give a real-world example of each.

7.9   Compare symmetric-key algorithms with public-key algorithms. What are the benefits and drawbacks of each type of algorithm? How are these differences manifested in the real-world uses of the two types of algorithms?

7.10   The Visa International Web Site includes an interactive demonstration of the Secure Electronic Transaction (SET) protocol that uses animation to explain this complicated protocol in a way that most people will understand. Visit Visa at **www.visa.com/nt/sec/no_shock/ intro_L.html** to view the demo. Write a short summary of SET. How does SET differ from SSL? Why are digital wallets important? How are they used? If you were asked to choose between the two protocols, which would you choose, and why?

7.11   Explain how, in a network using symmetric-key encryption, a key distribution center can play the role of an authenticator of parties.

7.12   Go to the VeriSign Web site, at **www.verisign.com**. Write an analysis of the features and security of VeriSign's digital certificates. Then go to five other certification authorities and compare the features and security of their digital certificates with that of VeriSign.

7.13   Research the Secure Digital Music Initiative (**www.sdmi.org**). Describe how security technologies such as digital watermarks can help music publishers protect their copyrighted work.

7.14   Distinguish between packet-filtering firewalls and application-level gateways.

7.15   Using steganography, hide the message "MERGER IS A GO" inside a seemingly unrelated paragraph of text. Insert your secret message as the second character of each word in the paragraph.

WORKS CITED

The notation <**www.domain-name.com**> indicates that the citation is for information found at the Web site.

1.   A. Harrison, "Xerox Unit Farms Out Security in $20M Deal," *Computerworld* 5 June 2000: 24.

2.   RSA Laboratories, "RSA Laboratories' Frequently Asked Questions About Today's Cryptography, Version 4.1," <**www.rsasecurity.com/rsalabs/faq**>, RSA Security, Inc., 2000.

3.   A. Harrison, "Advanced Encryption Standard," *Computerworld* 29 May 2000: 57.

4.   RSA Laboratories, "RSA Laboratories' Frequently Asked Questions About Today's Cryptography, Version 4.1," <**www.rsasecurity.com/rsalabs/faq**>, RSA Security, Inc. 2000.

5.   R. Yasin, "PKI Rollout to Get Cheaper, Quicker," *InternetWeek* 24 July 2000: 28.

6.   S. Abbot, "The Debate for Secure E-Commerce," *Performance Computing* February 1999" 37-42.

7.   T. Wilson, "E-Biz Bucks Lost Under the SSL Train," *Internet Week* 24 May 1999: 1,3.

8.   M. Bull, "Ensuring End-to-End Security with SSL," *Network World* 15 May 2000: 63.

9.   S. Machlis, "IBM Hedges its Bets on SET," *Computerworld* 20 July 1998: 4.

10.   J. McKendrick, "Is Anyone SET for Secure Electronic Transactions," *ENT* 4 March 1998: 44, 46.

11.   W. Andrews, "The Digital Wallet: A concept revolutionizing e-commerce," *Internet World* 15 October 1999: 34-35.

12. "Securing B2B," *Global Technology Business* July 200: 50-51.

13. S. Machlis, "MasterCard Makes SET More Attractive," *Computerworld* 12 January 1998: 3.

14. R. Marsland, "Hidden Cost of Technology," *Financial Times* 2 June 2000: 5.

15. F. Avolio, "Best Practices in Network Security," *Network Computing* 20 March 2000: 60-72.

16. H. Bray, "Trojan Horse Attacks Computers, Disguised as a Video Chip," *The Boston Globe* 10 June 2000: C1+.

17. A. Eisenberg, "Viruses Could Have Your Number," *The New York Times* 8 June 2000: E7.

18. R. Marshland, "Hidden Cost of Technology," *Financial Times* 2 June 2000: 5.

19. T. Spangler, "Home Is Where the Hack Is," *Inter@ctive Week* 10 April 2000: 28-34.

20. S. Gaudin, "The Enemy Within," *Network World* 8 May 2000: 122-126.

21. D. Deckmyn, "Companies Push New Approaches to Authentication," *Computerworld*, 15 May 2000: 6.

22. S. Katzenbeisser and F. Petitcolas, Ed., *Information Hiding: Techniques for Steganography and Digital Watermarking* (Norwood, MA: Artech House, Inc., 2000) 1-2.

RECOMMENDED READINGS

Berinato, S. "Feds Sign Off on e-Signatures." *eWeek* 29 May 2000: 20-21.

Deitel, H. *An Introduction to Operating System*s. Second Edition, Reading, MA: Addison Wesley, 1990.

DiDio, L. "Private-key Nets Unlock e-Commerce." *Computerworld* 16 March 1998: 49-50.

Ford, W., and M. Baum. *Secure Electronic Commerce: Building the Infrastructure for Digital Signatures and Encryption.* Upper Saddle River, NJ: Prentice Hall, 1997.

Garfinkel, S. and Spafford, G. *Web Security and Commerce.* Cambridge, MA: O'Reilly, 1997.

Ghosh, A. *E-Commerce Security: Weak Links, Best Defenses.* New York, NY: Wiley Computer Publishing, 1998.

Goncalves, M. *Firewalls: A Complete Guide.*New York, NY: McGraw-Hill, 2000.

Kippenhahn, R. *Code Breaking.* New York, NY: The Overlook Press, 1999.

Kosiur, D. *Understanding Electronic Commerce.* Redmond, WA: Microsoft Press, 1997.

Marsland, R. "Hidden Cost of Technology." *Financial Times* 2 June 2 2000: 5.

Pfleeger, C. *Security in Computing: Second Edition.* Upper Saddle River, NJ: Prentice Hall, 1997.

RSA Laboratories. "*RSA Laboratories' Frequently Asked Questions About Today's Cryptography, Version 4.1.*" <**www.rsasecurity.com/rsalabs/faq**> RSA Security Inc., 2000.

Sager, I. "Cyber Crime." *Business Week* 21 February 2000: 37-42.

Schneier, B. *Applied Cryptography: Protocols, Algorithms and Source Code in C.* New York, NY: John Wiley & Sons, Inc., 1996.

Sherif, M. *Protocols for Secure Electronic Commerce.* New York, NY: CRC Press, 2000.

Smith, R. *Internet Cryptography.* Reading, MA: Addison Wesley, 1997.

Spangler, T. "Home Is Where The Hack Is." *Inter@ctive Week* 10 April 2000: 28-34.

Wrixon, F. *Codes, Ciphers & Other Cryptic & Clandestine Communication* New York, NY: Black Dog & Leventhal Publishers, 1998.

Part 4

Internet Marketing

Outline

Chapter 8   Internet Marketing

Chapter 9   Affiliate Programs

Chapter 10   e-Customer Relationship
Management

8

Internet Marketing

Objectives

- To explore various Internet marketing strategies.
- To discuss online marketing research.
- To discuss e-mail marketing.
- To investigate different online advertising options.
- To discuss options for e-business promotions.
- To explore online public relations.
- To examine business-to-business marketing.
- To understand search engines and how to increase rankings on search result lists.

The new electronic independence re-creates the world in the image of a global village.
Marshall McLuhan

If we value the pursuit of knowledge, we must be free to follow wherever that search may lead us.
Adlai E. Stevenson

"Will you walk into my parlor?" said the Spider to the Fly; "Tis the prettiest little parlor that ever did you spy."
Mary Howitt

There are no dumb customers.
Peter Drucker

You can tell the ideals of a nation by its advertisements.
Norman Douglas

Advertisers are the interpreters of our dreams . . .
E. B. White

Outline

8.1   Introduction
8.3   Internet Marketing Research
8.4   e-Mail Marketing
8.5   Promotions
8.6   e-Business Advertising
    8.6.1   Banner Advertising
    8.6.2   Buying and Selling Banner Advertising
    8.6.3   Media-Rich Advertising
    8.6.4   Wireless Advertising
8.7   e-Business Public Relations
8.8   Business-to-Business (B2B) Marketing on the Web
8.9   Search Engines
    8.9.1   META Tags
    8.9.2   Search-Engine Registration
8.10 Internet and World Wide Web Resources

Summary • Terminology • Self-Review Exercises • Answers to Self-Review Exercises • Exercises • Works Cited

8.1 Introduction

In the early stages of electronic commerce, having the most efficient and creative site was enough for e-businesses to prosper. Today, competition is intense, and having a solid Internet marketing strategy can give a company an advantage.

The Internet and the World Wide Web provide marketers with new tools and added convenience that can increase the success of their marketing efforts. In this chapter, we explore various components of an *Internet marketing campaign*, such as marketing research, advertising, promotions and public relations. We also discuss the importance of understanding how search engines work, which can help a company increase traffic to its Web site. Affiliate programs, a form of advertising, are discussed in Chapter 9, Affiliate Programs. Customer service is covered in Chapter 10, e-Customer Relationship Management (e-CRM).

While generating Web-site traffic is important to the success of an e-business, it is not enough. Keeping user profiles, recording visits and analyzing promotional and advertising results are key to measuring the effectiveness of marketing campaigns. By discovering your *target market*—the group of people toward whom it is most profitable to aim your marketing campaign—you can focus your campaign and increase the number of visits, responses and purchases. Internet marketing should be used with traditional marketing to create the most effective corporate marketing strategy. This strategy includes a focus on attracting new customers to your site and bringing them back repeatedly.

This chapter provides an extensive number of Internet marketing resources, including many URLs, tutorials and demos. These resources will help you expand your knowledge and understanding of Internet marketing.

8.2 Branding

Brand is typically defined as a name, logo or symbol that helps one identify a company's products or services. A company's customers' experience can be considered part of its brand and includes the quality of customers' interactions with a company and its products or services.[1] *Brand equity* includes the value of tangible and intangible items, such as a brand and its monetary value over time, customer perceptions and customer loyalty to a company and its products or services. Businesses that already have a solid brand may find it easier to transfer their brand to the Web, while Internet-only businesses must strive to develop a brand that customers trust and value.

Uniformity of the brand as it is used across all channels of customer contact will increase brand recognition. By using offline and online advertising, e-mail marketing and public relations, e-businesses seek to create dominant brand awareness and encourage customer loyalty. In this chapter, we discuss Internet marketing techniques and how they can be used to increase brand recognition.

The Internet provides an opportunity for further branding a company and its products, but the Internet also makes it difficult to protect a company's brand from misuse. Rumors and customer dissatisfaction can spread quickly over the Internet and can show up on message boards and in chat rooms. It is not difficult for people to use other companies' logos on their sites or products illegally. Companies can attempt to protect their brands by hiring people to surf the Web and look for news, rumors and other instances of brand abuse. Such brand monitoring activities can be outsourced to companies such as eWatch (**www.ewatch.com**) and NetCurrents (**www.netcurrents.com**).

8.3 Internet Marketing Research

Marketing research can help a company develop its *marketing mix* which includes product or service details and development, effective pricing, promotion and distribution. Marketing research has traditionally consisted of focus groups, interviews, paper and telephone surveys, questionnaires and *secondary research*—findings based on previously collected data. Research can now be performed over the Internet, giving marketers a new, faster option for finding and analyzing industry, customer and competitor information. The Internet also provides a relaxed and anonymous setting to hold focus-group discussions and distribute questionnaires.

It is useful to learn about the demographics of Internet and World Wide Web users to target marketing campaigns more effectively. *Demographics* are statistics on the human population, including age, sex, marital status and income. To view some Internet demographics and e-commerce statistics, visit **www.wilsonweb.com/webmarket/ demograf.htm** and **www.commerce.net/research/stats/stats.html**. Knowing your customers' ages, incomes and locations can give you an idea of their buying power, but you will also need to evaluate and research further to find their *psychographics*, which can include family lifestyle, cultural differences and values.[2]

e-Fact 8.1

With ninety percent accuracy, Quova, a company developing technology to determine physical locations of Internet users, can provide browsers' city locations within one-fiftieth of a second.[3]

Once this information is collected, you may begin to segment the market into groups that have similar characteristics and interests. Segmentation, both online and offline, can be based on age, income, gender, culture and common needs and wants. This process will help you conduct further research and develop and target marketing campaigns more effectively. What does each group want? Which of their needs are not being met? Are they demanding a product or service that you can provide? Are they unhappy with current products or services? Answers to these questions can help you tailor product development and service management to fit the needs and wants of your target market.

Online focus groups can be conducted to allow current or potential consumers to present their opinions about your products, services or ideas. This feedback can be useful when you are making critical decisions on the launch of a new product, service or campaign. Note that although Internet focus groups do provide participants with a comfortable setting, the leader of the focus group cannot interpret a participant's body language as a form of communication.[4] Traditional focus groups can allow customers to touch, smell and experience products or services as compared to online methods.

SurveySite™ conducts online focus groups and surveys. Its groups usually consist of 8 to 10 participants and a moderator, who meet during a specific time in one of SurveySite's chat rooms that allows text, graphics and multimedia to be delivered. SurveySite then provides a transcript of the session and a report providing a qualitative analysis of the focus group. The company also provides demos of its online surveys at **www.surveysite.com**.

Online surveys can be conducted from your Web site or through e-mail. **Insight-Express.com** offers automated marketing research, including survey creation and delivery. Visit the site to view the demo of its service. GoGlobal Technologies (**www.goglobal.com**) also creates online surveys for corporations and marketing research firms. **QuickTake.com**™ is a Web-based online-survey solution that can assist in survey creation; it can locate your target market over the Internet and collect answers to the survey. It then analyzes the findings and provides reports in real time. It is important to test the design of your site and the aspects of your campaign to discover any flaws.

It is important to understand each culture and each target market. By testing your site and marketing campaign on a smaller scale with focus groups and trials, you can correct misconceptions and misunderstandings before you launch your site or campaign.

Data collected from your company's Web site can also provide you with valuable marketing research. Technologies that can reveal consumer preferences are available. To learn about log-file analysis and data mining, see Chapter 10, e-Customer Relationship Management. @Plan (**www.atplan.net**) provides Internet marketing research tools and support for using them. KVO (**www.kvo.com**) provides research for companies involved in the e-commerce and Web-advertising industries, and Macro Consulting, Inc. (**www.macroinc.com**) offers traditional and Internet marketing research and consultations. Quirk's *Marketing Research Review* (**www.Quirks.com**) is a marketing research magazine. Its site provides access to the *Researcher SourceBook*™, where you can find a listing of companies that specialize in marketing-research products and services.

Marketing research can also be used to evaluate campaign results. Measuring the costs and benefits of your campaign can help you determine its relative success or failure. These measurements can also help you develop a budget for the following year's marketing activities. You can use the results of marketing research to identify segments that may be growing or that may be the most profitable.

To understand current industry trends, you may want to view research on e-commerce. Some of the most popular marketing-research firms are now providing research results online. Forrester Research (**www.forrester.com**) gives you access to research findings on Internet and e-commerce activities. It also offers a free e-research demonstration and some free research reports.

Adknowledge has complete research solutions and free marketing-research information on the online-advertising industry. The free reports can be downloaded at **www.adknowledge.com**. Other popular research companies include Jupiter Communications (**www.jup.com**) and Media Metrix (**www.mediametrix.com**).

To keep current on news from different industries, try searching at **www.marketresearchinfo.com**. Market researchers can find free tools, such as tutorials for Web surveys, a market-research company directory and an *Employment Board* for the marketing-research industry, at **@ResearchInfo.com**. Also, you can find trials for software, *freeware* and *shareware* at **www.marketresearchinfo.com/public/software**. Freeware and shareware are both software distribution methods. Both are ways to offer software at no cost; however, shareware is distributed with the expectation of donations in return.

E-business pricing of products and services can be affected by marketing research. The Internet provides ways for buyers and sellers to meet. People tend to shop for the lowest prices, forcing companies to price products and services competitively. While some products can be priced to reflect competition, companies that want customers to perceive products as high-value and luxurious may decide to keep high prices. Companies can use prices to position their products and services on the Internet. Positioning includes affecting consumers' overall views of a company and its products and services as compared to the way those customers view competitors' products or services. *Positioning* strategies can be based on price, quality, use and competitors' positions in the market.

Research and segmentation can also assist marketers in determining a proper distribution system for products and services. When operating an e-business, distribution cost and time can contribute to success or failure. For example, **Amazon.com** did extensive research to determine an efficient distribution system and strategically built and placed warehouses to minimize the time it takes to deliver products. Fulfillment is also a concern of e-businesses, which must be able to execute orders correctly and ship products promptly.

8.4 e-Mail Marketing

E-mail marketing campaigns can provide an inexpensive and effective way to target potential customers. Before beginning an e-mail marketing campaign, a company must first decide on the goals of the campaign. These processes may include defining the *reach*, or the span of people you would like to target, including geographic locations and demographic profiles; and determining the level of personalization of the campaign. Personalized *direct e-mail* targets consumers with specific information. By using customer names, offering the right products at the right time and sending special promotions targeted to consumers' interests, the marketer makes a stronger connection with the people receiving the e-mails.

If companies plan to enter global markets, their personalization methods should include translating e-mails into the proper languages, for the convenience of international consumers. The Italian translation company Logos® (**www.logos.it**) offers free access to its online dictionary of more than 20 languages and will translate e-mails for a fee.[5]

AltaVista offers a free text and Web-site translation service that can be accessed through the **Translate** link at `www.altavista.com`. See Chapter 12, Globalization for more information on global marketing.

Personalization technology also allows the marketer to target campaigns to a specific market, which can improve the *response rate*—the percentage of responses generated from the target market. Products and services are available to help you personalize your e-mails and manage your e-mail campaigns. One option is to *outsource* e-mail marketing. Outsourcing means that parts of your company's operations are performed by other companies. Some service providers allow marketers to maintain control of content, mailing lists and campaign timing. Outsourcing services should be used when direct e-mail becomes too difficult to manage, because of e-mail volume and inadequate staff or technical support. `Boldfish.com` provides a tutorial on how its e-mail marketing-campaign system works. Other electronic-mail software and service sites are `www.messagemedia.com`, `www.digitalimpact.com`, `www.ilux.com`, `www.247media.com` and `www.econtacts.com`.

There are new, innovative ways to market through e-mail. Audio, video and graphics are becoming important aspects of creative e-mail marketing campaigns. Products such as MindArrow's *eCommercials®* (`www.mindarrow.com`) can be sent as self-playing e-mail attachments and do not require any software plug-ins to view the video or listen to the audio. The attachments do not require plug-ins because all the necessary components are sent along with the eCommercial, allowing it to execute without requiring the viewer to download any extras. A *plug-in* is a small application designed to extend the capabilities of another product, such as a Web browser. MindArrow's *eComTracker™* provides companies with information about the recipients of the messages and the number of e-mail forwards of a particular eCommercial. inChorus (`www.inChorus.com`) provides its clients with the capability to send media-rich e-mail. `MediaRing.com` offers its customers the opportunity to place streaming audio in e-mail and newsletters or on their Web sites. Customers can click on a link to hear a voice making the e-mail or newsletter more personal. Companies should be aware that people use different programs to read their e-mails, so not all users may be able to view e-mails with enriched content or handle the size of media-enriched e-mails. The e-mails should be customized based on receivers' preferences and their readers' capabilities. E-mail recipients may also be concerned about computer viruses sent in e-mails. Companies will have more successful e-mail campaigns if they have recognizable, trusted brand.

E-mail can also be used to improve your customer service. For example, adding an e-mail link to your Web site provides a convenient way for customers to voice their opinions and ask questions. Although this is a good idea, you should make certain that your business has the ability to handle the anticipated volume of e-mails. E-mail systems can be set up so that incoming e-mails will be sorted automatically and directed to the appropriate people.[6] E-mail can also help customers track the location of their orders, informing them of when to expect delivery and possible delays and providing information such as the carrier's name.

Internet mailing lists can help you target customers through personalized e-mail. *Opt-in e-mail* is sent to people who explicitly choose to receive offers, information and promotions.[7] Opt-in e-mail is part of *permission-based marketing*—a company can market its products and services to people who have granted permission. It is important not to abuse people who have given you permission to market to them; do not flood them with e-mails.

Excessive e-mailing can decrease the effectiveness of your e-mail campaign. NetCreation's Web site, **PostMasterDirect.com**, will send your campaign e-mail to those on a Net-Creations lists who have expressed interest in your business category. **Yesmail.com** and **Xactmail.com** are other companies that create lists of people who want to receive information on certain subjects.

It is important to avoid sending e-mail to people who have not shown interest in your products or services. *Spamming*—mass e-mailing to people who have not expressed interest in receiving e-mails from you—can give your company a poor reputation. Spamming, its ramifications and federal regulations are discussed in Chapter 11, Legal and Ethical Issues; Internet Taxation.

E-mail can be combined with *traditional direct marketing*—including sending information by mail and using telemarketers to contact prospective customers—to allow marketers to reach a large audience. Although traditional direct mailing can be more expensive, more difficult to analyze and can have a lower response rate than direct e-mailing, many companies, such as **www.eletter.com** and **www.mbsmm.com** can provide efficient direct-mailing services. Another option for targeting prospective customers is *telemarketing*. Telemarketing can offer the benefit of live interaction between customers and service representatives. Also, people may find it more difficult to ignore phone calls than e-mail. However, unlike telemarketing calls, e-mail messages can arrive even if the recipients are busy or away from their computers, and recipients can deal with the e-mail at their own convenience. By using both forms of marketing, you can experience the advantages—and, unfortunately, the disadvantages—of each.

8.5 Promotions

E-business *promotions* can attract visitors to your site and can influence purchasing. They can also be used to increase brand loyalty through reward programs. Promotions can include frequent-flyer miles, point-based rewards, discounts, sweepstakes, free trials, free shipping and coupons. Promoting products and services will attract visitors to your site and may influence their purchasing decisions. Promotions can provide your company with an economical way to establish contact with potential customers, but it is important to make sure that customers are actually becoming loyal to your company and not just to your promotions or rewards program. You must also carefully monitor the costs of the program.[8]

Offering frequent-flyer miles provides an incentive for customers to shop at your site. This can attract repeat visitors, by allowing them to view the number of miles they have accumulated; this information can be made available through a username and password system. Netcentives™ (**www.netcentives.com**) designs rewards programs for e-businesses. For example, Netcentives offers *ClickRewards*, a rewards program that allows your customers to accumulate frequent-flyer miles, called *ClickMiles*. *ClickRewards* requires that both your customer and your company are registered with the program.

With a *points-based promotion*, every time a customer performs a prespecified action, he or she can receive points redeemable for products, services, rebates, discounts, etc. MyPoints® (**www.mypoints.com**) allows members to receive points for browsing and shopping on the Internet. These points can be redeemed for products and services of various companies including airlines, restaurants and merchandise stores. Giving away items with your company's logo for redeemed points increases brand exposure. **Branders.com** allows you to upload your company's designs and logos to the site to view how the designs will look on t-shirts, mugs and other promotional items. **iSwag.com** offers brand management solutions. *eBuyer* allows a company to add its logos to selected promotional products from a catalog. The company can then attempt to fill this customized order through **iSwag.com**, which connects buyers, sellers and distributors online.

Offering discounts on products or shipping and handling is a good way to attract consumers. Advertising your discounts in magazines, newspapers, on other Web sites and through direct e-mail can bring both new and repeat customers to your Web site.

Sweepstakes can bring people to your site and can generate leads. Offering prizes can increase interest in your site. iPromotions (**www.ipromotions.com**) offers sweepstakes and development of incentive-based programs.

Allowing customers to sample your product or try your service for free can make customers feel comfortable about purchasing your product or using your service. For example, at **www.travelocity.com**, customers can sign up to be a member for free or can try the service as an anonymous guest. When signing up as a member, you can receive personalized information including airfare watches and promotional e-mails. This business helps customers plan their travel and purchase travel services, and it updates its site frequently with discount offers and special promotions.

Some Web sites offer *online coupons* for online shopping. Your company can place coupons on these sites to target consumers and bring them to your site. Some sites that advertise coupons are **www.directcoupons.com**, **www.coolsavings.com** and **www.valupage.com**. To offer free promotional items, visit and register with portals such as **free.com**, **free2try.com** and **freeshop.com**. You can also visit **www.promotionworld.com/tutorial/000.html** to view a tutorial on ways to promote your site.

8.6 e-Business Advertising

Today, a great deal of e-business advertising is conducted through traditional channels such as television, movies, newspapers and magazines, as well as the new online advertising channel. Many e-businesses advertise during prime-time television, which is the most expensive way to air commercials. Advertising gives e-businesses the opportunity to establish and strengthen branding. Your brand should be unique, recognizable and easy to remember.[9] Publicizing your URL on all direct mailings, business cards, billboards, print advertisements and other media helps increase brand awareness and bring more visitors to your site.

e-Fact 8.2

The amount of money spent on e-business commercials during Super Bowl XXXIV totaled approximately $135 million.[10]

While newspapers, magazines, television and films all provide effective promotional channels, online advertising is quickly becoming part of the promotional world. Online advertising can include placing your links and banners on other companies' Web sites and registering your site with search engines and directories. You can also charge other companies for placing their advertisements on your site, providing you with additional income. Affiliate programs, another method of advertising, are discussed in Chapter 9, Affiliate Programs.

e-Fact 8.3

By 2003, revenues for online advertising are expected to reach $13.3 billion, according to Jupiter Research.[11]

8.6.1 Banner Advertising

Web page *banner ads* act like small billboards containing graphics and an advertising message (Fig. 8.1). The benefits of banner advertising include increased brand recognition, exposure and revenues. Effective banner design and positioning will help determine the success of your banner ad campaign. Banners can be created in different sizes and placed in various positions on your Web site. Most ads provide a link to the home page of the product or service being advertised. A new style of banner ads, sometimes referred to as *side panel ads* or *skyscraper banners*, are advertisements that lie vertically on Web sites (Fig. 8.2).[12] These vertical advertisements provide a new look for traditional banner advertising and also allow the advertiser to display more products or content in the banner.

Fig. 8.1   Banner advertisements. (Courtesy of **GaryCohn.com** Marketing.)

Fig. 8.2   Example of a panel ad. (Courtesy of Venture Capital Online, Inc.)

When designing a banner advertisement, determining how you would like your company to be recognized plays an important role. For example, Deitel & Associates, Inc., could use its signature bug logo on every banner, enhancing brand recognition. Inventive color schemes and movement will also grab a viewer's attention. Movement can include flashing, scrolling text, pop-up boxes and color changes. A *pop-up box* is a window containing an advertisement that appears separately from the window the user is viewing. The box pops up randomly or as a result of specific user actions. These boxes can have a negative effect due to their intrusive nature.

Before placing banner ads on Web sites, note how many ads the sites already carry. Many consumers are annoyed by Web sites cluttered with ads. Try different positions on Web pages, and analyze the results to determine what position gets the greatest number of click-throughs.

After selecting where to place your banners, you will have to choose a method of payment. Some sites will post your banner advertisement during specific times. Advertising space is normally more expensive during peak traffic times. Exchanging banners with another site is also an option. Some sites will carry your banner ads for free.[13]

The industry has calculated click-through rates for banner advertisements to be around .5 percent and this rate is decreasing continuously.[14] Although recent studies have indicated that banner advertisements are losing their effectiveness,[15] these ads still lead to brand recognition and possible purchases and should be a part of your marketing strategy. Two of the many sites dedicated to banner advertising are **www.adbility.com** and **www.bannertips.com**.

8.6.2 Buying and Selling Banner Advertising

Buying advertising space on sites that receive a large number of hits and that target a market similar to yours can increase the number of hits on your site and lead to higher revenues. Selling advertising space on your own site can provide you with additional income.

It is important to distinguish a site's *unique visitors* from the total number of *hits* it receives. Visiting any site registers one unique visit. Hits are recorded for each object that is downloaded, and there could be many such objects per unique visit. For instance, if you were to visit a Web site with three images and background music, five hits would be recorded: one for each image, one for the audio and one for the page itself. This visit would still count as only one unique visit.

Companies have adopted different payment systems for advertising on their sites. Monthly charges for online advertising are rarely used today. Instead, some sites charge a designated fee for every 1,000 people who view the site on which your banner is located; this method of payment is called the *CPM (cost-per-thousand)* method. If the company hosting your ad has 50,000 visitors per month, your advertisement will cost 50 times the CPM rate. The problem with this form of payment is that many people may be at the site, but may not see the advertisement. This means that the advertiser would be paying for an advertisement based on the number of people who are viewing the site, but not necessarily the advertisement. Even though this measurement is consistent with other forms of advertising media, the Internet provides ways that users can interact with an advertisement, which may make paying for user actions more attractive.

With some advertising-payment schemes, you will be charged only if the customer performs an action predetermined by you and the Web site managers. *Pay-per-performance* fees include *pay-per-click, pay-per-lead* and *pay-per-sale.*[16] When using the pay-per-click method, you pay the site hosting your banner according to the number of click-throughs to your site. Pay-per-lead means that you pay the host for every lead generated from the advertisement, and pay-per-sale means that you pay the host for every sale resulting from a click-through. Affiliate programs, another form of advertising using these different advertising methods, is discussed in Chapter 9, Affiliate Programs.

Another advertising option involves exchanging advertising space on your site in return for advertising space on another site. This arrangement is effective for businesses that complement one another, and it is usually free.

If you wish to sell advertising space, provide the appropriate contact information on your Web site. You can also register with organizations that will sell your space for you. These companies typically charge a percentage of the revenue you receive from the advertisements placed on your site. Some advertising companies that offer banner advertising options include ValueClick (**www.valueclick.com**), DoubleClick (**www.doubleclick.com**), AdSmart (**www.adsmart.net**) and LinkExchange (**www.linkexchange.com**).

ValueClick: An Advertising Option[17]

ValueClick (**www.valueclick.com**) manages advertising campaigns. The company acts as a broker for people who want to buy and sell advertising space (Fig. 8.3). ValueClick has access to advertising space on thousands of Web sites and gives you the option of targeting specific markets.

To buy advertising through ValueClick, you must first design a banner. A representative of ValueClick can then help you determine what program best fits your advertising needs. Payment is made in advance and is based on the number of visitors you want to receive.

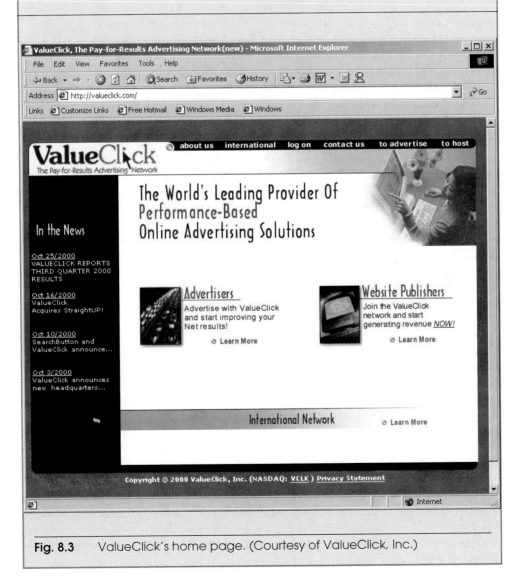

Fig. 8.3   ValueClick's home page. (Courtesy of ValueClick, Inc.)

ValueClick: An Advertising Option[17] (Cont.)

ValueClick offers many *segmented markets* for advertising. Segmented markets consist of people or companies with similar characteristics. You can select a particular segment or advertise on a variety of sites. ValueClick does not offer services to companies hosting illegal or questionable content.

When publishing advertisements on your site through ValueClick, your earnings will depend on the number of visitors resulting from the advertisements. ValueClick pays the publisher monthly as long as revenues are greater than a certain amount. If you do not meet that amount in one month, the balance rolls over to the next month.

ValueClick offers four options for publishing advertisements on your site: the ValueClick Affiliate, Premium, AdVantage and AdVantage Plus programs. Each program requires a certain minimum number of clicks before ValueClick starts paying the higher prices per click. Payments per click increase progressively as you move from the Affiliate program to the Premium program to the AdVantage programs. The AdVantage Plus program is for the largest Web sites.

8.6.3 Media-Rich Advertising

Webcasting uses streaming media to broadcast an event over the Web. *Streaming video* simulates television. Marketers must consider, however, that many people still have relatively slow Internet access; the slower the connection, the more disconnected the streaming video appears.[18]

Victoria's Secret's Webcast was the most popular Webcast ever.[19] The first time Victoria's Secret, a lingerie store for women, tried to Webcast a fashion show, the servers could not handle the volume of traffic to the site, and the show was unavailable to many individuals. These problems were corrected in the year 2000 fashion-show Webcast.[20] Visit **www.victoriassecret.com** to view the 2000 Victoria's Secret fashion show.

Some streaming media experts include Resource Marketing (**www.resource.com**), a company offering a variety of services for Internet marketing, and Clear Digital (**www.cleardigital.com**), a company that develops Web commercials and extensive Web sites. Navisite (**www.navisite.com**) offers consulting, development and implementation of a variety of streaming-media events. Cyber-Logics (**www.cyber-logics.com**) designs Web sites, e-commerce sites and develops streaming media. To find out about current streaming-media conferences, news, company directories and many other details on streaming media, visit **www.streamingmedia.com**. In addition, Macromedia® (**www.macromedia.com**) offers many media software products employing audio and visual technologies such as Macromedia Flash™, Dreamweaver™, Fireworks® and Director®.

Spinway™ (**www.spinway.com**) is a company that provides free dial-up Internet access and also performs media-rich advertising. The company hosts television-like commercials that air on your computer during wait times. For example, a commercial would be aired while you are waiting to establish a connection to the Internet. Spinway can target commercials to certain markets. Spinway requires user registration for its free Internet access. You provide Spinway with a video commercial and specify your target market for the video. Visit **www.spinway.com** to view an online demonstration of a commercial. You can also see the demographics of Spinway's consumers on the site. If you are having trouble viewing the sample commercial, you may have to download a technology used to view rich media, such as RealPlayer (**www.realplayer.com**), QuickTime (**www.apple.com/quicktime**) or Shockwave (**www.shockwave.com**), or, if you have Microsoft® Windows, you can use Windows Media Player.

Burst.com offers Burstware®, a client–server software package that delivers video and audio content through *bursting* (rather than streaming). Streaming delivers a flow of data in real time. In contrast, bursting delivers content faster, so that it builds up substantially at the receiving end, potentially enabling a smoother appearance. Visit the site **www.burst.com** for an explanation of the difference between streaming and bursting and to view some examples of bursting.

Cross-media advertising or *hybrid advertising* uses a combination of various media including rich media over the Internet (such as audio, video, images and animations) and traditional advertising forms (such as print, television and radio advertisements) to execute an advertising campaign. Involving consumers in the advertising process makes them more likely to remember your company. For example, Nike developed a campaign that included interactions between the consumer, television and Nike's Web site. In this campaign, Nike aired television commercials with an ending that directed viewers to **www.nike.com**. The site also offered a link to a Nike digital video. The consumer had the option to select various action pictures of an athlete and music to be played in the background. The consumer could then view the constructed video and send it to other people via e-mail, providing free advertising for Nike.

Another example of cross-media advertising is WebRIOT, a game show on MTV™. The game is aired on television, and viewers can join in the game at the same time by playing online. The top online players' screen names are then featured on TV. To try WebRIOT, visit **www.mtv.com** and download the game. You can also visit H₂O Design (**www.h2odesign.com**) and Lot21 (**www.lot21.com**), additional companies that specialize in cross-media advertising.

Interactive television advertising allows people viewing television to interact with what they are seeing on the screen. For example, when a television commercial is aired, there may be a question asked on the screen that a viewer can actually answer by using a remote control to click on an icon on the screen. Through this technology, consumers have the ability to choose to learn more about an offer, make a purchase or even request that customer service representatives contact them. RespondTV (**www.respond.com**), a company that provides technology to support interactive television, signed up major advertisers to try out interactive television advertising. PowerTV and WebTV are a few examples of platforms for interactive television that can run this type of advertisement.

e-Fact 8.4

Forrester Research predicts that iTV (interactive television) boxes in the United States will number 25 million by 2004.[21]

8.6.4 Wireless Advertising

The Internet can now be used anywhere with the new wireless technologies. Although the wireless Internet is in its early stages, advertising companies are preparing to take advantage of this new medium. SkyGo™ (**www.skygo.com**) is a wireless advertising company that provides wireless marketing solutions and infrastructure. It offers real-time wireless delivery and tracking of permission-based campaigns. Adbroadcast[SM] (**www.adbroadcast.com**) pays people who opt in to receive advertisements on their cell phones. The company sends no more than three advertisements in one day. Another company, GeePS (**www.geeps.com**), offers brick-and-mortar stores wireless advertising targeted toward specific markets. GeePS sends relevant wireless advertisements to customers as they enter the proximity of a store. In addition, this company can send targeted wireless advertising to customers as they are shopping in malls. AdForce (**www.adforce.com**) is also working with MediaPlex (**www.mediaplex.com**) to offer wireless advertising services. See Chapter 6, Wireless Internet and m-Business, and visit **www.wirelessnetnow.com**, **www.rcrnews.com**, **wirelesstoday.com**, **wirelessclick.com** and **www.fiercewireless.com** to learn more about the wireless industry and wireless advertising.

e-Fact 8.5

According to Jupiter Communications, the number of Internet-enabled cell phones in use will number more than 75 million by 2003.[22]

8.7 e-Business Public Relations

Public relations (PR) keeps your customers and your company's employees current on the latest information about products, services and internal and external issues, such as company promotions and consumer reactions. It includes communicating with your consumers and employees through press releases, speeches, special events, presentations and e-mail. The Web is a relatively new medium for public relations.

Chat sessions are one method of learning what people think about your company or products. Placing a bulletin board on your Web site will enable people to post comments. You can also involve consumers by organizing a special event or function on your Web site. *Brand awareness* and increased exposure can result from attending and participating in trade shows and exhibitions, at which you can speak with prospective customers.

Press releases, which announce current events and other significant news to the press, can be delivered over the Web. PR Web (**www.prweb.com**) allows you to submit a press release for free. The press release will be distributed to the contacts in PR Web's database. Its site also gives you access to public-relations firms, current press releases and newsletters. Another site that offers public-relations information and helps visitors find jobs in the field is **www.thePRnetwork.com**.

Video clips of news appearances, speeches, commercials and advertisements can be effective publicity for your company. Visit **www.prnewswire.com** and **www.businesswire.com** to view lists of recent press releases, including audio and video news.

PR specialists must be able to contact companies that will distribute and print the press releases. MediaMap is a company that provides PR contacts and software designed for PR. Visit **www.mediamaponline.com** to sign up for a free trial of MediaMap. The trial provides access to the company's database of contacts and allows users to create their own concentrated sample list of media contacts. MediaMap also offers white papers on its product and how to use it.

Outsourcing your public relations is an option. Future Works (**www.futureworks.com**) is a company that offers public-relations services such as press-release writing, news media relations and positioning. Visit **www.webcom.com/impulse/ prlist.html** to view a listing of PR agencies by geographical location and links to many PR resources.

   Crisis management, another aspect of PR, is conducted in response to problems the company is having. For example, many investors and consumers follow the financial news about Internet companies closely. When your company is doing well financially, this fact should be made public. However, if the company is doing poorly, your public-relations department must be ready to issue information about what is causing the problem and what will be done to correct it. For example, when Bridgestore/Firestone, Inc., had to recall 6.5 million tires, many people visited its Web site. The company had the opportunity to provide information that the public may not have been receiving from the news and other sources of information.[23]

8.8 Business-to-Business (B2B) Marketing on the Web

Business-to-business (B2B) marketing can be different from *business-to-consumer (B2C) marketing.* B2B marketers must consider their companies' distributors, resellers, retailers and partners when developing their marketing strategies. When you sell your product or service to another business, you may be selling to someone who is not the direct user of the product or service. Because the user of the product might have an opinion or comment different from what you are hearing from your business contact, ask your contact to speak with the end users. They may have suggestions that could improve your product or service.[24]

e-Fact 8.6

According to an estimate made by Forrester Research, B2B e-commerce will grow from $109 billion in 1999 to $2.7 trillion in 2004.[25]

   Usually more than one person is involved in a company's purchasing process. This is different from B2C marketing, where one customer is usually making the decision to buy. Therefore, marketing to another business requires the marketer to be conscious of all parties involved in the purchasing decision and to design a marketing strategy accordingly. Maintaining strong relationships is key to the growth and success of business-to-business companies. Businesses making large purchases depend on their suppliers and expect them to be reliable and to deliver quality products and services on time. B2B customer relationship management is discussed in Chapter 10, e-Customer Relationship Management.

   B2B marketers can use the Internet to market to other businesses. E-mails sent to companies should be addressed to all people involved in the purchasing decision and should be tailored to provide informative and personalized content. Personalization should include why and how your company's products and services will benefit the targeted business. It is a good idea to require registration when a site visitor requests more information about your company. The marketer can then research the company and design an e-mail response that will present relevant marketing materials that address the inquiring company in a more customized manner.

   B2B companies can also use intranets and extranets (see Chapter 5) for marketing purposes. To provide targeted marketing to their customers, B2B companies can offer special information and services through extranets developed for those with authorized access. This can include the introduction and promotion of additional services or products that these companies may find useful.

Industry *marketplaces* are good resources for companies that want to sell to other businesses. Searching marketplaces for potential clients can help you define your target market and generate customer leads more effectively. Business-to-business marketplaces for several industries are available on the Internet. For example, construction companies can find appropriate B2B marketplaces at **www.construction.com, www.e-cement.com** and **www.redladder.com**, while retailers can visit **www.globalnetxchange.com** and **www.worldwideretailexchange.com**.

Commerce One offers solutions for e-businesses. Its portal, **www.marketsite.net**, helps buyers and sellers find each other and relevant business-to-business exchange sites worldwide. Commerce One also helps companies build industry-specific marketplaces. Connect, Inc. (**www.connectinc.com**), Concur Technologies (**www.concur.com**) and Ariba (**www.ariba.com**) are a few other companies that provide technology and consulting for creating marketplaces for buyers and sellers.

8.9 Search Engines

A search engine is a program that scans Web sites and forms a list of relevant sites based on keywords or other search-engine ranking criteria. *Search-engine ranking* is important to bringing new visitors to your site. The method used by search engines to rank your Web site will determine how "high" your site appears on lists of search results. You can customize and register your site to improve the position in which your company appears in search-engine results.

8.9.1 META Tags

A *META tag* is an HTML tag that contains information about a Web page. The tag does not change how a Web page is displayed, but can contain a description of the page, keywords and the page's title. Search engines often use this information when ranking a site.

Some search engines rank your site by sending out a program, called a *spider*, to inspect the site. The spider reads the META tags, determines the relevance of the Web page's information and keywords and then ranks the site according to that visit's findings. You should examine your competitors' sites to see what META tags they are using. Ask yourself, "If I wanted to search for products or services that my company offers, what keywords would I type when using a search engine?" You want your site to appear in the top 10 results, because often people will not look further. For valuable information about keyword selection, visit **www.keywordcount.com** and **www.websearch.about.com/internet/web-search/insub2-m02.htm**.

8.9.2 Search-Engine Registration

When you register your site with a search engine, you submit keywords and a description of your business. The search engine will add your information to its database of Web sites. When someone uses that search engine, your Web site may appear in the list of results. Many search engines are constantly scouring the Web, visiting and ranking Web pages. Even if you do not register, the search engines may still find your page, if it is linked to another site. By registering, however, you eliminate the uncertainty.

Various companies will register your Web site with search engines for a fee. To view free information about some of the major search engines' requirements for registering, as well as general tips about search-engine registration and META-tag development, visit **www.searchenginewatch.com/Webmasters/index.html**. See Fig. 8.4 for a chart of some popular search engines' requirements and registration processes

Many search engines do not charge a fee for registering, although some require payment to use other services they provide. Excite[SM] is a search engine that allows people to register their sites for free. You also have the option to apply through *Excite Plus*, a quick way to submit your site to the LookSmart[SM] network. This service charges a one-time fee.[26] Popular search engines include **www.yahoo.com**, **www.lycos.com**, **www.excite.com**, **www.altavista.com**, **www.google.com** and **www.askjeeves.com**. Ask Jeeves[SM] uses *natural-language technology* that allows people to enter their search subjects in the form of full sentences, rather than just keywords. This system works well, because the engine maintains a database of question templates that it uses to match questions with possible answers.[27] Natural-language technology is discussed in Chapter 10, e-Customer Relationship Management.

Search Engine	Registration Requirements and Details
AltaVista **www.altavista.com**	In theory, you should not have to register with AltaVista. The search engine should be able to find your site on its own, because it sends out crawlers that find sites and add them to AltaVista's index. The crawler follows links from other pages it finds, and that is how AltaVista adds more URLs to its index. So, if many pages are linked to your site, your site is more likely to be found. If not, it will never be found. To register, enter your URL in the form located at **www.altavista.com/cgi-bin/query?pg=addurl**. After this process is complete, AltaVista sends out crawlers to find the site, learn what is included in the content and add the URL to the index. Submission is free.
Lycos® **www.lycos.com**	Lycos requires you to submit a URL for each page of your site, as well as your e-mail address. Lycos then sends a spider to your site. In approximately two to three weeks, your site will be entered into Lycos's catalog. Registration is free. If your site is not live for a certain amount of time, the spider cannot connect to it. Your site then gets deleted from the catalog.
Ask Jeeves™ **www.ask.com**	To submit a URL to Ask Jeeves' knowledge base, you send an e-mail including your URL and a short description of your site to Ask Jeeves. Human editors then review your request by visiting your site and checking if your site matches certain guidelines including quick loading time, regular updating of content and free features without the requirement of user registration. Ask Jeeves also uses its patented popularity search technology to determine which sites have provided the best answers to Ask Jeeves users. In addition to the previous guidelines, e-commerce sites should meet additional guidelines including security requirements, customer service and credibility as an e-commerce site.

Fig. 8.4   Search engines and their registration processes (part 1 of 2).

Search Engine	Registration Requirements and Details
Yahoo!® **www.yahoo.com**	Before registering with Yahoo!, you should first check if your site is already in Yahoo!'s database. It is possible that your site has been suggested to Yahoo! by another user. If your site is in a foreign language, it may be located in an International Yahoo!. If it is in an International Yahoo! it will not be added to **www.yahoo.com**. Once you have determined that your site is not in Yahoo!, you should find an appropriate category in the Yahoo! directory to list your site. You can do this by going to the bottom of the category page and clicking on the link for suggesting a site. Yahoo! provides suggestions to help you determine where your site should be placed. Suggesting sites is free. To suggest a site using the normal process, you are only required to provide the name, URL and short description of the site. When using the *Business Express* you are required to pay a fee, guaranteeing that your site will be reviewed within seven business days.
Google℠ **www.google.com**	Visit **www.google.com/addurl.html** to add a URL to Google. This search engine requests your URL and comments about your site (for Google's information), however it does not use the comments submitted for indexing purposes. Google does not index every site submitted. The engine only requires the submission of a site's main page because its crawler, *Googlebot*, will be able to find the rest of your pages as it searches all possible links. Google ranks pages by the number of connections between Web sites, with the theory that the more connections to a site, the more popular and useful the site.[28] This is different compared to other search engines that use META tags and site descriptions as a method of ranking.

Fig. 8.4   Search engines and their registration processes (part 2 of 2).

Metasearch engines aggregate results from a variety of search engines. For example, if you go to metacrawler® (**www.metacrawler.com**) and conduct a search, you will find a list of results derived from many different search engines. **FrameSearch.net** is another example of a metasearch engine. This engine allows you to indicate which engines you would like to search.

In this chapter we discuss the importance of tailoring a marketing strategy to include the online channel. Advertising, direct marketing and public relations can all be implemented on the Internet. E-businesses can increase brand awareness and traffic to their sites using the different methods of Internet marketing. In Chapter 9, we focus on affiliate programs.

8.10 Internet and World Wide Web Resources

Direct e-Mailing

www.radicalmail.com
Radicalmail.com is a company that performs streaming multimedia e-mailing services. Visit the site for demonstrations of its latest e-mail capabilities.

www.flonetwork.com
FloNetwork, Inc., manages direct e-mail campaigns. The company provides real-time tracking and analysis of e-mail campaigns.

www.clickaction.com
ClickAction offers e-mail campaign management.

Online Promotions

www.webpromote.com
WebPromote.com offers information on Internet marketing, including extensive coverage of promoting your Web site.

newapps.internet.com/appstopics/
Win_95_Web_Site_Promotion_Tools.html
This site is a resource listing tools to help a business conduct effective promotional campaigns. The tools include Web-tracking software and search-engine effectiveness software, some of which is free.

www.promotionworld.com/tutorial/000.html
Promotion World has an online promotional outline containing information on site-promotion services.

Internet Marketing Research

www.iconocast.com
ICONOCAST features a variety of marketing information, including a newsletter.

www.zonaresearch.com
Zona Research offers marketing-research reports.

www.idc.com
International Data Corporation offers specialized marketing research on the Internet, e-commerce and information technology.

Online Advertising

www.engage.com
Engage Media offers a variety of Internet marketing products and services.

www.adresource.com
Ad Resource offers Internet advertising resources, including information on software, events and articles.

www.burst.com
Burst.com uses bursting to deliver video content. Visit the site for a demonstration of the difference between bursting and streaming.

Webcasting and Interactive Advertising

www.streamingmedia.com
Streamingmedia.com is a site where you can learn about current streaming-media conferences, industry news, company directories and other information on streaming media.

www.digiknow.com
Digiknow.com offers interactive advertising, including online, on-disk and on-paper advertising. Visit the site to see demonstrations.

www.bluestreak.com
Bluestreak offers interactive banners. Visit the site to see demonstrations.

Business-to-Business Marketing on the Web

www.verticalnet.com

VerticalNet, Inc., provides a list of industry communities. It also has a variety of e-business solutions that help bring buyers and sellers together. Its resources give marketers options for B2B marketing.

www.commerceone.com

Commerce One offers a portal (**www.marketsite.net**) for businesses to exchange products around the world. *Commerce One* also assists companies in building industry marketplaces.

www.linkshare.com

Linkshare is one of the few companies offering business-to-business affiliate programs in addition to business-to-consumer affiliate programs.

Public Relations

www.mediarelations.com

Media Relations provides publicity, marketing and event management.

www1.internetwire.com/iwire/home

Internet Wire offers a free PR newsletter.

www.newsiq.com

NewsIQ offers a service that tracks when a client appears in the news.

Search-Engine Information

www.submiturl.com/metatags.htm

This site has a brief tutorial on META tags.

www.webdeveloper.com/html/html_metatags.html

The *Webdeveloper* provides a tutorial on **META** tags.

www.tiac.net/users/seeker/searchenginesub.html

This site offers direct links to the registration portions of many search engines.

General Internet Marketing Information

www.asknetrageous.com/AskNetrageous.html

Asknetrageous offers answers to questions on Internet marketing. You can subscribe to any of its e-mail newsletters for free.

www.eMarketer.com

eMarketer aggregates content on Internet marketing, including news, statistics, profiles and reviews.

www.channelseven.com

Channelseven is a news and information site that helps marketing and advertising professionals keep up to date with the Web.

www.roibotlibrary.com/index.htm

ROIbotlibrary is a listing of free resources on Internet marketing. The resources include a free five-day marketing course sent to you over the Internet. The Web site also provides free marketing software.

Total Internet Marketing Solutions and Services

www.wheelhouse.com

Wheelhouse consults and provides implementation assistance for various marketing strategies. It also implements marketing systems.

www.hyperlink.com
Hyperlink is a full-service company that offers customer-acquisition management tools and relationship marketing consultancy.

www.ilux.com
Ilux develops and sells software for Internet marketing solutions and also provides services, including evaluation of Web sites, outsourcing and assistance with the use of *Ilux* software.

SUMMARY

- A solid Internet marketing strategy can provide your company with an important advantage over competitors and can include e-mailing, advertising, promotions and public relations.

- Keeping user profiles, recording visits and analyzing promotional and advertising results are key to measuring the effectiveness of your marketing campaign.

- Brand is typically defined as a name, logo or symbol that helps one identify a company's products or services.

- A company's customers' experience can be considered part of its brand and includes the quality of customers' interactions with a company and its products or services.

- Brand equity includes the value of tangible and intangible items, such as a brand and its monetary value over time, customer perceptions and customer loyalty to a company and its products or services.

- Businesses that already have a solid brand may find it easier to transfer their brand to the Web, while Internet-only businesses must strive to develop a brand that customers trust and value.

- Uniformity of the brand as it is used across all channels of customer contact will increase brand recognition.

- The Internet provides an opportunity for further branding a company and its products, however the Internet also makes it difficult to protect a company's brand from misuse.

- Rumors and customer dissatisfaction can spread quickly over the Internet and can show up on message boards and in chat rooms.

- By discovering your target market, you can increase visits, responses and possible purchases.

- Internet marketing should be used with traditional marketing to enhance your marketing strategy.

- Marketing research can be performed over the Internet, giving marketers a new, faster option for finding and analyzing industry, customer and competitor information.

- Web sites should be designed with the consumers' preferences in mind.

- E-mail is a fast, cheap and far-reaching marketing tool.

- Organizations that plan to enter the global market must have the ability to send e-mail translated into the proper languages, demonstrating that they value international consumers.

- Personalized direct e-mail targets consumers with specific information and offers.

- Personalization technology allows the marketer to target campaigns to a specific market.

- Outsourcing services should be used when direct e-mailing gets too difficult to manage, because of e-mail volume and inadequate staff or technical support.

- Determining a goal for your campaign includes defining the reach, or the span of people you would like to target, including geographic locations and demographic profiles. Determining the level of personalization of the campaign is also important.

- Good Internet mailing lists include the contact information for people who have opted in to receive information by e-mail.

- Traditional direct marketing—which includes sending information by mail and using telemarketers to contact prospective customers—should be used with e-mailing to reach more people.

- Direct mailing is often more expensive, more difficult to analyze and has a lower response rate than direct e-mailing.

- To allow people to access your information, add your company's contact information to a list of companies or organizations related to your field of business.

- Placing a link on your Web site so that people can e-mail your company directly from the site is a good idea; however, you should be sure that your business has the ability to handle the anticipated volume of e-mail.

- Spamming—mass e-mailing customers who have not expressed interest in receiving these e-mails—can reflect poorly on your company.

- Offering something extra, such as frequent-flyer miles for participating airlines, to consumers when they purchase products or services online can increase brand loyalty.

- With a points-based promotion, points are awarded to customers every time they perform a designated action. These points can be accumulated and redeemed for products or services.

- Placing discount advertisements in magazines, newspapers, direct e-mail and on other Web sites can bring both new and repeat customers to your Web site.

- You can help consumers feel comfortable about using your site by offering a free trial.

- Your company can place your coupons on sites that offer online coupons to target consumers and bring them to your site.

- Today, most of the advertising for e-businesses is conducted through mainstream channels, such as television, movies, newspapers and magazines, as well as on the new online channel.

- E-businesses should establish and continually strengthen branding. A brand is a symbol or name that distinguishes your company and its products or services from its competitors. Your brand should be unique, recognizable and easy to remember.

- Publicizing your URL on all direct mailings, business cards and advertisements will bring people to your site. Placing your links on other companies' Web sites and registering your site with search engines and directories are other means of increasing traffic to your site.

- Banner ads, which act like small billboards, usually contain graphics and an advertising message and are located on Web pages. The benefits of banner advertising include increased brand recognition, exposure and possible revenue gained through purchases by consumers.

- Banner ads can be created in different sizes and placed in various positions on your Web site.

- A pop-up box is a window containing an advertisement that appears separately from the window the user is viewing. The box pops up randomly or as a result of user actions.

- Many consumers are annoyed by Web sites cluttered with ads. By trying different positions on Web pages and analyzing the results, you can determine what position gets the greatest number of click-throughs on your banner ads.

- Buying advertising space on sites that receive a large number of hits and that target a market similar to yours can increase the number of hits on your site and lead to higher revenues. Selling advertising space on your own site can provide you with additional income.

- Paying a designated fee for every 1000 people who view the site on which your banner is located is called the CPM (cost-per-thousand) method of payment.

- One unique visit registers when you visit a site. Hits are recorded for each object that is downloaded. To determine the value of a Web site for advertising purposes, one should use the number of unique visitors, not total hits.

- Advertising fees based on actions include pay per click, pay per lead and pay per sale. Under the pay-per-click method, you pay the host for click-throughs to your site. Under the pay-per-lead method, you pay the host for every lead generated from the advertisement. Under the pay-per-sale method, you pay the host for every sale resulting from a click-through.

- Another advertising option involves exchanging advertising space on your site for advertising space on another Web site. This is effective for businesses that complement one another.

- You can register with companies that sell your advertising space for you. These companies typically charge a percentage of the revenue you receive from the advertisements placed on your site.

- Webcasting involves using streaming media to broadcast an event over the Web. Streaming video simulates television.

- Bursting delivers content faster than streaming. Bursting causes a substantial buildup of content at the receiving end, potentially enabling a smoother appearance.

- Cross-media advertising includes using many forms of rich media (such as audio, video, images and animations) and traditional advertising forms (such as print, television and radio advertisements) to execute an advertising campaign.

- Although the wireless Internet is in its early stages, advertising companies are preparing to take advantage of this new medium.

- Public relations (PR) keeps your customers and your company current on the latest information about products, services and internal and external issues.

- PR includes communicating with your consumers and company through press releases, speeches, special events, presentations and e-mail.

- To learn what people think about your company or products, try hosting chat sessions. Consider using a bulletin board on your Web site to enable people to post comments. You can also involve consumers by organizing a special event or function on your Web site.

- Press releases can be delivered over the Web.

- Your Web site should contain a link that connects to all of your company's press releases.

- Video clips of news appearances, speeches, commercials and advertisements can be effective publicity for your company.

- Crisis management, another aspect of PR, is conducted in response to company problems.

- If the company is doing poorly, your public-relations department must be ready to issue information about what is causing the problem and what will be done to correct it.

- Registration—requiring visitors to fill out a form with personal information that is used to create a profile— is recommended when it will provide a benefit to the consumer. By obtaining information from registration forms, companies are able to evaluate who their consumers are and what they want.

- People are often reluctant to fill out a form requiring personal information. To encourage people to start building a consumer profile, you can require them to provide a minimal amount of information, such as a username, password and possibly an e-mail address.

- Personalization technology can help a company understand the needs of its customers and the effectiveness of its Web site.

- B2B marketing can be different from B2C marketing, because when you sell your product to another business, you may be selling to someone who is not the direct user of your product.

- Industry marketplaces are good resources for companies that want to sell to other businesses.

- Search-engine ranking is important to bringing consumers to your site.

- A META tag is an HTML tag that contains information about a Web page.

- Most search engines rank your site by sending out a spider to inspect the site. The spider reads the META tags, determines the relevance of the Web page's information and keywords, and then ranks the site according to that visit's findings.

- When you register your site with a search engine, you submit keywords and a description of your business to the engine. The search engine will add your information to its database of Web sites.

- Failing to submit your site to search engines does not mean that your site will not show up on various search engines, but registering will increase the probability of your site appearing in result listings.

- By understanding each culture to the best of your ability and by testing your site and marketing campaign on a smaller scale with focus groups and trials, you can correct misconceptions and misunderstandings before you launch your site for the world to see.

TERMINOLOGY

banner ads	pay-per-performance
brand	pay-per-sale
brand awareness	permission-based marketing
brand equity	plug-in
bursting	points-based promotion
business-to-business (B2B) marketing	pop-up box
business-to-consumer (B2C) marketing	points-based promotion
CPM (cost per thousand)	positioning
crisis management	press release
cross-media advertising	promotions
demographics	public relations (PR)
direct e-mail	psychographics
freeware	reach
hits	response rate
hybrid advertising	secondary research
interactive television advertising	segmented markets
Internet mailing list	shareware
Internet marketing campaign	side-panel ad
marketing mix	skyscraper banner
marketplace	spamming
metasearch engines	spider
META tag	streaming video
online coupons	target market
online focus group	telemarketing
opt-in e-mail	traditional direct marketing
outsource	unique visitor
pay-per-click	Webcasting
pay-per-lead	

SELF-REVIEW EXERCISES

8.1   State whether each of the following is true or false; if false, explain why.
  a) Spamming is soliciting consumers with unwanted e-mail.
  b) Registering with search engines will increase the probability of your site appearing in result listings.
  c) The more effective way to determine the value of a Web site for advertising purposes is to use the number of hits the site receives versus using the number of unique visitors.

     d) CPM is considered an action-based fee.

     e) Streaming delivers a flow of data in real time.

8.2   Fill in the blanks in each of the following statements:

     a) Keeping the public and your company's employees current on company news is called

     _____.

     b) A _____ is what a search engine sends out to rank a Web site.

     c) _____ delivers content faster than streaming; it causes a substantial buildup of content at the receiving end, potentially enabling a smoother appearance.

     d) _____ is used to make Webcasts appear like television.

     e) _____, an aspect of PR, is conducted in response to problems the company is having.

ANSWERS TO SELF-REVIEW EXERCISES

8.1   a) True. b) True. c) False. Finding unique visitors is more effective than determining the number of hits. Visiting any site registers one unique visit. Hits are recorded for each object that is downloaded, and there could be many such objects per unique visit. d) False. Action-based fees include pay per lead, pay per sale and pay per click. e) True.

8.2   a) public relations. b) spider. c) Bursting. d) Streaming video. e) Crisis management.

EXERCISES

8.3   State whether each of the following is true or false; if false, explain why.

     a) A target market is the group of people toward whom you direct a marketing campaign.

     b) Search-engine registration is important to increasing traffic to your site.

     c) CPM stands for Consumer Product Management.

     d) Direct mailing is often less expensive, easier to analyze and has a higher response rate than direct e-mailing.

     e) Using Webcasting for your online advertising can simulate television commercials.

8.4   Fill in the blanks in each of the following statements:

     a) A _____ is an HTML tag that contains information about a Web page.

     b) Online focus groups, surveys and interviews are all part of performing _____.

     c) A symbol or name that distinguishes your company and its products or services from its competitors is called a _____.

     d) Online and offline statistics based on age, income and gender are known as _____.

     e) By placing a _____ on your Web site, you will allow people to post their comments and questions about your company, products and services on the site.

8.5   Define each of the following terms:

     a) reach

     b) response rates

     c) spamming

     d) opt-in e-mail

     e) cross-media advertising

8.6   Research and compare three different online advertising agencies.

     a) What forms of media does each company offer for advertising?

     b) Do any of the sites offer demonstrations? Explain any demonstrations that you can view.

     c) Which company has the most appealing and navigable site? Which company would you choose for your advertising campaign. Why?

8.7   Explain the three common types of pay-per-performance advertising campaigns. For each type of pay-per-action advertising, give an example of what type of site should use it and why.

8.8   Visit SurveySite (`www.surveysite.com`) and explore its online demo of Internet-based surveys. Answer the following questions.
   a) What are switching questions? What switching questions did the demo give for examples?
   b) What does piping mean?
   c) What is the difference between skip pattern questions and branching questions?
   d) Visit `www.surveysite.com/newsite/newpop/showmenewx.htm` and describe SurveySite's pop-up survey software. At the bottom of this Web page, click on the Click Here link to see an example of the pop-up software. Answer the survey questions. Do you think that the survey will help a site? What questions do you feel are most important? Why? List additional questions that you would ask in an online survey.

8.9   (*Project*) Choose a traditionally marketed product or service, and create an Internet marketing strategy for it. Discuss how you would perform each of the following for the product or service, discuss the importance of each and give examples:
   a) direct e-mail
   b) cross-media advertising
   c) banner advertising
   d) target market
   e) public relations
   f) promotions
   g) Internet marketing research
   h) search-engine registration

WORKS CITED

The notation `<www.domain-name.com>` indicates that the citation is for information found at that Web site.

1. P. Seybold, "Broad Brand," *The Industry Standard* 6 November 2000: 214.
2. `<www.dictionary.com/cgi-bin/dict.pl?term=psychographics>`.
3. S. Wooley, "We Know Where You Live," *Forbes* 13 November 2000: 332.
4. "Getting Things In Focus," *The Industry Standard* 31 July 2000: 180.
5. T. Seibel and P. House, *Cyber Rules: Strategies for Excelling At E-Business* (New York: Random House, Inc., 1999) 78.
6. P. Seybold and R. Marshak, `Customers.com` (New York: Random House, Inc., 1998) 93.
7. D. Greening, "When Push Comes To Shove," *Webtechniques* April 2000: 20, 22, 23.
8. J. Black, "Dangle With Care," *Internet World* 15 October 2000: 39.
9. B. Warner and L. Schuchman, "Getting Heard Above the Noise," *The Industry Standard* 27 December 1999 - 3 January 2000: 53.
10. S. Eliot, "Not X'es, Not O's, It's the Dot-Coms that Matter. Marketers Suit Up For a Costly Race for Recognition," *The New York Times* 28 January 2000: C1.
11. S. Mulcahy, "On-line Advertising Poised To Explode; Learn Ropes Now," *Mass High Tech* 28 February-5 March 2000: 4.
12. J. Gaffney, "Smart Buy: `Ashford.com` on `NYTimes.com`," *Revolution* August 2000: 17.
13. L. Cunningham, "Marketing: Only Performance Counts," *Inter@ctive Week* 1 May 2000: 116.
14. T. Sweeney, "Advertisers Seek More Bang For Their Web Bucks," `informationweek.com` 2 October 2000: 130.

15. D. Lehman, "Privacy Policies Missing on 77% of Web Sites," *Computer World* 17 April 2000: 103.

16. L. Cunningham, "Marketing: Only Performance Counts," *Inter@ctive Week* 1 May 2000: 116.

17. K. Weisul, "ValueClick Could Live Up To Its Name," *Inter@ctive Week* 27 March 2000: 92. Information also collected from **www.valueclick.com**.

18. M. Smetannikov, "Perchance To Dream of Bannerless Ads," *Inter@ctive Week* 17 April 2000: 22.

19. M. McCarthy, "Webcast Show Fashion Success," *USA Today* 22 May 2000: 8B.

20. M. McCarthy, 8B.

21. A. Houston, "Advertisers Get Set to Try Interactivity on Television," *Revolution* August 2000:14.

22. P. Schaut, "Online Advertising Report: I Don't Think We're In Kansas Anymore," *Revolution* August 2000: 3.

23. K. Lundegaard, "The Internet is Playing a Principal Role In Recall of Bridgestone/Firestone Tires," *The Wall Street Journal* 16 August 2000: A14.

24. D. Peppers, et al., *The One To One Field Book: The Complete Toolkit for Implementing a 1 to 1 Marketing Program* (New York: Bantam Doubleday Dell Publishing Group, Inc., 1999) 42.

25. M. Boyle, "Anyone Up For a B-to-B Business-plan Bandwagon?" *Revolution* August 2000: 8.

26. <www.excite.com>.

27. <www.askjeeves.com>.

28. C. Taylor, "In Search of Google," *Time* 21 August 2000: 67.

RECOMMENDED READINGS

Amor, D. *The E-business (R)Evolution.* New Jersey: Prentice Hall, 2000.

Bond, J. "Marketers, Your Stock Has Never Been Higher." *Revolution* March 2000: 55-59.

Cunningham, L. "Marketing: Only Performance Counts." *Inter@ctive Week* 1 May 2000: 116.

Estabrook, A. "Drive Customers To Your Web Site." *e-Business Advisor* November 1999: 22-25.

Gray, D. *The Complete Guide To Associate and Affiliate Programs on the Net: Turning Clicks into Cash.* New York: McGraw-Hill, 2000.

Kuehl, C. "E-mail Marketing, Spam's Good Twin." *Internet World* 1 May 2000: 31-38.

Mann-Craik, F. "The Power of Advertising Your Internet Firm." *Tornado-Insider,* February 2000: 92-94, 96.

Mowrey, M. "Thank You, Please Come Again." *The Industry Standard* 27 March 2000: 196, 197.

Seybold, P. and R. Marshak. *Customers.com: How To Create A Profitable Business Strategy For The Internet and Beyond.* New York: Random House, Inc., 1998.

Siebel, T. and P. House. *Cyber Rules: Strategies for Excelling At E-Business.* New York: Random House, Inc., 1999.

"Special Report: CRM e-volves." *Global Technology Business* May 2000: 48+.

"Special Report: Online Marketing: Customer Conundrum." *Upside* April 2000: 145+.

Tiernan, B. *E-tailing.* Chicago: Dearborn Financial Publishing, Inc., 2000.

Walsh, B. "Building A Business Plan For An E-Commerce Project." *Network Computing* 15 September 1998: 69-71+.

Affiliate Programs

Objectives

- To learn how affiliate programs work.
- To understand the benefits and costs of affiliate programs.
- To comprehend the different reward structures.
- To review methods of affiliate tracking.
- To discuss various providers of affiliate-program solutions.

A banner with the strange device, Excelsior!
Henry Wadsworth Longfellow

All for love, and nothing for reward.
Edmund Spenser

One among a thousand.
Holy Bible: The Old Testament

When you stop talking, you've lost your customer.
Estée Lauder

A man travels the world over in search of what he needs and returns home to find it.
George Moore

Give me my golf clubs, fresh air, and a beautiful partner, and you can keep my golf clubs and the fresh air.
Jack Benny

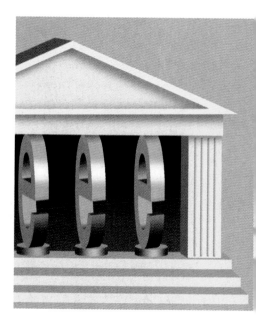

Outline

9.1   Introduction
9.2   How an Affiliate Program Works
9.3   Selecting An Affiliate-Program Reward Structure
       9.3.1   Pay-Per-Click Model
       9.3.2   Pay-Per-Lead Model
       9.3.3   Pay-Per-Sale Model
       9.3.4   Multi-Tiered Model
       9.3.5   Hybrid Model
       9.3.6   CPM (Cost-Per-Thousand) Model
9.4   Attracting Affiliates
9.5   Monitoring An Affiliate Program
9.6   Affiliate Solution Providers
       9.6.1   Commission Junction
       9.6.2   LinkShare
       9.6.3   Be Free
       9.6.4   ClickTrade
       9.6.5   PlugInGo.com
9.7   Web-site "Stickiness"
9.8   Becoming an Affiliate
9.9   Examples of Affiliate Programs
9.10   Examples of Affiliate Programs by Industry
9.11   Costs and Taxation of Affiliate Programs
9.12   Affiliate-Program Directories and Search Engines
9.13   Internet and World Wide Web Resources

Summary • Terminology • Self-Review Exercises • Answers to Self-Review Exercises • Exercises • Works Cited

9.1 Introduction

Affiliate programs have become a dominant and unique form of Internet marketing. An affiliate program is a form of partnership in which a company pays *affiliates* (other companies or individuals) for prespecified actions taken by visitors who *click-through* from an *affiliate site* to a *merchant site*. In this chapter, we discuss the costs, benefits and program reward structures of affiliate programs. We discuss program-building options, particularly *tracking* and *affiliate solution providers*. *Directories* and *search engines* that provide affiliate- and partnering-program resources are also discussed in this chapter.

9.2 How an Affiliate Program Works

New income streams can be established when companies host the advertising of merchant Web sites. This partnership is called an affiliate program. Affiliates act as an extended sales force, assisting in building traffic, awareness, leads or even sales for merchants.[1] This can lead to an increase in market share for the merchant. A *merchant* is the company that advertises on another company's site. The company hosting the advertising, in return for a *reward* based on predetermined terms, is called the *affiliate*. For example, if an online bookseller (merchant) sells computer science textbooks on its Web site and Deitel & Associates' Web site hosts content related to computer science, it might benefit that bookseller to have Deitel & Associates as an affiliate.

The merchant can place a banner advertisement on the affiliate's Web site. When a person clicks through to the merchant's site via the advertisement on the affiliate's site and makes a purchase, a commission on the sale is typically awarded to the affiliate (Fig. 9.1). This system creates a "win-win" situation; the merchant can be sure that its banner advertising campaign is developing new leads and revenue, and the affiliate can collect income for hosting a banner. Before operating an affiliate program, decisions must be made on which program model(s) to use and how to track affiliates and payments.

9.3 Selecting An Affiliate-Program Reward Structure

Affiliate programs vary among affiliate solution providers and merchants. These programs can use the *pay-per-click, pay-per-lead, pay-per-sale* and *CPM (cost-per-thousand)* models to reward their affiliates.[2] Other *reward structures* include *multi-level,* or *multi-tiered,* programs and a *hybrid model*, which combines a variety of reward models. Implementation of the appropriate reward structure(s) will depend on what type of site you operate and your product mix. For example, companies that sell products typically reward affiliates for sales made (pay-per-sale). Companies that want to increase the readership of their newsletters typically reward affiliates for visitors who sign up to receive the newsletters (pay-per-lead).

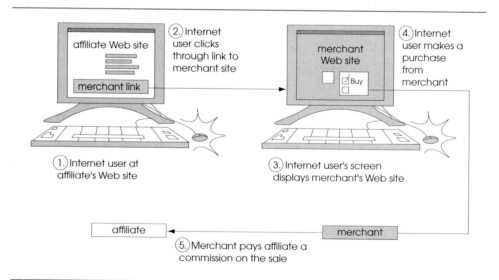

Fig. 9.1   Affiliate-program operation for a program that pays commissions on sales.

9.3.1 Pay-Per-Click Model

The pay-per-click model rewards an affiliate for each click-through that is generated from a banner ad hosted by the affiliate. A click-through is when a person clicks on the banner advertisement on the affiliate site and is taken to the merchant site. A problem with this model is that it is easy for affiliates to generate dishonest click-throughs to "run up the numbers." Sites that depend on advertising rates, such as some search engines, use this model to attract more traffic. Advertisers pay more to place their ads on high-traffic sites.[3] GoTo™ (**www.goto.com**) is a search engine that pays for every click-through made from an affiliate's site. Lycos® (**www.lycos.com**) is another search engine that uses the pay-per-click model. Lycos offers affiliates the option to carry *Content Boxes*. These boxes contain search options, product offerings and other information from the Lycos Network. Lycos pays the affiliate a designated amount for every visitor that clicks on a Content Box. Rewards vary, depending on which Content Box you choose to place on your site. Go to **www.lycos.com/affiliateprogram** to view the reward amount for each Content Box.

9.3.2 Pay-Per-Lead Model

Some affiliate programs use the *pay-per-lead model*, which rewards affiliates based on the number of qualified leads generated. *Qualified leads*—potential customers that have expressed interest in a product or service and meet requirements determined by the company—can include new customer registrations and having visitors sign up to receive a newsletter or use a free demo. **Mailsweeps.com** requires users to fill out surveys in return for entering sweepstakes to win prizes. It pays affiliates for each referred person who enters its sweeps program with a valid e-mail address.

9.3.3 Pay-Per-Sale Model

The *pay-per-sale model*, also known as the *commission-based model*, compensates its affiliates for each sale resulting from affiliate-hosted advertisements. The rewards to the affiliates based on sales are typically larger. **express.com**® sells entertainment products such as movies, games and electronics; it uses the pay-per-sale affiliate program. Some pay-per-sale affiliate programs allow the affiliate to set up a *virtual store* on its site to sell the merchant's products without requiring the visitor to leave the affiliate's site.

9.3.4 Multi-Tiered Model

With the *multi-tiered model*, also known as the *multi-level model*, new affiliates are recruited by current affiliates, who are then rewarded with a percentage of the new affiliates' revenues. A *two-tiered model* involves only the original affiliate and its recruits, also known as subaffiliates.[4] For example, ValueClick's two-tiered program pays an affiliate a designated amount per click-through generated from an affiliate-referred site that has become a host for ValueClick's services (see the ValueClick Feature in Chapter 8, Internet Marketing). See Fig. 9.2 for a two-tiered affiliate diagram.

For example, if a pay-per-sale affiliate program pays an affiliate a 15-percent commission on a sale, the affiliate is entitled to the full 15 percent. If a consumer buys a product through a subaffiliate link, the merchant still pays 15 percent of the sale; however, the subaffiliate might get 10 percent of the sale, and the original affiliate would then get 5 percent of the sale.

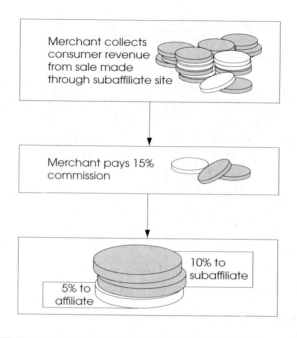

Merchant collects consumer revenue from sale made through subaffiliate site

Merchant pays 15% commission

10% to subaffiliate

5% to affiliate

Fig. 9.2   Diagram of a two-tiered affiliate-program model.

9.3.5 Hybrid Model

Some companies use a *hybrid model* to reward affiliates. Hybrid models combine features of multiple models. Combining models may make an affiliate program more competitive. However, it can increase the cost for the merchant, which could be paying affiliates for more than one action. **FreeShop.com®** is a site that offers an affiliate program that is a pay-per-click and pay-per-sale program. It rewards affiliates for each click-through and for each sale that results from a click-through. **FreeShop.com**   uses LinkShare (**www.linkshare.com**), an affiliate solution provider, to run its affiliate program. We discuss the services provided by LinkShare, as well as its competitors, in Section 9.6.

9.3.6 CPM (Cost-Per-Thousand) Model

The *CPM (cost-per-thousand) model* is rarely used in affiliate programs today. This model requires the merchant to pay the affiliate a fee for every 1000 visitors that simply view the merchant's banner on the affiliate site. A visitor may not even notice a banner on an affiliate site, yet under the CPM model the merchant is paying the affiliate for that person's page view. This model is not used as often as the other models because merchants prefer to pay for actions such as click-throughs, leads and purchases. However, CPM is often used to price traditional advertising methods, such as print and television. The differences of traditional and Internet advertising and the importance of incorporating both methods in a marketing strategy is discussed in detail in Chapter 8, Internet Marketing.

9.4 Attracting Affiliates

Affiliate programs can result in additional sales, *traffic generation*, *lead generation* and *customer acquisition.*[5] By placing links on an affiliate sites, merchants are advertising their companies, improving *brand recognition* and providing people with a direct channel to their sites. A pay-per-lead program will generate leads making it easier for merchants to target their marketing campaign toward a group of people who have shown interest in their companies' products or services. Attracting affiliates is important to help an affiliate program grow in size and increase profits.

e-Fact 9.1

Forrester Research estimates that by 2003, affiliates will generate 21 percent of online retailers' revenues, as compared with today's [1999] average of 13 percent.[6]

When a company wants to advertise its affiliate program to attract more affiliates, simply advertising the program on its site may not be enough to get the attention of potential affiliates. A company should try posting announcements on message boards that target an audience the company would like to have as affiliates. *Newsgroups* which are online discussion groups, are another potential source for finding affiliates for a program. However, mentioning an affiliate program in newsgroup discussions must be done carefully because spamming and unwanted advertising are unwelcome and may be against the rules of some of the groups. The company should participate in the group discussions to learn the rules and to establish the company as a legitimate member. A merchant could visit **Deja.com** to do a search of related newsgroups, and begin monitoring and participating in some of the newsgroups to see if it is acceptable to mention the affiliate program. There is also a directory of newsgroups at **tile.net/news** and **www.liszt.com/news**.

Merchants should also consider posting information about their affiliate programs in directories. A *directory* is a site that provides aggregated information and links to sites relevant to specific topics. The merchant should be sure to include words associated with affiliate programs in the description of its site. META tags should include words related to the affiliate program, in order to increase the possibility that the site will appear on affiliate-program search engine results. See Section 9.12 for more information on affiliate-program search engines and directories. META tags are discussed in Chapter 8, Internet Marketing.

Researching companies in the merchant's industry to see what kind of affiliate programs they may offer can help a merchant understand the industry market for affiliate programs. Determining what reward structures and amounts the companies in the merchant's industry are offering will help a merchant keep its program competitive.

9.5 Monitoring An Affiliate Program

Merchants can use affiliate program tracking information to analyze the effectiveness of their programs and make improvements. Information gained from tracking can also be used to monitor payment schedules and identify the strongest affiliates.

Companies with internal resources can consider creating their own tracking solutions. By creating duplicates of every Web page, each affiliate can link to an individually assigned page. This system can make it easy for a company to track each affiliate's progress because referred visitors will click through to only the *mirror page* (the duplicate page) designated for that specific affiliate, allowing companies to record these visits separately. For example, if Deitel & Associates, Inc. (**www.deitel.com**) created an affiliate program, one affiliate would link to a mirror page of this URL, such as **www.deitel.com/ affiliate1.html**. Only one affiliate would refer visitors to this page through its affiliate link.

Constructing mirror sites can be a time-consuming process, especially when there are multiple products. In this case, a company will need more than one mirror page per affiliate, because each product will require its own mirror page.[7] Other costs include hosting and updating mirror pages. Payments, marketing, credit-card processing and customer service costs also need to be considered when tracking a program in-house.

A company can also buy software to track its affiliate program. This software can be costly, depending on the level of functionality. **AffiliateZone.com** offers affiliate-tracking software called *Affiliate Link 1.6*. This software allows a company to track its affiliates and related purchases. The company and its affiliates can also access commission information at the same time. A demo of the product is available at **www.affiliate-zone.com/index4.htm**.

My Affiliate Program[TM] (**www.myaffiliateprogram.com**) is another affiliate-tracking software package that can be customized to fit a marketing strategy. The software keeps track of commissions and provides administrative capabilities such as registering affiliates. This program has a monthly fee for licensing, maintaining backup servers and other expenses. *Pro-TRACK* (**www.affiliatesoftware.net**) allows you to view a demo and take a tour of the *Administrative Side control panel*. The demo and tour enable you to view samples of the reports and options that the merchant has access to when using this software. Many software packages do not require the merchant to pay commissions on its program. This option can be cheaper compared with paying services to track the program or having the program run by an affiliate solution provider.

9.6 Affiliate Solution Providers

Affiliate solution providers are companies that can provide end-to-end solutions for a company's affiliate program. A solution provider can recruit affiliates and merchants to participate in programs, conduct accurate tracking, provide detailed reporting for merchants and affiliates and distribute commissions. Fees, such as a percentage of affiliate commissions or a monthly service fee, may be required for affiliate solution services.

9.6.1 Commission Junction

Commission Junction (**www.cj.com**) is an affiliate solution provider that offers design, implementation and management services for companies interested in business-to-business affiliations. There is no fee to become an affiliate. Commission Junction's application service is *Web based*, meaning that you do not have to download or upgrade any software. The service includes instant tracking and reporting in real time. Commission Junction charges merchants a network-access fee, an annual renewal fee and transaction fees based on the predetermined actions taken by visitors on the affiliate sites. The merchant is required to keep a minimum balance in an account that will be used to pay affiliates. The company makes monthly payments to the affiliates for the merchants. Commission Junction's *En-Context*[TM] solution offers content sites the opportunity to sell goods directly from their sites. Commission Junction also pays merchants to refer new affiliates to the program and gives merchants five percent of each of their recruited affiliates' earnings for as long as the affiliates remain in the program. A choice of operating or joining a pay-per-sale, pay-per-lead or pay-per-click program is given.

Commission Junction provides a variety of services to its merchants. *SmartMatch*™ connects products and services to appropriate content sites, providing a targeted offering to site visitors. *SmartTrack*™ provides tracking and reporting to users instantaneously. *SmartZones*™ and *SmartStats*™ update the advertisements and links on the sites and measure and monitor the program. *SmartServe*™ is a scalable technology that serves advertisements. *SmartPay*™ combines the payments from all of the programs that affiliates belong to into a monthly payment.

9.6.2 LinkShare

LinkShare (**www.linkshare.com**) offers affiliate programs for B2B and B2C companies (Fig. 9.3). It enables affiliates the opportunity to join pay-per-click, pay-per-lead and pay-per-sale programs through LinkShare for free. The affiliate can join as many programs as desired. A username and password are created to access affiliate information, including programs and tracking statistics. The code for the links for all affiliate programs is available on the LinkShare site.

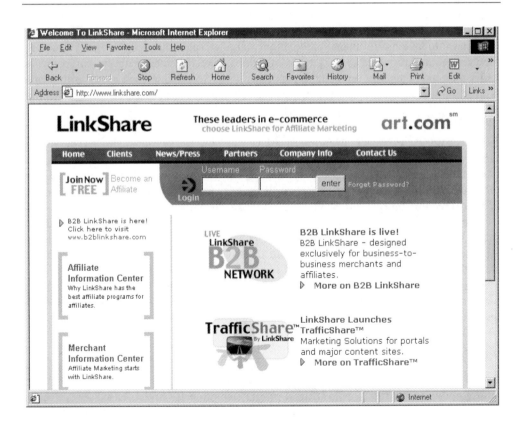

Fig. 9.3   LinkShare's home page. (Courtesy of LinkShare Corporation.)

Merchants that want to use LinkShare can use *The LinkShare Network*™, a *Private Label Network* or a combination of the two to develop their affiliate programs. The Link-Share Network provides merchants with access to companies that have become affiliates through LinkShare. Using *LinkShare Synergy*™ Web-based software, merchants can launch their programs quickly. Affiliates will be notified that the program is new; the program will be displayed as a "New Program" on the login page for affiliates. The merchant can also target marketing efforts towards segmented groups of affiliates. The *Private Label Network* is a LinkShare solution that allows merchants to sign up affiliates through their own Web sites.

Tools provided through the LinkShare Synergy include *CustomComp*, a function that allows merchants to customize compensation methods among different affiliates; *One-Click Updates*, which allows merchants to update links, graphics and product offerings with one click; *SmartChat*, which is an online chatting option that allows merchants and affiliates to arrange for a chat session in The LinkShare Network; and *SmartReports*, a function that provides merchants with focused reports that can be sent to their e-mail addresses automatically and at specific times.

9.6.3 Be Free

Another provider of affiliate-program management solutions is Be Free, Inc. (**www.be-free.com**) (Fig. 9.4). The *BFAST*^{SM} product is an affiliate-program enabler. The system is designed to build performance-based, highly targeted sales channels. BFAST runs on Be Free servers and provides over 75 types of reports. The system also allows companies to target their affiliates in a segmented manner, in order to provide each group with proper promotions and tips on how to sell their products better. *beFLEX*^{SM}, part of the architecture of the BFAST solution, allows companies to make changes to their sites without affecting their affiliate-program structures or links. Rewards and compensation are determined by the merchant. Be Free acts as an intermediary, tracking impressions, click-throughs and sales for both the merchant and its affiliate partners. Using Be Free, merchants can place promotions on affiliated Web sites that are relevant to their industry (Fig. 9.5). Be Free records each time a promotion is viewed. If the visitor clicks through the promotion, Be Free also records this action. When a sale is made, Be Free receives information through its connection with the merchant's site. Payment is collected when a lead is generated or a sale is completed. Affiliates are paid from each individual merchant with which they are affiliated. Be Free uses **Reporting.net** to provide performance information to affiliates. Affiliates can go to this site to discover which links have been performing the best. This site assists affiliates in creating the links to the merchants' sites. Be Free also has a product that uses personalization technology to market to consumers. Personalization is discussed in detail in Chapter 10, e-Customer Relationship Management.

9.6.4 ClickTrade

ClickTrade (**www.clicktrade.com**), part of Microsoft® bCentral (an end-to-end e-business solution provider), is an affiliate-program solution. This Web-based service tracks a company's program and provides payment services. It has an online wizard to help a company set up its program with no setup fee or contract to sign. It provides companies with the option of setting up a pay-per-lead, pay-per-sale or hybrid-model affiliate program.

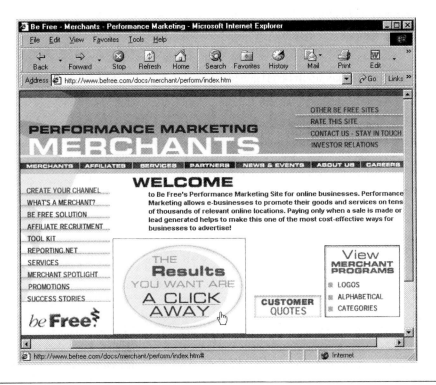

Fig. 9.4   Be Free's performance-marketing page for merchants. (Courtesy of Be Free, Inc.)

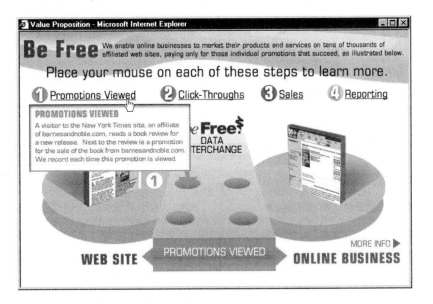

Fig. 9.5   Be Free demonstration: How promotions work, step 1. (Courtesy of Be Free, Inc.)

Merchants have control over the links, images and banners that affiliates can use to link to the merchants' sites. ClickTrade will also list a program in *Revenue Avenue*, its directory for affiliate programs. ClickTrade's only charge is 30 percent of any merchant payments to affiliates.

Companies can sign up to be affiliates for free through ClickTrade and can join a program as an affiliate by sending a request for the merchant's approval. Approvals can be done manually or automatically through an approval system.

Reports provided by ClickTrade include tracking of affiliates' clicks, sales and commissions. These reports can be generated for each individual affiliate. Reports can also be graphically represented, for easier interpretation. Visit **www.clicktrade.com** to take the "Quick Tour" of the program's features and benefits.

9.6.5 PlugInGo.com

The *PlugInGo.com Affiliate Network*™ is another Web-based solution for affiliate programs. **PlugInGo.com** provides merchants with a template for an affiliate sign-up page. The *Affiliate Mail Center* allows merchants to send notices and announcements to their affiliates after they have been approved by the **PlugInGo.com** Staff. There are also online message boards for members to discuss thoughts and ideas about the Network and technical questions.

PlugInGo.com rewards its members through *PlugInGo Points that Pay*. Members are rewarded points for different reasons, such as signing up a new merchant or checking statistics. For a complete list of actions that are rewarded with points, visit **www.plug-ingo.com/index.cfm?Action=M_Started**. The points accumulate and then can be used to bid in **PlugInGo.com**'s auction, which is held monthly. The points must be used within the month that they are earned, otherwise they become obsolete. Reports can be produced daily, weekly or monthly. **PlugInGo.com** also performs payment-processing services, including mailing paychecks to a company's affiliates. As with other providers, companies can join as affiliates for free. **PlugInGo.com** charges a one-time setup fee and then charges a commission of two percent of every sale or lead made through the network.

9.7 Web-site "Stickiness"

The ability to keep people at a site and interested in its content is often referred to as the *stickiness* of a site. The extra revenue generated from affiliate programs may not always compensate for the loss of visitors through links to other sites.[8] To increase stickiness, companies should update content frequently to keep information accurate and content interesting. Providing quality customer service for a site can also keep visitors browsing and shopping. If customers have questions about products or services, they may not stay at the site long if they can not find answers. Carefully organizing a site will also help to keep visitors at a site longer as navigation becomes easier. In this section, we discuss how some companies offer e-commerce capabilities to sites that want to participate in an affiliate program, but also want to keep visitors at their sites.

Nexchange™ (**www.nexchange.com**) offers a full-service solution for affiliate marketing, including e-commerce capabilities. The solution includes technology to host an online store where visitors can purchase products while remaining at the affiliate's site.

This solution adds value to sites by allowing them to sell products related to their target market's interest. The service also provides real-time sales reports. Merchants can change the prices of their products instantaneously, and the prices will be updated on every Web site at which their products are sold. Nexchange's service helps affiliates keep visitors at their sites. Vcommerce Corporation gives companies the option of providing e-commerce on their sites for free and allows them to make money from sales made from their sites (see the **vstore.com** feature). CrossCommerce™ (**www.crosscommerce.com**) is another company that adds e-commerce capabilities to content sites.

By offering virtual stores to affiliates, companies will be able to control the way their brands are presented on affiliate sites. A challenge when using these virtual stores is to make visitors aware that by clicking on the store, they will not be sent away from the site they are viewing.[10]

9.8 Becoming an Affiliate

With low barriers to entry, becoming an affiliate can be easy and is usually free. However, if a company joins too many programs, it will have banners and links covering its site, which will make the site look cluttered and unprofessional. This can diminish credibility with its customers.

Identifying a target market will help a company select the proper programs to join. Visitors will find affiliate links relevant to their interests, increasing the chance that they will click through the links.

Options for becoming an affiliate include signing up directly at the merchant's site or joining through an affiliate solution provider or affiliate directory. Becoming an affiliate is usually free, no matter how a company decides to join.

---

vstore.com: Store-hosting Opportunities[9]

Through **vstore.com**, Vcommerce Corporation provides sites with store-hosting opportunities. Vcommerce manages all credit-card transactions, order fulfillment, customer service and hosting of the storefront.

The site provides an easy step-by-step process to complete your store design and implementation. You first select a category from the listed choices, including electronics, gifts and jewelry, movies, superstore, sports and outdoors and video games. Then you select a subcategory to further concentrate on a particular market. After each selection, **vstore.com** gives a small description of the store, the number of products and a default commission range for that category. Next, you choose a store design, store colors and store typography. At this point, you can see previews of your choices. You then personalize your store with a name, slogan and logo. You have to provide a URL for your store, and you have the option of linking your store back to your home page. Finally, you provide your personal information such as your e-mail address, name, phone number and commission payment information including the name of the person to whom to make the check out and the address to which the commissions should be sent. See the sample store in Fig. 9.6.

vstore.com: *Store-hosting Opportunities*[9] (Cont.)

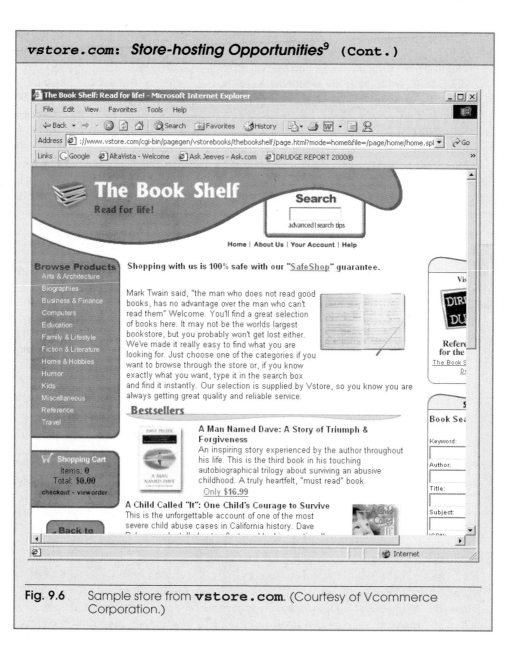

Fig. 9.6   Sample store from **vstore.com**. (Courtesy of Vcommerce Corporation.)

Adbility (**www.adbility.com**) offers information on various forms of marketing, including affiliate programs. The section of the site on affiliate programs is divided first by segments of the market and then by divisions within that segment (Fig. 9.7). Next, visitors can read about various programs within a particular category that pay fees according to the reward structure in which they have shown interest (Fig. 9.8). The descriptions of the programs provide customer reviews and recommendations. Visitors can also search for programs through directories and search engines.

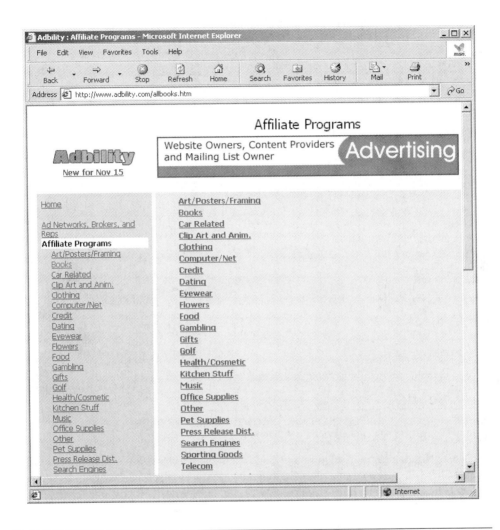

Fig. 9.7   Adbility's specific segments within an industry. (Courtesy of
Adbility.com.)

Some programs have requirements that must be met to become an affiliate. For example, they may require site statistics, such as the number of unique visitors per month, information about visitors and a tax identification number.

Hidden fees and restrictions, such as not allowing companies to join other affiliate programs, are among the limitations and obligations that appear in some affiliate contracts. Companies that want to be affiliates should note the reputation of the merchant offering the affiliate program. A company does not want to refer its visitors to a site that is inappropriate, has bad customer service or has overpriced products and services. Identifying the companies that have already joined the program as affiliates can provide information that may help a company determine whether the program is appropriate or not.

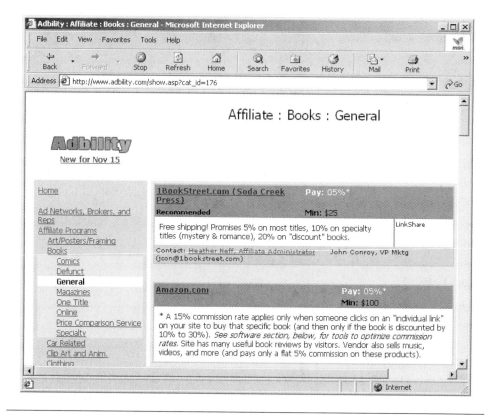

Fig. 9.8   Adbility's listing of affiliate programs for books in the "general" segment. (Courtesy of **Adbility.com**.)

Most affiliate programs require a person or company to have a Web site to participate as an affiliate. Some programs allow individuals to join by placing affiliate links on their personal sites. If a person does not have a Web site, many sites will host one for free, such as Yahoo!® (**www.yahoo.com**), GeoCities (**www.geocities.com**) and Tripod® (**www.tripod.lycos.com**).

9.9 Examples of Affiliate Programs

Amazon.com is a pioneer in affiliate marketing. Its *Associate Program* consists of over 500,000 sites that have linked to **Amazon.com**, including Yahoo!, **AOL.com**, MSN and Excite.[11] To become an **Amazon.com** Associate, an application must be completed. **Amazon.com** will review the application and notify the applicant of acceptance or rejection. A site will be rejected if it contains "amazon" or variations of the word in the domain names, promotes violence, is discriminatory or contains sexual material or other content deemed inappropriate. Once a site has been accepted, it simply provides a link to **Amazon.com**. All of the graphics and links needed can be found at a members-only section called *Associates Central*, where affiliates can also access their earnings and traffic information online at any time. An affiliate can provide an **Amazon.com** search box on its site or link to the home page or recommended books. **Amazon.com** pays referral fees on any sales made through affiliate links. Joining the **Amazon.com** Associates Program is free and pays up to 15 percent in referral fees. See the Barnes & Noble feature for another example of an online business that offers an affiliate program.

BabyCenter® (**www.babycenter.com**) offers information on pregnancy, parenting and health and sells products related to these topics. It also offers a commission-based affiliate program. Members are paid for all sales originating from their sites. Unlike many other affiliate programs, BabyCenter pays affiliates for their own personal shopping through the links on their sites. BabyCenter provides affiliates with the links, banners or images to place on their sites. Affiliates are paid on a quarterly basis. BabyCenter does not ship outside the United States; however, sites in other countries can join the program and earn commissions on sales made from customers in the United States. Earning reports are available through the *BabyCenter Affiliate Gateway*, a site that also has the images and links that can be downloaded to connect to the merchant site.

9.10 Examples of Affiliate Programs by Industry

There are companies that operate affiliate programs in almost all online industries. Affiliate programs benefit both merchants and their affiliates. Many companies, big and small, are starting affiliate programs or joining programs as affiliates. Some examples of companies that offer affiliate programs are listed in Fig. 9.9.

Barnes & Noble™: Affiliate Program[12]

Barnes & Noble (**www.bn.com**), a clicks-and-mortar bookstore that offers an e-commerce site, has developed a free affiliate program. To join its *Affiliate Network*, potential affiliates must complete an online application. The application requests a few statistics, such as the number of unique visitors to the affiliate site per month, the date the site was established, its business tax classification and the number of page views logged each month. An e-mail notification of acceptance or rejection should be received within 48 hours. After the application process has been completed and accepted, the affiliate can go to **www.affiliate.net** and find the "Getting Started" section. Barnes & Noble gives affiliates many options for links, banners and virtual storefronts (allowing affiliates to sell Barnes & Noble's products from their sites). Affiliates can go to **affiliate.net** when they want to view reports on sales or click-throughs. The company will send a commission check to affiliates every three months. Barnes & Noble even pays commissions on gift certificates. Members of the Barnes & Noble affiliate program include CNN, *USA TODAY*, *The New York Times*, Lycos, *Fortune*, Discover Card, MSN Shopping, Ebates and AT&T.

    Barnes & Noble.com's *MyB&NLink* program allows people to earn commissions by placing a link to the Web site in their e-mails. Every time someone buys a product through the e-mail link, the affiliate receives a commission on the sale. The affiliate can either accept the commission or have it sent to one of the charities listed by **Barnes & Nobles.com**. Program restrictions include spamming, pornography, hate mail and illegal activities. **Barnes & Noble.com**'s legal disclaimer must be included in each e-mail. Sample e-mails, participating charities and answers to frequently asked questions can be viewed at the Barnes & Noble Web site (**www.bn.com**).

Industry	Merchants that Host Affiliate Programs
Internet Services	**Ask Jeeves (`www.ask.com`)** Ask Jeeves's affiliate program pays a commission every time someone uses its search engine as a result of a search box you place on your site. **America Online (`www.americaonline.com`)** The AOLAffiliateNetwork^{SM} offers members a commission for every person that signs up for AOL service through your site and uses the service for 90 days or more.
Music	**CDNow (`www.cdnow.com`)** CdNow, which sells CDs, videos and other gifts, offers search boxes and links to its affiliate members. The program pays commissions based on net sales, and the commission percentage is based on a sliding scale. **`sheetmusicplus.com`** This company sells sheet music and other musical products. Its affiliate program allows members to earn commissions on all products. **`MP3.com`** This comp'any offers a wide variety of music and technology. Its affiliate program pays commission on sales of CDs from its affiliates' sites.
Sports	**`GolfStore.com`** This company sells golf equipment. It offers a commission on all sales. **`MVP.com`** This site sells sporting goods online. Its affiliate program offers commissions based on sales. The commission percentage increases as the amount of sales increases. **`ALLBLACKBELT.com`** This site sells martial arts supplies online. The company offers affiliates commissions on sales made to referred customers and all future orders made by these customers.
Flower Delivery	**`1-800-Flowers.com` (`www.1800flowers.com`)** This site sells flowers, plants, gift baskets and gourmet treats. This company pays commissions on sales made through links on affiliate sites. LinkShare tracks the affiliate program. **`Flower.com`^{TM}** This site sells flowers and related products. It offers a pay-per-sale affiliate program.
Food and Wine	**`NoMeat.com`** This site is an online grocer for vegetarian products. It offers a pay-per-sale affiliate program. **`AAAFruitbaskets.com`** This site sells fruit baskets and offers delivery within 24 hours. Tracking is done through Commission Junction.

Fig. 9.9   Companies that use affiliate programs.

Industry	Merchants that Host Affiliate Programs

Books

fatbrain.com
This site sells books online. Its referral program is commission based and free to join. You can select a reading list and set up your own virtual store with tools provided by the company.

Borders.com
This site sells books, music and videos. The tracking of the program is performed by LinkShare.

Automobiles

CarPrices.com™
This site provides resources and information for people who are researching new cars. You can also buy a new car by starting a PriceWar™ or buy or sell a used car. Its affiliate program is a two-tiered, pay-per-lead program. It is free to join.

Autobytel.com
This site is a complete resource for information on new cars, used cars, auctions, financing, insurance, maintenance and warranties. *AutoPartners* are paid based on qualified leads.

Travel

Travelocity.com™
This site provides visitors with travel information and sells travel accommodations, such as airline tickets, hotel rooms, cruises and car rentals. It pays affiliates a certain amount for air travel or VIA Rail Canada tickets sold through affiliate sites.

Lodging.com
This site provides booking for lodging accommodations, including hotels and ski lodges. Its affiliate program pays commissions for bookings made through affiliate sites.

Art

Art.com^SM
This site sells art online. Its affiliate program is commission based, and affiliates are allowed to earn revenue by purchasing art through their own links.

ArtMecca.com
This site is an online art community. Its affiliate program pays commissions on sales made through search boxes placed on affiliate sites.

Grocery Stores

onlinefood.com
This site is an online delivery service of international and local food and wines. Its affiliate program is commission-based.

Peapod.com
This online grocery store pays affiliates for new customers that place an order, and then again when the same customers place their third orders.

Fig. 9.9   Companies that use affiliate programs.

Industry	Merchants that Host Affiliate Programs
Real Estate	**MortgageSelect.com** This site allows visitors to shop for and compare mortgage loans from competing companies. Its affiliate program pays when a visitor completes a loan application. **Domainia.com** This site provides information and tools for people interested in buying or selling real estate. It pays affiliates per click-through.
Clothing	Gap (**www.gap.com**) The Gap sells clothing online and offers its affiliates a percentage of the sales. Lands' End® (**www.landsend.com**) This site sells clothing and accessories online. It pays its affiliates a commission for every sale made through the affiliate link and also rewards affiliates for referring new customers.
Computers	Dell® (**www.dell.com**) This site sells computer products online. **Dell®Host.com**™ offers affiliates a commission on sales of Web Hosting Solutions. IBM® (**www.ibm.com**) This company sells computers and computer-related products. It rewards affiliates with a commission on sales. The amount depends on the type of product.
Careers	**Career.com**™ This site provides a list of job openings and allows companies to post positions available. It pays a commission on sales of memberships. **Vault.com** This site provides tools, information and job postings for careers. It pays affiliates a commission for each visitor that signs up for its free membership.
Pets	**PETsMART.com**™ This site sells pet supplies and provides information on the care and ownership of pets. It pays affiliates a commission on all sales and gives an additional reward for purchases by new customers. Petopia™ (**www.petopia.com**) This site sells pet products online and offers affiliates a commission on every sale originating at the affiliate site.
Cards	Hallmark (**www.hallmark.com**) Hallmark sells gifts and flowers online and provides free e-cards. Higher commissions are paid on gifts and flowers than on business-to-business cards. **ecards.com** This site provides e-cards for different occasions. Its affiliate program allows affiliates to create a card shop on their site or simply add links to **ecards.com**. Affiliates are rewarded for each card sent through their site and for each visitor who signs up at **ecards.com**.

Fig. 9.9   Companies that use affiliate programs.

9.11 Costs and Taxation of Affiliate Programs

There are costs involved with affiliate programs. The merchant is required to pay the affiliate, with the amount depending on the prespecified terms of the program. Merchants should consider that these costs can rise with increases in the number of click-throughs, purchases or other specified actions. Losing visitors through affiliate links can also be considered a cost. Other costs are those of developing and implementing the program.

Internet taxation, discussed in detail in Chapter 11, has become an issue for affiliate programs. While it is clear that the commissions collected by affiliates are considered income and will be taxed, the issue of state taxation on sales made through affiliates in states other than the state where the merchant is located has not been settled. If it is decided that affiliates are considered as agents or vendors of online retailers' products, then online retailers may be required to collect state tax on the sales made through affiliates in other states.[13] For example, if a merchant in Massachusetts made a sale through an affiliate in New Jersey, then the merchant would be required to collect the New Jersey sales tax.

9.12 Affiliate-Program Directories and Search Engines

Affiliate-program directories and *search engines* provide parties who are interested in becoming affiliates with programs that match their interests, and parties who are interested in finding affiliates with the different options available to them. Associate-It™ (**www.associate-it.com**) offers a directory for affiliate programs, based on categories such as those listed on its *Affiliate Corner* page (**www.associate-it.com/html/main/affiliate_corner**). The page offers *Popular Programs*, *New Programs* and *Two-Tier Programs* lists as well as a free *Affiliate Tribune Newsletter*, among other affiliate resources (Fig 9.10). *Popular Programs* lists popular affiliate programs by category (e.g., finance, advertising and careers). *New Programs* lists the latest additions to the directory. *Two-Tier Programs* lists the affiliate programs that offer a two-tiered reward structure, such as **CarPrices.com**™ and Amazing Media (**www.amazingmedia.com**).

AssociatePrograms.com is another directory for affiliate programs. Refer-it™ (**www.refer-it.com**) and **AffiliateFind.com** are search engines designed for people interested in affiliate programs. Affiliate Announce (**www.affiliate-announce.com**) will submit your affiliate program to many of the affiliate directories for a fee. The submissions are done manually and are tailored to meet the submission requirements of each directory.

In this chapter, we discuss affiliate programs, a form of marketing and advertising. We cover different reward structures and the importance of stickiness when becoming an affiliate. This chapter offers many examples of companies hosting affiliate programs and affiliate solution providers. In Chapter 10, e-Customer Relationship Management we discuss why effective customer relationship management is important for e-businesses and various methods of tracking and analyzing customers on the Internet. The chapter also includes discussions on personalization, sales force automation, e-contact centers and e-CRM technologies.

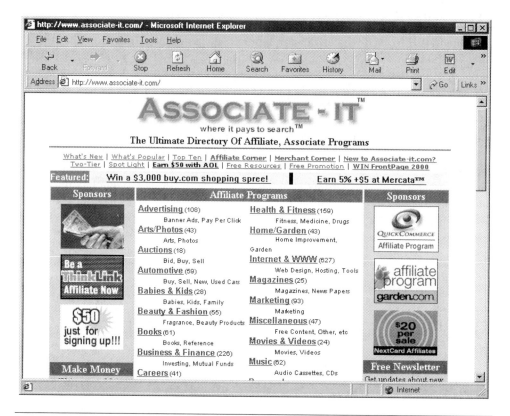

Fig. 9.10   Associate-It home page. (Courtesy of iSeed Inc.)

9.13 Internet and World Wide Web Resources

Directories and Search Engines for Affiliate Programs

www.associatesearch.com
This site is a directory for affiliate programs that allows you to search by category or topic.

www.referralmadness.com
This site provides a directory of affiliate programs and affiliate-program products.

www.affiliateadvisor.com
This site offers affiliate-program recommendations, a message board and information on tools and services.

www.webaffiliateprograms.com
This site is a directory for affiliate programs, listed by category.

www.clickquick.com
This site provides a free e-mail newsletter containing news and strategies related to affiliate programs. The site also provides reviews of many different affiliate programs.

www.associate-it.com
This site is an affiliate program directory. It offers lists of popular programs, new programs and two-tier programs, as well as a free newsletter. Its Top Ten List is published every two weeks.

www.associateprograms.com

This site is a directory of affiliate programs.

www.refer-it.com

This site offers a search engine for affiliate programs.

www.affiliatesdirectory.com

This site offers a directory for affiliates and merchants.

www.webmaster-programs.com

This site rates the top affiliate programs. It also offers tips on maximizing your program and the latest news about affiliate programs.

www.masterclick.8m.com

This site is a directory for affiliate and referral programs.

www.clickslink.com

This site provides a list of associate programs, a free newsletter, site promotion and discussion lists.

Affiliate-Program Solution Providers

www.quickclick.com

Visit this site for reviews of the top-paying and most effective affiliate and pay-per-action online advertising programs.

www.cashpile.com

This site aggregates information on affiliate programs. It also offers tutorials, news and links to top sites.

www.atWebsites.com/startaffiliate/index.html

This site provides a step-by-step explanation of how to set up an affiliate program.

www.plugingo.com

This company is an affiliate network provider.

Tracking Solutions

www.cybertrakker.com

This site offers software for tracking affiliates. It includes an integrated e-commerce system with a shopping cart and can support a two-tiered affiliate program.

www.affiliatezone.com

This company provides affiliate tracking software. Visit the Web site to see view an online example of the software's capabilities.

www.superscripts.com/scripts/agents.html

Agents of Fortune Software provides multilevel affiliate-program tracking.

SUMMARY

- An affiliate program is a form of partnership that is based on payment of commissions to affiliates for prespecified actions taken by visitors who click through from an affiliate site to a merchant site.
- Affiliates act as an extended sales force, assisting in building traffic, awareness, leads or even sales for merchants.
- The affiliate hosts advertising in return for a commission based on predetermined terms.
- The pay-per-click model rewards an affiliate for each click-through that is generated off a banner hosted by the affiliate. This system may not be accurate, because click-throughs can be generated falsely.

- The pay-per-lead model rewards affiliates based on the number of qualified leads generated.
- Qualified leads can include new customer registrations, having visitors sign up to receive a newsletter or having visitors use a free demo.
- The pay-per-sale model, also known as the commission-based model, compensates affiliates for each sale resulting from affiliate-hosted advertisements. Since a sale is normally more valuable than a lead or click-through for e-commerce sites, the reward to the affiliate is often larger than with the pay-per-lead and pay-per-click models.
- With the multi-tiered model, also known as a multi-level model, new affiliates are recruited by current affiliates, who are then rewarded with a percentage of the new affiliates' revenues.
- A two-tiered model involves only the original affiliate and its affiliate recruits.
- A hybrid model is a combination of models to reward affiliates.
- Combining different models may make an affiliate program more competitive with others, but it can also increase the cost, because merchants could be paying affiliates for more than one action.
- The CPM (cost-per-thousand) model requires the merchant to pay the affiliate a fee for every 1000 visitors that view the merchant's banner on the affiliate site.
- Information received from tracking an affiliate program can be used to analyze the program's effectiveness and to make improvements. Information gained from tracking can also be used to monitor payment schedules and identify the strongest affiliates.
- Affiliate solution providers provide accurate tracking and detailed reporting of your affiliates, recruit affiliates and merchants to participate in programs and distribute commissions. These providers may require a percentage of any commission paid to affiliates and can also require an annual or monthly fee.
- Web-site stickiness is the ability to keep people at a site and interested in its content.
- The extra revenue generated from affiliate programs may not be worth losing the visitors through links to other sites.
- Some companies are offering e-commerce capabilities to sites that want to participate in an affiliate program, but also want to keep visitors at their sites.
- If a company joins too many affiliate programs, it will have banners and links covering its site which will make it look cluttered and unprofessional, and diminish credibility with consumers.
- Knowing the target market can help a company choose related sites as affiliates.
- Options for becoming an affiliate include signing up directly at the merchant's site, using an affiliate solutions provider or joining through an affiliate directory.
- Becoming an affiliate is usually free when a company uses an affiliate solutions provider or when it joins individual affiliate programs.
- Note the reputation of the merchant; a company does not want people to be referred to a site that is inappropriate, has bad customer service or overprices its products or services.
- Determine what companies the merchant has already acquired as affiliates. This information can help a company determine whether the merchant's affiliate program is appropriate or not.
- With low barriers to entry, becoming an affiliate can be easy if a company does extensive research and creates a strategy that will generate income and not crowd its site.
- When placing your link on another site, an affiliate is advertising a company, therefore improving brand recognition and providing people with a direct channel to the company's site. By increasing traffic to its site, the company may be able to charge higher prices for advertising.
- When affiliates place merchant links on their sites, they are also providing an easy way for the visitors to leave their sites. Other merchant costs to consider include the costs of development and implementation of the program.

- The issue of state taxation on sales made through affiliates in states other than the state where the merchant is located has not been settled.
- Affiliate-program directories and search engines provide parties who are interested in becoming affiliates with programs that match their interests.

TERMINOLOGY

affiliate
affiliate program
affiliate solution provider
banner
brand recognition
click-through
commission-based model
CPM (cost-per-thousand) model
customer acquisition
directory for affiliate programs
hybrid model
lead generation
link
merchant
mirror page
multi-level model
multi-tiered model

newsgroups
partnering
pay-per-click model
pay-per-lead model
pay-per-sale model
qualified lead
reward structure
search engine for affiliate programs
stickiness
target market
taxation and affiliate programs
tracking
traffic generation
two-tiered model
virtual store
Web-based solution

SELF-REVIEW EXERCISES

9.1   State whether each of the following is true or false; if false, explain why.
   a) A two-tiered model is an affiliate-program structure involving pay-per-click and pay-per-lead models.
   b) It is usually free for companies and individuals to join affiliate programs through affiliate solution providers.
   c) CPM stands for Consumer Product Management.
   d) A hybrid model rewards affiliates on a pay-per-click basis.
   e) A reward structure determines how much revenue the merchant will receive.

9.2   Fill in the blanks in each of the following statements:
   a) _____ leads can include new customer registration, having visitors sign up to receive a newsletter or having visitors use a free demo.
   b) The model that rewards an affiliate for each click-through that is generated off a banner hosted by the affiliate is called the _____.
   c) A pay-per-sale model is also known as a _____.
   d) A _____ is a site that organizes and aggregates other sites and content.
   e) The _____ hosts advertising in return for a commission based on predetermined terms.

ANSWERS TO SELF-REVIEW EXERCISES

9.1   a) False. A two-tiered model is an affiliate structure that rewards affiliates for actions taken through their affiliate links and actions taken through new affiliates that have been recruited by the original affiliates. b) True. c) False. CPM stands for "cost per thousand" and is used in reference to advertising costs. d) False. A hybrid model is a model that uses a combination of models to reward its affiliates. e) False. A reward structure determines how much revenue the affiliate will receive.

9.2   a) Qualified. b) pay-per-click model. c) commission-based model. d) directory. e) merchant.

EXERCISES

9.3   State whether each of the following is true or false; if false, explain why.
a) An affiliate program is a form of public relations.
b) Few industries have companies that host affiliate programs.
c) Affiliate commissions are not taxable.
d) Creating mirror sites is a way to track your affiliates.
e) The company hosting the advertising in return for a commission based on predetermined terms is called the merchant.

9.4   Fill in the blanks in each of the following statements:
a) Allowing a company to advertise on your Web site in return for receiving money for users who click-through the advertisement to that company's site is an example of an _____ .
b) Another name for the pay-per-sale model is the _____ model.
c) _____ describes the ability to keep people at your site and interested in your content.
d) Companies that can fulfill all of your affiliate-program needs are called _____ .
e) Three major online affiliate solutions providers include _____ , _____ and _____ .

9.5   Define the following terms:
a) Web-based solution.
b) Commission-based model.
c) Pay-per-lead.
d) CPM.
e) Affiliate.

9.6   Research three Web sites that offer affiliate programs and that have not been discussed in this chapter. Discuss the similarities and differences between the programs.
a) Can companies join the affiliate programs for free? If not, how much does each cost?
b) What are the requirements for becoming an affiliate for each program?
c) What type of affiliate program model(s) does each use? Explain in detail. Are the rewards the same for each type of product or service?
d) For each of the companies, discuss which affiliate reward structure is most appropriate and why.
e) Which company offers the most rewarding affiliate program? Why? Which program do you think generates the most revenue for the merchant? Why?

9.7   Visit the following sites and state what affiliate program model(s) they use.
a) American Greetings (**www.americangreetings.com**).
b) NextCard® VISA (**www.nextcard.com**).
c) 1StopAuto (**www.1stopauto.com**).
d) Paytrust (**www.paytrust.com**).
e) **Mall.com**.

9.8   Visit two directories not discussed in the chapter. Evaluate the benefits of each and determine the better of the two.
a) Which site displays more affiliate program options?
b) Does each site recommend particular affiliate programs over others?
c) Does either site categorize the top affiliate programs? If so, what are the top three programs on the list?
d) Does each site provide useful information on affiliate programs? Explain.

e) How does a company get listed in these directories? How much does it cost?

f) Overall, which of the sites is better? What made you come to this conclusion?

9.9 (*Semester Project*) Try joining **BarnesandNoble.com**'s *MyB&NLink program*, which allows you to earn commissions by placing a link to **www.bn.com** in your e-mails.

a) Discuss the process of signing up. What fields were required?

b) What are the program restrictions?

c) How could this program be improved? Will you continue to participate?

d) Do you think that Barnes & Noble will profit from this type of advertising? Does the program help develop customer loyalty for Barnes & Noble? Why or why not?

9.10 Choose an industry (such as booksellers) and research companies online that belong to that industry. What kind of affiliate programs do they offer? Select three companies within a certain industry, and compare their programs and their contracts.

a) Which one has the best rewards?

b) Do the reward programs seem similar among companies within the industry? Compare these programs.

c) What industries do you think will profit the most from the use of affiliate programs? Which industries will pay higher commissions? Why?

WORKS CITED

The notation **<www.domain-name.com>** indicates that the citation is for information found at that Web site.

1. S. Sweeney, *101 Ways To Promote Your Web Site* (Gulf Breeze: Maximum Press, 2000) 269.

2. G. Helmstetter, G. and P. Metivier, *Affiliate Selling* (New York: John Wiley & Sons, Inc., 2000) 21.

3. D. Pescovitz, "Join The Club," *The Industry Standard* 8 November 1999: 172.

4. D. Gray, *The Complete Guide to Associate and Affiliate Programs on the Net* (New York: McGraw Hill, 2000) 61.

5. D. Gray, *The Complete Guide to Associate and Affiliate Programs on the Net* (New York: McGraw Hill, 2000) 5.

6. D. Pescovitz, "Join The Club," *The Industry Standard* 8 November 1999: 171.

7. S. Sweeney, *101 Ways to Promote Your Web Site* (Gulf Breeze: Maximum Press, 2000) 270.

8. D. Pescovitz, "Join The Club," *The Industry Standard* 8 November 1999: 174.

9. **<www.vstore.com>**.

10. B. Tedeschi, "E-Commerce Report," *The New York Times* 6 November 2000: C16.

11. **<www.amazon.com>**.

12. **<www.bn.com>**.

13. D. Hardesty, "Nexus from Affiliate Programs," *EcommerceTax.com* 9 April 2000.

10

e-Customer Relationship Management

Objectives

- To understand the importance of customer relationship management.
- To explore various ways to collect and analyze customer data.
- To discuss personalization efforts and opportunities.
- To examine the transformation of the call center.
- To explore the tools used for customer relationship management.

To write it, it took three months; to conceive it—three minutes; to collect the data in it—all my life.
F. Scott Fitzgerald

Friendship is one of the most tangible things in a world which offers fewer and fewer supports.
Kenneth Branagh

Well, if I called the wrong number, why did you answer the phone?
James Thurber

A friend may well be reckoned the masterpiece of Nature.
Ralph Waldo Emerson

Is it not rather what we expect in men, that they should have numerous strands of experience lying side by side and never compare them with each other?
George Eliot

Outline

10.1　Introduction
10.2　Tracking and Analyzing Data
　　10.2.1　Log-File Analysis
　　10.2.2　Data Mining
　　10.2.3　Customer Registration
　　10.2.4　Cookies
10.3　Personalization
　　10.3.1　Intelligent Agents
　　10.3.2　Personalization vs. Privacy
10.4　Contact Centers
　　10.4.1　Frequently Asked Questions (FAQs)
　　10.4.2　e-Mail
　　10.4.3　Online Text Chatting
　　10.4.4　Speech Synthesis and Recognition; Natural Language Processing
　　10.4.5　Voice Communications
　　10.4.6　Sales-Force Automation
10.5　Business-to-Business e-CRM
10.6　Complete e-CRM Solutions
10.7　Internet and World Wide Web Resources

Summary • Terminology • Self-Review Exercises • Answers to Self-Review Exercises • Exercises • Works Cited • Recommended Reading

10.1 Introduction

Today's world of e-business and e-commerce has become one of intense competition. It is often difficult to distinguish an e-business from its competitors. Offering customers convenience, personalization and excellent service plays a key role in the success and differentiation of many online businesses. *Customer relationship management (CRM)* focuses on providing and maintaining quality service for customers, by effectively communicating and delivering products, services, information and solutions to address customer problems, wants and needs. CRM can include *call handling* (the maintenance of outbound and inbound calls from customers and service representatives), *sales tracking* (the tracking and recording of all sales made) and *transaction support* (the technology and personnel used for conducting business transactions), as well as many other functions. eCRM is the application of CRM to an e-business' strategy and includes the personalization and customization of customers' experiences and interactions with a Web site, call center or any other method of customer contact with the e-business. The term iCRM (Internet customer relationship management) can be used interchangeably with eCRM for e-business customer relationship management. To provide quality CRM, a company must design a plan with defined goals and execute the plan with cooperation from the marketing and information technology departments. Business analysts should review all plan details and review data, such as drops in costs or increases in customer complaints, to refine the CRM system.

eCRM is essential to the success of an e-business because the relationship between the merchant and its customers is distant; you may never see or even talk to the other party. Therefore, it is important to know more about the other party to establish and maintain a relationship, one that will bring customers back for repeat purchases. It is far less expensive to keep current customers than it is to acquire new ones.

e-Fact 10.1

According to the Boston Consulting Group, the cost of acquiring a new online customer is approximately thirty-four dollars, while using the online channel to market to a current customer costs around seven dollars.[1]

Bain & Company's research demonstrated that repeat shoppers accounted for 57 percent more revenue than customers who purchased only one time.[2] Repeat customers can have a higher lifetime value than one-time buyers. A customer's *lifetime value* is the expected amount of profit derived from a customer over a designated length of time. If a company can turn a first-time buyer into a repeat customer, it can spread initial acquisition costs over the lifetime of the person as a customer. For example, it takes two-and-a-half years on average for a regular **Amazon.com** customer to yield a profit.[3] Customers can also have a negative lifetime value. This occurs when the acquisition and maintenance costs are greater than the revenue generated by the customer. Companies should evaluate the potential to profit from this customer to decide if the company should continue to invest more marketing and customer service dollars into this relationship. Visit **www.bah.com/viewpoints/insights/cmt_clv_2.html** for information on customer lifetime value. For more information on marketing to current and prospective customers, see Chapter 8, Internet Marketing.

10.2 Tracking and Analyzing Data

One of the principal methods used by online advertisers, online communities and online businesses to keep track of their visitors' behavior is to employ *tracking devices*. Data gathered through log-file analysis, data mining, customer registration, cookies and other tracking devices can be used to personalize each visitor's experience, find trends in customer use and measure the effectiveness of a Web site over time. These tracking devices are covered in detail in the following sub-sections. Proper analysis of data and the implementation of responsive measures can be used to increase marketing campaign efficiency and lead to greater customer satisfaction.

Advertisers and Web-site owners can use *ID cards*, *click-through banner advertisements* and *Web bugs* to track visitors. An ID card enables information to be sent to your computer from a Web site. Your name and e-mail address are not included. Only the numerical address of your PC on the Internet, your browser and your operating system are necessary for your computer to retrieve information.[4]

Click-through advertisements enable visitors to view a service or product by clicking the advertisement. This also serves as a tracking device, as advertisers can learn what sites generate the most click-through sales and which advertisements are most effective.[5] Advertising is also discussed in Chapter 8, Internet Marketing.

Web Bugs, or *clear GIFs* (a type of image file), are embedded in an image on the screen. Site owners allow companies, especially advertising companies, to hide these information-collecting programs on various parts of their sites. Every time a user requests a page with a Web bug on it, the Web bug sends a request to the Web bug's company's server, which then tracks where the user goes on the Web. This method of tracking allows affiliates to gather consumer information.[6] For example, imagine that an advertising company is allowed to place Web bugs on its client's Web sites. If you visited one of these sites with a Web bug, information would be recorded on the advertising company's server about your visit. Then, if you went to another site that had the advertising agency's Web bug on it, your visit would also be recorded. This allows the advertising company to build up customer profiles over time. The following sections cover tracking and analysis including log-file analysis, data mining, customer registration and cookies.

10.2.1 Log-File Analysis

When you visit a site, you are submitting a request for information from the site's server. The request is recorded in a log file. *Log files* consist of data generated by site visits, including each visitor's location, IP address, time of visit, frequency of visits and other information. *Log-file analysis* organizes and summarizes the information contained in the log files. For an example of log-file analysis products, see the WebTrends® feature.

The analysis of log files can be used to determine the number of unique visitors. This information is useful for advertising purposes (as discussed in Chapter 8, Internet Marketing). Log-file analysis can show you the Web-site traffic effects of changing your Web site or advertising campaign. Knowing your visitors' origins can assist in better defining your target markets. For example, if you notice that you have many international visitors but you market to local regions, you may want to consider defining a target market that includes these visitors and modifying your site accordingly. (For more on target markets, see Chapter 8, Internet Marketing.)

10.2.2 Data Mining

Although log-file analysis is a good way to determine Web-traffic statistics, eventually you will want to know more about your customers. *Data mining* uses algorithms and statistical tools to find patterns in data gathered from customer visits. Although businesses are "data rich," they often do not use their data to their best advantage. It would be extremely costly and time consuming to go through large amounts of data manually. Businesses can use data-mining to analyze trends within their companies or in the marketplace—information that in turn helps them market their products and run their businesses more effectively. Uncovered patterns can improve CRM and marketing campaigns by helping businesses better understand their customers. Businesses can also discover a need for new or improved services or products by studying the patterns of customers' purchases.

Log-file Analysis Products: WebTrends®[7]

WebTrends (**www.webtrends.com**) provides solutions for tracking visitors (Fig. 10.1). It offers products that allow you to profile site visitors and measure the effectiveness of each of your Web pages. After downloading a WebTrends product, the user must specify the source of the log files, types of reports and location where data is stored. Then the analysis is conducted automatically. The program can be scheduled to analyze data during non-business hours to maximize its efficiency. The collected information can be used to evaluate e-commerce methods, customer service and Web-site design.

WebTrends offers free-trial versions of many of its products. Once you have downloaded and installed a WebTrends product, it will use your log files to show you the effectiveness of your site. Figure 10.2 shows a graphical example of the analysis from a WebTrends product. If your log files are not available, you can access and manipulate sample log files provided by WebTrends. You can view the report in one of many applications including Microsoft Word, Excel, HTML and text format.

The WebTrends program reports its progress as it analyzes the data. Depending on the output format you have chosen, graphical interpretation of the log files will be presented. You can view demographic and geographic data, technical analysis of the Web site's effectiveness, *top-referring sites*—sites that most frequently refer visitors to your site—and many other analyses that can help you improve your site.

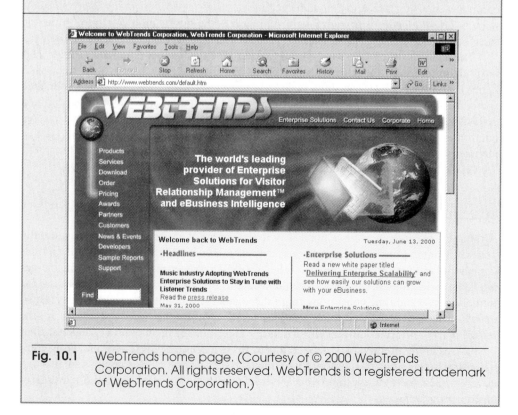

Fig. 10.1   WebTrends home page. (Courtesy of © 2000 WebTrends Corporation. All rights reserved. WebTrends is a registered trademark of WebTrends Corporation.)

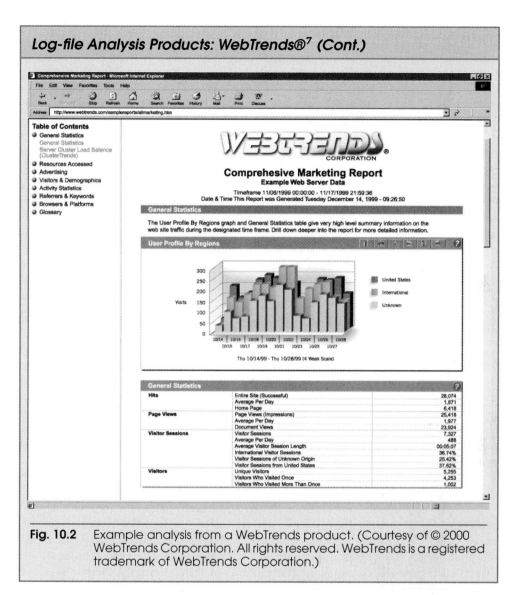

Fig. 10.2　Example analysis from a WebTrends product. (Courtesy of © 2000 WebTrends Corporation. All rights reserved. WebTrends is a registered trademark of WebTrends Corporation.)

HNC Software offers the *DataBase Mining® Marksman* (**www.hncmarksman.com**) product, which mines data to provide marketers with statistical models and analyses of their customers and marketing campaigns. For example, it can help you determine the correct target audience for a marketing campaign. HNC Software offers a thirty-day free trial for those who fill out a form and qualify. Data Distilleries (**www.datadistilleries.com**) also offers customer relationship management services and products, including its data mining software called *DD/Marketer*. Visit **www.angoss.com/ksprod/kspage.htm** to download a free educational version of *KnowledgeSEEKER*, a data mining product offered by ANGOSS Software Corporation. Other sites offering data mining services are **www.appliedmetrix.com**, **www.datainstincts.com** and **www.smart-drill.com**.

10.2.3 Customer Registration

Customer registration—requiring visitors to fill out a form with personal information that is then used to create a profile—is recommended when it will provide a benefit to the customer. Every time customers log on to a site using usernames and passwords, their actions can be tracked and stored in the company's database. This information helps businesses customize their Web sites, customer service and marketing strategies.

Getting customers to register can be difficult. People are often reluctant to fill out a form requiring personal information. The best way to start building a customer profile is to require minimal information, such as a username, password and e-mail address. You should give potential customers an incentive to register. If the site offers an online service, offer a free-trial or a free demonstration to familiarize the user with the service. To entice consumers to register, businesses selling products can offer promotions, such as free gift certificates, free calling cards or discounts on online purchases. The registration process should be quick and easy, otherwise the consumer may go elsewhere.

After potential customers have registered, you should send them e-mails including their usernames and welcoming them to your Web site. Some sites ask each user to provide a specific question to which only the user will know the answer—if users forget their passwords, they will be asked the questions. Upon receipt of the correct answers, the site e-mails users their passwords.

10.2.4 Cookies

A *cookie* is a text file stored by a Web site on an individual's personal computer that allows a site to track the actions of a visitor. The first time a user visits a Web site, the user's computer may receive a cookie. This cookie is reactivated each time the computer revisits that site. The information collected is intended to be an anonymous account of log-on times, the length of stay at the site, purchases made on the site, the site previously visited and the site visited next. Although the cookie resides on an individual's hard drive, it does not interact with other information stored on the system. Cookies can only be read by the host that sets them on a person's computer.

Cookies can be beneficial to the customer. They record passwords for returning visitors, keep track of shopping-cart materials and register preferences. Cookies also help businesses by allowing them to address their target markets with greater accuracy. However, these advantages may be gained at the expense of customer privacy. For a discussion of the inappropriate uses of cookies and the consequences of such actions, see Chapter 11, Legal and Ethical Issues; Internet Taxation.

Suppose you are browsing the Web for the lowest price on a digital camera. You might register for a contest or make a purchase, leaving your mailing address and some other personal information. As you travel from site to site, you might notice the advertisements are for companies that sell digital cameras. If you return to a former site, you might be welcomed by name. Potentially, the sites you have visited belong to a direct advertising network, and, rather than one site gathering this information about you and using it in the future, information from several sites will be used to create a *customer profile*.

This type of tracking also can be beneficial to the customer. After you complete your first purchase at **Amazon.com**, all subsequent purchases can be made without having to re-enter your mailing address and contact information. If you are looking for a specific item, advertisements that appear along the way can lead you in the right direction.

Cookies can be misleading to the site that places the cookie on a computer. Different people may use the same computer to surf the Web, and the cookie will not be able to differentiate the users. Therefore, some cookies may collect information from each user. The combination of information may give inaccurate information to the company that placed the cookie on the computer.

10.3 Personalization

Personalization uses information from tracking, mining and data analysis to customize a person's interactions with a company's products, services, Web site and employees. Consumers and companies can benefit from the unique treatment resulting from personalization. Providing content of special interest to your visitor can help establish a relationship that you can build upon each time that person returns to your site. By targeting consumers with personal offers, advertisements, promotions and service, customers will enjoy the individual attention and may become more loyal. Originally, the Internet lacked personal assistance when compared with the individual service often experienced in bricks-and-mortar stores. Sophisticated technology helps many Web sites offer a personal touch to their visitors. For example, **Amazon.com** offers customer registration and provides recommended products and a personalized greeting to its customers. Personalization is important for Internet marketing, and especially for managing customer relationships to increase customer loyalty.

Collaborative filtering compares ratings of a present user's interests and decisions with those of past users to offer content relative to the present user's interests. Music and book sites often use collaborative filtering to make recommendations to their customers. Visit **shadow.ieor.berkeley.edu/humor/info.html** to experience personalization resulting from collaborative filtering. Rate the jokes that are displayed, and then register for free to receive jokes recommended using collaborative filtering. This site also offers links to other sites containing collaborative filtering information. *Rules-based personalization* is the delivery of personalized content based on the subjection of a user's profile to set rules or assumptions.[8]

Many sites offer personalization features. Excite[SM] (**www.excite.com**) is a search engine that offers *My Excite Start Page*. This allows you to select the content and style that appears on your Excite home page. You can choose your Start Page greeting and colors as well as receive free e-mail, chatting and voicemail. Visit **www.excite.com** to sign up for free and see how personalization can deliver content relevant to your interests and specifications. Excite also offers the option to keep a planner and receive e-mails reminding you of important dates, events or other appointments. You can have your Excite information synchronized with Microsoft Outlook® and with wireless devices such as Palm™ hand-held computers.

HomePage.com offers outsourced home-page development. *ePage[SM]*, a solution from **HomePage.com**, works with a company and its customers to personalize their Web-interaction experiences. **HomePage.com** develops architecture that works with your infrastructure to implement personalization technology and services. Each customer's personal page provides access to your product and service information and customer support. Through these pages, you can offer personalized promotions and targeted marketing. Involving customers in the personalization process makes them feel more comfortable with, and more in control of, their Web-site visits. Other sites that provide personalization products include **www.allaire.com**, **www.blazesoft.com**, **www.netgen.com** and **www.personify.com**.

10.3.1 Intelligent Agents

An *intelligent agent* is a program that can be used on the Web to assist a user in the completion of a specified task, including searching for information and automating tasks. For example, this can save consumers time by helping them find the lowest price for a certain product. Without the use of an intelligent agent, the consumer would have to visit many sites that carry the product to determine which site offers the lowest price. Intelligent agents can also be used as personalization mechanisms by providing content related to the user's interests.

Some intelligent agents can observe your Web-surfing habits and purchasing behavior to recommend new products to buy or sites to visit. They can help e-businesses offer a level of customer service similar to person-to-person interaction. For example, suppose a customer in Boston is shopping for a new CD player and is looking at 5-disk CD players. In the past, this customer had purchased a receiver and a dual-cassette player, both top-of-the-line. The customer also bought a large number of CDs, including three Rolling Stones CDs. Based on the consumer's buying history, an intelligent agent could recommend a variety of top-of-the-line 5 disk CD players. It could also suggest a 100-disk CD changer that has just gone on sale and is now the same price as the 5-disk changer. Since the customer seems to be a fan of the Rolling Stones, who have just announced they are playing in Boston in a few months, the intelligent agent could inform the customer of the upcoming tour in Boston and provide an option for buying tickets to the show. For another example demonstrating the use of personalization agents, see the **Priceline.com** feature in Chapter 2, e-Business Models.

10.3.2 Personalization vs. Privacy

Some people feel that personalization represents an invasion of their privacy, whereas others may not even be aware that data is being collected and personalization is occurring at a site. At the heart of this debate are the technologies allowing personalization. For example, cookies allow e-commerce sites to record visitor behavior and identify more valuable customers. Many customers are not aware that cookies are being stored on their computers as these customers browse particular sites. Cookies and privacy are discussed in depth in Chapter 11, Legal and Ethical Issues: Internet Taxation. Marketers must be discrete about the way they use personal information gained from data research. The *Personalization Consortium*, a newly formed alliance of major Web sites, attempts to accommodate those individuals who prefer to have their Web experiences tailored. In June 2000, the Consortium released a study suggesting that most users actually prefer to have their information stored and actions tracked. The results of the study can be viewed at **www.personalization.org**.[9] While some users may want their Web experiences personally tailored, others consider having their actions recorded to be a violation of their privacy. If used properly and with consumers' privacy rights in mind, personalization technology can establish solid relationships with customers by giving them what they want, when they want it. Privacy and legal issues concerning personalization technology are discussed in detail in Chapter 11, Legal and Ethical Issues; Internet Taxation.

10.4 Contact Centers

Customers should also be able to conduct transactions and get answers to their questions through a call center. Traditional call centers house customer-service representatives who can be reached by an 800 number. Companies that have multimedia contact centers allow customers with Internet access to contact customer service representatives through e-mail, online text chatting or real-time voice communications. Whether called a *call center*, an *e-contact center* or a *multimedia contact center*, the purpose is the same—to provide a personal customer service experience that is individualized to each customer's needs and questions.

To provide customer service representatives with a comprehensive view of their consumers, companies are trying to integrate all customer service functions. In the past, customer service representatives were considered costly and encouraged to keep the length of their calls to a minimum.[10] Now the Internet can be used as an additional customer contact option, creating an opportunity to personalize a customer's experience, which can increase loyalty and sales.[11]

Multimedia contact centers will change the culture of customer service representatives, who will have to become more technically knowledgeable to handle all the forms of customer contact. The issue will no longer be to answer the question in the shortest amount of time. The customer service representative (CSR) will have to provide a highly personalized experience that provides customer satisfaction.[12] The new forms of customer contact can decrease costs by decreasing phone bills and increasing the number of customer inquiries that one service representative can handle.

3Com™ (**www.3com.com**) offers *Contact Advantage*™, a contact center solution. The solution offers *IP Contact* (voice, phone and fax services), *Web Contact* (Web chat, click-to-talk and call back) and *Ultimate Contact* (integrates all customer contact channels to provide comprehensive view of customer). This solution is targeted for small-to-medium-sized businesses.

Some companies may choose to outsource contact center services. This may be appropriate if a company cannot afford to implement a contact center due to the costs of equipment, office space, service representatives and technical support. Stream International, Inc. (**www.stream.com/Stream.nsf**) offers companies outsourced technical support.[13] Other companies offering outsourced contact center services include Sitel® Corporation (**www.sitel.com**) and TeleTech (**www.teletech.com**). Sitel Corporation has over seventy centers for customer management and handles customers from around the world. TeleTech uses its "multi-channel customer-interaction platform," *CyberCare*™, in its "customer-interaction centers." This gives service representatives a single view of a customer, regardless of the method used to contact the representative.

10.4.1 Frequently Asked Questions (FAQs)

A *Frequently Asked Questions (FAQ)* section on your Web site will help customers find answers to some of their questions, freeing up time for your customer-service representatives to handle questions that can not be answered without human interaction. Self-service FAQ software and Web FAQ software assist companies in providing helpful answers to common customer questions and track visitor usage of these services.[14] In addition to providing a FAQ section, you should place your phone numbers and appropriate e-mail addresses nearby, allowing people browsing the FAQ section to contact you for additional information if necessary because FAQs will not be able to answer every visitor's question. Another option to complement your FAQ section is to include a search engine on your site, allowing users to type in a word or phrase to find on your site information relevant to their particular question.

e-Fact 10.2

The average cost per customer interaction for customer service through an 800-number can range from ten dollars to thirty-five dollars. E-mail correspondence for customer service can cost from three dollars to ten dollars per contact, while self-service over the Web costs approximately one dollar per contact. These figures are according to Forrester Research and Giga Information Group.[15]

10.4.2 e-Mail

If a company is not ready to invest in a complete CRM solution, e-mail can provide a less expensive customer service solution. E-mails sent to thank consumers for their purchases and to offer new products will show your customers that you appreciate their patronage and are working hard to offer them the products they need. Customers can use e-mail to ask questions or comment on your company's services or products.

Using e-mail as part of your customer service is important, but it is only appropriate if you have the resources to handle the demands. The Internet creates fierce competition between companies, and customers may be not be willing to wait long for an e-mail reply.[16] Ideally, a response to a customer's e-mail inquiry should be completed within forty-eight hours.

e-Fact 10.3

Almost fifty percent of companies studied did not reply to e-mails sent from customers in five days or less, according to Jupiter Communications.[17]

Brightware® (**www.brightware.com**) offers many CRM tools. *Email Assistance* can be used to manage your e-mail customer service. *Brightware Answer*™ consists of automated and assisted-answer options. *Automated Answer* provides fast responses sent directly to the senders of e-mails containing typical questions. *Assisted Answer* is used for the more difficult inquiries. When an e-mail of this nature is received, Assisted Answer scripts a possible answer and sends it to someone within the company to review before it gets send to the inquirer. Other companies offering e-mail products and services include RightNow® Technologies (**www.rightnowtech.com**), Servicesoft® (**www.servicesoft.com**) and Delano (**www.delanotech.com**).

10.4.3 Online Text Chatting

Online text chatting provides a real-time form of communication between customers and service representatives. Customers that may have decided to leave a site because they could not get an answer will have the option to contact a service representative immediately if the company offers text chatting. Some service representatives may be able to handle more than one text chat at a time, while traditional service representatives could normally assist only one customer at a time.[18] By clicking on a button that brings up a small window for text chatting, customers can continue to view the Web site as they chat with a service representative. This can allow the service representative to see what the customers are looking at as they pose their questions. Text chatting is "instantaneous;" however, if representatives are busy with many chat sessions, a customer may experience a delay in the responses. Text chatting can also lose the dynamics of human communication because voice intonations and expressions are lost, and the meaning of a message may be misinterpreted when it is written in text and read by a customer service representative.

FaceTime Communications (**www.facetime.com**) offers the *FaceTime Instant Customer Suite* that includes chatting and e-mail management capabilities. Its Instant Messaging option enables e-businesses to register a *BizBuddy* name, allowing customers who use AOL Instant Messenger[SM] to add an e-business' *BizBuddy* name to their buddy lists. Customers can chat with service representatives, and the e-business can determine which customers are online. This allows the company to target online customers with specific offers. The suite also offers text-chatting capabilities, allowing customers who do not use AOL Instant Messenger to communicate over the Internet in real-time with the *FaceTime Chat* system. This system uses *FaceTime Messenger* which provides customers with a connection to service representatives from your site using Java or HTML versions of the chat service, depending on which is compatible with the customer's browser. To view a Flash® demo of the *FaceTime Message Exchange*, go to **www.facetime.com/products/ demo**. You can also try the service by chatting with FaceTime Communications customer service representatives. CLICKiCHAT (**www.clickichat.com**) also offers online text chatting capabilities and provides companies with the option to send a transcript of the text chat by e-mail, print or both to the visitor (Fig. 10.3). LivePerson[SM] (**www.liveperson.com**) offers text chatting in many languages including Finnish, Chinese, Dutch, Spanish, Italian, French and English. Visit these sites to try demonstrations of human-to-human communication using online text chatting over the Web.

With text chatting and streaming media becoming popular, the future of customer service chatting may include live video-conferencing, allowing the customer service representative and customer to see each other as they text chat or use voice communications. This will help create an extraordinary level of personalization. Voice-over IP, a technology allowing voice communications over the Internet, is discussed in Section 6.4.5, Voice Communications.

10.4.4 Speech Synthesis and Recognition; Natural Language Processing

Speech synthesis is the process of having a computer convert text to voice. The mechanical-sounding voices that result from speech synthesis have some human intonations; however, as technology improves, speech synthesis will sound more realistic. The costs of these services are relatively low. Visit **www.softseek.com/Utilities/ Voice_Recognition_and_Text_To_Speech** to try speech synthesis and speech recognition products and services. This page lists links for freeware, shareware and software. Visit **www.bell-labs.com/project/tts/voices.html** and **www.cstr.ed.ac.uk/projects/festival/userin.html** to try speech synthesis for free. You can type text into the designated box and click a button to hear your text read back to you. Each site gives you the choice of listening to your text read in different voices, such as male or female voice or in foreign accents.

Speech recognition is when a computer listens to speech and is able to convert what is being said into text. An example of the use of speech recognition can be found in some luxury vehicles which are equipped with voice-activated controls. The vehicle's computer system recognizes certain commands such as "radio on" or "air conditioning off" and responds to them appropriately. However, different pronunciations, accents, intonations and languages can create difficulties when using this technology.

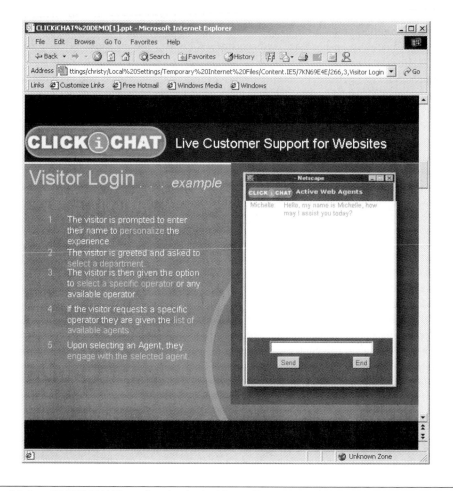

Fig. 10.3   CLICKiCHAT's online text chatting. (Courtesy of StartCall Corporation.)

Natural language processing attempts to understand text and respond with a proper answer or comment. Ask Jeeves™ (**www.ask.com**) uses natural language processing. This search engine allows you to submit requests in the form of typed-in questions. It then displays results that attempt to answer that question (Figs. 10.4 and 10.5).

Although Ask Jeeves narrows searches and allows you to search by submitting a natural-language question, the results are not always relevant to the questions asked. Ask Jeeves also offers sites the option to license its *Ask Jeeves Business Solutions*. Also visit **www-ai.ijs.si/eliza/eliza.html** to chat with a natural language-processing program named Eliza. Eliza attempts to respond to your comments and questions in a conversational manner. Artificial Life (**www.artificiallife.com**) is another company that uses artificial intelligence and natural-language processing to offer solutions such as *ALife e-CRM*™, which gives companies the option to add a bot to their sites that can provide answers and guidance to visitors questions and comments. Visit the site to view examples of their products (see the Microsoft® Agent feature for another example of a speech synthesis and recognition product).

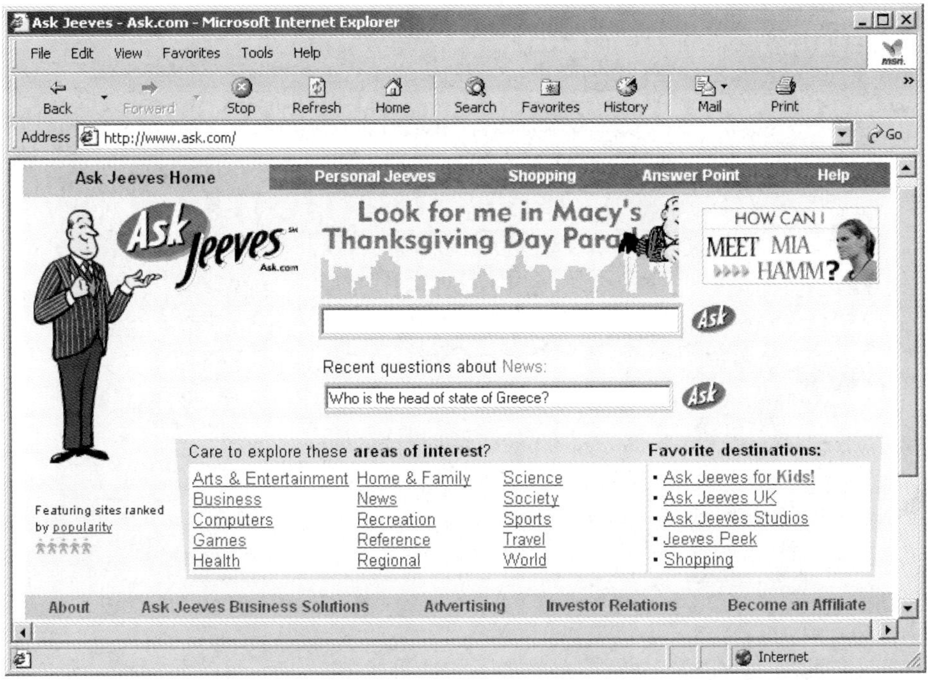

Fig. 10.4   Ask Jeeves™ home page with a sample query. (Courtesy of Ask Jeeves, Inc.)

When a natural language comment or question is posed to a computer over a phone or directly from a person, the audio must first be converted to text through *continuous speech recognition (CSR)*. CSR allows a person to speak fluently and quickly to a computer without losing the accuracy of the translation into text.

Speech technology will have a large impact on the future of CRM applications. Imagine having a question about a product or service at three o'clock in the morning, when customer-service representatives may not be available. What if you could go online, type in your question at the company's Web site and get a clear, concise answer? It would also be convenient to be able to pick up a phone, ask a question and get a correct reply from a computer using speech recognition and speech synthesis. This technology will provide more accurate automated answers to customers' inquiries and will allow companies to cut customer service costs as the technology advances.

10.4.5 Voice Communications

Although many forms of communication are used today for customer service (such as e-mail and text chatting), human-to-human voice communication is often preferred by a customer. The Internet provides another channel for human-to-human voice communication.

e-Fact 10.4

Without enough human interaction, sixty-three percent of Internet users will not make an online purchase, according to a study by Yankelovich Partners.[19]

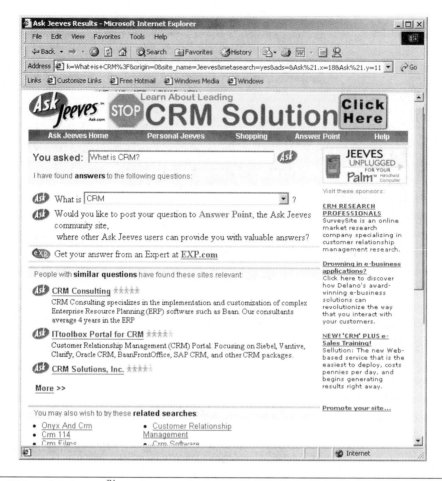

Fig. 10.5   Ask Jeeves™ results page from sample query. (Courtesy of Ask Jeeves, Inc.)

Voice over Internet Protocol (VoIP) products and applications allow people to communicate with speech over the Internet. *Internet telephony* allows people to make phone calls over the Internet (see Chapter 5, Internet Hardware, Software and Communications). The quality of the transmission has yet to match that of a regular telephone call; however many companies are using PC-to-phone communication because it is of higher quality than PC-to-PC (where a person speaks from a computer to another person who responds through another computer).

PC-to-phone (computer-to-phone) voice communication allows a visitor to a Web site to continue browsing while talking to a customer-service representative over the Internet. The customer-service representative speaks by phone to a visitor who listens through speakers or headphones connected to a computer. The visitor responds by speaking into a microphone connected to the computer. This allows dial-up Internet users who have only one phone line to chat with a customer-service representative without having to disconnect from the Internet. Companies can use current customer-service representatives who already service 800 numbers to assist online visitors using PC-to-phone technology.[20]

Microsoft® Agent: A Speech Synthesis and Recognition Product

Microsoft Agent is an exciting technology for adding interactive animated characters in a Windows application or World Wide Web page. You can choose from four different animated characters, including *Peedy the Parrot, Genie, Merlin* and *Robby the Robot*. These characters allow users to interact with the application using natural human-communication techniques. The character accepts both mouse and keyboard interactions, speaks (if a compatible text-to-speech engine is installed) and also supports speech recognition (i.e., hears—if a compatible speech recognition engine is installed). With these capabilities, your Web pages can "speak" to visitors and can actually respond to their voice commands. You can also create your own characters with the help of the *Microsoft Agent Character Editor* and the *Microsoft Linguistic Sound Editing tool* (both free for download from the Microsoft Agent Web site, **msdn.microsoft.com/workshop/imedia/agent**). A detailed exercise at the end of the chapter walks you through downloading and using the Microsoft Agent characters.

HearMe™ (**www.hearme.com**) offers e-businesses the opportunity to provide live-voice communication over the Web. Companies can add a *Click&Talk™* button to their site that allows customers to speak with representatives while continuing to browse the site. More than one customer-service representative can speak with the visitor at a time, if additional expertise on a certain customer comment or question is required. Customers can also experience the added convenience of having the service representatives call them back at a later time. Visit **www.hearme.com** for an interactive demonstration of HearMe's services.

RealCall® Alert™ is a service that allows customers to connect to your customer-service representatives from your Web site through a callback button that you place on your site.[21] This is done by using HTML and RealCall's *wizard*—a software program that walks you through the steps needed to complete a task on your computer. It requires no new equipment. When the user wants to speak to a person, the user clicks on the button. The request is sent through the Web to a RealCall server, which then sends the request to the Web-site owner's phone. From here, the owner can call the customer to assist them. Instead of calling the company and holding on the line for someone to help them, consumers can request that customer-service representatives call them immediately, or in fifteen minutes (Fig. 10.6). Visit **www.realcall.com** to try a live demonstration of RealCall Alert. Similar services are offered by Web Call Back (**www.webcallback.com**) and ITXC (**www.itxc.com/webtalknow**).

10.4.6 Sales-Force Automation

Sales-force automation assists companies in the sales process, including maintaining and discovering leads, managing contacts and other sales-force activities. Assuring salespeople that sales-force automation does not mean the loss of their jobs, but the improvement of sales efficiency, has been difficult for some companies.[22] Sales-force automation can lighten the administrative load on the sales force, allowing sales people to focus on important details and leads which can increase productivity and revenue. Important information about products and customers can be accessed in real time through sales-force automation, allowing salespeople to keep current on company and client information.[23]

Salespeople's relationships with customers can increase trust and loyalty. Customers will most likely want human contact at some point throughout the purchasing process, especially with higher-priced items.

e-Fact 10.5

According to Mercer Management Consulting, an average 37% increase in sales occurred when customers visited a company's Web site to find information on products and salespeople found and followed up on leads generated through the Internet.[24]

Services and products for sales-force automation are available over the Internet. **Salesforce.com** provides Internet-based sales-force automation. The service is provided online and fees are subscription based. The service allows salespeople to keep track of daily and upcoming appointments and gives them access to information regarding partners, customers and leads. Hoover's (**www.hoovers.com**) and Dow Jones (**www.dow-jones.com**) have become partners with **salesforce.com**. Hoover's provides users with company and industry information and Dow Jones provide users with financial information and current news on many companies and markets. Both companies offer some services on a subscription basis only. **Salesforce.com** offers its clients access to this information.

Salesforce.com also allows salespeople to view quarterly progress reports and forecast reports. The forecast reports can be adjusted to include each additional opportunity, such as possible new clients or revenue. Go to **www.salesforce.com** and follow the quick tour to view screens of what the sales force would see as they use this service. Activities for the week and messages from management can be delivered to the sales force using this service. Lead information can be imported from another program or can be entered manually and then routed to the appropriate person, depending on the nature of the lead. Customer account information can be shared with others within the company and can include past activities and contact information.

	Enter your information **and we will call you right back!**
telephone	_____ (direct phone or mobile # only, incl. area code & excl. country code)
name / ext.	_____ (optional)
country	United States ▾
call me	◉ Now ○ In 15 mins
	realcallme

Fig. 10.6   RealCall Alert Demonstration. (Courtesy of RealCall, Inc.)

Sales.com provides a similar service with added travel services, such as booking airline and hotel reservations or getting a map to your destination. Visit the site for a quick tour. Both companies provide offline synchronization with MS Outlook™ and other offline options allowing salespeople to carry important information with them when they are not connected to the Internet. Some other companies that offer sales-force automation products and services include Sales Logix® (**www.saleslogix.com**) and Clarify™ (**www.clarify.com**).

10.5 Business-to-Business e-CRM

The emerging key to business-to-business (B2B) e-commerce is effective customer relationship management (CRM). In the context of business-to-business commerce, B2B CRM can be different from business-to-consumer (B2C) CRM. When you sell your product to another business, you may be selling to someone who is not the direct user of your product. Because the user of the product might have an opinion or comment different from what you are hearing from your business contact, ask your contact to speak with the end users. You may find that end users have suggestions that could improve your product or service.[25] Maintaining relationships with current customers by listening to their suggestions and continuing to improve service will build loyalty.

Developing good *partner relationship management (PRM)* includes increasing efficiency in operations and processes between a business and its partners. Partners can include resellers, distributors and businesses that improve your product or service by supplying you with value-added services or product parts. Managing these relationships can include integrating systems to combine selling, buying and marketing operations of partners. The integration of systems between a company and its partners will streamline processes and provide technical conformity, improving efficiency and decreasing the amount of time it takes for placing orders and fulfillment.

ChannelWave Software, Inc. (**www.virtuflex.com**) offers Web-based solutions for partner relationship management. *ChannelWave 3.0* helps businesses manage their partners by providing *Partner Profiling* and *Channel Partner Recruitment*, in addition to other channel solutions. The product also provides tools for selling that assist in decreasing costs of sales for channel partners and vendors. This solution can also provide forecasting and reporting. Other companies offering PRM solutions include Allegis™ (**www.allegis.com**) and Partnerware® (**www.partnerware.com**).

10.6 Complete e-CRM Solutions

Solutions, software or services that use and integrate all the tools of CRM provide a single view of a customer, but doing so can be expensive. Costs include the price of the software or service itself, the integration into the current system, the maintenance of the system and employing the service representatives.[26] These solutions will continue to become more efficient.

E.piphany™ (**www.epiphany.com**) is a provider of customer relationship management solutions.[27] *E.piphany E.5* is a suite of Web-based CRM solutions that allows you to collect data from your present software systems and third parties. This data can include customers, visitors to the Web site, partners, affiliates and product revenues. E.piphany E.5 analyzes this data to determine the profitability of specific campaigns, return-on-investment, purchase patterns of your consumers, etc. The data analyses can be used to personalize a customer's visit. E.piphany E.5 can also provide recommendations in real time for a customer-service representative's course of action during an employee-to-customer interaction.

eGain (**www.eGain.com**), a leader in the customer relationship management software market,[28] offers an extensive program that implements a CRM system for a client. The *eGain Commerce*™ platform incorporates eGain's *Self-Service, eMail, Live Web* and *Call Center* solutions. *eGain Assistant*, part of the Self-Service, is an agent that allows customers to ask questions and take tours of your site. If it cannot provide the correct information, customers can be connected with a live agent. *k-Commerce Support Enterprise* connects all forms of customer contact together, so that CSRs can review customer history before making recommendations. The *eMail* solution provides e-mail customer-service options, in addition to e-mail marketing campaign management. Live Web provides text chatting and VoIP through *eGain Live*.

Siebel® Systems (**www.siebel.com**) offers solutions covering many aspects of CRM. *Siebel eService* is a Web-based solution allowing site visitors to receive assistance on their own or with the help of service representatives. *Siebel eMail Response* enables the routing of e-mails, the use of e-mail templates and the handling of a large volume of e-mail. *Siebel Call Center* provides customer-service representatives with a single view of customers, by integrating all points of customer contact, such as the Web, e-mail, fax and telephone. Companies offering similar services are Kana Communications (**www.kana.com**) and Oracle Systems (**www.oracle.com**).

In this chapter, we discussed the importance of managing relationships with customers effectively by providing proper customer relationship management. We covered various tracking methods including data mining and the use of cookies for personalization purposes. We discussed the elements of the e-contact center and the technologies, such as speech synthesis and recognition and natural-language processing, that will impact the future of e-CRM solutions. In Chapter 11, Legal and Ethical Issues; Internet Taxation, we discuss a number of major legal and ethical concerns that have developed from the introduction of the Internet and World Wide Web.

10.7 Internet and World Wide Web Resources

Log-file Analysis

www.uu.se/Software/Analyzers/Access-analyzers.html
This site offers a listing of URLs for various log-file analysis tools. The list is organized by platform, including Unix, Windows NT, Windows, Macintosh and platform independent.

www.sane.com
Sane Solutions offers *NetTracker*®, a log-file analysis product. Visit the site for an online demo.

www.activeconcepts.com
Active Concepts provides Internet analysis products for eBusiness, Web administration, online training and marketing.

Data Mining

www.sas.com
SAS® has many solutions for customer relationship management. Its *Balanced Scorecard* uses data warehousing and data management to analyze collected data.

www-4.ibm.com/software/data/iminer/fordata
IBM® offers *DB2 Intelligent Miner for Data.* This product mines high-volume data and also provides analysis results.

www.magnify.com
Magnify provides data-mining solutions including specific products for the financial industry.

Personalization

www.andromedia.com
Andromedia provides LikeMinds, a solution that allows you to personalize your customers' experiences on your Web site based on their previous visits.

www.bluemartini.com
The BlueMartini Customer Interaction Server allows businesses to manage the needs of individual customers by tracking and mining the customer's visits.

www.broadbase.com
Broadbase Software, Inc. provides solutions for all aspects of e-commerce. The E-Marketing product assists the marketer in planning, executing and analyzing personalized marketing campaigns.

Call Centers

www.cosmocom.com
CosmoCom™'s *CosmoCall Universe* is a communication platform that includes Internet, e-mail, voicemail, fax and telephone.

www.siebel.com
Siebel® offers a wide range of CRM solutions, including a call-center solution that includes coordinating all interactions with customers using telephone, fax, e-mail, the Web and VoIP.

www.clarify.com
Clarify™ offers many CRM products, including the *Clarify ClearCall Center.* This solution is used by salespeople, managers and customer service representatives, so all views of the customer can be linked into one system.

E-mail

www.echomail.com
EchoMail®, Inc. provides companies with *EchoMail,* a software application that routes e-mail to the proper people; it also warehouses and mines e-mail for analysis in real time and creates mailing lists and administers e-mail campaigns.

www.emailtoday.com
This portal provides e-mail industry news and articles.

www.clickaction.com
ClickAction™ ERM is a Web-based e-mail management solution designed for marketers and database managers. You can tailor the solution to be self-service (e-mails are sent automatically) or full service (e-mails are managed by employees), depending on your needs.

Online Text Chatting

www.humanclick.com
HumanClick offers companies the option to place on their sites buttons that connect to live customer-service representatives over the Internet. The customer can then speak with the CSR. Visit the site to view the demo.

www.webdialogs.com
WebDialogs offers online text chatting services as well as callback features and browsing synchronization between visitors and customer service representatives.

www.eshare.com
eshare™ offers *eshare Expressions®*, a turnkey solution for adding discussion forums, presentations and chatting capabilities to a Web site.

Speech Synthesis, Speech Recognition and Natural-Language Processing

www.askjeeves.com
AskJeeves[SM] offers *Jeeves Relevant Answers,* a product that uses "popularity-ranking technology" and "natural-language question answering" to help visitors find products and services relevant to their interests.

www.kanisa.com/espover.html
Kanisa's *ESP* solution allows a Web site to hold a dialog with visitors by asking questions to determine what the visitor is asking, to provide the correct answer.

www.speech.philips.com/ud/get/pages/pc_home.htm
Philips' *SpeechMania™* is a software package that performs "natural speech recognition" for transaction services and automating telephone information services.

Voice Communications

www.lipstream.com
The Lipstream Live Voice Service™ provides companies with the option to add VoIP to their sites. The service is PC to phone.

www.iec.org/tutorials/vfoip
This site offers an online tutorial for Voice over IP applications.

www.dialpad.com
This company provides users with free calls using VoIP.

Sales Force Automation

www.selectica.com
Selectica's *Internet Selling System™ (ISS)* is a solution that improves the sales process by assisting in product development, analysis, sales data management and other sales functions.

www.oraclesalesonline.com
Oracle® provides an online solution for sales-force automation. **OracleSalesOnline.com** gives a company's sales force access to sales force automation tools, including company updates and forecasts.

www.frontrange.com
FrontRange Solutions™ sells *GoldMine® 5.0*, an automation software for sales and marketing.

Complete CRM Solutions

www.peoplesoft.com
PeopleSoft® created the *Vantive Enterprise* and the *Web-based Vantive eBusiness application suites* to fulfill companies' customer relationship management needs. The modules of the solution can be used separately or together and include *Vantive Quality, Vantive Support, Vantive Sales, Vantive Field Service* and *Vantive HelpDesk.*

www.pegasystems.com
Pegasystem offers a full range of CRM solutions for service, marketing and sales, using various channels of contact with consumers.

www.crmcommunity.com

This site is a resource for customer relationship management. This site provides visitors with a listing of solutions, CRM events and a career center.

www.crm-forum.com

CRM Forum contains articles, tutorials, presentations, and white papers on improving the quality of customer relationship management on the Internet.

www.isky.com

iSky provides assistance for companies who need customer care systems. A company can outsource customer relationship management to *iSky*.

www.sychrony.net

Synchrony offers a product that integrates all forms of communication to provide one single profile of a customer's history.

www.acxiom.com

Acxiom® offers Abilitec™, a solution that integrates all forms of contact with customers, so a company can have a single view of each customer.

SUMMARY

- Offering customers convenience, personalization and service plays a key role in the success and differentiation of many online businesses.

- Customer relationship management (CRM) is a strategy that focuses on providing and maintaining quality service for customers by effectively communicating and delivering products, services, information and solutions to address their problems. It is sometimes referred to as eCRM or iCRM when used in discussions involving the Internet.

- CRM can include call handling (the maintenance of outbound and inbound calls from customers and service representatives), sales tracking (the tracking and recording of all sales activity) and transaction support (the technology and personnel used for conducting transactions), as well as many other functions.

- While acquiring new customers is important, it generally is less expensive to maintain current customers.

- Data gathered through log-file analysis, data mining, cookies and other tracking devices can be used to personalize each visitor's experience, find trends in customer use and measure the effectiveness of a Web site over time.

- Log files consist of data generated by site visits, including each visitor's location, IP address, time of visit, frequency of visits and other information. Log-file analysis organizes and summarizes the information contained in the logs.

- Data mining uses algorithms and statistical tools to find patterns in data gathered from customer visits. This can improve your CRM and marketing campaigns, by helping you better understand your customers and their behaviors.

- Data mining can help with visitor segmentation, allowing you to target promotions to the proper audience. You can also discover a need for new or improved services or products by studying the patterns of your customers' purchases.

- Customer registration—requiring visitors to fill out a form with personal information that is then used to create a profile—is recommended when it will provide a benefit to the consumer. It will also allow businesses to customize their Web sites, customer service and marketing strategies more effectively.

- Personalization uses information from the tracking, mining and analyzing of data to customize a person's interactions with a company's products, services, Web site and employees.

- Some people feel that personalization represents an invasion of their privacy, whereas others may not even be aware that personalization is occurring at a site.

- Marketers must be careful how they use the personal information gained from data research. If used properly and with consumers' privacy rights in mind, personalization technology can establish solid relationships with customers by giving them what they want, when they want it.

- Using the Internet as a customer contact option has provided the opportunity to personalize a customer's experience, which can increase loyalty and sales.

- Traditional call centers house customer-service representatives who can be reached by an 800 number. However, more customers now have Internet access and contact companies through e-mail, online text chatting or real-time voice communications.

- It may be appropriate to outsource contact center services if your company cannot afford to implement a contact center due to the costs of equipment, office space, service representatives and technical support.

- A Frequently Asked Questions (FAQ) section located on your Web site will help consumers find answers to some of their questions, freeing up time for your customer service representatives to handle customers' questions that cannot be answered without human interaction.

- Online text chatting provides a real-time form of communication between customers and service representatives.

- By offering text chatting, customers who may have decided to leave the site because of a question that could not be answered now have the option to contact a service representative immediately.

- Speech synthesis is the process of having a computer covert text to voice.

- Speech recognition converts speech into text.

- A problem that makes speech recognition difficult is that people pronounce words with different accents and speak in different intonations or languages.

- Natural language processing attempts to understand text and respond with a proper answer or comment.

- When a natural language comment or question is posed to a computer over a phone or directly from a person, the audio must first be converted to text through continuous speech recognition (CSR). Then the text can be interpreted with natural language processing.

- Although many forms of communication are used today for customer service—such as e-mail and text chatting—communication through speech is often preferred by customers.

- Voice-over Internet Protocol (VoIP) products and applications allow people to communicate via speech over the Internet.

- Internet telephony allows people to make phone calls over the Internet. The quality of the transmission, however, has yet to match that of regular telephone calls.

- PC-to-phone (computer-to-phone) voice communication allows a visitor to a Web site to continue browsing while talking to a customer service representative over the Internet. This allows dial-up Internet users that have only one phone line to chat with a customer service representative without having to disconnect from the Internet.

- Sales force automation assists companies in the sales process, including maintaining and discovering leads, managing contacts and other sales-force activities.

- Salespeople's relationships with customers are essential to increasing trust and loyalty. Customers will most likely want human contact at some point during the purchasing process, especially with higher-priced items.

- Maintaining relationships with current customers by listening to their suggestions and continuing to improve service will build loyalty.

- Managing relationships with partners can include integrating systems to combine selling, buying and marketing operations.

- Solutions, software or services that use and integrate all tools of CRM provide a single view of a customer, but they can be expensive. Costs include the price of the software or service itself, the integration into the current system, the maintenance of the system and employing the service representatives.

TERMINOLOGY

call center
call handling
clear GIF
click-through banner advertisement
collaborative filtering
continuous speech recognition (CSR)
cookie
customer profile
customer registration
customer relationship management (CRM)
data mining
e-contact center
FAQ (frequently asked questions)
ID card
intelligent agent
Internet telephony
lifetime value
log files
log-file analysis

multimedia contact center
natural-language processing
online text chatting
partner relationship management (PRM)
PC-to-phone (computer-to-phone)
   voice communication
personalization
Personalization Consortium
rules-based personalization
sales force automation
sales tracking
speech recognition
speech synthesis
top-referring sites
tracking devices
transaction support
Voice over Internet Protocol (VoIP)
Web Bugs
wizard

SELF-REVIEW EXERCISES

10.1 State whether each of the following is true or false; if false, explain why.
  a) When you sell your product to another business, you may be selling to someone who is not the direct user of your product.
  b) While acquiring new customers is important, it is less expensive to maintain current customers.
  c) A FAQ section on your Web site is sufficient for customer inquiries.
  d) Personalization uses information from the tracking, mining and analyzing of data to customize a person's interactions with a company's products, services, Web site and employees.
  e) Developing good partner relationship management (PRM) includes increasing efficiency in operations and processes between a business and its partners.

10.2 Fill in the blanks in each of the following.
  a) _____ occurs when you feed text to a computer that synthesizes the text into voice.
  b) _____ products and applications allow people to communicate with speech over the Internet.
  c) _____ uses algorithms and statistical tools to find patterns in data gathered from customer visits.

d) _____, requiring visitors to fill out a form with personal information that is then used to create a profile, is recommended when it will provide a benefit to the consumer.

e) Customers should also be able to conduct transactions and get answers to their questions through a _____ center.

ANSWERS TO SELF-REVIEW EXERCISES

10.1   a) True. b) True. c) False, you should provide another option for customers to contact you, including an e-mail address or a phone number that can be easily seen on your site. d) True. e) True.

10.2   a) Speech synthesis. b) Voice over Internet Protocol (VoIP). c) data mining. d) customer registration. e) call, contact or multi-media.

EXERCISES

10.3   State whether each of the following is true or false; if false, explain why.

a) Maintaining relationships with current customers by listening to their suggestions and continuing to improve service will build loyalty.

b) Sales force automation attempts to complete many tasks that are presently performed by salespeople.

c) The best way to start building a consumer profile is to require as much information as possible when customers make a purchase or even just visit the Web site.

d) Acquiring new customers is important, but it is generally more expensive to maintain current customers.

e) PC-to-phone allows dial-up Internet users that have only one phone line to chat with a customer-service representative without having to disconnect from the Internet.

10.4   Fill in the blanks in each of the following.

a) _____ products and applications allow people to communicate via speech over the Internet.

a) _____ provides a real-time text form of communication between customers and service representatives.

b) _____ uses algorithms and statistical tools to find patterns in data gathered from customer visits.

c) Integrating systems to combine selling, buying and marketing operations will help a company implement good _____.

d) Some people feel that _____ represents an invasion of their privacy, whereas others may not even be aware that it is occurring at a site.

e) The maintenance of outbound and inbound calls from customers and service representatives is known as _____.

10.5   Define the following:

a) Internet telephony

b) top-referring sites

c) personalization

d) transaction support

e) log file

10.6   Visit Excite^TM (**www.excite.com**) and sign up for *My Excite Start Page*. Select the personal options of your choice and visit this site once a day for a few days.

a) Name at least three personalization selections offered and describe the options for each.

b) Are the personaizationl options you selected a convenience or are they bothersome? Explain.

c) Was the delivered content personalized each day you returned? Discuss what you viewed at your Excite Start Page each day.

    d) Does this change your view of personalization's benefits? How did you regard it previously?

10.7   Visit **dialpad.com** and sign up for the free service. Then make a phone call to someone you know.

    a) Who did you call? Did you call long distance?

    b) What was the quality of the connection?

    c) What is the technology used to transmit the voices called?

    d) Comment on the registration field requirements and the overall service. Were you comfortable filling in the required fields?

    e) If you do not have a microphone and speakers, compare and contrast **dialpad.com** and two other companies offering similar services. Are there price differences? Can you call internationally? What kind of software is required?

10.8   (*Class Discussion*) After trying natural-language technology by using AskJeeves (**www.askjeeves.com**) and Eliza (**www-ai.ijs.si/eliza/eliza.html**), discuss the accuracy of this technology. Which one is more accurate? Is it a good idea to add a form of this technology to an e-business' site? Why or why not? Have you ever used this technology for customer service before?

10.9   In a group, discuss your experiences with customer services. What experiences went well and why? What obstacles did you encounter? Select two e-businesses of your choice and do a complete comparison of their customer relationship management tools, or lack thereof.

10.10   Visit **www.bell-labs.com/project/tts/voices.html** to try speech synthesis.

    a) First, write a paragraph about customer relationship management. Then, copy the paragraph into the box to be synthesized.

    b) Select a voice and speed and then synthesize your paragraph. What was the result?

    c) Could you understand the computer's voice?

    d) What words were not synthesized correctly? To what extent could you hear human intonations?

    e) Answer all questions and provide a copy of the paragraph you used. Try the same exercise at **www.cstr.ed.ac.uk/projects/festival/userin.html** and compare the results with the speech synthesis at **www.bell-labs.com/project/tts/voices.html**.

10.11   Visit the sites of Sitel Corporation (**www.sitel.com**) and TeleTech (**www.teletech.com**) and compare their CRM applications. Which Web site had more informative content? What services does TeleTech offer? Do both companies have global reach? Based on the company's Web sites, which company has the competitive advantage? Why? If your company was looking for CRM, which company would you choose? Prepare a detailed explanation.

10.12   (*Class Discussion*) Discuss the e-mail customer service in e-Fact 6.3. Is this finding relevant to your experience with customer service through e-mail? What are the consequences of not providing sufficient customer service through e-mail?

10.13   Visit **www.aol.com** and register to use *AIM Express* for free.

    a) Try chatting with someone from your class.

    b) Compare the timeliness of this service with the delays associated with e-mails.

    c) Describe the benefits of having online text chatting as a customer service option, as compared with e-mail. Would you recommend using both? Why or why not?

10.14   In this chapter we discussed online text chatting. Go to **www.facetime.com/products/demo** to view a demonstration of text chatting, and answer the following questions.

    a) What is Marcia's dilemma?

    b) Who helps her and what does he suggest for her to do while he is trying to find the solution to her problem?

    c) What is it called when someone suggests another product in addition to what the customer originally requests?

    d) Why does Janet not like the original wig sent to her?

    e) What method does Pete use to respond to Cyndee's request?

    f) What are the benefits of online text chatting? Would you use this service while visiting a site?

10.15 This exercise is designed to walk through downloading of Microsoft Agent, a speech synthesis and recognition product. There are a few steps that must be taken before you will be able to use Microsoft Agent. The process outlined in this section must be completed by anyone who wishes to use the technology. Keep in mind that if you decide to use Agent in any of your pages, visitors to your site will have to complete this process as well. The process varies depending on what aspects of Agent you wish to use. There are a total of three installations that must be completed to take full advantage of Agent. The first is the installation of the Microsoft Agent core files which are the heart of Agent's functionality. The second download is the text-to-speech engine. It converts text displayed in the word bubbles (like cartoon callouts) into computer-generated speech that you will hear. The last download is optional; it is the speech-recognition engine. Many developers choose not to add speech-recognition capabilities to their Agents, however the example will guide you through this download as well. It is important to note that this process has to be completed only once per computer. After completing this exercise, your computer will be ready to display Microsoft Agent enabled Web-sites. In fact, if you decide later that you wish to create your own Microsoft Agent enabled Web-sites, these three programs will have provided you with everything you need. Lastly, you must download each Agent character that you want to see. Once again, character downloads must be done only once, you will then be able to view any Web-site that uses that character. In this case we will download Peedy the Parrot. Microsoft offers four high-quality agent characters. There are many third-party vendors that offer Agent characters as well.

    a) Open a Web browser and go to the Microsoft Agent section of the Microsoft Developer Network at: `http://msdn.microsoft.com/workshop/c-frame.htm?/workshop/imedia/agent/default.asp` Once there, you will see a picture of Peedy the Parrot to the right of a link labeled **Download Microsoft Agent**. Click the link to continue.

    b) Clicking the link will advance you to the downloads section, where you will find the files you need to run Agent. This page has many links on it, however you will need to use only a few. First, download the core Agent files. To do so, click the first link, Microsoft Agent and language support. Next, click the link labeled **Download the Microsoft Agent core components (395 kb exe)**. When you see the dialog window, click the radio button labeled **Run this program from its current location**. Then click ok. This will run the program as soon as it is finished downloading.

    c) When the download is complete, read the licence agreement, and click **Yes** to continue. The files will then automatically be installed. Next, return to you browser window. Scroll down the page until you see the heading **Microsoft Agent character files**. Select **Peedy** from the pull-down list, then click the link labeled **Download selected character**. Once again click the radio button labeled **Run this program from its current location** and click **OK**. When the download is complete, follow the instructions to run the installation. Like the previous installation, the files will automatically be installed.

    d) Now you must install the speech engine. To do so, scroll down to the heading **Text-to-speech engines** and select **Lernout & Houspie(R) TruVoice Text-To-Speech Engine - American English (1 MB exe)** and click the link labeled **Download selected engine**. Just as before, click the radio button labeled **Run this program from it's current location** and click **OK**.

e) When the installation completes, return to the Web page, and scroll down to the **Speech recognition engines** heading. Click the link labeled **Download the Microsoft Speech Recognition Engine (6 MB exe)**. Repeat the download method used before. This time you will be asked to configure the recognition engine. Follow the step-by-step instructions. The installation is now complete.

f) To test Peedy, visit Peedy's Pizza Palace, a Microsoft Web site that demonstrates most of Peedy's capabilities. Use the flowering URL to get to the page. http://**agent.microsoft.com/agent2/sdk/samples/html/peedypza.htm** Your computer is now configured to use any Web page that uses Peedy the Parrot.

g) To try using Peedy, visit **www.msdn.microsoft.com/workshop/imedia/agent/TryMicrosoftAgent.htm**

WORKS CITED

The notation <**www.domain-name.com**> indicates that the citation is for information found at that Web site.

1. B. Thompson, "Keeping Customers is Smart and Profitable," *Business Week Special Advertising Section* 3 July 2000.

2. S. Baveja, "Making the Most of Customers," *The Industry Standard* 6 March 2000: 107.

3. S. Baveja, 107.

4. T.E. Weber, "Tricks of the Web Snoops Trade," *The Wall Street Journal* 23 February 2000: B1.

5. T.E. Weber, B1.

6. T.E. Weber, B1.

7. <**www.webtrends.com**>.

8. *E-Business Technology Forecast* (PricewaterhouseCoopers LLP: 1999) 83.

9. <**www.personalization.com**>.

10. E. Messmer, "Web Having Huge Impact On Call Centers," *Network World* 24 July 2000: 10.

11. E. Messmer, 10.

12. D. Radcliff, "The Web Meets The Call Center," *COMPUTERWORLD* 24 January 2000: 50.

13. R. Kerber, "Booming Stream International to Add Up to 12 Call Centers Worldwide," *The Boston Globe* 27 June 2000: E3.

14. E. Messmer, "Call Centers Feeling Web's Impact," *Network World* 21 August 2000: 36.

15. E. Messmer, 36.

16. J. King, "Answer Customer E-mail Fast!" *COMPUTERWORLD* 3 January 2000: S26.

17. D. Tweney, "Who Needs Customer Service Online? You Do." <***www.ecompany.com***> July 2000: 165.

18. W. Durr, "Turning Browsers Into Buyers Using Your Call Center," *C@LL CENTER CRM Solutions*™ September 2000: 71.

19. D. Pescovitz, "Hello, May I Help You?" *The Industry Standard* 22 May 2000: 230.

20. D. Pescovitz, 234.

21. <**www.realcall.net**>.

22. D. Drucker, "The Web: Hardly Death Of A Salesman," *InternetWeek* 25 October 1999: 73.

23. D. Drucker, 74.

24.   "Click, Then Call," *The Wall Street Journal* 20 July 2000.

25.   D. Peppers et al., *The One to One Field Book: The Complete Toolkit for Implementing a 1 to 1 Marketing Program* (New York: Bantam Doubleday Publishing Group, Inc., 1999) 42.

26.   D. Tweney, "Who Needs Customer Service Online? You Do." **<www.ecompany.com>** July 2000: 166.

27. <www.epiphany.com>.

28.   E. Cone, "EGain Reached Two Markets," *Inter@ctive Week* 29 May 2000: 38.

RECOMMENDED READINGS

Girishankar, S. "Customer Service For Business Partners." *Informationweek* 17 April 2000: 65+

Peppers, D., et al. *The One To One Field Book: The Complete Toolkit for Implementing a 1 to 1 Marketing Program.* New York: Bantam Doubleday Dell Publishing Group, Inc., 1999.

"Special Report: CRM e-volves." *Global Technology Business* May 2000: 48+.

Waters, J. "Getting Personal On The Web." *Application Development Trends* May 2000: 25-32.

Part 5

Legal, Ethical, Social and Global Issues

Outline

Chapter 11 Legal and Ethical Issues; Internet Taxation

Chapter 12 Globalization

Chapter 13 Social and Political Issues

Chapter 14 Accessibility

11

Legal and Ethical Issues; Internet Taxation

Objectives

- To explore the issues of online privacy.
- To review the current applications of traditional law to the Internet: defamation, intellectual property, unsolicited e-mail and sexually explicit speech.
- To understand the impact of traditional law on e-commerce.
- To understand the limitations of traditional law with respect to the Internet.
- To review issues regarding Internet taxation.

We deal with the right of privacy older than the Bill of Rights – older than our political parties, older than our school system.
William O. Douglas

He plants trees to benefit another generation.
Caecilius Statius

Truth is generally the best vindication against slander.
Abraham Lincoln

Taxes, after all, are the dues we pay for the privilege of membership in an organized society.
Franklin D. Roosevelt

Outline

11.1   Introduction
11.2   Legal Issues: Privacy on the Internet
    11.2.1   Right to Privacy
    11.2.2   Internet and the Right to Privacy
    11.2.3   Network Advertising Initiative
    11.2.4   Employer and Employee
    11.2.5   Protecting Yourself as a User
    11.2.6   Protecting Your Business: Privacy Issues
11.3   Legal Issues: Other Areas of Concern
    11.3.1   Defamation
    11.3.2   Sexually Explicit Speech
    11.3.3   Children and the Internet
    11.3.4   Alternative Methods of Regulation
    11.3.5   Intellectual Property: Copyright and Patents
    11.3.6   Trademark and Domain Name Registration
    11.3.7   Unsolicited Commercial e-Mail (Spam)
    11.3.8   Online Auctions
    11.3.9   Online Contracts
    11.3.10 User Agreements
11.4   Cybercrime
11.5   Internet Taxation
11.6   Internet And World Wide Web Resources

*Summary • Terminology • Self-Review Exercises • Answers to Self-Review Exercises • Exercises •
Works Cited • Recommended Reading*

11.1 Introduction

The Internet has posed significant challenges to the legal structure in the United States. Copyright infringement has come up against file-sharing technology, and privacy continues to be challenged by personalization mechanisms. In this chapter, we investigate the differences between our physical environment consisting of temporal and geographic boundaries, and *cyberspace*, the realm of digital transmission not limited by geography. We explore defamation, Spam (unsolicited electronic mail), trademarking, pornography and taxation as they relate to the Internet.

11.2 Legal Issues: Privacy on the Internet

The application of traditional law to the Internet is not always straightforward. In this section, we explore technologies that present new challenges to maintaining privacy.

11.2.1 Right to Privacy

An individual's right to privacy is not explicitly guaranteed by the Constitution, but protection from government intrusion is implicitly guaranteed through the First, Fourth, Ninth and Fourteenth Amendments.[1] Of these four amendments listed, the Fourth Amendment provides U.S. citizens with the greatest assurance of privacy, in that it protects them from illegal search and seizure by the government:

> *The right of the people to be secure in their persons, houses, papers, and effects, against unreasonable searches and seizures, shall not be violated, and no Warrant shall issue, but upon probable cause, supported by Oath or affirmation, and particularly describing the place to be searched, and the person or things to be seized.*

When the Fourth Amendment was drafted, trespassing by the government was the privacy issue of greatest concern. Problems with applying the Fourth Amendment began to appear when the right to individual privacy moved beyond private property. In the landmark case *Olmstead v. United States*, which involved the discussion of illegal alcohol sales over the telephone during the Prohibition era, the Supreme Court ruled that information obtained through the tapping of telephone wires fell outside the protection of the Fourth Amendment.

This example demonstrates the need for translation, or interpretation of the Constitution to protect the greater good.[2] At the time the Fourth Amendment was drafted, trespassing was the violation in question. The invention of the telephone required the regulation against trespassing to be reinterpreted so that it also included protection against wiretapping.

11.2.2 Internet and the Right to Privacy

The Internet is currently a *self-regulated medium*—the Internet industry essentially governs itself. This condition enables the Internet to flourish without the constraints of legislation, but it also creates problems because there are few specific guidelines to follow.

Many Internet companies collect users' personal information as the users navigate through a site. While privacy advocates argue that these efforts violate individuals' privacy rights, online marketers and advertisers disagree; they suggest that, by recording the likes and dislikes of online consumers, online companies can better serve their users. For example, if you visit an online travel site and purchase a ticket from Boston to Philadelphia, the travel site might record this transaction. In the future, when a ticket goes on sale for the same flight, the Web site can notify you. The advantages of collecting users' personal information as a marketing tactic and the methods used for collection are discussed in Chapter 10, e-Customer Relationship Management.

However, there are profound ramifications as well. Consider a different scenario. Suppose you are planning your first trip to Washington, D.C. You would like to visit the White House's Web site, so you type in `www.whitehouse.com`. Actually, the White House is a government entity, so the domain extension you need is `.gov` (`www.whitehouse.gov`). Before you realize this, you enter the address ending in `.com`, and, to your surprise, you are now browsing a pornography site. At the time, you may consider this situation a small inconvenience. You go and enjoy your trip.

Six months later, you are bidding on an apartment in a respectable neighborhood. The landlord, reviewing the applications, comes across documentation of your Internet activity, discovers that you have recently visited a pornography site (`www.whitehouse.com`) and decides that you are not eligible to rent the apartment. This situation is only one of many problems that privacy advocates fear.

This is a hypothetical scenario, but certainly not outside the realm of possibility, and not the scariest. In fact, most privacy protection legislation protects consumers against advertisers, but it does not mention content providers. In a report recently released by HealthCare Foundation, titled "Report on the Privacy Policies and Practices of Health Web Sites," suggests that sites providing health information to consumers could potentially share this information with third parties. For example, if you were you visit a Web site and download information on cancer, AIDS and other life-threatening diseases, this information could be distributed without your knowledge or consent. Now, rather than losing your apartment, you could be denied insurance coverage or a job.[3 , 4]

Privacy is one of the driving forces behind potential federal regulation. The Federal Trade Commission (FTC) found that 97 percent of Web sites studied collected personal information, but only 62 percent of those sites gave any indication to the consumer that information was being collected, and 57 percent of studied sites contained third-party *tracking devices*.[5] (Tracking devices collect consumer data. Log-file analysis, data mining, customer registration and cookies are examples of tracking devices. They are discussed in greater detail in Chapter 10, e-Customer Relationship Management.) In another survey, conducted by **Enonymous.com**, a Web company that provides privacy-sensitive marketing services and technologies, only 3.5 percent of the 30,000 Web sites studied earned a four-star rating (out of four stars) on their privacy policies. A four star rating signifies internal use only of user information and solicitation will be distributed when the user requests it.[6]

Recent studies show that 90 percent of consumers say that online security is a major concern, and 50 percent are hesitant to use their credit-card numbers for online transactions in the event that records are kept of what they purchased and where it was purchased.[7] These statistics are particularly significant, given the many advantages of conducting online sales versus doing business through traditional *brick-and-mortar establishments*.

The United States is establishing commissions to study online privacy. The *Financial Services Modernization Act of 1999* establishes a set of regulations concerning the management of consumer information. For example, businesses must provide consumers with the ability to *opt out* (actively choose not to have their information shared with third parties).

Many e-businesses are creating specific positions to manage consumer privacy. Chief Privacy Officers (CPOs) are responsible for maintaining the integrity of a Web site's privacy policy. This involves creating policies and serving as an intermediary to government officials regarding privacy issues. American Express, Doubleclick and Microsoft are among organizations that employ a CPO.[8]

e-Fact 11.1

Statistics indicate that there are currently 50-60 CPO in the United States.[9]

Microsoft is also making efforts to regulate the use of consumer information. Cookies, perhaps the most common of tracking devices, are concerning to consumers. Cookies are defined in Chapter 10, e-Customer Relationship Management, Section 10.2.4. In the beta version of Internet Explorer 5.5, Microsoft has included a *cookie management feature*, which does not allow cookies from third-party vendors, usually advertisers, to collect identifying information about Internet users without first receiving consent by the consumer. Consent is given via a pop-up window that is presented when the browser recognizes a third-party vendor.[10]

Many people are unaware that they can disable cookies. However, it must be noted that disabling cookies may exclude users from some Web sites. Cookie files can be viewed by searching the hard drive for the appropriate directory, called the cookie directory. To locate this file on your PC, go to **Find** (or **Search** depending on your version of Windows) on your **Start** menu and search for the cookie directory.

11.2.3 Network Advertising Initiative

In an effort to support self-regulation, the FTC approved the *Network Advertising Initiative* (NAI) in July 1999. NAI currently represents 90 percent of Web advertisers, including DoubleClick and 24/7 Media. The group was established to determine the proper protocols for managing a Web user's personal information on the Internet. While the Initiative prohibits the collection of consumer data from medical and financial sites, it allows the combination of Web-collected data and personal information (see the DoubleClick feature).[17] However, it has also taken steps to dictate how this information should be collected, including issues of user notification and allowing users access to their own records.[18]

DoubleClick: Marketing with Personal Information

While privacy advocate groups argue that the Web will not survive without some form of regulation, advertising organizations disagree. DoubleClick, an Internet advertising firm, suggests that advertising must be effective to minimize Internet-related costs. Regulation of the Internet could limit a company's efforts to buy and sell advertising. As with television and radio advertising, the money generated by Internet advertising can allow people of all economic means to use the medium.[11]

Web sites use a variety of tracking methods to record where visitors come from, where they go and what catches their interest along the way. This information is tied to your computer's IP address (i.e., the numerical address of your computer on the Internet), Web browser and operating system; it is used by marketers to target relevant advertisements at specific computers. DoubleClick has an advertising network of more than 1,500 sites where banner advertisements for 11,000 of its clients appear.[12] This network enables DoubleClick to combine data from many sites to target advertisements for particular computers.

However, targeting a specific IP address, browser and operating system is less effective than targeting a specific consumer. In 1999, DoubleClick acquired Abacus Direct Corporation, a direct-marketing organization. Abacus stores names, addresses, telephone numbers, age, gender, income levels and a history of purchases at retail, catalog and online stores. This acquisition enabled DoubleClick to attach personal information to the activities of what were once "nameless" personal computers.

One concern with this method of collecting and using data is termed *digital redlining*.[13] Digital redlining suggests that a company could skew an individual's knowledge of available products by basing the advertisements the user sees on past behavior. This practice could allow advertisers to influence consumers' habits by limiting the information they see to what the advertisers determine the consumers want to see.[14]

DoubleClick: Marketing with Personal Information (Cont.)

Direct marketing in the traditional sense affords a certain time lapse between an individual's purchases, the processing of that information and the use of that information to target the particular customer. However, users can be targeted instantly as they browse the Internet.[15]

Perhaps of greater concern is the recording of personal activities. The Internet is valued as a medium in which users can search for information and express opinions anonymously. Privacy advocates are concerned that such data could be used against individuals attempting to obtain housing, get a loan, apply for insurance coverage or even deal with spousal disagreement and divorce.[16] For example, a user visiting a Web site to learn more about an illness might not want that information to be made available to insurance companies. DoubleClick promises to uphold its privacy policy, which assures users that the company will not collect financial, sexually oriented or medical information. In response to concerns about privacy, DoubleClick has joined the Network Advertising Initiative, which we discuss in section 11.2.3.

Opponents to the NAI argue that what may appear to be good self-regulation to one group may be a violation of privacy to another. For example, **Toysmart.com**, an online retailer forced to declare bankruptcy, made plans to sell its consumers' personal information. This decision was in direct violation of its past privacy policy, which was in effect when the information was collected. **Toysrus.com**'s practice of outsourcing consumer-data analysis has also come into question. These companies, however, most likely considered these uses of consumer information to be good business practices. Both **Toysmart.com** and **Toyrus.com** are examples of self-regulated privacy decisions illustrating the ambiguity in determining the level of privacy preferred by consumers.[19]

The FTC plans to continue pursuing a method of regulating privacy on the Internet, but has agreed to offer the NAI a "safe harbor" provision provided that the Initiative acts according to FTC protocols.[20] For more information regarding consumer-protection laws, visit the FTC Web site at **www.ftc.gov/bcp/conline/pubs/buspubs/dotcom/index.html** for the downloadable guide "Dot-com Disclosures: Information about Online Advertising."

11.2.4 Employer and Employee

Many businesses monitor employee activities on corporate and communications equipment. One of the newest surveillance technologies, *keystroke cops*, are creating tension between employers and employees.[21] Keystroke software provides an inexpensive, easy-to-use method of monitoring productivity and the abuse of company equipment.[22] Products such as *Computer Usage Compliance Survey*, from Codex Data Systems (**www.codexdatasystems.com**), allow business owners to create a custom user's policy to define how the company will monitor Web surfing, e-mailing, visits to restricted sites, downloading of inappropriate images and use of encryption. Another company, **www.surfsecurity.com**, offers a variety of surveillance software that is available at a fee for download from its site (**www.softsecurity.com**). KCap TSR Keystroke Capture Utility 1.0,

Stealthlogger ProBot v1.0 and Ghost Keylogger v1.0 are available as free-trial downloads from **www.hotfiles.com**.

The surveillance software is loaded onto the hard drive of an employee's computer, or it can be sent to an unsuspecting employee as an e-mail attachment. Once activated, the software registers each keystroke before it appears on the screen. Many products also have scanning capabilities that enable them to search through documents for keywords such as "boss" and "union."[23]

The issue is most often one of company time and company equipment versus the employee's right of self expression. Situations may involve employees who neglect responsibilities to write personal e-mails, surf the Web or conduct online tirades against management in chat rooms.

In order to determine the outcome of court cases on these issues, the courts propose the determination of two criteria: (1) did the employee have a *reasonable expectation of privacy*, and (2) does the business have *legitimate business interests* that would reasonably justify the intrusion of an employee's privacy?

Companies do have legitimate reasons for monitoring their employees' activities on the Internet. Employees that use company time for irrelevant Web surfing not only waste time, but also attract unsolicited e-mail. Increased traffic to the server means slower access for those employees using the Web for legitimate purposes.[24]

E-mails can reach large groups of people quickly and easily, creating the possibility of harassment suits. For example, e-mails of a questionable nature could be used to argue that the workplace is an unfriendly environment. To see how this argument works, read the feature "Michael A. Smyth v. The Pillsbury Company: Viewing Expectations of Privacy and Reasonable Business Interests."

Letting your employees know what is expected of them will, in many cases, cut back on the amount of time wasted surfing the Internet and sending e-mail to family and friends. When implementing a surveillance mechanism, make it known. This way, surveillance takes on a preventive role, saving both parties time and energy.

Michael A. Smyth v. The Pillsbury Company: Viewing Expectations of Privacy and Reasonable Business Interests

Based on a series of unprofessional e-mail messages transmitted to his supervisor in October of 1994, Michael A. Smyth was dismissed as regional operations manager at The Pillsbury Company in February of 1995. After receiving his notification of termination, Mr. Smyth sued the company.

Mr. Smyth claimed that the Pillsbury Company had assured its employees that e-mail would not result in reprimand. However, under Pennsylvania law, "an employer may discharge an employee with or without cause, at pleasure, unless restrained by some contract."[25]

Having to give up his claim of wrongful termination, Mr. Smyth then restructured his argument. Mr. Smyth suggested that the use of his personal e-mail against him was a violation of public policy. Examples of public-policy violations condemned by the court include reprimanding an employee called for jury duty and denial of employment as a result of previous convictions.

> ### Michael A. Smyth v. The Pillsbury Company: Viewing Expectations of Privacy and Reasonable Business Interests (Cont.)
>
> However, the court did not find in favor of Mr. Smyth. It determined that there was no reasonable expectation of privacy, nor was Mr. Smyth made to share personal information. Rather, the court determined that The Pillsbury Company had legitimate business purposes for its actions against Mr. Smyth.

In an effort to regulate e-mail and Internet surveillance by employers, the *Notice of Electronic Monitoring Act* was proposed in 2000. The bill would require employers to notify employees of telephone, e-mail and Internet surveillance. Employees would be updated annually or when policy changes were made. The frequency of surveillance, the type of information collected and the method of collection would also be disclosed.

Proponents of notification argue that prevention would reduce the number of questionable transactions made over the Internet. However, opponents suggest that notification could result in lawsuits, as the recipients of the questionable e-mail or other communications could argue that the company knowingly allowed these transactions to be made.[26]

The government has also made use of Internet surveillance as a tool to locate criminals (see the feature "Carnivore: E-mail Surveillance by the FBI").

11.2.5 Protecting Yourself as a User

Users are able to take on falsified identities, *pseudonymity*, or use software to maintain anonymity on the Web. For example, **PrivacyX.com**, a free Internet service, allows users to surf the Web unidentified. To do this, **PrivacyX.com** creates a digital certificate for new users when they register. We discuss digital certificates and encryption in Chapter 7, Internet Security. What is unique to **PrivacyX.com**'s service is that anonymity can be maintained even in the digital certificate, which holds no personal information the user does not wish to include. **PrivacyX.com** then uses the digital certificate to return the requested information to the user, encrypted.

> ### Carnivore: E-mail Surveillance by the FBI
>
> *Carnivore*, an e-mail surveillance mechanism implemented by the FBI, was developed to scan e-mail transactions. The device is attached to an ISP that can regulate information transmitted through the ISP. The FBI claims that the mechanism searches only according to e-mail address. Opponents to the service argue that, while this might be the case now, it is possible to abuse the system. The searching capabilities could also provide IP addresses, e-mail subject titles, e-mail content and e-mail addresses. Visitors to a specific Web site could also be traced.[27] Several ISPs and companies specializing in encryption have raised objections to the use of the device. In a recent court battle, Earthlink, a popular ISP, was required to include the surveying capabilities to its service. Companies that specialize in encryption technologies are developing software and other services to circumvent e-mail scanning capabilities.[28]

The World Wide Web Consortium is introducing the *Platform for Privacy Preferences Project (P3P)*. The Consortium will release a questionnaire to users who have downloaded a newer version of the more popular browsers (e.g., Netscape Navigator and Internet Explorer) asking individual users about the level of privacy they desire. Then the browser will comply in accordance with users' answers by allowing them to interact in specific ways.[29] This method has been endorsed by the federal government as a means of avoiding legislation. The Web sites of many companies, including AOL, AT&T, Microsoft and IBM, already employ the P3P protocol.[30]

The P3P privacy policies are XML-based applications. XML technology is discusses and used in the programming appendices of this book. This system allows the user's preferences to be matched accurately to the site's standardized privacy protocols. While it will prompt users if the privacy policy of a particular Web site does not match the users' given preferences, it does not enforce Web sites to abide by their own policies. Opponents fear that this method will instead present Internet users with a false sense of security that their privacy is being protected.

e-Fact 11.2

According to Forrester Research, privacy concerns have had a significant impact on Web sales. An estimated $2.8 million dollars in potential revenue was lost in 1999 due to consumer concerns with the use of personal information.[31]

Sites such as **www.junkbusters.com** and **www.privacychoices.org**, run by DoubleClick, instruct visitors how to avoid receiving direct mail and how to disable cookies. To find more information on privacy issues, visit **www.cdt.org**, **www.eff.org**, **www.epic.org** and **www.privacyrights.org**.

11.2.6 Protecting Your Business: Privacy Issues

It is important to include a *privacy policy* on your Web site, respect the stated policy and treat your visitors' information with care. We provide an example of a privacy policy in Chapter 3, Building an e-Business. This means conducting regular audits to know exactly what information is being collected through your site. There are several services available over the Web that can generate a privacy policy according to your needs. For example, **PrivacyBot.com** features a questionnaire regarding your interest in collecting consumer information and how you plan to use the information you collect (Fig 11.1). For a fee, **PrivacyBot.com** issues an XML version of your privacy policy, authorizes the use of the official *Trustmark* seal to ensure users that you have an approved privacy policy and offers a mediation service, should problems arise.[32]

PriceWaterhouseCoopers offers a similar service through its *BetterWeb*[SM] Program. Based on the study of businesses, consumer input, current industry standards and the arguments of privacy-rights advocates, PriceWaterhouseCoopers created this program to assist developing and preexisting Web sites with their customer service programs. *The BetterWeb Standards*, as PWC has termed them, work for the benefit of both consumers and businesses by providing consumers with "what they can expect from an online business regarding sales terms, security and privacy policies and consumer complaint procedures."[33] For more information, visit **www.pwcbetterweb.com/betterweb/index.cfm**.

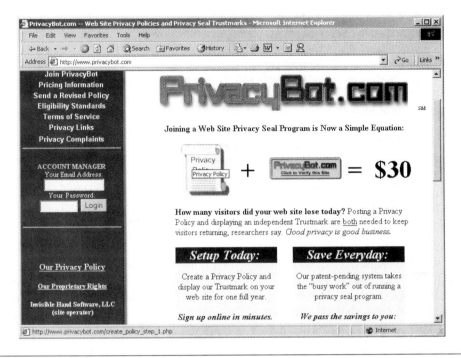

Fig. 11.1   PrivacyBot.com. (Courtesy of Invisible Hand Software, LLC.)

Not all sites carrying the mark of a security company make the effort to follow their privacy guidelines. **TRUSTe.com**, one of the most recognized auditing organizations, grants businesses its seal to signify a trustworthy privacy protection plan. When users visit a **TRUSTe.com** site, they can be reasonably sure that their information is being properly protected. However, it is still up to the organization to honor its stated privacy policies.

e-Fact 11.3

According to PriceWaterhouseCoopers, 76 percent of Web sites do not adhere to their own privacy policies.[34]

The Federal Trade Commission (FTC) has established five *Core Fair Information Practices* regarding online marketing tactics that involve gathering and using consumer information. They are: (1) Consumers should be made aware that personal information will be collected; (2) The consumer should have a say in how this information will be used; (3) The consumer should have the ability to check the information collected to ensure that it is complete and accurate; (4) The information collected should be secured; and (5) The Web site should be responsible for seeing that these practices are followed.[35]

11.3 Legal Issues: Other Areas of Concern

In this section, we will explore defamation, sexually explicit speech, copyrights, patents, trademarks, unsolicited e-mail and online auctions and how these issues are affected by the Internet and the First Amendment of the Constitution.

The First Amendment is designed to protect freedom of expression:

> *Congress shall make no law respecting an establishment of religion, or prohibiting the free exercise thereof; or abridging the freedom of speech, or of the press; or the right of the people peaceably to assemble and to petition the Government for a redress of grievances.*

11.3.1 Defamation

Defamation is the act of injuring another's reputation, honor or good name through false written or oral communication.[36] Because the First Amendment strongly protects the freedom of anonymous speech, it is often difficult to win a defamation suit.

Defamation consists of two parts, *libel* and *slander*. Slander is spoken defamation, whereas libelous statements are written or are spoken in a context in which they have longevity and pervasiveness that exceed slander. For example, broadcasting is considered libelous even though it is spoken.

To prove defamation, a plaintiff's case must meet five requirements: (1) The statement must have been published, spoken or broadcast; (2) there must be identification of the individual(s) through name or reasonable association; (3) the statement must, in fact, be defamatory; (4) there must be fault (for public persons, the statement must have been made in *actual malice*; for private persons, the statement needs only to have been *negligent*, or published, spoken or broadcast when known to be false); and (5) there must be evidence of injury or *actual loss*.[37]

Cubby v. Compuserve and Stratton Oakmont v. Prodigy

In the case *Cubby v. Compuserve*, an anonymous individual used a news service hosted by Compuserve to post an allegedly defamatory statement. As the provider of the bulletin board, Compuserve claimed that it could not be held liable for the defamatory statements, because Compuserve was not the publisher of the statement.

The deciding factor in this case rested on the distinction between *distributor* and *publisher*. In the court's opinion, a distributor cannot be held liable for a defamatory statement unless the distributor has knowledge of the content.

As a result, Compuserve and other providers cannot be held responsible for their users' statements. However, as we will discover when addressing the case *Stratton Oakmont v. Prodigy*, there was a fine line between claiming responsibility as a publisher of users' content and maintaining the "distance" of a distributor.

Prodigy differed from Compuserve in that it, as an ISP, claimed responsibility to remove potentially defamatory or otherwise questionable material when the material has been brought to its attention. Prodigy further claimed that it had an automatic scanning device that screens bulletin board postings before they are posted.

As a result, Prodigy assumed the role of a publisher by claiming control over specific statements made by its users. As a publisher, Prodigy was held liable for the posted statements. This decision later spurred Congress to pass Section 230 of the Telecommunications Act, which protects ISPs actively seeking to control the content of their sites.[40]

The responsibility of defamatory statements is addressed in the cases *Cubby v. Compuserve* and *Stratton Oakmont v. Prodigy* (see the feature "Cubby v. Compuserve and Stratton Oakmont v. Prodigy").

Congress has passed the *Good Samaritan* provision, *Section 230 of the Telecommunications Act*. This legislation protects ISPs from defamation lawsuits in the ISPs' attempts to control potentially damaging postings, including those that are "obscene, lewd, lascivious, filthy, excessively violent, harassing or otherwise objectionable." The Telecommunications Act further protects ISPs by excusing them from publisher status even after they have been informed of defamatory material posted on their site. This premise relieves ISPs of the time-consuming activity of exploring all defamation claims, and it protects freedom of expression by allowing unpopular opinions to appear. Without the added protection, an ISP, concerned about being charged with defamation, would remove all questionable material.

Because a plaintiff (the person bringing the argument to court) in a defamation suit cannot seek reward from the ISP, they must then seek out the author of the content. Most often, the speakers are anonymous and can remain so through bogus e-mail accounts and *anonymity indexes* (e.g., **PrivacyX.com** and **www.anonymizer.com**), through which the users can claim alternative identities. When plaintiffs pursue such cases, they create what is called a *John Doe suit*.[38] In an attempt to resolve the situation, the ISP will receive a request to provide the user's information. In the meantime, John Doe, whoever he or she might be, is being sued for what may or may not be a defamation case. To bring the case to court, John Doe's identity must be revealed, which is arguably a violation of John Doe's First Amendment right to anonymous free speech.[39]

11.3.2 Sexually Explicit Speech

As determined in *Miller v. California (1973)*, the *Miller Test* identifies the criteria used to distinguish between obscenity and pornography. Pornography is protected by the First Amendment. In order to be determined by the Miller Test to be obscene, material has to (1) appeal to the prurient interest, according to contemporary community standards, and (2) when taken as a whole, lack serious literary, artistic, political or scientific value.[41]

The Internet, with its lack of geographic boundaries, challenges the Miller Test. As we have discussed, the Test is dependent on contemporary community standards. In cyberspace, communities exist independently of geographic boundaries.

Cyberspace complicates jurisdiction by making it possible, for example, for a person in Tennessee, where the tolerance for pornography is relatively low, to view a site in California, where the tolerance is higher (see the feature "United States v. Thomas: Reviewing the Question of Jurisdiction").

The Internet has characteristics similar to those of broadcast media and print media; yet there are problems with applying traditional regulations to communications on the Web. Broadcasting is considered highly pervasive. The Internet resembles broadcasting in its ability to reach a broad audience with little or no warning.[42] Print, however, focuses more on the regulation of the audience and less on the content of the material. Defined as *non-content-related means* (an effort to control the audience rather than the material), print restrictions allow adults to view pornographic material while limiting an adolescent's ability to obtain that material. The Internet can mimic this method by requiring users to provide identification before entering specific sites.

United States v. Thomas: Reviewing the Question of Jurisdiction

Thomas, an Internet business owner in California, had established a pornographic Web site from which merchandise could be ordered. The Web site was membership based, and a review of all applications was conducted before passwords were distributed to users. By California community standards, the Web site was legitimate.

In court, Thomas was found guilty of distributing obscenity, even though his site was established in California, where the actions were considered legitimate. The determining factor, and Thomas's critical mistake, was in the application process. The court argued that Thomas knew that the applicant was from Tennessee; the applicant's address and phone number appeared on the application. It suggested that, having this knowledge, Thomas should have denied any individual from an area of less tolerant community standards access to his Web site.

How, then, should the Internet be regulated to protect individuals like Thomas? The site, however disagreeable, was legal as far as his resident state was concerned. To answer this question, the courts have looked at the regulation of broadcasting and print. This issue is discussed in Section 11.3.2.

11.3.3 Children and the Internet

Elementary and junior high schools implement Web-based learning in much the same way as do high schools and universities. Most public libraries provide visitors with Internet access. Often, younger Internet audiences are able to gain access to the same information as adults without the constraints that might be found in *real space* (our physical environment). The Internet is not subject to the same zoning laws that would prohibit a pornography store from situating itself near an elementary school.

e-Fact 11.4

Frederick Lane, author of Obscene Profits, *estimates that pornography sites on the Internet now number between 30,000 and 60,000.*[43]

Let us revisit a previous example. Suppose you are a parent whose fourth grader has been assigned to write a report on the White House. The teacher has requested that the students conduct their research on the Internet. While working on the project, your fourth grader stumbles across **www.whitehouse.com**, a pornography site, and other undesirable sites targeted toward unsuspecting viewers.

This example presents a complicated issue. Parents are concerned with protecting the well-being of their children. Yet, by limiting speech in an effort to protect younger audiences, we run the risk of infringing upon the constitutional right to the freedom of expression. For example, **www.whitehouse.com**, however distasteful, is protected under the First Amendment. It is the right of an adult to construct, own and visit a site of this nature.

The *Communications Decency Act of 1996 (CDA)* and the *Child Online Protection Act of 1998 (COPA)* were designed to restrict pornography on the Internet, particularly in the interest of children. Both CDA and COPA, however, have several flaws that have been pointed out by free-speech advocates. Both the CDA and COPA were accused of being *overbroad*—that is, reaching beyond the group they intended to protect. They attempted to enforce regulation when sites offered information that was "patently offensive," "indecent" and "harmful to minors." Arguments rested on the ambiguity of these defining terms. Opponents of CDA and COPA argue that decisions become arbitrary when the actual crime is too hard to define.[44] Thus, individuals may not violate the guidelines intentionally; or, of equal concern, individuals will limit their speech to avoid a lawsuit. This situation is commonly referred to as the *chilling effect.*[45]

Children's privacy is also a concern. The *Children's Online Privacy Protection Act of 2000* (COPPA) prohibits Web sites from collecting personal information from children under the age of 13 without parental consent. While COPPA may be effective in protecting younger children, studies have indicated that teenagers are more likely than children to divulge information and are, therefore, at greater risk.[46] Web sites will often target this group by running promotions and contests geared toward them.

11.3.4 Alternative Methods of Regulation

Software companies have developed *blocking and filtering* technologies to help parents and teachers protect children from questionable material. This software allows users to select what kinds of information can and cannot be received through their browsers. The technology is available at Web sites such as **www.surfwatch.com**, **www.cybersitter.com** and **www.netnanny.com** (Fig. 11.2).

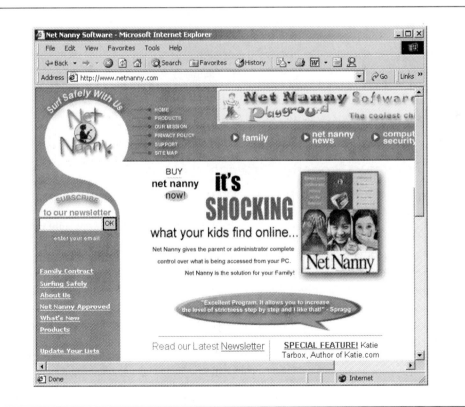

Fig. 11.2   Net Nanny home page. (Courtesy of Net Nanny Software International Inc.)

Although blocking software is an effective way of keeping children away from sites that may not be suitable for them, the software may also be considered a violation of First Amendment rights, because most filters do not give parents direct control of what can and cannot be viewed. Once users turn that responsibility over to the software, they have limited their knowledge of what information is available to them. Net Nanny (Fig 11.2), however, is a filter that makes NetNanny's list of objectionable sites open and can be customized to accommodate this issue. Parents are able to view this list and de-select sites that were marked as blocked.

Blocking technology often exceeds its purpose by blocking out sites that can be thought of as educational. The *Electronic Privacy Information Center* (EPIC), a privacy-rights group in Washington, D. C., found that "family-friendly" filtering technology blocked access to well over 90 percent of "decent material on the Internet." EPIC loaded up the family software and then used powerful Internet searching systems to find information about schools, charitable and political organizations and educational, artistic and cultural institutions, using search terms including "American Red Cross," the "San Diego Zoo" and the "Smithsonian Institution," as well as such concepts as "Christianity," the "Bill of Rights" and "eating disorders." Many sites including information based on these keywords was blocked by the software.[47]

Recently a congressional panel rejected the mandate that filtering software be installed in public libraries and school-owned computers, two locations where children could access harmful material regardless of blocking software installed on their computers at home. The rejection was based on reasons similar to the results found in EPIC's study. Rather than installing filtering software, members of the panel have suggested higher standards for self regulation.[48]

As an alternative to filtering software, Web sites are available to counsel parents on supervising their children on the Internet. Visit **www.cyberangels.com**, **www.get-netwise.com** and **www.parentsoup.com** for more information.

11.3.5 Intellectual Property: Copyright and Patents

Copyright, according to the U.S. Copyright Office, is the protection given to the author of an original piece, including "literary, dramatic, musical, artistic and certain other intellectual works," whether the work has been published or not. For example, copyright protection is provided for literature, music, sculpture and architecture. Copyright protects only the expression or form of an idea, and not the idea itself.

Copyright protection provides incentives to the creators of original material by guaranteeing them credit for their work for a given amount of time. Currently, copyright protection is guaranteed for the life of the author plus 70 years.

Because of the ease with which material can be reproduced on the Internet, and because *digital copies* are perfect duplicates of the original, concerns have been raised regarding the level of protection of intellectual property offered through traditional law (see the feature "File Sharing and the Copyright Debate".

 e-Fact 11.5

In one year, Napster's user list has grown to over 25 million, making it the fastest growing site in Internet history.[51]

In a study released by the Digital Media Association, 66 percent of users suggest that they are prompted to buy the album after downloading the MP3.[52] The software industry is also experiencing a loss in sales due to online copyright infringement. On a fact sheet about policy issues, Microsoft cites a 1998 study which indicates that an $11 billion loss in desktop application sales was the result of software piracy.[53] Losses can be the result of license sharing, differing cultural perspectives on copyrighting and ownership of information and counterfeit reproductions.

 e-Fact 11.6

According to the Business Software Alliance, approximately 33 percent of Microsoft software currently in use has been pirated.[54]

File Sharing and the Copyright Debate

File sharing, or *peer-to-peer networking* of information, have presented significant challenges to the traditional treatment of copyright protection. As technology progresses, services such as **Napster.com** and Gnutella create mechanisms by which information can be exchanged from one user to another for free.

Napster, a file-sharing service, offers software that allows users to download MP3 files from the hard drives of other members. *MP3* is a compression method used to substantially reduce the size of audio files, with no significant reduction in sound quality.[49] This compression method facilitates the exchange of audio files over the Internet.

Napster uses central servers to help users locate MP3 files stored on other Napster users' hard drives. After locating the files, Napster members are able to download these files to their own hard drives; the files are not stored on Napster's servers. Consequently, **Napster.com** suggests that it cannot control the use (or misuse) of those files, and therefore it is not violating copyright laws.[50]

Gnutella differs from Napster in that it is a *decentralized* service. Rather than passing information exchanges through a central server, individuals with Gnutella software installed on their computers operate as both a client and a server. This means that searches made by one user that cannot be fulfilled by another user are passed on until they are matched with a user containing the information. Gnutella also differs from Napster in that it allows text files, images, video, MP3 files, etc., to be exchanged.

Debate is currently centered on the freedoms that exchange systems of Gnutella's type allow versus the issue of copyright infringement. The distribution of information cannot be limited by censorship under these circumstances, and the potential audience size is larger than that of most traditional forums. For example, to distribute your opinion over television or to broadcast it on the radio requires that certain standards are met (see the feature "United States v. Thomas: Reviewing the Question of Jurisdiction"). However, as previously discussed, the original purpose of copyright was to protect creative efforts in order to provide incentives for further creative efforts; if copyrighted works are distributed over the system, creators will have less incentive to continue generating original works.

File Sharing and the Copyright Debate (Cont.)

In both cases, the concern lies in the assignment of responsibility. For example, Sony released the Betamax in 1984, enabling the taping of television programs and televised movies. The motion picture industry filed a suit suggesting that the release of this product would result in lost revenue. The courts awarded the victory to Sony, suggesting that the Betamax provided other uses, namely recording for personal viewing, that justified its existence; obeying copyright law was the responsibility of the user, and not of the technology. Napster's argument focused on the scores of unsigned artists represented. In addition, chat rooms and instant messenger services are also available through Napster.

`MP3.com`, which varies slightly from the exchange mechanisms employed by Napster, recently settled with the recording industry by agreeing to pay a licensing fee for use of the music. After much debate, Napster's legal proceedings approached a similar resolution. In the summer of 2000 the site received an injunction against a ruling that would have forced it off the Web. By Fall, 2000, Napster received funding from Bertelsmann, the third largest media company in the world, to legitimize its MP3 transactions. In short, Napster agreed to redesign itself to charge participants a small monthly fee for use of the service. If Napster complies, then Bertelmann (BMG) has agreed to drop its lawsuit and take an active role in developing Napster into a forum for trading a variety of media. This would include books, movies, DVDs and other copyright protected materials.

In a landmark case, *United States v. LaMacchia*, Congress recognized the inability of traditional copyright law in the United States to regulate the Internet. As a result, several attempts were made to ensure that creators (i.e., software developers, writers, artists, etc.) and resource providers could maintain the same protection for digitally transmitted material as is afforded for other material under traditional law.

United States v. Lamacchia: Copyright Infringement and the "Commercial Gain" Loophole

In 1994, the U.S. Court made a landmark decision that changed the face of copyright protection. The case involved an M.I.T. student by the last name of LaMacchia who had posted computer software on his Web site. Users could then access his site and download the copyrighted material for free, costing computer software companies lost sales.

Although the material posted was not original, the courts could not find LaMacchia guilty of copyright infringement according to the *Copyright Act of 1976*. In order to be guilty of copyright infringement under the Act, the violation must have been conducted "willfully and for purposes of commercial advantage or private financial gain."[55]

In this particular case, LaMacchia did not profit from the copyright violations and could not be tried as such. Consequently, LaMacchia was not convicted for his actions.

The *Digital Millennium Copyright Act of 1998* (DMCA) represents the rights of creative bodies to protect their work, as well as the rights of educators and resource providers to receive access to the work. The DMCA makes it illegal to delete or otherwise alter the identifying information of the copyright owner. It prevents the circumvention of protection mechanisms and/or the sale of such circumvention mechanisms, but limits this restriction to activity outside research, encryption, technological development and the testing of security measures. The DMCA protects the rights of ISPs by providing a *safe-harbor* provision in which the Webcasting of such property can be permitted by the purchase of license. Finally, the DMCA protects the *fair use* of copyrighted material.[56]

Fair use is defined as the use of a copyrighted work for education, research, criticism, etc. Four criteria have been established in order to determine whether fair use can be applied to the reproduction of a copyrighted work.

First, the purpose of the copyrighted work is examined. For example, was the reproduction of the copyrighted material for commercial use?

Second, the nature of the copyrighted work is taken into account. When determining the nature of a reproduction, the court looks at whether the original material was factual or fictitious. It is the expression of ideas that receives protection, not the ideas themselves.

Third, the amount of the material that has been reproduced is reviewed. This criterion creates a gray area, in that it is impossible to determine whether the amount of material reproduced is guaranteed copyright protection. So, it is the significance of the material that is examined here: How crucial was the piece of information to the whole work?

Fourth, the effect of the reproduction is taken into consideration: How does the reproduction of the copyrighted material affect the potential market?

However, the DMCA does not address all of the concerns facing copyright protection. For example, issues such as first sale, which allows an owner to sell a used item and permits the reproduction of material used in distance-learning programs, still need to be addressed.[57] Opponents of the legislation also feel that it is too restrictive, because it limits the progression of *open-source code*, or code that is able to be accessed and modified by anyone.

Patents, which grant the creator sole rights to the use of a new discovery, present another issue: There are opponents to the duration of patents. Given the growth rate of the Internet, some argue that the 20-year duration of patents discourages continuous software development and improvement.

In 1998, the federal regulations governing the distribution of patents increased the scope of patented discoveries to include "methods of doing business."[58] In order to be granted a patent for a method of doing business, the idea must be new and not obvious to a skilled person.[59]

To some, the inability to share information freely appears to be in opposition to the founding principles of the Internet, and the ability to restrict competition would hinder the growth of e-commerce (see the feature "**Amazon.com** and the 1-Click Patent"). Bounty/quest Corp., offers cash rewards to individuals or groups that can prove that a patent owner does not have rightful ownership of that patent.

Expedia.com is currently being sued by Priceline for its use of the "name-your-own price" technology, and British Telecommunications recently discovered that it had a patent, dating back to 1976, that claims ownership to hyperlinking technology. *Hyperlinks* are links from one electronic document to another electronic document (see the feature "Profitable Patents").

Amazon.com and the 1-Click^{SM} Patent

At the time of this book's publication, **Amazon.com** was at the forefront of the dispute over patent grants. The innovator of the 1-Click^{SM} system, **Amazon.com** received a patent on this new method of online purchasing in September 1999.[60] The 1-Click system allowed **Amazon.com** users to make purchases on the site without having to go through the checkout process.

This technology is significant, as studies show that approximately 65 percent of online shopping carts are abandoned before a purchase is complete. While there are several reasons that users typically abandon their shopping carts, the dominant theory suggests that the long and complicated checkout process tops the list.[61]

The 1-Click patent gave **Amazon.com** an advantage over its competitors, enabling **Amazon.com** to provide faster, more efficient service to its customers than was legally available at any other site. **Barnesandnoble.com** quickly discovered this situation after losing a legal dispute involving its check-out technology, *Express Lane.*[62]

According to the criteria for a method-of-doing-business patent, the 1-Click system was correctly protected by a patent. The system was unlike any checkout system on the Internet, and the patent's usefulness was adequately demonstrated by the similar version created by **Barnesandnoble.com**.

Profitable Patents

In many cases, organizations never realize the full potential of the patents they hold. For example, if you were to obtain a patent on a material and you used that material for your own production purposes, there might be other opportunities for other companies to use that material for something else. You could sell the use of your patent to those companies. Marketing patents, or selling rights to your patents to other groups, is a growing industry on the Internet. Several Web sites enable patent owners to post their patents and auction them to companies that need the technologies.

Yet2.com provides a searchable database of under-used patents. A 10-percent transaction fee is taken by the site when a sale is completed, but searching the database is free. **PatentAuction.com** offers auctions for several types of patents, including methods of doing business, and evaluates the present value of patents for interested buyers. Fees are charged to post patents, and the site takes a commission on its sales.[63],[64]

 e-Fact 11.7

According to the British Technology Group, only 3 percent of the commercial value of patents worldwide was met in 1999.[65]

11.3.6 Trademark and Domain Name Registration

There are several methods by which one can commit an alleged trademark infringement in cyberspace. One method is by becoming a *parasite*. A parasite selects a domain name based on common typos made when entering a popular domain name.

Another way in which trademark infringement can occur is called *cybersquatting*. A cybersquatter buys an assortment of domain names that are obvious representations of the names of brick-and-mortar companies. When these previously established companies make the transition to the Internet, they are forced to buy the domain names from the cybersquatter.

Congress enacted the *Anticybersquatting Consumer Protection Act of 1999* (ACPA) to protect traditional trademarking in cyberspace. Consumer fraud, decreased revenue for the trademark holder and the hindrance of e-commerce are among the reasons for the ACPA.

Trademarks belonging to a person or entity other than the person or entity registering or using the domain name are protected. Registering a domain name that is similar to an established trademark to cause confusion, to intentionally deceive or to dilute the established trademark is illegal. However, persons registering domain names are protected from prosecution if they have a legitimate claim to the domain name, such as if it is their first or last name or if the domain name was registered prior to the first use of the registered trademark.[66] In addition, domain names cannot be registered with the intention of resale to the rightful trademark owner.

Cybersquatting is not a cut-and-dry issue—there are legitimate cases in which a trademarked name can be used by a third party. This makes it imperative that when selecting a domain name for your organization, you think carefully about similar names that could be used to criticize you. In many cases, individuals will choose a domain name similar to yours. For example, if you own X Auto Body Parts, you might select **www.xauto.com** as your domain name. To many consumers, this might be the obvious domain name. However, suppose one of your mechanics makes a mistake one day, failing to fix a customer's car properly and this customer decides to establish a Web site to warn others against choosing you as their mechanic. The new Web site is named **www.xautoparts.com**. In this particular case, **www.xautoparts.com** is not competing with your business, but rather providing a legitimate service to other consumers, and many consumers may type **www.xautoparts.com** into their Web browser without verifying the correct address. In other cases, an individual or a group will choose a domain name that indicates it is a Web site for criticism. For example, the disgruntled customer may select **www.xautostinks.com**. This particular situation has cost large organizations significant amounts of money as they often must pay large fees to obtain ownership of these sites.

11.3.7 Unsolicited Commercial e-Mail (Spam)

E-mail is an exceedingly popular form of online communication. In 1996, an estimated 20,000,000 e-mail users in the United States sent an estimated 500,000,000 messages per day. By 2002, those numbers are expected to reach 105,000,000 users sending 1,500,000,000 messages per day.[67] AOL estimates that nearly one third of the messages sent daily can be categorized as unsolicited commercial e-mail (UCE), most commonly referred to as *spam*.[68]

Electronic mail is different from the direct mail you receive via the U.S. Postal Service. Direct mail printing, packaging and postage fees are absorbed by the advertiser. For unsolicited e-mail, a large part of the cost is incurred by the recipient through ISP access fees.

Often, organizations responsible for distributing large quantities of unwanted messages will either maintain anonymity or present themselves as legitimate companies. In the former case, receivers cannot request to be taken off the organization's mailing list. Consequently, they will continue to receive the unwanted messages. In the second case, the legitimate companies' reputations could be damaged, or they might have to waste valuable resources responding to the receivers' (often angry) replies.

The arguments in support of government regulation of e-mail transactions focus minimizing the cost and protecting the integrity of legitimate electronic communications. At the time of publication of this book, the federal government is reviewing the *Unsolicited Electronic Mail Act.*[69] This legislation would mandate that the nature of e-mails be made clear. For example, advertisements must be labeled as such. This would, in effect, require online marketers to know the policy of every ISP they encounter on the Web, as different ISPs have different rules governing the transmission of e-mail.[70]

In the meantime, there are alternative ways to protect your time and business against unwanted e-mail. Web sites such as **unitedmessaging.com** offer services that allow subscribers to control the information they receive. The service provided by **unitedmessaging.com**, *Message Control*, reduces the amount of spam received, and it also protects users against viruses and certain types of content. Other, similar services include **www.spambouncer.org** and **www.scambusters.org**.

Spammotel.com is a Web-based service that allows users to regulate the e-mail they receive. Through this service, users specify that future messages from particular senders be blocked. During the registration process at other sites, users can submit their Spammotel address in place of their regular e-mail address. Before sending a message, users are prompted to keep a record of the registration and its purpose. Any replies sent from the original site are collected by Spammotel and forwarded to the user with this record attached. This way, users can track unsolicited e-mail and can then block the senders. Screen shots that demonstrate the service are available at **www.spammotel.com/spammotel/screens.html**.[71]

The *Mail Abuse Prevention System* (MAPS) also protects users against spam. It receives consumer complaints regarding the distribution of unsolicited e-mail. After as few as three complaints about an address, MAPS places the address on its list of offenders. MAPS then provides a blocking service based on this list. ISPs such as Netscape and Juno subscribe to the service to protect their users from receiving e-mails from addresses on the list. The list includes both Hotmail and America Online (AOL) accounts.

While MAPS may seem to be a solution to the distribution of unsolicited e-mail, it is also prone to error, given the small number of complaints needed to add an e-mail address to the list. Opponents of the service further argue that MAPS also infringes on ISP subscribers who are rendered incapable of making their own decisions regarding incoming messages.

MAPS supports the *double-confirmation system*. Under this system, users would have to *opt in* (users choose to be solicited) when first prompted by the Web site and then opt in again by responding positively to a confirmation e-mail sent by the Web site. Other sites offering information and anti-spam services include the Network Abuse Clearinghouse (**spam.abuse.net**), which supports efforts to boycott spam, and the Coalition Against Unsolicited Commercial E-mail (**www.cauce.org**).[72,73]

11.3.8 Online Auctions

Sites such as eBay and Bidland allow Internet users to post and search for a wide variety of items available for auction. Auctions are regulated by government on several levels.

North Carolina, for example, has had a law in effect for several years requiring that auctioneers be licensed to conduct an auction. The state has decided to enforce the regulation of auctions on the Internet as well. This means that, to sell an item on an auction site, an individual must take a state certification exam and pay a series of fees. Anyone posting an item without a license is subject to a fine.[74]

Many countries, including Germany, France, Italy and the Netherlands, also restrict auctions to individuals certified to conduct them. At the time of publication of this book, France demanded that Yahoo! pay antiracist groups for allowing neo-Nazi merchandise to appear in online auctions. The site was given two months to discontinue access in France due to violations of French laws against racism.[75]

Copyright infringement is another pressing issue for online auction sites. eBay, the most popular auction site, earns commissions from transactions completed at its site. Comprehensive auction sites that use *intelligent agents*, or programs designed to search for information designated by the user and to compare auctions on a variety of auction sites, continually search the Web for this information. As a result, the livelihood of one site depends on taking information from others. In a recent court decision, the courts awarded eBay an injunction to protect its site against copyright infringement.[76]

Designed to protect the compiled lists of organizations like eBay, *The Collection of Information Antipiracy Act* (CIAA) makes it easier to prosecute any group that takes listings from one organization and, in doing so, harms the original business of the organization. A lack of protection of this sort, proponents argue, would cause sites like eBay to create restrictions for access to the sites. Opponents argue that the CIAA will limit the growth potential of the Internet, by limiting access to public information, making it more difficult to conduct comparison shopping.[77]

Fraudulent activity is another problem for online auction sites. Fraudulent activity can consist of bogus bidding, bids that are unsubstantiated and *shill bidding*, when sellers bid for their own items to increase the bid price.

11.3.9 Online Contracts

The *Electronic Signatures in Global and National Commerce Act of 2000*, otherwise known as the *E-Sign bill*, is designed to promote online commerce by legitimizing online contractual agreements. Under the bill, digital agreements receive the same level of validity as their hard-copy counterparts. The bill also allows cooperating parties to establish their own contracts. This provision is expected to reduce the time and expense of paperwork.

Security features, which are discussed in greater detail in Chapter 7, Internet Security, can be used to validate online contracts. Digital signatures, the electronic equivalent of handwritten signatures, are used to authenticate the participating parties and ensure the integrity of the message.

11.3.10 User Agreements

In many cases, a Web site will require users to agree to certain terms regarding the service or product provided by the site before entering. Prior to the advent of the Internet, this agreement was most commonly called a *shrink-wrap agreement*. The agreement was printed on the outside of the package holding the product and became binding when the consumer opened the package. In the Internet age, user agreements are often provided as *click-throughs* presented in a pop-up screen to which users must agree before they can continue.

Depending on their presentation, these types of agreements can be considered valid by the U. S. courts. They must be easy to find and understandable to Web users. Users must actively indicate their acceptance of the conditions of such agreements. This is usually done by clicking on an "I accept" or "I agree" icon. Web site owners should keep a record of each agreement, for reference purposes.[78]

11.4 Cybercrime

While the Internet provides a wide variety of opportunities, it is also a place to exercise skepticism. Auctions, chat rooms and bulletin boards are among the most popular forums for illegal activities. In this section, we explore cybercrimes and present resources for protecting your e-business and your customers from such occurrences.

Viruses, which often lead to denial of service or a loss of stored information, are among the most common cybercrimes. The Melissa virus and the ILOVEYOU virus, which recently cost corporations and organizations worldwide considerable sums, are discussed in Chapter 7, Internet Security. *Stock scams* (crimes in which individuals purchase stocks, then present false claims about the value of that stock in chat rooms or on bulletin boards to sell them back at a higher price) are common Internet crimes. Credit-card fraud, fabricated free offers, undeliverable purchases and false auctions are also among frequently occurring cybercrimes.

Web-page hijacking is another issue of concern. When a Web page is hijacked, it is used as a gateway (the intermediary between one site and another) to another site. Often, users who click on the link to the hijacked page are transferred to a pornography site. This can be costly to organizations that can lose both their customer base and their reputations.

In an effort to alert Internet users to Internet scams, the FTC has posted "dummy" sites on the Web. The Web sites appear to be online businesses, but when Internet users click to make payment or gain more information a warning page appears instead. The warning indicates to users the types of sites usually associated with online scams (Fig. 11.3 and 11.4).

The Federal Trade Commission (FTC) offers a Web site (**www.ftc.gov/ftc/consumer.htm**) on consumer protection practices, covering a wide range of issues including privacy, children on the Internet, telemarketing and identity theft. The U.S. Securities and Exchange Commission (SEC) also offers a site (**www.sec.gov/consumer/offertip.htm**) to avoid Internet investment scams.

11.5 Internet Taxation

Internet taxation is a monumentally controversial topic, and a highly complicated issue. While one side argues for a permanent ban on Internet taxation, the other maintains the necessity of fairly taxing Internet sales.

The geographic locations of the vendor, consumer, ISP, server and other participating parties present a major issue. If both a vendor and a consumer are located in the same state, a sales tax can be imposed. If the vendor and the consumer are not located in the same state, then the sale is subject to a *use tax*. The state in which the purchased property or service is used directly imposes this tax on the consumer. If the vendor has a physical presence, or *nexus*, in that state, then it is required to collect the tax; otherwise, the vendor must assess the tax and pay it directly to the state. This was determined by the 1992 Supreme Court case, *Quill Corp. vs. North Dakota* to address catalog/mail-order sales. This assessment is a voluntary responsibility, and although compliance often occurs in business-to-business transactions, it is far less common in business-to-consumer sales.

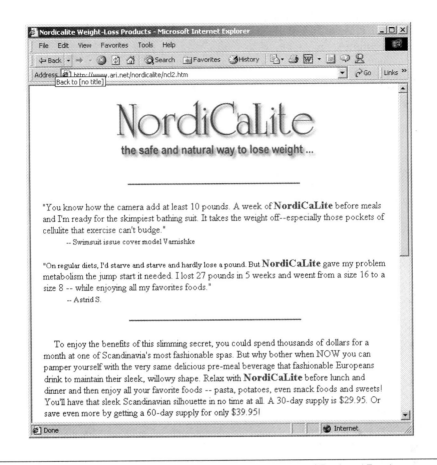

Fig. 11.3   FTC "dummy" site for NordiCaLite. (Courtesy of Federal Trade Commission.)

There are other problems with interstate taxation. Physical presence is proving to be a difficult term to define. Should it be determined by the location of the ISP, the location of the server or the location of the home page? Taxation policies vary by state. What is considered a taxable item in one state may be considered a necessity, and consequently non-taxable, in another.

Many state and local governments support remote taxation of the consumer based on the location of the vendor's physical presence. Sales tax revenues are the single largest source of a state's revenue and are used to fund government-subsidized programs, including fire departments, police departments and public education systems. It also allows the nation's wealthiest members to shop tax free, while those without Internet access must continue to pay sales tax. This is often referred to as the digital divide. The digital divide is discussed in Chapter 13, Social and Political Issues. Figures suggest that the amount of uncollected sales taxes from online shopping was $525 million in 1999.[80] State and local governments argue that removing taxation methods from their jurisdiction infringes upon state sovereignty, an element of the checks-and-balances system maintained by the U. S. Constitution.

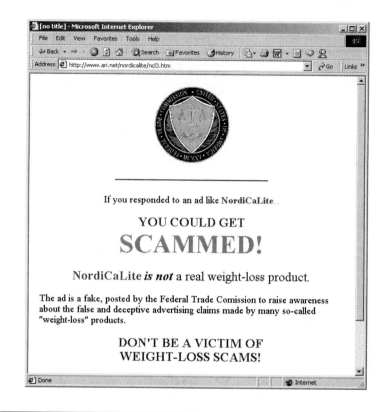

Fig. 11.4   FTC warning page. (Courtesy of Federal Trade Commission.)

Opponents to Internet taxation claim that it will inhibit the growth of the Internet. There are an estimated 7,500 different taxation methods.[81] To meet the taxation requirements of all parties in online transactions, e-businesses would be required to implement all these methods. Opponents to Internet taxation suggest that the real revenue for state and local governments will come as a result of the high-paying technical positions created by Internet growth. The higher salaries require higher income taxes and this money is used to boost the local economies. They further argue that brick-and-mortar businesses will continue to survive, despite the growth of online purchasing, because a brick-and mortar purchase provides instant gratification, and the sales personnel of brick-and-mortar businesses offer human-to-human communication.

The *Internet Tax Commission*, created by the *Internet Tax Freedom Act*, was developed to review the issue of Internet taxation and return a recommendation to Congress in April 2000.[82] Issues to be addressed by the commission included a revision of state and local taxes to make taxation a feasible process for Internet businesses, clearer definitions of the meaning of "physical presence" and universal taxation exemptions.

The panel included members of federal, state and local government, industry leaders and officials of trade organizations. Despite the lack of unanimity, the commission agreed on several recommendations, including an extension to the moratorium on Internet taxation and international e-commerce taxation and the elimination of taxes on digital content (e.g. music and software). The commission further recommended that a clear definition of "physical presence" be determined, taxation methods be simplified by each state and welfare money be allocated for Internet access. Consumer privacy and Internet access for the poor were also among the issues presented by the Commission to Congress.[83]

The *Streamlined Sales Tax Project* is yet another panel designed to resolve Internet taxation issues. The panel suggests that taxation should occur in the state where a product is delivered and that the state should determine the percentage taxed. Similarly, the National Academy of Science's National Research Center suggests a flat tax rate should be collected by the vendor and returned to the state in which the vendor resides.[84]

Taxation problems with regard to the Internet are as abundant internationally as they are in the United States. Each country in the European Union imposes a *value-added tax* (VAT) ranging from 15–25 percent on goods sold to consumers within the European Union. All E.U. companies are VAT registered, while non-E.U. companies are not. Under the current system, when a non-E.U. business sells to an E.U. business, the buyer is required to self-assess the VAT. However, when a non-E.U. business sells online to an individual consumer in the European Union, the VAT is not paid. This gives non-E.U. businesses an advantage, as their products are ultimately less expensive for the consumer.[85]

In addition to taxation, the global capabilities of the Internet raise many additional issues. These are discussed in Chapter 13, Globalization.

11.6 Internet And World Wide Web Resources

Legal References

www2.bc.edu/~herbeck/cyberreadings.html
Prof. D. Herbeck of Boston College has established this site to provide students with readings and court cases relevant to the development of cyberlaw. The site includes several landmark cases in the development of the freedom of expression in the United States, as well as more current debates over speech and the Internet.

www.fcc.gov
The Federal Communications Commission is the government body responsible for regulating interstate and international communications, including radio, television and satellite. The FCC plays an active role in determining the need for government regulation of the Internet.

www.findlaw.com
This site provides users with state and federal court decisions, as well as current law.

www.legalengine.com
This comprehensive Web site has links to federal, state, county and local laws. It includes world law, Supreme Court decisions and cyberlaw.

europa.eu.int
This site provides links to information regarding the European Data Protection Act and U.S. agreements for the management of international Web sites.

Online Privacy

www.privaseek.com
Now called Persona, this company provides users with the tools to protect their privacy online.

www.enonymous.com
A developer of privacy-oriented marketing strategies and services, **Enonymous.com** provides privacy ratings of various Web sites and presents them to users on a scale of 0 to 4 stars (0 being the lowest, 4 being the highest).

www.doubleclick.com

Doubleclick is an online advertising agency. The site was recently in the headlines for its consumer-tracking techniques.

www.codexdatasystems.com

Codex Data Systems manufactures tracking and surveillance software.

www.softsecurity.com

This private organization develops security software.

www.cdt.org

The *Center for Democracy and Technology* has expertise in the legal and technological development of the Web. Its mission is protecting privacy and free speech.

www.eff.org

The *Electronic Frontier Foundation* is a nonprofit organization concerned with privacy and the freedom of expression in the digital age.

www.privacyrights.org

The *Privacy Rights Clearinghouse* is a nonprofit organization designed to help consumers better understand and protect their privacy.

www.truste.com

This site is the leading provider of online privacy protection services. **Truste.com** audits member organizations to ensure consumers that the sites are upholding their privacy policies.

www.privacybot.com

This site generates privacy policies for Web sites. For a fee, users can enter information that is then incorporated into a policy. The service is supported by Trustmark.

www.privacyx.com

This free Internet service allows users to surf the Internet anonymously.

www.privacychoices.org

This site, operated by DoubleClick, aids users in understanding privacy policies, how to avoid receiving junk mail and how to disable cookies.

www.epic.org

The *Electronic Privacy Information Center* (*EPIC*) is concerned with the use of consumer information by online companies. The Web site allows users to register for regular e-mails that discuss updates on the current issues surrounding privacy and First Amendment rights.

www.junkbusters.com

Junkbusters is a privacy advocacy and consulting group that helps consumers and businesses reduce the amount of junk mail they receive. Although not a supplier of legal advice, the organization offers products designed to protect users from unsolicited e-mail.

www.getagriponit.com

WQuinn offers a software solution to monitor the material that is being stored on your server. The collection of outdated mail, sexually explicit images and otherwise sensitive material on your hard drive can lead to slow service or legal complications. The site offers a free 30-day trial of the software.

www.privaseek.com

Persona, formerly known as *Privaseek*, enables consumers to control their personal information through *MyPersona*. It provides material to alert users to privacy issues and provides a list of resources through which users can continue researching these issues.

www.netcoalition.com

A consortium of major Web sites, including **Amazon.com**, Yahoo! and Lycos. **Netcoalition.com** attempts to meet the needs of e-business while matching the demands of the consumer regarding online privacy.

www.ftc.gov/kidzprivacy
The Federal Trade Commission's site details the treatment of children's personal information on the Internet. The site includes the Child's Online Privacy Protection Act (COPPA), enacted in April 2000.

Regulation Methods

www.surfwatch.com
The first to enter the Internet filtering market in 1995, Surfwatch advertises a 90- to 95-percent success rate in filtering questionable content.

www.cybersitter.com
Cybersitter filtering software is available for a free trial or to buy as a download.

www.getnetwise.com
GetNetWise is an organization that provides and promotes a valuable Web experience. The site provides information on safe surfing.

www.unitedmessaging.com
This site aids users in managing incoming e-mail messages. Message Control, a service it provides, protects users from unwanted mail and viruses.

www.pwcbetterweb.com
This site is for PriceWaterhouseCoopers's auditing and privacy policy development program.

SUMMARY

- The application of traditional law to the Internet is not always a straightforward process.
- An individual's right to privacy is not explicitly guaranteed by the Constitution, but it is implicitly guaranteed through the First, Fourth, Ninth and Fourteenth Amendments.
- Translation is the interpretation of the Constitution to protect the greater good.
- The Internet is currently a self-regulated medium.
- The Financial Services Modernization Act of 1999 establishes a set of regulations concerning the management of consumer information.
- While having the Web experience tailored to their individual patterns appeals to some users, others consider having their every action recorded to be a violation of their privacy.
- Keystroke software provides an inexpensive, easy-to-use method of monitoring productivity and the abuse of company equipment. Keystroke software
- The courts propose two criteria to determine an employee's right to privacy: (1) Did the employee have a reasonable expectation of privacy, and (2) does the business have legitimate business interests that would reasonably justify the intrusion of an employee's privacy?
- Users are able to take on false identities to maintain anonymity on the Web.
- The World Wide Web Consortium has introduced the Platform for Privacy Preferences Project (P3P). This system enables a user to select the type of information to be accepted by the browser.
- It is important to include a privacy policy on your Web site, respect the stated policy and treat your visitors' information with care.
- Not all sites carrying a certified security trademark make the effort to follow their privacy guidelines. It is still up to the organization to honor its stated privacy policies.
- The Federal Trade Commission has established five Core Fair Information Practices regarding the use of online marketing tactics for gathering and using consumer information.
- Defamation is the act of injuring another's reputation or good name through written or oral communication.

- Slander is spoken defamation, whereas libelous statements are written or are spoken in a context in which they have longevity and pervasiveness exceeding that of slander.

- Without the added protection of Section 230 of the Telecommunications Decency Act, an ISP, concerned about being charged with defamation, would simply remove all questionable material.

- Pornography is protected by the First Amendment.

- In order to be determined by the Miller Test to be obscene, material has to: (1) appeal to the prurient interest, according to contemporary community standards, and (2) when taken as a whole, lack serious literary, artistic, political or scientific value.

- Broadcasting is considered highly pervasive. The Internet resembles broadcasting in its ability to reach a broad audience with little or no warning.

- Print focuses more on the regulation of the audience and less on the content of the material. For example, children are not permitted to buy pornographic material. This is regulating the audience. If the content were to be changed to allow children to buy the material, then the content would be regulated. This is often referred to as non-content-related means.

- The Communications Decency Act of 1996 (CDA) and the Child Online Protection Act of 1998 (COPA) were designed to restrict pornography on the Internet, particularly in the interest of children.

- Both the CDA and COPA were accused of being overbroad, reaching beyond the groups (children from pornographic or "harmful" material) they intended to protect.

- The Children's Online Privacy Protection Act of 2000 (COPPA) prohibits Web sites from collecting personal information from children under the age of 13 without parental consent.

- Software companies have developed blocking and filtering technologies to help parents and teachers protect children from questionable material.

- Blocking technology often exceeds its purpose by blocking out educational sites.

- Copyright, according to the U.S. Copyright Office, is the protection given to the author of an original piece, including "literary, dramatic, musical, artistic and certain other intellectual works," whether the work has been published or not.

- Copyright protection provides incentives to the creators of original material by guaranteeing them credit for their work for a given amount of time. Currently, copyright protection is guaranteed for the life of the author plus 70 years.

- In a landmark case, United States v. LaMacchia, Congress recognized the inability of traditional copyright law in the United States to regulate the Internet.

- The Digital Millennium Copyright Act of 1998 (DMCA) represents the rights of creative bodies to protect their work, as well as the rights of educators and resource providers to access this work.

- The DMCA protects the rights of ISPs by providing a safe-harbor provision in which the Webcasting of such property can be permitted by the purchase of a license.

- Fair use is defined as the use of a copyrighted work for education, research, criticism, etc.

- Patents grant the creator sole rights to the use of a new discovery.

- In 1998, the federal regulations governing the distribution of patents increased the scope of patented discoveries to include "methods of doing business."

- A parasite selects a domain name based on typos made when entering a popular domain name.

- A cybersquatter buys an assortment of domain names that are obvious representations of a brick-and-mortar company.

- Congress enacted the Anticybersquatting Consumer Protection Act of 1999 (ACPA) in an effort to protect traditional trademarking in cyberspace.

- Persons registering domain names are protected from prosecution if they have a legitimate claim to the domain name, such as if it is their first or last name, or if the domain name was registered prior to the first use of the registered trademark.

- Domain names cannot be registered with the intention of resale to the rightful trademark owner.

- AOL estimates that nearly one third of the messages sent daily can be categorized as unsolicited commercial e-mail (UCE), most commonly referred to as spam.

- Often, organizations responsible for distributing large quantities of unwanted messages will either maintain anonymity or falsely present themselves as a legitimate company.

- The federal government is reviewing the Unsolicited Electronic Mail Act; this legislation would mandate that the nature of e-mails be made clear.

- Many states have laws that requires that auctioneers be licensed to conduct an auction.

- The Collection of Information Antipiracy Act (CIAA) makes it easier to prosecute any group that takes listings from one organization and, in doing so, harms the original business.

- Fraudulent activity is a problem for online auction sites. Such activity can consist of bogus bidding, bids that are unsubstantiated and shill bidding (i.e., sellers bidding for their own items to increase the bid price).

- The E-Sign bill is designed to promote online commerce by legitimizing online contractual agreements.

- Many state and local governments support remote taxation of the consumer based on the location of the vendor's physical presence.

- Sales tax revenues are the single largest source of state revenue and are used to fund government subsidized programs, including the fire department, the police and the public education systems.

- State and local governments argue that to remove taxation methods from their jurisdiction infringes upon state sovereignty, an element of the checks and balances system maintained by the Constitution.

- Opponents to Internet taxation claim that it will inhibit the growth of the Internet.

- The Internet Tax Commission, created by the Internet Tax Freedom Act, was developed in order to review the issue of Internet taxation and return a recommendation to Congress in April 2000.

- Internet taxation problems are as common internationally as they are in the United States.

- The *Streamlined Sales Tax Project* suggests taxation should be the responsibility of the state where a product is delivered.

- The National Academy of Science's National Research Center suggests a flat tax rate on Internet sales should be collected by the vendor and returned to the state in which the vendor resides.

TERMINOLOGY

actual malice
actual loss
Americans with Disabilities Act
anonymity indexes
Anticybersquatting Consumer Protection Act
    of 1999
BetterWeb
blocking and filtering methods
brick-and-mortar business
Child Online Privacy Protection Act of 1999
Child Online Protection Act of 1998

chilling effect
clear GIFs
click-through banner advertisements
client–server networking model
Collections of Information Antipiracy Act
Communications Decency Act of 1996
Computer Usage Compliance Survey
consumer profile
cookie
copyright
Copyright Act of 1976

Core Fair Information Practices   Miller Test
cyberspace   negligence
cybersquatting   nexus
defamation   non-content-related means
digital copies   open-source code
Digital Millennium Copyright Act of 1998   opt in
digital redlining   opt out
distributor vs. publisher   overbroad
Electronic Privacy Information Center (EPIC)   parasite
Electronic Signatures in Global and   Personalization Consortium
    National Commerce Act of 2000   Platform for Privacy Preferences Project (P3P)
E-Sign Bill   privacy policy
European Union Directive on Data Protection   publisher
fair use of copyrighted material   real space
Financial Services Modernization Act of 1999   reasonable expectation of privacy
Good Samaritan provision   Section 230 of the Telecommunications
ID cards   Decency Act
intelligent agents   self-regulated medium
Internet Tax Commission   shill bidding
Internet Tax Freedom Act   slander
John Doe suit   spam
keystroke cops   Streamlined Sales Tax Project
legitimate business interests   tracking devices
libel   translation
Message Control   Unsolicited Electronic Mail Act
MPEG-1 Audio Layer 3   use tax
MP3   value-added tax

SELF-REVIEW EXERCISES

11.1 State whether the following are true or false. If the answer is false, explain why.

    a) Often, organizations responsible for distributing large quantities of unwanted messages will either maintain anonymity or falsely present themselves as a legitimate company.

    b) If a Web site has a posted privacy policy, it is reasonable to assume that the policy is being upheld.

    c) The *Streamlined Sales Tax Project* suggests taxation should be the responsibility of the state where a product is delivered.

    d) An Internet Service Provider (ISP) can be held accountable for a statement posted on a bulletin board by an anonymous user.

    e) Non-content-related means suggest that the medium by which a material is distributed receives regulation rather than the content of the material itself.

11.2 Fill in the blanks in each of the following statements:

    a) The five criteria that must be met in order to bring forth a defamation suit are: _____, _____, _____, _____ and _____.

    b) The two types of defamation are _____ and _____.

    c) The two criteria used to determine whether an intrusion into an employee's e-mail account by an employer was justifiable are _____ and _____.

    d) The three criteria that distinguish obscenity from pornography are as follows:_____, _____ and _____. The name of the U.S. Supreme Court case that determined this definition was _____.

    e) Copyright protection is guaranteed for the life of the author plus _____.

ANSWERS TO SELF-REVIEW EXERCISES

11.1 a) True. b) False. There are no regulatory bodies to guarantee that a Web site is upholding its privacy policy. c) True. d) False. Under the "Good Samaritan" provision of the Telecommunications Decency Act, ISPs are recognized as distributors and are consequently protected. e) True.

11.2 a) The statement must be defamatory, identify the plaintiff (this can be accomplished through allusions and descriptions), have been published or broadcast, have been done in negligence or actual malice and there must be evidence of injury or actual loss. b) libel and slander. c) a reasonable expectation of privacy and legitimate business interests. d) The material in question must appeal to the prurient interest, according to contemporary community standards and, when taken as a whole, lack serious literary, artistic, political or scientific value. e) 70 years.

EXERCISES

11.3 State whether the following are true or false. If the answer is false, explain why.
   a) Copyright protection is intended to protect an idea.
   b) To receive legitimate copyright protection an artist must have registered the material with the U.S. Copyright Office.
   c) An individual's right to privacy is guaranteed explicitly by the Constitution.
   d) Registering a domain name that is similar to an established trademark to cause confusion, intentionally deceive or to dilute the established trademark is considered illegal.
   e) Many state and local governments support remote taxation of the consumer by the location of the vendor's physical presence.

11.4 Fill in the blanks in each of the following:
   a) Limiting speech to avoid a lawsuit is commonly referred to as the _____.
   b) The _____ makes it easier to prosecute any group that takes listings from one organization and, in doing so, harms the original business.
   c) _____ and _____ were the cases that helped to define the difference between a distributor and a publisher on the Internet.
   d) The five _____ provide guidelines for the use of online marketing tactics for gathering and using customer information.
   e) The _____ provision of Section 230 of the Telecommunications Act protects ISPs from defamation lawsuits in their attempts to control potentially damaging postings, including those that are lewd, lascivious, filthy, excessively violent, harassing or otherwise objectionable.

11.5 Define the following.
   a) United States v. LaMacchia
   b) Digital Millennium Copyright Act of 1998
   c) parasite
   d) Unsolicited Electronic Mail Act

11.6 This chapter has discussed the use of cookies to track consumer activity and provide targeted advertising. Spend an hour surfing the Web, and record the sites you visit and the pattern of advertising that you find as you go along. Do the ads reflect the sites you have previously visited? Record any advertising agencies that sponsor the ads. (This information is available in the navigation bar located at the bottom of your screen.) Then, try to find the cookie file on your hard drive. Did it keep an accurate record of your travels? Write a brief summary describing your findings.

11.7 This chapter has discussed the issue of online privacy. According to the Personalization Consortium, there are many people who are in favor of targeted advertising. After reviewing the different sides of the argument, survey your friends and family to evaluate their stance on online privacy and summarize their thoughts and your own.

11.8   *(Class discussion)* File-sharing services, as offered through Napster, Gnutella, Freenet and other available downloads, suggest that these services protect individuals' freedom of expression. How does this argument work? Opponents argue that the services merely serve as a means to infringe on the copyrights of others. Which argument appeals to you? Why? Surf the Web for articles that argue either point to help you support your opinion. Prepare a summary of your evidence, and be prepared to offer quotes from various sources that address your point.

11.9   *(Class Discussion)* In this chapter, we discuss filtering software as a mechanism for blocking a child's access to "harmful materials." The Electronic Privacy Information Center (EPIC) found that many legitimate topics are blocked when filtering software is employed. Go to **Lycos.com** and activate the parental controls. Then, spend some time searching the Web. Try looking for questionable material, then spend some time looking for material that could be misinterpreted as questionable. Do you think this method is overbroad? Report your results.

WORKS CITED

The notation **<www.domain-name.com>** indicates that the citation is for information found at that Web site.

1.   D. Herbeck, Chair and Associate Professor of Communication, Boston College, 29 February 2000, lecture notes.

2.   L. Lessig, *Code and Other Laws of Cyberspace* (New York: Basic Books, 1999) 6.

3.   S. Herrera, "Hypocritic Oaths," *Red Herring* October 2000: 240.

4.   M. Stepanek, "Surf At Your Own Risk," *Business Week* 30 October 2000: 143.

5.   D. Hendrickson, "FTC Proposal for Web Privacy Guidelines Meets Mixed Reception," *Mass High Tech* 5 June -11 June 2000: 11.

6.   M. Nelson, "Majority of Web Sites Lack Privacy Policies," *Information Week* 17 April 2000: 173.

7.   R. Wright, "Can the Internet Ever Be Tamed," *Toronto Star News* 24 February 2000.

8.   F. Mogel, "Rise of the CPO," *Internet World* 1 November 2000: 36.

9.   F. Mogel, 36.

10.   S. Berinato and D. Callaghan, "Will Tool Crumble Cookies?" *eWeek* 7 August 2000: 36.

11.   "DoubleClick Advertisement: Commited to Privacy," *The New York Times* 14 February 2000: C19.

12.   B. Tedeschi, "In a Shift, Double Click Cuts Off Plan for Wider Use of Personal Data of Internet Consumers," *The New York Times* 3 March 2000: C5.

13.   R. Tomkins, "Cookies Leave a Nasty Taste: Marketing Internet Privacy," *Financial Times* 3 March 2000: 16.

14.   R. Tomkins, 16.

15.   "The DoubleClick Dilemma," *The Boston Globe* 2 March 2000: A16.

16.   J. Beauprez, "Giant Online Database Dropped DoubleClick, Yields to Privacy Concerns," *The Denver Post* 6 March 2000: C1.

17.   P. Thibodeau, "Web Advertisers Make Promises on Privacy," *Computer World* 14 August 2000: 37.

18.   D. Brown, "FTC Privacy Plan: What Does It Ad Up To?" *Inter@active Week* 31 July 2000: 14.

19.   K. Fogarty, "Be careful what you wish for," *Computer World* 14 August 2000: 36.

20. K. Perine, "Who Are the Privacy Police?" *The Industry Standard* 14 August 2000: 112.

21. M.J. McCarthy, "Thinking Out Loud: You Assumed 'Erase' Wiped Out That Rant Against the Boss? Nope," *The Wall Street Journal* 7 March 2000.

22. M.J. McCarthy, "Thinking Out Loud: You Assumed 'Erase' Wiped Out That Rant Against the Boss? Nope."

23. M.J. McCarthy, "Thinking Out Loud: You Assumed 'Erase' Wiped Out That Rant Against the Boss? Nope."

24. R. Beck, "Cyber Liability Updates Old Risks," *Mass High Tech* 31 January - 6 February 2000: 27.

25. Michael A. Smyth vs. The Pillsbury Company, C.A. No. 95-5712 (1996).

26. P. Thibodeau, "Employer Snooping Measure Nears Vote," *Computer World* 11 September 2000: 1.

27. A. Harrison, "Carnivore: How Much Bite Behind the Bark," *Computer World* 7 August 2000: 73.

28. M. French, "Surprise! The FBI may already be taking a bite of your e-mail," *Mass High Tech* 31 July - 6 August 2000: 18.

29. "The DoubleClick Dilemma," *The Boston Globe* 2 March 2000.

30. "White House back initiative for Net privacy," *The Boston Globe* 22 June 2000.

31. G. Erman, "Privacy, personalization: can the twain meet on the Net?" *Mass High Tech* 31 July - 6 August 2000: 41.

32. B. Machrone, "The Web Solves the Same Problem it Creates," *PC Week* 17 January 2000: 55.

33. <**www.pwcbetterweb.com**>.

34. S. Stoughton, "Who's Watching," *The Boston Globe* 18 September 2000: C6.

35. "Generic Code of Fair Information Practices," <**www.cdt.org/privacy/guide/basic/generic.html**>.

36. Webster's New World College Dictionary (USA: MacMillian, 1999).

37. <**www.abbotlaw.com**>.

38. M. France and D. Carney, "Free speech on the Web? Not Quite." *Business Week* 28 February 2000: 93-94.

39. R. Kerber, "Free Speech or Cyber-slander?" *The Boston Globe* 29 February 2000.

40. Cubby vs. Compuserve, 776 F. Supp. 135 at _ (1991) And Stratton Oakmont vs. Prodigy, 23 Media L. Rep 1794 at_ (1995).

41. Miller vs. California, 413 U.S. 15 at 24-25 (1973).

42. FCC vs. Pacifica Foundation 438 U.S. 726 (1978).

43. B. Headlam, "How the Web Changed the Smut Business," *The New York Times* 13 January 2000: D14.

44. D. Herbeck, Chair and Associate Professor of Communication, Boston College, 1 February 2000, lecture notes.

45. D. Herbeck, Chair and Associate Professor of Communication, Boston College, 1 February 2000, lecture notes.

46. K. Thomas, "For a 'Net Gift, Teens Will Share Wealth of Family Info," *USA Today* 15 March 2000: 7D.

47. S. Davies, "Make It Safe, But Keep It Free," *The Independent (London)* 4 September 1998: 5.

48. C. Johnson, "U.S. Panel Rejects Call for Software Filters on Children's Internet Use," *The Boston Globe* 21 October 2000: A8.

49. RIAA vs. Diamond Multimedia Systems, 180 F. 3d. 1072 at _ (9th Cir. 1999).

50. "Napster Closes 300,000 Music Accounts," *The New York Times* 12 May 2000: C6.

51. G. Heisler, "Meet the Napster," *Time* 2 October 2000: 62.

52. A. Mathews, "Music Samplers on the Web Buy CDs in Stores," *The Wall Street Journal* 15 June 2000: A3.

53. "2000 Policy Issue Fact Sheet," `<www.microsoft.com/freedomtoinnovate.policyissues.htm>`

54. M. Romano, "The Next Piracy Panic: Software," *The Industry Standard* 28 August 2000: 122.

55. U.S. vs. LaMacchia, 871 F. Supp. 535 at _ (D. Mass. 1994).

56. D. Young, "Congress Modifies Copyright Protection for the Digital Age," *Legal Backgrounder* Vol 14, No. 6.

57. D. Young, Vol 14, No. 6.

58. L. Lessig, "Patent Problems," *The Industry Standard* 31 January 2000: 47.

59. R. Libshon, "Madness In the Method: Will Method of Doing Business' Patents Undermine the Web?" *Net Commerce Magazine* March 2000: 8.

60. R. Libshon, 8.

61. R. Libshon, 8.

62. R. Libshon, 8.

63. `<www.yet2.com>`

64. `<www.patentauction.com>`

65. M. Stroud, "Invisible, Inc.," *Business 2.0* April 2000: 285.

66. Section 4, Anti-cybersquatting Consumer Protection Act.

67. D. Herbeck, Chair and Assoicate Professor of Communication, Boston College, 2 March 2000, lecture notes.

68. D. Herbeck, Chair and Assoicate Professor of Communication, Boston College, 28 March 2000, lecture notes.

69. P. Thibodeau, "Defining 'Spam' Technically Isn't Easy," *Computer World* 8 May 2000: 12.

70. P. Thibodeau, 12.

71. `<www.spammotel.com>`

72. `<maps.vix.com>`

73. F. Hayes, "Web Vigilantes," *Computer World* 14 August 2000: 82.

74. S. Collett, "States to Require License for Online Auctioneers," *Computer World* 6 December 1999: 4.

75. "French Court Says Yahoo Broke Racial Law," *The New York Times* 23 May 2000: C27.

76. B. Gruley and B. Simpson, "eBay Battles Yahoo! and Other Web Giants Over Privacy Protection," *The Wall Street Journal* 10 April 2000: B1.

77. B. Gruley and B. Simpson, B1.

78. J. Darby, "Drafting enforceable, understandable'click-wrap' agreements for the Web," *Mass High Tech* 8 May 2000: 51.

79. K. Murphy, "Costly Tax Showdown," *Internet World* 15 April 2000: 41-42.

80. "States Lose Millions of Tax Dollars to Internet," *Computer World* 6 March 2000: 62.

81. D. Brown, "Will E-Commerce Stay a Tax Free Haven?" *Inter@ctive Week* 27 March 2000: 14.

82. D. Brown, "Gilmore's Commission Issues E-Tax Report," *Inter@ctive Week* 17 April 2000: 20.

83. D. Brown, 20.

84. D. Callaghan, "The States Want a Fair Share," *eWeek* 16 October 2000: 49.

85. `<www.ecommercetax.com and www.eurovat.com>`

RECOMMENDED READING

It is important to be able to read the information provided below properly. The name of the case is presented first. Following the comma, is the volume number, the reader where the case is located and the page number. (Note: at_ indicates that the case is continued). The information in the parenthesis denotes where and when the case was determined

American Civil Liberties Union of Georgia vs. Miller, 1:96-cv-2475-MHS (N.D. Ga. 1997).

Basic Books, Inc. vs. Kinko's Graphics Corp., 758 F. Supp. 1522 (S.D.N.Y. 1991).

Blumenthal vs. Drudge, 992 F. Supp. 44 at _ (1998).

Child Online Protection Act of 1998 (COPA).

Children's Online Privacy Protection Act of 2000 (COPPA).

Communications Decency Act of 1996 (CDA).

Compuserve vs. Cyber Promotions, 962 F. Supp. 1015 at _ (S.D. Ohio 1997).

Cubby vs. Compuserve, 776 F. Supp. 135 at _ (1991).

Cyber Promotions Inc. vs. America Online, 948 F. Supp. 436 at _ (Ed. Pa. 1996).

Digital Millenium Copyright Act (DMCA).

Encyclopedia Britannica Educational Corp. vs. Crooks, 542 F. Supp. 1156 (W.D.N.Y. 1982).

FCC vs. Pacifica Foundation, 438 U.S. 726 at 748-751 (1978).

"German Compuserve Judgment," `<www.qlinks.net/comdocs/somm.html>`.

Ginsberg vs. New York, 390 U.S. 629 at _ (1968).

Harper and Row Publishers, Inc. v. Nation Enterprises, 471 U.S. 539 (1985).

Intermatic vs. Toeppen (N.D. Ill. 1996).

Internet Tax Freedom Act.

Miller vs. California, 413 U.S. 15 at 24-25 (1973).

MTV vs. Curry (S.D. N.Y. 1994).

Playboy Enterprises, Inc. vs. Frena, 839 F. Supp. 1552 at _ (1993).

Reno vs. American Civil Liberties Union, 117 S Ct. 2329 at _ (1997).

RTC vs. Netcom, 907 F. Supp. 1361 at _ (N.D. Cal. 1995).

Sable Communications vs. FCC, 492 U.S. 115 at _ (1989).

Section 230 of the Telecommunications Act.

Sega Enterprises Ltd. vs. MAPHIA, 857 F. Supp. 679 at _ (N.D. Cal. 1994).

Smyth v. Pillsbury Co., 914 F. Supp. 97 at _ (Ed. Pa. 1996).

Steve Jackson Games, Inc. v. U.S. Secret Service (5th Cir. 1994).

Stratton Oakmont vs. Prodigy, 23 Media L. Rep. 1794 at _ (1995).

United States Constitution.

U.S. vs. LaMachiaa, 871 F. Supp. 535 at _ (D. Mass. 1994).

United States v. Thomas, 74 F3d 701 at _, cert.denied, 117 S Ct. 74 (1996).

Zeran vs. America Online, Inc., 129 F. 3d 327 at _ (1997).

Zippo Mfg. Co. vs. Zippo Dot Com, Inc. (W. Pa. 1997).

12

Globalization

Objectives

- To discuss the development of the global economy.
- To discuss the challenges and opportunities involved in e-business globalization.
- To explore the marketing obstacles in the development of the global economy.
- To understand the legal and cultural challenges of globalization.
- To review taxation, distribution and payment in the global economy.

Humour is the first of the gifts to perish in a foreign tongue.
Virginia Woolf

Merchants have no country. The mere spot they stand on does not constitute so strong an attachment as that from which they draw their gains.
Thomas Jefferson

The country that is more developed industrially only shows, to the less developed, the image of its own future.
Karl Marx

If the world were good for nothing else, it is a fine subject for speculation.
William Hazlitt

The world is a beautiful book, but of little use to him who cannot read it.
Carlo Goldoni

Outline

12.1   Introduction
12.2   Regulating the Internet on an International Level
        12.2.1   Accounting for Legal and Cultural Differences
        12.2.2   International Internet Regulations
12.3   Creating an e-Business with Global Capabilities
        12.3.1   Choosing an International Market
        12.3.2   Obtaining a Local Internet Address
        12.3.3   Internationalization and Localization
        12.3.4   Partnering and Hiring
        12.3.5   Payment Systems
        12.3.6   Distribution
        12.3.7   Legal and Taxation Systems
        12.3.8   Promotions
12.4   Canada
12.5   Mexico and Central and South America
12.6   Europe
12.7   Africa
12.8   Middle East
12.9   Asia
12.10   Australia
12.11   Future of Global e-Business
12.12   Internet and World Wide Web Resources

Summary • Terminology • Self-Review Exercises • Answers to Self-Review Exercises • Exercises • Works Cited

12.1 Introduction

Today, we live in a world that seems smaller and more unified because of advances in information technology. Through the Internet, we can communicate with people in different countries at a speed that was unimaginable even 20 years ago. This creates unprecedented opportunities for conducting business globally. When you create a Web site, you potentially reach Internet users in every corner of the world, and, as more and more people become connected to the Web, an ever-increasing customer base is generated. This kind of universal access generates increased responsibilities for e-businesses, their owners and managers. International laws must be complied with, and linguistic and cultural variances must be addressed. In this chapter, we explore the opportunities and challenges associated with conducting e-business in an international market, and we develop basic guidelines for managing international projects.

12.2 Regulating the Internet on an International Level

The global reach of the Internet poses challenges to a world composed of different cultures, attitudes, languages, codes of conduct and government authorities. As more people access the Web worldwide, users can be exposed to products, services or information that are considered offensive or that are illegal in their countries of residence. In addition, the transnational nature of Internet activity raises questions concerning the application of national laws to cyberspace. Political, legal and corporate leaders see a need for global Internet policies that protect Internet users from potentially illegal or offensive material while allowing for the future growth of e-business and e-commerce. Differences among nations and cultures must be addressed, and international Internet laws may need to be established.

12.2.1 Accounting for Legal and Cultural Differences

Government regulation affects the growth rate of the Internet and has the potential to cause major problems as the volume of international e-business transactions increases. Countries have different laws and varying viewpoints. For example, Americans are extremely protective of copyright. Intellectual property in the U.S. cannot be used substantially without gaining the creator's permission or citing the source of the information. The United States also reacts differently to the use of personal information than many other countries. In Europe, respect for privacy is much greater. These differences of opinion point to an important issue arising in relation to the Internet. How do we create a global communication forum while maintaining respect for different cultures and codes of conduct?

The American Bar Association released a report from the group's *Global Cyberspace Jurisdiction Project* in July, 2000 (this report can be found at **www.abanet.org/ buslaw/cyber/initiatives/prospect.html**). The report represents the culmination of two years of research relating to international legal questions introduced by the Internet and global e-commerce.[1] In the report, legal experts point out many of the unresolved issues that surround the application of national laws to international e-businesses. International organizations and leaders must decide when national governments can apply or create laws that will affect parties and transactions that fall partially or completely outside their jurisdiction (the range of legal control). For example, who should determine taxation methods for businesses that conduct transactions on a global scale? When a copyrighted work on a computer in one country is accessed in another, which country's copyright laws should be applied? Similar jurisdiction issues include privacy laws, the transmission of offensive or illegal content, advertising and marketing restrictions, the enforcement of electronic contracts and the use of computers to detect and monitor criminal activity.

In relation to jurisdiction, governments must determine whether an e-business that maintains a Web site is subject to the laws of all the countries from which the site can be accessed. In the United States, this is called *minimum contacts*. Jurisdiction rules in other countries can be quite different from those of the United States. In cases where more than one court claims jurisdiction, standards must be developed to determine the most appropriate forum for settling the dispute. Factors include the relevance of the case to a particular court and the defendant's level of burden to present the case in that location.

Questions regarding courts' jurisdiction to enforce laws and regulations add to the complexity of international legal issues. For example, is a court responsible for informing people of the charges against them, or can it determine their right to speak when the individual lives and works outside the normal jurisdiction of the court? Can a court in one country or region require the presence at trial of a party residing outside of that country or region? If a monetary award is granted in a case, can a defendant's assets that are located outside of the jurisdiction of the court be seized to pay the award?

None of these questions have easy answers, and governments continue to struggle with issues of jurisdiction in relation to the Internet and e-commerce (see Felix Somm and International Perspective on Privacy feature).

12.2.2 International Internet Regulations

Because national governments are composed differently, businesses and legal experts are calling for the creation of worldwide e-commerce laws and standards. The American Bar Association's (ABA) report recommends forming a "global online standards commission" to govern Internet-related legal disputes involving parties from two or more countries. Universally adopted laws would likely address cybercrimes such as copyright infringement, cybersquatting, cyber terrorism, fraud, hacking and computer viruses. In May 2000, the destructive ILOVEYOU virus was spread via e-mail to computer systems around the world. Although the virus led to billions of dollars in damages, the citizen of the Philippines suspected of creating the virus could not be prosecuted because of a lack of applicable laws in his home country. Many point to this incident as an argument for Internet regulation at a global level.[3] Viruses and Internet security are discussed in Chapter 7, Internet Security.

Felix Somm and International Perspective on Privacy

Privacy issues present the world with some difficult questions. How are standards to be developed, and who will develop them? Under whose jurisdiction will violations of legal, ethical and social code be reviewed? Who should be held responsible? The case involving Felix Somm offers insight into the ways that governments are addressing international privacy concerns.

Felix Somm, an overseas agent for Compuserve, an American Internet service provider, was held accountable under German law for providing German subscribers access to sexually explicit material. Because Compuserve is an internationally operating Internet Service Provider (ISP), material posted in the United States was also accessible to Compuserve's international members.

Germany has a lower tolerance of pornography than the United States does. The content found on Compuserve was, according to German mandates, bestial and obscene, and, because of his role as an international representative of Compuserve, Felix Somm was found guilty in the German courts.

The courts determined that Compuserve had knowledge of the material available through the server and, disregarding the sensitivity of its subscribers, failed to remove the material or effectively block its accessibility. They further determined that Compuserve was acting for commercial gain. Due to Somm's position in the company, he was held personally responsible.

Felix Somm and International Perspective on Privacy (Cont.)

The case went to the court of appeals in Germany, and the decision was overturned in favor of Somm. Recognizing the distinction between a distributor and a publisher and Felix Somm's technical inability to block German access to specific content on the site, the court reasoned that Somm could not be held accountable. The case, however, raised important issues regarding the global aspects of the Internet and international jurisdiction.[2]

Some international standards have been set to regulate crime on the Internet. The *World Intellectual Property Organization (WIPO)* is a special agency that is part of the United Nations' system of organizations (**www.wipo.int**). WIPO has created an international forum for regulating Internet issues related to trademarks and cybersquatting (see Chapter 11, Legal and Ethical Issues; Internet Taxation). In an attempt to eliminate the illegal use of trademarked names in Web-site addresses, WIPO established an arbitration service to settle cybersquatting controversies. The relatively fast and inexpensive arbitration service has been popular; six months after the service was created, more than 2000 cases had been filed. WIPO is considering expanding the scope of the service to deal with disputes concerning the misuse in Web addresses of trade names, geographical locations, international organization names and pharmaceutical compounds. In the future, similar international legal services may be created to address other Internet-related legal controversies.[4]

Other multinational groups have begun efforts to establish comprehensive standards pertaining to Internet security and cyber crime. *The Organization for Economic Cooperation and Development* (**www.oecd.org**) is a club created as a forum for its 29 member countries to communicate ideas, share experiences and develop policy. In 2000, the OECD acknowledged that cyber crime is a growing problem worldwide and must be dealt with on an international level. The club suggests increasing the scope of its jurisdiction to include collecting data pertaining to computer-related security breaches and supervising the creation of national policies on digital certificates.[5] Digital certificates and other security issues are discussed further in Chapter 7, Internet Security.

After three years of research and discussion, the *Council of Europe* (**www.coe.int**) released in 2000 a draft of the world's first international treaty relating to cyber crime. Composed of 41 member countries, the Council of Europe is a ruling body that develops policy pertaining to human rights, democracy and law. Although the COE is primarily a European initiative, the Council is writing its treaty in collaboration with representatives from Canada, Japan, South Africa and the U.S. and plans to invite other countries to sign the completed version. The treaty mandates that all signatories establish laws prohibiting the unauthorized accessing of computers, intercepting of computer data, and exchange or possession of equipment used in hacking. Countries who sign the treaty would also be required to pass laws against computer-enabled fraud, forgery and child pornography and to grant law enforcement agents the right to search computers and seize data relevant to computer crime. Although cyber crime is generally acknowledged as an important global problem, many privacy advocates argue that the treaty sacrifices personal freedom and privacy to security concerns; they and others suggest that cyber crime can be countered most efficiently through the development of improved security technology.[6]

When countries and cultures have different legal attitudes toward an issue, creating global solutions becomes more complex. For example, the United States is negotiating with the European Union to create mutually acceptable standards for international e-commerce.

The *European Union Directive on Data Protection* (`europa.eu.net`) is an agreement among its members on the regulations that apply to information exchange. The directive includes mandates that personal information be kept current and used in a lawful manner for its designated purpose. Because of the different treatment of privacy in the United States, many U.S. sites could be in violation of this directive. To address the issue of international differences, the U.S. and the European Union have a pending agreement in which the U.S. will compile a list of American Web sites that meet the criteria designated by the directive. In the case of a violation, the case will be tried in the United States. In the future, similar agreements are expected to be made between different countries and regions concerning Web-site content, marketing and consumer privacy.

In some cases, extensive international regulation may conflict with national laws and impede the growth of e-business.[7] This argument is particularly relevant in discussions of regulation of content. At the *Internet Content Summit (2000)*, a report entitled "Self-regulation of Internet Content" was presented by Bertelsmann Foundation and a panel of industry experts. Although parts of the report were not unanimously supported by its authors, the report favors self-rating and filtering over third-party regulation. The proposal suggests that Web content providers rate their sites, that filters for possibly offensive content be made available and that a network of national hot lines be established so that Internet users can register complaints about site content.[8] Although many decisions have yet to be made, the final method of global Internet regulation is likely to be a combination of industry self-regulation, voluntary filtering, improved security, national laws and international treaties.

12.3 Creating an e-Business with Global Capabilities

Globalization is an excellent opportunity for many e-businesses, but it is also an ambitious and expensive investment that does not guarantee increased revenue. Before you decide to operate overseas, you should ask yourself whether the revenues you gain from expansion will cover the costs involved and whether other cultures will react positively to what you sell. Once you commit to entering foreign markets, you must make important strategic decisions as to when, where and how the business will operate. Although the Internet provides easy access to customers around the world, technology alone cannot eliminate linguistic and cultural barriers. In this section, we begin to develop guidelines for evaluating international opportunities and transforming e-businesses into global e-businesses.

e-Fact 12.1

According to Jupiter Communications, two-thirds of America's biggest e-businesses continue to ignore the needs of non-English-speaking Internet users.[9]

12.3.1 Choosing an International Market

Once a business has chosen to pursue globalization, it must locate the international market or markets it wishes to enter. Initially, it is advisable to focus your time and money in one or two key markets until you experience some success.[10] While researching various possibilities, you should check with your current Web host and ask for a copy of your site's access logs; these can tell you whether Web surfers from foreign domains have recently accessed your site.[11] You should also investigate companies that offer goods or services comparable to your own. In locations where other companies have already entered the market, visit their Web sites and evaluate the status of their efforts. If you notice that the market is already saturated with the goods or services you promote, you may want to search for country or region with a less developed Internet economy. However, if you feel that your offerings are unique in some way and that your company can compete among local and foreign competition, consider expanding your business to the location. When deciding on a market, factors such as the number of people online, Internet usage growth rates, per capita income and consumers' probable expectations of your business must be considered.

Determining future e-commerce demand requires more extensive research than determining current demand. However, many resources are available on the Web and through other media. Visit Web sites such as **www.nua.ie**, which publishes two Internet business-related newsletters and offers links to other relevant information to learn more about the development of e-business on the Web. Internet and technology statistics by country or language are available at the Global Reach site (Fig. 12.1) (**www.glreach.com/glob-stats/index.php3**). Idiom Inc.'s site (**www.idiominc.com**) contains a *Resource Library* that allows users to search for articles and information pertaining to specific foreign markets and topics. Other possible sources include data from the U.S. Department of Commerce, the United Nations and various research firms. Be aware that smaller, less obvious markets are sometimes better choices for marketing-specific products. For example, Russia is predicted to be a strong emerging market for golf supplies.[12] An analysis of various global markets and the pros and cons of doing business in those parts of the world is included later in this chapter.

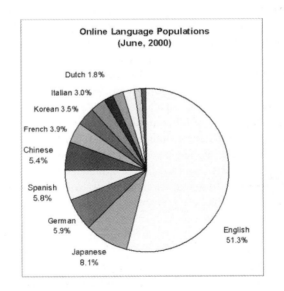

Fig. 12.1   Type of information found at Global Reach's Web site. (Courtesy of Global Reach.)

12.3.2 Obtaining a Local Internet Address

To create an e-business with a truly global reach, separate Web sites geared toward different countries and cultures should be developed. The `.com` domain name is the most universally recognized address on the Web, and some companies connect foreign sites as links to their main site. This option can make your e-business seem truly global. However, foreign consumers will locate your Web site more easily and access it more quickly if it is registered and hosted in their own country. In some cases, search capabilities are affected by the accuracy of the location. For these reasons, registering a new domain name ending with the local country name extension is often advisable.[13]

Domain-name registration in foreign countries is often more complex than registering a `.com` domain and may require owning a trademark or incorporating your business in the foreign country.[14] Even if you are not planning to launch international Web sites immediately, registering a domain name for your company in foreign markets can help you avoid cybersquatters and problems obtaining the domain name later. For information on registering foreign domain names, visit the Web site of the *Internet Assigned Numbers Authority (IANA)* at **www.iana.org/cctld.html**. NetNames (**www.netnames.co.uk**) is the largest global registrar of domain names; their site allows users to search for the availability of specific domain names and register those names in domains worldwide.

12.3.3 Internationalization and Localization

Globalizing your Web site comprises two major steps: internationalization and localization. *Internationalization* involves restructuring the software used by your e-business so that it can process foreign languages, currencies, date formats and other variations involved in conducting business globally.[15] To accept and fulfill orders in German or Japanese, your database will have to be restructured to accommodate those languages. International software must be compatible with 16-bit character encoding systems and other international computing standards. Unicode (**www.unicode.org**), a 16-bit encoding system that assigns a unique number to almost every character in every language, enables your system to handle iconic languages such as Chinese, Japanese or Korean.[16]

Localization includes the translation and cultural adaptation of your site's content and presentation. A variety of translation options is available for companies with different expectation and budgets. Some services and software are designed to translate for you. The *Enterprise Translation Server* from Transparent Language (**www.transparentlanguage.com**) allows your customers to click on a link from your Web site and view your site translated into various languages. Transparent Language's Web site offers a free demonstration that allows you to view any Web site in the language you specify. Alis Technologies (**www.alis.com**) offers a similar solution called *AutoTranslate*. Netscape Navigator 6 uses this solution; users can go to the **View Menu** and select **Translate** to view any Web site in another language. Logos (**www.logos.it**) (see the Logos Group, Italy feature) and AltaVista's *Babelfish* (**www.babelfish.altavista.com**) also offer fast translations. This technology can be useful, especially for real-time translation of customer-service inquiries or e-mails. However, you must be aware that translations will not be perfect, and mistakes could result in misunderstandings.

e-Fact 12.2

Providing information in more than one language is key to conducting business globally; according to Forrester Research, consumers are three times more likely to purchase products or services from a Web site presented in their native language.[17]

Logos Group, Italy [18]

Logos, an Italian translation company, provides assistance for those who are in need of translations. Logos also provides an online language translation dictionary. This *multilingual e-translation portal* will instantly translate any typed word or phrase into many different languages (Figs. 12.2 and 12.3). You can also click on a button to hear how the word is pronounced. If you are not sure how one of the translated words is used, *Logos' Wordtheque* demonstrates the use of the word in context. From here, you can click on the *Word Exchange Forum*, where professionals around the world are willing to help you with a difficult word or phrase. For further information or to try a translation, visit `www.logos.it`.

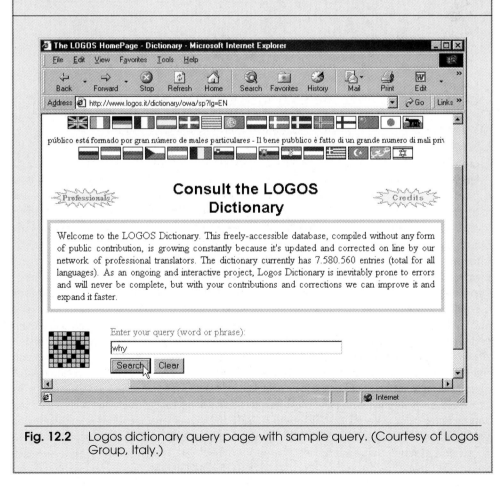

Fig. 12.2   Logos dictionary query page with sample query. (Courtesy of Logos Group, Italy.)

Logos Group, Italy (Cont.) [18]

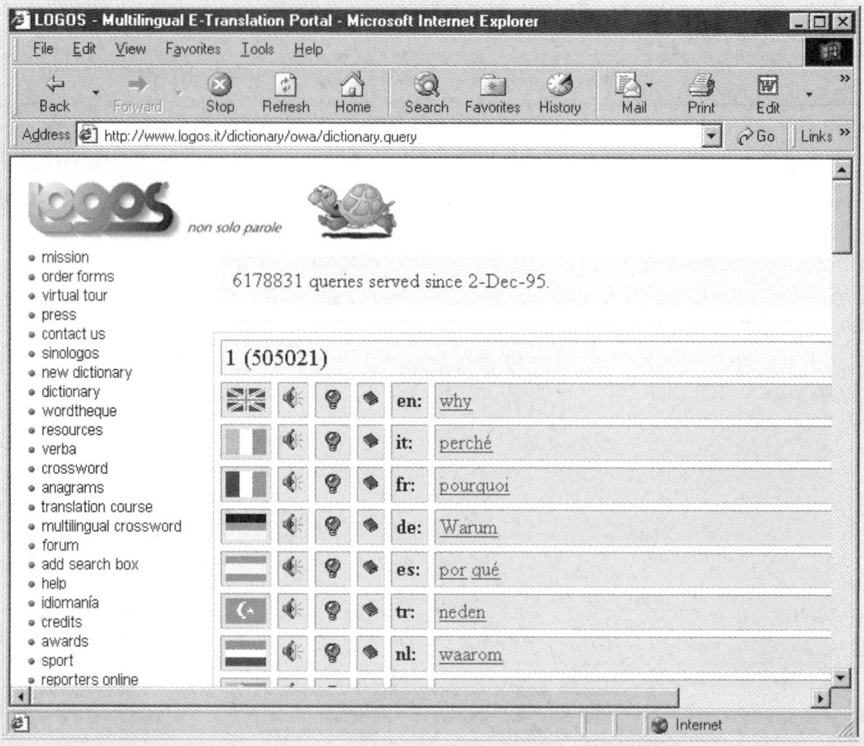

Fig. 12.3   Logos query results page with sample query result. (Courtesy of Logos Group, Italy.)

Because machines cannot be relied upon to translate grammar, idioms and humor perfectly, human translators are necessary to create a complete foreign language Web site. A bilingual translator and an editor should be employed, preferably ones living abroad and aware of cultural variations, terminology, market trends and other regional issues.[19] Translators that are familiar with the context of the information to be translated are also desirable, especially if the content is technical in nature. Present translatable content to a translator as an HTML file or as a text file, and be sure to have him or her translate any META tags and text within graphic images (META tags are discussed in Chapter 8, Internet Marketing).[20] Aquarius (**www.aquarius.net**), an e-marketplace that connects businesses with freelance translators and translation agencies, is an excellent place to locate translators for most foreign languages (Fig. 12.4).

Even trained translators may not solve all the problems that result in localizing the content and design of a Web site. When considering the layout of your foreign-language site, you should be aware that translation into European languages can expand English text up to 40 percent in length, whereas translation into Asian languages requires slightly less space than equivalent English text.[21] Site layout must be adapted to accommodate languages which are read vertically, such as Chinese, or those which read right to left, such as Hebrew. The language in which text appears also affects the appropriate font size. For example, although you can reduce the font of text in many European languages to fit more information on a page, languages such as Japanese are difficult to read clearly in 8-point font.[22]

Localization must also consider the cultural associations of colors in different parts of the world (Fig. 12.5). Because cultures and religions view colors differently, the use of color can affect the way consumers view your Web site and make their purchasing decisions. For example, if you are creating a Web site for a Chinese audience, you might want to include red, which signifies celebration and good luck in Chinese culture. Although Americans commonly relate green with money, people from countries where money is printed differently will not make the same connection. Blue is viewed positively in most cultures and is the best choice for a globally accessible Web site.[23]

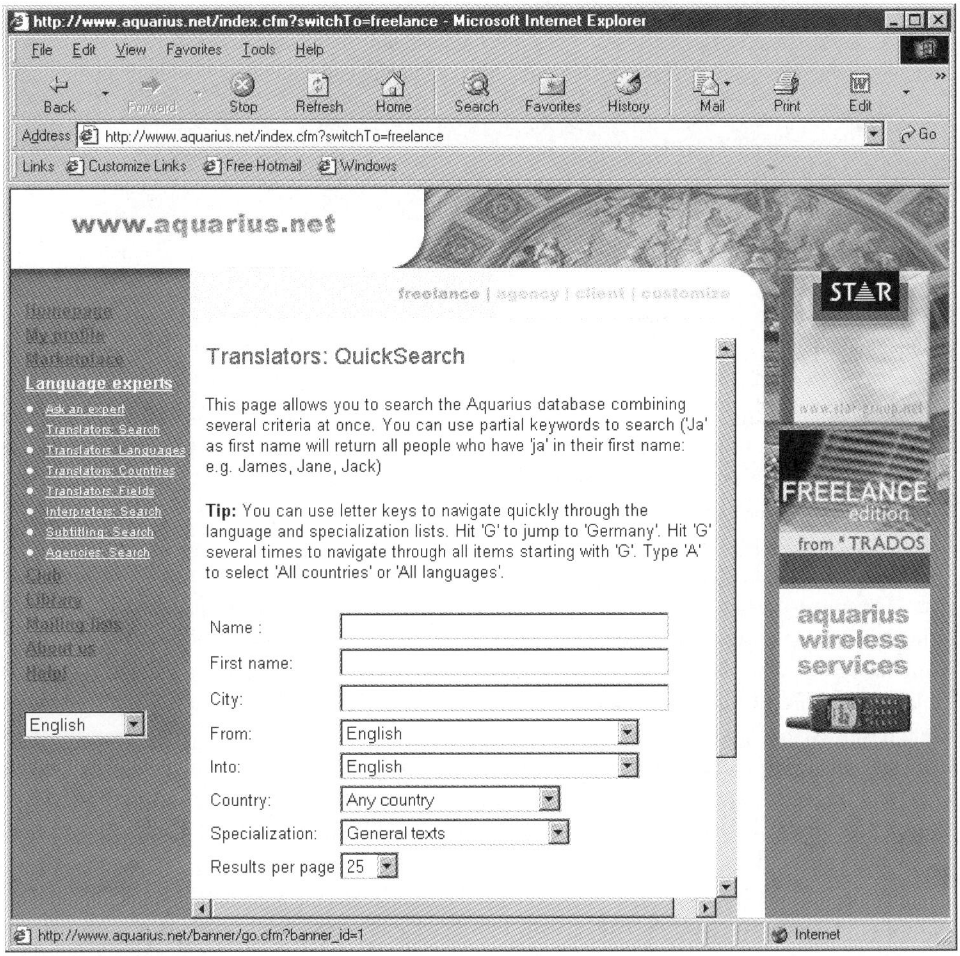

Fig. 12.4 **Aquarius.net** translator search. (Courtesy of Language Networks BV.)

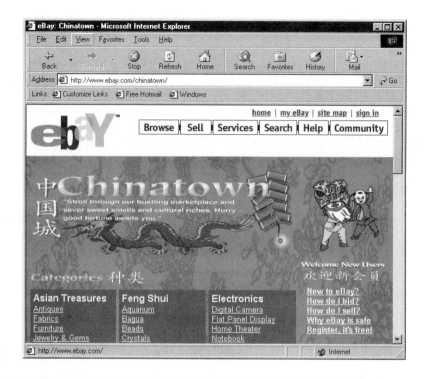

Fig. 12.5   eBay's Chinatown site uses a red background signifying celebration and good luck. (These materials have been reproduced with the permission of eBay Inc. COPYRIGHT © EBAY INC. ALL RIGHTS RESERVED.)

It is also important to localize the content available on global sites. Try to make writing for foreign sites as linguistically and culturally neutral as possible.[24] It is better not to use American slang, idioms, and specific examples from American or Western culture; for example, if you are selling hot dogs in China, avoid content about eating hot dogs at a football game or at the mall.

Companies should also consider adapting icons and logos for the targeted foreign culture. The most common example of an e-business that uses a culturally specific icon is America Online (**www.aol.com**), whose trademark mailbox icon is understood by Americans to signify mail, but it is not a recognized symbol in all cultures. As a result, America Online has replaced the mailbox logo with a more universally recognized envelope on its French site (**www.aol.fr**) and with a picture of a typical European mail box on their German site (**www.aol.de**) (Fig. 12.6). However, other international America Online sites, such as that servicing Japan (**www.jp.aol.com**), retain the original mailbox logo. Companies must weigh the benefits of offering recognizable symbols to their customers against the costs of sacrificing brand association.

International customers will be hesitant to buy from your Web site if they do not understand the pricing information. Make sure that prices are available in the local currency or that the exchange-rate information is available on your site. You can offer your customers current and accurate exchange rate information by linking your site to an online currency conversion service. For an example, visit Olsen & Associates' s (**www.oanda.com**).[25]

Fig. 12.6   Various America Online icons. (AOL screenshots copyright © 2000 America Online, Inc. Used with permission.)

Researching the predominant culture, customs and business practices of the area for which you are creating the Web site is important to localization. However, in order to create a truly global brand, your localized Web sites should retain the overall look and feel of your company. If you intend to use complex graphics and streaming media, you should be aware of your visitor's ability to download this material.[26] In general, consumers in developing countries will have less complex technology. Streaming media is discussed in Chapter 5, Internet Hardware, Software and Communications.

IKEA's foreign Web sites demonstrate localization. IKEA has created 14 localized sites for different national markets, including one for Italy (**www.ikea.it**) and one for Saudi Arabia (**www.ikea.com.sa**). Italians both accept and respond to sexy advertising—it is common for sexually charged images and even nudity to appear on network television or in mainstream advertising campaigns in Italy.[27] In response to this, IKEA has included photographs of young women in pajamas and bathing suits on their Italian Web site. By contrast, the Saudi Arabian IKEA site markets the store as a place for "good values and fun for your family" and contains photos of a man in Arab clothing shopping with his son. This more conservative approach is more appropriate for Saudi Arabia's Islamic culture.[28] In addition, IKEA maintains a generic global Web site at **www.ikea.com/content**. This site contains minimal amounts of culturally specific content and features models from a variety of cultures to appeal equally to all customers.

Experts often categorize information available on global Web sites as global, regional or local content. *Global content* refers to information and design that requires translation, but is essentially the same for all cultures. This typically includes logos, trademarks and company history and mission. *Regional content*, such as product and marketing information, is usually written once in English and then adapted for various markets. Material on specific regional pages that appears only on that Web site, such as regional promotions, pricing, delivery and store or office locations, is called *local content*.[29] This division can help you balance cultural adaptation with consistency throughout all markets. It is also a useful tool in managing and distributing responsibility for updates of site content. If certain sections of a foreign Web site have not been localized, it is advisable to inform users of this by creating a pop-up notice explaining the transition.[30]

For businesses that prefer to outsource localization, several companies offer translation and localization solutions. Localization services specialize in adapting Web sites and content for other cultures, and they are able to address a range of issues that extend beyond simple translation. eTranslate specializes in end-to-end globalization solutions. e-businesses can outsource the entire globalization process to eTranslate (**www.etranslate.com**), which consults with the client to create customized technology integration, translation and content adaptation for the client's foreign Web sites. After the foreign site is created, eTranslate translates the site directly back into English, allowing clients to see how localization has affected the content.[31] General Electric Co., one of eTranslate's clients, has experienced a 27-percent increase in lead generation for its information portal since eTranslate created Web sites for the portal in German, Japanese, Chinese and Korean.[32] Other companies that offer similar globalization software and services include Bowne Global Solutions (**www.bowneglobal.com**), GlobalSight (**www.globalsight.com**), Idiom (**www.idiominc.com**), Lionbridge Technologies (**www.lionbridge.com**) and WorldPoint Interactive (**www.worldpoint.com**).

12.3.4 Partnering and Hiring

A local, brick-and-mortar presence gives your company an important advantage. Many foreign businesses partner with existing companies in foreign markets. Local partners can provide many advantages, including a physical presence in the target country, a recognized brand, extensive knowledge of the target market and localized content and customer service. Partnering with local companies also can also decrease the cost to your business of international Web hosting. Yahoo (**www.yahoo.com**) is an American Internet portal that has successfully penetrated many foreign markets. Yahoo is currently ranked first in Internet traffic in Japan and the United Kingdom, and the portal attributes its popularity to the more than 300 partnerships it has created with local content providers worldwide.[33,34] Other popular U.S. e-businesses, such as America Online and eBay, partner with local businesses in each targeted foreign market. For example, when eBay decided to expand into the European market, the company partnered with German **alando.de** and restructured the preexisting auction site as an eBay site.[35]

If you choose to build your own local presence and hire foreign employees to work with your partners, try to educate yourself about local employment practices. Many consulting firms are available online that specialize in employee relations. If you plan to expand your business beyond a single country or region, hiring employees who are proficient in more than one language is advisable. This provides a means to communicate with customers from a variety of markets.

Many countries and regions offer online resources to help foreign businesses find employees and partners. First Tuesday (**www.firsttuesday.com**) helps Internet entrepreneurs and companies make business connections. Potential partners and employees gather at monthly meetings or online job markets, which occur on the first Tuesday of every month (Fig. 12.7). First Tuesday operates globally in 45 countries and 107 cities. DJR Associates (**www.djr.co.uk**) offers similar services targeted specifically toward foreign companies expanding into the European market. To find talent in other foreign markets, investigate possible resources online and consult with local employment agencies.

Fig. 12.7   First Tuesday provides jobs in the European Information Technology
             market. (Courtesy of First Tuesday, Ltd.)

12.3.5 Payment Systems

When doing business in another part of the world, it is important to localize your payment
system in order to accommodate your foreign customers. In the United States, many online
goods and services are bought with credit cards; some e-businesses do not offer alternatives
to credit-card payment. However, credit cards are less common in other parts of the world,
even among the upper and middle classes in industrialized areas. Credit cards are rare
among customers in developing nations, because of infrastructure and trust issues. When
planning expansion into a particular market, investigate the payment systems used by the
most established e-businesses there. What percentage of online sales at these sites are made
with credit cards? What alternative payment methods are used?

e-Fact 12.3

*Only approximately 30 percent of Europeans have credit cards, and many feel uncomfortable
revealing credit card numbers over the telephone or Internet.*[36]

e-Businesses in Europe should offer a c.o.d. (cash on delivery) option and should consider other means of monetary transfer that do not involve credit cards. *Giros* (wire trans-

fers between bank accounts) offer an alternative for companies that work in some northern European countries.[37] However, giros sometimes require that customers send authorizations through the mail, which slows the transaction process. *DirectDebit*[TM], a new e-payment service from an American company called EuroDebit, enables electronic debits from European customers' bank accounts to be sent to merchants' bank accounts for a small fee. DirectDebit is currently available only in Germany, but the company is negotiating with banks to offer the service in Austria, Belgium, the Netherlands, Switzerland, Luxembourg, Sweden and the United Kingdom.[38] Additionally, forms of electronic cash have been developed for use in e-commerce transactions (see Chapter 4, Online Monetary Transactions). In the near future, one or more of these systems may be used internationally and enable simpler monetary exchange between parties involved in global e-commerce.

12.3.6 Distribution

Conducting international business successfully often depends on distribution methods. Does the country have the infrastructure in place to support your e-business on a broad scale? What kind of distribution channels reach your consumers? It is also important to consider shipping costs to the various countries.

If you are focusing your globalization efforts in a small number of key markets, it is usually more efficient to ship goods from a local distribution center, rather than from the United States. When shipping within foreign countries or regions, investigate local distribution options. For example, because there is no integrated postal system serving the European continent, choosing the most appropriate delivery system for European customers can be confusing. Companies such as FedEx and UPS offer integrated networks that service most European nations, but such carriers charge significantly more than they do in the United States.[39] If you are shipping within one European country, the best solution may be offered by that country's national postal service. Even when shipping between countries, national postal services often have partnerships with other companies and services that ensure fast and affordable delivery. You can review the offerings of the British Post Office at **www.postoffice.co.uk** and the Deutsche Post at **www.post-ag.de**, which can be viewed in either German or English. To locate shipping options in other areas of the world, research national postal services and local couriers.

If you choose to do business in a large number of international markets, creating regional distribution centers may prove to be impractical. In this case, a volume deal from a well-established international shipping and handling company may offer the best solution for your e-business. Two of the world's most popular shipping companies are UPS (**www.ups.com**) and Federal Express (**www.fedex.com**), both of which are based in the United States. The United States Postal Service (**www.usps.com**) also offers international shipping services. UPS delivers to over 200 countries around the world and offers next-day or two-day delivery to most locations. To find out more about UPS's services in any particular area of the world, go to the UPS Web site and click on your area of interest in the box headed "Global Regions." Federal Express provides comparable fast delivery to locations around the world. The company's site also includes the "Global Trade Manager," a database of online resources for businesses who ship internationally that includes international shipping news, export/import guidelines, downloadable customs documents, a universal currency converter, and information on international time zones and holidays. For a free tour of Federal Express's "Global Trade Manager," go to **www.fedex.com/us/**

`international` and click on the "tour" option. To make sure that you are receiving the best shipping price, you can utilize InterShipper (`www.intershipper.com`), a free service that compares the shipping prices and arrival times of eight different shipping companies according to a specific package's weight and destination. Intershipper also offers free integration tools so that its technology can be added to any online store.

It is important to be honest with your customers about the costs of various distribution options. When shipping internationally, indicate to buyers that your distribution center is located outside their home country. Customers will want to know that additional taxes levied by their country's customs house will be added to the cost of their purchases, and that goods may potentially be held up at customs. Although you want your e-business to come across as localized and efficient, misrepresentation of shipping costs or time frames will not help you generate a loyal customer base.

12.3.7 Legal and Taxation Systems

Every government has a unique strategy when it comes to regulating business and the Internet, and every nation has a different set of laws relating to these topics. In some countries, including the United States, laws may even vary by state or region. Companies that wish to buy or sell products in the global market must obey both the export laws of their own country and the import laws of the country in which they wish to do business. Failure to comply with these laws is treated as a serious offense; governments may seize goods when they pass through customs and even press charges against offenders.

Since international commerce laws are confusing, shipping companies and customs agencies that process internationally distributed goods often facilitate compliance with regulations.[40] However, when international commerce is conducted on the Web, transactions can be completed quickly without the involvement of third parties. The relative ease with which e-businesses can buy and sell internationally is a major advantage, but it makes violating import and export laws much simpler. For this reason, e-businesses must be particularly aware of the laws that limit commerce between nations.

Every government places restrictions on international trade. Most nations require a special permit to sell animals, plants, products made from endangered species, arms and explosives, bulletproof clothes, toy guns, weapons of any kind, toy coins, pornography, controlled substances and poisons.[41] Other rules are more specific, and your business might only learn of them through extensive research. For example, distributing Viagra is prohibited in the United Kingdom, and selling items related to the Nazi era is illegal in France and Germany.[42,43] Exporting countries also have their own sets of regulations; for example, due to national security concerns, the United States prohibits the sale of certain software and computer technology to other areas of the world.[44] The United States also maintains lists of embargoed countries, sanctioned countries, denied persons (people who are not allowed to buy any goods or services from the U.S.) and debarred parties (people or groups who are not allowed to buy specific goods or services from the U.S.).[45]

In addition to the already extensive list of international commerce regulations, e-businesses must comply with each country's Internet regulations. Some of these regulations and the problems they pose for global e-commerce have already been discussed in section 14.2. For example, the European Union's privacy laws forbid the unauthorized collection of personal data from Internet users. Other governments, such as that of Saudi Arabia, have strict regulations on content that they view as offensive or pornographic.[46] Because of the complexity of the rules and regulations that govern international e-commerce, you should research local laws and consult with legal experts before you begin exporting goods or services to a particular foreign market.

Taxation also creates difficulties for global e-businesses. Before you begin processing sales in another country, investigate international tax laws in that country as they apply to Internet sales and to the specific products you wish to market. In many countries, including all members of the European Union, a value-added tax (VAT) is added all goods sold to consumers. If significant taxes are placed on the goods or services you offer, evaluate whether your prices will remain competitive once those taxes are added. Ideally, your e-business should include all applicable taxes in listed product prices so that customers know the total amount they are spending before they commit to purchasing from your Web site. Commercial tax software such as that offered by Taxware International, Inc. (**www.tax-ware.com**) can help your e-business calculate applicable taxes more quickly and easily.

Several companies provide solutions that can simplify the entire process of calculating international taxes and fees and complying with international distribution regulations. myCustoms™ (**www.mycustoms.com**) offers an online backend service that provides landed costs for an e-businesses' international customers in real time. The landed cost of a product is the total cost as delivered to a customer, which includes the price of the product, shipping costs, insurance, taxes, duties, and import/export fees. myCustoms guarantees its cited landed costs and ensures that international transactions authorized by its system comply with all international trade laws. In addition, myCustoms automatically generates the documents needed to ship goods internationally and pays any fees involved. A similar service is provided by World Tariff (**www.worldtariff.com**), a company that tracks customs duty and tax information for global businesses. Although World Tariff does not provide landed costs for specific transactions, it offers e-businesses the information necessary to calculate landed costs accurately. Vastera (**www.vastera.com**) and ClearCross (**www.clearcross.com**) are other companies that provide information about the costs and documentation involved in international distribution.[47]

12.3.8 Promotions

Creating an internationally established e-business is contingent on successful global marketing. When writing promotional material for foreign audiences, investigate the interpretation of your company and product names in the language or languages in which you are advertising. Do they translate appropriately (i.e. does the literal meaning change when translated), or should they be adapted for your target market? Often, product names and advertising slogans cannot be directly translated.

For example, both Pepsi and Coke have had problems marketing in foreign nations. Pepsi's "Choice for the next generation" slogan translated into "Pepsi brings your ancestors back from the grave" in Chinese. The name Coca-Cola means "Bite the wax tadpole" in one Chinese dialect and "female horse stuffed with wax" in another. It was eventually resolved to translate into "happiness in the mouth." To view these and other marketing errors, visit **www.the-net-effect.com/articles/multiculture.html**. Other companies' names and advertisements did not create such blatant misunderstandings but were modified for other reasons. When America Online expanded to Europe and Asia, the company changed the official name of their overseas operations to AOL in an attempt to seem more inclusive and less American. In addition, many American advertising tactics, such as the "hard sell", do not come across well in other cultures and should be avoided. Other advertising tactics are strictly prohibited in other countries; for example, it is illegal to use foreign languages when advertising in France or to directly mention competitors when advertising in Germany.[48] The sending of unsolicited commercial e-mail, or Spam, is also restricted in many countries.

Once promotional material has been culturally adapted, you must select the media through which you want to advertise your business. Investigate various options such as billboards, print advertisements, radio and television spots, and various forms of online promotion. Which channels will allow you to reach the largest number of potential customers at the lowest possible cost in the particular country or region that you are targeting? Answers to this question will vary considerably from market to market, so it is important to reevaluate your advertising strategy each time you enter a new foreign market.

If you choose to advertise on foreign Web sites, be aware that site performance data in most foreign markets is less reliable and more difficult to obtain than in the U.S. However, some Internet ratings firms have begun to offer performance information on international sites. The American ratings firm Media Matrix has partnered with German GfK and British Ipsos to form MMXI (**www.mmxi.com**), a company that provides Internet ratings for the U.S., Canada, the United Kingdom, France, Germany, Sweden, Australia and New Zealand. The company plans to offer data on Japanese, Chinese and other European sites in the near future. Other companies that offer international Internet ratings are Paris-based NetValue (**www.netvalue.com**) and ACNielsen **eRatings.com**.[49] In markets where there is little or no site performance information available, you may want to look for advertising space on sites of companies that sell products similar or complementary to your own.

Many issues relating to international advertising and promotions are complex, and the best way to assure that your efforts will be successful is to consult with experts. Companies that offer comprehensive localization solutions will assist you with promotions in foreign markets. A list of companies that offer such services is included at the end of section 14.3.3.

12.4 Canada

Because Canada abuts the United States and shares many cultural similarities, Canada is a natural market for American e-businesses (and vice versa). Canada's population is much smaller than that of the United States (31 million in 1999 versus the U.S.'s 273 million).[50] Furthermore, Canada's Internet users are spending ever-increasing amounts of time online, averaging 8.6 hours per week in December 1999.[51]

e-Fact 12.4

The Winter 2000 CyberTrends report by ComQuest estimates that 54 percent of Canadians have Internet access, and one-third use the Internet at least once a week.[52]

Despite the popularity of the Web in Canada, e-commerce Web sites have been slower to appear than in the Unites States. The canadian government's opposition to regulating the Internet in the way that they restrict broadcasting opens the e-business market to foreign competitors.[53]

e-Fact 12.5

In 1999, online shopping was offered by only 26 percent of Canada's 200 largest retailers, whereas half of America's biggest stores offered some form of e-commerce.[54]

Many U.S. companies are focused on the Canadian market's e-commerce potential. For example, in 1999, online toy store eToys Inc. began a Canadian advertising campaign and published large advertisements in Canadian newspapers.[55] In general, Canadians have been receptive to the foreign companies. Over half of Canadian online purchases are made from American Web sites.[56] Web shoppers say that, although they would prefer to buy from domestic merchants, U.S. sites often offer lower prices and better selection. However, marketers should remember that many citizens of Montreal, one of Canada's largest and most populated cities, list French as their primary language. Offering a French-language option on a Canadian e-commerce site or a U.S. site that services Canada is crucial to addressing Montreal consumers.

In addition to Canadian traffic on U.S. retail sites, other connections have been made between the American and Canadian Internet markets. U.S.-based portals, such as America Online, have launched special Canadian services, and others, such as Lycos, have partnered with Canadian content providers. The Sympatico-Lycos portal, which is available in both French and English with localized Canadian content, is one of the most popular Web sites among Canadians. Interest from American investors and the U.S.'s less restrictive tax laws have convinced many Canadian e-businesses to relocate to the United States. Online grocery store **HomeGrocer.com**, virtual pet supply store **Petopia.com** and golfing portal **Book4golf.com** are among the Canadian companies that have chosen to move their operations to the United States.[57]

Canadian businesses have nevertheless been advancing Canada's Internet and e-commerce capabilities. Canada is ahead of the United States in terms of the development of wireless technology (see Chapter 6, Wireless Internet and m-Business). In an attempt to create domestic e-businesses, Canadian venture capitalists are funding dot-com start-ups and high-risk companies. Some successful Canadian e-businesses have launched international campaigns targeted at the United States. Montreal-based Peachtree Network (**www.peachtree.ca**), Canada's leading online grocer, already operates five American centers and hopes to offer services in 10 major U.S. markets in the near future.[58]

 e-Fact 12.6

12 percent of Canadians have purchased products or services online, and 11 percent use Internet banking services.[59]

12.5 Mexico and Central and South America

Latin America has the fastest growth rate of Internet usage in the world.[60] Although only 2 percent (10 million) of Latin America's 500 million citizens are currently connected to the Web, Internet populations are expected to number between 29.6 and 40 million by 2003. Also, since the Latin Americans who are going online tend to represent the wealthiest segment of the population, Web-based sales are predicted to reach as much as $8 billion by 2003.[61]

The spread of the Internet has been advantageous for Latin American businesses. Considering the explosive growth rate of the Latin Web, the positive economic atmosphere will likely generate countless opportunities for entrepreneurs and workers during the coming years. Already, Latin American ISPs and portals are experiencing success; in some markets, such as Brazil, local companies are even outperforming U.S.-based corporations such as America Online's AOL Latin America.[62] These companies generate money and jobs in this area of the world. Because of the region's geographic diversity and dispersed population,

Web-based business models allow companies to target much broader markets than would be possible through brick-and-mortar institutions.[64] The Internet also enables Latin American businesses to serve the Spanish-speaking American population. U.S. Latino consumers, who usually spend more money online than Latin Americans do, have shown growing interest in purchasing Latin American goods online, both for themselves and to send as gifts to friends and relatives who live in Mexico and in Central and South America.[64]

Admittedly, many obstacles must be surmounted before the Internet can reach all of Latin America. Because computers and Internet service in most parts of Latin America cost the same or more than they do in the United States, gaining access to the Web is financially impossible for many. The high cost of local phone calls compounds this problem.

Some governments and private companies have started initiatives to help citizens reach the Web. Free Internet access is now widely available in Brazil, and this has led to drastic increases in the online population there. In parts of Mexico, businesses and local governments have worked together to provide secondary schools with computers and Web access.[65] Affordable Internet service is appearing in Argentina. In 2000, the Argentinian president allocated $1 billion for low-cost loans to private citizens to buy computers; the Argentinian government has also established a special low-cost phone rate for calls to ISPs.[66] Internet access through televisions and cellular phones is also becoming more popular, which means that users will not be excluded from the Web because they cannot afford to purchase a computer.[67] Experts hope that these and other initiatives will help the Internet continue to grow in Latin America so that, in the long term, technology can facilitate economic and social change.

12.6 Europe

Europe has been hailed by many as the next Internet and e-commerce frontier. Europe is also a predominately industrialized and technology-savvy society with much of the needed infrastructure in place to support widespread adoption of the Internet and e-commerce. This growth is expected to continue over the next few years. By 2003, one in three Europeans will use the Internet, according to a "Techno-graphics Europe Report" by Forrester Research B.V.[68]

e-Fact 12.7

During 1999, the number of Europeans online increased 100 percent.[69]

European e-businesses have been launched in all areas of the continent, and new e-businesses are receiving more venture capital than has been previously available to European technology companies. According to the European Venture Capital Association, VC investments in technology have risen significantly over the last few years.[70] Europeans, who have previously hesitated at high-risk investments and entrepreneurial activity, especially in the realm of technology, are accepting Internet companies as tomorrow's possible corporate leaders and are supporting them accordingly.

Driven by the development of Internet economy, many European countries have taken steps to make their national stock exchanges more e-business friendly. Traditionally, the European stock exchanges have enforced rigorous requirements that barred the public trading of newer and riskier companies. For example, the *Amsterdam Exchange* usually requires that a company exist for three years to be traded there.[71] However, in an attempt to attract Internet companies to their floors, many exchanges have established alternate trading markets with more flexible requirements, similar to the *Nasdaq* in the United States. The *Alternative Investment Market* in London, the *Neuer Markt* in Frankfurt, the *Nuovo Mercato* in Milan and *Le Nouveau Marche* in Paris are examples of the new, high-risk markets.[72] Though these markets are experiencing limited success, the German Neuer Markt is considered the premier trading platform for technology stocks in Europe. The Neuer Markt and the proposed *Nasdaq Europe*, set to open in late 2000, are inspiring other exchanges to bend or alter their rules to keep pace with the Internet and the global economy. The *London Stock Exchange* waived some of its rules in order to list Freeserve, a British ISP, and the Milan exchange is considering after-hours trading to accommodate online traders.[73] In the spring of 2000, the fall of Internet stock prices in the United States decreased European excitement over e-businesses and Internet stocks, but the Web continues to expand its reach in Europe, and investors and stock exchanges realize the need to keep the pace.

The European Internet market still lags behind the United States by an estimated one to four years.[74] The most commonly cited reasons for Europe's late arrival to the Web are the predominance of English-language content and the high cost-per-minute of local phone calls in most parts of Europe.[75] Internet connection media are discussed in Chapter 5, Internet Hardware, Software and Communications. For e-businesses, Europe's hesitation means that there are fewer consumers to target. However, the European user base is growing steadily, and the sellers' market remains less crowded than that of the United States. Companies that move quickly to market their goods or services in Europe could increase their chances of becoming major players in the European market and creating globally recognized brands.[76] Many American companies have expanded their businesses to include the European market, with varying degrees of success. American e-businesses' globalization efforts in Europe as a whole, however, can be seen as progress; at the beginning of 2000, one-third of the top Web sites in Europe were run by American companies.[77]

e-Fact 12.8

At the beginning of the year 2000, only 13 percent of Europeans used the Internet at home, whereas 43 percent of Americans had home access.[78]

Europe is actually a compilation of many markets. Although it is the second smallest continent in the world, Europe is composed of many countries whose inhabitants speak over 60 languages.[79] One globalization strategy cannot be used to target the entire continent. Markets should be strategically chosen within Europe, and one or more localized Web sites should be created to service these regions. As a general rule, Northern Europe has a greater per-capita income, is more Americanized and has higher Internet penetration levels than Southern Europe.[80]

12.7 Africa

Internet access in Africa is rising, but its growth is challenged by regulation and limited infrastructure. The continent has few Internet Service Providers (ISPs). *Africa Online* (Fig. 12.9) is the only transcontinental service.[81]

Few Africans own telephones, and even fewer own computers. Africa Online has operations in eight African countries, with a total dial-up customer base of 26,000. Over 600 *E-Touch* centers (public centers that offer a means for more people to access the Internet) have been established in six countries, serving another 30,000 users (Fig. 12.8).

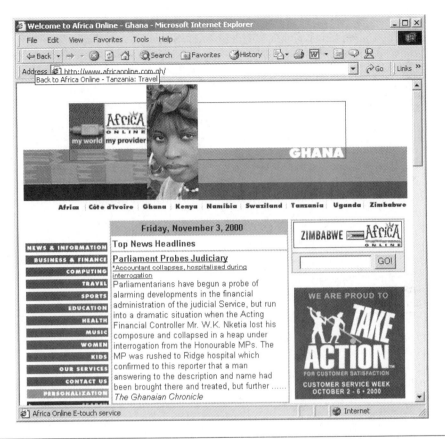

Fig. 12.8　Africa Online Ghana site. (Courtesy of Africa Online, Inc.)

In 1996, the *African Information Society Initiative* was adopted to build national communication standards. These include reducing the number of regulations limiting the development of communications, increasing accessibility particularly in rural areas and providing human resources in the development and implementation of Internet access.[82]

e-Fact 12.9

Between 1996 and 2000, the number of African countries with Internet access increased from 11 to 51.[83]

12.8 Middle East

Countries such as Egypt, Kuwait, Israel, Jordan and the United Arab Emirates have already begun growing their Web presence. Other countries, such as Iran and Saudi Arabia, are extending full Internet capabilities to government institutions and educational facilities. Individual citizens have access to a limited number of Internet resources, but efforts toward expansion continue. Libya, Syria and Iraq have yet to establish Internet access.[84]

Most Internet access in the Middle East is government regulated, although the level of regulation varies from nation to nation. The discussion of government policies, officials and challenges to moral code are heavily regulated.

12.9 Asia

Asia, including China, Japan, Korea, Vietnam, India, Singapore and Taiwan, appears on the Web, through both natively hosted Web sites and localized presence of foreign ventures. The Web presents both challenges and opportunities to traditional Asian cultural identities. In this section, we will explore the Internet and the effects it is having in the Asian regions.

In China, Internet access is limited; approximately one in 2000 individuals own computers.[85] As we discuss in Chapter 4, Online Monetary Transactions, the most common form of payment over the Web is via credit card. However, most Chinese citizens do not own credit cards, reducing the amount of online transactions, or even an interest in shopping on the Internet. Internet taxation is carefully monitored in China. In addition, supply-chain mechanisms are not in place to support e-commerce (supply-chain management is discussed in Chapter 3, Building an e-Business). The Internet in China is mostly a means of acquiring information and communicating (Fig. 12.10).[86]

The situation is similar in Japan. Statistics demonstrate that there are fewer Japanese Internet users than American users. Like China, credit-card use is limited, reducing the number of transactions conducted online. In Japan, receiving payment is a cumbersome effort on the merchant's part.[87,88]

e-Fact 12.10

According to the Computer Industry Almanac, 14 percent of Japan's population uses the Internet, of which 29 percent of access occurs from the home. In the United States, 40 percent of Americans use the Internet, of which 51 percent of access occurs from the home.[89]

Cell phone use in Japan is relatively high. Approximately 58 percent of Japanese families have cellular phones and Japan's wireless technology is advanced as well.[90] This provides a market for e-businesses that have sites accessible through wireless devices. DoCoMo (Japan's NTT Mobile Communications Network) utilizes *Code Division Multiple Access (CDMA)* technology, which provides substantial bandwidth, allowing streaming audio and video to be presented through wireless devices.[91] Wireless Internet access is discussed in Chapter 6, Wireless Internet and m-Business.

India is also adopting Web technology into its culture. Its Web population is expected to grow from four million in 1999 to 23 million in 2003. Several of the major U.S. portals, including Altavista, Lycos, MSN and Yahoo! offer, or are planning to offer, access in India.[92] Several India-based portals offer access as well.

In 2000, India began distributing ISP licenses to private organizations. Prior to this, Internet access was government regulated. Researchers suggest that this action will make India the fastest-growing nation in the Asian–Pacific region in terms of Internet access.[93] Competition has reduced access costs and increased service quality.

The Internet has had a significant impact in Asia outside corporations as well. It is causing cultural changes in Japan. For example, in the United States, it is not unusual for an individual to change careers many times. In Japan, however, the majority of the workforce not only finds a single career, but often a single employer. Japanese education systems are accommodating those who want to participate in the New Economy by adding new business schools with classes such as Internet Business Management and Financial Management of Ventures.[94]

In China, the effects of the Internet are largely related to government control over the distribution of information. Similar to several of the Middle Eastern countries, access to political and moral discussion is discouraged, and in some cases, prohibited. Often, access to Western sites is restricted by firewalls (firewalls are discussed in Chapter 7, Internet Security).[95]

12.10 Australia

In Australia, a country disconnected by large stretches of barren territory and vast amounts of water, the Internet presents an opportunity for national communication. It is currently among the most connected nations in the world.[96]

e-Fact 12.11

According to the Australian Bureau of Statistics, in 1999 farms with an Internet presence increased from 11 percent to 20 percent.[97]

Given its large dependency on agriculture, approximately one-fifth of Australian exports are composed of livestock, grain and minerals, Australia's Internet presence is largely designed to accommodate the farming industry (Fig. 12.9).[98] Australia ranks in the top five nations an online consumer of groceries, hygiene products and hardware.[99] Connection costs are high in more rural areas like the outback.

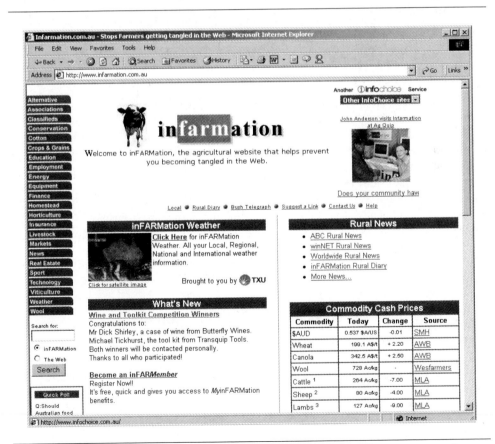

Fig. 12.9   Australia's InFARMation. (Courtesy of **inFARMation.com.au**.)

12.11 Future of Global e-Business

The Internet was, in its earliest stages, an American medium. E-commerce Web sites marketed themselves primarily to domestic consumers, and few companies adapted their Web sites to accommodate foreign audiences. The vast majority of Web sites catered to English-speaking audiences. New developments in technology and infrastructure must be made before the Web can be considered truly global. The World Bank recently released a study suggesting that the digital divide continues to widen between developed and underdeveloped countries. The imbalance of information technology is recognized as a global economic problem, and it was a top agenda item at the 2000 United Nation's Millennium Summit.

e-Fact 12.12

Although only 8 percent of the world's population are native English speakers, 78 percent of all Web sites and 96 percent of all e-commerce sites are presented primarily in English.[100]

The importance of addressing the global Internet community becomes more apparent as more people gain access to the Web worldwide. E-businesses that do not accommodate international users exclude as many as half their potential visitors. Furthermore, Internet populations outside of North America are growing explosively. The widespread availability of Web access on mobile phones and handheld devices is expected to cause even larger user increases.

e-Fact 12.13

According to Gartner Group, by 2004, 61 percent of business-to-consumer online transactions and 63 percent of business-to-business online transactions will originate outside the United States.[101]

What do these growth rates and statistics mean for the future of e-business? The adoption of Internet technology is a driving force in the movement toward a singular global economy. The Web enables activities ranging from worldwide stock trading to global supply-chain networks. Web-based companies are springing up in nearly every corner of the globe. Using the Internet, businesses can communicate quickly and efficiently with suppliers and customers anywhere in the world. American e-businesses realize that if they do not continue to provide and expand services aimed at an international customer base, competitors will.[102] Globalization is major part of the future of some e-business, and survival is contingent on implementing intelligent and thorough globalization strategies.

e-Fact 12.14

In 2000, 66 percent of Internet users are non-Americans, compared with 44 percent in 1998.[103]

12.12 Internet and World Wide Web Resources

General

www.globalcrossing.com
GlobalCrossing provides a fast, secure global network, IP services and rich content, applications and Web hosting.

`www.abanet.org/buslaw/cyber/initiatives/prospect.html`
The full text of this report can be found of the American Bar Association *Global Cyberspace Juris-diction Project.* The report represents the culmination of two years of research relating to international legal questions introduced by the Internet and global e-commerce.

`europa.eu.net`
This site provides additional information on the European Union Directive on Data Protection.

`www.info.uu.net/vpn`
UUNet offers reliable global VPN service and end-to-end management. It is part of MCI WorldCom.

`www.telecomitalia.it`
Sea-Bone is Telecom Italia's solution for telecommunication operators and ISPs that want to upgrade their network to Global Internet.

`www.From2.com`
This site offers complete solutions for international e-commerce (IT trade compliance, custom bro-kerage, global logistics etc.) and helps with taxation, customer service and shipping.

`www.nua.ie`
This site hosts two Internet business-related newsletters and offers links to other relevant information to learn more about the development of e-business on the Web.

`www.glreach.com/globstats/index.php3`
Internet and technology statistics by country or language are available at the Global Reach site.

`www.idiominc.com`
This site contains a *Resource Library* that allows users to search for articles and information pertain-ing to specific foreign markets and topics.

`www.firsttuesday.com`
This site connects potential business partners and employees to gather at the group's monthly meet-ings or online job marketplace.

Domain Names

`www.iana.org/cctld.html.`
The Internet Assigned Numbers Authority (IANA) Web site. This site provides information on regis-tering foreign domain names.

Translation Services

`www.ilanguage.com`
This site offers dynamic Internet translation and globalization services for Internet companies, in-house translations, global promotion of your Web site and e-mails to customers in their native language.

`www.etranslate.com`
eTranslate specializes in end-to-end globalization solutions.

`www.logos.it`
This site provides an online language translation dictionary, helps users pronounce words correctly and demonstrates the use of the word in context.

`www.aquarius.net`
This site provides online translation services.

`www.wholetree.com`
Wholetree offers integrated multi-language support for customer service

www.RSL.com
RSL is the telecom's first multi-national e-services platform with a real-time language translator.

www.teltrust.com
Teltrust offers seamless integrated multilingual support services and one-touch support.

Internationalization and Localization
The following sites provide internalization and localization services.

www.bowneglobal.com
Bowne Global Provides localization services for businesses in a variety of industries.

www.globalsight.com
This site provides software for internationalization and localization intergration.

www.lionbridge.com
LionBridge Technologies provides globalization solutions for technology, telecommunications, life sciences and financial services industries.

www.worldpoint.com
This site provides translation services and content management for e-businesses.

Distribution

www.postoffice.co.uk
Web site of the British Post Office

www.post-ag.de
Web site of the German post office

SUMMARY

- When you create a Web site, you potentially reach Internet users in every corner of the world, and, as more and more people become connected to the Web, an ever-increasing customer base is generated.

- The global reach of the Internet also poses challenges to a world composed of different cultures, attitudes, languages, codes of conduct and government authorities.

- As more people access the Web worldwide, users can be exposed to products, services or information that are considered offensive or that are illegal in their countries of residence. Government regulation affects the growth rate of the Internet and has the potential to cause major problems as the volume of international e-business transactions increases.

- Americans are extremely protective of copyright. Intellectual property in the United States. cannot be used substantially without gaining the creator's permission or citing the source of the information.

- In relation to jurisdiction, or the range of legal control, governments must determine whether an e-business that maintains a Web site is subject to the laws of all the countries from which the site can be accessed.

- The American Bar Association's (ABA) report recommends forming a "global online standards commission" to govern Internet-related legal disputes involving parties from two or more countries. Universally adopted laws would likely address cybercrimes such as copyright infringement, cybersquatting, cyber terrorism, fraud, hacking and computer viruses.

- In May 2000, the destructive "Love Bug" or "I-Love-You" virus was spread via e-mail to computer systems around the world.

- The World Intellectual Property Organization (WIPO) has created an international forum for regulating Internet issues related to trademarks and cybersquatting

- In an attempt to eliminate the illegal use of trademarked names in Web-site addresses, WIPO established an arbitration service to settle cybersquatting controversies.

- The European Union Directive on Data Protection (**europa.eu.net**) is an agreement among its members on the regulations that apply to information exchange. The Directive mandates that personal information be kept current and be used in a lawful manner for its designated purpose.

- Before you decide to operate overseas, you should ask yourself whether the revenues you gain from expansion will cover the costs involved and whether other cultures will react positively to what you sell.

- When deciding on a market, factors such as the number of people online, Internet usage growth rates, per capita income and consumers' probable expectations of your business must be considered.

- Domain-name registration in foreign countries is often more complex than registering a **.com** domain and may require owning a trademark or incorporating your business in the country.

- Globalizing your Web site is composed of two major steps: internationalization and localization.

- Internationalization involves restructuring the software used by your e-business so that it can process foreign languages, currencies, date formats and other variations involved in conducting business globally.

- Unicode (**www.unicode.org**), a 16-bit encoding system that assigns a unique number to almost every character in every language, enables your system to handle iconic languages such as Chinese, Japanese or Korean.

- Localization includes the translation and cultural adaptation of your site's content and presentation.

- Because machines cannot be relied upon to translate grammar, idioms and humor perfectly, human translators are necessary to create a complete foreign language Web site. A bilingual translator and an editor should be employed, preferably those living abroad and aware of culture terminology, market trends and other regional legal issues.

- When considering the layout of your foreign language site, you should be aware that translation into European languages can expand text up to 40 percent in length, whereas translation into Asian languages slightly decreases text length.

- Site layout must be adapted to accommodate languages which are read vertically, such as Chinese, or those which read right to left, such as Hebrew.

- When creating a regional site, investigate the interpretation of your company and product names in the language or languages for which you are creating the site.

- Global content refers to information and design that requires translation, but is essentially the same for all cultures. This typically includes logos, trademarks and company history and mission.

- Regional content, such as product and marketing information, is usually written once in English and then adapted for various markets.

- Material on specific regional pages that appears only on that Web site, such as regional promotions, pricing, delivery and store or office locations, is called local content.

- Local partners can provide many advantages, including a physical presence in the target country, a recognized brand, extensive knowledge of the target market and localized content and customer service.

- Credit cards are less common in other parts of the world, even among the upper and middle classes in industrialized areas. Credit cards are rare among consumers in developing nations.

- E-businesses in Europe should offer a c.o.d. (cash on delivery) option and should consider other means of monetary transfer that do not involve credit cards.

- Giros (wire transfers between bank accounts) offer an alternative for companies that work in some northern European countries.

- It is best to ship goods from a local distribution center, rather than from the U.S.

- Every government has a unique strategy when it comes to regulating business and the Internet, and every nation has a different set of laws relating to these topics. In some countries, including the United States, laws may even vary by state or region.

- Most nations require a special permit to sell animals, plants, products made from endangered species, arms and explosives, bulletproof clothes, toy guns, weapons of any kind, toy coins, pornography, controlled substances and poisons.

- E-businesses must comply with each country's Internet regulations.

- Before you begin processing sales in another country, investigate international tax laws in that country as they apply to Internet sales and to the specific products you wish to market.

- Canada's Internet users are spending ever-increasing amounts of time online, averaging 8.6 hours per week in December 1999.

- In general, Canadians have been receptive to the foreign companies. Over half of Canadian online purchases are made from American Web sites.

- Latin America has the fastest growth rate of Internet usage in the world.

- Latin American ISPs and portals are experiencing success; in some markets, such as Brazil, local companies are even outperforming U.S.-based corporations such as America Online's AOL Latin America.

- Europe is a predominately industrialized and technology-savvy society with much of the needed infrastructure in place to support widespread adoption of the Internet and e-commerce.

- European e-businesses have been launched in all areas of the continent, and new e-businesses are receiving more venture capital than has been previously available to European technology companies.

- Driven by the development of Internet economy, many European countries have taken steps to make their national stock exchanges more e-business friendly. Traditionally, the European stock exchanges have enforced rigorous requirements that barred the public trading of newer and riskier companies.

- Europe is actually a compilation of many markets. Although it is the second-smallest continent in the world, Europe is composed of many countries whose inhabitants speak over 60 languages.

- Markets should be strategically chosen within Europe, and one or more localized Web sites should be created to service these regions.

- Internet access in Africa is rising, but its growth is challenged by regulation and limited infrastructure.

- Few Africans own telephones, and fewer still own computers. Public centers offer a means for more people to access the Internet.

- In 1996, the African Information Society Initiative was adopted to build national communication standards. These include reducing the number of regulations limiting the development of communications, increasing accessibility particularly in rural areas and providing human resources in the development and implementation of Internet access.

- Countries such as Egypt, Kuwait, Israel, Jordan, the United Arab Emirates, Morocco and Tunisia have already begun growing their Web presence. Other countries, such as Iran and Saudi Arabia, are extending full Internet capabilities to government institutions and educational facilities. Libya, Syria and Iraq have yet to establish Internet access.

- Most Internet access in the Middle East is government regulated, although the level of regulation varies from nation to nation. Issues such as the discussion of government policies and officials or challenges to moral code are heavily regulated.

- Asia, including China, Japan, Korea, Vietnam, India, Singapore and Taiwan, appear on the Web, through both natively hosted Web sites and localized presence of foreign ventures. Most Chinese citizens do not own one, reducing the amount of online transactions or even an interest in shopping on the Internet.

- Both Japan and China are expected to be leading users of wireless Web access.

- In 2000, India began distributing ISP licenses to private organizations. Prior to this, Internet access was government regulated.

- In Australia, a country disconnected by large stretches of barren territory and vast amounts of water, the Internet presents an opportunity for connectivity. Australia is currently among the most connected nations in the world.

- The Internet in its earliest stages, catered to English-speaking audiences.

- The adoption of Internet technology is a driving force in the movement toward a singular global economy.

TERMINOLOGY

Africa Online
African Information Society Initiative
Alternative Investment Market
Amsterdam Exchange
Council of Europe
E-Touch
European Union Directive on Data Exchange
European Venture Capital Association
giros
global content
Global Cyberspace Jurisdiction Project
global economy
globalization
hate speech
imminent lawless action
Internet Content Summit

internalization
jurisdiction
Le Nouveau Marche
local content
localization
London Stock Exchange
minimum contacts
multilingual e-translation portal
Neuer Markt
Nuovo Mercato
regional content
spam
The Organization for Economic Cooperation
    and Development
World Intellectual Property Organization (WIPO)

SELF-REVIEW EXERCISES

12.1   State whether the following are true or false. If the answer is false, explain why.
a) Approximately 50 percent of the content of the Internet is available only in English.
b) American law is less protective of copyright than most nations.
c) Generally, it is advisable to register international versions of your Web site under a foreign domain name.
d) Consumers are approximately 10 times more likely to purchase a product if it is presented in their native language.
e) Translations from English to European languages can increase the amount of text by 40 percent.
f) Europe has an integrated postal service similar to that of the United States.

12.2   Fill in the blanks in each of the following statements:
a) The _____ is a pending agreement between the United States and the European Union that addresses the issue of international differences, particularly regarding the issue of privacy.

b) In some countries, a Web-site owner must also apply for a _____ when registering a domain name.

c) _____, a 16-bit encoding system that assigns a unique number to almost every character in every language, enables your system to handle iconic languages, such as Chinese, Japanese or Korean.

d) Most cultures view the color _____ more positively than other colors.

e) _____ content refers to information and design that requires translation, but is essentially the same for all cultures.

ANSWERS TO SELF-REVIEW EXERCISES

12.1 a) False. The majority of content on the Internet is available in English; however, 50 percent of the world's population is unable to understand it. b) False. American law is often more protective. To use copyrighted material in the United States, permission must be obtained to use the material, or a citation of the original creator must be indicated. c) True. d) False. Consumers are approximately three times more likely to purchase a product if it is presented in their native language. e) True. f) False. Europe does not have an integrated postal service.

12.2 a) European Union Directive on Data Protection. b) Trademark. c) Unicode. d) Blue. e) Global content.

EXERCISES

12.3 State whether the following are true or false. If the answer is false, explain why.
  a) The global reach of the Internet also poses challenges to a world composed of different cultures, attitudes, languages, codes of conduct and government authorities.
  b) When deciding on a market, factors such as the number of people online, Internet usage growth rates, per capita income and consumers' probable expectations of your business must be considered.
  c) Domain-name registration in foreign countries is often easier than registering a .com domain.
  d) Presentation includes the translation and cultural adaptation of your site's content and presentation.
  e) Because machines cannot be relied upon to translate grammar, idioms and humor perfectly, human translators are necessary to create a complete foreign language Web site.

12.4 Fill in the blanks in each of the following statements:
  a) In relation to _____, or the range of legal control, governments must determine whether an e-business that maintains a Web site is subject to the laws of all the countries from which the site can be accessed.
  b) In an attempt to eliminate the illegal use of trademarked names in Web-site addresses, _____ established an arbitration service to settle cybersquatting controversies.
  c) Globalizing your Web site is composed of two major steps: _____ and _____.
  d) When considering the layout of your foreign language site, you should be aware that translation into European languages can expand text up to _____ in length, whereas translation into Asian languages slightly decreases text length.
  e) Site layout must be adapted to accommodate languages which are read _____, such as Chinese, or those which read right to left, such as Hebrew.

12.5 Define the following:
  a) Internalization
  b) The World Intellectual Property Organization (WIPO)
  c) Global content

  d) Regional content
  e) Minimum contacts

12.6 (*Class Discussion*). In Section 14.2.1, Accounting for Legal and Cultural Differences, we discuss the American Bar Association's treatment of international Internet law. Visit the Web site at **www.abanet.org/buslaw/cyber/initiatives/prospect.html** to learn more about privacy, copyright, taxation, etc., when applied internationally. How do you think these issues can be resolved? What are some of the obstacles? Prepare a statement on one issue. Come to class prepared to present your opinion. Be prepared to support your statement with evidence.

12.7 (*Class Discussion*). In the chapter, we present the question, "How do we create a global communication forum while maintaining respect for different cultures and codes of conduct?" Divide the class into groups, giving each group a specific region of the world to investigate. Teams should gather information regarding each nation's perspective on the Internet and be prepared to discuss the challenges this will present in forming a global economy. For example, how do these nations regard privacy? Intellectual property? Free speech? Pornography?

12.8 (*Semester Project*). In this chapter, we mentioned the Enterprise Translation Server from Transparent Language (**www.transparentlanguage.com**), which converts Web sites into your language of choice. We also discussed how various colors, layouts and logos are interpreted differently from culture to culture. Choose a domestic site with text and images on the Internet. Discuss the aspects of that site that should be redesigned to make the site more approachable internationally.

WORKS CITED

The notation <**www.domain-name.com**> indicates that the citation is for information found at the Web site.

1. T. R. Weiss, "ABA Panel Calls for Global Internet Laws," *Computer World* 17 July 2000: 6.

2. "German Compuserve Judgement," <**www.qlinks.net/comdocs/somm.html**>.

3. "Indian industry calls for global Internet law," <**news.findlaw.com/legalnews/s/20000821/dl164641.html**>.

4. F. Williams, "Squatters in cyberspace face rights crackdown," *Financial Times* 11 July 2000: 6.

5. C. Grande, "Crime Leaves Websites Rushing to Fill the Breach," *Financial Times* 19 October 2000: 10.

6. J. Gruenwald, "Europeans Defining the Long Arm of the Cyberlaw," *Inter@ctive Week* 25 September 2000: 10-11.

7. V. Cerf and J. Patrick, "A better way to police the Internet," *Financial Times* 28 June 2000: 13.

8. M. L. D'Amico, "Who Polices the Net," <**www.pcworld.com/shared/printable_articles/0,1440,12745.html**>.

9. D. Depalma, 2 9

10. T. Mccollum, "Foreign Affairs," *The Industry Standard* 7 August 2000: 175.

11. S. Tapper, "Is Globalization Right for You?" *Webtechniques* September 2000: 26.

12. D. DePalma, 30.

13. S. Tapper, 26

14. L. Hakan Sjoo, "Set Up Shop in Europe," *e-Business Advisor* February 2000: 21.

15. H. Schwartz, "Going Global," *Webtechniques* September 2000: 54.

16. J. DiSabitino, "Web Site Globalization," *Computer World* 10 July 2000: 56.

17. H. Schwartz, "Going Global," *Webtechniques* September 2000: 54.

18. <**www.logos.it**>.

19. H. Schwartz, 57.

20. J. Yunker, "Speaking in Charsets," *Webtechniques* September 2000: 62.

21. J. Yunker, 62.

22. J. DiSabatino, 56.

23. M. E. Holzschlag, "Color My World," *Webtechniques* September 2000: 38-40.

24. J. DiSabatino, 56

25. B. Sawyer, D. Greely and J. Cataudella: 314.

26. S. Tapper, 26

27. O. Lagon, "Culturally Correct Site Design," *Webtechniques* September 2000: 51.

28. O. Lagon, 51.

29. H. Schwartz, 56.

30. O. Lagon, 50

31. P. Musich, "A Small World, After All," *eWeek* 21 August 2000: 27.

32. P. Musich, 27.

33. S. Syre and C. Stein, "Crossing the Ocean Still a Crucial Test," *The Boston Globe* 21 July 2000: C10.

34. B. McCarthy, "All E-Business is Global," *InformationWeek* 5 June 2000: 204.

35. L. Hakan Sjoo, 23.

36. T. Mullen, "Service Aids Selling to Europeans," *InternetWeek* 17 July 2000: 13.

37. L. Hakan Sjoo, 20

38. T. Mullen, 13.

39. L. Hakan Sjoo, 21

40. B. Sawyer, D. Greely and J. Cataudella. *Creating Stores on the Web*: 2nd Edition. Berkeley, CA: Peachpit Press, 2000: 472.

41. S. Tapper, 30.

42. S. Tapper, 30.

43. D. DePalma, 31.

44. B. Sawyer, D. Greely and J. Cataudella, 473.

45. J. Shen, "The Commerce Diplomats: Enabling the Free Flow of Goods," *Webtechniques* November 2000: 48.

46. DePalma, 31.

47. J. Shen, 48-49.

48. S. Sawyer, D. Greely and J. Cataudella, 473.

49. S. Lawrence, "Measuring Up: The Race is on to Deliver Internet Ratings in Europe," *The Industry Standard* 14 February 2000: 212.

50. S. Lawrence, "The Internet World in Numbers," *The Industry Standard* 14 February 2000: 219.

51. "Home-Based Net Usage Up in Canada," `<cyberatlas.Internet.com/big_picture/demographics/article/0,1323,5911_331361,00.html>`, 30 March 2000.

52. "Home-Based Net Usage Up in Canada."

53. F. Sheikah, "Canadian Portals Patriot Play," *The Industry Standard* 1 May 2000: 149.

54. R. Ricklefs, "U.S. E-Tailers Expand Efforts North of the Border," *The Wall Street Journal* 31 January 2000: A21.

55. Ricklefs, A21.

56. Ricklefs, A21.

57. F. Sheikh, "Too Little, Too Late For Canadian VCs?" *The Industry Standard* 3 April 2000: 143.

58. F. Sheikh, "Putting Its Eggs in Too Many Baskets?" *The Industry Standard* 17 April 2000: 151

59. "Home-Based Net Usage Up In Canada," `<cyberatlas.Internet.com/big_picture/demographics/article/0,1323,5911_331361,00.html>`

60. J. T. Mulqueen, "Latin American Online: Overcrowded Field?" *Inter@ctive Week* 14 August 2000: 56.

61. S. M. Ferdandez, "Latin America Logs On," *Time* 8 May 2000: B3.

62. T. Jackson, "AOL's Perilous Journey South," *Financial Times* 25 July 2000: 27. S. M. Fernandez: B3.

63. S.M. Fernandez, B3.

64. M. Yeomans, "Chasing the Latin American Shopper," *The Industry Standard* 6 March 2000: 148.

65. S. M. Fernandez, B3.

66. "Latin America: Wiring the Southern Hemisphere," *Global Technology* Business June 2000: 14.

67. Fernandez, B4.

68. L. Hakan Sjoo, 17.

69. S. Baker and W. Echikson, "Europe's Internet Bash," *Business Week* 7 February 2000: EB40.

70. J. Evans, "Old World, New Economy," *The Industry Standard* 14 February 2000: 186. P. Sprenger, "A Change of Heart for Euro Exchanges," *The Industry Standard* 7 February 2000: 150.

71. P. Sprenger, 150.

72. P. Sprenger, 150.

73. P. Sprenger, 150.

74. L. Hakan Sjoo, 17.

75. S. Baker and W. Echikson, EB 42.

76. L. Hakan Sjoo, 16.

77. L. Hakan Sjoo, 17.

78. S. Baker and W. Echikson: EB42

79. "Europe: Physical and human geography," `<britannica.com www.britannica.com/bcom/eb/article/50,5716,108575+2+106055,00.html>`

80. L. Hakan Sjoo, 18.

81. M. Yeomans, "Africa Online," *The Industry Standard* 14 February 2000: 135.

82. "African Information Society Initiative," <**www.bellanet.org/partners/aisi**>.

83. M. Jensen, "African Internet Status," <**www3.sn.apc.org/africa/afstat.htm**> May 2000: 1.

13

Social and Political Issues

Objectives

- To address the impact of the Internet on society.
- To understand the so-called digital divide.
- To discuss specific online communities.
- To explore how the Internet is affecting the workplace.
- To explore how the Internet is playing an active role in political and social activities.

It contributes greatly towards a man's moral and intellectual health, to be brought into habits of companionship with individuals unlike himself, who care little for his pursuits, and whose sphere and abilities he must go out of himself to appreciate.
Nathaniel Hawthorne

The only fence against the world is a thorough knowledge of it.
John Locke

The ballot is stronger than the bullet.
Abraham Lincoln

The freeman, casting with unpurchased hand
The vote that shakes the turrets of the land.
Oliver Wendell Holmes, Sr.

Outline

13.1   Introduction

13.2   Health, Social Interaction and the Internet

   13.2.1   Social Health

   13.2.2   Children and the Internet

13.3   Socio-Economic Segregation

13.4   New Economic Workplace

13.5   Online Communities

   13.5.1   Online Communities: Defining the Difference

   13.5.2   Communication Tools

   13.5.3   Online Activism

13.6   Online Charities and Non Profit Organizations on the Web

13.7   Internet and World Wide Web Resources

Summary • Terminology • Self-Review Exercises • Answers to Self-Review Exercises • Exercises •
Works Cited

13.1 Introduction

The Internet is proving to be a valuable learning, business and communications tool. Its influence has affected our commercial, political and social lives. It has provided a forum for addressing important issues, supporting causes and meeting new individuals.

In this chapter, we explore the effects of the Internet on our personal and professional lives. We discuss the complexities of the *digital divide* (the socio-economic segregation between those who can afford Internet technology and those who cannot), and what countries, cities and school districts are doing to make Internet access universally available. The advantages and disadvantages of online communities and social interaction on the Web are also discussed.

13.2 Health, Social Interaction and the Internet

Many sociologists argue that life is becoming too dependent on the Internet. Studies show that many users are spending more time on the Internet and, as a result, less time is devoted to interpersonal communication. Internet enthusiasts disagree, suggesting that the Internet provides alternatives to the traditional forms of communication. E-mailing, video-conferencing, chat rooms, electronic forums and message boards are all new communications channels created by the Internet and World Wide Web. In this section, we explore the role of the Internet in our social development.

13.2.1 Social Health

In February, 2000, Stanford University released a study indicating that the Internet was causing its users to become socially isolated. Statistics from the study revealed that as a result of the Internet, 34 percent of Americans spent less time reading newspapers, 25 percent worked more hours while at home, 25 percent spent less time in stores and 13 percent reduced time spent with their friends and family.[1]

Being one of the first of its kind, this study received a considerable amount of attention. Further studies suggested that the sampling pool and questioning method in the study were biased. For example, both Internet users and nonusers were questioned; however, all of the questioning was conducted via the Internet.[2]

Pornography, gambling, Internet scams and violence are readily available on the Web, and the tolerance for this material varies from one region of the world to another. Pornography, as we discuss in Chapter 11, Legal and Ethical Issues; Internet Taxation, is legal in the United States. Prohibiting this and other forms of speech is a violation of the Constitution. Yet, the ability for individuals of all age groups to access this material quickly and easily can be considered harmful. Other issues include Web sites containing violent speech and virus attacks hindering airport, hospital and government communications.[3] Illegal gambling is also an issue. Several of the Caribbean Islands and Costa Rica host online gambling sites—legal in their own countries—in an effort to generate revenue and bring in new business. These sites, because of their large numbers, enable individuals to gamble online from remote locations.

e-Fact 13.1

A Scottish programming group discovered that access to pornographic material was growing at 20,000 hosts per day.[4]

13.2.2 Children and the Internet

The way the Internet affects the development of children is a debated issue. Proponents suggest that giving children access to the Internet gives them a head-start in their education. Companies like JumpStart (**www.education.com/jumpstart**) offer learning games and assessment tests tailored to various age groups. Alphabetization, mathematics, sentence construction and matching are among the skill sets tested.

e-Fact 13.2

According to PC Data, the software market for children under 3 years of age is worth approximately $30 million.[5]

Others disagree, questioning the benefits of dependency on the Internet as a learning tool, especially when young children are learning communication skills. Distracting children from outdoor activity and explicit speech with the Web are also of concern. As we discussed in the previous section, much Web content may not be suitable for children. Unsupervised Web access leaves children "one URL away" from accessing graphic material of a violent and sexual nature. In addition, children may also be subjected to adult conversations when entering chat rooms, or may encounter individuals posing under a false identity. Filtering software and other methods for restricting access to some Web sites are discussed in Chapter 11, Legal and Ethical Issues; Internet Taxation.

e-Fact 13.3

According to Money magazine, the average amount of time American children (ages 10-17) will spend on the Internet is 23 years.[6]

Home schooling (teaching children in the home versus sending them to public or private schools) is increasingly popular. Advocates of home schooling suggest it offers an optimal learning environment, because children receive personal attention from the people who care about them most—their parents and guardians. Lessons can be tailored to the aptitude of the student. Opponents find faults in home schooling, suggesting that it limits the opportunity for social interaction and learning to work with others. Another issue is the ability of parents and guardians to convey the learning material. At what level do the parents and guardians become less effective than trained teachers?

The Internet provides several options for enhancing home schooling, as well as other school students. In addition to learning from parents and guardians, students can turn to the Internet for online tutors, classes and supplementary information. Online text chatting and message boards allow students to interact with other students and teachers. (Online education, sometimes referred to as *e-learning*, is discussed in depth in Chapter 17, e-Learning.)

13.3 Socio-Economic Segregation

The *"digital divide,"* a common term for socio-economic segregation created by the Internet, is a growing problem.[7] It involves the cost of acquiring Internet access, the technical support to maintain it and the proper instructions to bring it into homes and schools. The digital divide is, in large part, about education and training.

e-Fact 13.4

The digital divide extends far beyond the United States. For example, in Bangladesh a computer costs approximately 8 years' salary. By comparison, in the United States a computer costs one month's salary, on average.[8]

However, the inability to access the Internet is not limited to cost. Other circumstances directly limit portions of the population. For example, approximately a quarter of U.S. households do not own a credit card, a primary form of payment over the Web. Further, approximately 18 million Americans receive food stamps, yet many of the major online grocers do not accept food stamps as a form of payment. As a result, many e-businesses lose potential customers.[9]

The U.S. Department of Commerce released "Falling Through the Net: Defining The Digital Divide" in July, 1999. The report indicates that in 1998, households with incomes of $75,000 or higher were 20 times more likely to have Internet access than those of lower income. The divide also applies to certain minority groups, inner-city and rural areas as opposed to more affluent neighborhoods. These numbers, when compared with those of 1997, indicate that the gap is increasing.

The impact of the digital divide is profound. The lack of Internet access and consequent lack of network skills limit the number of applicants for the growing number of technical positions in the United States. The inability for companies to fill these positions could affect the growth of the economy.

Internet advocates suggest that the Internet does not differ greatly from the technological advancements of the past. Electricity, the telephone and other inventions now widely available, were, at one point, luxuries that few could afford. As technology advances, computers and the cost of connecting to the Internet could become more commonplace.[10]

In the meantime, government agencies, nonprofit organizations and corporations are making efforts to bridge the gap (see 3Com Urban Challenge feature). Lawmakers are also trying to work a tax break into the system to reward participating groups. AOL launched *AOL@School* (`www.school.aol.com`) in May 2000, in an effort to bring Internet tools

(Instant Messenger and e-mail) and filtering mechanisms to schools.[11] The government is sponsoring PeoplePC, which offers Internet access at a low cost, with a proposed $100 million budget.[12] *Computers For Youth* is a nonprofit organization that teaches parents and students how to operate a computer and use the Internet. Based in New York, the organization brings students and their parents to the schools on Saturday mornings and, at the close of the class, students are given their computers and three months of free Internet access.[13]

13.4 New Economic Workplace

The advent of the Internet has created new job requirements. In some cases people have more job flexibility. However, starting an e-business is demanding—perhaps more than any other business, given the intense competition. In addition, technology savvy employees often are required to work longer hours, because finding employees to fill all technical positions can be difficult. In this section, we explore how the new economy is changing the dynamics of the workplace.

e-Fact 13.5

Job loyalty is a concern felt by many business owners. The average person changes jobs seven times.[18]

3Com Urban Challenge[14,15]

In an effort to support equal Internet opportunities, 3Com and AmeriCorps*VISTA announced the 3Com Urban Challenge in 2000. The Urban Challenge is designed to provide 10 American cities with the finances and the personnel to acquire and maintain Internet access.

3Com, the leading provider of networks to schools, is providing a total of $1 million in equipment, network design, consulting and training, in an effort to educate students in network management. The Urban Challenge is the result of previously successful efforts to enable cities in the United States to offer students Internet access. Boston, with the help of 3Com, reduced their computer-to-student ratio from 1:63 to 1:6 for 1999.[16]

Volunteers in Service to America (AmeriCorps*VISTA) is a program hosting individuals who wish to work toward equal opportunity in the United States. Each of the cities awarded an Urban Challenge Grant will be eligible to receive three AmeriCorps*VISTA members to provide support services at a cost-share amount.[17]

Applications and additional information can be found at **www.3com.com/government/urbanchallenge/americorps.html**. Students can view the full-length video announcement of 3Com's Urban Challenge ar **www.3com.com/government/urbanchallenge** and by following the links to the CSPAN National Press Club. The RealPlayer G, necessary for viewing, is also available for download. The full report is available for download at **www.ntia.doc.gov/ntiahome/digitaldivide**.

The growth of the Internet and the use of digital transmission is changing the workplace. As Internet use increases, employees are no longer required to spend all of their time in the office. Personal computers and handheld devices allow work to be completed and communications to be conducted from remote locations. Professionals can use the Internet to employ themselves as outside contractors (see Chapter 20, Online Career Services). Streaming media—which offers video conferencing and Web-based demonstration further enhances long distance communications. These technologies are discussed in Chapter 5, Hardware, Software and Communications.

While the Internet and wireless technologies may create opportunities for people to migrate to more rural areas, it is also at least partly responsible for the increase in rent in formerly low rent areas. This has lead to a significant backlash from the native communities. Vandalism is a continually growing problem, and antitechnology groups such as Mission Yuppie Eradication Project are pushing to move the dot-coms out of their neighborhoods.[19]

e-Fact 13.6

According to Money magazine, the average cost of a home in the United States is $133,300. In Silicon Valley, the cost of a 792 square foot home can cost up to a half-million dollars.[20]

For families, Internet start-ups can be particularly challenging. Federal Law protects expectant mothers through the Family and Medical Leave Act of 1993, requiring employers to grant them 12 weeks of unpaid leave. This is only mandatory in companies with more than 50 employees, however, and many Internet start-ups have fewer than 50 employees.[21]

Job stability is also an issue with Internet-related careers. In the summer of 2000, the dot-com phenomenon slowed considerably, causing many Internet companies to downsize their staffs. As more companies downsize and reduce their budgets, Internet-related jobs are becoming more difficult to find.[22]

e-Fact 13.7

In a review of 55 companies from January through June (2000) 4,425 employees were laid-off from companies such as **ToySmart.com**, **Boo.com** *and* **PetStore.com**, *according to The Industry Standard.*[23]

13.5 Online Communities

The Internet is redefining the notion of communities. On the Internet, communities are not formed by geographic boundaries; they are formed by shared interests. By enabling people to form communities outside of a geographic setting, the Web allows larger groups to communicate, share information and exchange opinions. Many Web sites accommodate a variety of individuals with different backgrounds, interests and ideas (Fig. 13.1 and 13.2). In this section, we will explore how the Internet is developing communities and facilitating discussion.

13.5.1 Online Communities: Defining the Difference

The Internet alters the ways people meet and interact. In cyberspace we do not notice a person's appearance first, unless they have posted a picture or are communicating through a video camera. In cyberspace, it is not our appearance that draws people to us; rather, we learn about each other through text communication.[24]

Web sites

```
www.blackvoices.com
www.migente.com
www.asianavenue.com
www.blackplanet.com
www.celt.net
```

Fig. 13.1   Ethnic Web communities.

Community	URL	Purpose
Agri-Ville: Online Farming Community	`www.agri-ville.com`	To connect farmers online and provide relevant current events. Online seminars and discussion are also available.
The Learning Space	`www.learningspace.org`	To connect educators and provide discussion and information on educational issues.
Green Communities Association	`www.gca.ca`	To provide a forum for individuals interested in protecting the environment.

Fig. 13.2   Interest-based online communities

Virtual communities also allow individuals with many different likes, dislikes, ambitions and hobbies to foster their interests, despite hindrances that might occur in real space (see the AOL feature). For example, a visitor of any demographic make-up can visit an online cooking portal and be identified only as an Internet user who is interested in cooking. Gender, race, creed, age and sexual orientation play no role in the user's experience. The online user is free to move about the site and browse products undisturbed. This is not necessarily the experience that the same individual would have in a brick-and-mortar establishment, where a shopper's physical appearance is evident to the merchant.

Ethnic communities serve as a forum where members can exchange information, read about current events and chat. Like other online communities, they allow these groups to act on issues that concern them. For example, these groups may want to stop an advertisement or television show that portrays them in a stereotypical way, or they may want to present an idea or opinion in the political sphere.[25]

Online relationship services have provided new options for meeting people. For example, when meeting people in the physical world, our initial reaction often is to formulate an opinion about them on the basis of their physical appearance. Unfortunately, in many cases, we might make these judgments too quickly and miss the opportunity to form relationships with other people.

AOL: Super Community

America Online, one of the largest communities on the Web, began this century with its highly publicized planned merger with Time Warner Entertainment. Just 16 years after Steve Case started the company in his dorm room, AOL has become the leading media organization on the Web. The network of AOL companies includes CompuServe, Netscape, DigitalCity, ICQ and AOL Movie Fone. On the Web, AOL has succeeded by offering a user-friendly way to access the Internet and communicate with other AOL members. According to AOL's Web Site, AOL's 24-million-plus users are able to conduct all of their browsing, email, chatting and downloading within the AOL format.

Age-oriented sites can also be found on the Web. Teenagers are among the most popular target audience due to high levels of spending online. Shopping, entertainment, sports and fashion are among the topics discussed. Teen sites include **www.alloy.com** and **www.bolt.com**. The elderly population is also using the Internet at a growing rate, and sites such as **www.elderweb.com** and **www.seniornet.org** are designed to meet their needs.

Gender-specific sites (Fig. 13.3), especially those designated for the female Internet user, are increasingly popular. Sites such as **www.oxygen.com** and **www.ivillage.com** allow women to gather online and discuss issues pertaining particularly to them, such as pregnancy and breast cancer. Similar online services are available to men. **Crosswalk.com** provides a men's site that offers current events at (**men.crosswalk.com**); there are a variety of sites providing information on men's health issues.

Gender-Specific Sites	URL	Purpose
The Men's Issues Page	**www.vix.com/pub/men/index.html**	Offers information on men's issues, such as fatherhood and physical health.
Victorian AIDS Council/ Gay Men's Health Centre	**www.vicaids.asn.au**	Provides health and treatment information for men with AIDS.
Men's Health	**www.menshealth.com**	Presents health information, current events and interactive chat opportunities.
Women.com	**www.women.com**	Provides women's health information, current events and interactive opportunities.
Advancing Woman	**www.advancing-women.com**	An online career advancement center for women in technology.

Fig. 13.3   Sample of gender-specific sites on the Internet (part 1 of 2).

Gender-Specific Sites	URL	Purpose
Ms. Foundation for Women	`www.ms.foundation.org`	The Web site for the National Women's Fund. Presents women's issues, events and contribution opportunities.
African American Women's Network	`members.tripod.com/ ~AAWN1`	Provides access to cultural, personal and professional development. News articles, classes and directories are available on the site.

Fig. 13.3   Sample of gender-specific sites on the Internet (part 2 of 2).

The gay and lesbian population is another demographic group that is well represented on the Internet. Web sites include **www.planetout.com**, **gay.com** and **www.youth-pride.com**. These sites provide individuals with health information, promote gay rights and offer interactive chat opportunities.

13.5.2 Communication Tools

In this section, we discuss some of the technologies that provide people with communication tools. Chatting is an increasingly popular method of online communication. In Chapter 10, e-Customer Relationship Management, we discuss *online text chatting* and its role in customer service. However, online chatting also enables social interaction on the Web.

Firetalk™ Communication Through the Web

Firetalk Communications Inc. provides several different Web-based communications techniques. Users can make worldwide person-to-person calls for free over the Internet (Fig. 13.4), or invite as many as 100 different Firetalk members for an online conference call. Users select the person they wish to call from their contact list. Additional contacts can be added to conduct conference calls. Users speak into the computer's microphone and listen through headsets.

Firetalk also offers text-based chatting through its Instant Messaging service. Users select the person they wish to communicate with from their list of contacts, and they type a message into the dialog box (Fig. 13.5).

Firetalk users can also create discussion groups using the **Forum** feature. When initiating the feature, users are prompted to select a forum category. These include computers and technology, family, games, hobbies, sports, etc. Once the forum has been created, up to 1,000 users can participate in a *Virtual Auditorium*. Once in the Virtual Auditorium, a moderator, the owner and participants who request to speak by clicking on the **Raise Hand** button can participate in the discussion.

Firetalk™ Communication Through the Web (Cont.)

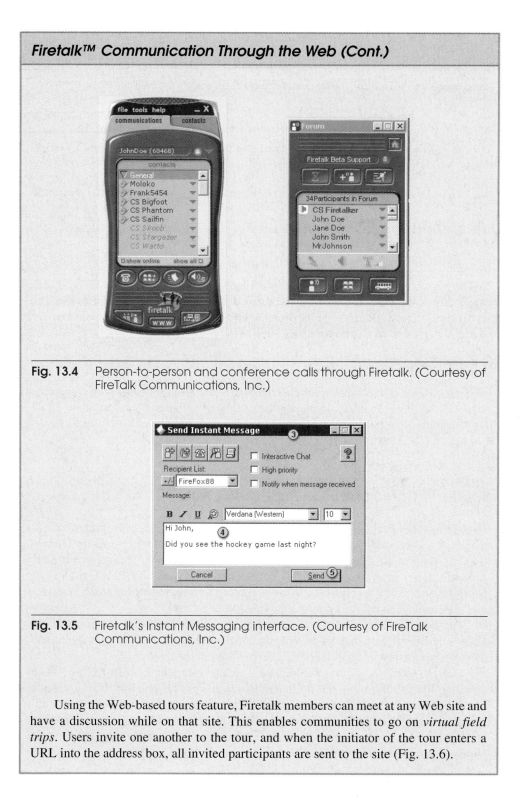

Fig. 13.4   Person-to-person and conference calls through Firetalk. (Courtesy of FireTalk Communications, Inc.)

Fig. 13.5   Firetalk's Instant Messaging interface. (Courtesy of FireTalk Communications, Inc.)

Using the Web-based tours feature, Firetalk members can meet at any Web site and have a discussion while on that site. This enables communities to go on *virtual field trips*. Users invite one another to the tour, and when the initiator of the tour enters a URL into the address box, all invited participants are sent to the site (Fig. 13.6).

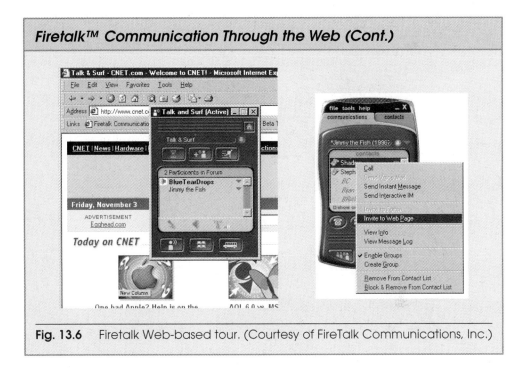

Fig. 13.6   Firetalk Web-based tour. (Courtesy of FireTalk Communications, Inc.)

EGroups.com allows users to join e-mail groups with people having interests similar to their own. When an e-mail is submitted it is distributed to the whole group. Users can start their own groups and select members. The site also features a calendar for event scheduling. An online demonstration of the eGroup services is available at **www.eGroups.com**.

Other community-enhancing services include Crowdburst (**www.crowdburst.com**), which allows groups to tour the Web together; **www.participate.com**, which helps e-businesses build online communities and Talk City (**www.talkcity.com**), an online community center where users can join chat groups of a variety of topics. AOL Instant Messenger and MSN Messenger Service are also popular communication tools. We discuss how these, and other communication tools are used in customer relationship management in Chapter 10.

13.5.3 Online Activism

Through the Internet we are able to learn more about the issues that concern us. In this section, we explore online activism, social awareness and the ability to build online communities around these issues.

Some communities organize around political and social action. For example, **www.youthactivism.com** (Fig. 13.7) has created a forum for individuals under the age of 18 to discuss and debate issues that concern them. The site provides young adults with information on picking a cause, team organization and decision-making to implement change. The site also features success stories, advice to adults who want to participate and resources for getting publicity and financial support.

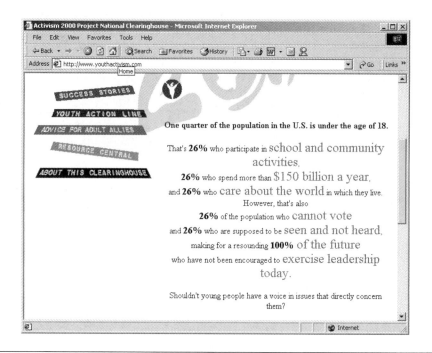

Fig. 13.7   YouthActivism home page. (Courtesy of Activism Project 2000.)

www.igc.org is a portal of a progressively political nature, hosting sites concerned with human rights, racism and sexism.[26] The site is divided into four categories—WomenNet, EcoNet, PeaceNet and Anti-RacismNet—and is home to such groups as the National Organization for Women and the Hunger Project.

Resourcelink.org, a project developed and managed by Hewlett Packard, links America's Second Harvest with surplus food supplies, then locates shipping opportunities to bring the food to locations in the United States where it is needed most.[27] This is a good example of how communication capabilities of the Internet can be used for social action.

e-Fact 13.8

In the United States today, approximately 35 million people do not have enough to eat. Simultaneously, one billion pounds of food gets wasted per year.[28] The Internet, through its communication technologies, can help people locate and distribute surplus food.

During election years, voters can use the Internet to learn more about the candidates and their stance on a particular issue. During the 2000 election campaign, Internet users could visit **AlGore.com**, **GeorgeWBush.com** and **NaderTrader.org** to learn more about them as candidates. **Voter.com** offers voter-registration services, links to activist groups and information about the candidates.[29]

e-Fact 13.9

*During the 2000 Presidential Election, **CNN.com** received one-hundred million hits on election day as viewers monitored the poll results.[30]*

In the future, voting online could potentially change the political structure of the United States. Under a *representative democracy*, each state's citizens are represented by the Electoral College, or a group of individuals who formally choose the President and the Vice President of the United States. California and Arizona beta tested the service during the 2000 Presidential Election.[31] If voting on the Internet was employed successfully, each citizen would vote directly for the candidate of their choice, creating a *pure democracy*. The Internet would provide better accuracy and more timely results. Some believe that voter turnouts would be greater, as the Internet would provide many additional locations from which voters could participate. Further, the traditional decision-making mechanisms (Representatives and Senators) employed by the U.S. government could also change significantly. Through the Internet, people could regularly log on and vote directly on the issues that interest them.

e-Fact 13.10

According to The Federal Election Commission, of the 140 million voters registered in 1998, less than 40 percent participated in the election. The most common reason cited was lack of time to get to the polls.[32]

There are obstacles to online voting. For example, if a Web site were to crash during a voting session, then votes could be lost during the transmission. Computer hackers are another area of concern, as votes could be altered. Some systems have built in protections against this, but absolute security on the Internet has yet to exist (see VoteHere feature).

Individuals can also support a number of causes by donating their unused computer time. SETI@home is perhaps the best known project that utilizes this resource, called a *collaborative-computing network*. Because computers are connected through the Internet, it becomes possible to deliver data to them for analysis. After logging on to a collaborative-computing network, your machine, when unused, will analyze data distributed to it by the server of your chosen cause's Web site. Finding the cure for AIDS and the study of the human genome are among projects now seeking computer power.[35]

Other organizations that promote their causes on the Internet include The Student Environmental Action Coalition (`www.seac.org`), Amnesty International (`www.amnestyusa.org`) and the Peace Corps (`www.peacecorps.gov`).

`VoteHere.net`: *Voting on the Internet* [33]

Beginning in 1996, `VoteHere.net` has been working toward secure online voting. Through `VoteHere.net`, Internet voting can occur in two ways. *Poll-site voting* allows individuals to vote using the Internet at traditional polling sites. This reduces election costs. Voting from home, work, etc. is called *remote voting*. Remote voting would enable individuals to vote from any location with Internet access, or through a wireless device.

To address voter authentication, voters submit their registration in a method similar to the absentee ballot. Once certified, the voter receives a digital certificate. Digital certificates are discussed in Chapter 7, Internet Security. Votes are digitally encrypted during transmission, and when received, the digital signature is used to verify the voter. Once the vote is received, no other vote can be made using that digital signature. This eliminates the potential of repeat voting. To prevent hackers from adding or deleting vote counts, votes are permanently stored, so the vote count is always protected.[34]

13.6 Online Charities and Non Profit Organizations on the Web

The reach of the Internet has a profound impact on businesses of all types. Because of the relative ease of designing and maintaining a content-based Web site, nonprofit organizations can take advantage of this medium as well (see CharityAmerica feature). In this section, we explore some of the organizations that are using the Web to promote their cause.

Web of Hope (**www.webofhope.com**) is an online nonprofit organization. Recognizing the need for adequate funding for medical research, the foundation is raising money through contributions. In addition to this, the foundation will also distribute information and services in urban areas. Applications for grants, fellowships and scholarships will also be available on the site in the future. Web of Hope is a division of Hopelink, a for-profit organization designed to encourage private enrollment in clinical trials.[37]

Other nonprofit organizations concerned with a variety of issues and interests can be found on the Internet (Fig. 13.8). Stop It Now! (**www.stopitnow.com**) is a helpline for sexual offenders. The site suggests that many people would seek help if they knew where to begin. The site offers information about the organization's cause, as well as a forum to collect information from former abusers. It also provides resources for additional information and contacts.

CharityAmerica.com: Providing Through the Web [36]

CharityAmerica connects donating individuals and groups with charitable organizations. The site features nonprofit organizations that can be searched by geographic location, name and category. Site visitors can donate tickets to sporting events, an items such as clothes or even cars, or money (via credit card). Events, information and volunteer opportunities can also be searched. The site also provides a list of businesses that make a donation to a charitable organization for every purchase made. Non-profit groups can apply to become members of the site, provided no less than two-thirds of their expenses are used for their designated cause and they have been a non-profit organization for a minimum of three years.

Organization	URL	Cause
The Hunger Site	**www.thehungersite.com**	Internet surfers can initiate corporate donations by clicking on their advertisements.
Big Brother Association	**www.bigbroboston.org**	Provides information and applications for becoming a big brother in the Boston area.
American Rivers Online	**www.amrivers.org**	Learn more about endangered rivers in the United States.

Fig. 13.8   Non-profit organizations online (part 1 of 2).

Organization	URL	Cause
Favors Unlimited	`www.favorsunlimited.com`	Web surfers can visit this site and look through postings of people in need.
Drug-Free America	`www.drugfreeamerica.org`	Provides parents and their children with information.
Elton John AIDS Foundation	`www.ejaf.org`	Lists fundraisers and facilitates auctions.

Fig. 13.8   *Non-profit organizations online (part 2 of 2).*

Individuals interested in starting a nonprofit organization can find help on the Internet. The Internet Nonprofit Center (**`www.nonprofit-info.org`**) provides information on how to obtain a bulk mailing permit, how to register your organization as a non-profit and how to collect donations legally.

In this chapter, we discuss how the World Wide Web and the Internet are changing our social structures, and how individuals and groups are using this medium to address issues that concern them. The relative low-cost and large audience provide high visibility to individuals and organizations they might not otherwise have had. We explore online communities, the digital divide and the Internet's effect on human-to-human communication. Chapter 14, Accessibility examines the World Wide Web Consortium's (W3C) Web Accessibility Initiative (WAI) which makes the Web accessible to people with disabilities. We also take an extensive tour of Microsoft's Windows 2000 accessibility features.

13.7 Internet and World Wide Web Resources

Social Issues

`www4.nscu.edu/unity/users/j/jherkert/index.html`
The Society on Social Implications of Technology (SSIT) provides information regarding the effects of technology on society. The environment, health, safety, ethics and responsibility are the foundational topics. The SSIT is a division of the Institute of Electrical and Electronic Engineers (IEEE).

`www.cpsr.org`
Computer Professionals for Social Responsibility (CPSR) is an organization concerned with the development and use of computers and the effects they have on society. The group has addressed issues including the national information infrastructure, civil liberties and privacy, computers in the workplace and technology policy and human needs. CPSR serves as an advisory board to policy makers and the public.

`www.igc.com`
The Institute for Global Communications is a progressively political portal acting as home to Web sites dedicated to addressing racism, gender, the environment, human rights and international disputes.

`www.ekidnetwork.com`
This portal operates with many of the same features available to adults on the Internet today, yet safeguards children from accessing questionable material on the Internet or conducting an unsupervised conversation through e-mail or in a chat room.

www.youthactivism.com
This site is targeted towards political activists under the age of 18. It provides younger audiences with information and advice to initiate political change.

www.planetout.com
A leading Web site for the gay population, PlanetOut provides users with headline news and other relevant information.

www.gay.com
This is a popular Web site targeted to the gay community.

www.match.com
This site, one of the leaders in online dating services, provides users with access to hundreds of potential significant others. For a fee the site will pair members according to their areas of interest.

www.oxygen.com
This site is targeted toward female audiences, providing information on health, motherhood, relationships, entertainment and fashion.

Communication Technologies

www.firetalk.com
This service allows Firetalk members to conduct online communications, gather in discussion groups and tour the Web together.

Digital Divide

www.3com.com/government/urbanchallenge/americorps.html
3Com's initiative to bring Internet access technologies and training into urban schools.

www.school.aol.com
This site provides information about AOL's effort to bring Internet tools into urban schools.

Activism

www.youthactivism.com
This site is designed to help young adults get involved in the issues that concern them most.

www.algore.com
Users can visit this site to learn more about the Democrat presidential nominee.

www.georgewbush.com
Users can visit this site to learn more about the Republican presidential nominee.

www.voter.com
Web users can visit this site to learn more about the presidential election, the issues, the funding and the candidates.

www.opensecrets.com
This site informs users about campaign funding—how much the candidates receive and from what source.

www.seac.org
This is the Web site for the Student Environmental Action Coalition.

www.amnestyusa.org
The Web site for Amnesty International.

www.peacecorps.org
Visit this Web site to learn more about the Peace Corps and the causes it serves.

Charities and Non-Profit Organizations

www.charityamerica.com
This site offers Web surfers the ability to shop at charity-sponsoring businesses, donate items and money, and learn more about charitable organizations.

www.webofhope.com
This site is designed to raise awareness and funding for medical research and health support in urban areas.

www.stopitnow.com
This organization provides information and resources for abusers.

www.thehungersite.com
Web surfers can visit this site and click on participating advertisements. The proceeds from advertisement dollars are donated according to the number of visitors to the ad.

www.bigbroboston.org
The site hosts the Boston chapter of Big Brother. Interested users can submit a request for an application and learn more about the organization.

www.amrivers.org
This site hosts American Rivers Online, an organization making an effort to clean up and preserve the polluted rivers in the United States.

www.nonprofit-info.org
This site provides extensive information for users interested in starting a non-profit organization on-line.

Online Communities

www.bolt.com
This Web site is designed to target the teenage audience. It offers advice columns, the option to build your own home page and vote in a daily poll.

www.alloy.com
This teenage site provides e-mail accounts, online chatting and shopping.

www.blackvoices.com
This portal serves the African American community

www.blackplanet.com
This site is designed to meet the needs of the Black community.

www.celt.net
The following are interest-based community sites.

www.agri-ville.com
An online community for agriculturalists, providing information on produce, livestock and equipment.

www.learningspace.com
An online community for educators to meet and share ideas.

www.gca.ca
The following are gender-specific communities

www.vicaids.asn.au
This site provides information regarding gay health and the AIDS virus.

www.menshealth.com
This is the online version of the popular magazine.

`www.women.com`
Women can find information of health, style and childbirth.

`www.advancingwoman.com`
This site is designed for women in careers.

SUMMARY

- The Internet is proving to be a valuable learning, business and communications tool, providing a forum for gathering around issues, supporting causes and meeting new individuals.

- Many opponents argue that life is becoming too dependent on the Internet. New studies show that many users are spending more time on the Internet and, as a result, less time devoted to interpersonal communication.

- Internet enthusiasts suggest that the Internet provides alternatives to the traditional forms of communication. E-mailing, video-conferencing, chat rooms, forums and message boards are all new means of interacting that were developed from the Internet.

- The Internet can be a gateway to questionable material and illegal activity. Pornography, gambling, Internet scams and violence all are readily available on the Web, and the levels of tolerance for this material vary from one region of the world to another.

- Data transactions on the Web can also (with the addition of encryption) promote, and even plot, violence. Virus attacks on airport, hospital and government communications are one example.

- The Internet, given its unique structure, challenges the boundaries of geographic space, making it possible for people to gamble out of their homes.

- Some suggest that exposing children to the Internet and similar technologies gives them a head start in their education.

- Some disagree with dependency on the Internet as a learning tool, especially at young ages when children are learning communication skills.

- Recent studies indicate that competition and efficiency have become children's primary goals, potentially at the expense of creativity and imagination.

- Unsupervised Web access leaves children one URL away from accessing graphic material of a violent and sexual nature. In addition, children are also subject to adult conversation when entering a chat room.

- The Internet provides several options for enhancing home schooling. In addition to learning from parents and guardians, students can turn to the Internet for online tutors, classes and supplementary information.

- Often referred to as the *digital divide*, socio-economic segregation is becoming an apparent problem with regard to the Internet. It involves the cost of acquiring Internet access, the technical support to maintain it and the proper instruction to bring in into homes and schools.

- The U.S. Department of Commerce released "Falling Through the Net: Defining The Digital Divide" in July, 1999. The study indicated that the gap is increasing rather than decreasing.

- Electricity, the telephone and other inventions now widely available to all were at one point, luxuries that not all could afford. As technology continues to advance rapidly, computers and the cost of connecting to the Internet could become commonplace.

- The advent of the Internet has created new job structures. In some cases people have more job flexiblity.

- Starting an e-business is demanding—perhaps more so than any other business, given the intense competition to be first, to investors, then to market.

- Technology-savvy employees are in high demand, often requiring currently employed techies to work longer hours.

- In time, personal computers and handheld devices will allow work to be completed and communications to be conducted from remote locations. Further enhancements are provided through the use of streaming media—which offers video conferencing and Web-based demonstrations.

- The rise in living costs due to the growth of the Internet industry has lead to a significant backlash in certain areas.

- Federal Law protects expectant mothers through the Family and Medical Leave Act of 1993, which mandates that employers grant them 12 weeks unpaid of leave. However, this is only mandatory for companies that have more than 50 employees, and many Internet start-ups do not.

- On the Internet, communities are not formed by geographic boundaries, but rather by shared interests.

- By enabling people to form communities outside of a geographic setting and the limits it imposes, the Web allows larger and more diverse groups to communicate, share information and exchange opinions.

- In cyberspace we do not notice a person's appearance first, unless they have posted a picture or are communicating through a video camera. In cyberspace, it is not our appearance that draws people to us; rather, we learn about each other through text communication.

- Gender, race, creed, age and sexual orientation play a much less significant role in the user's experience when visiting an online store. This is not necessarily the experience that the same individual would have in a brick-and-mortar establishment.

- Gender-specific sites, especially those designated for women, are increasingly popular.

- In the future, voting online could potentially change the political structure of the United States.

- In addition to learning more about a given issue on the Internet, individuals can also support these causes by donating their unused computer time. SETI@home is perhaps the best known project that utilizes this resource, called a *collaborating-computing network*.

- Because of the relative ease of designing and maintaining a content-based Web site, nonprofit organizations can take advantage of this medium as well.

- Endangered species also may be preserved with the help of the Internet. There are a variety of Web sites designed to teach people about these animals and generate interest in protecting them.

TERMINOLOGY

age-oriented communities
AOL School
collaborating-computing network
Computers For Youth
digital divide
e-learning
gender-oriented communities

home schooling
online communities
online text chatting
pure democracy
remote voting
representative democracy
virtual field trip

SELF-REVIEW EXERCISES

13.1 State whether the following are true or false. If the answer is false, explain why.
   a) Pornography, gambling, Internet scams and violence are inaccessible to children on the Web.
   b) The U.S. Department of Commerce released "Falling Through the Net: Defining The Digital Divide" in July, 1999. The study indicated that the gap is decreasing rather than increasing.

c) The digital divide could lead to the inability for companies to fill positions, leading to a slowing of economic development.

d) Electricity, the telephone and other inventions now widely available to all, were, at one point, luxuries that not all could afford.

e) All areas, particularly those where dot-coms have chosen to put their office buildings, are embracing the industry, because of the wealth it brings to the area.

13.2   Fill in the blanks in the following statements:

a) The _____ involves the cost of acquiring Internet access, the technical support to maintain it and the proper instruction to bring in into home and schools.

b) Federal Law protects expectant mothers through the Family and Medical Leave Act of 1993, issuing them 12 weeks of leave. This however, is only mandatory for companies that have greater than _____ employees, and many Internet start-ups do not.

c) In addition to learning more about a given issue on the Internet, individuals can also support specific causes by donating their unused computer time. SETI@home is perhaps the best known project that utilizes a _____.

d) In the future, _____ could potentially change the political structure of the United States.

e) Internet enthusiasts suggest that the Internet provides alternatives to the traditional forms of communication. _____, _____ and _____ are examples of the new means of interacting developed from the Internet.

ANSWERS TO SELF-REVIEW EXERCISES

13.1   a) False. There are some filtering methods available to help block "harmful" information from reaching children, but there is no complete protection. b.) False. Studies showed that the gap was increasing rather than decreasing. c) True. d) True. e) False. Many areas are experiencing a backlash due to higher rents.

13.2   a) Digital divide. b) 50. c) distributed-computing network. d) voting online. e) E-mailing, video-conferencing, chat rooms, forums and message boards.

EXERCISES

13.3   State whether the following are true or false. If the answer is false, explain why.

a) Starting an e-business is demanding—perhaps more so than any other business, given the intense competition to be first to market.

b) Endangered species also may be preserved with the help of the Internet.

c) The Internet, given its unique structure, challenges the boundaries of geographic space, making it possible for people to gamble out of their homes.

d) Some disagree with dependency on the Internet as a learning tool, especially at young ages when children are learning communication skills.

13.4   Fill in the blanks in the following statements:

a) On the Internet, communities are not formed by _____, but rather by shared interests.

b) As technology continues to advance rapidly, computers and the cost of connecting to the Internet could become _____.

c) Data transactions on the Web can also (with the addition of encryption) promote, and even plot, violence. _____ attacks on airport, hospital and government communications are one example.

d) Recent studies indicate that competition and efficiency have become children's primary goals, potentially at the expense of _____ and _____.

13.5   Define the following:
   a) 3Com Urban Challenge
   b) Mission Yuppie Eradication Project
   c) representative democracy vs. pure democracy
   d) Computers For Youth
   e) ResourceLink.org

13.6   (*Class Discussion*). In this chapter, we discuss the issue of social health and the Internet? Using the material provided in this book and three supplementary resources (use the Internet to find additional commentary), determine your opinion on this issue. Do you think Americans spend too much time on the Internet? In your opinion, what are the potential effects of this? How do you regard children and the Internet? At what age should children be given access, and how many hours per week? When should children be allowed to use the Internet unsupervised? Be prepared to discuss your answers.

13.7   (*Class Discussion*). In this chapter, we discuss the Internet and how it affects social interaction. While some argue that we spend less time interacting with others (i.e. going to a party, chatting in the grocery store, having dinner with friends, etc.) because of the Internet, others consider the exchanging of e-mail, online text chatting and message boards to be an adequate substitute that actually allows us to keep in better touch with others. After reading through the text and conducting some of your own research (poll your friends and family), what is your opinion? Why? Be prepared to discuss your answers.

13.8   In the chapter, we discuss the continuous growth of the digital divide. Go to the U.S. Department of Commerce Web site and view "Falling Through the Net: Defining the Digital Divide" (**www.ntia.doc.gov/ntiahome/fttn99/contents.html**). Based on the information in this chapter and this document, answer the following questions.
   a) Name the four groups particularly subject to the digital divide (paragraph two, Introduction).
   b) According to the first bulleted point in the Executive Summary, urban households are how many times more likely to have Internet access? What is the minimum household income for this statistic?
   c) According to Part I, the digital divide has increased according to what three criteria (paragraph 4)?
   d) According to the first bulleted point in Part II: Internet Access and Usage, what percentage of Americans have access to the Internet? What percentage have access at home?

WORKS CITED

The notation <**www.domain-name.com**> indicates that the citation is for information found at the Web site.
1.   G. Koretz, "The Web's Chilling Trend," *Business Week* 5, June 2000: 36.

2.   J. Fallows, "Feeling Sociable," *The Industry Standard* 22 May 2000: 51.

3.   M. Gibson, "Uncovering the Dark Side of the World Wide Web," *Financial Times* 21-22 October 2000: IX.

4.   M. Gibson, IX.

5.   J. Sandberg, "Multimedia Childhood," *Newsweek* Fall/Winter 2000: 78.

6.   "The Margin-Debt Hole: How Deep is too Deep," *Money* April 2000: 136.

7.   J. Fallows, "The Other Divide," *The Industry Standard* 10 January-17 January 2000: 47.

8.   L. Kappelman, "Closing the Digital Divide," *Information Week* 8 May 2000: 262.

9.   A. Lazarus, "Food Stamps Not Accepted Here," *The Industry Standard* 10 January - 17 January 2000: 39.

10.   J. Fallows, "The Other Divide," *The Industry Standard* 10 January-17 January 2000: 47.

11.   N. Wingfield, "AOL to Announce This Week the Launch of Free Online Service Aimed at Schools," *The Wall Street Journal* 16 May 2000: B6.

12.   "Should Government Solve the Digital Divide?" *Upside* May 2000: 60.

13.   B. Warner, "Spreading the Net," *The Industry Standard* 3 April 2000: 150-174.

14.   `<www.3com.com/government/urbanchallenge/cspan.ram>`

15.   `<www.3com.com/government/urbanchallenge>`

16.   David Katz, 3Com Director of Global Market Developments, CSPAN 12 June 2000.

17.   `<www.3com.com/government/urbanchallenge/americorps.html>`

18.   B. Hall, "eLearning," *Forbes Special Advertising Section* 2 October 2000: 2.

19.   L. Anderson, "There Goes the Neighborhood," *The Industry Standard* 10-17 July 2000: 142-146.

20.   "The Margin-Debt Hole: How Deep is too Deep?" *Money* April 2000: 137.

21.   T. Ehrenfeld, "The Parent Trap," *The Industry Standard* 3 July 2000: 222.

22.   K. Dunham. "Laid-Off Internet Workers Find Dot-Com Aren't Quick to Hire," *The Wall Street Journal* 18 July 2000: B12.

23.   K. Motta, "Internet Layoffs Pile Up," *The Industry Standard* 3 July 2000: 188.

24.   L. Lessig, *Code and Other Laws of Cyberspace* (New York: Basic Books, 1999) 65.

25.   K.T.L. Tran, "Group Think," *The Wall Street Journal* 23 October 2000: R53.

26.   M. Richtel, "Promoting Peace through Portals," *Yahoo! Internet Life* March 2000: 86, 88.

27.   Hewlett Packard Advertisement

28.   Hewlett Packard Advertisement

29.   T. Mullaney, "League of Web Voters," *Business Week* 23 October 2000: 20.

30.   "E-Decision," *The Wall Street Journal* 9 November 2000: B6.

31.   A. Harrison, "Online Voting Moves Closer to Acceptance," *Computer World* 30 October 2000: 70.

32.   `<www.votehere.net>`.

33.   `<www.votehere.net>`.

34.   A. Harrison, "Threats and Defenses," *Computer World* 30 October 2000: 70.

35.   U. Kher, "Science by Screensaver," *Time* 16 October 2000: 102.

36.   `<www.charityamerica.com>`.

37.   J. Lerner, "Giving at the Office," *Boston Business Journal* 28 July-3 August 2000: 28.

14

Accessibility

Objectives

- To understand the importance of making your Web site accessible to people with disabilities.
- To explore Web accessibility legal requirements.
- To introduce the World Wide Web Consortium's Web Content Accessibility Guidelines 1.0 (WCAG 1.0).
- To use the **ALT** attribute of the **<IMG>** tag to describe images to blind and vision impaired people, to mobile Web device users, to search engines, etc.
- To introduce the various accessibility aids offered in Windows 2000.

I once was lost, but now am found,
Was blind, but now I see.
John Newton

'Tis the good reader that makes the good book...
Ralph Waldo Emerson

Outline

14.1   Introduction
14.2   Web Accessibility
14.3   Web Accessibility Initiative
14.4   Providing Alternatives for Multimedia Content
    14.4.1   Readability
    14.4.2   Using Voice Synthesis and Recognition with VoiceXML™
    14.4.2   Using Voice Synthesis and Recognition with VoiceXML™
14.5   Accessibility in Microsoft® Windows® 2000
    14.5.1   Tools for Visually Impaired People
    14.5.2   Tools for Hearing-Impaired People
    14.5.3   Tools for Users Who Have Difficulty Using the Keyboard
    14.5.4   Microsoft Narrator
    14.5.5   Microsoft On-Screen Keyboard
    14.5.6   Accessibility Features in Microsoft Internet Explorer 5.0
14.6   Other Accessibility Tools
14.7   Internet and World Wide Web Resources

Summary • Terminology • Self-Review Exercises • Answers to Self-Review Exercises • Exercises • Works Cited • Recommended Reading

14.1 Introduction

Enabling your Web site to meet the needs of individuals with disabilities is an issue relevant to all businesses. Persons with disabilities make up a significant portion of the population, and legal ramifications exist for Web sites that discriminate by not providing adequate and universal access to the site's resources. In this chapter, we explore the *Web Accessibility Initiative* and its requirements, various laws regarding businesses are their availability to people with disabilities and how some companies have developed their systems, products and services to meet the needs of this demographic.

14.2 Web Accessibility

In 1999, a lawsuit was filed by the National Federation for the Blind (NFB) against AOL for not supplying access to its services to people with visual disabilities, a mandate of the Americans with Disabilities Act of 1990.[1] Many other efforts have been made to address this issue (Fig. 14.1).

    WeMedia.com™ (Fig. 14.2) is a Web site dedicated to providing disabled individuals with the same opportunities as the general population. The site serves 54 million disabled consumers with an estimated $1 trillion in purchasing power.[4] The screen capture below also demonstrates the use of ALT tags to identify an image to a screen reader. ALT tags are discussed in section 14.4. We Media also provides online educational opportunities for people with disabilities (see Chapter 17, e-Learning).

Act	Purpose
Americans with Disabilities Act	The ADA prohibits discrimination on the basis of disability in employment, state and local government, public accommodations, commercial facilities, transportation, and telecommunications.[2]
Telecommunications Act of 1996	The Telecommunications Act of 1996 contains two amendments to Section 255 and Section 251(a)(2) of the Communications Act of 1934. These amendments require that communication devices, such as cell phones, telephones and pagers, be accessible to individuals with disabilities.[3]
Individuals with Disabilities Education Act of 1997	Educational materials in the school setting must be made accessible to children with disabilities.

Fig. 14.1 Acts designed to protect access to the Internet for people with disabilities.

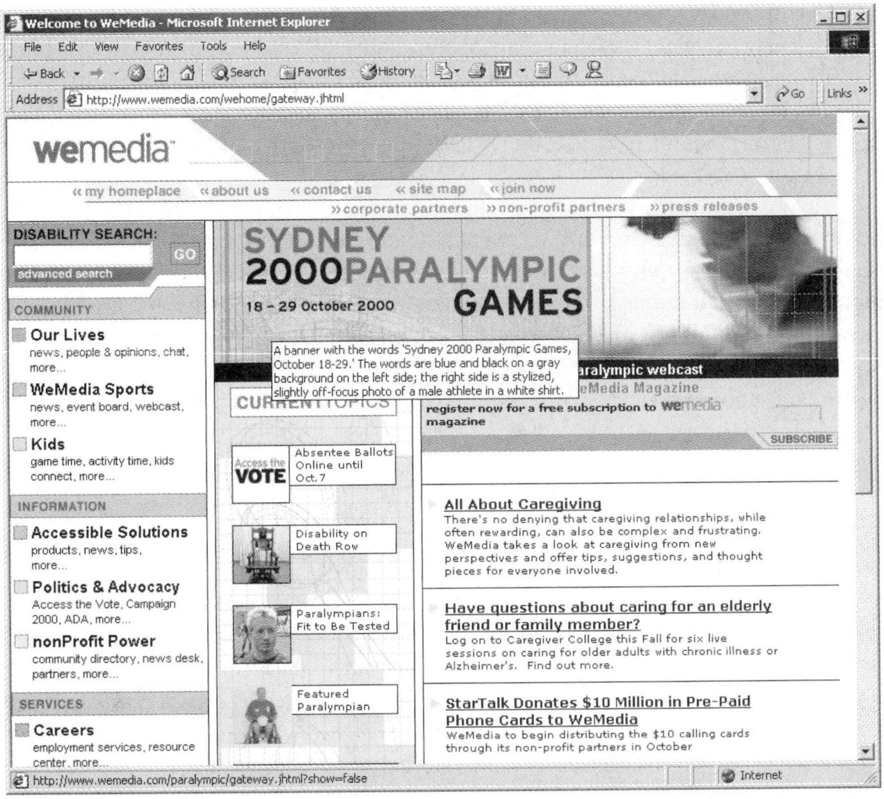

Fig. 14.2 We Media home page. (Courtesy of We Media Inc.)

The Internet has also enabled disabled individuals to work in a vast array of new fields. Prior to its advent, 25 percent of the 15 million Americans with disabilities found employment as a result of the *Americans with Disabilities Act* (ADA).[5] Technologies such as voice activation, visual enhancers and auditory aids afford disabled individuals with more work opportunities. For example, visually impaired people might use computer monitors with enlarged text or electronic equipment with braille operating controls.

Within the next year, information provided through technology will have to be equally accessible to individuals with disabilities.[6] For example, federal regulations similar to the disability ramp mandates will be applied to the Internet to meet the needs of those with impaired hearing, sight and speech. In the future, sites heavily laden with graphic images might have to simplify their appearance.[7] In the following sections, we explore a variety of products and services that provide Internet access to people with disabilities.

14.3 Web Accessibility Initiative

On April 7, 1997, the World Wide Web Consortium (W3C) launched the *Web Accessibility Initiative* (WAI™). *Accessibility* refers to the level of usability of an application or Web site for people with disabilities. The vast majority of Web sites are considered inaccessible to people with visual, learning or mobility impairments. A high level of accessibility is difficult to achieve, because there are many different disabilities, language barriers, hardware and software inconsistencies, etc. As greater numbers of people with disabilities begin to use the Internet, it is imperative that Web-site designers increase accessibility to their sites. The WAI is an attempt to make the Web more accessible; its mission is described at **www.w3.org/WAI**.

The Web Content Accessibility Guidelines 1.0 (**www.w3.org/TR/WCAG10**) are divided into a three-tier structure of checkpoints according to their priority. *Priority-one checkpoints* are those that must be met to ensure accessibility. *Priority-two checkpoints*, though not essential, are highly recommended. *Priority-three checkpoints* improve accessibility slightly. The WAI also presents a supplemental list of *quick tips*—this list contains checkpoints aimed at solving priority one problems. More information on the WAI Quick Tips can be found at **www.w3.org/WAI/References/Quicktips**.)

14.4 Providing Alternatives for Multimedia Content

One important WAI requirement is to ensure that every image, movie and sound used on a Web page is accompanied by a description called an **ALT** *tag* that clearly defines its purpose. It is intended to provide a short description of an HTML object which may not load properly on all user agents. For example, if the **ALT** attribute describes a sales growth chart, it should specify the chart's title. Specialized *user agent*s, such as *screen readers* (programs that allow users to hear what is being displayed on their screen) and *braille displays* (devices that receive data from screen-reading software and output the data as braille) allow blind and visually impaired people to access text-based information that is normally displayed on the screen. A user agent is an application that interprets Web-page source code and translates it into formatted text and images. Web browsers such as Microsoft Internet

Explorer and Netscape Communicator and the screen readers mentioned throughout this chapter are examples of user agents.

Web pages with large amounts of multimedia content are difficult for user agents to interpret, unless they are designed properly. Images, movies and other non-HTML objects cannot be read by screen readers. Providing multimedia-based information in a variety of ways (i.e., using the **ALT** attribute or providing online descriptions of images) helps maximize the content's accessibility. Boldface titles and *image maps* (images with areas designated as hyperlinks) also present challenges to some Web users—particularly those who cannot use a mouse (visit the Web Content Accessibility Guidelines 1.0 at **www.w3.org/TR/WCAG** for further examples). When accessing an image map, users are required to click to initiate their actions. User-agent technology is unable to make image maps accessible to blind people or to others who cannot use a mouse. If equivalent text links are not provided when a server-side image map is used, some users will be unable to navigate the site. User agent manufacturers will provide accessibility to server-side image maps in the future. For more information on image maps, visit **www.w3.org/TR/REC-html40/struct/objects.html#h-13.6**.

Using a screen reader to navigate a Web site can be time consuming and frustrating as screen readers are unable to interpret pictures and other graphical content. One method of combatting this problem is to include a link at the top of each Web page that provides easy access to the page's content. Users can use the link to bypass an image map or other inaccessible element, jumping to another part of the page or to a different page.

14.4.1 Readability

Another accessibility issue is *readability*. When creating a Web page intended for the general public, it is important to consider the reading level at which it is written. Website designers can make their site more readable through the use of shorter words, as some users may have difficulty reading longer words. Also users from other countries may have difficulty understanding slang and other nontraditional language, so these should also be avoided. Building an e-business with a global reach is discussed in Chapter 12, Globalization.

In the *Web Content Accessibility Guidelines 1.0*, it is suggested that a paragraph's first sentence convey its subject. Immediately stating the point makes finding crucial information easier and allows those unable to comprehend large amounts of text to bypass unwanted material.

A good way to evaluate a Web site's readability is by using the *Gunning Fog Index*— a formula that produces a readability grade when applied to a text sample. For more information on the Gunning Fog Index see **www.trainingpost.org/3-2-inst.htm**.

14.4.2 Using Voice Synthesis and Recognition with VoiceXML™

A joint effort by AT&T, IBM®, Lucent and Motorola has created an XML application that uses *speech synthesis* to enable the computer to speak to the user (see Programming Appedices B through H).This technology, called *VoiceXML*, has tremendous implications for visually impaired people and for people who cannot read. Not only does VoiceXML read

Web pages to the user, but it also includes *speech recognition* technology—which enables computers to understand words spoken into the microphone, enabling them to interact with users. An example of a speech recognition tool is IBM's *ViaVoice* (`www-4.ibm.com/software/speech`).

VoiceXML is processed by a VoiceXML interpreter or VoiceXML browser; Web browsers might incorporate these interpreters in the future. Because VoiceXML is derived from XML, it is platform independent. When a VoiceXML document is loaded, a *voice server* sends a message to the VoiceXML browser and begins a conversation between the user and the computer.

Voice Server SDK, developed by IBM, is a free beta version of a VoiceXML interpreter and can be used for desktop testing of VoiceXML documents. Visit `www.alphaworks.ibm.com` for hardware and software specifications and for more information on Voice Server SDK. Instructions on how to run VoiceXML documents can be obtained along with the software.

14.5 Accessibility in Microsoft® Windows® 2000

Beginning with Microsoft Windows 95, Microsoft has included accessibility features in its operating systems and many of its applications, including Office 97, Office 2000 and Netmeeting. In Microsoft Windows 2000, the accessibility features have been significantly enhanced. The accessibility options provided by Windows 2000 are available through the **Accessibility Wizard**, which guides a user through the Windows 2000 accessibility features and configures their computer according to the chosen specifications. This section guides the user through the configuration of their Windows 2000 accessibility options using the **Accessibility Wizard**.

To access the **Accessibility Wizard**, you must be using Microsoft Windows 2000. Click the **Start** button and select **Programs** followed by **Accessories**, **Accessibility** and **Accessibility Wizard**. When the wizard starts, the **Welcome** screen is displayed. Click **Next >**. The next dialog (Fig. 14.3) asks the user to select a text size. Click **Next >**.

Figure 14.4 shows the next dialog displayed. This dialog allows the user to activate the text-size settings chosen in the previous window, change the screen resolution, enable the *Microsoft Magnifier* (a program that displays an enlarged section of the screen in a separate window) and disable personalized menus (a feature that hides rarely used programs from the **Start** menu), which can be a hindrance to disabled users. Make selections and click **Next >**.

The next dialog (Fig. 14.5) displayed asks questions about the user's disabilities, which allows the **Accessibility Wizard** to customize Windows to better suit the user's needs. We selected everything for demonstration purposes. Click **Next >** to continue.

14.5.1 Tools for Visually Impaired People

Because we checked all of the options, in Fig. 14.5, the wizard begins by configuring Windows for visually impaired people. As shown in Fig. 14.6, this dialog box allows the user to resize the scroll bars and window borders to increase their visibility. Click **Next >** to proceed to the next dialog.

Figure 14.7's dialog allows the user to resize icons. Users with poor vision—as well as users who have trouble reading—benefit from large icons.

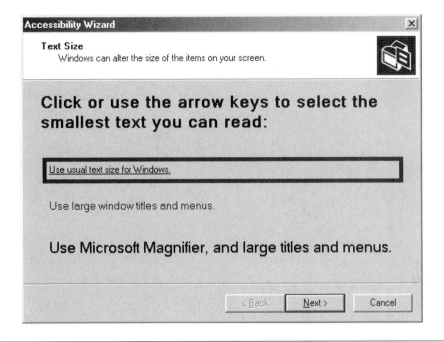

Fig. 14.3   Text Size dialog.

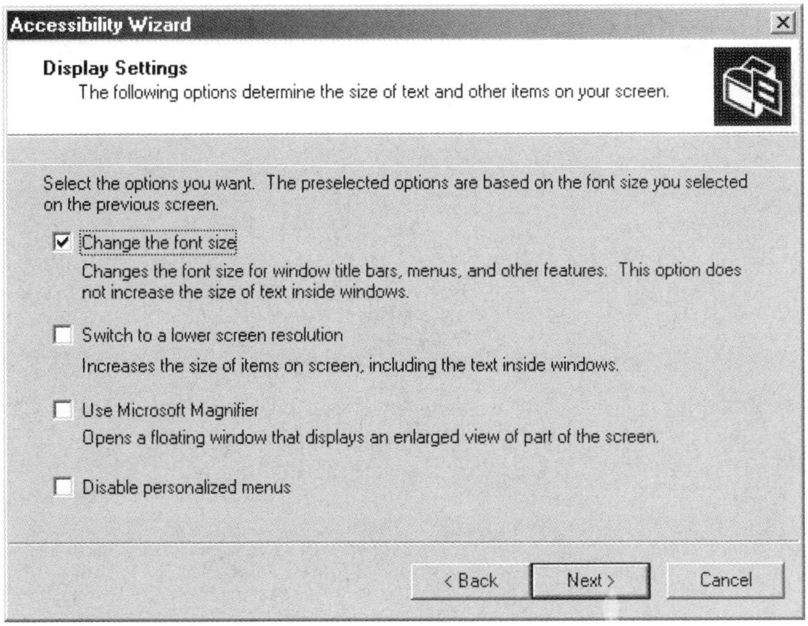

Fig. 14.4   Display Settings dialog.

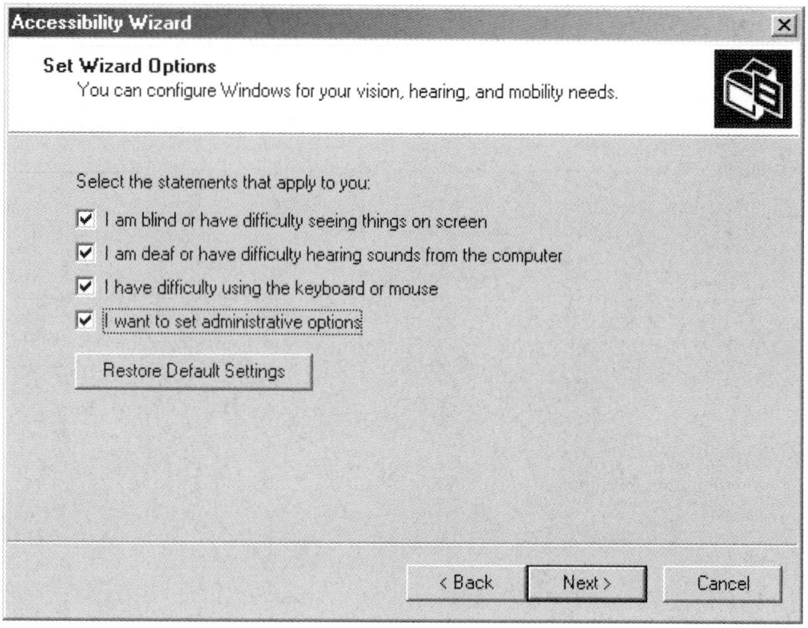

Fig. 14.5   Accessibility Wizard initialization options.

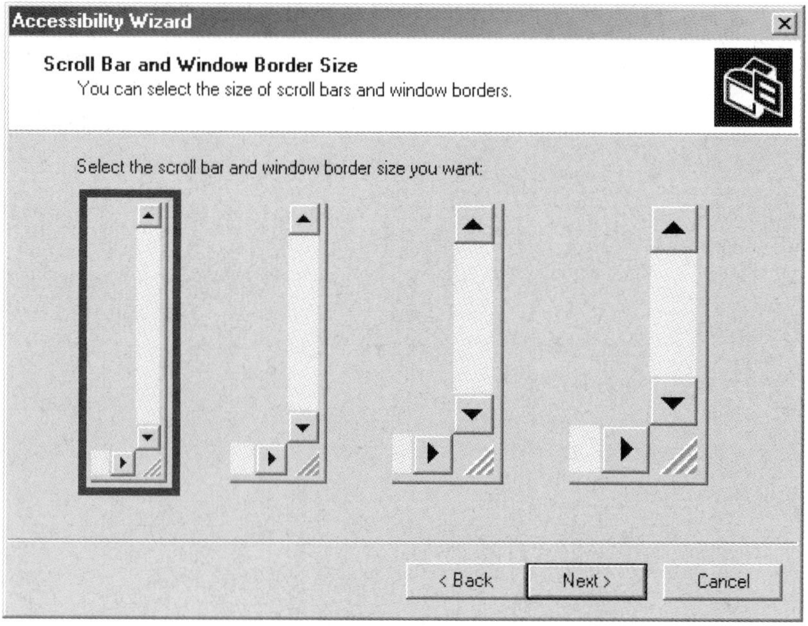

Fig. 14.6   Scroll Bar and **Window Border** Size dialog.

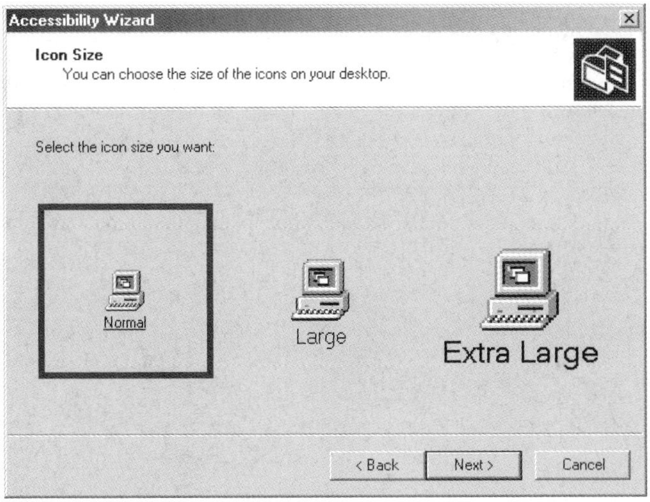

Fig. 14.7 Setting window element sizes.

Clicking **Next >** displays the **Display Color Settings** dialog (Fig. 14.8). These settings allow the user to change Windows' color scheme and to resize various screen elements. Click **Next >** to view the dialog (Fig. 14.9) for customizing the mouse cursor.

Anyone who has ever used a laptop computer knows how difficult it can be to see the mouse cursor. This is an especially serious problem for visually impaired people. To help solve this problem, the wizard offers the user the choice of using larger cursors, black cursors and cursors that invert the colors of objects underneath them. Click **Next >**.

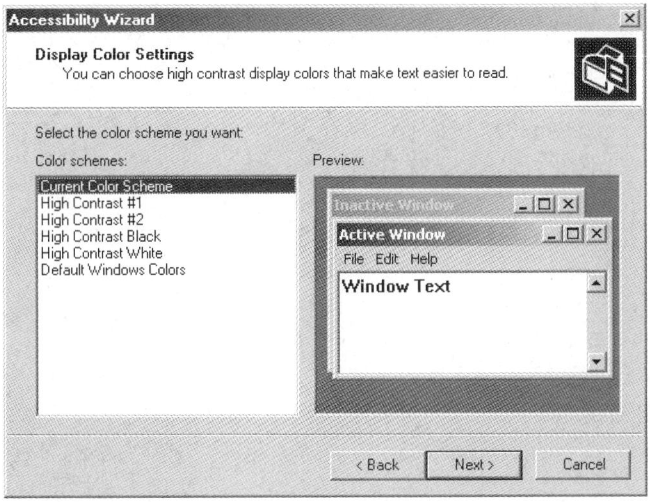

Fig. 14.8   Display Color Settings options.

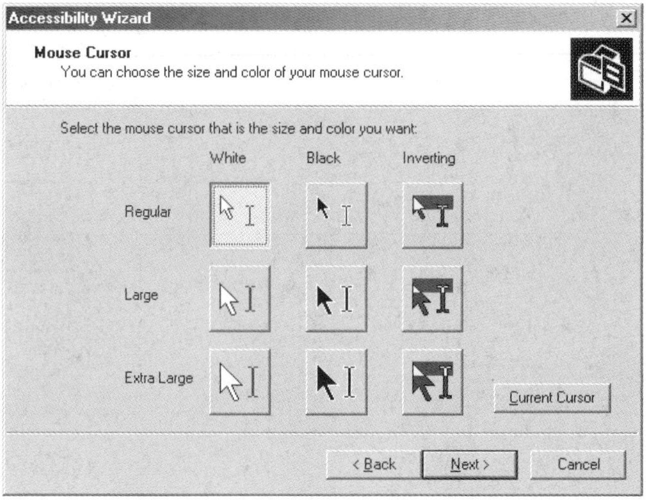

Fig. 14.9   **Accessibility Wizard** mouse cursor adjustment tool.

14.5.2 Tools for Hearing-Impaired People

This section, which focuses on accessibility for deaf and hearing-impaired people, begins with the **SoundSentry** window (Fig. 14.10). **SoundSentry** is a tool that creates visual signals when system events occur. For example, since hearing-impaired people are unable to hear the beeps, which normally warn users, **SoundSentry** flashes the screen when a beep occurs. To continue on to the next dialog click **Next >**.

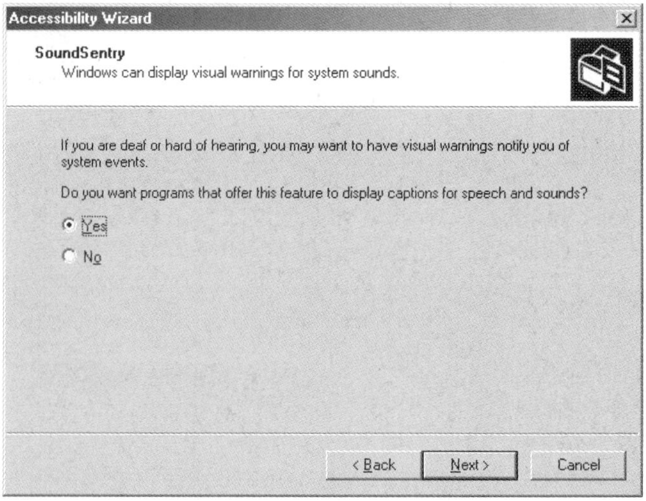

Fig. 14.10 **SoundSentry** dialog.

The next window is the **ShowSounds** dialog (Fig. 14.11), which enables you to add captions to spoken text and other sounds produced by today's multimedia-rich software. For **ShowSounds** to work, software developers must specifically provide the captions and spoken text within their software. Make selections and click **Next >**.

14.5.3 Tools for Users Who Have Difficulty Using the Keyboard

The next dialog is **StickyKeys** (Fig. 14.12)—a program that helps users who have difficulty pressing multiple keys at the same time. Many important computer commands can only be invoked by pressing specific key combinations. For example, the reboot command requires pressing *Ctrl+Alt+Delete simultaneously.* **StickyKeys** allows the user to press key combinations in sequence rather than at the same time. Click **Next >** to continue to the **BounceKeys** dialog (Fig. 14.13). Another common problem for certain users with disabilities is accidentally pressing the same key more than once. This problem is typically caused by holding a key down too long. **BounceKeys** forces the computer to ignore repeated keystrokes. Click **Next >**. **ToggleKeys** (Fig. 14.14) alerts the user that they have pressed one of the lock keys (i.e., *Caps Lock*, *Num Lock* and *Scroll Lock*), by sounding an audible beep. Make selections and click **Next >**.

Next, the **Extra Keyboard Help** dialog (Fig. 14.15) is displayed. This section is used to activate a tool that displays information, such as keyboard shortcuts and tool tips, when they are available. Like **ShowSounds**, this tool requires that software developers provide the content to be displayed. Clicking **Next >** will load the **MouseKeys** (Fig. 14.16) customization window.

MouseKeys is a tool that uses the keyboard to emulate mouse movements. The arrow keys direct the mouse, while the *5* key sends a single click. To double click, the user must press the + key, and to simulate holding down the mouse button, the user must press the *Ins* (Insert) key. To release the mouse button, the user must press the *Del* (Delete) key. To continue to the next screen in the **Accessibility Wizard**, click **Next >**.

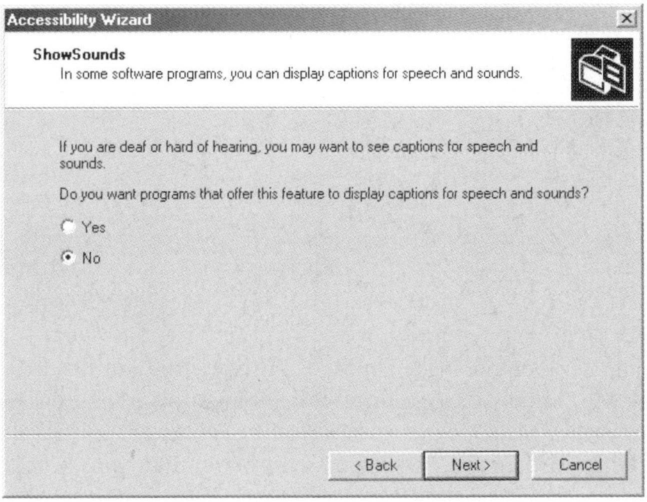

Fig. 14.11 Show Sounds dialog.

Accessibility Wizard

StickyKeys
You do not have to hold down two keys at once.

If you find it difficult to hold down several keys at once, you may have trouble with key combinations (such as CTRL+ALT+DELETE). Instead of pressing and holding several keys at once, you can press each key one at a time. This applies to key combinations that use SHIFT, CTRL, or ALT.

Do you want to press keys in key combinations one at a time?

   ○ Yes

   ⦿ No

              < Back   Next >   Cancel

Fig. 14.12 StickyKeys dialog.

Accessibility Wizard

BounceKeys
You can set Windows to ignore repeated keystrokes.

If you have motion disabilities, You might accidentally press a key too many times.

Do you want Windows to ignore repeated keystrokes?

   ○ Yes

   ⦿ No

              < Back   Next >   Cancel

Fig. 14.13 BounceKeys dialog.

Today's computer tools are made almost exclusively for right-handed users, including most computer mice. Microsoft recognized this problem by adding the **Mouse Button Settings** window (Fig. 14.17) to the **Accessibility Wizard**. This tool allows the user to create a virtual lefthanded mouse, by swapping the button functions. Click **Next >**.

Mouse speed is adjusted using the **MouseSpeed** (Fig. 14.18) section of the **Accessibility Wizard**. Dragging the scroll bar changes the speed. Clicking the **Next** button sets the speed and displays the wizard's **Set Automatic Timeouts** window (Fig. 14.19).

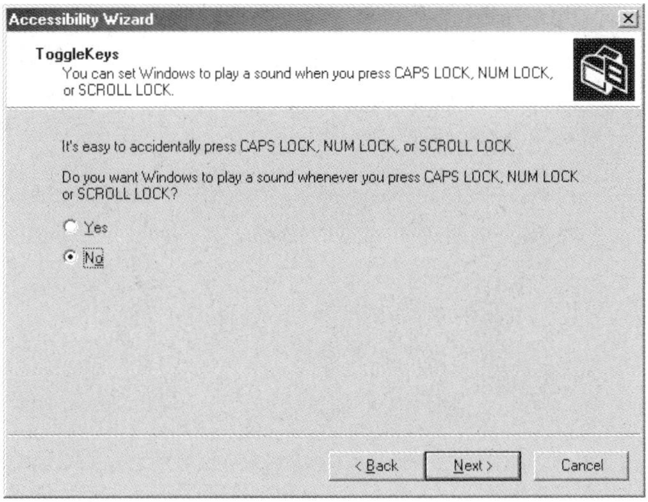

Fig. 14.14   ToggleKeys dialog.

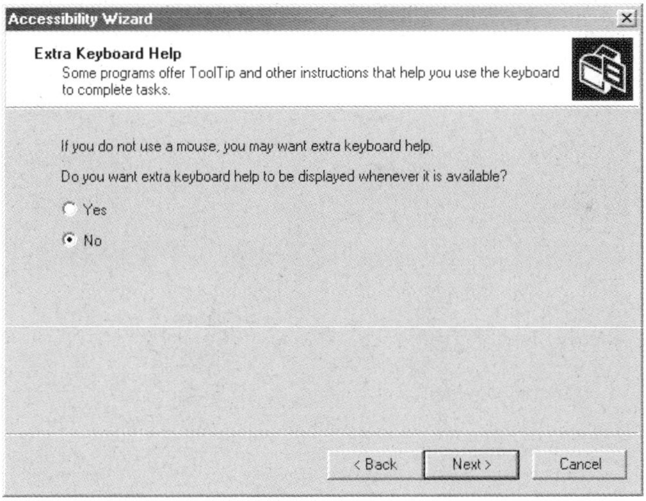

Fig. 14.15   Extra Keyboard Help dialog.

Although accessibility tools are important to users with disabilities, they can be a hindrance to users who do not need them. In situations where there are varying accessibility needs, it is important that the user be able to turn the accessibility tools off and on as necessary. The **Set Automatic Timeouts** window specifies a *timeout* period for the tools. A timeout either enables or disables a certain action after the computer has idled for a specified amount of time. A screen saver is a common example of a program with a timeout period. Here, a timeout is set to toggle the accessibility tools.

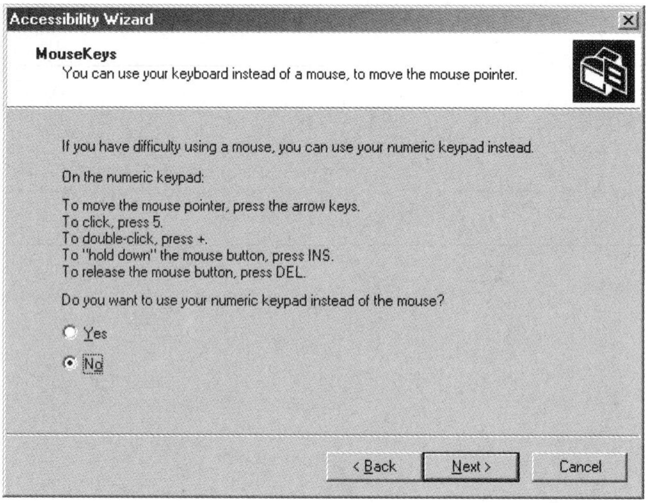

Fig. 14.16 MouseKeys window.

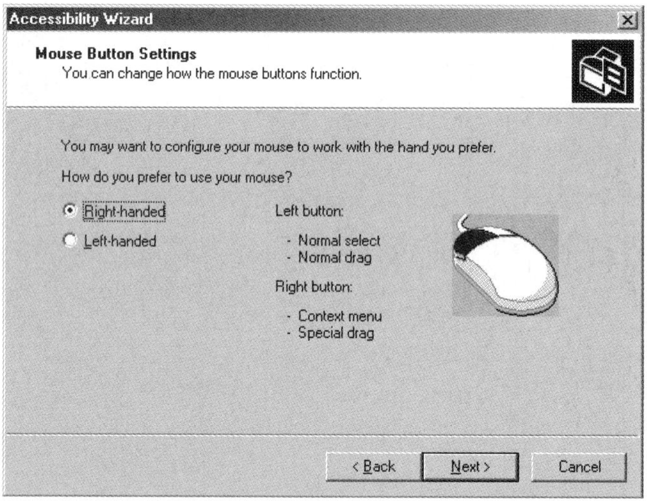

Fig. 14.17 Mouse Button Settings window.

After clicking **Next >** you will be brought to the **Save Settings to File** dialog (14.20). This dialog determines whether the accessibility settings should be used as the *default settings*, which are loaded when the computer is rebooted or after a timeout. Set the accessibility settings as the default if the majority of users need them. You can also save the accessibility settings. The user can create an **.acw** file, which, when clicked, automatically activates the saved accessibility settings on any Windows 2000 computer.

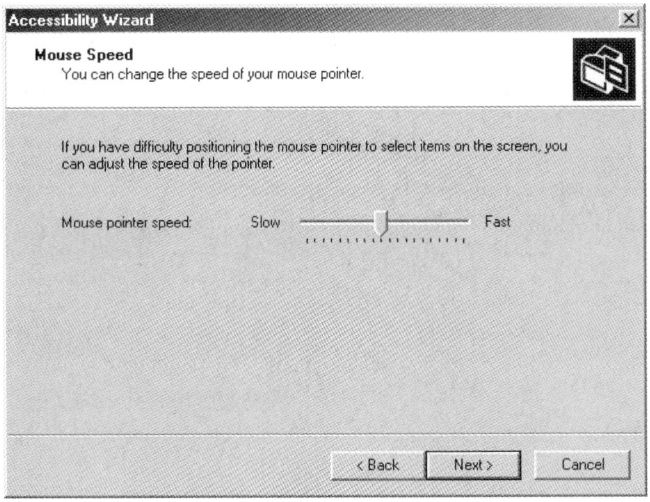

Fig. 14.18   Mouse Speed dialog.

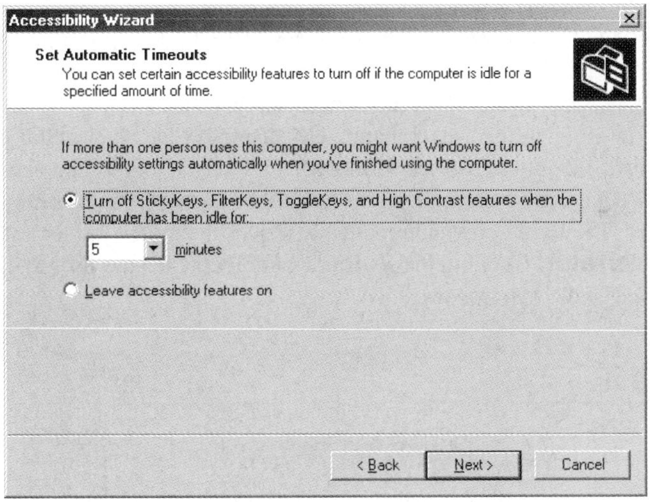

Fig. 14.19   Set Automatic Timeouts.

14.5.4 Microsoft Narrator

*Microsoft **Narrator*** is a *text-to-speech* program for visually impaired people. It reads text, describes the current desktop environment and alerts the user when certain Windows events occur. **Narrator** is intended to aid in configuring Microsoft Windows. It is a screen reader that works with Internet Explorer, Wordpad, Notepad and most programs in the **Control Panel**. Though it is limited outside these applications, **Narrator** is excellent at navigating the Windows environment.

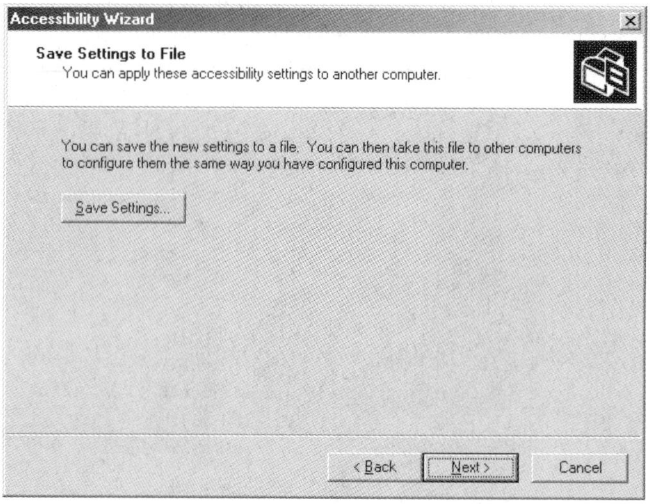

Fig. 14.20 Saving new accessibility settings with the **Save Settings to File** dialog.

We explain how to use **Narrator** with various Windows applications. Click the **Start** button and select **Programs** followed by **Accessories**, **Accessibility** and **Narrator**. Once **Narrator** is open, it describes the current foreground window. Then it reads the text inside the window aloud to the user. Clicking **OK** displays Fig. 14.21 dialog.

Checking the first option instructs **Narrator** to describe menus and new windows when they are opened. The second option instructs **Narrator** to speak the characters you are typing as you type them. The third option automatically moves the mouse cursor to the region that is being read by **Narrator**. Clicking the **Voice...** button enables the user to change the pitch, volume and speed of the narrator voice.

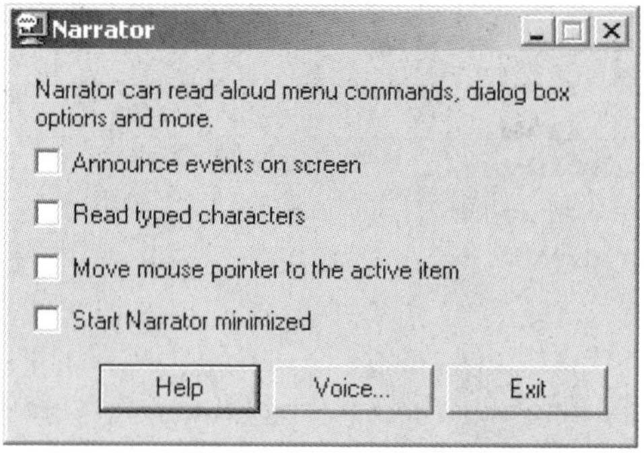

Fig. 14.21 **Narrator** window.

With **Narrator** running, open **Notepad** and click the **File** menu. **Narrator** announces the opening of the program and begins to describe the items in the **File** menu. When scrolling down the list, **Narrator** reads the current item to which the mouse is pointing. Type some text and press *Ctrl-Shift-Enter* to hear **Narrator** read it (Fig. 14.22). If the **Read typed characters** option is checked, **Narrator** reads each character as it is typed. The direction arrows on the keyboard can be used to make **Narrator** read. The up and down arrows cause **Narrator** to speak the lines adjacent to the current mouse position, and the left and right arrows cause **Narrator** to speak to the characters adjacent to the current mouse position.

14.5.5 Microsoft On-Screen Keyboard

Some computer users lack the ability to use a keyboard, but have the ability to use a pointing device such as a mouse. For these users, the *On-Screen Keyboard* is helpful. To access the On-Screen Keyboard, click the **Start** button and select **Programs** followed by **Accessories**, **Accessibility** and **On-Screen Keyboard**. Figure 14.23 shows the layout of the Microsoft On-Screen Keyboard.

Users who still have difficulty using the **On-Screen Keyboard** should purchase more sophisticated products, such as *Clicker 4* by Inclusive Technology. Clicker 4 was developed as an aid for people who cannot effectively use a keyboard. It has excellent customization features. Keys can have letters, numbers, entire words or even pictures on them.

14.5.6 Accessibility Features in Microsoft Internet Explorer 5.0

Internet Explorer 5.0 offers a variety of options to improve usability. To access Internet Explorer 5.0's accessibility features, launch the program, click the **Tools** menu and select **Internet Options....** From the **Internet Options** menu, press the button labeled **Accessibility...** to open the accessibility options (Fig. 14.24).

The accessibility options in Microsoft Internet Explorer 5.0 augment the user's Web browsing. Users are able to ignore Web colors, Web fonts and font-size tags. This eliminates problems that arise from poor Web-page design and allows users to customize their Web browsing. Users can even specify a *style sheet* that formats every Web site the user visits, according to that user's personal preferences.

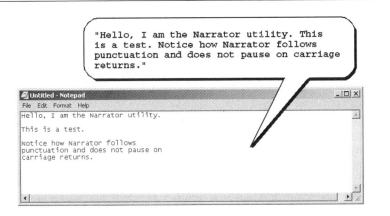

Fig. 14.22   Narrator reading **Notepad** text.

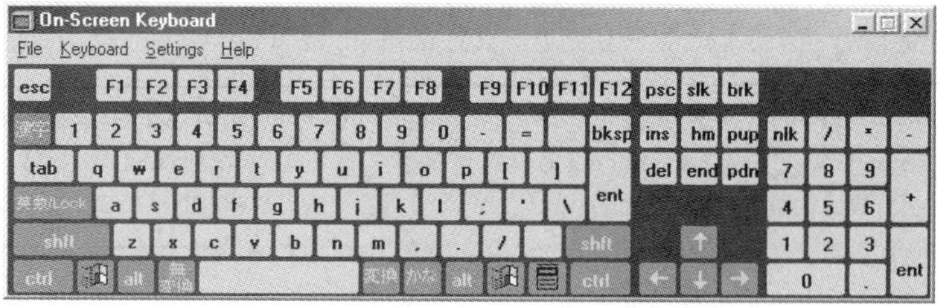

Fig. 14.23 Microsoft **On-Screen Keyboard**.

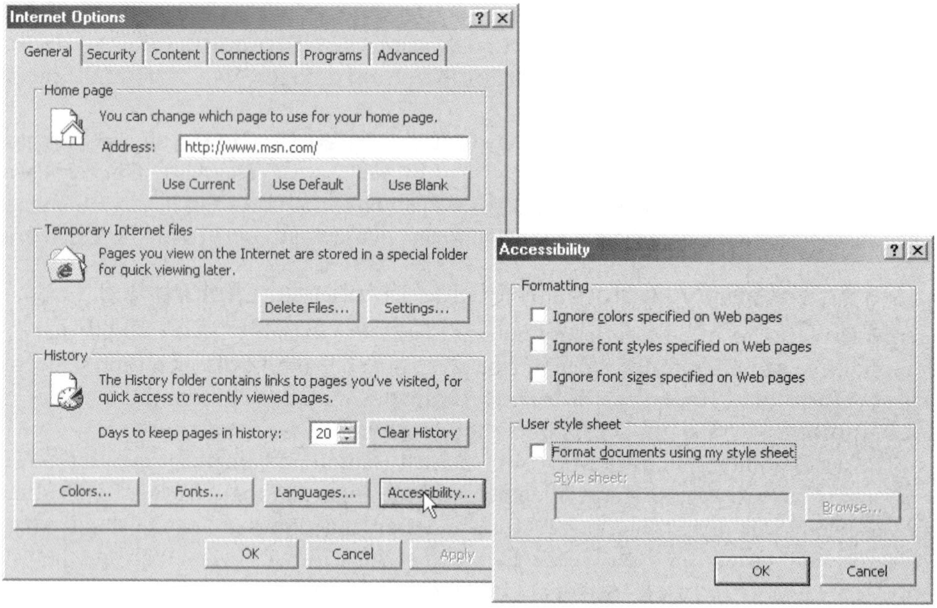

Fig. 14.24 Microsoft Internet Explorer 5.0's **Accessibility** options.

There are additional accessibility options in Internet Explorer 5.0. In the **Internet Options** dialog, click the **Advanced** tab. This opens the dialog shown in Fig. 14.25. The first option that can be set is labeled **Always expand ALT text for images**. By default, Internet Explorer 5.0 hides some of the **<ALT>** text, if it exceeds the size of the image it describes. This option forces all of the text to be shown. The second option reads **Move system caret with focus/selection changes**. This option is intended to make screen reading more effective. Some screen readers use the *system caret* (the blinking vertical bar associated with editing text) to decide what is read. If this option is not activated, screen readers may not read Web pages correctly.

Web designers often forget to take accessibility into account when creating Web sites and use fonts that are too small. Many user agents have addressed this problem, by allowing the user to adjust the text size. Click the **View** menu and select **Text Size** to change the font size using Internet Explorer 5.0. Figure 14.26 shows the resulting sub-menu. By default, the text size is set to **Medium**.

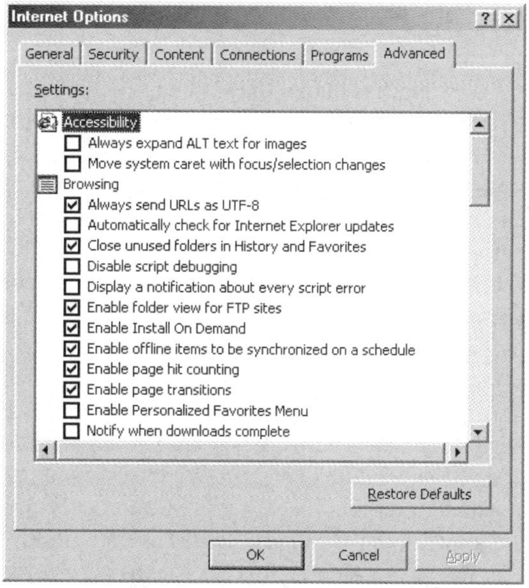

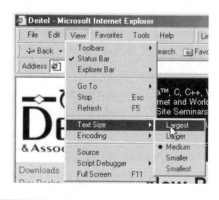

Fig. 14.25 Advanced accessibility settings in Microsoft Internet Explorer 5.0.

Fig. 14.26 Accessing the **Text Size** menu in Microsoft Internet Explorer 5.0.

14.6 Other Accessibility Tools

Most of the accessibility products offered today are aimed at helping hearing and visually impaired people. However, software does exist to help those with other types of disabilities (see JAWS® for Windows feature). This section describes some other accessibility products we have not yet discussed.

One such product is the *braille keyboard*. A braille keyboard is similar to a standard keyboard except that in addition to having the letters written on every key it has the equivalent braille symbol. Most often, braille keyboards are combined with a speech synthesizer or a braille display, so users are able to interact with the computers and verify that their typing is correct.

JAWS® for Windows

JAWS (Job Access With Sound) is one of the leading screen readers on the market today. It was created by Henter-Joyce, a division of Freedom Scientific™ and a company that tries to help visually impaired people use technology.

To download a demonstration version of JAWS, visit `www.hj.com/JAWS/JAWS37DemoOp.htm` and click the **JAWS 3.7 FREE Demo** link. This demo will run for 40 minutes, after which it will terminate.

The JAWS demo is fully functional and includes an extensive help menu that is highly customized. The user can select which voice to utilize, the rate at which text is spoken and create keyboard shortcuts. Although the demo is in English, the full version of JAWS 3.5 allows the user to choose one of several supported languages.

JAWS also includes special key commands for popular programs, such as Microsoft Internet Explorer and Microsoft Word. For example, when browsing in Internet Explorer, JAWS' capabilities extend beyond just reading the content on the screen. If JAWS is enabled, pressing *Insert + F7*, in Internet Explorer, opens a **Links List** dialog, which displays all the Web page links. For more information about JAWS and the other products offered by Henter-Joyce, visit `www.hj.com`.

Speech synthesizers are not new to the computer world. They have been used for many years to aid those who are unable to communicate verbally. However, the growing popularity of the Web has prompted a great deal of work in the field of speech synthesis and speech recognition. These technologies are allowing people with disabilities to utilize computers more than ever before. The development of speech synthesizers is also enabling other technologies, such as VoiceXML and *AuralCSS* (`www.w3.org/TR/REC-CSS2/aural.html`) to improve. These tools allow visually impaired people and those who cannot read to access Web sites.

Visually impaired people are not the only beneficiaries of the effort being made to improve *markup languages*—languages such as HTML and XML, which are designed to layout and link text files. The deaf also have a great number of tools to help them interpret auditory information delivered over the Web. Hearing-impaired Web users are already benefitting from what is called *Synchronized Multimedia Integration Language* (SMIL™). This markup language is designed to add extra *tracks*—layers of content found within a single audio or video file. The additional tracks can contain data, such as closed captioning.

Products are also being designed to help severely handicapped persons, such as those with quadriplegia, a form of paralysis affecting the body from the neck down. One such product, *EagleEyes*, developed by researchers at Boston College, (`www.cs.bc.edu/~eagleeye`), is a system that recognizes a user's eye movements and translates them to move the cursor.

The company CitXCorp is developing new technology that translates information over the Web through the telephone. Information on a specific topic will be accessed by dialing the designated number. The new software is expected to be made available to users for $10 per month.[8] For more information on regulations governing the design of Web sites to accommodate people with disabilities, visit `www.access-board.gov`.[9]

In alliance with Microsoft, GW Micro and Henter-Joyce, Adobe Systems Inc. is also working on software to aid people with disabilities. Adobe Acrobat and Adobe's PDF will be manufactured to comply with Microsoft's application programming interface (API), allowing businesses to reach a disabled audience. JetForm Corp is also meeting the needs of disabled persons with the development of their server-based XML software. The new software will allow users to download a format modified to best meet their needs.[10]

There are also many services on the Web that assist e-business owners in properly designing their Web sites to be accessible to individuals with disabilities. For additional information, The U.S. Department of Justice (**www.webable.com**) provides extensive resources detailing legal issues and current technologies related to people with disabilities.

In this chapter, we take a detailed look the efforts being put forth to make the Internet accessible to people with disabilities. Chapter 15, Online Industries begins a sequence of chapters that identify the industries that have been revolutionized by the Web.

14.7 Internet and World Wide Web Resources

www.w3.org/WAI
The World Wide Web Consortium's *Web Accessibility Initiative (WAI)* site promotes design of universally accessible Web sites. This site will help you keep up-to-date with current guidelines and forthcoming standards for Web accessibility.

www.w3.org/TR/WCAG10
This page is a note published by the WCAG working group. It discusses techniques that can be used to comply with the WAI. This is a great resource and can be used to find additional information on many of the topics covered in this chapter.

deafness.about.com/health/deafness/msubmenu6.htm
This is the home page of **deafness.about.com**. It is an excellent resource to find information pertaining to deafness.

www.cast.org
CAST stands for the Center for Applied Special Technology. They offer software intended to help individuals with disabilities use a computer, including a valuable accessibility checker—free of charge. The accessibility checker is a Web based program used to validate the accessibility of Web sites.

www.trainingpost.org/3-2-inst.htm
This site presents a tutorial on the Gunning Fog Index. The Gunning Fog Index is a method of grading text on its readability.

www.w3.org/TR/REC-CSS2/aural.html
This page discusses Aural Style Sheets, outlining the purpose and uses of this new technology.

laurence.canlearn.ca/English/learn/newaccessguide/indie
INDIE is an acronym which stands for "Integrated Network of Disability Information and Education." This site is home to a powerful search engine which help users find out information about disabilities.

java.sun.com/products/java-media/speech/forDevelopers/JSML
This site outlines the specifications for JSML, Sun Microsystem's Java Speech Markup Language. This language, like VoiceXML, could drastically improve accessibility for visually impaired people.

www.slcc.edu/webguide/lynxit.html
Lynxit is a development tool that allows users to view any Web site just as a text-only browser would. The site's form allows you to enter a URL and returns the Web site in text-only format.

www.trill-home.com/lynx/public_lynx.html
This site allows you to use browse the Web using a Lynx browser. Doing so will allow you to see how your page will load for users without the most current technologies.

www.wgbh.org/wgbh/pages/ncam/accesslinks.html
This site provides links to other accessibility pages across the Web.

ocfo.ed.gov/coninfo/clibrary/software.htm
This is the U.S. Department of Education's Web site for software accessibility requirements. It is aimed at helping developers produce accessible products.

www.alphaworks.ibm.com
This is the home page for IBM Alphaworks. It provides information on VoiceXML and offers a download of the beta version of Voice Server SDK.

www-3.ibm.com/able/access.html
This is the homepage of IBM's accessibility site. It provides information on IBM products and their accessibility and also discusses hardware, software and Web accessibility.

www.microsoft.com/enable/dev/guidelines/software.htm
This Web site presents Microsoft's guidelines to designing accessible software.

www.w3.org/TR/voice-tts-reqs
This page explains the speech synthesis markup requirements for voice markup languages.

deafness.about.com/health/deafness/msubvib.htm
This site provides information on deafness; it outlines vibrotactile devices. These devices allow deaf people to experience audio in the form of vibrations.

web.ukonline.co.uk/ddmc/software.html
This site provides links to software for people with disabilities.

www.hj.com
Henter-Joyce a division of Freedom Scientific provides software for the blind and visually impaired people. It is the home of JAWS.

www.abledata.com/text2/icg_hear.htm
This page contains a consumer guide that discusses technologies for hearing-impaired people.

www.washington.edu/doit
The University of Washington's DO-IT (Disabilities, Opportunities, Internetworking and Technology) site provides information and Web development resources for creating universally accessible Web sites.

www.webable.com
The WebABLE site contains links to many disability-related Internet resources and is geared towards those looking to develop technologies for people with disabilities.

www.speech.cs.cmu.edu/comp.speech/SpeechLinks.html
The Speech Technology Hyperlinks page has over 500 links to sites related to computer-based speech and speech recognition tools.

www.islandnet.com/~tslemko
The Micro Consulting Limited site contains shareware speech synthesis software.

www.chantinc.com/technology
This is the Chant Web site, which discusses speech technology and how it works. Chant also provides speech synthesis and speech recognition software.

SUMMARY

- Enabling your Web site to meet the needs of individuals with disabilities is an issue relevant to all business owners.

- In addition to comprising a significant portion of the population, legal ramifications exist for Web sites that discriminate against people with disabilities, by not providing them with adequate access to the site's resources.

- Technologies such as voice activation, visual enhancers and auditory aids enable disabled individuals to work in a large number of positions.

- Within the next year, information provided through technology will have to be equally accessible to individuals with disabilities

- On April 7, 1997, the World Wide Web Consortium (W3C) launched the Web Accessibility Initiative (WAI™).

- The vast majority of Web sites are considered inaccessible to people with visual, learning or mobility impairments.

- A high level of accessibility is difficult to achieve because there are many different disabilities, language barriers, hardware and software inconsistencies, etc.

- The Web Content Accessibility Guidelines 1.0 (**www.w3.org/TR/WCAG10**) are divided into a three-tier structure of checkpoints according to their priority.

- One important WAI requirement is to ensure that every image, movie and sound used on a Web page are accompanied by a description that clearly defines their purpose; this is called an **ALT** tag.

- Specialized user agents, such as screen readers (programs which allow users to hear what is being displayed on their screen) and braille displays (devices that receive data from screen reading software and output the data as braille) allow blind and visually impaired people to access text-based information that is normally displayed on the screen.

- Web pages with large amounts of multimedia content are difficult for user agents to interpret unless they are designed properly. Images, movies and other non-HTML objects cannot be read by screen readers.

- Bolded titles and image maps (images with areas designated as hyperlinks also present challenges to some Web users—particularly those who cannot use a mouse.

- Using a screen reader to navigate a Web site can be time consuming and frustrating, because screen readers are unable to interpret pictures and other graphical content. One method of combatting this problem is to include a link at the top of each Web page that provides easy access to the page's content.

- When creating a Web page intended for the general public, it is important to consider the reading level at which it is written. Web-site designers can make their site more readable by using smaller words, as some users may have difficulty reading large words.

- Users from other countries may have difficulty understanding slang and other non traditional language; hence, these should be avoided.

- *Web Content Accessibility Guidelines 1.0* suggests using a paragraph's first sentence to convey its subject.

- VoiceXML, has tremendous implications for visually impaired people and for the illiterate. Not only does VoiceXML read Web pages to the user, but it also includes speech recognition technology—a technology that enables computers to understand words spoken into the microphone—enabling it to interact with users.

- Beginning with Microsoft Windows 95, Microsoft has included accessibility features in its operating systems and many of its applications, including Office 97, Office 2000 and Netmeeting.

- A braille keyboard is similar to a standard keyboard, except that in addition to having the letters written on every key, it has the equivalent braille symbol.

- Hearing-impaired Web users will soon benefit from what is called synchronized Multimedia Integration Language (SMIL™). This markup language is designed to add extra *tracks*—layers of content found within a single audio or video file. The additional tracks can contain data such as closed captioning.

- EagleEyes, developed by researchers at Boston College, (`www.cs.bc.edu/~eagleeye`) is a system that translates eye movements into mouse movements. The user moves the mouse cursor by moving their eyes or head, through the use of electrodes.

TERMINOLOGY

ALT tag
Americans with Disabilities Act (ADA)
braille displays
braille keyboard
default settings
Gunning Fox Index
image maps
mark-up languages
Microsoft Magnifier
On-Screen Keyboard
Priority-one checkpoints
Priority-three checkpoints
Priority-two checkpoints
readability
screen readers
speech recognition

speech synthesis
style sheet
Synchronized Multimedia Integration
    Language (SMIL)
system caret
text to speech
timeout
user agents
ViaVoice
voiceserver
Voice Server SDK
VoiceXML
Web accessibility
Web Accessibility Initiative (WAI)
Web Content Accessibility Guidelines 1.0

SELF-REVIEW EXERCISES

14.1 State whether each of the following is true or false. If the statement is false, explain why.
   a) Screen readers have no problem reading and translating images.
   b) The Windows Accessibility Wizard has a feature that changes the on-screen appearance and the speed of the mouse.
   c) When writing pages for the general public, it is important to consider the reading difficulty level of the text you are writing.
   d) The Windows 2000 **Accessibility Wizard** can, among other things, help you modify the appearance of your system by changing colors, fonts, sizes, etc.
   e) Left-handed people have been helped by the improvements made in speech-recognition technology more than any other group.

14.2 Fill in the blanks in each of the following.
   a) Technologies such as _____, _____ and _____ enable disabled individuals to work in a large number of positions.
   b) On April 7, 1997, the World Wide Web Consortium (W3C) launched the _____.
   c) The Web Content Accessibility Guidelines 1.0 (`www.w3.org/TR/WCAG10`) are divided into a _____ of checkpoints according to their priority.
   d) One important WAI requirement is to ensure that every _____, _____ and _____ used on a Web page are accompanied by a description that clearly defines their purpose; this is called an **ALT** tag.

e) Specialized user agents, such as _____ (programs which allow users to hear what is being displayed on their screen) and braille displays (devices that receive data from screen reading software and output the data as braille) allow blind and visually impaired people to access text-based information that is normally displayed on the screen.

ANSWERS TO SELF-REVIEW EXERCISES

14.1 a) False. Screen readers have no way of telling a user what is shown in an image. If the programmer includes an **ALT** attribute inside the **<IMG>** tag, the screen reader will read this to the user. b) True. c) True. d) True. e) False. Although left-handed people can utilize speech-recognition technology like everyone else, speech-recognition technology has the largest impact on the blind and those who have trouble typing.

14.2 a) Voice activation, visual enhancers and auditory aids. b) Web Accessibility Initiative (WAI™). c) Three-tier structure. d) Image, movie and sound. e) Screen readers.

EXERCISES

14.3 State whether each of the following is true or false. If the statement is false, explain why
a) Enabling your Web site to meet the needs of individuals with disabilities is an issue relevant to all business owners.
b) Within the next year, information provided through technology will have to be equally accessible to individuals with disabilities.
c) The vast majority of Web sites are considered accessible to people with visual, learning or mobility impairments.
d) A high level of accessibility is difficult to achieve because there are many different disabilities, language barriers, hardware and software inconsistencies, etc.
e) Web pages with large amounts of multimedia content are easy for user agents to interpret. Images, movies and other non-HTML objects can also be read by screen readers.
f) Beginning with Microsoft Windows 95, Microsoft has included accessibility features in its operating systems and many of its applications, including Office 97, Office 2000 and Netmeeting.

14.4 Fill in the blanks in each of the following
a) Bolded titles and image maps (images with areas designated as hyperlinks) also present challenges to some Web users—particularly those who cannot use a _____.
b) *Web Content Accessibility Guidelines 1.0* suggests using a paragraph's _____ to convey its subject.
c) Not only does VoiceXML read Web pages to the user, but it also includes _____—a technology that enables computers to understand words spoken into the microphone—enabling it to interact with users.
d) A _____ is similar to a standard keyboard, except that in addition to having the letters written on every key, it has the equivalent braille symbol.
e) Hearing-impaired Web users will soon benefit from what is called _____. This markup language is designed to add extra *tracks*—layers of content found within a single audio or video file. The additional tracks can contain data such as closed captioning.
f) _____ is a system that translates eye movements into mouse movements. The user moves the mouse cursor by moving their eyes or head, through the use of electrodes.

14.5 Define the following terms.
a) W3C
b) WAI
c) JAWS

  d) SMIL
  e) Americans with Disabilities Act
  f) Telecommunications Act of 1996
  g) Individuals with Disabilities Education Act of 1997

14.6   Create a set of accessibility options for yourself using the Windows **Accessibility Wizard** and save them to a floppy disk. Use these new settings for half an hour and describe how they affect your computer usage.

WORKS CITED

The notation <**www.domain-name.com**> indicates that the citation is for information found at that Web site.

1.   D.Z. "They Oughta Pass A Law, And They Did, But Is It Working," *Presentations* September 2000: 45.

2.   *Americans with Disabilities Act.*

3.   <**www.usdoj.gov/crt/ada/cguide.htm#anchor63109**>

4.   <**www.wemedia.com**>

5.   M. Conlin, "The New Workforce," *Business Week* 20 March 2000:65.

6.   M. Conlin, 65.

7.   S. Tillet, "E-Commerce for the Blind," *Internet Week* 8 May 2000: 31.

8.   S. Tillet, 31.

9.   "Web Disability," *Inter@ctive Week* 10 April 2000: 92.

10.   S. Lais, "Coming Soon: Easier-to-Use Software for the Disabled," *Computer World* 1 May 2000: 70.

Part 6

e-Business and e-Commerce Case Studies

Outline

Chapter 15 Online Industries

Chapter 16 Online Banking and Investing

Chapter 17 e-Learning

Chapter 18 e-Publishing

Chapter 19 Online Entertainment

Chapter 20 Online Career Services

15

Online Industries

Objectives

- To review the major industry segments on the Web.
- To explore the ways the Internet and the Web have improved business practices.
- To evaluate the business models being implemented by companies on the Web.
- To discuss the challenges facing online businesses.
- To examine the successful methods of conducting business in the Internet economy.

I have found out that there ain't no surer way to find out whether you like people or hate them than to travel with them.
Mark Twain

Down went the owners—greedy men whom hope of gain allured:
Oh, dry the starting tear, for they were heavily insured.
W. S. Gilbert

Outline

15.1   Introduction
15.2   Retailing on the Web
15.3   Medical Services Online; Health and Nutrition
15.4   Online Travel
15.5   Transportation and Shipping
15.6   Online Automotive Sites
15.7   Energy Online
15.8   Selling Brainpower Online
15.9   Online Art Dealers
15.10   Online Grocery Stores
15.11   Online Real Estate
15.12   Online Legal Services
15.13   Government Online
15.14   Insurance Online
15.15   Children Online
15.16   Purchasing Event Tickets Online
15.17   Genealogy Online
15.18   Internet and World Wide Web Resources

Summary • Terminology • Self-Review Exercises • Answers to Self-Review Exercises • Exercises • Works Cited

15.1 Introduction

In Chapter 2, we discussed the many business models implemented on the Web. In this chapter, we discuss the notion of business models in an industry-specific manner. We feature many leading e-businesses and major industry categories. Each industry uses the Web effectively to improve current business practices and to diversify into new areas. Each of these industries understands the importance of providing unique and highly targeted information.

15.2 Retailing on the Web

A retail store purchases goods from a wholesaler, marks up the price and then offers the products to consumers. On the Web, the retail process works the same way, however consumers cannot touch, feel or taste the products they are viewing, but if they know what they are looking for, the Web can save them time and money.

Retail is one of the most widely implemented forms of e-commerce. Online retailers can communicate easily with suppliers, shipping companies and customers. Online systems are available that enable merchants to bill customers and accept payment (Chapter 4, Online Monetary Transactions). A large majority of retailers on the Web use the *shopping-*

cart model exclusively, while others integrate other models such as the *auction model* or *price-comparison model*. Retail Web sites often endure losses to offer lower prices to their consumers. Many e-tailers feel that this will build brand awareness and customer loyalty. In the long term these sites will rely on the profit margins generated by advertising sales and partnering arrangements. Online retailers that fulfill orders in a timely manner while serving customers effectively can succeed on the Internet.

Compusa.com is a retail outlet that has used the Web to grow its business. The company sells computers, software and peripherals online and off-line. Its product catalog appears on its Web site. Once you have found the product you are looking for, you can order it through the Web site or visit a CompUSA store to make your purchase. Clicks-and-mortar businesses like CompUSA give customers a chance to see the product in the store and then make their final purchase on the Web, or vice versa. Having an online and off-line presence will generate brand awareness and loyalty, but it can require substantially more resources than purely online businesses.

Some of the world's most successful clothing designers offer their products on the Web. Designers Kenneth Cole (**www.kennethcole.com**), French Connection (**www.frenchconnection.com**™), BCBGMaxAzria (**www.bcbg.com**) and Vera Wang (**www.verawang.com**) have all brought their products to the Web. Victoria's Secret (**www.victoriassecret.com**) Webcasts an annual fashion show showcasing their lingerie and models. The Victoria's Secret Web Fashion Show of 2000 was the most widely viewed Internet event in history to that point.

15.3 Medical Services Online; Health and Nutrition

People can learn about and discuss medical issues at a variety of Web sites (see the feature, WebMD). The Web gives consumers access to case studies, medical journal articles and doctors who can answer questions. The Web also acts as a forum where people discuss the issues currently affecting the health-care industry.

The *Health Insurance Portability and Accountability Act (HIPAA)* of 1996 will soon require medical offices and other healthcare related agencies to perform many of their administrative tasks online. This will save the healthcare industry billions of dollars.[1] If the system is successful, we may see similar legislation passed for other major industries.

Sickbay.com is a full-service medical site focusing on the issues that affect doctors and their patients. The *doctors* section consists of a practice center where doctors can submit articles to help their peers. The site also offers discounts on medical supplies and administrative services to medical professionals. These services include patient background information retrieval and online billing. The site also provides information and advice for health and wellness, fitness, retirement and nutrition, and includes an encyclopedia of medical terms, suggested physical exercises and a pharmacy. Other medical portal sites include Medscape (**www.medscape.com**) and **Selfcare.com** and **DrKoop.com**.

The Medical industry is constantly changing. New discoveries often revolutionize the way people are medicated and treated. The Internet will help medical professionals make discoveries and share their findings with physicians and regulatory agencies worldwide. Although the Web is a vast and dynamic store of medical information, it will never take the place of physicians. Web users should consult their doctors regularly. Another concern among individuals is privacy. People with serious illnesses may be reluctant to use the Web fearing that their employers or friends might have access to their personal data.

WebMD℠: Using the Web to Improve Your Health[2]

Healtheon WebMD (`www.Webmd.com`) is a *vertical portal*, a portal offering a great depth on a small amount of subjects, that offers a repository of documentation relating to the medical field (Fig. 15.1). WebMD can also help you find doctors and medical professionals. A free database of medical information is available. Users can access tips on combating common ailments.

WebMD realizes the importance of using both online and offline media to reach its target audience. It now offers content on television. WebMD TV is broadcast on the Fox network and is available for download on the WebMD site. The broadcast features medical professionals discussing the latest healthcare issues. Membership is free and entitles you to additional services. *MyHealthRecord* is a free service that allows you to keep track of your medical history. You can store information about past illnesses, current prescriptions and anticipated health risks. Once you have filled out your profile, you can print personal identification cards that include emergency contact information. Consumer members can participate in live events, post messages on the discussion boards and customize content to their interests. *Health-E-Tools* is a listing of free calculators and guidelines to help visitors determine their ideal body weight, calorie counts and nutrition.

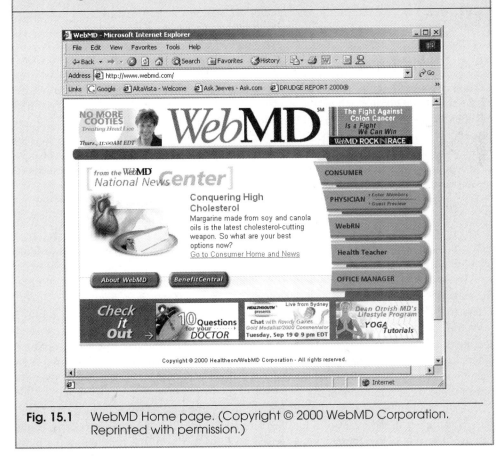

Fig. 15.1   WebMD Home page. (Copyright © 2000 WebMD Corporation. Reprinted with permission.)

WebMD℠: Using the Web to Improve Your Health[2] (Cont.)

Physicians can become members of WebMD to gain access to additional services. Joining the specialized practice portal allows members to keep current with medical announcements, read the latest medical journals and communicate with other members of the medical community. Templates are available for physicians who wish to establish Web sites. Medical office managers can access financial and customer management tools. They can also order office supplies from a catalog of hundreds of thousands of products. Medical professionals have access to labs that process samples and record results.

WebRN is a segment of the site dedicated to nurses. This site offers drug databases, clinical research, tools and tips, discussion groups and access to supplies. WebRN was created by nurses as a way to provide fellow nurses with up-to-date news and developments in their field, as well as improve present practices with time-saving tools and patient-management advice.

WebMD is a specialized portal that generates traffic with high-quality content. The site generates revenue from advertising, retail sales and support services. They also receive help from sponsors and strategic partners.

15.4 Online Travel

Companies like Boeing (**www.boeing.com**™) and Airbus Industries (**www.airbus.com**) build civilian and military aircraft. Many planes take off without being filled to capacity. Since the relatively fixed overhead expenses are spread over fewer people, ticket prices are higher. The Internet helps the commercial airline industry to fill more seats and reduce costs. Electronic ticketing lowers overhead by reducing printing costs and lost-ticket processing costs. Given that air travel is traditionally a high-cost, low-margin business, these savings can have a profound effect on an airline's profits.

People can often save time and money by booking their travel arrangements on the Web, which gives them access to much of the same information previously accessible only to travel agents (**Travelocity.com** feature). You can search for the lowest prices, best times and the best accommodations available using the resources and search capabilities available on many of the online travel sites.

There is a great deal of competition among travel Web sites. Each one is struggling to increase site traffic by offering better service, lower prices and more features. Microsoft offers travel services through **www.expedia.com**®, which allows you to book all of your travel arrangements, including transportation and lodging. Membership is free and members are given access to a database of information offering the best travel options. Once they have found a flight they wish to take, they can purchase it directly from the Web site. This is essentially a storefront model, but rather than buying a book or a CD, the customer is buying accommodations.

A site with an interesting business premise is **BizTravel.com**®, which will reimburse customers in the event of a late or cancelled flight, lost luggage or poor in-flight service. The rate of reimbursement is based on the severity of the problem. All flights that are cancelled or arrive more than two hours late are reimbursed in full. Lost luggage is also paid for in full. The site offers incremental refunds for other travel inconveniences. For example, if you feel that the travel agent who helped you book your travel has behaved in an unprofessional manner, you will be refunded $50 for the inconvenience. Similar refunds are offered for lengthy waiting times for phone services, slow e-mail response and an inadequate choice of meals. **Biztravel.com** also offers wireless services that keep you posted on the status of your flight by sending frequent updates to your cellular phone or wireless handheld device. The wireless service allows you to request an upgrade using frequent-flyer miles and will soon allow you to book a flight. We will discuss wireless technology further in Chapter 6, Wireless Internet and m-Business. As an additional service to the business traveler, **Biztravel.com** will keep a log of your travels and calculate the appropriate miles earned for your trip. *BizAlerts* is a free service that reminds travelers of their impending travel arrangements, so they never miss a flight. They also inform travelers about gate changes, weather conditions and other important travel data. Membership to the site is free. BizTravel makes a small commission on all transactions processed through the site.

Another site designed for business travelers, **GetThere.com**™ helps corporate clients cut travel costs by connecting them directly to airlines, hotels and rental cars through its site. **GetThere.com** also outsources its technology, allowing portal sites to offer similar services. **GetThere.com** has products targeting various areas of the travel industry. *DirectCorporate*™ allows corporations to integrate a travel management system into their current infrastructure. Corporations using the product can integrate their current travel protocols into the system. Past travel data, preferred vendor information and other company preferences can be added to the system. Employees can store their frequent flyer information as well as seating and meal preferences within the *DirectCorporate* system. The product allows users to get up-to-the minute flight, hotel and rental car data. *DirectAirline*™ allows airlines to post flight data within the **GetThere.com** system and on their own Web sites. Airline customers can use the system to search and book flights, store personal mileage information and request upgrades. *Direct Portal*™ can give any Web site the ability to offer up-to-the-minute flight information to its visitors. National attractions such as amusement parks and museums may want to provide this type of data on their sites to encourage visitors.

Site59.com is a travel and entertainment site that allows you to find low prices at the last minute. Often when booking travel at the last minute, you find yourself paying exorbitant rates for the same seats you could have had for much less. Site59 works with airlines, hotels, ticket agencies and entertainment vendors to help you find the lowest rates on your vacation. The site offers complete weekend getaways that are prepackaged to save you planning time. Site59 can also make arrangements for special events such as bachelor parties or anniversaries. Trips include broadway excursions and weekends in the Orient.

Cheaptickets (**www.cheaptickets.com**™) helps customers find discount fares for airline tickets, hotel rooms, cruise vacations and rental cars. Users are given access to a database of up-to-the-minute flight schedule data.

15.5 Transportation and Shipping

Transportation and shipping is an estimated $1.3 trillion industry.[4] Major shipping vendors, including UPS (**www.ups.com**®), DHL (**www.dhl.com**™) and Federal Express (**www.fedex.com**®) have built Web sites to enhance their services. Each of the sites allows customers to track their shipments as they pass checkpoints en route to their final destination. Payment processing and account management are also available.

The trucking industry uses the Web to keep trucks fully loaded and to ensure timely delivery. Web sites match available truck capacity with the shipping needs of many companies that are willing to split the cost of full truckloads.[5] This process called *load matching* lowers costs by reducing the number of trucks needed to fulfill an order.

Layover.com© is a trucking portal that allows drivers to find maps, chat and match loads with available space. The site posts stories and advice from truckers worldwide. Other trucking Web sites include **trucking.net**™ and **getloaded.com**.

Commercial freight shipping is a complex process. A company operating worldwide will have to manage shipments with multiple airlines, shipping companies and trucking firms. Tradient (**www.tradient.com**) helps businesses manage the shipping segments of the supply chain by keeping tabs on shipments as they travel. The site connects shippers with suppliers and customers. The Global Freight Exchange (**www.gf-x.com**) specializes in shipping air freight through the major airlines.

Travelocity.com™: Making Travel Arrangements[3]

Consumers are booking their travel itineraries online, often at lower prices than those available through travel agents. **Travelocity.com** is an online travel service that enables you to make all of your travel arrangements with a single visit to its Web site (Fig. 15.2). You can book flights, rental cars, hotel rooms and vacation packages without utilizing a travel agent.

Travelocity uses *shopping-bot technology*, which scans databases and Web sites to find certain prespecified criteria. For example, a customer who wishes to fly from New York to Los Angeles enters a time frame for the trip and airport codes to receive current fare information. The shopping bot scans airline rates and scheduling databases for matches. The site then displays the flights that meet the criteria you have submitted. Once you have decided on the fare, you proceed to the checkout and book an electronic ticket for the flight. An *electronic ticket* serves the same purpose as a paper ticket. Once a person arrives at the departure gate, a representative confirms the customer's arrival and issues a boarding pass. No paper ticket is issued. All pertinent information is stored in the airline's computer system when the customer initially purchases the ticket. Customers no longer have to worry about losing their paper tickets. However, electronic ticket holders run the risk of losing a spot due to a computer failure or the accidental deletion of their reservation. It is important to document your purchase with a confirmation number and any other proof of purchase.

Travelocity has formed strategic partnerships with airlines, hotels and rental car agencies. These partnerships give Travelocity access to flight information and pricing data in real time. Travelocity hopes to generate a profit by selling advertising and through cash flows generated on ticket brokering services.

Travelocity.com™: Making Travel Arrangements[3] (Cont.)

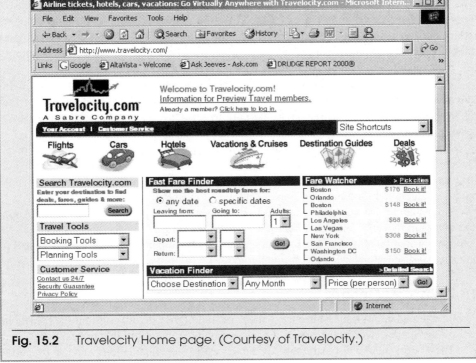

Fig. 15.2   Travelocity Home page. (Courtesy of Travelocity.)

15.6 Online Automotive Sites

Many sites allow Web users to research and purchase new and used cars. Whether or not you make your final arrangements for the purchase of a vehicle online, many of the preliminary steps can be completed on the Web. Users can explore options more efficiently than by traveling to geographically dispersed dealerships. Online automobile appraisers offer instant value estimates to help users negotiate prices. The Web empowers consumers by giving them easy access to information that may have been hard to find previously. This data may include crash-test data, maintenance estimates and insurance quotes. All of this information can be used as leverage when negotiating a better price on an automobile.

Dealers can search online databases for cars to boost their inventories. Traditionally this process is handled by dealers attending local auctions to find specific automobiles. These cars are then shipped to the dealerships and resold. Using the Web is much more efficient than sending dealers to auctions. Since the Web is a worldwide database, dealers have access to many more cars than they would locally.[6]

By improving communication between all departments responsible for automobile production, the Internet helps improve the way cars are manufactured. DaimlerChrysler, for example, recently introduced the *FastCar system,* which uses the Internet to speed up and improve the quality of production. The system prevents significant errors by ensuring that every member of the production team is aware of the status of a project from its design stages until the product is shipped.[7]

DaimlerChrysler has also used the Web to form partnerships with competitors. In 2000, GM, Ford and DaimlerChrysler announced plans to build the world's largest Internet-based, business-to-business automotive exchange, *Covisint*. The exchange is designed to help reduce the costs of automobile production by linking raw materials, parts suppliers and production plants.[8] Customers using Covisint may someday be able to design a custom automobile from top to bottom and drive it home within a week of placing the order.[9]

Autobytel (**www.autobytel.com**) is a one-stop shop where users buy, sell, maintain and learn more about automobiles. You can search classified ads for used cars or find the best price on a new car. If you are looking to service your car, you can contact local service stations for estimates. You can also locate the best values on car insurance.

Autoparts.com is an online auction site for people buying and selling auto parts. Once you register, you can begin searching through the auto parts database. You can search for parts by year, make and model. The auctions are posted by individuals who have spare parts—even engines and transmissions—and wish to sell them to the highest bidder.

AutoChannel (**www.autochannel.com**) is a site for both automotive enthusiasts and common drivers. The site offers news on the automotive and racing industries. An automobile auction allows visitors to sell old cars and auto parts. Visitors can also listen to automotive discussions using streaming audio.

15.7 Energy Online

People often take for granted the energy they consume. They do not consider the enormous behind-the-scenes effort it takes to make energy available at affordable prices.

The energy market is extremely dynamic, with price fluctuations created by subtle changes in supply, foreign affairs or even the weather. In the past, energy was regulated by the U.S. government and distributed by a few large companies. Regulation allowed the companies producing and distributing the energy to control the market. One example of this is the famous Standard Oil Case of 1911. Since Standard Oil had no real competition in the oil industry, the company could control pricing and distribution. The courts determined Standard Oil to be a monopoly and broke it into independent companies to stimulate fair pricing.[10]

Energy products are traded in a complex set of distribution channels. For instance, oil travels from the well, to a refinery, through a pipeline, to the distributor and then to its eventual consumer. This supply change system can be made more efficient when it is managed through Web-based systems. The synchronization of accounting and distribution practices expedite and reduce the cost of this process.

Large energy conglomerates will benefit from the standardization the Web can offer. Given the complex relationships these companies must manage, there is an enormous cost to document each transaction and manage the commodities as they are sold. The Web offers a standard way for energy businesses to communicate. Companies that use the Internet to manage their supply chains can reduce operating costs and gain access to group discounts and wholesale pricing. Small businesses can use the Web to reach a broader base of clients and provide better customer service. Customers are now able to pay bills and track their energy consumption online.[11]

Businesses both large and small will benefit from the B2B exchanges being created by the larger energy providers. Since demand drastically affects pricing in the energy market, it is important to have up-to-the-minute pricing data to determine the maximum profit opportunity for a given commodity. For instance, when demand for a product is high its price will increase. Energy exchanges allow buyers to search for the best prices and wholesalers to make the highest profit margins (see Enron feature). Each day a listing of available energy is posted. It is then valued against the demand and other economic factors to determine its final selling price. The initial price is determined and then fluctuates with demand as the trading day progresses.[12]

Enron: Selling Energy on The Web[13]

Enron has established itself as the leader of online energy distributors. The site, created in 1999, connects energy buyers and sellers anonymously. Each of these customers has access to almost 800 different energy commodities on a daily basis. Energy products include oil, gas and electricity as well as emissions allowances.[14]

Enron offers 13 separate B2B marketplaces that connect buyers and sellers in the energy, water, pulp/paper and international energy markets. `EnronOnline.com` focuses on energy commodities trading. Since the value of energy products is dynamic, profits can be made by purchasing them at a low cost and later selling the same energy at a higher rate. For instance, a barrel of oil may be bought at $30 today and sold for $35 dollars tomorrow. This could represent a $5 return on investment per barrel.

Customers of Enron Online must first register with the company before they can participate in the trading area of the site. EnronOnline offers a demo explaining the registration and trading processes. Once registered, the customers has access to a listing of commodities. This listing is color coded to represent the status of each offering. If the price is rising on a particular commodity, the offering is colored green. If prices are falling, it is colored red. Customers who wish to know more about a particular offering need only click on its name. This will open a new window with an extended description. This information includes geographic information and the most recent pricing data. Enron makes its money by brokering deals between two parties, In order to maintain their position as broker, they withhold the identities of each member in a transaction. Once a commodity is located, the customer must click on the price. A dialog box will then appear giving the customer a number of options. The customer must then set a buy price and hope that the price eventually becomes available. If the transaction is successful, it will be posted on the screen; if not, a message describing the failed transaction will be posted. A full demonstration of the Enron system is available at `www.enrononline.com`.

Enron now offers residential energy services through a partnership with IBM and AOL called `NewPowerCompany.com`. The company offers discounted energy to select markets across the country. Enron sees the Internet as a means of both strengthening its core business and diversifying.[15]

Other Enron marketplaces include `water2water.com`, a B2B marketplace for the purchase and sale of water and water-related services and `Clickpulp.com` a similar marketplace for the paper industry. Enron makes a commission on transactions that occur on its Web site.

Altranet (**www.altranet.com**) also sells energy commodities. Utility companies can buy natural gas, electricity and heating oil directly from the site. About 10 percent of U.S. natural gas is sold through the Altranet system. The site operates as a trading floor where wholesalers can offer excess capacity to markets in demand of the energy. This site competes directly with Enron, but operates in fewer markets.[16]

beMANY!© **(beMANY.com)** uses the demand-sensitive pricing model to get the best energy prices for its consumers. The site uses its large customer base to get bulk discounts from energy providers. Deregulation has caused an increase in the number of energy providers. This competitive market stimulates price competition and therefore lower prices for the buyer. **beMANY.com** helps its customers locate the lowest rates available for electricity and natural gas.

Retail Energy (**www.retailenergy.com**) is a directory for the energy industry. This site was designed by the *Power Marketing Association* and offers a comprehensive listing of energy providers. Current energy prices for both electricity and natural gas are available.

15.8 Selling Brainpower Online

Finding people qualified enough to turn a good business idea into a reality is often a major challenge. In many cases, businesses are started by technically adept individuals with little business management experience. Sometimes it is the opposite; the management team has business savvy but little technical expertise. Either way, the need for a qualified work force has generated one of the best career markets in recent times. Online career services are discussed in detail in Chapter 20, Online Career Services. One way that businesses are attracting talent is through consulting and contract hiring. Independent contracting offers experts in a particular field a chance to work in a constantly changing environment with a greater degree of flexibility. It is often more feasible for a business to outsource the talent than to hire an expert full time. *Outsourcing* is the process of hiring another company or individual to do a job when there is a lack of qualified resources within a company (see **Hello-Brain.com** feature). The Internet has given small-business owners a huge talent pool that is willing to contract its services. Contracting fees vary by project and contractor. This option can often be more cost effective than hiring new full-time employees.

HelloBrain.com *has Answers to Difficult Questions*

In the past, employers wishing to hire contractors selected from a limited pool of applicants, and often had to pay temp agencies large sums of money to hire a contractor. Today companies that do not have the human resources to complete complex projects can find help at **HelloBrain.com**. HelloBrain acts as the middleman offering free job and project postings for merchants. The site lists projects and potential compensation. HelloBrain then searches for contractors that may be able to handle the jobs.

A recent posting offered $63,000 for a consultant willing to develop a software product for a company in Chicago. The contractor would be paid the same whether the project was completed in three months or six. This open-ended offer motivates the contractor to work quickly to meet the final goal.

`HelloBrain.com` *has Answers to Difficult Questions (Cont.)*

Project listings range from applications programming to network design. If you are not a contractor, but know of someone with appropriate skills to complete a project, you can refer that person and possibly receive a referral fee.

`HelloBrain.com` employs intelligent-agent technology that searches project postings to determine which contractors are best fit for a given job or project. Once the potential contractors have been determined, HelloBrain sends e-mail to them describing the opportunities. `HelloBrain.com` retains a commission on the sale of all products and intellectual-property sales.

Question Exchange (`www.questionexchange.com`) allows businesses and individuals to access programming-specific troubleshooting as well as customer service. Companies pay a subscription fee to access the system. In exchange, users are able to ask programming-related development questions and access a database of 10,000 archived questions.

It is often said that one person's trash is another person's treasure. Yet2 (`www.yet2.com`) has turned this saying into a business model. Companies around the world have employed research and development departments to improve existing products and invent new ones. It has been estimated that 90 percent of these innovations go unused.[17] `Yet2.com` is an e-business designed to help companies raise capital by selling unused intellectual property such as patents and trademarks. `Yet2.com` is backed by industry-leading companies that wish to sell or license intellectual property. You can see a sample listing of potential properties on the site. `yet2.com` charges an annual subscription fee for the search service and a one-time commission fee on any sale.

15.9 Online Art Dealers

Art is traditionally sold in galleries or through mall vendors. The Internet gives artists a chance to showcase their work and reach a global audience. Although viewers cannot see each brush stroke, they can get an idea of the composition and quality of each work. Since customers cannot see the actual art before they make a purchase, often online art dealers provide certificates of authenticity to make customers feel more comfortable about making purchases online.

`Art.com`SM sells fine art, photography, posters and prints, animations and many other media. You can search the `Art.com` database by artist, medium, decor, size, subject and genre. Artists also list their favorites for you to peruse. The framing shop is a section of the site that allows customers to view their pieces in a variety of frames before making a final decision. `Art.com` uses a shopping-cart model and can have a piece delivered to a customer in a few days.

`Guild.com`™is another art dealer offering more than 7,000 products online including paintings, sculpture, basketry, metalwork and many other popular art forms. `Guild.com` realizes the value of printed media, and also offers their full product line in printed form. You can order their printed catalog on the site for free. Pieces range in price from a few hundred dollars to over a million depending on the artist and the work. *Visual galleries,* sections of the site each dedicated to a particular artist, feature up-and-coming artists and offer commentary by celebrity curators. **Guild.com** keeps its product listings current and is constantly adding new features to its Web site to engage visitors with new and interesting content.

Sothebys (**www.sothebys.com**) recently began offering online art auctions. Sothebys opened its doors as a bookseller in London in 1744. Today, it offers works from the world's most revered artists. Auctions are held daily and generate thousands of dollars in sales. Sothebys has been successful in transitioning its auction services to the Web. Customers recognize the Sothebys brand and trust that products will be of high quality. Sothebys hopes to attract new customers to their auction by offering instructions and explanations of the process and the benefits of buying art at auction.

Christies (**www.christies.com**), a competing auction house, also offers services on the Web. Although visitors cannot participate in auctions directly online, they can scan the company's catalog and find out where the next auction will be held and which lots will be auctioned.

15.10 Online Grocery Stores

Buying groceries online, especially staple items, is a time saver (see Webvan feature). You can create an electronic shopping list and make small edits to reflect your special needs each week. Many people prefer to go to the supermarket to examine perishables, such as fresh fruits, vegetables and meats. People feel more comfortable buying canned goods and packaged products online. Once a shopping list has been arranged and your purchases are made, the supermarket will send a delivery truck to your door with your groceries. The delivery company that can provide the fastest, most reliable service will have no trouble diversifying its delivery service into other product categories.[18]

 e-Fact 15.1

Jupiter Communications predicts that by 2003 over seven billion dollars will be spent on groceries purchased on the Web.[19].

Webvan™: Ordering Groceries on the Web

Webvan.com (Fig. 15.3) recently purchased competitor **Homegrocer.com** in a billion-dollar stock swap to become the largest home grocery delivery company on the Web.[20] The merger gave Webvan access to more products, locations, and equipment.

Once you have registered with Webvan you can begin to use its search engine to fill your shopping cart with grocery products. The site provides pictures of the products in its catalog. Webvan uses secure servers to protect your personal information. Online security is discussed in Chapter 7, Internet Security. Once you are finished shopping you can proceed to the checkout, where you pay and arrange delivery. The site allows you to pick your delivery times, which are scheduled in 30-minute segments—all available times for the current week are displayed.

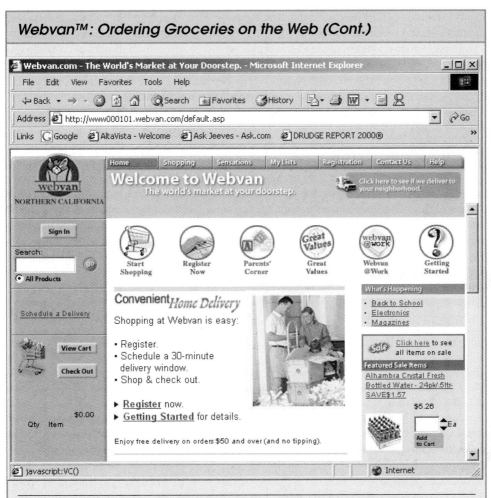

Fig. 15.3   Webvan Home page. (Courtesy of Webvan Group, Inc.)

Parent's Corner helps you plan a healthy diet for your child and have the products delivered to your door. *The Pampers Parenting Institute* helps parents of infants. This section of the site offers advice on planning for and raising babies. Other services include, *Webvan@work,* which will deliver food and supplies to your workplace. Customers can order traditional groceries or prepared meals.   `Homeruns.com,` `peapod.com, homegrocer.com, Kozmo.com` and many other online companies will deliver groceries and convenience goods to your door.

15.11 Online Real Estate

A real estate transaction conducted off-line can involve dozens of people. The buyer and seller each work with a broker, bank, mortgage lender, moving company and other supporting agencies. When a home is placed on the market, it is usually offered through a realty company. That company helps the owners market and sell their home and manage the paperwork that is generated in the process. At the same time they help the seller find a new home and set up the financing to afford it. It is a process that most people are happy to give to a broker.

Even in today's Internet-enabled world it would be virtually impossible to handle the entire real estate transaction yourself. Buying a home online is much more difficult than buying a new book or even a car on the Web when you consider the dynamics of the real estate market. There are millions of property listings available to people on the Web. Each of those listings is unique in style, location, price range and amenities. Would you be comfortable picking a house and buying it without ever physically opening the door? This is a question being asked by real estate brokers across the country. They realize the potential of the Internet but also know that they are an essential part of the process.

A broker usually charges a 6 percent transaction fee on the sale of a home.[21] Brokers can post their listings at hundreds of locations with a single entry using the *Multiple Listing System* (MLS). MLS gives customers a chance to see everything available to them rather than the properties that happen to be favorites of a particular broker.[22] Most realty Web sites offer full descriptions, photos and sometimes a *virtual tour*. Virtual tours offer potential buyers 360-degree views of the interior and exterior of a property. You can demo a virtual tour at **www.ipix.com**. The Web may not yet be the one-stop shop for buying and selling a home, but it does give users a head start in their search and gives brokers a new venue for selling their products.

Homes.com will help you buy, sell and mortgage your property. The site hosts listings and offers search for people buying or selling homes. Calculators are available to help new buyers budget for their purchase. The site helps buyers find the best mortgage terms, builders find the best architects and contractors and sellers find movers and other logistical help. **Propertyfirst.com** and **Rent.net** also offer residential real estate services over the Web.

Some online realty companies offer their listings in an auction. **Rbuy.com** is a online realty auction offering residential, investment and distinctive estate properties. After an undisclosed target selling price has been determined by the realtor on a given property, the property is listed in the online auction. Buyers can then bid on the property, however, if the predetermined price is not met, the property will not be sold. For example, if the target price for the home is set at $200,000 the seller may post the opening bid at $100,000 to generate interest in the property. If the bids never reach $200,000, then the property is not sold. However, in the instance of a bidding war, the selling price may actually exceed the target price.

eBay™ (**www.ebay.com**) recently began offering real estate auctions after partnering with **ZipRealty.com**. Listings range from multimillion-dollar estates to small mobile homes. eBay, **ZipRealty.com** and **Rbuy.com** receive a commission on the sale of any property through their auctions.

The average real estate transaction is a lengthy process requiring each party to read and sign many documents. Digital signatures are now being used to speed up the process by allowing a single signature to be transferred to many documents with the approval of each party. The U.S. government recently passed a bill making digital signatures legally binding. Digital signatures are discussed in detail in Chapter 7, Internet Security.[23]

OpenMLS (**www.openmls.com**) is a company using XML technology to improve the real estate industry's presence online. Through Multiple Listing Services (MLS), real estate listings can be posted and updated quickly and easily. In the past a real estate agent would have to post an individual listing at multiple real estate Web sites. MLS allows the postings to be made once and implemented at any number of sites designated by the realtor. The agent need only type a description of the listing in a text editor (Microsoft Word, note pad, etc.) and upload it into the OpenMLS system. A Web site is then dynamically generated for the listing. This does not require any technical expertise on the part of the realtor. Real estate listing updates can also be managed through the service, reducing the number of outdated listings (XML is discussed in the optional case study, Building an E-business: Introduction to Internet Programming). You can demo the OpenMLS system at (**www.openMLS.com**)

The recent boom in e-business has generated a high demand for commercial real estate. Given that supply does not currently meet demand in most major real estate markets, commercial space is often at a premium. Searching for real estate can be a time-consuming and costly process for many business owners. They must often neglect their daily operations in order to find a space that will fit their needs. These needs include the accommodation of future growth, Internet, telephone, electricity, heating and cooling. Many commercial real estate Web sites have emerged to help business owners and real estate investors improve their efforts. Business owners can run property searches based on specific criteria and find utilities and other service providers on the Web.

LoopNet© (**www.loopnet.com**) will send an e-mail to registered users when properties that fit the customer's preset preferences become available. They provide free Web page templates to brokers who want to mass market their properties. When a seller and a buyer complete a transaction, LoopNet makes a small profit. For five years, LoopNet has been building one of the largest databases of commercial properties on the Web. It has formed partnerships with the country's leading off-line brokers including RE/MAX and Coldwell Banker. They have created multiple revenue streams through value-added services available to customers and brokers. LoopNet plans on making a profit not only on the sale of homes and commercial properties, but also by helping off-line brokers find their way onto the Web. A business owner looking to relocate can search the LoopNet database for a wide variety of criteria. The user can search based on size, location, price, property type (high-rise v. low-rise), and age of the property. Once the owner has located the property, a viewing is arranged and financing can begin.

B2B exchange sites can offer better service to their clients and help property owners save money. In one B2B exchange, property owners serve as a network of incubators for commercial businesses that provide products and services targeted to the property owners' tenants. Simon Property Group, the country's largest holder of mall property recently partnered with Equity Residential Properties Trust, Equity Office Properties Trust and eight other industry leaders. As business incubators, the partners will build an internal network of suppliers, which reduces operating costs. For instance, the partnership might incubate a maintenance company to serve their properties. Since the company would be Internet, costs would be kept to a minimum. The venture, called *Project Constellation*, will incubate companies that the group feels will best target their current customers. The venture has made over 20 investments in companies, offering a wide range of products and services including e-tailing ventures, broadband providers and other technical service companies. Once an incubated company is officially launched, it is given access to the buildings and malls currently owned and operated by the Project Constellation group. Many incubators cannot guarantee that the companies they incubate will find a market. Project Constellation gives the market to their companies.[24]

Apartments.com: Finding an Apartment on the Web [25]

Apartments.com helps people find apartments based on the criteria they desire (Fig. 15.4). **Apartments.com** has access to the same listings available through these real estate agents as well as private offerings. A national database of listings is available free to site visitors. If you are looking for something such as a fireplace or enclosed parking, you can include these amenities in your search. The listings resulting from your search range from private homes to large multistory apartment complexes. Each listing offers a description of the property. Some listings include photographs, floor plans and virtual tours.

    Apartments.com can help you manage the apartment-hunting process from beginning to end. The site can connect you to realtors, moving companies, storage companies, renters insurance and furniture rental companies.

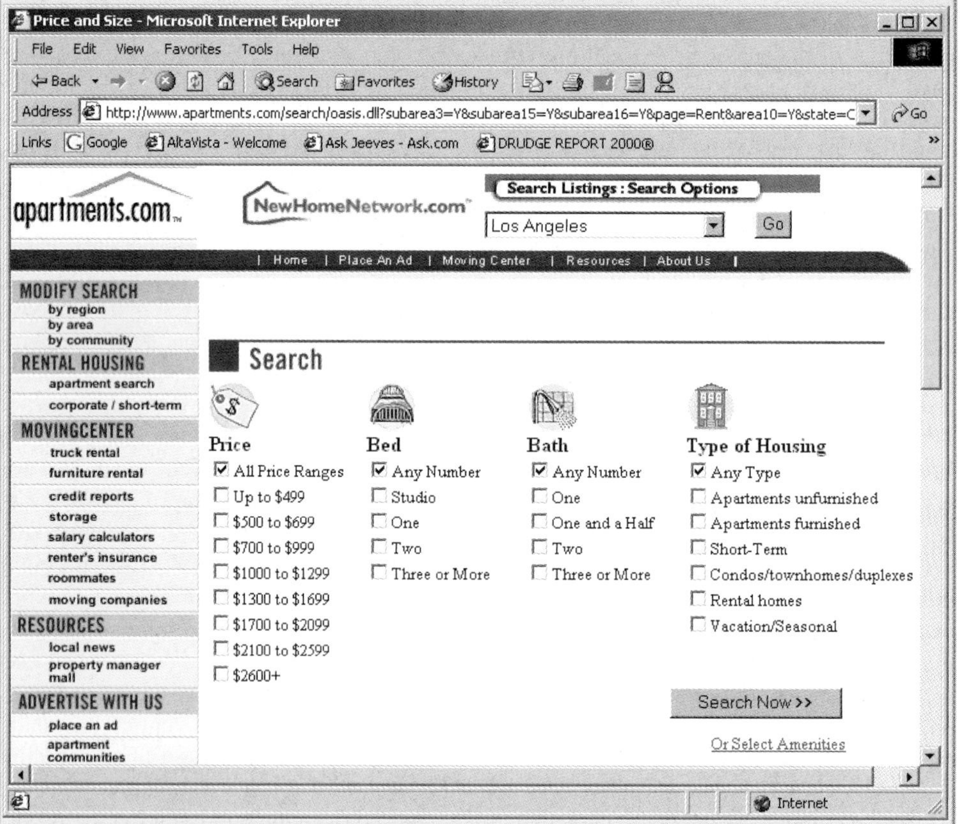

Fig. 15.4 **Apartments.com** can help you find an apartment. (Courtesy of Apartments.com.)

15.12 Online Legal Services

Legal professionals spend much of their time doing research. In the past, law firms had to assemble libraries of case-law directories, trade journals and client data to research each case effectively. Today, a majority of this research can be done online.

The range of Web sites targeted to the legal profession is growing. Sites are available for people looking for legal representation, lawyers looking for a better way to administer their services and law students looking to improve their studies (see Cybersettle feature). Many of these sites are e-commerce enabled offering a wide range of products to the legal community.

There are many legal portals on the Web. The services provided by LEXIS (**www.lexis.com**) and its partner site NEXIS (**www.nexis.com**) are fee based and usually purchased on a subscription basis by law firms. LEXIS provides access to cases and other legal data, as well as relevant news articles. LEXIS speeds the research process. NEXIS is a searchable archive of articles, news and statistical data that can be used to support legal cases. Both sites derive their content from the leading trade journals and case law resources.

Loislaw® (**www.loislaw.com**) is a competitor to LEXIS. It offers many of the same services including case-law databases and news archives. LoisLaw offers a free ten-day trial. Loislaw also offers *GlobalCite^{sm}*, a legal citation service that allows users to hyperlink to cited case law and other documentation with a few mouse clicks. GlobalCite is a search engine that allows users to access all cases and other documentation that cite a particular case instantly. For instance, a person could search for all documents citing Roe v. Wade. Users can also use *LawWatch*™, a system that searches the Loislaw databases for documents related to a lawyer's areas of expertise or current clients.

Cybersettle.com®: *Settling disputes online.* [26]

Cybersettle modifies the online auction business model to resolve various claims and disputes over the Web (Fig. 15.5). Specializing in insurance and workers compensation claims, Cybersettle will mediate any dispute for a small fee paid by both parties. In a traditional dispute both parties must meet with one or more mediators, lawyers and other administrators. This is a costly process for everyone involved. Cybersettle completely automates the process with the Web. A demo of the process is available at **www.cybersettle.com**

The settlement process begins when the claimant enters bids for three rounds of negotiation. Each member of the dispute enters three potential settlement bids. Neither has any knowledge of the others' bids. If a match is made, the settlement is paid. For instance, if a person feels they are entitled to $100,000 in compensation, they may enter their three bids as $200,000, $150,000 and $100,000. The opponent, unaware of these bids, enters three bids. Each round of bids is compared. If the two bids in any given round are within $5000 or 30 percent of one another, the median settlement is paid to the claimant. This process may take a few rounds of negotiation, but will lead to a mutually accepted settlement. The system is available 24 hours every day. The process saves each party in a dispute a great deal of time and money.

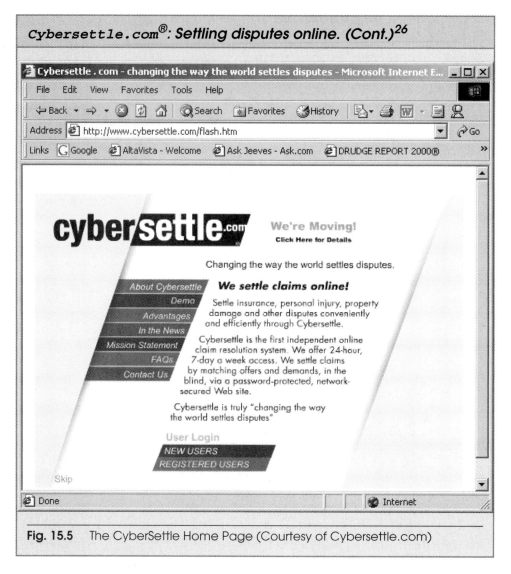

Fig. 15.5   The CyberSettle Home Page (Courtesy of Cybersettle.com)

15.13 Government Online

The Internet began as a government project and now serves as a tool for worldwide communication and trade. The Web is a fast and direct way to interact with local and national politicians. It is a medium that can be used to promote change. You can use the Web to discuss issues with your peers and special interest groups. E-mail, newsgroups and discussion boards are effective means of communicating about political issues.

The U.S. government offers documentation, news and reports over the Web. **Firstgov.com** is a portal dedicated to the United States Government. The portal offers links to various areas of the government and a search engine to help you find government resources. Each of the government's major branches has established a presence on the Web to inform constituents and to conduct research. **Whitehouse.gov** is the online "home" of the president and vice president of the United States. A list of U.S. senators and their contact information is available at **www.senate.gov**. Web users can review recent and archived federal legislature information using *Thomas* (**thomas.loc.gov**). Visitors can access bills passed since 1989, recent roll-call votes, congressional records and transcripts of hearings. The Supreme Court (**www.supremecourtus.gov**) also has a Web site where users can research case law and learn about the federal judicial system and the process of bringing a case to the U.S. Supreme Court.

The government now uses the Web to enhance its crime fighting efforts. **FBI.com** posts news bulletins on unsolved cases. The ten most-wanted criminals are listed with photographs and descriptions of their crimes. The FBI offers rewards for information leading to the capture of fugitives. The Central Intelligence Agency (CIA) Web site (**www.cia.gov**) keeps the public informed about its operations. Although many CIA documents are still classified, visitors to the site can access documentation on some of the most spectacular cases in history. The *Freedom of Information Act* requires all U.S. government agencies to release this information to the public. The act originally passed in 1966 was revised in 1996 to include electronic documentation. Visitors can read formerly classified documents on the *Bay of Pigs*, spy missions and UFO investigations. The site also disseminates information concerning the role of the CIA and its importance to the United States government,

People wishing to conduct business with the United States government should visit the General Services Administration (GSA) at **www.gsa.gov**. The GSA uses the Web and e-commerce to empower government buyers. The GSA Advantage!™ (**www.gsadavantage.gov**) is an e-commerce-enabled government site that allows government purchasing agents and individuals to buy products and services from government vendors.

The Small Business Administration (**www.sba.gov**) is a government agency that provides assistance and guidance to small-business owners. The site provides links to every government agency on the Internet. The SBA offers training courses to small-business owners who wish to improve their practices. Small-business owners seeking answers about legal, financial or operations issues will find them at **www.sba.gov**

15.14 Insurance Online

The insurance industry uses the Internet to inform potential customers about the insurance options that exist for individuals and businesses. These sites act as information repositories to help consumers make more informed decisions about their insurance (**ebix.com** feature). Insurance is traditionally sold by brokers, who build a base of customers and help them decide their level of coverage. Given the number of insurance options that exist across the country, it would be difficult to meet with a broker from every major insurance company. The Internet makes this possible for the average consumer. People can use the Web to receive price quotes and product descriptions from all of the leading insurance companies. They can then make a decision based on this information.

e-Fact 15.2

According to Cyber Dialog, 78 percent of people who own insurance want to be able to reach their carriers online.[27]

Buying insurance is a complex process for both the broker and consumer. The insurance market is competitive and customers tend to be loyal. Prudential Insurance (**www.pruden-**

tial.com) and Metropolitan Insurance (**www.getmet.com**) are two of the major insurance companies that have made an effort to reach customers online. Each of the sites offers informative data to help their customers understand the many different types of insurance available to them. These brick-and-mortar insurance agencies have the advantage of a recognizable brand. Many online insurance companies do not have brand recognition. They must drive customers to their sites with price breaks and other value-added features.

Large insurance firms are facing increased competition from InsWeb® (**www.insweb.com**) and **YouDecide.com**™ which aggregate price quotes from many insurance companies to help visitors comparison shop. **YouDecide.com** will help you search for the lowest car insurance rate available to you based on your driving record and coverage preferences. It searches for the lowest rate among 21 vendors. Both sites offer areas where customers can learn more about other options. These sites do not sell their own insurance. They direct customers to other companies and collect a commission.

15.15 Children Online

Unfortunately, much of the media coverage regarding children and the Web revolves around the less desirable content available. Although pornography and violent content are prevalent, there are also many positive Web sites for children to visit. This topic is discussed further in Chapter 13, Social and Political Issues.

EBIX.com™: Online Insurance Exchange [28]

B2B and B2C exchanges have been created for many industries and business categories (Fig. 15.6). **ebix.com** is an exchange for the insurance community. The site offers products and services for brokers and their customers. Visitors will find informative research and account management features along with company profiles to help people make informed decisions about their insurance.

The site gives brokers 42 different templates to help them build personalized Web sites. *E-agency* is designed to help nontechnical people gain access to the Web. These templates are prebuilt designs that can be used to create an effective e-business site quickly. Insurance carriers can connect with their agents in the B2B exchange section of the site titled **ebix.link**. Consumers can search the **ebix.mall** to find the best insurance options available to them from more than 1000 brokers. Each of these brokers is available to provide quotes and additional services. Once a purchase has been made, customers can manage their policies with the *My Insurance* feature. Customers using this feature can view their recent insurance statements and manage their next payments. The site offers insurance coverage in all major areas including home, life, auto, dental, long-term care and vision insurance.[29]

Customers can learn about their many options in the research center. Tools include a calculator for determining payments and a database of recall information for automobiles of all makes and models. When an automobile company discovers a flaw with an automobile they often recall the car or parts in question. Instructional demos are available on the site. These streaming-video explanations cover the basics of buying and selling insurance on the Web and off-line.

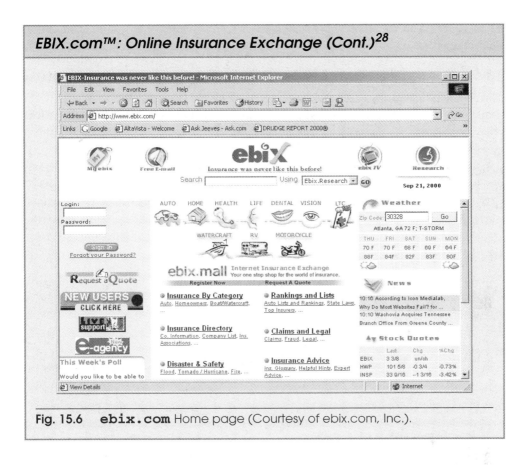

Fig. 15.6   ebix.com Home page (Courtesy of ebix.com, Inc.).

Sesamestreet.com™is an example of a site targeting children in a positive way. The site allows children to read about their favorite Sesame Street characters and learn about the Internet. Children can also send *e-cards* from the site—electronic greeting cards sent via e-mail. The messages are prewritten allowing younger children to send the e-cards. **Sesamestreet.com** is also dedicated to helping parents. Articles on parenting and advice from experts are available on the site. An activity planner helps parents arrange "quality time" activities with their children. The activity planner includes arts and craft projects and games.

Lycos.com™ is a Web portal offering links and news from all areas of the Web. It has recently introduced **LycosZone.com**™, a site designed to keep children interested in the Web. The content consists of games and puzzles, homework help, stories and comics. *The Homework Zone* gives kids access to dictionaries, encyclopedias, atlases and links to Web sites to help them learn a specific subject such as math or English.

Before the Web, children could use their computers to practice their reading, writing and mathematics skills by playing educational games. While this is still possible today, the Internet adds a global element to education. Students can now compete against children at other schools worldwide. A geography lesson can be enhanced through chat sessions with people located in the area the children are studying. Teachers can communicate with parents via e-mail and chat to keep the parents up to speed with their child's development. Education Planet™ (**www.educationplanet.com**) is dedicated to the advancement of the Web in the classroom. The site offers quiz-maker software and prewritten courseware for teachers. Students can chat with students and teachers in their same grade level in the forums.

15.16 Purchasing Event Tickets Online

Ticket purchasing has also been revolutionized be the Web. Users can now search for ticket availability online, eliminating long lines and time consuming telephone calls. (See Ticketmaster feature.)

Ticketmaster™: Selling Tickets Online[30]

Ticketmaster online (**www.ticketmaster.com**) was able to transition its ticket offering services onto the Web, which improved its service and increased its business. Customers looking for tickets to concerts, sporting events, theater and family events will probably find them at **Ticketmaster.com** (Fig. 15.7). Ticketmaster online customers have access to seating charts, arena information and directions to the shows. In the past, if a customer was not familiar with the arena, they had no way of knowing how good the available seats were. Customers can also purchase CDs and other entertainment-related merchandise directly from the site.

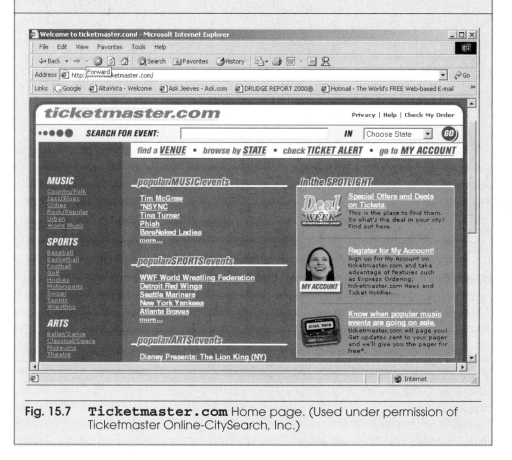

Fig. 15.7   Ticketmaster.com Home page. (Used under permission of Ticketmaster Online-CitySearch, Inc.)

> ## *Ticketmaster™: Selling Tickets Online*[30] *(Cont.)*
>
> Customers who know which event they want to attend can locate their tickets by using the search bar. The site allows you to search by artists, venue and category. The site also runs special offers and discounts for some of these events.

e-Fact 15.3

According to Forrester research, by 2003 one-fifth of all event tickets will be purchased on the Internet.[31]

Other ticket vendors offering online services include **Tickets.com**™, **tixx.com** and **TicketWeb.com**™. **Pollstar.com** allows you to search for upcoming events by venue, artists and location. **TicketCity.com**™ and **culturefinder.com**® also offer ticketing services.

15.17 Genealogy Online

In the past, people had to track their ancestry using traditional outlets such as the local library and city hall. This process can be extremely time consuming and can lead to many dead ends. The Web hosts many sites for people looking to trace their lineage. These sites aggregate ancestry data and simplify the process with searching capabilities.

Genealogy.com™ helps people find their ancestors and build family trees. The site also offers a free search, which can help you trace your lineage. **Genealogy.org** lists almost 2000 genealogy sites based on their popularity. These sites range from individual-families sites to broad databases of families seeking information on relatives. **Ancestry.com**® provides death notices, phone numbers, address listings and family-tree information. Many of its services are free.

Imagine discovering that your ancestors had invested in land in the 1850s and you might now own the rights! Imagine a great uncle leaving a valuable collection of wines in a bank vault with you as the closest heir. **Missingmoney.com**™ has formed a partnership with the National Association of Unclaimed Property Administrators (Naupa) (**www.naupa.com**) to help connect people with long-lost valuables. A recent visitor to the site found that she was owed money from two separate insurance companies. Her parents had taken out insurance policies 30 years ago and never informed their daughter. The site collects listings of unclaimed property left in bank accounts, safe deposit boxes, insurance claims and similar areas.[32] The *National Unclaimed Property Database*© (**www.nupd.com**) also provides a free unclaimed property search.

15.18 Internet and World Wide Web Resources

Law

lawlinks.com
This site is a legal portal with links, legal forms and a directory of attorneys.

www.ilrg.com
This is one of the most comprehensive legal resources on the Web with over 4000 links to law-related resources.

www.findlaw.com

FindLaw is one of the premier legal portals on the Web. The site hosts content pertaining to attorneys, students, the public and businesses.

Medicine

www.medlineplus.com

Created by the national library of medicine, this site hosts information on health and nutrition and offers dictionaries, drug information and medical directories.

MDchoice.com

This is an information resource for medical professionals and consumers. The site offers a search capability that gives users access to 6000 medical journals, the latest news in medicine and career-opportunity listings.

www.ama-assn.org

The American Medical Association is the professional association for the healthcare industry. The site monitors the industry and provides news and resources for medical professionals.

Insurance

www.quickeninsurance.com

One of the leaders in online insurance, Quicken offers free quotes on home, auto, life and medical insurance.

www.insure.com

This site is an insurance portal that offers links to various insurance carriers and brokers.

Government

www.Webgov.com

This is the official portal of the U.S. Government, offering links to its agencies and departments of the United States government.

www.firstgov.com

Visit this site for comprehensive listing of government Web sites.

Online Grocery Services

www.kozmo.com

Kozmo delivers movies, DVDs, food, magazines and many other convenience items to your doorstep. The site hosts a catalog of products that will typically be dropped off by a messenger within an hour of your purchase.

www.homeruns.com

Homeruns is a grocery delivery service exclusive to the greater Boston area.

www.peapod.com

Peapod, and online grocery store, was founded in 1996 and is a partner of Stop & Shop.

Tickets

NATB.org

The National Association of Ticket Brokers is dedicated to keeping the ticketing industry fair and ethical.

moviefone.com

Visitors can learn about films which are currently playing, and purchase tickets in advance.

tixx.com
You can order tickets to your favorite sporting events, concerts, theater productions and more at this site.

culturefinder.com
Dance, opera, theater and visual arts are some of the categories available on Culturefinder. This site offers a nationwide database of ticketing information.

Real Estate

propertyfirst.com
This site specializes in commercial-property sales and leasing across the United States. News and updates on recent purchases are also listed.

foxtons.com
This real estate site serves the United Kingdom, providing information about buying and selling homes, leasing property and moving.

Travel

www.revelex.com
This online service allows user to book reservations for airline tickets, car rental and hotels in a dynamic market. The prices change based on the volume of people bidding.

www.savvio.com
This online travel agency allows users to pick a personal itinerary and a travel provider and then decide the price they would like to pay, all while earning mileage and traveler points. As time passes the ticket prices drop until all tickets are sold.

www.lowestfare.com
Lowestfare is more than an online fare finder. This site also includes a currency converter, links to world events and news, weather and maps.

www.fareagent.com
Fareagent is a search engine designed to help consumers find the lowest airfares. An e-mail newsletter updates customers if their desired fare becomes available.

www.trip.com
This is an online travel agency that includes customized flight planning for corporate or personal travel, a trip planner and city destination guide.

Retail Products

www.cribs2go.com
This site is a one-stop shop for parents with infant children. Household items such as barricades, cabinet locks, formula and diapers are available.

www.iderive.com
iDerive is a unique retail product site that offers discounts on automobiles, hotel reservations, airline tickets and consumer electronics. When a customer puts in an order, iDerive searches for a vendor willing to sell the product. If the product is not available, iDerive will pay the customer a small reward.

www.overstock.com
This online shopping site offers electronics, computers, sporting goods, gifts, jewelry, housewares and apparel.

www.e-centives.com
E-centives offers digital coupons tailored to your shopping needs. Coupons can be redeemed from participating vendors.

SUMMARY

- Consumers cannot touch, feel or taste the products they are viewing on the Web.

- Some of the world's most successful clothing designers have set up shop on the Web to offer their products. Many of these retailers attract customers by offering discounts and rebates.

- The Internet is improving the healthcare industry by empowering consumers and members of the medical community. They can discuss medical issues and seek information about their ailments at a variety of Web sites.

- As a medical community site, Healtheon WebMD (`www.Webmd.com`) offers a repository of documentation relating to the medical field. WebMD can also help you find doctors and medical professionals.

- MyHealthRecord is a free service for all members that allows you to keep track of your medical history. You can use it to store information about past illnesses, current prescriptions and anticipated health risks.

- WebRN offers drug databases, clinical research, tools and tips, discussion groups and access to supplies.

- Web surfers can save time and money by booking their travel arrangements over the Web. The Web gives people access to much of the same information previously accessible only to travel agents.

- Travelocity uses shopping-bot technology. This technology scans databases and Web sites to find travel arrangements.

- Web sites that match empty truck capacity with the shipping needs of many companies now exist. So, companies can split the cost of a full truckload.

- Automotive Web sites help users explore options more efficiently than by traveling among dealerships. Online automobile appraisers offer users leverage in negotiating a price on a new car by giving them access to instant value estimates.

- The Internet improves the way cars are manufactured by improving communication among departments responsible for producing automobiles.

- GM, Ford and DaimlerChrysler recently announced their plans to build the world's largest business-to-business automotive exchange, Covisint. The exchange is designed to help reduce the cost of producing automobiles by linking raw materials suppliers, parts suppliers and production plants.

- Customers using Covisint will someday be able to design a custom automobile and drive it home within a week of placing the order. Internet communication will make this type of rapid customization possible.

- A number of companies have set up energy exchanges where buyers and sellers come to communicate, buy, sell and distribute energy. These companies sell crude oil, electricity and the products and systems for distributing them.

- Emissions allowances are traded by different nations based on the needed level of emissions for that particular country.

- Outsourcing refers to the process of hiring a another company to do a job or project.

- Art is traditionally sold in galleries or through mall vendors. The Internet gives artists a chance to reach the world with virtual galleries.

- The range of Web sites targeted to the legal profession is growing. Sites are available for people looking for legal representation. Some sites help lawyers administer their services. Others help law students improve their studies.

- The U.S. government recently passed a bill making digital signatures, signatures encoded for a specific individual and processed within a computer, legally binding.

- The U.S. government offers documentation, news and reports over the Web. It is possible to find information from almost every segment of the federal government on the Web. You can also connect with your state and local governments online.

- E-mail, newsgroups and discussion boards are effective means of communication when discussing political issues.

- The Internet also helps solve crimes. **FBI.com** posts news bulletins on famous and unsolved cases. The ten most-wanted criminals are listed with photographs and descriptions of their crimes. The FBI offers rewards for information leading to the capture of fugitives.

- You can review recent and archived federal legislature information online using *Thomas* (**thomas.loc.gov**) at no charge. You can access bills passed since 1989, recent roll-call votes, congressional records and transcripts of hearings.

- If you are interested in doing business with the U.S. government you can visit **GSA.gov**. The General Services Administration (GSA) uses the Web and e-commerce to empower government buyers.

- The Small Business Administration (**www.sba.gov**) is a government agency that provides assistance and guidance to small-business owners. The site provides links to every government agency on the Internet.

- The insurance industry uses the Internet to inform potential customers about the insurance options that exist for individuals and businesses. Whether you are looking to insure your life, home, automobile or business, these sites act as information repositories to help you make more informed decisions about their insurance.

- Ticketmaster online (**www.ticketmaster.com**) was able to translate its ticket offerings onto the Web, instantly improving service and increasing business. Ticketmaster online customers have access to seating charts, arena information and directions to the shows.

- According to Forrester Research, by 2003 one-fifth of all event tickets will be purchased on the Internet.

- The Internet makes it easy to learn the history of your lineage. **Genealogy.com** is a site that helps you discover your history. The site helps you find your ancestors and will also help you build a family tree that can be accessed by people worldwide.

- **Genealogy.org** lists almost 2000 genealogy sites based on their popularity. These sites range from individual-families sites to broad databases of families seeking information on relatives. **Ancestry.com** provides death notices, phone numbers, address listings and family tree information gathered from across the country. Many services are free.

TERMINOLOGY

digital signature	load matching
e-cards	Multiple Listing Service (MLS)
electronic ticket	name-your-price home delivery service
FastCar system	outsourcing
Freedom of Information Act	shopping-bot technology
genealogy	Small Business Administration (SBA)
General Services Administration (GSA)	vertical portal
Health Insurance Portability and	visual galleries
Accountability Act (HIPAA)	

SELF-REVIEW EXERCISES

15.1   State whether the following are *true* or *false*. If the answer is *false*, explain why.
   a)   The General Services Agency is designed to help small business owners improve their business practices.
   b)   **Pollstar.com** allows you to research politics and cast votes in various polls.
   c)   LycosZone is a portal site designed for young professionals in the real estate industry.
   d)   **Lexis.com** is an automotive Web site featuring product descriptions and news.
   e)   Load matching refers to the practice of filling a partially empty truck with loads from multiple companies.

15.2   Fill in the blank in each of the following statements:
   a)   Covisint is a B2B exchange site for the _____ industry.
   b)   Airline passengers no longer need to worry about losing their paper tickets. Many airlines now book flights electronically using _____.
   c)   **ebix.com** is a exchange for the _____ industry.
   d)   _____ is the name of a joint partnership that will incubate businesses to serve the residential and commercial real estate industry.
   e)   The _____ industry benefits from sites such as Site59.

ANSWERS TO SELF-REVIEW EXERCISES

15.1   a) False. The General Services Agency promotes and supports government commerce. b) False. Pollstar is a live-music search engine that will help you find an upcoming concert. c) False. **LycosZone**, is a segment of the Lycos portal dedicated to education and entertainment for children. d) False. **Lexis.com** is one of the most widely used legal Web sites. e) True.

15.2   a) automotive b) electronic tickets c) insurance d) Project Constellation e) travel

EXERCISES

15.3   State whether the following are true or false. If the answer is false, explain why.
   a)   A bill making digital signatures, signatures encoded for a specific individual and processed within a computer, legally binding was passed.
   b)   The small business association is a government agency designed to aid entrepreneurs which advice, financial assistance, and consulting.
   c)   e-cards are used by members of a B2B exchange to verify the identity of other suppliers.
   d)   The Web gives people access to much of the same information previously accessible only to travel agents.
   e)   The insurance industry created the General Services Agency as a way of linking the many individual insurance companies into a single database companies.

15.4   Fill in the blank in each of the following statements:
   a)   The process of hiring an outside firm or another internal division to complete specific tasks is referred to as _____.
   b)   _____ is the study of family and lineage.
   c)   The _____ was passed to improve the standards of the medical industry.
   d)   The _____ gave the U.S. public access to formally classified government documentation.
   e)   Many online art dealers showcase the work of artists in _____.

15.5   Categorize each of the following items as it best relates to the medical, legal, government or automotive industries.
   a)   Lexis
   b)   **Medscape.com**

c) **autobytel.com**

d) SBA

e) Healtheon

f) Thomas

15.6   Trace your lineage at **Ancestry.com**, **genealogy.com** and **genealogy.org**. Search both your surname and your mother's maiden name. Try your friends, maybe they will give you a reward! Document your findings. Next use your findings to search for lost money at **missing-money.com**. Are you or any of your ancestors entitled to money or valuables? Describe the effect the Web has had on our ability to learn more about our past.

15.7   Visit **propertyfirst.com**, **realty.com** and **foxtons.com**. Conduct a search for a two-bedroom apartment with covered parking and an elevator in your home state. Search for an apartment with a monthly rent of $500 dollars. Critique each Web site based on ease of use. Describe each site and include an explanation of your findings.

15.8   **Yet2.com** aggregates information on patents and other intellectual property that has been listed for sale by various vendors. These intellectual property rights can be bought or licensed. Visit the **Yet2.com** Web site and search the listing for energy, health, entertainment and law. Build a spreadsheet to document the result. Describe at least one piece of property for each key word. What are the benefits of the **Yet2.com** system?

15.9   Visit **Homes.com** and find the calculators section. There are a number of calculators in this section designed to help home buyers and sellers make informed decisions. Use the mortgage calculator to determine the monthly payment necessary to mortgage a home costing, $100,000, $250,000, $750,000 and $1,000,000. Make a list of the payments as provided by the calculator. Conduct the test again after changing the interest rate to 10 percent and then to 6 percent. How do your responses differ?

15.10   Visit the GSA Advantage! at **www.gsaadvantage.gov**. Search the database for five different items. Include keywords food, clothing, transportation, training and e-commerce. The site serves a broad range of agencies within the government and must therefore store many varying products in its database. Make a list of the top five results from each search.

WORKS CITED

The notation <**www.domain-name.com**> indicates that the citation is for information found at that Web site.

1.   I. Svete, "A Shock to the System," *The Industry Standard* 10 April 2000: 243.

2.   <**www.webMD.com**>.

3.   <*www.travelocity.com*>.

4.   <**www.tradiant.com/about**>.

5.   S. Lais "Still a World Wild Web in Trucking Industry," *Computerworld* 3 April 2000: 36.

6.   J. Smolka, "Used Cars, New Model" *Fast Company* July 2000: 322.

7.   L. Copeland "DaimlerChrylser Drives FastCar Web Initiative," *ComputerWorld* 14 August 2000: 12.

8.   T. Burt "Industry Faces Up To Challenge of E-Commerce," *Financial Times* 14 June 2000: I.

9.   S. Konicki "Covisint's Rough Road," *InformationWeek* 7 August 2000: 42.

10.   E. Conces, "Energy Industry," <**www.hoovers.com**> 2000.

11.   D. Radcliff, "Power Struggle," <**www.computerworld.com**>, 25 Oct. 1999.

12.   M. Hamblin, "Intranet Enables More Competitive Bids for Wholesalers," <**www.computer-world.com**> 5 June 2000.

13. <www.enron.com>

14. T. Mull, "Energy Companies Draw Internet Battle Lines," *Internet Week* 24 July 2000: 13.

15. W. Zellner, "Enron Electrified," *Business Week*, 24 July 2000:54-58.

16. J. Mullich "Altranet Serves as a Natural Resource," *Information Week* 12 June 2000: 152.

17. C. Adler, et. al., "the FSB 25," 24 April 2000, <www.fsb.com>.

18. D. Tapscot, D. Ticoll, "Retail Evolution" *The Standard*, 24 July 2000: 220.

19. T. Monroy, "Online Grocery Shopping: A Way Of Life," *Inter@ctive Week* 10 July 2000: 52.

20. D. Tapscot, D. Ticoll, 220.

21. M. Hamblen, "Real Estate Agents Can Tap in to MLS Listing on the Net," <www.computer-world.com> 20 May 1999.

22. M. Hamblen

23. T. Burney "Real Estate Industry Seeks to Make Home-Buying Paperless," *Chattanooga Times* 3 September 2000: I5.

24. B. Martinez, "Big Property Owners Team Up for E-Commerce," *The Wall Street Journal* 4 May 2000: A3.

25. <www.apartments.com>.

26. <www.cybersettle.com>.

27. C. Le Beau, "Insurance Online," *The Industry Standard* 10 April 2000: 235.

28. <www.ebix.com>.

29. G. Du Bois, "Suite Puts Agencies Online," *eWeek* 14 August 2000: 38.

30. <www.Ticketmaster.com>.

31. M. Wagner "Taking on Ticketmaster," *InternetWorldNews* 1 October 1999: 46.

32. G. W. Weinstein, "Lost Family Fortunes Found on the Web," *Financial Times* 3 September 2000: XXIII.

16

Online Banking and Investing

Objectives

- To discuss online banking services.
- To understand the differences between hybrid and Internet-only banks.
- To examine online lending.
- To discuss the ways in which online trading is changing the investment industry.
- To examine the advantages and disadvantages of trading online.
- To review Web sites that provide online investing.
- To understand the impact of the Web on financial planning.
- To explore online tutorials, demonstrations and stock market games.

Put not your trust in money, but put your money in trust.
Oliver Wendell Holmes, Sr.

'Tis money that begets money.
English Proverb

We estimate the wisdom of nations by seeing what they did with their surplus capital.
Ralph Waldo Emerson

The propensity to truck, barter and exchange one thing for another . . . is common to all men, and to be found in no other race of animals.
Adam Smith

Outline

16.1   Introduction
16.2   Online Banking Services
    16.2.1   Hybrid Banks
    16.2.2   Internet-Only Banks
16.3   Online Loans
16.4   How the Web Is Changing the Investment Community
    16.4.1   Electronic Communication Networks (ECNs)
    16.4.2   Online Trading
    16.4.3   Online Bond Trading
16.5   Merging Financial Services
16.6   Financial Aggregation Services
16.7   Wireless Banking and Trading
16.8   Financial Planning Online
16.9   Internet and World Wide Web Resources

Summary • Terminology • Self-Review Exercises • Answers to Self-Review Exercises • Exercises • Works Cited

16.1 Introduction

Banking and investing have been revolutionized by the Internet. The ability to manage, buy, sell, trade, lend and aggregate funds has had a profound impact on the development of Web-based and traditional brick-and-mortar online financial services. Intense competition continues to drive these businesses to add new products and services and improve those already existing.

In this chapter, we discuss online banking services provided by Internet-only banks (i.e., those with only a Web presence) and click-and-mortar banks (i.e., those with both a physical and an online presence) and the advantages and disadvantages of each model. We also explore the impact of the Internet on Wall Street and give a detailed explanation of online stock and bond trading, electronic communication networks (ECNs) and financial aggregators. Online lending and mortgage services and financial planning are also discussed.

16.2 Online Banking Services

One of the fastest growing online service industries is online banking, either as an extension of services from a traditional bank or as a pure online entity.[1] To maintain and capture market share, many brick-and-mortar banks have become click-and-mortar by adding the Internet as a method to deliver their services. *Internet-only banks* are attempting to establish a presence, but lack the brand awareness and recognition of the click-and-mortar banks. As the struggle for market share intensifies, banks will have to find ways to differentiate themselves from their competitors. Internet banking services can reduce a bank's expenses. Offering customers access to account information online decreases printing costs and the number of customer service phone calls.

Enabling customers to pay their bills and write checks online decreases the *float*—the time it takes for checks to clear after they have been sent for payment or deposited. For example, if you deposit your check at an ATM, the float would be the amount of time it takes for the bank to receive your check from the ATM, process the check and send it to the bank it was drawn upon to collect the funds (this same process can be applied to companies accepting payment for products or services). Because the Internet delivers payments faster than the mail does, money can be transferred more quickly. This frees up cash and decreases *accounts receivable*—the expected amount of payments owed to a company for products and services sold to customers. Having funds delivered faster also allows the person or institution receiving the funds to earn interest on them for a longer period of time.

Online banking services can also be beneficial to customers, who thereby can avoid buying stamps and do not have to send bills out early to make sure they get to their destinations on time. Account information is available 24-by-7, allowing individuals to review their account history and make transfers. People can view a detailed account history at one time online instead of listening to each individual transaction over the phone from an automated teller.

Despite the convenience of online banking, there are risks. Customers should be aware of security breaches. The *Office of the Currency (OCC)* has warned people that sites mimicking bank sites can scam them for their account information.[2]

In this section, we examine the similarities and differences of both Internet-only and click-and-mortar banks. We also discuss how each type of bank and its customers are affected by online banking.

e-Fact 16.1

International Data Corporation expects that by 2003, there will be over 32 million people doing online banking.[3]

16.2.1 Hybrid Banks

The *hybrid bank model* (brick-and-mortar banks offering online services) has found much success, with nine of the nation's 10 leading commercial banks offering online services.[4] Brick-and-mortar banks are adding the Web as a channel of service to remain competitive in the banking industry. Fleet, Citibank, Bank of America, Chase Manhattan Bank and many others now offer online banking services. The prominence of brick-and-mortar brand names increase customers' comfort levels when banking online.

e-Fact 16.2

Giga Information Group's research reveals that Wells Fargo has approximately 1 million consumers banking online, while Net.Bank, the largest Internet-only bank, has approximately 100,000 members.[5]

Banks such as Wells Fargo and Bank of America offer online banking and other financial services (see feature Wells Fargo). Despite the growing number of Internet-only banks, customers still like to know that there is a physical branch to visit in case they need to speak with a representative.[6] The physical presence also includes the large network of ATMs that exist for many of the major click-and-mortar banks. Many brick-and-mortar banks offering online banking charge monthly fees to use online bill-paying services.[7]

e-Fact 16.3

According to Jupiter Communications, by 2005, the number of households paying bills on-line will exceed 40 million.[8]

Offering services online has also become important to the survival and growth of small local banks that have traditionally relied on customer relations skills to attract customers. By going online, small banks can offer competitive services and attract national customers. Smaller banks sometimes partner with third-party service providers to make the transition to the Internet. Overall, this is cheaper than larger banks' attempts to implement electronic banking from scratch.[11]

Busey Bank, based in the college town of Urbana, Illinois, went online in an effort to retain college customers who were away for the summer months. In a year it doubled its online customers, citing the customer-service opportunities available through e-mail as a major factor in its success.[12]

Salem Five Cents Savings Bank, a small bank in Salem, Massachusetts, started its virtual bank and eventually changed the virtual bank's name to **directbanking.com**™ (originally **salemfive.com**). The virtual bank's 40,000 customers bring in about 15 percent of the bank's deposits.[13] Salem Five Cents Bank plans to open New England "cyberbranches" for **directbanking.com** to provide Internet kiosks (allowing customers to interact with a customer service representative through video-conferencing over the Internet) and virtual ATM machines.[14] Salem is also considering employing live tellers in the future. Visit **www.salemfive.com/homebanking/homebankingdemo/4/v/p1index.htm** to view a demo of **directbanking.com**'s banking services.

Bricks-and-Mortar turned Clicks-and-Mortar: Wells Fargo[9]

Wells Fargo (**www.wellsfargo.com**) is a leading provider of online banking services. The bank has achieved a large online clientele based on the strength of its traditional banking services.

Services are broken into three main sectors: personal finance, small business and commercial banking. Wells Fargo promotes itself as a financial resource center, offering personal banking customers free bill-paying and checking-account comparisons, as well as a help center for paying taxes.

Wells Fargo also plans to unveil a portal site that will offer financial services, such as stock trading, news, weather and other services.[10] The site will send e-mail alerts of price changes in customers' stocks. The bank is also planning to use its portal site as a *financial aggregator*, which would allow people to view information from all of their financial accounts.

In addition to the portal service, Wells Fargo is establishing specialized resource centers for students, retirees and those looking to purchase cars or homes. Such centers offer financial information and support. The retirement center, for example, offers education and interactive tools on retirement planning, featuring special reports from outside sources. Customers can also open IRAs online and seek financial counseling. The student center features information on student checking and credit, as well as links to outside loan and scholarship information.

Bricks-and-Mortar turned Clicks-and-Mortar: Wells Fargo[9] (Cont.)

The Wells Fargo site cross-markets the products and services of other companies, such as Internet access from Pacific Bell.

16.2.2 Internet-Only Banks

Internet-only banks offer convenience and often lower fees and higher interest rates to their customers (see feature NetBank).[15] Using the Internet to offer banking can lower costs of buildings and equipment and can decrease the payroll as traditional bank employee roles are eliminated.

These banks have to accept deposits by mail because they lack physical branches. This kind of transaction can take longer, especially if the customer is located in another state, unless the customer is making electronic deposits. Internet-only banks also have little brand recognition compared to brick-and-click banks and will have to develop and invest in a strong marketing strategy to attract customers (see Chapter 8, Internet Marketing). Even though Internet-only banks are insured by the FDIC, customers may not feel comfortable because they cannot visit a physical branch or teller.

Claritybank.com is an Internet-only bank that specializes in loans to new-economy firms.[16] **Claritybank.com**'s marketing and Web site stress the speed of online banking as a selling point to technology firms. **Claritybank.com** offers a customized portal service and a B2B center. If customers keep a navigation bar with **Claritybank.com**'s logo on their screens, they are eligible for free Internet access. After only two weeks in operation, the bank had collected $6 million in deposits and enjoyed strong loan-application volume.[17]

Another online bank that has enjoyed success is OneCore (**www.onecore.com**), which targets small businesses at different stages of growth by offering customized packages. OneCore can provide customized services and personalized customer service to its clients. OneCore offers financial-overview services that are compatible with leading financial software packages and can provide payroll and 401(k) services for its clients. Merchants can use OneCore solutions to facilitate credit-card processing and to streamline payables (simplifying bill payment by providing the process online). Additionally, an "electronic financial officer" is available to answer business financial questions via e-mail.[18]

NetBank®: An Internet-Only Bank[19]

NetBank began offering lending, investing and high-interest checking services on the Web in 1996. NetBank is the largest bank operating solely on the Internet. Customers have the ability to open checking, savings and credit accounts that can be managed from their desktop. They can also plan for retirement using IRAs and other types of investment accounts, as well as conduct online trading.

NetBank®: An Internet-Only Bank[19] (Cont.)

NetBank customers can obtain mortgage, car and business loans by applying directly online. All details of this process are outlined on the NetBank Web site. Rates and calculators are also available to help you make an informed decision. Customers have the choice of using money-market funds, buying certificates of deposit (CDs), trading stocks and bonds and investing in their retirement.

Customers can also obtain a line of credit, free online bill payment and presentment, an ATM card and a Visa credit card. For a demonstration of online bill payment and presentment visit **www.netbank.com/demo/demo_index.htm**. This demo shows the customer log-in process and services, including viewing one's account history, making transfers, making payments and finding loan payments.

Some Internet-only banks are attempting to establish a physical presence. For example, E*TRADE's online banking service has placed interactive kiosks that can accept deposits in stores.[20] Other Internet-only banks allow customers to use specially designed cards at existing ATMs, and some banks will reimburse customers for the fees paid to use these ATMs.[21] To appeal to customers, Internet-only banks may also offer lower minimum balances. See Fig. 16.1 for examples of other Internet-only banks and online-banking information sites.

Internet-Only Banks	Description
BankAtlantic.com	Offers services in Spanish. Provides trading services through ShareBuilder™. Offers customers personal, small-business and commercial banking.
CompuBank® (www.compubank.com)	Offers clickrewards™ (www.clickrewards.com), allowing customers to earn rewards for direct-deposit and check-card purchases. Pays above-average interest on checking accounts and offers free online bill payment.
SFNB® (www.sfnb.com)	Offers its customers the *Share the Wealth* program, which rewards customers for referring new customers. This bank also offers advice on managing your money and provides budget, savings and retirement calculations.
nBank (www.nbank.com)	Provides personal and business banking. Business services include merchant credit-card processing and business-credit inquiry. nBank also offers Internet service to local areas in Atlanta and Georgia.

Fig. 16.1   Internet-only banks and online banking information sites.

Internet-Only Banks	Description
`everbank.com`	Offers free online bill payment, mortgage services, the *everCard*™ *Visa® Platinum* credit card with free credit-card management online and trading services through EverTrade Direct Brokerage, Inc.
`Gomez.com`™	Evaluates e-commerce customer experiences. Coverage includes banks, brokers, credit cards, home buying, travel and shopping services and health sites. This site provides its opinion of the best online banks and allows visitors to rate and review the banks.
`CyberInvest.com`	Offers information on and evaluations of different financial service providers. Visitors can check out sections such as the *Bond Center, Brokerage Center, Educational Center, Mortgage Center* and *Global Investing Center.*
`bankonline.com`	Helps visitors find institutions that offer online banking, insurance comparison shopping, financial planning and loan and credit applications

Fig. 16.1   Internet-only banks and online banking information sites.

16.3 Online Loans

Traditionally, when seeking a loan, companies and individuals would deal with a few different lenders to locate financing. Filling out the documents and comparing options was a time-consuming process. Through the Internet, this process can be more efficient, sometimes returning loan approvals within minutes. The Internet also gives people access to many lending institutions, enabling those seeking loans to shop for the best deals.

E-LOAN (**www.eloan.com**) is an online loan services company that offers home, auto and small-business loans and credit cards. The company provides professional service throughout the complete loan process and allows customers to contact customer service representatives to ask questions or make comments about their loans while they are viewing their accounts. E-LOAN, like many other online loan services, allows people to compare and apply for loans from multiple lenders. Customers can monitor the process from start to finish by signing up for E-TRACK℠. This service provides customers with a continuously updated timeline showing when E-LOAN received necessary documents, when paperwork is due and other details of the loans (Fig. 16.2). Customers can also receive details of the closing costs of their loans. To view the E-TRACK demo, visit **www.eloan.com/s/ etrack?stage=login&loginnow=true**.

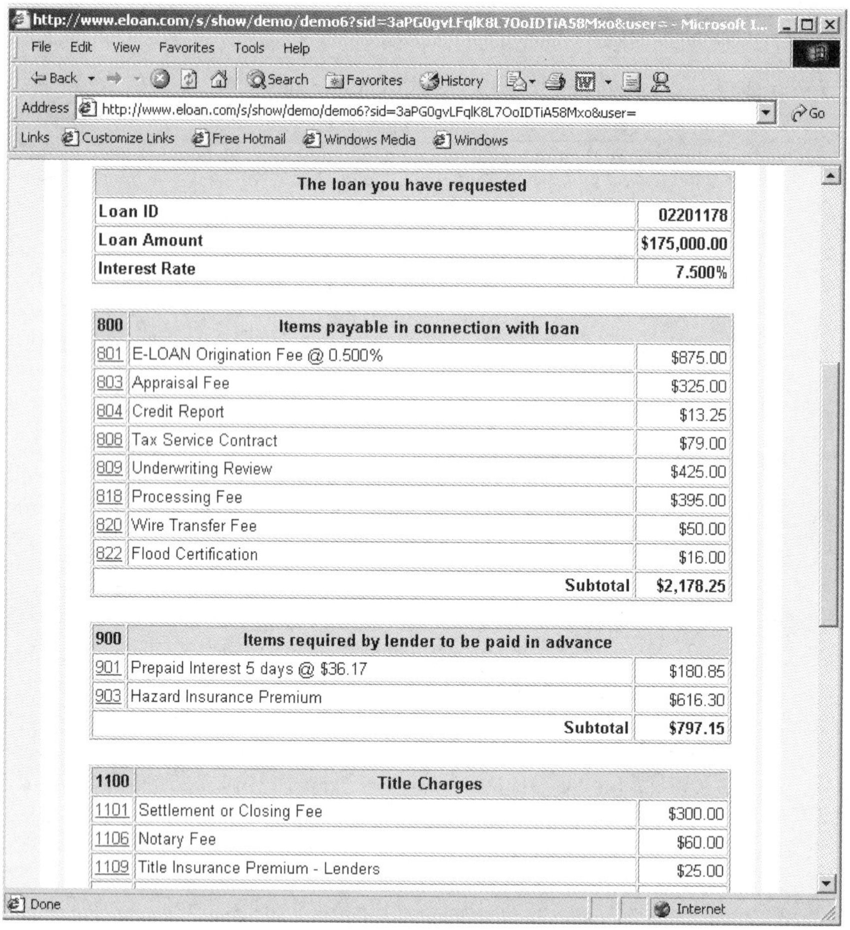

The loan you have requested	
Loan ID	02201178
Loan Amount	$175,000.00
Interest Rate	7.500%

800	Items payable in connection with loan	
801	E-LOAN Origination Fee @ 0.500%	$875.00
803	Appraisal Fee	$325.00
804	Credit Report	$13.25
808	Tax Service Contract	$79.00
809	Underwriting Review	$425.00
818	Processing Fee	$395.00
820	Wire Transfer Fee	$50.00
822	Flood Certification	$16.00
	Subtotal	$2,178.25

900	Items required by lender to be paid in advance	
901	Prepaid Interest 5 days @ $36.17	$180.85
903	Hazard Insurance Premium	$616.30
	Subtotal	$797.15

1100	Title Charges	
1101	Settlement or Closing Fee	$300.00
1106	Notary Fee	$60.00
1109	Title Insurance Premium - Lenders	$25.00

Fig. 16.2 E-LOAN's E-TRACK demo. (Courtesy of E-LOAN, Inc.)

PrimeStreet™ (**`www.primestreet.com`**) is an online lending source for small businesses that also provides solutions for financial institutions and loan brokers. Businesses can use the *Financing Adviser* to get a quick suggestion of the type of financing needed (term/installment loans, credit cards, leases and lines of credit). Information on starting a business, marketing products, managing finances or retiring or selling the business is available at PrimeStreet's *Financial Library & Links* section. A free *Credit Check-Up* informs businesses of their financial standings. This can be used to estimate the likelihood of receiving a loan. It does not guarantee acceptance for loans, but it can give a business an idea of how its profile appears. Credit reports can also be purchased from the site.

To begin searching for the best loan to fit your needs, you can use PrimeStreet's *Loan Auctions*. First you must complete an application designating the type and terms of a loan. Then the application is sent to the various lenders that work with PrimeStreet. The results of the loan application can be monitored through a URL link sent from PrimeStreet. A bid can be selected at any point in time.

LiveCapital™ (`www.livecapital.com`) is another company that offers online financing for businesses. The *LiveCapital Finance Platform*™ enables companies to offer financing services from their Web sites. `companyfinance.com` also offers online lending services for businesses. The *Small Business Administration Office of Advocacy* lists legitimate commercial institutions that make loans to small businesses at `www.sba.gov/advo/stats/lending`.

In addition to personal, business and automobile loans, Internet users can search the Web to find mortgages online. Online mortgage services decrease the time it takes to find a mortgage, however many online companies still need standard paperwork that cannot be completed over the Internet.[22] However, digital signatures may allow these companies to accept documents legally over the Web. See Chapter 7, Internet Security, and Chapter 11, Legal and Ethical Issues; Internet Taxation, for in-depth discussions of digital signatures.

`Ditech.com`[SM] is an online mortgage service company. The loan application process can be completed over the phone and computer through `Ditech.com`. The company offers money management calculators and free *e-Appraisals* allowing users to find approximate values of their homes. Users can also specify the interest rates and fees they want for a loan, and `Ditech.com` will alert them for free by e-mail when loans fitting these requirements are found. Other sites offering online mortgage services include `MortgageRamp.com`[SM] and LoopNet (`www.loopnet.com`).

Sites differ in the way they offer mortgages. Some sites provide mortgages directly from the lenders. Others act as brokers and allow customers to search for the best mortgage (out of the group of lenders with which the site is affiliated). Just as in sales force automation (see Chapter 10, e-Customer Relationship Management), there is the concern that these online mortgage services may mean a reduction in available broker jobs.[23] This concern will be addressed as online mortgage services evolve and become more popular. Another issue with online lending is the stability of the lender. The online mortgage service is relatively new and some companies are experiencing difficulty in maintaining operations. For example `Mortgage.com`, an online mortgage company, had to end operations close and sell some loans.[24]

16.4 How the Web Is Changing the Investment Community

The Internet and World Wide Web continue to change the financial services industry. In this section, we discuss the techniques, advantages and disadvantages of trading on the Internet and the ways in which online trading has affected stock exchanges.

16.4.1 Electronic Communication Networks (ECNs)

Electronic communication networks (ECNs)—electronic networks that facilitate electronic trading by listing securities order sizes and prices, connecting buyers and sellers and processing digital orders—will change the structure of the traditional stock market.[25] *Securities* can represent ownership, such as stocks, or debt, such as bonds. Transactions are completed faster using ECNs than in the traditional stock market trading system, because buyers and sellers communicate directly. When there is movement in the market, faster trading helps to lock in a buy or sell price.[26] ECNs offer before and after-hours trading and increase price *transparency* by listing prices from more than one exchange. This allows investors to come as close as possible to buying and selling at the best market price. While ECNs attempt to create a more efficient marketplace for trading, they may mean the loss of the middlemen and the trading floors, as they make trading easier for investors to do without brokers.

The electronic communication network Instinet (**www.instinet.com**) does not own stocks, but acts strictly as an agent, thereby providing neutral trading grounds for its clients (brokers and institutions). Instinet allows its clients to interact with each other and trade 24 hours a day in many different markets. Costs of trading can be reduced, allowing brokers or institutions to pass savings along to individual investors by lowering commission or transaction costs or reinvesting the savings in the investors' securities. *Instinet Research* offers institutional investors news and research. Real-time costs of trading are also provided. E*TRADE, an online trading company, uses Instinet as its ECN to provide extended-hours trading. Other ECNs include Island® (**www.island.com**), REDIBook® (**www.redibook.com**) and Archipelago® (**www.tradearca.com**) (see feature ECN: Archipelago).

ECNs will benefit from *decimalization*—the change of stock prices from fractions to decimals.[29] Decimalization saves investors money because the buy and sell prices are more accurate using decimals than when using fractions (the smallest fraction used in the traditional system is 1/16).[30] The electronic communication networks are designed to make this transition, potentially attracting investors away from more traditional markets.[31]

Nasdaq and the NYSE do not currently use ECNs, although the pressure is building as Archipelago has joined with the Pacific Exchange to offer an electronic stock market. With the benefits of ECNs and the competition they have provided, Wall Street must incorporate the technology into the present stock exchange models.[32] The NYSE is attempting to address the ECN competition by offering many of the ECN advantages. It will offer instant and anonymous electronic trading and the option to trade without a broker.[33] Anonymous trading will create more fair trading by eliminating trading that occurs before the completion of large trades can dramatically affect the market.[34]

e-Fact 16.4

In the course of a 10-year period (1989–1999), discounted trading services have reduced traditional, full-service trading service's control of the market from 84 percent to 55 percent.[35]

ECN: Archipelago®[27]

Archipelago (**www.tradearca.com**) is an electronic communications network providing anonymity to it clients. Its *SmartBook*™ software executes orders by searching internally (within Archipelago) and externally (outside of Archipelago's system, including other ECNs) for the best price. Once a match is made, the order is executed in real time. Archipelago has trading hours from 8 A.M. to 8 P.M. Eastern Time and has clients that include brokers and dealers, institutions and Nasdaq market makers. Clients can trade, buy and sell listed, Nasdaq National Market and Nasdaq SmallCap stocks. Figure 16.3 shows an example of how Archipelago executes and routes orders.

Subject to the Securities and Exchange Commission (SEC), Archipelago has partnered with the Pacific Exchange (PCX) to create the first U.S. electronic stock exchange.[28] If the SEC approves, the *Archipelago Exchange* will permit the trading of stocks from the *American Stock Exchange (AMEX)*, *New York Stock Exchange (NYSE)* and *Nasdaq*. This new exchange will be in direct competition with current exchanges (AMEX, NYSE and Nasdaq).

ECN: Archipelago®[27] (Cont.)

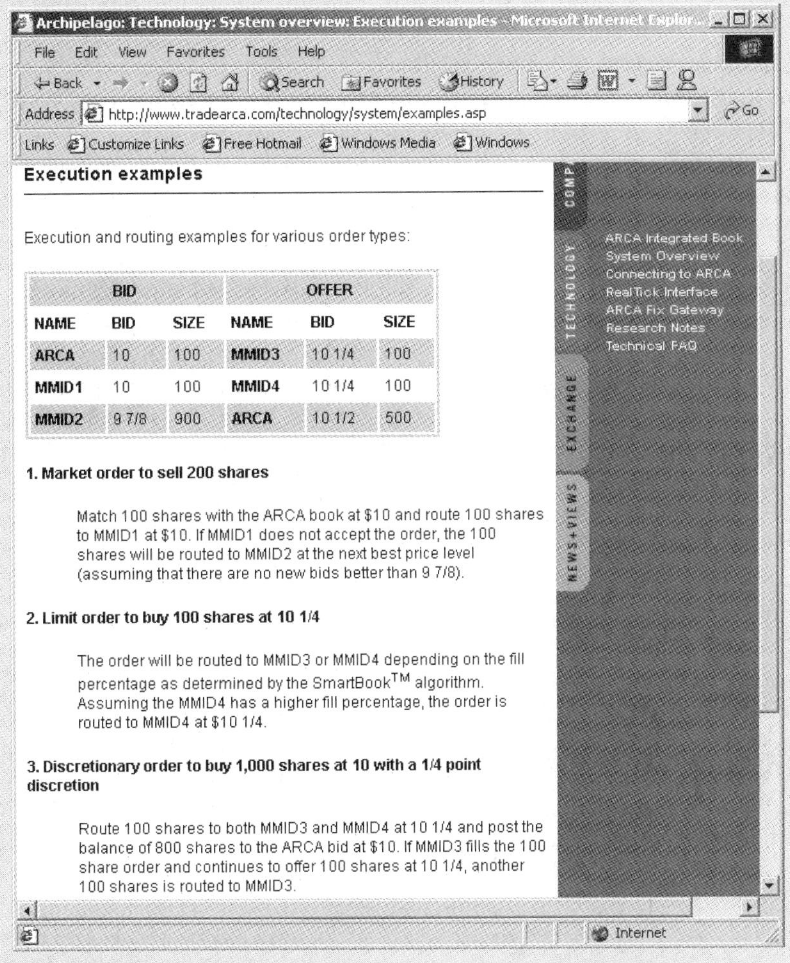

Archipelago: Technology: System overview: Execution examples - Microsoft Internet Explor...

File Edit View Favorites Tools Help

Address http://www.tradearca.com/technology/system/examples.asp

Links Customize Links Free Hotmail Windows Media Windows

Execution examples

Execution and routing examples for various order types:

BID			OFFER		
NAME	BID	SIZE	NAME	BID	SIZE
ARCA	10	100	MMID3	10 1/4	100
MMID1	10	100	MMID4	10 1/4	100
MMID2	9 7/8	900	ARCA	10 1/2	500

1. Market order to sell 200 shares

Match 100 shares with the ARCA book at $10 and route 100 shares to MMID1 at $10. If MMID1 does not accept the order, the 100 shares will be routed to MMID2 at the next best price level (assuming that there are no new bids better than 9 7/8).

2. Limit order to buy 100 shares at 10 1/4

The order will be routed to MMID3 or MMID4 depending on the fill percentage as determined by the SmartBook™ algorithm. Assuming the MMID4 has a higher fill percentage, the order is routed to MMID4 at $10 1/4.

3. Discretionary order to buy 1,000 shares at 10 with a 1/4 point discretion

Route 100 shares to both MMID3 and MMID4 at 10 1/4 and post the balance of 800 shares to the ARCA bid at $10. If MMID3 fills the 100 share order and continues to offer 100 shares at 10 1/4, another 100 shares is routed to MMID3.

Fig. 16.3 Archipelago order routing and execution example. (Courtesy of Archipelago Holdings, L.L.C.)

16.4.2 Online Trading

Investing is one of the most popular industries on the Internet, significantly altering both the number of investors and the means by which they invest. There are a variety of sites providing full-service and discount brokerage online trading services. *Full-service brokers*, such as Merrill Lynch and Salomon Smith Barney, offer the speed and convenience of online trading together with the advice of a broker. While there are fees for such services, online investors also receive the benefit of research and account management. A *discount-*

brokerage service, such as E*TRADE, requires self-sufficiency, leaving the investor responsible for making and executing investment decisions. Discount brokerage services require investors to manage their own accounts and conduct their own research. By taking on these responsibilities, investors can reduce the cost of commission. Similar to the online banking industry, there are Internet-only brokerages and hybrid brokerages.

Before trading online, there are many things to consider. If you do not have a sufficient amount of time to devote to managing your investments or if you are not knowledgeable in the field, then it may be wise to use traditional services, such as a a full-service broker, to assist you in making the proper investment decisions. If you are knowledgeable in the investment field, you may decide that you are capable of investing online. Factors to consider when choosing to invest online include the type of investments you wish to make (stocks, bonds, mutual funds, 401(k) plans, etc.), the quality of site navigation tools and customer service. Can you keep current on market activities at the site? You may want to compare the cost of transactional fees versus the number of trades per year. Online companies usually charge a fee for every purchase or sale of securities made. Sometimes the fee is lower if an investor makes more trades. If you are investing over the long term and do not plan on trading many times a year, your fees may be higher. You should search around to find the right fee structure for your investment plans.

e-Fact 16.5

The average online trading transaction fee is $23.35.[36]

The Internet serves as a valuable learning tool for new and seasoned investors. The aggregation of financial information can assist those who know little about finance and can provide the information needed by serious investors in real time. Visit The Motley Fool® (`www.fool.com`) for a comprehensive financial information site that includes discussion boards, definitions of investment terms, *Fool's School* (an educational section), a section dedicated to personal finance decisions, market news and other information. MSN's *MoneyCentral* (`moneycentral.msn.com/home.asp`) also provides financial information on different categories, such as taxes, loans, saving, spending, insurance and financing college.

`Money.com` is dedicated to providing information to assist people with their financial strategies. This site gives visitors the option to listen to live conference calls on earnings reports from different companies, participate in chat sessions with professionals, view current market updates and stock charts and learn about investing and planning. Visit `www.money.com/money/101/lessons/1/intro.html` to take over 20 lessons on various subjects, including the basics of investing and banking, buying a home and controlling debt. Each lesson gives a visitor the "Top 10 Things To Know." From here, the visitor can click on any of the "The Details" to learn more. There are calculators and interactive features throughout the lessons. A glossary is provided to define unknown terminology, and there is an interactive test for each lesson. After answering the questions, the visitor can find out which answers are right, which are wrong and why.

Companies offering online services, such as Quick & Reilly (`www.quickandreilly.com`), `SureTrade.com`® and E*TRADE (`www.etrade.com`), have made investing in stocks and options accessible to a larger audience. (See the E*TRADE feature.) Online services also provide real-time market information.

Online Trading: E*TRADE[37]

One of the leaders in online trading is E*TRADE. The company was founded in 1982 to offer online stock quotes to the nation's major investment firms. With the advent of the Web, E*TRADE created a Web site (**www.etrade.com**) where individual investors could manage their own investments without the need for brokers. E*TRADE now offers investing and financial services with a community section in which users can chat with others and view *Live Events* over the Web. Investing can include buying or selling mutual funds, stocks, bonds and options. E*TRADE offers extended hours for trading (you can trade before and after the stock market has closed for the day) and a *Knowledge Center* that provides users with tools and information on the basics and strategies of investing. You can also sign up to receive news on investing by e-mail.

E*TRADE's financial services include banking, insurance, taxes, retirement and real estate (Fig. 16.4). E*TRADE BANK^{SM} is FDIC insured and offers competitive rates, ATMs (use its ATM Locator to find one near you), checking, savings, money market accounts and bill payment options. See **www.etradebank.com/services/demo/vbm_demo1.cfm** for an online demo of *E*TRADE BANK*.

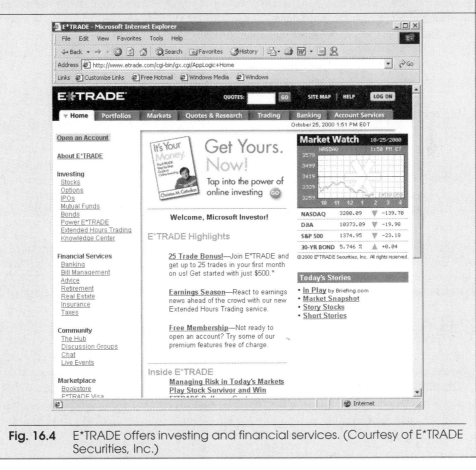

Fig. 16.4　　E*TRADE offers investing and financial services. (Courtesy of E*TRADE Securities, Inc.)

Online Trading: E*TRADE[37] (Cont.)

If you have little knowledge about buying and selling stocks, E*TRADE offers two games in which you use "game money" to carry out stock and options trades. Each player is given $100,000 in virtual trading dollars to start. Game players have access to charts, graphs and recent news articles to help them choose their investments. There is no risk of losing real money, so the players can feel free to experiment with different trading strategies. Each trade takes approximately one minute to process. The goal of each game is, of course, to increase the value of your portfolio. The E*TRADE games are a friendly, no-risk way for beginners to experiment with online trading. Players compete for real cash prizes. The trading game lasts one month.

Ameritrade® (**www.ameritrade.com**) is an e-business offering online trading. Its services include real-time quotes and company profiles. The company can provide you with stock alerts that can be delivered to your e-mail and pager. Customer service is available 24-by-7, and you can trade using your wireless device as well. Ameritrade offers a stock game similar to E*TRADE. Ameritrade Investors Cup[SM] is a free competition for people interested in investing. The participants receive $50,000 of play money to invest in a portfolio. The goal is to have the most valuable portfolio. Ameritrade offers various prizes for the winners. See the Sharebuilder feature (Figs. 16.5 and 16.6) and the online trading table (Fig. 16.7) for more companies offering trading services online.

Dollar-Based Investing[38]: ShareBuilder™

ShareBuilder (**www.sharebuilder.com**), offers *dollar-based investing*—investors can purchase stock based on a dollar amount, not a whole number of shares. This service provides a simple and affordable way for people to invest online. For example, if an investor wants to buy a share of stock that costs $100, but wants to invest only $50 per month, the investor would own one-half a share the first month and a whole share the second month for a nominal flat transaction fee.

This type of investing is possible because ShareBuilder Securities Corp., a registered broker-dealer, collects the money and purchases the stocks once a week in a lump sum at the market price of the stock. ShareBuilder then notifies investors of their pro-rated portion. If investors want to purchase stock in real time, they can do so through this service by paying a somewhat higher flat fee. To sell your stock, you pay the real-time fee per transaction.

Investors can choose to periodically invest a designated amount of money or make a one-time investment. Payment can be made by automatic payroll deductions, check, wired money or transfers from bank accounts. No minimum investment is required. The investor can select from more than 3,500 stocks and 68 *Index shares* (shares of a portfolio of stocks). The fee is higher for lump-sum investments compared to recurring investments. See the chart in Fig. 16.6 for an example of investing over time and its results.

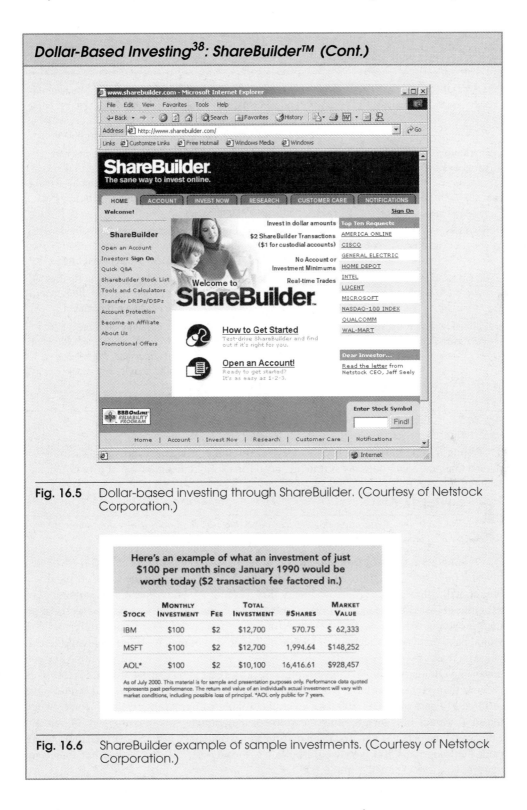

Fig. 16.5   Dollar-based investing through ShareBuilder. (Courtesy of Netstock Corporation.)

Here's an example of what an investment of just $100 per month since January 1990 would be worth today ($2 transaction fee factored in.)

STOCK	MONTHLY INVESTMENT	FEE	TOTAL INVESTMENT	#SHARES	MARKET VALUE
IBM	$100	$2	$12,700	570.75	$ 62,333
MSFT	$100	$2	$12,700	1,994.64	$148,252
AOL*	$100	$2	$10,100	16,416.61	$928,457

As of July 2000. This material is for sample and presentation purposes only. Performance data quoted represents past performance. The return and value of an individual's actual investment will vary with market conditions, including possible loss of principal. *AOL only public for 7 years.

Fig. 16.6   ShareBuilder example of sample investments. (Courtesy of Netstock Corporation.)

Online Trading	Description
Datek Online (www.datek.com)	Offers trading commission free if an order is not administered within 60 seconds, updates portfolios in real time and provides free check-writing services. If necessary, Datek routes orders to the Island ECN to be traded.
Charles Schwab (www.schwab.com)	Provides online trading services, stock quotes and research. If an investor has an account of $10,000 or more, Schwab will give the investor a Web phone and a few commission-free trades through its wireless PocketBroker™ trades.
Scottrade (www.scottrade.com)	Provides online trading services and allows investors to locate nearby branches by using *Branch Locator*. These branches allow investors to have a personal broker.
Merrill Lynch Direct (www.mldirect.com)	Offers online trading and investing (mutual funds, bonds, CDs). Customers can take part in e-IPOs. Merrill Lynch Direct also offers online bill payment.
National Discount Brokers (www.ndb.com)	Offers *Flat-Fee Trading*®, allowing customers to pay only one fee independent of the amount of stock traded. Provides research, account status and *StockPulse*—a graphing tool that graphs the activity of a stock throughout the trading day.

Fig. 16.7   Online Brokerages.

While trading online has been successful for some, it has also proven disastrous for others. Online trading does not negate the need for a solid understanding of investment and strategy.

 e-Fact 16.6

The Consumer Federation of America found that less than half of investors know that the price of bonds decreases with an increase in interest rates.[39]

A temptation faced by online traders is the easy access to *trading on margin*—when an investor buys stock and borrows money from the broker to invest in the stock. Typically, a broker will allow you to borrow up to fifty percent of your investment amount. For example, if you were going to invest $5,000 in a company and you wanted to trade on margin, you could borrow $2,500 more from your broker to invest in the company. You would have then invested a total of $7,500 dollars in that company. If the company's stock value increases by 30 percent, the value of your investment is now worth $9,750. After you pay back your loan of $2,500 (and any other dues you owe) you can net around $7,250. This is more than you would have made if you had invested only $5,000, which would have resulted in a gain of just $1,500. However, the trouble with trading on margin comes when the stock values fall. Imagine that the value of the company's stock dropped 30 percent. This would mean that if you traded on margin, you would have lost $5,250, and after paying back the loan of $2,500, you would be left with only $2,750. If you had not traded on margin, you would be left with $3,500.

Potentially, a stock's value could fall to a price that, when sold at the market price, will not cover the loan. When this happens, the broker can issue a *margin call*—the broker requires the investor to invest more cash or securities or sell the stock to pay back the loan. When the margin between what the investor has invested and what is owed to the broker reaches a certain point, the broker has the right to sell the securities without notifying the investor. People can end up repeatedly investing money to cover the margin, making it easy to lose more money continuously as the stock falls.

Trading on margin over the Internet has attracted many investors because it is easy to qualify. Opening a margin account online requires a relatively low minimum balance, answering a questionnaire (which sometimes replaces a credit check) and being qualified electronically, with no assessment made by a human broker.[40]

e-Fact 16.7

There is $242 billion of margin debt on Nasdaq and New York Stock Exchange stocks, an increase of 64 percent in one year.[41]

Day trading—making short-term trades in an attempt to profit off of *market inefficiencies* (e.g. news affecting the market, disproportionate risk to price value of a stock or *arbitrage*, wherein someone profits by converting money from one currency to another)—has also become prevalent on the Internet. This type of trading is easier on the Internet because people can access their accounts and make trades with a click of the mouse. When trading online, the trader must realize that transactions will be limited by modem speed and server-side transaction speed. Traders may think that they made trades at a certain price, however the trades may have suffered a small delay which could result in a price change. The fees associated with trading online can make day trading an expensive activity, especially if multiple trades are executed in a day. Day traders still bear the same risks as other traders. Many people who are not knowledgeable about the stock market and the risks entailed have lost money trying to make quick profits through day trading. Some day trading sites are **CareerDayTrader.com**, **DayTradingOnline.com** and **OnlineTradingAcademy.com**.

People have been cautioned by the *Federal Trade Commission*, the *Commodity Futures Trading Commission* and the *Securities and Exchange Commission* about the exaggerations and counter factual claims made by some online trading firms, such as the possibility of incredible profits with no risk.[42] Online investors must realize that using the Internet to trade does not reduce the risk involved with the stock market.

Online trading has also affected the global investment industry. The reach of the Internet has allowed investors around the world to receive real-time information and conduct trades from any location. Foreign-exchange banks have begun to move their services to the Internet to remain competitive. Many banks have their own foreign exchange systems and have joined existing systems to facilitate clients' currency trading.[43] Foreign exchange systems allow traders to find the best deals on foreign currency, and this creates smaller margins between the prices of different currencies.[44] The online foreign exchange market is one of the most underdeveloped financial services online.

The Internet facilitates trading commodities globally. EnronOnline™ (**www.enrononline.com**) is an e-commerce site for trading commodities globally. Transactions occur in real time, and market information is made available at the site. Commodities are priced in real time. Traders can set a specific price and quantity of a commodity that they are looking for, and when the volume and price match, the purchase is executed. See the EnronOnline feature in Chapter 15, Online Industries.

The Internet affords a competitive field for firms providing International investment opportunities to their clients. Investors can trade securities in other stock markets, invest in foreign countries and follow other markets closely, with information instantly updated on the Web. Electronic trading is being implemented globally. It will soon be introduced in Japan as that country's economy strengthens and the market grows.[45] Europe has online stock-trading platforms, although Goldman Sachs Group, Inc., plans to found a competitive platform. This platform will allow the execution of trades on different exchanges, including the U.S. markets, in addition to providing brokerages with the option to allow clients to trade stocks globally.[46] For more information on the effects of the Internet worldwide, see Chapter 12, Globalization.

16.4.3 Online Bond Trading

A *bond* is a written promise that an entity will repay a debt that is sold to an investor. The Investor receives its original investments and a dividend for a certain period of time. Traditionally, someone would check the newspapers and call different institutions to buy or sell a bond. The broker that helps someone trade bonds usually charges a commission. Online companies offer these bonds with the claim that the process is easier and cheaper. The Internet can also cut the cost of issuing bonds. Bear Stearns used its *Dutch Auction Internet Syndicate System* to sell $600 million worth of bonds. Investors could watch the bond auction in real time and make bids.[47] Harvard University also offered bonds worth $170 million over the Internet to refinance its debt.[48]

Tradebonds.com™ enables people to buy and sell bonds through its electronic system. The site provides access to research and news on the bond markets. The site allows you to search for a variety of bonds, including treasury, municipal, zero coupons and corporate bonds (Fig. 16.8). Other bond-trading sites include bondsonline (**www.bondsonline.com**) and MuniDirect™ (**www.munidirect.com**).

Some people have found the online process to be technically complex, and each site has a different purchasing and selling process. A standardized system for the bond sales process will help improve this situation.[49]

16.5 Merging Financial Services

Merging financial services is the major trend affecting brick-and-mortar and online banking and financial institutions of all sizes. Since the repeal of the *Glass–Steagle Act*—which prohibited financial institutions from engaging in multiple financial operations (i.e.,one institution offering banking services and trading services)—banks, brokerages and insurance companies are permitted to offer a wide range of financial services. **Excite.com** has partnered with Bank One to add various financial services to its general Web portal, while E*TRADE has developed online banking in addition to its brokerage services. Most online financial services offer *electronic bill presentment and payment* (*EBPP*) as well, and the vast majority use CheckFree's *Technology through Partnerships*.[50] This is discussed further in Chapter 4, Online Monetary Transactions. It is crucial for financial institutions to offer a wide variety of services to remain competitive.

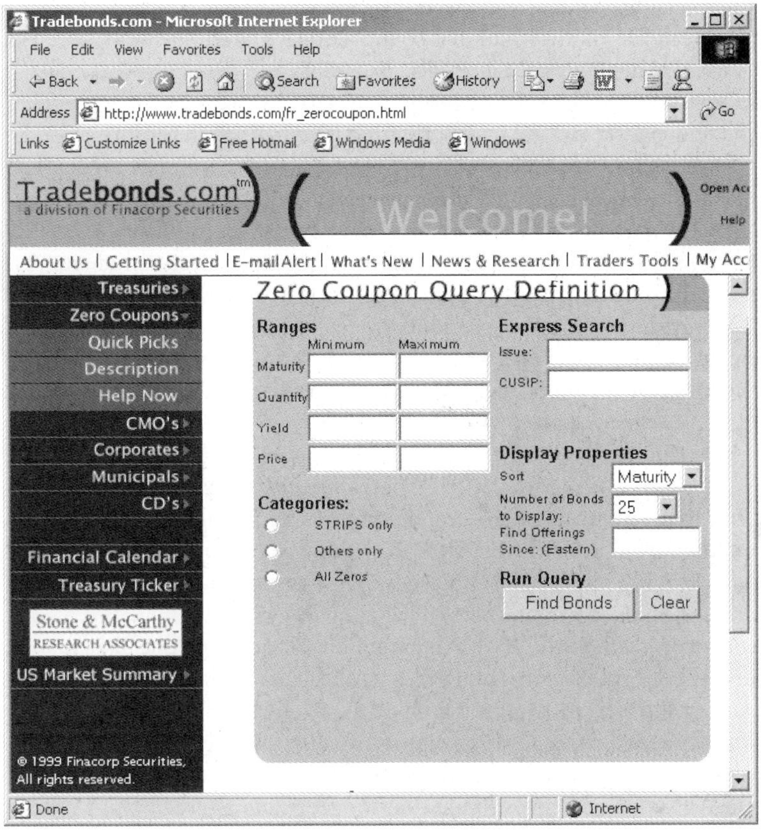

Fig. 16.8   `Tradebonds.com`'s zero coupon bond query. (Courtesy of
             `Tradebonds.com`.)

Prudential (**www.prudential.com**) is an example of a company offering a wide
variety of online and offline services, allowing it to reach a large market and provide different methods of customer service. The firm's extensive insurance, banking, brokerage,
real-estate, business-to-business and financial-planning services make it a competitive and
successful company. Visitors to the site can request to have a local Prudential representative contact them in person. Prudential provides online loan applications and financial planning tools, including Prudential's Roth IRA calculator, a retirement-planning quiz, an
estate-planning worksheet and a college cost calculator. Its *Prudential Advisor*[SM] program
enables investors to access market information and investment tools and a personal Financial Advisor, who provides additional knowledge and recommendations for investment
decisions. The service also offers *PruTrade*[SM] for online trading.

16.6 Financial Aggregation Services

Online *aggregation services* give users the option of keeping all their financial information
in one location on the Internet. Instead of remembering many usernames and passwords
and visiting different sites to view and manage their finances, users can experience the con-

venience of "one-stop" financial management by registering with an aggregator and using only one password for all information (see the Yodlee feature).

To use a financial aggregation service, you must register and provide all of your usernames and passwords. Then, the aggregation service uses *screen scraping*, a process whereby the aggregator visits the sites that have your financial information and services and uses your usernames and passwords to log in. The information is then downloaded and stored in one place, where the user can then access the information.

Aggregator VerticalOne[SM] (**www.verticalone.com**) offers a service similar to that of Yodlee. VerticalOne's service is offered through its destination site partners, such as **SmartMoney.com** and **CNBC.com**, and is free to end users. VerticalOne charges the destination site partners for the opportunity to use its service on their sites. Other aggregation companies include ebalance™ (**www.ebalance.com**), 1View Network (**www.1ViewNetwork.com**), ezlogin (**www.ezlogin.com**) and GainsKeeper[SM] (**www.GainsKeeper.com**).

Many banks do not authorize aggregators to screen scrape, although the aggregators are not required to have authorization. The *Financial Services Technology Consortium (FSTC)* is trying to stop the screen-scraping process and implement another form of gathering information from the different sites to create a standard.[52] One possibility for eliminating screen scraping and increase the security of aggregation is to develop a direct feed of information from the financial sites to the aggregators.[53]

Major concerns among users of aggregation services include privacy and security. People who are concerned with giving their credit-card and account information over the Web will have a difficult time entering all of their information into one Web site that has the ability to aggregate personal financial information. If a hacker manages to break into the aggregator's system, identity theft and complete destruction of someone's finances could result.[54] The federal government does not regulate aggregators, so the aggregators are not required to compensate users if security is compromised by a hacker.[55] While many aggregators require that the companies using the aggregation technology on their sites agree not to sell users' personal information, this does not limit the information from being used internally by the companies.[56] Despite the security and privacy factors, some people find these services to be convenient and worthwhile.

e-Fact 16.8

Aggregation services are used by almost half a million Americans. Celent Communications' study predicts that, by 2003, the number of aggregation users will reach 7 million.[57]

As the number of aggregation services and users of these services increase, they pose a threat to the traffic at online banking and investing sites. Banks have reacted by implementing the services on their own sites. Chase Manhattan Bank announced that it intended to launch an aggregation service for its customers. The service is to be backed by Yodlee's *e-Personalization Platform*.[58] Financial aggregation services will become more common and efficient as banks try to remain competitive.

16.7 Wireless Banking and Trading

Wireless Internet technology is improving, creating a growth in wireless applications for banking and trading. Even though the market demand for wireless banking is not overwhelming, many institutions are beginning to offer wireless services. These companies can use wireless technology to offer their customers a value-added service that can create customer loyalty.

Aggregation Services: Yodlee[51]

Yodlee (**www.yodlee.com**) is one of the leaders in financial aggregation. Its service brings all of a user's financial information together and allows transactions through partnerships with financial institutions and providers (such as Paytrust and Check-Free® for bill-payment functionality). Yodlee also offers aggregation of non-financial content such as travel reservations, e-mail, news, shopping accounts, frequent-flyer and reward programs, etc. People can access Yodlee's services from one of Yodlee's partners, including AltaVista (**www.altavista.com**), AOL (**www.aol.com**), Citibank (**www.myciti.com**) (Fig. 16.9), Chase Manhattan Bank (**www.chase.com**) and Morgan Stanley Dean Witter (**www.msdw.com**). The company's personalized aggregation solution can be delivered over the Web, personal digital assistants (PDAs) and Web-enabled wireless phones. *Yodlee2Go* is a solution that allows users to access real-time personal account information, including investments, banking and e-mail, on their wireless phones and PDAs.

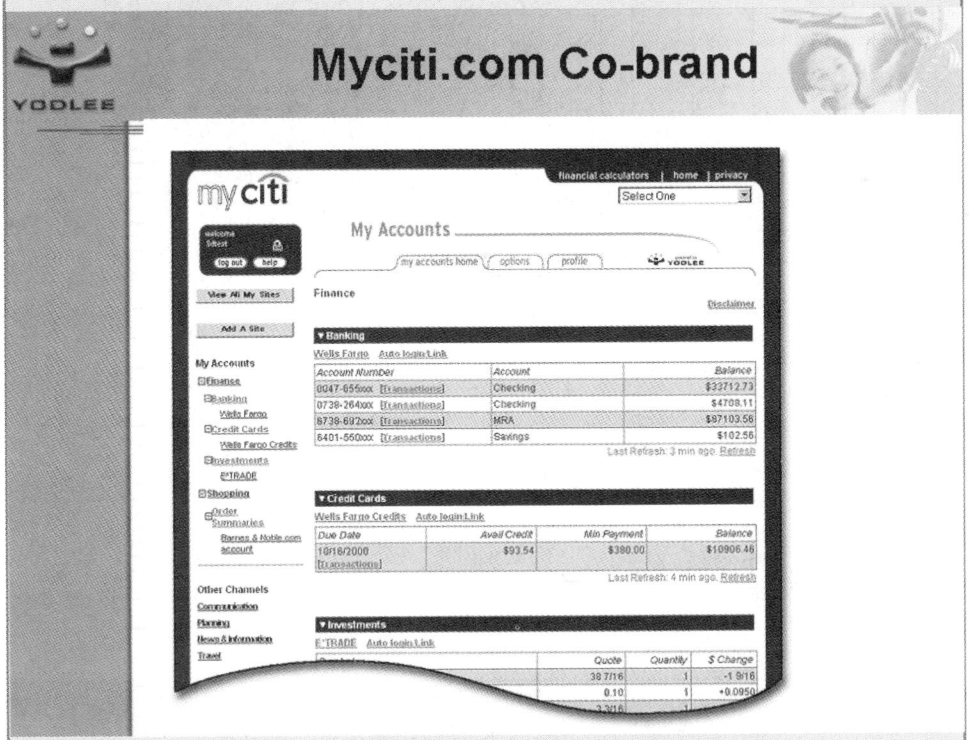

Fig. 16.9 Example of Yodlee's service through Citibank's myciti. (Courtesy of Yodlee, Inc.)

Aggregation Services: Yodlee[51] (Cont.)

Yodlee's service provides customers with personalized alerts. For example, Yodlee can notify you of a bank account balance change or a bill due date. Yodlee also provides users with a view of their bank and credit-card balances, stock portfolio, retirement funds, frequent-flyer miles and e-mail accounts. This information can be sent to your wireless devices as well. You can act on your accounts and view transaction histories. Yodlee can also track and chart account activity (Fig. 16.10). Visit **www.yodlee.com** to view an online demonstration.

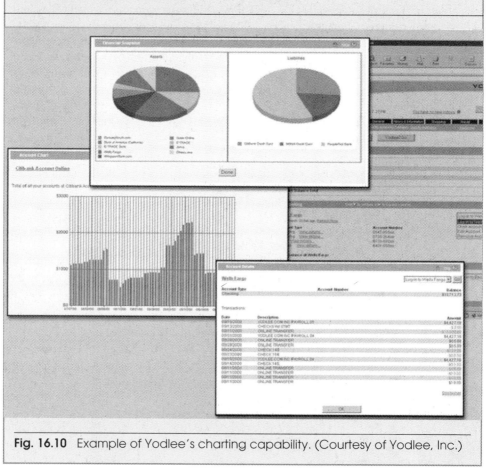

Fig. 16.10 Example of Yodlee's charting capability. (Courtesy of Yodlee, Inc.)

e-Fact 16.9

According to the American Banker/Gallup consumer survey, approximately 72 percent of people surveyed do not find completing financial transactions using their wireless Internet devices to be appealing.[59]

Wireless banking allows users to pay bills from anywhere. In addition to making payments, people can transfer funds between accounts and can check their account activity.

TD Bank Financial Group (**www.tdbank.ca**), one of Canada's largest banks, offers wireless banking service to its customers. TD Bank allows customers to view a summary of their financial status, transfer funds and check their account history and credit-card activity. The company also provides wireless services for TD Waterhouse, a brokerage company. Netbank, an Internet-only bank, offers wireless access for its banking customers as well.

While the market may be adopting wireless banking slowly, wireless securities trading is growing rapidly. Traders need to make quick decisions in real time. Using wireless technologies, traders can receive important information and news about the market or their investments. They can then react by making a trade immediately.

e-Fact 16.10

According to Celent Communications, by 2004, 150 million people worldwide will use personal digital assistants to make trades, get stock quotes and view their bank accounts.[60]

Fidelity Investments® (**www.fidelity.com**) provides financial services, including discount brokerage, life insurance, investment management and estate planning. Fidelity Investments also offers online trading and investment information through Powerstreet[SM]. This service provides personalized content and account information, allowing its users to make better informed trading decisions. Customers that sign up for Fidelity InstantBroker[SM] have access to their account activity and market information from their wireless devices, including RIM™ handheld devices, Palm™ handheld computers and Internet-enabled phones. InstantBroker allows investors to make trades from anywhere using their wireless devices. The service also enables customers to receive notifications of changes in account balances, margin calls, maturation of bonds and securities and newly issued securities.

Trade.com[SM] offers wireless trading and account information through its partnership with w-Technologies™ (**www.w-technologies.com**), a company that provides wireless solutions for e-commerce, financial institutions and communications companies. w-Technologies' financial solutions include *w-Trade*, *w-Bank*, *w-401k*, *w-Cash*, *w-Alert* and *w-Research*. These solutions can be used together or separately and can be integrated with a company's current system to offer wireless services to its customers. **Trade.com** uses w-Trade, which enables customers to use wireless devices, including Smart Cellular Phones, Nokia™ Communicators, PDAs and Windows CE™ palm-sized PCs. w-Technologies offers wireless banking solutions through w-Bank, allowing a bank's customers to transfer money between their accounts, pay bills and access their account histories.

Wireless access to financial information may grow more slowly in the United States than in Europe and Asia, because the United States has more technical standards and wireless devices in use.[61] Until there is an accepted standard for these services, customers will be required to have the appropriate wireless device to access their information and make trades. Companies offering wireless trading services include Ameritrade® (**www.ameritrade.com**), DLJ Direct™ (**www.dljdirect.com**), **SureTrade.com**® and Morgan Stanley Dean Witter Online (**www.msdwonline.com**). For more information about wireless technology, see Chapter 6, Wireless Internet and M-Business.

16.8 Financial Planning Online

The Internet has made the task of *financial planning* easier for service providers and customers. With the abundance of financial content available, people can educate themselves about financial-planning options. People can search for better rates on loans and bank accounts or read about retirement programs. Estate-planning information and services can also be found on the Internet.

Companies can use the Internet as another way to service customers. They can offer applications, account histories, new-product offerings, investment tracking and other services online. This can reduce the number of phone calls to customer service representatives and increase customer satisfaction. By offering a wider variety of financial-planning options, companies can also increase customer loyalty.

For example, 401kafe (**www.401kafe.com**) is a site that offers information regarding *401(k) plans*—investing vehicles for employee retirement. An employee and the company can make contributions to the plan. 401kafe is a free community Web site provided by mPower (**www.mpower.com**), which offers retirement-planning advice to employees of member companies that sign up for the subscription-based service. 401kafe is an informative site for individuals to learn more about how a 401(k) plan works.

ihatefinancialplanning.com is a site providing information on all financial-planning topics. Visitors can select the topic of interest, view *The Basics* and try some of the *Common Tools*. There is also a *Pop Quiz* at the end of each topic discussion. Topics include retirement and estate planning, budgeting, tax planning, college funding, surviving divorce, stocks, bonds and mutual funds and buying a home. The site also offers free downloadable forms to help visitors get financially organized.

Library.thinkquest.org/10326/investment_lessons gives the basics of investing, including individual lessons on each topic. The site also provides a glossary of investment terminology. Many financial institutions offer free financial-planning information to add value to their products and services. For example, Salomon Smith Barney Access® gives financial-planning information at **www.smithbarney.com/fin_pln**. Other sites offering financial-planning information and tools include **Kiplinger.com** and the American Association of Individual Investors® (AAII) (**www.aaii.com/finplan/index.shtml**).

This chapter discusses the ways the Internet has affected the financial industry including banking, trading and financial planning. Financial services will continue to take advantage of the online channel as they increase marketing efforts to gain online customers. In Chapter 17, e-Learning, we will cover how the Internet impacts corporate training and traditional education. By using online training, corporations can reduce costs. Traditional education will be revolutionized as students can take online university classes and receive degrees.

16.9 Internet and World Wide Web Resources

Hybrid Banks

www.fleet.com
FleetBoston Financial offers a physical presence, as well as online banking services. The company also offers online brokerage services through Quick & Reilly.

www.wellsfargo.com
Wells Fargo is an online branch of a California-based commercial bank.

www.citibankonline.com
Citibank® offers *Citibank Online*, its online banking service offering customers free bill payment online and personal finance research tools.

www.pnc.com
PNC offers online banking services, and online mortgage and investment services for personal and corporate accounts.

Internet-Only Banks

www.netbank.com
NetBank an Internet-only bank offering a variety of banking services.

www.clarity.com
This is an online bank that specializes in helping technology firms.

www.onecore.com
This is an online bank that specializes in helping small businesses.

www.bankrate.com
This site aggregates financial information and financial rates.

www.compubank.com
CompuBank® offers clickrewards™, allowing customers to earn rewards for direct deposits and check-card purchases. The company pays above-average interest on checking accounts and offers free online bill payment.

everbank.com
This bank offers free online bill payment, mortgage services and the *everCard*™ *Visa*® *Platinum* credit card with free credit-card management and trading services through everTrade Direct Brokerage, Inc.

Online Loans

www.fanniemae.com
FannieMae offers its loan services online, including mortgages.

www.loansdirect.com
LoansDirect™ is an online lending site providing refinancing, home-buying and home equity services.

www.countrywide.com
Countrywide® offers direct lending for home purchasing, refinancing and home equities.

www.quickenloan.com
This site offers online mortgage services, including refinancing and home buying.

www.netcredit.net/connect
This site connects lenders with Internet loan-application resources.

capital.com
This site is a business marketplace where financial companies compete to offer loans.

www.primestreet.com
PrimeStreet™ is an online lending source for small businesses that also provides solutions for financial institutions and loan brokers.

Electronic Communications Networks (ECNs)

www.island.com
Island® is a privately held ECN that offers securities trading to brokerage firms.

www.redibook.com
REDIBook® offers trading grounds for AMEX, NYSE and NASDAQ securities.

www.tradearca.com

Archipelago is an ECN that allows the buying and selling of NASDAQ securities. Pending SEC approval, its joint efforts with the Pacific Stock Exchange could create an electronic stock exchange.

Online Trading

www.etrade.com

E*TRADE is an online brokerage firm. This company also offers online banking services.

www.tradeweb.com

This site provides a market for online bond buying and selling. A free 60-day trial is available at the site.

www.quickandreilly.com

Quick & Reilly is a FleetBoston Financial Company that offers online trading services and provides access to Personal Financial Consultants either by phone or at one of its centers.

www.unx.com

Universal Network Exchange provides a Web-based trading technology that accesses different ECNs for trading.

www.datek.com

Datek Online offers trading commission free if an order is not administered within 60 seconds, updates portfolios in real time and provides free check-writing services. If necessary, Datek routes orders to the Island ECN to be traded.

www.ameritrade.com

Ameritrade® is an e-business offering online trading. Its services include real-time quotes and company profiles. Stock alerts can be delivered to your e-mail (wireless e-mail, too) and pager.

www.enrononline.com

EnronOnline™ is an e-commerce site for trading commodities globally.

Financial Aggregation Services

www.ebalance.com

ebalance™ offers aggregation services and can collect bank and brokerage information. The company collects information from over 1,800 service providers.

www.1ViewNetwork.com

1View Network™ aggregates content for individuals and also provides aggregation technology for financial institutions.

www.ezlogin.com

ezlogin.com is a free service that aggregates personal information and tracks online accounts. It also allows users to surf the Web together.

www.verticalone.com

VerticalOne^{SM} offers aggregation services through its destination site partners such as **Smart-Money.com** and **NBC.com** and is free to end-users.

Wireless Trading

www.dljdirect.com

DLJ Direct™ *Anywhere*™ *Wireless Services* offers trading, real-time quotes and portfolio tracking.

www.suretrade.com

This site offers wireless trading through w-Technologies' *w-Trade* solution.

www.msdwonline.com

Morgan Stanley Dean Witter Online offers *TradeRunner*^{SM} to provide wireless trading, quotes, market information and notifications.

Financial Planning Online

www.investorguide.com
This site provides market information, stock research, quotes, charts and a tracking service for investors' portfolios.

www.morningstar.com
This site provides mutual fund, stock and insurance information for those seeking finance education. It also offers *Morningstar*^{SM} *ClearFuture*^{SM} to assist users in planning their 401(k)s.

ihatefinancialplanning.com
This site provides information on retirement and estate planning, budgeting, tax planning, college funding, surviving divorce, stocks, bonds, mutual funds and buying a home.

www.401kafe.com
401kafe is an informative site for individuals to learn more about how a 401(k) plan works.

www.money.com
This site gives visitors the option to listen to live conference calls on earnings reports from different companies, participate in chat sessions with professionals, view current market updates and stock charts, and learn about investing and planning.

SUMMARY

- One of the fastest growing online service industries is online banking, either as an extension of services from a traditional bank or as a purely online entity.

- To maintain and capture market share, many brick-and-mortar banks have become click-and-mortar by using the Internet as a method to deliver their services.

- Internet-only banks are attempting to establish a presence, but lack the brand awareness and recognition of the click-and-mortar banks.

- Enabling customers to pay their bills and write checks online decreases float—the time it takes for checks to clear after they have been deposited.

- Because the Internet delivers payments faster than the mail, money can be transferred more quickly. This frees up cash and decreases accounts receivable.

- Online banking services are also beneficial to customers, who can avoid buying stamps and do not have to send bills out early to make sure they get to their destinations on time.

- Despite the convenience of online banking, there are risks. Be aware of security breaches.

- Despite the growing number of Internet-only banks, customers still like to know that there is a physical branch to visit in case they need to speak with a representative.

- Many click-and-mortar banks charge monthly fees to use their online bill paying and banking services.

- Smaller banks sometime partner with third-party service providers to transition to the Internet.

- To appeal to customers, Internet-only banks often offer convenience, lower fees and higher interest rates to their customers and may also offer lower minimum balances.

- Using the Internet to offer banking can lower costs, such as the costs of employees salaries, buildings and equipment.

- Internet-only banks have to accept deposits by mail because they lack physical branches.

- Through the Internet, the loan application process can be more efficient, sometimes returning loan approvals within minutes. The Internet gives people access to many different lending institutions, enabling those seeking loans to shop for the best deals.

- Users can find personal, business and automobile loans and even mortgages online.

- Some sites provide mortgages that are directly from lenders. Others act as brokers and allow customers to search for the best mortgage.

- Transactions are completed faster using ECNs than in the traditional stock market trading system because buyers and sellers are in direct contact. When there is movement in the market, faster trading helps to lock in a buy or sell price.

- ECNs offer before and after-hours trading and increase price transparency by listing prices from more than one exchange.

- ECNs will benefit from decimalization—the change of stock prices from fractions to decimals. Decimalization will save investors money because the buy and sell prices are more accurate using decimals than when using fractions (the smallest fraction used in the traditional system is 1/16).

- Full-service brokers offer the speed and convenience of online trading, together with the advice of a broker. While there are fees for such services, online investors also receive the benefit of research and account management.

- A discount brokerage service requires self-sufficiency, leaving the investor responsible for making and executing investment decisions. Discount brokerage services requires investors to manage their own accounts and conduct their own research. By taking on these responsibilities, investors can reduce the cost of commission.

- Online companies usually charge a fee for every purchase or sale of securities. Sometimes the fee is lower if an investor makes more trades. If you are investing over the long term and do not plan on trading many times a year, your fees may be higher.

- The Internet serves as a valuable learning tool for new and seasoned investors. The aggregation of financial information can assist those who know little about finance and can provide the information needed by serious investors in real time.

- A temptation faced by online traders is the easy access to trading on margin—when an investor buys stock and borrows money from the broker to invest further in the stock.

- The problem with trading on margin is that the stock's value can fall close to a price that would not raise enough money to cover the loan if the stock were sold.

- Day trading—making short-term trades in an attempt to profit off of market inefficiencies—has also become prevalent on the Internet. This type of trading is made easier by the Internet because people can access their accounts and make trades with a click of the mouse.

- Day trading can be expensive if a lot of trades are made in a day, due to the costs the brokers or sites charge for each transaction. Day traders still bear the same risks as other traders.

- People have been cautioned by the Federal Trade Commission, the Commodity Futures Trading Commission and the Securities and Exchange Commission about the exaggerations and counterfactual claims made by some online trading firms, such as the possibility of earning incredible profits with no risk.

- Online investors must realize that using the Internet to trade does not reduce the risk involved with the stock market.

- The reach of the Internet has allowed investors around the world to receive real-time information and conduct trades from any location.

- Foreign exchange banks have begun to move their services to the Internet to remain competitive. Foreign exchange systems allow traders to find the best deals on foreign currency, and this could create smaller margins between the prices of different currencies.

- The Internet offers a competitive field to firms providing international investment opportunities to their clients. Investors can trade securities in other stock markets, invest in foreign countries and follow other markets closely with information frequently updated on the Web.

- Online marketplaces attempt to make it easier and less expensive to buy and sell bonds.

- A bond is a written promise that an entity will repay a debt that is sold to an investor. The investor receives its original investment and a dividend for a certain period of time.

- Some people have found the online bond-trading process to be technically complex, and each site has a different purchasing and selling process. A standardized system for the bond sales process will help improve this situation.

- Since the repeal of the Glass–Steagle Act—which prohibited financial institutions from engaging in multiple financial operations—banks, brokerages and insurance companies are permitted to offer a wide range of financial services.

- Online aggregation services give users the option of keeping all their financial information in one location on the Internet.

- Aggregation services use screen scraping, a process wherein the aggregator visits the sites that have your financial information and services and uses your usernames and passwords to log in. The information is then downloaded and stored in one place, where the user can then access the information.

- Major concerns among users of aggregation services include privacy and security. If a hacker manages to break into an aggregator's system, identity theft and the complete destruction of someone's finances could result. The federal government does not regulate aggregators, so the aggregators are not required to compensate users if security is compromised by a hacker.

- As the number of aggregation services and users of these services increases, they pose a threat to the traffic at online banking and investing sites. Banks have reacted by implementing the services on their own sites.

- Wireless Internet technology is improving, creating a growth in wireless applications for banking and trading. Even though the market demand for wireless banking is not overwhelming, many institutions are beginning to offer wireless services. These companies can use wireless technology to offer their customers a value-added service that can create customer loyalty.

- Wireless banking will allow users to pay bills from anywhere. In addition to making payments, people can make transfers and check their account activity.

- Wireless access to financial information may grow more slowly in the United States than in Europe and Asia, because the United States has more technical standards and wireless devices in use. Until there is an accepted standard for these services, customers will be required to have the appropriate wireless device to access their information and make trades.

- The Internet has made the task of financial planning easier for service providers and customers. With the abundance of financial content, people can educate themselves about financial planning options.

- Companies can use the Internet as another way to service customers. They can offer applications, account histories, new products, investment tracking and other services online. By offering a wider variety of financial planning options, companies can also increase customer loyalty.

TERMINOLOGY

accounts receivable
aggregation service
American Stock Exchange (AMEX)
arbitrage
bond
Commodity Futures Trading Commission
day trading

decimalization
discount-brokerage service
dollar-based investing
electronic bill presentment and payment (EBPP)
electronic communications network (ECN)
Federal Trade Commission (FTC)
financial aggregator

financial planning
Financial Services Technology
    Consortium (FSTC)
float
full-service broker
Glass–Steagle Act
hybrid-bank model
Index share
Internet-only bank
margin call
market inefficiencies

Nasdaq
New York Stock Exchange (NYSE)
Office of the Currency (OCC)
screen scraping
Securities and Exchange Commission (SEC)
securities
Small Business Administration
trading on margin
transparency
401(k) plan

SELF-REVIEW EXERCISES

16.1 State whether each of the following is *true* or *false*; if *false*, explain why.
  a) Internet-only banks have greater brand awareness and recognition than click-and-mortar banks.
  b) Enabling customers to pay their bills and write checks online increases float.
  c) Wireless access to financial information is growing faster in the United States than in Europe and Asia.
  d) Since the repeal of the Glass-Steagle Act, banks, brokerages and insurance companies are permitted to offer a wide range of financial services.
  e) A 401(k) plan is a written promise that an entity will repay debt that is sold to an investor.

16.2 Fill in the blanks in each of the following statements:
  a) Online _____ give users the option of keeping all their financial information in one location on the Internet.
  b) _____ means that investors can own stock based on a dollar amount, not a whole number of shares.
  c) _____ banks offer convenience and, often, lower fees and higher interest rates to their customers.
  d) _____, such as Merrill Lynch and Salomon Smith Barney, offer the speed and convenience of online trading, together with the advice of a broker.
  e) _____ is when an investor buys stock and borrows money from the broker to invest further in the stock.

ANSWERS TO SELF-REVIEW EXERCISES

16.1 a) False. Internet-only banks lack brand awareness and recognition compared with click-and-mortar banks. b) False. Enabling customers to pay their bills and write checks online decreases float. c) False. Wireless access to financial information is growing slowly in the United States because of the many different technical standards. d) True. e) False. A bond is a written promise that an entity will repay a debt that is sold to an investor.

16.2 a) Aggregation services. b) Dollar-based investing. c) Internet-only. d) Full-service brokers. e) Trading on margin.

EXERCISES

16.3 State whether each of the following is true or false; if false, explain why.
  a) Investors are subject to less risk when trading online compared with traditional trading.
  b) Discount brokerage services require investors to manage their own accounts and conduct their own research.

c) Online companies usually charge a fee for every purchase or sale of securities.

d) ECNs open and close trading hours at the same time as the traditional markets.

e) The federal government does not regulate aggregators, so the aggregators are not required to compensate users if security is compromised by a hacker.

16.4 Fill in the blanks in each of the following statements:

a) A _____ requires self-sufficiency, leaving the investor responsible for making and executing investment decisions.

b) _____ will allow traders to find the best deals on foreign currency, and this could create smaller margins between the prices of different currencies.

c) A _____ is a written promise that an entity will repay debt that is sold to an investor.

d) ECNs will benefit from _____, the change of stock prices from fractions to decimals.

e) _____, making short-term trades in an attempt to profit off of market inefficiencies, has become prevalent on the Internet.

16.5 Define the following:

a) screen scraping

b) margin call

c) electronic communications network (ECN)

d) transparency

e) decimalization

16.6 E*TRADE offers a stock- and options-trading simulation at www.etrade.com. Each player is allocated an initial $100,000 in order to make his or her trades. As the round progresses, a player's stocks will gain or lose value, reflecting the actual stock market activity. Players compete to earn the greatest return on their investment (i.e., profits) for the round. Each new round begins on the first day of each month. At the end of the month, all portfolios are compared, and the 32 highest finishers receive a prize. The E*TRADE game is free for your use and gives potential investors a chance to see how their stock picks would perform without actually putting their money at risk. For this exercise, the class will be divided into teams. Each team should decide on a name and use it to register for the "stock-trading only" version of the game. This exercise will let the teams compete over a period of three days to see which can create the most valuable stock portfolio. Each team should begin the game on the same day. Teams should be aware that investing all of the available funds will not necessarily give them a more profitable portfolio: A market downturn could spell disaster for a fully invested team! (Note: E*TRADE automatically resets the game at the end of each month. Be sure to start this exercise at least three days prior to the end of the month, so that you do not lose your data.) In order to begin trading, you should complete the tasks that follow. Please let us know if you win a prize!

a) Create a written log of your stock choices.

b) Record the initial purchase value of each stock.

c) If a stock is sold, make a note of its sale in the log. How much was it sold for?

d) Record the value of your portfolio at least twice a day. Include the time it was recorded.

e) Record the final value of each stock and of the overall portfolio at the end of three days.

f) How did your stocks perform?

g) What rank did your portfolio achieve in the competition?

16.7 Visit **www.money.com/101** and take lesson number 4, on the basics of investing.

a) List the "Top Ten Things To Know" for this lesson.

b) Read the details for each section.

c) What occurred in 1997 that affected the stock market?

d) When the interest rates go up (with everything else held the same), investors tend to do what? Why?

e) What kind of bonds generally have higher coupons? Why?

f) What are growth funds?

g) Take the test at the end of the lesson. What is your score? Which questions did you get wrong? Was this lesson useful?

16.8 Print and fill out the form found at **www.ihatefinancialplanning.com/topics/ content/Financial_Plan/networth.pdf**. What is your approximate net worth? How do you stand financially? Now visit **www.ihatefinancialplanning.com/topics/calc/ applets/Loan.jsp**, and calculate the monthly payment of a $20,000 loan for a new car. Assume that the length of the loan is six years and the interest rate is nine percent.

16.9 Visit **www.401kafe.com/tools/calc.html** and use the 401(k) calculator. Use a current 401(k) balance of zero dollars, an annual salary of $40,000, an annual contribution of 10 percent, an employer match of 4 percent, an average rate of return of 6 percent, an inflation rate of 3 percent, your age now and a retirement age of 60. What is the future value of your contributions? Will you be able to retire comfortably with this retirement plan? Why or why not?

16.10 Select three Internet-only banks and discuss the following:
   a) Which bank offers the best rates on checking, savings and CDs?
   b) Do any of the banks offer credit-card services? Which ones? Explain.
   c) Which banks offer trading services? Explain each service. How much does it cost to make a trade?
   d) What are the main differences between hybrid and Internet-only banks?

WORKS CITED

The notation **<www.domain-name.com>** indicates that the citation is for information found at that Web site.

1.   G. Gottlieg, "Big Changes in the Banking Industry," *Net Commerce Magazine* March 2000: 16.

2.   M. Trombley, "Bankers Group Pushes Its Seal of Approval," *Computerworld* 14 August 2000: 20.

3.   K. Kirkpatrick, "Banking On The Net," *Computer Shopper* May 2000: 189.

4.   S. Junnakar, "Web Banks Look to Branch Out," **<news.cnet.com/news/0-1007-200-1551999.html>** 16 February 2000.

5.   K. Kirkpatrick, "Banking on The Net," *Computer Shopper* May 2000: 190.

6.   J. Labate and G. Silverman, "World Wide Web is not Wide Enough," *Financial Times* 6 April 2000: 20.

7.   K. Thomas, "Millions Turn PCs Into Personal Tellers," *USA Today* 3 October 2000: 3D.

8.   K. Thomas, 3D.

9.   **<www.wellsfargo.com>**.

10. D. Levine, "Wells Next Stage," **TheStandard.com** 8 May 2000.

11. J. Sapsford, "Smaller Institutions Make Web Inroads Via Outsourcing," *The Wall Street Journal* 21 January 2000: C1.

12. L. Berlin, "Small Change," **TheStandard.com** 8 May 2000.

13. J. Hechinger, "A Tiny Bank Turns Big Player On The Internet," *The Wall Street Journal* 20 July 2000: B1.

14. J. Hechinger, B12.

15. S. Rose, "The Truth About Online Banking," *Money* April 2000: 119.

16. K. Weisul, "Wingspan Causes Online Banking Flap," *Inter@ctive Week* 27 March 2000: 24.

17. B. Menniger, "Small or Not At All," **TheStandard.com** 8 May 2000.

18. **<www.onecore.com>**.

19. **<www.netbank.com>**.

20. P. Patsuris, "Veterans From First USA, Wingspan Form New Net Bank," **Forbes.com** 25 May 2000.

21. K. Thomas, "Millions Turn PCs Into Personal Tellers," *USA Today* 3 October 2000: 3D.

22. D. Kong, "Home Buyers In Their Sites," *The Boston Globe* 13 February 2000: C5.

23. D. Kong, C5.

24. **<www.mortgage.com/pressrelease.htm>**.

25. **<www.tradearca.com>** and J. Labate, "Wall Starts To Crack As Pressure Intensifies," *Financial Times* 31 March 2000: 7.

26. C. Murphy "Biz Model: Archipelago," **Informationweek.com** 26 June 2000: RB24.

27. **<www.tradearca.com>**.

28. **<www.tradearca.com/news_and_views/releases/ releases_07_13_00.asp>**.

29. W. Watts, "Stocks To Trade In Decimal Increments," **CBS.MarketWatch.com** 13 June 2000.

30. W. Watts, "Stocks To Trade In Decimal Increments."

31. S. Ginsberg, "The Decimal Debacle," **www.theindustrystandard.com** 26 June 2000.

32. J. Labate, "Wall Starts To Crack As Pressure Intensifies," *Financial Times* 31 March 2000: 7.

33. N. Weinberg and D. Kruger, "The Big Board Comes Back From The Brink," *Forbes* 13 November 2000: 276.

34. N. Weinberg and D. Kruger, 276.

35. G. Smith, "On the Web—But With A Broker on Standby," *Business Week* 22 May 2000: 150.

36. C. Farrell, "Online or Off, the Rules Are the Same," *Business Week* 22 May 2000: 148.

37. **<www.etrade.com>**.

38. **<www.sharebuilder.com>**.

39. M. Vickers and G. Weiss, "Wall Street's Hype Machine," *Business Week* 3 April 2000: 115.

40. L. Reilly, "The Margin-Debt Hole: How Deep Is Too Deep?" *Money* April 2000: 136.

41. L. Reilly, 136.

42. "Web Trading Firms' Claims Curbed," *The Boston Globe* 2 May 2000: E6.

43. C. Swann, "Foreign Exchange Banks Charge Into Online Battle," *Financial Times* 15 August 2000: 19.

44. C. Swann, 19.

45. A. Schmertz, "JGB Market In Scramble To Introduce Electronic Trading," *Financial Times* 25 October 2000: 30.

46. S. Ascarelli, "Online Stock-Trading Platform Planned For Europe by Goldman Sachs Group," *The Wall Street Journal* 29 September 2000: C12.

47. S. Calamba and J. Dooley, "Online Corporate-Bond Sales by Bear Stearns, Deutsche Bank Get Mixed Reviews From Investors," *The Wall Street Journal* 14 August 2000: C21.

48. B. Healy, "Harvard Selling Bonds On The Web," *The Boston Globe* 3 November 2000: C5.

49. S. Calamba and J. Dooley, "Online Corporate-Bond Sales by Bear Stearns, Deutsche Bank Get Mixed Reviews From Investors," *The Wall Street Journal* 14 August 2000: C21.

50. E. Buckley, "Green Revolution," **TheStandard.com** 8 May 2000.

51. <www.yodlee.com>.

52. M. Trombley, "Group Seeks Web Banking Standard," *Computer World* 12 June 2000: 20.

53. M. Trombley, 20.

54. H. Timmons, "Look, There's Your Portfolio," *Business Week* 12 June 2000: 166.

55. H. Timmons, 168.

56. J. Sapsford, "Personalized Financial Web Sites Spread, Amid Privacy Concerns," *The Wall Street Journal* 19 July 2000: C1.

57. S. Nelson, "Aggregation Services Put All of Your Financial Stuff In One Place," *The Boston Globe* 16 July 2000: H7.

58. <www.chase.com>.

59. C. Power, "Wireless Banking Fails to Attract The Masses," **AmericanBanker.com** <www.americanbanker.com/supplements/CS2000/wireless.html>.

60. E. Batista, "Wireless Banking: Bust In U.S." *Wired News* 25 July 2000 <www.wired-news.com/news/wireless/0,1382,37639,00.html>.

61. E. Batista, "Wireless Banking: Bust In U.S."

17

e-Learning

Objectives

- To understand the concept of e-learning.
- To understand the effects of e-learning on traditional education.
- To discuss how e-learning is affecting corporate and information-technology training.
- To explore test-taking and online book suppliers.
- To predict the future of e-learning.

The medieval university looked backwards; it professed to be a storehouse of old knowledge. . . . The modern university looks forward, and is a factory of new knowledge.
Thomas Henry Huxley

You must train the children to their studies in a playful manner, and without any air of constraint, with the further object of discerning more readily the natural bent of their respective characters.
Plato

The only fence against the world is a thorough knowledge of it.
John Locke

What sculpture is to a block of marble, education is to an human soul.
Joseph Addison

'Tis education forms the common mind,
Just as the twig is bent, the tree's inclined.
Alexander Pope

Outline

17.1   Introduction
17.2   e-Learning Technologies and Infrastructure.
17.3   e-Learning Overview
17.5   Training Marketplaces
17.6   Information Technology (IT) Training Online
17.7   Traditional Education Online
17.8   Studying Online
17.9   Educational Supplies and Resources Online
17.10 Internet and World Wide Web Resources

Summary • Terminology • Self-Review Exercises • Answers to Self-Review Exercises • Exercises • Works Cited

17.1 Introduction

E-learning—the use of the Internet and related technologies for the development, distribution and enhancement of learning resources—has enormous potential as a new medium for education. It provides an efficient means for undergraduates, graduate students, postgraduates, international students and professionals to obtain a degree in a variety of disciplines. It provides students and professional with skills for career advancement, enabling busy people to learn new technologies. Corporations are also implementing Web-based training to keep employees up-to-date on new products, services and protocols. Experts believe it to be the fastest growing education industry, expecting it to double in size from 2000 to 2002.[1]

e-Fact 17.1

In July, 2000, the e-learning industry was estimated to be a $250 billion dollar market.[2]

In this chapter, we explore e-learning in the academic and corporate world. We discuss current technologies and the potential uses of e-learning. We provide an analysis of the strengths, weaknesses, opportunities and threats of e-learning as it continues to become more popular (Fig. 17.1). We also review the various services on the Web that offer courses, solutions, resources and supplies.

e-Learning SWOT Analysis	
Strengths	Ability to offer education to large numbers of students from distant locations.
	Lower costs (travel, instructor fees).
	Shorter courses mean less time commitment necessary from corporate students.

Fig. 17.1   e-Learning SWOT analysis (part 1 of 2).

	e-Learning SWOT Analysis
	Lower cost means education is more accessible to people with limited financial resources.
	Use best instructors making best courses available to all.
Weaknesses	Large commitment to technology needed from universities, corporations offering e-learning courses.
	Lack of face-to-face contact with students.
	Current technology does not support low-cost, high-bandwidth, synchronous student-teacher interaction.
Opportunities	Ability to reach the world instantaneously with the latest news and technologies.
	Ability to train sales force and employees about product advancements.
	Access to courses from a variety of universities.
	Decrease long-term education expenses by shifting learning programs to the Web.
Threats	Lack of student interest.
	Equipment and technology requirements restrict adoption of e-learning.
	Lack of human interaction deters the learning process.
	Most corporate instructor-led courses last 4-5 days, comprehensive coverage of some topics could be lost in a shorter e-course.

Fig. 17.1   e-Learning SWOT analysis (part 2 of 2).

17.2 e-Learning Technologies and Infrastructure.

E-learning relies heavily on technology and will only improve as bandwidth, multimedia technologies advance (See Chapter 5, Hardware, Software, and Communications). Corporations looking to offer e-learning programs will have to invest a great deal of resources in technology infrastructure which may include video-conferencing technology, streaming audio and video, redundant storage space and high-bandwidth to broadcast courses over the Web.

Less multimedia-intensive products can also be effective and can provide a productive learning experience for students. *Computer-based-training* (CBT) is not new. Corporate employees and students have been using interactive educational software for many years. Floppy disks and CDs helped facilitate the learning process by making educational software readily available. CD-ROM computer-based-training products allow students to take a self-paced course in any number of subjects. Since no downloading is necessary, bandwidth is not a concern with CBT courses.

CBT and Web-based-training developers must consider that their courses will be used on varying operating systems and platforms. XML and Java technology offer portability and hence scalability to developers, making the process of creating courseware more efficient. [*Note: XML is discussed in the programming appendices in the back of the book.*] The Internet gives e-learning solution providers the ability to reach a global market instantaneously. *Cross-platform* products are accessible by many different operating systems and are a necessity when trying to reach markets using varying information systems.

Web-based training (WBT) requires many additional technologies. Students taking *asynchronous* courses (which can be taken any time and are self-paced) will not have the benefit of a live instructor. These courses must minimize student confusion by providing a basic interface and clear, concise content. Students should have the ability to communicate with each other using chat programs and message boards. Electronic whiteboards that can be seen by every student will make the learning process easier, helping to illustrate concepts. To keep the students' interest, it is important to keep each course reasonably short. Courses lasting more than a few hours might lose a students' attention before the course is completed. Streaming audio and video are also tools that can help keep students interested and solidify difficult concepts. However, these technologies require substantial bandwidth, and should be made optional to the user. Voice recognition capabilities, animation and voice-chatting capabilities will also add significant value to a course.

Storage space is a major concern for e-learning vendors. Each course requires a database of information that can be downloaded by the students. Audio and video require additional server space. Storage space is expensive with high-capacity servers potentially costing millions of dollars. *Redundancy* is important to prevent costly downtime. Courses offering *synchronous* (occurring in real time) audio and video with live instructors will require even more resources to ensure that systems function properly when the courses are delivered.

Universities and corporations that offer e-learning must also have an organized way to offer these courses to their students. *Learning Management Systems* (LMS) allow these e-learning solutions providers to offer courses to students in an efficient manner. An LMS is a database which can be accessed by employees and students, providing course outlines, explanations, pre-requisite information and the courses themselves. The e-learning provider has the option of charging the user per course or offering the courses for free. The LMS can also be used to offer the course to the general public by integrating an e-commerce infrastructure.

Despite the costs of integrating education and the Web, the benefits are unquestionable. The average instructor-led corporate-training course lasts four-to-five days and between 30-40 hours. This represents a major resource commitment for a company, including lost productivity by a group of employees for an extended period of time. This lost productivity can be a considerable expense. Instructor travel and course materials add to this expense. Although the short-term technology expense is great, the long-term savings offer a valuable alternative. It is unlikely that Web-based training will make traditional instructor-led training obsolete, but it will offer corporations, universities and students a valuable, lower-cost alternative.

17.3 e-Learning Overview

Many companies have taken different approaches to the e-learning business model. A *learning marketplace* connects students and teachers to courses on the Internet. Some businesses design e-learning opportunities to supplement their current products and services. Online universities offer both accredited and non-accredited courses. The sale of supplementary educational materials is another popular form of online-learning services.

The advantages of instant communication and global accessibility over the Internet and the decreasing cost of hardware and communications have fostered a growth in e-learning.[4] E-learning also reduces time and travel expenses, allowing people to complete courses from their homes and offices, further increasing their ability to fit learning into their schedules. It allows businesses to educate their employees on new technologies and reduces the amount of time it takes to train instructors. This helps to accelerate *time to market*, the speed at which a company can begin to sell its products or services. In some cases, such as asynchronous learning, fewer classes need to be arranged as a larger number of employees can be accommodated at one time via e-learning. Further, the cost of updating information is greatly reduced by using content-management tools. Businesses can implement changes to their materials in one central location, ensuring instructional consistency. Offering online courses is also an effective way to attract customers to your site and increase the length of their stay, often called a site's *stickiness*. Stickiness is discussed in Chapter 10, e-Customer Relationship Management.

Online learning also includes classes for people interested in developing new skills or entertaining hobbies. For example, Barnes & Noble (**www.bn.com**) offers online courses in nutrition and money management. The courses suggest readings that users can then purchase from the Web site. Powered (**www.powered.com**), formerly **notHarvard.com**, offers *eduCommerce* services and **SmartPlanet.com** provides a variety of online courses.

e-Fact 17.2

Organizations save an estimated 50–70 percent when implementing online learning in place of traditional instructor-led classroom training.[5]

However, e-learning also has its skeptics. Since e-learning will not be immediately available to a worldwide market, some fear that a gap will be created between the rich and poor. People in developing nations will be at a disadvantage to wealthier nations with more technology resources. Copyright infringement is of particular concern, as proprietary information posted on the Web can easily be downloaded, copied and distributed. Copyright issues are discussed in Chapter 11, Legal and Ethical Issues; Internet Taxation. Teaching young children over the Internet is also a divided issue. Some individuals maintain that e-learning, when used in controlled settings, can supplement traditional education. Others suggest that learning online reduces social interaction among children. Regardless of discussion that occurs in a chat room, students in a Web-based program will lack the socialization aspects of a traditional education. Further, Web-based training is not always designed by skilled educators. These issues are discussed in Chapter 13, Social and Political Issues.

17.4 E-Learning Solution Providers

E-learning solution providers build customized courses for businesses (Fig. 17.2). In addition to building the e-learning program, many of these companies monitor the success of the training to determine the company's *return on investment* (ROI), the ratio of cost savings and increased revenue to money. In this section, we explore e-learning solution providers.

DigitalThink (**www.digitalthink.com**) is an end-to-end solution provider, offering a series of previously constructed Web-based courses (Java, e-commerce, databases, etc.) and the ability to build Web-based training according to the specifications of an organization. E-learning solutions developed by DigitalThink are self-paced, accommodating student's schedules. Interested users can experiment with DigitalThink courses by taking a sampler course at **www.digitalthink.com/els/sampler/html**. Courses include *e-Commerce Fundamentals Sampler*, *Elements of the e-Business Solution* and *Introduction to Analyzing Financial Statements Sampler.*

Centra's e-learning platforms (**www.centra.com**) offer Web-based training solutions through *Centra Symposium 4.0™*, a virtual classroom, that can manage up to 250 users at one time and *Centra Conference 3.0™*, which enables businesses to conduct demonstrations and presentations via the Internet. *Centra Meeting 3.0™* offers a secure forum for making meeting arrangements and conducting conferences.

e-Learning Solution Provider	URL	Features
Saba™	**www.saba.com**	Offers consulting services, solutions implementation, hosting services, scalable corporate education services and performance management.
WBT Systems	**www.wbtsytems.com**	*TopClass*, WBT System's signature product, offers design and development services for Web-based training.
VCampus®	**www.vcampus.com**	Provides e-learning platform with customizing capabilities. A tour of VCampus and a demonstration course are available through the site.
SmartForce	**www.smartforce.com**	Offers customized e-learning solutions and support services.
THINQ	**www.thinq.com**	Provides customized Web-based training through Thinq *Learning Consulting* services.
Click2Learn	**www.click2learn.com**	A database of products and services to help individuals and companies find the courses they need. This site also has a skills assessment feature that helps customers evaluate their e-learning needs. Companies wishing to develop their own training can use the *Click2Learn Toolbook* product to develop and sell courses on the Click2Learn site.
Headlight.com	**www.headlight.com**	Design, development and deployment of training courses based on corporate needs. Consulting services are also available.

Fig. 17.2   e-learning solution providers.

e-Learning Solution Provider	URL	Features
PBS Adult Learning Service	**www.pbs.org/adultlearning**	Licenses and distributes online learning courses to colleges, universities, etc.
Caliber™	**www.caliberlearning.com**	Builds online courses to meet corporate needs, provides distribution methods and consulting services.

Fig. 17.2   e-learning solution providers.

17.5 Training Marketplaces

Training marketplaces serve as forums for companies that need training but do not want to pay the development and implementation costs of designing their own program. Marketplaces allow them to select the material they need and pay per course. In this section, we review several training marketplaces and the variety of services they provide.

THINQ (**www.thinq.com**), formerly known as **Trainingnet.com**, connects businesses to training through the THINQ *eCatalog*. Companies can browse through course offerings of approximately 3000 training providers to select a course that best suits their needs. They can also post for training providers through the THINQ *RFP (request for proposal) Exchange*. Here, companies can post training opportunities to be viewed by qualified training providers.

In addition to providing e-learning solutions, **KnowledgePlanet.com** also operates as a training marketplace. Interested companies can browse the list of **Knowledge-Planet.com**'s partners, searching according to general categories or specific industries. Other training marketplaces include Docent™ (**www.docent.com**)—which integrates businesses, enterprises and professional communities into marketplaces—and Hungry Minds (**www.hungryminds.com**). EduPoint™ (**www.edupoint.com**) offers over one million educational options through 4000 different providers, and **TrainSeek.com** links trainers and organizations to educational resources.

17.6 Information Technology (IT) Training Online

Web-based training (WBT) provides a new means for corporate learning. As previously discussed, the expense of training employees can be greatly reduced by implementing e-learning. In this section, we explore information technology (IT) and management training, how they affect business processes and various companies that are offering e-learning courses.

Web-based IT training provides the advantage of hands-on experience, an important element when approaching certification exams. Students can learn new languages and techniques and apply them directly while at the computer. There are currently over 200 IT training Web sites (Fig. 17.3).[9]

URL	Products and Services
www.knowledgenet.com	View demonstrations of KnowledgeNet including *KnowledgeNet Live* (e-learning classroom setting, dual-band communication, etc.); *KnowledgeNet Express* (experience Microsoft and Cisco training sessions); *KnowledgeNet Custom* (view custom designed training session); *KnowledgeNet Mentor* and *KnowledgeNet Labs*.
gocertify.earthweb.com	Provides IT training and certification from a variety of vendors.
www.wavetech.com	Offers instructor-led training, self-paced study, computer-based training, certification, etc.
www.ameritrain.com	Provides hands-on computer training.

Fig. 17.3   Online IT training.

CyberStateU.com, founded in 1994, offers Web-based IT training for individuals and corporations. CyberStateU provides 24-hour access to its online training "facilities" as well as its *Practice Lab*, where students can receive hands-on training experience. The Lab allows students to work through similar technologies, whereas traditional classroom styles are often complicated by access (or lack thereof) to various types of equipment.[10] The site offers stand-alone courses and complete training courses. Classes generally run four to five months. Courses taught through **CyberStateU.com** are no less expensive than a traditionally taught course at a local university, but they do offer the reduced expense of time and travel.

Students can browse available class schedules to find a time that works best for them. Registration deadlines generally close 10 days before the class begins. Through the use of books, video, online lectures and reviews, **CyberStateU.com**'s Practice Lab and a comprehensive support system, students can work toward certification. *Professor Wire*, **CyberStateU.com**'s online lecturer allows students to ask questions.[11] A free sample class is available at **CyberStateU.com**.

CodeWarriorU.com, another online education site, offers users access to programming courses including Java, XML and C++. Registered students (registration takes just a few minutes) can view course offerings, prerequisites and the course syllabus. Supplementary materials are recommended and usually cost $80–$100.

Corporate management and product development e-learning is a growing industry, and some organizations employ a *Chief Learning Officer* (CLO) to design the corporate learning strategy. To stay competitive, organizations must constantly inform their employees about developing products, services and technologies (see Quisic feature). Distance learning drastically cuts the cost of corporate training by reducing time and travel expenses. Web-based trainers suggest that, having eliminated the need for a hotel stay, airfare, rental car and meals, in addition to the cost of the course itself, corporations reduce the cost of training their employees by 60 percent.[12]

e-Fact 17.3

Between 1988 and 2000, the number of corporate universities quadrupled. At this pace, there are expected to be more corporate universities than traditional educational institutions by 2010.[13]

Businesses can also choose to build their own Web-based e-learning services. Net-Scene (**www.net-scene.com**) allows businesses to build streaming-media presentations from PowerPoint slides using its *PointPlus Maker*. The *PointPlus Viewer* enables the PowerPoint slides to be viewed with RealAudio synchronization.

Quisic^{SM}: Corporate Education Online

Launched in 1997, Quisic (**www.quisic.com**) offers online corporate training for undergraduates, graduate students and those already in the corporate sector. Quisic has several different offerings. Businesses can choose to enroll their employees in pre-MBA and Corporate MBA programs, allowing employees to advance their skills while staying on the job (Fig. 17.4). A demonstration of the pre-MBA program is available at **www.quisic.com/demo/graduate/pre_mba_demos/index.htm** (Fig. 17.5). The demonstration walks the user through a sample class, indicating objectives and providing examples.

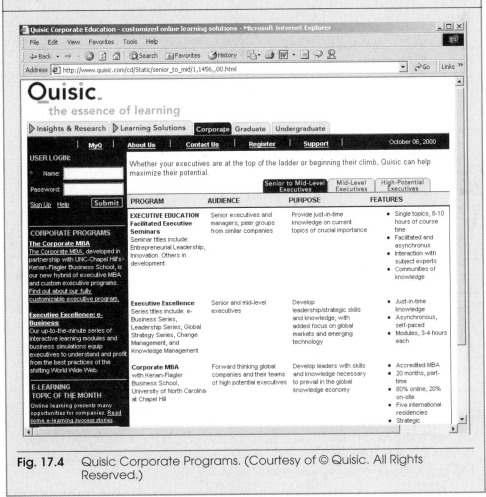

Fig. 17.4   Quisic Corporate Programs. (Courtesy of © Quisic. All Rights Reserved.)

Quisic^{SM}: Corporate Education Online (Cont.)

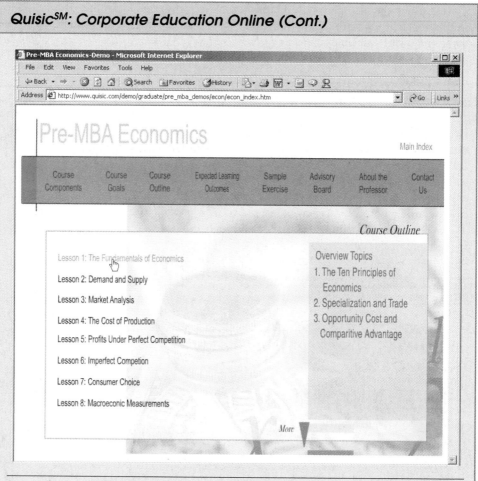

Fig. 17.5   PreMBA Course Outline. (Courtesy of © Quisic. All Rights Reserved.)

The Corporate MBA program demonstration (**www.quisic.com/cmba/demo/ index.htm**) walks the user through an example interactive exercise and case study. The undergraduate programs demonstration (**www.quisic.com/demo/under-grad/index.htm**) allows the user to review course offerings and requirements.

Quisic also offers the *Executive Excellence: e-Business series*, consisting of seven short, interactive modules. Students are introduced to basic e-business principles and then have the opportunity to apply them to real situations. E-business models, e-business strategies, legal issues and infrastructure are among the topics covered.

Quisic is affiliated with the Tuck School of Business at Dartmouth College, London Business School, Kenan-Flagler Business School at the University of North Carolina at Chapel Hill, the Marshall School of Business at the University of Southern California, and professors from Duke University, the University of Chicago and the University of California at Los Angeles.

e-Fact 17.4

According to PricewaterhouseCoopers, the lack of properly trained employees is the primary hindrance to the growth of 70 percent of the world's top businesses.[14]

17.7 Traditional Education Online

Elementary, high school, college and adult students also have educational opportunities through the Internet (see **Gen.com** feature). For adults continuing their education, Web-based training can be structured around their work schedules, allowing people to log on from home, business or travel anytime. In the future, wireless applications will allow people to take classes while commuting to and from the office (see Chapter 6, Wireless Internet and m-Business).

While many elementary and high schools use the Web as a supplement to classroom teaching (see Learning Network feature), higher education including undergraduate, graduate and professional programs offer full-length courses and degree programs via the Web (Fig. 17.6). For example, Stanford University and Duke University offer fully accredited MBA programs online, and The University of Phoenix is an accredited *virtual university*.[7]

Gen.com: Liberal Arts Online

The Global Education Network (**www.gen.com**) offers online courses and seminars via the Web. Interested users can view the course catalog online, which includes AIDS, Calculus, Mythology, Politics, etc. The courses, usually 10–18 one-hour lectures and related assignments, are taught by professors from well-known colleges and universities, such as Williams College, Wellesley College and Brown University.

While browsing the course catalog, interested users have the opportunity to view a QuickTime video of the course. These are usually a few minutes long and are given by the professor teaching the course.

Registered students who are auditing a course have one year to complete the requirements. Those completing the course for a grade are expected to follow the requirements set forth by the instructor. A transcript of official grades is given to the student upon completion.

Learning Network: Supplementing Education

The Learning Network offers learning resources categorized by subject and age group. This includes software, books, games and other resource materials to enhance the learning experience. Parents and teachers can also consult the site for information regarding children's education.

FamilyEducation, a division of the Learning Network, is a combined effort among parents and educators to bring online tools into children's education. *TeacherVision*, also part of the *Learning Network*, serves as a forum for educators and administrators. *InfoPlease* provides the Learning Network with a database of resources covering over 60 years of published material, and *FactMonster* provides a fun way for students to research projects.

University	URL	Programs Offered
University of Dallas	`imba.udallas.edu`	e-Commerce, Telecommunications Management, Information Technology and Sport Management
Colorado State	`www.biz.colostate.edu`	MBA and Management of Technology
East Carolina University	`www.dcs.ecu.edu`	MS Industrial Technology, MS Occupational Safety, graduate and undergraduate courses
Concord University	`bw.concordlawschool.com`	Juris Doctorate, Executive JD^{SM}
Suffolk University	`www.suffolkemba.org`	MBA
Jones International University	`www.educationalbenefit.com`	MBA
Kaplan	`www.kaplancollege.com`	MBA, Paralegal Studies, Legal Nurse Consulting, Criminal Justice and Law.
Capella University	`www.capellauniveristy.com`	MS, MBA, PhD

Fig. 17.6 Graduate and professional degrees available online.

`eCollege.com`^{SM} provides students with access to a variety of courses offered online. Course searches can be conducted according to degree, discipline and institution or by searching for available online course offerings. Links to scholarship opportunities are also available through the site.

e-Fact 17.5

In 2000, nearly 30 percent of colleges and universities were offering distance learning programs; this is expected to increase to 80 percent by the year 2002.[8]

eCompanion^{SM}, a feature of `eCollege.com`, allows educators to post grades online, provide supplementary course material and relevant links and organize group activities. An online tour of eCompanion is available at `www.ecollege.com/faculty/products/teach.html`. Online tours for `eCollege.com`'s other education service, *eCourse*^{SM}, demonstrates how the service allows teachers to design and manage online courses. *eToolkit*^{SM}, which provides administrative tools such as posting office hours and announcing events, is also available on the site.

Recognizing their academic resources as a potential source of capital, traditional institutions are also taking the initiative to offer e-learning programs (Fig. 17.7). These initiatives include degree-earning distance learning classes as well as the use their expertise and resources to create new businesses. For example, Stanford, Carnegie Mellon, University of Chicago, Columbia and the London School of Economics and Political Science are contributing parties to Cardean (`www.cardean.com`). Cardean is the first online business university built by UNext (**www.unext.com**) an online education provider. Courses offered through Cardean are sponsored by the contributing universities. They are asynchronous, allowing students to move at their own pace. A course demo and catalog are available through the site.

As we discussed in Chapter 13, Social and Political Issues, many secondary and elementary schools lack the proper funding to implement new technologies and the professional training to support them. Further, schools will need to be rewired and, in some cases, redesigned to accommodate the effects of the new economy. However, the addition of the Internet to the learning process is important. Nearly all businesses use computers, and an increasing number are developing an online presence to enhance communications and procedures.

 e-Fact 17.6

According to the Higher Education Research Institute, approximately 83 percent of first-year college students use the Internet when conducting research.[6]

17.8 Studying Online

In addition to taking classes, earning a degree or becoming certified online, Internet users can also take advantage of test-prep and tutoring services. College graduates and graduating high school students can find practice tests and test-taking advice online for standardized tests.

TestU (**www.testu.com**) is geared toward high school students preparing for the college entrance exams. Asynchronous test preparation is available for the SAT, PSAT, ACT and TOEFL. Full-length practice tests enable students to familiarize themselves with the material and time limits. In addition, TestU, through its *SMART Curriculum*™ (Self-Modifying, Ability-Reactive Training) feature, modifies its practice program to focus on the areas where students need the most help.

For younger students and their parents, online tutoring services can provide students with an enhanced learning experience (see the **Tutor.com** feature). Some of these sites link students and tutors so they can meet person-to-person, while others facilitate tutoring services over the Web.

School	URL	Purpose
Stanford	**eskolar.com**	Designed for healthcare professionals, allowing them to meet patient needs and continue their education.
NYU	**NYUOnline.com**	Delivers customized content packages to business organizations.
Columbia	**Fathom.com**	Provides articles, interviews, lectures and additional resources in technology, business, law, etc.
UCLA	**OnlineLearning.net**	Offers both accredited and nonaccredited continuing education courses.
UPenn	**Pensare.com**	Hosts an e-learning center, now offering "Strategic Business Plan Analysis."

Fig. 17.7   Examples of online ventures by college and universities.

Tutor.com: *Enhancing Learning Online*

Tutor.com is an online service that connects students with qualified tutors in 375 different subjects. Students and tutors can choose to meet personally, or they can meet at the online whiteboard that allows them to communicate lessons over the Internet. The tutoring forum offers voice interaction (Chapter 10, e-Customer Relationship Management), drawing tools, math tools, chatting capabilities and file uploads (Fig. 17.8).

Tutors can register themselves online. Payment amounts are determined by the tutor. For online tutors, **Tutor.com** establishes online payment and distributes a check twice per month. **Tutor.com** then keeps a percentage of the fee based upon the amount of time spent online and the rate charged by the tutor.

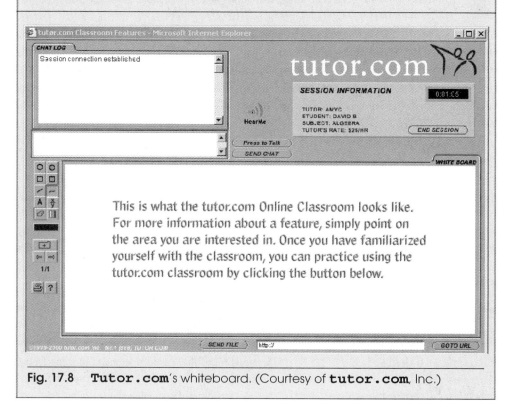

Fig. 17.8   Tutor.com's whiteboard. (Courtesy of **tutor.com**, Inc.)

Thomson Learning™ (**www.itped.com**) offers test-preparation products and services. Using Testing Tools, teachers can create, administer and grade practice tests and exams. The site also offers *Web Tutor*™, which allows teachers and students to communicate via the Web. Course design, links to supplementary content, flashcards and multimedia further enhance the learning experience. Online tutorials and animated demos are available on the site.

Well-known test-preparation services also offer online services and courses. Visit **www.princetonreview.com** to learn more about studying for the SAT and GMAT online. Kaplan allows interested students to enroll online for private tutors and offline and online classes, including test-preparation as well as topic-specific training. Visit **www.kaplan.com** for a listing of course offerings and services.

17.9 Educational Supplies and Resources Online

Educational supplies can also be purchased online. Many sites offer books, videos and other materials at a low cost. Designed to meet the needs of the college student, **eCampus.com** was launched in 1999. Through **eCampus.com**, students can purchase many of the same items they would find in a campus store at a reduced cost with free shipping. In addition to buying books and collegiate merchandise, students are also able to sell used books back and participate in **eCampus.com**'s online auction. A "backpack" (**eCampus.com**'s version of a shopping cart) enables multiple purchases to be made in a single transaction. Other online resources allowing students to buy and sell books and other materials include, **Varsitybooks.com** and Bigwords (**www.bigwords.com**).

Addall.com searches a variety of online educational resource providers to find the lowest cost on books. Searches can be conducted by keyword, author, title and ISBN number. Similar services are provided by **Bookfinder.com**. Virtual books can be purchased through **ibooks.com**. *Public domain* works, such as classic novels can be downloaded for free. E-publishing and associated electronic devices are discussed in Chapter 18, e-Publishing.

Financial aid, often a necessity for students interesting in attending college, can also be researched on the Internet. Web sites such as **FreeScholarships.com** allows students to "earn" funding by playing games. U.S. News and World Report (**www.usnews.com**) also offers financial-aid resources in addition to its well-known annual rankings of educational institutions.

17.10 Internet and World Wide Web Resources

Online Learning Opportunities

www.bn.com
Barnes and Noble offers several online courses for areas of general interest. Courses include literature, history and many other liberal arts.

www.cardean.com
This online university of business has affiliations with Stanford University, Carnegie Mellon University, University of Chicago, and others.

www.eskolar.com
This site is an affiliate of Stanford University designed to provide healthcare professionals with information and continuing education.

www.nyuonline.com
New York University (NYU) delivers customized content packages to businesses and organizations through this site.

www.fathom.com
This site (developed by Columbia University) provides articles, interviews, lectures and additional resources in technology, business, law, etc.

www.onlinelearning.net
This UCLA-affiliated site offers both accredited and non-accredited continuing education courses.

`www.pensare.com`
Affiliated with the University of Pennsylvania, this site hosts an e-learning center, now offering "Strategic Business Plan Analysis."

Solutions Providers

`www.unext.com`
UNext is the online education solutions provider responsible for the development of Cardean.

`www.powered.com`
Powered offers *eduCommerce*, a service that supplies online businesses with e-learning opportunities.

`www.digitalthink.com`
This solution provider offers a series of pre-designed and customizable courses.

`www.centra.com`
Centra offers a Web-based classroom, conferencing capabilities and online meeting options.

`www.wbtsystems.com`
TopClass, WBT System's signature product offers design and development services for Web-based training.

`www.vcampus.com`
VCampus provides an e-learning platform with customizing capabilities. Visit this site to check out the demonstration courses.

`www.saba.com`
Saba offers consulting services, solutions implementation, hosting services, scalable corporate education services and performance management solutions.

`www.caliberlearning.com`
Caliber builds online courses and provides distribution methods and consulting services.

`www.pbs.org/adultlearning`
The Public Broadcasting System's adult education services licenses and distributes online learning courses to colleges, universities, etc.

`www.headlight.com`
This site offers design, development and deployment of training courses for corporations. Consulting services are also available.

`www.click2learn.com`
Click2Learn offers a database of products and services to help individuals and companies find the education they need.

`www.thinq.com`
Thinq provides customized Web-based training through Thinq *Learning Consulting* services.

`www.smartforce.com`
This site offers customized e-learning solutions and support services.

Traditional Education Online

`www.gen.com`
The Global Education Network offers a variety of online courses and seminars. Its affiliates include Williams College, Brown University and Wellesley College.

`imba.udallas.edu`
Students can take courses in e-commerce, telecommunications management, information technology and sports management.

`www.biz.colostate.edu`

Colorado State offers MBA and Management of Technology online programs.

`www.dcs.ecu.edu`

Students can enroll in online MS Industrial Technology, MS Occupational Safety, graduate and undergraduate courses.

`bw.concordlawschool.com`

This site offers Juris Doctorate and Executive JD[SM] degrees.

`www.suffolkemba.org`

Students can earn their MBA from Suffolk University online.

`www.educationalbenefit.com`

Students can enroll online to earn their MBA.

`www.kaplancollege.com`

Kaplan College offers MBA, Paralegal Studies, Legal Nurse Consulting, Criminal Justice and Law programs online.

`www.capellauniveristy.com`

Students can earn their MS, MBA and PhD.

`www.ecollege.com`

This site is an online marketplace for traditional education.

IT Training Online

`www.knowledgenet.com`

Visit this site to view demonstrations of KnowledgeNet products and services.

`gocertify.earthweb.com`

GoCerify provides IT training and certification from a variety of vendors.

`www.wavetech.com`

This site offers instructor-led training, self-paced study, computer-based training, certification and more.

`www.ameritrain.com`

Ameritrain provides hands-on computer training online.

`www.cyberstateu.com`

CyberStateU provides IT training in Cisco networks, Microsoft products and Linux.

`CodeWarriorU.com`

This site offers programming courses in Java, XML and C++.

Corporate Training

`www.quisic.com`

Quisic offers online business training for undergraduates, graduates and professionals.

`www.net-scene.com`

Net-Scene allows businesses to build streaming-media versions of their PowerPoint presentations.

Online Test Preparation

`www.testu.com`

This site provides asynchronous training for students studying for college entrance exams.

`www.tutor.com`

This site links students and parents to tutors both online and offline.

www.itped.com
Thomson Learning offers online test-preparation services to teachers who wish to design and administer tests and quizzes online.

www.princetonreview.com
The Princeton Review provides information and online courses for SAT and GMAT test prep.

www.kaplan.com
Kaplan offers a search feature to help students locate tutors and test-preparation classes. Courses are also offered online.

www.ecampus.com
This site allows students to purchase school supplies and sell their used text books.

www.varistybooks.com
VarsityBooks offers school supplies online. Students can also sell their used text books through the site.

www.addall.com
This site allows students to search over 40 different book providers to find the lowest price.

www.eplyon.com
This site links educational institutions and resource suppliers.

www.ibooks.com
Students can purchase electronic course materials on this site.

www.usnews.com
U.S. News and World Report provides graduates and undergraduates with yearly school rankings as well as financial aid and other relevant information.

SUMMARY

- E-learning provides an efficient means for undergraduates, graduate students, postgraduates international students, professionals and programmers to obtain a degree in a variety of disciplines.

- Experts believe e-learning to be the fastest growing education industry, expecting it to double in size from 2000 to 2002.

- E-learning provides skills for career advancement, an additional service provided on the Web.

- Online training portals and supplementary materials are also a popular form of online learning businesses.

- The advantages of information transactions over the Internet and the decreasing cost of the hardware necessary to support this have fostered a growth in e-learning.

- E-learning also reduces time and travel expenses, especially when connected to corporate training, as it often requires the student to relocate for a given amount of time and allows all students and employees to learn from the best teachers.

- E-learning provides individuals and corporations with the ability to take courses on a schedule that best suits their, or their employees', needs.

- Asynchronous Web-based learning enables students to move through material at their own pace, ask questions when they become apparent and participate in a classroom discussion by addressing other students in designated chat rooms.

- E-learning reduces the amount of time it takes to train instructors to teach material and the time it takes to train all employees on the material.

- Offering online courses is an effective way to attract customers to your site and increase the length of their stay, often called a site's stickiness.

- One fear related to e-learning is a lack of accessibility, and, therefore, a growing gap between the rich and the poor, postindustrial nations and preindustrial nations, the technologically affluent and those less-technologically inclined.

- Some individuals maintain that e-learning, when used in controlled settings, can supplement traditional education. Others suggest that learning online reduces social interaction among children.

- Recognizing their academic resources as a potential source of capital, traditional institutions are also making efforts online.

- Many online courses and degree programs cost approximately the same as they might when taken in a traditional classroom.

- Companies adding e-learning to increase the stickiness of their sites can charge students on a per-course basis, and professors can leverage their own expertise by charging per student attending a lecture.

- In its earliest stages, e-learning was delivered through computer-based training (CBT) usually delivered to the desktop via CD ROM.

- With synchronous learning students and teacher meet on the Web at predetermined times and classes are conducted much like they would be in classroom settings.

- A Learning Management System (LMS) serves as a database from which employees can quickly and easily find training and information.

- Course registrations, posted scores and payment mechanisms are among the services available through LMSs.

- Skills assessment can also be implemented through LMS, allowing companies to customize training sessions for specific employees.

- Web-based training providers build company-specific courses, allowing a company to apply its own information, look and feel to the e-learning program.

- In addition to building the e-learning program, many of these Web-based training providers monitor the success of the training to determine the company's return on investment (ROI), cost savings and increased revenues to money spent.

- Training marketplaces serve as forums for companies needing training to find training providers.

- Training marketplaces are a valuable resource to companies that need training but do not want to pay the development and implementation costs of designing their own.

- Elementary, high school and college students have educational opportunities through the Internet.

- Wireless technology allows people to take classes while commuting to and from their offices.

- Many secondary and elementary schools lack the proper funding to implement new technologies and the professional training to support them.

- Full-length undergraduate degrees, graduate degrees and professional programs are offered via the Web.

- Web-based training (WBT) provides a new means for IT instruction. In addition to course lectures and reading materials, Web-based training provides the advantage of hands-on experience, an important element when approaching certification exams.

- Many organizations employ a Chief Learning Officer (CLO) to design the corporate learning strategy.

- Organizations must constantly inform their employees about developing products, services and technologies to stay competitive.

- It has been suggested that Web-based training can help corporations reduce the cost of training their employees by 60 percent over comparative instructor-led training programs.

TERMINOLOGY

asynchronous learning   redundancy
Chief Learning Officer (CLO)   request for proposal
code   return on investment (ROI)
cross-platform   stickiness
e-learning   synchronous learning
Learning Management System (LMS)   training marketplaces
learning marketplace   time to market
public domain   virtual university

SELF-REVIEW EXERCISES

17.1   State whether each of the following is true or false; if false, explain why.
   a) E-learning provides individuals the ability to take courses on a schedule that best suits their needs.
   b) Experts believe e-learning to be the fastest-growing education industry.
   c) The Internet is largely a forum for adult education. There are few opportunities for children to use the Internet as a learning tool.
   d) Recognizing their academic resources as a potential source of capital, traditional institutions are also making efforts online.
   e) Many online courses and degree programs cost approximately twice the amount of classes taken in a traditional classroom.

17.2   Fill in the blanks in each of the following statements.
   a) E-learning also reduces _____ and _____ expenses, especially when compared with corporate training, which often requires students to relocate for a given amount of time.
   b) Offering online courses is an effective way to attract customers to your site and increase the length of their stay, often called a site's _____.
   c) One fear related to e-learning is a lack of _____, and, therefore, a growing gap between the rich and the poor, postindustrial nations and preindustrial nations, the technologically affluent and those less-technologically inclined.
   d) In its earliest stages, e-learning was delivered through _____ usually delivered to the desktop via CD ROM.
   e) During _____ learning students and the teacher meet on the Web at a predetermined time and class is conducted much like it would be in a classroom setting.

ANSWERS TO SELF-REVIEW EXERCISES

17.1   a) True. b) True. c) False. Elementary, high school, college students and others all have educational opportunities through the Internet. d) True. e) False. The actual cost of the course is generally about the same as those taken in a traditional classroom.

17.2   a) Time and travel. b) Stickiness. c) accessibility. d) Computer-based training (CBT). e) Synchronous.

EXERCISES

17.3   State whether each of the following is true or false; if false, explain why.
   a) Training marketplaces serve as a forum for companies needing training to find individuals or companies that provide training.
   b) Full-length undergraduate degrees, graduate degrees and professional programs are offered via the Web.

c) E-learning increases the amount of time it takes to train instructors to teach material and the time it takes to train all employees on the material.

d) Web-based training providers can build company-specific courses, allowing a company to apply its own information, look and feel to the e-learning program.

e) Voice recognition software and animation can make learning more dynamic and more effective.

f) Organizations must constantly inform their employees on developing products, services and technologies to stay competitive.

17.4 Fill in the blanks in each of the following statements.

a) Students who want to move through a module at their own pace, skipping from area to area according to their current skill sets, would probably prefer self-paced classes, also called _____.

b) A _____ serves as a database from which employees can quickly and easily find training and information.

c) In addition to building e-learning programs, many Web-based training providers monitor the success of the training to determine the company's _____, the ratio cost savings and increased revenues to money spent.

d) In the future, _____ applications will allow people to take classes while they are commuting to and from the office.

e) _____ provides a new means for IT instruction. In addition to course lectures and reading materials, Web-based training provides the advantage of hands-on experience, an important element when approaching certification exams.

f) Many organizations employ a _____ to design the corporate learning strategy.

g) It has been suggested that Web-based training can help corporations reduce the cost of training their employees by _____ percent over comparative instructor-led training programs.

17.5 Define the following:

a) e-learning
b) training marketplace
c) e-learning solution provider
d) request-for-proposal

17.6 (*Class Discussion*). In this chapter we discuss the conflict surrounding online education. For some, an online education is a convenient, effective way to continue and supplement traditional education. Others view this as a threat to the educational process. Using the information provided in this text and supplementary resources, answer the following questions. Be prepared to discuss your answers.

a) What are some of the issues involved?
b) How do these affect the learning process?
c) What types of online learning do you think are beneficial, and which are not?

17.7 Visit **eCollege.com** and take the eCompanion Online Tour. Then, answer the following questions.

a) What is the central location for all course information called?
b) Describe the features available through the **Calendar** feature.
c) The **Threaded Discussion** is an asynchronous tool. What does this mean?
d) The **Chatroom** is a synchronous tool. What does that mean?
e) Describe the **Document Sharing** feature.

17.8 Sample the Introduction to Business undergraduate course demo at **www.quisic.com/demo/undergrad/index.htm** and answer the following questions.

a) Read through the **Course Components** section. How many lessons make up the course?

    b) List five of the course goals.

    c) Visit the **Expected Learning Outcomes** page. Name three outcomes in the Human Resources lesson.

17.9 View the KnowledgenetLive demonstration (`www.knowledgenet.com/products-andsolutions/demosandguidedtours/index.jsp`) and answer the following questions.

    a) Name the four components of KnowledgeNet Live.

    b) What is delivered as part of the Tool Kit?

    c) The e-Learning Classroom offers what feature? How is this beneficial to the student?

    d) The labs can be accessed in what two ways?

WORKS CITED

The notation `<www.domain-name.com>` indicates that the citation is for information found at that web site.

1. B. Hall, "E-Learning," *Forbes* 2 October 2000: 38.

2. A. Grimes, "A Matter of Degree," *The Wall Street Journal* 17 July 2000: R29.

3. T. Hernandez, "e-Learning: A Buyer's Market," *Certification Magazine* August 2000: 27.

4. G.M. Farrell, Ed., *The Development of Virtual Education: A Global Perspective* (Vancouver: The Commonwealth of Learning, 1999) 4.

5. B. Hall, "E-Learning," *Forbes* 2 October 2000.

6. M. Franklin, "Computer Age," *The Boston Globe* 13 February 2000: H8.

7. A. Grimes, "A Matter of Degree," *The Wall Street Journal* 17 July 2000: R29.

8. J. Steinberg and E. Wyatt, "Boola, Boola: E-Commerce Comes to the Quad," *The New York Times* 13 February 2000: 1.

9. A. Crowley, "IT Training, certification go online," `<eWeek.com>` 23 August 1999 `<www.zdnet.com>`.

10. K. Ferguson, "Getting into Training," `Forbes.com` 29 December 1999 `<www.forbes.com/tool/smallbus/99/dec/1229/feat.htm>`.

11. S. Holt, "Mentor's Corner: Web-based training helps one family man move up," `Info-World.com` 7 June 1999 `<www.infoworld.com/cgi-bin/displayArchive.pl?/99/23/z03-23.80.htm>`

12. S. Kossen, "Web-Based IT Training Comes of Age," *Network Computing* 24 January 2000: 109.

13. B. Hall, "E-Learning," *Forbes* 2 October 2000.

14. B. Hall, "E-Learning: Building Competitive Advantage Through People and Technology," *Forbes: Special Advertising Section* 2 October 2000: 6.

18

e-Publishing

Objectives

- To explore e-Publishing and its affect on the traditional publishing industry.
- To introduce the technologies currently used to create and display electronic publications.
- To explore opportunities for content creators.
- To review existing online news services.
- To introduce leading e-content enablers and creators.

The book is here to stay. What we're doing is symbolic of the peaceful coexistence of the book and the computer.
Vartan Gregorian

A big leather-bound volume makes an ideal razorstrap. A thin book is useful to stick under a table with a broken caster to steady it. A large, flat atlas can be used to cover a window with a broken pane. And a thick, old-fashioned heavy book with a clasp is the finest thing in the world to throw at a noisy cat.
Mark Twain

Everything in the world exists to end up in a book.
Stéphane Mallarmé

The mind can store an estimated 100 trillion bits of information—compared with which a computer's mere billions are virtually amnesiac.
Sharon Begley

The love of learning, the sequestered nooks,
And all the sweet serenity of books.
Henry Wadsworth Longfellow

Outline

18.1   Introduction
18.2   Electronic Publishing
18.3   Self-Publishing
18.4   Print on Demand
18.5   e-Publishing: Related Hardware and Technologies
        18.5.1   XrML
        18.5.2   e-Books
18.6   Online News Sources
18.7   e-Zines and Online Magazines
18.8   Future of e-Publishing
18.9   Internet and World Wide Web Resources

*Summary • Terminology • Self-Review Exercises • Answers to Self-Review Exercises • Exercises •
Works Cited*

18.1 Introduction

The Internet is changing the way content is created, edited, distributed, bought and sold. Authors are self-publishing their work, booksellers are beginning to offer publishing services and publishers are selling beginning books directly to consumers.[1]

E-publishing is the digital creation and distribution of electronic content, including printed materials, music, video and software. In this chapter, we will introduce the many forms of e-publishing. We discuss the e-publishing companies and the best methods of publishing original material online.

Many best-selling authors use the Internet to distribute their work. Some work with their publishers and editors to convert their material to the Web, while other authors have self-published their material. We review these efforts in detail. We will also review the options for freelance writers made available through e-publishing technology.

The Internet helps researchers and academics speed up the peer-review process by making content and reviews readily available through e-mail and on the Web. The traditional review process can take months and often continues after a document has been published.

Some of the world's most successful news organizations have created Web presences to supplement their offline efforts. Other news and information sites were born on the Web and now compete for an audience with the leading news and information providers such as *CNN* and the *New York Times.*

In Chapter 11, Legal and Ethical Issues; Internet Taxation, we discussed copyright infringement issues. In this chapter, we discuss the issue further and explain XrML, the technology that allows content creators to assign strictly enforced usage rights to a given item.

18.2 Electronic Publishing

Many major publishing companies, including Pearson (**www.pearson.com**), Simon & Shuster (**www.simonsays.com**) and Random House (**www.atrandom.com**) have invested in electronic publishing. The transition to e-publishing is a technical and financial challenge. Traditionally, when a book is published, it must pass through a rigorous editing, printing and distribution process. This requires substantial financial resources. Many publishing companies have spent years developing a cost-effective system that best utilizes their property, equipment and human resources. They have all benefited from the early efforts of Xerox and Project Gutenberg who created the first e-text in the early 1970's (see Project Gutenberg feature).

In publishing, break-even sales volumes are determined as a way of measuring the success or failure of a book. A *break-even point* is the lowest sales volume where total revenues first equals total expenses. E-publishing threatens traditional pricing and product marketing efforts by giving customers a low-cost alternative to paper texts. For instance, a publisher might estimate that it must sell 20,000 copies of a particular hard-copy publication to break even. In a traditional system, the publisher could use historical sales data and consumer-buying indicators to determine if such sales goals were feasible. In electronic publishing, there are fewer indicators, because e-publishing technology is still evolving. In the future, it may be easier to predict sales of electronic publications as consumers accept the medium on a grander scale.

Traditional publishing companies have to consider a number of issues when transitioning to e-publishing. Publishing companies have to make large investments in technology in order to begin publishing the materials securely and with high quality. They must purchase storage equipment, set up an e-commerce infrastructure and integrate their online and offline efforts.

Once the infrastructure for e-publishing is in place, publishers must consider *cannibalization*—a decrease in sales of one or more products in a line, when a new product is released. It is unlikely that a person will buy both an electronic and a hard copy of the same book. This creates an interesting problem, because publishing benefits from *economies of scale*—a decrease in cost as supply increases. It is less costly to mass produce 10 thousand books in a single print run, than to generate 10 thousand books in multiple print runs. As the number of books printed in a single run decreases, the cost of operating the machinery remains the same, spreading the cost over fewer books, increasing the cost per book. A publisher that releases a book in both paper and electronic format must consider this phenomenon. As the number of electronic sales of a book increases, the sales of paper editions of the same book will probably decrease. This in turn increases printing expenses and overall production costs for the books.[2] If the e-books are strategically priced, publishers may be able to offset the increase in printing costs. Since an e-book does not have to be printed, bound and distributed through traditional channels, an estimated 25% of production costs can be saved per book.[3] Retailers can use this savings to price the e-books lower to foster growth of the medium. E-publishing offers many opportunities for publishers and authors, but there are also a number of negatives to consider (Fig. 18.1).

In publishing, material is generated by a *content creator*, sent to a publisher for final edits and then distributed to various wholesalers and retailers. This process is protected by copyright laws and governed by a series of contracts and user agreements. Copywritten materials cannot be reproduced and distributed without the permission of the author and publisher. Music, film and software are protected by similar rules and regulations. This issue will be discussed further in Section 18.5.1, XrML.

Strengths	Weaknesses	Opportunities	Threats
More control over final material	Hard to read	Greater chance of being published Ability to add multimedia to a publication	Piracy
Better for the environment	Electronic readers are expensive	Books-on-demand will make every publication readily available in printed form	Copyright infringement
Higher royalties	Amateur material is so abundant, it is difficult to get noticed	Easy, less expensive distribution	Few sales in a saturated market
Shorter publication times	Consumers reluctant to read from their computer screen	Subsidy e-publishing allows authors the chance to be published for a fee	
Global availability			

Fig. 18.1   Analysis of e-publishing.

Project Gutenberg converts classic texts.

In 1971, Xerox was looking for a way to track and improve the proficiency of its computer operators. The company had an abundance of computers and related technology, but needed to learn more about the way people used them. To solve this problem, four computer operators were given $100,000,000 in computer time for research and development.[4] It was up to the group to decide how the time should be spent. The operators chose a project that would not only serve the needs of Xerox, but generate a database useful to future generations. They named their endeavour *Project Gutenberg*™ and set out to convert 10,000 texts to digital format. Each one of these texts is considered *public domain* (free to the public) and do not have a copyright.[5] Since storage technology was still in its infancy in 1971, it was difficult to convert large volumes of text into the Project Gutenberg *e-text* format. To address this issue, the group used ASCII, a basic scripting language to convert the materials. ASCII allows the Project Gutenberg volunteers keep file size small and reusable. Reuse is an essential aspect of Project Gutenberg, named after Johannes Gutenberg, inventor of the printing press.

The first task of the group was to covert the Declaration of Independence and send it to other computer operators across the primitive network. This successful effort paved the way for Project Gutenberg as it currently exists. Today, hundreds of volunteers convert an average of one major book per day into electronic format. Technological improvements in storage and file-transfer technology give the world easy access to these texts. This has had major implications for the new e-publishing companies. Many retailers selling e-published material offer classics formatted from Project Gutenberg e-texts.

Copyright issues have arisen many times in the past. The photocopy machine and the VCR allow people to make duplicates of copywritten material without the express written permission of the content owner. However, both of these technologies are limited in the level of quality they can recreate. Today, the Internet and World Wide Web allow the easy transfer of data, including music, video and written content without any significant loss in quality. For instance, MP3 technology allows for the rapid transfer of near CD-quality audio without any significant distortion of the material. We discuss the copyright issue surrounding the MP3 format in Chapter 11, Legal and Ethical Issues; Internet Taxation.

18.3 Self-Publishing

The Internet and the Web give freelance writers access to a global audience. These writers have a number of *self-publishing* options. One option is to set up a Web site featuring original content such as short stories, poetry and commentary on a variety of issues. Some content creators offer their material for free. Writers that wish to charge for their work can set up an e-commerce infrastructure and sell their products independently. We discuss Building an e-Business in Chapter 3, Online Monetary Transactions in Chapter 4 and Internet Marketing in Chapter 8. This process is considerably more expensive and offers no guarantees that a writer's content will be sold. However, a well-designed and implemented e-commerce site that hosts high-quality content can be profitable (see the Stephen King feature).

Stephen King: e-Publishing Pioneer

After Stephen King released *Ride the Bullet* with Simon & Shuster in March 2000, publishers began to see the potential for the Internet as a major distribution channel. They were even more convinced when the book sold over 400,000 copies in the first week of its release. *Ride the Bullet* also raised questions about the security of the medium, as digital copies of the book were available for free on the Internet a few days after its release.[6]

Stephen King surprised the publishing community once again, when he decided to self-publish his second e-book, *The Plant*. (Fig 18.2) For Stephen King, *The Plant* is less about profit and more about testing the medium. The book, released in multiple installments is available to readers on the honor system. Readers can choose to pay for the installments (between $1–$2 for approximately 30 pages) before they download them, or defer payment until a later date. King's system is simple, if 75% of the readers pay for the material, the story will continue. If not, *The Plant* will not be released in its entirety. At the time of publication, *The Plant* was in its fourth installment.[7]

Steven King worked with `Amazon.com` to attain the e-commerce infrastructure necessary to distribute the book. He used his own Web site `stephenking.com` to promote the book and explain the honor system. By self-publishing his material, Stephen King works with an editor to ensure that the text is ready for publication, but he has the final word on the content and the royalties resulting from its sales.

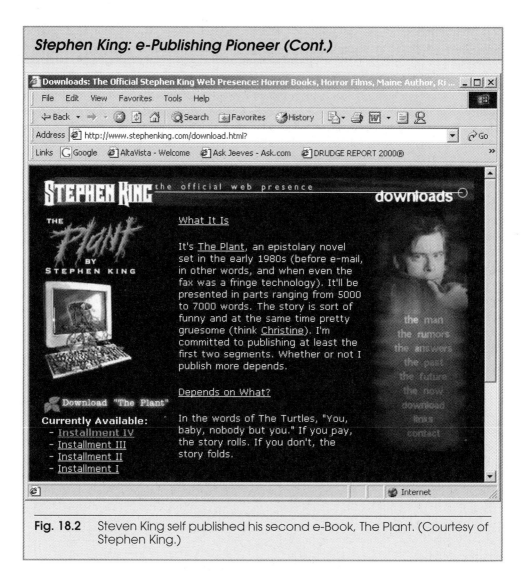

Fig. 18.2   Steven King self published his second e-Book, The Plant. (Courtesy of Stephen King.)

Many writers do not have the technical expertise or business savvy to sell their work on the Web. One option for these writers is subsidy e-publishing. *Subsidy e-publishers* charge writers a small fee in return for providing marketing and technical services. Authors using this method must be sure to copy edit their work before submission to a subsidy publisher, as the work is usually published as submitted. Xlibris[SM] (**www.xlibrix.com**) offers a full range of subsidy e-publishing services to help authors transfer their content to the Web and begin selling it at various locations online. Service fees range from a few hundred dollars to a few thousand dollars and include access to template body pages, covers, posting services, ISBN retrieval and assignment and other supportive efforts. Xlibris will market your material for an additional charge. Authors that do not have their content in digital form can pay Xlibris to convert the text. 1stBooks Library™ (**www.1stbooks.com**) also offers e-publishing and marketing services. For a fee, 1stBooks will publish your material. The author retains the rights to the material, but 1stBooks takes a portion of the royalties. **IUniverse.com** also offers a full range of subsidy e-publishing and marketing services.

Some e-publishers do not charge a fee for their publishing services, but retain a portion of the royalties. These companies are generally more selective about the material they accept. Since they do not charge a fee for their publishing services, they must cover their expenses with revenues generated through book sales. These e-publishers include Mightywords (**www.mightywords.com**) (see Mightywords feature), @random, (**www.atrandom.com**) and Fiction Works **www.fictionworks.com.**

Mightywords: Helps Authors Publish Their Content Online

Mightywords publishes original works online (Fig. 18.3). The e-publishing site specializes in *eMatter*—short stories, single chapters and other small works. Mightywords also publishes full length e-books. The site has made publishing deals with famous authors and up-and-coming authors.

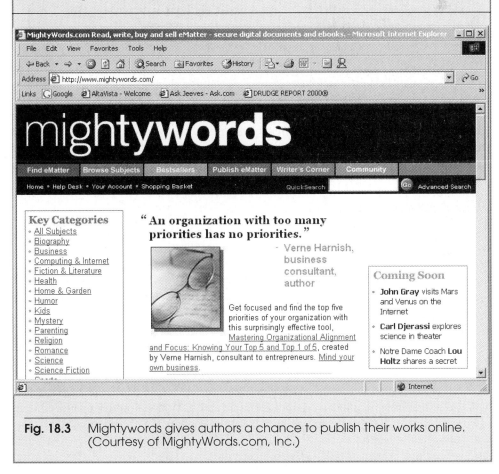

Fig. 18.3   Mightywords gives authors a chance to publish their works online. (Courtesy of MightyWords.com, Inc.)

Mightywords: Helps Authors Publish Their Content Online (Cont.)

Authors who wish to publish on Mightywords must first register with the site. Mightywords does not provide editing services, therefore it is essential to check and work carefully before submission. All materials must be between 7,000 and 95,000 words. The site only accepts material pertaining to business & management, computing & technology, health and self-help. All submissions must be accompanied by a detailed proposal explaining the authors interest in e-publishing their material with Mightywords. Authors must prepare their documents in Adobe® Acrobat®, Microsoft Word, Adobe Postscript® or in or other acceptable text formats. Once you have prepared your file and determined your selling price, you can upload your work to the site. When the document is fully uploaded, and accepted by Mightywords you can consider yourself a published author. If your content sells, you will receive commissions. As a Mighty-Words author, you retain full copyright on your material. Each author receives a percentage of the list price when an item is sold.

MightyWords recently published a book titled *Heavenly Miracles*. The book was cowritten by a woman who, after being diagnosed with terminal cancer, realized she would probably never see the hard-copy release of her book. e-Publishing gave her the chance to release her work in time to hear her readers reactions.[8]

Many e-publishers operate for the advancement of the electronic medium alone and do not accept payment for their services. **agoodbook.com** is a site run by an author looking to showcase the work of talented writers that cannot find traditional publishers for their work. **Chapbooks.com** specializes in publishing chapbooks which are often only a few pages long. Bookface (**www.bookface.com**) will publish your electronic book at their site and offer it to registered users for free.[9]

18.4 Print on Demand

As consumers adopt electronic books over printed books, there could be a profound decrease in demand for paper. This could have major implications for the paper industry. A decrease in demand for paper books could help the environment by reducing the rate of *deforestation*—the loss of forest land over time. The transition will also reduce the need for complex printing systems and the overhead at major publishing houses. Unfortunately, a transition to e-publishing might also reduce jobs in the paper and printing industries.

Despite the new electronic medium, the demand for paper books will not disappear. However, given that printing expenses per paper book increases as the number of units printed decreases, publishers will have to find a more cost-effective alternative as e-published materials begin to sell in larger volumes. Bookstores and libraries can offer *print-on-demand* services, allowing customers to convert electronic text to paper and have it bound and sold to them within minutes. Barnes & Noble and IBM have formed a partnership to offer print-on-demand systems in Barnes & Noble bookstores.[10] Print-on-demand systems will be especially helpful to people looking for an out-of-print text or less popular titles such as academic papers or back issues of magazines.

18.5 e-Publishing: Related Hardware and Technologies

One of the major complaints among electronic content users is its inconvenience. It is unlikely that you will curl up in bed with a lap top or a full-size computer to read your favorite novel. One alternative is the e-book. *E-book* technology allows consumers to read digital content on a device about the size of the average paperback book. In this section, we discuss various e-book options available to consumers. We also discuss the ways the publishing industry is combatting piracy. In the first section, XrML, we discuss the XML-based technology designed to protect digital content. XML is discussed in the optional case study, Building an E-business: Introduction to Internet Programming.

18.5.1 XrML

Many people feel that the answer to piracy protection is the *eXtensible Rights Markup Language (XrML)*.[11] This XML-based language will help to define policies, rights and permissions for digital content. XrML is designed to prevent the illegal use of copyrighted materials by standardizing the technology used to protect these materials. XrML is an XML extension of *DPRL (Digital Property Rights Language)*, a technology created by Xerox to prevent the illegal use of copywritten material.[12]

Digital content creators work with publishers and distributors to make sure that their content is protected with XrML. The process begins when the content creator submits material to the publisher. Once the content is determined to be complete, the rights policy, pricing data and restrictions are encoded into the file using XML. The rights holder determines the rights assigned to a given product. The product is then sent to distributors, who price the product based on the guidelines set by the publisher in the XrML code.

XrML defines the usage rules for the content. For instance, a document protected with XrML will define the transfer, printing and resale restrictions. A person will be prevented from copying and redistributing the material to others without the express permission of the rights holder. In the past, publishers put trust in the consumer, often relying on honesty and ethics to prevent the piracy of materials. XrML places the control in the computer itself. A user will not be able to manipulate a document that is designated as "unalterable" by the XrML code.

Publications authored with XrML will rely on trusted systems to protect and present the data. *Trusted systems* are designed to read and execute XrML data. These system will be developed for all types of published media. They will include e-books, computers, radios, VCRs, DVD players and other platforms that provide consumer access to copyrighted material. Trusted systems will operate according to the rights and restrictions encoded in the document.[13] Trusted systems are programmed to assign the appropriate rules to a given consumer. For instance, if a consumer buys the right to print a document, the trusted system would then allow the consumer to print. If the printing rights are not licensed, than the trusted system will restrict the consumer.[14]

The music industry has tried to eliminate piracy of its content by preventing the unauthorized transfer of high-quality music over the Internet in the form of MP3 files. If an XrML document is encoded into a particular MP3 file, this type of transfer can be prevented. For instance. If a musician wanted to send a copy of a new song to all fan club members, but did not want to give access to the general public, the musician could offer selective access using XrML.

18.5.2 e-Books

To accommodate the recent surge in digital content creation, many of the leading electronics manufacturers have created electronic readers or *e-book readers*. These products resemble a personal digital assistant (PDA) with a rectangular shape and LCD screen. E-book users simply download the digital materials to begin reading. This can be done by linking your e-book to your home computer or a phone line and downloading the material. Readers are billed when content is downloaded. Using wireless technology, users will be able to download e-books from remote locations to their handheld device. Imagine sitting on your lawn and downloading the latest best-sellers to your palm-sized e-book reader.

e-Fact 18.1

The Association of American Publishers estimates that by 2005, the consumer market for electronic books will reach $3.5 billion.[15]

The *Open eBook Forum* (**www.openebook.org**) is an association of publishers, book sellers, manufacturers and industry supporters who wish to advance the technology and use of electronic books. The group is working to set standards for e-books. Their accomplishments include a text formatting standard based in HTML and XML. The standard allows authors and publishers to format a document once for use on a wide range of devices.[16]

Gemstar Corporation (**www.gemstarebook.com**) offers one of the most widely used electronic books (Fig. 18.4). This product, the Gemstar e-book, is about the size of a paperback novel and can hold 4000 pages of text and graphics.

Fig. 18.4   eBook is one of many electronic book readers available. (Courtesy of Gemstar-TV Guide International.)

Many people complain that the resolution on an LCD screen limits the appeal of e-books. In response to these complaints, Microsoft® introduced *Cleartype*™, which offers three times the resolution of traditional LCD screens. Microsoft recently released its *Microsoft Reader*, allowing consumers to read digital content from computers, e-books or personal digital assistants. The product formats text so that it is easier on the eyes by using Microsoft Cleartype technology.

PeanutPress (`www.peanutpress.com`) offers e-books for your Palm™ and Handspring™ Visor handhelds and Pocket PCs. The site offers e-content from leading authors at traditional retail-book prices.

18.6 Online News Sources

As we move into the information age, there is no question that the Web will play a major role in the publishing and news industries. Well-known news organizations such as *CNN* (`www.cnn.com`) (see CNN Interactive feature), *The Wall Street Journal* (`www.wsj.com`) and *Newsweek* (`www.newsweek.com`) use the Web to feature their news stories.

The Wall Street Journal, one of the most widely read newspapers in the world, offers an online edition that includes full text and 24-hour updates. You can start by trying the online version on a free-trial basis, and if you choose to subscribe, you will receive full access to the Barrons (`www.barrons.com`) database—an online database of commentary and articles by leading investment analysts.

`ESPN.com` provides the latest sporting news and allows users to get in-depth information on their favorite players, teams, etc. `ESPN.com` offers live text, audio and video of games and highlights. Visitors to this site can also enroll in fantasy sporting games, such as football, baseball and golf.

`Rivals.com`™ an online competitor to ESPN, offers a collection of Web sites for professional, college, amateur and high school leagues in every major sports. The sites often include recruiting information, interviews with players and coaches, and scores and highlights. Much of the content available on `Rivals.com` has been written by freelance authors.

`Salon.com` has also built a large online audience for its news service. Salon.com is a collection of sites covering a broad range of topics including politics, sports, health, books, motherhood, sex and people. Slate (`www.slate.msn.com`), a competing site, offers content in the same subject areas. Neither Slate nor `Salon.com` have an offline presence.

18.7 e-Zines and Online Magazines

E-zines, or *electronic magazines*, can be broadly defined as collections of digital content covering a wide range of topics distributed electronically over the Web. E-zines give independent writers the chance to vocalize their opinions about their favorite hobbies, special interests and the latest news. Thousands of e-zines feature content about entertainment, politics, science and mathematics, pets and celebrities. Many business have begun offering e-zines to their customers as a way of keeping them informed of new product offerings and other developments.

Some e-zines are digital copies of print magazines. These e-zines supplement articles with multimedia, user polls, discussion boards, live chat etc. Other e-zines use many of the same technologies, but were born on the Web and do not have print counterparts.

CNN Interactive: A leader in Online News

CNN Interactive (**www.cnn.com**) is one of the most visited and most interactive sites on the Web. CNN has a network of sites designed to give current, highly targeted news and information to its visitors. Each of these sites offers streaming audio and video taken from broadcasts on television networks.

CNNallpolitics is a site offering more in-depth articles about politicians and their campaigns, public policy and global political coverage. *CNNSI* is the all-sports section of the CNN network. You can follow teams in every league or just catch up on the latest scores and highlights. *CNNFN* allows you to track financial news and securities data from your Web browser. *MyCNN* allows you to personalize the news and information that appears on your browser. Visitors can choose text, audio and video in any category. They can then customize the way CNN appears when you visit the site.

CNN also has sites that offer information in foreign languages. These sites include news and information specific to each country and region. The network of sites that make up CNN Interactive uses the highest quality multimedia and content to add value to customers' experiences.

E-zines are often run by small teams of people writing highly specialized information. Many of these sites rely solely on advertising to survive. Given the competition among these Web sites, many e-zines are seeking alternative revenue sources such as subscriptions and retailing. Other e-zine sites collect customer data and use it to generate marketing research reports. The reports are then sold to interested parties.

Perhaps the best example of an independent e-zine is the *Drudge Report* (**www.drudgereport.com**). The *Drudge Report* is an aggregation of articles gathered from leading publications across the Web and reposted as links on his Web site. The now infamous Monica Lewinski story was first released by the site's operator Matt Drudge. The *Drudge Report* has found success by combining the global reach of the Internet, close contacts in media and politics and good writing skills. The site has received both praise and criticism from traditional journalists who claim Drudges' efforts to get the story first often make him the first to get it wrong. Although this has proven true on a number of occasions, Drudge has used the speed of the Internet to break such stories as "Jack Kemp for Vice President" and the Kathleen Willey story. The content featured on the Drudge Report is often controversial, but nonetheless important to society.[17]

Drudge himself provides some of the site's most interesting and high-profile coverage. The site began as a collection of personal postings on various newsletters and quickly evolved into a newsletter that is delivered by email. The *Drudge Report* is now a full-scale Web site featuring up-to-the minute news and receiving over a million hits per day.[18] The success of the Drudge Report is an example of one individual's ability use the Web to reach the World, as well as a warning that the Web is still governed by the same laws as traditional media. Defamation, libel and other legal issues related to e-publishing are discussed in Chapter 11, Legal and Ethical Issues; Internet Taxation.

Infojump (**www.infojump.com**) is an e-zine portal. The site connects its visitors to over 4,000 publications and millions of articles. Infojump updates its articles daily and estimates that 10,000 new articles are created each day. Infojump sells advertising to support its services.

Magazines such as *U.S. News & World Report* (**www.usnews.com**), *The Economist* (**www.economist.com**) and *Fortune* (**www.fortune.com**) all supplemented their print editions with an online presence. Many online magazines syndicate the print stories onto the Web and offer them for free. Fortune Magazine offers stories from its latest issue, free for download.

Many digital publishers offer their content in paper form. Yahoo! publishes a hard-copy magazine focusing on Internet life and the digital economy called *Yahoo! Life*. Inside **www.inside.com**, E*TRADE (**www.etrade.com**) and **thestreet.com** are all working on paper versions of their electronic content. These efforts will increase branding and produce new income streams and advertising opportunities.

18.8 Future of e-Publishing

E-publishing is still in its infancy. As technology advances, we will read digital content from e-books that are smaller, faster and easier to use than the products currently available. However, readers will not be confined to their computer screens or e-books. They will be able to read content from a wide variety of digital surfaces. *Digital Paper*, a digital surface that can be manipulated with electronic data, will drastically change the way we purchase our reading material (see the E Ink feature). For instance, readers might use the same newspaper for a week or a month, as the text will change dynamically each day. Wireless technology will make this possible anywhere in the world.[19]

E Ink Makes Electronic Ink.

Imagine opening the newspaper you purchased yesterday, and having the text change dynamically to reflect today's news. This will soon be possible with electronic ink. Researchers at MIT have discovered a way to create digital surfaces, as thin as a piece of paper, that will accept data from the Internet and format it to look like printed text. The technology, called *electronic ink*, relies on simple electric fields to change the content of a newspaper, billboard or even text on clothing dynamically.

Electronic ink is essentially a collection of tiny fluid-filled balls called *microcapsules*. Each one of these capsules contains tiny white disks, called *pigment chips* (Fig 18.5). The pigment chips have a positive charge. An electronic ink panel, whether it is a sign, sheet of paper or an item of clothing, appears blue. However, if a negative charge is applied to the top of the microcapsule, the tiny white pigment chips will be drawn to the surface, making the electronic ink panel appear to be white. By selectively applying positive and negative charges to each of the microcapsules, a person can create letters, numbers or virtually any design they choose. Since these electrical signals can be sent via a computer, the Internet and wireless technology will allow electronic ink users to manipulate the panels from anywhere in the world. For example, if a company using electronic Ink technology decides to change their product line, electronic Ink billboards could be manipulated to reflect the product changes in an instant.

E Ink Makes Electronic Ink. (Cont.)

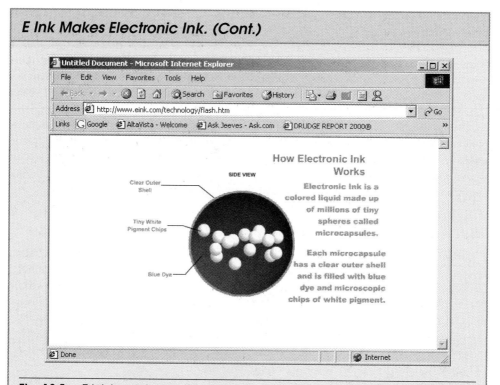

Fig. 18.5   E Ink is made up of microcapsules. (Courtesy of E Ink Corporation - October 2000.)

E Ink is marketing its first commercial application, which is called *Immedia*™ Displays. Safeway, a west-coast supermarket chain and the Phoenix newspaper, *Arizona Republic,* have signed deals to use the electronic ink displays in stores.[21] A demo of the product can be found at **www.eink.com**. Alternative surfaces are currently being developed using electronic ink. In the future, it will be possible to publish a newspaper or a magazine and have it automatically update itself each day by downloading the new material from the Internet.

Researchers at Xerox's Palo Alto Research Center recently invented a form of digital printing. The technology is designed to print tiny coded messages onto a sheet of paper. The small codes called *dataglyphs*, appear as standard text symbols and can be coded to represent complete data files such as a text document, personal identification information or a computer command. A group of dataglyphs the size of a postage stamp could store the entire Gettysburg address. Dataglyphs could be printed onto ID badges in a given company to provide selective access to restrictive areas.[20]

By combining text-based publications with multimedia, new forms of interactive media will become a reality. For instance, children's books enhanced with artificial intelligence might give children the chance to communicate with the characters. When struggling to solve a problem, students may be able to contact other students by using an e-book with video conferencing technology. It will be possible to update older editions of a text by sending an automatic update to the electronic reader.

As we discussed in the previous chapter, formal education will include more e-learning, with instructors offering Web-based curricula. Students will be able to takes notes, read text books, and communicate with instructors from their computers, handheld devices and even via interactive television.

In this chapter, we introduced the basic concepts of e-publishing and offered examples of the many products and services currently available to authors. Many of the e-publications created in the future will be used in the classroom. In the next chapter, we will review the changes that have occurred in education as a result of technology. We will discuss the concepts of e-learning in detail.

18.9 Internet and World Wide Web Resources

e-Books

www.microsoft.com/reader
Microsoft Reader is a free technology that enables users to read electronic books on their computer, handheld device or electronic book reader.

Self-publishing

www.bananafish.com
This site specializes in publishing the work of unknown authors. The site will review original materials and post them to the site.

www.onlineoriginals.com
This site will review and edit original work and post it to their site in digital format. They are pure e-publishers.

www.inkspot.com
This site offers tips and techniques for writers of all ages and skill levels who wish to publish their materials online. The site also aggregates news related to e-publishing.

Subsidy e-Publishing

www.xlibris.com
This site publishes original material for a small administrative fee. All materials must be edited before submittal.

www.IUniverse.com
This site posts, distributes and markets original materials. A processing fee is paid by the author. IUniverse has access to multiple distribution channels and will customize content for these channels.

www.iPublisher.com
This subsidy e-publisher offers a full range of e-publishing services. This site also distributes and markets original material.

Online News Sources

www.prnewswire.com
Immediate business news from corporations worldwide is posted on this site. This site is free for general use. Listings are updated instantly as news is released.

www.Reuters.com

This service is used by many of the news organizations to find breaking news. The site offers the information for free.

www.upi.com

United Press International is an online news resource. Specializing in breaking news, it offers its content free on their site. Visitors also have free access to the sites extensive photo library.

SUMMARY

- e-Publishing is the digital creation and distribution of electronic content, including printed materials, music, video and software.

- In publishing, break-even sales volumes are determined as a way of measuring the success or failure of a book. A break-even point is the lowest sales volume where total revenues equal total expenses.

- Publishing companies have to make large investments in technology to begin publishing the materials securely and with a high degree of quality in electronic formats. They must purchase storage equipment, set-up an e-commerce infrastructure and integrate their online and offline efforts.

- Since an e-book does not have to be printed, bound and distributed through traditional channels, an estimated 25% of production costs can be saved per book.

- Copywritten materials cannot be reproduced and distributed without the permission of the author and publisher.

- The Internet and the Web give freelance writers instant access to a global audience.

- People who want to self-publish can set up an e-commerce infrastructure and sell their products independently.

- By self-publishing material, you are able to keep full control of your product. You can work with an editor to ensure that your text is ready for publication, but you have the final word on the content and the royalties resulting from its sales.

- Many writers do not have the technical expertise or business savvy to sell their work on the Web. Subsidy e-publishers charge writers a fee in return for their marketing and technical services.

- Many online publishers operate for the advancement of the electronic medium alone and do not accept payment for their services.

- A decrease in demand for paper books would reduce the rate of *deforestation*—the loss of forest land over time.

- A transition to e-publishing could reduce jobs in the paper and printing industries.

- One alternative to traditional printing is a print-on-demand system. Bookstores could offer print-on-demand services that would allow customers to convert an electronic text to paper and have it bound and sold to them in a few minutes.

- E-book technology allows consumers to read digital content on a device about the size of the average paperback book.

- XrML, an XML-based markup language, will help to define policies, rights and permissions for digital content.

- XrML is an XML extension of *DPRL (Digital Property Rights Language)*, a technology created by Xerox to prevent the illegal use of copywritten material.

- Trusted systems are designed to read and execute XrML data. These systems will be developed for all types of published media to provide consumer access to copyrighted material. Trusted systems will execute the rights and restrictions encoded in the document.

- e-Book readers resemble a personal digital assistant (PDA), with a rectangular shape and LCD screen. e-book users need only download the digital materials to begin reading.

- The Open eBook Forum (**www.openebook.org**) is an association of publishers, book sellers, manufacturers and industry supporters who wish to advance the technology and use of electronic books.

- Microsoft introduced Cleartype™ to improve the readability of electronic text. Cleartype offers users three times the resolution of traditional LCD screens.

- E-zines, or electronic magazines, can be broadly defined as collections of digital content, covering a wide range of topics distributed electronically over the Web.

- Some e-zines are digital copies of print magazines. These e-zines supplement articles with multimedia, user polls, discussion boards, live chat, etc.

- Many e-zines rely solely on advertising to survive. Given the competition among these Web sites, many e-zines are looking for alternative revenue sources such as subscriptions and retailing.

- E-publishing is still in its infancy. As technology advances, we will read digital content from e-books that are smaller, faster and easier to use than the products currently available.

- Researchers at MIT have discovered a way to create digital surfaces, as thin as a piece of paper, that will accept data from the Internet and format it to look like printed text. The technology, called Electronic Ink (E Ink), relies on simple magnetism to change the content of a newspaper, billboard or even text on clothing dynamically.

TERMINOLOGY

break-even point	eXtensible Rights Markup Language (XrML)
cannibalization	e-zines (electronic magazines)
Cleartype™ (from Microsoft)	microcapsules in E Ink
content creator	Microsoft Reader
deforestation	open ebook forum
DPRL (Digital Property Rights Language)	pigment chips in E Ink
e-book	print-on-demand
economies of scale	Project Gutenberg™
electronic ink (E Ink)	public domain
eMatter	self-publishing
e-publishing	subsidy e-publishers
e-text	trusted systems

SELF-REVIEW EXERCISES

18.1 State whether the following are true or false. If the answer is false, explain why.
   a) e-Publishing is the digital creation and distribution of electronic content.
   b) Independent authors must work with a publishing company to publish content to the Web.
   c) E Ink is used to improve the quality of print and ease of use of electronic readers.
   d) Project Gutenberg began as a contest to create the first e-book.
   e) E-zines are electronic magazines.

18.2 Fill in the blanks in each of the following:
   a) Many leading electronics firms have developed electronic reader products called _____.
   b) E-publishers that offer their services for a fee are called _____.

c) The process of creating electronic content and distributing it over various channels, including the Internet, is called _____.

d) _____ systems make paper version of an electronic text readily available.

e) _____ and their containers, _____ are the two basic elements of E Ink technology.

ANSWERS TO SELF-REVIEW EXERCISES

18.1   a) True. b) False. It is not necessary to work with a publisher when posting your work to the
Web; you can self-publish c) False. E Ink is an electronic writing technology used to digitize messages on a variety of surfaces. d) False. Project Gutenberg produce electronic versions of texts in the public domain. e) True.

18.2   a) e-book readers. b) subsidy e-publishers. c) e-publishing. d) Print-on-demand. e) Pigment
chips, microcapsules.

EXERCISES

18.3   State whether the following are true or false. If the answer is false, explain why.

a) E Ink is used to create electronic book readers.

b) Cleartype technology improves the readability of electronic text.

c) XrML is a XML specification designed to modify electronic text for disparate electronic
reader systems.

d) Project Gutenberg was initiated at Xerox to produce the first electronic book reader.

e) Public domain publications do not have a copyright.

18.4   Fill in the blanks in each of the following:

a) XrML is an extension of _____ which was developed by Xerox.

b) the term _____ is often used to describe electronic text that is shorter than an e-
book. but still a substantial publication.

c) _____ describes the phenomenon when a new product introduction has a negative
effect on other products in a companies product line.

d) Systems that are designed to protect copyright of a given product are called _____.

e) The creation distribution and sale of electronic texts is referred to as _____.

18.5   Define the following terms:

a) e-matter

b) e-zine

c) e-book

d) XrML

e) cannibalization

f) trusted system

18.6   (Class Discussion) Electronic publishing is reinventing the way content is created and distributed. E-Publishing will profoundly affect the way content is created. Discuss the implications of
e-publishing as they effect the way we read and understand content. Discuss e-books, print on demand, copyright and XrML and the use of multimedia.

18.7   Visit Xlibris (**www.xlibris.com**)and Mightywords (**www.mightywords.com**).
Compare and contrast the two sites.

a) How do their product offerings differ?

b) How does an author get published through each site?

c) Does the site charge a fee for its publishing services?

d) Does the site provide any additional services (copy edit, marketing, etc.)?

e) Write a paragraph describing each site.

f) Write a third paragraph answering the questions "Which site would you publish your material with? and Why?"

18.8 Visit the E Ink home page (**www.eink.com**), and view the demo. According to the demo, what charge does each pigment chip carry? What happens to the microcapsule when a negative charge is applied to the top electrode? To which electrode is a positive charge applied?

WORKS CITED

The notation <**www.domain-name.com**> indicates that the citation is for information found at the Web site.

1. K. Li, "Publish Online or Perish?" 3 *Industry Standard* 3 April 2000: 60.

2. B. D. Reimers, "New Technology Transforms Digital Publishing," *Information Week* 27 March 2000: 140.

3. G. Landers et. al., "E-Books: A Challenge to Paper Books?, *Gartner Group Research Note* 5 September 2000, <**www.gartnerweb.com**>.

4. <**www.gutenberg.net**>.

5. **Kushal, D. "The Future of Publishing," <promo.net/pg/kushal.html>.**

6. G. Saunders, W. Roush, "Cracking the Bullet: Hackers Decrypt PDF Version of Stephen King eBook," <**www.ebooknet.org**> 23 March 2000.

7. J. Kornblum, "Online Honesty is King's Policy," *USA Today* 13 June 2000: 3D.

8. J. KornBlum, "E-publishing gives dying author a boost," *USA Today* 26 July 2000: 3D.

9. J. Berrett, "Can't Stop the Presses," *Industry Standard* 1 May 2000: <**www.thestandard.com**>.

10. J. Harding, "New Chapter as Internet Kicks In," *Financial Times* 18 May 2000: VI.

11. S. Sanborn, "Protecting Intellectual Property on the Web," *Infoworld* 19 June 2000: <**www.infoworld.com**>.

12. <**www.XrML.org**>.

13. M. Stefik, A. Silverman, "The Bit and the Pendulum: Balancing the Interests of Stakeholders in Digital Publishing," White paper (Palo Alto: Xerox Palo Alto Research Center, 1997) 4-7.

14. R. Cover, "The XML Cover Pages," <**www.oasis-open.org/cover/xrml.html**> 4 August 2000.

15. D. Brady, "Story of E," *Business Week* 24 July 2000: 47.

16. M. Berber, "E-Book of Tomorrow," *Upside* September 2000: 54.

17. M. Drudge, *Manifesto* (New York: New American Library, 2000)11-15.

18. M. Drudge, "Anyone With a Modem can Report on the World," Address Before the National Press Club, 2 June 2000 <**www.frontpagemag.com/archives/drudge/drudge.htm**>.

19. S. Outing, "Milestone on the Road to Digital Paper," <**www.mediainfo.com/ephome**> 7 May 1999.

20. S. Rupley, "Digital Paper," *PC Magazine Online* 4 March 1999: <**www.zdnet.com/pcmag**>.

21. M. French, "E Ink pens deal with Phoenix Paper, Safeway," *Mass High Tech Journal* 18-24 September 2000: 9.

19

Online Entertainment

Objectives

- To explore how the Internet and World Wide Web have affected the entertainment industry.
- To discuss the various multimedia technologies necessary to make the Web a premier entertainment medium.
- To discuss the convergence of technologies occurring today and the effect this will have on the future of entertainment.
- To showcase the leading entertainment sites on the Web.
- To consider some exciting possibilities for the future of the entertainment industry.

Imagination is the eye of the soul.
Joseph Joubert

Music has charms to soothe a savage breast,
To soften rocks, or bend a knotted oak.
William Congreve

Outline

19.1   Introduction
19.2   Online Entertainment
19.3   Entertainment and Technology
19.4   MP3 and File-Transfer Technology
19.5   Amateur and Independent Artist Opportunities
19.6   Interactive Web TV
19.7   Music and the Web
19.8   Web Radio
19.9   Sports on the Web
19.10   Comedy on the Web
19.11   Online Games
19.12   Online Hollywood
        19.12.1 Talent Scouting
        19.12.2 Screen Writing
        19.12.3 Distribution and Supplies
19.13   The Future of Entertainment
19.14   Internet and World Wide Web Resources

Summary • Terminology • Self-Review Exercises • Answers to Self-Review Exercises • Exercises • Works Cited

19.1 Introduction

In this chapter, we will discuss the effect the Internet and the World Wide Web have had on entertainment. File-transfer technology, streaming audio and video, bandwidth advancements, set-top boxes and video-on-demand are just a few examples of how technology is changing the way people are entertained. We cover each of these topics in further detail and explore how each will affect the future of entertainment.

Every aspect of the entertainment industry has been affected by technology, and each is struggling to use it most effectively. Advancements in bandwidth, the capacity for data exchange over the Internet and data processing have made the Internet a viable source of streaming-media-based entertainment. *Streaming media* is often used to describe video and audio as it is streamed digitally to the audience. Before streaming technology was available, people had to wait for full audio and video of a particular file to download before the content could be viewed. At the same time, connection speeds were extremely slow. A video lasting a few seconds would take many minutes to download. Streaming media begins playing even before the entire file is downloaded. This process reduces viewer waiting time. Streaming media has also made television an outlet for Internet-based video-on-demand entertainment. *Video-on-demand* will allow consumers to scan databases of filmed entertainment and play videos at their leisure. Once a film with video-on-demand has been purchased, it is stored on a hard drive within the consumers set-top box, a device that combines the funcionality of a cable television converter box with the interactivity of the Internet. Technology is currently limited and only allows for choppy video in a small viewing area. As technology advances, so will the quality of the video image, the clarity of sound and the overall quality of the multimedia content. It will soon be possible to play full-length feature films on a full screen using streaming media technology.

The Web itself is a form of entertainment that is constantly evolving and influencing traditional media. The relationships between the Internet, film, music and television are becoming more closely intertwined. In the future, we will see a *media convergence* that allows consumers to design their own television channels, pick their own sound tracks and surf the Internet over a wireless network. Digital cellular phones will double as personal music players, personal digital assistants, and video conferencing devices (see Chapter 6, Wireless Internet and m-Business).

19.2 Online Entertainment

Entertainment has been a major part of the Web since the Web's inception. Previously, text-only browsers allowed users to exchange conversation, images and data, but the transfer rate was slow as bandwidth was narrow, and images often took hours to download. However, the ability to send and receive text messages instantly still held the interest of early adopters. Today, the Web is a dynamic environment offering users a variety of entertainment options. Creative designers have turned the Web into a virtual world where we can buy, sell, play, chat and explore. The entertainment industry recognizes the potential of the Internet as a new distribution channel for film, music, books and other forms of entertainment.

Web surfing is a form of entertainment in itself. The Web is essentially an immense database of information created by individuals and organizations worldwide. The Internet has created a global community where Web surfers can communicate with their peers using chat programs, message posting and e-mail. Recent studies have shown that chat is the most popular form of Web-based entertainment, followed by streaming video, Internet radio, gaming and movie clips (see Fig. 19.1).[1]

Online gaming is another form of online entertainment. Online games have existed since the early days of the Web. Offering games is a way to attract visitors to a site and increase Web stickiness. Sony's `station.sony.com` site allows visitors to play some of their favorite television game shows against people anywhere in the world. Once you have registered at the site, you can play *Jeopardy*, *Wheel of Fortune* and *The Dating Game*, among others.

Many radio stations and amateur radio enthusiasts are turning to the Web to broadcast their favorite music. It is now possible to tune into radio shows broadcasted from around the world using an Internet browser. Record companies, film studios and other traditional entertainment outlets recognize the important role the Internet and the Web will have on their industries. Many of them are trying to determine exactly what type of role they will play. Recent *Nielsen ratings*, which are used to predict trends and popularity in the entertainment industry, show a promising future for entertainment on the Web. Recent ratings showed half of the top 10 audience gainers on the Web were entertainment sites.[2]

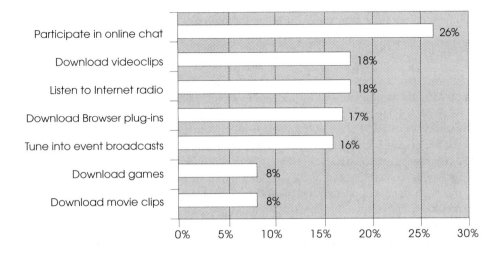

Fig. 19.1   Entertainment activities have varied among online adults in the summer of 2000. Note: chat data reflects the period beginning 30 days prior to initial publication. All other data reflects the three month period prior to publication.[3] (Reprinted by permission of The Industry Standard.)

19.3 Entertainment and Technology

Entertainment and technology have always been closely tied. When one area of entertainment is improved with technology, the rest of the industry races to catch up. For instance—when the VCR was first introduced, cable television responded with *pay-per-view* TV, a system that allows viewers to order premium programming at times prespecified by the cable provider—to keep people from turning to video cassettes. Since traditional TV relies on advertising revenues, pay-per-view offers people the opportunity to watch feature-length films without leaving their homes and without the commercials.

As the Internet draws people away from traditional forms of entertainment, television, radio and film executives are rushing to include the Internet in their businesses. This has led to a convergence of television, film, radio and the Internet that may one day lead to a universal entertainment system. This device would combine the leading characteristics of each of these media and offer them to the viewer in a single machine. We are beginning to see the first phase of this convergence with *set-top boxes*. Set-top boxes combine the interactivity of the Web with the visual quality and usability of television. Set-top boxes also give the viewer VCR-like controls to pause, rewind and fast forward their television programs. By storing digitally-broadcast programming on an internal hard drive, these boxes will allow people to skip commercials. This will force broadcasters to seek new revenue streams. Users will be able to communicate via e-mail and chat while watching television and feature-length films on their TVs with the use of a set-top box.[4]

Filmed entertainment has probably benefitted the most from advancements in technology. Special effects have improved as computer technology has advanced. Filmmakers are able to bring dinosaurs to life and raise the Titanic using the latest computer graphics technologies. These efforts will help the average e-business owner produce high-quality special effects for their personal Web site in the future.

19.4 MP3 and File-Transfer Technology

The Internet and file-transfer technology are changing the way music is distributed and purchased. *MP3* technology allows for the rapid and substantial compression of vast amounts of data. With MP3 technology, individuals can play CD-quality audio from their computer without the use of a CD. The MP3 format is an effective way of transferring digital audio over the Web (see Chapter 11, Legal and Ethical Issues; Internet Taxation). Companies like **MP3.com** and **Farmclub.com** (**www.farmclub.com**) act as distribution channels through which consumers can exchange MP3 audio files. Similar file types are available for videos, allowing people to transfer short films and video snippets quickly. As compression methods and bandwidth improve, it will be possible to transfer large forms of media, such as feature-length films, with minimal file corruption.

Wireless technology will eventually allow for the rapid transfer of data over a wireless network. Media files are too large to transfer over a wireless network at this point, but as the standards improve, you will be able to download and listen to your favorite music on your wireless devices. Imagine downloading and listening to your favorite new album using your cellular phone and a set of headphones.[5]

File transfer technology, a technology that enables the rapid and secure transfer of large-format media files over the Web, has been controversial. For example, the ability to transfer high-quality multimedia securely and anonymously has had profound effects on the music industry. If listeners are turning to their computers for free music and not paying for the content, then the record companies are losing revenue. Recent lawsuits against Napster (**www.napster.com**) and **MP3.com** have caused many of the companies that provide this technology to shut down their services or restructure their offering policies. Many of these file-transfer enablers are now offering access to media files on a subscription basis. Napster recently partnered with German media conglomerate Bertelsmann, to begin offering their technology on a subscription basis.[6] A file format similar to MP3 standard is being developed for video files. This format may result in similar litigation within the film entertainment industry.

19.5 Amateur and Independent Artist Opportunities

If you are an amateur musician, aspiring actor, fledgling film maker or a struggling artist, there are opportunities for you on the Web. The major motion picture studios, record companies and publishing houses are always looking for budding talent. The Web can be a fast track to success. Web sites across the Internet need interesting content. An artist who is willing to make an effort has a good chance of being noticed. Many content producers are using the Web as a testing ground for new material (see the Icebox feature). By offering short clips of potential programming, executives and artists can preempt a show's failure and make changes to a flawed script.

Farmclub.com is a Web site designed by music executives to showcase top-of-the-charts artists, as well as to give up-and-coming artists an opportunity for success. Developing bands can upload their material to the site in digital format, where it is then made available to the listening public at no cost.

Icebox: Internet Based Entertainment

Icebox (**www.icebox.com**) was launched in June of 2000 with the leadership of former ICM executive Steve Stanford. Icebox has assembled the talents of some of Hollywood's most successful producers, writers and animators. Executive producers from *The Simpsons*, *King of the Hill*, *South Park* and many other successful programs, contribute content to the site. Budding artists and animators can contribute their own content as well. The cartoons are limited to short episodes that are easy to download.

How will Icebox make money? The Web will not be a primary source of revenue for Icebox, at least in its early stages. Icebox hopes that it can create high-quality content that can be sold to network television programs and as feature films (see Fig. 19.2).[7]

Original series on the site include *Superhero Roommate*, *Zombie College*, *Rock n' Roll Dad* and *Starship Regulars*, among many others. *Zombie College* is the story of a boy who heads off to a college full of zombies and leaves his friends and family behind. *Starship Regulars* is a cartoon set on a spaceship in a distant galaxy. This short animation was recently sold to the cable television channel Showtime. It is the first content sale for the site.

Most of the site's content is view only; however, if you desire a more hands-on approach to the content, you can make your own cartoon using the cast and settings of Zombie College by using the *Reanimator*. The reanimator allows the user to select the characters, settings, and conversation in a given cartoon.

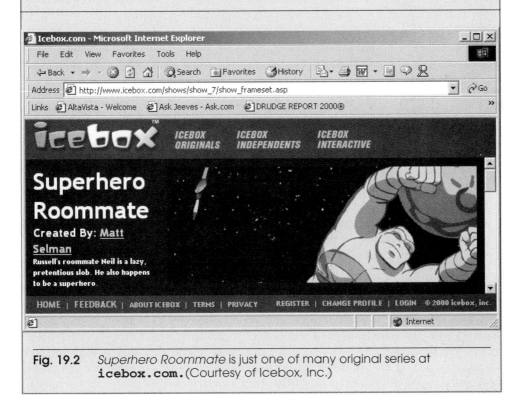

Fig. 19.2 *Superhero Roommate* is just one of many original series at **icebox.com.** (Courtesy of Icebox, Inc.)

19.6 Interactive Web TV

Television has evolved rapidly since its mass distribution beginning in the 1950s. Today, it is possible to select from hundreds of channels. Using *satellite technology*, people can gain access to worldwide television broadcasts. Satellite-television subscribers can choose from hundreds of channels and can purchase additional packages that cover sporting events, concerts and other premium programming.

Television viewers can now interact with their favorite shows by accessing the World Wide Web. MTV (`www.mtv.com`) has recently integrated the Internet into its network with online chats, contests and a fully interactive game show. MTV recently introduced *WebRIOT*, a television game show that allows Internet users to play along from home. Home contestants need only download the game from the MTV Web site to play online with the TV contestants. The leading scorers receive prizes. The screen names are displayed on *WebRIOT* as you play. ABC, the American Broadcasting Company (`www.abc.com`), recently scored major ratings with its runaway hit *Who Wants to Be a Millionaire?* ABC has added interactivity to the show that allows viewers to play along at home and possibly win prizes.[8]

Other channels hold chat sessions and provide supplementary material on their Web sites following broadcasts. News channels such as **CNN.com** (`www.cnn.com`) add video footage and streaming audio to enhance their online content. CNN uses the Internet to gather user data, opinion polls and research to support its off-line efforts.

Computer users that have access to a *Web cam* (a video camera that connects to your computer) can begin broadcasting their own short programs over the Web. Web cams can also be used to communicate with other Web cam users in video conference.

In the near future, we will see the convergence of the Internet and cable television with the introduction of set-top boxes capable of storing vast amounts of information on an internal storage device.[9] Many of the technologies needed to create this convergence already exist. Microsoft, Sun Microsystems and leading electronics manufacturers are building the first-generation boxes that will incorporate many of these features. WebTV (`www.webtv.com`) allows people to access the Internet, send e-mail and surf the Web from their television. A wireless keyboard can be used to navigate the Web from your television. WebTV gives people the opportunity to discover the Web if they do not have access to a computer.

Tivo (`www.tivo.com`) is a device that downloads analog signals from your favorite channels and saves them as digital data on an internal hard drive. This technology allows users to pause, fast forward and rewind live television. Since the system is always downloading data, you can pause the programming and resume it at a later point. Tivo will record the rest of the programming on its internal hard drive for later viewing. ReplayTV (`www.replaytv.com`) offers similar features.

As bandwidth widens and the cost of high speed data transfer decreases, the number of people adopting interactive TV will increase. Set-top boxes and video-on-demand are a threat to VHS distributors and retailers. As the number of consumers using set-top boxes increases, the number of people renting and buying videos on VHS will decrease. Blockbuster Video is already addressing this threat by partnering with video-on-demand providers. The Blockbuster Video of the future may exist only as a channel on the television. Consumers will be able to download feature-length films to their Internet compatible device (television, cellular telephone, PDA, etc.) when they want. Search capabilities will allow consumers to search for their favorite films, actors and actresses, by genre or any other related characteristic.

19.7 Music and the Web

As with film and television, music is establishing itself on the Internet. Studio executives, start-up bands and up-and-coming hip-hop acts are all using the Web. Amateur artists now have a chance to reach new fans worldwide by posting their music on the Web. Artists such as Russell Simmons, Chuck D. and Will Smith have all made investments in high-tech music. Chuck D., the founder of the successful rap group Public Enemy, has started a site, **rapstation.com**, to feature new rap artists, discuss politics and present the latest news. New rap artists can showcase their material on the site and possibly be "discovered." Russell Simmons, among the most successful entrepreneurs in hip-hop music, offers a music site, **360HipHop.com**, that presents the latest news in urban music.

The Web is home to every form of music. If your are looking for your favorite artists, there is a good chance they have a Web site of their own. If not, their record label probably does. Other sites aggregate the work of a wide variety of artists and allow you to choose which you choose the artist by name. **Music.com** is a site that aggregates news, reviews and actual music from the world's most popular musicians. You can download a new song by your favorite artist or trade your music with other **music.com** members. The site offers free e-mail to those who wish to use it. The site has an affiliation with **quick-music.com** that allows you to purchase your favorite CDs directly from the site.

19.8 Web Radio

The Internet has introduced many new forms of entertainment. It has also refined and presented older forms in new ways. For instance, Internet radio gives users access not only to their local stations, but also to stations worldwide (see the **Windowsmedia.com** feature). A computer with audio capabilities and a recently upgraded browser should have no problem downloading the live radio feed. Streaming audio allows you to begin listening to the feed before it has completely downloaded, decreasing user wait time. Many companies have banned the use of Internet radio in the work place do to its high bandwidth demands.

Aspiring deejays and ejays can get their start by broadcasting shows on the Web. SHOUTcast (**www.shoutcast.com**) allows music fans to start radio stations in a matter of minutes. Users must have the ability to play MP3 files to start broadcasting their own radio show. SHOUTcast suggests using the WinAMP player (**www.winamp.com**). It is important, but not essential, to have a high speed connection to the Internet. The faster the connection, the more likely the broadcast will be clear and easily accessible by multiple users. Broadcasters with a microphone will be able to introduce songs and provide commentary live over the Internet. SHOUTcast provides all of the necessary user documentation at their Web site.

Givemetalk.com also allows members to set up their own talk-radio stations. all broadcasts are then made available to listeners at **www.Givemetalk.com**. The service is free for broadcasters and listeners. Listeners are able to download your broadcasts and rate them against the broadcasts of other deejays. Most of the content on the **Give-metalk.com** site is pure talk radio.

e-Fact 19.1

In the year 2000, 63 percent of home-computer users listened to online radio stations, compared with 33 percent in 1999.[10]

National Public Radio's Web site (**www.npr.com**) features supplementary materials supporting the talk-radio programming it offers over the airwaves. The site also offers 24-hour live programming on the Web. **Spinner.com** offers its radio player free for download giving users access to 150 separate music channels and 375,000 songs playing at one time. RadioTower (**www.radiotower.com**) aggregates over 1300 streams of Internet radio. You can choose from every type of music from stations broadcasting worldwide. Each station is categorized by genre, call letters and location. Most of the audio is streamed using *Real Audio*—a Web-based application that decodes the digital audio information. The Real Media Player plays both digital audio and video and can be downloaded for free at **www.real.com**.

19.9 Sports on the Web

The Web offers a number of interesting sports resources. Sporting enthusiasts can find their favorite sports news providers on the Web. ESPN (**www.espn.com**), Sporting News (**www.sportingnews.com**) and the New England Sports Network (**www.nesn.com**) have all established a presence on the Web. The major leagues including the NFL (**www.nfl.com**), NHL (**www.nhl.com**) NBA (**www.nba.com**), MLB (**www.MLB.com**), PGA (**www.pga.com**) and WNBA (**www.wnba.com**) have all created Web sites. These sites offer audio and video of past games and players. The sites also feature expert analysis and commentary by some of the best writers in sports.

SportingNews.com offers the latest information and highlights in sports. It gives you recaps of recent sporting events as well as predictions for upcoming events. The site also provides scores of video and audio snippets for free.

ESPN.com is a leader on television and the Web. The site features the latest headline news in professional, college, high school and amateur sports. The site also offers editorials and predictions by some of the world's top sports writers and analysts. Sports fans can discuss their favorite players, teams and plays in the **ESPN.com** chat rooms. If you are looking to see that great play from last night's game one more time, you will probably find it at **ESPN.com**.

Rivals.com is an *independent site* (i.e., it is not affiliated with a network) that covers most professional and college team in popular sports. The site reports the latest recruiting information in college football and basketball. You can see video footage of the previous season's action and leave messages on the bulletin boards.

Quokka.com is an extreme sporting site that uses high quality streaming audio and video to enhance its content. Formula One racing, Motocross and mountain climbing are among the many sports found on **quokka.com**.

If you want to participate in sports and games online, you can join a *fantasy league*. Fantasy leagues are created at the beginning of a new season. For instance, fantasy football commences at the beginning of the NFL season. In a fantasy league, whether it is football, baseball, golf, hockey or any other sport, players assemble teams by drafting the names of existing players. After each game, the player's statistics are analyzed and recorded as points for each fantasy league member. At the end of the season, the member with the most overall points wins. Fantasy sporting leagues were in existence before the Web became popular, but the Web has made major improvements on the traditional method. For example, in the past, statistics had to be calculated by hand, while today they are done within a computer. This system allows individuals to become members of enormous leagues that span the globe. You can join fantasy sporting leagues for free at Yahoo! (**www.yahoo.com**) and **ESPN.com**.

WindowsMedia.com *and Internet Radio*

WindowsMedia.com offers visitors a way to organize their favorite radio stations (see Fig. 19.3). The WindowsMedia radio tuner allows listeners to search for their favorite stations by location, call numbers, frequency and name. Once you have found a station you like, you can save it in your presets. You can play the stations directly from the radio toolbar on the Microsoft Internet Explorer browser.

    WindowsMedia.com also hosts streaming video from the site. Listeners can enjoy music, talk radio, sports, weather and even streaming police scanners. CDs can be purchased directly from the site as well.

Fig. 19.3   **WindowsMedia.com** allows you to find your favorite radio station. (Courtesy of FNX Radio Network and Microsoft Corporation).

19.10 Comedy on the Web

Anyone who uses e-mail to communicate has probably received a joke or two. The Internet is a place to learn and research, but it is also a place to laugh. (see Onion feature) In fact, some of the world's funniest comedians recently introduced **laugh.com**. Veteran comedians, including Phyllis Diller, George Carlin, Jonathan Winters and Red Buttons have invested in the site. The site features free streaming audio and video of veteran and up-and-coming comics performing.[11] The Modern Humorist (**www.modernhumorist.com**) offers political satire, sports humor and pokes fun at almost all aspects of popular entertainment. The site features audio downloads and accepts submissions from freelance writers.

The Onion and Comedy Online

Onion.com, based on the book series, offers satirical headlines covering politics, sports, entertainment and the workplace. A recent headlines included "Oatmeal Variety Pack Has Only Regular Flavor Left" and "My Tattoo Will Rock Your World" (see Fig. 19.4). The site is designed to look like a traditional news portal, but it is far from serious. *The Onion* uses the Web as a way to sell branded merchandise such as tee shirts and other gift items. Visitors can subscribe to print editions of *The Onion* from their Web site.

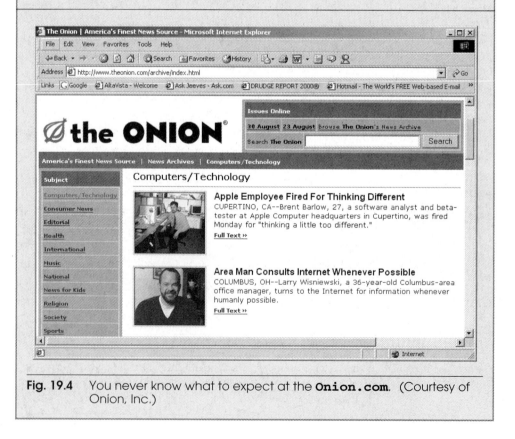

Fig. 19.4   You never know what to expect at the **Onion.com**. (Courtesy of Onion, Inc.)

Comedy Central Online (**www.comcentral.com**) supplements the TV comedy network Comedy Central. Visitors can read information on their favorite shows, play games like South Park Pinball (based on the popular cartoon series), read their horoscope and send Comedy Central e-cards.

19.11 Online Games

The Web is an endless resource of free gaming opportunities. Many of the leading game makers offer demo versions of their retail products on the Web. The games are as simple as jigsaw puzzles and as complex as the latest arcade style shoot'em up. Many online gaming sites allow you to play against other Web surfers. (see the **HSX.com** feature)

Mplayer (**www.mplayer.com**) is a free service that allows you to play online games or your own games with competitors online. Once you have registered, you can access traditional games like backgammon and spades, as well as contemporary games like *Age of Empires*™. Many of the games can be played directly from the Web, while others require the users to have a CD. Mplayer supports its gaming site with an online store selling hardware software and other consumer electronics.

You Don't Know Jack (**www.flipside.com**) is a trivia game that can be played directly over the Web. Visitors are presented with advertisements during short intermissions. Up to three people can play at a time. The categories are written around holidays, seasons and important events. The game is simple: the first one to buzz in gets the points. If you do not know the answer to a question and are pretty sure your opponents are stumped, then you get a chance to force them to answer, you can do this twice a game. *You Don't Know Jack* is also available in a CD-ROM version. The online version can be played for free, if you do not mind watching the advertisements.

If you look hard enough, you will find a number of free games online. Many of them are demos of retail products, while others are small freeware games used to attract people to a site. **Longbowdigitalarts.com** (**www.longboxdigitalarts.com/dxball2.html**) offers *DX-BALL 2*. The object is to use a paddle and bouncing ball to eliminate the blocks that keep you captive. You can play the first 24 stages for free.

HSX.com: the Hollywood Stock Exchange

The Hollywood Stock Exchange (**www.HSX.com**) is a game that allows you to trade Movie Stocks and Star Bonds. The concept is simple: once you have filled out the free registration forms, you are given $2,000,000 in digital-gaming dollars (see Fig. 19.5). This currency can be used to buy movie stocks and celebrity bonds. The value of these securities fluctuates as they are bought and sold by other players. Each member's portfolio is tracked and ranked by the Hollywood Stock Exchange system. The leading scorers are listed on the Web site and qualify for awards. The Hollywood Stock Exchange sells advertising space to movie studios, record companies and other entertainment vendors who wish to increase awareness of upcoming films, artists or pieces of music. The site uses traditional trading methods, which makes it a good way to develop a basic understanding of securities trading.

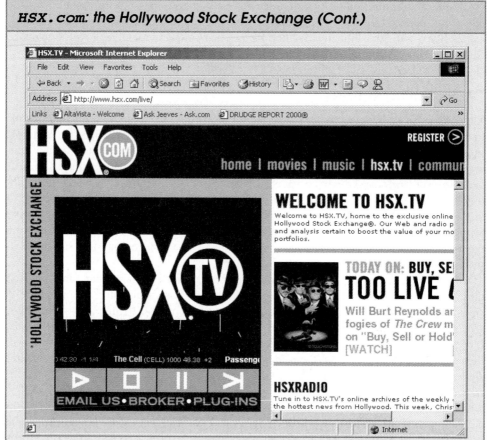

Fig. 19.5   The Hollywood Stock Exchange. (Courtesy of the Hollywood Stock Exchange®. Copyright © 1996-2000. All Rights Reserved.)

Most computer gamers are aware of the classic simulation game *Sim City*. In Sim City, you are the mayor and have to zone, plan and build your city. The better you plan, the happier and more productive your city will become. Beware of natural disasters; your whole town could be destroyed by a tornado or an earthquake. Sim City is now in its third version, Sim City 3000. You can play the classic version online for free at **Maxis.com**.

If you are interested in playing classic games, Activision (**www.activision.com**) offers its original role-playing series Zork for free download at its Web site. Yahoo! has also created a directory of games that can be searched by type. You can find this listing at **games.yahoo.com**. You must register to play. Games include card games, sports games and board games.

19.12 Online Hollywood

Film is an extremely powerful art form that shapes public opinion and promotes change. The best filmmakers recognize the power of film as a medium for communication and change. Anyone with the talent and drive in this field can reach the world with the Internet. The Internet is an open opportunity waiting to be capitalized upon. (see the **Inside.com** feature) For example, scores of *Star Wars* fans have created fan films since the re-release of the *Star Wars* series. Joseph Nussbaum, a film student in California, impressed George Lucas, the *Star Wars* films' writer and director, with his parody film *George Lucas in Love*. His nine-minute short film is now being sold on **Amazon.com**. Special effects experts Bruce Branit and Jeremy Hunt were recently signed to representation by Creative Artists Agency after posting their three-minute short action film on **iFilm.com**. The artists created their film, *405*, using *CGI, computer-generated imaging*, to create the dramatic emergency landing of a jumbo jet onto the 405 freeway in San Diego.

Movie buffs benefit from the Web with movie databases, free short-film downloads and fan sites dedicated to their favorite celebrities, films, and filmmakers. The Internet Movie Database (**www.imdb.com**) is one of the most comprehensive movie sites on the Web. The site is a source of film information, including full cast and crew listings of almost every major blockbuster and small independent film ever made. The design of the site allows you to search through each film by date, cast and crew, production company, filming locations, etc. Links are provided which allow users to research the work of various people in a given movie or television program. Internet users are asked for their input and often provide quality reviews.

Inside: an Entertainment E-zine

Publishing industry veterans Kurt Andersen, Michael Hirschorn and Deanna Brown have joined forces to create a full service news and information site for the entertainment industry. *Inside* (which includes the web site **inside.com**, the magazine *Inside: The Business of Entertainment, Media, and Technology*, and a conference business) describes its audience as entertainment industry leaders, up-and-coming industry players and participants in the convergence economy of entertainment, media, and technology (see Fig 19.6). The site offers the latest news and information in all areas of media and entertainment including film, TV, music, media, and books, with a specific focus on how digital technology is transforming the creation, marketing, distribution, and consumption of entertainment and information. Visitors will find insider news, photos, discussion boards and Ask Bernie—a feature that allows visitors to send entertainment questions to Hollywood producer Bernie Brillstein.

Inside.com also offers key industry data and analysis including the latest advertising rates, merger and acquisition information and proprietary databases that track, among other things, book sales, album sales, and radio airplay. Site members also have access to analysis of the latest Nielson ratings, breakdowns of the nightly television programs and updates on top stories. Members can choose to have content updates sent to their email, pager and personal digital assistant. Individuals looking to start a career in the entertainment industry or continue in their current entertainment career will find job listings at the site. Inside.com will begin offering a print version of its content called *[INSIDE] Magazine* in December of 2000. The magazine is being produced in conjunction with *The Industry Standard*, and is targeted at entertainment/media industry professionals and IT professionals who deal with web content, broadband, wireless and other digital technologies.

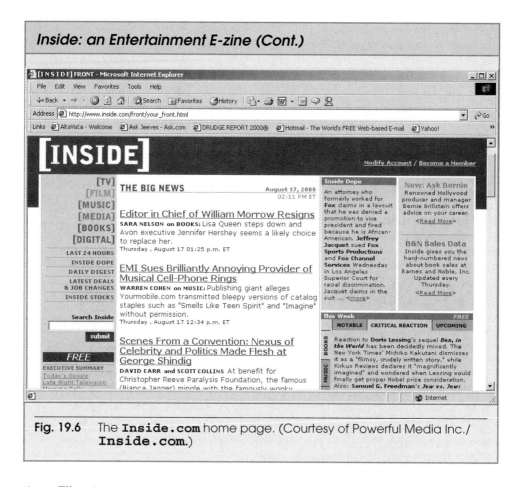

Fig. 19.6   The **Inside.com** home page. (Courtesy of Powerful Media Inc./
Inside.com.)

Atom Films (**www.atomfilms.com**) is a Web site designed to bring attention to independent short films. Many of the short films featured on AtomFilms have won awards. Some of the films on the site have even been nominated for the Academy Awards. The site features work from amateur filmmakers as well as established artists. **FilmFilm.com** and **Hypnotic.com** also offer free short films over the internet.

19.12.1 Talent Scouting

The Internet gives artists the opportunity to present their work to the world, and many artists have found success by using the Web. The Web can be used to research potential jobs, post resumes and portfolios, make contact with industry executives and get your foot in the door—of Hollywood, for example—from across the country. Streaming video allows studio executives to view the *dailies*, the day's film from a given production, from their computers without waiting for a VHS cassette to arrive by mail. Casting calls can be conducted via streaming media. Actors and actresses can submit their past work to potential employers via e-mail, MP3 audio and streaming video.

　　Casting.com is a good way to get yourself noticed if you are a struggling actor. It is also a good place to scope out the competition. The advanced-search function allows you to search for talent by gender, eye color, hair color, ethnicity, age and experience. The site currently hosts talent in Los Angeles and San Francisco.

One way to get your start is to try your luck at **Moviextras.com**. You can post a short description of yourself or a full resume on their site. There are no guarantees, but it could land you a job.

19.12.2 Screen Writing

Screenwriting is a complex process. A *screenwriter* must often conceptualize each relationship and setting before he or she even begins writing a screenplay. Consider the effect that changing the name of a character would have on a completed script if traditional writing tools were used. Screenwriters can get advice and feedback, take writing workshops and courses and chat with other writers on web sites. One such site, **Screenwriters.com**, hosts chats with award-winning screenwriters, studio executives and other Hollywood insiders. Emerging screenwriters can also use the site to submit their work for review and contact other writers for help on a project.

Screenwriters Ted Elliot and Terry Rossio have created a Web site dedicated to the art of screenwriting. Together, they have written many major motion pictures, including *Aladdin*, *The Mask of Zorro* and *Little Monsters*. Visit their site, **Wordplayer.com**, to read articles about screenwriting, answers to specific questions and complete scripts as written by Ted and Terry.

Discussion groups on Web sites relevant to screenwriting and the film industry can be a valuable source of contacts. You never know who will be reading the boards. You also never know who you are actually chatting with. Someone who says they are an insider may only be a fan, but this situation can also work in reverse.

19.12.3 Distribution and Supplies

Film is distributed in many ways. First-run films are usually printed, placed on reels and sold to individual theaters. Films are released on specific dates for a reason. For example, the release of a film with a lot of similarities to a film debuting in July may be pushed up a week or two to reach audiences first. A film that is released in the United States may not be shown in foreign markets for a few months after the U.S. opening. However, digital technology and video-on-demand may change this situation. It is reasonable to assume that feature films will be delivered to theaters and cinemas electronically at some point in the future. Although a fully secure transfer system may never exist, electronic film distribution will rely on a high degree of security to prevent fraud (see Chapter 7, Internet Security). Films will be released domestically and internationally at the same time. It will be possible to order first-run movies from your living room. Distribution, printing and marketing expenses could be reduced tremendously.

19.13 The Future of Entertainment

The Internet and the World Wide Web have already transformed the way we communicate, conduct business and entertain ourselves. As technology advances, electronic components get smaller, memory and storage space increase and bandwidth expands and new opportunities are created. People will one day have near infinite computer power, memory and storage space, for a fraction of the cost they are currently paying. These inexorable trends will have a profound effect on the way entertainment is created, distributed and presented to consumers.

As the number of entertainment options increases, media moguls will compete for our time, making the consumer more important than ever. Companies will be forced to cater to the needs of the individual rather than a large demographic. This drive for personalization will give consumers more freedom than ever before, but paradoxically, it will also threaten their privacy. To personalize an individuals experience, the entertainment providers will have to know intimate details about a person (see Chapter 10 e-Customer Relationship Management.

Personalization will play a major role in interactive television and video-on-demand. Interactive TV and set-top-box technology will make it possible to watch over 500,000 channels on demand. Instead of using a traditional remote control, we may have a television portal similar to Yahoo! and Google that will allow people to find the programming they wish to view. Interactive television will allow us to play along with our favorite game shows and actually compete from home for real prizes. Talk shows could offer live audience participation in real time using Webcam technology. This technology is currently used on a limited basis, but in the future, every home viewer will be able to participate with the show in real time. Living rooms will be transformed into multimedia centers where people can access the Internet, watch television, telecommunicate and conduct business. Advertising will be accurately personalized to the individual user, based on purchases and interest settings.

In the future, home entertainment will expand to give people an even greater range of entertainment options. Musicians will be able to broadcast their music live over the Internet to wireless devices, television, and the radio with ease. We can expect that copyright will continue to be a controversial issue as file transfer technology becomes widely available. It will soon be possible to transfer any type of file anonymously and with little loss of quality. Feature films will be distributed to the theater and to the home simultaneously. Films will open worldwide within the same weekend, reducing marketing expenses, distribution costs and printing costs. People who enjoy the theater will be able to view the latest Broadway show from their living-room television. People will have VCR-like control over their televisions. Tivo and ReplayTV are a few ways of doing this today. In the future, Tivo technology will be standard with televisions. Communication will be possible though multimedia. Text-based chat and live audio will be available over the television, the Web and handheld wireless programs. Advancements in language translation technology could give viewers the ability to switch the dialog to their native language. Many TV's and VCRs currently have the ability to subtitle or provide audio in three to four languages, in the future it will be possible to be entertained in any language. Voices of important speakers that have passed away could be used in presentations and advertising. This technology could also enable celebrity voice endorsements to be created digitally without having the person actually speaking the words.

As technology continues to evolve, three-dimensional video may become a reality. This would open the door for theater-in-the-round entertainment (entertainment offering 360 degree views of the action) in the living room. In film and television it will be possible to generate a 3D digital image of a person or object that appears to be an actual person or object. It will be possible for a silent film star from the 1920's to costar in a film with a mega-star from the year 2020. Imagine watching a film starring Jim Carrey, and digital reproductions of the Marx Brothers. Characters would appear life size, transforming the living room into the setting of an action adventure film, a drama or a popular sitcom. This technology could be used to provide a virtual reality experience and allow people to visit distant countries from their living rooms. We will one day be able to experience history in our living rooms by traveling to a virtual ancient Rome, or prehistoric Africa. If people have access to such a high-quality entertainment experience in the home, it is less likely that people will travel to the local cinema to see a film.

The Internet and Web have added a new dimension to entertainment which changes everything. Roles held by producers, directors, musicians, record companies, movie studios, agents and actors have all been profoundly changed by the Internet. People can create, distribute, market and sell their own work to the world on the Web. In the future, we will continue to see these roles evolve and new forms of entertainment emerge.

In this chapter, we reviewed the key aspects of the entertainment industry and the effects of the Internet and World Wide Web on entertainment. In Chapter 20, Online Career Services, we discuss the new recruiting and employment options created by the Internet. We will review the options to both employers looking to setup recruitment efforts online, and people seeking work in the new economy.

19.14 Internet and World Wide Web Resources

General Entertainment

www.inside.com
This site offers the latest news in popular entertainment, plus content from the film, music, publishing and electronic media industries.

www.entertaindom.com
Entertaindom features downloadable music, streaming media and free downloads of popular artists, movies, animations and original content. The site recently Webcasted a full concert by the Barenaked Ladies.

www.checkout.com
If you are looking for reviews on the latest movies, music and games, visit Checkout. The site profiles artists and content creators and their latest material.

www.x-entertainment.com
This site is dedicated to entertainment of the past. Daily articles discuss toys, games and media of the past. Recent articles include "The Top 8 Transformer Figures of All Time" and "Nintendo: Kung-Fu! Hyyya!". The site also includes a photo gallery, video downloads and games.

www.intertainer.com
This site uses broadband technology to provide streaming audio and video over the Web. It also hosts movie trailers, music videos, and other high-quality multimedia.

Film

www.Rottentomatoes.com
This is a movie review site that aggregates film reviews from leading reviewers and rates movies as either "rotten" or "fresh." This site is a great resource when you are trying to decide on what film to watch.

www.Aintitcool.com
Ain't It Cool News is one of the most successful film entertainment sites on the Web. Harry Knowles, a well-known Hollywood gossip reporter, developed the site and publishes the latest news and gossip related to the entertainment industry. The site is filled with interesting rumors and back-lot gossip.

www.filmthreat.com/
Film Threat is designed to bring attention to lesser-known independent and underground films. The site's publisher, Chris Gore, has been creating content for over a decade and has created a valuable resource for fans of alternative and independent films.

www.icebox.com
Icebox was launched in June of 2000 with the support of Hollywood's leading animators. Visitors can download animations for free and submit their own content. If the content is accepted, it will be placed on the Web. Icebox accepts artwork, writing and full animations.

www.wordplayer.com
This site is the home of Hollywood screenwriters Ted Elliot and Terry Rossio. They have assembled a database of questions and answers for the fledgling screenwriter.

www.ifilm.com
This site is one of the leading short-film cinemas on the Web. The site is a mixture of professional and amateur work assembled from filmmakers worldwide. The films are free once you register.

www.upcomingmovies.com
This site is a collections of insider tips and rumors assembled from individuals across the Web. Each upcoming film that is listed includes the latest casting rumors, on-set gossip and location information.

Music

www.music.com
This site aggregates news and content about popular music. You can download clips of songs and read about your favorite performers.

www.winamp.com
WinAmp is a free application that can be downloaded and used to play MP3 music files. The player includes a playlist organizer and an equalizer. Add-ons allow you to use animated visualizations that perform to the music.

www.MP3.com
MP3.com has become well known since its highly publicized litigation with leading record companies. The site allows you to store your personal MP3 files on its servers. You can then listen to them without the use of a CD.

www.mplayer.com
Mplayer hosts multiplayer gaming across the Web. The site allows you to play some of your CD-ROM-based games and some of its own games over its multiplayer server for free. Games include backgammon, poker and bingo.

www.farmclub.com
Farmclub is a site designed by music industry executives to promote their own artists, as well as unsigned musicians. If you have a band and would like to post your music to the Web, Farmclub will allow you to post your music for free.

Games

www.Jibjab.com
This site is a combination of games and animated short films. The site features rapping politicians and musical food.

www.Amused.com
This site is full of free games. They range from harmless to extreme.

games.yahoo.com
Once you have registered at this site, you can play scores of games for free. Games include poker, backgammon, chess, checkers, memory games, crosswords and more.

`www.microsoft.com/games`
This site is dedicated to the Microsoft games series. It offers patches, add-ons and multiplayer forums for the many of the Microsoft games.

Entertainment Careers

`www.laactorsonline.com`
The goal of the site is to empower the amateur acting community. The site aggregates studio lot maps, personal bios, headshots and resumes and a searchable database of casting directors, agents and other professionals in the field.

`www.hollywoodnetwork.com/hn/acting/index.html`
The Hollywood network is another resource for the Hollywood acting community. Visitors can improve their careers by chatting with other actors, searching the directories and databases and building their own Web site.

`www.Showbizjobs.com`
If you are looking to break into the entertainment industry, `showbizjobs.com` is a good place to start. The database allows you to search for jobs in a wide range of categories and locations.

SUMMARY

- Every aspect of the entertainment industry has been affected by technology, and each is struggling to use it most effectively.
- Advancements in bandwidth, the capacity for data exchange over the Internet, and data processing have made the Internet a viable source of streaming-media-based entertainment.
- The term streaming media is often used to describe video and audio as it is streamed electronically to the viewer.
- Video-on-demand will allow consumers to scan databases of filmed entertainment and play videos at their leisure.
- In the future, we will see a media convergence that will allow consumers to design their own television channels, pick their own sound tracks and surf the Internet over a wireless network.
- Recent studies have shown that chat is the most popular form of Web-based entertainment, followed by streaming video, Internet radio, gaming and movie clips.
- Half of the top 10 audience gainers on the Web were entertainment sites in 2000.
- Set-top boxes combine the interactivity of the Web with the visual quality and usability of television. Set-top boxes also give the viewer VCR-like controls to pause, rewind and fast forward their television programs.
- MP3 Technology allows for the rapid and substantial compression of vast amounts of data. With MP3 technology, individuals can play CD-quality audio from their computer without the use of a CD.
- Using satellite technology, people can gain access to worldwide television broadcasts.
- Tivo is a product that downloads analog signals from your favorite channels and saves them as digital data on an internal hard drive. This system allows users to pause, fast forward and rewind live television.
- `Givemetalk.com` allows members to set up their own talk-radio stations. Their content is then served from the `Givemetalk.com` Web site.
- In the year 2000, 63 percent of home-computer users listen to online radio station, compared with 33 percent in 1999.

- **WindowsMedia.com** offers visitors a way to organize their favorite stations. The radio tuner allows listeners to search for their favorite stations by location, call numbers, frequency and name.

- Each of the major leagues has a Web site that allows you to view each team and player in professional sports. The NFL (**www.nfl.com**), NBA (**www.nba.com**), MLB (**www.MLB.com**), PGA (**www.pga.com**) and WNBA (**www.wnba.com**) have all created Web sites.

- **Onion.com** is site based on the best-selling book. The site offers satirical headlines covering politics, sports, entertainment and the workplace.

- Comedy Central Online (**www.comcentral.com**) supplements the TV network Comedy Central. Visitors can read information on their favorite shows, play games like *South Park* pinball (based on the popular cartoon series), get their horoscope and send Comedy Central e-cards.

- The Web is an endless resource of free gaming opportunities. Many of the leading game makers offer demo versions of their retail products on the Web.

- The Internet Movie Database (**www.imdb.com**) is one of the most comprehensive movie sites on the Web. The site is a source of film information that includes full cast and crew listings of almost every major blockbuster and small independent film ever made.

- **Inside.com** (**www.inside.com**) is a news and information resource for people working in the entertainment industry, as well as for fans looking to learn more.

- Atom Films (**www.atomfilms.com**) is a Web site designed to bring attention to independent short films. Many of the short films featured on Atom Films have won awards; some have even been nominated for the Academy Awards.

- **Screenwirters.com** hosts chats with award-winning screenwriters, studio executives and other Hollywood insiders. Emerging screenwriters can submit their work for review and contact other writers for help on a project. Classes are also available on the site.

- Although a fully secure transfer system may never exist, electronic film distribution will rely on a high degree of security to prevent fraud.

- In the future, feature films will be distributed to the theater and to the home simultaneously. Films will open world wide within the same weekend, reducing marketing expenses, distribution costs and printing costs.

- In the future, communication will be possible though multimedia. Text-based chat and live audio will be available over the television, the Web and handheld wireless programs.

TERMINOLOGY

animation	multimedia
computer-generated imaging (CGI)	Nielsen rating
convergence	pay-per-view
dailies	real audio
entertainment	satellite technology
fantasy league	screenwriter
file-transfer technology	set-top box
independent site	streaming media
media convergence	VHS
MP3	video-on-demand

SELF-REVIEW EXERCISES

19.1   State whether the following are true or false. If the answer is false, explain why.

    a) A set-top box combines television and Internet technology to form a single entertainment solution.

     b) Bandwidth is a measure of capacity used to determine how much information can travel over a given wire at a given time.

     c) Streaming media refers to the transfer of electronic books over the Internet.

     d) Pay-per-view is the same as video-on-demand.

     e) Convergence refers to the joining of multiple technologies, such as the Internet with television, radio and wireless technology.

19.2   Fill in the blanks in each of the following statements.

     a) Napster was recently in the news for allowing individuals to trade _____ using Napster's software product without paying for the service.

     b) _____ refers to the combination of multiple technologies to form a new generation of products and services.

     c) Television viewers are now able to pause, rewind and fast forward live television broadcasts by using _____.

     d) Technology used to pass compressed data over the Web securely is referred to often as _____.

     e) The convergence of the Internet and television will soon make _____ possible; people will be able to choose which movie they want to see and when they want to see it.

ANSWERS TO SELF-REVIEW EXERCISES

19.1   a) True. b) True. c) False. Streaming media could be audio, video or animation files that are played as they download. d) False. Pay-per-view is a service that allows consumers to view content that is available only at certain times of the day. Video-on-demand will allow users to download and view any content they desire at any point in time, within the limitations of their hard-drive capacity. e) True. f) False. Most films are distributed using traditional printing and shipping methods. g) True. h) False. Multimedia refers to the multiple media forms used to create content. These forms can include graphic design, video, audio, etc. i) False. Mplayer is a free gaming site on the Web. j) True.

19.2   a) MP3 files. b) Convergence. c) Tivo. d) File-transfer technology. e) Video-on-demand. f) gaming. g) electronically. h) set-top box.

EXERCISES

19.3   State whether the following are true or false. If the answer is false, explain why.

     a) Most films are distributed electronically via a secure connection to the Internet.

     b) MP3 is a compression standard used to transfer CD-quality audio over the Web.

     c) Multimedia is a company that allows people to post their content to the Web.

     d) Mplayer is used to play MP3 music files over the Internet.

     e) Nielsen ratings are used to measure consumer demographic and usage data within a certain audience or group.

19.4   Fill in the blanks in each of the following statements.

     a) Mplayer and the Station are examples of online _____ sites.

     b) It is possible that feature films will one day be distributed _____, which will cut down on marketing, printing and distribution expenses.

     c) In the future, we will be able to watch TV, surf the Web, write e-mail and shop using a single machine referred to as a _____.

     d) Internet radio is made possible in part by the _____ file format.

     e) _____ will allow filmed content viewers to select the exact film or television program they would like to watch whenever they want to watch it.

19.5   Categorize each of the following items as relating mainly to film, music, television or a combination of them, and give a short explanation of each:

      a) Tivo
      b) **IceBox.com**
      c) WebRIOT
      d) Ask Bernie
      e) MP3
      f) Streaming media

19.6   Define each of the following terms:
      a) set-top box
      b) streaming video
      c) screenwriter
      d) animation
      e) MP3

19.7   Convergence is defined as the combination of multiple technologies and ideas to create a new product or concept. Give a few examples of convergence of technology as it has occurred in the past. How do you think technology will effect our future. In the Future of technology section we describe a number of possibilities. Can you think of any other applications of technology for the future.

19.8   Visit **AtomFilms.com** and **iFilm.com**. Watch a short film. Write a short description of the film you watched and describe your experience? What do you think of the benefits of How do these companies earn their revenues?

19.9   Visit Two online radio stations, **Radiotower.com** and **Spinner.com**. How many individual songs does each broadcast? How many different genres of music does each one broadcast? Which makes it easier to find your favorite music? Which site do you prefer?

19.10   Visit Tivo (**www.tivo.com**) and take the tour. Tivo allows users to rate programs before viewing them, what ratings system is used in the demo? What are the benefits of Tivo? Are there any drawbacks to the system? Write a one-page summary of your opinion on this technology.

WORKS CITED

The notation <**www.domain-name.com**> indicates that the citation is for information found at the Web site.

1.   D. Lake, "The Road to Convergence," *The Standard* September 2000: 151.

2.   A. Oldenburg, "In a Wired World Multimedia is the Message," *USA Today* 22 August 2000 <**www.usatoday.com**>.

3.   D. Lake, 151.

4.   A. Oldenburg, <**www.usatoday.com**>.

5.   T. Weber, "Web Music's Future Turning Cell Phone Into Wireless Walkman," *Wall Street Journal* 7 November 2000: C1.

6.   J. Harding, C. Grimes, "Online Music Rebel Napster in Alliance with Bertelsmann," *Financial Times* 1 November 2000: 1.

7.   L. Hatlestad, "The Icebox Cometh," *eCompany* September 2000: 61.

8.   A. Somers, "Media Merger," *Computer Shopper* November 2000: 186.

9.   R. Tomkins, "A Brainier Box," *Financial Times* 1 November 2000: 18.

10. J. Townley, "Survey: Internet Radio Doubles," *Internet News* 20 March 2000 <**www.internetnews.com**>.

11. "'Dot-Comic Relief': Web Venture to Offer Legends' Work Online," *Wall Street Journal* 1 September 2000: B7.

20

Online Career Services

Objectives

- To explore the various online career services.
- To examine the advantages and disadvantages of posting and finding jobs online.
- To review the major online career services Web sites available to job seekers.
- To explore the various online services available to employers seeking to build their workforces.

What is the city but the people?
William Shakespeare

A great city is that which has the greatest men and women,
If it be a few ragged huts it is still the greatest city in the
whole world.
Walt Whitman

To understand the true quality of people, you must look into
their minds, and examine their pursuits and aversions.
Marcus Aurelius

The soul is made for action, and cannot rest till it be
employed. Idleness is its rust. Unless it will up and think and
taste and see, all is in vain.
Thomas Traherne

Outline

20.1   Introduction
20.2   Resources for the Job Seeker
20.3   Online Opportunities for Employers
        20.3.1   Posting Jobs Online
        20.3.2   Problems with Recruiting on the Web
        20.3.3   Diversity in the Workplace
        20.3.4   Recruiting Services
        20.3.5   Testing Potential Employees Online
20.4   Career Sites
        20.4.1   Comprehensive Career Sites
        20.4.2   Technical Positions
        20.4.3   Contracting Online
        20.4.4   Executive Positions
        20.4.5   Students and Young Professionals
        20.4.6   Other Online Career Services
20.5   Internet and World Wide Web Resources

Summary • Terminology • Self-Review Exercises • Answers to Self-Review Exercises • Exercises • Works Cited

20.1 Introduction

There are approximately 40,000 career-advancement services on the Internet today.[1] These services include large, comprehensive job sites, such as **Monster.com** (see the upcoming feature), as well as interest-specific job sites such as **JustJavaJobs.com**. Companies can reduce the amount of time spent searching for qualified employees by building a recruiting feature on their sites or establishing an account with a career site. This results in a larger pools of qualified applicants, as online services can automatically select and reject resumes based on user-designated criteria. Online interviews, testing services and other resources also expedite the recruiting process.

Applying for a position online is a relatively new method of exploring career opportunities. Online recruiting services streamline the process and allow job seekers to concentrate their energies in careers that are of interest to them. Job seekers can explore opportunities according to geographic location, position, salary or benefits package.

Job seekers can learn how to write a resume and cover letter and post them online and search through job listings to find the jobs that best suit their needs. *Entry-level positions*, or positions commonly sought by individuals who are entering a specific field or the job market for the first time; contracting positions; executive-level positions and middle-management-level positions are all available on the Web.

Job seekers will find a number of time-saving features when searching for a job online. These include storing and distributing resumes digitally, e-mail notification of possible positions, salary and relocation calculators, job coaches, self-assessment tools and information on continuing education.

In this chapter, we explore online career services from the employer and employee's perspective. We suggest sites on which applications can be submitted, jobs cans be searched and applicants can be reviewed. We also review services that build recruiting pages directly into your e-business.

20.2 Resources for the Job Seeker

Finding a job online can greatly reduce the amount of time spent applying for a position. Instead of searching through newspapers and mailing resumes, job seekers can request a specific position in a specific industry through a search engine. Some sites allow job seekers to setup intelligent agents to find jobs that meet their requirements. When the agent finds a potential match, it sends it to the job seeker's inbox. Resumes can be stored digitally, customized quickly to meet job requirements and e-mailed instantaneously. Potential candidates can also learn more about a company by visiting its Web site. Most employment sites are free to job seekers. These sites typically generate their revenues by charging employers for posting job opportunities and by selling advertising space on their Web pages (see the **Monster.com** feature).

Career services, such as **FlipDog.com**, search a list of employer job sites to find positions. By searching links to employer Web sites, **FlipDog.com** is able to identify positions from companies of all sizes. This feature enables job seekers to find jobs that employers may not have posted outside the corporation's Web site.

Monster.com

Super Bowl ads and effective marketing have made **Monster.com** one of the most recognizable online brands (see Fig. 20.1). In fact, in the 24 hours following Super Bowl XXXIV, 5 million job searches occurred on **Monster.com**.[2] The site allows people looking for jobs to post their resumes, search job listings, read advice and information about the job-search process and take proactive steps to improve their careers. These services are free to job seekers. Employers can post job listings, search resume databases and become featured employers.

Posting your resume at **Monster.com** is simple and free. **Monster.com** has a resume builder that allows you to post a resume to its site in 15–30 minutes. You can store up to 5 resumes and cover letters on the **Monster.com** server. Some companies offer their employment applications directly through the **Monster.com** site. **Monster.com** has job postings in every state and all major categories. You can limit access to your personal identification information. As one of the leading recruiting sites on the Web, **Monster.com** is a good place to start your job search or to find out more about the search process.

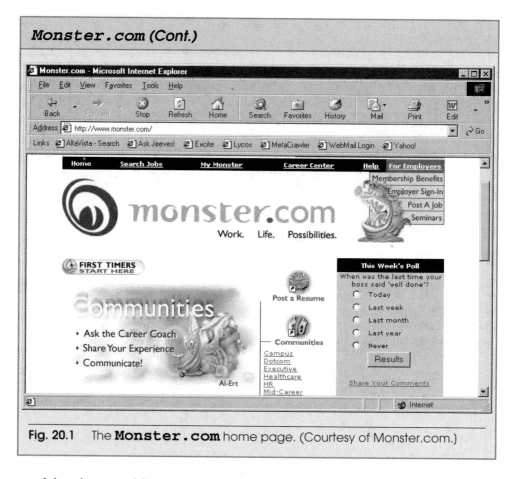

Fig. 20.1   The **Monster.com** home page. (Courtesy of Monster.com.)

Job seekers can visit **FlipDog.com** and choose, by state, the area in which they are looking for a position. Applicants can also conduct worldwide searches. After a user selects a region, **FlipDog.com** requests the user to specify a job category containing several specific positions. The user's choice causes a list of local employers to appear. The user can choose a specific employer or request that **FlipDog.com** search the employment databases for jobs offered by all employers (see Fig. 20.2).

Other services, such as employment networks, also help job seekers in their search. Sites such as **Vault.com** (see the **Vault.com** feature) and **WetFeet.com** allow job seekers to post questions about employers and positions in designated chat rooms and bulletin boards.

20.3 Online Opportunities for Employers

Recruiting on the Internet provides several benefits over traditional recruiting. For example, Web recruiting reaches a much larger audience than posting an advertisement in a local newspaper. Given the breadth of the services provided on most online career services Web sites, the cost of posting online can be considerably less expensive than posting positions through traditional means—even newspapers, which depend greatly on career opportunity advertising, are starting online career sites.[4]

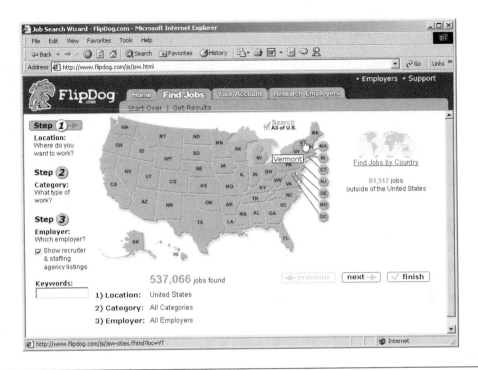

Fig. 20.2   **FlipDog.com** job search. (Courtesy of **FlipDog.com**.)

Vault.com: Finding the Right Job on the Web [3]

Vault.com allows potential employees to seek out additional, third-party information for over 3000 companies. By visiting the *Insider Research* page, Web users have access to a profile on the company of their choice, as long as it exists in **Vault.com**'s database. In addition to **Vault.com**'s profile, there is also a link to additional commentary by company employees. Most often anonymous, these messages can provide prospective employees with potentially valuable, decision-making information. However, users must also consider the integrity of the source. For example, a disgruntled employee may leave a posting that is not a good representation of the corporate culture of his or her company.

The **Vault.com** *Electronic Watercooler*™ is a message board that allows visitors to post stories, questions and concerns and to advise employees and job seekers. In addition, the site provides e-newsletters and feature stories designed to help job seekers in their search. Individuals seeking information on the best business, law and graduate schools can also find information on **Vault.com**.

Job-posting and career-advancement services for the job seeker are also featured on **Vault.com**. These services include *VaultMatch*, a career service that e-mails job postings as requested, and *Salary Wizard*™, which helps job seekers determine what they are worth. Online guides with advice for fulfilling your career ambitions are also available.

> ### Vault.com: Finding the Right Job on the Web (Cont.)[3]
>
> Employers can also use the site. *HR Vault*, a feature of **Vault.com**, provides employers with a free job-posting site. It also features career-management advice, employer-to-employee relationship management and recruiting resources.

e-Fact 20.1

According to Forrester Research, 33 percent of today's average company's hiring budget goes toward online career services, while the remaining 66 percent is used toward tradition-al recruiting mechanisms. Online use expected to increase to 42 percent by 2004, while tra-ditional mechanisms will be reduced to 10 percent.[5]

Generally, jobs posted online are viewed by a larger number of job seekers than jobs posted through traditional means. However, it is important not to overlook the benefits of combining these efforts with human-to-human interaction. There are many job seekers who are not yet comfortable with the process of finding a job online. Often, online recruiting is used as a means of freeing up a recruiter's time for the interviewing process and final selection.

e-Fact 20.2

Cisco Systems cites a 39 percent reduction in cost-per-hire expenses, and a 60 percent re-duction in the time spent hiring.[6]

20.3.1 Posting Jobs Online

When searching for job candidates online, there are many things employers need to consid-er. The Internet is a valuable tool for recruiting, but one that takes careful planning to get the best results. It provides a good supplementary tool, but should not be considered the complete solution for filling positions. Web sites, such as WebHire (**www.web-hire.com**), enhance a company's online employment search (see the Webhire feature).

There are a variety of sites that allow employers to post jobs online. Some of these sites require a fee, which generally runs between $100–$200. Postings typically remain on the Web site for 30–60 days. Employers should be careful to post to sites that are most likely to be visited by eligible candidates. As we discovered in the previous section, there are a variety of online career services focused on specific industries, and many of the larger, more comprehensive sites have categorized their database by job category.

When designing a posting, the recruiter should also consider the vast number of post-ings already on the Web. Defining what makes your position unique, including information such as benefits and salary, might convince a qualified candidate to further investigate the position (see Fig. 20.3).[8]

HotJobs.com career postings are cross-listed on a variety of other sites, thus increasing the number of potential employees that see the job listings. Like **Mon-ster.com** and **jobfind.com**, **hotjobs.com** requires a fee per listing. Employers also have the option of becoming **HotJob.com** members. Employers also receive access to HotJob's *Private Label Job Boards* (private corporate employment sites), online recruiting technology and online career fairs.

WebHire™[7]

Designed specifically for recruiters and employers, WebHire is a multifaceted service that provides employers with *end-to-end recruiting solutions*. The service offers job-posting services as well as candidate searches. The most comprehensive of the services, *WebHire™ Enterprise*, locates and ranks candidates found through resume-scanning mechanisms. Clients will also receive a report indicating the best resources for their search. Other services, available through the *WebHire™ Employment Services Network*, include preemployment screening, tools for assessing employees' skill levels and information on compensation packages. An employment law advisor helps organizations design interview questions.

WebHire™ Agent is an intelligent agent that searches for qualified applicants, based on your job specifications. When WebHire Agent identifies a potential candidate, an e-mail is automatically sent to that candidate to generate interest. WebHire Agent then ranks applicants according to the skills information it gains from the Web search; the information is stored, so that new applicants are distinguished from those who have already received an e-mail from the site.

Yahoo!® Resumes, a feature of WebHire, allows recruiters to find potential employees by typing in keywords to the Yahoo! Resumes search engine. Employers can purchase a year's membership to the recruiting solution for a flat fee; there are no per-use charges.

Job Seeker's Criteria

Position (responsibilities)

Salary

Location

Benefits (health, dental, stock options)

Advancement

Time Commitment

Training Opportunities

Tuition Reimbursement

Corporate Culture

Fig. 20.3   List of a job seeker's criteria.

Boston Herald *Job Find* (`www.jobfind.com`) also charges employers to post on its site. The initial fee entitles the employer to post up to three listings. Employers have no limitations on the length of their postings.

Other Web sites providing employers with employee recruitment services include **CareerPath.com**, America's Job Bank (`www.ajb.dni.us/employer`), CareerWeb (`www.cweb.com`), **Jobs.com** and **Career.com**.

20.3.2 Problems with Recruiting on the Web

The large number of applicants presents a challenge to both job seekers and employers. On many recruitment sites, matching resumes to positions is conducted by *resume-filtering software*. The software scans a pool of resumes for keywords that match the job description. While this software increases the number of resumes that receive some attention, it is not a foolproof system. For example, the resume-filtering software might overlook someone with similar skills to those listed in the job description, or someone whose current abilities would enable them to learn the skills required for the position. Digital transmissions can also create problems as certain software platforms are not always acceptable by the recruiting software. This sometimes results in an unformatted transmission, or a failed transmission.

Confidentiality is another disadvantage of online career services. In many cases, a job candidate will want to search for job opportunities anonymously. This reduces the possibility of offending the candidate's current employer. Posting a resume on the Web increases the likelihood that the candidate's employer might come across it when recruiting new employees. The traditional method of mailing resumes and cover letters to potential employers does not impose the same risk.

According to recent studies, the number of individuals researching employment positions through other means, such as referrals, newspapers and temporary agencies, far outweighs the number of job seekers researching positions through the Internet.[9] Optimists feel, however, that this disparity is largely due to the early stages of e-business development. Given time, online career services will become more refined in their posting and searching capabilities, decreasing the amount of time it takes for a job seeker to find jobs and employers to fill positions.

20.3.3 Diversity in the Workplace

Every workplace inevitably develops its own culture. Responsibilities, schedules, deadlines and projects all contribute to a working environment. Perhaps the most defining elements of a *corporate culture* are the employees. For example, if all employees were to have the same skills and the same ideas, then the workplace would lack diversity. It might also lack creativity and enthusiasm. One way to increase the dynamics of an organization is to employ people of all backgrounds and cultures.

The Internet hosts demographic-specific sites for employers seeking to increase diversity in the workplace. Increasing diversity enhances organizations in many ways. By recruiting people from different backgrounds, new ideas and perspectives are brought forth, helping businesses meet the needs of a larger, more diverse target audience.[10]

Blackvoices.com and **hirediversity.com** are demographic-specific Web sites (see Fig. 20.4). BlackVoices™, which functions primarily as a portal, features job searching capabilities and the ability for prospective employees to post resumes. HireDiversity is divided into several categories, including African American, Hispanic and opportunities for women. Other online recruiting services place banner advertisements on ethnic Web sites for companies seeking diverse workforces.

The Diversity Directory (**www.mindexchange.com**) offers international career-searching capabilities. Users selecting the **Diversity** site can find job opportunities, information and additional resources to help them in their career search. The site can be searched according to demographics (African American, Hispanic, alternative lifestyle, etc.) or by subject (employer, position, etc.) through hundreds of links. Featured sites include **BilingualJobs.com**, *Latin World* and *American Society for Female Entrepreneurs.*

The Internet also provides people with disabilities opportunities for career advancement. Many sites have sections dedicated to job seekers with disabilities. In addition to providing job-searching capabilities, these sites include additional resources, such as equal opportunity documents and message boards. The *National Business and Disability Council (NBDC)* provides employers with information on employing people with disabilities, such as integration and accessibility, as well as opportunities for job seekers.

Fig. 20.4   Career opportunities at BlackVoices. (Courtesy of **BlackVoices.com**.)

20.3.4 Recruiting Services

There are many services on the Internet that help employers match individuals to positions. The time saved by conducting preliminary searches on the Internet can then be dedicated to interviewing qualified candidates and making the best matches possible.

Advantage Hiring, Inc. (**www.advantagehiring.com**) provides employers with a resume-screening service. When a prospective employee submits a resume for a particular position, Advantage Hiring, Inc., presents *Net-Interview*™, a small questionnaire to supplement the information presented on the resume. The site also offers *SiteBuilder*, a service that helps employers build an employee recruitment site. An online demonstration can be found at **www.advantagehiring.com**. The demonstration walks the user through the Net-Interview software, as well as a number of the other services offered by Advantage Hiring (see Fig. 20.5).

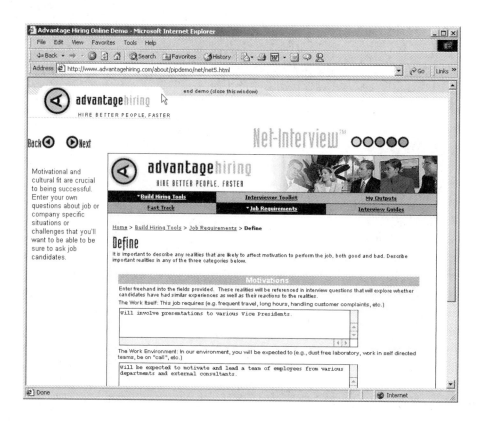

Fig. 20.5   Advantage Hiring, Inc.'s Net-Interview™ service. (Courtesy of Advantage Hiring, Inc.)

Recruitsoft.com is an application service provider (ASP) that offers companies recruiting software on a *pay-per-hire* basis (Recruitsoft receives a commission on hires made via its service). ASPs are discussed in Chapter 5, Internet Hardware, Software and Network Communications. *Recruiter WebTop*™ is the company's online recruiting software. It includes a host of features, such as Web-site hosting, an employee-referral program, skill-based resume screening, applicant-tracking capabilities and job-board posting capabilities. A demonstration of Recruiter WebTop's *Corporate Recruiting Solutions* can be found at **www.recruitsoft.com/process**. The demonstration shows how recruiting solutions find and rank potential candidates. More information about Recruitsoft's solution can be viewed in a *QuickTime* media player demonstration, found at **www.recruitsoft.com/corpoVideo**.[11]

Peoplescape.com is an online service that help employers recruit employees and maintain a positive work environment once the employee has been hired. In addition to searches for potential candidates, Peoplescape also offers *PayCheck*™, *LegalCheck*™ and *PeopleCheck*™. These services help to ensure that compensation offers are adequate, legal guidelines are met and candidates have provided accurate information both on their resumes and during the hiring process. For job seekers, Peoplescape offers searching capabilities, insights to career transitions, a job compensation calculator that takes benefits and bonuses into consideration when exploring a new job possibility and a series of regularly posted articles relevant to the job search.[12]

To further assist companies in their recruiting process, Web sites such as **Refer.com** reward visitors for successful job referrals. Highly sought-after positions can earn thousands of dollars. If you refer a friend or a family member and he or she is hired, you receive a commission.

Other online recruiting services include **SkillsVillage.com**, **Hire.com**, **MorganWorks.com** and **Futurestep.com**™.

20.3.5 Testing Potential Employees Online

The Internet has also provided employers with a cost-effective means of testing their prospective employees in such categories as decision making, problem solving and personality. Services such *eTest* help to reduce the cost of in-house testing and to make the interview process more effective. Test results, given in paragraph form, present the interested individual's strengths and weaknesses. Based on these results, the report suggests interview methods, such as asking *open-ended questions*, or questions that require more than a "yes" or "no" response. Sample reports and a free-trial test can be found at **www.etest.net**.

Employers and job seekers can also find career placement exercises at **www.advisorteam.net/AT/User/kcs.asp**. Some of these services require a fee. The tests ask several questions regarding the individual's interests and working style. Results help candidates to determine the best career for their skills and interests.

20.4 Career Sites

Online career sites can be comprehensive or industry specific. In this section, we explore a variety of sites on the Web that accommodate the needs of both the job seeker and the employer. We review sites offering technical positions, free-lancing opportunities and contracting positions.

20.4.1 Comprehensive Career Sites

As mentioned previously, there are many sites on the Web that provide job seekers with career opportunities in multiple fields. **Monster.com** is the largest of these sites, attracting the largest number of unique visitors per month. Other popular online recruiting sites include **JobsOnline.com**, **HotJobs.com**, **www.jobtrak.com** and **Headhunter.net**.

Searching for a job online can be a conducted in a few steps. For example, during an initial visit to **JobsOnline.com**, a user is required to fill out a registration form. The form requests basic information, such as name, address and area of interest. After registering, members can search through job postings according to such criteria as the number of days posted, category and location. Contact information is provided for additional communication. Registered members are offered access to XDrive™ (**www.xdrive.com**), which provides 25 MB of storage space for resumes, cover letters and additional communication. Stored files can be shared through any Web browser or Wireless Application Protocol (WAP) enabled device.[13] We discuss the wireless Web in depth in Chapter 6, Wireless Internet and m-Business. **Driveway.com** offers a similar service, allowing individuals to store, share and organize files online. An online demonstration of the service can be found at **www.driveway.com**. The animated demo walks the user through the features offered by the service. **Driveway.com** offers 100 MB of space, and the service is free.[14] Other sites, such as Cruel World (see the Cruel World feature), allow you to store and send your resume directly.

Cruel World[15]

Cruel World is a free, online career advancement service for job seekers. After becoming a registered member, your information is matched with available positions in the Cruel World database. When an available job matches your criteria, *JobCast*®, a feature of Cruel World, sends an e-mail alerting you of the available position. If you are interested, you can send your resume to the employer that posted the position, customized to the job's requirements. If you do not wish to continue your search, you can simply send a negative response via e-mail.

The client list, or the list of companies seeking new employees through Cruel World, can be viewed at **www.cruelworld.com/corporate/aboutus.asp** (Fig. 20.6). Additional features on the site include hints for salary negotiation; a self-assessment link to **CareerLeader.com**, where, for a small fee, members can reassess their career goals under the advisement of career counselors and a relocation calculator for job seekers who are considering changing location.

Employers seeking to hire new talent can post opportunities through Cruel World. posting positions requires a fee. A demonstration of the service can be viewed at **www.cruelworld.com/clients/quicktour1.asp**. The demonstration is a three-step slide of JobCast.

Cruel World[15] *(Cont.)*

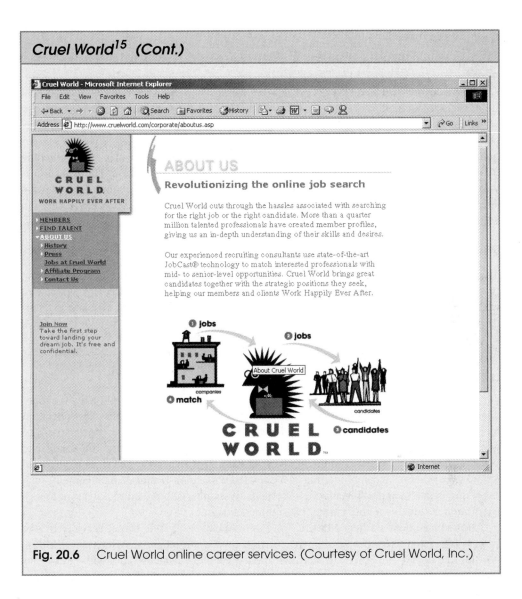

Fig. 20.6   Cruel World online career services. (Courtesy of Cruel World, Inc.)

20.4.2 Technical Positions

Technical positions are among the most widely available as the Internet becomes more pervasive. Limited job loyalty and high turnover rates allow job seekers to find the job that best suits their needs and skills, and requires employers to rehire continuously to keep positions filled and productivity levels high. The amount of time for an employer to fill a technical position can be greatly reduced by using an industry-specific site. Career sites designed for individuals seeking technical positions are among the most popular online career sites. In this section, we review several sites that offer recruiting and hiring opportunities for technical positions.

e-Fact 20.3

It costs a company 25 percent more to hire an new technical employee than it does to pay a currently employed individual's salary.[16]

Dice.com (**www.dice.com**) is a recruiting Web site that focuses on technical fields. Fees to companies are based on the number of jobs they post and the frequency with which the postings are updated. Job seekers can post their resumes and search the job database for free. **JustComputerJobs.com** directs job seekers toward 39 specific computer technologies for their job search. Language-specific sites include **JustJavaJobs.com**, **JustCJobs.com** and **JustPerlJobs.com**. Hardware, software and communications technology sites are also available. Other technology recruiting sites include **HireAbility.com**, **Bid4Geeks.com**, **HotDispatch.com** and **www.cmpnet.com/careerdirect**.

20.4.3 Contracting Online

The Internet also serves as a forum for job seekers to find employment on a project-by-project basis. *Online contracting services* allow businesses to post positions for which they want to hire outside resources, and individuals can identify projects that best suit their interests, schedules and skills.

e-Fact 20.4

Approximately six percent of America's workforce falls into the category of independent contractor.[17]

Guru.com (**www.guru.com**) is a recruiting site for contract employees. Independent contractors, private consultants and trainers use **guru.com** to find short-term and long-term contract assignments. Tips, articles and advice are available for contractors who wish to learn more about their industry. Other sections of the site teach you how to manage your business, buy the best equipment and deal with legal issues. **Guru.com** includes an online store where you can buy products associated with small-business management, such as printing services and office supplies. Companies wishing to hire contractors need to register, but individuals seeking contract assignments do not.

Monster.com's Talent Market™ offers online auction-style career services to free agents. Interested users design a profile, listing their qualifications. After establishing a profile, free agents "Go Live" to start the bidding on their services. The bidding lasts for five days during which users can view the incoming bids. At the close of five days, the user can choose the job of their choice. The service is free for users, bidding employers pay a commission on completed transactions.

eLance.com is another site where individuals can find contracting work. Interested applicants can search eLance's database by category, including business, finance and marketing (see Fig. 20.7). These projects, or *requests for proposals* (RFPs), are posted by companies worldwide. When you find a project for which you feel you are qualified, you submit a bid on the project. Your bid will contain your required payment, a statement detailing your skills and a feedback rating drawn from other projects on which you have worked. If your bid is accepted, you are given the project, and the work is conducted over eLance's file-sharing system, enabling both the contractor and the employer to contact one another quickly and easily. For an online demonstration, visit **www.elance.com** and click on the **demonstration** icon.

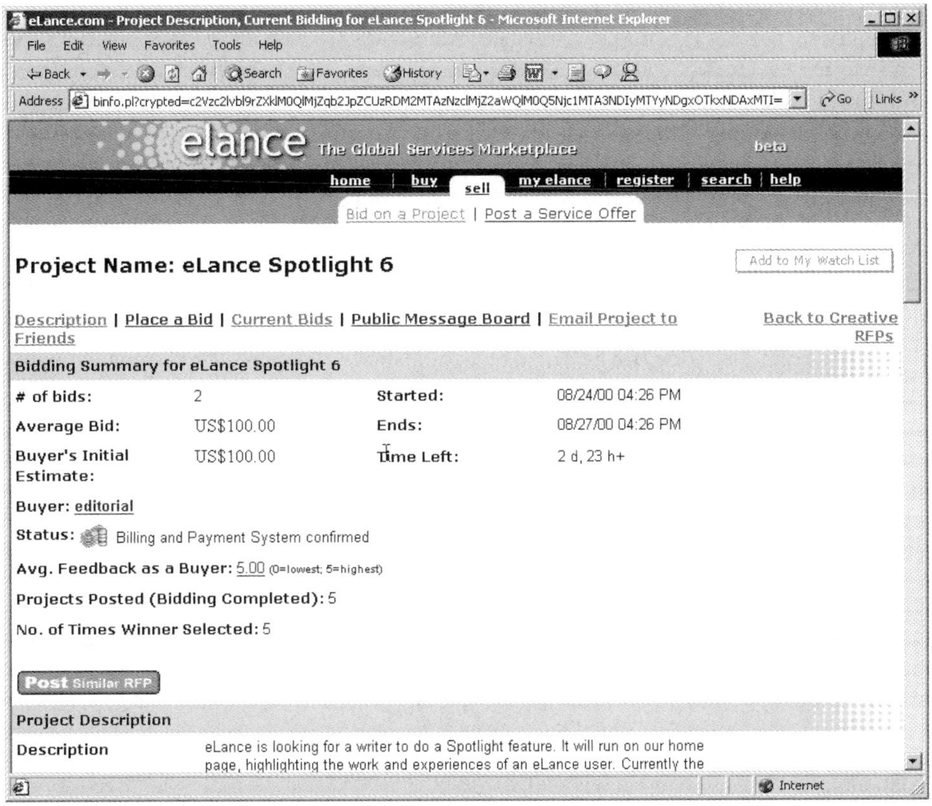

Fig. 20.7   **eLance.com** request for proposal (RFP) example. (Courtesy of
eLance, Inc.)

FreeAgent (**www.freeagent.com**) is another site designed for contracting
projects. Candidates create an *e.portfolio* that provides an introductory "snapshot" of their
skills, a biography, a list of their experience and references. An interview section of the
portfolio lists questions and the applicant's answers. Examples of e.portfolios can be found
at **www.freeagent.com/splash/models.asp**. Free Agent's *e.office* offers a benefits package to outside contractors, including health insurance, a retirement plan and reimbursement for business-related expenses, among other features.

Other Web sites that provide contractors with projects and information include
eWork® Exchange (**www.ework.com**), **MBAFreeAgent.com**, **Aquent.com** and
WorkingSolo.com.

20.4.4 Executive Positions

In this section, we discuss the advantages and disadvantages of finding an executive position online. Executive career advancement sites usually include many of the features that
you might find on a comprehensive job-search site. Searching for an executive position on-

line differs from finding an entry-level position online. The Internet allows individuals to continually survey the job market. However, candidates for executive-level positions must exercise a higher level of caution when determining who is able to view their resume. Applying for an executive position online is an extensive process. Because of the high level of scrutiny passed on a candidate during the hiring process, the initial criteria presented by an executive level candidate are often more specific than the criteria presented by the first-time job seeker. Executive positions are often difficult to fill, due to the high demands and large amount of experience required for the jobs.

SixFigureJobs (**www.sixfigurejobs.com**) is a recruitment site designed for experienced executives. Resume posting and job searching is free to job seekers. Other sites including, **www.execunet.com**, **Monster.com**'s ChiefMonster™ (**www.chief-monster.com**) and **www.nationjob.com** also are designed for helping executives find positions

20.4.5 Students and Young Professionals

The Internet provides students and young professionals with many tools to get them started in the job market. Individuals still in school and seeking internships, individuals who are just graduating and individuals who have been in the workforce for a few years make up the target market. Additional tools specifically designed for this *demographic*, or a population defined by a specific characteristic, are also available. For example, journals kept by previous interns provide prospective interns with information regarding what to look for in an internship, what to expect and what to avoid. Many of these sites will provide information to start young professionals in the right direction, such as matching positions to college or university major.

Experience.com is a career services Web site geared toward the younger population. Members can search for positions according to specific criteria, such as geographic location, job category, keywords, commitment (i.e. full time, part time, internship), amount of vacation and amount of travel time. After applicants register, they can send their resumes directly to the companies posting on the site. In addition to the resume, candidates also provide a personal statement, a list of applicable skills and their language proficiency. Registered members also receive access to the site's *Job Agent*. Members can set up to three Job Agents. The agents search for available positions, based on the criteria posted by the member. If a match is made, the site contacts the candidate via e-mail.[18,19]

Internshipprograms.com helps students find internships. In addition to posting a resume and searching for an internship, students can also use the relocation calculator and read through information and tips on building resumes and writing essays. The *City Intern* program provides travel, housing, entertainment and guides to interns interviewing or accepting a position in an unfamiliar city, making them feel more at home in a new location.

In addition to its internship locators, undergraduate, graduate, law school, medical school and business school services, the Princeton Review's Web site (**www.review.com**) offers career services to graduating students. While searching for a job, students and young professionals can also read through the site's news reports or even increase their vocabulary by visiting the "word for the day." Other Web sites geared toward the younger population include **campuscareercenter.com, brassring-campus.com** and **collegegrads.com**.

20.4.6 Other Online Career Services

In addition to Web sites that help you find and post jobs online, there are a number of Web sites that offer features that will enhance your search, prepare you for searching online, help you design your resume or help you calculate the cost of relocating.

Salary.com helps job seekers gauge their expected income, based on position, level of responsibility and years of experience. The search requires job category, ZIP code and specific job title. Based on this information, the site will return an estimated salary for an individual living in the specified area, and employed in the position described. Estimates are returned based on the average level of income for that position.

In addition to being a resource for finding employment, **www.careerpower.com** also provides individuals with tests that will help them realize their strengths, weaknesses, values, skills and personality traits. Based on the results, which can be up to 10–12 pages per test, users can best decide what job category they are best qualified for and what career choice will be best suited to their personal ambitions. The service is available for a fee.

InterviewSmart™ is another service offered through CareerPower that prepares job seekers of all levels for the interviewing process. The service can be downloaded for a minimal fee or can be used on the Web for free. Both versions are available at **www.careerpower.com/CareerPerfect/interviewing.htm#is.start.anchor**.

Additional services will help you find a position that meets your unique needs, or design your resume to attract the attention of employers. **Dogfriendly.com**, organized by geographic location, helps job seekers find opportunities that allow them to bring their pets to work, and **cooljobs.com** is a searchable database of unique job opportunities.

20.5 Internet and World Wide Web Resources

Information Technology (IT) Career Sites

www.dice.com
This is a recruiting Web site that focuses on the computer industry.

www.peoplescape.com
This site provides career advancement services for both employers and job seekers. Its services include PayCheck™, LegalCheck™ and PeopleCheck™, to assist employers in the hiring process.

www.guru.com
This is a recruiting site for contract employees. Independent contractors, private consultants and trainers can use **guru.com** to find short-term and long-term work.

www.hallkinion.com
This is a Web recruiting service for individuals seeking IT positions.

www.techrepublic.com
This site provides employers and job seekers with recruiting capabilities and information regarding developing technology.

www.justcomputerjobs.com
This site serves as a portal with access to language-specific sites, including Java, Perl, C and C++.

www.bid4geeks.com
This career services site is geared toward the technical professional.

www.hotdispatch.com
This forum provides software developers with an opportunity to share projects, discuss code and ask questions.

Career Sites

www.careerbuilder.com

A network of career sites, including IT Careers, *USA Today* and MSN, CareerBuilder attracts 3 million unique job seekers per month. This site also provides resume-builder and job-searching agents.

www.recruitek.com

This free site caters to jobs seekers, employers and contractors.

www.monster.com

This site, the largest of the online career sites, allows people looking for jobs to post their resumes, search job listings and read advice and information about the job-search process. It also provides a variety of recruitment services for employers.

www.jobsonline.com

Similar to **Monster.com**, this site provides opportunities for job seekers and employers.

www.hotjobs.com

This online recruiting site offers cross-listing possibilities on additional sites.

www.jobfind.com

This job site is an example of locally targeted job-search resources. **JobFind.com** targets the Boston area.

www.flipdog.com

This site allows online job candidates to search for career opportunities. It employs intelligent agents to scour the Web and return jobs matching the candidate's request.

www.cooljobs.com

This site highlights unique job opportunities.

Executive Positions

www.sixfigurejobs.com

This is a recruitment site designed for experienced executives.

www.leadersonline.com

This career services Web site offers confidential job searches for mid-level professionals. Potential job matches are e-mailed to job candidates.

Diversity

www.latpro.com

This site is designed for Spanish and Portuguese-speaking job seekers. In addition to provide resume-posting services, the site enables job seekers to receive matching positions via e-mail. Advice and information services are also available.

www.blackvoices.com

This portal site hosts a career center designed to match African American job seekers with job opportunities.

www.hirediversity.com

In addition to services for searching for and posting positions, resume-building and up-dating services are also available at this site. The site targets a variety of demographics including African Americans, Asian Americans, people with disabilities, women and Latin Americans.

People with Disabilities

www.halftheplanet.com

This site represents people with disabilities. The site is large and includes many different resources and information services. A special section is dedicated to job seekers and employers.

`www.wemedia.com`
This site is designed to meet the needs of people with disabilities. It also includes a section for job seekers and employers.

`www.disabilities.com`
This site provides users with a host of links to information resources on career opportunities.

`www.rileyguide.com`
This site includes a section with opportunities for people with disabilities, which can be viewed at `www.dbm.com/jobguide/vets.html#abled`.

`www.mindexchange.com`
The diversity section of this site provides users with several links to additional resources regarding people with disabilities and employment.

`www.usdoj.gov/crt/ada/adahom1.htm`
This is the Americans with Disabilities Act home page.

`www.abanet.org/disability/home.html`
This is the Web site for The Commission on Mental and Physical Disability Law.

`janweb.icdi.wvu.edu`
The Job Accommodation Web site offers consulting services to employers regarding the integration of people with disabilities in the workplace.

General Resources

`www.vault.com`
This site provides potential employees with "insider information" on over 3000 companies. In addition, job seekers can search through available positions and post and answer questions on the message board.

`www.wetfeet.com`
Similar to **vault.com**, this site allows visitors to ask questions and receive "insider information" on companies that are hiring.

Free Services

`www.sleuth.com`
On this site job seekers can fill out a form that indicates their desired field of employment. Job Sleuth™ searches the Internet and returns potential matches to the user's inbox. The service is free.

`www.refer.com`
This site rewards visitors for successful job referrals. If you refer a friend or family member and he or she is hired, you receive a commission.

`www.ajb.org`
America's Job Bank is an online recruiting service provided through the Department of Labor and the state employment service. Searching and for posting positions on the site are free.

`www.xdrive.com`
This free site provides members with 25 MB of storage space for housing documents. XDrive is able to communicate with all browser types and has wireless capabilities.

`www.driveway.com`
Similar to **XDrive.com**, this Web site provides users with 100 MB of storage space. Users can back up, share and organize the information. **Driveway.com** works on all platforms.

Special Interest

`www.eharvest.com/careers/index.cfm`
This Web site provides job seekers interested in agricultural positions with online career services.

www.opportunitynocs.org
This career services site is for both employers and job seekers interested in non-profit opportunitites.

www.experience.com
This Web site is designed specifically for young professionals and students seeking full-time, part-time and internship positions.

www.internshipprograms.com
Students seeking internships can search job listings on this site. It also features City Intern, to help new interns become acquainted with a new location.

www.brassringcampus.com
This site provides college grads and young professionals with less than five years of experience with job opportunities. Additional features help users buy a car or find an apartment.

Online Contracting

www.ework.com
This online recruiting site matches outside contractors with companies needing project specialists. Other services provided through eWork include links to online training sites, benefits packages and payment services and online meeting and management resources.

www.elance.com
Similar to **eWork.com**, eLance matches outside contractors with projects.

www.freeagent.com
Similar to other sites in this category, FreeAgent matches contractors with projects.

MBAFreeAgent.com
This site is designed to match MBAs with contracting opportunities.

Aquent.com
This site provides access to technical contracting positions.

WorkingSolo.com
This site helps contractors start working for themselves.

Recruiting Services

www.advantagehiring.com
This site helps employers screen resumes.

www.morganworks.com
MorganWorks.com is an online recruiting-services provider.Its services include outsourced recruiting, searchable candidate databases, career-site-building services, career-searching capabilities and international executive searches.

www.etest.net
This site provides employers with testing services to assess the strengths and weaknesses of prospective employees. This information can be used for better hiring strategies.

www.hire.com
Hire.com's eRecruiter is an application service provider that helps organizations streamline their Web-recruiting process.

www.futurestep.com
Executives can register confidentially at **Futurestep.com** to be considered for senior executive positions. The site connects registered individuals to positions. It also offers career management services.

www.webhire.com
This site provides employers with end-to-end recruiting solutions.

SUMMARY

- The Internet can improve your ability to recruit employees and find career opportunities from around the world.

- Job seekers can learn how to write a resume and cover letter, post them online and search through job listings to find the jobs that best suit their needs.

- Employers can post jobs that can be searched by an enormous pool of applicants.

- Job seekers can store and distribute resumes digitally, receive e-mail notification of possible positions, use salary and relocation calculators, consult job coaches and use self-assessment tools when searching for a job on the Web.

- There are approximately 40,000 career-advancement services on the Internet today.

- Finding a job online can greatly reduce the amount of time spent applying for a position. Potential candidates can also learn more about a company by visiting its Web site.

- Most sites are free to job seekers. These sites typically generate their revenues by charging employers to post their job opportunities and by selling advertising space on their Web pages.

- Sites such as **Vault.com** and **WetFeet.com** allow job seekers to post questions about employers and positions in designated chat rooms and bulletin boards.

- On many recruitment sites, the match of a resume to a position is conducted by resume filtering software.

- Confidentiality is disadvantage of online career services.

- According to recent studies, the number of individuals researching employment positions through means other than the Internet, such as referrals, newspapers and temporary agencies, far outweighs the number of Internet job seekers.

- Career sites designed for individuals seeking a technical position are among the most popular online career sites.

- Online contracting services allow businesses to post positions for which they want to hire outside resources, and individuals can identify projects that best suit their interests, schedules and skills.

- The Internet provides students and young professionals with some of the necessary tools to get them started in the job market. The target market is made up of individuals still in school and seeking internships, individuals that are just graduating and individuals who have been in the workforce for a few years.

- There are a number of Web sites that offer features that will enhance your job search, prepare you for searching online, help design your resume or help you calculate the cost of relocating.

- Web recruiting reaches a much larger audience than posting an advertisement in the local newspaper.

- There are a variety of sites that allow employers to post jobs online. Some of these sites require a fee, which generally runs between $100–$200. Postings remain on the Web site for approximately 30–60 days.

- Employers should try to post to sites that are most likely to be visited by eligible candidates.

- When designing a job posting, defining what makes your position unique and including information such as benefits and salary might convince a qualified candidate to further investigate the position.

- The Internet hosts demographic-specific sites for employers seeking to increase diversity in the workplace.

- The Internet has also provided employers with a cost-effective means of testing their prospective employees in such categories as decision making, problem solving and personality.

TERMINOLOGY

corporate culture

demographic

end-to-end recruiting solutions

entry-level position

online contracting services

open-ended questions

pay per hire

recruiter

requests for proposals (RFPs)

resume filtering software

SELF-REVIEW EXERCISES

20.1   State whether each of the following is true or false; if false, explain why.

a) Online contracting services allow businesses to post job listings for specific projects which can be viewed by job seekers over the Web.

b) Other services, such as employment networks, are Web sites designed to provide information on a selected company to better inform job seekers of the corporate environment.

c) The large number of applications received over the Internet is considered an advantage by most online recruiters.

d) There is a greater number of individuals searching for work on the Web than through all other mediums combined.

e) Sixteen percent of America's workforce is categorized as independent contractors.

20.2   Fill in the blanks in each of the following statements.

a) There are approximately _____ online career services Web sites on the Internet today.

b) The Internet hosts demographic-specific sites for employers seeking to increase _____ in the workplace.

c) In the 24 hours following the Super Bowl, _____ job searches occurred on **Monster.com**.

d) Many recruitment sites use _____ to filter through received resumes.

e) Employers should try to post to sites that are most likely to be visited by _____ candidates.

ANSWERS TO SELF-REVIEW EXERCISES

20.1   a) True. b) True. c) False. The large number of applicants reduces the amount of time a recruiter can spend interviewing and making decisions. Despite screening processes, many highly qualified applicants can be overlooked. d) False. The number of individuals researching employment positions through other means, such as referrals, newspapers and temporary agencies, far outweighs the number of Internet job seekers. e) False. Six percent of America's workforce is categorized as independent consultants.

20.2   a) 40,000. b) diversity. c) 5 million. d) resume-filtering software. e) eligible.

EXERCISES

20.3   State whether each of the following is true or false; if false, explain why.

a) RFP is the acronym for request for proposal.

b) The Internet has also provided employers with a cost-effective means of testing their prospective employees in such categories as decision making, problem solving and personality.

c) Online job recruiting can completely replace other means of hiring employees.

d) Posting a job online is less expensive than placing ads in more traditional media.

e) Confidentiality is disadvantage of online career services.

20.4   Fill in the blanks in each of the following statements.

    a) Finding a job online can greatly _____ the amount of time spent applying for a position.

    b) _____ is an example of a Web site in which contractors can bid on projects.

    c) When designing a job posting, defining what makes your position unique and including information such as _____ and _____ might convince a qualified candidate to further investigate the position.

    d) The Internet hosts _____ for employers seeking to increase diversity in the workplace.

    e) The Internet has also provided employers with a cost-effective means of testing their prospective employees in such categories as _____, _____ and _____.

20.1   Define the following

    a) corporate culture

    b) pay per hire

    c) requests for proposals (RFPs)

    d) resume filtering software

20.1   (*Class discussion*). In this chapter, we discuss the short-comings and the advantages of recruiting on the Internet. Using the text, additional reading material and personal accounts answer the following questions. Be prepared to discuss your answers.

    a) Do you think finding a job is easier on the Web? Why or why not?

    b) What disadvantages can you identify?

    c) What are some of the advantages?

    d) What online recruiting services do you think will be most successful? Why?

20.1   Many of the career services Web sites we have discussed in this chapter offer resume-building capabilities. Begin building your resume, choosing an objective that is of interest to you. Think of your primary concerns. Are you searching for a paid internship or a volunteer opportunity? Do you have a specific location in mind? Do you have an opportunity for future employment? Are stock options important to you? Find several entry-level jobs that meet your requirements. Write a short summary of your results. Include any obstacles and opportunities.

20.2   In this chapter, we have discussed online contracting opportunities. Visit FreeAgent (`www.freeagent.com`) and create your own e.portfolio, or visit eLance (`www.elance.com`) and search the requests for proposals for contracting opportunities that interest you.

20.3   In this chapter, we have discussed many career services Web sites. Choose three sites. Explore the opportunities and resources offered by the site. Visit any demonstrations, conduct a job search, build your resume and calculate your salary or relocation expenses. Answer the following questions.

    a) Which site provides the best service? Why?

    b) What did you like? Dislike?

    c) Write a brief summary of your findings, including descriptions of any features that you would add.

WORKS CITED

The notation <`www.domain-name.com`> indicates that the citation is for information found at the Web site.

1.   J. Gaskin, "Web Job Sites Face Tough Job," *Inter@ctive Week* 14 August 2000: 50.

2.   J. Gaskin, 50.

3.   <`www.vault.com`>.

4.   M. Berger, "Jobs Supermarket," *Upside* November 2000: 224.

5. M. Berger, 224.

6. Cisco Advertisement, *The Wall Street Journal* 19 October 2000: B13.

7. <**www.webhire.com**>.

8. M. Feffer, "Posting Jobs on the Internet," <**www.webhire.com/hr/spotlight.asp**> 18 August 2000.

9. J. Gaskin, "Web Job Sites Face Tough Job," *Inter@ctive Week* 14 August 2000: 51.

10. C. Wilde, "Recruiters Discover Diverse Value in Web Sites," *Information Week* 7 February 2000: 144.

11. <**www.recruitsoft.com**>.

12. <**www.peoplescape.com**>.

13. <**www.jobsonline.com**>.

14. <**www.driveway.com**>.

15. <**www.cruelworld.com**>.

16. A. K. Smith, "Charting Your Own Course," *U.S News and World Report* 6 November 2000: 58.

17. D. Lewis, "Hired! By the Highest Bidder," *The Boston Globe* 9 July 2000: G1.

18. <**www.experience.com**>.

19. M. French, "Experience, Inc., e-recruiting for jobs for college students," *Mass High Tech* 7 February - 13 February 2000: 29.

Part 7

Appendices

Outline

Appendix A Microsoft® Internet Explorer 5.5

Appendix B Building an e-Business: Internet and Web Programming

Appendix C Introduction to HyperText Markup Language 4 (HTML 4)

Appendix D Intermediate HTML 4

Appendix E Introduction to HTML, ASP, XML and JavaScript Syntax

Appendix F The Client Tier: The User Interface

Appendix G The Middle Tier: Business Processes

Appendix H The Bottom Tier: The Database

Appendix I Accessibility Programming

Appendix J Installing a Web Server

Appendix K Setting Up a Microsoft ODBC Data Source

Microsoft® Internet Explorer 5.5

Objectives

- To become familiar with the Microsoft Internet Explorer 5.5 (IE5.5) Web browser's capabilities.
- To be able to use IE5.5 to search the "world of information" available on the World Wide Web.
- To be able to use Microsoft Outlook Express to send and receive e-mail.
- To be able to use Microsoft NetMeeting to have online conferences with friends and colleagues.
- To feel comfortable using the Internet as an information tool.

Give us the tools, and we will finish the job.
Sir Winston Spencer Churchill

We must learn to explore all the options and possibilities that confront us in a complex and rapidly changing world.
James William Fulbright

Outline

A.1   Introduction to the Internet Explorer 5.5 Web Browser
    A.1.1   Connecting to the Internet
    A.1.2   Features of Internet Explorer 5.5
    A.1.3   File Transfer Protocol (FTP)
    A.1.4   Outlook Express and Electronic Mail
    A.1.5   Outlook Express and Newsgroups
    A.1.6   NetMeeting and MSN Messenger Service
    A.1.7   Controlling the Details

Summary • Terminology • Self-Review Exercises • Answers to Self-Review Exercises • Exercises

A.1 Introduction to the Internet Explorer 5.5 Web Browser

Prior to the explosion of interest in the Internet and the World Wide Web, if you heard the term *browser,* you probably would have thought about a person browsing for a book at a bookstore. Today, "browser" has a whole new meaning. Now a browser is an important piece of software that enables you to look around the Internet ("surf" the Web). You have a world of information, services and products to browse. The two most popular browsers are *Microsoft's Internet Explorer* and *Netscape's Communicator*—we will study Internet Explorer in depth.

The Internet is also a wonderful medium for exchanging information. Using tools that are part of Internet Explorer 5.5, we discuss how to use the Web. These tools include the Internet browser, e-mail, newsgroups, chat and much more.

A.1.1 Connecting to the Internet

To connect to the Internet, you need a computer, a modem or network card, Internet software and knowledge of how to install and run programs.

The first step to getting on the Internet, which we cannot cover here (because the method differs widely, depending on your situation), is registering with an *Internet Service Provider* (ISP). As described earlier in the chapter, an ISP connects your computer to the Internet through a modem or a network connection. If you are living on a college campus, you may have a free network connection available; contact your college computer support staff for more information on getting a network hookup. If you do not have a network connection available, then you will have to connect through a commercial ISP, such as America Online, CompuServe and many others.

Once you have signed up for your account (with your ISP), you should start the **Internet Connection Wizard** (ICW). This program should be located in the **Start** menu under **Programs-Accessories-Communications**. The screen that appears upon starting this program should look like Fig. A.1.

Simply follow the instructions in the **Internet Connection Wizard** to make the appropriate settings for the Internet connection with your computer. The settings will help the connection run more smoothly and will also help you reconnect to the Internet if you are ever disconnected accidentally.

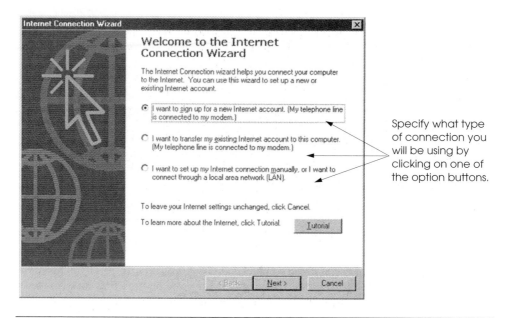

Specify what type of connection you will be using by clicking on one of the option buttons.

Fig. A.1   Using the **Internet Connection Wizard** to get on the Internet.

If you are interested in learning more about the Internet and its features, click on the button labeled **Tutorial**, located in the first ICW screen. Once your connection has been set up, you are ready to communicate over the Internet.

A.1.2 Features of Internet Explorer 5.5

The browser is a program that showcases certain files on the Internet in an accessible, visually pleasing way. Figure A.2 shows the main browser window in Microsoft's Internet Explorer 5.5 (IE5.5).

A *URL* (*Uniform Resource Locator*, or *Universal Resource Locator; both terms are* both commonly used) is displayed in the **Address** bar, toward the top of the browser window. The URL describes the location of the file your browser is displaying or loading. If you are viewing a page on the Web, then the URL will usually begin with *http://*. The acronym **http** stands for *HyperText Transfer Protocol*. This is the format of most URLs you will be viewing. We discuss additional types of URLs later in this chapter.

To go to a new URL, click anywhere inside the address bar. Once the text of the current URL is highlighted, type in the URL for the site you would like to visit (this overwrites the highlighted URL), and press the **Enter** key.

A *hyperlink* is a visual element on a Web page that, when clicked, loads a specified URL into the browser window. By clicking on this hyperlink (also known as an *anchor*), you will make your browser automatically load the new URL. Your mouse's icon appears as a pointer (or arrow) by default. When it is passed over a hyperlink, it is transformed into a hand with the index finger pointing upward (to indicate that this is indeed a link). Originally used as a publishing tool for scientific texts, hyperlinking has been crucial to making the Internet a more interesting and dynamic environment for sharing information.

Address Bar   Toolbar items   E-mail link   Scroll bar

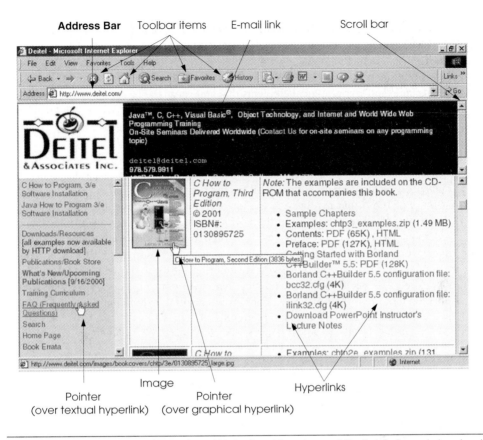

Pointer   Image   Pointer   Hyperlinks
(over textual hyperlink)   (over graphical hyperlink)

Fig. A.2   Deitel & Associates, Inc., Web site. (Courtesy of Deitel & Associates, Inc.)

IE5.5 has built-in controls that record the URLs your browser has loaded. This record is called your *history* and is stored in chronological order by date. We discuss several ways to access this history. The simplest method is to use the **Forward** and **Back** buttons, located at the top of your browser window (Fig. A.2). If you click on **Back**, then your browser will reload the last page you viewed in the browser. The **Forward** button loads the next page in your history (you can use the **Forward** button only after you have gone backward in your history). On pages that are frequently updated, you may want to on click the **Refresh** button from time to time. This will cause your browser to reload an up-to-the-minute version of the current URL.

You can skip forward or backward several entries in your history at a time by clicking on the small arrow pointing down, located directly to the right of both the **Back** and **Forward** buttons. This will display a list of the last/next five sites in your history. You can go directly to one of these sites by highlighting and clicking its entry in the list.

As mentioned earlier, hyperlinks are used to direct your browser toward a specified URL. The URL could be another Web page, or it could lead to an e-mail address or a file. If the hyperlink is targeted to an e-mail address, clicking it will not load a new Web page. Instead, it will load your default e-mail program and open a message addressed to the specified recipient's e-mail address. We will discuss e-mail in greater detail later in this chapter.

If a URL is targeted towards a file that the browser is incapable of displaying, then you will be given the option to *download* the file. When you download a file, you are making a copy of it on your computer. Examples of downloadable files are programs, documents and sound files.

The browser interface also enables you to download all of the elements of a Web page, including its code and any graphical elements that appear on the page. You save images on the page by right clicking, choosing **Save Picture As...** from the options box that pops up, and then specifying a location on your hard drive to save the image (Fig. A.3). You can have the browser save the image as your background wallpaper by clicking on the **Set as Wallpaper** option located in the right-click menu (*wallpaper* is the background for your main operating system screen). To save the code of the page, click **Save As...** in the **File** menu and specify a location on your system for the file.

A feature of IE5.5 that is related to the history function is the address-bar *AutoComplete*. AutoComplete remembers all of the URLs you have visited for a set time span (30 days by default). When you start typing a URL stored in the history, a scrollable drop-down menu like the one in Fig. A.4 appears beneath the address bar, listing all URLs in the history that are potential matches for the URL you are entering. To go to one of these URLs, highlight the desired address in the AutoComplete bar (with your mouse or arrow keys), and either click on it or press the Enter key. Your browser will then load the file at the selected URL as if you had clicked a hyperlink targeting that URL.

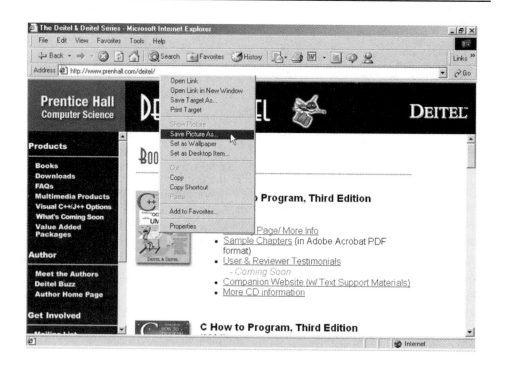

Fig. A.3   Capturing a picture from a Web site. (Courtesy of Pearson Education.)

Partial address   AutoComplete address options

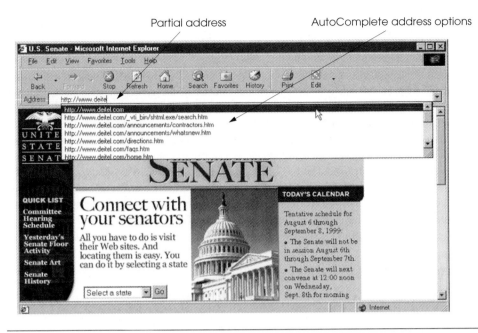

Fig. A.4   AutoComplete address-bar options.

There is also an extension of the AutoComplete feature for use with *forms* (i.e., areas on Web sites where you can enter information). While browsing the Web, you will often encounter forms for entering and dispatching information. Examples of forms you might use are a username and password form to enter a site, or an address and credit-card form for buying a book online. AutoComplete gives you the option (which you can decline, if you like) of having it remember some of your common entries to forms. It will then provide an AutoComplete drop-down menu when you go to an area in a form where these commonly typed terms might be placed, thus saving you time. For security reasons, AutoComplete does not remember passwords.

The interactive history bar (Fig. A.5) can be activated by clicking the button marked **History** in the row of buttons at the top of your browser window. The interactive history bar will show you your history over the past 30 days (or whatever length of time you specify). It has heading levels ordered chronologically by week, by day, alphabetically by site directory name and by individual URL. You can choose directories and URLs to visit with your mouse. This tool is useful for returning to a recently visited site for which you have forgotten the URL.

A.1.3 File Transfer Protocol (FTP)

Earlier in this chapter, we touched upon downloading—the process of copying a file from the Internet to your hard drive. You will normally be downloading programs, or compressed versions of programs (i.e., programs that have been reformatted to take up less space), to install on your computer. Downloading is typically initiated on a Web page by clicking a hyperlink targeted at a file on a Web site or *FTP* site. FTP stands for *File Transfer Protocol*, an old, but still popular, method for transporting information over the Internet.

An FTP site URL begins with **ftp://**, rather than **http://**, which is used with Web page addresses.

FTP sites are typically accessed via hyperlinks. You can also access FTP sites through the IE5.5 Web browser interface (see Fig. A.6).

When you point your browser to the URL of an FTP site, you see the contents of the specified site directory. Two types of objects appear in the directory: files available for download and other directories to open. You can download a file by right clicking on its icon, choosing the option **Save target as...** and specifying the location to which you would like to download the file. To enter another directory, double click on its folder icon.

When you log on to an FTP site, IE5.5 automatically sends your e-mail address and your name (which is set by default to **anonymous**) to the site. This occurs on FTP sites with *public access*. Many FTP sites on the Internet have *restricted access*; only people with authorized usernames and passwords are allowed to access such sites. If you try to enter a restricted-access FTP site, a dialog box like the one in Fig. A.6 appears, prompting you to enter your user information.

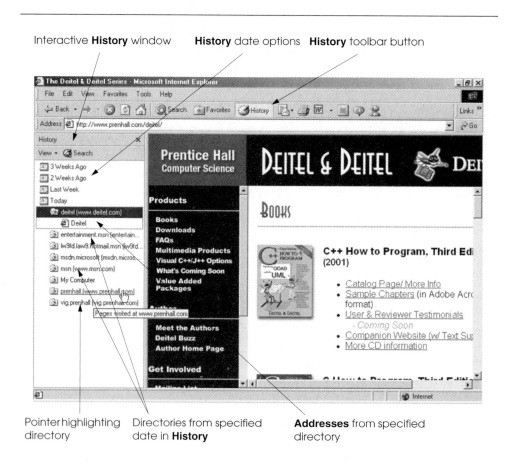

Interactive **History** window   **History** date options   **History** toolbar button

Pointer highlighting directory   Directories from specified date in **History**   **Addresses** from specified directory

Fig. A.5   **History** options. (Courtesy of Pearson Education.)

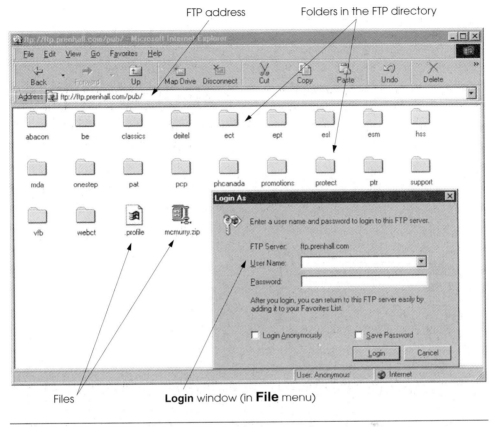

Fig. A.6   Using IE5.5 to access FTP sites.

Sending a file to another location on the Internet is called *uploading* and can be done through the FTP protocol. To place a page on a Web site, you will usually have to upload it to a specific restricted-access FTP server (this is dependent on your ISP). The process involves uploading the file to a directory on the FTP site that is accessible through the Web.

A.1.4 Outlook Express and Electronic Mail

Electronic mail (*e-mail* for short) is a method of sending formatted messages and files over the Internet to other people. Depending on Internet traffic, an e-mail message can go anywhere in the world in as little as a few seconds. E-mail is one of the most heavily used Internet services. Your Internet Service Provider will give you an e-mail address in the form *username@domainname* (e.g., `deitel@deitel.com`). To learn more about domain names, see Chapter 3, Building and e-Business.

Popular e-mail programs such as Microsoft Outlook, Netscape Messenger and Eudora are available on the Internet for free download or for sale. Microsoft *Outlook Express* installs with IE5.5 (included on the CD). The opening screen of Outlook Express is shown in Fig. A.7. The figure also shows the **Internet Accounts** dialog box, for adding e-mail and news accounts to Outlook Express.

Tools menu   Account setup   Outlook welcome screen

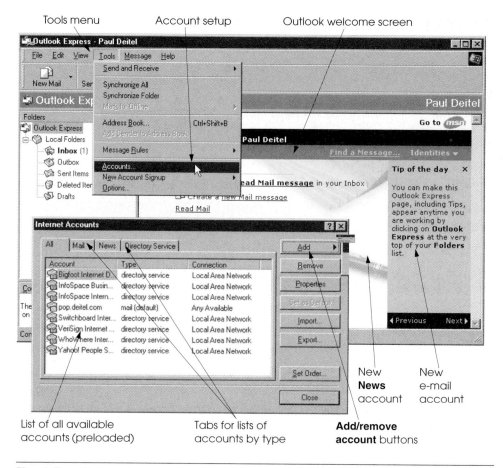

List of all available   Tabs for lists of   Add/remove
accounts (preloaded)   accounts by type   account buttons

Fig. A.7   Outlook Express opening screen and the **Internet Accounts** dialog box.

When you start Outlook Express for the first time, you will have to enter information about your connection to the Internet and about your e-mail account. You will provide this information in the dialog box that appears the first time the program is run. You will be asked for the names of your incoming and outgoing *e-mail servers*. These are addresses of servers located at your ISP that administer your incoming and outgoing e-mail. You should obtain the server addresses from your network administrator.

You can manage more than one e-mail account with Outlook Express. To add new accounts, click on the **Accounts** option in the **Tools** menu; this will bring up a dialog box listing all of your accounts (there are a number of built-in accounts, as you will see). To add a new account, click the **Add** button in the upper right corner of the dialog box, and select either a **Mail** or a **News** account. Figure A.8 shows the account sign-up dialog box at various points in the sign-up process. We will discuss **News** accounts later in the chapter, but the sign-up process for new accounts is nearly the same.

Outlook Express provides a straightforward interface for managing your accounts and messages. When you receive messages, you can save them on your hard drive for later access. Outlook Express also allows you to create folders for saving messages.

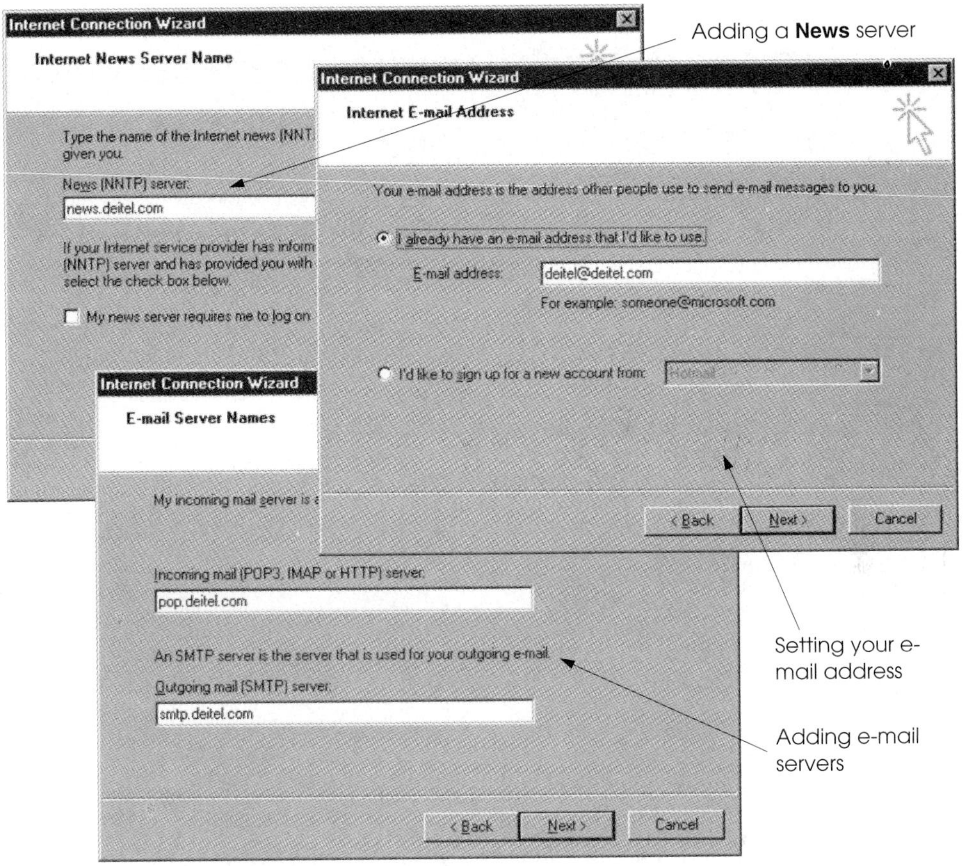

Internet Connection Wizard

Internet News Server Name

Type the name of the Internet news (NNT given you.

News (NNTP) server:

|news.deitel.com|

If your Internet service provider has inform (NNTP) server and has provided you with select the check box below.

☐ My news server requires me to log on

Adding a **News** server

Internet Connection Wizard

Internet E-mail Address

Your e-mail address is the address other people use to send e-mail messages to you.

⦿ I already have an e-mail address that I'd like to use.

    E-mail address: |deitel@deitel.com|

    For example: someone@microsoft.com

○ I'd like to sign up for a new account from: |Hotmail ▾|

                                        [< Back] [Next >] [Cancel]

Internet Connection Wizard

E-mail Server Names

My incoming mail server is

Incoming mail (POP3, IMAP or HTTP) server:

|pop.deitel.com|

An SMTP server is the server that is used for your outgoing e-mail.

Outgoing mail (SMTP) server:

|smtp.deitel.com|

                        [< Back] [Next >] [Cancel]

Setting your e-mail address

Adding e-mail servers

Fig. A.8   Adding e-mail and news accounts in Outlook Express.

Outlook Express automatically checks for new messages several times per hour (this frequency can be changed). When a new message arrives, it is placed in your **Inbox**. The **Inbox** layout is shown in Fig. A.9.

The layout of the **Inbox** screen is fairly simple. Across the top of the window are buttons you can use to start **New Mail** messages and to **Reply** to, **Forward**, **Print**, **Delete** and **Send/Recv** messages. The right side of the window contains a list of messages in your inbox (listed by date and time received), the message subjects and the senders. Below this is a content preview of the selected message. To view the message in its entirety, double click its entry in the **Inbox**. To do other things with the message (such as reply to its sender or print the message), highlight the message and click on the appropriate button at the top of the screen. To move the message from the **Inbox** to another folder, highlight and drag the message to the left side of the screen and drop it into the selected folder.

The left side of the screen contains your folder structure and your **Address Book**. To add a new folder, right click on **Local Folders** and select the **New Folder** option. In your address book, you can store the names and e-mail addresses of people with whom you communicate frequently.

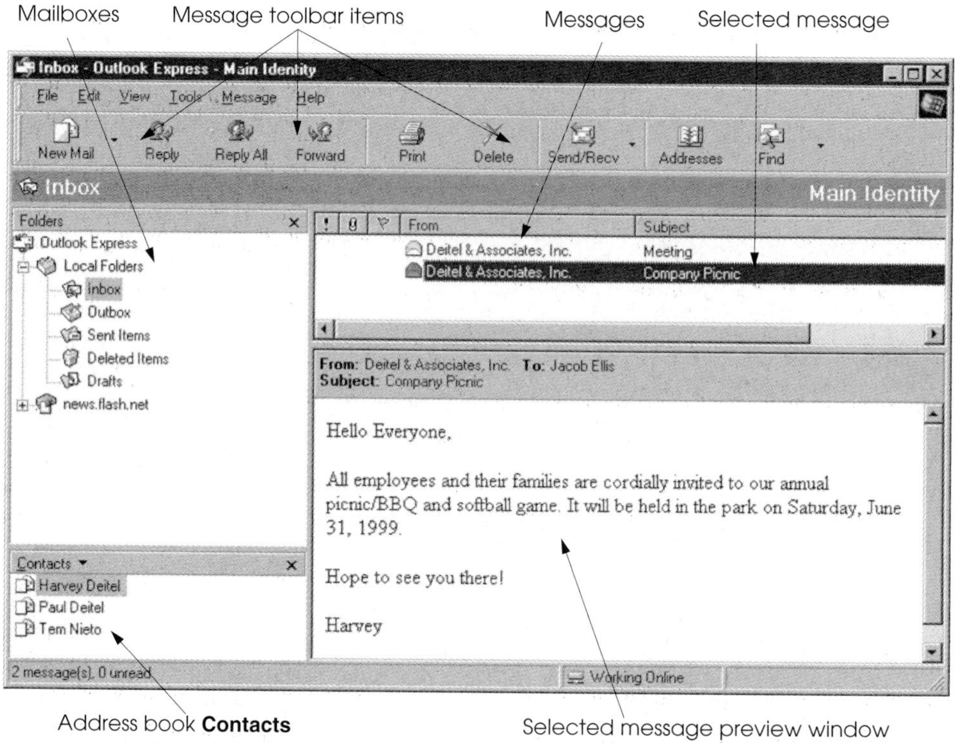

Mailboxes   Message toolbar items   Messages   Selected message

Fig. A.9   Outlook Express e-mail main screen.

To enter a new contact into the address book, click on the **Addresses** button at the top of the window, or click on the **Address Book...** entry in the **Tools** menu. The **Address Book** is shown in Fig. A.10.

All entries in the **Address Book** are listed in the main dialog box. You can send a message to anyone in your list by highlighting that person's entry, clicking on the **Action** button and then clicking on the **Send Mail** button. This sequence will open a blank message addressed to the selected recipient. To add an entry to the list, click on the **New** button and then click on the **Contact** button. This sequence will open a dialog box like the one in Fig. A.11 and will give you a place to insert information on that person. You can also enter personal information, such as addresses and phone numbers, for reference and use outside of Outlook Express.

When you initiate a new message through any source, a message box like the one in Fig. A.11 opens. There are several properties that can be associated with a message. The only mandatory property is the e-mail address of the recipient, which should be put in the form described earlier in this chapter and placed in the field labeled **To:**. To send your message to more than one recipient, you can type in multiple e-mail addresses in the **To:** field, separated by semicolons. You should always enter a subject in the **Subject** field. The **Subject** should give the recipient an idea of the message's contents before it is opened. The **Cc:** (carbon copy) field is for sending messages to people who, although the message is not addressed to them directly, may be interested in the message. If you want to change the *priority* of the message, click on the **Priority** button on the toolbar. High-priority messages will be flagged to get the attention of their recipients.

Finally, your message gets entered in the main window of the message box. You can format the text (e.g., by changing the font size, colors, styling) with the buttons above the message area. After you have entered your message, click on the **Send** button, and your message will be on its way to the designated recipient(s).

A.1.5 Outlook Express and Newsgroups

Newsgroups allow people to post messages to a shared online viewing area. Other people can then view these messages, reply to them and post new messages. Imagine newsgroups as a way of sending e-mail not to anyone in particular, but to a place where people interested in the e-mail's subject can read it. Tens of thousands of newsgroups are available, on virtually any topic, and new groups are created daily.

Outlook Express has a built-in capability to view newsgroups. An Outlook Express newsgroup screen is shown in Fig. A.12.

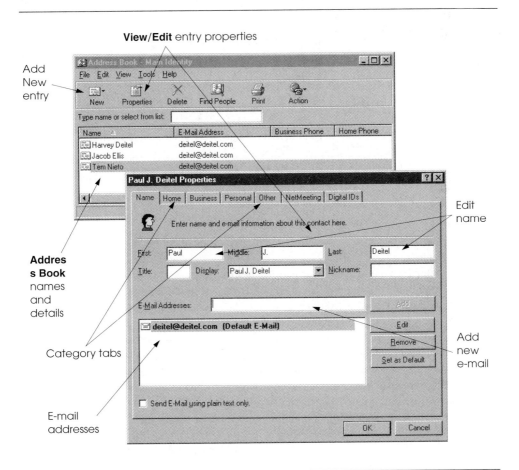

Fig. A.10   Adding and modifying names in your **Address Book**.

Send message   Tools menu

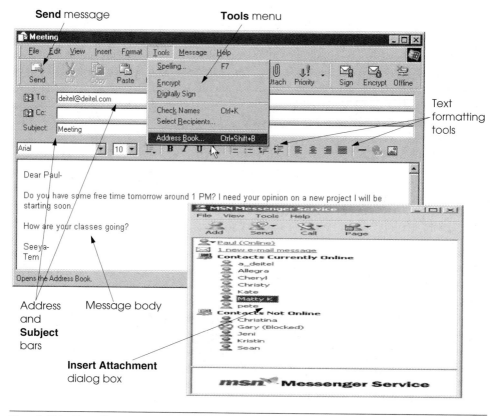

Text formatting tools

Address and **Subject** bars

Message body

Insert Attachment dialog box

Fig. A.11   E-mail message in **Outlook Express**.

To be able to view newsgroups, you must first register your server settings with Outlook Express. Use the same process illustrated in A.7, but select **News...** instead of **Mail...** on the popup menu.

After entering your server information, you can access newsgroups by clicking the **Newsgroups** button on the toolbar or by clicking on the **Read News** hyperlink in the main Outlook screen. This action brings you to the main newsgroups screen, which ordinarily lists the groups to which you have subscribed. A subscribed newsgroup is comparable to a favorite site in IE5.5. The program will remember its location and give you easy access to its contents at the click of a button.

To search through and subscribe to newsgroups, click on the **Newsgroups** button at the top of the main screen. Outlook Express will then download a list of all the available newsgroups (this search can take several minutes, as there are often tens of thousands of newsgroups available on a server). Use the search bar to search the list by typing in keywords pertaining to your interests. When you find a group you like, double click on its entry, and you will be "subscribed" to it. All of the groups to which you have subscribed are listed underneath the mail folders on the left side of the screen and on the main newsgroups screen. To view the contents of a newsgroup, double click on its entry.

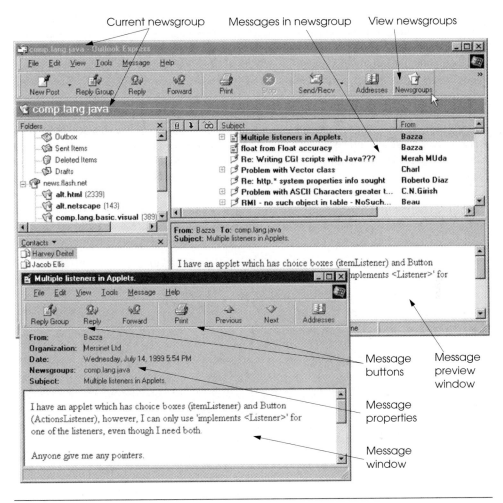

Fig. A.12 Using **Outlook Express** to browse newsgroups.

The look and functionality of the individual newsgroup view is similar to that of the e-mail message box. You will find message lists and previews in the same places. Posting a message to the group is done in the same way as you write a new e-mail message, and likewise for replying to a message and printing and reading messages.

You can use a newsgroup to find information, to correspond with a group, to exchange news or to learn new subjects. Be cautious about entering too much personal information about yourself, however, because newsgroups are public forums.

A.1.6 NetMeeting and MSN Messenger Service

Internet Explorer 5.5 is packaged with two programs for communicating with people over the Internet via live written text and other media, including audio and video. The first of these programs is *NetMeeting*. NetMeeting is designed for business and for work-related collaborations.

You can use NetMeeting to communicate with groups of people via textual and visual aids. These include sound (you can use a microphone to speak with people) and video (you can use video cameras to transmit live video). You can also use NetMeeting to share files; there are built-in mechanisms for group editing of files and for sharing of diagrams via the *whiteboard*, a drawing application that allows you to share visual effects with other people in the meeting.

When you open NetMeeting for the first time, you are prompted to set your initial options such as your contact information, security preferences, etc. Next, a screen appears that displays a list of the people who are available to chat using NetMeeting (Fig. A.13). You can also initiate a one-on-one meeting with an individual by using the **Call** button on the toolbar at the top of the screen. You can use the **Address Book** feature in NetMeeting to save commonly used addresses.

Once you begin a meeting, buttons appear on your screen and options become available on the toolbar for using the various communications media. You should experiment with these tools to determine how to use NetMeeting to its fullest potential.

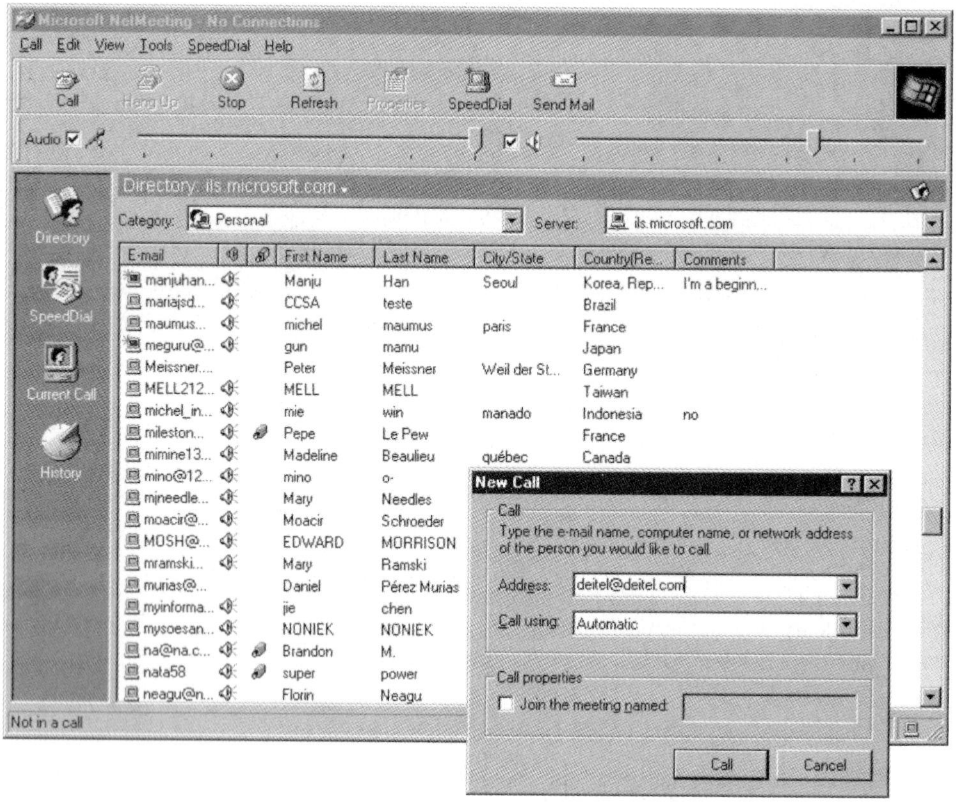

Fig. A.13 Using NetMeeting to "speak" with people on the Internet.

MSN Messenger Service is a new feature that has been included with Microsoft Internet Explorer 5.5. To begin using MSN Messenger, you must first sign up for a *passport* with Microsoft. This passport entitles you to the free messaging service and a free e-mail account. Once registered, users can link their MSN Messenger to that of friends, family and business associates also running MSN Messenger. MSN Messenger users can communicate only with other MSN Messenger users. However, users can send automated e-mail messages to invite others to download the service.

MSN Messenger offers a direct link that allows users to communicate in a text-based chat. Users can initiate text and audio chat sessions with other users through the MSN Messenger interface. The service is compatible with Microsoft NetMeeting and offers easy access to the conferencing tool. A user need only select the **Invite** option to initiate a conference using Microsoft NetMeeting.

To begin a chat session, double click on the name of a contact that is currently online (Fig. A.14). A chat box will open, allowing two-way text communication. Once a chat session has been initiated, other contacts can be added to the conversation by using the **Invite** feature. Users can transfer files over the MSN messenger, eliminating the need to send an e-mail.

A contact can be blocked if the users desires, by using the **Block** feature. After selecting this option, you will appear to be offline to the blocked user. Have fun chatting with and meeting new people, but be cautious about revealing your identity and contact information.

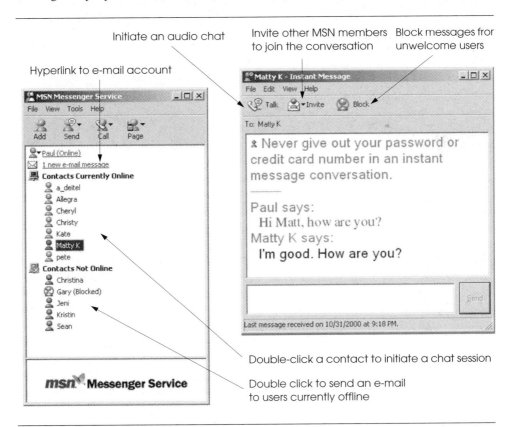

Fig. A.14 Chatting using MSN Messenger.

A.1.7 Controlling the Details

Internet Explorer 5.5 is installed with a myriad of default settings that affect the way in which sites are displayed, the security measures browsers take and the way browser outputs appear. Most of these settings are modifiable in the **Internet Options** dialog box (Fig. A.15).

Let us consider some of the more significant options that affect your browsing experience. If you have a slow connection and do not mind less colorful pages being displayed in your browser, you might want to consider toggling off the **Load Pictures** setting, located under the **Advanced** tab. Toggling off this setting stops the browser from loading images on a Web page. Images can require long load times, so this toggle can save precious minutes during every browsing session. Under the **Programs** tab, you can specify the default programs you want IE5.5 to use for such common Internet procedures as viewing newsgroups and sending e-mail. Specifying these causes the designated programs to be accessed when there is a need for their respective technologies in your browsing. For example, if you designate **Outlook Express** as your default e-mail program, then when you click on an e-mail hyperlink, **Outlook Express** will open a new e-mail message for you to compose.

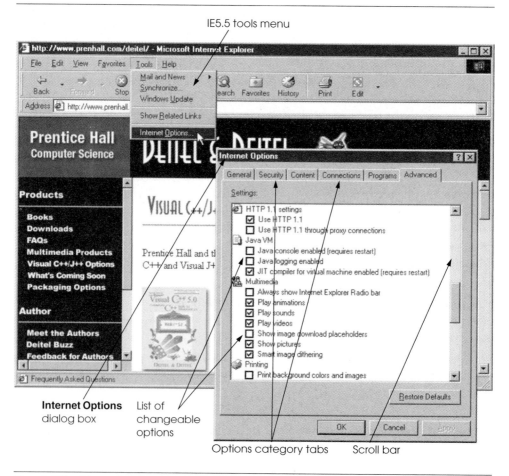

Fig. A.15 Changing your **Internet Options** in IE5.5. (Courtesy of Pearson Education.)

Under the **Security** tab, you can specify the level of caution IE5.5 should exercise when browsing sites in general, as well as for specific sites. There are four levels of security. The most lenient level will not provide you with many alerts about downloading and *cookies* (files that are placed on your computer by Web sites to retain or gather information between sessions); the most secure level will provide you with a constant flow of alerts and alarms about the security of your browsing. You should find a setting that balances your comfort level with the Internet against your tolerance for interruptions while browsing.

Finally, in the **General** options tab, you can specify a home page, which is the Web site that is loaded when the browser starts and that appears when you click on the **Home** button on top of the browser window. You can designate here the length of time for which you would like to keep a history of URLs you have visited. By clicking on the **Settings...** button, you can set the amount of disk space you would like to reserve for your Web page *cache*. The cache is an area on your hard drive that a browser designates for automatically saving Web pages and their elements for rapid, future access. When you view a page that you have visited previously, IE5.5 checks the cache to see if it already has some elements on that page saved in the cache and thereby save some download time. Having a large cache can considerably speed up Web browsing, whereas having a small cache can save disk space. However, caching can be a problem, as Internet Explorer does not always check to make sure that the cached page is the same as the latest version residing on the Web server. Clicking on the **Refresh** button on top of the browser window will remedy this problem by making Internet Explorer get the latest version of the Web page from the site. You can also remedy the problem by holding the shift key while clicking **Refresh**; this forces the browser to ignore the cache and access the server to get the most current version of the site.

Once your **Internet Options** are set, click on the **Apply** button and then click on the **OK** button. This sequence will apply your changes and will once again display the main browser window.

As useful as HTML is for transferring information, it is still a rather primitive markup language. The *Adobe Acrobat Reader* plug-in reads documents with advanced formatting. Figure A.16 shows a file displayed with the Adobe Acrobat Reader plug-in.

The Acrobat reader is a multi-platform software plug-in (i.e., it works on many operating systems) that is capable of showing documents online without changing the original format of the document. Many manuals and forms are available for download in the Acrobat format (**.pdf**, or *Portable Data Format*). When you visit a site that requires the Acrobat reader, there will normally be a link to download the plug-in.

Macromedia Shockwave is a software plug-in used to add audio, video and animation effects to a Web site. When you visit a Web site using Shockwave, you will be prompted to download the plug-in (if it is not already installed on your system) in order to view the effects. You can also download the plug-in directly at **www.shockwave.com**. To view sites enabled with Shockwave effects, visit **www.shockwave.com**.

In most cases, you are given an option or a link to download a plug-in whenever you visit a site that requires you to use the plug-in for the most effective browsing experience. Plug-ins may also be downloaded from **www.download.com** or **www.shareware.com**. These sites have large, searchable indexes and databases of almost every program available for download on the Internet.

Adobe Acrobat controls   Browser area   Document area

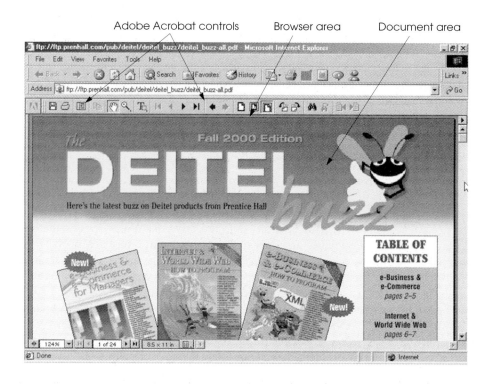

Fig. A.16 "The Deitel Buzz" newsletter, displayed with Adobe Acrobat. (Courtesy of Pearson Education.)

SUMMARY

- To connect to the Internet, you need a computer, a modem or network card, Internet software and knowledge of how to install and run programs.

- An ISP connects your computer to the Internet through a modem or a network connection.

- The browser is a program that showcases certain files on the Internet in an accessible, visually pleasing way.

- A URL (Uniform Resource Locator, or Universal Resource Locator; both terms are commonly used) describes the location of the file your browser is displaying or loading.

- A hyperlink is a visual element on a Web page that, when clicked on, loads a specified URL into the browser window.

- Internet Explorer 5.5 has built-in controls that record the URLs sites your browser has loaded. This record is called your history and is stored in chronological order by date.

- If a hyperlink is targeted to an e-mail address, clicking o it will load your default e-mail program and open a message addressed to the specified recipient e-mail address.

- When you download a file, you are making a copy of it on your computer.

- FTP stands for File Transfer Protocol, an old, but still popular, method for transporting information over the Internet. An FTP site's URL begins with `ftp://`, rather than `http://`, (which is used with Web-page addresses).

- Sending a file to another location on the Internet is called uploading and can be done through the FTP protocol.

- Electronic mail (e-mail for short) is a method of sending formatted messages and files over the Internet to other people.

- You can use a newsgroup to find information, to correspond with a group, to exchange news or to learn new subjects.

- NetMeeting is designed for business and for work-related collaborations.

- You can use NetMeeting to communicate with groups of people via textual and visual aids. You can also use NetMeeting to share files.

- The Acrobat reader is a multiplatform software plug-in (i.e., it works on many operating systems) that is capable of showing documents online without changing the original format of the document.

TERMINOLOGY

Address Book
Adobe Acrobat Reader
anchor
AutoComplete
browser
cache
cookies
download
electronic mail (e-mail)
e-mail server
File Transfer Protocol (FTP)
forms
history
hyperlink
HyperText Transfer Protocol (HTTP)
Inbox
Internet Accounts
Internet Explorer 5.5 (IE5.5)

Macromedia Shockwave
Microsoft Internet Explorer
Microsoft Outlook Express
MSN Messenger Service
NetMeeting
Netscape Communicator
newsgroup
passport
Portable Data Format (PDF)
priority
public access
restricted access
uploading
URL (Uniform Resource Locator and
    Universal Resource Locator)
wallpaper
whiteboard

SELF-REVIEW EXERCISES

A.1 Fill in the blanks in each of the following statements:
   a) The two most popular browsers are _____ and _____.
   b) A browser is used to view files on the _____.
   c) The location of a file on the Internet is called its _____.
   d) The element in a Web page that, when clicked on, causes a new Web page to load is called a _____; when your mouse passes over this element, the mouse pointer changes into a _____ in IE5.5.
   e) The record IE5.5 keeps of your Web travels is called your _____.
   f) You can save an image from a Web page by right clicking it and selecting _____.
   g) The feature of IE5.5 that provides options for completing URLs is called _____.
   h) The feature of IE5.5 that lets you save URLs of sites you visit often is called_____.

A.2 State whether each of the following is *true* or *false*. If the statement is *false*, explain why.
   a) There are about 1000 newsgroups on the Internet.
   b) You will have to download and install most plug-ins in order to use them.
   c) NetMeeting and MSN Messenger are identical programs that do the same thing, but look different.

d) FTP is a popular Internet mechanism by which files are uploaded and downloaded.

e) You can access any FTP site by logging in as **anonymous**.

ANSWERS TO SELF-REVIEW EXERCISES

A.1   a) Internet Explorer, Netscape Navigator. b) Internet and the Web c) URL. d) hyperlink, hand. e) history f) **Save Picture as...** g) AutoComplete. h) **Favorites**.

A.2   a) False. There are tens of thousands of newsgroups, and more are added every day. b) True. c) False. NetMeeting is geared more for business use, and includes many features that facilitate the sharing of information. MSN Messenger is intended for more casual "chat" use. d) True. e) False. Many FTP sites are private and do not admit the general public.

EXERCISES

A.3   Expand the following acronyms and include a description of each:
   a) HTTP
   b) FTP
   c) URL
   d) WWW

A.4   Use Internet Explorer's FTP capability to access both **ftp.cdrom.com** and **sunsite.unc.edu**. List the directory output for both sites.

A.5   Log on to a NetMeeting server and initiate a conversation with a friend.

A.6   Use Outlook Express to subscribe to the newsgroup **alt.html**.

Building an e-Business:
Internet and Web
Programming

Objectives

- To understand the concept of a multitier application model.
- To understand the top-tier and its role in a three-tier Web-based application.
- To understand the middle-tier and its role in a three-tier Web-based application.
- To understand the bottom-tier and its role in a Web-based application.
- To understand how documents used in the **Bug2Bug.com** bookstore are related to each other.

Outline

B.1   Introduction
B.2   Problem Statement
B.3   Three–Tier Architecture
       B.3.1   Top Tier: The User Interface
       B.3.2   Middle Tier: Business Processes (The Server)
       B.3.3   Bottom Tier: Database
B.4   Introduction to the `Bug2Bug.com` Bookstore

B.1 Introduction

In the following case study, we present an e-commerce Web site that employs the shopping-cart model introduced in Chapter 2. This optional case study carefully introduces the reader to Web programming using nine appendices. Two of these appendices are located at the Deitel & Associates, Inc. Web site (**www.deitel.com**) and are provided for those readers who wish to run the case study. This case study is loaded with leading-edge technologies that are used to build real-world systems. After completing this case study, the reader will have a solid understanding of many of today's hottest technologies and their role in e-business.

In this case study, we walk through the concepts surrounding a shopping-cart model and the tasks involved in the construction of this technology. After presenting an overview in this appendix, we introduce HTML (HyperText Markup Language) in the next two appendices, which is used to build the majority of the Web pages in our case study. Once we have introduced some of the introductory programming concepts, we use a live-code™ approach to show how the shopping cart is constructed in Appendices F through H.

B.2 Problem Statement

A fictitious e-business named **Bug2Bug.com** sells books online. They have a small inventory of books—*Visual Basic 6 How to Program*, *C++ How to Program: Third Edition* and *Java How to Program: Third Edition.*

Each of these books are stored in a database. **Bug2Bug.com** publishes the contents of its database (i.e., book descriptions) on the Web. Visitors to the Web site can purchase any one of these books. **Bug2Bug.com** uses a storefront model for their bookstore. Customers can add books to their shopping cart with the simple click of a button. In this case study, we examine **Bug2Bug.com**'s implementation of an online bookstore.

B.3 Three–Tier Architecture

Bug2Bug.com's online bookstore uses a *multitier application model*. A multitier application—sometimes called an *n-tier application*—is divided into several modular parts, called *tiers*, each of which may be located either on the same, or on a different, physical computer. This architecture is illustrated in Fig. B.1.

In the *top tier* or *client tier*, we use HTML to define the interface through which the user interacts with the bookstore. The client is Internet Explorer 5, which renders the HTML. In the client tier, we validate client input with *client-side scripting*—programs written in *JavaScript* and embedded in the HTML documents. Appendix F discusses the client tier in detail. The *middle tier* interacts with both the *client tier* and the bottom tier. In the middle tier, **Bug2Bug.com** dynamically creates the HTML markup sent to the client using *Microsoft Active Server Pages (ASP)* on the server. Appendix G discusses the middle tier in detail. The *bottom tier,* or *database tier,* stores the bookstore's data. **Bug2Bug.com** uses ASP to interact with a Microsoft Access database. Appendix H discusses the bottom tier in detail.

B.3.1 Top Tier: The User Interface

In this case study, the client tier consists of Microsoft Internet Explorer 5 (IE5) which renders the HTML documents it receives from the middle tier. The majority of **Bug2Bug.com**'s HTML documents are generated by Active Server Pages (ASP) on the server. In addition to HTML, **Bug2Bug.com** also uses both the *Extensible Markup Language (XML)* and *Extensible Stylesheet Language (XSL)* on the client. We will say more about what these two technologies are momentarily.

In this case study, two types of HTML documents are sent to the client. The first type—called a *static HTML document*—is created using a text editor (such as Notepad) or a software program such as FrontPage 2000 and saved as a file with either the **.htm** or **.html** file extension. Static HTML pages do not change unless they are edited manually by a person or a computer program. The HTML document **welcome.html** used at the **Bug2Bug.com** Web site is an example of a static HTML page. The second type are dynamically created HTML documents. Active Server Pages, such as **books.asp**, dynamically create these HTML documents. Using ASP in this manner allows customers to see the most up-to-date information.

B.3.2 Middle Tier: Business Processes (The Server)

The middle tier of a multitier application acts as a "middleman" between the data in the bottom tier and users of the application. All user requests for data (e.g., a request to view the contents of the shopping cart) go through the middle tier, which interacts with the database. Likewise, responses to requests travel back through the middle tier before reaching the user. The middle tier implements *business logic* and *presentation logic* to control interactions between users and data.

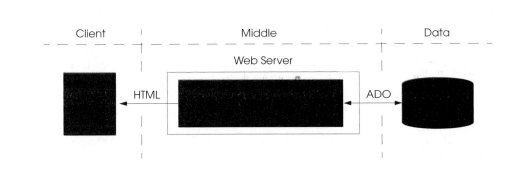

Fig. B.1   Three-tier architecture for the **Bug2Bug.com** online bookstore.

602 Building an e-Business: Internet and Web Programming

Business logic enforces *business rules*, which ensure proper manipulation of the data in the database on behalf of the user. For example, an online store may have a business rule requiring that a customer's credit card be verified with the credit card issuer before the customer's order is shipped. Business logic might implement this business rule by obtaining the credit-card number and expiration date from the user and performing the verification. If verification is successful, the business logic updates the database to reflect the customer's order. In this case study, simple business rules validate form data submitted by the user to ensure that the user inputs a last name and a proper state abbreviation.

B.3.3 Bottom Tier: Database

The bottom tier is responsible for providing data to the middle tier. **Bug2Bug.com** uses a Microsoft Access database to store information about three Deitel books available for sale. From this database, the book information is retrieved and marked up as HTML. We use Microsoft Active Server Pages and a programming technology called ActiveX Data Objects to access and retrieve book information from the database.

B.4 Introduction to the **Bug2Bug.com** Bookstore

Bug2Bug.com employs a number of technologies for its online bookstore, which we introduce in this section. We briefly summarize each of these technologies in Fig. B.2.

We now present an overview of the top tier, showing how the site is navigated by the user. **Bug2Bug.com**'s home page is **welcome.html** (Fig. B.3). This page represents the electronic front door of the store. In addition to providing access to the store, it also greets visitors. In this case study, **welcome.html** is the first document the user requests. When the user makes a request, that request is processed by the Web server (see the feature on Web Servers). This page is requested by typing the address

```
Bug2Bug.com/webpub/store/welcome.html
```

Web Servers

Web servers—such as Internet Information Services and Personal Web Server (PWS)—publish (i.e., serve) HTML documents, connect to data sources (i.e., databases) and process *Active Server Pages (ASP)*, which is a technology further discussed in Appendix G.

Web servers deliver content over the Internet using the *Hypertext Transfer Protocol (HTTP)*, which handles the specific details of sending and receiving information over the Internet. The Web server accepts HTTP requests from browsers, such as Internet Explorer, and returns the appropriate resources (i.e., documents, images, etc.). Although almost any computer may be used, Web servers tend to be machines with large amounts of memory and hard disk space. A machine is "turned into" a Web server by installing specialized software such as Microsoft Personal Web Server. [*Note*: readers installing and executing the case study will learn more about Personal Web Server.]

Technology	Description
Client Side	
HTML	Hypertext Markup Language (HTML) marks up text, audio, images and video for the Web. At present, HTML is the most popular technology for marking up Web content. HTML defines the structure and layout of a Web page.
JavaScript	JavaScript is a programming language (also called a *scripting language*) that is often used to make Web pages more interactive and dynamic. JavaScript programs are embedded in HTML documents and interpreted by the Web browser. **Bug2Bug.com** uses JavaScript to validate user input at check out.
XML	Extensible Markup Language (XML) is a markup language for describing and structuring data. XML differs from HTML in many ways, including its use. **Bug2Bug.com** uses XML to markup a list of books on back order (i.e., not available yet). We discuss XML in Appendix F.
XSL	XML documents are not intended to be rendered directly by a Web browser. Extensible Stylesheet Language (XSL) defines the rules for transforming an XML document's data into renderable data. **Bug2Bug.com** uses XSL to transform the XML document into an HTML document.
Server Side	
ASP	Active Server Pages (ASP) are server-side text files that are executed in response to a client request from a Web server. **Bug2Bug.com** uses Active Server Pages to process client requests for documents. We discuss Active Server Pages in Appendix G.
VBScript	Microsoft VBScript is a programming language used in Active Server Page documents. VBScript is the most popular language for programming Active Server Pages. **Bug2Bug.com** uses VBScript to implement its Active Server Pages.
ADO	ASP does not provide any features for accessing a database. Microsoft provides a collection of objects—called *ActiveX Data Objects (ADO)*—that ASP documents use to access databases. **Bug2Bug.com** uses ADO in its ASP pages to retrieve each book's information.
SQL	*Structured Query Language (SQL)* describes a database interaction such as querying for data or updating existing data..
Database	
Microsoft Access	Microsoft Access is a database management system that **Bug2Bug.com** uses to store book information. This database contains a single table that is populated with book information such as title, price, etc.

Fig. B.2   Technologies used by **Bug2Bug.com** and their descriptions.

into the browser's address field. [*Note:* Remember, **Bug2Bug.com** is a fictitious company we created for this case study. If you enter this URL into your browser, you will receive an error message.] This address, which is called a *Uniform Resource Locator (URL)*, specifies where this document is located. In this particular case, the document is located at **Bug2Bug.com** in the **webpub/store** directory. Clicking the **Enter** button requests the Active Server page **books.asp** (Fig. B.4).

Fig. B.3   Bug2Bug.com's home page (**Welcome.html**).

The ASP page **books.asp** (Fig. B.4) presents the user with a list of Deitel books available for purchase. The HTML rendered by Internet Explorer actually is created by **books.asp**. This works as follows:

1. The user clicks **Enter** which is programmed to request **books.asp**.

2. The Web server executes **books.asp**, which retrieves the book information from the database and fomats the data with HTML. Then, the HTML is sent to the client.

3. The client (Internet Explorer) renders the HTML.

Each book title is a hyperlink that, when clicked, requests an Active Server Page which describes the book.

When the user clicks a book title, one of three ASP pages—**book1.asp**, **book2.asp** or **book3.asp**—is requested. Each page displays a different book and its respective information, which includes the title, authors, image, price, ISBN number, description, edition and date published. Figure B.5 shows the HTML rendered when **book1.asp** is requested. The user can either click the **Add To Cart** button to add the book to their shopping cart or click the **View Cart** button to view the contents of their shopping cart.

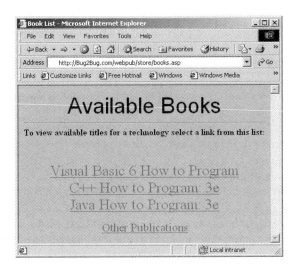

Fig. B.4   List of available books (**books.asp**).

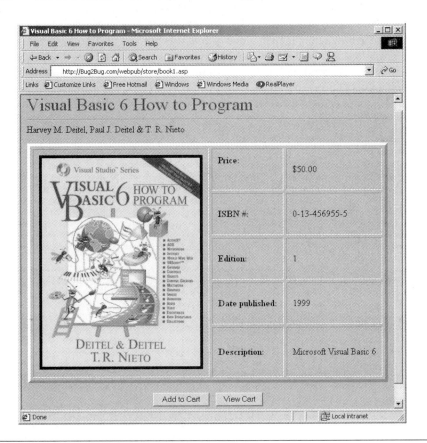

Fig. B.5   Visual Basic information page (**book1.asp**).

The shopping cart is managed by two Active Server Pages—**addToCart.asp** and **viewCart.asp**. The document **addToCart.asp** is requested when **Add to Cart** is clicked. This Active Server Page writes the book information to a text file—called a *cookie*—on the client machine. This cookie stores the items that the user adds to the shopping cart. If the cookie file already exists, it is updated. If the cookie file does not exist, it is created. This ASP does not write any HTML to the client—it simply adds a book to the cookie and redirects (i.e., changes the Web page displayed in the browser) the user to **viewCart.asp**. Clicking **View Cart** on either **book1.asp**, **book2.asp** or **book3.asp** results in **viewCart.asp** being displayed.

The document **viewCart.asp** (Fig. B.6) retrieves the cookie's contents and creates HTML to render the shopping cart. Subtotals are displayed for each book in the cart as well as a total for all books in the shopping cart. In Fig. B.6, the user has six books in their shopping cart for a total of $300. From this page, the user can either check out by clicking **Check Out** or return to the book list by clicking **Book List**. As its name implies, **Check Out** allows the user to purchase the books by requesting the **order.html** document.

Document **order.html**, shown in Fig. B.7, is a form that the user fills out to complete the order. The form prompts the user for their first name, last name, address, phone number, credit card number and credit card expiration date. Like other e-businesses, **Bug2Bug.com** is concerned about getting a customer's order correct. To ensure smooth processing of the order, **Bug2Bug.com** requires that the user provide a last name and a valid U.S. state abbreviation. HTML alone cannot validate that the user has provided all the proper information. For this reason, JavaScript code is embedded into this HTML document. Clicking the **Submit** button executes this JavaScript. If the user does not fill in the form completely and correctly, dialogs—called *alert boxes*—are displayed informing the user of the problem (Figs. B.7–B.9). If the input is valid, the form is sent as part of the request for ASP **process.asp**.

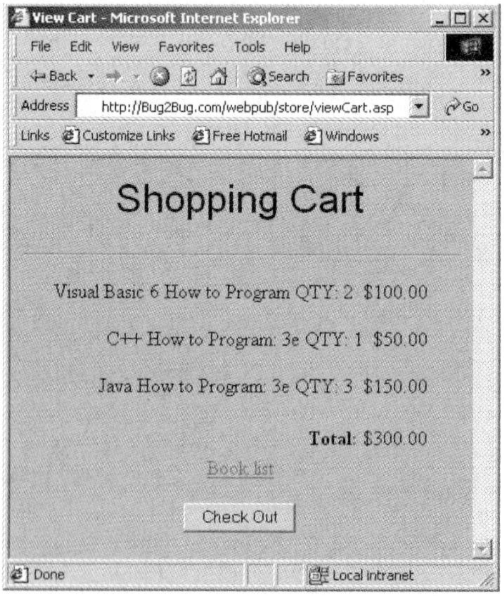

Fig. B.6   Contents of the shopping cart (**viewCart.asp**).

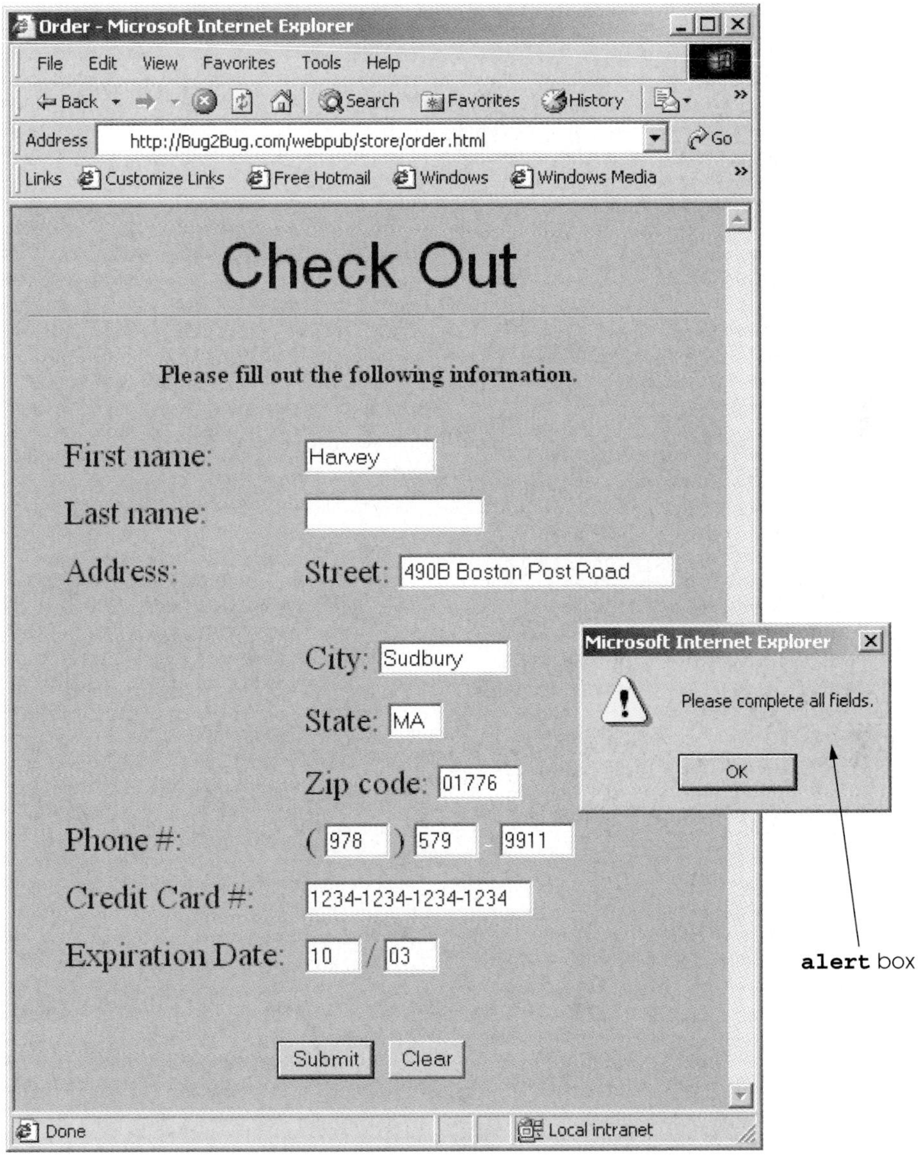

Fig. B.7   User attempting to submit order with empty field (**order.html**).

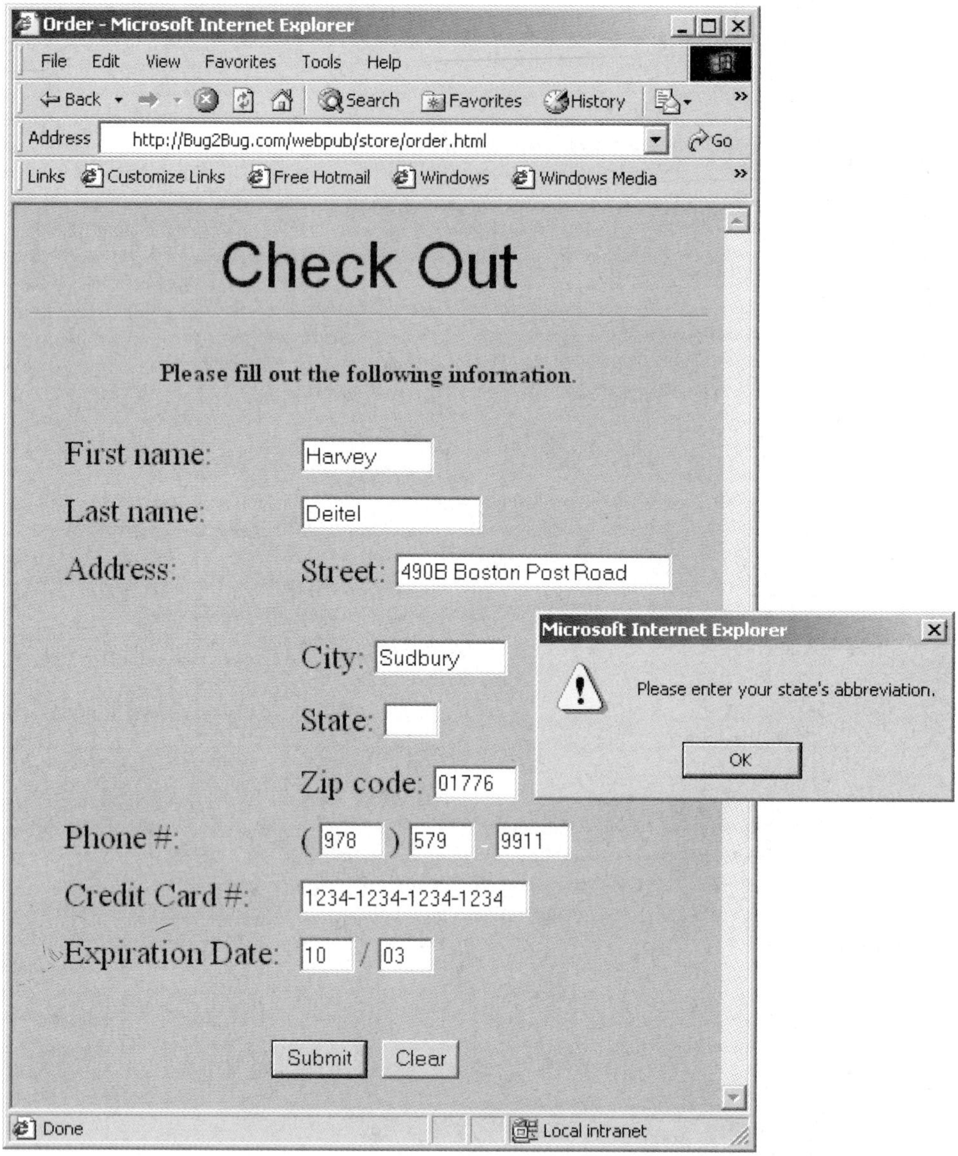

Fig. B.8   User trying to submit order with State field empty (`order.html`).

Active Server Page `process.asp` (Fig. B.10), is a simple ASP page that displays the total amount that `Bug2Bug.com` will bill to the customer's credit card, along with a short thank-you message.

Like many e-businesses, `Bug2Bug.com` is beginning a gradual transition to an XML-based Web site. Their first step in the process is to maintain their back ordered books as an XML document.

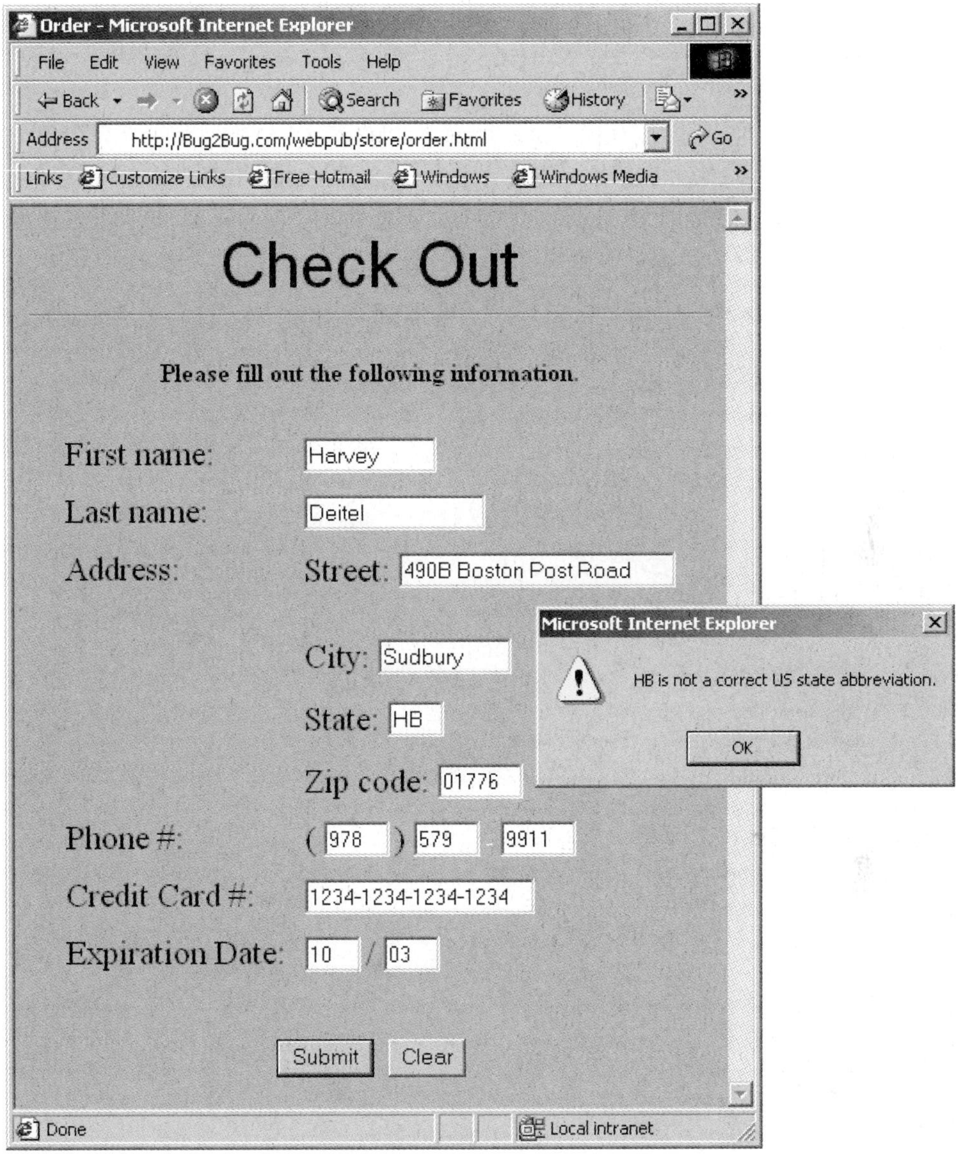

Fig. B.9   User attempting to check-out form with an invalid state abbreviation (`order.html`).

The last link of **books.asp** (Fig. B.4), labeled **Other Publications**—requests **backOrder.xml** (Fig. B.11)—an XML document that marks up a few of the publications that are currently not available.

Figure B.12 shows the key interactions between **Bug2Bug.com**'s documents. You will find this diagram useful as you study this example.

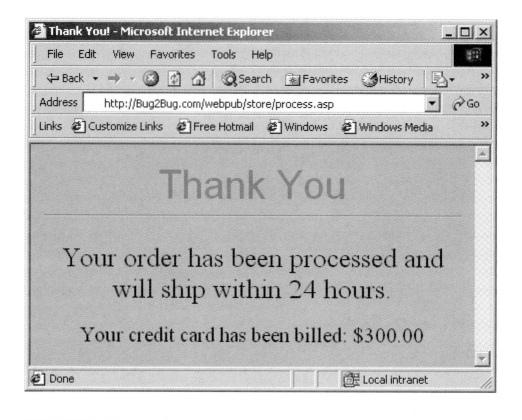

Fig. B.10   Order confirmation (`process.asp`).

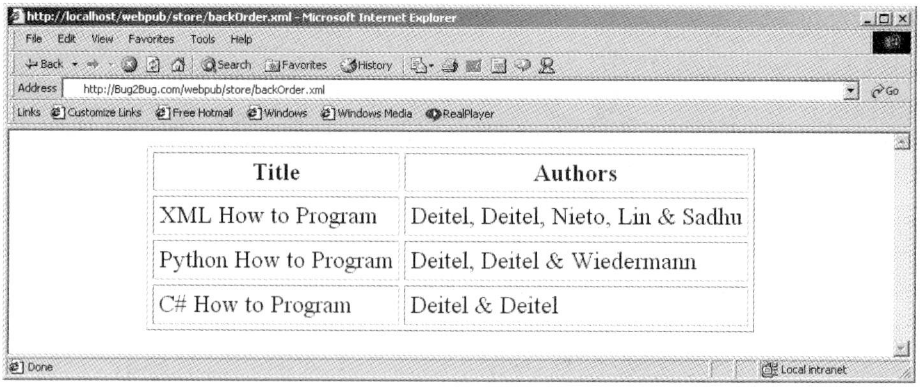

Fig. B.11   Table of books on back order (`backOrder.xml`).

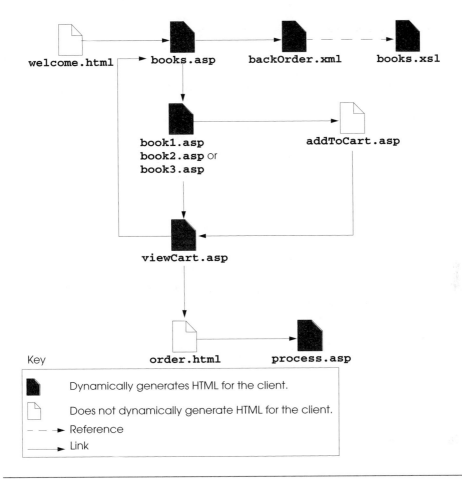

Fig. B.12   Shopping cart documents and their interactions.

The dashed line between **backOrder.xml** and **books.xsl** indicates that **back-Order.xml** references **book.xsl**. This simply means that when **backOrder.xml** is requested, **books.xsl** will automatically be requested as well. In this particular case, the browser uses **books.xsl** to transform the XML data to HTML that can be rendered by a Web browser. Figure B.13 summarizes the documents used in this case study.

File	Description
welcome.html	**Bug2Bug.com**'s home page. This is the first document requested by the user.
books.asp	ASP document that dynamically creates a hyperlinked list of book titles.

Fig. B.13   Summary of **Bug2Bug.com**'s documents.

File	Description
`backOrder.xml`	XML document containing the books on back order.
`books.xsl`	The stylesheet used to format `backOrder.xml`.
`book1.asp`, `book2.asp`, `book3.asp`	ASP documents that retrieve and format book information from the database.
`addtocart.asp`	Adds a book to the user's shopping cart by updating a cookie.
`viewcart.asp`	Displays the contents of the shopping cart, the quantities of each book, the total price of each book and the total order as HTML.
`order.html`	An HTML document consisting of an HTML form. Gets and validates the customer's information before redirecting to `process.asp`.
`process.asp`	Calculates order total and displays it along with a thank-you message.

Fig. B.13   Summary of **Bug2Bug.com**'s documents.

In the next two appendices, we take a brief diversion from **Bug2Bug.com** to study HTML. In Appendix E, we resume our study of **Bug2Bug.com**.

TERMINOLOGY

Access database
Active Server Pages (ASP)
ADO (ActiveX Data Objects)
alert box
bookstore
business logic
business rules
client computer
client side
cookie
data tier
database
database management system
e-business
e-commerce application
HTML (HyperText Markup Language)
HTTP (HyperText Transfer Protocol)
interface

Internet Explorer 5 (IE5)
JavaScript
middle tier
n-tier
presentation logic
request
response
server
server-side script
shopping cart
Structured Query Language (SQL)
three-tier architecture
Uniform Resource Locator (URL)
VBScript
Web browser
Web server
XML (Extensible Markup Language)
XSL (Extensible Stylesheet Language)

SUMMARY

• A multitier application—sometimes called an n-tier application—is divided into several modular parts, called tiers, each of which may be located either on the same, or on a different, physical computer.

• In the top tier or client tier, HTML displays the interface through which the user interacts with the bookstore.

- In the client tier, client-side scripting (e.g., JavaScript) is an effective way to validate client input.
- The middle tier interacts with both the top tier and the bottom tier.
- The bottom tier, or database tier, stores the bookstore's data.
- The main purpose of the client is to display the content, the majority of which is HTML, sent from the Active Server Pages (ASP) on the server.
- A static HTML document is created using a text editor (such as Notepad) or a program such as FrontPage 2000 and saved as a file with either the `.htm` or `.html` file extension.
- Static HTML pages do not change unless they are manually edited by a person or a computer program.
- The middle tier of a multitier application acts as a "middleman" between the data in the data tier and users of the application.
- All user requests for data (e.g., a request to view the contents of the shopping cart) go through the middle tier, which interacts with the database.
- Likewise, responses to requests for data travel back through the middle tier before reaching the user.
- The middle tier implements business logic and presentation logic to control interactions between users and data.
- Business logic enforces business rules and is used to ensure data is accurate before it is updated in the database or retrieved from the database for the user.
- Business rules dictate how data can and cannot be accessed and updated.
- The bottom tier is responsible for providing data to the middle tier.
- A Uniform Resource Locator (URL) specifies where a document is located.

Introduction to HyperText Markup Language 4 (HTML 4)

Objectives

- To understand the key components of an HTML document.
- To be able to use basic HTML tags to write World Wide Web pages.
- To be able to use HTML to format text.
- To be able to add images to your Web pages.
- To understand how to create and use hyperlinks to transit between Web pages.

To read between the lines was easier than to follow the text.
Henry James

Mere colour, unspoiled by meaning, and annulled with definite form, can speak to the soul in a thousand different ways.
Oscar Wide

High thoughts must have high language.
Aristophanes

I've gradually risen from lower-class background to lower-class foreground.
Marvin Cohen

Outline

C.1   Introduction
C.2   Markup Languages
C.3   Editing HTML
C.4   Common Tags
C.5   Headers
C.6   Text Styling
C.7   Linking
C.8   Images
C.9   Formatting Text With <FONT>
C.10   Special Characters, Horizontal Rules and More Line Breaks
C.11   Internet and WWW Resources

Summary • Terminology • Self-Review Exercises • Answers to Self-Review Exercises • Exercises

C.1 Introduction

Welcome to the wonderful world of opportunities being created by the World Wide Web. The Internet is now three decades old, but it was not until the World Wide Web became popular in the 1990s that this current explosion of opportunities began. It seems that exciting new developments occur almost daily—a pace of innovation unlike what we have seen with any other technology. In this appendix, you will begin developing your own Web pages.

We begin unlocking the power of the Web in this appendix with *HTML*—the *Hypertext Markup Language*. HTML is not a procedural programming language like C, Fortran, Cobol or Pascal. Rather it is a *markup language* for identifying the elements of a page so that a browser, such as Microsoft's Internet Explorer or Netscape's Communicator, can render that page on your computer screen.

In this appendix, we take a diversion from our study of the **Bug2Bug.com** Web site and introduce the basics of creating Web pages in HTML. We write many simple Web pages. In Appendix D, we introduce more sophisticated HTML techniques, such as *tables*, which are particularly useful for presenting and manipulating information from databases.

In this appendix we introduce basic HTML *tags* and *attributes*. A key issue when using HTML is the separation of the *presentation of a document* (i.e., how the document is rendered on the screen by a browser) from the *structure of that document*.

C.2 Markup Languages

HTML is a *markup language*. It is used to format text and information. This "marking up" of information is different from the intent of traditional programming languages, which is to perform actions in a designated order. In this appendix and Appendix D, we discuss HTML markup in detail. (Note that we are specifically not doing action-oriented programming.)

In HTML, text is marked up with *elements*, delineated by *tags* that are keywords contained in pairs of angle brackets. For example, the HTML *element* itself, which indicates that we are writing a Web page to be rendered by a browser, begins with a start tag of `<HTML>` and terminates with an end tag of `</HTML>`, as shown in Fig C.1.

Good Programming Practice C.1

HTML tags are not case sensitive. However, keeping all the letters in one case improves program readability. We choose uppercase, which we believe helps make the tags stand out from the surrounding code.

Common Programming Error C.1

Forgetting to include closing tags for elements that require them is a syntax error and can grossly affect the formatting and look of your page. However, unlike in conventional programming languages, a syntax error in HTML does not usually cause page display in browsers to fail completely.

These elements format your page in a specified way. In this appendix, as well as appendix D, we introduce many of the commonly used tags and how to use them.

C.3 Editing HTML

In this appendix we show how to write HTML in its *source-code form*. We create *HTML files*—also called *HTML documents*—using a text editor. A software package like *FrontPage Express* is used to create Web pages visually, without the need for the page developer to code with HTML directly.

A text editor called **Notepad** is built into Windows. It can be found inside the **Accessories** panel of your **Program** list, inside the **Start** menu.

You can also download a free HTML source-code editor called HTML-Kit at `www.chami.com/html-kit`. Programs like this can perform useful tasks, such as validating your code and speeding up some repetitive tasks.

All HTML files typically have either the `.htm` or the `.html` file name extension (this is dependent on the server software). When HTML was first developed, most personal computers were running the Windows 3.1/DOS operating system, which allowed only three-character file name extensions. Current versions of Windows allow more characters in the extension, so the common usage has switched to `.html`. We recommend that you name all of your HTML files with the `.html` extension.

Good Programming Practice C.2

Assign names to your files that describe their functionality. This practice can help you identify pages faster. It also helps people who want to link to your page, by giving them an easier-to-remember name for the file. For example, if you are writing an HTML document that will display your products, you might want to call it `products.html`.

Making errors while coding in conventional programming languages like C, C++ and Java often produces a fatal error, preventing the program from running. Errors in HTML code are usually not fatal. The browser will make its best effort at rendering the page, but will probably not display the page as you intended. In our *Common Programming Errors* and *Testing and Debugging Tips,* we highlight common HTML errors and how to detect and correct them.

The file name of your *home page* (the first of your HTML pages that a user sees when browsing your Web site) should be *`index.html`*, because when a browser does not request a specific file in a directory, the normal default Web server response is to return

index.html (this may be different for your server) if it exists in that directory. For example, if you direct your browser to **www.deitel.com**, the server actually sends the file **www.deitel.com/index.html** to your browser.

C.4 Common Tags

Fig. C.1 shows an HTML file that displays one line of text. Line 1

```
<HTML>
```

tells the browser that everything contained between the opening **<HTML>** tag and the closing **</HTML>** tag (line 15) is HTML. The **<HTML>** and **</HTML>** tags should always be the first and last lines of code in your HTML file, respectively.

Good Programming Practice C.3

*Always include the **<HTML>...</HTML>** tags in the beginning and end of your HTML document. Place comments throughout your code. Comments in HTML are placed inside the **<!--...-->** tags. Comments help other programmers understand the code, assist in debugging and list other useful information that you do not want the browser to render. Comments also help you understand your own code, especially if you have not looked at it for a while.*

```
1   <HTML>
2
3   <!-- Fig. C.1: main.html -->
4   <!-- Our first Web page   -->
5
6   <HEAD>
7   <TITLE>e-Business & e-Commerce for Managers - Welcome</TITLE>
8   </HEAD>
9
10  <BODY>
11
12  <P>Welcome to Our Web Site!</P>
13
14  </BODY>
15  </HTML>
```

e-Business & e-Commerce for Managers - Welcome - Microsoft Internet Explorer

File   Edit   View   Favorites   Tools   Help

Back   Forward   Stop   Refresh   Home   Search   Favorites   History   Mail   Print

Address C:\books\2000\ebecmC\ebecmC_examples\appC\01\main.html   Go

Welcome to Our Web Site!

Done   My Computer

Fig. C.1   Basic HTML file.

We see our first comments on lines 3 and 4:

```
<!-- Fig. C.1: main.html -->
<!-- Our first Web page    -->
```

Comments in HTML always begin with **<!--** and end with **-->**. The browser ignores any text and/or tags inside a comment. We place comments at the top of each HTML document file giving the figure number, the file name and a brief description of the file being coded. We also include abundant comments in the code, especially when we introduce new features.

Every HTML file is separated into a header element, which generally contains information about the document, and a body, which contains the page content. Information in the header element is not generally rendered in the display window but may be made available to the user through other means.

Lines 6 through 8

```
<HEAD>
<TITLE>Internet and WWW How to Program - Welcome</TITLE>
</HEAD>
```

show the header section of our Web page. Including a title is mandatory for every HTML document. To include a title in your Web page, enclose your chosen title between the pair of tags **<TITLE>**...**</TITLE>**, which are placed inside the header.

Good Programming Practice C.4

Use a consistent title naming convention for all pages on your site. For example, if your site is called "Al's Web Site," then the title of your links page might best be "Al's Web Site - Links," etc. This practice presents a clearer picture to those browsing your site.

The **TITLE** element names your Web page. The title usually appears on the colored bar at the top of the browser window, and will also appear as the text identifying your page if a user adds your page to his or her list of **Favorites**. The title is also used by search engines for cataloging purposes, so picking a meaningful title can help the search engines direct a more focused group of people to your site.

Line 10

```
<BODY>
```

opens the **BODY** element. The body of an HTML document is the area where you place all content you would like browsers to display. This includes text, images, links, forms, etc. We discuss many elements that can be inserted in the **BODY** element later in this appendix. These include backgrounds, link colors and font faces. For now, we will use **<BODY>**...**</BODY>** in its simplest form. Remember to include the closing **</BODY>** tag at the end of the document right before the closing **</HTML>** tag.

Various elements enable you to place text in your HTML document. We see the *paragraph element* on line 12:

```
<P>Welcome to Our Web Site!</P>
```

All text placed between the **<P>**...**</P>** tags forms one paragraph. This paragraph will be set apart from all other material on the page by a line of vertical space both before and after the paragraph. The HTML in line 12 causes the browser to render the enclosed text as shown in Fig. C.1.

Our code example ends on lines 14 and 15 with

```
</BODY>
</HTML>
```

These two tags close the body and HTML sections of the document, respectively. As discussed earlier, the last tag in any HTML document should be **</HTML>**, which tells the browser that all HTML coding is complete. The closing **</BODY>** tag is placed before the **</HTML>** tag because the body section of the document is entirely enclosed by the HTML section. Therefore, the body section must be closed before the HTML section.

C.5 Headers

Headers are a simple form of text formatting that vary text size based on the header's "level." The six header elements (**H1** through **H6**) are often used to delineate new sections and subsections of a page. Figure C.2 shows how they are used and their relative display sizes. Note that the actual size of the text of each header element is selected by the browser and can in fact vary significantly between browsers. Later in the book we discuss how you can "take control" of specifying these text sizes and other text attributes as well.

 Good Programming Practice C.5

Adding comments to the right of short HTML lines is a clean-looking way to comment code.

```
1   <HTML>
2
3   <!-- Fig. C.2: header.html -->
4   <!-- HTML headers          -->
5
6   <HEAD>
7   <TITLE>e-Business & e-Commerce for Managers - Headers</TITLE>
8   </HEAD>
9
10  <BODY>
11
12  <!-- Centers everything in the CENTER element -->
13  <CENTER>
14  <H1>Level 1 Header</H1>    <!-- Level 1 header -->
15  <H2>Level 2 header</H2>    <!-- Level 2 header -->
16  <H3>Level 3 header</H3>    <!-- Level 3 header -->
17  <H4>Level 4 header</H4>    <!-- Level 4 header -->
18  <H5>Level 5 header</H5>    <!-- Level 5 header -->
19  <H6>Level 6 header</H6>    <!-- Level 6 header -->
20  </CENTER>
21
22  </BODY>
23  </HTML>
```

Fig. C.2   Header elements **H1** through **H6** (part 1 of 2).

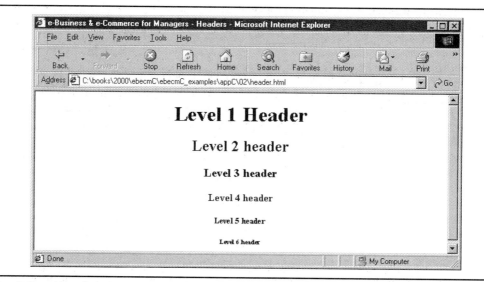

Fig. C.2   Header elements **H1** through **H6** (part 2 of 2).

Line 13

```
<CENTER>
```

introduces element ***CENTER*** which centers horizontally in the browser window all the material between its **<CENTER>** and **</CENTER>** tags. Most elements of an HTML page are left adjusted on the screen by default. Later, we discuss how to align individual elements.

Line 14

```
<H1>Level 1 Header</H1>
```

introduces the **H1** header element, with its opening tag ***<H1>*** and its closing tag ***</H1>***. Any text to be displayed is placed between the two tags. All six header elements, **H1** through **H6**, follow the same patterns but in successively smaller type font sizes.

 Look-and-Feel Observation C.1

Putting a header at the top of every Web page helps those viewing your pages understand what the purpose of each page is.

C.6 Text Styling

In HTML, text can be highlighted with bold, underlined and/or italicized styles (Fig. C.3). Our first style, the *underline*, appears on line 11

```
<H1 ALIGN = "center"><U>Welcome to Our Web Site!</U></H1>
```

Notice the statement ***ALIGN = "center"*** inside the **<H1>** tag. This is the method by which any single element of the page can be aligned. This same attribute can be used in the **<P>** tag and in other elements such as images and tables. To right-align the element, include the statement **ALIGN = "right"** inside the opening tag of the element. The HTML 4.0 convention is to enclose the **ALIGN** value (**left**, **center**, or **right**) in quotation marks. This convention applies to most attribute values.

Good Programming Practice C.6

When you have nested tags, always close them in the reverse order from that in which they were started. For example, if you have a word both italicized and underlined: <EM><U>Hello!</U></EM>, then close the U element before the EM element.

As you can see, all text enclosed in the **<U>**...**</U>** tags is displayed underlined. A second style, the *emphasis* or *italic* style, is shown on line 14

```
about the wonders of <EM>HTML</EM>. We have been using
```

and is used in the same manner as the underline tag. The last style, the *strong* or *bold* style is shown on line 15:

```
<EM>HTML</EM> ever since <U>version<STRONG> 2.0</STRONG></U>,
```

<STRONG> and **<EM>** are used instead of the tags **<B>** and **<I>** (the old standard usages for *bold* and *italic*). This is because the purpose of HTML is simply to mark up text, while the question of how it is presented is left to the browser itself. Therefore, the tags **<B>** and **<I>** are *deprecated* (i.e., their use in valid HTML is discouraged and their support in browsers will eventually disappear), because they overstep this boundary between content and presentation.

For example, people who have difficulty seeing can use special browsers that read aloud the text on the screen. These *text-based browsers* (which do not show images, colors or graphics) might read **STRONG** and **EM** with different inflections to convey the impact of the styled text to the user.

```
1    <HTML>
2
3    <!-- Fig. C.3: main.html -->
4    <!-- Stylizing your text -->
5
6    <HEAD>
7    <TITLE>e-Business & e-Commerce for Managers - Welcome</TITLE>
8    </HEAD>
9
10   <BODY>
11   <H1 ALIGN = "center"><U>Welcome to Our Web Site!</U></H1>
12
13   <P>We have designed this site to teach
14   about the wonders of <EM>HTML</EM>. We have been using
15   <EM>HTML</EM> since <U>version<STRONG> 2.0</STRONG></U>,
16   and we enjoy the features that have been added recently. It
17   seems only a short time ago that we read our first <EM>HTML</EM>
18   book. Soon you will know about many of the great new features
19   of HTML 4.0.</P>
20
21   <H2 ALIGN = "center">Have Fun With the Site!</H2>
22
23   </BODY>
24   </HTML>
```

Fig. C.3   Stylizing text on Web pages (part 1 of 2).

Fig. C.3   Stylizing text on Web pages (part 2 of 2).

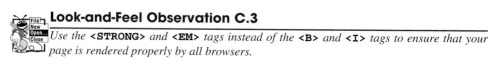

Look-and-Feel Observation C.2

Be cautious when underlining text on your site, because hyperlinks are underlined by default in most browsers. Underlining plain text can be confusing to people browsing your site.

Look-and-Feel Observation C.3

Use the `<STRONG>` and `<EM>` tags instead of the `<B>` and `<I>` tags to ensure that your page is rendered properly by all browsers.

You should also notice inside line 15

```
<U>version <STRONG>2.0</STRONG></U>
```

Here, the **U** and **STRONG** elements overlap each other. This causes the text included in both elements ("**2.0**") to have both styles applied.

You should also observe the order of the closing tags in the above example from line 15. Because the **STRONG** element started after the **U** element, the **STRONG** element's closing tag appears before that of **U**. Although the order of the closing tags does not always matter to the browser, it is good practice to close them in the reverse order from the order in which they were started.

C.7 Linking

The most important capability of HTML is its ability to create hyperlinks to documents elsewhere on the server and on different servers and thereby make possible a world-wide network of linked documents and information. In HTML, both text and images can act as *anchors* to *link* to other pages on the Web. We introduce anchors and links in Fig. C.4.

```
1    <HTML>
2
3    <!-- Fig. C.4: links.html        -->
4    <!-- Introduction to hyperlinks -->
5
6    <HEAD>
7    <TITLE>e-Business & e-Commerce for Managers - Links</TITLE>
8    </HEAD>
9
10   <BODY>
11
12   <CENTER>
13   <H2>Here are my favorite Internet Search Engines</H2>
14   <P><STRONG>Click on the Search Engine address to go to that
15   page.</STRONG></P>
16
17   <!-- Hyperlink form: <A HREF = "address"> -->
18   <P>Yahoo: <A HREF = "http://www.yahoo.com">
19   http://www.yahoo.com</A></P>
20
21   <P>AltaVista: <A HREF = "http://www.altavista.com">
22   http://www.altavista.com</A></P>
23
24   <P>Ask Jeeves: <A HREF = "http://www.askjeeves.com">
25   http://www.askjeeves.com</A></P>
26
27   <P>WebCrawler: <A HREF = "http://www.webcrawler.com">
28   http://www.webcrawler.com</A></P>
29   </CENTER>
30
31   </BODY>
32   </HTML>
```

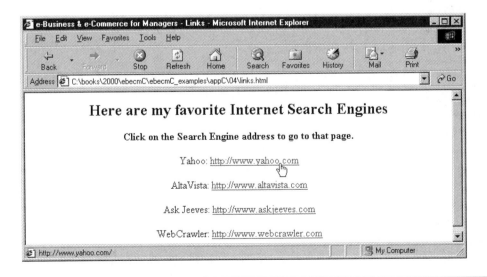

Fig. C.4   Linking to other Web pages.

The first link can be found on lines 18 and 19:

```
<P>Yahoo: <A HREF = "http://www.yahoo.com">
http://www.yahoo.com</A></P>
```

Links are inserted using the **A** *(anchor) element*. The anchor element is unlike the elements we have seen thus far in that it requires certain attributes inside its opening tag in order to activate the hyperlink. The most important attribute is the location to which you would like the anchoring object to be linked. This location can be any accessible page, file or email URL. To specify the address you would like to link to, insert the **HREF** *attribute* into the anchor tag as follows: **<A HREF = "***address***">**. In this case, the address we are linking to is **http://www.yahoo.com**. The hyperlink created on line 18 activates the text on line 19, **http://www.yahoo.com** as an anchor to link to the indicated address.

Anyone who loads your page and clicks on the hyperlinked word(s) will have their browser go to that page. Figure C.4 contains several other examples of anchor tags.

Figure C.4 also further demonstrates element **P**. Recall that the paragraph element adds vertical space around the paragraph area. On lines 18 through 28, there are four complete paragraph tags. Each one is a new paragraph and therefore has vertical space around it.

Anchors can also link to email addresses. When someone clicks on this type of anchored link, their default email program initiates an email message to the linked address. This type of anchor is demonstrated in Fig. C.5.

Email links use a syntax almost identical to that for links to other Web pages. We see an email link on lines 14 and 15:

```
<P>My email address is <A HREF = "mailto:deitel@deitel.com">
deitel@deitel.com</A>.
```

The form of an email anchor is **<A HREF = "mailto:***emailaddress***">...</A>**. It is important that this whole attribute, including the **mailto:**, be placed in quotation marks.

```
1    <HTML>
2
3    <!-- Fig. C.5: contact.html  -->
4    <!-- Adding email hyperlinks -->
5
6    <HEAD>
7    <TITLE>e-Business & e-Commerce for Managers - Contact Page</TITLE>
8    </HEAD>
9
10   <BODY>
11
12   <!-- The correct form for hyperlinking to an email address -->
13   <!-- is <A HREF = "mailto:address"></A>                     -->
14   <P>My email address is <A HREF = "mailto:deitel@deitel.com">
15   deitel@deitel.com</A>. Click on the address and your browser
16   will open an email message and address it to me.
17   </P>
18
19   </BODY>
20   </HTML>
```

Fig. C.5   Linking to an email address (part 1 of 2).

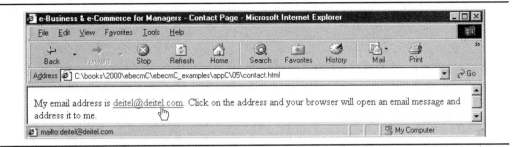

Fig. C.5   Linking to an email address (part 2 of 2).

C.8 Images

We have been dealing exclusively with text. We now show how to incorporate images into Web pages (Fig. C.6).

```
1    <HTML>
2
3    <!-- Fig. C.6: picture.html  -->
4    <!-- Adding images with HTML -->
5
6    <HEAD>
7    <TITLE>e-Business & e-Commerce for Managers - Welcome</TITLE>
8    </HEAD>
9
10   <BODY BACKGROUND = "bckgrnd.gif">
11
12   <CENTER>
13   <!-- Format for entering images: <IMG SRC = "name"> -->
14   <IMG SRC = "deitel.gif" BORDER = "1" HEIGHT = "144"
15       WIDTH = "200" ALT = "Harvey and Paul Deitel">
16   </CENTER>
17
18   </BODY>
19   </HTML>
```

Fig. C.6   Placing images in HTML files.

For this page, an image background has been inserted in line 10:

```
<BODY BACKGROUND = "bckgrnd.gif">
```

As mentioned earlier, attributes can be added to the **BODY** tag to set certain characteristics of the page, one of which is *BACKGROUND*. A background can consist of an image or a color. In this case, we are using an image. To use an image as a background, include the attribute **BACKGROUND = "***filename***"** inside the opening **<BODY>** tag. The filename of the image in this case is **bckgrnd.gif**.

An image used as a background does not need to be large In fact, large background images greatly increase the time it takes for a page to load. The image used for the background in Fig. C.6 is only 325 *pixels* wide and 85 *pixels* high—the browser *tiles* the image across and down the screen. The term pixel stands for "picture element". Each pixel represents one addressable dot of color on the screen.

Look-and-Feel Observation C.4

Using an image for your background can be visually appealing. Make sure, however, that the image does not have any sharp color changes, as they can be disorienting to the user, making the text on top hard to read. Also try to use an image that tiles, that is, blends smoothly with the surrounding repetitions of itself.

The image in this code example is inserted in lines 14 and 15:

```
<IMG SRC = "deitel.gif" BORDER = "1" HEIGHT = "144"
    WIDTH = "200" ALT = "Harvey and Paul Deitel">
```

You specify the location of the image file in the **<*IMG*>** tag. This is done by adding the **SRC = "***location***"** attribute. You can specify the *HEIGHT* and *WIDTH* of an image, measured in pixels. This image is 200 pixels wide and 144 pixels high.

Good Programming Practice C.7

*Always include the **HEIGHT** and **WIDTH** of an image in the **IMG** tag. When the browser loads the HTML file, it will know immediately how much screen space to give the image and will therefore lay out the page properly, even before it downloads the image.*

Common Programming Error C.2

Entering new dimensions for an image that change its inherent width-to-height ratio distorts the appearance of the image. For example, if your image is 200 pixels wide and 100 pixels high, you should always make sure that any new dimensions have a 2:1 width-to-height ratio.

You can add a border (black by default) to images with attribute *BORDER* = x. If x is a number larger than 0, the width of the border will be that number of pixels. The image in this example has a border of 1 pixel, as indicated by the image attribute **BORDER = 1**.

An important image attribute is *ALT*. In Fig. C.6, the value of this attribute is

```
ALT = "Harvey and Paul Deitel"
```

ALT is provided for browsers that have images turned off, or that cannot view images (i.e., text-based browsers). The value of the **ALT** attribute will appear on-screen in place of the image, giving the user an idea of what was in the image.

Good Programming Practice C.8

*Include a description of every image using the **ALT** attribute in the **IMG** tag.*

Now that we have discussed placing images on your Web page, we will show you how to transform images into anchors to link your site to other sites on the Internet (Fig. C.7).

We add a background on line 10 with

```
<BODY BGCOLOR = "#CDCDCD">
```

This is similar to the method we used in Fig. C.6. The difference is that instead of using a background image, we use a solid background color. Because of this, the attribute name is *BGCOLOR* instead of **BACKGROUND**.

```
1    <HTML>
2
3    <!-- Fig. C.7: navigationbar.html -->
4    <!-- Using images as link anchors -->
5
6    <HEAD>
7    <TITLE>e-Business & e-Commerce for Managers - Nav Bar</TITLE>
8    </HEAD>
9
10   <BODY BGCOLOR = "#CDCDCD">
11   <CENTER>
12
13   <A HREF = "main.html">
14   <IMG SRC = "buttons/about.jpg" WIDTH = "65" HEIGHT = "50"
15      BORDER = "0" ALT = "Main Page"></A><BR>
16
17   <A HREF = "links.html">
18   <IMG SRC = "buttons/links.jpg" WIDTH = "65" HEIGHT = "50"
19      BORDER = "0" ALT = "Links Page"></A><BR>
20
21   <A HREF = "list.html">
22   <IMG SRC = "buttons/list.jpg" WIDTH = "65" HEIGHT = "50"
23      BORDER = "0" ALT = "List Example Page"></A><BR>
24
25   <A HREF = "contact.html">
26   <IMG SRC = "buttons/contact.jpg" WIDTH = "65" HEIGHT = "50"
27      BORDER = "0" ALT = "Contact Page"></A><BR>
28
29   <A HREF = "header.html">
30   <IMG SRC = "buttons/header.jpg" WIDTH = "65" HEIGHT = "50"
31      BORDER = "0" ALT = "Header Page"></A><BR>
32
33   <A HREF = "table.html">
34   <IMG SRC = "buttons/table.jpg" WIDTH = "65" HEIGHT = "50"
35      BORDER = "0" ALT = "Table Page"></A><BR>
36
37   <A HREF = "form.html">
38   <IMG SRC = "buttons/form.jpg" WIDTH = "65" HEIGHT = "50"
39      BORDER = "0" ALT = "Feedback Form"></A><BR>
40   </CENTER>
41
42   </BODY>
43   </HTML>
```

Fig. C.7   Using images as link anchors (part 1 of 2).

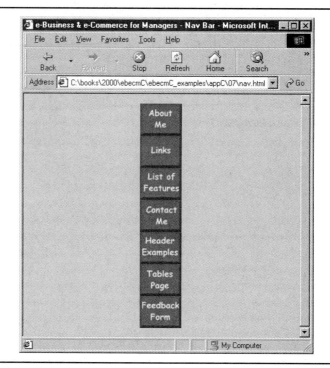

Fig. C.7   Using images as link anchors (part 2 of 2).

To indicate the color for your background, you can use either a preset color name, of which there are more than 100, or you can use a *hexadecimal* code to tell the browser what color you want to use (see the code **#CDCDCD** above). This method is also used to change your font color, as we show you in the next section. All colors are composed of varying shades of red, green and blue (so-called *RGB* colors). The first two characters in the "hex" color code represent the amount of red in the color, the second two represent the amount of green and the last two represent the blue. **00** is the weakest a color can get and **FF** is the strongest a color can get. Therefore, **"#FF0000"** is red, **"#00FF00"** is green, **"#0000FF"** is blue, **"#000000"** is black and **"#FFFFFF"** is white.

We see an image hyperlink in lines 13 through 15:

```
<A HREF = "main.html">
<IMG SRC = "buttons/about.jpg" WIDTH = "65" HEIGHT = "50"
    BORDER = "0" ALT = "Main Page"></A>
```

Here we use the **A** element and the **IMG** element. The anchor works the same way as when it surrounds text; the image becomes an active hyperlink to a location somewhere on the Internet, indicated by the **HREF** attribute inside the **<A>** tag. Remember to close the anchor element when you want the hyperlink to end.

If you direct your attention to the **SRC** attribute of the **IMG** element,

```
SRC = "buttons/about.jpg"
```

you will see that it is not in the same form as that of the image in the previous example. This is because the image we are using here, **about.jpg**, resides in a subdirectory called

buttons, which is in our main directory for the site. We have done this so that we can keep all our button graphics in the same place, making them easier to find and edit.

You can always refer to files in different directories simply by putting the directory name in the correct format in the **SRC** attribute. If, for example, there was a directory inside the **buttons** directory called **images**, and we wanted to put a graphic from that directory onto our page, we would just have to make the source attribute reflect the location of the image: **SRC = "buttons/images/filename"**.

You can even insert an image from a different Web site into your site (after obtaining permission from the site's owner, of course). Just make the **SRC** attribute reflect the location and name of the image file.

We introduce the *line break* element in line 15:

```
BORDER = "0" ALT = "Main Page"></A><BR>
```

The *BR* element causes a line break to occur. If the **BR** element is placed inside a text area, the text begins a new line at the place of the **
** tag. We are using **
** here so that we can skip to the line below the image.

C.9 Formatting Text With <FONT>

We have seen how to make pages visually richer using backgrounds and images. Figure C.8 shows how to add color and formatting to text.

We demonstrate the common methods of formatting in lines 15 through 17:

```
<P><FONT COLOR = "red" SIZE = "+1" FACE = "Arial">We have
designed this site to teach about the wonders of
<EM>HTML</EM>.</FONT>
```

Here, several attributes of the *FONT* element are demonstrated. The first attribute is *COLOR*, which indicates the color of the formatted text in the same manner in which you indicate a background color: You enter either a preset color name or a hex color code. Remember to include the quotation marks around the color name.

Note that you can set the font color for the whole document by putting a *TEXT* attribute into the **BODY** element and indicating the color in the same manner as above.

```
1    <HTML>
2
3    <!-- Fig. C.8: main.html              -->
4    <!-- Formatting text size and color -->
5
6    <HEAD>
7    <TITLE>e-Business & e-Commerce for Managers - Welcome</TITLE>
8    </HEAD>
9
10   <BODY>
11
12   <H1 ALIGN = "center"><U>Welcome to Our Web Site!</U></H1>
13
```

Fig. C.8   Using the **FONT** element to format text (part 1 of 2).

```
14    <!-- Font tags change the formatting of text they enclose -->
15    <P><FONT COLOR = "red" SIZE = "+1" FACE = "Arial">We have
16    designed this site to teach about the wonders of
17    <EM>HTML</EM>.</FONT>
18
19    <FONT COLOR = "purple" SIZE = "+2" FACE = "Verdana">We have been
20    using <EM>HTML</EM> since <U>version<STRONG> 2.0</STRONG></U>,
21    and we enjoy the features that have been added recently.</FONT>
22
23    <FONT COLOR = "blue" SIZE = "+1" FACE = "Helvetica">It
24    seems only a short time ago that we read our first <EM>HTML</EM>
25    book.</FONT>
26
27    <FONT COLOR = "green" SIZE = "+2" FACE = "Times">Soon you will
28    know about many of the great new features of HTML 4.0.</FONT></P>
29
30    <H2 ALIGN = "center">Have Fun With the Site!</H2>
31
32    </BODY>
33    </HTML>
```

Fig. C.8   Using the **FONT** element to format text (part 2 of 2).

The second attribute in the example is **SIZE**, which is used to change the size of the text being formatted. To make the text larger, set **SIZE="+x"**. To make the text smaller, set **SIZE="-x"**. In each case, *x* is the number of font point sizes by which you want to enlarge or diminish the text.

The last font attribute shown in our example is **FACE**. This attribute is used to change the font of the text you are formatting. Enter a font name in quotation marks, and the text will be changed to that font.

Common Programming Error C.3

When using the font face attribute, be careful to only use common fonts like Times, Arial, Courier and Helvetica (just to name a few). Avoid more obscure fonts, because the browser default will be displayed instead (usually Times New Roman).

C.10 Special Characters, Horizontal Rules and More Line Breaks

In HTML, the old QWERTY typewriter setup no longer suffices for all our textual needs. HTML 4.0 has a provision for inserting special characters and symbols (Fig. C.9).

There are some *special characters* inserted into the text of lines 18 and 19:

```
<P>All information on this site is <STRONG>&copy;</STRONG>
Deitel <STRONG>&amp;</STRONG> Associates, 1999.</P>
```

All special characters are inserted in their code form. The format of the code is always &*code*;. An example of this is **&**, which inserts an ampersand. Codes are often abbreviated forms of the character (like **amp** for ampersand and **copy** for copyright) and can also be in the form of *hex codes*. (For example, the hex code for an ampersand is 38, so another method of inserting an ampersand is to use **&**.).

```
1    <HTML>
2
3    <!-- Fig. C.9: contact.html        -->
4    <!-- Inserting special characters -->
5
6    <HEAD>
7    <TITLE>e-Business & e-Commerce for Managers - Contact Page</TITLE>
8    </HEAD>
9
10   <BODY>
11
12   <!-- Special characters are entered using the form &code; -->
13   <P>My email address is <A HREF = "mailto:deitel@deitel.com">
14   deitel@deitel.com</A>. Click on the address and your browser
15   will automatically open an email message and address it to my
16   address.</P>
17
18   <P>All information on this site is <STRONG>&copy;</STRONG>
19   Deitel <STRONG>&amp;</STRONG> Associates, 1999.</P>
20
21   <!-- Text can be struck out with a set of <DEL>...</DEL>   -->
22   <!-- tags, it can be set in subscript with <SUB>...</SUB>, -->
23   <!-- and it can be set into superscript with <SUP...</SUP> -->
24   <DEL><P>You may copy up to 3.14 x 10<SUP>2</SUP> characters
25   worth of information from this site.</DEL><BR> Just make sure
26   you <SUB>do not copy more information</SUB> than is allowable.
27
28   <P>No permission is needed if you only need to use <STRONG>
29   &lt; &frac14;</STRONG> of the information presented here.</P>
30
```

Fig. C.9   Inserting special characters into HTML (part 1 of 2).

```
31    </BODY>
32    </HTML>
```

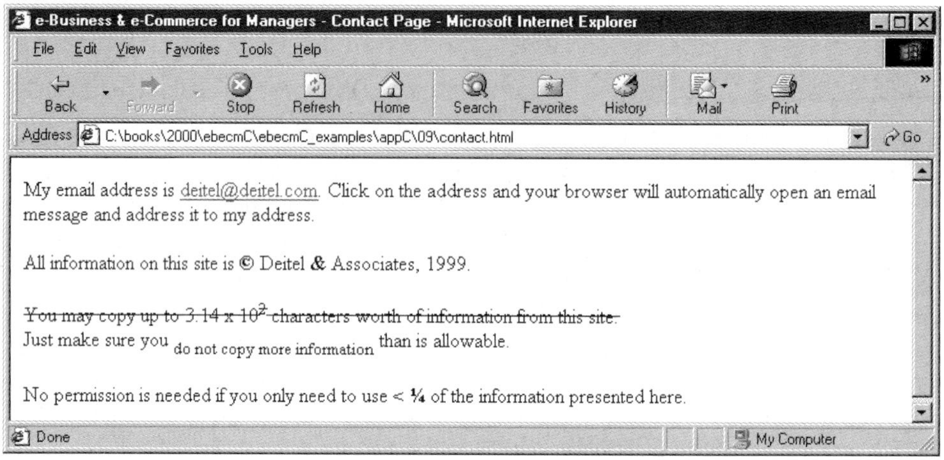

Fig. C.9   Inserting special characters into HTML (part 2 of 2).

In lines 24 through 26, we introduce three new styles.

```
<DEL><P>You may copy up to 3.14 x 10<SUP>2</SUP> characters
worth of information from this site.</DEL><BR> Just make sure
you <SUB>do not copy more information</SUB> than is allowable.
```

You can strike-through text with a horizontal line by including it in a **DEL** element. This could be used as an easy way to communicate revisions of an online document. To turn text into *superscript* (i.e., raised vertically to the top of the line and made smaller) or to turn text into *subscript* (the opposite of superscript, lowers text on a line and makes it smaller), use the **SUP** and **SUB** elements, respectively.

We touched on line breaks in Fig. C.8. We now provide an example of a textual line break with a horizontal rule (Fig. C.10).

```
1    <HTML>
2
3    <!-- Fig. C.10: header.html          -->
4    <!-- Line breaks and horizontal rules -->
5
6    <HEAD>
7    <TITLE>
8        e-Business & e-Commerce for Managers - Horizontal Rule
9    </TITLE>
10   </HEAD>
11
12   <BODY>
13   <!-- Horizontal rules as inserted using the format: -->
14   <!-- <HR WIDTH = ".." SIZE = ".." ALIGN = "..">      -->
```

Fig. C.10   Using horizontal rules (part 1 of 2).

```
15   <HR WIDTH = "25%" SIZE = 1>
16   <HR WIDTH = "25%" SIZE = 2>
17   <HR WIDTH = "25%" SIZE = 3>
18
19   <P ALIGN = "left"><STRONG>Size:</STRONG>4
20   <STRONG>Width:</STRONG>75%
21   <HR WIDTH = "75%" SIZE = "4" ALIGN = "left">
22
23   <P ALIGN = "right"><STRONG>Size:</STRONG>12
24   <STRONG>Width:</STRONG>25%
25   <HR WIDTH = "25%" SIZE = "12" ALIGN = "right">
26
27   <P ALIGN = "center"><STRONG>Size:</STRONG>8
28   <STRONG>Width:</STRONG>50%
29   <STRONG><EM>No shade...</EM></STRONG>
30   <HR NOSHADE WIDTH = "50%" SIZE = "8" ALIGN = "center">
31
32   </BODY>
33   </HTML>
```

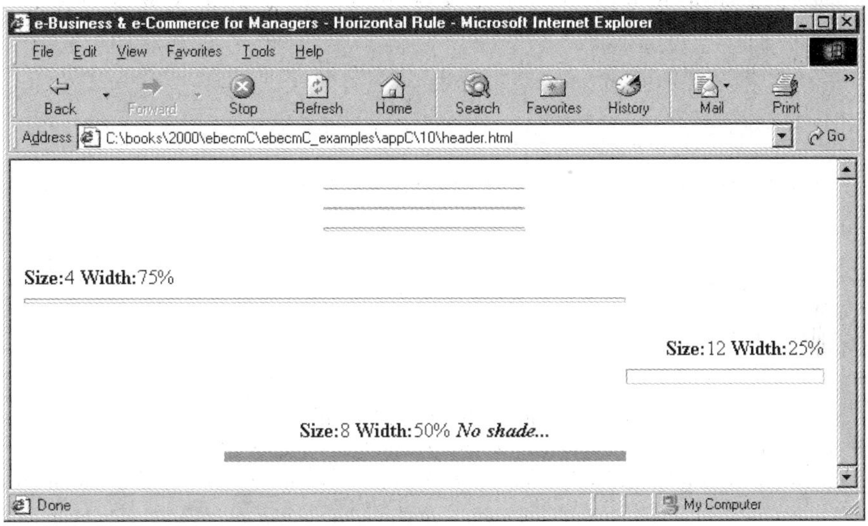

Fig. C.10   Using horizontal rules (part 2 of 2).

Line 15

```
<HR WIDTH = "25%" SIZE = 1>
```

inserts a horizontal rule, indicated by the **<HR>** tag. A horizontal rule is a straight line going across the screen horizontally. The **HR** element also inserts a line break directly below it.

You can adjust the width of the horizontal rule by including the **WIDTH** attribute in the **HR** tag. You can set the width either by entering a number, which will indicate the width in pixels, or by entering a percentage, which indicates that the horizontal rule will occupy that percent of the screen width. For example, if you enter **WIDTH = "50%"**, and your screen resolution is 640 pixels, then the **HR** will measure 320 pixels across.

Look-and-Feel Observation C.5

Inserting horizontal rules into your document can help break text up into meaningful units and so make the text easier to read.

This method of entering the width of an element is used with other elements in HTML 4, the most common being the *TABLE* element.

The **SIZE** attribute determines the height of the horizontal rule, in pixels. The **ALIGN** attribute, as we used with the **IMG** element, aligns the **HR** element horizontally on the page. The value of **ALIGN** can be either left, center or right. One final attribute of the **HR** element is *NOSHADE*. This eliminates the default shading effect and instead displays the horizontal rule as a solid-color bar.

C.11 Internet and WWW Resources

There are many resources available on the World Wide Web that go into more depth on the topics we cover. Visit the following sites for additional information on these topics.

www.w3.org/
The *World Wide Web Consortium* (W3C), is the group that makes HTML recommendations. This Web site holds a variety of information about HTML—both its history and its present status.

www.w3.org/TR/REC-html40/
The *HTML 4.0 Specification* contains all the nuances and fine points in HTML 4.0.

www.freewebpromotion.com/harvillo/index.htm
Harvillo's Finest HTML Help. This site contains step-by-step instructions for beginners on building a Web page.

www2.utep.edu/~kross/tutorial
This University of Texas at El Paso site contains another guide for simple HTML programming. The site is helpful for beginners, because it focuses on teaching and gives specific examples.

SUMMARY

- HTML is not a procedural programming language like C, Fortran, Cobol or Pascal. It is a markup language that identifies the elements of a page so a browser can render that page on the screen.

- HTML is used to format text and information. This "marking up" of information is different from the intent of traditional programming languages, which is to perform actions in a designated order.

- In HTML, text is marked up with elements, delineated by tags that are keywords contained in pairs of angle brackets.

- Create HTML files—also called HTML documents—using a text editor. A text editor called Notepad is built into Windows. You can also download an HTML shareware source-code editor or use Microsoft's Visual InterDev.

- All HTML files require either the **.htm** or the **.html** file name extension.

- Making errors while coding in conventional programming languages like C, C++ and Java often produces a fatal error, preventing the program from running. Errors in HTML code are usually not fatal. The browser will make its best effort at rendering the page but will probably not display the page as you intended. In our Common Programming Errors and Testing and Debugging Tips we highlight common HTML errors and how to detect and correct them.

- The filename of your home page should be **index.html**. When a browser requests a directory, the default Web server response is to return **index.html**, if it exists in that directory.

- **<HTML>** tells the browser that everything contained between the opening **<HTML>** tag and the closing **</HTML>** tag is HTML.

- Comments in HTML always begin with **<!--** and end with **-->** and can span across several source lines. The browser ignores any text and/or tags placed inside a comment.

- Every HTML file is separated into a header section and a body.

- Including a title is mandatory for every HTML document. Use the **<TITLE>...</TITLE>** tags to do so. They are placed inside the header.

- **<BODY>** opens the **BODY** element. The body of an HTML document is the area where you place all content you would like browsers to display.

- All text between the **<P>...</P>** tags forms one paragraph. This paragraph will be set apart from all other material on the page by a line of vertical space both before and after the paragraph.

- Headers are a simple form of text formatting that typically increase text size based on the header's "level" (**H1** through **H6**). They are often used to delineate new sections and subsections of a page.

- The **CENTER** element causes all material between its **<CENTER>** and **</CENTER>** tags to be centered horizontally in the browser window.

- The attribute **ALIGN** is the method by which any single element of the page can be aligned. The HTML 4.0 convention is to enclose the **ALIGN** value (**left**, **center** or **right**) in quotation marks. This convention applies to most attribute values.

- The purpose of HTML is simply to mark up text; the question of how it is presented is left to the browser itself.

- People who have difficulty seeing can use special browsers that read the text on the screen aloud. These browsers (which are text based and do not show images, colors or graphics) might read **STRONG** and **EM** with different inflections to convey the impact of the styled text to the user.

- You should close tags in the reverse order from that in which they were started.

- The most important capability of HTML is creating hyperlinks to documents on any server to form a world-wide network of linked documents and information.

- Links are inserted using the **A** (anchor) element. To specify the address you would like to link to, insert the **HREF** attribute into the anchor tag, with the address as the value of **HREF**.

- Anchors can link to email addresses. When someone clicks on this type of anchored link, their default email program initiates an email message to the linked address.

- Attributes can be added to the **BODY** tag to set certain characteristics of the page. To use an image as a background, include the attribute **BACKGROUND = "file.ext"** inside the opening **<BODY>** tag.

- Large background images greatly increase the time it takes for a page to load. The browser tiles the image across and down the screen.

- The term pixel stands for "picture element". Each pixel represents one dot of color on the screen.

- You specify the location of the image file with the **SRC = "location"** attribute in the **<IMG>** tag. You can specify the **HEIGHT** and **WIDTH** of an image, measured in pixels. You can add a border by using the **BORDER = "x"** attribute.

- **ALT** is provided for browsers that cannot view pictures or that have images turned off (text-based browsers, for example). The value of the **ALT** attribute will appear on-screen in place of the image, giving the user an idea of what was in the image.

- **<BODY BGCOLOR = "#CDCDCD">** adds a solid background color. To indicate the color to use specify either a preset color name or a hexadecimal code.

- All colors are composed of varying shades of red, green and blue (i.e., so-called RGB colors). The first two characters in the "hex" color code represent the amount of red in the color, the second two represent the amount of green and the last two represent the blue. **00** is the weakest a color can get, and **FF** is the strongest a color can get.

- You can refer to files in different directories by including the directory name in the correct format in the **SRC** attribute. You can insert an image from a different Web site onto your site (after obtaining permission from the site's owner). Just make the **SRC** attribute reflects the location and name of the image file.

- The **BR** element forces a line break. If the **BR** element is placed inside a text area, the text begins a new line at the place of the **
** tag. Attribute **COLOR** indicates the color of the formatted text in the same manner in which you indicate a background color; you enter either a preset color name or a hex color code. Remember to include the quotation marks around the color name.

- Use **SIZE** to change the size of the text being formatted with **<FONT>**. To make the text larger, set the **SIZE = "+x"**. To make the text smaller set **SIZE = "-x"**. Use **FACE** to change the font of the text you are formatting.

- HTML 4.0 has a provision for inserting special characters and symbols. All special characters are inserted in the format of the code, always &code;. An example of this is **&**, which inserts an ampersand. Codes are often abbreviated forms of the character (like **amp** for ampersand and **copy** for copyright) and can also be in the form of hex codes. For example, the hex code for an ampersand is 38, so another method of inserting an ampersand is to use **&**.

- You can strike-through text with a horizontal line by including it in a **DEL** element. To turn text into superscript or subscript, use the **SUP** and **SUB** elements respectively.

- **<HR>** inserts a horizontal rule, a straight line going across the screen. You can adjust the width of it by including the **WIDTH** attribute, using a number of pixels or a percentage of screen width. **NOSHADE** will remove the 3D shading, rendering the **HR** as a solid-color bar. This method of entering the width of an element is used with other elements in HTML 4, for example the **TABLE** element.

TERMINOLOGY

<!--...--> (comment)	content of an HTML element
<BODY>...</BODY>	**DEL** element
<HR> element (horizontal rule)	**EM** element (**<EM>...</EM>**)
A element (anchor; **<A>...</A>**)	emphasis
ALIGN = "center"	**FACE =** in **<FONT>**
ALIGN = "left"	**FONT** element (**<FONT>...</FONT>**)
ALIGN = "right"	**FORM** element (**<FORM>...</FORM>**)
ALT	FrontPage Express
&	**H1** element (**<H1>...</H1>**)
anchor	**H2** element (**<H2>...</H2>**)
attributes of an HTML tag	**H3** element (**<H3>...</H3>**)
BACKGROUND attribute of **BODY** element	**H4** element (**<H4>...</H4>**)
BGCOLOR attribute of **BODY** element	**H5** element (**<H5>...</H5>**)
bold	**H6** element (**<H6>...</H6>**)
border of an image	**HEAD** element (**<HEAD>...</HEAD>**)
CENTER element (**<CENTER>...</CENTER>**)	height
CLEAR = "all" in ** **	hexadecimal color codes
closing tag	horizontal rule
color	**HREF** attribute of **<A>** element
COLOR in **<BODY>**	**.htm**
comments	**.html**

HTML (HyperText Markup Language)
HTML document
HTML element (**<HTML>**...**</HTML>**)
HTML file
HTML tags
HTML-Kit
hyperlink
hypertext
image
IMG element
index.html
italic
line break element (**
...</BR>**)
link
link attribute of **BODY** element...
mailto:
Markup Language
Name attribute of **FRAME** element
opening tag
P element (paragraph; **<P>**...**</P>**)
paragraph element (**<P>**...**</P>**)
presentation of a Web Page

RGB colors
SIZE = in **<FONT>**
source-code form
special characters
SRC attribute in **IMG** element
STRONG element (**<STRONG>**...**</STRONG>**)
structure of a Web page
SUB (subscript)
SUP (superscript)
tags in HTML
TEXT in **BODY**
text-based browser
tiling an image across the screen
TITLE element (**<TITLE>**...**</TITLE>**)
U element
unordered list (**<UL>**...**</UL>**)
Web site
WIDTH attribute
width by percentage
width by pixel
World Wide Web

SELF-REVIEW EXERCISES

C.1   State whether the following are *true* or *false*. If *false*, explain why.
   a) You can specify the background of the page as an attribute in the **<HTML>** tag.
   b) The use of the **EM** and **STRONG** elements is deprecated.
   c) The name of your site home page should always be **homepage.html**.
   d) It is a good programming practice to insert comments into your HTML document that explain what you are doing.
   e) A hyperlink is inserted around text with the **LINK** element.

C.2   Fill in the blanks in each of the following:
   a) The _____ element is used to insert a horizontal rule.
   b) Superscript is formatted with the _____ element and subscript is formatted with the _____ element.
   c) The _____ element is located within the **<HEAD>**...**</HEAD>** tags.
   d) The smallest text header is the _____ element and the largest text header is _____.
   e) The _____ element is used to format the size and color of text.
   f) You can center a section of your page by enclosing it between _____ tags.

C.3   Identify each of the following as either an element or attribute.
   a) **HTML**
   b) **WIDTH**
   c) **ALIGN**
   d) **BR**
   e) **SIZE**
   f) **H3**
   g) **A**
   h) **SRC**

ANSWERS TO SELF-REVIEW EXERCISES

C.1   a) False. You specify the background with either the **BACKGROUND** or the **BGCOLOR** attribute in the **BODY** element. b) False. The use of the **I** and **B** elements is deprecated. **EM** and **STRONG** should be used instead. c) False. The name of your homepage should always be **index.html**. d) True. e) False. A hyperlink is inserted around text with the **A** (anchor) element.

C.2   a) **HR**. b) **SUP, SUB**. c) **TITLE**. d) **H6, H1**. e) **FONT**. f) **<CENTER>**…**</CENTER>**.

C.3   a) Tag. b) Attribute. c) Attribute. d) Tag. e) Attribute. f) Tag. g) Tag. h) Attribute.

EXERCISES

C.4   Mark up the first paragraph of this appendix. Use **H1** for the section header, **P** for text, **STRONG** for the first word of every sentence, and **EM** for all capital letters.

C.5   Mark up the first paragraph again, this time using left-aligned horizontal rules to separate sentences. The size of each horizontal rule should be the same as the number of words in the preceding sentence. Every alternate horizontal rule should have the **NOSHADE** attribute applied.

C.6   Why is this code valid? (*Hint*: you can find the W3C specification for the **P** element at **www.w3.org/TR/REC-html40/struct/text.html**.)

```
<P>Here's some text...
<HR>
<P>And some more text...</P>
```

C.7   Why is this code invalid? (*Hint*: you can find the W3C specification for the **BR** element at the same URL given in Exercise C.6.)

```
<P>Here's some text...<BR></BR>
And some more text...</P>
```

C.8   Given: We have an image named **deitel.gif** that is 200 pixels wide and 150 pixels high. Use the **WIDTH** and **HEIGHT** attributes of the **IMG** tag to a) increase image size by 100%; b) increase image size by 50%; c) change the width-to-height ratio to 2:1, keeping the width attained in a).

C.9   Create a link to each of the following: a) **index.html**, located in the **files** directory; b) index.html, located in the **text** subdirectory of the **files** directory; c) **index.html**, located in the **other** directory in your *parent directory* [*Hint*: **..** signifies parent directory.]; d) A link to the President's email address (**president@whitehouse.gov**); e) An **FTP** link to the file named **README** in the **pub** directory of **ftp.cdrom.com** [*Hint*: remember to use **ftp://**].

Intermediate HTML 4

Objectives

- To be able to create lists of information.
- To be able to create tables with rows and columns of data.
- To be able to control the display and formatting of tables.
- To be able to create and use forms.
- To be able to create and use image maps to aid hyperlinking.
- To be able to make Web pages accessible to search engines.

Yea, from the table of my memory
I'll wipe away all trivial fond records.
William Shakespeare

Outline

D.1   **Introduction**
D.2   **Basic HTML Tables**
D.3   **Intermediate HTML Tables and Formatting**
D.4   **Basic HTML Forms**
D.5   **More Complex HTML Forms**
D.6   **Internet and WWW Resources**

Summary • Terminology • Self-Review Exercises • Answers to Self-Review Exercises • Exercises

D.1 Introduction

In Appendix C, we discussed some basic HTML features. We built several complete Web pages featuring text, hyperlinks, images, backgrounds, colors and such formatting tools as horizontal rules and line breaks.

In this appendix, we discuss more substantial HTML elements and features. We will see how to present information in *lists* and *tables*. We discuss how to use forms to collect information from people browsing a site. We explain how to use *internal linking* and *image maps* to make pages more navigable.

By the end of this appendix, you will be familiar with most commonly used HTML tags and features. You will then be able to create more complex and visually appealing Web sites and have a much better understanding of the HTML Web pages used by **Bug2Bug.com**, which we continue studying in Appendix E.

D.2 Basic HTML Tables

Another way to format information using HTML 4.0 is to use *tables*. The table in Fig. D.1 organizes data into rows and columns.

```
1    <HTML>
2
3    <!-- Fig. D.1: table.html -->
4    <!-- Basic table design    -->
5
6    <HEAD>
7    <TITLE>e-Business & e-Commerce for Managers - Tables</TITLE>
8    </HEAD>
9
10   <BODY>
11
12   <CENTER><H2>Table Example Page</H2></CENTER>
13
14   <!-- The <TABLE> tag opens a new table and lets you put in -->
15   <!-- design options and instructions                       -->
16   <TABLE BORDER = "1" ALIGN = "center" WIDTH = "40%">
17
```

Fig. D.1   HTML table (part 1 of 2).

```
18   <!-- Use the <CAPTION> tag to summarize the table's contents -->
19   <!-- (this helps the visually impaired)                       -->
20   <CAPTION>Here is a small sample table.</CAPTION>
21
22   <!-- The <THEAD> is the first (non-scrolling) horizontal       -->
23   <!-- section. Use it to format the table header area.          -->
24   <!-- <TH> inserts a header cell and displays bold text         -->
25   <THEAD>
26   <TR><TH>This is the head.</TH></TR>
27   </THEAD>
28
29   <!-- All of your important content goes in the <TBODY>.        -->
30   <!-- Use this tag to format the entire section                 -->
31   <!-- <TD> inserts a data cell, with regular text               -->
32   <TBODY>
33   <TR><TD ALIGN = "center">This is the body.</TD></TR>
34   </TBODY>
35
36   </TABLE>
37
38   </BODY>
39   </HTML>
```

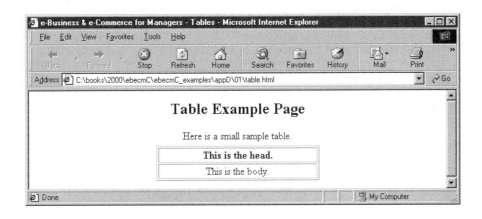

Fig. D.1   HTML table (part 2 of 2).

All tags and text that apply to the table go inside the **<TABLE>**...**</TABLE>** tags, which begin on line 16

```
<TABLE BORDER = "1" ALIGN = "center" WIDTH = "40%">
```

There are a number of attributes that can be applied to the **TABLE** element. The **BORDER** *attribute* lets you set the width of the table's border in pixels. If you want all lines to be invisible, you can specify **BORDER = "0"**. You should experiment to find the best "look" for each table. In the table shown in Fig. D.1, the value of the border attribute is set to **1**.

The horizontal alignment we saw before also applies to tables (**ALIGN = "left"**, **"center"** or **"right"**). The *WIDTH* attribute sets the width of the table, and is used exactly as in the **HR** element— you specify either a number of pixels or a percentage of the screen width.

Line 20

```
<CAPTION>Here is a small sample table.</CAPTION>
```

inserts a *caption* element into the table. The text inside the *<CAPTION>...</CAPTION>* tags is inserted directly above the table in the browser window. The caption text is also used to help *text-based browsers* interpret the table data.

Tables can be split into distinct horizontal and vertical sections. The first of these sections, the head area, appears in lines 25 through 27

```
<THEAD>
<TR><TH>This is the head.</TH></TR>
</THEAD>
```

Put all header information (for example, the titles of the table and column headers) inside the *<THEAD>...</THEAD>* tags.

The **TR**, or *table row element*, is used for formatting the cells of individual rows. All of the cells in a row belong within the *<TR>...</TR>* tags of that row. In the next section we discuss how to use **TR** for row formatting.

The smallest area of the table we are able to format is the *data cell*. There are two types of data cells, located in the header (*<TH>...</TH>*) or in the table body (*<TD>...</TD>*). The code example above inserts a header cell. Header cells, which are usually placed in the **<THEAD>** area, are suitable for titles and column headings.

The second grouping section, the **TBODY** element, appears in lines 32 through 34

```
<TBODY>
<TR><TD ALIGN = "center">This is the body.</TD></TR>
</TBODY>
```

Like the **THEAD**, the *TBODY* is used for formatting and grouping purposes. Although there is only one row and one cell in the above example, most tables will use **TBODY** to house the majority of their content. In this code example, **TBODY** includes only one row and one data cell. The cell is marked by the *<TD>...</TD>* tags.

Regular data cells are left aligned by default. In the above example, notice that there is an **ALIGN** attribute included inside the opening **<TD>** tag. This attribute affects the horizontal alignment (we will see how to set vertical alignment in the next code example). The **ALIGN** attribute is used here in the same way as it is used to align other HTML tags.

Look-and-Feel Observation D.1

Use tables in your HTML pages to organize data attractively and effectively.

Common Programming Error D.1

Forgetting to close any of the area formatting tags inside the table area can distort the table format. Be sure to check that every element is opened and closed in its proper place to make sure that the table appears as intended.

D.3 Intermediate HTML Tables and Formatting

In the previous section and code example, we explored the structure of a basic table. In Fig. D.2, we extend our table example with more formatting attributes.

The new table begins on line 32. The **COLGROUP** element, used for formatting groups of columns, is shown on lines 39 through 42

```
<COLGROUP>
   <COL ALIGN = "right">
   <COL SPAN = "4" ALIGN = "center">
</COLGROUP>
```

The *COLGROUP* element can be used to group and format columns. Each *COL* element in the **<COLGROUP>...</COLGROUP>** tags can format any number of columns (specified with the **SPAN** attribute). Any formatting to be applied to a column or group of columns can be specified in both the **COLGROUP** and **COL** tags. In this case, we align the text inside the leftmost column to the right and center the text in the remaining four columns. Another useful attribute to use here is **WIDTH**, which specifies the width of the column.

```
1    <HTML>
2
3    <!-- Fig. D.2: table.html      -->
4    <!-- Intermediate table design -->
5
6    <HEAD>
7    <TITLE>e-Business & e-Commerce for Managers - Tables</TITLE>
8    </HEAD>
9    <BODY>
10
11   <H2 ALIGN = "center">Table Example Page</H2>
12
13   <TABLE BORDER = "1" ALIGN = "center" WIDTH = "40%">
14      <CAPTION>Here is a small sample table.</CAPTION>
15
16      <THEAD>
17      <TR>
18         <TH>This is the Head.</TH>
19      </TR>
20      </THEAD>
21
22      <TBODY>
23      <TR>
24         <TD ALIGN = "center">This is the Body.</TD>
25      </TR>
26      </TBODY>
27
28   </TABLE>
29
30   <BR><BR>
31
32   <TABLE BORDER = "1" ALIGN = "center">
33
```

Fig. D.2   A complex table with formatting and color (part 1 of 3).

```
34        <CAPTION>Here is a more complex sample table.</CAPTION>
35
36        <!-- <COLGROUP> and <COL> are used to format entire   -->
37        <!-- columns at once. SPAN determines how many columns -->
38        <!-- the COL tag effects.                              -->
39        <COLGROUP>
40           <COL ALIGN = "right">
41           <COL SPAN = "4" ALIGN = "center">
42        </COLGROUP>
43
44        <THEAD>
45
46        <!-- ROWSPANs and COLSPANs combine the indicated number -->
47        <!-- of cells vertically or horizontally                -->
48        <TR BGCOLOR = "#8888FF">
49           <TH ROWSPAN = "2">
50              <IMG SRC = "deitel.gif" WIDTH = "200" HEIGHT = "144"
51                 ALT = "Harvey and Paul Deitel">
52           </TH>
53
54           <TH COLSPAN = "4" VALIGN = "top">
55              <H1>Camelid comparison</H1><BR>
56              <P>Approximate as of 8/99</P>
57           </TH>
58        </TR>
59
60        <TR BGCOLOR = "khaki" VALIGN = "bottom">
61           <TH># of Humps</TH>
62           <TH>Indigenous region</TH>
63           <TH>Spits?</TH>
64           <TH>Produces Wool?</TH>
65        </TR>
66
67        </THEAD>
68
69        <TBODY>
70
71        <TR>
72           <TH>Camels (bactrian)</TH>
73           <TD>2</TD>
74           <TD>Africa/Asia</TD>
75           <TD ROWSPAN = "2">Llama</TD>
76           <TD ROWSPAN = "2">Llama</TD>
77        </TR>
78
79        <TR>
80           <TH>Llamas</TH>
81           <TD>1</TD>
82           <TD>Andes Mountains</TD>
83        </TR>
84
85     </TBODY>
86     </TABLE>
```

Fig. D.2   A complex table with formatting and color (part 2 of 3).

```
87
88    </BODY>
89    </HMTL>
```

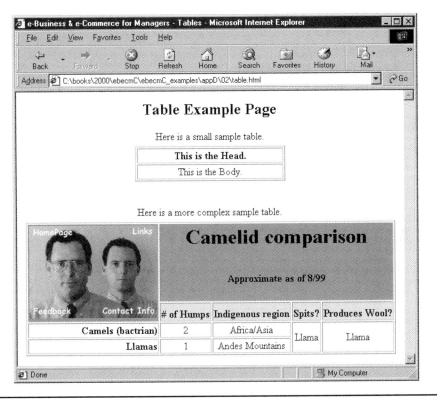

Fig. D.2   A complex table with formatting and color (part 3 of 3).

Lines 48 and 49

```
<TR BGCOLOR = "#8888FF">
   <TH ROWSPAN = "2">
```

introduce several more table formatting capabilities. You can add a background color or image to any row or cell with the **BGCOLOR** and **BACKGROUND** attributes, which are used in the same way as in the **BODY** element.

It is possible to make some data cells larger than others. This effect is accomplished with the **ROWSPAN** and **COLSPAN** attributes, which can be placed inside any data cell opening tag. The attribute value extends the data cell to span the specified number of cells. Using our line of code, for example, **ROWSPAN = "2"** tells the browser that this data cell will span the area of two vertically adjacent cells. These cells will be joined vertically (and will thus span over two rows). An example of **COLSPAN** appears in line 53:

```
<TH COLSPAN = "4" VALIGN = "top">
```

where the header cell is widened to span four cells.

We also see here an example of vertical alignment formatting. The **VALIGN** attribute accepts the following values: **"top"**, **"middle"**, **"bottom"** and **"baseline"**. All cells in a row whose **VALIGN** attribute is set to **"baseline"** will have the first text line occur on a common baseline. The default vertical alignment in all data and header cells is **VALIGN = "middle"**.

The remaining code in Fig. D.2 demonstrates other uses of the table attributes and elements outlined above.

Look-and-Feel Observation D.2

Using the **COLSPAN** *and* **ROWSPAN** *attributes in your tables adds a nice look and can help you format the data cells to contain your information more effectively.*

Common Programming Error D.2

When using **COLSPAN** *and* **ROWSPAN** *in table data cells, consider that the modified cells will cover the areas of other cells. Compensate for this in your code by reducing the number of cells in that row or column. If you do not, the formatting of your table will be distorted, and you may inadvertently create more columns and/or rows than you originally intended.*

D.4 Basic HTML Forms

HTML provides several mechanisms to collect information from people viewing your site; one is the *form* (Fig. D.3).

```
1   <HTML>
2
3   <!-- Fig. D.3: form.html      -->
4   <!-- Introducing Form Design -->
5
6   <HEAD>
7   <TITLE>e-Business & e-Commerce for Managers - Forms</TITLE>
8   </HEAD>
9
10  <BODY>
11  <H2>Feedback Form</H2>
12
13  <P>Please fill out this form to help us improve our site.</P>
14
15  <!-- This tag starts the form, gives the method of sending -->
16  <!-- information and the location of form scripts.         -->
17  <!-- Hidden inputs give the server non-visual information  -->
18  <FORM METHOD = "POST" ACTION = "/cgi-bin/formmail">
19
20  <INPUT TYPE = "hidden" NAME = "recipient"
21     VALUE = "deitel@deitel.com">
22  <INPUT TYPE = "hidden" NAME = "subject"
23     VALUE = "Feedback Form">
24  <INPUT TYPE = "hidden" NAME = "redirect"
25     VALUE = "main.html">
26
```

Fig. D.3   Simple form with basic fields and a text box (part 1 of 2).

```
27   <!-- <INPUT type = "text"> inserts a text box -->
28   <P><STRONG>Name:</STRONG>
29   <INPUT NAME = "name" TYPE = "text" SIZE = "25"></P>
30
31   <!-- Input types "submit" and "reset" insert buttons -->
32   <!-- for submitting or clearing the form's contents  -->
33   <INPUT TYPE = "submit" VALUE = "Submit Your Entries">
34   <INPUT TYPE = "reset" VALUE = "Clear Your Entries">
35   </FORM>
36
37   </BODY>
38   </HTML>
```

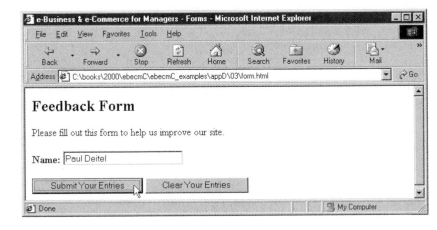

Fig. D.3   Simple form with basic fields and a text box (part 2 of 2).

The form begins on line 18

```
<FORM METHOD = "POST" ACTION = "/cgi-bin/formmail">
```

with the **FORM** element. The **METHOD** attribute indicates the way the *Web server* will organize and send you the form output. Use **METHOD = "post"** in a form that causes changes to server data, for example when updating a database. The form data will be sent to the server as an *environment variable,* which scripts are able to access. The other possible value, **METHOD = "get"**, should be used when your form does not cause any changes in server-side data, for example when making a database request. The form data from **METHOD = "get"** is appended to the end of the URL (for example, **/cgi-bin/form-mail?name=bob&order=5**). Because of this, the amount of data submitted using this **METHOD** is limited to 4K. Also be aware that **METHOD = "get"** is limited to standard characters, and can not submit any special characters.

A *Web server* is a machine that runs a software package such as Microsoft's PWS (Personal Web Server), Microsoft's IIS (Internet Information Server), Apache or Jigsaw. Personal Web Server is described later in the Appendix J. Web servers handle browser requests. When a browser requests a page or file somewhere on a server, the server processes the request and returns an answer to the browser. In this example, the data from the form goes to a CGI (Common Gateway Interface) script, which is a means of interfacing an HTML page with a script (i.e., a program) written in Perl, C, Tcl or other languages. The script then handles the data fed to it by the server and typically returns some information for the user. The **ACTION** attribute in the **FORM** tag is the path to this script; in this case, it is a common script which emails form data to an address. Most Internet Service Providers will have a script like this on their site, so you can ask your system administrator how to set up your HTML to use the script correctly.

There are several pieces of information (not seen by the user) that you need to insert in the form. Lines 20 through 25

```
<INPUT TYPE = "hidden" NAME = "recipient"
   VALUE = "deitel@deitel.com">
<INPUT TYPE = "hidden" NAME = "subject"
   VALUE = "Feedback Form">
<INPUT TYPE = "hidden" NAME = "redirect"
   VALUE = "main.html">
```

obtain this information by the use of *hidden input elements*. The **INPUT** element is common in forms and always requires the **TYPE** attribute. Two other attributes are **NAME**, which provides a unique identification for the **INPUT** element, and **VALUE**, which indicates the value that the **INPUT** element sends to the server upon submission.

As shown above, hidden inputs always have the attribute **TYPE = "hidden"**. The three hidden inputs shown are typical for this kind of CGI script: An email address to which to send the data, the subject line of the email and a URL to which the user is redirected after submitting the form.

Good Programming Practice D.1

Place hidden **INPUT** *elements in the beginning of a form, right after the opening* **<FORM>** *tag. This makes these elements easier to find and identify.*

The usage of an **<INPUT>** element is defined by the value of its **TYPE** attribute. We introduce another of these options in lines 28 and 29:

```
<P><STRONG>Name: </STRONG>
<INPUT NAME = "name" TYPE = "text" SIZE = "25"></P>
```

The input **TYPE = "text"** inserts a one-line text box into the form. The value of this **INPUT** element and the information that the server sends to you from this **INPUT** is the text that the user types into the bar. A good use of the textual input element is for names or other one-line pieces of information.

We also use the **SIZE** attribute, whose value determines the width of the text input, measured in characters. You can also set a maximum number of characters that the text input will accept by inserting the **MAXLENGTH = "***length***"** attribute.

Good Programming Practice D.2

When using **INPUT** *elements in forms, be sure to leave enough space for users to input the pertinent information.*

It is important to note here the placement of text relative to the **INPUT** element. You must make sure to include a textual identifier (in this case, **Name:**) adjacent to the **INPUT** element, to indicate the purpose of the element.

Common Programming Error D.3

Forgetting to include textual labels for a form element is a design error. Without these labels, users will have no way of knowing what the function of individual form elements is.

There are two types of **INPUT** elements in lines 33 and 34

```
<INPUT TYPE = "submit" VALUE = "Submit Your Entries">
<INPUT TYPE = "reset" VALUE = "Clear Your Entries">
```

that should be inserted into every form. The **TYPE = "submit"** **INPUT** element places a button in the form that submits data to the server when clicked. The **VALUE** attribute changes the text displayed on the button (the default value is **"submit"**). The input element **TYPE = "reset"** inserts a button onto the form that, when clicked, clears all entries the user entered into the form. This can help the user correct mistakes or simply start over. As with the **submit** input, the **VALUE** attribute of the **RESET** input affects the text of the button on the screen, but does not affect functionality at all.

Good Programming Practice D.3

*Be sure to close your form code with the **</FORM>** tag. Neglecting to include this can affect the actions of other forms on the same page.*

Common Programming Error D.4

*When your form has several checkboxes with the same **NAME**, you must make sure that they have different **VALUEs**, or else the script will have no way of distinguishing between them.*

D.5 More Complex HTML Forms

We introduce additional form input options in Fig. D.4.
    Line 29

```
<TEXTAREA NAME = "comments" ROWS = "4" COLS = "36">
    </TEXTAREA>
```

introduces the **TEXTAREA** element. This type of form component has its own element name. The **TEXTAREA** element inserts a box into the form. You specify the size of the box (which is scrollable) inside the opening **<TEXTAREA>** tag with the **ROWS** attribute, which sets the number of rows appearing in the **TEXTAREA**. With the **COLS** attribute, you specify how wide the **TEXTAREA** should be. This **TEXTAREA** is four rows of characters tall and 36 characters wide. Any default text that you want to place inside the **TEXTAREA** should be contained within the **<TEXTAREA>...</TEXTAREA>** tags.
    The input **TYPE = "password"** in line 35

```
<INPUT NAME = "email" TYPE = "password" SIZE = "25"></P>
```

inserts a text box with the indicated size. The only difference between a password input and a text input is that, when data is entered into a password area, it appears on the screen as asterisks. The password is used for submitting sensitive information which the user would not want others to be able to read. It is just the browser that displays asterisks—the real form data is still submitted to the server.

Lines 40 through 49 introduce another form input **TYPE**.

```
Site design
<INPUT NAME = "things" TYPE = "checkbox" VALUE = "Design">
Links
<INPUT NAME = "things" TYPE = "checkbox" VALUE = "Links">
Ease of use
<INPUT NAME = "things" TYPE = "checkbox" VALUE = "Ease">
Images
<INPUT NAME = "things" TYPE = "checkbox" VALUE = "Images">
Source code
<INPUT NAME = "things" TYPE = "checkbox" VALUE = "Code">
```

Every **INPUT** element with **TYPE = "checkbox"** creates a new checkbox in the form. Checkboxes can be used individually or in groups. Each checkbox in a group should have the same **NAME** (in this case, **NAME = "things"**). This notifies the script handling the form that all of the checkboxes are related to one another, and are typically listed in the same output line in the email generated by the form.

```
1   <HTML>
2
3   <!-- Fig. D.4: form.html    -->
4   <!-- Form Design Example 2 -->
5
6   <HEAD>
7   <TITLE>e-Business & e-Commerce for Managers - Forms</TITLE>
8   </HEAD>
9
10  <BODY>
11  <H2>Feedback Form</H2>
12
13  <P>Please fill out this form to help us improve our site.</P>
14
15  <FORM METHOD = "POST" ACTION = "/cgi-bin/formmail">
16
17  <INPUT TYPE = "hidden" NAME = "recipient"
18     VALUE = "deitel@deitel.com">
19  <INPUT TYPE = "hidden" NAME = "subject"
20     VALUE = "Feedback Form">
21  <INPUT TYPE = "hidden" NAME = "redirect"
22     VALUE = "main.html">
23
24  <P><STRONG>Name: </STRONG>
25  <INPUT NAME = "name" TYPE = "text" SIZE = "25"></P>
26
27  <!-- <TEXTAREA> creates a textbox of the size given -->
28  <P><STRONG>Comments:</STRONG>
29  <TEXTAREA NAME = "comments" ROWS = "4" COLS = "36"></TEXTAREA>
30  </P>
31
32  <!-- <INPUT TYPE = "password"> inserts a textbox whose    -->
33  <!-- readout will be in *** instead of regular characters -->
34  <P><STRONG>Email Address:</STRONG>
```

Fig. D.4   Form including textareas, password boxes and checkboxes (part 1 of 2).

```
35    <INPUT NAME = "email" TYPE = "password" SIZE = "25"></P>
36
37    <!-- <INPUT TYPE = "checkbox"> creates a checkbox -->
38    <P><STRONG>Things you liked:</STRONG><BR>
39
40    Site design
41    <INPUT NAME = "things" TYPE = "checkbox" VALUE = "Design">
42    Links
43    <INPUT NAME = "things" TYPE = "checkbox" VALUE = "Links">
44    Ease of use
45    <INPUT NAME = "things" TYPE = "checkbox" VALUE = "Ease">
46    Images
47    <INPUT NAME = "things" TYPE = "checkbox" VALUE = "Images">
48    Source code
49    <INPUT NAME = "things" TYPE = "checkbox" VALUE = "Code">
50    </P>
51
52    <INPUT TYPE = "submit" VALUE = "Submit Your Entries">
53    <INPUT TYPE = "reset" VALUE = "Clear Your Entries">
54    </FORM>
55
56    </BODY>
57    </HTML>
```

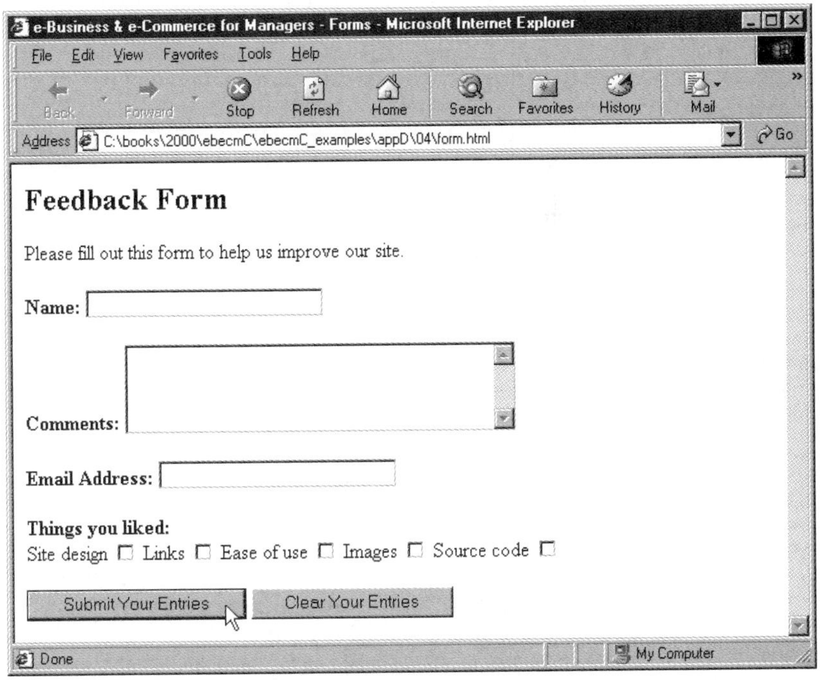

Fig. D.4   Form including textareas, password boxes and checkboxes (part 2 of 2).

Yet more form elements are introduced in Fig. D.5. In our final form code example, we introduce two new types of input options. The first of these is the *radio buttons*, introduced in lines 53 through 67

```
Search engine
<INPUT NAME = "how get to site" TYPE = "radio"
    VALUE ="search engine" CHECKED>
Links from another site
<INPUT NAME = "how get to site" TYPE = "radio"
    VALUE = "link">
Deitel.com Web site
<INPUT NAME = "how get to site" TYPE = "radio"
    VALUE = "deitel.com">
Reference in a book
<INPUT NAME = "how get to site" TYPE = "radio"
    VALUE = "book">
Other
<INPUT NAME = "how get to site" TYPE = "radio"
    VALUE = "other">
```

Inserted into forms with the **INPUT** attribute *TYPE = "radio"*, radio buttons are similar in function and usage to checkboxes. Radio buttons are different in that only one in the group may be selected at any time. All of the **NAME** attributes of a group of radio inputs must be the same and all of the **VALUE** attributes different. Insert the attribute *CHECKED* to indicate which radio button you would like selected initially. The **CHECKED** attribute can also be applied to checkboxes.

 Common Programming Error D.5

When you are using a group of radio inputs in a form, forgetting to set the **NAME** *values to the same name will let the user select all the radio buttons at the same time: an undesired result.*

```
1   <HTML>
2
3   <!-- Fig. D.5: form.html   -->
4   <!-- Form Design Example 3 -->
5
6   <HEAD>
7   <TITLE>e-Business & e-Commerce for Managers - Forms</TITLE>
8   </HEAD>
9
10  <BODY>
11  <H2>Feedback Form</H2>
12
13  <P>Please fill out this form to help us improve our site.</P>
14
15  <FORM METHOD = "POST" ACTION = "/cgi-bin/formmail">
16
17  <INPUT TYPE = "hidden" NAME = "recipient"
18      VALUE = "deitel@deitel.com">
19  <INPUT TYPE = "hidden" NAME = "subject"
```

Fig. D.5   HTML form including radio buttons and pulldown lists (part 1 of 3).

```
20        VALUE = "Feedback Form">
21   <INPUT TYPE = "hidden" NAME = "redirect"
22        VALUE = "main.html">
23
24   <P><STRONG>Name: </STRONG>
25   <INPUT NAME = "name" TYPE = "text" SIZE = "25"></P>
26
27   <P><STRONG>Comments:</STRONG>
28   <TEXTAREA NAME = "comments" ROWS = "4" COLS = "36"></TEXTAREA>
29   </P>
30
31   <P><STRONG>Email Address:</STRONG>
32   <INPUT NAME = "email" TYPE = "password" SIZE = "25"></P>
33
34   <P><STRONG>Things you liked:</STRONG><BR>
35
36   Site design
37   <INPUT NAME = "things" TYPE = "checkbox" VALUE = "Design">
38   Links
39   <INPUT NAME = "things" TYPE = "checkbox" VALUE = "Links">
40   Ease of use
41   <INPUT NAME = "things" TYPE = "checkbox" VALUE = "Ease">
42   Images
43   <INPUT NAME = "things" TYPE = "checkbox" VALUE = "Images">
44   Source code
45   <INPUT NAME = "things" TYPE = "checkbox" VALUE = "Code">
46   </P>
47
48   <!-- <INPUT TYPE="radio"> creates a radio button. The      -->
49   <!-- difference between radio buttons and checkboxes is     -->
50   <!-- that only one radio button in a group can be selected -->
51   <P><STRONG>How did you get to our site?:</STRONG><BR>
52
53   Search engine
54   <INPUT NAME = "how get to site" TYPE = "radio"
55        VALUE = "search engine" CHECKED>
56   Links from another site
57   <INPUT NAME = "how get to site" TYPE = "radio"
58        VALUE = "link">
59   Deitel.com Web site
60   <INPUT NAME = "how get to site" TYPE = "radio"
61        VALUE = "deitel.com">
62   Reference in a book
63   <INPUT NAME = "how get to site" TYPE = "radio"
64        VALUE = "book">
65   Other
66   <INPUT NAME = "how get to site" TYPE = "radio"
67        VALUE = "other">
68   </P>
69
70   <!-- The <select> tag presents a drop down menu with -->
71   <!-- choices indicated by the <option> tags          -->
72   <P><STRONG>Rate our site (1-10):</STRONG>
```

Fig. D.5   HTML form including radio buttons and pulldown lists (part 2 of 3).

```
73   <SELECT NAME = "rating">
74   <OPTION SELECTED>Amazing:-)
75   <OPTION>10
76   <OPTION>9
77   <OPTION>8
78   <OPTION>7
79   <OPTION>6
80   <OPTION>5
81   <OPTION>4
82   <OPTION>3
83   <OPTION>2
84   <OPTION>1
85   <OPTION>The Pits:-(
86   </SELECT></P>
87
88   <INPUT TYPE = "submit" VALUE = "Submit Your Entries">
89   <INPUT TYPE = "reset" VALUE = "Clear Your Entries">
90   </FORM>
91
92   </BODY>
93   </HTML>
```

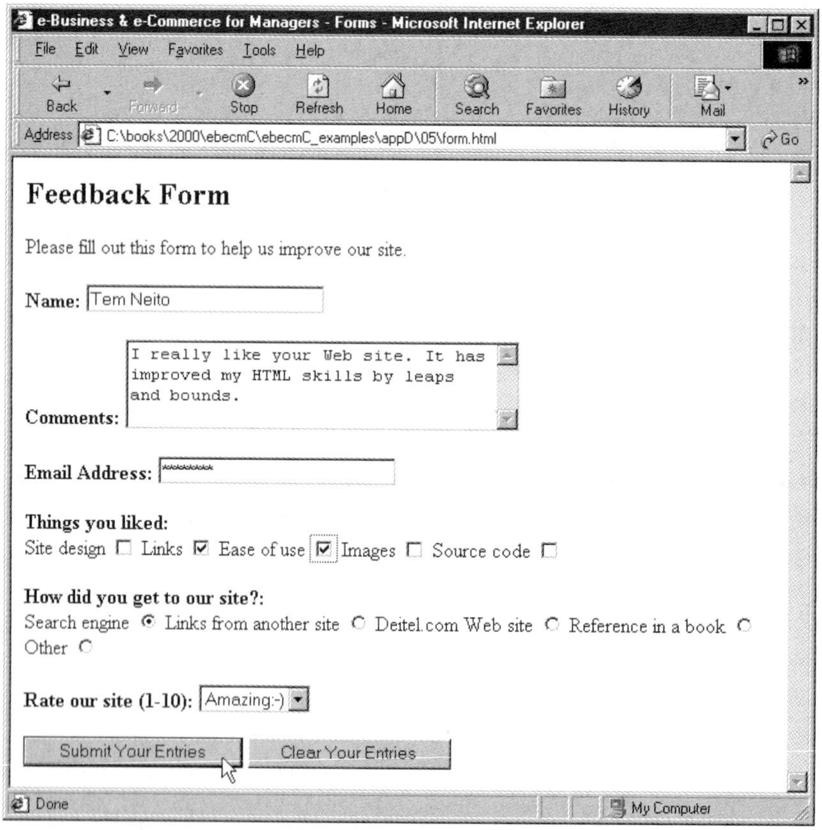

Fig. D.5   HTML form including radio buttons and pulldown lists (part 3 of 3).

The last type of form input that we introduce here is the ***SELECT*** element, on lines 73 through 86 of our code. This will place a selectable list of items inside your form.

```
<SELECT NAME = "rating">
<OPTION SELECTED>Amazing:-)
<OPTION>10
<OPTION>9
<OPTION>8
<OPTION>7
<OPTION>6
<OPTION>5
<OPTION>4
<OPTION>3
<OPTION>2
<OPTION>1
<OPTION>The Pits:-(
</SELECT>
```

This type of type of form input is inserted using a **SELECT** element instead of an **INPUT** element. Inside the opening ***<SELECT>*** tag, be sure to include the **NAME** attribute.

To add an item to the list, insert an ***OPTION*** element in the ***<SELECT>…</SELECT>*** area, and type what you want the list item to display on the same line. If an option is selected, this text will be sent to you in the form output email. Although a closing tag for the **OPTION** element is optional, its use is deprecated, and it is generally not included. When you have completed the list of **OPTION**s, close the **SELECT** area. The **SELECTED** attribute, like the **CHECKED** attribute for radio buttons and checkboxes, applies a default selection to your list.

The preceding code will generate a pull-down list of options, as shown in Fig. D.5. There is another attribute that can be included in the opening **<SELECT>** tag which changes the appearance of the list: You can change the number of list options visible at one time by including the ***SIZE = "*x*"*** attribute inside the **<SELECT>** tag. Use this attribute if you prefer an expanded version of the list to the one-line expandable list.

D.6 Internet and WWW Resources

There are many Web sites that cover the more advanced and difficult features of HTML. Several of these sites are featured here.

markradcliffe.co.uk/html/advancedhtml.htm
This site gives pointers on techniques that can be used in addition to knowledge of basic HTML tags. The site mainly focuses on frames and tables.

www.geocities.com/SiliconValley/Orchard/5212/
Adam's Advanced HTML Page is geared to those looking to master the more advanced techniques of HTML. It includes instructions for creating tables, frames and marquees and other advanced topics.

www.webdeveloper.com
An excellent resource for creating and maintaining Web pages. This site contains extensive coverage of almost all topics related to creating Web pages and keeping them running. Its clean examples make learning even advanced topics very easy.

SUMMARY

- HTML tables organize data into rows and columns. All tags and text that apply to a table go inside the **<TABLE>**...**</TABLE>** tags. The **BORDER** attribute lets you set the width of the table's border in pixels. The **WIDTH** attribute sets the width of the table—you specify either a number of pixels or a percentage of the screen width.

- Tables can be split into distinct horizontal and vertical sections. Put all header information (such as table titles and column headers) inside the **<THEAD>**...**</THEAD>** tags. The **TR** (table row) element is used for formatting the cells of individual rows. All of the cells in a row belong within the **<TR>**...**</TR>** tags of that row.

- The smallest area of the table that we are able to format is the data cell. There are two types of data cells: ones located in the header (**<TH>**...**</TH>**) and ones located in the table body (**<TD>**...**</TD>**). Header cells, usually placed in the **<THEAD>** area, are suitable for titles and column headings.

- Like **THEAD**, the **TBODY** is used for formatting and grouping purposes. Most tables use **TBODY** to house the majority of their content.

- **TD** table data cells are left aligned by default. **TH** cells are centered by default.

- Just as you can use the **THEAD** and **TBODY** elements to format groups of table rows, you can use the **COLGROUP** element to group and format columns. **COLGROUP** is used by setting in its opening tag the number of columns it affects and the formatting it imposes on that group of columns.

- Each **COL** element contained inside the **<COLGROUP>**...**</COLGROUP>** tags can in turn format a specified number of columns.

- You can add a background color or image to any table row or cell with either the **BGCOLOR** or **BACKGROUND** attributes, which are used in the same way as in the **BODY** element.

- It is possible to make some table data cells larger than others by using the **ROWSPAN** and **COLSPAN** attributes. The attribute value extends the data cell to span the specified number of cells.

- The **VALIGN** (vertical alignment) attribute of a table data cell accepts the following values: **"top"**, **"middle"**, **"bottom"** and **"baseline"**.

- All cells in a table row whose **VALIGN** attribute is set to **"baseline"** will have the first text line on a common baseline.

- The default vertical alignment in all data and header cells is **VALIGN="middle"**.

- HTML provides several mechanisms—including the **FORM**—to collect information from people viewing your site.

- Use **METHOD = "post"** in a form that causes changes to server data, for example when updating a database. The form data will be sent to the server as an *environment variable,* which scripts are able to access. The other possible value, **METHOD = "get"**, should be used when your form does not cause any changes in server-side data, for example when making a database request. The form data from **METHOD = "get"** is appended to the end of the URL. Because of this, the amount of data submitted using this **METHOD** is limited to 4K. Also be aware that **METHOD = "get"** is limited to standard characters, and cannot submit any special characters.

- A Web server is a machine that runs a software package such as Apache or IIS; servers are designed to handle browser requests. When a user uses a browser to request a page or file somewhere on the server, the server processes this request and returns an answer to the browser.

- The **ACTION** attribute in the **FORM** tag is the path to a script that processes the form data.

- The input element is common in forms, and always requires the **TYPE** attribute. Two other attributes are **NAME**, which provides a unique identification for the **INPUT**, and **VALUE**, which indicates the value that the **INPUT** element sends to the server upon submission.

- The input **TYPE="text"** inserts a one-line text bar into the form. The value of this **INPUT** element and the information that the server sends to you from this **INPUT** is the text that the user types into the bar. The **SIZE** attribute determines the width of the text input, measured in characters. You can also set a maximum number of characters that the text input will accept by inserting the **MAXLENGTH="***length***"** attribute.

- You must make sure to include a textual identifier (in this case, "**Name:**") adjacent to the **INPUT** element to indicate the function of the element.

- The **TYPE="submit" INPUT** element places a button in the form that submits data to the server when clicked. The **VALUE** attribute of the **submit** input changes the text displayed on the button.

- The **TYPE="reset"** input element places a button on the form that, when clicked, will clear all entries the user has entered into the form.

- The **TEXTAREA** element inserts a box into the form. You specify the size of the box (which is scrollable) inside the opening **<TEXTAREA>** tag with the **ROWS** attribute and the **COLS** attribute.

- Data entered in a **TYPE="password"** input appears on the screen as asterisks. The password is used for submitting sensitive information that the user would not want others to be able to read. It is just the browser that displays asterisks—the real form data is still submitted to the server.

- Every **INPUT** element with **TYPE="checkbox"** creates a new checkbox in the form. Checkboxes can be used individually or in groups. Each checkbox in a group should have the same **NAME** (in this case, **NAME="things"**).

- Inserted into forms by means of the **INPUT** attribute **TYPE="radio"**, radio buttons are different from checkboxes in that only one in the group may be selected at any time. All of the **NAME** attributes of a group of radio inputs must be the same and all of the **VALUE** attributes different.

- Insert the attribute **CHECKED** to indicate which radio button you would like selected initially.

- The **SELECT** element places a selectable list of items inside your form. To add an item to the list, insert an **OPTION** element in the **<SELECT>...</SELECT>** area and type what you want the list item to display on the same line. You can change the number of list options visible at one time by including the **SIZE="***size***"** attribute inside the **<SELECT>** tag. Use this attribute if you prefer an expanded version of the list to the one-line expandable list.

- A location on a page is marked by including a **NAME** attribute in an **A** element. Clicking on this hyperlink in a browser would scroll the browser window to that point on the page.

TERMINOLOGY

MAXLENGTH="#"
<!DOCTYPE...>
<META> Tag
<OPTION>
ACTION attribute in **FORM** element
BORDER property of **TABLE** element
cell of a table
CELLSPACING property of **TABLE** element
CGI script
CHECKED
COLGROUP element
COLS attribute of **TABLE** element
COLSPAN attribute of **TD** element
column of a table
data cell

DATAFIELD property of **TD** element
environment variable
form
header cell
indenting lists
INPUT element (**<INPUT>...</INPUT>**)
INPUT Type="button"
INPUT Type="checkbox"
INPUT Type="password"
INPUT Type="radio"
INPUT Type="reset"
INPUT Type="submit"
INPUT Type="text"
INPUT Type="textarea"
internal linking

list
METHOD="get"
METHOD="post"
NAME attribute in INPUT element
NAME="recipient" in INPUT element
NAME="redirect" in INPUT element
NAME="subject" in INPUT element
nested lists
OL (ordered list) element (<OL>...</OL>)
row of a table
ROWSPAN attribute of TD element
SCROLLING attribute in FRAME

SELECT element (<SELECT>...</SELECT>)
SIZE attribute in SELECT
table
TABLE element (<TABLE>...</TABLE>)
TBODY
TD (table data) element (<TD>...</TD>)
text-based browser
TH (header cell) element (<TH>...</TH>)
THEAD element (<THEAD>...</THEAD>)
TR (table row) element (<TR>...</TR>)
VALUE attribute of INPUT element
Web server

SELF-REVIEW EXERCISES

D.1   State whether the following are *true* or *false*. If *false*, explain why.
   a) The width of all data cells in a table must be the same.
   b) The **THEAD** element is mandatory in a **TABLE**.

D.2   Fill in the blanks in each of the following statements.
   a) The _____ attribute in an **INPUT** element inserts a button that, when clicked, will clear the contents of the form.
   b) The _____ element inserts a new item in a list.

D.3   Write HTML tags to accomplish the following.
   a) Insert an ordered list that will have numbering by lowercase Roman numerals.
   b) Insert a scrollable list (in a form) that will always display four entries of the list.

ANSWERS TO SELF-REVIEW EXERCISES

D.1   a) False. You can specify the width of any column either in pixels or as a percentage of the total width of the table. b) False. The **THEAD** element is used only for formatting purposes and is optional (but it is recommended that you include it).

D.2   a) TYPE = "reset". b) LI.

D.3   a) <OL TYPE = "i">...</OL>. b) <SELECT SIZE = "4">...</SELECT>.

EXERCISES

D.4   Categorize each of the following as an element or an attribute:
   a) SIZE
   b) OL
   c) LI
   d) CAPTION
   e) SELECT
   f) TYPE

D.5   Write the HTML code that produces the following Web page. The width of the table is 400 pixels and the border is one pixel wide. The header is enclosed in an H2 element.

Average Grades by Year - Microsoft Internet Explorer

File Edit View Favorites Tools Help

Back   Forward   Stop   Refresh   Home   Search   Favorites   History

Address C:\books\2000\ebecmC\ebecmC_examples\appD\Exercises\06.htm

Average Grades by Year

Report Card

	1997	1998	1999
History	B+	B	A-
English	C+	B-	C
Math	A-	A	A+

Done   My Computer

Introduction to HTML, ASP, XML and JavaScript Syntax

Objectives

- To become familiar with basic Active Server Pages (ASP) syntax.
- To become familiar with the Extensible Markup Language (XML) and the Extensible Stylesheet Language (XSL).
- To become familiar with JavaScript syntax.

Outline

E.1   Introduction
E.2   Introduction to HTML
E.3   Introduction to ASP
E.4   Introduction to XML
E.5   Introduction to JavaScript

E.1 Introduction

In Appendix B, we introduced the technologies used by the **Bug2Bug.com** bookstore. In this appendix, we provide more in-depth technology discussions. Specifically, we highlight key portions of code taken from the actual Web documents used in the case study. Each technology is carefully presented by showing a small amount of code with screen captures. This allows the reader to become comfortable with the look and feel of these technologies. In Appendices F and G, we present the complete code listings with detailed discussions. This technology-preview appendix also provides features that contain additional information about a given technology.

E.2 Introduction to HTML

After studying Appendices C and D, the reader should be comfortable with HTML, which comprises the bulk of this case study. In this section, we provide a brief discussion of HTML in the context of **Bug2Bug.com**'s Web site.

The **Enter** button (Fig. E.1) is created using HTML **form** and **input** tags. The attributes **method** (**post**) and **action** (**books.asp**) on line 3 indicate that when this form is submitted to the server, **books.asp** is requested. Line 4 creates an **input** element of type **submit** (a button). The **name** of this button is **"enterButton"** and the **value** displayed on the button is **"Enter"**.

E.3 Introduction to ASP

In Appendix B, we briefly introduced Active Server Pages (ASP)—a technology for interacting with the middle and bottom tiers. In this section, we show a portion of ASP code that generates the book list (Fig. E.2). The HTML document created by **books.asp** contains a list of books available for purchase. Notice the familiar HTML look and feel. We use VB-Script in our ASP pages to retrieve information such as book title, price and ISBN number from the Access database and place the data in the HTML sent to the client.

```
1   <!-- The following form creates a button that is -->
2   <!-- used to send the user to books.asp          -->
3   <form method = "post" action = "books.asp">
4      <input type = "submit" name = "enterButton" value = "Enter">
5   </form>
```

Fig. E.1   **Enter** button of **welcome.html**.

Fig. E.1   **Enter** button of `welcome.html`.

```
1   <!-- Create a link to each page that describes -->
2   <!-- the book                                   -->
3   <a href = "book<% =data( "productid" ) %>.asp">
4       <font color = "green" size = "6">
5           <% =data( "title" ) %>
6       </font>
7   </a>
```

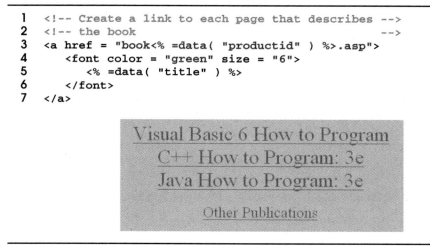

Fig. E.2   List of available books from `books.asp`.

ASP page **viewCart.asp** (Fig. E.3) retrieves the contents of the shopping cart from a cookie placed on the client and dynamically inserts those values into HTML elements. The HTML is sent to the browser where it is rendered (see the screen capture in Fig. E.3). An Active Server Page is able to respond to a client's request using the **Response** object (line 1). In this case, **write** is called to write HTML mark up to the client. Notice the use of the **Request** object (line 1) which contains information sent as part of the request to the server. In this particular case, the cookie which contains the shopping cart contents is retrieved. We will discuss these objects and this code in greater detail in Appendix G.

Figure E.3 uses the data from the database to dynamically create hyperlinks. The figure also introduces an important new topic—ActiveX Data Objects (ADO). We use ADO to get the current **productID** number and title from a Microsoft Access database. The **productID** number is used to create a specific URL for that book and the title becomes that link's text. Lines 1 and 2 are HTML comments that are part of the HTML sent to the client. Line 3 uses an **a** element to create an anchor and line 4 uses a **font** element to set the font. However, some features are syntactically different than what was presented in Appendices C and D. For example, the *scripting delimiters* (**<%** and **%>**) are used to specify blocks of ASP code. Anything enclosed in these delimiters is executed on the Web server—the client never sees these statements. The code segments **=data("productid")** and **=data("title")** take the information retrieved from the database and write it to the client. This block of code is executed once for each individual link shown in Fig. E.5. The specifics of this are discussed in greater detail in Appendix G.

VBScript is the most common scripting language used with ASP. For more information on VBScript please see the "Introduction to VBScript" feature.

```
1   Call Response.write( Request.Cookies( "shoppingCart" ) _
2      ( "book" & counter ) & "  QTY: " & quantity & "  " _
3      & formatCurrency( CCur( quantity * price ) ) _
4      & "<br/><br/>" )
5   total = CInt( total ) + CInt( quantity * price )
```

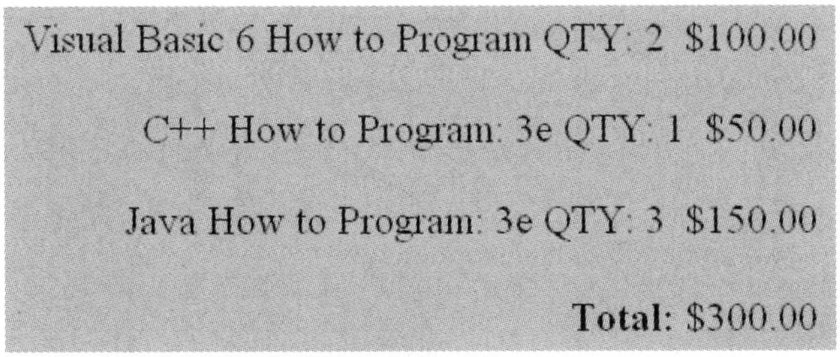

Visual Basic 6 How to Program QTY: 2 $100.00

C++ How to Program: 3e QTY: 1 $50.00

Java How to Program: 3e QTY: 3 $150.00

Total: $300.00

Fig. E.3   View of shopping cart contents from **viewCart.asp**.

Introduction to VBScript

Visual Basic Script (VBScript) is a subset of Microsoft Visual Basic® used in *server-side documents* with Microsoft Web servers to create *Active Server Pages (ASP)*—a technology that allows a *server-side script* to create dynamic content that is sent to the client's browser. Although other scripting languages can be used, VBScript is the most popular language for ASP.

VBScript can be used to manipulate strings—a series of characters. The *ampersand*, **&**, operator is used for string concatenation as follows:

```
s1 = "Pro"
s2 = "gram"
s3 = s1 & s2
```

The ampersand is more formally called the *string concatenation operator*. The above statements would concatenate (or join) **s2** (**"gram"**) to the end of **s1** (**"Pro"**) to create an entirely new string, **s3**, containing **"Program"**. Note that neither **s1** nor **s2** is modified.

Data Types and Control Structures
VBScript has only one data type, *variant*—that is capable of storing different kinds of data (e.g., strings, integers, etc.). The data types (or *variant subtypes*) a variant stores are listed in Fig. E.4. VBScript interprets a variant in a manner that is suitable to the type of data it contains. For example, if a variant contains numeric information, it will be treated as a number; if it contains string information, it will be treated as a string.

Introduction to VBScript (Cont.)	
Subtype	Range/Description
Boolean	**True** or **False**
Currency	–922337203685477.5808 to 922337203685477.5807
Empty	Uninitialized. This value is 0 for numeric types (e.g., double), **False** for booleans and the empty string (i.e., **""**) for strings.
Integer	–32768 to 32767
String	0 to ~2000000000 characters.

Fig. E.4   Some VBScript variant subtypes.

Some VBScript variant subtypes

A variable is a location in the computer's memory where a value can be stored for use by a program. Variable names cannot be keywords (e.g., **Dim**, **Call**) and must begin with a letter. The maximum length of a variable name is 255 characters containing only letters, digits (0-9) and underscores. Variables can be declared simply by using their name in the VBScript code. The optional **Option Explicit** statement is often used to force all variables to be declared before they are used. It is a good practice to use **Option Explicit** to avoid subtle errors.

Control structures are used to dictate the path taken in executing the code. VBScript provides control structures such as **If/Then/End If**, **If/Then/Else/End If** and **While/Wend** or **Do While/Loop** for controlling program execution. Syntactically, every VBScript control structure terminates with one or more keywords (e.g., **End If**, **Loop**, etc.).

VBScript Functions

VBScript's predefined functions simplify the programmer's job by providing powerful features. Some VBScript functions are listed in Fig. E.5.

Line-Continuation Character

Often, when writing code, long statements need to be separated into multiple lines to maintain clarity. The *underscore character*, _, is VBScript's *line-continuation character*. A statement cannot extend beyond the current line without using this character. A statement may use as many line-continuation characters as necessary.

String Manipulation

One of VBScript's most powerful features is its string-manipulation functions. VBScript strings are case sensitive (i.e., uppercase letters are considered to be different characters than their lowercase equivalents). The first character in a string has index 1 (as opposed to arrays, discussed in Appendix G, which begin at index 0). [*Note*: Almost all VBScript string-manipulation functions do not modify their string argument(s); rather, they return new strings containing the results.]

Introduction to VBScript (Cont.)	
Function	**Description**
`Right`	Returns a string containing characters from the right side of a string argument. For example, the call `Right("Web", 2)` returns "eb."
`Split`	Returns an array containing substrings. The default delimiter for `Split` is a space character. For example, the call `Split("I met a traveler")` returns an array containing elements "`I`", "`met`", "`a`" and "`traveler`" and `Split("red,white,and blue", ",")` returns an array containing elements "`red`", "`white`" and "`and blue`."
`FormatCurrency`	Formats a value as a currency string. For example, the call `FormatCurrency("-1234.789")` returns "`($1,234.79)`" and the call `FormatCurrency(123456.789)` returns "`$123,456.79`." Note the rounding to the right of the decimal place.

Fig. E.5   Some VBScript functions.

E.4 Introduction to XML

The *Extensible Markup Language (XML)* is a technology for structuring data. XML gives document authors the ability to create their own markup. This is quite different from the set of markup tags provided by HTML. Figure E.6 shows the markup created by **Bug2Bug.com** to describe their list of back ordered books. Notice that the elements in this document are completely different from HTML introduced in Appendices C and D. As mentioned in Appendix B, XML documents simply mark up data and are not intended to be directly rendered. Figure E.7 shows the Extensible Stylesheet Language (XSL) document that transforms (i.e., converts) the XML to HTML. Notice that this document contains HTML comments and elements. Other parts are distinctly non-HTML. This stylesheet takes the XML of Fig. E.6 and formats it as an HTML table. We will discuss the specifics of this in Appendix G.

```
1   <?xml:stylesheet type = "text/xsl" href = "books.xsl"?>
2
3   <backOrder>
4
5      <book>
6         <title>XML How to Program</title>
7         <authors>Deitel, Deitel, Nieto, Lin &amp; Sadhu</authors>
8      </book>
9
10     <book>
11        <title>Python How to Program</title>
```

Fig. E.6   Listing of **backOrder.xml** (part 1 of 2)

```
12        <authors>Deitel, Deitel &amp; Wiedermann</authors>
13     </book>
14
15     <book>
16        <title>C# How to Program</title>
17        <authors>Deitel &amp; Deitel</authors>
18     </book>
19
20  </backOrder>
```

Fig. E.6   Listing of **backOrder.xml** (part 2 of 2)

```
1   <!-- select each book element -->
2   <xsl:for-each select = "backOrder/book">
3
4      <!-- select each book's title and authors value -->
5      <tr>
6         <td>
7            <font size = "5">
8               <xsl:value-of select = "title"/>
9            </font>
10        </td>
11
12        <td>
13           <font size = "5">
14              <xsl:value-of select = "authors"/>
15           </font>
16        </td>
17     </tr>
18
19  </xsl:for-each>
```

Title	Authors
XML How to Program	Deitel, Deitel, Nieto, Lin & Sadhu
Python How to Program	Deitel, Deitel & Wiedermann
C# How to Program	Deitel & Deitel

Fig. E.7   HTML table created by values from **backOrder.xml**.

E.5 Introduction to JavaScript

In this section, we discuss the *JavaScript scripting language,* which enables programmers to write programs that enhance the functionality and appearance of Web pages. The feature, "A JavaScript Program: Printing a Line of Text in a Web Page," introduces a basic Java-Script program. The section then continues with a discussion of the **orders.html** document, which uses JavaScript to validate the contents of an HTML form submitted from the client Web browser.

A JavaScript Program: Printing a Line of Text in a Web Page

JavaScript is a programming language that adds interactivity to Web pages. It uses notations that may appear strange to non-programmers. We begin by considering a simple *script* (or *program*) that displays the line of text "**Welcome to JavaScript Programming!**" in the body of an HTML document. Internet Explorer contains a built in *JavaScript interpreter,* which executes (or interprets) the commands in the JavaScript code. The script and its output are shown in Fig. E.8.

This program illustrates several important JavaScript features. Lines 11 and 12 do the "real work" of the script, namely displaying the text **Welcome to JavaScript Programming!** in the Web page. Let us consider each line in order.

The **DOCTYPE** element in lines 1 and 2 indicates that the document type is an HTML 4.0 document. Line 4

```
<!-- JavaScript Example -->
```

```
1   <!DOCTYPE html PUBLIC
2       "-//W3C//DTD HTML 4.0 Transitional//EN">
3
4   <!-- JavaScript Example -->
5
6   <HTML>
7   <HEAD>
8   <TITLE>A First Program in JavaScript</TITLE>
9
10  <SCRIPT LANGUAGE = "JavaScript">
11    document.writeln(
12       "<H1>Welcome to JavaScript Programming!</H1>" );
13  </SCRIPT>
14
15  </HEAD><BODY></BODY>
16  </HTML>
```

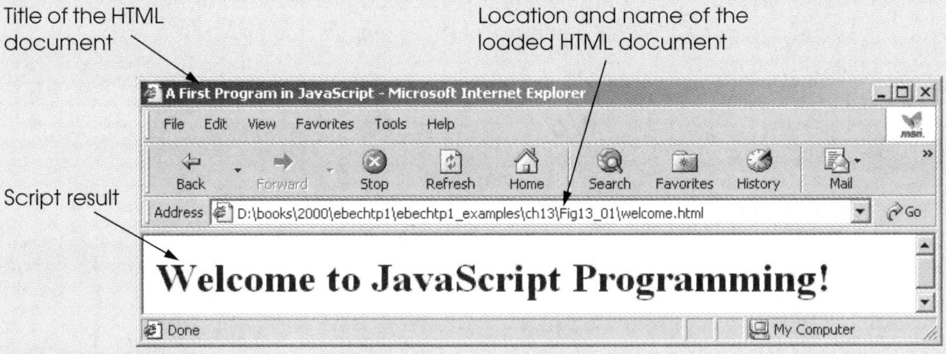

Fig. E.8   A first program in JavaScript.

A JavaScript Program: Printing a Line of Text in a Web Page (Cont.)

is an HTML comment describing this document. Recall that programmers insert HTML comments to document or describe the purpose of parts of an HTML document and to improve the readability of the code. Comments also help other people read and understand your HTML documents.

Lines 3 and 5 are simply blank lines. Blank lines and space characters are often used throughout HTML documents and scripts to make them easier to read. Blank lines, space characters and tab characters are known as *whitespace* (space characters and tabs are known specifically as *whitespace characters*). Such characters are generally ignored by the browser. In many cases, such characters are used for readability and clarity. The spacing displayed by a browser in a Web page is determined by the HTML elements used to format the page. Line 10

```
<SCRIPT LANGUAGE = "JavaScript">
```

uses the ***<SCRIPT>*** tag to indicate to the browser that the text that follows is part of a script. The ***LANGUAGE*** attribute specifies the *scripting language* used in the script—in this case, **JavaScript**.

Lines 11 and 12

```
document.writeln(
    "<H1>Welcome to JavaScript Programming!</H1>" );
```

instruct the browser's JavaScript interpreter to display in the Web page the *string* of characters contained between the *double quotation (") marks*.

Lines 11 and 12 use the browser's ***document*** *object,* which represents the HTML document currently being displayed in the browser. The **document** object allows a script programmer to specify HTML text to be displayed in the HTML document.

In the preceding statement, we call the **document** object's ***writeln*** *method* to write a line of HTML text in the HTML document being displayed. The parentheses following the method name **writeln** contain the *arguments* that the method requires to perform its task (or its action). Method **writeln** instructs the browser to display the argument string. If the string contains HTML elements, the browser interprets these elements and renders them on the screen.

Line 13

```
</SCRIPT>
```

indicates the end of the script.

The check out page, **order.html**, is an HTML document that includes an HTML form where the user's name, address and credit card information are entered for billing and shipping purposes. In the HTML markup for this page, JavaScript is used to validate the data the user enters (e.g., to ensure the user enters a correct state abbreviation). If the user enters incorrect input into a field and then tries to check out by clicking the **Submit** button, the script is run and an *alert* box opens to notify the user of the error (Fig. E.9).

```
1   // Create the function checkState to validate the input of
2   // the form
3   function checkState( form )
4   {
5      // Declare the variable string and set it equal to the
6      // input in the state text box
7      var string = form.state.value;
8
9      // The regular expression abbr lists all possible values for
10     // the state field
11     var abbr = new RegExp( "AL|AK|AZ|AR|CA|CO|CT|DE|FL|GA|" +
12                            "HI|ID|IL|IN|IA|KS|KY|LA|ME|MD|" +
13                            "MA|MI|MN|MS|MO|MT|NB|NV|NH|NJ|" +
14                            "NM|NY|NC|ND|OH|OK|OR|PA|RI|SC|" +
15                            "SD|TN|TX|UT|VT|VA|WA|WV|WI|WY",
16                            "i" );
17
18     // Declare the variable check and set it equal to the input
19     // in the last name text box
20     var check = form.lastname.value;
21
22     // Check to see if the Last name field is empty
23     if ( check == "" ) {
24        alert( "Please complete all fields." );
25        return false;
26     }
27
28     // Check to see if the state value is empty
29     if ( form.state.value == "" ) {
30        alert( "Please enter your state's abbreviation." );
31        return false;
32     }
33
34     // Check to see if the value entered into the state field
35     // matches one of the acceptable values
36     if ( abbr.test( string ) ) {
37        form.state.value = string.toUpperCase();
38        location.href = "process.asp";
39        return false;
40     }
41
42     // Alert the user that the input is not an acceptable value
43     alert( "" + string + "
44        is not a correct US State abbreviation" );
45        form.state.select();
46        return false;
47  }
```

Fig. E.9   Validation script and output windows from **order.html** (part 1 of 2).

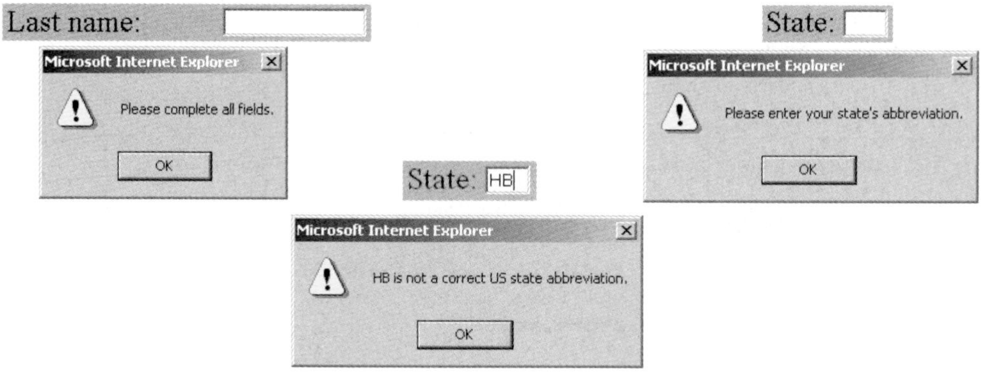

Fig. E.9   Validation script and output windows from **order.html** (part 2 of 2).

SUMMARY

- Active Server Pages (ASP) interact with the other two tiers.
- An Active Server Page is able to respond to a client's request using the **Response** object.
- The **Request** object contains information sent as part of the request to the server.
- Visual Basic Script (VBScript) is a subset of Microsoft Visual Basic® used in server-side documents to create Active Server Pages (ASP)—a technology that allows a server-side script to create dynamic content that is sent to the client's browser.
- Although other scripting languages can be used, VBScript is the most popular language for ASP.
- VBScript can be used to manipulate series of characters called strings.
- The ampersand, **&**, operator is used for string concatenation.
- VBScript has only one data type, variant—that is capable of storing different kinds of data (e.g., strings, integers, etc.).
- A variable is a location in the computer's memory where a value can be stored for use by a program.
- Variable names cannot be keywords (e.g., **Dim**, **Call**) and must begin with a letter.
- The maximum length of a variable name is 255 characters containing only letters, digits (0-9) and underscores.
- Variables can be declared simply by using their name in the VBScript code.
- The optional **Option Explicit** statement is often used to force all variables to be declared before they are used.
- Control structures are used to dictate the path taken in executing the code.
- The underscore character, _, is VBScript's line-continuation character.
- The first character in a string has index 1 (as opposed to arrays, which begin at index 0).
- The scripting delimiters (**<%** and **%>**) are used to specify blocks of ASP code.
- Anything enclosed in these delimiters is executed on the Web server—the client never sees these statements.
- The Extensible Markup Language (XML) is a technology for structuring data.
- XML gives document authors the ability to create their own markup.

- JavaScript is a programming language that adds interactivity to Web pages.
- Blank lines and space characters are often used throughout HTML documents and scripts to make them easier to read.
- Blank lines, space characters and tab characters are known as whitespace (space characters and tabs are known specifically as whitespace characters).
- The **LANGUAGE** attribute specifies the scripting language used in the script.
- The **document** object allows a script programmer to specify HTML text to be displayed in the HTML document.
- Method **writeln** instructs the browser to display the argument string.

TERMINOLOGY

Active Server Pages (ASP)
ActiveX Data Object (ADO)
ampersand
Call
client-side scripting
cookie
data type
Dim
Do While/Loop
DOCTYPE element
document object
dynamic content
End If
Extensible Markup Language (XML)
Extensible Stylesheet Language (XSL)
HTML comment
If/Then/Else/End If
If/Then/End If
integer
JavaScript interpreter

LANGUAGE attribute of **SCRIPT** element
line continuation character
Loop
method arguments
Microsoft Visual Basic
Microsoft Web servers
Option Explicit
program
script
scripting delimiters
scripting language
server-side scripting
Split
string
variant
variant subtypes
Visual Basic Script (VBScript)
While/Wend or **Do While/Loop**
whitespace
writeln method

The Client Tier:
The User Interface

Objectives

- To understand the role of the client tier in a three-tier architecture.
- To use the Hypertext Markup Language (HTML) on the client tier.
- To use the Extensible Markup Language (XML) and Extensible Stylesheet Language (XSL) on the client tier.
- To see dynamically generated HTML sent to the client tier by the middle tier.

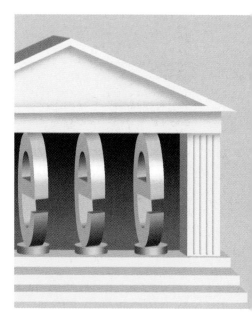

Outline

F.1   The Client Tier

F.2   HTML

F.3   XML and XSL

Self Review Exercises • Answers to Self Review Exercises

F.1 The Client Tier

This appendix discusses the **Bug2Bug.com** Web site's client tier, which provides the user interface for the three-tier application. Microsoft Internet Explorer 5 is used to render the HTML documents sent to the client. **Bug2Bug.com** uses HTML, XML and XSL in this tier. In this appendix and the next, we present complete code listings for each **Bug2Bug.com** Web document. Each code listing is followed by a detailed discussion and one or more screen captures illustrating the Web document. Each code listing is followed by a detailed inline discussion of the code. The documents discussed in this appendix are highlighted in Fig. F.1.

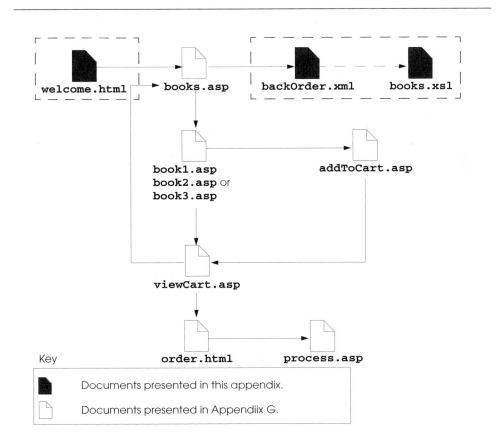

Fig. F.1   Bug2Bug.com documents presented in this appendix.

F.2 HTML

The **welcome.html** (Fig. F.2) document is a simple HTML page that includes tags to format text and link to **books.asp**, which displays a list of books available for purchase. This document is **Bug2Bug.com**'s home page. We expect that most readers will be comfortable with the HTML presented in this section after having studied Appendices C and D.

```
1   <!-- Fig. F.2: welcome.html -->
2
3   <!DOCTYPE HTML PUBLIC "-//W3C//DTD HTML 4.01//EN"
4            "http://www.w3.org/TR/html4/strict.dtd">
5
6   <html>
7   <head>
8
9      <!-- The text placed between the title tag is what    -->
10     <!-- is displayed in the title bar at the top          -->
11     <!-- of the browser                                    -->
12     <title>Shopping Cart Case Study</title>
13  </head>
14
15  <!-- The bgcolor attribute sets the background color -->
16  <!-- of the page.                                    -->
17  <body bgcolor = "lightskyblue">
18
19     <!-- Everything placed between the center tags is -->
20     <!-- justified in the middle of the page, or in   -->
21     <!-- some cases, the cell of a table.             -->
22     <center>
23
24     <!-- Setting the attributes of the font tag changes -->
25     <!-- the way the text between the font tags is       -->
26     <!-- rendered by the browser.  The face attribute   -->
27     <!-- sets the style of font                          -->
28     <font size = "10" color = "blue" face = "helvetica">
29          Bug2Bug.com
30     </font>
31
32     <!-- The horizontal (hr) rule tag places a -->
33     <!-- line across the screen                -->
34     <hr>
35
36     <!-- The break (br) tag is the equivalent -->
37     <!-- of a return character                -->
38     <br/><br/><br/>
39
40     <font size = "10" color = "red" face = "arial">
41
42        <!-- The italic (em) tag italicizes -->
43        <!-- the font between it             -->
44        <em>Deitel & Associates, Inc.</em><br/>
45     </font>
```

Fig. F.2   Listing for **welcome.html** (part 1 of 2).

```
46
47      <font size = "8" color = "green">
48         Shopping Cart Case Study
49      </font>
50
51      <br/><br/><br/>
52
53      <font size = "5" face = "arial">
54         Click here to enter the store.
55      </font>
56
57      <!-- The following form creates a button that is -->
58      <!-- used to send the user to books.asp        -->
59      <form method = "post" action = "books.asp">
60         <input type = "submit" name = "enterButton" value = "Enter">
61      </form>
62
63      </center>
64
65   </body>
66
67   </html>
```

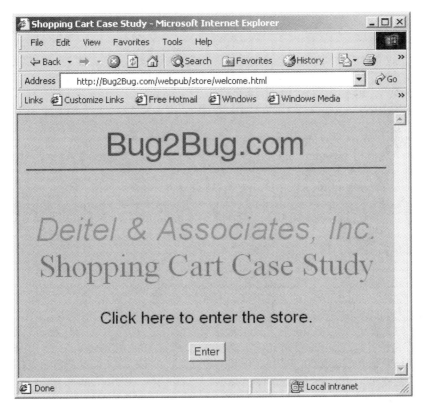

Fig. F.2   Listing for **welcome.html** (part 2 of 2).

Lines 3 and 4

```
<!DOCTYPE HTML PUBLIC "-//W3C//DTD HTML 4.01//EN"
    "http://www.w3.org/TR/html4/strict.dtd">
```

are the document's required **DOCTYPE** declaration, which specifies the version of HTML used by the document.

Lines 7–13

```
<head>

    <!-- The text placed between the title tags is what   -->
    <!-- is displayed in the title bar at the top          -->
    <!-- of the browser                                    -->
    <title>Shopping Cart Case Study</title>
</head>
```

are the document's required **head** section, which describes the document. The most common elements placed in the **head** section are the **title** tag and any scripts (e.g., JavaScript, VBScript, etc.) used by the document.

Line 17

```
<body bgcolor = "lightskyblue">
```

sets the document's background color. Attribute **bgcolor** is assigned a preset color name, of which there are over 100 (i.e., **red**, **blue**, etc.). If the **bgcolor** attribute is absent, the background of the page is set to white.

The **center** tag starts on line 22. Everything between the start tag and end tag is centered horizontally, but not vertically in the browser window. Most elements, when rendered, are *left justified* on the screen by default.

Lines 28–55 format the text (e.g., **Bug2Bug.com** and **Deitel & Associates, Inc.**, etc.) that is displayed at the top of the page. The text is formatted using the **font** tag and its **color**, **size** and **face** attributes. The **face** attribute specifies the font name (e.g., **helvetica**). The other tags used that format text are the **strong** tag, which applies a bold style and the **emphasis** (**<em>**) tag, which applies an italic style.

On line 34, the horizontal rule tag places a horizontal line across the browser window. By default, the length of the line is the width of the browser window.

The remaining elements mark up the **Enter** button (lines 59–61). When clicked, the document **books.asp** is requested. The attribute **method** is assigned a value of **post**, which indicates that this document communicates with the Web server using an HTTP post—a popular way of encoding information sent to the server. Attribute **action** specifies the resource (e.g., document, image, etc.) that is requested when the form is **post**ed to the Web server. The name of the resource requested (i.e., **books.asp**) is part of this information that is encoded and sent to the server. The server is then able to retrieve this resource and send it to the client. The **input** tag (line 60), within the **form** tags, is what is displayed on the screen. Setting attribute **type** to **submit** creates a button. The **name** attribute specifies the button name. The **value** attribute specifies the text that the button displays to the user.

Active Server Pages often generate HTML that is sent to the client for rendering. ASP **books.asp** generates an HTML document containing a list of books. Figure F.3 shows the HTML document sent to the browser by **books.asp**. [*Note:* We have edited the code for presentation purposes.] We will discuss the ASP **books.asp** in Appendix G.

```
1    <!-- Fig. F.3: booksOutput.html>
2
3    <!DOCTYPE HTML PUBLIC
4       "-//W3C//DTD HTML 4.0 Transitional//EN">
5
6    <html>
7       <head>
8
9          <!-- Book List is placed in the title bar -->
10         <!-- of the browser                        -->
11         <title>Book List</title>
12      </head>
13
14      <!-- The bgcolor attribute changes the background -->
15      <!-- color of the page                            -->
16      <body bgcolor = "lightskyblue">
17
18      <center>
19
20      <!-- Change the font size and the style -->
21      <!-- (face attribute)                   -->
22      <font size = "8" face = "arial">
23         Available Books
24      </font>
25
26      <!-- Place a horizontal line across the screen -->
27      <hr>
28
29      <!-- Use the font tag to change the size and the -->
30      <!-- strong tag to make the text bold            -->
31      <font size = "4"><strong>To view available titles for a
32         technology select a link from this list:</strong></font>
33
34      <br/><br/><br/>
35
36         <!-- Create a link to each page that describes -->
37         <!-- the book                                  -->
38         <a href = "book1.asp">
39            <font color = "green" size = "6">
40               Visual Basic 6 How to Program
41            </font>
42         </a>
43
44      <br/>
45
46         <!-- Create a link to each page that describes -->
47         <!-- the book                                  -->
```

Fig. F.3   HTML output generated by **books.asp** (part 1 of 2).

```
48           <a href = "book2.asp">
49              <font color = "green" size = "6">
50                 C++ How to Program: 3e
51              </font>
52           </a>
53
54        <br/>
55
56           <!-- Create a link to each page that describes -->
57           <!-- the book                                    -->
58           <a href = "book3.asp">
59              <font color = "green" size = "6">
60                 Java How to Program: 3e
61              </font>
62           </a>
63
64        <br/><br/>
65
66           <!-- Create a link to backOrder.xml-->
67           <a href = "backOrder.xml">
68              <font color = "green" size = "5">
69                 Other Publications
70              </font>
71           </a>
72
73        </center>
74
75     </body>
76
77     </html>
```

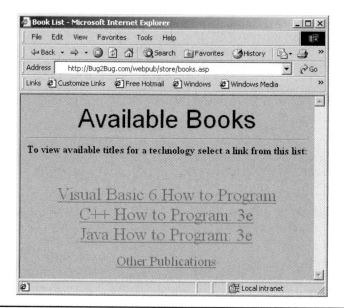

Fig. F.3   HTML output generated by **books.asp** (part 2 of 2).

Lines 1–32 use HTML elements to format the heading of the page. Lines 36–42

```
<!-- Create a link to each page that describes -->
<!-- the book                                   -->
    <a href = "book1.asp">
        <font color = "green" size = "6">
            Visual Basic How to Program
        </font>
    </a>
```

Lines 46–52

```
<!-- Create a link to each page that describes -->
<!-- the book                                   -->
    <a href = "book2.asp">
        <font color = "green" size = "6">
            C++ How to Program: 3e
        </font>
    </a>
```

and lines 56–62

```
<!-- Create a link to each page that describes -->
<!-- the book                                   -->
    <a href = "book3.asp">
        <font color = "green" size = "6">
            Java How to Program: 3e
        </font>
    </a>
```

create hyperlinks to each book's information page. Recall that in Appendix E, we provided the lines

```
<!-- Create a link to each page that describes -->
<!-- the book                                   -->
<a href = "book<% =data( "productid" ) %>.asp">
    <font color = "green" size = "6">
        <% =data( "title" ) %>
    </font>
</a>
```

from **books.asp**. The scripting code enclosed in the delimiters (**<%** and **%>**) is executed and the results of **=data("productID")** and **=data("title")** replace **<% =data("productID") %>** and **<% =data("title") %>**. The contents of scripting delimiters are always executed on the server.

F.3 XML and XSL

Like many companies, **Bug2Bug.com** is beginning to use XML on its Web site. XML is a complex technology. For simplicity, **Bug2Bug.com** is using it to mark up books that are on back order (i.e., currently not available). The XML is rendered using an XSL stylesheet. XML document **backOrder.xml** (Fig. F.4) contains the list of back ordered books. The XSL stylesheet **books.xsl** (Fig. F.5) transforms the XML to HTML. Recall that XML documents are not intended to be directly rendered. A complimentary technology, such as

XSL, converts the XML to another format for rendering. Internet Explorer 5 has built in capabilities to process XSL documents.

Line 1 of the XML document

```
<?xml version = "1.0"?>
```

specifies the **version** of XML to which the document conforms.

Because XML documents do not include any formatting information, an additional technology such as XSL is needed to format the document. To specify the XSL document that formats the XML document, a special instruction (line 8)—called a *processing instruction*—must be inserted into the XML document. Line 8

```
<?xml:stylesheet type = "text/xsl" href = "books.xsl"?>
```

references the stylesheet (**books.xsl**). This processing instruction is executed by Internet Explorer 5—which uses the value of **type** to determine what to do with the resource assigned to **href**. Because **text/xsl** is specified as the **type**, Internet Explorer 5 can processes **books.xsl** as an XSL document.

The element **backOrder** (line 10) is the *root element* of **backOrder.xml**. Every XML document must contain a minimum of one element—the root element.

```
1   <?xml version = "1.0"?>
2
3   <!-- Fig. F.4 : backOrder.xml                              -->
4   <!-- XML document that contains a list of books that       -->
5   <!-- are currently on back order.                          -->
6
7   <!-- Processing instruction that references an XSL document -->
8   <?xml:stylesheet type = "text/xsl" href = "books.xsl"?>
9
10  <backOrder>
11
12     <book>
13        <title>XML How to Program</title>
14        <authors>Deitel, Deitel, Nieto, Lin &amp; Sadhu</authors>
15     </book>
16
17     <book>
18        <title>Python How to Program</title>
19        <authors>Deitel, Deitel &amp; Wiedermann</authors>
20     </book>
21
22     <book>
23        <title>C# How to Program</title>
24        <authors>Deitel &amp; Deitel</authors>
25     </book>
26
27  </backOrder>
```

Fig. F.4   Listing for **backOrder.xml**.

Element **book** (lines 12, 17 and 22) is called a *container element* because it contains other elements such as **title** and **authors**. The **title** element contains the text that describes the book's title and the **authors** element contains the text that describes the book's authors.

When marking up data as XML, certain characters such as ampersand (**&**), less than (**<**), greater than (**>**), etc., cannot be written as is. This is because XML syntax uses these characters for other purposes, such as marking up the start and end of tags. Occasionally, the document author needs to use these characters in their markup. For example, each book's author list contains ampersands. XML provides a special notations—called *entity references*—for representing ampersands, less-than symbols, etc. Entity references are preceded by an ampersand and terminated with a semicolon. Between the ampersand and semicolon is a series of predefined characters that represent a given symbol. In this case, **amp** specifies an ampersand.

Figure F.5 shows the listing for **books.xsl**, a XSL stylesheet that transforms an XML document into HTML. Line 2

```
<xsl:stylesheet xmlns:xsl = "http://www.w3.org/TR/WD-xsl">
```

starts the ***stylesheet*** *element*, which is the root element for this XSL document. Prefix **xsl** is defined using attribute **xmlns**. This prefix identifies XSL elements. The value assigned to **xmlns:xsl** is used by Internet Explorer to specify which version of XSL is being used. [*Note:* XSL is an evolving technology and many different version exist.]

```
1    <?xml version= "1.0" ?>
2    <xsl:stylesheet xmlns:xsl = "http://www.w3.org/TR/WD-xsl">
3
4    <!-- Fig. F.5 : books.xsl                          -->
5    <!-- XSL document that transforms XML into HTML -->
6
7
8    <!-- specify the root of the XML document -->
9    <!-- that references this stylesheet          -->
10   <xsl:template match = "/">
11
12      <html>
13
14      <body>
15
16         <center>
17
18         <table border = "1" cellspacing = "5" cellpadding = "5">
19
20            <thead>
21
22               <tr>
23                  <th><font size = "5">Title</font></th>
24                  <th><font size = "5">Authors</font></th>
25               </tr>
26
27            </thead>
```

Fig. F.5   Listing for **books.xsl** (part 1 of 2).

```
28
29            <!-- select each book element -->
30            <xsl:for-each select = "backOrder/book">
31
32               <!-- select each book's title and authors value -->
33               <tr>
34                  <td>
35                     <font size = "5">
36                        <xsl:value-of select = "title"/>
37                     </font>
38                  </td>
39
40                  <td>
41                     <font size = "5">
42                        <xsl:value-of select = "authors"/>
43                     </font>
44                  </td>
45               </tr>
46
47            </xsl:for-each>
48
49         </table>
50
51         </center>
52
53      </body>
54
55      </html>
56
57   </xsl:template>
58
59   </xsl:stylesheet>
```

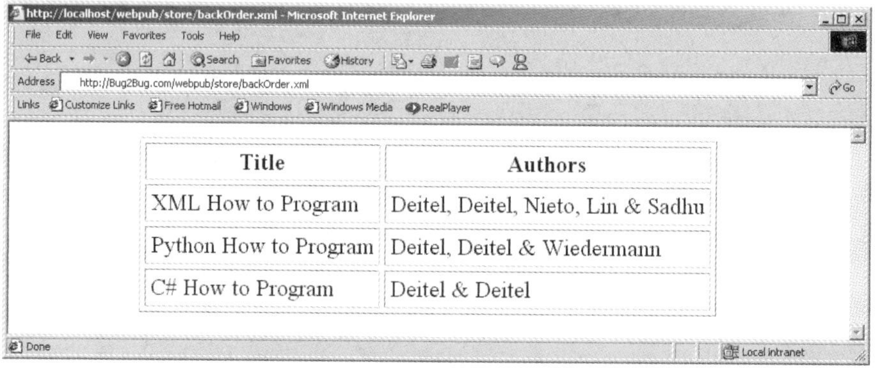

http://localhost/webpub/store/backOrder.xml - Microsoft Internet Explorer
Address http://Bug2Bug.com/webpub/store/backOrder.xml
Title
Authors
XML How to Program
Deitel, Deitel, Nieto, Lin & Sadhu
Python How to Program
Deitel, Deitel & Wiedermann
C# How to Program
Deitel & Deitel
Done
Local intranet

Fig. F.5 Listing for **books.xsl** (part 2 of 2).

XSL uses *templates* to define how a particular element should be laid out. The template (lines 10–57) is applied automatically by Internet Explorer. Element **xsl:template**'s ***match*** *attribute* specifies the element in an XML document for which the template rule should be applied.

In line 10

```
<xsl:template match = "/">
```

the **match** attribute is set to value **"/"**, which indicates that the **xsl:template** applies to the root element of the XML document that references this stylesheet. In this case, **backOrder.xml**'s **backOrder** element.

Lines 12–55 define the HTML that will be sent to the browser for rendering. This HTML includes a table, which is populated with **title** and **authors** information.

Line 30

```
<xsl:for-each select = "backOrder/book">
```

uses the **for-each** element, to repeatedly iterate through the XML document selecting **book** elements. When a **book** element is found, lines 36 and 42

```
<td><xsl:value-of select = "title"/></td>
<td><xsl:value-of select = "authors"/></td>
```

select the values of elements **title** and **authors** using *xsl:value-of*'s **select** attribute.

SUMMARY

- The client tier provides the user interface for a three-tier application.
- Microsoft Internet Explorer 5 renders the HTML documents sent to the client.
- The **head** section of an HTML document is used to describe the document.
- The most common elements placed in the **head** section are the **title** tag and any scripts (e.g., JavaScript) used by the document.
- The default background color of an HTML document is white.
- Attribute **bgcolor** is assigned a preset color name, of which there are over 100 (i.e., **red**, **blue**, etc.).
- Most elements, when rendered, are left justified on the screen by default.
- The **face** attribute specifies the font name (e.g., **helvetica**).
- Active Server Pages often generate HTML that is sent to the client for rendering.
- The actual formatting of the XML document is performed by a related technology called the Extensible Stylesheet Language (XSL).
- Internet Explorer 5 has built in capabilities to process XSL.
- To specify the XSL document that formats the XML document, a special instruction—called a processing instruction—must be inserted into the XML document.
- When marking up data as XML, certain characters such as ampersand (**&**), less than (**<**), greater than (**>**), etc., cannot be written as is. Entity references must be used.
- XSL uses templates to define how a particular element should be laid out.
- Element **xsl:template**'s **match** attribute specifies the element in an XML document for which the template rule should be applied.

TERMINOLOGY

& entity

entity references

for-each element

match attribute

processing instruction

root element

scripting delimiters (<% and %>)

select attribute

template

XML (Extensible Markup Language)

xmlns

XML document

XSL (Extensible Stylesheet Language)

XSL document

XSL prefix

xsl:value-of element

SELF REVIEW EXERCISES

F.1   Fill in the blanks for each of the following statements.

a) The _____ tier provides a user interface for the application.

b) All HTML documents are required to have a _____ declaration.

c) To include a title in an HTML document, enclose the title text between the _____ tags.

d) The default background color of an HTML document is _____.

e) Every XML document must contain at least one element called the _____ element.

f) Because XML documents do not include formatting information, _____ are used to format them.

F.2   Add the **bgcolor** attribute to the **body** tag to change the color of the background to red.

F.3   Using the **font** tag and the **color** attribute, change the color of the text Deitel & Associates, Inc. to orange.

F.4   Add the necessary attribute to the **table** tag to add a **border** 5 pixels wide.

ANSWERS TO SELF REVIEW EXERCISES

F.1   a) client. b) **DOCTYPE**. c) **title**. d) white. e) root. f) XSL stylesheets.

F.2   `<body bgcolor = "red">`

F.3   `<font color = "orange">Deitel & Associates, Inc.</font>`

F.4   `<table border = "5">`

The Middle Tier:
Business Processes

Objectives

- To understand the role of the middle tier in a three-tier application.
- To implement Active Server Pages (ASP) using VBScript in the middle tier.
- To access a database from the middle tier using ASP and ActiveX Data Objects (ADO).
- To understand how JavaScript can be used on the top tier to perform validation before submitting information to the server.

Outline

G.1   Introduction

G.2   Active Server Pages (ASP)

G.3   Adding and Viewing Cart contents

G.4   Check Out

Self Review Exercises • Answers to Self Review Exercises

G.1 Introduction

In this appendix, we study the middle tier of **Bug2Bug.com**. This tier is responsible for interacting with the other two tiers. The middle tier accepts a user request for data from the top tier (i.e., the client), retrieves the data from the bottom tier (i.e., the database) and then responds to the client's request. A typical response is to send HTML to the client. As a general rule, the middle tier is the most complex tier. **Bug2Bug.com** uses ASP to query their database for data, mark it up as HTML and send it to the client. The documents discussed in this appendix are highlighted in Fig. G.1. As with the previous appendix, we present the document code for each Web document, followed by a screen capture of Internet Explorer 5 rendering the HTML. After we present a code listing, we carefully walk the reader through the code.

G.2 Active Server Pages (ASP)

Active Server Pages are a Microsoft technology for enhancing server-side functionality. **Bug2Bug.com** uses ASP technology (see How Active Server Pages Work) to create HTML documents dynamically (i.e, at the time the request is made) for the client that marks up book information. In this section we examine each Active Server Page used in the middle tier of **Bug2Bug.com**.

ASP documents have the file extension **.asp** and can contain both HTML markup and scripting code. Although other languages like JavaScript can be used for ASP scripting, VBScript is the most widely used language for ASP scripting.

How Active Server Pages Work

The Active Server Pages in this appendix demonstrate communication between clients and servers via the HTTP protocol (discussed in Chapter 5). When a server receives a client's HTTP request, the server loads the document (or page) requested by the client. HTML documents are *static documents*—all clients see the same content when requesting the same HTML document. ASP is a Microsoft technology for sending dynamic Web content to the client. The Active Server Page processes the request (which often includes interacting with a database because the client wants data), and returns the results to the client—normally in the form of an HTML document.

A common *HTTP request type* (also known as *request method*) is **POST**. This request is frequently used to send client form data to a Web server. A **POST** request *posts* form contents to the end of an HTTP request. An HTTP request contains information about the server, client, connection, authorization, etc.

Active Server Pages provide several built-in objects to allow programmers to communicate with both the client and Web server. Figure G.2 provides a short description of three commonly used ASP objects. We will discuss exactly how these objects are used momentarily.

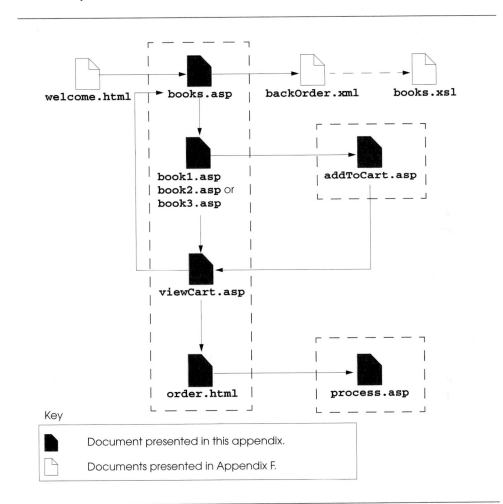

Key

Document presented in this appendix.

Documents presented in Appendix F.

Fig. G.1   Bug2Bug.com documents presented in this appendix.

Object Name	Description
Request	Used to access information passed by an HTTP request.
Response	Used to send information to the client.
Server	Used to interact with the server.

Fig. G.2   Some built-in ASP objects.

The **Request** *object* is commonly used to access the information sent to the server by the client. This information usually consists of data posted by the user in an HTML form. The **Request** object provides access to information, such as cookies, that are stored on a client's machine. The **Response** *object* sends information such as HTML, text, etc., to the client. The **Server** *object* allows an ASP document to interact with the server.

The first ASP we study is **books.asp** (Fig. G.3), which is requested when the user clicks the **Enter** button on **welcome.html**. This ASP dynamically generates a list of book titles by retrieving the book titles from an Access database. The data is marked up as HTML and sent to the client to create the list of available books.

On line 1, we declare the scripting language for this ASP page as VBScript using the **@LANGUAGE** *directive*. We set **Option Explicit** in line 2 to force all variables to be explicitly declared by the programmer. Using **Option Explicit** is a good programming practice because it alerts the programmer to many subtle errors. When used, the **Option Explicit** statement must immediately follow the **@LANGUAGE** directive

```
1    <% @LANGUAGE = VBScript %>
2    <% Option Explicit %>
3
4    <% ' Fig. G.3 : books.asp %>
5
6    <!DOCTYPE HTML PUBLIC
7       "-//W3C//DTD HTML 4.0 Transitional//EN">
8    <html>
9    <head>
10
11       <!-- Book List is placed in the title bar -->
12       <!-- of the browser                       -->
13       <title>Book List</title>
14    </head>
15
16    <!-- The bgcolor attribute changes the background -->
17    <!-- color of the page                            -->
18    <body bgcolor = "lightskyblue">
19
20    <center>
21
22    <!-- Change the font size and the style -->
23    <!-- (face attribute)                    -->
24    <font size = "8" face = "arial">
25       Available Books
26    </font>
27
28
29    <!-- Place a horizontal line across the screen -->
30    <hr>
31
32    <!-- Use the font tag to change the size and the -->
33    <!-- strong (strong) tag to make the text bold   -->
34    <font size = "4"><strong>To view available titles for a
35       technology select a link from this list:</strong></font>
```

Fig. G.3   Listing for **books.asp** (part 1 of 3).

```
36
37        <br/><br/><br/>
38
39   <%
40        Dim connection, query, data
41
42        ' Create an ADODB Connection object
43        Set connection = Server.CreateObject( "ADODB.Connection" )
44
45        ' Open a connection to the database referenced
46        ' with the Dname booklist
47        Call connection.Open( "booklist" )
48
49        ' Create the SQL query and record set object
50        query = "SELECT * FROM Products"
51        Set data = Server.CreateObject( "ADODB.Recordset" )
52
53        ' Execute query against the database
54        ' Record set data is populated with all the records
55        ' that match
56        Call data.Open( query, connection )
57
58        ' Declare array to store each book's data
59        Dim allBookData( 3 )
60
61        ' Begin a while loop that iterates through each record
62        ' in the record set
63        While Not data.EOF
64           Dim oneBooksInformation
65
66           oneBooksInformation = data( "productID" ) & "|" & _
67                                 data( "title" ) & "|" & _
68                                 data( "publishDate" ) & "|" & _
69                                 data( "edition" ) & "|" & _
70                                 data( "isbn" ) & "|" & _
71                                 data( "coverart" ) & "|" & _
72                                 data( "description" ) & "|" & _
73                                 data( "price" )
74
75
76   %>
77
78           <!-- Create a link to each page that describes -->
79           <!-- the book                               -->
80           <a href = "book<% =data( "productid" ) %>.asp">
81              <font color = "green" size = "6">
82                 <% =data( "title" ) %>
83              </font>
84           </a>
85   <br/>
86
87   <%
88           ' Place the current book's data into the array
```

Fig. G.3   Listing for **books.asp** (part 2 of 3).

```
89            ' allBookData which is used to store each book's
90            ' data. The productID is used for the array's index
91            allBookData( CInt( data( "productID" ) ) ) = _
92               oneBooksInformation
93
94            Call data.MoveNext()    ' Move to the next record
95         Wend
96
97         ' Close the record set and database connection
98         Call data.Close()
99         Call connection.Close()
100
101        ' Create a Session variable that each book ASP page
102        ' (e.g., book1.asp, book2.asp, etc.) can use to
103        ' get its book data
104        Session( "bookDataArray" ) = allBookData
105    %>
106
107    <br>
108
109        <!-- Create a link to backOrder.xml -->
110        <a href = "backOrder.xml">
111           <font color = "green" size = "5">
112              <% ="Other Publications" %>
113           </font>
114        </a>
115    </center>
116
117    </body>
118
119    </html>
```

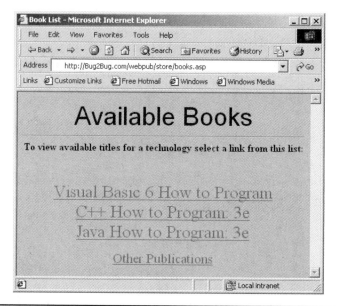

Fig. G.3   Listing for **books.asp** (part 3 of 3).

In lines 24–26, we use the **font** tag to increase the size and change the style of the heading, **Available Books**. On line 30, a horizontal line is placed across the document using the **hr** tag. This creates a consistent look and feel for **Bug2Bug.com**'s Web site. Line 37 contains three consecutive break (**
**) tags, which create space between the heading of the page and the list of books.

Line 39 begins the server-side VBScript, which is delimited by the script delimiters (**<%** and **%>**). Content enclosed in these tags are executed on the server. The client never receives the server-side VBScript.

Line 40

```
Dim connection, query, data
```

declares the variables **connection**, **query** and **data** used in the VBScript.

Line 43

```
Set connection = Server.CreateObject( "ADODB.Connection" )
```

calls **Server** method **CreateObject** to create an ***ADODB.Connection*** *object* and **Set**s it to reference **connection**. An **ADODB.Connection** object contains the functionality necessary to connect to a database. This object is an ActiveX Data Object (see the feature ActiveX Data Objects).

Line 47

```
Call connection.Open( "booklist" )
```

calls method ***Open*** to open the database named **booklist**. The name **booklist** is the name—called a *system data source name*—that the server uses to identify the database.

Line 50

```
query = "SELECT * FROM Products"
```

assigns the SQL query (see the feature Databases and SQL) that **SELECT**s everything in the **products** table. This line simply defines the query. The query is executed in line 56.

Lines 51 and 56

```
Set data = Server.CreateObject( "ADODB.Recordset" )
Call data.Open( query, connection )
```

set **data** to an **ADODB.Recordset** object and call method **Open** to execute the query (from line 50) against the database (i.e., **booklist**) referenced by **connection**. When **Open** finishes executing, the **ADODB.Recordset** object **data** contains all records that match the SQL query and points to either the first record or *end of file* (***EOF***) if no records were found. The **While** loop (lines 63 through 95) iterates through **data**'s records.

Line 63

```
While Not data.EOF
```

tests for the end of the record set. This loop ensures that all records inside **data** are processed.

As each record is processed, a link to each page book's description is created. Line 80

```
<a href = "book<% = data( "productID" ) %>.asp">
```

embeds a server-side scripting statement inside the anchor tag's **href** attribute value. The code **=data("productID")** inserts the value of the current record's **productID** field between the word **book** and **.asp**. The result is a string, such as **book1.asp**, **book2.asp** or **book3.asp**, being assigned to **href**. This final string is what the client receives.

Lines 66–73

```
oneBooksInformation = data( "productID" ) & "|" & _
                      data( "title" ) & "|" & _
                      data( "publishDate" ) & "|" & _
                      data( "edition" ) & "|" & _
                      data( "isbn" ) & "|" & _
                      data( "coverart" ) & "|" & _
                      data( "description" ) & "|" & _
                      data( "price" )
```

assigns a string to **oneBooksInformation**. Each field (e.g., **productID**, **title**, **publishDate**, etc.) is concatenated together to form one string. The *pipe character* (|) separates each field name. This is done so that the beginning and ending of each field is delimited. This allows the programmer to quickly retrieve the field values from the string. We discuss how this is done momentarily.

Lines 91–92

```
allBookData( CInt( data( "productID" ) ) ) = _
    oneBooksInformation
```

take all of the book's data and places it into an array (see the feature Arrays). When referencing the array, the **productID** is used as the array's index. Notice that the VBScript function ***CInt*** is called to convert the **productID** returned from the record set to an integer. This is done to avoid subtle errors that can occur when using variables.

Line 94

```
Call data.MoveNext()
```

calls method **MoveNext** to refer to the next record in the record set.

Lines 98 and 99 close the connection to the database and to the record set. Line 104

```
Session( "bookDataArray" ) = allBookData
```

creates a ***Session*** *variable* that each book's information page (i.e., **book1.asp**, **book2.asp** and **book3.asp**) uses to get data about their respective book. **Session** variables provide a means for sharing information between Active Server Pages.

Finally, in lines 110–114, we create a link to **backOrder.xml**, which is the XML page that references the XSL stylesheet **books.xsl**. Recall that the XSL stylesheet formats the books contained in the XML document as HTML.

ActiveX Data Objects

ActiveX Data Objects allow Active Server Pages to interact with a database. Figure G.4 summarizes two ADO objects used in the appendix examples.

Object/Collection	Description
Connection object	The connection to the database.
Recordset object	Contains zero or more records that match the database query. Collectively this group of records is called a *record set*.

Fig. G.4   Two ADO object and collection types.

Databases and SQL

A *database* is an integrated collection of data. A *database management system (DBMS)* involves the data itself and the software that controls the storage and retrieval of data. Database management systems provide mechanisms for storing and organizing data in a manner that facilitates satisfying sophisticated queries and manipulations of the data.

The most popular database systems in use today are *relational databases*—a database where data is organized using rows and columns of data that are collectively called *tables*.

A language called *Structured Query Language* (*SQL*—pronounced "sequel") is almost universally used with relational database systems to make *queries* (i.e., to request information that satisfies a given criteria) and manipulate data. Some popular relational database systems used in industry include Microsoft SQL Server, Oracle, Sybase, DB2 and Informix. A popular personal relational database is Microsoft Access (which is used by **Bug2Bug.com**).

A relational database is composed of tables, which in turn are composed of *records* (or *rows*) and *fields* (or *columns*). **Bug2Bug.com**'s database contains one table: **products**. Within this table there are multiple fields. The **products** table has eight fields, **productID**, **title**, **publishDate**, **edition**, **isbn**, **coverart**, **description** and **price**. A *primary key* is a unique field that is used to identify a record. The records of the **products** table are ordered by a primary key (**productID**). We will examine the records and fields for this database when we study Appendix H.

Different database users are often interested in different data and different relationships between those data. SQL statements are commonly used to specify which data to *select* from the table. SQL provides keywords (Fig. G.5) that enable programmers to define complex queries for retrieving data from a table. Query results are commonly called *record sets*.

Databases and SQL (Cont.)

Figure G.5 lists two SQL keywords for querying a database and updating existing records in a database. For more information on SQL keywords, visit `www.aspin.com/home/references/database/sql`.

A typical SQL query selects information from one or more tables in a database. Such selections are performed by **SELECT** *queries*. The simplest form of a **SELECT** query is

```
SELECT * FROM TableName
```

In the preceding query, the asterisk (*****) indicates that all rows and columns (fields) from table *TableName* should be selected. To select specific fields from a table, replace the asterisk (*****) with a comma-separated list of the field names to select. For example,

```
SELECT FieldName1, FieldName2, FROM TableName
```

selects all the *FieldName1* and *FieldName2* fields from the records in the *TableName* table.

SQL Keyword	Description
SELECT	Select (retrieve) fields from one or more tables.
FROM	Tables from which to get fields. Required in every **SELECT**.

Fig. G.5   Two SQL keywords.

Arrays

Arrays are data structures consisting of related data items of the same type. The declaration

```
Dim numbers(2)
```

instructs the VBScript interpreter to reserve three elements for array **numbers**. The value **2** defines the *upper bound* (i.e., the highest valid index) of **numbers**. The *lower bound* (the lowest valid index) of **numbers** is **0**.

The programmer can explicitly initialize the array with assignment statements. For example, the lines

```
numbers(0) = 77
numbers(1) = 68
numbers(2) = 55
```

Arrays (Cont.)

initialize **numbers**. Individual array elements are referred to by giving the array name followed by the element position number in parentheses, **()**. The first array element is always at position zero. The position number contained within parentheses following an array reference is more formally called an *index*. An index must be in the range 0 to 2,147,483,648. Repetition statements can also be used to initialize arrays. For example, the statements

```
Dim h( 11 ), x, i
For x = 0 To 10
    h( i ) = CInt( x )
    i = CInt( i ) + 1
Next
```

initializes the elements of **h** to the values 0, 1, 2, 3, ..., 10.

Figure G.6, **book1.asp**, is one of the book information pages. Because these pages are similar, we list only **book1.asp**. The differences between the three pages are found in the index value of **bookDataArray** in line 11, the authors in line 46 and the value of the **alt** tag in line 72.

The page **book1.asp** is a book information page that displays all of the Visual Basic book's data, such as **title**, **price**, etc., including a graphic image of the book cover.

We begin by setting **Option Explicit** on line 1 and then declaring variables used by the VBScript on line 7.

Line 11

```
bookInformation = Split( Session( "bookDataArray" ) _
    ( 1 ), "|" )
```

calls VBScript function **Split** to retrieve each individual book's data from the **Session** variable **bookDataArray**. Because **bookDataArray** contains an array, an index must be provided. In this particular case, the value **1** is provided because this is **book1.asp**—the first book. **Session("bookDataArray") (1)** evaluates to the string

```
"1|Visual Basic How to Program|1999|1|0-13-465955-5|Microsoft
    Visual Basic 6|$50.00"
```

Split places each pipe-separated piece of data into an array that is assigned to **bookInformation**. Each data value of **bookInformation** can be referenced by its index value, where **title** has an index of **1** and **price** has an index of **7**.

Lines 14–16

```
Session( "bookToAdd" ) = bookInformation( 1 )
Session( "Price" ) = bookinformation( 7 )
Session( "bookID" ) = bookInformation( 0 )
```

create new **session** variables for the book title **bookToAdd**, its price (**price**) and the book ID (**bookID**). This information is placed in **Session** variables for **addToCart.asp** and **viewCart.asp**—both of which we discuss momentarily.

```
1   <% Option Explicit %>
2
3   <!-- Fig. G.6 : book1.asp    -->
4
5   <%
6       ' Declare all variables to be used
7       Dim bookInformation, counter
8
9       ' Split string into pieces such that we can display
10      ' the book's information as HTML
11      bookInformation = Split( Session( "bookDataArray" )( 1 ), "|" )
12
13      ' Store the book title and price in Session variables
14      Session( "bookToAdd" ) = bookInformation( 1 )
15      Session( "Price" ) = bookInformation( 7 )
16      Session( "bookID" ) = bookInformation( 0 )
17  %>
18
19  <!DOCTYPE HTML PUBLIC "-//W3C//DTD HTML 4.01//EN"
20      "http://www.w3.org/TR/html4/strict.dtd" >
21
22  <html>
23  <head>
24
25      <!-- By calling the book title from the asp page, we can   -->
26      <!-- display in the title bar of the browser by placing it -->
27      <!-- between the title tags                                -->
28      <title><% =bookInformation( 1 ) %></title>
29  </head>
30
31  <!-- Change the background color -->
32  <body bgcolor = "lightskyblue">
33
34      <!-- Change the font size to 8 and -->
35      <!-- the color of the text to blue -->
36      <font size = "8" color = "blue">
37         <% =bookInformation( 1 ) %>
38      </font>
39
40      <!-- Place a horizontal line across the screen -->
41      <hr>
42
43      <!-- The database does not have the authors data. Thus, -->
44      <!-- VBScript cannot be used to generate this info       -->
45      <font size = "5">
46         Harvey M. Deitel, Paul J. Deitel & T. R. Nieto
47      </font>
48
49      <br/><br/>
50
51      <!-- Center the table in the middle of the page -->
52      <center>
53
```

Fig. G.6   Listing for **book1.asp** (part 1 of 4).

```
54        <!-- The following table contains three columns and five -->
55        <!-- rows. The border is set to 5 which places a border  -->
56        <!-- around each cell and the entire table. Cellpadding   -->
57        <!-- is the amount of space between the text in each       -->
58        <!-- cell and its border. Cellspacing is the amount of     -->
59        <!-- space between cell borders                            -->
60        <table border = "5" cellpadding = "10" cellspacing = "5">
61        <tr>
62
63           <!-- The rowspan attribute sets the amount -->
64           <!-- of rows a cell occupies                -->
65           <td rowspan = "5">
66
67              <!-- The image (img) tag is used to place an image -->
68              <!-- on a page. The src attribute defines the path -->
69              <!-- where the image is located. The alt attribute -->
70              <!-- is used to label the image                    -->
71              <img src = "<% =bookInformation( 5 ) %>" border = "5"
72                 alt = "Visual Basic book cover">
73           </td>
74
75           <td valign = "top">
76              <font size = "5"><strong>Price:</strong></font>
77           </td>
78
79           <td>
80
81              <!-- Each of the values for the price, edition, etc. -->
82              <!-- are generated using VBScript to get the data     -->
83              <!-- from the array bookInformation                   -->
84              <font size = "5">$<% =bookInformation( 7 ) %>.00</font>
85           </td>
86        </tr>
87
88        <tr>
89           <td>
90              <font size = "5"><strong>ISBN #:</strong></font>
91           </td>
92
93           <td>
94              <font size = "5"><% =bookInformation( 4 ) %></font>
95           </td>
96        </tr>
97
98        <tr>
99           <td>
100             <font size = "5"><strong>Edition:</strong></font>
101          </td>
102
103          <td>
104             <font size = "5"><% =bookInformation( 3 ) %></font>
105          </td>
106       </tr>
```

Fig. G.6   Listing for **book1.asp** (part 2 of 4).

```
107
108        <tr>
109           <td>
110             <font size = "5"><strong>Date published:</strong></font>
111           </td>
112
113           <td>
114              <font size = "5"><% =bookInformation( 2 ) %></font>
115           </td>
116        </tr>
117
118        <tr>
119           <td>
120              <font size = "5"><strong>Description:</strong></font>
121           </td>
122
123           <td>
124              <font size = "5"><% =bookInformation( 6 ) %></font>
125           </td>
126        </tr>
127
128     </table>
129
130     <br/>
131
132     <table>
133        <tr>
134           <td>
135              <!-- The form tag is used to create a submit button -->
136              <!-- which will request addToCart.asp                -->
137              <form method = "post" action = "addToCart.asp">
138                 <input type = "submit" value = "Add to Cart">
139              </form>
140           </td>
141
142           <td> </td>
143
144           <td>
145              <!-- Here, the submit button is used to -->
146              <!-- requests viewCart.asp              -->
147              <form method = "post" action = "viewCart.asp">
148                 <input type = "submit" value = "View Cart">
149              </form>
150           </td>
151        </tr>
152     </table>
153
154     </center>
155
156  </body>
157
158  </html>
```

Fig. G.6   Listing for **book1.asp** (part 3 of 4).

Fig. G.6   Listing for **book1.asp** (part 4 of 4).

Again, a title is added to the page with the markup (line 28)

```
<title><% =bookInformation( 1 ) %></title>
```

This time, VBScript is used to place the text contained in index **1** of **bookInformation** between the **title** tags. This syntax is short for

```
Call Response.write( bookInformation( 1 ) )
```

which calls **Response** method **write** to write data to the client.

Because the authors of each book are not stored in the database, they are listed inline in the HTML (line 46).

Lines 60–128 present an HTML table containing 3 columns and 5 rows, which formats the layout of the book information and the book cover. Each of the values in this table uses VBScript to retrieve the data from array **bookInformation**.

Line 60

```
<table border = "5" cellpadding = "10" cellspacing = "5">
```

sets the **border** attribute to **5**, which places a border 5 pixels wide around each cell of the table. The **cellpadding** attribute is set to **10** and the **cellspacing** attribute is set to **5**. Attribute **cellpadding** creates space between the cell borders and **cellspacing** creates space around the cell contents.

The first cell of the table contains the book cover image. Because of the size of the image and the layout of the page, the **rowspan** attribute is set in line 65 to **5**. This tells the browser that this data cell will span 5 vertically adjacent cells.

Lines 71 and 72

```
<img src = "<% =bookInformation( 5 ) %>" border = "5"
    alt = "Visual Basic Book cover">
```

use the **img** tag to place the graphic of the book cover image in a cell of the table. The **src** attribute specifies the location of the graphic. In this case, VBScript retrieves the name of the image, which is contained in array **bookInformation** at index **5**. Setting the **border** attribute to **5** gives the image a border that is 5 pixels wide. The **alt** attribute's text is displayed if the image is not found. The **alt** attribute value is also shown as a *tooltip*— a label that displays the **alt** attribute value—when the mouse is placed over an image.

The last two items on the page are **Submit** buttons that give users two options—add a book to their shopping cart or view their shopping cart. When the **Add to Cart** button is clicked, the book information (e.g., the book **title** and **price**) is sent to **addToCart.asp**, where the information is written as a text file—called a *cookie* (see the feature Cookies)—on the client's computer. When the user is redirected to **viewCart.asp**, the cookie's contents are displayed on the screen. When the **View Cart** button is clicked, **viewCart.asp** is requested.

Cookies

In this section, we will introduce a technology called cookies that enables a Web server to distinguish between clients.

Many Web sites provide custom Web pages and/or functionality on a client-by-client basis. For example, some Web sites allow you to customize their home page to suit your needs. An excellent example of this is the *Yahoo!* Web site (**my.yahoo.com**), which allows you to customize how the Yahoo! site appears. [*Note:* You need to get a free Yahoo! ID first.]

Another example of a service that is customized on a client-by-client basis is a *shopping cart* for shopping on the Web. Obviously, the server must distinguish between clients so the business can assign the proper items and charge each client the proper amount. A popular way to customize Web pages is via cookies. Cookies can store information on the client's computer for retrieval later in the same browsing session or in future browsing sessions. For example, **Bug2Bug.com** uses cookies in their shopping cart application to keep track of the client's shopping-cart items.

A third example of customizing on a client-by-client basis is marketing. Companies often track the pages you visit so they can display advertisements based upon your browsing trends. Many people consider tracking to be an invasion of their privacy, an increasingly sensitive issue in our information-based society. See Chapter 11 for more information on this and other legal, ethical and moral issues.

There are a number of popular techniques for uniquely identifying clients. For the purpose of this appendix, we introduce a technique used to track clients individually, called cookies.

Cookies (Cont.)

Cookies are files sent by an Active Server Page (or another similar technology such as Perl) as part of a response to a client. Every HTTP-based interaction between a client and a server includes a *header* that contains information about either the request (when the communication is from the client to the server) or the response (when the communication is from the server to the client). When an Active Server Page receives a request, the header includes information such as the request type (e.g., **POST**) and cookies stored on the client machine by the server. When the server formulates its response, the header information includes any cookies the server wants to store on the client computer.

Depending on the *maximum age* of a cookie, the Web browser either maintains the cookie for the duration of the browsing session (i.e., until the user closes the Web browser) or stores the cookie on the client computer for future use. When the browser makes a request to a server, cookies previously sent to the client by that server are returned to the server (if the cookies have not expired) as part of the request formulated by the browser. Cookies are automatically deleted when they *expire* (i.e., reach their maximum age) by the Web browser.

G.3 Adding and Viewing Cart contents

The document **addToCart.asp** (Fig. G.7) writes information about a book as a cookie on the client's computer. This page does not include any HTML to send to the browser, thus the user never sees this page. After the cookie is written, the user is redirected to **view-Cart.asp** (Fig. G.8).

```
1   <% Option Explicit %>
2
3   <!-- Fig. G.7 : addToCart.asp -->
4
5   <%
6      Dim numberOfBooks, counter, inCart, quantity
7
8      inCart = False
9
10     ' Get the total number of items. Divide by 3 because
11     ' each item has three parts: book, numberOfbooks and
12     ' bookPrice
13     numberOfBooks = Request.Cookies( "shoppingCart" ).Count / 3
14
15     If Request.Cookies( "shoppingCart" )( "book" _
16        & Session( "bookID" ) ) = Session( "bookToAdd" ) Then
17        inCart = True
18     End If
19
```

Fig. G.7   Listing for **addToCart.asp** (part 1 of 2).

```
20        ' If the book is in the shopping cart update its
21        ' quantity. Otherwise, add the book to the shopping
22        ' cart
23        If inCart = True Then
24           quantity = Request.Cookies _
25              ( "shoppingCart" )( "numberOfbooks" _
26                 & Session( "bookID" ) )
27           quantity = quantity + 1
28           Response.Cookies( "shoppingCart" ) _
29              ( "numberOfbooks" & Session( "bookID" ) ) = quantity
30        Else
31           Response.Cookies( "shoppingCart" ) _
32              ( "numberOfbooks" & Session( "bookID" ) ) = 1
33           Response.Cookies( "shoppingCart" )( "book" _
34              & Session( "bookID" ) ) = Session( "bookToAdd" )
35        End If
36
37        ' Add the price to the cookie
38        Response.Cookies( "shoppingCart" ) _
39           ( "bookPrice" & Session( "bookID" ) ) = Session( "Price" )
40
41        ' Send the user to viewCart.asp
42        Call Response.Redirect( "viewCart.asp" )
43     %>
```

Fig. G.7   Listing for **addToCart.asp** (part 2 of 2).

Line 6

```
Dim numberOfBooks, counter, inCart, quantity
```

declares the variables used in this script.

On line 8

```
inCart = False
```

initializes the variable **inCart** to **False**. This variable is used to indicate whether the book being added to the cart is already in the cart. **False** is used to indicate that the book is not in the cart. If the book already exists in the cart, the quantity is updated, otherwise, a new instance of the book is added. If it is, **inCart** is assigned **True**.

Line 13

```
numberOfBooks = Request.Cookies( "shoppingCart" ).Count / 3
```

retrieves the total number of items in the cart. This number is divided by 3 because each book in the shopping cart has three parts: **book**, **numberOfBooks** and **bookPrice**.

In lines 15–18, a test is made to determine if the book being updated is already in the cart. Lines 23–35 manipulate the cart based on the value of **inCart**. If the book is already in the cart, its quantity is increased by one. Otherwise, the quantity is set to **1** and the book is added to the shopping cart.

Lines 38 and 39

```
Response.Cookies( "shoppingCart" ) _
   ( "bookPrice" & Session ( "bookID" ) ) = Session( "Price" )
```

adds the price for the book to the cookie file. Recall that **Session** variable **Price** is set on the appropriate book page (i.e., **book1.asp**, **book2.asp** and **book3.asp**). Each book is uniquely identified within the shopping cart as either **bookPrice1**, **bookPrice2** or **bookPrice3**. These names are used in a manner similar to an array index. The left side of the assignment

```
Response( "ShoppingCart" )( "bookPrice2" ) =
    Session( "Price" )
```

indicates that the item identified as **bookPrice2** in the **ShoppingCart** should be modified.

On line 42, the user is redirected to **viewCart.asp**. This is done without interaction by the user.

Fig. G.8 shows **viewCart.asp**, which displays the contents of the shopping cart. The contents include book titles, the quantity of each book in the cart, the price per book and the total price for the order.

The layout of the HTML page generated by **viewCart.asp** is similar to that of the other pages presented so far.

Line 26 declares the variables used in this script, **counter**, **cartCounter** and **total**. Line 32 begins the construction of a table. All values that are to be displayed to the user are placed in a table. This is done to present the items in a neat, tabular manner.

Line 29

```
cartCount = Request.Cookies( "shoppingCart" ).Count
```

retrieves the number of items in the cart using the same techniques discussed in **addTo-Cart.asp**. This value is used in line 38 to determine if there is anything in the cart. If the value of **cartCount** is equal to 0, then **Response** prints the string, "**Your shopping cart is currently empty.**" as HTML on line 45.

Lines 62 and 63

```
If Request.Cookies ( "shoppingCart" ) _
    ( "numberOfBooks" & counter ) <> Empty Then
```

```
1   <% Option Explicit %>
2
3   <!-- Fig. G.8: viewCart.asp -->
4
5   <html>
6   <head>
7
8      <!-- Place View Cart in the title bar of the browser. -->
9      <title>View Cart</title>
10  </head>
11
12  <!-- Change the background color of the page. -->
13  <body bgcolor = "lightskyblue">
14
15     <center>
16
17        <font size = "8" face = "arial">
```

Fig. G.8   Listing for **viewCart.asp** (part 1 of 4).

```
18              Shopping Cart
19      </font></p>
20
21      <hr>
22
23      <br/><br/>
24
25  <%
26      Dim counter, cartCount, total
27
28          ' Get the number of items in the cart
29          cartCount = Request.Cookies( "shoppingCart" ).Count
30  %>
31
32      <table>
33        <tr>
34           <td>
35
36  <%
37      ' Test if cart is empty
38      If cartCount = 0 Then
39  %>
40
41              <font size = "5">
42
43  <%
44          ' If the cart is empty, modify the user
45      Call Response.write( "Your shopping cart is currently empty." )
46      Else
47  %>
48
49           </font>
50           </td>
51        </tr>
52
53        <tr>
54           <td align = "right">
55
56  <%
57      ' Retrieve shopping cart contents and display them
58      For counter = 1 To 3
59        Dim quantity, price
60
61          ' Display information only if the Cookie variable exists
62          If Request.Cookies( "shoppingCart" ) _
63             ( "numberOfBooks" & counter ) <> Empty Then
64             quantity = Request.Cookies( "shoppingCart" ) _
65                ( "numberOfBooks" & counter )
66             price = Session( "Price" )
67  %>
68
69              <font size = "5">
70
```

Fig. G.8   Listing for **viewCart.asp** (part 2 of 4).

```
71   <%
72                Call Response.write( Request.Cookies( "shoppingCart" ) _
73                   ( "book" & counter ) & "  QTY: " & quantity _
74                    & "  " _
75                    & formatCurrency( CCur( quantity * price ) ) _
76                    & "<br/><br/>" )
77                  total = CInt( total ) + CInt( quantity * price )
78             End If
79
80       Next
81
82     End If
83
84     Session( "Total" ) = total
85   %>
86
87                </font>
88           </td>
89        </tr>
90
91        <tr>
92           <td align = "right">
93              <font size = "5"><strong>Total: </strong>
94                 <% =FormatCurrency( Session( "Total" ) ) %></font>
95           </td>
96        </tr>
97     </table>
98     </center>
99
100    <br/><br/>
101
102    <center>
103
104    <!-- Create a link back to books.asp -->
105    <a href = "books.asp">
106       <font color = "green" size = "5">
107          Book list
108       </font>
109    </a>
110
111    <br/>
112
113    <form>
114       <input type = "button" value = "Check Out"
115          onclick = "location.href = 'order.html'">
116    </form>
117
118    </center>
119
120    </body>
121
122    </html>
```

Fig. G.8   Listing for **viewCart.asp** (part 3 of 4).

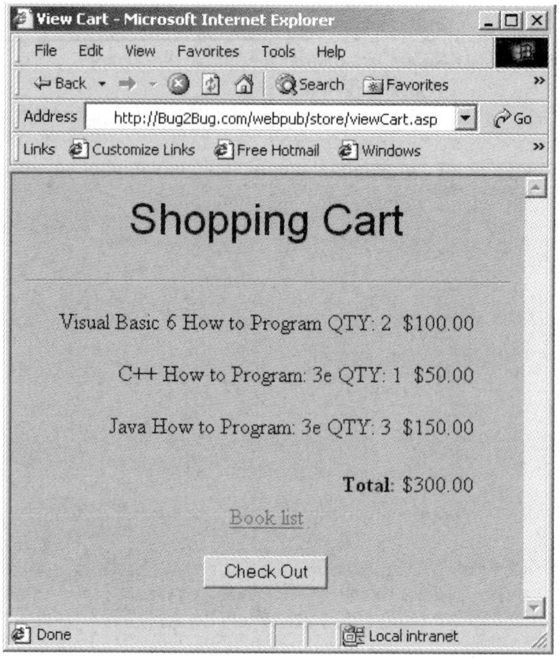

Fig. G.8   Listing for **viewCart.asp** (part 4 of 4).

tests if **"numberOfBooks" & counter**'s value, which stores the quantity ordered for a
specific book in the cart, is not empty. Essentially, this test is determining if a book exists
in the cart. If we use the same Java book example, **numberOfBooks3** would exist and
therefore not be **Empty**. If **numberOfBooks1** was used—it would not exist and by definition would be considered **Empty**. If the value is **Empty**, **False** is returned and the
cookie is not modified. If the value exists, lines 64–66

```
quantity = Request.Cookies( "shoppingCart" ) _
    ( "numberOfBooks" & counter )
price = Session( "Price" )
```

retrieve the books quantity and **Price** and store them in variable **quantity** and **price**.
    Lines 72–77

```
Call Response.write( Request.Cookies( "shoppingCart" ) _
    ( "book" & counter ) & "  QTY: " & quantity _
    & "  " _
    & formatCurrency( CCur( quantity * price ) ) _
    & "<br/><br/>" )
total = CInt( total ) + CInt( quantity * price )
```

print the title of the book (**"book" & counter**), the quantity (**quantity**) of the book
and the total price for the book by calling function **formatCurrency**. Function **CCur** is
called to convert the result of multiplying **quantity** by **price**.

Lines 93 and 94

```
<strong>Total: </strong>
   <% =FormatCurrency( Session( "Total" ) ) %>
```

format **session** variable **Total** as a currency value.

The last two items on the page are a link back to the list of available books (**books.asp**) and a **Check Out** button. The **Book List** link sends the user back to **books.asp**. The **Check Out** button (lines 114 and 115) is created using the **form** and **input** tags, and when clicked, requests **order.html**.

G.4 Check Out

In this section, we present a client-side document that allows the user to check out. We have intentionally placed this document in this appendix because of its relationship to the other documents. This HTML document (**order.html**—Fig. G.9) is more complex then the ones presented previously because it contains JavaScript code. This document is used by **Bug2Bug.com** to get the user's name, address and credit-card information for shipping and billing purposes. It consists of input fields in an HTML **form**. JavaScript is used to validate the contents of the last name and state fields.

```
1   <!-- Fig. G.9: order.html -->
2
3   <!DOCTYPE HTML PUBLIC "-//W3C//DTD HTML 4.01//EN"
4             "http://www.w3.org/TR/html4/strict.dtd">
5
6   <html>
7   <head>
8   <title>Order</title>
9
10  <!-- Although the default scripting language is JavaScript, -->
11  <!-- there is a possibility the standard may change, it is  -->
12  <!-- a good habit to always declare it                      -->
13  <script language = "JavaScript">
14
15  <!-- The JavaScript is placed inside an HTML comment in -->
16  <!-- case the browser does not support it               -->
17  <!--
18
19  // Create the function checkState to validate the input of
20  // the form.
21  function checkState( form )
22  {
23     // Declare the variable string and set it equal to the
24     // input in the state text box
25     var string = form.state.value;
26
27     // The regular expression abbr lists all possible values for
28     // the state field
```

Fig. G.9   Listing for **order.html** (part 1 of 6).

```
29          var abbr = new RegExp( "AL|AK|AZ|AR|CA|CO|CT|DE|FL|GA|" +
30                                 "HI|ID|IL|IN|IA|KS|KY|LA|ME|MD|" +
31                                 "MA|MI|MN|MS|MO|MT|NB|NV|NH|NJ|" +
32                                 "NM|NY|NC|ND|OH|OK|OR|PA|RI|SC|" +
33                                 "SD|TN|TX|UT|VT|VA|WA|WV|WI|WY",
34                                 "i" );
35
36          // Declare the variable check and set it equal to the input
37          // in the last name text box
38          var check = form.lastname.value;
39
40          // Check to see if the Last name field is empty.
41          if ( check == "" ) {
42             alert( "Please complete all fields." );
43             return false;
44          }
45
46          // Check to see if the state value is empty.
47          if ( form.state.value == "" ) {
48             alert( "Please enter your state abbreviation." );
49             return false;
50          }
51
52          // Check to see if the value entered into the state field
53          // matches one of the acceptable values.
54          if ( abbr.test( string ) ) {
55             form.state.value = string.toUpperCase();
56             location.href = "process.asp";
57             return false;
58          }
59
60          // Alert the user that the input is not an acceptable value.
61          alert( "" +
62             string + " is not a correct abbreviation of a US State." );
63             form.state.select();
64          return false;
65       }
66
67    // -->
68
69    </script>
70
71    </head>
72
73    <!--Change the background color of the page -->
74    <body bgcolor = "lightskyblue">
75
76       <center>
77
78       <!-- Place the page heading in the top center of the page -->
79       <font size = "10" face = "arial">
80          Check Out
81       </font>
```

Fig. G.9   Listing for **order.html** (part 2 of 6).

```
82
83    <!-- Place a horizontal line across the page. -->
84    <hr>
85
86       <!-- The remaining elements of the page are form elements -->
87       <!-- The onSubmit attribute is used here to call function -->
88       <!-- checkState and run the validation                   -->
89       <form onSubmit = "return checkState(this);">
90
91       <font size = "4"><p><strong>
92          Please fill out the following information.</strong></p>
93       </font>
94
95       <!-- This table consists of two columns and nine rows -->
96       <!-- Cellspacing separates the cells by the number of -->
97       <!-- pixels specified                                 -->
98       <table cellspacing = "10">
99          <tr>
100            <td>
101               <font size = "5">
102                  First name:
103               </font>
104            </td>
105
106            <td>
107
108               <!-- The text boxes in this form are given a name -->
109               <!-- for reference purposes and a size to limit   -->
110               <!-- the size of the box                          -->
111               <input type = "text" name = "firstname" size = "10">
112            </td>
113          </tr>
114
115          <tr>
116            <td>
117               <font size = "5">
118                  Last name:
119               </font>
120            </td>
121
122            <td>
123               <input type = "text" name = "lastname" size = "15">
124            </td>
125          </tr>
126
127          <tr>
128            <td valign = "top">
129               <font size = "5">
130                  Address:
131               <font>
132            </td>
133
```

Fig. G.9   Listing for **order.html** (part 3 of 6).

```
134            <td>
135               <font size = "5">
136                  Street:
137               </font>
138
139               <input type = "text" name = "street" size = "25">
140 <br/><br/>
141
142               <font size = "5">
143                  City:
144               </font>
145
146               <input type = "text" name = "city" size = "10">
147 <br/><br/>
148
149               <font size = "5">
150                  State:
151               </font>
152
153               <input type = "text" name = "state" size = "2">
154 <br/><br/>
155
156               <font size = "5">
157                  Zip code:
158               </font>
159
160               <input type = "text" name = "zipcode" size = "5">
161            </td>
162         </tr>
163
164         <tr>
165            <td>
166               <font size = "5">
167                  Phone #:
168               </font>
169            </td>
170
171            <td>
172               <font size = "5">
173                  (
174               </font>
175
176               <input type = "text" name = "phone" size = "3">
177
178               <font size = "5">
179                  )
180               </font>
181
182               <input type = "text" name = "phone2" size = "3">
183
184               <font color = "white" size = "4">
185                  -
186               </font>
```

Fig. G.9   Listing for **order.html** (part 4 of 6).

```
187
188                    <input type = "text" name = "phone3" size = "4">
189                </td>
190          </tr>
191
192          <tr>
193              <td>
194                  <font size = "5">
195                      Credit Card #:
196                  </font>
197              </td>
198
199              <td>
200                  <input type = "text" name = "creditcard" size = "20">
201              </td>
202          </tr>
203
204          <tr>
205              <td>
206                  <font size = "5">
207                      Expiration Date:
208                  </font>
209              </td>
210
211              <td>
212                  <input type = "text" name = "expdate" size = "2"
213                      value = "MM">
214
215                  <font size = "5">
216                      /
217                  </font>
218
219                  <input type = "text" name = "expdate2"
220                      size = "2" value = "YY">
221              </td>
222          </tr>
223
224      </table>
225
226  <br/><br/>
227
228
229      <!-- The Submit button calls function checkState and the -->
230      <!-- reset button clears all the text in the form fields -->
231      <input type = "submit" value = "Submit">  
232      <input type = "reset" value = "Clear">
233
234      </center>
235
236      </form>
237
238  </body>
239
```

Fig. G.9   Listing for **order.html** (part 5 of 6).

240 </html>

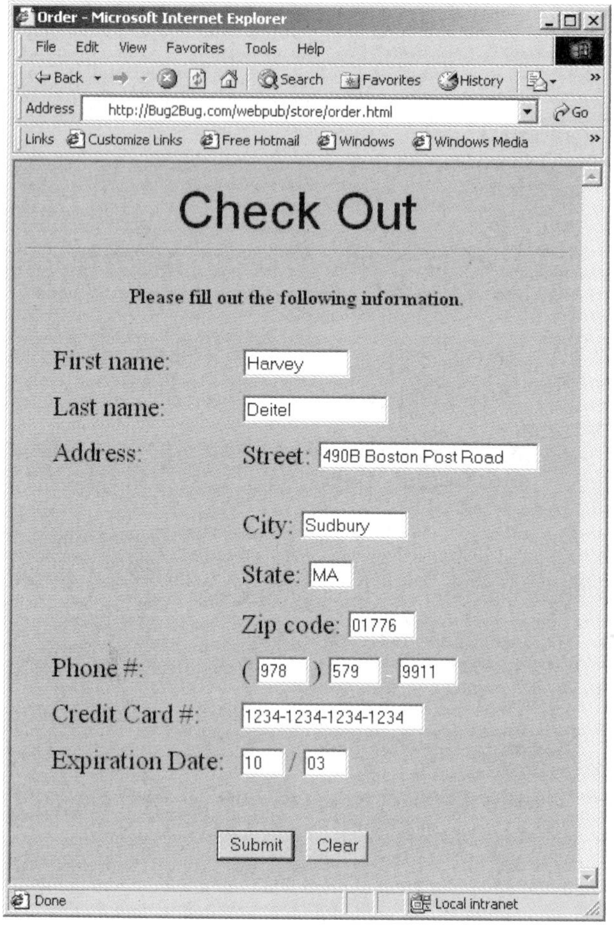

Fig. G.9   Listing for **order.html** (part 6 of 6).

The layout of this page is similar to the other **Bug2Bug.com** Web site pages. Between the **head** tags is the JavaScript that validates the form fields. Specifically, this JavaScript validates the last name field to ensure that it is not empty and that a valid state abbreviation has been input.

Line 21

```
function checkState( form )
```

begins the function definition for **checkState**. This function (see the feature Programmer-Defined Functions) is called when the user clicks the **Submit** button (line 231) at the bottom of the page. The **Submit** button requests **process.asp**, which processes the order. Before the request is made, the JavaScript function **checkState** is called.

Programmer-Defined Functions

Functions are used in programming to execute a specific task when called. Functions allow the programmer to modularize (i.e., break down into smaller pieces) a program—this makes programs easier to write and debug (i.e., find and correct program errors). All variables declared in function definitions are *local variables*—they are known only in the function in which they are defined. Most functions have a list of *parameters* that provide the means for communicating information between functions via function calls. A function's parameters are also considered to be local variables. When a function is called, the arguments in the function call are assigned to the corresponding parameters in the function definition.

The format of a function definition is

```
function function-name( parameter-list )
{
    declarations and statements
}
```

The *function-name* can be anything. The *parameter-list* is a comma-separated list containing the names of the parameters received by the function when it is called (the arguments in the function call—when the function is called to execute—are assigned to the corresponding parameter in the function definition—where the function tasks are defined). There should be one argument in the function call for each parameter in the function definition. If a function does not receive any values, the *parameter-list* is empty (the function name is followed by an empty set of parentheses). The *declarations* and *statements* within braces form the *function body*.

Line 25

```
var string = form.state.value;
```

assigns variable **string** state's value.

One of the most powerful features available to the programmer is *regular expressions*, which allow patterns of characters to be matched quickly and efficiently. Lines 29–34

```
var abbr = new RegExp( "AL|AK|AZ|AR|CA|CO|CT|DE|FL|GA|" +
                       "HI|ID|IL|IN|IA|KS|KY|LA|ME|MD|" +
                       "MA|MI|MN|MS|MO|MT|NB|NV|NH|NJ|" +
                       "NM|NY|NC|ND|OH|OK|OR|PA|RI|SC|" +
                       "SD|TN|TX|UT|VT|VA|WA|WV|WI|WY",
                         "i" );
```

creates a regular expression that includes all of the valid state abbreviations. Each valid state abbreviation in **RegExp** is separated by a pipe character (|). Unlike our discussion for **book1.asp**, where the pipe character was used in a call to function **split**, the pipe character separates the values passed to **RegExp**. The first argument passed to **RegExp** is a string containing the patterns to match. The second argument specifies a case–insensitive match. For example, valid matches for TX would be Tx, tx, TX and tX. When the script is run, the text that is input into the **state** field is compared to the values listed here. If a match is not found, an **alert** window is displayed stating that either the field is empty or the input is invalid. Line 48

```
alert( "Please enter your state's abbreviation." );
```

and lines 61–62

```
alert( "" + string +
    " is not a correct US state abbreviation." );
```

call function **alert** to display messages to the user.

Before either of the validation checks are done, the script determines if anything has been input into the last name field. The testing is done using an **if** JavaScript control structure (see the feature on Control Structures). This is tested in line 41

```
if ( check == "" ) {
```

where variable **check** (declared in line 38) is tested against the *empty string (" ")*. If something has been input into the field, the script returns **false**. Otherwise, the script opens an **alert** box that notifies the user to complete all fields.

If all checks return **false**, the user is redirected to **process.asp** (line 56). Otherwise, an **alert** box containing an error message is displayed. The user must comply before continuing.

Line 89 starts an HTML form that contains input fields for the customer's billing and shipping information. In line 89, we set the value of the **onSubmit** attribute to the function **checkState**. Thus, clicking the **Submit** button calls the function **checkState** and the validation is executed. The **input** tags throughout the table (lines 111–219) create text fields. The **type** attribute of the **input** tag is given the value of **text** to create the text field and the **size** attribute is used to define the size of the text field. Line 111

```
<input type = "text" name = "firstname" size = "10">
```

sets **size** attribute's value to **10**. This creates a text box that is 10 characters wide. The **name** attribute provides a name for the text field for identification purposes. For example, we reference the **lastname** field in the JavaScript in line 38,

```
var check = form.lastname.value
```

Line 232

```
<input type = "reset" value = "clear">
```

creates a form button which is used to clear the form. The **type** attribute value **reset** specifies that all of the fields in the form are to be cleared when the button is clicked.

Control Structures

Normally, statements in a program are executed one after the other in the order in which they are written. This is called *sequential execution*. Various JavaScript statements we will soon discuss enable the programmer to specify that the next statement to be executed may be one other than the next one in sequence. This is called *transfer of control*.

JavaScript provides three types of selection structures. The **if** selection structure performs an action if a condition is true or skips the action if the condition is false. The **if/else** selection structure performs an action if a condition is true and performs a different action if the condition is false.

The **if** structure is called a *single-selection structure* because it selects or ignores a single action (or, as we will soon see, a single group of actions). The **if/else** structure is called a *double-selection structure* because it selects between two different actions (or groups of actions).

Pseudocode is an artificial and informal language that helps programmers develop algorithms. Pseudocode is similar to everyday English; it is convenient and user-friendly although it is not an actual computer programming language. Pseudocode programs are not actually executed on computers. Rather, they help the programmer "think out" a program before attempting to write it in a programming language. A carefully prepared pseudocode program can be converted easily to a corresponding program. This is done in many cases simply by replacing pseudocode statements with their programming language equivalents.

The *if* Selection Structure

A selection structure is used to choose among alternative courses of action in a program. For example, suppose that the passing grade on an examination is 60 (out of 100). Then the pseudocode statement

> *If student's grade is greater than or equal to 60*
> > *Print "Passed"*

determines if the condition "student's grade is greater than or equal to 60" is true or false. If the condition is true, then "Passed" is printed, and the next pseudocode statement in order is "performed" (remember that pseudocode is not a real programming language). If the condition is false, the print statement is ignored, and the next pseudocode statement in order is performed. Note that the second line of this selection structure is indented. Such indentation is optional, but it is highly recommended because it emphasizes the inherent structure of structured programs. The JavaScript interpreter ignores whitespace characters: blanks, tabs and newlines used for indentation and vertical spacing. Programmers insert these whitespace characters to enhance program clarity.

The preceding pseudocode *If* statement may be written in JavaScript as

```
if ( studentGrade >= 60 )
    document.writeln( "Passed" );
```

Control Structures (Cont.)

Notice that the JavaScript code corresponds closely to the pseudocode. This similarity is why pseudocode is a useful program development tool. The statement in the body of the **if** structure outputs the character string **"Passed"** in the HTML document.

The if/else Selection Structure

The **if** selection structure performs an indicated action only when the condition evaluates to **true**; otherwise, the action is skipped. The **if/else** selection structure allows the programmer to specify that a different action is to be performed when the condition is true than when the condition is false. For example, the pseudocode statement

> *If student's grade is greater than or equal to 60*
>> *Print "Passed"*
> *else*
>> *Print "Failed"*

prints *Passed* if the student's grade is greater than or equal to 60 and prints *Failed* if the student's grade is less than 60. In either case, after printing occurs, the next pseudocode statement in sequence (the next statement after the whole **if/else** structure) is "performed." Note that the body of the *else* is also indented.

The indentation convention you choose should be carefully applied throughout your programs (both in pseudocode and in JavaScript). It is difficult to read programs that do not use uniform spacing conventions.

The preceding pseudocode *If/else* structure may be written in JavaScript as

```
if ( studentGrade >= 60 )
   document.writeln( "Passed" );
else
   document.writeln( "Failed" );
```

A Note on Data Types

JavaScript does not require variables to have a type before they can be used in a program. A variable in JavaScript can contain a value of any data type, and in many situations JavaScript automatically converts between values of different types for you. For this reason, JavaScript is referred to as a *loosely typed language*.

When a variable is declared in JavaScript but not given a value, that variable has an *undefined* value. Attempting to use the value of such a variable is normally a logic error.

When variables are declared, they are not assigned default values unless specified otherwise by the programmer. To indicate that a variable does not contain a value, you can assign the value **null** to the variable.

Figure G.10 is the last server-side document to present. This document is requested as part of the validation script when all of the validation tests return **False**. This document sends HTML to the client that informs that their order has been processed.

```asp
1    <% Option Explicit %>
2
3    <!-- Fig. G.10 process.asp -->
4
5    <%
6       ' Remove shopping cart because it has been processed
7       Response.Cookies( "shoppingCart" ) =    Empty
8    %>
9
10   <!DOCTYPE HTML PUBLIC "-//W3C//DTD HTML 4.01//EN"
11           "http://www.w3.org/TR/html14/strict.dtd">
12   <html>
13
14   <head>
15      <title>Thank You!</title>
16   </head>
17
18   <body bgcolor = "lightskyblue">
19
20      <center>
21
22      <table>
23         <tr>
24            <td align = "center">
25               <font size = "8" color = "red" face = "arial">
26                  Thank You</font><br/><hr><br/>
27            </td>
28         </tr>
29
30         <tr>
31            <td align = "center">
32               <font size = "6">Your order has been processed and will
33                  ship within 24 hours.</font><br/><br/>
34            </td>
35         </tr>
36
37         <tr>
38            <td align = "center">
39               <font size = "5">Your credit card has been billed:
40
41               <!-- Get and display the total amount of the order. -->
42                  <% =FormatCurrency( Session( "Total" ) ) %></font>
43            </td>
44         </tr>
45
46      </table>
47
48   </body>
```

Fig. G.10 Listing for **process.asp** (part 1 of 2).

49
50   `</html>`

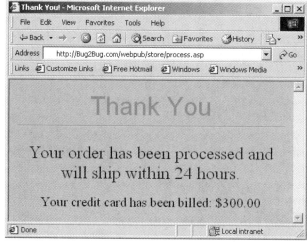

Fig. G.10   Listing for **`process.asp`** (part 2 of 2).

Line 7

```
Response.Cookies( "shoppingCart" ) = Empty
```

empties the shopping cart because the user has checked out and the order has been processed. The next time the customer visits the site, they will have an empty shopping cart.

Besides an HTML table to define the page layout and the **font** tag to format the text, VBScript is used in line 42

```
<% =FormatCurrency( Session( "Total" ) ) %>
```

to format and display the total amount of the order.

SUMMARY

- The middle tier accepts a user request for data from the top tier, retrieves the data from the bottom tier (i.e., the database) and then responds to the client's request.
- Active Server Pages are a Microsoft technology for enhancing server-side functionality.
- An ASP file has the file extension **.asp** and can contain both HTML markup and scripting code.
- Although other languages like JavaScript can be used for ASP scripting, VBScript is the most widely used language for ASP scripting.
- When a server receives a client's HTTP request, the server loads the document (or page) requested by the client. HTML documents are static documents—all clients see the same content when requesting the same an HTML document. ASP is a Microsoft technology for sending dynamic Web content to the client.
- A common HTTP request type (also known as request method) is **POST**.
- The **Request** object is commonly used to access the information sent to the server by the client.

- The **Request** object provides access to information, such as cookies, that are stored on a client's machine.
- The **Response** object sends information such as HTML, text, etc., to the client.
- The **Server** object allows an ASP document to interact with the server.
- When used, the **Option Explicit** statement must immediately follow the **@LANGUAGE** directive.
- Content enclosed in delimiter tags are executed on the server.
- A database is an integrated collection of data.
- A database management system (DBMS) involves the data itself and the software that controls the storage and retrieval of data.
- The most popular database systems in use today are relational databases—a database where data is organized using rows and columns of data that are collectively called tables.
- A language called Structured Query Language (SQL—pronounced "sequel") is almost universally used with relational database systems to make queries (i.e., to request information that satisfies a given criteria) and manipulate data.
- A relational database is composed of tables, which in turn are composed of records (or rows) and fields (or columns).
- A typical SQL query selects information from one or more tables in a database.
- ActiveX Data Objects allow Active Server Pages to interact with a database.
- A popular way to customize Web pages is via cookies.
- Cookies can store information on the client's computer for retrieval later in the same browsing session or in future browsing sessions.
- Cookies are small files sent by an Active Server Page (or another similar technology such as Perl) as part of a response to a client. Every HTTP-based interaction between a client and a server includes a header that contains information about either the request (when the communication is from the client to the server) or the response (when the communication is from the server to the client).
- Functions are used in programming to execute a specific task when called.
- Functions allow the programmer to modularized (i.e., break down into smaller pieces) a program—this makes programs easier to write and debug (i.e, find and correct program errors).
- All variables declared in function definitions are local variables—they are known only in the function in which they are defined.
- One of the most powerful features available to the programmer is regular expressions, which allow patterns of characters to be matched quickly and efficiently.
- The **if** structure is called a single-selection structure because it selects or ignores a single action (or, as we will soon see, a single group of actions).
- The **if/else** structure is called a double-selection structure because it selects between two different actions (or groups of actions).
- Pseudocode is an artificial and informal language that helps programmers develop algorithms.
- The JavaScript interpreter ignores whitespace characters: blanks, tabs and newlines used for indentation and vertical spacing.
- The **if** selection structure performs an indicated action only when the condition evaluates to **true**; otherwise, the action is skipped.

- The **if/else** selection structure allows the programmer to specify that a different action is to be performed when the condition is true than when the condition is false.

- JavaScript does not require variables to have a type before they can be used in a program.

- When a variable is declared in JavaScript but is not given a value, that variable has an undefined value.

TERMINOLOGY

Active Server Pages (ASP)
Open method
ADODB.Connection object
ADODB.Recordset
alert box
alt attribute
array
border attribute
cellpadding attribute
cellspacing attribute
client
column
cookie file
database
database management systems (DBMS)
double-selection structure
EOF (end of file)
field
form tag
FROM
function parameter
head tag
horizontal line
HTML form
HTTP header
HTTP **POST** request
HTTP protocol (HyperText Transfer Protocol)
if/else selection structure
img tag
index value
input tag
JavaScript
local variable
logic error
Microsoft Access
Microsoft SQL Server

modularize
name attribute
null
Option Explicit
parameters
POST
primary key
pseudocode
queries
record
record set
regular expression
relational database
Request method
Response object
rowspan attribute
script
SELECT
sequential execution
Server method
session variable
shopping cart
size attribute
SQL (Structured Query Language)
src attribute
table
text fields
transfer of control
type attribute
variable
VBScript
While loop
whitespace characters
XML (Extensible Markup Language)
XSL stylesheet

SELF REVIEW EXERCISES

G.1   Fill in the blanks for each of the following.

      a)   The _____ tier of a multitier application acts as a sort of "middleman" between the data in the data tier and users of the application.

b) When using the script (**<script>**) tag within an HTML document, the default language is _____.

c) Whenever VBScript is used within an ASP document, it is wrapped in _____ tags.

d) _____ forces all variables in a VBScript to be declared.

e) By setting the _____ attribute of the **paragraph** (**<p>**) tag, we can justify the text that populates this tag.

f) The _____ at the end of a regular expression denotes that the value which is eventually matched against these values can be lowercase or uppercase.

g) The _____ attribute is used to define the size of the text box.

G.2   On line 7 of **book1.asp** (Fig. G.6),

```
Dim bookinformation, counter
```

we declare the variables **bookInformation** and **counter**. Use the same syntax to declare variables **book** and **author**.

G.3   On line 42 of **order.html** (Fig. G.9),

```
alert( "Please complete all fields." );
```

the caption of the **alert** box is set. Use the same syntax to set the caption of the an **alert** box to "**Welcome to Deitel & Associates, Inc.**"

G.4   In line 50 of **books.asp** (Fig. G.3).

```
query = "SELECT * FROM Products"
```

a query is specified to select everything (*****) from the **Products** table. Write a SQL statement that selects everything from a table named **Payroll**.

ANSWERS TO SELF REVIEW EXERCISES

G.1   a) middle. b) JavaScript. c) delimiter. d) **Option Explicit**. e) **align**. f) **i**. g) **size**.

G.2   Dim book, author

G.3   alert("Welcome to Deitel & associates, Inc.");

G.4   query = SELECT * FROM Payroll

The Bottom Tier:
The Database

Objectives

- To become familiar with the bottom tier.
- To understand the roles that databases have in e-business.
- To understand fundamental database concepts.
- To become familiar with the structure of an Access database table.

Outline

H.1   Introduction

H.2   Bottom Tier: Database

H.3   Access Database

Self Review Exercises • Answers to Self Review Exercises

H.1 Introduction

In this appendix, we discuss the bottom tier of a three-tier architecture—the database. A database stores an e-business' data. Most databases are relational databases—databases where the data is organized in tables. A variety of different database products exist, ranging from small products like Microsoft Access to large-scale database products such as Microsoft SQL Server 2000.

H.2 Bottom Tier: Database

The bottom tier maintains all of the data (organized in tables) needed for an e-business. The database that stores this data may contain product data, such as a description, price and quantity in stock; and customer data, such as a user name, shipping information, etc.

Databases are an integral piece of applications. Databases give an e-business the ability to update data in real time. As soon as a piece of data is entered into the database, it is accessible to users and programs. Because data is stored electronically, it can be accessed and manipulated much faster than paper copies. Databases also allow reports to be generated in an automated way.

H.3 Access Database

`Bug2Bug.com` uses an Access database to store the data about books it sells. This data is retrieved from the database using Active Server Pages (ASP) and ActiveX Data Objects (ADO). One table, named **Products**, stores each book's information.

The **Products** table contains eight fields (i.e., columns): **productID**, **title**, **publishDate**, **edition**, **isbn**, **coverart**, **description** and **price**. These fields contain the title, date published, edition number, ISBN number (a unique number used to reference a book), image name, description and price of each book, respectively.

Labeled in the figure are a few of the table fields and three records. Although only three fields are labeled, every column in the table is a field. Additionally, a record is an entire table row.

Record   Fields

	productID	title	publishDate	edition	isbn	coverart	description	price
▶	1	Visual Basic 6 How to Program	1999	1	0-13-456955-5	vbcover.jpg	Microsoft Visual Basic 6	$50.00
	2	C++ How to Program	2000	3	0-13-089571-7	cpphtp3.jpg	Generic C++	$50.00
	3	Java How to Program: 3e	1999	3	0-13-012507-5	jhtp3.jpg	Introduces Swing	$50.00
*	toNumber)							$0.00

Fig. H.1   **Products** table for the **Bug2Bug.com** Access database.

TERMINOLOGY

Active Server Pages (ASP)	Microsoft Access
ActiveX Data Objects (ADO)	Microsoft SQL Server 2000
bottom tier	real time
data	record
database	relational database
e-business	row
field	table
large-scale database	three-tier architecture

SELF REVIEW EXERCISES

H.1   Fill in the blanks for each of the following.
   a) The _____ tier of a multitier application maintains all of the information needed for an application.
   b) Data may be retrieved from a database using _____ and ActiveX Data Object (ADO).
   c) Query languages such as _____ are used to retrieve data from a database.

H.2   When answering the following questions, refer to Fig. H.1.
   a) How many fields are in the **Products** table?
   b) What is the name of the second field?

ANSWERS TO SELF REVIEW EXERCISES

H.1   a) data. b) Active Server Pages. c) SQL (Structured Query Language).

H.2   a) eight. b) title.

Accessibility Programming

Objectives

- To understand how to use the **alt** attribute of the **img** tag to describe images to blind and vision-impaired people, mobile-Web-device users, search engines, etc.
- To understand how to make tables more accessible to page readers by using the **headers** attribute in HTML 4.01.
- To understand how to verify that HTML tags are used properly and to ensure that Web pages are viewable on any type of display or reader.
- To better understand how VoiceXML™ will change the way people with disabilities access information on the Web.

I once was lost, but now am found,
Was blind, but now I see.
John Newton

'Tis the good reader that makes the good book...
Ralph Waldo Emerson

Outline

I.1	Introduction
I.2	Providing Alternatives for Multimedia Content
I.3	Maximizing Readability by Focusing on Structure
I.4	Accessibility in HTML Tables
I.5	Accessibility in HTML Frames
I.6	Accessibility in XML
I.7	Using Voice Synthesis and Recognition with VoiceXML™

Summary • Terminology • Self-Review Exercises • Answers to Self-Review Exercises

I.1 Introduction

The World Wide Web Consortium (W3C) launched the *Web Accessibility Initiative* (WAI™) on April 7, 1997. The initiative was launched with the goal of adapting standards for Web page development to ensure that everyone, including people with disabilities, can use the Web equally. *Accessibility* refers to the level of usability of an application or Web site for people with disabilities. Currently the Web is largely inaccessible to people with visual, learning, and mobility impairments. Factors such as the large variety of disabilities, language barriers, hardware and software inconsistencies, and others make achieving total Web accessibility difficult. As greater numbers of people with disabilities begin to use the Internet, it is imperative that Web site designers work to improve the accessibility of their sites. The mission of the WAI is described at **www.w3.org/WAI**.

As a member of the World Wide Web Consortium, Deitel & Associates, Inc., is committed to supporting the WAI. This appendix offers a closer look at what common practices make HTML and XML code inaccessible.

I.2 Providing Alternatives for Multimedia Content

Because current software used to interpret HTML is not able to describe image files automatically, it is essential that a description of the image be provided by the developer. Doing so with HTML requires the developer to use the **alt** tag. Web designers should be sure to provide useful descriptions in the **alt** attribute for use in nonvisual user agents. For example, if the **alt** attribute describes a sales growth chart, it should not describe the data in the chart. Instead, it should specify the chart's title. The chart's data should be included in the Web site's text. Web designers may also use the *longdesc attribute*, which is intended to augment the **alt** attribute's description. The value of the **longdesc** attribute is a URL that links to a Web page describing the image or multimedia content. [*Note:* If an image is used as a hyperlink and the **longdesc** attribute is also used, there is no set standard as to which page is loaded when the image is clicked.]

You will notice that the example in Fig. I.1 introdcues a new concept on lines 11 through 16. We begin with the **style** element on line 11. That element starts a new in-line style sheet, its attribute **type** which is set to **text/css** is what is called a *mime type*. A mime type indicates to the browser that a specific type of element, in this case, a cascading style sheet, will follow. Style Sheets are used to define the appearance of a Web-page or an entire Web site. The topic of style sheets goes beyond the scope of this appendix, however, separating a pages content from its appearance is a very important part of the WAI. For more information on how style sheets can improve a Web sites accessibility please visit `http://www.w3.org/TR/WCAG10-CORE-TECHS/#structure`

```
1   <!DOCTYPE HTML PUBLIC "-//W3C//DTD HTML 4.0 Transitional//EN">
2   <html>
3
4   <!-- Fig. 18.1 : altattribute.html                    -->
5   <!-- Using The alt attribute to Make an Image Accessible -->
6
7   <head>
8
9      <title>How To Use the alt Attribute</title>
10
11     <style type = "text/css">
12        body { background: powderblue; }
13        h1 { text-align: center; }
14        p { margin-top: 1em; text-align: center; }
15        p.description { text-align: left; }
16     </style>
17
18   </head>
19
20   <body>
21      <h1>How to use the <strong>alt</strong> attribute</h1>
22
23      <p class = "description">Below we compare two images,
24         one with the <strong>alt</strong> attribute present,
25         and one without. The <strong>alt</strong> appears as
26         a tool tip in most Web browsers, but, more importantly,
27         will help users who cannot view information conveyed
28         graphically.</p>
29
30      <p>This image has the <strong>alt</strong> attribute</p>
31
32      <p><img width = "182" height = "238"
33         src = "advjhtp1cov.jpg"
34         alt = "This is a picture of the cover of Advanced Java
35              How to Program">
36      </p>
37
38      <p>
39         This image does not have the <strong>alt</strong> attribute
40      </p>
41
42      <p>
43         <!-- This markup should be changed     -->
44         <!-- to include the alt attribute.     -->
45         <img src = "advjhtp1cov.jpg" width = "182" height = "238">
46      </p>
47
```

Fig. I.1   Using the **alt** attribute of the **img** tag (part 1 of 2).

```
48    </body>
49    </html>
```

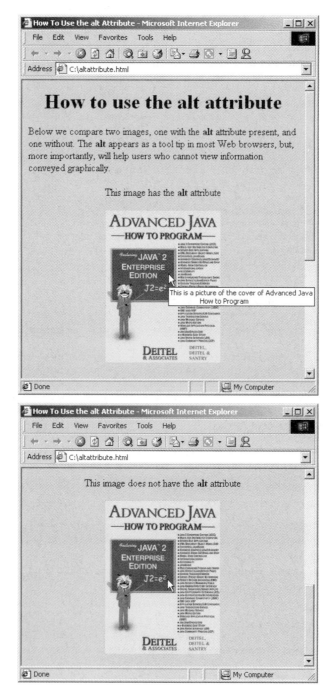

Fig. I.1   Using the **alt** attribute of the **img** tag (part 2 of 2).

Server-side image maps (images stored on a Web server with areas designated as hyperlinks) are another troublesome technology for some Web users, particularly those who cannot use a mouse. Server-side image maps require clicks of the mouse to initiate their actions. User agents are unable to make server-side image maps accessible to blind people or to users who cannot use a mouse. If equivalent text links are not provided when a server-side image map is used, some users will be unable to navigate the site. User-agent manufacturers will provide accessibility to server-side image maps in the future. Until then, if image maps are used, we recommend using client-side image maps (image maps whose links are designated in the Web page's source and thus can be understood by non-graphical user agents). For an example of the use of client-side image maps, see Fig. I.7 in Appendix D, "Introduction to HyperText Markup Language 4: Part II." For more information regarding the use of image maps, visit **www.w3.org/TR/REC-html40/struct/objects.html#h-13.6**.

 Good Programming Practice I.1

Always provide generous descriptions and corresponding text links for all image maps.

I.3 Maximizing Readability by Focusing on Structure

Many Web sites use tags for aesthetic purposes, rather than the purpose for which they were intended. For example, the **h1** heading tag is often erroneously used to make text large and bold. The desired visual effect may be achieved, but it creates a problem for screen readers: When the screen reader software encounters the **h1** tag, it may verbally inform the user that a new section has been reached, which may confuse the user. Only use tags such as **h1** in accordance with their HTML specification (e.g., as headings to introduce important sections of a document). Instead of using **h1** to make text large and bold, use Cascading Style Sheets (discussed in Appendix D) to format and style the text. Please refer to the *Web Content Accessibility Guidelines 1.0* at **www.w3.org/TR/WCAG** for further examples. [*Note:* the **strong** tag may also be used to make text bold; however, the inflection with which the text is spoken by screen readers may be affected.]

I.4 Accessibility in HTML Tables

Complex Web pages often contain tables for formatting content and presenting data. Tables cause problems for many screen readers, which are often incapable of translating tables in an understandable manner unless the tables are designed properly. For example, the *CAST eReader*, a screen reader developed by the Center for Applied Special Technology (**www.cast.org**), starts at the top-left-hand cell and reads, from top to bottom, columns from left to right. This procedure is known as reading a table in a *linearized* manner. The CAST eReader would thus read the table in Fig. I.2 as follows:

```
Price of Fruit Fruit Price Apple $0.25 Orange $0.50 Banana
$1.00 Pineapple $2.00
```

This reading does not adequately present the content of the table. The Web Content Accessibility Guidelines 1.0 recommend using Cascading Style Sheets (discussed in Appendix D) instead of tables unless the content in your tables, linearizes in an understandable way.

If the table in Fig. I.2 were large, the screen reader's linearized reading would be even more confusing to the user. By modifying the **td** tag with the **headers** attribute and modifying *header cells* (cells specified by the **th** tag) with the **id** attribute, you can ensure that a table is read as intended. Figure I.3 demonstrates how these modifications change the way a table is interpreted.

This table does not appear to be different from a standard HTML table. However, to a person using a screen reader, this table is read in a more intelligent manner. A screen reader would vocalize the data from the table in Fig. I.3 as follows:

```
1   <!DOCTYPE HTML PUBLIC "-//W3C//DTD HTML 4.0 Transitional//EN">
2
3   <html>
4   <!-- Fig. I.2 : withoutheaders.html -->
5
6   <head>
7      <title>HTML Table Without Headers</title>
8
9      <style type = "text/css">
10        body { background: limegreen;
11              text-align: center; }
12     </style>
13  </head>
14
15  <body>
16
17     <p>Price of Fruit</p>
18
19     <table border = "1" width = "50%">
20
21        <tr>
22           <td>Fruit</td>
23           <td>Price</td>
24        </tr>
25
26        <tr>
27           <td>Apple</td>
28           <td>$0.25</td>
29        </tr>
30
31        <tr>
32           <td>Orange</td>
33           <td>$0.50</td>
34        </tr>
35
36        <tr>
37           <td>Banana</td>
38           <td>$1.00</td>
39        </tr>
40
41        <tr>
42           <td>Pineapple</td>
```

Fig. I.2   HTML table without accessibility modifications (part 1 of 2).

```
43              <td>$2.00</td>
44          </tr>
45
46      </table>
47
48  </body>
49  </html>
```

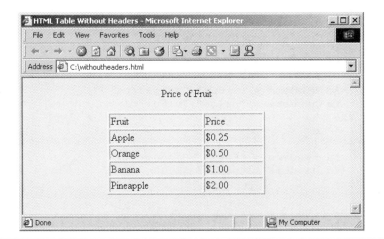

Fig. I.2   HTML table without accessibility modifications (part 2 of 2).

```
1   <!DOCTYPE HTML PUBLIC "-//W3C//DTD HTML 4.0 Transitional//EN">
2
3   <html>
4   <!-- Fig. I.3 : withheaders.html -->
5
6   <head>
7       <title>HTML Table With Headers</title>
8
9       <style type = "text/css">
10          body { background: limegreen;
11               text-align: center; }
12      </style>
13  </head>
14
15  <body>
16
17  <!-- This table uses the id and headers attributes to   -->
18  <!-- ensure readability by text-based browsers. It also -->
19  <!-- uses a summary attribute, used screen readers to    -->
20  <!-- describe the table.                                 -->
21
22      <table width = "50%" border = "1"
23          summary = "This table uses th elements and id and headers
24          attributes to make the table readable by screen readers">
```

Fig. I.3   Table optimized for screen reading using attribute **headers** (part 1 of 2).

```
25
26          <caption><strong>Price of Fruit</strong></caption>
27
28          <tr>
29             <th id = "fruit">Fruit</th>
30             <th id = "price">Price</th>
31          </tr>
32
33          <tr>
34             <td headers = "fruit">Apple</td>
35             <td headers = "price">$0.25</td>
36          </tr>
37
38          <tr>
39             <td headers = "fruit">Orange</td>
40             <td headers = "price">$0.50</td>
41          </tr>
42
43          <tr>
44             <td headers = "fruit">Banana</td>
45             <td headers = "price">$1.00</td>
46          </tr>
47
48          <tr>
49             <td headers = "fruit">Pineapple</td>
50             <td headers = "price">$2.00</td>
51          </tr>
52
53       </table>
54
55    </body>
56    </html>
```

Fig. I.3   Table optimized for screen reading using attribute `headers` (part 2 of 2).

```
Caption: Price of Fruit
Summary: This table uses th and the id and headers attributes
to make the table readable by screen readers.
Fruit: Apple, Price: $0.25
Fruit: Orange, Price: $0.50
Fruit: Banana, Price: $1.00
Fruit: Pineapple, Price: $2.00
```

Every cell in the table is preceded by its corresponding header when read by the screen reader. This format helps the listener understand the table. The **headers** attribute is specifically intended for tables that hold large amounts of data. Most small tables linearize fairly well as long as the **th** tag is used properly. It also helps to use the **summary** and **caption** attributes.

For more examples demonstrating how to make tables more accessible, visit **www.w3.org/TR/WCAG**.

I.5 Accessibility in HTML Frames

Web designers often use frames to display more than one HTML file in a single browser window. Frames are a convenient way to ensure that certain content is always on screen. Unfortunately, frames often lack proper descriptions, which prevents users with text-based browsers, or users who lack sight, from navigating the Web site.

The most important part of documenting a site with frames is making sure that all of the frames are given a meaningful description in the **title** tag. Examples of good titles are "*Navigation Frame*" and "*Main Content Frame.*" Users with text-based browsers, such as Lynx, a UNIX-based Web browser, must choose which frame they want to open, and the use of descriptive titles can make this choice much simpler for them. However, giving titles to frames does not solve all of the navigation problems associated with frames. The **noframes** tag allows Web designers to offer alternative content to users whose browsers do not support frames.

Good Programming Practice I.2

Always give a text equivalent for frames to ensure that user agents, which do not support frames, are given an alternative.

Good Programming Practice I.3

*Include a description of each frame's contents within the **noframes** tag.*

The Web Content Accessibility Guidelines 1.0 suggest using Cascading Style Sheets as an alternative to frames, because Cascading Style Sheets can provide similar functionality to that of frames and are highly customizible. Unfortunately, the ability to display multiple HTML documents in a single browser window requires the second generation of Cascading Style Sheets (CSS2), which is not yet fully supported by many user agents.

I.6 Accessibility in XML

Because of the freedom that XML gives developers in creating new markup languages, it is possible that many of these languages might not incorporate accessibility features. To prevent the proliferation of inaccessible languages, the WAI created guidelines for creating accessible XML. The specification focuses only on languages used to mark up data for user-interface rendering, such as the Extensible Hypertext Markup Language (XHTML). Accessible DTDs and schemas result in accessible XML documents, so the requirements for accessible DTDs and schemas have been defined. Reuse of existing accessible DTDs and schemas prevents developers from having to reinvent the wheel. In addition, the Guidelines recommend including a text description, similar to HTML's **alt** tag, for each nontext object on a page. XSL, rather than presentational elements, should be used to format XML documents for presentation. To further facilitate accessibility, element types should allow grouping and classification and should identify important content. Without an accessible user interface, other efforts to implement accessibility are much less effective, so it is essential to create stylesheets that can produce multiple outputs, including document outlines. To ensure that hyperlinks are accessible, XLink should be used.

Many XML languages follow the WAI guidelines, including Synchronized Multimedia Integration Language (SMIL) and Scalable Vector Graphics (SVG). The WAI XML Accessibility Guidelines can be found at **www.w3.org/WAI/PF/xmlgl.htm**.

I.7 Using Voice Synthesis and Recognition with VoiceXML™

Figures I.4 and I.5 show examples of VoiceXML for a Web site. The document's text is spoken to the user, and the text embedded within the VoiceXML tags allow for interactivity between the user and the browser. The output included in Fig. I.5 demonstrates a conversation that might take place between the user and the computer when this document is loaded.

```
1   <?xml version = "1.0"?>
2   <vxml version = "1.0">
3
4   <!-- Fig. I.4: main.vxml -->
5   <!-- Voice page            -->
6
7   <link next = "#home">
8       <grammar>home</grammar>
9   </link>
10
11  <link next = "#end">
12      <grammar>exit</grammar>
13  </link>
14
15  <var name = "currentOption" expr = "'home'"/>
16
17  <form>
18      <block>
19          <emp>Welcome</emp> to the voice page of Deitel and
20          Associates. To exit any time say exit.
21          To go to the home page any time say home.
22      </block>
23      <subdialog src = "#home"/>
24  </form>
25
```

Fig. I.4   A home page written in VoiceXML (part 1 of 3).

```
26    <menu id = "home">
27       <prompt count = "1" timeout = "10s">
28          You have just entered the Deitel home page.
29          Please make a selection by speaking one of the
30          following options:
31          <break msecs = "1000 "/>
32          <enumerate/>
33       </prompt>
34
35       <prompt count = "2">
36          Please say one of the following.
37          <break msecs = "1000 "/>
38          <enumerate/>
39       </prompt>
40
41       <choice next = "#about">About us</choice>
42       <choice next = "#directions">Driving directions</choice>
43       <choice next = "publications.vxml">Publications</choice>
44    </menu>
45
46    <form id = "about">
47       <block>
48       About Deitel and Associates, Inc.
49       Deitel and Associates, Inc. is an internationally
50       recognized corporate training and publishing organization,
51       specializing in programming languages, Internet and World
52       Wide Web technology and object technology education.
53       Deitel and Associates, Inc. is a member of the World Wide
54       Web Consortium. The company provides courses on Java, C++,
55       Visual Basic, C, Internet and World Wide Web programming
56       and Object Technology.
57          <assign name = "currentOption" expr = "'about'"/>
58          <goto next = "#repeat"/>
59       </block>
60    </form>
61
62    <form id = "directions">
63       <block>
64          Directions to Deitel and Associates, Inc.
65          We are located on Route 20 in Sudbury,
66          Massachusetts, equidistant from route
67       <sayas class = "digits">128</sayas> and route
68       <sayas class = "digits">495</sayas>.
69       <assign name = "currentOption" expr = "'directions'"/>
70       <goto next = "#repeat"/>
71       </block>
72    </form>
73
74    <form id = "repeat">
75       <field name = "confirm" type = "boolean">
76          <prompt>
77             To repeat say yes. To go back to home, say no.
78          </prompt>
```

Fig. I.4   A home page written in VoiceXML (part 2 of 3).

```
79
80          <filled>
81             <if cond = "confirm == true">
82                <goto expr = "'#' + currentOption"/>
83             <else/>
84                <goto next = "#home"/>
85             </if>
86          </filled>
87
88       </field>
89    </form>
90
91    <form id = "end">
92       <block>
93          Thank you for visiting Deitel and Associates voice page.
94          Have a nice day.
95          <exit/>
96       </block>
97    </form>
98
99    </vxml>
```

Fig. I.4   A home page written in VoiceXML (part 3 of 3).

```
100  <?xml version = "1.0"?>
101  <vxml version = "1.0">
102
103  <!-- Fig. I.5: publications.vxml       -->
104  <!-- Voice page for various publications -->
105
106  <link next = "main.vxml#home">
107     <grammar>home</grammar>
108  </link>
109  <link next = "main.vxml#end">
110     <grammar>exit</grammar>
111  </link>
112  <link next = "#publication">
113     <grammar>menu</grammar>
114  </link>
115
116  <var name = "currentOption" expr = "'home'"/>
117
118  <menu id = "publication">
119
120     <prompt count = "1" timeout = "12s">
121       Following are some of our publications. For more
122       information visit our web page at www.deitel.com.
123       To repeat the following menu, say menu at any time.
124       Please select by saying one of the following books:
125       <break msecs = "1000 "/>
126       <enumerate/>
127     </prompt>
```

Fig. I.5   Publication page of Deitel's VoiceXML page (part 1 of 4).

```
128
129    <prompt count = "2">
130      Please select from the following books.
131      <break msecs = "1000"/>
132      <enumerate/>
133    </prompt>
134
135    <choice next = "#java">Java.</choice>
136    <choice next = "#c">C.</choice>
137    <choice next = "#cplus">C plus plus.</choice>
138  </menu>
139
140  <form id = "java">
141    <block>
142      Java How to program, third edition.
143      The complete, authoritative introduction to Java.
144      Java is revolutionizing software development with
145      multimedia-intensive, platform-independent,
146      object-oriented code for conventional, Internet,
147      Intranet and Extranet-based applets and applications.
148      This Third Edition of the world's most widely used
149      university-level Java textbook carefully explains
150      Java's extraordinary capabilities.
151      <assign name = "currentOption" expr = "'java'"/>
152      <goto next = "#repeat"/>
153    </block>
154  </form>
155
156  <form id = "c">
157    <block>
158      C How to Program, third edition.
159      This is the long-awaited, thorough revision to the
160      world's best-selling introductory C book! The book's
161      powerful "teach by example" approach is based on
162      more than 10,000 lines of live code, thoroughly
163      explained and illustrated with screen captures showing
164      detailed output.World-renowned corporate trainers and
165      best-selling authors Harvey and Paul Deitel offer the
166      most comprehensive, practical introduction to C ever
167      published with hundreds of hands-on exercises, more
168      than 250 complete programs written and documented for
169      easy learning, and exceptional insight into good
170      programming practices, maximizing performance, avoiding
171      errors, debugging, and testing. New features include
172      thorough introductions to C++, Java, and object-oriented
173      programming that build directly on the C skills taught
174      in this book; coverage of graphical user interface
175      development and C library functions; and many new,
176      substantial hands-on projects.For anyone who wants to
177      learn C, improve their existing C skills, and understand
178      how C serves as the foundation for C++, Java, and
179      object-oriented development.
180      <assign name = "currentOption" expr = "'c'"/>
```

Fig. I.5   Publication page of Deitel's VoiceXML page (part 2 of 4).

```
181        <goto next = "#repeat"/>
182      </block>
183   </form>
184
185   <form id = "cplus">
186      <block>
187         The C++ how to program, second edition.
188         With nearly 250,000 sold, Harvey and Paul Deitel's C++
189         How to Program is the world's best-selling introduction
190         to C++ programming. Now, this classic has been thoroughly
191         updated! The new, full-color Third Edition has been
192         completely revised to reflect the ANSI C++ standard, add
193         powerful new coverage of object analysis and design with
194         UML, and give beginning C++ developers even better live
195         code examples and real-world projects. The Deitels' C++
196         How to Program is the most comprehensive, practical
197         introduction to C++ ever published with hundreds of
198         hands-on exercises, roughly 250 complete programs written
199         and documented for easy learning, and exceptional insight
200         into good programming practices, maximizing performance,
201         avoiding errors, debugging, and testing. This new Third
202         Edition covers every key concept and technique ANSI C++
203         developers need to master: control structures, functions,
204         arrays, pointers and strings, classes and data
205         abstraction, operator overloading, inheritance, virtual
206         functions, polymorphism, I/O, templates, exception
207         handling, file processing, data structures, and more. It
208         also includes a detailed introduction to Standard
209         Template Library containers, container adapters,
210         algorithms, and iterators.
211         <assign name = "currentOption" expr = "'cplus'"/>
212         <goto next = "#repeat"/>
213      </block>
214   </form>
215
216   <form id = "repeat">
217      <field name = "confirm" type = "boolean">
218
219         <prompt>
220            To repeat say yes. Say no, to go back to home.
221         </prompt>
222
223         <filled>
224            <if cond = "confirm == true">
225               <goto expr = "'#' + currentOption"/>
226            <else/>
227               <goto next = "#publication"/>
228            </if>
229         </filled>
230      </field>
231   </form>
232   </vxml>
```

Fig. I.5   Publication page of Deitel's VoiceXML page (part 3 of 4).

```
Computer:
Welcome to the voice page of Deitel and Associates. To exit any time
say exit. To go to the home page any time say home.

User:
Home

Computer:
You have just entered the Deitel home page. Please make a selection by
speaking one of the following options: About us, Driving directions,
Publications.

User:
Driving directions

Computer:
Directions to Deitel and Associates, Inc.
We are located on Route 20 in Sudbury,
Massachusetts, equidistant from route 128
and route 495.
To repeat say yes. To go back to home, say no.
```

Fig. I.5   Publication page of Deitel's VoiceXML page (part 4 of 4).

A VoiceXML document is made up of a series of dialogs and subdialogs, which result in spoken interaction between the user and the computer. The tags that implement the dialogs are the **form** and **menu** tags. A **form** element presents information and gathers data from the user. A **menu** element provides options to the user and transfers control to other dialogs, based on the user's selections.

Lines 7–9

```
<link next = "#home">
    <grammar>home</grammar>
</link>
```

use element *link* to create an active link to the home page. Attribute *next* holds the URI that is navigated to when the link is selected. Element *grammar* provides the text that the user must speak in order to select the link. In this **link** element, we navigate to the element with **id home** when the user says the word **home**. Lines 11–13 use element **link** to create a link to **id end** when the user says the word **exit**.

Lines 17–24 create a form dialog using element *form*, which collects information from the user. Lines 18–22

```
<block>
    <emp>Welcome</emp> to the voice page of Deitel and
    Associates. To exit any time say exit.
    To go to the home page any time say home.
</block>
```

present introductory text to the user. Element **emp** is used to add emphasis to a section of speech.

The **menu** element on line 26 enables the user to select the page to which they would like to link. The **choice** element, which is always part of either a **menu** or a **form**, presents these options to the user. The **next** attribute indicates the page to be loaded when the user makes a selection. The user selects a **choice** element by speaking the words contained in the element into a microphone. In this example, the first and second **choice** elements on lines 41 and 42 transfer control to a *local dialog* (i.e., a location within the same document) when they are selected. The third **choice** element transfers the user to the document **publications.vxml**. Lines 27–33

```
<prompt count = "1" timeout = "10s">
   You have just entered the Deitel home page.
   Please make a selection by speaking one of the
   following options:
   <break msecs = "1000" />
   <enumerate/>
</prompt>
```

use element ***prompt*** to instruct the user to make a selection. Attribute ***count*** is used to provide multiple prompts for a task. VoiceXML keeps track of the number of prompts given and matches them to attribute **count**. The closest **prompt** with attribute **count** that is less than the current number of prompts is output. Attribute **timeout** provides a length of time to wait after the output of the prompt. In case the user does not respond before the timeout period expires, lines 35–39 provide a second, shorter prompt to remind the user that a selection is required.

The **publications.vxml** (Fig. I.5) is loaded into the browser when the user chooses the **publications** option. Lines 106–111 define **link** elements that provide links to **main.vxml**. Lines 112–114 provide links to the **menu** element (lines 118–138), which asks the user to select one of the publications. Java, C and C++ are the three options the user can select. Each of the books on these topics is described in the **form** elements (lines 140–214). Once the browser speaks out the description, the control is transferred to the **form** element with **id** attribute whose value equals **repeat** (lines 216–231).

Figure I.6 provides a brief description of each of the VoiceXML tags used in the previous example (Fig. I.5).

VoiceXML Tag	Description
`<assign>`	Assigns a value to a variable.
`<block>`	Presents information to the user without any interaction between the user and the computer (i.e., the computer does not expect any input from the user).
`<break>`	Instructs the computer to pause its speech output for a specified period of time.
`<choice>`	Specifies an option in a **menu** element.
`<enumerate>`	Lists all of the available options to the user.
`<exit>`	Exits the program.

Fig. I.6   Elements in VoiceXML.

VoiceXML Tag	Description
`<filled>`	Contains elements to be executed when the computer receives input for a **form** element from the user.
`<form>`	Gathers information from the user for a set of variables.
`<goto>`	Transfers control from one dialog to another.
`<grammar>`	Specifies grammar for the expected input from the user.
`<if>`, `<else>`, `<elseif>`	Control statements used for making logic decisions.
`<link>`	A transfer of control similar to the **goto** statement, but a **link** can be executed at any time during the program's execution.
`<menu>`	Provides user options and transfers control to other dialogs, based on the selected option.
`<prompt>`	Specifies text to be read to the user when a selection is needed.
`<subdialog>`	Calls another dialog. Control is transferred back to the calling dialog after the subdialog is executed.
`<var>`	Declares a variable.
`<vxml>`	The top-level tag which specifies that the document should be processed by a VoiceXML interpreter.

Fig. I.6   Elements in VoiceXML.

6.6 Internet and World Wide Web Resources

There are many accessibility resources on the Internet and World Wide Web, and this section lists a variety of them.

www.w3.org/WAI
The World Wide Web Consortium's *Web Accessibility Initiative* (*WAI*) site promotes design of universally accessible Web sites. This site will help you keep up to date with current guidelines and forthcoming standards for Web accessibility.

www.w3.org/TR/WCAG10
This page is a note published by the WCAG working group. It discusses techniques that can be used to comply with the WAI. This page is a great resource and can be used to find additional information on many of the topics covered in this chapter.

deafness.about.com/health/deafness/msubmenu6.htm
This site is the home page of **deafness.about.com**. It is an excellent resource to find information pertaining to deafness.

www.cast.org
CAST stands for the Center for Applied Special Technology. CAST offers software intended to help individuals with disabilities use a computer, including a valuable accessibility checker—free of charge. The accessibility checker is a Web-based program used to validate the accessibility of Web sites.

www.trainingpost.org/3-2-inst.htm
This site presents a tutorial on the Gunning Fog Index. The Gunning Fog Index is a method of grading text on its readability.

www.w3.org/TR/REC-CSS2/aural.html
This page discusses Aural Style Sheets, outlining the purpose and uses of this new technology.

laurence.canlearn.ca/English/learn/newaccessguide/indie
INDIE is an acronym that stands for "Integrated Network of Disability Information and Education." This site is home to a powerful search engine that help users find out information about disabilities.

java.sun.com/products/java-media/speech/forDevelopers/JSML
This site outlines the specifications for JSML, Sun Microsystem's Java Speech Markup Language. This language, like VoiceXML, could drastically improve accessibility for visually impaired people.

www.slcc.edu/webguide/lynxit.html
Lynxit is a development tool that allows users to view any Web site just as a text-only browser would. The site's form allows you to enter a URL and returns the Web site in text-only format.

www.trill-home.com/lynx/public_lynx.html
This site allows you to use browse the Web using a Lynx browser. Doing so will allow you to see how your page will load for users without the most current technologies.

www.wgbh.org/wgbh/pages/ncam/accesslinks.html
This site provides links to other accessibility pages across the Web.

ocfo.ed.gov/coninfo/clibrary/software.htm
This page is the U.S. Department of Education's Web site for software accessibility requirements. It is aimed at helping developers produce accessible products.

www.alphaworks.ibm.com
This site is the home page for IBM Alphaworks. It provides information on VoiceXML and offers a download of the beta version of Voice Server SDK.

www-3.ibm.com/able/access.html
This site is the homepage of IBM's accessibility site. It provides information on IBM products and their accessibility and also discusses hardware, software and Web accessibility.

www.microsoft.com/enable/dev/guidelines/software.htm
This Web site presents Microsoft's guidelines for designing accessible software.

www.w3.org/TR/voice-tts-reqs
This page explains the speech synthesis markup requirements for voice markup languages.

deafness.about.com/health/deafness/msubvib.htm
This site provides information on vibrotactile devices. These devices allow deaf people to experience audio in the form of vibrations.

web.ukonline.co.uk/ddmc/software.html
This site provides links to software for people with disabilities.

www.hj.com
Henter-Joyce a division of Freedom Scientific that provides software for blind and visually impaired people. It is the home of JAWS.

www.abledata.com/text2/icg_hear.htm
This page contains a consumer guide that discusses technologies for hearing-impaired people.

www.washington.edu/doit
The University of Washington's DO-IT (Disabilities, Opportunities, Internetworking and Technology) site provides information and Web development resources for creating universally accessible Web sites.

`www.webable.com`

The WebABLE site contains links to many disability-related Internet resources and is geared towards those looking to develop technologies for people with disabilities.

`www.speech.cs.cmu.edu/comp.speech/SpeechLinks.html`

The Speech Technology Hyperlinks page has over 500 links to sites related to computer-based speech and speech recognition tools.

`www.islandnet.com/~tslemko`

The Micro Consulting Limited site contains shareware speech synthesis software.

`www.chantinc.com/technology`

This page is the Chant Web site, which discusses speech technology and how it works. Chant also provides speech synthesis and speech recognition software.

SUMMARY

- Accessibility refers to the level of usability of an application or Web site for people with disabilities. The vast majority of Web sites are considered inaccessible to people with visual, learning or mobility impairments.

- Web designers should avoid misuse of the **alt** attribute; it is intended to provide a short description of an HTML object that may not load properly on all user agents.

- The value of the **longdesc** attribute is a text-based URL that is linked to a Web page which describes the image associated with the attribute.

- User agents are unable to make server-side image maps accessible to blind people or to others who cannot use a mouse. If equivalent text links are not provided when a server-side image map is used, some users will be unable to navigate the site.

- Web designers often use frames to display more than one HTML file at a time and are a convenient way to ensure that certain content is always on screen. Unfortunately, frames often lack proper descriptions, which prevents users with text-based browsers, or users who lack sight, from navigating the Web site.

- The **noframes** tag allows the designer to offer alternative content to users whose browsers do not support frames.

- A VoiceXML document is made up of a series of dialogs and subdialogs, which result in spoken interaction between the user and the computer.

- Open-source software for the visually impaired already exists and is often superior to most of its proprietary, closed-source counterparts, but it still does not use the Linux OS to its fullest extent.

- Visually impaired people are not the only beneficiaries of the effort being made to improve mark-up languages. The deaf also have a great number of tools to help them interpret auditory information delivered over the Web.

TERMINOLOGY

a division of Freedom Scientific
accessibility
alt attribute
assign tag in VoiceXML
AuralCSS
b tag (bold)
block tag in VoiceXML
break tag in VoiceXML

caption
Cascading Style Sheets (CSS)
choice tag in VoiceXML
client-side image map
CSS2
default settings
enumerate tag in VoiceXML
exit tag in VoiceXML

field variable
filled tag in VoiceXML
form tag in VoiceXML
frames
goto tag in VoiceXML
grammar tag in VoiceXML
h1
header cells
headers attribute of **td** tag
id attribute
img tag
linearized reading of a table
link tag in VoiceXML
longdesc attribute
Lynx
markup language
menu tag in VoiceXML
noframes tag
priority 2 checkpoint
priority 3 checkpoint
prompt tag in VoiceXML
quick tips

readability
screen reader
server-side image map
speech recognition
speech synthesizer
strong tag
subdialog tag in VoiceXML
summary attribute
Synchronized Multimedia Integration
     Language (SMIL)
tables
td tag
text-to-speech
th tag
timeout
title tag
user agent
var tag in VoiceXML
Voice Server
Voice Server SDK
VoiceXML
vxml tag in VoiceXML

SELF-REVIEW EXERCISES

I.1   Spell out the following acronyms:
   a) W3C.
   b) WAI.
   c) JAWS.
   d) SMIL.
   e) CSS.

I.2   Fill in the blanks in each of the following statements.
   a) The highest priority of the Web Accessibility Initiative is to ensure that each _____,
      _____ and _____ is accompanied by a description that clearly defines its pur-
      pose.
   b) Although they can be used as a great layout tool,_____ are difficult for screen read-
      ers to interpret and convey clearly to a user.
   c) In order to make your frame accessible to the handicapped, it is important to include
      _____ tags on your page.
   d) Blind people using computers are often assisted by_____ and _____.

I.3   State whether each of the following is *true* or *false*. If *false*, explain why.
   a) Screen readers have no problem reading and translating images.
   b) Image maps are no problem for screen readers to translate, so long as the programmer has
      made changes to their code to improve accessibility.
   c) When writing pages for the general public, it is important to consider the reading diffi-
      culty level of the text you are writing.
   d) The **alt** tag helps screen readers describe images in a Web page.
   e) Left-handed people have been helped by the improvements made in speech-recognition
      technology more than any other group of people.

        f)   VoiceXML lets users interact with Web content using speech recognition and speech synthesis technologies.

ANSWERS TO SELF-REVIEW EXERCISES

I.1   a) World Wide Web Consortium. b) Web Accessibility Initiative. c) Job Access with Sound. d) Synchronized Multimedia Integration Language. e) Cascading Style Sheets.

I.2   a) image, movie, sound. b) tables. c) **noframes**. d) braille displays, braille keyboards.

I.3   a) False. Screen readers have no way of telling a user what is shown in an image. If the programmer includes an **alt** attribute inside the **img** tag, the screen reader will read this description to the user. b) False. Screen readers have no way of translating image maps, no matter what programming changes are made. The solution to this problem is to include text-based links alongside all image maps. c) True. d) True. e) False. Although left-handed people can use speech-recognition technology as everyone else can, speech-recognition technology has had the largest impact on the blind and on people who have trouble typing. f) True.

Installing a Web Server

This appendix (located on our Web site—**www.deitel.com**) discusses the setup and configuration of a Web server for use with the case study in Appendices B through H.

Setting Up a Microsoft ODBC Data Source

This appendix (located on our Web site—**www.deitel.com**) discusses the setup and configuration of a Microsoft Open Database Connectivity (ODBC) Data Source for use with the case study in Appendices B through H.

Glossary

Numerics

24-by-7 24 hours per day, seven days per week.

3G Third generation technology.

401(k) plan An investing vehicle for employee retirement.

A

Abeline The high-speed network currently used by Internet2 consortium members.

accounts receivable The realistic and expected amount of payments owed to a company for products and services sold to customers.

actual loss One of the criteria used to prove defamation. The defendant must be able to prove that the defamatory statement resulted monetary loss, or will result in monetary loss.

actual malice One of the criteria used to prove defamation. The defendant must be able to prove that defamatory statements were made when known to be false.

address book A feature of e-mail that stores names and e-mail addresses.

advanced encryption standard (AES) A new, more secure standard for symmetric encryption.

affiliate The company hosting another company's advertising in return for a reward based on predetermined terms.

affiliate program A form of partnership where a merchant pays affiliates for pre-specified actions taken by visitors who click-through from an affiliate site to a merchant site.

affiliate solution provider Companies that can provide end-to-end solutions for a company's affiliate program.

African Information Society Initiative A program developed to build national communication standards in Africa.

Age of Knowledge A phrase often used to describe the Internet era.

aggregation service Collects users' financial information and keeps it in one location on the Internet.

ALT tag Provides a short text description of an HTML object.

Americans with Disabilities Act (ADA) Prohibits businesses from discriminating against people with disabilities.

analog signal   As opposed to a digital signal which is sent in discrete intervals, this is sent as a stream of continuous data.

anchor   A term used interchangeably with hyperlink.

animation   This often refers to a series of still images played in sequence to simulate movement.

anonymity indexes   Users can acquire a false identity under which to surf the Internet.

Anticybersquatting Consumer Protection Act of 1999   Enacted by Congress in an effort to protect traditional trademarking in cyberspace.

application service provider (ASP)   Provide customized business software applications over the Internet.

application-level gateway   A type of firewall that screens the actual data.

ARPANet   The predecessor to the modern Internet.

asymmetric algorithms   Use inversely related key pairs (a public key and a private key) to encrypt and decrypt messages. If the public key is used to encrypt the message, only the inversely related private key can decrypt it.

asymmetric digital subscriber line (ADSL)   ADSL connections are asymmetric because the connection speed for sending data to the Internet (upstream) is slower than the connection speed for receiving data from the Internet (downstream).

asynchronous learning   Self-paced learning.

attribute   Each field or column in a table.

authentication   Proving the identity of an individual.

authoring tools accessibility guidelines (ATAG)   Contains specifications for software developers to follow to meet the needs of people with disabilities.

automated clearing house (ACH)   Processes electronic monetary transfers.

automatic number identification (ANI)   Used to verify the identity of the customer and the purchases they make.

availability   Allowing authorized users in a network to access information and services while keeping unauthorized users out.

B

back-end systems   Portions of the Web site that service functionality, usually including database management, payment processing and logistics.

bandwidth   The capacity for data exchange over the Internet. Indicates how much data can be transferred through the medium in a fixed amount of time.

banner advertisement   Appears on a Web site as a small billboard containing graphics and an advertising message.

bartering   Offering one item in exchange for another.

basic rate interface (BRI)   ISDN bandwidth is divided into three channels that each perform different tasks, using Basic Rate Interface (BRI). Two bearer (B) channels each support data transfers at 64 Kbps, while the data (D) channel is used to transmit routing information. Each B channel can be used for either voice or data communications. The B channels may also be combined to provide the maximum ISDN transfer rate of 128 Kbps.

bearer channel   A type of channel in ISDN bandwidth used for either voice or data communications. The B channels may also be combined to provide the maximum ISDN transfer rate of 128 Kbps.

binary string   A computer stores data as such; a sequence of ones and zeros.

biometrics   Uses unique personal information such as fingerprints, eyeball iris scans or face scans to identify a user.

bit   Each digital sequence of a binary string.

blocking and filtering methods   Technologies that help parents and educators limit children's access to "harmful" material on the Web.

bond   A written promise that an entity will repay debt that is sold to an investor.

braille displays   Devices that receive data from screen-reading software and output the data as braille.

braille keyboard   Has the letters written on every key and its equivalent braille symbol.

brand   A symbol or name that distinguishes a company and its products or services from its competitors.

break-even point   The exact sales volume where total revenues equal total expenses.

brick-and-mortar business   A business that has only a physical presence.

broadband   A category of high-bandwidth Internet service provided mainly by cable television and telephone companies to home users.

browser   An important piece of software that enables you to browse the Internet.

bursting   Delivers video and audio content faster so that it builds up substantially at the receiving end, potentially enabling a smoother appearance.

business plan   Enables you to see your business on paper for evaluation purposes. Usually includes the layout, an overview of the business premise, etc.

business verify   Allow businesses to access information databases that check the credit and validity of new customers.

business-to-business (B2B)   Refers to the relationship between two or more companies.

business-to-business integrators (B2Bi)   Companies that use XML and similar technologies to help other companies integrate their current systems with the Web.

business-to-consumer (B2C)   Refers to the relationship between a business and the end consumer. Businesses that market towards consumers, as opposed to other businesses.

C

cable modem   A cable modem allows you to access the Internet using cable TV lines.

cache   Automatically saves Web pages and their elements for rapid, future access.

call handling   The maintenance of out-bound and in-bound calls from customers and service representatives.

cannibalization   Decrease in sales of one or more products in a line, when a new product is released.

cards (in WML)   Static parts in a WML document (or deck). Each card consists of one user interaction, providing the WML browser with a small, self-contained document for browsing.

central processing unit (CPU)   That part of the computer where calculations are done.

CERT security improvement modules   Tutorials on network security.

certificate authority hierarchy   A chain of certificates.

certificate repository   Where digital certificates are held available to the public.

certificate revocation list (CRL)   A list of canceled and revoked certificates.

Certification Authority (CA)   Issues digital certificates and takes responsibility for authentication.

channel   A communications path that carries data between a computer and the Internet.

Chief Learning Officer (CLO)   Employed to design the corporate learning strategy in corporate industries.

Children's Online Protection Act of 1998   Designed to restrict pornography on the Internet.

Children's Online Privacy Protection Act of 2000   Requires e-businesses to receive parental consent before acquiring personal information from a child.

chilling effect   When individuals limit their speech to avoid a lawsuit.

cipher   A technique or algorithm for encrypting messages; also called cryptosystem.

ciphertext   Encrypted data.

clear GIFs   See Web bugs.

click-and-mortar business   Has both physical and online presence.

click-through banner advertisements   A banner advertisement with an embedded link that allows users to click on it and be brought to another site.

client side   Refers to the computer and information systems employed by the user, or consumer.

client/server application   Using a database on the server side which allows customers on the client side to search for products in a variety of ways.

code-division multiple access (CDMA)   A technology with increased bandwidth used for digital, wireless communications.

collaborative filtering   Compares ratings of a present user's interests and decisions with those of past users in order to offer content relative to the present user's interests.

Collections of Information Antipiracy Act   Makes it easier to prosecute any group which takes listings from one organization and, in doing so, harms the original business.

collision   Occurs when multiple messages have the same hash value.

co-location   Provide a secure physical locations for a business' server hardware. Typical co-location services include dedicated Internet connections and protection from power outages, fire and other disasters.

column   A field or attribute in a table.

commission-based model   Compensates its affiliates for each sale resulting from affiliate-hosted advertisements.

Commodity Futures Trading Commission   Federal Regulatory Agency for Futures Trading.

Communications Decency Act of 1996   Designed to restrict pornography on the Internet.

communications medium   Connects computers and other digital equipment together.

comparison-pricing model   Allows customers to search a variety of merchants and find a desired product or service at the lowest price.

computer emergency response team (CERT)   Responds to reports of viruses and denial-of-service attacks. Provides information on network security.

computer usage compliance survey   Allow business owners to create a custom user's policy to define how the company will monitor Web surfing, e-mailing, visits to restricted sites, downloading of inappropriate images and use of encryption.

computer-generated imaging (CGI)   Used to create special effects in film.

consolidation service   Services any biller and presents consumers with all their bills in one interactive online environment.

consumer profile   Collected personal information on a consumer, usually for marketing purposes.

contact smart card   Card that enables secure online payments when used with a smart-card reader.

contactless smart card   Contains a coiled antenna and a computer chip inside, enabling the card to transmit information. Enables faster information exchange than is possible using a contact smart card.

content delivery service   Manages, updates and distributes Web site content.

content management   Frequent and efficient updating of Web site content.

continuous speech recognition (CSR)   A program that allows a person to speak fluently and quickly to a computer without losing the accuracy of the translation into text.

continuous-availability computing   Attempts to eliminate downtime.

convergence   Refers to the joining of multiple technologies such as the Internet with television, radio and wireless technology to create a new and improved group of products.

cookies   Files that are placed on your computer by Web sites to retain or gather information between sessions

copyright   The protection given to the author of an original piece, including "literary, dramatic, musical, artistic and certain other intellectual works," whether the work has been published or not.

Copyright Act of 1976   Determines copyright infringement based on the criteria that the violation must have been conducted "willfully and for purposes of commercial advantage or private financial gain."

core fair information practices   Established by the Federal Trade Commission regarding online marketing tactics that involve gathering and using consumer information.

corporate culture   The general feeling or identity of an organization that is a reflection of the environment and the employees.

cost-per-thousand model (CPM)   A fee for every one thousand visitors that view an advertisement.

crisis management   A response to a problematic situation of a company or organization.

cross-media advertising   Uses a combination of rich media and traditional advertising forms to execute an advertising campaign.

cross-platform   Can be accessed by many different operating systems.

cryptanalysis   Trying to decrypt ciphertext without knowledge of the decryption key.

cryptography   Transforms data by using a key to make the data incomprehensible to all but the sender and the intended receivers.

cryptosystem   A technique or algorithm for encrypting messages; also called cipher.

customer acquisition   Additional sales which can result from having affiliates.

customer registration   Requiring visitors to fill out a form with personal information that is used to create a profile.

customer relationship management (CRM)   A strategy that focuses on providing and maintaining quality service for customers by effectively communicating and delivering products, services, information, and solutions to address their problems.

cyberspace   The realm of digital transmission not limited by geography.

cybersquatting   A form of trademark infringement that occurs when a cybersquatter buys an assortment of domain names that are obvious representations of a brick-and-mortar company.

D

dailies   The days film from a given production.

data channel   Used to transmit routing information.

data encryption standard (DES)   One of the most commonly used symmetric encryption algorithms.

data mining   Uses algorithms and statistical tools to find patterns in data gathered from customer visits.

data packets   Individual message pieces.

database   Stores and reports on large amounts of customer information, such as names, addresses, credit-card information and past purchases.

database management system (DBMS)   Provides mechanisms for storing and organizing data in a manner that facilitates satisfying sophisticated queries and manipulations of the data.

database server   A networked computer used for storing databases.

day trading   Making short-term trades in an attempt to profit off of market inefficiencies.

debit card   Gives card-holders access to their savings, checking and other accounts. Funds are instantly deducted from the customer's checking account.

decimalization   The change of stock prices from fractions to decimals.

deck (in WML)   A WML document.

decryption   Decoding information.

dedicated connection   Typically a high-speed Internet connection that is always connected.

defamation   The act of injuring another's reputation, honor or good name through false written or oral communication.

default settings   Standard settings in a hardware or software product as defined by the manufacturer.

deforestation   The loss of forest land over time.

demand-collection system   Priceline's patented business mechanism, called the demand-collection system, is an intelligent agent that takes customers' bids to the Priceline partners to see whether they will accept the prices for the requested products and services.

demodulation   Converts light into an electrical signal.

demodulator   Translates digital signals from a computer into light.

demographics   Statistics of the human population such as size, growth and income.

denial-of-service attack   Causes networked computers to crash or disconnect from the network.

deployment   To initiate, as in launching an e-business.

destination address   Indicates the house or business to which the letter or e-mail should be delivered.

Diffie-Hellman key agreement protocol   In 1976 Whitfield Diffie and Martin Hellman developed public key cryptography. Developed to solve the problem of exchanging keys securely.

digital cash   Cash stored electronically that is used for online purchases, can be used to make online electronic payments.

digital cellular phone   A wireless, handheld phone that currently uses second generation wireless technology.

digital certificate   A document which includes relevant information about the identity of information sent over the Internet.

digital copies   Perfect duplicates of original material.

digital divide   The socio-economic segregation between those who can afford Internet technology and those that cannot.

digital envelope   The most common key agreement protocol.

digital IDs   Allows user to digitally sign e-mail messages for security purposes.

digital libraries   Stores audio and video and text files.

Digital Millennium Copyright Act of 1998   Represents the rights of creative bodies to protect their work as well as the rights of educators and resource providers to receive access to this work.

digital payment authentication (DPA)   Online payments are digitally signed, secured and authenticated.

digital property rights language (DPRL)   A technology created by Xerox to prevent the illegal use of copywritten material.

digital redlining   Suggests that a company could skew an individual's knowledge of available products by basing the advertisements the user sees on past behavior.

digital signature   Signatures encoded for a specific individual and processed within a computer; electronic equivalent of written signatures.

digital signature algorithm (DSA)   The U.S. government's digital-authentication standard.

digital subscriber line (DSL)   Offers high-bandwidth Internet access over existing copper telephone lines.

digital wallet   Stores credit (or debit) card information for multiple cards, as well as a digital certificate verifying the cardholder's identity for payment of online transactions.

digital watermarking   Used most commonly for intellectual property protection, a digital watermark can be either visible or invisible. It is usually a company logo, copyright notification or other mark or message that indicates the owner of the digital document. The owner of a document could show the hidden watermark in a court of law, for example, to prove that the watermarked item was stolen.

direct e-mail   Sending e-mail for marketing purposes including advertising products and sending special promotions.

directory   A site that provides aggregated information and links to sites relevant to specified topics.

disabilities issues task force (of the FCC)   Ensures that hearing and speech-impaired people have access to 911 using mobile devices.

discount-brokerage service   Requires self-sufficiency, leaving the investor responsible for making and executing investment decisions. Requires the investor to manage their own accounts and conduct their own research.

distributed denial-of-service attack   Occurs when a network's resources are taken up by an unauthorized party, leaving the network unavailable for legitimate users; typically, the attack is performed by flooding servers with data packets sent by many computers simultaneously. This action greatly increases the traffic on the network, overwhelming the servers and making it impossible for legitimate users to download information.

distributed-computing network   Enables individuals to support a number of causes by donating their unused computer time.

distributor   The supplier who acts as a middleman to manufacturers and vendors.

dollar-based investing   Allows investors to invest smaller monetary amounts and own fractions of stocks.

domain name   A combination of your ISP's name and an extension specifying the email address type.

domain name system (DNS)   Translates fully-qualified host names into IP addresses.

download   Making a copy of a file on a computer.

downstream   Used to identify the flow of information received by a personal computer from the Web server.

E

E911 Act   Designed to standardize and enhance 911 service across mobile devices.

e-book   Digitally formatted content that appears like a book.

e-book reader   A device about the size of the average paperback book that allows consumers to read digital content.

e-business   A company that has an online presence. Involves all business functions, both inter- and intra-organizational.

ebXML   An XML specification designed to standardize e-book formatting across disparate electronic publishing media.

e-cards   Electronic greeting cards sent via e-mail.

e-commerce   Selling, trading, bartering and conducting transactions over the Web.

economies of scale   A decrease in cost as supply increases.

e-contact center   Uses online methods of customer service. Same as multimedia contact center.

e-Customer Relationship Management (eCRM)   the application of CRM to an e-business' strategy and includes the personalization and customizing of customers' experiences and interactions with a Web site, call center or any other method of customer contact with the e-business.

e-learning   Education as facilitated by the Internet, World Wide Web and various technologies.

electronic benefits transfer (EBT)   The electronic transfer of government funds to retailers for the benefit of the needy.

electronic bill presentment and payment (EBPP)   Offers the ability to present a company's bill on multiple platforms online, an execute payment processes.

electronic commerce modeling language (ECML)   Standardized the technology of eWallets. At the point of online checkout, a universal format for buyers and sellers.

electronic communication network (ECN)   Provide an electronic network for trading securities by revealing order sizes and prices and connecting buyers and sellers.

electronic data interchange (EDI)   Business forms are standardized so that companies can share information with customers, vendors and business partners electronically.

electronic funds transfer (EFT)   Used to transfer money between accounts electronically.

electronic mail (e-mail)   The digital transmission of a message.

electronic payment (e-payment)   Currency that is stored electronically and used to make payments to online merchants who do not accept credit cards.

Electronic Signatures in Global and National Commerce Act of 2000   Legislation, also known as the e-Sign bill, designed to promote online commerce by legitimizing online contractual agreements.

electronic ticket (e-ticket)   An electronic reservation service that stores all customer registration data within a computer system making paper tickets unnecessary.

e-mail assistance   Used to manage e-mail customer service.

e-mail server   Administer incoming and outgoing e-mail.

eMatter   A collection of short stories, single chapters and other small works not considered a full-length e-book.

end-to-end e-business solutions   Services to build Web sites from conception to implementation.

enterprise application integration (EAI)   The process of integrating traditional EDI systems with the Web.

enterprise resource planning (ERP)   A software system that integrates and automates manufacturing, distribution, management issues, projects and employees.

entry-level position   Positions commonly sought by individuals who are entering a specific field or the job market for the first time.

e-publishing   The digital creation and distribution of electronic content, including printed materials, music, video and software.

e-text   Project Gutenberg defines their electronic material as e-text.

European Union Directive on Data Exchange   Mandates that personal information be kept current and used in a lawful manner for its designated purpose.

e-wallet   Electronically stores purchasing information.

eXtensible markup language (XML)   A specification developed by the W3C to allow the customization of Web documents. XML allows for the custom definition, transmission, validation, and interpretation of data over the Internet.

eXtensible rights markup language (XrML)   An XML specification designed to prevent the illegal use of copyrighted materials by standardizing the technology used to protect these materials.

e-zine   Electronic magazine.

F

fair use   The use of a copyrighted work for education, research, criticism, etc.

fault-tolerant systems   Systems that implement multiple levels of back-up to prevent the loss of important data.

Federal Trade Commission (FCC)   Government body that regulates antitrust and consumer-protection laws.

fiber optics   Allows for unlimited speed of data transfers over the Internet.

fiber-optic cable   Cables composed of flexible glass fiber that have much wider bandwidth than traditional copper wire. Fiber-optic cables use short bursts of light to represent bits.

file server   A networked computer used for storing files.

file transfer protocol (FTP)   A method for making data available over the Internet.

file-transfer technology   Technology used to pass compressed data over the Web securely.

financial aggregator   Allows people to view information from all of their financial accounts in one place on the Internet, regardless of holding institution.

financial planning   A financial strategy for investing and reaching set goals.

Financial Services Modernization Act of 1999   Establishes a set of regulations concerning the management of consumer information.

Financial Services Technology Consortium (FSTC)   Attempts to set a standard for aggregation methods.

firewall   Protects a local area network (LAN) from intruders outside the network.

float   The time it takes for checks to clear after they have been deposited.

forms   Areas on Web sites where a user can enter information.

Freedom of Information Act   Requires all U.S. government agencies to release information on CIA operations and historical cases to the public.

freeware   Free software distribution methods.

frequently asked questions (FAQ)   A list of common questions or concerns regarding a service of product, usually compiled and posted on a Web site to manage consumer questions.

front-end system   The portion of your e-business that is visible to the consumer.

fulfillment   Distribution and shipping.

full-service broker   A broker that provides full assistance to investors. When online trading, it offers speed and convenience, with the advice of a broker.

G

gateway   Sends voice data across the standard telephone system.

genealogy   Family structure, lineage.

General Services Administration (GSA)   A government agency set up to help people wishing to conduct business with the United States government.

gigabits per second (gbps)   A billion bits per second.

giros   Wire transfers between bank accounts; offer an alternative for companies that work in some northern European countries.

Glass-Steagle Act   Prohibited financial institutions from engaging in multiple financial operations.

global content   Refers to information and design that requires translation but is essentially the same content for all cultures.

global cyberspace jurisdiction project   Contains a report on research relating to international legal questions introduced by the Internet and global e-commerce.

global economy   The worldwide balance of finance, politics and resource management.

global financing network   Enables eCredit customers to have access to automated credit approval and financing.

global positioning system (GPS)   Give handheld devices the ability to pinpoint the latitude and longitude of a user's location.

globalization   The phenomenon that occurs when new lines of communication are introduced allowing the world to interact more effectively.

Gnome Foundation   Founded to develop a free Linux-based desktop environment and a free application framework to compete against Microsoft Office on the desktop.

GNU public license (GPL)   A public license to distribute content and code for the free use of others.

good samaritan provision   Protects ISPs from defamation lawsuits.

Gunning Fog Index   Produces a readability grade when applied to a text sample.

H

hacker   A skilled programmer responsible for viruses and denial-of-service attacks.

hash function   The algorithm that converts textual information into digits for secure transmission.

hash value   The number representing the string of text used for transmitting data securely.

hate speech   That which induces imminent lawless action, provoking another individual to act in an immediate and violent way.

Health Insurance Portability and Accountability Act (HIPAA)   Will soon require medical offices and other health care related agencies to perform many of their administrative tasks online.

high-availability computing   Redundant servers used to minimize network downtime.

high-speed digital subscriber line (HDSL)   Provides equal bandwidth for upstream and downstream transfers at rates of up to 1.544 Mbps.

hits   Recorded for each object that is downloaded on a Web page, there could be many such objects per unique visit.

horizontal portal   Portals with a general focus. These portals aggregate information on a broad range of topics.

HTML   Acronym for Hypertext Markup Language, a language used to create documents on the World Wide Web.

HTTP   (Hypertext Transfer Protocol) Used to define how messages are transmitted across the Internet.

hybrid model   A business model that includes both an online presence and a physical establishment. Also called clicks-and-mortar.

hyperlink   Loads a specified URL into the browser window.

I

ID cards   A tracking device that enables information to be sent to your computer from a Web site.

illuminated statement   Allows offers from retail merchants to correspond with the itemized charges on a credit-card statement.

ILOVEYOU Virus   A computer virus sent by e-mail that caused billions of dollars of damage worldwide.

image maps   Images with areas designated as hyperlinks.

imminent lawless action   Hate speech provoking another individual to act on it in an immediate and violent way.

inbox   Stores e-mail messages.

incubator   A company that specializes in the development of Internet businesses.

independent site   Not affiliated with a network.

index shares   Shares of a portfolio of stocks.

industry to industry (ItoI)   An exchange site designed for interindustry trading and offers services in the chemical, retail, construction and energy industries.

information technology (IT)   Department or subject concerned with managing business processes and information.

infrared   Technology that can be used to create wireless networks within an office or even between nearby offices.

integrated access device (IAD)   Provides network connections for high-speed Internet access as well as connections for multiple voice telephone lines.

integrated services digital network (ISDN)   Provides high-speed connections to the Internet over both digital and standard telephone lines with transfer speeds of up to 128 Kbps.

integrity   When the information you send or receive has not been compromised or altered.

intelligent agents   Programs that search and arrange large amounts of data, and report answers based on that data.

internalization   Involves restructuring the software used by an e-business so that it can process foreign languages, currencies, date formats and other variations involved in conducting business globally.

Internet   A global network of computers used to exchange data.

Internet Corporation for Assigned Names and Numbers (ICANN)   Regulates domain names and IP addresses.

Internet mailing list   Lists helping a company target personalized e-mail for consumers who have either expressed interest in your business category or who want to receive information on certain subjects.

Internet marketing campaign   Applying traditional marketing techniques to the Internet and incorporating Internet-only marketing techniques such as banner advertisements and e-mail into your marketing strategy. Marketing research advertising, promotions and public relations all should be addressed.

Internet payment provider (IPP)   Network operators, ISPs, payment-card companies, banks or utility companies who aggregate the sum payment of content transactions, billing the consumer periodically.

Internet Policy Registration Authority (IPRA)   Signs certificates using the root key.

Internet service provider (ISP)   Connects your computer to the Internet through a modem or a network connection.

Internet Tax Commission   Developed to review the issue of Internet taxation.

Internet Tax Freedom Act   Imposed a moratorium on Internet Taxation.

Internet telephony   Enables users to make phone calls over the Internet.

Internet2   A consortium working to develop the next generation of the Internet.

Internet-only bank   A bank offering its services only over the Internet.

IP address   Used to locate other computers on the Internet.

J

JavaScript   A scripting language designed by Netscape similar to the Java programming language developed to be used with HTML.

John Doe suit   When a plaintiff pursues a case against and anonymous or otherwise unknown author in a defamation suit.

jurisdiction   The range of legal control.

just-in-time (JIT) inventory management   A resource management system that processes information and delivers raw materials and products as they are needed.

K

Kerberos   Employs symmetric secret-key cryptography to authenticate users inside a network, and to maintain the integrity and privacy of network communications.

kernel   The core of the operating system of Linux.

key   A string of digits that acts as a password.

key agreement protocol   The process by which two parties can exchange keys over an insecure medium.

key distribution center   A way to exchange the symmetric secret key securely. This central authority shares a different symmetric secret key with every user in the network.

key generation   The process by which keys are created.

key length   Determines the strength of an encryption. Longer keys have stronger encryption.

key management   Maintaining the secrecy of private keys.

keystroke cops   Surveillance technology used to monitor productivity and the abuse of company equipment.

kilobits per second (Kbps)   A communications speed of approximately 1000 bits per second.

L

laser   Technology that is used for building-to-building wireless network connections.

lead generation   Includes new customer registrations and having visitors sign in to receive a newsletter or use a free demo.

lead time   The time it takes to receive a product from a supplier after an order has been placed.

learning management system (LMS)   Serves as a database from which employees can quickly and easily find training and information.

legitimate business interests Determines whether a business had reasonable interest in invading an employee's privacy.

libel Statements written or spoken in a context in which they have longevity and pervasiveness that exceed slander.

lifetime value The expected amount of profit derived from a customer over a designated length of time.

Linux An open-source operating system commonly used for server-side applications.

load matching This process called load matching lowers costs by reducing the number of trucks needed to fulfill an order.

local area network (LAN) An internal network that allows employees to share files and access company information.

local content Material on specific regional pages that appears only on that Web site, such as regional promotions, pricing, delivery and store or office locations.

localization Includes the translation and cultural adaptation of your site's content and presentation.

log file Consist of data generated by site visits, including each visitor's location, IP address, time of visit, frequency of visits and other information.

log-file analysis Organizes and summarizes the information contained in the logs, can also show you the Web-site traffic effects of changing your Web site or advertising campaign. Data gathered can be used to demonstrate the effectiveness of a Web site over time.

logic bombs Viruses which trigger when a given condition is met.

logistics A portion of back-end responsibilities; managing the details of an organization.

M

Mac OS X The newest Apple Macintosh Operating System.

manufacturer The direct producer of the product.

margin call The broker requires the investor to invest more money or sell the stock to pay back the loan.

marketplace A term often used to describe B2B exchange.

mark-up languages Designed to layout and link text files.

megabits per second (Mbps) A communications speed of approximately one million bits per second.

merchant When used in discussion of affiliate programs, it is the company that advertises on an affiliate's site and rewards the affiliate based on pre-determined visitor actions.

merchant account Allows merchants to accept credit-card payments.

merchant server The merchant server is the data storage and management system employed by the merchant.

message digest see hash value.

message integrity When the message has not been altered in transmission.

META tag An HTML tag that contains information about a Web page.

microbrowsers Access the Web via the wireless Internet. Without graphics and animations, the transmission consumes less bandwidth and memory, and becomes easier to view on the small screens of wireless devices.

micropayment Payments that generally do not exceed $10.

Miller test Identifies the criteria used to distinguish obscenity and pornography.

minimum contacts In relation to jurisdiction, or the range of legal control, governments must determine whether an e-business that maintains a Web site is subject to the laws of all the countries from which the site can be accessed.

mirror site A duplicate page of an existing Web site.

mobile business (m-business) E-business using wireless devices accessing the Internet any time, anywhere.

mobile Internet   Internet access over wireless devices.

mobile payment   Allows customers to make payments using a mobile phone.

modem   Takes digital signals from the computer and turns them into sound.

modulation   A process through which digital signals from computers are translated into light.

MPEG-1 Audio Layer 3 (MP3)   Technology allowing the rapid and substantial compression of vast amounts of data.

MS-DOS   The older operating system on which Microsoft Windows is based.

multi-level model   New affiliates are recruited by current affiliates who are then rewarded with a percentage of the new affiliates' revenues. Also multi-tiered model.

multimedia   Refers to the multiple media used to create content.

multimedia contact center   Allows customers with Internet access to contact customer-service representatives through various methods including e-mail, online text chatting and real-time voice communications in addition to fax, phone and other traditional methods.

multiple listing service (MLS)   Allows realty postings to be made once and implemented at any number of sites designated by the realtor. In the past, a real estate agent would have to post an individual listing at multiple real estate Web sites.

multi-processing   Controls a computer that has many hardware CPUs (Central Processing Units).

multi-tasking   Allows multiple applications to run simultaneously.

multi-threading   Allows an individual program to specify that several activities should be performed in parallel.

multi-tiered model   New affiliates are recruited by current affiliates who are then rewarded with a percentage of the new affiliates' revenues. Also multi-level model.

multiuser   Allows more than one user to run a program at the same time.

N

name-your-price model   Empowers customers to state the price they are willing to pay for products and services.

National Institute of Standards and Technology   An organization which sets the cryptographic standards for the U.S. government.

natural language processing   A computer attempts to understand text and respond with a proper answer or comment.

negligence   Used to determine fault in a defamation case, defendant must have failed to responsibly justify claims.

network security   Allows authorized users to access information and services, while preventing unauthorized users from gaining access to, and possibly corrupting, the network.

newsgroups   Online discussion groups.

nexus   Physical presence in a geographical location.

Nielson rating   Used to predict trends and popularity in the entertainment industry.

non-content-related means   An effort to control the audience rather than the material.

non-repudiation   Providing substantial proof that an explicit action happened, as in the transmission of digital information.

O

Office of Foreign Assets Control (OFAC)   Responsible for enforcing international trade sanctions.

one-way hash functions   A mathematical calculation that gives the message a hash value. It is called a "one-way" hash function because you cannot determine the contents of the original message based on the hash value and the hash function.

online contracting services   Allow businesses to post positions for which they want to hire outside resources, and individuals can identify projects that best suit their interests, schedules and skills.

online coupons   Offer rebates and discounts for use while shopping online.

online text chatting   Provides a real-time form of text communication between customers and service representatives.

Open eBook Forum (OeBF)   An association of publishers, book sellers, manufacturers and industry supporters who wish to advance the technology and use of electronic books.

Open Financial Exchange (OFE)   Serves as a standard mechanism for the exchange of financial information.

open-ended questions   Questions that require more than a "yes" or "no" answer.

open-source code   Freely available code that may be accessed and modified by anyone.

Operating System (OS)   The OS allows the monitor, keyboard, mouse and other peripherals to work together. In some cases the operating system manages all peripherals in a network allocating the appropriate memory and storage resources to maximize the efficiency of the system.

optical modem   Translates digital signals from a computer into light through a process called modulation.

opt-in e-mail   Explicit consent from the user to receive offers, information and promotions by e-mail.

opto-chip   Capable of converting the most basic particle of light, the photon, into an electric current.

opt-out   Explicit refusal to accept solicitation.

outsourcing   The process of hiring another company or individual to do a job when there is a lack of qualified resources within a company.

overbroad   Reaching beyond the group intended.

overhead cost   The cost of operation including rents, utilities and taxes.

P

packet switching   Allows multiple users to send and receive information at the same time over the same communications paths (such as phone lines). A technique in which digital data is sent in small packages called packets.

packet-filtering firewall   Examines all data sent from outside the LAN and automatically rejects any data packets that have local network addresses.

parasite   Selects a domain name based on common typos made when entering a popular domain name.

partner relationship management (PRM)   Increasing efficiency in operations and maintaining and improving relationships between a business and its partners.

pay-per-click model   Rewards an affiliate for each click-through that is generated off a banner hosted by the affiliate.

pay-per-hire   Recruiting organizations pay recruiting service for every individual hire.

pay-per-lead model   Rewards affiliates based on the number of qualified leads generated.

pay-per-performance   Fees based on pay-per-click, pay-per-lead and pay-per-sale.

pay-per-sale method   Compensates its affiliates for each sale resulting from affiliate-hosted advertisements.

pay-per-view   A service requiring consumers to pay to view content that is available at certain times of the day.

PC-to-phone (computer-to-phone)   Speech communication between a person on a phone and a person on a computer.

peer-to-peer payment   Transactions that allow online monetary transfers between consumers.

personal communications services (PCS)   Networks that enable wide-area wireless data communication.

personal digital assistants (PDAs)   Enabled with Internet access; allow users to manage their information while away from their desktop computers.

personalization　　Uses information from the tracking, mining and analyzing of data to customize a person's interactions with a company's products, services, Web sites and employees.

Personalization Consortium　　An alliance of major Web sites defending the use of personalization mechanisms.

plain old telephone system (POTS)　　Used for voice-telephone calls around the world and was built with copper wire.

plaintext　　Unencrypted data.

platform　　Provides the basic services that applications need to run.

Platform for Privacy Preferences Project (P3P)　　Matches a user's privacy preferences to the privacy policy of a Web site.

point-of-sale (POS) transactions　　Those that occur when you present your credit card at a store.

points-based promotion　　Points are awarded to customers every time they perform a pre-designated action. These points can be accumulated and redeemed for products or services.

point-to-point tunneling protocol (PPTP)　　Creates a secure channel of communication between the customer and the ASP.

policy creation authorities　　Organizations that set policies for obtaining digital certificates.

pop-up box　　A window containing an advertisement that appears separate from the window the user is viewing.

portable data format (PDF)　　Format for downloading manuals and forms.

post office protocol (POP)　　A protocol for receiving e-mail.

precise positioning service (PPS)　　The level of service in GPS available to the military. Is not available to the public for security reasons.

press release　　Announces current events and other significant news to the press.

pretty good privacy (PGP)　　A freely-available e-mail encryption program written in 1991.

primary key　　Used to identify a record.

print-on-demand　　Allows customers to convert an electronic text to paper and have it bound and sold to them.

privacy　　Ensuring that the information transmitted over the Internet has not be captured or passed on to a third party without knowledge of sender.

privacy policy　　A company's statement of protection of consumer privacy relating to the content accessed on their Web site.

private key　　When used to encrypt a message only the corresponding public key can decrypt it. The key is kept secret by its owner.

processor speed　　The optimal operating speed of a computer's internal processor.

procurement　　Acquiring goods or services.

Project Gutenberg™　　A Xerox initiative designed to convert classic texts in the public domain into electronic form.

promotions　　Attract visitors to your site and can influence purchasing. Can include frequent-flyer miles, point-based rewards, discounts, sweepstakes, free trials, free shipping and coupons.

protocol　　Defines the steps necessary for computers to communicate over the Internet.

proxy server　　Responds to queries for Web pages.

public domain　　Free to the public.

public key　　Publicly available encryption key.

public relations (PR)　　A management function concern with public opinion and awareness. A PR departments primary function is to support an organization by making people aware of the organizations efforts. This is done by through traditional media such as print, radio and television, as well as through special events. PR departments often work with the media to announce the release of new products, handle crises and develop consumer awareness.Keeps a company's customers and your company's employees current on the latest information about products, services and internal and external issues, such as its promotions and consumer reactions.

public-key algorithms   One that is computationally infeasible to deduce the private key from the public key.

public-key cryptography   Used to solve the problem of exchanging keys securely. Is asymmetric.

public-key infrastructure (PKI)   Integrates public-key cryptography with digital certificates and certification authorities to authenticate parties in a transaction.

publisher   The printer and many times the copyright owner of a publication.

pure democracy   Each citizen could vote directly on issues that concern them.

Q

qualified lead   Enables visitors sign up to receive a newsletter or to use a free demo.

R

radio frequency WLAN (RF WLAN)   A Wireless local Area Network that uses radio frequencies to distribute data across the network. Since radio frequencies can travel through solid objects it is often used over long distances. Interference, a lack of available frequencies and security concerns limit its use.

RAM   Random access memory. The most common type of memory found in computers and related devices.

reach   The number of target consumers exposed to a particular marketing effort. A national radio campaign would have a much greater reach than a quarter page ad in a local newspaper.

readability   An accessibility issue that considers the reading level at which a Web site intended for the general public is written.

real audio   A Web-based application that decodes the digital audio information.

real space   Physical environment consisting of temporal and geographic boundaries.

real time   Refers to actions occurring over the web with no delay. Live broadcasts are considered to occur in real-time.

reasonable expectation of privacy   Criteria to determine an employee's right to privacy.

record   Any particular row of the table.

recruiter   The person or group that seeks out potential employees.

redundancy   An attempt to minimize down time or eliminate it completely.

redundant servers   Identical servers for back up in case of failure.

regional content   Information that is usually written once in English and then adapted for various markets.

registrar   Responsible for managing the registration of domain names with individuals and businesses.

relational database   A database that stores information in related tables.

remote-voting   Voting via the Internet from any location with Internet access, or through a wireless device.

repeater   Amplify and retransmit signals across segments of copper wire or fiber-optic cable.

representative democracy   Under a representative democracy, each state's citizens are represented by the Electoral College, or a group of individuals who formally choose the President and the Vice President of the United States.

request for proposal   A project poseted by a company that is requesting bids from an outside contractor.

reserve price   The lowest price a seller will accept in an auction.

resident virus   Once loaded into the memory of a computer, operates for the duration of the computer's use.

response rate   The percentage of responses generated from the target market.

restricted access   Only people with authorized user names and passwords are allowed to access such sites.

restricted algorithms   Keep certain ciphers secure by relying on the sender and receiver to remember the key and keep it secret.

resume filtering software   Filters through submitted resumes using pre-determined terms to select the applicant pool.

return on investment   The ratio of cost savings and increased revenues to money spent.

reverse-auction model   Auctions that allow buyers to set a price as sellers compete to match, or even beat it.

reward structure   Determines how much revenue the affiliate will receive.

root certification authority   Part of the chain of certificates which is the Internet Policy Registration Authority (IPRA).

root key   Used to sign certificates by the IPRA.

router   Used to move packets across the Internet in an efficient way. Responsible for redirecting packets around any areas of the network that may have failed and ensuring that packets are delivered to the proper destination hosts.

routing tables   Essentially the road map of a network, providing directions for data to get from one computer to another.

rules-based personalization   The delivery of personalized content based on the subjection of a user's profile to set rules or assumptions.

S

sales force automation   Assists companies in the sales process, including maintaining and discovering leads, managing contacts and other sales-force activities.

sales tracking   The tracking and recording of all sales made.

satellite technology   A communications device that orbits the earth and relays messages from various locations. Satellite technology is currently used to broadcast all forms of digital and analog data signals.

s-business   Secure e-business.

scalability   The ability for the infrastructure to handle growth. Also a measure of how well hardware and software can handle increased demands.

screen readers   Programs that allow users to hear what is being displayed on their screen.

screen scraping   A process where the aggregator visits the sites that have your financial information and services and uses your user names and passwords to log-in and collect the information.

search engine   A Web site that helps Web users navigate the Web using keywords and phrases.

search-engine ranking   Determines how "high" a site appears in search results.

secondary research   Findings based on previously conducted investigations.

secret key   Used to encrypt data.

Section 230 of the Telecommunications Decency Act   Protects ISPs from being responsible for material that is posted by users.

secure electronic transactions (SET)   A security protocol designed specifically to protect e-commerce payment transactions.

secure sockets layer (SSL)   A non-proprietary protocol commonly used to secure communication on the Internet and the Web.

Securities and Exchange Commission (SEC)   Regulatory agency that attempts to protect investors and regulate trading activities.

segmented markets   People or companies with similar characteristics.

self-publishing   Gives writer ability to keep full control over material.

self-regulated medium   Self-governed.

sequencing information   Used to rearrange data into its proper order.

server   A host on the Internet that manages network resources and fulfills requests from clients.

server side   Refers to the computer and communications equipment that manages all data for a particular Web site, FTP server or any other interface accessed by outside users (clients). Computers and information systems on the merchant-side.

service ticket   Authorizes client access to specific network services.

session keys   Secret keys used during public-key cryptography to communicate securely.

SET secure electronic transaction LLC   An organization formed by Visa and MasterCard to manage and promote the SET protocol.

set-top box   Combine the interactivity of the Web with the visual quality and usability of television.

shill bidding   When sellers bid for their own items to increase the bid price.

shopping cart   Allows customers to accumulate items they wish to buy as they continue to shop online.

shopping-bot technology   Used to scour data contained within a single database or across the Web to find answers to specific questions.

short messaging service   Mobile data.

side panel ad   Advertisement that lays vertically on a Web site.

simple mail transfer protocol (SMTP)   A protocol used for sending e-mail.

slander   Spoken defamation.

small business administration (SBA)   A government agency that provides assistance and guidance to small business owners.

smart card   Holds more information that an ordinary credit card, with added security and activity.

smart card reader   Reads the information on a smart card and updates the information on the computer chip.

software platform   Provides the basic services that applications need to run.

spamming   Mass e-mailing to people who have not expressed interest in receiving e-mails.

speech recognition   Technology which enables computers to convert voice to text.

speech synthesis   The process of having a computer convert text to voice.

spider   An intelligent agent often used by search engines to rank and categorize Web sites based on specific key words and phrases.

standard positioning service (SPS)   The level of service in GPS available for public use. Is accurate to approximately 100 meters horizontal and 156 meters vertical.

steganography   The practice of hiding information within other information.

stickiness   The ability to keep people at a site and interested in its content.

storage area network (SAN)   Provides high-capacity, reliable data storage and delivery on a network.

storage devices   Machines used to store massive amounts of information.

streaming media   Audio and video that are played as they download onto the user's system. By using streaming media, users minimize wait times.

streamlined sales tax project   A panel designed to resolve Internet taxation issues.

style sheet   Formats every Web site the user visits, according to that user's personal preferences.

subsidy e-publishing   Fee-based e-publishing services.

symmetric digital subscriber line (SDSL)   Transfers data at the same speed both upstream and downstream.

symmetric encryption algorithms   Encryption algorithms that uses the same secret key to encrypt and decrypt a message.

synchronized multimedia integration language (SMIL)   A markup language designed to add extra tracks (layers of content found within a single audio or video file), which contain data such as closed captioning.

synchronous e-learning   Step-by-step learning designed to work toward a goal or certification completed in real time.

system caret   The blinking vertical bar associated with editing text.

T

table   Used to store information in a relational database. A table consists of records and fields (or attributes).

target market   a group of people to whom a company directs its marketing campaign, products or services. Usually based on certain demographics and psychographics.

TCP/IP   Transmission Control Protocol/Internet Protocol (TCP/IP), the standard set of protocols used for communication between computers on the Internet. Most Internet transmissions are sent as sets of individual message pieces, called packets. At the sending side, the packets of one message are numbered sequentially, and error-control information is attached to each packet. TCP/IP routes packets to avoid traffic jams, so each packet might travel a different route over the Internet. At the receiving end, TCP/IP makes sure that all of the packets have arrived, puts them in sequential order and determines if the packets have arrived without alteration. If the packets have been altered, TCP/IP retransmits them.

tele-immersion   Allows users in different locations to share information real-time.

terabyte   Equal to one trillion bytes.

terminal adapter (TA)   A device that connects a computer to an ISDN line.

third-party logistics service provider   Industry terminology for a shipping company.

Tim Berners-Lee   Developed the World Wide Web.

time bombs   Triggered when the clock on the computer matches a certain time or date.

Time Division Multiple Access (TDMA)   A method of distributing wireless massages over radio frequencies, in which frequencies are divided into multiple time slots. Messages are then allocated to specific time slots to maximize the efficiency of the wireless network.

time to market   The speed at which a company can begin to sell its product or service.

timeout   Enables or disables a certain action after the computer has idled for a specified amount of time.

timestamping   Binds a time and date to a digital document.

timestamping agency   Digitally timestamps documents after signed by the contractor.

timofonica   A worm propagated through e-mail to the cellular phone network in Spain.

top level domain   Usually describes the type of organization that owns the domain name.

top-referring sites   Sites that most frequently refer visitors to another site.

tracking   Monitoring visitor's behavior or a program's result. Information obtained can be used to analyze the effectiveness of a site or program.

trading on margin   When an investor buys stock and borrows money from the broker to further invest in the stock.

traditional call center   Houses customer-service representatives who can be reached by an 800 number.

traditional direct marketing   Includes sending information by mail and using telemarketers to contact prospective customers.

traffic generation   Bringing more visitors to a site.

training marketplaces   Serve as forums for companies needing training to find individuals or companies that provide training.

tranceiver   a radio transmitter and receiver that uses the same components to send and receive messages.

transaction support   The technology and personnel used for conducting transactions.

transient virus   A virus that attaches to a specific computer program and is activated when the program is run and deactivated when the program is terminated.

translation   Interpreting the meaning of a word or phrase.

transmission control protocol (TCP)   One of two main protocols in TCP/IP networks, TCP creates the connection through which IP sends packets of data in a network.

transparency   Decreasing the spread between buy and sell prices of securities.

triangulation   Any trigonometric operation for finding a time or location by means of mathematical coordinates.

triple DES   The current standard of symmetric encryption, encrypts data three times.

Trojan horse virus   A malicious program that hides within a friendly program or simulates the identity of a legitimate program or feature, while actually causing damage to the computer or network in the background.

trusted systems   Devices such as VCR, DVD players, computers, e-books and similar technologies modified to read XrML documents. Trusted systems use XrML to dictate usage of a particular copyright protected product.

turnkey solution   A pre-packaged solution.

two-tiered model   An affiliate structure that rewards an affiliate for actions taken through its links to merchants' sites and actions taken through the merchant links on affiliates' sites that have been recruited by the original affiliates.

two-way pager   A wireless communications device that allows users to send text alphanumeric messages over wireless connections. E-mails can be sent and retrieved automatically without the need to dial into a provider for access.

U

uniform resource locator and universal resource locator (URL)   The global address of documents and other resources on the World Wide Web.

unique visitor   One is registered every time a user visits a site.

Universal Mobile Telecommunications Standard (UMTS)   A Third Generation (3G) mobile technology that will deliver broadband information at speeds up to 2Mbits/sec.

Unix   An open standards operating system.

Unsolicited Electronic Mail Act   This would mandate that the nature of the e-mail be made clear.

upload   To transfer information from a computer to a network, mainframe or bulletin board service or other remote location.

upstream   The term used to describe information sent from a user's computer to the Web server.

use tax   If the vendor and the consumer are not located in the same state, then the sale is subject to a use tax. The state in which the purchased property or service is used directly imposes this tax upon the consumer.

user agents   An application that interprets Web-page source code and translates it into formatted text and images.

V

value-added network   In traditional electronic Data Interchange (EDI), value-added networks (VANs) are firms that helped a company manage its EDI.

value-added tax   A tax, passed on to the consumer, based on the estimated market value added to a product at each level of its manufacture and distribution.

venture capitalist   Individuals or groups that generate the financial support of a growing enterprise, usually claiming a certain degree of ownership in the company.

vertical portal   A specialized Web site offering a great deal of information, links and news about a specific subject.

very high-speed digital subscriber line (VDSL)   Offers symmetric data transfer rates of between 13 Mbps and 55 Mbps.

video-on-demand   Allows users to download video and view any content they desire at any point in time within the limitations of the storage capacity.

virtual private network (VPN)   Allows customers to connect to their applications securely over the Internet.

virtual university   A university that is completely online.

virus   Computer programs that attach to, or overwrite, other programs to replicate themselves. They can corrupt files or even wipe out entire hard drives.

visual galleries   Sites dedicated to particular artists and their works.

voice over digital subscriber line (VoDSL)   Uses a standard cost-efficient technology for managing data and voice services for small businesses and home offices.

voice over internet protocol (VoIP)   Set of hardware devices that allow people to transmit telephone call of the Internet.

voice server   Sends a message to the VoiceXML browser and begins a conversation between the user and the computer.

voiceXML   Allows people to mark up text so that it can be read aloud by special programs that convert text to speech. Applications include automated telephone systems and the Web. Voice XML may prove to be particularly helpful to web accessibility efforts.

W

wallpaper   The background for your main operating system screen.

WAP forum™   The industry association working to develop a standard for communication on wireless devices.

Web accessibility   The level at which the Web is able to be utilized by people with disabilities.

Web Accessibility Initiative (WAI)   Provides guidelines on how to make Web sites accessible to people with disabilities.

Web bug   A graphic that can reside on a Web page or in an e-mail that can track the user or e-mail recipient.

Web conferencing   Allows businesses to meet and collaborate online, in real time from anywhere in the world.

Web content accessibility guidelines 1.0   Developed by the W3C, accessibility guidelines divided into a three-tier structure of checkpoints according to their priority.

Web defacing   When hackers illegally enter an organization's Web site and change its contents.

Web server   Stores Web pages and delivers those pages to clients upon request.

Web-based solution   A solution that is offered and managed over the Web with no downloads necessary.

Webcasting   Uses streaming media to broadcast an event over the Web.

whiteboard   A drawing application that allows you to share visual effects with other people over the Internet.

Windows   The most popular operating system in the world, currently used on approximately 90 percent of all desktop computers.

wireless application protocol (WAP)   A set of communication protocols for wireless devices that enable different kinds of wireless devices to communicate and access the Internet. The goal is to standardize development across different wireless technologies worldwide.

wireless local area network (WLAN)   A localized network of computers that are connected via wireless devices.

wireless markup language (WML)   The scripting language used to design Web content to be delivered to wireless handheld devices.

World Wide Web   a group of Internet servers that work together to support HTML documents, graphics, audio and video.

worm Similar to a virus except that it can spread and infect files over a network on its own; worms do not need to be attached to another program to spread.

X

xDSL Used to describe the many types of digital subscriber lines available.

Z

zooming Technology used to focus on one part of an element at a close range.

Index

Symbols

238
& 631
© 631
.NET 135
@Plan 221
@ResearchInfo.com 222

Numerics

1-800-FLOWERS 46
128-bit encryption systems 184
1-Click system 31, 320
1View Network 474
24-by-7 9, 22, 29
3Com Urban Challenge 379
3G 153, 156
401(k) 459, 478
401kafe 478

A

A element (anchor; <A>...</A>)
    622, 624, 628
Abeline 131
AbleCommerce's AuctionBuilder
    1.0 66
About.com 35, 36
abracad.us-
    ers.netlink.co.uk/
    emoney.html 113
Access database 602

accessibility 400, 401, 402, 409,
    410, 413, 414, 415, 417,
    418, 419, 726, 729, 741
Accessibility Wizard 402, 406,
    408
Accessories panel of your
    Program list 616
account settlement 74, 100
Accounts option in the Tools
    menu 586
accounts receivable 457
accredited 492
ACH (Automated Clearing
    House) 108
ACPA 321
ACTION attribute 648
Action button 588
action-oriented programming 615
Active Server Pages (ASP) 601,
    602, 613, 663, 670, 723
ActiveShield 198
ActiveX Data Objects (ADO) 723
actual loss 312
actual malice 312
actual payment process 108
ActualSoft 159
.acw 410
Addall.com 503
adding a News server 587
adding email servers 587
Address bar 580
Address Book 587, 588, 589,
    592

Addresses button 588
addToCart.asp 701
Adknowledge 222
Adleman, Leonard 187
Adobe Acrobat Reader plug-in
    595
Adobe Postscript® 518
Adobe® Acrobat® 518
ADODB Open method 691
ADODB.Connection object
    691
ADODB.Recordset 691
ADSL 129
AdSmart 228
advanced application 131
Advanced Encryption Standard
    (AES) 186
Advanced tab 594
Advancing Woman 382
Advantage Hiring, Inc. 562
advertising 40, 56, 60, 155, 219,
    221, 225, 227, 229, 230,
    231, 251, 275, 279, 341,
    351
AES 186
affiliate marketing 95
affiliate program 66, 247, 248,
    249, 250, 251, 252, 254,
    256, 257, 258, 259, 261,
    265, 289
Affiliate Selling 4
affiliate solution provider 247,
    250, 252, 257

affiliate.net 261
AffiliateFind.com 265
AffiliateZone.com 252
Africa 360
Africa Online 360
African American Women's
      Network 383
African Information Society
      Initiative 361
Age of Knowledge 7, 21
aggregation service 473, 474
agoodbook.com 518
AIX 134
Akamai 77
alando.de 352
alert box 606
alert box 714
algorithm 275
ALIGN = "center" 642
ALIGN = "left" 642
ALIGN = "right" 642
ALIGN = "center" 620
ALIGN = "right" 620
ALIGN attribute 634, 642
Alis Technologies 346
<ALT> 414
ALT attribute 626, 700
AltaVista 35, 36, 37, 112, 222,
      362
Alternative Investment Market
      360
altranet.com 434
Amazon.com 28, 30, 31, 68,
      260, 320, 328, 515, 543
Amendment 304
America Online 350, 352, 579
America's Job Bank 559
American Association of
      Individual Investors®
      (AAII) 478
American Bar Association 341,
      364
American Society for Female
      Entrepreneurs 561
American Stock Exchange
      (AMEX) 464
AmeriNet 100
Ameritrade 468, 477
ampersand **&** 631
ampersand (**&**) 663, 670
Amsterdam Exchange 359
analog modem 128
analog signal 128
Ancestry.com 447
anchor 580, 628
Andersen Consulting 79

angle brackets (<…>) 615
ANI (Automatic Number
      Identification) 102
anonymity 309, 321
anonymity indexes 313
anonymous 584
ANSI (American National
      Standards Institute) 186
Answerthink Consulting Group
      79
Anticybersquatting Consumer
      Protection Act of 1999 321
anti-virus software 198
AOL.com 260
AOL@School 378
Apache 136, 647
Apartments.com 440
Apple Computer, Inc. 136
application 133
application service provider (ASP)
      69, 131, 563
applications 163, 166
Apply button 595
Aqua 137
Aquarius 348
Aquent.com 567
Archipelago 464
argument 668
Arial font 631
Ariba 234
ARPAnet 5, 6, 21
array 692
Art.com 435
ASCII 514
Asia 362
Ask Jeeves 37, 235
.asp 686
ASP (Active Server Pages) 663,
      670
<assign> tag (**<assign>…</
      assign>**) 740
AssociatePrograms.com
      265
asterisk (*****) 694
asymmetric DSL (ADSL) 128
asymmetric keys 186
asynchronous learning 501
AT&T 134
AT&T SecureBuy 104
ATAG (Authoring Tools
      Accessibility Guidelines) 12
atrandom.com 517
attribute 615
auction 28, 43, 101, 108, 322
auctions.yahoo.com 35
AuctionWeb 32

audio 166, 232, 591
Aural Style Sheet 742
Aural Style Sheets 417
AuralCSS 416
Austria 354
authentication 168, 182, 184,
      186, 187, 189, 191
AuthentiDate.com 190
authorization 74, 100, 104
Autobytel 432
AutoComplete 582, 583
Automatic Location Identification
      (ALI) 169
Automatic Number Information
      169
automatic recurring payment 108
Automatic Teller Machines
      (ATMs) 99
Automatic Timeout 409
automobile loan 463
automotive industry 44
Autoparts.com 432
AutoTranslate 346
availability 183

B

B element 621
B2Bi 43
Babelfish 346
Back button 581
back-end operations 289
back-end systems 74
BACKGROUND 626, 627
background color 627
background image 627
background wallpaper 582
backOrder.xml 680
backup 35
bandwidth 6, 21, 126, 130, 131,
      153, 160, 166, 168, 362,
      531
bank card 104
Bank of America 457
Bank One 99, 472
BankAtlantic.com 460
bankonewallet 99
bankonline.com 461
banner advertisement 226, 227,
      229, 248, 257
Barnes & Noble 45
barnesandnoble.com 98,
      261, 320
barriers to entry 257
barter 38, 40
Basic HTML file 617

Basic Rate Interface (BRI) 130
bCentral 75
Be Free 254
bearer (B) channel 130
beenz 98
before and after-hours trading 463
Belgium 354
Bell Laboratories 133
BeMany.com 434
Berners-Lee, Tim 6, 21
Bertelsmann Foundation 344
BetterWebSM 310
BGCOLOR attribute 627
bgcolor attribute (**body**) 676
bid 34
Bid4Geeks.com 566
Bidland 322
Bigstep.com 66
Bigwords.com 503
BilingualJobs.com 561
bill 475
bill paying 92
bill payment 459, 460, 470, 475
bill payment portal 108
billing 36, 457, 459, 460, 467,
      476
billing and shipping information
      98
billing systems 155
BillPoint 101
binary string 183
Biometric Application
      Programming Interface
      (BAPI) 201
bits 183
bits per second (bps) 126
BizTravel.com 428
black 628
BlackBerry 153, 154, 155
Blackvoices.com 560
blank line 668
<block> tag (**<block>...</
      block>**) 740
blocking and filtering
      technologies 315
Blocking technology 316, 336
blue 628
Blue Spike 202
Bluetooth 14, 166, 167, 168,
      170
Bluetooth Special Interest Group
      167
BODY element 618
Boeing 428
bold 620, 621
Boldfish.com 223

bond 463, 467, 470, 472, 477,
      478
bondsonline 472
book1.asp 696
Book4golf.com 358
bookface.com 518
Bookfinder.com 503
books.asp 688
books.xsl 681
BORDER attribute 626, 641
border attribute 699
Boston Business Journal 4
bottom tier 602, 723
BottomDollar.com 39
BounceKeys 407
Bowne Global Solutions 352
BR element 629
braille display 400, 415
braille keyboard 415
brand 220
brand awareness 232, 456
brand recognition 226, 251
Branders.com 224
branding 58, 75, 351
Brassringcampus.com 568
<break> tag (**<break>...</
      break>**) 740
break-even point 513
brick-and-mortar 10, 22, 44, 45,
      456, 457, 472
British Post Office 354
broadband 58, 130
broadcasting 312, 313
broker 462, 463, 464, 467, 470,
      471, 472
brokerage 472, 477
Brown University 499
browser 579
browser requests 647
budgeting 478
*Building Cyberstores (McGraw-
      Hill)* 4
bulletin board 69
Burst.com 231
bursting 231
Burstware® 231
Busey Bank 458
business 38
Business 2.0 4
Business communication 138
business intelligence 80
business logic 601, 613
business plan 13, 56, 58
business rules 602, 613

business-to-business (B2B) 10,
      35, 41, 58, 66, 104, 105,
      106, 108, 155, 289
business-to-business (B2B)
      exchange 42, 234
business-to-business integrators
      (B2BI) 43
business-to-business (B2B)
      marketplace 234
business-to-business (B2B)
      marketing 233
business-to-business sale 253
business-to-consumer 10, 22
business-to-consumer (B2C) 10,
      22, 45, 104, 108
business-to-consumer (B2C)
      marketing 233
business-to-consumer sale 253
business transaction process 107
Business Week 4
business-to-business (B2B) 41,
      43, 101
business-to-consumer (B2C) 29,
      155
BusinessVerify 105
buying advertising space 228
**bw.concordlaw-
      school.com** 500

C

C 134
C++ 496
*C@LL CENTER CRM
      Solutions*™ 4
cable modem 130
cache 595
Caldera 136
Caldera Systems 137
Caliber 495
Call 663
Call button 592
call center 280, 281
call handling 273
callback button 287
CampusCareerCenter.com
      568
Campusfood.com 8
Canada 357
cannibalization 513
Capella University 500
caption attribute 733
caption element 642
capturing a picture from a Web
      site 582
card 162

Cardean 500
cards 161
Career.com 559
CareerDayTrader.com 471
CareerLeader.com 564
CareerPath.com 559
CareerWeb 559
Carnegie Mellon 500
CarPrices.com™ 265
Cascading Style Sheets 20
Cascading Style Sheets (CSS)
    729, 733
case sensitive 664
case-sensitive 616
cash on delivery (COD) 99, 353
CashRegister 95, 96
CAST eReader 729
Casting.com 544
catalog 30, 39, 65, 67
CC: (Carbon Copy) field 588
CDMA 156
cdma2000 156
cellpadding attribute 699
cellspacing attribute 699
cellular phone 152
CENTER attribute 620
CENTER element 620
Center for Applied Special
    Technology 417, 729, 741
central processing unit (CPU) 133
centralized control 6, 21
CERN 6, 21
certificate authority hierarchy 192
certificate repositories 191
certificate revocation list (CRL)
    192
certification authority 191, 192,
    195
Certification Magazine 4
CGI (Common Gateway
    Interface) 648
CGI script 648
changes in server-side data 647
channels 130, 139
Chapbooks.com 518
CharlesSchwab 470
Chase Manhattan Bank 457, 474
chat rooms 376
chat sessions 232
Chattanooga Times 4
chatting 254
check 92, 99, 101, 104, 108
checkbox 650
CHECKED attribute 652
CheckFree 108, 111
chemical industry 44

Chief Learning Officer (CLO)
    496
ChiefMonster™ 568
Child Online Protection Act of
    1998 (COPA) 314
Children's Online Privacy
    Protection Act of 2000
    (COPPA) 315
chilling effect 315
China 346, 349, 362
<choice> tag (**<choice>…</
    choice>**) 740
CIAA 323
cipher 183
ciphertext 183, 193
CircuitCity 46
circumvention 319
Citibank 457
Clareon 106, 107
Claritybank.com 459
Clear Digital 230
click-through 227, 228, 254
Click2Learn 494
click-and-mortar bank 456, 457
Clicker 4 413
ClickMiles 224
Clickpulp.com 433
ClickRewards 224
click-through 247, 249, 250,
    257, 265, 269
client 126, 686, 700
client side 135
client/server application 30
client-side image maps 729
CNBC.com 474
CNN 512, 522
Coca-Cola 356
*Code and Other Laws of
    Cyberspace (Basic Books)* 4
Code Division Multiple Access
    (CDMA) 156, 157, 362
CodeWarriorU.com 496
Coface 105
COL element 643
COLGROUP element 643
collaborative business 80
Collegegrads.com 568
collision 190
co-location 64, 74
COLOR attribute 629
color name 628, 629
color of text 629
Colorado State 500
COLS attribute 649
COLSPAN attributes 645, 646
Columbia 500

column 640, 693
column heading 642
com 60
Comedy Central Online 541
comma 694
comment 668
comments in HTML 617
Commerce One 234
commercial banking 458
commission 466, 470
commission-based 249, 261
Commodity Futures Trading
    Commission 471
Common Programming Errors
    616
communication protocols 160
communications channels 35
Communications Decency Act of
    1996 (CDA) 314
communications medium 126
companyfinance.com 463
comparison pricing 39
comparison pricing model 39
complement 228
comprehensive job sites 554
CompuBank 460
compusa.com 426
CompuServe 579
computer generated imaging
    (CGI) 543
Computer Reseller News 4
computer security 182
Computer Shopper 4
Computer World 4
computer-generated imaging
    (CGI) 543
Computers For Youth 379
Concord University 500
Concur Technologies 234
Connect Inc. 234
connect to the Internet 579
Connection object in ADO
    693
consolidation service 108
Constitution 304, 311
construction industry 44
consulting 78, 230
consumer preference 221
consumer profile 110
consumer reaction 232
Contact 588
contact information 69, 228
contact smart card 101
contactless smart card 101
contemporary community
    standards 313

content delivery service 77
continuous-availability computing 34
continuous speech recognition (CSR) 285
contract 254, 259
cookie 274, 280, 595, 606, 662, 700
cookie file 700
Cooljobs.com 569
copper wire 126
copyright 311, 316, 318, 319, 323
Copyright Act of 1976 318
copyright infringement 317, 342
Core Fair Information Practices 311
corporate bond 472
corporate culture 557, 560
corporate marketing strategy 219
correspond with a group 591
coupons 224
Covisint 432, 450
CPM (cost per thousand) 228, 248, 250
credit card 92, 95, 98, 99, 101, 104, 110, 362
credit-card fraud 92
credit-card management 461
credit-card payments 67
credit-card processing 459, 460
crisis management 233
CRL 192
cross marketing 110
cross-border data management and payment 105
cross-media advertising 231
Crowdburst 385
Cruel World 564
cryptanalysis 193
cryptanalysts 186
cryptanalytic attack 193
Cryptographic ciphers 183
cryptographic standards 186
cryptography 183, 186
cryptologists 193
cryptosystem 183
CSS2 733
Cubby v. Compuserve 312, 313
culturefinder.com 447
Custom E-Commerce Planning 58
customer acquisition 251
customer loyalty 478
customer profile 278
customer registration 278
customer relations 45

customer relationship management (CRM) 56, 80, 273, 277, 289
customer satisfaction 45, 77
customer service 28, 45, 75, 100, 103, 223, 252, 278, 280, 285, 457, 466, 468
customer service representative 281, 285, 286, 458, 478
Customers.com 4
customize a home page 700
Cyber-Logics 230
Cyber Rules
  Strategies for Excelling At E-Business (Doubleday) 4
cyber terrorism 342
CyberCash 13, 95, 104
cybercrime 342
CyberInvest.com 461
CyberSource® 104
cyberspace 313
cybersquatting 321, 342, 346
CyberStateU.com 496

D

dailies 544
Darwin 137
data 723
data (D) channel 130
data cell 642
data compliance engine 105
Data Encryption Standard (DES) 186
data management 74
data mining 274, 275, 277, 305
data tier 613
data type 663, 670
database 29, 30, 33, 38, 74, 131, 132, 232, 234, 615, 686, 693, 699, 723
database management system (DBMS) 132, 603, 693
database server 126
databases 155, 493
dataglyphs 524
DataTAC Network 154
Datek Online 470
day trading 471
DayTradingOnline.com 471
DBMS 132
DB2 693
DD/Marketer 277
Dealtime.com 39
debit card 99, 104
debt 463, 466, 472

debugging 617
decimalization 464
decipher 184
DecisionDesktop 105
deck 161
decryption 183, 184, 186, 188
decryption key 186
dedicated communications lines 6
dedicated server 64
defamation 311, 313
default settings 410, 594
Defense Department 134
DeimlerCrysler 431
deitel@deitel.com 585
Deja.com 39, 251
Delete 587
Dell 75, 136
demand-collection system 38
demand-sensitive pricing 40
demodulation 126
demographic 220, 276
Dennis Ritchie 134
deprecated 621
Derivion 110
DES 186
describe 668
destination address 125
Deutsche Post 354
Development and Managed E-Commerce Services 58
Dice.com 566
differentiation 273
Digital Age 4
digital cash 13, 97, 98, 100
digital cellular phone 153, 156, 160, 161, 170
digital certificate 14, 191, 192
digital copies 316
digital currency 98
digital divide 16, 376, 378
digital envelope 188
Digital libraries 131
Digital Media Association 317
digital payment 106
digital payment authentication (DPA) 106
digital payment system 101
digital signal 128
digital signature 14, 96, 189, 190
Digital Signature Algorithm (DSA) 190
digital steganography 14
Digital Subscriber Line (DSL) 128
digital transaction 97
digital video 231

digital wallet 97, 99
digital watermark 202
digital watermarking software 202
digital-authentication standard 190
digital-signature legislation 190
DigitalThink 493
Dim 664
direct e-mail 223, 225
directbanking.com 458
DirectDebit 354
directory 247, 251, 256, 257, 258, 265
Disabilities Issues Task Force 169
discount 39, 224
discount-brokerage service 465
Discover 95
disk space 595
disks 35
Display Color Settings 405
distance learning 496
distribution 74, 100, 107, 354
distribution channel 41
distributor 289, 312
Ditech.com 463
diversity 560
dividend 472
DJR Associates 352
DLJ Direct 477
Do While/Loop 664
Docent 495
DoCoMo 362
DOCTYPE element 667
document 616, 668
document object 668
Document Object Model 20
document.writeln 668
Dogfriendly.com 569
dollar-based investing 468
DOM 20
domain extension 304
domain name 13, 45, 60, 74, 88, 260, 320, 346
DoS attacks 14
dot-com 61
dot-net 61
double-click 584
double quotation (') marks 668
DoubleClick 228, 306
double-selection structure 715
download a plug-in 595
download file 582
Download Now link 139
download time 595
downloading 583, 585, 595

downstream 129
DPRL 519
Driveway.com 564
Drudge Manifesto (New American Library) 4
Drudge Report 522
Drug-Free America 389
DSL 74, 129
Duke University 498, 499
Dutch Auction Internet Syndicate System 472
dynamic content 663, 670
dynamic pricing 28

E

e-billing 104, 110
e-book 7, 21, 519, 520, 527
e-book reader 520
e-business 12, 29, 35, 40, 77, 723
e-check 98
e-commerce 12, 29, 35, 43, 68, 342, 493
e-consulting 73
e-contact center 281
E Ink 523
e-Intelligence Quiz 79
e-learning 378, 490, 492
E-LOAN 461
e-mail 282, 321, 442
e-mail server 126, 586
e-matter 517
e-publishing 503, 512, 513, 526
e-retailers 45
e-text 514
e-wallet 13
E*TRADE 460, 464, 466, 467, 472, 523
E.piphany 289
E911 Act 169
EagleEyes 416
EAI 43
East Carolina University 500
ebalance 474
eBates 40
eBay 28, 32, 33, 35, 101, 322, 323, 352
eBay.com 68
eBRobot 77
eBSure Inc 77
EBT (Electronic Benefits Transfer) 104
eBTracker 77
e-Business Advisor 4
eBWatch 77

ebXML 42
eCampus.com 503
eCash 97, 100
eCashPad 102
eCharge 102
eCollege.com 500
e-commerce defined 79
eCompany 4
eConnect 102
economies of scale 513
economist.com 523
eCredit 105
EDGE 156
EDI 41
Edit Symbols button 581
education 67, 83
EduPoint 495
eGain 290
eGain Commerce platform 290
EGroups.com 385
Egypt 361
eIssuer 95
eLance.com 566
electronic banking 458
Electronic Bill Presentment and Payment (EBPP) 108, 110, 472
electronic billing 108
Electronic Commerce Modeling Language (ECML) 99
electronic communications network (ECN) 456, 463, 464
electronic contracts 341
Electronic Data Interchange (EDI) 29, 41, 108
electronic financial officer 459
Electronic Funds Transfer (EFT) 29
electronic ink 523
electronic mail 585
electronic merchant 101, 104
electronic monetary transfer 108
electronic payment 99, 101, 107
electronic piracy 11
Electronic Privacy Information Center 316
Electronic Signatures in Global and National Commerce Act of 2000 323
electronic stock exchange 464
electronic ticketing 428
electronic transaction 95
electronic transfer 108
electronics industry 44
elements 615

Elton John AIDS Foundation 389
EM (emphasis) element 621, 624
EM element 621
emazing.com 41
employee relations 352
employee-to-customer interaction
  290
encipher 184
Encirq 110
encryption 96, 102, 168, 183,
  184, 185, 186, 187, 319
encryption algorithm 188
encryption key 183, 186, 193
encyclopedia 426
End If 664
end of a script 668
end-to-end e-business solutions
  58, 74
end-to-end solution provider 493
energy industry 44, 434, 450
English 354
Enonymous.com 305
EnronOnline 471
EnronOnline.com 433
ENT 4
Enter key 580
enterprise 132
Enterprise Application Integration
  43
Enterprise Translation Server 346
entertainment 163, 165
entertainment industry 532
entity references 681
entry-level position 554
Entrypoint.com 99
<enumerate> tag (**<enu-
  merate>…</enumer-
  ate>**) 740
environment variable 647
EOF (end of file) 691
Epage.com 279
EPIC 316
ePocketPay 102
Ericsson 167
error-control information 125
E-Sign bill 323
eskolar.com 501
ESPN.com 521, 539
estate planning 478
ethical issues 15
eTime Capital 107
eToys 358
eTranslate 352
EuroDebit 354
europa.eu.int 327
europa.eu.net 344, 365

Europe 341, 348, 359
European Laboratory for Particle
  Physics 6, 21
European Union 344
European Venture Capital
  Association 359
everbank.com 461
eWeek 4
eWork® Exchange 567
Examples
  A first program in JavaScript
    667
  addToCart.asp 701
  backOrder.xml 680
  Basic HTML file 617
  book1.asp 696
  books.asp 688
  books.xsl 681
  Bug2Bug.com documents
    presented in this appendix.
    673
  Check-out form, **order.ht-
    ml** with an invalid state
    abbreviation. 609
  Check-out form, **order.ht-
    ml** with the last name field
    incomplete. 607
  Check-out form, **order.ht-
    ml** with the state field
    incomplete. 608
  Contents of the shopping cart,
    viewCart.asp 606
  Form including textareas,
    password boxes and
    checkboxes 650
  HTML form including radio
    buttons and pulldown lists
    652
  HTML table 640
  Inserting special characters
    into HTML 631
  Linking to an email address
    624
  Linking to other Web pages
    623
  List of available books,
    books.asp 605
  Listing for **addTo-
    Cart.asp**. 701
  Listing for **book1.asp**. 696
  Listing for **books.asp**. 688
  Listing for **order.html**.
    707
  Listing for **process.asp**.
    717

  Listing for **viewCart.asp**.
    703
  order.html 707
  Placing images in HTML files
    625
  process.asp 717
  Simple form with basic fields
    and a text box 646
  Some built-in ASP objects.
    687
  Stylizing text on Web pages
    621
  Table of books on back order,
    backOrder.xml 610
  Technologies used in this case
    study and their descriptions
    603
  Three-tier architecture for the
    Deitel online book store. 601
  Using horizontal rules 632
  Using images as link anchors
    627
  Using the **FONT** element to
    format text 629
  viewCart.asp 703
  Visual Basic information
    page, **book1.asp** 605
  welcome.html 674
Excel 276
exchanging advertising space 228
exchanging banners 227
exchanging symmetric secret keys
  184
Excite.com 472
<exit> tag (**<exit>…</ex-
  it>**) 740
Experience.com 568
expire 701
exporting cryptosystems 184
Express Lane 320
express.com® 249
eXtensible Markup Language 42
Extensible Markup Language
  (XML) 665
eXtensible Rights Markup
  Language (XrML) 519
Extensible Stylesheet Language
  20
Extensible Stylesheet Language
  (XSL) 665
external issue 232
Extra Keyboard Help 407
extranet 138
e-Zine 521, 527
ezlogin 474

F

face attribute 631
FactMonster 499
fair use 319
Falling Through the Net
    Defining The Digital Divide
    378
Family and Medical Leave Act of
    1993 380
FamilyEducation 499
Farmclub 534
Fast Company 4
fatal error 616
Fathom.com 501
fault-tolerant systems 35
Favorites 618
FBI.com 443, 451
Federal Communications
    Commission (FCC) 167,
    169
Federal Trade Commission (FTC)
    169, 311, 471
FedEx 354
Felix Somm 342
fiber 127
Fiber optic cable 126
fictionworks.com 517
Fidelity Investments 477
field 693, 707, 723
file server 126
File Transfer Protocol (FTP) 583
file transfer protocol (FTP) 126
file-transfer technology 531, 534
<filled> tag (**<filled>...</
    filled>**) 741
film 532
filtering mechanisms 379
financial 56, 80
financial aggregator 456, 458
financial aid 503
financial institution 462
financial operation 472
financial planning 456, 477, 478
financial resource center 458
financial service 467, 471, 472
financial services industry 463
Financial Services Modernization
    Act of 1999, 305
Financial Services Technology
    Consortium (FSTC) 474
financial strategy 466
Financial Times 4
Firetalk Communications Inc.
    383
firewall 78, 363

First Amendment 311, 313, 314,
    316
first sale 319
First Tuesday 352
first-generation wireless
    technology 152
flashing 227
Fleet 457
FlipDog.com 555
float 457
Flooz 98
focus group 220
font color 628
font point size 630
food and beverage industry 44
Forbes 4
for-each element 683
foreign-exchange bank 471
<form> tag (**<form>...</
    form>**) 739, 741
form 583, 640, 646, 649
FORM element 647, 649
form fields 712
form input 655
form tag (**<form>...</form>**)
    707
Forrester Research 32, 222
Fortune Small Business 4
fortune.com 523
Forward button 581, 587
frames 733
FrameSearch.net 236
fraud 101, 342
free 700
free download 585
free Internet access 128
free-programs.com 41
free shipping 224
free speech 313, 314
free trials 224
free.com 225
free2try.com 225
FreeAgent 567
freedom of expression 313, 314
FreeFlow Streaming 77
Freemerchant.com 41, 65
freeshop.com 225
FreeShop.com® 250
freestuffcenter.com 41
freight shipping 430
French 350
frequent-flyer miles 224
frequently asked question 69,
    261, 281
FROM 689
front-end operations 289

FrontPage Express 616
FTP (File Transfer Protocol) 583,
    584
FTP address 584
FTP directory 584
FTP server 585
FTP site 584
ftp:// 584
fulfillment 74, 100
full-service broker 465
Function 713
function body 713
function parameter 713
Futurestep.com 563

G

GainsKeeper 474
gambling 377
games.yahoo.com 542
**ganges.cs.tcd.ie/me-
    peirce/Project/on-
    internet.html** 112
gateway 129
Gen.com 499
gender-specific sites 382
Genealogy.com 447, 451
General Electric 133, 352
General options tab 595
general packet radio services
    (GPRS) 168
General Services Administration
    443
geographic data 276
German 346, 350, 352, 354
getloaded.com 430
GetThere Direct Portal™ 429
GetThere DirectAirline™ 429
GetThere DirectCorporate™ 429
GetThere.com 429
gift cash 98
gigabits per second (gbps) 126
Giovanni™ 202
giros 354
Givemetalk.com 537
Glass-Steagle Act 472
Global Business Technology 4
global content 351
Global Cyberspace Jurisdiction
    Project 341
Global Education Network 499
Global Financing Network TM
    105
Global Freight Exchange 430
global online standards
    commission 342

Global Positioning System (GPS) 168, 169, 170, 171
Global Reach 345, 365
Global System for Mobile Communications (GSM) 156
globalization 360, 371, 471, 472
GlobalSight 352
Gnome Foundation 136
GNU 136
GNU General Public License (GPL) 136
Go.Web 158
Go2systems.com 168
GoAmerica 157, 158
gocertify.earthweb.com 496
GoGlobal Technologies 221
Goldman Sachs 43
Gomez.com 461
Good Samaritan provision 313
Google.com 36
<goto> tag (**<goto>…</go-to>**) 741
GoTo.com 36
government 341, 342
GPL 136
GPS 168
<grammar> tag (**<grammar>…</grammar>**) 741
graphic 226
graphical user interface (GUI) 134, 135, 136
graphics 67
green 628
GSA.gov 443
GuideSite 36
Guild.com 435
Gunning Fog Index 401, 417, 742

H

H2O Design 231
hacker 182, 474
hand 580
handheld devices 160
hardware 35, 75
harmful to minors 315
hash function 189
hash value 189, 192
HDSL 129
head section 676
head tag (**<head>…</head>**) 712

header cell 642
Header element 619
Header elements 618
headers attribute 730, 733
Headhunter.net 564
Headlight.com 494
Health Insurance Portability and Accountability Act 426
Healtheon WebMD 427, 450
hearing impaired 401, 406, 418
hearing-impaired 742
Hebrew 349
HEIGHT attribute 626
HelloBrain.com 434
Helvetica font 631
Henter-Joyce JAWS 16
Henter-Joyce 416, 418, 742
hexadecimal color code 628, 629, 631
hidden 652
hidden input elements 648
hiding information 201
high-availability computing 34
high priority messages 589
high speed DSL (HDSL) 128
high-bandwidth 126
Hire.com 563
HireAbility.com 566
Hirediversity.com 560
History 583
history 581
history of URLs visited 595
History options 584
hit 228
Holistix Inc 78
Holistix Remote Monitor 78
Holistix Web Manager 78
Hollywood 544
Home button 595
home page 595, 616
home schooling 377
home.verio.com 132
HomeGrocer.com 358
homegrocer.com 437
HomePage.com 279
Homeruns.com 437
Homes.com 438
Honeywell 133
horizontal line 691
horizontal portal 35, 36, 37
host 125
hosting 252
Hotbot.com 35
HotDispatch.com 566
HotJobs.com 558, 564
HR element 633

HREF attribute 624, 628
HTML 20, 161, 164, 234, 276, 520
.htm file name extension 616
HTML (Hypertext Markup Language) 600, 603, 615
HTML comment (**<!--…-->**) 617
HTML comment (**<--…-->**) 668
HTML document 616
.html file name extension 616
HTML form 714
HTML markup 615
HTML table 640
HTML tag (**<HTML>…</HTML>**) 615, 617
HTML-Kit 616
HTTP 20
HTTP (HyperText Transfer Protocol) 580
HTTP header 701
HTTP **POST** request 701
HTTP protocol (HyperText Transfer Protocol) 686
HTTP request type 686
http:// (Hypertext Transfer Protocol) 580
human capital management 80
human contact 288
human-to-human communication 283
Hungry Minds 495
hybrid bank model 457
hybrid model 248, 250, 254
hyperlink 580, 628
hyperlinks 622
Hypertext Markup Language 20, 42
hypertext transfer protocol 126
HyperText Transfer Protocol (HTTP) 580
hypertext transfer protocol (HTTP) 126

I

I (italic) tag (**<I>…</I>**) 621
IBM 167, 186
ibooks.com 503
ICANN (Internet Corporation for Assigned Names and Numbers) 61
iCat 95
Icebox 535
Idiom Inc. 345, 352, 365
<if> tag (**<if>…</if>**) 741

if/else selection structure 715
If/Then/Else/End If 664
If/Then/End If 664
iFilm.com 543
**ihatefinancialplan-
    ning.com** 478
IKEA 351
illegal 230
illuminated statement 110
image for background 626
image hyperlink 628
ImagePump 69
images in Web pages 625
imba.udallas.edu 500
IMG element 626, 628, 634
img tag (**<img>...</img>**) 700
incubator 58
indecent 314
indentation convention 716
index 695
index 0 664, 670
index 1 664, 670
index value 695
indexed array 692
India 362
industry marketplace 234
industry solutions 80
industry trend 222
iNetBiller 110
Infojump.com 523
InfoPlease 499
Information Hiding
    Techniques for Steganography
    and Digital Watermarking
    (Artech House) 4
Information Week 4
Informix 693
Infoworld 4
infrared 166
infrastructure 354
INPUT element 648, 649
input fields 707, 714
input tag (**<input>**) 707, 714
INPUT TYPE = "reset" 649
INPUT TYPE = "submit" 649
input/output devices (I/O) 133
Insert Attachment dialog box
    590
Inserting special characters into
    HTML 631
 543
Inside Technology Training 4
Inside.com 523
inside.com 543
InsightExpress.com 221
Instant Messenger 379

Instinet 464
insurance 466, 467, 472
insurance premium 108
integer 663, 670
integrated access device (IAD)
    129
Integrated Services Digital
    Network (ISDN) 130
integrity 182, 184, 189
Intel 75, 167
intelligent agent 38, 39, 323, 555
Intelligent Enterprise 4
Inter@ctive Week 4
interactive history bar 583
Interactive television advertising
    231
internal issue 232
international law 344
International Telecommunications
    Union (ITU) 156, 175
Internationalization 346
Internet 5, 6, 7, 11, 13, 20, 21,
    29, 32, 39
Internet access 230
Internet Accounts dialog 585
Internet appliances 137
Internet Assigned Numbers
    Authority (IANA) 346
Internet Connection Wizard
    579
Internet Content Summit 344
Internet domain name 60
Internet Explorer 16
Internet Explorer 5 673
Internet Explorer 5 (IE5) 601
Internet Explorer 5.5 593
Internet mailing list 223
Internet marketing 219
Internet marketing campaign 219
Internet marketing strategy 219
Internet-only bank 456, 457,
    459, 460, 477
Internet Options dialog 594,
    595
Internet payment provider 111
Internet Protocol 125
Internet radio programs 139
Internet Security 132
Internet Service Provider (ISP)
    127, 579, 585, 648
Internet taxation 265
Internet telephony 139, 140, 286
Internet.com 4
Internet2 131
Internetcash.com 98

**internetra-
    dio.about.com** 139
InternetWeek 4
Internetworking Protocol (IP) 6,
    21
Internshipprograms.com
    568
interpersonal communication 376
interview 220
InterviewSmart™ 569
Intranet 6
intranet 138
Intuit 111
inventory 39, 40
IP address 125, 275
iPAQ Home Internet Appliance
    137
iPlanet 79
IRA 458, 459
Iran 361
Iraq 361
iSharp 78
island 464
iSolve 40
ISP 130
ISP (Internet Service Providers)
    648
Israel 361
iSwag.com 225
Italian 347, 351
italic style 621
IUniverse.com 517
iWon.com 41

J

Jalda 111
Japan 346, 349, 350, 362
Japanese 362
Java 493, 496
JavaScript 603, 676, 686
JavaScript interpreter 667
JavaScript scripting language 666
JAWS 416, 418, 742
Jigsaw 647
JIT 43
jobfind.com 558
Jobs.com 559
JobsOnline.com 564
Johannes Gutenberg 514
John Doe suit 313
Jones International University
    500
Jordan 361
JSML 417, 742
JumpStart 377

Jupiter Communications 222
jurisdiction 341
JustCJobs.com 566
JustComputerJobs.com 566
just-in-time inventory
       management 43, 50
JustJavaJobs.com 554, 566

K

Kana Communications 290
Kaplan 500, 502
Ken Thompson 133
Kenan-Flagler Business School at
       the University of North
       Carolina at Chapel Hill 498
kernel 136
key 183, 189
key agreement protocol 188
key algorithms 192
key distribution center 185
key exchange 185
key generation 189
key length 184, 186
key management 188, 193
key theft 188
Keynote 79
keystroke cops 307
keyword 36, 234
kilobits per second (Kbps) 126
Kintana 79
Kiplinger.com 478
KnowledgePlanet.com 495
Korea 346, 352, 362
KPMG Consulting 79
Kuwait 361
KVO 221

L

Laboratory for Computer Science
       5
LANGUAGE 667
@LANGUAGE tag 688
large cache 595
large-scale database 723
laser 166
Latin World 561
laugh.com 540
layover.com 430
Le Nouveau Marche 360
lead 248, 250, 256, 287
lead generation 251
lead time 43
Learn the Net 20
Learning Network 499

lease 462
legal 341, 342
Legal Backgrounder 4
legal issues 15
legitimate business interests 308
legitimate business purposes 309
lending 38
lending institution 461
levels of security 595
LEXIS 441
libel 312
line break element (**
…</
       BR>**) 629, 633
linearized 729
<link> tag (**<link>…</
       link>**) 741
link 707
linked documents 622
LinkExchange 228
Linus Torvalds 135
Linux 14, 133, 135, 136
Linux vendors 137
Liquidprice.com 32
list 640
live code approach 600
LiveCapital 463
Load Pictures setting 594
loading images 594
loan 460, 461, 466, 471, 478
loan application 462
local content 351
Local Folders 587
local variable 713
localization 346, 349, 352
location tracking 168, 169
log file 275, 276
log-file analysis 274, 275, 305
logic error 716
logo 224
Logos 347
Logos Group, Italy 347
Logos' Wordtheque 347
London Business School 498
London School of Economics and
       Political Science 500
London Stock Exchange 360
Longbowdigitalarts.com
       541
longdesc attribute 726
Loop 664
Lot21 231
low-bandwidth 126
lower bound 694
loyalty 281
Luxembourg 354
Lybia 361

Lycos 362
Lycos.com 445
LycosZone.com 445
LYNX 418
Lynx 733

M

Mac OS X 137
MacIntosh 14
Macintosh 133, 136, 137
Macro Consulting Inc. 221
Macromedia 230
Macromedia Shockwave 595
Magazine 543
magazine 225
Mail... 590
mailto attribute 624
mainstream channel 225
Mall.com 31
margin call 471, 477
marketing 56, 73, 74, 258, 341,
       344
marketing campaign 219, 251,
       275
marketing research 219, 220,
       222
marketing strategy 228, 278
markup language 416, 615
Marshall School of Business at the
       University of Southern
       California 498
Martin Hellman 186
Mass High Tech 4
Mastercard 95, 99
match attribute
       (**xsl:template**) 682,
       683
maximum age of a cookie 701
Maxis.com 542
MAXLENGTH attribute 648
MBAFreeAgent.com 567
MBNA 99
m-business 152, 153, 155, 171
McAfee 198
m-Commerce 58
media contact 232
media convergence 532
Media Metrix 222
media software 230
MediaMap 232
MediaRing.com 223
megabits per second (Mbps) 126
**members.tripod.com/
       ~AAWN1** 383
men.crosswalk.com 382

Men's Health 382
\<menu\> tag (**\<menu\>...\</ menu\>**) 739, 741
merchant 39, 247, 248, 249, 252, 254, 256, 257, 259, 265
merchant account 94
Merchant Connection Kit (MCK) 95
merchant server 29
Mercury Interactive 77
merging financial services 472
Merrill Lynch 465
Merrill Lynch Direct 470
message board 251, 256
message body 590
Message Control 322
message digest 190
message integrity 190
Messaging Magazine 4
META tag 234, 251
metasearch engines 236
METHOD = "get" 647
METHOD = "post" 647
METHOD attribute 647
method of doing business 319
Michael A. Smyth v. The Pillsbury Company 308
microbrowsers 160
microcapsules 523
micropayment 13, 102
Microsoft 14, 75, 111
Microsoft .NET 135
Microsoft Access 603, 693, 723
Microsoft Chat 593
Microsoft Cleartype™ 521, 527
Microsoft Exchange 155
Microsoft Internet Explorer Web 579
Microsoft Magnifier 402
Microsoft Narrator 411, 413
Microsoft NetMeeting 593
Microsoft On-Screen Keyboard 413
Microsoft Outlook Express 585
Microsoft Reader 521
Microsoft SQL Server 693
Microsoft SQL Server 2000 723
Microsoft Visual Basic 663, 670
Microsoft Web servers 663
Microsoft Word 276, 518
middle tier 601, 613
MightyWords.com 517, 518
mii.siterock.com/ home.html 79
Miller Test 313

Miller v. California 313
minimum contacts 341
mirror page 252
Missingmoney.com 447
Mission Yuppie Eradication Project 380
MIT 523, 527
MIT's Project Mac 5
mobile business 152, 153
mobile communications 165
mobile Internet 156
Mobile Internet Kit 159
mobile payments 95
Mobitex Network 154
MobShop 40
modem 157, 579
modularize 713
modulation 126
modulator and demodulator 126
monetary transaction 92
monetary transfer 95
Money 4
money order 99, 101
Money.com 466
MoneyCentral 466
moneycentral.msn.com/ home.asp 466
Monster.com 554, 558, 564, 566
Montreal 358
More.com 29
Morgan Stanley Dean Witter Online 477
MorganWorks.com 563
Morocco 361
mortgage 108, 456, 460, 461, 463
MortgageRamp.com 463
Mouse Button Settings 408
mouse cursor 405
MouseKeys 407
movie 225
Moviextras.com 545
MP3 11, 171, 317, 515, 519
MP3 technology 534
MP3.com 534
Mplayer 541
mPower 478
Ms. Foundation for Women 383
msdn.microsoft.com/ workshop/imedia/ agent 287
MSN 362
MSN Messenger 593
MTV 231, 536
multi-processing 133

multi-tasking 133
multi-threading 133
multi-tiered model 248, 249
multi-user 133
Multics 133
multi-level model 248, 249
multi-lingual e-translation portal 347
Multimail 159
multimedia 73, 74, 165
multimedia contact center 281
municipal bond 472
MuniDirect 472
music 532
Music.com 537
mutual fund 467, 470, 478
MyGo.Web 158
MyHealthRecord 427, 450
mySAP 79, 80
mysap.com/solutions/ crm/index.htm 80
mysap.com/solutions/e- commerce/index.htm 80
mysap.com/solutions/ hr/index.htm 80
mysap.com/solutions/ mobile_workplace/ index.htm 80
mysap.com/solutions/ plm/index.htm 80
mysap.com/solutions/ workplace/in- dex.htm 80

N

NAME attribute 648
name attribute 714
name recognition 45
name-your-price 38
Name: 648
Nasdaq 360, 464
Nasdaq Market Maker 464
National Discount Brokers 470
National Institute of Standards and Technology (NIST) 186
National Security Agency (NSA) 186
natural language processing 284
navigation 67, 75
Navisite 230
nBank 460
NEAR Magazine 168
negligent 312
nested tags 621

Net Commerce Magazine 4
Net2Phone 139, 140
Netbank 459
Netcentives 224
NetCreations 224
Netherlands 354
NetMeeting 591, 592
Netpliance i-opener 137, 138
Netscape Navigator 6 346
Netscape's Communicator 579
Net-Scene 497
network administrator 586
network card 579
network of networks 6, 21
network security 182
Network World 4
network-related site 61
Neuer Markt 360
New button 588
New Economy 501
new economy 379
New Folder option 587
New Mail message 587
New York Stock Exchange
    (NYSE) 464
New York Times, The 103, 512
newapps.internet.com/
    appstopics/
    Win_95_Web_Site_Pro
    motion_Tools.html
    237
News account 586
News server 586
News... 590
newsgroups 251, 589, 594
Newsgroups button on the
    toolbar 590
newsgroups screen 590
newsletter 232, 248
newspaper 225
Newsweek 4
newsweek.com 521
NEXIS 441
Nielsen rating 532
Nike 231
Nokia 163, 167
Nokia WAP Developer Toolkit
    161
non-content-related means 313
non-repudiation 182, 190
Norton™ Internet Security 198
NOSHADE attribute 634
Notepad 616
notHarvard.com 493
NTT DoCoMo 156
null 716

Nuovo Mercato 360
NYUOnline.com 501

O

oasis-open.org/cover/
    wap-wml.html 163
Office of Foreign Assets Control
    (OFAC) 105
Office of the Currency (OCC) 457
Olmstead v. United States 304
OmniSky 159
one-click shopping 99
OneCore 459
Onion.com 540
online advertising 222, 225, 228
online auction 32, 65, 311
online banking 13, 456, 457,
    458, 460, 474
online banking services 45
online bill payment and
    presentment 460
online billing 426
online chatting 383
online communities 376, 380
online contracting services 566
online coupon 225
online financial services 13
online language translation
    dictionary 347
online lending 462
online marketing 230
online marketing research 221
online natural-language
    technology 235
online payment 13, 56, 74, 97,
    100
online purchase 92
online recruiting 67, 556
online shopping malls 31
online store 256
online survey 221
online text chatting 281, 282,
    283, 285
online trading 465, 468, 470
online transactions 152
OnlineLearning.net 501
OnlineTradingAcade-
    my.com 471
Open eBook Forum 520, 527
Open Financial Exchange (OFX)
    111
open platform 166
open source code 319
open source software 136
openebook.org 520

operating system 131, 133, 134,
    135
*Operating Systems, Second
    Edition* 4
opt-in e-mail 223
optical modem 126
option 466
OPTION element 655
Option Explicit 664, 670,
    688, 695
opto-chip 126
Oracle 136
Oracle (database product from
    Oracle Corporation) 693
Oracle Systems 290
order of closing tags 622
order-processing technology 29
order.html 707
order-fulfillment provider 107
org 60
original equipment manufacturers
    41
Outlook 585
Outlook Express 585, 586, 587,
    588, 594
Outlook Express newsgroups 589
outsource 281
outsourcing 77, 223, 232
overbroad 314
overhead cost 40, 45
overlapping elements 622
overstock 40

P

P element 618, 621, 624
Pacific Bell 459
Pacific Exchange (PCX) 464
packet 5, 21, 125
packet switching 5, 21
PacketVideo 163, 165, 166
packetvideo.com 165
page content 618
pagers 160
Palm 158, 159, 167
Palm handheld computer 153
Palm Query Applications (PQAs)
    159
Palm Web clipping 158
palm.com/devzone/palm-
    vii/tutorials/
    tutorial_palm.html
    159
palm.net 159
paper survey 220
parameters 713

parasite 320
partner relationship management (PRM) 289, 295
partnership 75, 247, 289
passport 593
password 36, 253, 278, 473
password 651, 653
password boxes 650
password input 650
patently offensive 314
patents 311, 319
path to a script 648
pattern 275
pay everyone service 108
pay-per-click 103, 228, 248, 249, 250, 253
pay-per-download 103
pay-per-lead 228, 248, 249, 253, 254
pay-per-performance 228
pay-per-sale 228, 248, 249, 250, 253, 254
pay-per-sale model 249
pay-per-view TV 533
payment 252, 254, 256
payment management system 103
payment model 13
payment solution provider 104
Paymentech 104
PaymentNet 104
PayPal 101
payroll 459
Paytrust 108
Payware® 95
PBS Adult Learning Service 495
PC 4
PC Magazine 4
PC Novice 4
PC Week 4
PCS 154, 156, 157, 167
PC-to-PC 286
PC-to-PC calls 138, 140
PC-to-phone 286
PC-to-phone calls 138
PC-to-telephone calls 140
.pdf (Portable Document Format) 595
Peachtree Network 358
peanutpress.com 521
peapod.com 437
peer-to-peer payment 92
Pensare.com 501
people with disabilities 170
PeoplePC 379
Peoplescape.com 563

PeopleSoft Mobile Company Directory 157
peoplesoft.com 157
Pepsi 356
per capita income 345
percent of screen width 634
Performance Computing 4
permission-based marketing 223
personal communications services (PCS) 154
personal digital assistant (PDA) 73, 153, 156, 157, 158, 163, 167, 170, 475, 520, 521, 527
personal finance 458
personal information 304, 309, 311
personalization 11, 22, 222, 223, 254, 273, 274, 279, 280, 289
Petopia.com 358
Pez® 32
pharmacy 426
physical branch 459
physical presence 457, 460
picture 582
picture element (pixel) 626
Pierre Omidyar 32
pigment chips 523
pixel 626
PKI 191, 192
plain old telephone system (POTS) 126
plaintext 183, 193
Platform for Privacy Preferences Project (P3P) 310
playback controls 139
plug-in 223
PlugInGo.com 256
Pocket Internet Explorer 158, 164
Pocket PC 153, 164
point to point tunneling protocol (PPTP) 132
point-based rewards 224
point-of-sale transaction 94, 104, 118
points-based currency system 98
points-based promotion 224
points-based reward 98
policy creation authorities 192
political 341
poll 39
Pollstar.com 447
pop-up box 227
pornography 313, 314, 377

Portable Data Format (**.pdf**) 595
portal 28, 35, 36, 225, 234
portfolio 468, 470, 476
position zero 695
positioning 222
POST 701
post office protocol (POP) 126
postal system 354
PostMasterDirect.com 224
Power Marketing Association 434
Powerstreet 477
PowerWallet 103
PQA 159
PR Web 232
Precise Positioning Service (PPS) 169
predefined functions 664
preferences 69
prescriptions 427, 450
presentation 232
presentation logic 601, 613
Presentations 4
press release 232
Pretty Good Privacy (PGP) 11
Priceline.com 38, 39
PriceWaterhouseCoopers 310
primary key 132, 693
PrimeStreet 462
Princeton Review 568
Principles of Internet Marketing (South-Western College Publishing) 4
Priority button on the toolbar 589
privacy 14, 75, 110, 169, 182, 184, 186, 190, 280, 303, 307, 308, 310, 316, 341, 344, 474
privacy invasion 11, 22
privacy policy 72, 310, 311
Privacy Wizard 75
PrivacyBot.com 310
PrivacyX.com 309, 313
PrivacyX.com 309
private key 186, 187, 188, 190, 192
process.asp 717
processing instruction 680
product lifecycle management 80
Programming Application With the Wireless Application Protocol (John Wiley and Sons) 4
Programs tab 594
progress bar 139

Progressive Casualty Insurance Company 155
Project Gutenberg 514
Project MAC 133
Project Mac 5
promotion 219, 222, 224, 232, 278, 279
promotional program 224
<prompt> tag (**<prompt>**…**</ prompt>**) 741
Propertyfirst.com 438
protecting copyrighted material 202
protocol 126, 188
proxy server 158
pseudocode 715
pseudocode **If statement** 715
pseudocode **if/else struc- ture** 716
psychographics 220
public access 584
public domain 503
public key 186, 187, 188, 190, 192
public-key algorithm 186, 188
public Key cryptography 14
public key cryptography 186
public-key cryptography 191, 192, 193
public-key encryption 187, 188
Public-key Infrastructure (PKI) 191
public policy 308
public relations (PR) 219, 232
publicity 232
publisher 312
pulldown lists 652
purchase pattern 289
PVAuthor 166
PVPlatform 166
PVPlayer 166
PVServer 166
PWS (Personal Web Server) 647

Q
Qpass 103
Qualified lead 249
queries 132, 693
Query Application Builder (QAB) 159
querying a database 694
question template 235
questionnaire 220
Quick & Reilly 466

Quicken 108
quickmusic.com 537
QuickTake.com 221
Quisic 497, 498
Quokka.com 538
quotation (') mark 668

R
radiation 153
radio 139, 231
radio 652
radio button 652
radio frequency 166, 167
radio frequency WLANs 167
random access memory (RAM) 133
Rare Medium 58
reach 222
Read News hyperlink 590
readability 401, 417, 668, 729, 742
reading messages 591
real estate 467
Real Networks 139
real time 101, 290, 723
RealAudio Channels 139
RealCall Alert 287
RealPlayer 139
RealPlayer dialog 139
realtime voice communication 281
Reanimator 535
reasonable expectation of privacy 308, 309
rebate 38, 40
recognition 228
record 132, 691, 693, 723
record set 689
Recordset object in ADO 693
Recruitsoft.com 563
red 628
Red Hat 136, 137
REDIBook 464
redundancy 35
redundant server 96
Refer.com 563
referrals 75
Refresh button 581, 595
regional content 351
registering 61, 228
registration 34, 36
regular expression 713
relational database 132, 693, 723
relational database model 132
relational database systems 132

reliability 39
reload the last page you viewed 581
Rent.net 438
Repeater 127
ReplayTV 536
Reply to 587
replying to a message 591
reporting 252, 256, 257
Reporting.net 254
request 601, 613
request for proposal 43, 495, 566
request method 686
Request object 688
research 220
Research In Motion (RIM) 153, 154, 155, 158
Research in Motion (RIM) 154
resellers 289
reserve price 32
reset 651, 654, 714
Resource Marketing 230
response 601, 613
Response object 703
Response object 688
response rate 223
restricted access FTP site 584
restricted algorithms 183
resume 555, 560, 564
resume-filtering software 560
retail 38, 39
Retail Energy 434
retirement 460, 467, 476, 478
return on investment (ROI) 289, 493
reverse auctions 32
revoked certificates 192
Revolution 4
reward structure 247, 248, 250, 251, 254, 258, 265
reward structures 75
RF WLANs 167
RGB colors 628
rich media 231
Ride the Bullet 515
Right 665
right attribute value (**align**) 620
right-click 582, 584
RIM 158
RIM Developer Zone 155
risk 471
Rivals.com 538
Rivest, Ron 187
ROIDirect's ECommerce solution 75

root certification authority 192
root key 192
router 125
row 132, 723
ROWS attribute 649
ROWSPAN attribute 646
rowspan attribute 700
RSA Security, Inc. 4, 187
Russia 345

S

Saba 494
safe-harbor 319
Salary.com 569
Salem Five Cents Savings Bank 458
salemfive.com 458
sales force automation 287, 288, 463
sales tracking 273
Salesforce.com 288
Salomon Smith Barney 465, 478
Salon.com 521
SAP (Systems, Applications and Products in Data Processing) 80
satellite technology 536
satellites 169
Saudi Arabia 351, 361
Saunders, Michael 8
Save As... in the file menu 582
save disk space 595
Save Picture As... 582
Save target as... 584
SBA 443
s-business 183
scholarship 500
Scottrade 470
screen reader 400, 401, 411, 414, 416, 729
screen scraping 474
Screenwriters.com 545
screenwriting 545
script 667, 702, 703
scripting language 668, 671
scrolling text 227
SDSL 129
search capabilities 67
search engine 219, 234, 247, 249, 251, 258, 618
search-engine ranking 234
search engine registration 235
searching 234
second generation wireless technology 152

secondary research 220
secret key 184, 186
secret-key cryptography 184
Section 230 of the Telecommunications Act 312, 313
Secure Electonic Transaction (SET) 111
Secure Socket Layer (SSL) 111
secure transactions 185
securing communication 184
Securities and Exchange Commission (SEC) 464, 471
security 13, 28, 56, 97, 102, 132, 168, 182, 342, 344, 463, 466, 472, 474, 477
security attacks 182
security measures browsers take 594
Security tab 595
segmented market 230
Seibel 157
seibel.com 157
SELECT 689, 691, 694
Selfcare.com 426
self-regulated medium 304
self-regulation 344
selling advertising 228, 229
Send 589
Send/Recv message 587
sensitive information 649
sequencing information 125
sequential execution 715
server 126
Server method **CreateObject** 691
Server object 688
server settings 590
server side 135
server software 616
Server-side image maps 729
server-side image maps 401
Sesamestreet.com 445
Session variable 692, 695
SET 14, 73
Set as Wallpaper 582
Settings... button 595
settlement service 106
set-top box 533
sexually explicit speech 311
SFNB 460
Shamir, Adi 187
Sharebuilder 468
shill bidding 323
shipping 74, 100, 425

Shopnow.com 31
shopping bot 38, 39
shopping cart 29, 65, 72, 95, 600, 700
shopping cart technology 36
shopping online 29
shopping.altavista.com/home.sdc 112
short messaging service (SMS) 156
ShowSounds 407
sickbay.com 426
Siliconindia 4
Simon & Shuster 515
simple mail transfer protocol (SMTP) 126
Singapore 362
single-selection structure 715
site directory 584
Site59.com 429
SiteBuilder 66, 83
SiteRoc 79
SixFigureJobs 568
SIZE attribute 630, 634, 648
size attribute 714
SkillsVillage.com 563
slander 312
slate.com 521
slow connection 594
small business 458
Small Business Administration 443
Small Business Administration Office of Advocacy 463
small cache 595
smart card 13, 101
Smart Card Industry Association 102
smart card reader 101, 116
SmartForce 494
SmartMoney.com 474
social 376
social interaction 376, 378, 383
socio-economic segregation 376, 378
socket 193
software 75
software platform 133
Solaris 134
sound file 139
SoundSentry 406
source address 125
source-code form 616
SPAM 321
spamming 224, 251
SPAN attribute 643

special characters 631, 647
special event 232
speech 232
speech recognition 283, 287, 402, 416, 418, 743
speech synthesis 283, 284, 416, 418, 742, 743
speed up Web browsing 595
spider 234
Spinner.com 538
Split 665, 695
SportingNews.com 538
Sprint PCS 156, 157
SQL 132
SQL (Structured Query Language) 693, 694
SQL query keywords 694
SQL Server 132
SRC = "location" 626
src attribute 700
SRC attribute of the **IMG** element 628
SSL 14, 73
standard accessibility 160
standard characters 647
Standard Positioning Service (SPS) 169
Stanford University 376, 499, 500
Staples 72
Start menu 616
Startsampling.com 41
static document 686
station.sony.com 532
statistical tool 275
steganography 11, 201
Stephen King 515
stephenking.com 515
stickiness 256, 493
StickyKeys 407
stock 463, 464, 466, 468, 470, 478
stock exchange 360, 464
stock market 463, 472
stock trading 458
storage 74
storage area network (SAN) 127
store.Yahoo.com 65
store-builder 65
storefront 65, 74
storefront model 28
strategic planning 58
Stratton Oakmont v. Prodigy 312, 313
Stratus 35
streaming audio 138, 362, 531

streaming event 230
streaming media 230, 351, 380, 531
streaming video 73, 77, 138, 165, 230, 531
string 663, 668, 670
strong tag (****…****) 621
strongest color 628
structure of that document 615
Structured Query Language (SQL) 132, 603
style sheet 413
Stylizing text on Web pages 621
SUB element 632
subaffiliate 249
<subdialog> tag (**<subdialog>**…**</subdialog>**) 741
Subject bar 590
Subject field 588
submit 651, 654
Submit button 700, 712
submit input 649
SubmitOrder.com 107
subscribed newsgroup 590
subscript 632
subsidy e-publishing 516
substitution ciphers 183
suffix 61
Suffolk University 500
summary attribute 733
Sun Microsystems 79, 134
SunOS 134
superscript 632
supply chain management 28, 58
SureTrade.com 466, 477
"surf" the Web 579
SuSE 137
Sweden 354
sweepstakes 224, 225
switching cost 68
Switzerland 354
Sybase 693
Symantec 198
symmetric 129
symmetric cryptography 184
symmetric DSL (SDSL) 128
symmetric encryption 186
symmetric key algorithms 188
symmetric secret key 184, 185, 188, 203
synchronization 289
synchronized communication 74

Synchronized Multimedia Integration Language (SMIL) 416
syntax error in HTML 616
Syria 361
system caret 414

T

T-1 130
T-3 line 130
table 132, 615, 640, 699, 703, 714, 723, 729, 730
TABLE element 634, 641
TableName 694
tag 615
tags 160, 161
Taiwan 362
talent scouting 544
Talk City 385
target market 219, 221, 229, 257, 275
targeted advertising 166
tax 466, 467, 478
taxation 15, 341, 362
TBODY 642
TCP 6, 21
TCP/IP 6, 21, 138
TD Bank Financial Group 477
TD element 642
TDMA 156
TeacherVision 499
Technology Review 4
tele-immersion 131
telephone survey 220
television 225, 230, 231
Testing and Debugging Tips 616
TestU 501
testyourlimits.mercuryinteractive.com 77
text 714
TEXT attribute 629
text box 646
text editor 616
text fields 714
text format 276
text messaging 158
<TEXTAREA> tag 649
TEXTAREA element 649
text-based browser 621, 626
text-based browsers 642
text-to-speech 411
textual identifier 648
textual labels for a form element 649
TH element 642

th tag (`<th>...</th>`) 730
Thawte 192
The Boston Globe 4
The Collections of Information
    Antipiracy Act 323
*The Complete Guide to Associate
    and Affiliate Programs on
    the Net (McGraw-Hill)* 4
The Denver Post 4
The Diversity Directory 560
The Hollywood Stock Exchange
    541
The Independent (London) 4
The Industry Standard 4
The Internet Movie Database 543
The Men's Issues Page 382
The Motley Fool 466
The National Business and
    Disability Council (NBDC)
    561
The New York Times 5
The One to One Field Book
    The Complete Toolkit for
    Implementing a 1 to 1
    Marketing Program (Bantam
    Doubleday Dell Publishing
    Group) 5
The Open Group 134
The Portable MBA 5
The Standards 310
The Wall Street Journal 5
THEAD element 642
THINQ 494, 495
third-party logistics services
    provider (3PL) 105
THOMAS 443
Thomas Cook 105
thomas.loc.gov 443, 451
**thomas.loc.gov/cgi-
    bin/bdquery/
    z?d106:hr.01714:** 190
**thomas.loc.gov/cgi-
    bin/bdquery/
    z?d106:s.00761:** 190
Thomson Learning 502
three-tier application 673
three-tier architecture 600, 723
Ticketmaster 29
Ticketmaster.com 29, 46
Tickets.com 447
TicketWeb.com 447
tile.net/news 251
tiles an image 626
Tim Berners-Lee 6, 21
Time 5

Time Division Multiple Access
    (TDMA) 156
time to market 493
timeout 409
Times font 631
Timestamping 190
timestamping agency 190
title tag (`<title>...</ti-
    tle>`) 733
TITLE element 618
title tag 676
Tivo 536
tixx.com 447
To: field 588
ToggleKeys 407
toolbar menu 592
top-referring sites 276
top tier 601
top-level domain (TLD) 88
Toronto Star 5
Toshiba 167
Toyota 156
Toyota InfoTechnology Center
    156
toysrus.com 98
TR element 642
tracking 247, 251, 252, 253,
    254, 256
tracks 416
Trade.com 477
Tradebonds.com 472
trademark 311, 320, 343, 351
Tradesafe.com 101
Tradient 430
trading on margin 470
traditional advertising form 231
traditional direct marketing 224
traditional education 493
traditional marketing 219
traditional marketing research
    221
traffic 219, 227
traffic generation 249, 251
training marketplace 495
Trainingnet.com 495
TrainSeek.com 495
transaction support 273
transactional fee 466
transceivers 167
transfer of control 715
translation 346, 348
Transmission Control Protocol 6,
    21
transmiting messages securely
    186
transparency 463, 482

Transparent Language 346
transposition ciphers 183
travel 38
travel industry 429
Travelocity.com 428, 430,
    430, 450
treasury bond 472
triangulation 169
Trintech 95
Triple DES 186
tripod.com 66
Trojan Horse 14
trucking.net 430
TRUSTe.com 311
Truste.com 328
Trusted systems 519
Trustmark 310
Tuck School of Business at
    Dartmouth College 498
Tunisia 361
TurboLinux 137
turnkey solution 65, 74, 83
Tutor.com 501, 502
Tuvala 61
two-tiered model 249, 265
two-way pagers 153, 157, 170
two-way video 166
TYPE = "checkbox" 651
TYPE = "hidden" 648, 652
TYPE = "password" 649, 651,
    653
TYPE = "radio" 652, 653
TYPE = "reset" 649, 651, 654
TYPE = "submit" 649, 651,
    654
TYPE = "text" 648, 653
TYPE attribute 648
type attribute 714

U

U (underline) element 621
U.S. Department of Commerce
    345, 378
U.S. government 43
U.S. News and World Report 503
Ubarter.com 40
uDecide.com 444
ultimate wireless device 171
undefined 716
underline 620
*Understanding WAP (Artech
    House)* 5
UNext 501
Unicode 346
unique visitor 228, 259, 275

United Arab Emirates 361
United Kingdom 354
United Nations 345
United States 6
United States v. LaMacchia 318
unitedmessaging.com 322
universal mobile
    telecommunications
    standard (UMTS) 168
University of California at
    Berkeley 134
University of California at Los
    Angeles 498
University of Chicago 498, 500
University of Dallas 500
University of Illinois at Urbana-
    Champaign 5
University of Phoenix 499
University of Utah 5
UNIX 133, 134, 135, 137
Unix 14
UNIX Time-Sharing System 134
Unsolicited Electronic Mail Act
    322
unsolicited e-mail 311
UP.Browser 157
updating a database 647
updating existing records in a
    database 694
uploading 585
upper bound 694
UPS 354
Upside 5
upstream 129
URL (Uniform Resource Locator
    or Universal Resource
    Locator) 580
USA Today 5
user agent 400, 401, 414, 729
user profile 219
username 36, 253, 473
usnews.com 523

V

VA Linux 136
VA Linux Systems 135, 137
validation 95
VALIGN = "middle" 646
VALIGN attribute 646
Value added network 41
VALUE attribute 649
ValueClick 228, 229, 230
ValueClick AdVantage 230
ValueClick AdVantage Plus 230
ValueClick Affiliate 230

ValueClick Premium 230
<var> tag (**<var>...</var>**)
    741
variable 702, 703, 713, 714
variant 663, 670
variant subtype 663, 664
variant treated as a number 663
Varsitybooks.com 503
Vault.com 557
VBScript 583, 603, 663, 670,
    676, 686
VCampus 494
venture capital 358
**ventures@raremedi-
    um.com** 58
verification 14
VeriSign 191, 192
vertical alignment formatting 646
vertical portal 35
VerticalOne 474
very high speed DSL (VDSL)
    128, 129
ViaPay 105
ViaVoice 402
Victoria's Secret 230
Victorian AIDS Council/ Gay
    Men's Health Centre 382
victoriassecret.com 426
video 139, 591
video e-mail 166
video games 163
video-conferencing 74, 376, 380
video-on-demand 531, 545
Vietnam 362
viewCart.asp 703
viewing newsgroups 594
violence 377
Virtual Auditorium 383
virtual classroom 494
virtual credit card 95
virtual laboratory 131
virtual private networks (VPNs)
    132
virtual university 499
virus 14, 371, 377
VirusScan® 198
Visa 95, 99, 102, 460
Visa Cash 102
Visual Basic 663, 670
visually impaired 402, 411, 416,
    418
voice and data communication
    167
Voice over Internet Protocol
    (VoIP) 286
Voice Server SDK 402, 418, 742

voice synthesis 401, 734
voice-over-DSL (VoDSL) 129
VoiceXML 20, 401, 416, 417,
    418, 734, 739, 742
volume control 139
voluntary filtering 344
Volunteers in Service to America
    (Americorps*VISTA) 379
<vxml> tag (**<vxml>...</
    vxml>**) 741

W

W3C 20, 400
WAI 400, 417
WAI Quicktips 400
Wall Street 456
Wall Street Journal, The 103
wallpaper 582
WAP 158, 160, 161, 163
WAP Developer Toolkit 161
WAP gateway 161
water2water.com 433
wavelength 127
WBT Systems 494
W-CDMA 156
Web 13, 20, 36, 38, 39
Web Accessibility Guidelines 401
Web Accessibility Initiative
    (WAI) 12, 16, 22, 400,
    417, 726, 741
Web clipping 158, 159
Web commercials 230
Web Content Accessibility
    Guidelines 400, 729, 733
Web hosting 62
Web page cache 595
Web server 126, 647
**web.mit.edu/network/
    pgp.html** 187
Web-based course 493
Web-based CRM solution 289
Webcasting 230
WebHire 558
WebMD 427, 450
WebMD TV 427
WebRIOT 231, 536
WebRN 428, 450
Websiteforfree 67
Webtechniques 5
Webtechniques.com 68
WebTrends 275, 276
WEBtropolis ORDERnet 74
WebTV 128, 167, 536
Webvision 74
welcome.html 674

Wellesley College 499
Wells Fargo 101, 457, 458, 459
While loop 691
While/Wend or **Do While/ Loop** 664
whitespace 668, 671
whitespace characters 715
Whitfield Diffie 186
WIDTH element 626, 633, 634
width in pixels 634
width of text input 648
width-to-height ratio 626
Williams College 499
Windows 133
Windows 2.0 134
Windows 3.0 134
Windows 95 135
Windows 98 135
Windows NT 135
WindowsMedia.com 539
wire transfer 101
wireless 14, 58, 69, 110, 231, 380, 468, 475, 476, 477
Wireless Application Protocol (WAP) 14, 73, 158, 160
wireless applications 155
wireless banking 474, 476
wireless communication 160
wireless devices 153, 155, 160, 163, 167, 168, 170
wireless e-mail 155
wireless handhelds 154
wireless Internet 152, 160
wireless Internet access 152, 153, 156, 157
wireless Internet service provider 153, 155, 157, 158
wireless LAN 167
wireless location 168
Wireless Markup Language (WML) 160, 161, 163
Wireless Minstrel V 159
wireless multimedia 166
wireless networks 167
wireless office 152, 167
wireless technology 155, 156, 163, 167, 168, 170
wireless trading 474
wireless transmissions 153
wireless video 165, 166
Wireless Web Browser 157
Wireless Web Connection Kit 157
Wireless Web Messaging 157
Wireless Web Updates 157
wirelessclick.com 232
wirelesstoday.com 232

wmbr.mit.edu/stations/ list.html 139
WML 160
WML browser 161
WML document 161
WMLScript 161
Women.com 382
Word Exchange Forum 347
Wordplayer.com 545
WorkingSolo.com 567
World Intellectual Property Organization (WIPO) 343
World Wide Web 6, 7, 10, 13, 16, 20, 21, 22
World Wide Web Consortium (W3C) 12, 16, 20, 22, 400, 417, 419, 420, 726, 741
WorldPoint Interactive 352
writeln method 668
w-Technologies 477
www 60
www.1800flowers.com 46
www.1stbooks.com 516
www.1ViewNetwork.com 474
www.247media.com 223
www.3com.com/govern- ment/urbanchal- lenge/ americorps.html 379
www.401kafe.com 478
www.abanet.org/buslaw/ cyber/initiatives/ prospect.html 341, 364
www.abc.com 536
www.ac.com/ecommerce/ define.html 79
www.activision.com 542
www.adarus.com/html/ demos.html 56
www.adbility.com 228, 258
www.adbroadcast.com 232
www.address.com 129
www.adforce.com 232
www.adgrafix.com 132
www.adknowledge.com 222
www.adobe.com 203
www.adresource.com 237
www.adsmart.net 228
www.advancingwomen.com 382
www.advantagehir- ing.com 562
www.advisorteam.net/ AT/User/kcs.asp 563
www.affiliate-an- nounce.com 265

www.affiliatesoft- ware.net 252
www.akamai.com 77
www.alis.com 346
www.allaire.com 279
www.allegis.com 289
www.altavista.com 223, 235, 475
www.amazingmedia.com 265
www.amazon.com 35
www.ameritrade.com 468, 477
www.ameritrain.com 496
www.andromedia.com 291
www.anonymizer.com 313
www.aol.com 350, 475
www.aol.de 350
www.apache.org 136
www.apple.com 68
www.apple.com/macosx 137
www.apple.com/macosx/ technologies/ aqua.html 137
www.apple.com/quick- time 231
www.appliedmetrix.com 277
www.aquarius.net 348
www.ariba.com 234
www.ask.com 37
www.askjeeves.com 235, 284
www.asknetrageous.com/ AskNetrageous.html 238
www.associate-it.com 265
www.astroterra.com 167
www.atomfilms.com 544
www.atplan.net 221
www.atrandom.com 512
www.auctionbuilder.com 66
www.authentidate.com 190
www.autobytel.com 432
www.av.com 37
www.babelfish.altavis- ta.com 346
www.babycenter.com 261
www.bannertips.com 228
www.bcentral.com 75
www.beenz.com 98, 113
www.befree.com 254
www.bell-labs.com/ project/tts/voic- es.html 283
www.bidland.com 66

www.bigstep.com 89
www.bigstep.com/foyer/
    examples.jhtml 66
www.bigwords.com 503
www.billpoint.com 113
www.blazesoft.com 279
www.bluemartini.com 291
www.bluestreak.com 237
www.bluetooth.com 168
www.bn.com 45, 261, 493
www.bondsonline.com 472
www.breakaway.com 132
www.brightware.com 282
www.broadbase.com 291
www.burst.com 237
www.businesstown.com/
    mindspring/plan-
    ning/creating-de-
    veloping.asp 56
www.businesswire.com 232
www.caldera.com 136, 137
www.caliberlearn-
    ing.com 495
www.campsix.com 59
www.campusfood.com 8
www.capellauniver-
    isty.com 500
www.cardean.com 500
www.careerpower.com 569
www.cashpile.com 267
www.cdnow.com 31
www.cdt.org 310, 328
www.centra.com 494
www.chami.com/html-kit
    616
www.channelseven.com 238
www.chase.com 475
www.cheaptickets.com 429
www.checkfree.com 108,
    115
www.chiefmonster.com 568
www.cj.com 252
www.clareon.com 114
www.clarify.com 289
www.cleardigital.com 230
www.click2learn.com 494
www.clickaction.com 237
www.clickichat.com 283
www.clicktrade.com 254
www.cnn.com 536
www.codexdatasys-
    tems.com 307, 328
www.cognicity.com 203
www.comcentral.com 541
www.commerceone.com 66,
    238

www.compubank.com 460
www.concur.com 234
www.connectinc.com 234
www.construction.com 234
www.corio.com 132
www.cpsr.org 389
www.crayola.com 68
www.crm-forum.com 293
www.crosscommerce.com
    257
www.crowdburst.com 385
www.cstr.ed.ac.uk/
    projects/festival/
    userin.html 283
www.curcuitcity.com 46
www.cyberangels.com 316
www.cybercash.com 112
www.cyber-logics.com 230
www.cybersitter.com 315,
    329
www.datadistiller-
    ies.com 277
www.datainstincts.com
    277
www.datek.com 470
www.dcs.ecu.edu 500
www.DealShop.com 31
www.dealtime.com 39
www.debit-it.com 100, 113
www.deitel.com 251, 617
www.deitel.com/in-
    dex.html 617
www.dell.com 136
www.derivion.com 110, 115
www.developers.rim.net
    155
www.dhl.com 429
www.dialfree.net 129
www.digiknow.com 237
www.digimark.com 203
www.digitalimpact.com
    223
www.digitalthink.com 493
www.directcoupons.com
    225
www.djr.co.uk 352
www.dljdirect.com 477
www.docent.com 495
www.domainit.com 61
www.doubleclick.com 228,
    328
www.dowjones.com 288
www.download.com 595
www.driveway.com 564
www.drudgereport.com 522
www.drugfreeamerica.org 389

www.ebalance.com 474
www.ebsure.com 77
www.ecash.net 97, 113
www.e-cement.com 234
www.echarge.com 114
www.econtacts.com 223
www.ecorporation.com 59
www.ecredit.com 105, 114
www.education.com/
    jumpstart 377
www.educationalbene-
    fit.com 500
www.edupoint.com 495
www.eff.org 310, 328
www.eGain.com 290
www.eGroups.com 385
www.ehatchery.com 59
www.ekidnetwork.com 389
www.eletter.com 224
www.eloan.com 461
www.eMarketer.com 238
www.encirq.com 110, 115
www.engage.com 237
www.enonymous.com 327
www.enrononline.com 471
www.entrypoint.com 99,
    112
www.epic.org 310, 328
www.epiphany.com 289
www.eprise.com 67
www.espn.com 538
www.etest.net 563
www.etimecapital.com
    107, 115
www.etoys.com 31
www.etrade.com 466, 467
www.etranslate.com 352
www.everythingt1.com
    130, 142
www.ework.com 567
www.excite.com 235, 279
www.execunet.com 568
www.expedia.com 428
www.ezlogin.com 474
www.facetime.com 283
www.farmclub.com 534
www.fcc.gov 327
www.fcc.gov/Bureaus/
    Wireless/
    Public_Notices/
    2000/da002099.html
    170
www.fcc.gov/e911 170
www.fedex.com 430
www.fidelity.com 477

www.fiercewireless.com 232

www.findlaw.com 327

www.firsttuesday.com 352

www.flipside.com 541

www.flonetwork.com 237

www.flooz.com 98, 113

www.fool.com 466

www.forrester.com 222

www.freeagent.com 567

www.freeinternet.com 129

www.fsf.org/copyleft/gpl.html 136

www.ftc.gov/kidzprivacy 329

www.future-works.com 232

www.GainsKeeper.com 474

www.gay.com 390

www.gccgroup.com/internet/facts1.htm 9

www.geeps.com 232

www.geocities.com 260

www.getagriponit.com 328

www.getnetwise.com 316, 329

www.gf-x.com 430

www.giftcertificates.com 113

www.globalnetxchange.com 234

www.globalsight.com 352

www.glreach.com/globstats/index.php3 345, 365

www.gnome.org 136

www.goamerica.com 158

www.goglobal.com 221

www.gomez.com 37

www.google.com 37, 235

www.goto.com 249

www.h20design.com 231

www.headlight.com 494

www.hearme.com 287

www.hncmarksman.com 277

www.holistix.net/products/solutions2.htm 78

www.homestead.com 67

www.hoovers.com 288

www.hotfiles.com 308

www.HSX.com 541

www.hungryminds.com 495

www.hut.fi/~jkytojok/micropayments 114

www.hyperlink.com 239

www.iana.org/cctld.html 346

www.ibidlive.com 35

www.ibm.com/db2 132

www.icat.com 112

www.icebox.com 535

www.iconocast.com 237

www.idc.com 237

www.idealab.com 59

www.idiominc.com 345, 352, 365

www.igc.com 389

www.ikea.com.sa 351

www.ikea.com/content 351

www.ikea.it 351

www.ilux.com 223, 239

www.imdb.com 543

www.inChorus.com 223

www.informix.com 132

www.instinet.com 464

www.intellicharge.com 112

www.internet2.edu 131

www.internetcash.com 113

www.internetindicators.com 112

www.ipin.com 114

www.ipromotions.com 225

www.isdnzone.com 130

www.isfree.com 129

www.isharp.com 90

www.isky.com 293

www.island.com 464

www.isolve.com 40

www.itaa.org/infosec/ 190

www.itoi.com 43

www.itped.com 502

www.itu.org 156

www.itxc.com/webtalknow 287

www.jobfind.com 559

www.jobtrak.com 564

www.jolt.co.il 167

www.junkbusters.com 310, 328

www.jup.com 222

www.kana.com 290

www.kaplan.com 503

www.kaplancollege.com 500

www.keynote.com/services/downloads/downloads_demos.html 79

www.keywordcount.com 234

www.knowledgenet.com 496

www.kvo.com 221

www.learnthenet.com/english/index.html 20

www.legalengine.com 327

www.levcom.co.il/olencom/navigator/index.htm 167

www.lexis.com 441

www.linkexchange.com 228

www.linkshare.com 238, 250, 253

www.linux.com 135

www.linux.org 135

www.lionbridge.com 352

www.liszt.com/news 251

www.livecapital.com 463

www.liveperson.com 283

www.logos.it 222, 346, 347, 365

www.loopnet.com 463

www.lot21.com 231

www.lsainc.com/products/connectivitysolutions/highperflacomm/products.html 167

www.lycos.com 235, 249

www.macroinc.com 221

www.macromedia.com 230

www.marketresearchinfo.com 222

www.marketresearchinfo.com/public/software 222

www.marketsite.net 234

www.match.com 390

www.mbsmm.com 224

www.mcafee.com 198

www.mediamaponline.com 232

www.mediametrix.com 222

www.mediaplex.com 232

www.medscape.com 426

www.menshealth.com 382

www.mercata.com 40

www.messagemedia.com 223

www.metacrawler.com 37, 236

www.mgisoft.com 69

www.microsoft.com/exchange 155

www.microsoft.com/mobile/pocketpc/features/pie.asp 164

www.microsoft.com/net 135
www.microsoft.com/windows2000/default.asp 135
www.mindarrow.com 223
www.mindexchange.com 560
www.MLB.com 538
www.mldirect.com 470
www.mobshop.com 40
www.modernhumorist.com 540
www.moneyzap.com 114
www.mplayer.com 541
www.mpower.com 478
www.ms.foundation.org 383
www.msdw.com 475
www.msdwonline.com 477
www.mtv.com 231, 536
www.munidirect.com 472
www.myaffiliateprogram.com 252
www.myciti.com 475
www.mysimon.com 39
www.napster.com 534
www.nationjob.com 568
www.navisite.com 230
www.nba.com 538
www.nbank.com 460
www.ndb.com 470
www.nearmagazine.com 168
www.nesn.com 538
www.net2phone.com 140
www.net2phone.com/ecommerce/clicktogether.html 140
www.netcentives.com 224
www.netchex.com 113
www.netcoalition.com 328
www.netgen.com 279
www.netnanny.com 315
www.netpliance.com 138
www.net-scene.com 497
www.networksolutions.com 61
www.netzero.com 129
www.newsiq.com 238
www.nexchange.com 256
www.nexis.com 441
www.nextcard.com 114
www.nfl.com 538
www.nhl.com 538
www.nike.com 231

www.nokia.com/corporate/wap/sdk.html 161
www.npr.com 538
www.npr.org 139
www.ntia.doc.gov/ntiahome/digitaldivide 379
www.nua.ie 345
www.nuvomedia.com 520
www.omnisky.com 159
www.onecore.com 459
www.onlineorders.net 112
www.oracle.com 132, 290
www.oxygen.com 382, 390
www.packetvideo.com/products_overview.html# 166
www.palm.com/products/palmvii/webclipping.html 158
www.palm.net/apps/index.html 158
www.parentsoup.com 316
www.participate.com 385
www.partnerware.com 289
www.paymentech.com 104
www.paypal.com 101
www.paypal.com/cgi-bin/webscr?cmd=index 113
www.paytrust.com 115
www.pbs.org/adultlearning 495
www.peachtree.ca 358
www.pearson.com 512
www.personify.com 279
www.pga.com 538
www.plaintree.com/wire_pro.htm 167
www.planetout.com 383, 390
www.post-ag.de 354
www.powered.com 493
www.primestreet.com 462
www.princetonreview.com 502
www.privacybot.com 328
www.privacychoices.org 310, 328
www.privacyrights.org 310, 328
www.privacyx.com 328
www.privaseek.com 327, 328
www.prnewswire.com 232

www.progressive.com 155
www.promotionworld.com/tutorial/000.html 225, 237
www.prweb.com 232
www.pwcbetterweb.com 329
www.pwcbetterweb.com/betterweb/index.cfm 310
www.qpass.com 103, 114
www.questionexchange.com 435
www.quickandreilly.com 466
www.quickclick.com 267
www.Quirks.com 221
www.quisic.com 497
www.radicalmail.com 236
www.radiotower.com 538
www.raremedium.com 58
www.rcrnews.com 232
www.real.com 139, 538
www.realcall.com 287
www.realplayer.com 231
www.recruitsoft.com/corpoVideo 563
www.recruitsoft.com/process 563
www.redhat.com 136, 137
www.redibook.com 464
www.redladder.com 234
www.refer-it.com 265
www.register.com 61
www.replaytv.com 536
www.resource.com 230
www.respond.com 231
www.retailenergy.com 434
www.review.com 568
www.rightnowtech.com 282
www.rim.net/products/handhelds/service.html#Exchange 155
www.roibotlibrary.com/index.htm 238
www.roidirect.com/ecommerce/tour01.htm 75
www.rsasecurity.com 187
www.saba.com 494
www.sales.com 289
www.saleslogix.com 289
www.sba.gov 443, 451
www.sba.gov/advo/stats/lending 463
www.scambusters.org 322

www.school.aol.com 378
www.schwab.com 470
www.scia.org 102
www.scottrade.com 470
www.searchengin-
    ewatch.com/Webmas-
    ters/index.html 235
www.senate.gov 443
www.servicesoft.com 282
www.sfnb.com 460
www.sharebuilder.com 468
www.shareware.com 595
www.shockwave.com 157,
    231, 595
www.shoutcast.com 537
www.siebel.com 290
www.simonsays.com 512
www.sitel.com 281
www.sixfigurejobs.com
    568
www.skygo.com 232
www.smart-card.com 114
www.smartdrill.com 277
www.smartforce.com 494
www.softsecurity.com
    307, 328
www.softseek.com/Util-
    ities/
    Voice_Recognition_a
    nd_Text_To_Speech
    283
www.spambouncer.org 322
www.spinway.com 230, 231
www.sportingnews.com 538
www.sprint.com/e-com-
    merce 156
www.sprintpcs.com/
    aboutsprintpcs/
    buzz/articles/
    092200_wwforbiz_sum
    mary.html 157
www.sprintpcs.com/
    wireless/wwbrows-
    ing.html 157
www.storagenet-
    works.com 127
www.stratus.com 35
www.stream.com/
    Stream.nsf 281
www.streamingmedia.com
    230, 237
www.submiturl.com/
    metatags.htm 238
www.suffolkemba.org 500
www.surfsecurity.com 307

www.surfwatch.com 315,
    329
www.surveysite.com 221
www.suse.com 137
www.sybase.com 132
www.sychrony.net 293
www.symantec.com 198
www.synrgistic.com/
    busplan/bus-
    plan.htm 56
www.talkcity.com 385
www.tandem.com 35
www.tawte.com 192
www.tdbank.ca 477
www.teletech.com 281
www.testu.com 501
www.the-net-ef-
    fect.com/articles/
    multiculture.html
    356
www.thePRnetwork.com 232
www.thestandard.net 112
www.thinq.com 494
www.tiac.net/users/
    seeker/search-
    enginesub.html 238
www.ticketmaster.com 446
www.tivo.com 536
www.tradearca.com 464
www.tradecard.com 105,
    115
www.tradesafe.com 114
www.tradient.com 430
www.transparentlan-
    guage.com 346
www.travelocity.com 225
www.trimble.com/gps 169
www.trintech.com 112
www.tripod.com 89
www.tripod.lycos.com 260
www.trivnet.com 114
www.truste.com 328
www.turbolinux.com 137
www.unext.com 501
www.unicode.org 346, 367
www.unitedmessag-
    ing.com 329
www.unix-systems.org 134
www.ups.com 429
www.usnews.com 503
www.valinux.com 136, 137
www.valueclick.com 228
www.vcampus.com 494
www.verisign.com 192
www.verticalnet.com 238
www.verticalone.com 474

www.viapay.com 105
www.vicaids.asn.au 382
www.victoriasse-
    cret.com 230
www.virtualspin.com 66
www.virtuflex.com 289
www.visa.com/nt/chip/
    info.html 114
www.visa.com/pd/ewal-
    let/main.html 112
www.vix.com/pub/men/
    index.html 382
www.w3.org 20
www.w3.org/WAI 12
www.wapforum.org 163
www.wavetech.com 496
www.wbtsystems.com 494
www.webcallback.com 287
www.webcom.com/im-
    pulse/prlist.html
    233
www.webdeveloper.com/
    html/
    html_metatags.html
    238
www.webhire.com 558
www.webmd.com 427, 450
www.webpromote.com 237
www.web-
    search.about.com/
    internet/websearch/
    insub2-m02.htm 234
www.websitefor-
    free.website/
    forfree2/1-fs.asp 67
www.webtrends.com 276
www.webtv.com 128, 536
www.webvision.com 74
www.wellsfargo.com 458
www.wheelhouse.com 238
www.winamp.com 537
www.wirelessnetnow.com
    232
www.wnba.com 538
www.women.com 382
www.worldcallex-
    change.com 35
www.worldpoint.com 352
www.worldwideretailex-
    change.com 234
www.wsj.com 521
www.w-technologies.com
    477
www.xdrive.com 564
www.xippix.com 69
www.xlibrix.com 516

www.xml.com/pub/Guide/
    WML 163
www.yahoo.com 235, 352
www.yet2.com 435
www.yodlee.com 475
www.youthactivism.com
    390
www.youthpride.com 383
www.zdnet.com/pcmag/
    features/windows98/
    history2.html 135
www.zonaresearch.com 237
www1.internetwire.com/
    iwire/home 238
www2.bc.edu/~herbeck/
    cyberreadings.html
    327
www4.nscu.edu/unity/
    users/j/jherkert/
    index.html 389

www5.compaq.com/prod-
    ucts/iPAQ 137
www-ai.ijs.si/eliza/
    eliza.html 284

X

Xactmail.com 224
XDrive™ 564
xDSL 128
XML 20, 42, 106, 160, 164,
    496, 519, 520, 526
XML (Extensible Markup
    Language) 603, 692
XrML 512, 513, 519
XSL 20
XSL (Extensible Stylesheet
    Language) 603
XSL stylesheet 692

Y

Yahoo 5, 700
Yahoo! 28, 36, 108, 352, 362,
    559
Yahoo! Internet Life 5
Yahoo! Shopping 36
Yahoo.com 35
Yesmail.com 224
Yodlee 475, 476

Z

ZDNet 5
zero coupon bond 472
zoning 314
ZOOM Server software 69

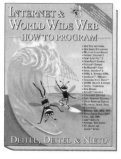

XML How to Program

©2001, 1000 pp., paper
(0-13-028417-3)

This new book in the Deitels' *How to Program* series is a comprehensive guide to programming in XML. It explains how to use XML to create customized tags and includes several chapters that address standard custom markup languages for science and technology, multimedia, commerce and other fields. The authors include concise introductions to Java, VBScript, Active Server Pages and Perl/CGI, providing readers with the essentials of these programming languages and server-side development technologies to enable them to work effectively with XML. The book also includes cutting-edge topics such as XQL, SMIL and VoiceXML as well as a real-world e-commerce case study. A complete chapter on Web accessibility that addresses Voice XML is also included. It also includes tips such as valuable insights into Common Programming Errors, Software Engineering Observations, Portability Tips and Debugging Hints.

Perl How to Program

©2001, 1000 pp., paper
(0-13-028418-1)

This comprehensive new guide to programming with Perl emphasizes the use of the Common Gateway Interface (CGI) with Perl to create powerful dynamic Web content for e-commerce applications. The book begins with a clear and careful introduction to the concepts of structured programming at a level suitable for beginners, and proceeds through advanced topics such as references and complex data structures. Key Perl topics such as regular expressions and string manipulation are covered in detail. The authors address important and topical issues such as object-oriented programming, the Perl database interface (DBI), graphics and security. Also included is a treatment of XML, a bonus chapter introducing the Python programming language, and a complete chapter on Web accessibility that addresses programming and technologies relevant to accessibility for people with disabilities. The text also includes tips such as valuable insights into Common Programming Errors, Software Engineering Observations, Portability Tips and Debugging Hints.

e-Business & e-Commerce for Managers

©2001, 900 pp., paper
(0-13-032364-0)

This innovative new text is a comprehensive overview of building and managing an e-business. It explores topics such as the decision to bring a business online, choosing a business model, accepting payment, marketing strategies and security, as well as many other important issues. Features, Web resources and online demonstrations supplement the text and direct readers to additional materials. The book also includes an appendix that develops a complete Web-based shopping cart application using HTML, VBScript, Active Server Pages and an Access database. Plus, company-specific sections provide "real-world" examples of the concepts presented in the book.

Advanced Java How to Program

©2001, 1100 pp., paper
(0-13-089560-1)

Expanding on the world's best-selling Java text, *Advanced Java How to Program* includes an in-depth discussion of advanced topics, aiding developers in producing significant, scalable Java applications and distributed systems. The book integrates such technologies as Swing, multithreading, RMI, JDBC, servlets, Java XML and Enterprise JavaBeans into a complete, rigorous, production-quality system, thus allowing developers to take better advantage of the leverage and platform-independence provided by the Java 2 platform.

Java How to
Program
Third Edition

BOOK / CD-ROM

©2000, 1360 pp., paper bound w/CD-ROM (0-13-012507-5)

This edition of the world's best-selling Java textbook incorporates Sun Microsystems' latest version of Java, the Java 2 Software Development Kit (J2SDK). The introduction of new functionality in this upgrade has made Java a friendlier and more accessible programming language. Reviewers of the book were unanimous in praising the Deitels for making the best use of these enhancements and writing the introductory chapters in an engaging and accessible style. Designed for beginning through intermediate readers, it uses the Deitels' proven "live-code" approach with hundreds of complete working programs, valuable programming tips, more than 16,000 lines of code and over 1400 interesting and challenging exercises. The graphical user interface examples use Sun's new Swing GUI components. The authors have added significant coverage of JDBC, JavaBeans, RMI, Servlets, Java 2D, Java Media Framework, Collections, Serialization, Inner Classes and other topics. Includes several examples and projects on multi-tier, client/server systems development. The CD-ROM contains a complete Java Integrated Development Environment, source code for all examples in the text, and hyperlinks to valuable Java demos and resources on the Internet.

C++ How to
Program
Third Edition

BOOK / CD-ROM

© 2001, 1168 pp., paper (0-13-089571-7)

The world's best-selling C++ text teaches programming by emphasizing structured and object-oriented programming, software reuse and component-oriented software construction. This comprehensive book uses the Deitels' signature "live-code" approach, presenting every concept in the context of a complete, working C++ program followed by a screen capture showing the program's output. It also includes a rich collection of exercises and valuable insights into Common Programming Errors, Software Engineering Observations, Portability Tips and Debugging Hints. The Third Edition includes a new case study that focuses on object-oriented design with the UML and illustrates the entire process of object-oriented design from conception to implementation. In addition, it adheres to the latest ANSI/ISO C++ standards. The accompanying CD-ROM contains Microsoft® Visual C++ 6.0 Introductory Edition software, source code for all examples in the text and hyperlinks to C++ demos and Internet resources.

C How to Program
Third Edition

BOOK / CD-ROM

©2001, 1253 pp., paper (0-13-089572-5)

Highly practical in approach, the Third Edition of the world's best-selling C text introduces the fundamentals of structured programming and software engineering and gets up to speed quickly. This comprehensive book not only covers the full C language, but also reviews library functions and introduces object-based and object-oriented programming in C++ and Java, as well as event-driven GUI programming in Java. The Third Edition includes a new 346-page introduction to Java 2 and the basics of GUIs, and the introduction to C++ has been condensed to 298 pages and updated to be consistent with the most current ANSI/ISO C++ standards. Plus, icons throughout the book point out valuable programming tips such as Common Programming Errors, Portability Tips and Testing and Debugging Tips.

Getting Started with Microsoft® Visual C++™ 6
with an Introduction to MFC

BOOK / CD-ROM

©2000, 163 pp., paper (0-13-016147-0)

This exciting book is intended to be a companion to the ANSI/ISO standard C++ best-selling book, *C++ How to Program, Second Edition.* Learn how to use Microsoft's Visual Studio 6 integrated development environment (IDE) and Visual C++ 6 to create Windows programs using the Microsoft Foundation Classes (MFC). The book includes 17 "live-code" Visual C++/MFC programs with screen captures, dozens of tips, recommended practices and cautions and exercises accompanying every chapter. It includes coverage of Win32 and console applications, online documentation and Web resources, GUI controls, dialog boxes, graphics, message handling, the resource definition language and the debugger.

Visual Basic® 6
How to Program

BOOK / CD-ROM

©1999, 1015 pp., paper bound w/CD-ROM (0-13-456955-5)

Visual Basic 6 is revolutionizing software development for conventional and Internet/Intranet-based applications. This text explains Visual Basic 6's extraordinary capabilities. Part of the Deitels' *Visual Studio* series, this book uses the Deitels' "live-code" approach to cover Internet/Intranet, World Wide Web, VBScript, ActiveX, ADO, multimedia, animation, audio, video, files, database, networking, graphics, strings, data structures, collections, GUI and control creation. The accompanying CD-ROM contains Microsoft's *Visual Basic 6 Working Model Edition* software, source code and hyperlinks to valuable Visual Basic resources.

BOOK/MULTIMEDIA PACKAGES

These complete packages include books and interactive multimedia CD-ROMs, and are perfect for anyone interested in learning Java, C++, Visual Basic, Internet/World Wide Web and e-commerce programming. They are exceptional and affordable resources for college students and professionals learning programming for the first time or reinforcing their knowledge.

The Complete Internet & World Wide Web Programming Training Course

BOXED SET

©2000, boxed book and software
(0-13-085611-8)

Includes the book *Internet & World Wide Web How To Program* and the fully interactive browser-based *Internet & World Wide Web Programming Multimedia Cyber Classroom* CD-ROM that features:

- Fully searchable, electronic version of the textbook, complete with hyperlinks
- Hundreds of programs that can be run inside a browser
- Over 12 hours of audio explaining key Internet programming concepts
- Hundreds of exercises—many solved
- An integrated course completion and assessment summary feature to help you monitor your progress
- Practice exams with hundreds of short-answer test questions
- Hundreds of tips, terms and hints
- Master client- and server-side programming, including JavaScript, VBScript, ActiveX, ASP, SQL, XML, database and more!

Runs on Windows 95, 98, NT and Windows 2000

The Complete e-Business & e-Commerce Programming Training Course

BOXED SET

©2001, boxed book and software
(0-13-089549-0)

Includes the book *e-Business & e-Commerce How To Program* and the fully interactive *e-Business & e-Commerce Programming Multimedia Cyber Classroom* CD-ROM that features:

- Fully searchable, electronic version of the textbook, complete with hyperlinks
- Over 13 hours of detailed audio descriptions of more than 15,000 lines of fully tested "live code"
- Hundreds of example programs that readers can run with the click of a mouse button
- Practice exams with hundreds of short-answer test questions
- Hundreds of self-review questions, all with answers
- Hundreds of programming exercises, half with answers
- Hundreds of tips, marked with icons, that show how to write code that is portable, reusable and optimized for performance
- An intuitive browser-based interface

Runs on Windows 95, 98, NT and Windows 2000

The Complete C++ Training Course Third Edition

BOXED SET

©2001, boxed book and software
(0-13-089564-4)

Includes the complete, best-selling introductory book *C++ How to Program, Third Edition* and the fully interactive *C++ Multimedia Cyber Classroom* CD-ROM that features:

- Fully searchable, electronic version of the textbook, complete with hyperlinks
- 248 complete C++ programs that readers can edit and run with a click of the mouse in the Microsoft® Visual C++™ 6 Introductory Edition IDE included in the package
- Over 13 hours of detailed, expert audio descriptions of more than 13,000 lines of fully tested "live code"
- Hundreds of programming exercises, half with answers
- Practice exams with hundreds of short-answer test questions
- Hundreds of self-review questions, all with answers
- Hundreds of tips, marked with icons, that show how to write C++ code that is portable, reusable and optimized for performance
- An intuitive browser-based interface

Runs on Windows 95, 98, NT and Windows 2000

www.phptr.com/phptrinteractive

Coming Fall 2000, the award-winning Deitel & Deitel Cyber Classroom Series will be available from Prentice Hall over the World Wide Web. This is an ideal solution for students and programming professionals who prefer the convenience of Internet delivery to CD-ROM delivery, or who work on platforms not supported by the CD-ROM version of the Cyber Classrooms.

The Web-based Cyber Classrooms will run on any computer that supports version 4 of either Netscape Navigator or Internet Explorer and the free Real Networks RealPlayer version 7 or higher. The Web-based version will require a 56K modem or higher connection to the Internet.

The Web-based Cyber Classrooms will contain all of the features of the CD-ROM versions, including the Deitels' signature "live code" approach to teaching programming languages. All of the audio will be available through the Web, as will the sample program code, programming tips, exercises and so forth.

We are excited to announce enhanced Web-based versions of the Deitel & Deitel Cyber Classroom Series coming in 2001. The enhanced versions will attempt to recreate the experience of being in a live programming seminar. They will contain substantially more media than the current Cyber Classrooms, including extensive use of both audio and video. The enhanced versions will also include synchronous and asynchronous communications tools to support sophisticated instructor-to-student and student-to-student communication.

For more information, please visit **www.phptr.com/phptrinteractive**.

Turn back one page for details on the Cyber Classroom CD-ROMs and Complete Training Courses!

FORTHCOMING PUBLICATIONS FROM THE DEITELS

For those interested in
C++

Advanced C++ How to Program: This book builds on the pedagogy of *C++ How to Program, Third Edition*, and features more advanced discussions of templates, multiple inheritance, and other key topics. We are co-authoring this book with Don Kostuch, one of the world's most experienced C++ educators.

For those interested in
Microsoft® Visual C++

Visual C++ 7 How to Program: This book combines the pedagogy and extensive coverage of *C++ How to Program, Third Edition* with a more in-depth treatment of Windows programming in Visual Studio 7. We have carefully culled the best material from each of these areas to produce a solid, two-semester, introductory/intermediate level treatment.

Getting Started with Microsoft® Visual C++™ 7 with an Introduction to MFC, Second Edition: This book builds on the first edition introduced for Visual Studio 6. It features a much enhanced, yet still introductory, treatment of MFC.

For those interested in
C#

C# How to Program: This book discusses Microsoft's brand new C# language being introduced in Visual Studio 7.

Ms. Kito

Turn the page to find out more about Deitel & Associates!

For those interested in
Python

Python How to Program: This book introduces the increasingly popular Python language which makes many application development tasks much easier to accomplish than with traditional, recent object-oriented languages.

For those interested in
Flash

Flash 5 How to Program: Hundreds of millions of people browse Flash-enabled Web sites daily. This first book in our Multimedia series introduces the powerful features of Flash 5 and includes a detailed introduction to programming with the completely revamped Flash 5 scripting language.

For those interested in
Java

Java How to Program, Fourth Edition, Volume I and **Java How to Program, Fourth Edition, Volume II:** These books build on the pedagogy of *Java How to Program, Third Edition,* expanding our intermediate-level treatment of Java to two 1000-page volumes. The volumes include extensive treatments of XML and object-oriented design with UML.

For those interested in
Microsoft® Visual Basic

Visual Basic 7 How to Program, Second Edition: This book builds on the pedagogy of the first edition, which was developed for Visual Studio 6. It has a much enhanced treatment of developing Web-based e-business and e-commerce applications. The book includes an extensive treatment of XML.

New & Improved Deitel Web Site!

Deitel & Associates, Inc. is in the process of upgrading www.deitel.com. The new site will feature Macromedia Flash® enhancements and additional content to create a valuable resource for students, professors and professionals. Features will include FAQs, Web resources, e-publications and online chat sessions with the authors. We will include streaming audio clips where the authors discuss their publications. Web-based training demos will also be available at the site.